# Information Technology Law

The fifth edition of *Information Technology Law* continues to be dedicated to a detailed analysis of, and commentary on, the latest developments within this burgeoning field of law. It provides an essential read for all those interested in the interface between law and technology and the effect of new technological developments on the law. The contents have been restructured and the reordering of the chapters provides a coherent flow to the subject matter. Criminal law issues are now dealt with in two separate chapters to enable a more focused approach to content crime. This new edition contains both a significant amount of incremental change as well as substantial new material and, where possible, case studies have been used to illustrate significant issues.

In particular, new additions include:

- Social media and the criminal law;
- The impact of the decision in *Google Spain* and the 'right to be forgotten';
- The *Schrems* case and the demise of the Safe Harbour agreement;
- The judicial reassessment of the proportionality of ICT surveillance powers within the UK and EU after the Madrid bombings;
- The expansion of the ICANN gTLDs and the redesigned domain name registration and dispute resolution processes.

**Diane Rowland** is an Emeritus Professor of Law at Aberystwyth University, UK.

**Uta Kohl** is a Senior Lecturer in Law at Aberystwyth University, UK.

**Andrew Charlesworth** is a Reader in IT Law at the University of Bristol, UK.

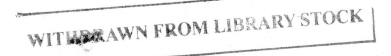

# Information Technology Law

FIFTH EDITION

Diane Rowland, Uta Kohl and
Andrew Charlesworth

Routledge
Taylor & Francis Group

LONDON AND NEW YORK

Fifth Edition published 2017
by Routledge
2 Park Square, Milton Park, Abingdon, Oxon, OX14 4RN

and by Routledge
711 Third Avenue, New York, NY 10017

*Routledge is an imprint of the Taylor & Francis Group, an informa business*

First edition published by Cavendish Publishing 1997
Fourth edition published by Routledge 2011

*British Library Cataloguing in Publication Data*
A catalogue record for this book is available from the British Library

*Library of Congress Cataloging-in-Publication Data*
Names: Rowland, Diane, author editor. | Kohl, Uta, author editor. |
    Charlesworth, Andrew, 1966– author editor.
Title: Information technology law / edited by Diane Rowland, Uta Kohl and
    Andrew Charlesworth.
Description: Fifth edition. | Abingdon, Oxon ; New York, NY : Routledge, 2017. | Includes
    bibliographical references and index.
Identifiers: LCCN 2016003406 | ISBN 9780415870153 (hbk) | ISBN 9780203798522 (ebk)
Subjects: LCSH: Computers—Law and legislation—Great Britain. | Internet—Law and
    legislation—Great Britain. | Data protection—Law and legislation—Great Britain. |
    Electronic commerce—Law and legislation—Great Britain. | Copyright—Computer
    programs—Great Britain. | Computer software—Law and legislation—Great Britain. |
    Information technology—Great Britain.
Classification: LCC KD667.C65 R69 2017 | DDC 343.4109/99—dc23
LC record available at http://lccn.loc.gov/2016003406

ISBN: 978-0-415-87015-3 (hbk)
ISBN: 978-0-415-87016-0 (pbk)
ISBN: 978-0-203-79852-2 (ebk)

Typeset in Joanna
by Apex CoVantage, LLC

Printed and bound in Great Britain by
TJ International Ltd, Padstow, Cornwall

# Contents

# Preface

Soon after the last edition of this book was published I came across the following:

> The good thing with the internet is that nobody really knows what exactly will happen next. Twenty years ago there were no search engines, 15 years ago there was no YouTube. Ten years ago there were no social networks. And five years ago we had only little experiences with cloud computing. Who knows what will be in 2017 or 2022?[1]

Whether or not you share the view that this is a good thing, it certainly means that there is no shortage of issues to consider but, inevitably, we have had to be selective in our choice of both subject matter and examples, so we apologise if we have not covered an issue in which you have a particular interest. In common with the previous editions, this book attempts to respond both to new developments which may not have even been anticipated when the previous edition was written, and also to reflect on more longstanding legal issues. We are grateful to the editorial team at Routledge and to reviewers for their comments on previous editions and have tried to take these into account in preparing this edition as we continued to overhaul and restructure the contents. One specific change is that the original chapter on criminal law has now been split into two to allow a separate consideration of content crime. Where possible we have also used case studies to illustrate significant issues.

As before, the book is primarily aimed at undergraduate and postgraduate law students. Against that background, it will hopefully provide reassurance that a detailed knowledge of the technology is unnecessary to an understanding of the legal issues. Where some rudimentary understanding is helpful, minimum technical explanations have been included. The book may also prove both useful and of interest to computer scientists, who increasingly have to consider the wider implications for their discipline. We remain excited by the challenges which information communications technology continues to pose for established legal frameworks and regulation and are hopeful that we have communicated this to the reader.

Diane Rowland
January 2016

---

1 Kleinwachter, W, 'Internet governance outlook 2012: cold war or constructive dialogue?' (2012) 17(1) Comms L 14, 18.

# Table of cases

# Table of statutes

## International statutes

### *Australia*

## France

### C

Code of Civil Procedure –
  Art 808 . . . 30
  Art 809 . . . 30
Creation and Internet Law 2009 (HADOPI) . . .
  159, 160, 167
Criminal Code . . . 30

## Germany

### C

Civil Code –
  § 145 . . . 225
Criminal Code . . . 31

### L

Law on the restriction of the privacy of posts
  and telecommunications, Gesetz zu Artikel
  10 Grundgesetz v 26 June 2001 (BGBl I S
  1254), as amended 9 January 2002 (BGBl I
  S 361) . . . 415

### P

Penal Code –
  s 184 . . . 312
Penal Law . . . 35

## Italy

### L

Law No 401 of 13 December 1989—
  Art 4 . . . 47

## New Zealand

### G

Gambling Act 2003 . . . 35
  s 4 . . . 35
  s 9(2)(b) . . . 35
  s 16 . . . 35
  s 16(1) . . . 47
  s 19 . . . 35

### S

Sale of Goods Act 1908 . . . 496
Sale of Goods (Amendment) Act 2003 . . .
  496

## Singapore

### B

Broadcasting Act 1994 . . . 314
Broadcasting Authority Act 1994 . . . 314

### C

Computer Misuse (Amendment) Act 1998 . . .
  288
Copyright Act 1988 . . . 465
  s 35 . . . 465
  s 35(5) . . . 465

### I

Internet Code of Practice . . . 314

## Spain

### L

Law 34/2002—
  Art 17 . . . 112

## Sweden

### C

Criminal Code . . . 150

## USA

### A

Anti-cybersquatting Consumer Protection Act
  1999 . . . 64, 186, 188, 189, 190, 191,
  192, 193, 194, 195, 196, 209
Espionage Act 1917 . . . 7, 10

### C

Californian Commercial Code –
  § 2204(1) . . . 233
Child Obscenity and Pornography Protection Act
  2003 . . . 327
Child Online Protection Act 1998 . . . 309, 310,
  311
Child Pornography Protection Act 1996 . . . 327
Collections of Information Antipiracy Act . . .
  483
Communications Decency Act 1996 . . . 117,
  308, 309
  s 230 . . . 48, 99, 117, 118, 119, 120, 123,
  125

# Table of statutory instruments

# Table of European legislation

## Regulations

## Treaties and Conventions

# Table of abbreviations

| | |
|---|---|
| ACLU | American Civil Liberties Union |
| ACMA | Australian Communications and Media Authority |
| ACPA | Anticybersquatting Consumer Protection Act 1999 |
| ACPO | Association of Chief Police Officers |
| ADR | Alternative Dispute Resolution |
| AGP | Affero General Public Licence |
| AI Lab | Artificial Intelligence Laboratory |
| ALI | American Law Institute |
| APIG | All Party Internet Group |
| ASCII | American Standard Code for Information Interchange |
| ASP | Application Service Provision |
| ATCSA | Anti-terrorism, Crime and Security Act 2001 |
| ATM | Automated Teller Machine |
| B2B | Business-to-Business |
| B2C | Business-to-Consumer |
| BCR | Binding Corporate Rules |
| BCS | British Computer Society |
| BEREC | Body of European Regulators for Electronic Communications |
| BERR | Business, Enterprise and Regulatory Reform |
| BSD | Berkeley Software Distribution |
| C2C | Consumer-to-Consumer |
| C & L | Computers and Law |
| CA | Communications Act 2003 |
| CCRO | Community Charge Registration Officer |
| CDA | Communications Decency Act 1996 (US) |
| CDPA | Copyright, Designs and Patents Act 1988 |
| CEO | Chief Executive Officer |
| CEOP | Child Exploitation and Online Protection Centre |
| CIP | Centre for Information Policy Leadership |
| CJEU | Court of Justice of the European Union |
| CL | Computer Law |
| CL & P | Computer Law and Practice |
| CLR | Commonwealth Law Reports |
| CMA | Computer Misuse Act 1990 |
| Comms L | Communications Law |
| COPA | Child Online Protection Act 1998 (US) |
| CPA | Consumer Protection Act 1987 |
| CPS | Crown Prosecution Service |
| CPU | Central Processing Unit |
| CRM | Customer Relationship Management |
| CSA | Common Services Agency |

| | |
|---|---|
| CSP | Certification Services Provider |
| Cth | Commonwealth of Australia |
| DDoS | Distributed Denial-of-Service |
| DEA | Digital Economy Act 2010 |
| DERs | Data Retention (EC Directive) Regulations 2009 (SI 2009/9870) |
| DMCA | Digital Millennium Copyright Act 1998/2000 (US) |
| DNS | Domain Name Server |
| DoS | Denial-of-Service |
| DPA | Data Protection Act 1984/1998 |
| DPP | Director of Public Prosecutions |
| DRM | Digital Rights Management |
| DTI | Department of Trade and Industry |
| DVR | Digital Video Recorder |
| EBA | Enlarged Board of Appeal |
| ECA | Electronic Communications Act 2000 |
| ECHR | European Convention on Human Rights |
| ECJ | European Court of Justice |
| ECR | European Court Reports |
| ECtHR | European Court of Human Rights |
| EEA | European Economic Area |
| EFF | Electronic Frontier Foundation |
| EIPR | European Intellectual Property Review |
| EPC | European Patent Convention |
| EPIC | Electronic Privacy Information Center |
| EPO | European Patent Office |
| ERP | Enterprise Resource Planning |
| EU | European Union |
| EULA | End-User Licence Agreement |
| FCC | Federal Communications Commission |
| FD | Free Document Licence |
| FHA | Fair Housing Act 1968 (US) |
| FIPR | Foundation for Information Policy Research |
| FOISA | Fraudulent Online Identity Sanctions Act 2004 |
| F/OSS | Free and Open Source Software Licensing |
| FSA | Financial Services Authority |
| FSF | Free Software Foundation |
| FSFE | Free Software Foundation Europe |
| FSMA | Financial Services and Markets Act 2000 |
| FSR | Fleet Street Reports |
| FTC | Federal Trade Commission |
| FTDA | Federal Trademark Dilution Act 1996 |
| GATT | General Agreement on Tariffs and Trade |
| GCHQ | Government Communications Headquarters (UK) |
| GDP | Gross Domestic Product |
| GDPR | General Data Protection Regulation |
| GMC | General Medical Council |
| GNSO | Generic Names Supporting Organization |
| GP | General Practitioner |
| GP | General Public Licence |
| HADOPI | Haute Autorité pour la Diffusion des Oeuvres et la Protection des Droit sur Internet |

| | |
|---|---|
| HL | High-Level Languages |
| HMRC | HM Revenue and Customs |
| HTM | Hypertext Mark-Up Language |
| IANA | Internet Assigned Numbers Authority |
| ICANN | Internet Corporation for Assigned Names and Numbers |
| ICCPR | International Covenant on Civil and Political Rights |
| ICO | Information Commissioner's Office |
| ICT | Information and Communications Technologies |
| IDN | Internationalised Domain Names |
| IDNA | Internationalising Domain Names in Applications |
| IEE | Institution of Electrical Engineers |
| IMEI | International Mobile Equipment Identity |
| IMSI | International Mobile Subscriber Identity |
| Int JLIT | International Journal of Information Technology |
| IOC | Initial Obligations Code |
| IOC | International Olympic Committee |
| IOCA | Interception of Communications Act 1985 |
| IP | Internet Protocol |
| IPT | Investigatory Powers Tribunal |
| ISCI | Independent Surveillance and Intelligence Commission |
| ISP | Internet Service Provider |
| ISSP | Information Society Service Provider |
| IT | Information Technology |
| ITU | International Telecommunication Union |
| IWF | Internet Watch Foundation |
| JANET | Joint Academic Network |
| JB | Journal of Business Law |
| JIC | Joint Intelligence Committee |
| JMRI | Java Model Railroad Interface Project |
| LBPR | Telecommunications (Lawful Business Practice) (Interception of Communications) Regulations 2000 |
| LGP | Lesser General Public Licence |
| LICRA | League against Racism and Ant-Semitism |
| LPP | Legally Privileged Communications |
| LRO | Legal Rights Objections |
| MDA | Media Development Authority (Singapore) |
| MDU | Medical Defence Union |
| MEP | Member of the European Parliament |
| MIT | Massachusetts Institute of Technology |
| MP | Member of Parliament |
| NHTCUS | National Hi-Tech Crime Unit Scotland |
| NLA | Newspaper Licensing Agency |
| NSA | National Security Agency (US) |
| NTAC | National Technical Assistance Centre |
| NTIA | National Telecommunications and Information Administration |
| OECD | Organisation for Economic Co-operation and Development |
| OFCOM | Office of the UK Communications Regulator |
| OFT | Office of Fair Trading |
| OSCE | Organization for Security and Co-operation in Europe |
| OSD | Open Source Definition |

| | |
|---|---|
| OSI | Open Source Initiative |
| OTC | Over-the-counter |
| P2P | Peer-To-Peer |
| PABX | Private Automated Branch Exchange |
| PACE | Police and Criminal Evidence Act 1984 |
| PCIJ | Permanent Court of International Justice |
| PCP | Parliamentary Control Panel |
| PECR | Privacy and Electronic Communications (EC Directive) Regulations 2003 |
| PIA | Privacy Impact Assessment |
| PNC | Police National Computer |
| PROTECT | Prosecutorial Remedies and Tools against the Exploitation of Children Today Act 2003 |
| RIAA | Recording Industry Association of America |
| RIPA | Regulation of Investigatory Powers Act 2000 |
| RRDRP | Registry Restriction Dispute Resolution Procedure |
| RRPRS | Registry Restriction Problem Report System |
| RPC | Report of Patent Design and Trademark Cases |
| RTR | Road Traffic Reports |
| SaaS | Software as a Service |
| SCM | Supply Chain Management |
| SCPA | Semiconductor Chip Protection Act 1984 (US) |
| SFLC | Software Freedom Law Center |
| SGA | Sale of Goods Act 1893 |
| SGSA | Supply of Goods and Services Act 1982 |
| SLA | Service Level Agreement |
| SLD | Second-Level Domain Name |
| SME | Small-To-Medium-Sized Enterprise |
| SOCA | Serious Organised Crime Agency |
| SoGA | Sale of Goods Act 1979 |
| SSGA | Sale and Supply of Goods Act 1994 |
| SSO | Structure, Sequence and Organisation |
| TBA | Technical Board of Appeal |
| TDNA | Truth in Domain Names Act 2003 |
| TDRA | Trademark Dilution Revision Act 2006 |
| TFEU | Treaty on the Functioning of the European Union |
| TLD | Top-level domain |
| TMA | Trade Marks Act 1994 |
| TMCH | Trademark Clearinghouse |
| TPDDRP | Trademark Post-Delegation Dispute Resolution Procedure |
| TPM | Technological Protection Mechanisms |
| TRIPS | Trade-Related Aspects of Intellectual Property Rights |
| TTP | Trusted Third Party |
| UCC | Uniform Commercial Code (US) |
| UCE | Unsolicited Commercial Emails |
| UCITA | Uniform Computer Information Transactions Act (US) |
| UCTA | Unfair Contract Terms Act 1977 |
| UDHR | Universal Declaration of Human Rights |
| UDRP | Uniform Domain Name Dispute Resolution Policy |
| UDRP | Uniform Dispute Resolution Policy |
| UEJF | French Jewish Students Union |

| | |
|---|---|
| UKIPO | UK Intellectual Property Office |
| UNICITRAL | United Nations Commission on International Trade Law |
| URS | Uniform Rapid Suspension |
| USC | United States Code |
| Web JCLI | Web Journal of Current Legal Issues |
| WHO | World Health Organization |
| WIPO | World Intellectual Property Organization |
| WLAN | Wireless Local Area Network |
| WTO | World Trade Organization |

# Chapter 1

# Regulating information technologies

## Chapter contents

## Information technology law?

Since its inception, the internet has metamorphosed from a minority research tool to a globally utilised communications instrument which exerts a profound effect on the world we live in be it socially, politically, economically and culturally. To many of its users it is far more than a mere tool but provides an environment for personal interaction with other users across the globe whether for business or pleasure. This revolution has been facilitated by the evolution of a plethora of devices from which the internet can be accessed and a multitude of programs and applications which enable and support that access. Together these developments have created dramatic changes in the ways in which people communicate via the internet and other information and communications technologies (ICT). Many of us now access the internet via mobile devices and may rarely use a static desktop PC. The internet has often been heralded as a democratising medium and the increased use of both mobile devices and social media has arguably fuelled that democratising effect. These smaller and often cheaper devices are also eroding the digital divide; for instance, many disadvantaged and displaced people learnt about Europe from Facebook. It has also created more government concerns about the circulation of information perceived to threaten the social order – such as in relation to terrorism and radicalisation – leading to calls for increased interception and surveillance.

These are merely a few of the developments which have had an impact on the legal response to ICT. Nevertheless and despite the fact that 40% of the global population now have an internet connection,[1] researching and teaching in the area of information technology (IT) law can occasionally lead to charges of dilettantism being levelled at an academic by his or her colleagues. Certainly, to work effectively in the field, one needs to be able to draw upon a range of knowledge and skills from across the legal sphere, whether the criminal law, contract and tort law, intellectual property law, constitutional and administrative law, European Union (EU) law, human rights law or public and private international law.

Yet it is that breadth of interaction with other academic legal domains that makes the subject such an involving and vibrant arena in which to participate. It has not been unusual for IT law to be the proving ground for developing jurisprudential thought on issues not yet sufficiently mainstream to merit a place within more established subject areas. Indeed, within university law courses, such issues often migrate between the IT curriculum and more familiar surroundings. For example, in the early to mid-1990s, the question of the admissibility of computer-generated evidence in criminal and civil cases exercised IT lawyers, but as the relevant civil and criminal issues have now been clarified this, in IT law terms at least, is only of historical interest. At one time most people rarely even travelled to other countries much less concluded cross-border contracts. Now, not only is foreign travel commonplace but the majority of internet shoppers will conclude cross-border contracts; defamatory comments on the internet can be read anywhere; and copyright material can be downloaded in another state without the creator's authority making IT law a significant forum for developing discussion of questions of jurisdiction and choice of law.

Equally importantly, the changing nature of the subject means that academic writers constantly enter and leave the field, as their interests intersect with topics in the IT law limelight. For some, their interaction is transitory and fleeting (an article here, a book chapter there); for others, the relationship may develop into a rather longer-lasting one. This access to ideas from other jurisprudential areas, however, is key to the way in which the subject has developed, and is developing, over time. The nature of the subject also invites cross-disciplinary input, both from the information sciences and from the social sciences (notably political science), which provides broader context for consideration of the potential and actual legal responses to developing issues. Finally, the influence of writers from other jurisdictions has been crucial in the process of evaluating and re-evaluating

---

1 See www.internetlivestats.com/internet-users/

national legal responses to IT developments. This additional cross-fertilisation has been enhanced significantly by the increased access to international materials brought by the internet, and the international legal databases such as Westlaw, HeinOnline, and LEXIS.[2] Each new technological development thus encourages a plethora of perspectives drawing on different jurisprudential, jurisdictional, and cross-disciplinary viewpoints.

This, however, leads to questions about the role of IT law as a legal discipline:[3] is it simply a holding area, or talking shop, for subject matter that does not yet fit comfortably within the established legal corpus? Or is there a more purposive role that it can play? The answer to these questions depends largely on whether the subject is treated as:

- a set of discrete topics linked solely by virtue of their transient novelty and relationship to information technologies; or
- a set of topics that raises new political, social, and economic issues, and thus requires consideration of appropriate legal and regulatory approaches to tackling them, outside of traditional legal paradigms.

To pose those questions another way: is IT law simply a collection of legal areas that happen to touch upon IT? Or is it greater than the sum of its parts, with some unifying underlying themes allowing for unique insights into law and society? Arguably, during its early years, IT law was probably closer to the former model, being driven as it was primarily by practitioner interests. This pragmatic influence resulted in a discipline concerned with short-term perspectives on legal changes in given areas. The aim was essentially to understand what impact those changes might have on existing practices, rather than why the law was developing in a particular way, and whether there might be longer-term advantages in plotting a different legal/regulatory path to that being taken.

Over the last decade or two, as the discipline has matured, the approach in academia has increasingly shifted towards the latter model. The black-letter, piecemeal perspective remains a significant element, but legal inquiries now also feature broader, more theoretical analyses: for example, about new methods of combining legal and non-legal regulatory techniques to achieve more efficient and effective outcomes.[4] The subject of IT law has been embraced as a worthy independent field of legal inquiry, with courses and books that lend themselves to wider reflections upon the information age, and its threats and opportunities – for lawyers and regulators, as well as society at large. In fact, to the extent that some of the former IT law subject matters are being absorbed by the traditional legal disciplines, IT law – to have legitimacy in itself – has to carve out a new identity that can only come in the form of inquiries into the special features and effects of IT and its interaction with the established legal order.

# The information age, IT law, and their paradoxes

The information age and the regulator's response to it are beyond bare infancy; yet we are still far removed from a time that would allow a detached account of technological and regulatory happenings. Both are peppered with tensions and fractions between multiple interest groups, with

---

2 This is often regarded by academics and students alike as being both a blessing and a curse: the blessing is that there is so much more material available upon which to draw for ideas and inspiration; the curse is that there is so much more through which to search in order to find relevant material.

3 See, e.g., Brian Napier, 'The future of information technology law' (1992) 51(1) CLJ 46; Stephen Saxby, 'A jurisprudence for information technology law' (1994) 2(1) IntJLIT 1; Lawrence Lessig, 'The law of the horse: What cyberlaw might teach' (1999b) 113 Harv L Rev 501; and Andres Guadamuz González, 'Attack of the killer acronyms: The future of information technology law' (2004) 18(3) IRLCT 411.

4 See, e.g., Lawrence Lessig, *Code: And Other Laws of Cyberspace*, 1999a, New York: Basic Books; Andrew Murray, *The Regulation of Cyberspace: Control in the Online Environment*, 2007, Abingdon: Glasshouse.

starkly contrasting narratives, with paradoxes and curiosities – some of these simply mirror, albeit more sharply, offline society; others are truly peculiar to the technological age; some are to be resolved; and others are likely to remain permanent fixtures. The internet is amorphous, fluid and constantly evolving. Where the future will lead us remains obscure, not the least because – taking a non-determinist view – it is in our hands: we are the makers of our future; it is our choices that will shape the information age of the future. So how far have we come to date? What are some of the emerging themes, trends, and paradoxes?

## Information as a source of power

A key issue in the information age is the use and abuse of information by economic and political actors as a means of control. It is possible, for instance, for those who provide the gateway to ICT – the information service providers (ISPs) – to exert significant and not necessarily consistent impediments by blocking access to certain material or by allowing content providers to pay a premium for a priority service. Such a practice would inevitably favour commercial providers over others. Although prejudicial behaviour against smaller content providers and consumers could, in principle, be dealt with by competition law, in both the US and EU, this led to calls to ensure net neutrality; the principle that 'internet service providers should enable access to all content and applications regardless of the source and without favouring or blocking particular products or websites'.[5] In other words it is not for ISPs to discriminate between different types of content, services and applications.

## Net neutrality

Net neutrality has been described as 'a deceptively simple phrase hiding a multitude of meanings'.[6] Originally the term arguably referred to a design principle that the network was itself 'neutral' and so it made no difference who was the provider, the user, what content was being made available and so on. Any departure from this general principle such as ISPs providing preferential rates or services for specific users or types of content has the propensity to be detrimental to more general access to the internet. 'Open access' and 'net neutrality' are thus very closely related and are often used interchangeably. In early discussions of the issues, Wu argued that the best way to ensure net neutrality in practice was by means of a non-discrimination rule.[7] Marsden distinguishes 'backward-looking net neutrality' which merely seeks to ensure that users are not disadvantaged as a result of a prejudicial ISP practice and 'forward-looking' net neutrality which permits a higher priced service with associated higher quality as long as it is offered on the same, fair, reasonable and non-discriminatory basis to all users. Overall net neutrality is likely to be difficult to achieve in practice without a more uniform approach to content regulation. The societal importance of the internet as the 'delivery mechanism for the Global Information Society' means that the matter cannot just be regarded as an issue for economic regulation of the market and Marsden advocates a co-regulatory approach 'to ensure oversight and remove the most obvious abuses by fixed and mobile ISPs'.[8] Other commentators have assessed whether or not specific rules are needed to ensure net neutrality or whether abuses of the market by providers could be dealt with by existing legal regimes, notably competition law.[9]

---

5 See www.oxforddictionaries.com/definition/english/net-neutrality
6 Christopher T. Marsden, 'Network Neutrality and Internet Service Provider Liability Regulation: Are the Wise Monkeys of Cyberspace Becoming Stupid?' (2011) 2 Global Policy 53, 54.
7 Tim Wu, 'Network Neutrality, Broadband Discrimination' (2003) 2 J Telecomm & High Tech L 141.
8 Marsden above and see discussion on co-regulation below at p 20.
9 See, e.g., Pablo Ibáñez Colomo, 'Discriminatory Conduct in the ICT Sector: A legal framework' pp 63–79 in G G Surblyté (ed), *Competition on the Internet*, 2015, Springer Verlag at p 64 suggesting that net neutrality is an example of issues relating to competition.

The regulatory debate over net neutrality began in the US where the US Communications Act gave the FCC general powers to regulate providers of information services and specific net neutrality rules were also originally included in the Open Internet Order 2010 which contained rules requiring transparency, no blocking and no unreasonable discrimination. As a result of the FCC reclassifying broadband as an 'information service' rather than a 'communication service', Verizon alleged that the FCC had exceeded its authority under the statute and in *Verizon v FCC*,[10] the first two of the net neutrality rules were held to fall outside the FCC's competence; in effect the FCC were impermissibly regulating broadband service providers as common carriers which it had no authority to do under the Communications Act. Although the net neutrality rules as initially drafted were invalid as they were not made under the correct legal framework, the court rejected Verizon's assertion that the FCC had no jurisdiction over broadband providers and the decision led to the FCC drafting new net neutrality rules which took into account the points made in the *Verizon* ruling as well as the more general objectives and rationales behind the need to ensure net neutrality. As an aside, in something of a volte-face for ISPs which previously had both argued strenuously that they were not to be regarded as 'speakers' and had taken advantage of immunity from suit on the basis of being a 'mere conduit', Verizon was effectively trying to establish that it had free speech rights and that there was an analogy between the provision of high speed internet access and newspaper publication.[11]

An apparently similar discussion concerning net neutrality was almost simultaneously taking place in Europe.[12] As early as 2011, the Body of European Regulators for Electronic Communications (BEREC) were charged with assessing the issues necessary to ensure an open and neutral internet including a consideration of the barriers to changing provider, blocking of internet traffic and issues surrounding the transparency and quality of service.[13] Then, in 2013 the European Commission put forward a proposal for a telecoms single market which referred to support for clear rules on net neutrality.[14] This eventually led to a Regulation being adopted in October 2015 although the term 'net neutrality' was lost as a result of various amendments along the way.[15] Nevertheless, the first recital states that the regulation 'aims to establish common rules to safeguard equal and non-discriminatory treatment of traffic in the provision of internet access services and related end-users' rights.' Articles 3 and 4 of the Regulation then refer to open internet access' but otherwise contain provisions which appear to relate to aspects of net neutrality.[16] Further, Article 5 gives BEREC a role in enforcement and will produce net neutrality guidelines by August 2016.[17] It appears that BEREC is treating open internet access as synonymous with net neutrality and it remains to be seen whether there are any nuances of definition which might affect what happens in practice.

---

10 740 F.3d 623 DC Cir (2014).

11 For further discussion see, e.g., T. Stephen Jenkins, 'Testing the privacy waters: Does recent FCC privacy enforcement signal the reclassification of broadband internet providers as common carriers?' (2015) 27 No. 3 Intell Prop & Tech LJ 3; Meredith Shell, 'Network neutrality and broadband service providers' First Amendment Right to Free Speech' (2014) 66 Fed Comm LJ 303; and Susan Crawford, 'First Amendment Common Sense' (2014) 127 Harv L Rev 2343. See also further discussion of net neutrality and ISPs in Chapter 3.

12 For general discussion of the net neutrality issues in Europe see, e.g., Jasper P. Sluijs, 'From competition to freedom of expression: introducing Article 10 ECHR in the European network neutrality debate' (2012) 12 HR LRev 509.

13 See https://ec.europa.eu/digital-agenda/en/eu-actions

14 Proposal for a Regulation of the European Parliament and of the Council laying down measures concerning the European single market for electronic communications and to achieve a Connected Continent, and amending Directives 2002/20/EC, 2002/21/EC and 2002/22/EC and Regulations (EC) No 1211/2009 and (EU) No 531/2012 COM (2013) 627 final p 6.

15 See http://eur-lex.europa.eu/procedure/EN/1041202 for a timeline of the legislative procedure.

16 Regulation (EU) 2015/2120 of the European Parliament and of the Council of 25 November 2015 laying down measures concerning open internet access and amending Directive 2002/22/EC on universal service and users' rights relating to electronic communications networks and services and Regulation (EU) No 531/2012 on roaming on public mobile communications networks within the Union (Text with EEA relevance) [2015] OJ L/310 pp 1–18.

17 See http://berec.europa.eu/eng/document_register/subject_matter/berec/press_releases/5588-statement-on-berec-work-to-produce-guidelines-for-the-implementation-of-net-neutrality-provisions-of-the-tsm-regulation.

## The surveillance society

Generally, once information is available online there is, on the one hand, the state seeking to use data, often generated by private communications, as a way in which to enhance law and order – recently under the guise of anti-terrorism measures. The initial helplessness of the state vis-à-vis activities on the internet has given way to the recognition of its unique potential for keeping a tab on the connections, whereabouts, and moves of everyone – on the premise that everyone harbours the risk of delinquencies. On the other hand, there are the large multinational companies scrambling for control over consumers through pinning down their preferences, shopping habits, lifestyle choices, and general web behaviour. The surveillance interests of these commercial actors sometimes overlap with those of consumers, but this is by no means always the case, as is illustrated, for example, by the debate surrounding 'cookies'.

The threat and, to some extent, the reality of a surveillance society driven by both private and public actors has prompted a heightened interest by civil society in data protection and privacy. Thus a large chunk of IT law can be understood as the conflict of the legitimate boundaries of surveillance with the legitimate expectation of a private life away from the prying eyes of government or business. How these legal boundaries have been shifting in recent years provides a wider commentary about our society in general. The privacy paradigm is not only in juxtaposition to the surveillance state, but equally to the relatively recent phenomenon of data accessibility. As data protection shields private information from government, the data accessibility movement pushes for greater transparency of public data – thus the information age has led to a sharpening of the private–public divide in terms of data management.

Of interest in this area – from a sociological, as well as a legal, perspective – is also the seeming paradox between the calls for privacy and the widespread bare-all attitudes on social networking sites. How can the very users who happily reveal the most personal information to the world at large still claim certain privacy entitlements in respect of that information? Legally, the solution to this paradox may draw upon notions of property/ownership:[18] personal information is a type of property the use of which is within the individual's control: he or she possesses it, can use and dispose of it as he or she sees fit, can transfer it – with or without payment – and may attach conditions to such transfers. In short, the individual is the ultimate arbiter of how, when, and why any information about himself or herself is used. Whether such proprietary notions are appropriate and valid in this personal-information context leaves much room for speculation, as did previous borderline property controversies, such as those concerning the human body: can and should the human body or any of its parts, such as genetic material, be treated in law like commodities?[19] Likewise, can and should we be able to commodify personal information? Interestingly, in the case of genetic material, it is also 'personal' information over which the person claims ownership.

But the issues relating to personal information relate not just to the information we think we control, such as that voluntarily placed on social media, but about the increasing use of personal information over which we have neither control nor even knowledge. Invisible personal data recording and surveillance is common, whether by commercial actors allegedly providing us with a service based on our perceived interests as revealed by our online activity, or by governments with a variety of motivations but frequently dressed up in the catch all of prevention of terrorism and preservation on national security. The extent of this type of activity was revealed when, in June 2013, Edward Snowden leaked documents which showed that the US National Security Agency (NSA) and UK GCHQ were accessing, storing and processing vast quantities of communications.

---

18 Other than copyright, because the use of the information by commercial or state actors may not actually entail any copying of the information.

19 Rohan Hardcastle, *Law and the Human Body: Property Rights, Ownership and Control*, 2007, Oxford: Hart Publishing. Traditionally under common law, the human body is not property: *Haynes' case* (1614) 77 ER 1389; *R v Lynn* (1788) 2 TR 733; *R v Price* (1884) 12 QB 247; *Williams v Williams* (1882) 20 Ch D 659.

These included phone calls, emails, messages on social media, browsing history; nothing was sacrosanct. A legal challenge brought by the ACLU was successful.[20] The court acknowledged that the case raised 'one of the most difficult issues in Fourth Amendment jurisprudence: the extent to which modern technology alters our traditional expectations of privacy'.[21] Although it noted that traditional notions of privacy could appear 'quaint' in the current technological environment, it acknowledged the perceived threat from sharing and collecting increasing amounts of information and decided that the scale of the data collection 'exceeds the scope of what Congress has authorized'.[22] Congress responded by passing the Freedom Act which is intended to stop the bulk collection of communications.[23] Although the ACLU referred to this as a 'testament to the significance of the Snowden disclosures',[24] it also pointed out that the amendments introduced are relatively modest. It thus seems doubtful that there will be significantly greater transparency as to what communication data are collected and how they are processed. In addition, despite these developments, Snowden himself is still wanted on charges under the Espionage Act. Although arguably, the vitriol directed at him has abated somewhat there are still calls from both ends of the political spectrum for him to stand trial in the US. The fallout from these revelations thus seems likely to continue for some time. In Europe, it has led to an action attempting to prevent personal data being transferred from the EU to the US which, as discussed further in Chapter 9, led to the CJEU declaring invalid the longstanding Safe Harbour agreement regulating the transfer of personal data between the EU and the US.

These questions go to the heart of foundational concepts such as personhood and property, including intangible property. They also touch upon wider issues about the legal status that should be attached to 'information' in the information age. This latter issue has been at the centre of possibly one of the most visible legal controversies concerning the internet – namely, the role and continued viability of copyright law. The pervasiveness of online piracy has forced regulators and commercial actors to re-evaluate accepted wisdoms and strategies regarding to how to protect intangible goods, and ultimately the feasibility and legitimacy of holding onto those goods.

## Empowerment through abundance of information?

Further trends of the information age with repercussions for IT law arise out of the sheer abundance of information. This has made possible the rise both of organised terrorist and other subversive groups and also to an increased amount of 'trolling' on social media and blogging sites. Whereas the use of the internet to peddle scurrilous invective and to incite and organise others to criminal and anti-social activities is not a recent phenomenon, the sheer amount of online information makes such behaviour more difficult to control. To start with, such abundance challenges the traditional information establishment and thereby creates challenges for the regulator. Information is no longer channelled through a few bottlenecks, such as the traditional print and broadcasting media companies, but can be produced and accessed by anyone from anywhere. The rise of the man-on-the-street publisher challenges traditional regulatory models, not least because of the internet's global nature. Furthermore, it is no longer only the acquisition of information that is problematic, but also its use after acquisition.

20 *ACLU v Clapper* 785 F.3d 787 (2nd Cir. 2015) – and see further discussion in Chapter 10.
21 *Ibid*, p 822.
22 *Ibid*, p 826.
23 Sabrina Saddiqui, 'Congress passes NSA surveillance reform in vindication for Snowden' (2015) *The Guardian*, 2 June, available online at: www.theguardian.com/us-news/2015/jun/02/congress-surveillance-reform-edward-snowden. The Freedom Act, although ending the NSA's collection of bulk telephone metadata, provided for a 180-day transition period which permitted the continued collection of data during this period. The Second Circuit subsequently denied a permanent injunction and allowed bulk collection of data to continue during this period on the grounds that an abrupt end to the programme would be contrary to public interest in effective surveillance of terrorist threats. See *ACLU v Clapper* 804 F.3d 617 (2nd Cir. 2015).
24 www.aclu.org/news/senate-passes-usa-freedom-act.

Paradoxically, an abundance of information does not necessarily equal empowerment. The traditional wisdom that 'information is power' is based on an assumption of scarcity of information. When information is no longer scarce, it is those who can most effectively filter, extract, prioritise, and discriminate who have a head start. In the same vein, Barry Schwartz, in *The Paradox of Choice: Why More is Less*,[25] argues that, from a psychological perspective, excessive choice or 'choice overload' does not lead to a happier life, but conversely may lead – in the search for perfection, the best deal, the best answer, etc – to anxiety, stress, dissatisfaction and depression, and (in the long term) the paralysis of decision-making. Then choice – a perceived prerequisite for personal freedom and self-determination – stifles the achievement of the very values that it is designed to underpin. For similar reasons, the abundance of information in the information age is, from a regulatory perspective, not an entirely positive phenomenon. For example, although consumers appear to have a greater online choice of products, as well as access to tools such as price comparison sites, and feedback and review sites, it is questionable whether these actually allow for better, more efficient decision-making and a more responsive, consumer-friendly market. More likely than not, even in the online age, consumer protection regulation is likely to retain its value.

Similarly, the abundance of information to which the regulator has access will not necessarily allow for greater regulatory efficiency. First, the instances in which a huge amount of information has been accidentally lost or made public by public servants show that the informational abundance also significantly multiplies the risk for the management of that data, with breaches of confidentiality and data protection and security threats looming large in the background.[26]

Second, by the same token, the retention of information as part of a regulatory agenda must be coupled with intelligent systems that allow for the efficient use of the information; otherwise, it is worthless. For example, there is evidence that the growing DNA database in the UK has not lived up to expectation in terms of delivering more convictions.[27]

Third, more information in the hands of the regulator may also lead to unexpected forms of overregulation, or what is referred to in medical terms as 'iatrogenic' illness – that is, the exacerbation of a disease or medical condition by the doctor's activity. For example, surveillance powers given initially to certain public authorities to fight terrorism and internet crime[28] have been hijacked by local councils to uncover relatively minor offences, such as dog fouling, fly-tipping, smoking in certain places, repairing vehicles in the street, or misrepresenting residence status within a certain school catchment area.[29] Whether such regulatory growth indeed achieves greater compliance or simply generates more and costly enforcement activity is debatable.[30] Certainly, more information may simply slow down regulatory efforts in key areas by creating regulatory activities in the margins.

The general point of all of the above examples is that it would be foolish to believe that the new abundance of information is delivering us a better regulatory environment. It creates at least as many regulatory problems as it resolves, and further research on this subject matter is long overdue.

---

25 2003, New York: Ecco.

26 One of the powerful reasons against a one-stop governmental 'superdatabase': Afua Hirsch, 'Superdatabase tracking all calls and emails legitimate, says DPP' (2009) *The Guardian*, 9 January, available online at: www.guardian.co.uk/uk/2009/jan/09/dpp-keir-starmer-superdatabase

27 Home Affairs Committee, *Eighth Report: The National DNA Database* (2010) HC 222-I, Session 2009–10, para 7, available online at: www.publications.parliament.uk/pa/cm200910/cmselect/cmhaff/222/22202.htm

28 Regulation of Investigatory Powers Act 2000.

29 Richard Ford, 'Smokers and tramps join 8,000 council surveillance targets' (2010) *Timesonline*, 25 May, available online at: www.timesonline.co.uk/tol/news/politics/article7134529.ece

30 That this is part of a more general trend can be seen from the discussion in the context of anti-cartel law enforcement in Christopher Harding, 'The Anti-Cartel Enforcement Industry: Criminological Perspectives on Cartel Criminalisation' in Caron Beaton-Wells and Ariel Ezrachi (eds), *Criminalising Cartels: Critical Studies of an International Regulatory Movement*, 2011, Oxford: Hart Publishing.

## Disembodied information

Another regulatory 'trauma' caused by the information age arises out of the nature of online information and, more specifically, its digital nature: its easy alterability, reproduction, and transport. Information on paper is relatively stable – it can be 'caught', locked up, and relied upon; digital information is slippery and ephemeral – one moment you see it, the next it is gone. Owners of intangible properties – that is, the music, software, and film industries, as well as the media – have felt the blow of this new type of information and are still struggling to imbue digital information with software characteristics that mimic their offline counterparts, or to find alternative avenues to protect their value. Also, both governmental agencies and commercial players have had to find new mechanisms to ensure the authenticity and reliability of digital information – because data may be quickly and, to all intents and purposes, untraceably amended, concepts such as 'original' or 'copy' make no real sense in the digital context.

## The alleged democratisation effect of the internet

The information age also challenges many established power parameters, but often in ways that are not immediately obvious and which at times appear counterintuitive. For example, in the mid-1990s, there were those who argued that the internet was a democratising force that would spell the end of authoritarian regimes. This view is encapsulated in some of the judicial comment in *ACLU v Reno I*,[31] for instance, with its reference to the 'never ending worldwide conversation'; 'a far more speech enhancing medium than print'; 'the most participatory marketplace of mass speech that . . . the world has yet seen' in which all can have a voice and all can be heard. The 'vast democratic forums of the internet' referred to by the US Supreme Court might have been taken to herald an egalitarian Utopia. But this has certainly not been realised, if indeed it was ever very likely. Although it is undeniably true that the rise of social media has certainly contributed to giving anyone who wants 'a voice that resonates farther than it could from any soapbox'; the internet is a forum where both good and bad things happen. Far from encouraging open and democratic debate, there are many examples of individuals refraining from making online comment and discussion because of the threat or the reality of abusive and malicious responses. A downside of the increased ability to communicate on the internet is the rise and rise of internet 'trolling'. The ability to speak freely and often anonymously has been abused since the early days of computer networks as evidenced by some of the early defamation cases. But the rise of social networks and the proliferation of mobile devices leading to many users being almost permanently connected have exacerbated this tendency. Some such messages, although unpleasant, may be hasty and/or ill-advised, some may threaten the social order, some may be intended as a joke – the dividing line between all of these may not always be easy to discern in other than extreme cases and the legal response is patchy and sometimes inconsistent.[32]

Despite the rhetoric of the 'borderless world', within their geographical borders, states have also responded in the ways which might be expected depending on their political, cultural and legal traditions. Many authoritarian regimes have remained perfectly intact despite the internet. Within some of these regimes, however, the internet has given a voice to dissent albeit often at great personal cost to the speaker; many cyberdissidents have been imprisoned in the more restrictive regimes.[33] In the meantime, the internet has been utilised by terrorist and criminal elements to organise their activities, which has prompted countries with long democratic traditions, such as the UK, to make significant inroads into well entrenched civil liberties, such as privacy or the

---

31 929 F Supp 824 (US DC Penn 1996). See further discussion in Chapter 8.
32 See www.eff.org/deeplinks/2013/07/manning-verdict-and-hacker-madness-prosecution-strategy. Hitoshi Nasu, 'State secrets law and national security' (2015) 64 ICLQ 365.
33 At the time of writing, the organisation Reporters without Borders stated that 173 netizens were imprisoned in a number of countries; most in China but with significant numbers in Iran, Vietnam and Syria and other states. See https://rsf.org/en/news/rsfs-2015-round-54-journalists-held-hostage-worldwide

presumption of innocence, in the name of anti-terrorist measures – thus perhaps weakening, rather than strengthening, democratic traditions.[34] On the other hand, it can be argued that the internet is fostering bottom-up democracy on a worldwide level by stimulating vast public debates on political news and often mobilising political activism. There has been an astonishing rise in citizen journalism – the BBC apparently receives up to 10,000 pieces of user-generated content each day.[35] In countries where the press is the mouthpiece of the state, citizen journalists are often the preferred source of news and political comment. So, overall there has been a dramatic rise in speech of all types from a whole range of sources but, in tandem, there is also evidence of significant government repression of that speech.

Democratic principles do not just relate to freedom of expression but also to freedom of information. The Snowden revelations had wider ramifications than the collection of personal communications; they showed that particular targets included international summits, embassies and EU offices. While Snowden sought refuge in Russia, at the same time Bradley Manning was prosecuted under the US Espionage Act for passing documents containing a range of material from specific information relating to the war in Afghanistan to more blanket release of US diplomatic cables.

From a commercial perspective, it was initially assumed that the internet would benefit businesses by opening world markets to them, and benefit consumers by giving them access to worldwide businesses. Again, while this expectation may not be entirely unrealised, on some levels, the possible benefits have clearly not been fulfilled. A UK consumer who would have previously bought books or music from a variety of mainly local or national businesses now buys online, mainly from international powerhouses such as Amazon or iTunes with which few national businesses can effectively compete. So rather than creating a more level playing field, the internet encourages monopolies or, at least, gravitates towards global market leaders. National competition law is hard pressed to rise to the challenge.

## IT law as a trigger for regulatory re-evaluations

Last, but not least, the internet also provokes fundamental questions about regulation: generally, what are the appropriate forms of regulation for online activities, how much regulation is required, and who should regulate? Regulation of and on the internet has been considered and examined in many different situations. For example, when it comes to the protection of minors from online adult material, the question is whether it is the state or the parent who should assume the protective role? Should the internet herald a new age of governmental paternalism, or a new age of personal responsibility? Should it be the state that protects us from online villains as well as from ourselves (for example, in respect of online gambling) and, if so, how should it go about doing it? These are not issues that can, in any meaningful way, be neatly contained within the world of technology. Overall as expressed by Joyce:

> It is remarkable how unregulated the Internet is at the level of international law and how regulation is viewed through lenses as various as crime, security, child protection, morality, development, culture, speech or privacy. Ideas of infrastructural equality (net neutrality) and broader notions of democratic freedom (to communicate, exchange, compete for market access and even to be anonymous or forgotten) have flavoured much of the discourse regarding Internet regulation, but so too have more authoritarian notions of government control, surveillance and punishment. On the one hand, the Internet and associated digital media technologies are presented as revolutionary, emancipatory and even as tools for democratization

---

34 For example the Data Retention and Investigatory Powers Act 2014 which was fast-tracked through Parliament in July 2014 and, at the time of writing, is the subject of a legal challenge – see further discussion in Chapter 10.
35 Vicky Baker, 'How far can you trust citizen journalism on the internet?' *New Statesman* (25 March 2015).

and the rebranding of liberal internationalism. On the other hand, the Internet represents information overload, the 'deluge' of big data, mass privacy and copyright violation and the resurgence of surveillance culture and control.[36]

As IT, with all of its peculiarities, becomes integrated with every facet of our lives, it is no longer simply the traditional law that gets transplanted to the technological world, but it is also the legal parameters that emerge from that world that shape our ordinary law. This means that the information age forces us to fundamentally re-evaluate law and regulation in our society: its function or role, its efficiency, its costs and benefits, and any alternative avenues for shaping behaviour.

# Regulatory theory

Regulatory theory – in the socio-legal sense of that term, rather than the political economy and economics sense – is a relatively new arrival to IT law, although it has a considerable history in areas such as environment law and utilities law. 'Regulation' is a commonly used term, but one that, as Baldwin and Cave note, may be utilised in several ways. It can refer to a specific set of commands devised for a particular purpose. More broadly, it can cover all government action designed to respond to a particular type of behaviour or activity. Finally, it can refer to any form of influence that affects behaviour, whether or not this emanates from the state or from other sources, such as the market.[37] The last of these definitions is considered here, in the context of the interrelationship of various factors, including the law, which are combined to 'regulate' the uses of IT.

## Lessig's regulatory model

In his book *Code: And Other Laws of Cyberspace*,[38] Lawrence Lessig talks of the above factors, or 'modalities of regulation', as being law, norms, market, and architecture. His main thesis is simple and applicable beyond the technological realm – which perhaps explains Lessig's popular success. According to Lessig, law – popularly understood as a command coupled with the threat of an *ex post* sanction for a violation – is only one of the ways in which behaviour may be regulated, and not necessarily the most efficient one. He lists other factors or restraints that may have an impact on our behaviour: social norms; markets; and what he refers to as 'architecture'.[39] Social norms will control how we behave in different circumstances and therefore exert a regulatory effect. Prices within a market can, for example, regulate the extent to which people are able to travel and therefore impact on their lifestyle. By 'architecture', Lessig means 'the physical world as we find it', which obviously has consequences for the way in which we are able to behave.

Importantly, the state cannot only use 'law' (direct regulation) to achieve a certain desired result, but can also influence and change the other three factors via regulation. Here, the regulation is indirect and often invisible to the subject, because it is channelled through the non-legal modalities. As an illustration, Lessig uses the example of the regulation of smoking and the consumption of cigarettes: the law may ban smoking (that is, the direct regulation of behaviour); it may tax cigarettes (that is, market regulation); it may provide a public education programme (that is, an attempt to regulate social norms); or it may control the amount of nicotine in cigarettes (that is, changing the 'architecture' of cigarettes). Clearly, all of these may have an effect on the consumption of cigarettes, the benefit of the regulation, but each also has a cost attached. Given the value that society places on autonomy, it may be that the education approach is preferred to the

---

36 Daniel Joyce, 'Internet freedom and human rights' (2015) 26 E.J.I.L 493, 496.
37 Robert Baldwin and Martin Cave, *Understanding Regulation: Theory, Strategy and Practice*, 1999, Oxford: Oxford University Press, p 2.
38 1999, New York: Basic Books. The same ideas are more succinctly put in Laurence Lessig 'The law of the horse: What Cyberlaw might teach' (1991) 113 Harv L Rev 501, 506ff.
39 *Ibid*, 507. Lessig also calls architecture 'code'; hence the title of his book.

'architectural' regulation.[40] A common feature of regulation by architecture is that it removes the individual's ability to choose whether or not to comply.

Alternatively, 'norms', 'market', and 'architecture' can be left untouched by the regulator, who may leave it to the individuals to protect themselves as well as they can. For example, having reliable locks and security alarms (that is, architecture or code) provides the individual with greater protection against burglary than any offence written in a statute book. In the IT context, code comes to the forefront of the regulatory debate, because the entire regulatory domain is man-made and thus relatively easily manipulated by private or public actors:

> Many believe that cyberspace simply cannot be regulated. Behavior in cyberspace . . . is beyond government's reach. The anonymity and multijurisdictionality of cyberspace makes control by government in cyberspace impossible. The nature of the space makes behavior there *unregulable*. This belief about cyberspace is wrong, but wrong in an interesting way. It assumes either that the nature of cyberspace is fixed – that its architecture, and the control it enables, cannot be changed – or that government cannot take steps to change this architecture. Neither assumption is correct. Cyberspace has no nature; it has no particular architecture that cannot be changed.[41]

Thus influencing the architecture of the internet to achieve a regulatory objective becomes a highly attractive option for the regulator. A classic example would be the creation of a criminal offence prohibiting the circumvention of digital rights management technology (technologically embedded copyright protection) or requiring internet service providers (ISPs) to block illegal sites.

The advantages of regulation by code are numerous. Code (used to implement legal provisions) generally leaves users – other than the technologically savvy – no choice whether to comply with the law or not, because they are physically prevented from non-compliance. Thus the compliance rate of indirect regulation via code is often close to 100 per cent.[42] In addition, code is self-enforcing – thus saving significant costs that would be associated with ordinary law enforcement. Finally, to comply with code, the subject need not have any awareness of it nor of the legal duties that the code implements. In contrast, to ensure compliance with direct regulation (that is, a norm backed by a sanction), it is necessary for the government to raise awareness of the law, because such awareness is a prerequisite for the subject's decision to comply with it.

This then brings us to the disadvantages of code as a regulatory tool. Because code does not need visibility to be effective, the state can easily influence code – and thereby behaviour – without attracting much attention. So regulation through code may therefore lack transparency and proper democratic accountability. Lessig argues that the 'government gets an effect at no political cost. It gets the benefit of what would be an illegal and controversial regulation, that is, without even having to admit any regulation exists'.[43] In other words:

> Indirection misdirects responsibility. When a government uses other structures of constraint to effect a constraint it could impose directly, it muddies the responsibility for that constraint and so undermines political accountability. If transparency is a value in constitutional government, indirection is its enemy.[44]

---

40  113 Harv L Rev 501, 512.

41  *Ibid*, 505 (internal marks omitted).

42  Although, as Lessig notes, the modalities interact with each other, and the use of indirect regulation via code may result in negative social or market responses. For example, regional coding on DVDs – a form of regulation by code imposed by manufacturers – created a thriving industry in mod chips and software hacks: a market-based response.

43  Lessig Code is Law, p 98.

44  *Ibid*, p 96.

A second problem of regulation through code is that it removes 'moral agency' or personal autonomy. We do not need to decide whether we want to comply with the 'law' or not, because that decision is forced upon us through the physical restraint. Some may argue that this cannot be a bad thing: the habitual compliers simply do what they would have done anyway and those that might have broken the law are forced to comply with it. The result is an end to freeloading and thus greater fairness all around. However, as Brownsword convincingly argues, liberal society gives people on the whole the freedom to comply or not to comply with the law.[45] This is not simply legal indulgence, but an essential attribute of liberal society in which personal choices (even if they are bad and later penalised) are respected as a requirement of human dignity and being an autonomous actor. In Brownsword's words:

> a fully techno-regulated community is no longer an operative moral community . . . [I]f techno-regulators know how to stop us from being bad only by, at the same time, stopping us from being good . . . [then ordinary law] for all its imperfections, has something going for it.[46]

Beyond these two main reasons, technological solutions to regulatory problems may (depending on their sophistication) also be too effective. Too effective? Legal restrictions in the case of direct regulation are invariably accompanied by defences or exceptions. Yet code tends to be better at implementing the main restriction, without taking into account any of the exceptions. This makes it a 'blunt force tool', inflexible and insensitive to other interests and values. For example, digital rights management technology has frequently been accused of trumping the 'fair dealing' or 'fair use' defence to copyright infringement.[47]

Last, but by no means least, code — as employed by private or public actors in cyberspace to protect certain values — often involves the recreation of characteristics from the physical world, given that these characteristics are essential for the proper functioning of the traditional law. For example, in the copyright law context, the perfection of digital copies is problematic because it gives users with access to a copy no incentive to buy the official product — because the official product would in no way be distinguishable from the 3,056th copy of that product. A regulatory solution to this dilemma would be to program digital data in such a way that their quality degrades with an increasing number of copies:

> With the code changed, when a machine is used to copy a particular CD, a serial number from the CD is recorded in the tape machine's memory. If the user tries to copy that tape more than a limited number of times, the machines adjusts the quality of the copy. As the copies increase, the quality is degraded.[48]

Of course code is, of itself, neutral and as well as constraining behaviour can equally well be used to facilitate infringement. While the use of technical protection mechanisms to protect copyright may raise issues of over-regulation, code used to enable file sharing provides a very efficient way of breaching copyright; it has been suggested that 'P2P filesharing represents the most ambitious effort to undermine an existing legal regime using computer code.'[49]

---

45 Roger Brownsword, 'Code, control, and choice: Why east is east and west is west' (2005) 25 Legal Studies 1.
46 Ibid, 20.
47 See further discussion in Chapter 4.
48 Lessig Code is Law, p 128.
49 Timothy Wu, 'When Code isn't Law' (2003) 89 Va L Rev 679, 683 and see discussion in Chapter 4.

## Moving on from Lessig

The virtue of Lessig's approach is its simplicity and the reality is much more complex. Mayer-Schönberger's critique of Lessig's theory leads him to conclude that the premise that code is law 'suffers from devastating structural weaknesses.'[50] Two specific reasons which he identifies for this are that a view of the market as based on information symmetries is not the only way of conceptualising the market and it also portrays a relatively simplistic view of the relationship between technology and society which has now become 'much more complex and multi-directional'.[51] In the internet environment as in other regulatory spheres, it is rarely the case that effective regulation can be achieved by only one method and in practice a more nuanced approach is likely to be required. Regulatory scholars have developed other approaches such as responsive regulation, smart regulation and risk regulation as ways of accommodating many variables within the regulatory mix.[52] Scott and Murray, for example, have developed Lessig's ideas in a more detailed fashion.[53] They propose four top-level categories, which broadly correspond to Lessig's four 'modalities of regulation'. In their terminology, these are 'control systems' (that is, methods of controlling or modifying behaviour):

- hierarchical control (Lessig's 'law');
- competition-based control (Lessig's 'market');
- community-based control (Lessig's 'norms'); and
- design-based control (Lessig's 'architecture').

However, Scott and Murray elaborate on these 'control systems' by identifying three stages in the regulatory process in respect of each of the above four modalities:

(1)   *Standard setting* – that is, what is the source and content of the restraint?
(2)   *Information gathering* – that is, how does the restraint interact with its subject? how is its compliance monitored?
(3)   *Behaviour modification* – that is, how is the restraint enforced or made effective vis-à-vis the potential violator/wrongdoer?

Each of these control systems may operate alone or in conjunction with one or more of the other three to provide a regulatory matrix.[54]

Murray and Scott note that even where there may appear to be a 'pure basis of regulation' (that is, where legal or other hierarchical measures alone appear to be the sole method of regulation), it may still be influenced indirectly by other control systems.

An example from data protection demonstrates that there may be overlaps between, for instance, hierarchical control in the legislative framework and community-based control based on general expectations of responsible data processing. Thus a subject access request that discovers a breach of the DPA 1998 by a data controller may trigger both a hierarchical control response, such as an audit by the ICO, and a community control response, such as a boycott of the data controller. Additionally, in a business environment, the information about the breach may be seized upon by competitors of the breaching data controller and used by them to create competitive advantage in the marketplace: for example, in terms of attracting customers who would otherwise have gone

---

50  Viktor Mayer-Schönberger, 'Demystifying Lessig' (2008) Wis L Rev 713, 745.
51  Ibid, 746.
52  See, generally, Robert Baldwin, Martin Cave and Martin Lodge, *Understanding Regulation: Theory, Strategy and Practice* 2nd edn, 2011, OUP.
53  Andrew Murray and Colin Scott, 'Controlling the new media: Hybrid responses to new forms of power' (2002) 65(4) MLR 491.
54  Ibid, 504. See also Ian Brown and Christopher Marsden, *Regulating Code: Good Governance and Better Regulation in the Information Age*, 2013, Cambridge, MA: MIT Press.

to the breaching data controller, or in terms of justifying their higher prices by virtue of claiming more effective data privacy practices. Thus competition-based control is also likely to play a role in some circumstances.

Given the potential complexity of the interaction between the control systems, it is clear that those wishing to regulate a particular sphere of activity need to consider very carefully the context of the regulatory goal that they are seeking to achieve, and seek not only to achieve the best approach available from the combination of the control systems, but also to be careful not to create 'perverse incentives' for those affected by the regulatory approach eventually adopted.

An example of such a 'perverse incentive' would be a scenario in which the regulatory goal was to prevent obscene material being displayed on websites. Obvious chokepoints for such content are the internet intermediaries that host the websites. A regulator seeking to use those chokepoints might thus decide to require those intermediaries to address the issue, by making them legally liable for not ensuring its removal. However, would it not be unfair if an intermediary were to be held responsible in the absence of knowledge about the content? A regulatory solution might be that the liability falls on an intermediary only if it is, or should have been, aware of the obscene material within its control.

What are the implications of this for an intermediary? Does it make it more or less likely that the intermediary will take proactive measures to prevent obscene content being made available, through exercising editorial control? As discussed elsewhere in this book,[55] an intermediary that takes proactive measures (rather than simply waiting for someone to complain about the material) is potentially opening itself up to greater liability, because exercising editorial function makes it more likely that it should have known about the material. Setting up an editorial process that then fails in some circumstances is thus more likely to have serious consequences for the intermediary than having no editing process at all. In such circumstances, a pragmatic intermediary might very well decide to do less screening of material on its hosted websites, because it could then more plausibly claim that it was unaware of the unwanted content.[56] An alternative solution might be to grant all intermediaries immunity from liability – but they are then only likely to be proactive in responding to unwanted content if they are provided with sufficient incentive to do so. It would appear therefore that the achievement of the regulatory goal of controlling certain forms of internet content will take more than a simple hierarchical control system.

# Regulatory strategies

Another way of viewing the types of process outlined above is to think of them in terms of regulatory strategies variously involving legal authority, the deployment of wealth, the use of markets, the provision of information, direct action, or the conferment of rights.[57] These capabilities or resources can be utilised by government to fashion a range of basic strategies. There are many examples of the use of such regulatory strategies in IT law and this section will briefly consider some of the key regulatory strategies. It does not aim either to be an exhaustive overview of possible strategies or to explore the concepts in great depth, both of which have been done at length elsewhere,[58] but rather to provide the reader with a basic introduction to the area. Examples of the

---

55 See Chapter 3.
56 See, e.g., the US case *Stratton Oakmont, Inc v Prodigy Services Co*, 1995 WL 323710 (NY Sup Ct, 1995); cf *Cubby, Inc v CompuServe Inc*, 776 F Supp 135 (SDNY 1991).
57 Baldwin and Cave, above, 34, citing Christopher C Hood, *The Tools of Government*, 1983, London: Macmillan, p 5; Terence C Daintith, 'The techniques of government' in J Jowell and D Oliver (eds), *The Changing Constitution*, 3rd edn, 1994, Oxford: Oxford University Press.
58 For example, Baldwin and Cave, above; Anthony Ogus, *Regulation: Legal Form and Economic Theory*, 1994, Oxford: Oxford University Press; Robert Baldwin, Colin Scott, and Christopher Hood (eds), *A Reader on Regulation*, 1998, Oxford: Oxford University Press.

use of different approaches in the regulation of IT are used as illustrations, but the general points raised in the subsequent discussion should be kept in mind when considering any of the topics that are discussed in the rest of the book.

## Criminal and administrative law: Command and control

A common regulatory technique is often referred to as 'command and control',[59] defined by Baldwin as 'the exercise of influence by imposing standards backed by criminal sanctions'.[60] In command-and-control regulation, therefore, legal rules are imposed by government and failure to meet the standards imposed in these provisions can result in the imposition of standards – usually criminal, but sometimes also administrative. The reactive nature of command-and-control regulation encourages highly prescriptive and inflexible rules. It engenders a view that problems will be identified by central government and that rules created will then be dealt with by a suitable regulatory agency. Thus, despite any particular knowledge and expertise that they may possess, the role of the regulated is essentially passive. Command-and-control regulation is very popular with governments, and sometimes also with the public too: '. . . there is a powerful and radical segment of opinion which, seeing a social evil, recommends a law of strict liability as the best legislative panacea.'[61] Such rules can be presented as evidence that action is being taken on issues of concern – that 'something is being done'. This can give the impression of an immediate and beneficial effect, even though, as we shall see, there may be adverse effects that only gradually come to light. As well as being popular with some, command-and-control regulation has some other important advantages: it can be both clear and straightforward both for the regulated and the regulator;[62] and, once formulated, there is usually very little discretion available to either side to deviate from the required standard. However, command-and-control regulation may not be uniformly effective and may be more suitable for use in some circumstances than others. In particular, although it may be fairly easy to enforce against corporations and other large institutions, it is much more difficult to apply to more diffuse and transitory operators, of which there are many examples on the internet. Enforcement of command-and-control regulation can also be problematic because there are considerable costs associated with compliance, inspection, detection, and enforcement.[63] Again in terms of activity on the internet, the difficulties in enforcement can be one of the major problems for the effective use of command-and-control regulation.

The Data Protection Act 1998 provides an example of rules of the command-and-control type. Data controllers are required to undertake particular actions, such as notification, and refrain from other actions, such as processing for the purposes of direct marketing. Further, there are both criminal and administrative sanctions that can be imposed for failure to comply with these requirements.[64] Restrictions are also placed on other third parties in particular circumstances. Adherence to these standards is overseen by a specific regulator: in the UK, this is the Information Commissioner's Office (ICO). Unlike some regulators,[65] this office does not have its own rule-making capacity, but both provides guidance on, and enforces, the regulatory standards set out in the legislation. The

---

59 See, e.g., Anthony Ogus, above, p 5; Baldwin, Scott, and Hood, above, p 24.
60 Robert Baldwin, 'Regulation: After "command and control"' in K Hawkins (ed), *The Human Face of Law*, 1997, Oxford: Clarendon, ch 3, p 65.
61 Charles D Drake and Frank B Wright, *Law of Health and Safety at Work: The New Approach*, 1983, London: Sweet and Maxwell, p 14.
62 Neil A Gunningham and Peter Grabosky, *Smart Regulation: Designing Environmental Policy*, 1998, Oxford: Oxford University Press, p 41.
63 See, e.g., ibid, pp 42–5. Interestingly, when discussing firms that are readily identifiable and accessible, the authors cite Robert A Kagan, 'Regulatory enforcement' in DH Rosenbloom and RD Schwartz (eds), *Handbook of Regulation and Administrative Law*, 1994, New York: Dekker, as referring to 'the difference between regulating "elephants" and "foxes": it is harder for elephants to hide' – a clear foreshadowing of Peter P Swire's later analysis of the Data Protection Directive, 'Of elephants, mice, and privacy: International choice of law and the internet' (1998) 32 International Lawyer 991.
64 For further details, see Chapter 9.
65 For example, the old Financial Services Authority: see Andromachi Georgosouli, 'The nature of the FSA policy of rule use: A critical overview' (2008) 28(1) Legal Studies 119.

use of the command-and-control approach in the data protection regulatory regime illustrates a number of the general problems with this type of regulation. In practice, the reliance placed on the ability of data subjects to question data controllers about the use of their personal data is difficult to apply both generally and in relation to use on the internet or in m-commerce. If data subjects see no benefit in engaging with the regulatory process, then the overall effectiveness of the regulatory regime will be significantly reduced. In addition, as the technology develops, the rules may no longer be so easily applicable to the new environment.[66] This is very apparent in data protection legislation: the original rules were developed for large, centralised databanks, and have not proved easy to translate to the amorphous and diffuse use of personal data on the internet.[67]

## Self-regulation and 'enforced' self-regulation

In IT law, the standard answer to the question posed above is 'self-regulation'. The difficulty with that answer lies in determining what exactly 'self-regulation' means. At one level, self-regulation can be used in a literal sense to refer to the individual's ability to control his or her own behaviour. More broadly, it may be used to refer to any regulatory activity that is not initiated by the state, whether originating in individual or collective actions. In the general field of corporate and business regulation, it is frequently used to describe the rules and codes of conduct imposed on their members by trade and professional organisations. Self-regulation is thus a fluid and amorphous concept that it has been suggested has 'no accepted definition'.[68] It is frequently merely one element of an overarching centralised regulatory scheme, but, within that context, can run right across the spectrum from informal, non-binding, and voluntary procedures, to rules that are enforceable through the courts. As this suggests, there is no accepted model of self-regulation: self-regulatory schemes may exhibit varying degrees of formality; and the extent to which third parties participate in rule formulation, enforcement, or supervision may differ, as may whether or not they have any legal effect. In many cases, self-regulation is 'much better seen not as a pervading regulatory approach, but as part of a shifting set of regulatory techniques, the mix depending on external political, economic, and social factors'.[69]

The availability of appropriate sanctions and rewards for good compliance records may also be issues in the comparison between the desirability and efficacy of self-regulation vis-à-vis those available in relation to command-and-control regulation. Violations may be dealt with relatively informally – for example, without necessarily having recourse to external legal procedures. This may be both quicker, less resource-intensive, and more effective, but will also be less publicly visible, raising both problems of perceived leniency and the spectre of lack of accountability. Cynics might also suspect the level of achievement to be significantly lower than that for traditionally enforced command-and-control rules, and this may well be so if there is no motivation towards compliance with self-regulatory standards. On the other hand, it is also possible for the reverse to be the case and for self-regulation to raise standards by inspiring 'ethical standards of conduct which extend beyond the letter of the law'.[70]

One particular reason why self-regulation has the propensity to be effective is that those directly involved with the activity themselves become the repository of the relevant expertise and information. Proponents would further suggest that, in consequence, self-regulators have a special appreciation of what will be seen as reasonable regulatory demands, and that this will, inevitably,

---

66 Andrew Charlesworth, 'The future of UK data protection regulation' (2006) 11(1) Inform Secur Tech Rep 46, 47 and 50, with regard to 'instrument failure', 'information failure', 'implementation failure', and 'motivation failure'; Julia M Black, 'Decentring regulation: Understanding the role of regulation and self regulation in a "post-regulatory" world' (2001) 54 CLP 103.

67 For a consideration of the development of data protection legislation in this context, see Chapter 9.

68 Baldwin, Scott, and Hood, above, p 27.

69 Tony Prosser, 'Self-regulation, co-regulation and the Audio-visual Media Services Directive' (2008) 31(1) J Consum Pol 99, 100.

70 Neil Gunningham and Joseph Rees, 'Industry self-regulation: An institutional perspective' (1997) 19 Law & Pol 363, 366.

lead to higher levels of voluntary compliance and consequent regulatory efficiency. Capture theorists, on the other hand, would say that this is precisely the mechanism that allows the industry to influence the regulatory process in its favour. Certainly, the public perception – and, in many cases, this may be confirmed by the reality – is that self-regulators do not have the commitment to regulate in the public interest unless that interest happens to coincide with their private interests. On occasion, this fear may not be realised if the alternative to administering a self-regulatory scheme is external regulation and state intervention. Although there are some powerful and vocal advocates of self-regulation, there is probably an equal level of scepticism amongst those who doubt that it has any positive attributes, as summed up by the comment that 'self-regulation is a euphemism which means no regulation at all'.[71] This polarisation of views is summed up eloquently by Black:

> . . . self-regulation is such a normatively loaded term. For some it denotes regulation that is responsive, flexible, informed, targeted, and which at once stimulates and draws on the internal morality of the sector or organization being regulated. For others it is self-serving, self-interested, lacking in sanctions, beset with free rider problems and simply a sham. The rhetoric affects policy attitudes and decisions and can result in poor regulatory design.[72]

Ogus notes that 'lawyers and economists have been equally scathing in their criticisms of self-regulation',[73] and that these criticisms have been based on the lack of accountability, the potential for abuse, etc. He goes on to point out, however, that a number of traditional criticisms are 'based on a narrow, stereotyped conception of the phenomenon'. Although the criticisms can certainly be justified in some cases, it is possible to conceive of systems that take these drawbacks into account and also benefit from the perceived advantages.

The UK's Internet Watch Foundation (IWF) provides an interesting example of a number of the above issues. The IWF was established in 1996 by a variety of internet companies as a mechanism to allow the public and IT professionals to report criminal online content in a secure and confidential way. Initially envisaged as a means to tackle the dissemination of child sexual abuse images online anywhere in the world, its remit has since expanded to include the reporting of criminally obscene adult content and incitement to racial hatred content hosted in the UK.

The IWF describes itself as 'an independent regulatory body funded by the EU and the online industry' and that its self-regulatory partnership approach is widely recognised as a model of good practice in combating the abuse of technology for the dissemination of criminal content.[74] So how does this 'self-regulation' operate in practice? Clearly the involvement, cooperation and financial support of the online industry is indicative of self-regulation, as is the fact that it receives no direct government funding. However, a few years after it was established, changes were made to its role and structure following a governmental review of its operation[75] suggesting that it cannot be regarded as entirely independent of government scrutiny. More recently a human rights audit of its operation[76] concluded that although it was funded by private industry, it carried out public acts and so its policies and decisions were susceptible to judicial review.

---

71 Paul Rose, *Hansard* HC, vol 871, col 1323 (1974).
72 Black, above, p 115.
73 Ogus, above, p 108.
74 See www.iwf.org.uk/about-iwf
75 For a summary of the work and history of the IWF, see https://www.iwf.org.uk/about-iwf/iwf-history/iwf-highlights
76 Petley, above, and see Wills, *Hansard* HC, vol 325, col 207–8W (9 February 1999). For a more recent examination of the operation of the IWF see Christopher Marsden, Steve Simmons, Ian Brown, Lorna Woods, Adam Peake, Neil Robinson, Stijn Hoorens and Lisa Klautzer, *Options for and Effectiveness of Internet Self- and Co-Regulation Phase 2: Case Study Report* (15 January 2008). Prepared for European Commission DG Information Society & Media. Available at SSRN: http://ssrn.com/abstract=1281374, pp 81–97. *A Human Rights Audit of the Internet Watch Foundation* Lord Macdonald of River Glaven (2014) available online at: www.iwf.org.uk/accountability/human-rights-audit

Additionally, without the panoply of UK illegal content legislation,[77] the IWF would have a much harder time gaining compliance from its full members. Indeed, despite explicit government pressure, some ISPs still resist utilising its blacklist.[78] Further, the 'notice and takedown' process, with provisions in the Electronic Commerce (EC Directive) Regulations 2002[79] giving information society service providers (ISSPs) a limited immunity from liability for hosting illegal content in certain situations, provides the IWF with significant additional leverage in its role as a private sector regulator. This would be lacking if ISSPs were to have full immunity from content liability. Finally, the IWF obtains additional powers through its memorandum of understanding with the Crown Prosecution Service (CPS) and the Association of Chief Police Officers (ACPO), linked to s 46 of the Sexual Offences Act 2003, which permits its staff to investigate criminal child sexual abuse content without being prosecuted for looking at/making illegal content in the course of their duties.[80]

Given all the foregoing, it can be seen that the IWF's claim to a self-regulatory role places a particularly broad interpretation upon the term 'self-regulation'. What it does do though is carry out a regulatory function at virtually no public cost; it has access to far more technical expertise than could reasonably be expected of a government department; together with other recognised advantages of self-regulation, namely being more readily accepted by regulatees and being able to respond quickly to changing circumstances. Nonetheless there are potential downsides. Unless the regulatory process is legally enforceable, potential regulatees will still be able to opt out. As noted above, some ISPs do refuse to use the IWF blacklist. The rules applied by the self-regulatory body may be designed more to benefit the regulated than the public interest. The use of the blacklist and 'notice and takedown' is designed to protect the ISPs and, although there is a right of appeal, there is no explicit onus to balance these actions with other interests such as freedom of expression. Finally, notwithstanding the possibility of judicial review, there is no general requirement of openness, transparency, accountability, and acceptability to the public generally, or to users of ISP services specifically. Both regulatees and government can thus implement policy goals without direct public scrutiny.

The potential downsides to the self-regulatory process may be overcome by what is sometimes termed 'enforced self-regulation', or 'regulated self-regulation'.[81] Under such a process, the government might, for example, allow the IWF (or possibly its full members as individual entities) to make its own rules, but require those rules to be approved by a government agency in conjunction with public-interest groups. Conformity with the approved rules would be monitored, via the IWF (or possibly by a company's own internal inspectors), which would then be subject to external scrutiny – again in conjunction with public-interest groups. Breach of the approved rules would result in legal sanction.

An example of a regulatory process similar to this model, developing organically, can be seen in the case of website data privacy protection policies in the USA. In the USA, there is no overarching data privacy regime, as there is in the UK. However, many US websites saw having a privacy policy as a useful mechanism through which to build trust with their customers. Despite having made such commitments to their customers through their privacy policies, some firms then breached, or sought to breach, those promises. At this point, the Federal Trade Commission (FTC) became involved – not in the role of a data privacy regulator, but rather in its role as a consumer protection regulator. The justification for the FTC's involvement was that the breach of privacy policies by

---

77 Including the Obscene Publications Acts 1959 and 1964, Protection of Children Act 1978, Sexual Offences Act 2003, and Public Order Act 1986, discussed further in Chapter 8.
78 Vernon Coaker (Parliamentary Under-Secretary, Home Office), HC Deb, 15 May 2006, c715W; see also HC Deb, 16 June 2008, c683W.
79 Electronic Commerce (EC Directive) Regulations 2002, SI 2002/2013, reg 19.
80 See Chapter 8 for discussion of the 'making' of child pornography.
81 See, e.g., Thorsten Held and Wolfgang Schulz, *Regulated Self-regulation as a Form of Modern Government*, 2004, Eastleigh: University of Luton Press and see below for discussion of co-regulation.

companies was a breach of their consumer protection obligations. As a result, the FTC became the de facto regulatory body for website data privacy, by virtue of its ability to enforce what websites had, up to that point, considered to be merely self-regulatory and non-legally binding policies.[82]

## Co-regulation

The division of regulatory strategy into discrete categories, while useful for theoretical discussion of particular regulatory techniques, is less helpful when engaging in actual regulation. As already noted, the regulatory problem is not, in practice, a stark choice between the big stick of command-and-control regulation and the vagaries of self-regulation – an argument described by Ayres and Braithwaite as 'a debate between those who favor regulatory shotguns and those who favor no guns at all'.[83] The level of this debate between these two regulatory extremes can, on occasion, foster the presumption that the two regulatory extremes of government regulation and pure self-regulation are mutually exclusive – that is, entirely opposing mechanisms that are impossible to reconcile or amalgamate.[84] The reality is that discussing types of regulatory practice in terms of 'strict' command and control, or 'pure' self-regulation clearly oversimplifies the complex reality of the real world, in which circumstances will often necessitate the use of a mix of regulatory techniques in order to achieve an effective solution. Command-and-control legislation is located at one extreme; at the other is pure self-regulation. In fact, even these extremes are, in practice, often ameliorated by elements drawn from other parts of the spectrum. As Brownsword has commented: 'smart regulators know that traditional command and control interventions, however tempting to politicians, are not always an effective or efficient form of response';[85] instead, a regulatory 'mix' is needed and the task for a regulator becomes one of selecting the appropriate point on the regulatory continuum for the activity in question.[86] Thus a consideration of the UK data protection regulatory framework, premised on the DPA 1998, shows that although many of its provisions fall within the 'command and control' paradigm, it clearly contains several other regulatory elements, not least an attempt to utilise a rights and liabilities-based approach. The limited powers originally granted to the ICO resulted in light-touch regulation, heavy emphasis on the education of data controllers, and a focus on cooperative problem-solving with data controllers and data subjects and the use of social-based strategies, such as 'name and shame'. The 'self-regulatory' model of the IWF can also be seen to lean heavily on what appear to be elements of command and control, or shades of enforced self-regulation. Without those elements – that is, if it were a 'pure' self-regulatory regulator – the IWF's regulatory activity would be much less likely to be perceived as a necessary service by its membership. That would significantly diminish its ability, via the provision of that service, to effectively control the availability of illegal content within the UK.

An approach that combines different categories of regulatory practice may be described as 'co-regulation' – although the use of this term, like 'self-regulation' itself, varies between authors. Closs and Nikoltchev view the term as 'particularly ambiguous. The concept is not clearly defined and does not refer to any one particular regulatory model.'[87] On the other hand it may be that the concept is not ambiguous *per se*, merely that there is no one type of co-regulatory model. A feature of all models is that they combine elements of government and self-regulation:

---

82 See Steven A Hetcher, 'The de facto Federal Privacy Commission' (2000) 19 John Marshall J of Comp & Info Law 109.
83 Ayres and Braithwaite, above, p 157.
84 For further discussion on this point, see, e.g., Darren Sinclair, 'Self-regulation versus command and control? Beyond false dichotomies' (1997) 19(4) Law & Policy 529, 530–3.
85 Brownsword, above, p 3.
86 See Sinclair, above.
87 Wolfgang Closs and Susanne Nikoltchev (eds), *Co-Regulation of the Media in Europe*, 2003, Strasbourg: European Audiovisual Observatory, p 4.

A co-regulatory scheme combines elements of self-regulation (and self-monitoring) as well as of traditional public authority regulation to form a new and self-contained regulatory system. In this perspective, there are conceivably many different forms of co-regulatory models, depending on the combination of public authority and private sector elements.[88]

Prosser thus argues (in the context of the EU Audio-visual Directive) that the use of the term 'co-regulation' allows a recognition not only of a continuum of regulatory approaches, but also of a mix of regulatory regimes that can take account of differing contextual factors including, for example, issues of effective enforcement.[89] Co-regulation was explicitly recognised at the EU level in the Interinstitutional Agreement of 2003:[90]

Co-regulation means the mechanism whereby a Community legislative act entrusts the attainment of the objectives defined by the legislative authority to parties which are recognised in the field (such as economic operators, the social partners, non-governmental organisations, or associations).[91]

This and subsequent paragraphs envisages a situation in which the framework and extent of the co-regulation is contained in a legislative act and the parties concerned then conclude voluntary agreements to ensure the objectives of the regulation are realised. In line with general principles of EU law, doctrines such as proportionality will apply to the authorising legislation. Although this type of co-regulation seems now to be well recognised in the EU, in December 2015, the European Commission endorsed a new agreement with the European Parliament and Council which will replace that of 2003 once it has been formally agreed by all institutions.[92] It makes no mention of alternative forms of regulation but is primarily focused on the legislative acts of the EU albeit stressing the need for stakeholder consultation and involvement.[93]

In principle, co-regulation could provide many of the advantages of self-regulation without the associated disadvantages. The central involvement of stakeholders leads to greater legitimacy and the fact of government involvement means that it may be more capable of integrating with existing regulatory regimes. The regulated target group is more likely to be aware of the regulation and understand its content when they have been involved in its creation, as well as potentially being more willing and able to comply. Co-regulation may have very tightly drawn objectives – as recommended by the Human Rights Audit for the IWF discussed above – and this can increase effectiveness for a number of reasons relating to expertise, focused enforcement, involvement of regulatees and so on. As the detail of the regulation is not set out in legislation it is capable of responding more quickly to changes in circumstances than legislation, which can be an important factor in a rapidly changing technological environment. On the other hand there can be a potential lack of transparency and accountability concerning the actual co-regulatory rules.[94]

---

88 Carmen Palzer, 'Self-Monitoring v. Self-Regulation v. Co-Regulation' in ibid at p 30. See also general discussion of co-regulation in OECD, *Regulatory Policies in OECD Countries: From Interventionism to Regulatory Governance*, 2002, Annex II, p 137 available online at: www.oecd.org/gov/regulatory-policy/35260489.pdf and in NZ Law Commission IP27, 'The News Media meets 'New Media': Rights, Responsibilities and Regulation in the Digital Age' (2011), Ch 6, paras 6.34–6.40 available online at: http://ip27.publications. lawcom.govt.nz/

89 Prosser, above, p 111.

90 Interinstitutional Agreement on better law-making [2003] OJ C 321/01, see generally Linda Senden, 'Soft Law, Self-regulation and Co-regulation in European Law: Where do they meet?' (2005) 9.1 EJCL available online at: www.ejcl.org/91/art91-3.html

91 Ibid, [18].

92 'Interinstitutional Agreement on Better Law Making' – provisional text available online at: http://ec.europa.eu/smart-regulation/index_en.htm

93 Ibid, [14]

94 For a detailed analysis of the operation of co-regulation see, e.g., Christopher T Marsden, 'Internet co-regulation and constitutionalism: Towards European judicial review' (2012) 26 Int Rev LCT 211.

Both the data protection regulatory framework and the IWF 'self-regulatory' model also attempt to involve the public and public-interest groups in the regulatory process, with varying degrees of success. The former's primary process for public involvement, the principle of 'subject access', is an inefficient (and arguably ineffective) means of involving the public in the regulatory process; the latter has yet to overcome effectively the problems of legitimacy in regard to the transparency of its administrative and decision-making functions, and the public scrutiny of its actions. However, regardless of their weakness, they still embody an assumption that public participation is a required element in their particular regulatory strategies.

## Looking forward (and backward and sideways)

It is instructive when approaching a new area of law – whether IT law, environmental law, or any of the other numerous subjects available in the modern law school curriculum – to consider not only what the law in that area used to be, and what it is now, but why it has developed in that way. Such an analysis needs to consider not only the context surrounding the subject matter of the law, but also the contemporary regulatory context: the regulatory options available to legislators and regulators.

For example, the UK current data protection law is an artefact not only of the social, political, and technological context in which the Data Protection Directive and the resulting DPA 1998 were forged, but also of historical approaches in the European Union and UK to regulatory strategy. As a result, if we were to seek today to develop a wholly new data protection framework, it would undoubtedly look very different from that which currently exists, even if it were still to reflect the same fair information practice principles that have underpinned data protection laws around the world since the 1970s. Our social attitudes towards privacy may have changed; the political balance between privacy and other interests, such as commerce or openness, may have shifted; the technologies in use have certainly changed: all of these factors would undoubtedly influence the nature of the law. What is also clear, however, is that there is an increasing range of regulatory possibilities available to today's legislators and regulators, and that there is, through practice and research across a range of fields, considerably greater understanding of how such strategies might be combined to produce a more flexible, efficient, and effective regulatory regime.

Regulatory theory and practice has developed apace since the early days of IT law, and innovation is not unique to this area of law. This means that, as we look to develop the IT law of the future, we need not only to consider the historical lessons derived from the successes and failures of past and present IT-related laws, but also to cast our net wider and to consider what lessons can be learned from current regulatory theory, and from current practice in other developing areas of law.

## Further reading

Robert Baldwin, Martin Cave and Martin Lodge, *Understanding Regulation: Theory, Strategy, and Practice*, 2nd edn, 2011, Oxford University Press

Lawrence Lessig, *Code: Version 2*, 2006, New York: Basic Books

Andrew Murray, *The Regulation of Cyberspace: Control in the Online Environment*, 2007, Glasshouse

Christopher T Marsden, *Internet Co-regulation: European Law, Regulatory Governance and Legitimacy in Cyberspace*, 2011, Cambridge University Press

Christopher T Marsden, *Net Neutrality: Towards a Co-regulatory Solution*, 2010, Bloomsbury

Eric Brousseau, Meryem Marzouki and Cécile Méadel (eds), *Governance, Regulation and Powers on the Internet*, 2012, Cambridge University Press

# Chapter 2

# Regulatory competence over the internet

## Chapter contents

# Introduction

Before answering the question of *how* online activity is or should be regulated, the first question is *who*, i.e. which state, has or should have an entitlement to do so.[1] In the purely domestic legal context the answer is too obvious to require further thought: where an activity falls within the territory of only one state, it is that state which regulates it. On an international level states are the main players sharing regulatory space between them and each state has regulatory control over its respective territory. The internet complicates this otherwise simple allocation rule as online activity seems to occur everywhere and nowhere in particular. The question then is which state has the right to regulate which site or online activity? The underlying generic issue is by no means new; allocating competence (or jurisdiction) over transnational activity to national regulators has been done for centuries. In the more recent past, transnational trade and environmental pollution, international travel and migration have all had to be accommodated within national legal regimes. Yet, the explosion of online activity has added a new level of acuteness to the inherent conflict between transnational activity and national law. And this issue of deciding who has competence over what affects the whole spectrum of online activities and attached legal concerns. The regulatory palette that has triggered primary questions of regulatory entitlement is wide-ranging from criminal or regulatory law on pornographic, gambling, pharmaceutical, banking and terrorist sites to civil law disputes concerning defamation, data protection and privacy, contracts and intellectual property rights.

Undisputedly states have a right to regulate sites hosted on their territory. The controversial issue is to what extent states can regulate 'foreign' sites, i.e. sites created and hosted elsewhere. States have an interest in doing so, as foreign sites have an effect on their territories which *prima facie* is in no way distinguishable from that of local sites. But can they regulate them? Principally yes, but as the discussion below shows, the precise answers to that question – found in national and international jurisdiction rules – vary, for example, depending on the civil or criminal nature of the dispute. Certainly states have sought – more or less successfully – to accommodate online activity within traditional legal frameworks: if it is regulated offline, so shall it be online. They have rejected the early proposition by some academics that the internet should be treated as a space apart and that online activity is beyond their regulatory control.[2] This proposition was made, and persuasively so, because online activity defies the sensible sharing of regulatory space between territorial sovereigns. As online activity occurs everywhere to the same degree (a view which has been challenged, see below), no one state seems more strongly linked to it than any other state and thus no state could make out a regulatory claim superior to that of any other state. Therefore it is either no state

---

1 See, generally, Uta Kohl, *Jurisdiction and the Internet – Regulatory Competence over Online Activity*, 2007, Cambridge: Cambridge University Press; Jonathan L Zittrain, *Jurisdiction*, 2005, New York: Foundation Press. On jurisdiction generally, see Cedric Ryngaert, *Jurisdiction in International Law*, 2008, Oxford: Oxford University Press; and Alex Mills, *The Confluence of Public and Private International Law*, 2009, Cambridge: Cambridge University Press; and Hannah L Buxbaum, 'Territory, territoriality, and the resolution of jurisdictional conflict' (2009) 57 American Journal of Comparative Law 631.

2 David R Johnson and David Post, 'Law and borders – The rise of law in cyberspace' (1996) 48 Stanford Law Review 1367.

or all states that can regulate any online activity, and this in turn would lead to unacceptable under-regulation or overregulation of the online world. Although states have principally 'voted' for the latter option, the regulatory concurrency to which that option gives rise is problematic. Can website providers really be expected to comply with hundreds of sets of different laws simultaneously and in any event, are states able to enforce their laws against foreign content providers? Alternatively, are we willing to accept a territorially fragmented cyberworld in which sites are restricted to a particular state out of fear of legal repercussions elsewhere? These are not simply academic questions, but have been serious concerns for governments, online actors and civil society.

If applying location-centric law to online activity is fraught with difficulties and does not really fit the bill, why have states not simply relinquished control over the internet, as suggested by those early academics? Despite the obvious attractions of the hands-off proposition, entirely surrendering regulatory control over online activity to a global body[3] or online corporations or the wider online community itself has not been acceptable to states and their constituents. The repercussions of this would be less authority within their territory more generally. By not regulating online activity, the regulation of the equivalent offline activity is also compromised. For example, if a state prohibits the sale of a particular drug because of concerns about its safety, this prohibition is undermined generally if people of that state can freely acquire that forbidden drug online. The prohibition loses its force and credibility. Yet, even though states have not relinquished control over the internet, on the whole they have not succeeded in policing their laws online particularly effectively. Suffice to say: while states have limited success in enforcing their prohibitions against foreign online content providers, it appears that the political costs of not even attempting to do so would be too great. Finally, the problems of deciding who should regulate what online activity is as alive today as it was in the early days of the internet, recently with particular focus on data protection and on enforcement through online intermediaries.

## Substantive legal harmonisation

Related to the above internet governance debate on uniform non-state rules is the debate on uniform state rules in the form of substantive legal harmonisation. Online publications are not by default limited to one state; by default they are global. Is it not imperative that these global publications are governed by a global set of rules – both for the sake of online publishers and users as well as the national regulators? Currently, the same publications may attract very different legal status in different states – ranging from being perfectly legal to being subject to civil sanctions or even criminal prosecutions. Like beauty, legality and crime is in the eye of the beholder. What may be under the laws of one state criminalised terrorist activity may be in the eyes of another state entirely legal political or religious speech. Conversely, what may be in one state a reasonable exercise of the right to free speech may amount to criminalised seditious or blasphemous speech under the laws of another state.[4] Such legal divergence creates huge theoretical and practical problems for users and regulators.

Of course, strong divergence is not present across the regulatory board. States are broadly in agreement in respect of significant areas of criminal activity aimed at the protection of the

---

3 See, e.g., ICANN (The Internet Corporation for Assigned Names and Numbers), which has the authority to coordinate the internet's global naming system and oversees certain domain name/trade mark disputes globally and is a private, not-for-profit US corporation, set up on the authority of a number of 'understandings' with the US Department of Trade. Its independent international status, as a multistakeholder or multilateral organisation, is still under negotiation. Anna Edgerton, 'At NETmundial, the U.S. Kept Its Companies on the Global Stage' (30 April 2014) Bloomberg. http://www.bloomberg.com/news/articles/2014-04-30/at-netmundial-the-u-dot-s-dot-kept-its-companies-on-the-global-stage

4 The most notorious example is the controversy caused by the cartoons featuring the Prophet Muhammad in a Danish newspaper in 2005 and its subsequent publication on YouTube. Viewed as legitimate political debate on criticism of Islam and self-censorship in Denmark, the cartoon was violently decried in the Muslim world, leading to attacks on Danish embassies and Muslim leaders offering rewards to anyone who killed the cartoonist responsible.

person and property. Such relative consensus explains why the Council of Europe Convention on Cybercrime (2001, Budapest) could be agreed upon in record time by international standards.[5] By limiting its ambit to matters such as hacking, viruses, fraud, child pornography and copyright, the Convention covers relatively 'safe' subject-matters – safe in terms of international consensus. Differences of opinion emerge in areas of regulation designed to protect the stability of the government and political order, but regulatory divergence is most pronounced in respect of those rules that seek to protect the moral fabric of society.[6] Thus, for example, hate speech had to be put into the optional Additional Protocol to the Convention.[7]

The existence and absence of international legal consensus is crucial for the jurisdiction debate. Where states take a relatively harmonised approach to the regulation of a particular online activity (whether this is formally reflected in a treaty or simply evident in relatively similar national legal standards), the competence question is of much lesser significance.[8] Each state, by regulating activity originating on its territory, effectively also upholds the laws of all other states insofar as that activity may have had an impact on those states.[9] Conversely, where states insist on their very different laws, it matters very much how exactly online activity is 'shared out' between states – with each state trying to get as big a slice as possible. Inevitably, the cases that have given rise to competence disputes are those where the laws of states vary strongly. For the moment, the point to be stressed is that substantive legal harmonisation and effective competence regimes generally present alternative answers to globalisation generally and internet transnationality more specifically. Although substantive legal harmonisation appears instinctively the superior and natural option to online governance, it has its problems. Apart from the practical and political difficulties of achieving it, it comes at a high price: states would have to surrender their distinct legal systems reflecting distinct cultural, political and social values, in favour of a one-size-fits-all legal order. And at least for the time being, legal diversity seems a good worthy of retention.

Last but not least, even in areas where there is substantive global harmonisation, e.g. copyright, nationally based protection of globally recognised right may still create significant barriers to transborder data flows. Typically, the arrangement of licensing agreements has meant that media services such as Netflix, BBC iPlayer, Amazon Instant Video and YouTube have implemented geoblocking which makes these services available in some places but not others, often with very different content.[10]

## Competence under public and private international law

The rules that allocate regulatory control in the transnational setting are rules of jurisdiction. 'Jurisdiction' (deriving from the Latin *juris dictio*, meaning the 'administration of justice') refers in its broadest sense to a state's right to regulate persons, property and events. The rules which govern the right to regulate have broadly two provenances. On the one hand, public international law governs the rights of states to impose criminal or regulatory sanctions on transnational or extra-territorial

---

5 Marc D Goodman and Susan W Brenner, 'The Emerging Consensus on Criminal Conduct in Cybercrime?' (2002) 10 International Journal of Law and Information Technology 139, 177ff. For another area of consensus, see WHO Framework Convention on Tobacco Control (2003, Geneva), esp Art 13(4)(e) on tobacco advertising on different media, including the internet.

6 Ibid, 177–9.

7 Additional Protocol to the Convention on Cybercrime, concerning the Criminalisation of Acts of a Racist and Xenophobic nature committed through Computer Systems (2003, Strasbourg).

8 For this reason, crimes covered by the Cybercrime Convention are not further discussed in this chapter on competence.

9 A residual question may be to what extent each state takes its responsibility for enforcing the harmonised area of law seriously.

10 Loek Essers, 'EU Parliament takes strong stance against geoblocking' (10 July 2015) CIO, available online at: http://www.cio.com/article/2946773/eu-parliament-takes-strong-stance-against-geoblocking.html

activity and actors.[11] On the other hand, private international law or conflict of laws governs private or civil transnational disputes. These latter rules are not international, but ordinary national law and thus vary from state to state unless harmonised in a regional or international treaty. These sets of competence rules for civil matters, and criminal matters are contained within separate legal disciplines despite a number of basic commonalities.[12]

The broad agenda underlying both regimes is arguably similar. They lay down rules to determine when a state or legal system is sufficiently *closely linked or connected* to a transnational event, person or dispute so as to make it fair to give the state regulatory control. More specifically, first, with focus on the interests of states, the rules aim at the *'juste partage de souveraineté'* (the just sharing of control) between states, at the protection of states from interferences by other states, and overall internationally at an orderly and effective regulatory structure. Second, both sets of rules aim at the fair and just treatment of individuals within these orders, protecting individuals from conflicting and compounding obligations. No doubt, this second objective dominates in the private international law context, while the first one assumes greater relevance in relation to state regulation through criminal or public law. But ultimately both objectives must guide new legal developments in the allocation of regulatory power in either discipline. Importantly, particularly in the internet context, the strength of any link conferring regulatory entitlement must always be judged against potential concurrent links/claims. A link with an event that is so weak that it could also be relied upon by many other states in the same instance is theoretically and practically dubious. It would give rise to a high level of regulatory concurrency and thereby defeat the above mentioned aims, i.e. the notion that regulation is most efficient when *divided or shared* between different regulators; the notion that individuals must be protected from overregulation. Thus the strength of a link is relative; it should be assessed *vis-à-vis* potentially competing links by other states or legal systems.

On a structural level there also parallels. Both private and public international law distinguish between three types of regulatory activity requiring different competence rules: adjudicating, legislating, and enforcing – broadly in line with the three arms of government.[13] The first type concerns the question whether a state court has the right to adjudicate a dispute; in private international law this is referred to as the jurisdictional enquiry ('jurisdiction' in a more narrow sense than used above). The next question is whether a state has the right to 'legislate' in relation to a transnational event; can it apply its substantive law to it, which – in private international law – is called the choice-of-law inquiry. In the civil context, a court may adjudicate a dispute without 'legislative jurisdiction'. In such cases it will apply foreign law to it.[14] In contrast, in the criminal context, once a court has decided it will hear a case, it will apply local law, never foreign law; so adjudicative and legislative jurisdiction effectively collapse into one inquiry. Finally, the third type of regulatory activity refers to 'executive jurisdiction': can a state enforce the judgment or conviction against the defendant or accused. Unlike with respect to the former two inquiries, enforcement jurisdiction is strictly territorial, or as Lombois put it: 'The law may very well decide to cast its shadow beyond its borders; the judge may well have a voice so loud that, speaking in his house, his condemnations

11 The assumption is that when activity is purely within the territory of one state, no issue of jurisdiction arises, although implicitly it is the territoriality principle that grants regulatory power in such cases.
12 Very few writers have examined both sets of rules as related and comparable legal phenomena, e.g. Michael Akehurst, 'Jurisdiction in international law' (1972–73) 46 British Yearbook of International Law 145; FA Mann, 'The doctrine of international jurisdiction revisited after twenty years' (1984) 186 Recueil des Cours 9 and 'The doctrine of jurisdiction in international law'(1964) 111 Recueil des Cours 1. See also Alex Mills, 'The private history of international law' (2006) 55 International and Comparative Law Quarterly 1 and 'Rethinking jurisdiction in international law' (2014) 84 The British Yearbook of International Law 187.
13 Akehurst, above n 12; see also Luc Reydams, *Universal Jurisdiction – International and Municipal Legal Perspectives*, 2003, Oxford: Oxford University Press, 25f.
14 Having said that, there is a homeward trend in choice of law inquiry, i.e. courts asserting adjudicative jurisdictions also often assert that forum rather than foreign substantive law is applicable to the case.

are heard outside; the reach of the police officer is only as long as his arm . . . he is a constable only at home.'[15] So a state can never enforce its law on the territory of another state, by for example sending its police officers there, except with the consent of the other state.

What gives a law or dispute a criminal rather than a civil character has at times been hotly debated,[16] but broadly when the state, rather than individuals, assumes responsibility over the rule's enforcement the dispute acquires a 'public' character. Scarce public resources are diverted to the systematic monitoring and penalisation of certain behaviour by agents of the state, in contrast to the ad hoc enforcement of civil law which is instigated and financed by the private parties to the dispute. The criminalisation or public regulation of activity reflects a value judgement by the state on the relative importance of the norms in question: the more important compliance with a norm in question, the more likely criminal sanctions are preferred over civil ones to encourage such compliance.

## Transnational online crime

The limits of regulatory competence in criminal matters are set by public international law and thus they are, in principle, the same for all states. Like many rules of customary international law the jurisdictional principles have blurry boundaries and are no more than signposts.[17] Given their permissive nature,[18] it is perhaps not surprising that national courts rarely mention them as a source of their jurisdiction in transnational criminal cases. Instead, in common law jurisdictions, national courts rely on the maxim that 'all crime is local' (unless there is specific statutory authority to the contrary) or on the presumption against the extra-territorial effect of legislation.[19] But such national legal concepts cannot detract from the fact that jurisdiction as assumed by national courts or legislatures must ultimately be consistent with public international law which delimits the criminal jurisdiction of states.

The jurisdictional rules under public international law specify which links with a person, property or an event are sufficiently strong to give a state regulatory power over that person, property or event. In *Lotus* (1927),[20] the seminal case on jurisdiction, a French and a Turkish steamer collided on the high seas resulting in the death of eight Turkish sailors and passengers. The issue was whether Turkey could institute criminal proceedings against a French lieutenant for his acts on the French ship, based on the effects of those acts on the Turkish steamer – which according to international law is an extension of Turkish territory. The Permanent Court of International Justice upheld Turkey's right to do so:

> the first and foremost restriction imposed by international law upon a State is that . . . it may not exercise its power in any form in the territory of another State. In this sense jurisdiction is certainly territorial . . . It does not however, follow that international law prohibits a State from exercising jurisdiction in its own territory, in respect of any case which relates to acts which have taken place abroad . . . Such a view would only be tenable if international law contained a general prohibition to States to extend the application of their laws and the jurisdiction of their

---

15 Claude Lombois, *Droit Penal International*, 2nd edn, 1979, Paris: Daloz, p 536 cited in Pierre Trudel, 'Jurisdiction over the internet: A Canadian perspective' (1998) 32 The International Lawyer 1027, 1047.
16 This discussion is mainly found within private international law concerning the non-application of foreign 'revenue, penal or other public laws' as well as the non-enforcement and non-recognition of foreign judgments of that nature.
17 Reydams, above n 13, 23ff.
18 The rules lay down when a state may exercise adjudicative/prescriptive jurisdiction rather than when it may *not* do so.
19 Matthew Goode, 'The Tortured Tale of Criminal Jurisdiction' (1997) 21 Melbourne University Law Review 411
20 *The Case of the SS 'Lotus' (France v Turkey)* (1927) PCIJ Reports, Series A, No 10.

courts to persons, property and acts outside their territory . . . But this is certainly not the case under international law as it stands at present.'[21]

So *Lotus* confirmed that – while states are strictly prohibited from enforcing their laws on foreign territory (enforcement jurisdiction) – they can attach legal consequences to extra-territorial events (adjudicative/legislative jurisdiction). To do so, they must bring the claim under one of the recognised links or 'heads of jurisdiction'. Of course that regulatory freedom over extra-territorial events is less valuable when not coupled with enforcement power.

So what are these recognised heads of jurisdiction under international law? The main heads are the territoriality principle, the nationality principle, the protective principle and the universality principle. The principle most frequently relied upon by states to make regulatory claims over transborder online events is – in some ways counterintuitively – the territoriality principle.[22] The territoriality principle which also allows a state to regulate what is or occurs on its territory, has over the years been adapted to accommodate the increasing incidence of activity spanning over numerous state territories. Already *Lotus* affirmed the legitimacy of concurrent regulatory claims, both by the state in which a crime commenced (subjective territoriality principle) as well as by the state or *states* in which it finished (objective territoriality principle).

## The objective territoriality principle – the destination approach

The objective territoriality principle allows a state to regulate a foreign actor when the impact of his/her act is felt on the state's territory. As the Permanent Court of Justice said in *Lotus*:

'it is certain that the courts of many countries, even of countries which have given their criminal legislation a strictly territorial character, interpret criminal law in the sense that offences, the authors of which at the moment of commission are in the territory of another State are nevertheless to be regarded as having been committed in the national territory, if one of the constituent elements of the offence, and more especially its effects, haven taken place there.'[23]

This principle has gone through different incarnations under different labels: it underlies the concept of 'result' crime (versus 'conduct' crime) traditionally used by common law courts;[24] it provides the basis of the US 'effects doctrine' in the anti-trust context in the 1970s to 1990s[25] and is, in the internet context, referred to as the destination or receipt rule or approach (in contrast the origin rule).[26] Common to all these concepts or labels is the focus on the *impact* of a foreign act on a state's territory and that impact provides the basis for subjecting the foreign actor to that state's law. In *Lotus* this impact was the physical impact on the Turkish vessel; in the US anti-trust cases it was the economic effects of the foreign cartels on the US market and in the online world it is the impact of foreign websites accessible in a state. The problem of extending *Lotus* to non-physical effects is

21 *The Case of the SS 'Lotus' (France v Turkey)* (1927) PCIJ Reports, Series A, No 10, 18. In fact the PCJ asserts that states can always claim regulatory competence unless there was a restrictive rule to the contrary, a view not commonly accepted today.

22 It is the primary basis in terms of quantity but not necessarily being of a higher order, i.e. a territorial connection with the to-be-regulated event does not trump a concurrent claim by another state based on the nationality of the offender.

23 *The Case of the SS 'Lotus' (France v Turkey)* (1927) PCIJ Reports, Series A, No 10, 23.

24 DPP v Stonehouse [1978] AC 55; R v Treacy [1971] AC 557; R v Markus [1975] 1 ALL ER 958; Brownlie v State Pollution Control Commission (1992) 27 NSWLR 78; R v Toubya [1993] 1 VR 226; cf Air India v Wiggins [1980] 2 All ER 593; discussed in Goode, above n 19, 437ff.

25 AV Lowe (ed), *Extraterritorial Jurisdiction*, 1983, Cambridge: Grotius Publications Ltd. The difference between the effects doctrine and the objective territoriality principle, if there is one, is that the former appears to have no explicit requirement that the effects on the territory must be a 'consistent element' of the crime in question, although in fact this is invariably established and can be provided for by framing the offence appropriately.

26 Graham Smith (ed), *Internet Law and Regulation*, 4th edn, 2007, London: Sweet and Maxwell, ch 12, p 507f. On German jurisprudence on 'Handlungs- und Erfolgsort' in the online context, see *Arzneimittelwerbung im Internet* (BGH, 30 March 2006, I ZR 24/03), para 10.

that innumerable states may be affected by the same foreign event, thus giving rise to innumerable concurrent regulatory rights by destination states, and this is precisely the dilemma caused by the internet. The examples below illustrate the objective territoriality principle in the online context, the economic, moral, political reasons behind states asserting regulatory control over online activity, including foreign online activity with an effect on their territory.[27]

## National political values (e.g. online hate and inflammatory speech)

One of the earliest illustrations of the destination approach is provided by the French case of LICRA & UEJF v Yahoo! Inc & Yahoo France (2000).[28] In Yahoo two French organisations – LICRA (The League against Racism and Anti-Semitism) and UEJF (The French Jewish Students Union) – sued Yahoo! Inc, a US corporation, and its French subsidiary for allowing surfers from France to buy Nazi artefacts from third parties via auction and other sites of Yahoo! Inc. While the action was in form a private action similar to a nuisance action,[29] in fact it was based on a 'manifest' violation of the French Criminal Code, i.e. the prohibition on distributing Nazi-memorabilia. Thus, the action could not easily be characterised as either private/civil or public/criminal, and thus whether the jurisdictional limits under public international law apply is debatable.[30]

The problem with the French action concerning the yahoo.com website (as opposed to the yahoo.fr site) was that the site seemed so much more clearly connected with the US than France: it was set up and maintained by a US corporation on a server situated in the US and it was in English with the vast majority of its users coming from the US. So should this site not be governed exclusively by US law where distributing Nazi-memorabilia is legal? The Paris court disagreed: it held that because 'harm was suffered on the territory of France' by virtue of the site's accessibility in France, French law was applicable (whatever else law may also govern it). The fact that Yahoo! Inc operated a separate .fr site, dedicated to French surfers and complying with French law, did not relieve it of accountability under French law in respect of its .com site. As that latter site was also accessible in France, it also had to comply with French law.

Once it is decided that local law is applicable to the foreign site, the next question is how the site could comply with it. If Yahoo! Inc complied with French law by removing all material offending French law from its site (as it was not required to do, but in fact did), all users worldwide would also be subjected to the legal standards of France. So, all US users of yahoo.com would forego the benefits of the more lenient US law on hate speech. If the French approach to extending its laws to foreign online material based on the site's accessibility within the state is followed by other states (as in fact it is), Yahoo! Inc would also have to remove material offending the laws of Mongolia, China, Saudi Arabia and so on. Yahoo! Inc could only operate the site legally by removing all material illegal worldwide, i.e. by complying with the most restrictive law, i.e. the highest common legal denominator.[31] Not surprisingly, regulatory claims by destination states have been criticised for a number of reasons. First, they impose a too high and unrealistic regulatory burden on individual and corporate online publishers. Second, the superimposition of one state's law on all other states amounts to strong censorship and deprives the online community of valuable content (or would do so if it were effective). Bland content would be all there is left. Third, if all states are entitled to regulate all online activities, regulatory space is no longer shared between states.

---

27  Thomas Schulz, 'Carving up the internet: Jurisdiction, legal orders, and the private/public international law interface' (2008) 19 European Journal of International Law 799, 805.

28  LICRA v Yahoo! Inc & Yahoo France (Tribunal de Grande Instance de Paris, 22 May 2000), affirmed in LICRA & UEJF v Yahoo! Inc & Yahoo France (Tribunal de Grande Instance de Paris, 20 November 2000) http://www.foruminternet.org/

29  Arts 808 and 809 of the New Code of Civil Procedure.

30  As illustrated by the divergent judicial assessments in Yahoo! Inc v LICRA & UEJF 433 F 3d 1199 (9th Cir 2006).

31  Conflicts can generally be resolved by the site provider adopting the highest common legal denominator, i.e. the most restrictive law. Only rarely would it be impossible for a content provider to comply with two or more sets of laws simultaneously which would only be the case where one law forbids what another law demands.

Avoiding some of these criticisms, the French court ordered an alternative compliance strategy, in fact the only alternative. It ordered Yahoo! Inc to prevent access to the artefacts and hate speech sites in question from French territory,[32] i.e. make the site territorially sensitive. By avoiding contact with French territory, Yahoo! Inc could not fall foul of French law. While it was disputed whether Yahoo! Inc was technically capable of identifying and excluding surfers from France,[33] an expert group concluded that it could do so. Even in 2000 website operators could identify the physical whereabouts of 70% of their users and exclude them, and that in addition to self-identification was considered sufficient to comply with the French order. Today geo-identification technology has advanced significantly and is often used for more specific commercial targeting of users from different states.[34] Such technology also enables website operators to seal their sites from being accessed from legally inhospitable states, although very few do so. But this alternative compliance strategy is also not unproblematic. As it encourages the creation of territorially limited websites, content providers, consumers and states forego the economic, social and political benefits derived from uninhibited open transnational online communications, as shown in the European right-to-be-forgotten *Google Spain* case in 2014 (see below). In the final analysis, however, *Yahoo* is a reminder that even where states make wide regulatory claims such as the French court, often they cannot or only with difficulty enforce these claims. Yahoo! Inc complied with the French order voluntarily without any real threat of French enforcement action.[35]

*Yahoo* made headlines at the time, but the same approach to competence has been taken again and again by states in different legal contexts. The German Federal Court in R v *Töben* (2000)[36] also adjudicated on the issue of hate speech criminalised under German law. Frederick Töben, a German-born Australian citizen, published anti-Semitic material, denying the Holocaust, on his Australian site. While on holiday in Germany, he was arrested and charged with an offence under the German Criminal Code, *inter alia*, in respect of his website. The German court claimed regulatory competence based on the objective territoriality principle: the offence had been completed in Germany by creating a real possibility of disturbing the public peace through the website's publication in Germany. The German court made some attempt to show why Germany had a stronger claim than other states to apply its criminal laws to the foreign site, thereby avoiding the legal position that all states can regulate all sites. It held that, given the historic connection between the subject-matter of the site and Germany, Germany was objectively closely linked to the site, and this link also meant that German users were clearly the intended and actual addressees of the site. However whether this link between Germany and the site was indeed special is less clear when one considers that the site was in English and its subject-matter of universal interest. Also it is doubtful whether a site by a self-appointed historian from a dubious Australian institute was indeed capable of having the effect of disturbing the public peace, required for the commission of the offence in Germany.[37] In fact there was no evidence that anyone, other than the investigating police officer had accessed the site from Germany. The English Court of Appeal in R v *Sheppard and Whittle* (2010)[38] upheld two

---

32 Backed by a penalty of 100,000 Francs per day for non-compliance. There were also orders against Yahoo! France to remove 'negationist' index headings and links to 'negationist' sites as well as to post a warning on fr.yahoo.com to any users that viewing 'negationist' websites is illegal and subject to penalties under French legislation.
33 The court ordered an inquiry into the feasibility of its order, which confirmed its feasibility: LICRA & UEJF v *Yahoo! Inc & Yahoo France* (Tribunal de Grande Instance de Paris, 11 August 2000).
34 Dan Jerker B Svantesson, 'Borders on, or border *around* – the future of the internet' (2006) 16 Albany Law Journal of Science and Technology 343 and 'Geo-location technologies and other means of placing borders on the "borderless" internet' (2004) 23 John Marshall Journal of Computer and Information Law 101
35 The most likely explanation for Yahoo! Inc's compliance is the bad publicity generated by the French litigation which seem to suggest that it tolerated anti-Semitic attitudes which is likely to have affected its reputability and respectability.
36 R v *Töben* (BGH, 12 December 2000, 1 StR 184/00, LG Mannheim) (2001) 8 Neue Juristische Wochenschrift 624 discussed in Yulia A Timofeeva, 'Worldwide prescriptive jurisdiction in internet content controversies: A comparative analysis' (2005) 20 Connecticut Journal of International Law 199, 206f.
37 Irini E Vassilaki, 'Anmerkung' (2001) 4 Computer und Recht 262, 265.
38 R v *Sheppard and Whittle* [2010] EWCA Crim 65.

convictions of publishing and distributing online racially inflammatory material contrary to the Public Order Act 1986, even though the offending material was hosted on a foreign server and there was no evidence that the material was accessed in England by anyone other than the police. However, as a matter of establishing a nexus with Britain, the court held that a 'substantial measure' of the offences had occurred in Britain (i.e. the material was generated, edited, uploaded and controlled in Britain) and the material was 'primarily aimed at a British public' (see further below 'moderate destination approach' and 'subjective territoriality principle'). Whilst this case might appear to suggest that the material must be created locally for a local audience to be subjected to local criminal law, *Yahoo* (above) and *Google Spain* (below) and many other cases show neither local origin of the material nor local targeting is needed for the assumption of jurisdiction; of course, the local presence of the offenders makes it easier and more worthwhile to prosecute them, as opposed to convicting foreign offenders in *absentia* against whom the convictions could not be enforced.

In more recent years extremist terrorist speech has become the focal point of regulatory concern falling under this heading. For example, in the UK the Counter Terrorism Internet Referral Unit[39] with a mandate to identify and take down extreme graphic material, e.g. beheadings, and material that glorifies, incites and radicalises has 'instigated the removal of over 55,000 pieces of on line content, including 34,000 pieces since December 2013'[40] based on s 3 of the Terrorism Act 2006 (see below and Chapter 3 on Intermediaries). Whilst here executive rather than judicial power is exercised over online material, it rests on the same jurisdictional basis, namely the effects of foreign online activity on local territory. But, unlike the judicial exercise of power, the executive action of removing illegal sites does not in itself create any obligation on the foreign parties.

### National moral values (e.g. online pornography)

Online pornography raises much the same issues as inflammatory online speech, as different states take very different attitudes to its acceptability. (In contrast, the despicability of child pornography is fairly undisputed,[41] and thus in jurisdictional terms less controversial.) 'Normal' pornography has not proved susceptible to international agreement.[42] There is room for disagreement: is it harmless entertainment for adults who should enjoy the autonomy and liberty to choose their pastimes without state interference, or is it a practice exploitive of women, that degrades and corrupts society, particularly its more vulnerable members? Even liberal societies disagree to what extent the rights of adults ought to be compromised to protect children.[43] Again, the internet challenges the parallel existence of such regulatory diversity; the danger is that either the more liberal regimes undermine the more restrictive ones or, conversely, that the restrictive regimes set the tone for the rest of the world.

An example of the latter scenario was the German *CompuServe* case, one of the first cases causing an international outcry concerning the clash of state laws online. In 1995 German police raided *CompuServe*'s German offices in an investigation concerning online pornography (some of it was said to contain child pornography). In response, CompuServe temporarily suspended all of its 200-plus

---

39 See https://www.herts.police.uk/advice/counter_terrorism.aspx
40 Patrick Wintour, 'UK ISPs to introduce jihadi and terror content reporting button' (2014) *The Guardian*, 14 November, available online at: http://www.theguardian.com/technology/2014/nov/14/uk-isps-to-introduce-jihadi-and-terror-content-reporting-button; Mark Townsend and Toby Helm, 'Jihad in a social media age: how can the west win an online war?' (2014) *The Guardian*, 23 August, available online at: http://www.theguardian.com/world/2014/aug/23/jihad-social-media-age-west-win-online-war
41 See Art 9 of the European Council Convention on Cybercrime (2001, Budapest) or the Optional Protocol to the Convention on the Rights of the Child on the Sale of Children, Child Prostitution and Child Pornography (2000). A borderline scenario in this area concerns computer-generated child pornography.
42 Uta Kohl, 'Barbarians in Our Midst: "Cultural Diversity" on the Transnational Internet' (2014) 5 European Journal of Law and Technology, available online at: http://ejlt.org/article/view/304/426
43 Karsten Bremer, *Strafbare Internet-Inhalte in International Hinsicht – Ist der Nationalstaat wirklich überholt?*, 2001, Frankfurt am Main: Peter Lang Verlag, available online at: http://ub-dok.uni-trier.de/diss/diss60/20000927/20000927.pdf, 134ff, noting the different emphasises placed in different societies on protecting the moral fabric of society on the one hand or vulnerable actors or viewers on the other hand in the context of obscenity regulation.

newsgroups (hosted in the US and accessible worldwide) for its 4 million users because it was technically incapable of blocking only Germans. This caused controversy as it effectively meant that if material could not be viewed in Germany, it could not be viewed anywhere.[44] A few years later, with the benefit of more advanced geo-identification technology, the French court in *Yahoo* was able to order territorially more select blocking.

Focus on the effects of foreign online activity on British soil provided the basis of the prosecution in R v *Perrin* (2002)[45] against Perrin, a French director of a US company operating a US hosted pornography website. Perrin, resident in the UK, was convicted of the offence of publishing an obscene article contrary to the Obscene Publications Act 1959 in relation to the freely accessible preview site of his pornography subscription site. He appealed on the basis that the site had been uploaded on a server abroad and that jurisdiction should only lie with the state where the 'major steps' in relation to the publication were taken.[46] He argued that applying English obscenity standards extraterritorially, i.e. to his foreign site, would be inconsistent with his right to freedom of expression under the European Convention on Human Rights. The Court of Appeal rejected that sites could only be regulated by the state from which they originated, as this would encourage online publishers to go forum-shopping for the most lenient legal standards. Like in *Yahoo* and *Töben*, English law was applied to the site on the basis that it was accessible in England – although again, there was no evidence that it had been accessed in Britain other than by the police. As Perrin was resident in England and admitted responsibility for the publication, it might equally have been argued that the offence had commenced in England and that, contrary to Perrin's argument, the 'major steps' towards the publication had been taken in England[47] – much like in *Sheppard and Whittle* (2010) (above). Thus jurisdiction over his activities could equally have been based on their origin.

## National safety concerns (e.g. online medicine & pharmaceutical products)

In many states abortions are illegal or severely restricted. Post-internet such restrictions matter less: women can go online and, for example, womenonweb.org supplies – after an online medical consultation with a doctor – the pills that allow them to have a relatively safe abortion at home. In ten per cent of the cases, complications which require surgical procedures develop.[48] Whether you think the wrong lies with the state that prohibits abortions or the woman who wants an abortion or the online provider that provides them, for competence purposes this scenario illustrates another reason why states often seek to apply their regulation to locally accessible sites, whether originating at home or not. Although, not unlike in gambling, the pharmaceutical industry raises high financial stakes, most states take a keen regulatory interest in the marketing and sale of drugs and the provision of medical procedures in order to protect their residents. Of course, at times, as in the case of abortion, regulation is also designed to protect the moral stance of the particular society. In either event, evasion of such legal restrictions through the easy resort to foreign online suppliers undermines and discredits local law.

---

44 In 1998 CompuServe's local manager in Germany, Felix Somm, was convicted under German obscenity laws in relation to CompuServe's Usenet newsgroups, hosted in the US and accessible in Germany and received a two-year suspended sentence; his conviction was overturned on appeal as there was no blocking technology available to CompuServe: R v *Somm* (Amtsgericht München, 17 November 1999).

45 R v *Perrin* [2002] EWCA Crim 747. Perrin's application to the European Court of Human Rights – arguing that the UK Regulation breached his right to freedom of expression – was rejected: *Perrin v UK* (ECHR 18 October 2005, No 5446/03).

46 It appears he admitted being a director and majority shareholder of one or more US companies involved in operating the website from the US.

47 R v *Waddon* [1999] Masons CLR 396, [2000] All ER (D) 502, where the Court of Appeal implicitly foreshadowed that possibility when it stated that a separate 'publication' for the purposes of s 1(3) the Obscene Publications Act 1959 occurs when a defendant uploads obscene material from England onto a foreign server (in addition to any 'publication' that occurs on downloading that material in England).

48 CNN, 'Women buy pills online for 'home abortions' (11 July 2008), available online at: http://edition.cnn.com/2008/HEALTH/07/11/abortion.pills/index.html?eref=edition_europe

In *Deutscher Apothekerverband eV v 0800 Doc Morris NV* (2003)[49] an injunction against a Dutch online pharmacy in respect of its supply of certain drugs in Germany – based on a German legal requirement of 'presence' sales, i.e. that certain drugs can only be sold in pharmacies – was challenged as being inconsistent with the internal market rule of free movement of goods. The CJEU held that the 'presence' requirement was only justified for prescription drugs where confusion over language or labelling could lead to harmful consequences, but not to over-the-counter drugs, the online sale of which could not be restricted by the destination state. Since then the Electronic Commerce Directive[50] has come into force and *prima facie* the regulation of drugs is not excluded from the scope of the origin rule required by Art 3 (see below).[51] Yet in *Arzneimittelwerbung im Internet* (2006)[52] the question arose whether a Dutch site advertising and selling drugs to Germans had to comply with German licensing requirements even though the drugs were perfectly legal in the Netherlands. The German Federal Court held that the origin rule in the Directive was not applicable to national legal requirements concerning the delivery of goods[53] and furthermore could be excluded if it fell within the exception in Art 3(4)(a)(i), the protection of public health.[54] Thus the application of German licensing requirements to the foreign Dutch site was legitimate. The court further stated that a disclaimer that products will not be delivered to certain states would be effective to avert accountability under the laws of the excluded states – *provided* the disclaimer was unequivocal and the provider did not act contrary to his stated intentions. In other words, it is deeds and not just words that count.

So even within the EU which seeks to limit the regulatory claims of destination states in order to facilitate a single market, states have resisted or severely circumscribed the origin rule in areas such as gambling or pharmaceutical products – either to protect national fiscal interests or national perceptions of health and safety. Yet, there is one critical caveat: even though the destination approach allows states in principle to apply local law to accessible foreign sites, in reality they can only with great difficulty enforce their laws against foreign providers. Providers in turn are subjected to so many compounding legal obligations making compliance with all of them impossible. Providers may decide to forgo the benefits of foreign markets on the off-chance that their sites might be in conflict with the foreign rules because actually ascertaining the content of all these rules would be an insurmountable task. Such risk averse approach or self-censorship would not just be a loss for the providers but also for states and the online community as a whole.

### National economic interests (e.g. online gambling, Airbnb and Uber)

Regulatory assertions over foreign online activity are not only, or even mainly, about political or moral issues, but frequently designed to protect significant local economic stakes. The activities of a number of popular IT companies mainly from the US, e.g. Uber and Airbnb, have met with hostility, first from industry and then from regulators, as they undermine established local industries, i.e. taxi and hotel.[55] Similarly, actions brought by rights holders based on copyright or trade marks (as discussed below under civil disputes) are about economic agendas.

---

49 *Deutscher Apothekerverband eV v 0800 Doc Morris NV* Case C-322/01 [2003] ECR I-14887.
50 Art 3(2) of the Electronic Commerce Directive, 00/31/EC.
51 See also Arts 1(5)(d) and 2(h) of the Electronic Commerce Directive, 00/31/EC.
52 *Arzneimittelwerbung im Internet* (BGH, 30 March 2006, I ZR 24/03), para 27–30.
53 See Recital 21 and Art 2(h)(ii) of the Electronic Commerce Directive, 00/31/EC.
54 Consistent with the German marketing prohibition in accordance with Art 2(1) of the Advertising of Medicinal Products Directive, 92/28/EC, and Art 87(1) of the Community Code for Medicinal Products for Human Use Directive, 2001/83/EC (prohibition on the marketing of drugs for which there is no authorisation in accordance with Community law). Note too, that Art 13(7) of the Framework Convention on Tobacco Control (Geneva, 2003) allows states to ban cross-border tobacco advertising (including advertising via the internet).
55 Eric Auchard, Christoph Steitz, 'UPDATE 3- German court bans Uber's unlicensed taxi services' (13 March 2015, *Reuters*), available online at: http://www.reuters.com/article/2015/03/18/uber-germany-idUSL6N0WK22J20150318; Will Coldwell, 'Airbnb's legal troubles: what are the issues?' (2014) *The Guardian*, 8 July, available online at: http://www.theguardian.com/travel/2014/jul/08/airbnb-legal-troubles-what-are-the-issues

One such economic area that has attracted significant regulatory activity is online gambling. Again regulatory responses have varied, ranging from outright prohibitions to toleration to positive encouragement. These variations have again created the danger that the toleration or encouragement of online gambling by one state undermines its prohibition in another. Gambling, more than any other regulatory area of the internet, highlights another reason why states have so readily applied their national laws to foreign sites that affect their territory. On the one hand, gambling can have very positive economic repercussions for the state where the gambling provider is established – through the creation of employment and through being a source of significant revenue from the profits made by the provider. These benefits are lost if the gambling services are provided by a foreign operator, who may also to a varying extent undermine the local industry. On the other hand, gambling creates significant social and economic problems flowing from gambling addiction, and these may be exacerbated by less regulated foreign providers. As foreign providers offer none of the advantages associated with gambling and all its disadvantages, they have received significant regulatory hostility and aggressive jurisdictional responses by many states, e.g. the US, Germany, Australia, Italy, the Netherlands, New Zealand, and lately the UK.[56] One US commentator explains: 'The fierceness . . . in this area is puzzling until one realises the one factor at stake in . . . traditional gambling, but not at stake in Internet gambling: Money . . . Internet gambling, hosted by foreign operators, not only generates zero governmental revenue and zero jobs, it also threatens traditional gambling.'[57]

There are many examples of states applying gambling restrictions to foreign online gambling providers. A Dutch court in *National Sporttotaliser Foundation v Ladbrokes Ltd*[58] ordered the defendant, Ladbrokes, based in England and Gibraltar, to make its gambling site inaccessible to Dutch residents as it did not comply with Dutch licensing requirements. Similarly, a German court found in 2004 that an Austrian company breached German penal law by offering online sport-betting services in Germany without a local licence; its licence under Austrian law did not relieve it of any responsibility under German law.[59] Australia (with a very lively offline gambling scene) prohibits anyone, whether local or foreign,[60] from offering online gambling services to people in Australia by virtue of ss 8 and 15 of the Interactive Gambling Act 2001 (Cth). Yet, local providers are free to offer their gambling services to punters abroad.[61] In other words, Australia seeks to obtain the benefits derived by gambling operators without any of its losses. The New Zealand Gambling Act 2003 also prohibits remote interactive gambling,[62] but excludes from this prohibition 'gambling by a person in New Zealand conducted by a gambling operator located outside New Zealand.'[63] Whilst this means foreign online providers may undermine the prohibition applicable to local businesses, New Zealand addresses this problem by prohibiting local intermediaries (such as ISPs and local sites) and offline publishers from advertising foreign gambling services in New Zealand.[64] This approach is smart: instead of seeking to control gambling through prohibitions on foreign gambling providers or local users that are difficult to enforce, it targets local intermediaries (that may provide knowledge of, and access to, the foreign services) over which full enforcement power is present.

---

56 Section 1 of the Gambling (Licensing and Advertising) Act 2014 amends s 33 of the AVMs 2005 (previously gambling providers with no equipment in the UK were not subject to the licensing requirements, but now it is sufficient if the gambling facilities are used in the UK).
57 Christine Hurt, 'Regulating public morals and private markets: Online securities trading, internet gambling and the speculation paradox' (2005) 86 Boston University Law Review 371, 375f.
58 (District Court, The Hague, 27 January 2003), see also *Holland Casino v Paramount Holdings et al* (District Court, Utrecht, 27 February 2003).
59 *Unzulässiges Online-Glücksspielangebot* (OLG Hamburg, 19 August 2004, 5 U 32/04) (2004) 12 Computer und Recht 925; following *Schöner Wetten* (BGH, 1 April 2004, I ZR 317/01).
60 Section 14 of the Interactive Gambling Act 2001 (Cth): 'this Act extends to acts, omissions, matters and things outside Australia'.
61 Unless the foreign country has been declared a 'designated country' (ss 15A, 9A, 9B). As of May 2009 no country had been declared a 'designated country'.
62 Sections 9(2)(b) and 19 of the Gambling Act 2003.
63 Section 4 of the Gambling Act 2003, see definition of 'remote interactive gambling'.
64 See s 16 of the Gambling Act 2003.

Also, if the foreign gambling sites are not known or not easily used, then the likelihood of them being used is relatively small.

The provision of transnational online gambling services has also been at the centre of free trade disputes, at the EU and the WTO levels. In each case, the attempt by states to regulate gambling services offered by foreign online providers was challenged as being inconsistent with free trade commitments. In the EU, gambling was specifically excluded from the Electronic Commerce Directive.[65] EU Member States were not comfortable with extending the Directive's origin rule (see below) to online gambling services. Yet that origin rule exists already to some extent in the form of free trade commitments. In Gambelli[66] in 2003 the CJEU was presented with a challenge to Italy's attempt to impose criminal sanctions on Italian agencies which, contrary to local licensing requirements, acted as online intermediaries for the UK bookmaker Stanley International Betting Ltd. Effectively, Italy wanted to protect its very lucrative national monopoly in the sports betting and gaming sector. This protectionist policy was challenged as being an unjustified restriction on the freedom of establishment and freedom to provide services of foreign providers, contrary to Arts 43 and 49 of the EC Treaty (now Arts 49 and 56 of the Treaty on the Functioning of the EU). These freedoms demanded, it was argued, that Member States take a regulatory hands-off approach to gambling providers from other Member States and regulated by those other states. The CJEU held that Italy's criminal sanctions presented a restriction on the two freedoms and that those restrictions could only be justifiable 'for reasons of overriding general interest' – for example, if they were intended to reduce the incidence of gambling. A fear of losing revenue did not justify restrictions on foreign operators. Thus EC free trade commitments do not prevent Member States from seeking to regulate foreign gambling providers. States can extend their laws to online providers from other EU states only for legitimate, non-economic reasons, but cannot operate protectionist policies.

The WTO Appellate Body had to decide similar issues and came to a similar conclusion in *United States – Measures Affecting the Cross-Border Supply of Gambling and Betting Services* (2005).[67] Antigua and Barbuda lodged a complaint against the US with the WTO in 2003, alleging that the US prohibition on the cross-border supply of gambling and betting services was inconsistent with 'market access' commitments made by the US under Art 16 of the *General Agreement on Trade in Services* (GATS). Antigua blamed the increasingly aggressive US strategy (enforced with the help of local US intermediaries) towards the operation of cross-border gaming activities in Antigua for the significant decline of gambling operators in Antigua: 'from a high of up to 119 licensed operators, employing around 3,000 and accounting for around ten per cent of GDP in 1999, by 2003 the number of operators has declined to 28, employing fewer than 500.'[68] The WTO Appellate Body rejected the US claim that by excluding sporting services from its GATS commitments, it had also excluded gambling and betting services, and held that various US Acts were inconsistent with its GATS commitments. However, as in *Gambelli*, the Appellate Body held that 'public moral' or 'public order' may exceptionally justify market access barriers, provided there were no other reasonable alternative measures. However, in this case the US could not rely on these exceptions as it had exempted domestic providers from the very restrictions it sought to apply to foreign providers. Its free trade commitments

---

65 Recital 16 and Art 1(5)(d) of the Electronic Commerce Directive, 00/31/EC.

66 *Criminal Proceedings against Piergiorgio Gambelli* C-243/01 [2003] ECR I-13031. In *Criminal Proceedings against Massimiliano Placanica and Others* C-338/04, C359/04 and C-360/04 [2007] CJEU ECR I-0000 it was again held that Italy's licensing regime which excluded companies listed on a stock exchange from tendering for a betting licence violated the freedom of establishment and the freedom to provide services as it went beyond what is necessary to achieve the objective of preventing the exploitation of the industry for criminal proposes. See also, *Zeturf Ltd v Premier Minister* C-212/08, [2011] ECR I-5633.

67 *United States – Measures Affecting the Cross-Border Supply of Gambling and Betting Services* first heard by the WTO Dispute Settlement Panel (WTO Panel, 10 November 2004, WT/DS285/R) and then by the Appellate Body (WTO Appellate Body, 7 April 2005, WT/DS285/AB/R). In 2007 the WTO panel concluded 'that the United States has failed to comply with the recommendations and rulings of the DSB in this dispute' (WTO Panel, 30 March 2007, WT/DS285/RW) which paved the way for a compensation claim and then trade sanction by Antigua, see http://www.wto.org/english/tratop_e/dispu_e/cases_e/ds285_e.htm

68 *United States – Measures Affecting the Cross-Border Supply of Gambling and Betting Services* (WTO Panel, 10 November 2004, WT/DS285/R), para 3.5.

prevented the US from imposing restrictions on foreign providers solely as a protectionist measure to safeguard the local industry, rather than as a regulation designed to reduce the incidence of gambling. A similar complaint against the US was lodged in 2007 by the Remote Gambling Association with the European Commission which came to very similar conclusion as the WTO Panel.[69]

## The 'reasonable' effects doctrine – the moderate destination approach

Whether the objective territoriality principle ought to be interpreted as to allow any state to assert regulatory control over foreign conduct based on *any* effects, however slight, of the conduct on the state's territory is disputable. In *Lotus* the effect in question was physical, thus the number of potential regulators was circumscribed. Once intangible effects, such as economic ones, are allowed to justify competence, concurrency of regulation spirals exponentially, defeating in its wake the aims of the competence regimes. Yet, this is precisely the position taken in the above instances: states assert the right to regulate every accessible site. Online providers are accountable to the wishes of hundreds of concurrent 'kings', ruling one and the same 'empire' but all expressing different wishes. In the end, the 'king' with enforcement power is the only one worth taking seriously.

Historically, there have been attempts to refine the objective territoriality principle, especially in the context of economic effects, in order to reduce the incidence of overlapping regulatory claims and mitigate interferences by states in each other affairs.[70] States have not been entirely insensitive to the problem of concurrency. A classic example of such attempts is the effects doctrine as formulated in the US Restatement (Third) of Foreign Relations Law (1986) in response to the international disapproval of the wide antitrust claims made by the US against foreign companies. Paragraph 403 of the Restatement states that 'a state may not exercise jurisdiction . . . with respect to a person or activity having connections with another state when the exercise of such jurisdiction is unreasonable.'[71] Whether such exercise is 'reasonable' is made dependent on a number of factors, such as the extent to which the activity has a substantial, direct or foreseeable effect upon the territory, the character of the activity, the degree to which the desirability of regulation is generally accepted, the existence of justified expectations, the importance of regulating the activity, the consistency with traditions of the international systems, the interest of other states in regulating the activity and the likelihood of conflicting regulation. This test is not easily implemented in any given situation, but in substance its aims are spot on. It goes beyond single-mindedly seeking to uphold a state's authority over its territory by also trying to protect individuals, the interests of other states and the coherence of the allocation system as a whole. Despite wide-spread approval of this moderated effects doctrine at the time,[72] the above examples show that moderation has often not guided the internet competence debate – at least not in the criminal or regulatory sphere. Otherwise the question whether the 'offending' foreign site is accessible from the would-be regulating state's territory would be replaced by the question whether the foreign site has had a *substantial* effect on that state's territory and whether that effect was foreseeable or intended – in short, whether the site was directed at the state. A moderate effects test would allow *only* those states which are targeted by the foreign conduct to assert regulatory rights, rather than all states (mildly) affected.

69 European Commission, *Report to the Trade Barriers Regulation Committee: Examination Procedure concerning an Obstacle to Trade, within the Meaning of Council Regulation (EC) No 3286/94, consisting of Measures Adopted by the United States of America Affecting Trade in Remote Gambling Services* (Brussels, 10 June 2009).

70 Bernard H Oxman, 'Jurisdiction of States' in Rudolf Bernhardt (ed), Encyclopaedia of Public International Law (1987) Vol 10, 277, 278, on the objectives of jurisdictional rules under public international law.

71 See also Reydams, above nn 13, 17: 'applications of the principles to a specific problem will require further balancing of interest of the States involved and the requirements of justice. Moreover, in some cases the question will not be posed in terms of whether a State's claim to jurisdiction is illegal *per se*, but whether it is a proper exercise of jurisdiction, given the conflicting interests of two or more States as well as the consequences for the individual defendant.'

72 See for example, AV Lowe, *Extraterritorial Jurisdiction – An Annotated Collection of Legal Materials*, 1983, Cambridge: Grotius Publications Ltd, 207ff.

As shown below, this moderate destination approach is endorsed in some civil internet disputes and might even be said to emerge as the dominant approach there. Even in criminal law there are some cases advocating a 'significant' nexus. In England and Wales, for example, *Sheppard and Whittle* (2010) (above) concerning inflammatory online speech followed the 'substantial measure' test adopted in R v Smith *(Wallace Duncan)* (No 4) (2004):

> The English courts have decisively begun to move away from definitional obsessions and technical formulations aimed at finding a single situs of a crime by locating where the gist of the crime occurred or where it was completed. Rather, they now appear to seek by an examination of relevant policies to apply the English criminal law where a *substantial measure of the activities* constituting a crime take place in England, and restrict its application in such circumstances solely in cases where it can seriously be argued on a reasonable view that these activities should, on the basis of international comity, be dealt with by another country.[73]

The court in *Sheppard and Whittle* (2010) also noted that the offending site *targeted* a British audience which is resonant with the approach taken in some civil law disputes (see below). Of course, the reality in the criminal context is that it generally would make little sense to prosecute internet offences unless the offending parties are local and then the chances are that a 'substantial measure' of their offensive acts were committed locally, primarily for a local audience. So whenever a prosecution is brought the 'substantial measure' test is bound to be satisfied as would the 'targeting' test be. For example, the case of *Donner* (2012)[74] concerned a German copyright prosecution[75] arising out of sales transactions in Germany, carried out by Italian companies, but controlled and masterminded by Mr Donner who was a German and conducted his business from his place of residence in Germany. The CJEU held that the German prosecution of Mr Donner was legitimate as he was responsible for the distribution of the offending products to the German public[76] given that 'he specifically targeted the public of the State of destination and must have been aware of the actions of that third party.'[77] According to the CJEU 'factors such as the existence of a German-language website, the content and distribution channels of Dimensione's advertising materials and its cooperation with Inspem, as an undertaking making deliveries to Germany, may be taken as constituting evidence of such targeted activity.'[78] So, much like in *Sheppard and Whittle*, the CJEU found in *Donner* a strong connection between Donner's activities and Germany, focusing on who was actually targeted by the online activities, i.e. the moderate destination approach. Yet, taking the targeting approach in cases where it is satisfied is easy; the real test will be whether the targeting approach would be taken when it requires regulatory forbearance where the effects on the state seeking to regulate it are not strong. States have not been very good at regulatory forbearance.

Finally, let us return to the US where a reasonable effects test was a response to criticisms of its global anti-trust enforcement. Although the US Supreme Court later backtracked from the 'reasonable effects' test,[79] US competence jurisprudence is still infused with moderate rhetoric. Part of the reason is that the US, unlike other states, even in criminal cases, treats adjudicative and legislative jurisdiction as two distinct inquiries. And as adjudicative jurisdiction is generally based

---

73 R v Smith *(Wallace Duncan)* (No 4) [2004] QB 1418, para 55 [emphasis added]. The court also explicitly rejected that criminal jurisdiction would in any way be resolved by jurisdictional concepts that might govern transnational private disputes: 'From a jurisdictional point of view it is unsatisfactory for a question of jurisdiction to be determined by an artificial concept designed for resolving contractual disputes' (para 52). See also Donner C5/11, para 25.

74 *Donner (Free movement of goods)* C-5/11, [2012] EUECJ (21 June 2012).

75 Copyright in the Information Society Directive 2001/29.

76 Article 4(1) of the Copyright in the Information Society Directive 2001/29.

77 *Donner (Free movement of goods)* C-5/11, [2012] EUECJ (21 June 2012), para 27.

78 Ibid, para 29.

79 *Hartford Fire Insurance Co v California*, 509 US 764 (1993) confined the moderate approach to situations where there is a true conflict between domestic and foreign law which is very rare indeed.

on the court's personal jurisdiction over the defendant, the 'due process' requirement under the US Constitution comes into play. This imports the requirement that the defendant must have purposefully (i.e. knowingly) availed himself of the privilege of conducting activity within the state, which in relation to online activity is established, for example, by evidence that the foreign site 'targeted' the state.[80] Thus the expansive objective territoriality principle gives way to a more moderate version that focuses on the substantiality of the effects of the foreign online activity, that is the site, on the state in addition to a 'mental element'.

For example, in People v World Interactive Gaming Corporation (1999)[81] the question was whether the state of New York could prohibit an Antiguan corporation licensed to operate a casino in Antigua from offering its online gambling services to New Yorkers. As in this case the foreign company was in fact the wholly owned subsidiary (and, according to the court, the alter ego) of a local company which had total control over the unauthorised activities, personal jurisdiction by the court over both companies could easily be established based on their 'presence' within the territory.[82] However, the court also examined the nature and quality of the defendants' internet activities and concluded that New York territory had been targeted by their activities; amongst other things, they had 'engaged in an advertising campaign all over the country to induce people to visit their website and gamble. Knowing that these ads were reaching thousands of New Yorkers, respondents made no attempt to exclude identifiable New Yorkers from the propaganda.'[83] This approach is very different from that adopted by other states in criminal cases, where states have rarely engaged with the relative strength of their claim, i.e. to what extent is their claim to regulate a site in any way stronger than that of any other state. The French court in Yahoo never expressly asked whether yahoo.com was specifically targeted at France (although it made a brief reference to the fact that the advertising was tailored to French users). Even in US jurisprudence in criminal cases, it is not entirely clear to what extent targeting would be required if it was not in fact present. Currently given the size of the US economy, the US is a very attractive market for many internet businesses and thus the targeting element can in many suits easily be proven.

Certainly the targeting approach does not feature in the US respect of prescriptive jurisdiction, i.e. when it comes to deciding on the territorial scope of the legislation, which would be the more important context for moderation as it determines the liability for the activities in question. In People v World Interactive Gaming Corporation the court – having to decide on the territorial scope of the New York gambling legislation – clearly endorsed the wide version of the objective territoriality principle: 'under New York Penal Law, if the person engaged in gambling is located in New York, then New York is the location where the gambling occurred.'[84] Although the court relied on actual gambling activity in its territory via the foreign site, rather than the site's mere accessibility there, it did not insist that New Yorkers must have been a particular target of that site, albeit in this case they were. The court stated that not regulating the site 'would immunize from liability anyone who engages in any activity over the Internet which is otherwise illegal in this state. A computer server cannot be permitted to function as a shield against liability, particularly in this case where respondents actively targeted New York as the location where they conducted many of their allegedly

---

80 The same approach as adopted in the US in civil matters, see below.
81 714 NYS 2d 844 (1999) [emphasis added]. For other Internet gambling cases, see US v Cohen 260 F 3d 68 (2d Cir 2001); State of Missouri v Coeur D'Alene Tribe 164 F 3d 1102 (1999); State of Missouri v Interactive Gaming & Communications Corp WL 33545763 (MoCir 1997); State of Minnesota v Granite Gate Resorts Inc 568 NW 2d 715 (1997). See also American Bar Association, 'Achieving Legal and Business Order in Cyberspace: A Report on Global Jurisdiction Issues Created by the Internet' (2000) 55 The Business Lawyer 1801. See http://www.kentlaw.edu/cyberlaw/docs/drafts/draft.rtf, 144ff
82 The parent company was in fact incorporated in Delaware, but as it operated its entire business from its corporate headquarters in New York, the court could rely on its actual physical presence to assert personal jurisdiction over it.
83 People v World Interactive Gaming Corporation 714 NYS 2d 844, 849 (1999).
84 People v World Interactive Gaming Corporation 714 NYS 2d 844, 850 (1999).

illegal activities.'[85] The term 'particularly' suggests that the court would have come to the same conclusion even if New York had not been targeted.

The targeting requirement also plays no part in cases where courts do not rely on personal jurisdiction over the defendant to assert their right to hear the claim. An alternative basis is provided by in rem jurisdiction where a court's adjudicative power is based on the fact that an object connected to the illegality is within its territory. Thus the formal defendant in the action is the object, not the person.[86] In rem jurisdiction provides a good testing ground for the reality of moderation in the regulatory assertions of the US, given that in in rem cases the state has the actual physical power to enforce the court's judgment by seizing the object in question. Thus it would be all the harder to abstain from hearing a dispute in the name of lofty notions such as reasonableness and moderation. In US v $734,578.82 in US Currency[87] the US government brought a civil in rem forfeiture action against local bank accounts used in the process of allegedly illegal gambling activity by a local corporation on behalf of an English gambling house, fully licensed in England. Most of its betting business, promoted through the Internet and carried out via the telephone, derived from North-American sports and most customers came from Canada and the US. Although this action was formally civil, in jurisdictional terms it would likely be categorised as 'criminal' or 'public' as the claimant was the government seeking to indirectly enforce a criminal prohibition on unauthorised gambling. The government asserted the right to seize the funds in these accounts as they were connected with the illegal gambling activity, as promoted contrary to New Jersey law by a local corporation. The court rejected that the foreign aspect of the case had in fact any bearing upon it:

> We therefore find no merit in Claimants' jurisdictional challenge to this *in rem* proceeding over New Jersey property based upon conduct occurring in New Jersey. It may well be true that British citizens and British companies will be affected by this *in rem* action in New Jersey. This does not mean that the law of New Jersey or the law of the United States is being applied to those citizens or companies.[88]

As these British companies were the holders and beneficiaries of the accounts, it is disingenuous to deny that US law was being applied to them when their funds were seized. This case shows that in in rem actions there is less need to justify the extraterritorial application of a state's law on foreign conduct given that competence can be based (or hide behind) the territorial application of the law to the local property that 'has done the wrong.'

## The subjective territoriality principle and the exclusive origin approach

The subjective territoriality principle presents the other side of the coin of the objective territoriality principle. It allows states to assume competence over a crime commenced on their territory even if it takes effect elsewhere. In the internet context this translates into the fairly uncontroversial position that states are entitled to regulate sites which are hosted on their territories or sites which – although hosted elsewhere – are created by locals.[89] In either case, the cause or source or origin of the criminalised activity is within state borders. An equivalent pre-internet case is *Treacy*

---

85 *People v World Interactive Gaming Corporation* 714 NYS 2d 844, 850 (1999) [emphasis added].
86 *United States v US Coin and Currency* 401 US 715, 719 (1971): 'the theory has been that if the object is "guilty", it should be held forfeit. In the words of a medieval English writer, "Where a man killeth another with the sword of John at Stile, the sword shall be forfeit as deodand, and yet no default is in the owner."' In *United States v Sandini* 816 F2d 869, 872 (1987): 'Civil forfeiture is an in rem proceeding. The property is the defendant in the case . . . The innocence of the owner is irrelevant – it is enough that the property was involved in a violation to which forfeiture attaches.'
87 286 F 3d 641 (2002).
88 *US v $734,578.82 in US Currency* 286 F 3d 641, 660 (2002).
89 See *R v Perrin* [2002] EWCA Crim 747.

v DPP (1971)[90] concerning a charge of blackmail where the letter demanding money was posted in England to a recipient in Germany. Nonetheless, Lord Diplock held that the conviction under English law would stand: 'There is no rule of comity to prevent Parliament from prohibiting under pain of punishment persons who are present in the United Kingdom and so owe local obedience to our law, from doing physical acts in England notwithstanding that the effects of those acts take place outside the United Kingdom.'[91] As shown above, a classic internet example of this approach, highlighting its practical advantages, is *Sheppard and Whittle* (2010).[92]

While the application of the subjective territoriality principle to the internet is fairly undisputed, online providers have persistently argued that the subjective territoriality principle should be the only basis of establishing competence over online activity – to the exclusion of regulatory claims by destination states. Allowing exclusively the country of origin to govern online conduct has significant merits. Online providers would only have to comply with one set of familiar laws, rather than innumerable foreign ones, and the origin states could easily enforce their claims as such enforcement would be directed against local sites or providers. How the 'origin state' is defined depends on the court or legislation in question; certainly there is no one single formula for the origin approach. It may focus on the location of the actor, the action or any 'tools' used in the process. Especially in the corporate context, there is also the choice between the seat of the management of the company, the seat of any of its editorial offices or the place of the server where the material is uploaded.[93] For example, under the Electronic Commerce Directive, the origin of the online service is determined by reference to where 'a service provider . . . pursues an economic activity using a fixed establishment for an infinite period. The presence and use of the technical means and technologies required . . . do not, in themselves, constitute an establishment of the provider.'[94] While the notion of a fixed establishment of the provider seems straightforward, the wording of the section is the end-product of significant litigation before the CJEU.[95] Nevertheless, relatively speaking definitional problems of the origin rule are minor compared to the uncertainties arising out of the destination rule. Assuming a definition of 'origin' is agreed upon, the online publisher can order his/her affairs fairly straightforwardly; he/she knows where it uploads its data or where it has a fixed establishment, can control those locations and would not face any unexpected legal exposure.

But the very reasons which have made states so eager to extend their laws to foreign sites, are also the reasons that have dictated against the exclusive country-of-origin approach becoming a mainstream solution to competence over internet activity. The exclusive origin approach to competence has the main disadvantages that it undermines the laws of the destination states. It also encourages forum-shopping for the state with the most lenient law by online providers and leads overall to the lowest common denominator setting the legal standards worldwide. Finally, although it reduces the regulatory burden for online content providers, in actual fact this burden of ascertaining foreign legal standards is often shifted to online users. Given these disadvantages, the question is when it would ever prove to be acceptable.

---

90 *Treacy v DPP* [1971] AC 537.
91 *Treacy v DPP* [1971] AC 537, 561f; but contrast R v *Manning* [1999] QB 980 which followed R v *Harden* [1963] 1 QB 8 insisting that the 'terminatory theory' of jurisdiction was the common law of England and Wales, also known as 'results crimes'; this approach was not followed in R v *Smith (Wallace Duncan) (No 4)* [2004] QB 1418, which followed Rose LJ's judgment in R v *Smith (Wallace Duncan)* [1996] 2 Cr App R 1.
92 R v *Sheppard and Whittle* [2010] EWCA Crim 65.
93 In *Dow Jones & Co Inc v Gutnick* [2002] HCA 56 the editorial office was in New York and the server New Jersey; see also para 41 for other possible connections: the location where the material was initially composed or the place of incorporation of the provider. Discussed in Australian Law Reform Commission, *Choice of Law* (Report No 58, 1992), 57.
94 Article 2(c) of the Electronic Commerce Directive 00/31/EC.
95 Julia Hörnle, 'country of origin regulation in cross-border media: one step beyond the freedom to provide services?' (2005) 54 International and Comparative Law Quarterly 89, 113; and *Commission v UK* C-222/94, [1996] ECR I-4025, concerning Art 2(1) of the Television Without Frontiers Directive 89/552/EC (later revised by 97/36/EC).

The Electronic Commerce Directive is a prime example of the exclusive origin approach in the online context, but exclusively within the EU (See further Chapter 6 on Electronic Commerce).[96] Article 3(2) provides that Member States 'may not . . . restrict the freedom to provide information society services from another Member State.'[97] This means that they may not impose their regulation on online providers from other Member States.[98] The rule applies to any legal requirements within 'the coordinated field', such as legal prerequisites for carrying out the activity or requirements concerning the content or quality of the service.[99] Despite some uncertainty as to what exactly falls within the 'coordinated field', there is no doubt that the rule has 'a very wide scope as it applies across all sectors [bar a few exceptions including gambling] and not just to the areas harmonized by the Directive.'[100] The exclusive origin rule in the Electronic Commerce Directive falls within the peculiar EU single market context and its attendant removal of internal economic borders through the grant of freedoms such as the free movements of goods and the freedom to provide services. Thus EU Member States are long used to restrictions being imposed on their natural inclination to regulate incoming goods and services – for the greater good of an open market. However, the exclusive origin rule in the Electronic Commerce Directive goes a step further than the above freedoms in that it prevents destination states from regulating foreign incoming services altogether, and not just when that regulation would be discriminatory or amount to an obstacle.[101] While that extra step has also been taken before, for example in the EU Television without Frontiers Directive,[102] there the origin rule was restricted to the areas of law harmonised in the Directive,[103] unlike its open-ended application to 'coordinated fields' in the Electronic Commerce Directive. Broadly speaking though, the exclusive origin rule in the Electronic Commerce Directive falls within, and is a natural progression of, the EU tradition of mutual recognition and a climate of mutual respect for each other's legal regimes.

What then may be regarded as pre-requisites or fertile ground for the acceptability of the exclusive origin rule, as illustrated by the Electronic Commerce Directive? First of all, as the exclusive origin rule requires destination states to abstain from regulating foreign conduct that affects them in deference to the regulatory claim by the origin state, it helps if the legal rules of that origin state are broadly in tune with those of the abstaining destination state. Then the destination state need not fear that local rules would be undermined by the foreign conduct. Legal harmonisation or at least approximisation, such as within the EU, makes the exclusive origin rule less threatening than it would be in respect of widely diverging legal standards. This explains why in previous Directives the origin was tied to the harmonised areas covered by the Directive. Second, reciprocity – as opposed to the unilateral adoption of the origin approach – makes the exclusive origin rule much easier to bear for states. Such reciprocity of regulatory abstinence entails that states can be assured that their forbearance in respect of foreign providers and any economic or other loss suffered due to such forbearance is recompensed by local providers gaining unhindered access to foreign markets. Again

---

96  See Hörnle ibid; Moerel, Lokke, 'The Country-of-Origin Principle in the E-Commerce Directive: The Expected One Stop Shop' (2001) 7 Computer and Telecommunication Law Review 184. See also, Arts 2 and 3 of the Audiovisual Media Services Directive 2010/13/EU.

97  For the interaction of this section with private international law, see Joined Cases eDate Advertising and Martinez C-509/09 and C-161/10, [2011] ECR I-10269.

98  *eDate Advertising GmbH v X and Olivier Martinez and Robert Martinez v MGN Limited* Joined cases C-509/09 and C-161/10, ECR 2011 I-10269, para 67, where the CJEU held Art 3(2) does not supply a jurisdiction rule, but 'caps' the substantive law of the host state to the strict standard of the home state of the provider.

99  Article 2(h) of the Electronic Commerce Directive, 00/31/EC.

100  Julia Hörnle, 'The UK Perspective on the Country of Origin Rule in the E-commerce Directive – A Rule of Administrative law Applicable to Private Law Disputes?' (2004) 12 International Journal of Law and Information Technology 333, 337; Joakim ST Oren, 'International jurisdiction over consumer contracts in e-Europe' (2003) 52 International and Comparative Law Quarterly 665, 668.

101  In respect of the freedom of movement of goods the CJEU held in *Deutscher Apothekerverband eV v 0800 Doc Morris NV* Case C-322/01, [2003] ECR I-14887, that the requirement under German law that certain drugs must be sold in pharmacies was in this case an unjustified restriction on the online activities of the Dutch pharmacy. Such requirement was only justified for prescription drugs. Since then the Directive has come into force, with the online sale of drugs being within the scope of the 'coordinated fields'.

102  Article 2a(1) of the Television without Frontiers Directive 89/552/EEC (revised by 97/36/EC). Other Directives that adopt the origin rule are 89/646/EEC, 93/22/EEC, 92/49/EEC and 92/96/EEC.

103  Article 2(1) of the Television without Frontiers Directive 89/552/EEC.

such reciprocity is provided for in the Electronic Commerce Directive as states mutually agree to abide by the origin rule amongst each other. Last but not least, the origin approach in a reciprocal setting must be understood not merely as an agreement *not to regulate* foreign providers or sites, but equally as the responsibility *to regulate* local providers. The deference to the origin state in the EU goes hand in hand with an expectation that that state takes its regulatory responsibility in respect of activities originating from its territory seriously. Consistently Art 3(1) of the Electronic Commerce Directive imposes an obligation on origin states to regulate: '[e]ach Member State shall ensure that the information services provided by a service provider established on its territory comply with the national provisions in the Member State in question which fall within the coordinated field.' This duty is coupled with various remedies in the hands of the destination state, should the duty not be fulfilled.[104] Thus, internationally an exclusive origin rule would rarely be acceptable to states – other than by way of an international agreement covering clearly delineated subject-matters amongst relatively homogenous legal systems with mutual respect for, and confidence in, each other.

## The universality principle

### Quasi-universal jurisdiction over online activity

As most online activity can easily be linked *territorially* to any states, there has been little need for states to rely on any other head of jurisdiction under public international law. Nevertheless the universality principle has some bearing on the internet competence debate, if only in so far as it indirectly comments on the current jurisdictional practices of states.

The universality principle is the only head of jurisdiction which dispenses with the need for any link between the state seeking to assert jurisdiction and the act, actor or victim in question, and in very limited circumstances gives *prima facie* all states competence.[105] Initially it only applied to piracy on the high seas; thus concerning an area beyond the territorial reach of any particular state while at the same time attaching to a phenomenon in which all states shared a common or *universal* interest in its suppression. The ambit of the principle later expanded to include slave trade and, after World War II, war crimes and crimes against humanity and has since been applied, at least in treaties, to torture, genocide, hijacking, hostage taking and terrorist activity. The assumption underlying all these instances is that in relation to particular heinous crimes that are universally condemned, it is in the interest of the international community for any state to have the right, and possibly a duty,[106] to prosecute if the offender is within the state's actual control.[107]

Relevant to the online competence debate is that the application of the universality principle, despite its expansion in the last half century, still remains strictly delimited. This could not be otherwise, as the principle runs – in its very design – counter to the very purpose of having competence rules and the notion of *sharing* regulatory space; under it all states have in theory a concurrent regulatory entitlement, which is only in practice resolved by the state who has apprehended the wrongdoer. But this exceptional position seems not so far removed from the normal state practice pertaining to websites. Although states have invariably based their regulatory claims over internet

---

104 The destination state can first of all request the origin state to fulfil its duty and then take measures to restrict incoming services, after notifying the Commission and the origin state of its intention under Art 3(40)(b) of the Directive; or initiate infringement proceedings.

105 See Reydams, above at n 13; and Kenneth C Randall, 'Universal jurisdiction under international law' (1988) 66 Texas Law Review 785, 991ff.

106 Under traditional customary international law the universality principle was merely permissive, allowing, but not requiring, them to exercise universal jurisdiction in respect of some offences. However, many treaties make such exercise of jurisdiction mandatory where the offender is within the state's custody. This position may now also apply to some very grave offences under customary international law. Robert Kolb, 'The exercise of criminal jurisdiction over international terrorists' in Andrea Bianchi, *Enforcing International Law Norms Against Terrorism*, 2004, Oxford: Hart, 227, 250, 260f.

107 Arguably universal jurisdiction may be exercised even in *absentia*, Reydams, above at n 13, 38ff.

activity on the territorial link between the site and the state (i.e. its territorial effect), given that this is generally universally true for all states, the effect of these regulatory claims has been the creation of a *de facto* type of universal jurisdiction over websites. Yet unlike universal jurisdiction proper, the impact of this quasi-universal jurisdiction is not contained by strict limits on its material application and also unlike universal jurisdiction proper, the subject-matters covered are not universally condemned as crimes against mankind – quite the reverse. Finally, the right to regulate the activity in question by the state is and could not be conceived as a corresponding duty to other states to do so. In short, all the conditions of the universality principle that legitimise its exceptional existence generally are absent in respect of all those regulatory claims over websites that could be made by all states. Thus their legitimacy is also dubious.

## Express universal jurisdiction over online activity – UK Terrorism Act 2006

Terrorist activity is an area to which the universality principle may apply under customary international law, and does apply under treaty law.[108] In the wake of 9/11 there has been a flurry of national and international legislative activity dealing with terrorist activities, including those on the internet. In the UK the Terrorism Act 2006 makes it an offence to publish statements, extending to internet publications, that encourage or induce the commission, preparation or instigation of terrorist acts.[109] The offence is extremely far reaching and requires no territorial connection with the UK at all: 'If (a) a person does anything outside the United Kingdom, and (b) his action, if done in a part of the United Kingdom, would constitute an offence . . . , he shall be guilty in that part of the United Kingdom of the offence.'[110] Section 17(3) then additionally dispenses with a nationality connection: 'Subsection (1) applies irrespective of whether the person is a British citizen, or in the case of a company, a company incorporated in a part of the United Kingdom.' Thus the Act asserts competence over terrorist publications by anyone anywhere – a classic example of universal jurisdiction. The Explanatory Memorandum confirms this when it states that '[t]he overall effect of the section is that if, for example, an individual were to commit one of these offences in a foreign country, they would be liable under UK law in the same way as if they had committed the offence in the UK.'[111]

The section seeks to give effect to the Council of Europe Convention on the Prevention of Terrorism (2005, Warsaw). Article 14(1) and (2) provide a fairly long list of specific heads of jurisdiction when states must or may – depending on the circumstances – assume control over the alleged terrorist activity. Broadly those heads focus on territorial and nationality connections of the state with the offence, offender or victim. They are supplemented by a catch-all provision in Art 14(3) which requires states to assume jurisdiction over terrorist offences whenever the alleged offender is within its territory and the state has not extradited him to a requesting party whose request is based on a valid head of jurisdiction.[112] The idea is that states cannot, wittingly or unwittingly, become safe havens for offenders, whenever they have no jurisdiction under Art 14(1) and (2) and

---

108 Randall, above at n 105, 790.
109 See ss 1–3. Section 1 creates the main offence of encouraging terrorism; s 2 criminalises the dissemination of terrorist publications; s 3 extends these provisions to internet intermediaries and provides for a notice-and-take-down defence to any secondary electronic publisher who would otherwise be caught by the offences under ss 1 and 2. For the definition of 'terrorism' see s 1 of the Terrorism Act 2000, which was considered by the Supreme Court in R v Gul [2013] UKSC 64.
110 Section 17(1) which goes much further than the Electronic Commerce Directive (Terrorism Act 2006) Regulations 2007 which in reg 3(1) provides: 'If (a) in the course of providing information society services, a service provider *established in the United Kingdom* does anything in an EEA state other than the United Kingdom, and (b) his action, if done in a part of the United Kingdom, would constitute a relevant offence, he shall be guilty in that part of the United Kingdom for the offence.' This provides for variation of the nationality principle given that the offence may be wholly committed elsewhere, but the offender is linked to the UK by his fixed establishment in the UK.
111 *Explanatory Notes* to the Terrorism Act 2006, para 82.
112 The validity of that assertion is assessed by the standards of the requested state, i.e. has the requested state a rule of jurisdiction which would have justified the requesting state's claim (also known as the double-jurisdiction rule).

decided to refuse, for whatever reasons, a valid extradition request. Nevertheless the insistence on the initial list of heads suggests that jurisdiction ought to lie first and foremost with those states that *have* a link to the offence and only on a secondary basis with an 'un-connected' state. In short, the universality principle is – consistent with its original design – a fall-back provision. Insofar as s 17 of the UK Terrorism Act 2006 provides for universal jurisdiction, it is formally in line with the Convention; however in so far as it gives no indication of the exceptional nature of such claims, it is not within its spirit.

Having said that, in respect of foreign online terrorist publications hosted by foreigners resort to universal jurisdiction under s 17 would rarely, if ever, be necessary as a basis for a prosecution. Such publications are already within the ambit of the territoriality principle, and particularly the objective territoriality principle, if they are accessible in the UK. For example, a person can be said to 'publish' a terrorist statement on UK soil under s 1 of the Act whenever such statement can be read online on UK soil – in line with the criminal case law discussed above. But as also noted above, given that most offenders are outside the UK, this area is dominated by the practical blocking measures instigated by the Counter Terrorism Internet Referral Unit.[113]

# Enforcement

## Non-intervention and non-cooperation

The anything-goes law-defying reality of the internet seems to belie the above proposition that online providers are severely overregulated through the compounding regulatory claims made by states over both home-grown and foreign sites. This apparent contradiction between the legal and actual reality of the internet is explicable by reference to the strict territorial limits on states' enforcement jurisdiction. A fundamental principle of public international law designed to protect the independence of states and their orderly co-existence with each other is the principle of non-intervention: a state may not engage in public acts on the territory of another state.[114] As the Permanent Court of Justice said in *Lotus*: 'the first and foremost restriction imposed by international law upon a State is that . . . it may not exercise its power in any form in the territory of another state. In this sense jurisdiction is certainly territorial.'[115] While states may attach legal consequences to foreign acts or actors under local law, they can never compel compliance with it by, for example, sending a local police officer or any public official into the territory of another state to effect an arrest or seize property. Consequently, many a time when foreign websites violate local law, states can do nothing about it.

This lack of enforcement is, in the criminal context, accompanied by a long-standing profound unwillingness of states to cooperate in the enforcement of each other's criminal, revenue and other public laws.[116] This uncooperative stance finds expression in two ways: on the one hand, states never apply foreign public/criminal law in local prosecutions and on the other hand, they never enforce foreign public/criminal law judgments against local offenders.[117] A recent inroad into this uncooperative stance has been made by an inconspicuous provision in the UK and

---

113 See text accompanying nn 39 and 40.
114 Examples of violations of that principle are the kidnapping of Nazi officer Adolf Eichmann by Israeli agents in Argentina in 1960, the sinking of the *Rainbow Warrior* by French government agents in New Zealand territorial waters in 1985 and the kidnapping of Alvarez-Machain by US agents in Mexico (*US v Alvarez-Machain*, 504 US 655 (1992)).
115 *The Case of the SS 'Lotus' (France v Turkey)* (1927) PCIJ Reports, Series A, No 10, 18.
116 Limited cooperation exists at the peripheries of criminal regulation, as for example under treaties in respect of the investigation of crimes and the production of evidence or concerning the extradition of offenders. Within the EU significant inroads into this non-cooperative stance have been made, e.g. European Arrest Warrant, see: Simon Chalton, 'E-commerce and the European Arrest Warrant' (2003) 8(4) Communications Law 329. In *Yahoo! Inc v LICRA and UEJF*, 433 F 3d 1199 (9th Cir. 2006) the US court refused to formally rule on the enforceability of the French judgment in the US but in *obiter* a majority of the judges stated that it would not have been enforced if they had to decide the issue.
117 Even in formally civil cases, such as *Yahoo*, a state may refuse to enforce a judgment if it would indirectly enforce a criminal or public law (see 'Enforcement in Transnational Civil Cases').

Australian online gambling legislation, aptly named the 'good neighbour' clause. Section 44 of the UK Gambling Act 2005 provides: 'A person commits an offence if he does anything in Great Britain, or uses remote gambling equipment situated in Great Britain, for the purpose of inviting or enabling a person in a prohibited territory to participate in remote gambling.' A territory is prohibited territory if the Secretary of State has made an order to that effect,[118] presumably following a request by a foreign state. The effect of the section is that a local provider may be penalised in the UK for breaching foreign criminal law on online gambling, even though the provision of gambling is legal at home. So far neither the UK nor Australia have made use of the good neighbour clause, despite clear evidence many states do not look kindly upon online gambling.[119] Thus perhaps these cooperative provisions are more rhetoric than reality.

The strict territorial limit of enforcement jurisdiction coupled with the unwillingness by states to cooperate in the enforcement of each other's criminal or public laws means that states have to find avenues within their borders, however imperfect, to make their expansive regulatory claims over foreign online providers more meaningful.

## Symbolic and educative prosecutions

One avenue chosen by states to try to induce respect for their laws in foreign providers are symbolic and educative prosecutions. States have prosecuted foreign providers in the rare circumstances when they could apprehend them as they happen to be on their soil, for example, on a visit. Let it be a warning to others! One such example is the German *Töben* (discussed above) where Töben, resident in Australia, was arrested while visiting Germany. Similarly, in the US foreign online gambling providers have been arrested in connection with their online activities by US border controls while trying to enter the country.[120] Alternatively, as in US v $734,578.82[121] (discussed above), the state's access to relevant property (e.g. local bank accounts) connected with the foreign illegal activity has been exploited by them as a lever to impose their rule on foreign online activities. While in these cases the state in question was able to penalise the particular offender in respect of his/her particular activities, the broader objective of such actions – as is the case for any criminal prosecution and to some extent for civil cases – cannot but be that of wider deterrence, that is inducing voluntary compliance in others. Of course, it may simply have signalled to, for example, Antiguan gambling providers that they should not book a holiday in the US, when they could be arrested. Sometimes, even in the absence of any enforcement power, the highly unfavourable damaging publicity arising from a court hearing and judgment may induce companies to voluntarily comply with the foreign law, as appears to have been the case in *Yahoo*.[122] This certainly holds true for those highly visible companies for whom their clean public image and respectability are important parts of their brand.

Last but not least, the occasional prosecution of foreign website providers serves another function, namely education. To the extent that law-imposing obligations can only be complied with if they are known, these cases 'inform' the online community that their legal obligations generally do not stop at their home borders and that states will not simply resign to their inability to catch foreign offenders if they can help it.

---

118 Section 44(2) of the Gambling Act 2005. The equivalent section in Australia is s 15A of the Interactive Gambling Act 2001 (Cth), also referred to as the 'Good Neighbour Clause'.

119 Addisons Lawyers, *Australia: Online Gaming Regulation* (November 2014) 3, available online at: http://www.addisonslawyers.com.au/knowledge/assetdoc/035009f0cbbf237e/1334198_1%20Australia%20Online%20Gaming%20Regulation.pdf. See also What-DoTheyKnow, Section 44 of 2005 Gambling Act – Orders (7 May 2014), available online at: https://www.whatdotheyknow.com/request/section_44_of_2005_gambling_act (dealing the Freedom of Information Requests).

120 Roy Mark, 'Feds Arrest Offshore Gambling CEO' (18 July 2006) *Internetnews.com*, available online at: http://www.internetnews.com/bus-news/article.php/3620731

121 US v $734,578.82 286 F 3d 641 (2002).

122 *Yahoo! Inc v LICRA and UEJF*, 433 F 3d 1199, 1205 (9th Cir. 2006), discussed in Kohl, above n 1, 206f.

## Prohibitions on end-users and intermediaries and blocking orders

Another avenue states increasingly rely upon to protect their regulatory sphere is to enforce parallel prohibitions on a local intermediary or a local end-user if the primary wrongdoer is outside the enforcement reach. With regard to end-users, for example, it is not just an offence under the French Criminal Code to sell Nazi-memorabilia as was in issue in *Yahoo*, but also to view it. Thus the downloading of Nazi items by an end user would be equally caught by the criminal prohibition. Similarly, under Italian law the participation by local consumers in illegal gambling constitutes an offence.[123] As a final example, many states have tried to stem the flood of music and film piracy by taking highly publicised prosecutions against the offending local end-users as a deterrent example, given that the foreign facilitators are often beyond their reach.[124] This strategy goes hand in hand with the three or six strikes out rule which limits internet access to individual pirates after repeated warnings and which has proven popular with regulators in a number of countries,[125] albeit controversial otherwise. Although such actions against a few of the innumerable individual users cannot but have some impact, they are clearly not as effective and efficient in suppressing illegal activity as dealing with its source. The approach against users also has other shortcomings. First, the selection of offending end-users for prosecution cannot but be arbitrary and thus is (rightly) perceived as unfair. Also, prohibitions against end-users would often not meet the regulatory aim. For example, while it might be an offence to offer pornographic material online without any age verification mechanism, it would not be an offence for an adult to access such material. Nor would it make sense to prosecute a child who accessed such material, as under the regulation the child is the victim and not the wrongdoer. Similarly, the sale of unlicensed pharmaceuticals by a foreign provider could not be 'enforced' by targeting local consumers who unwittingly buy the drugs. Again, they are meant to benefit from the regulation, rather than being burdened by it.

Focusing on (local) intermediaries to suppress foreign illegal sites is a more promising avenue, as they are fewer, often larger and thus more visible than end-users. Such intermediaries may be ISPs, the financial institutions used in the course of the transaction (such as PayPal or credit card providers) or advertisers (whether local print, broadcast or sites with hyperlinks) as well as search engines which often have a presence in the country through a local subsidiary (such as Google or Yahoo) as well as content hosts of various descriptions, e.g. YouTube, Facebook, Twitter or Blogger. Reliance on these actors by states to enforce regulatory standards (for their 'communities') is common and on the increase (see Chapter 3). For example, the US has, for a long time, dealt with foreign gambling providers by focusing on local financial intermediaries, such as banks and credit card providers, making it an offence to transmit funds to online gambling sites.[126] A similar treatment has been applied to actors that might advertise offshore gambling services.[127] In New Zealand the strategy to deal with offshore gambling providers centres squarely on the prohibition on local actors to advertise those services in any way.[128] Google has been required to take down 'offending' material on a number of its platforms and not just in the obvious non-democratic states, such as China or Middle

---

123 Art 4 of Law No 401 of 13 December 1989, see *Criminal Proceedings against Piergiorgio Gambelli* Case C-243/01, [2003] ECR I-13031, para 9.

124 In France, those guilty of internet piracy may be barred from broadband access for up to a year. Charles Bremer, 'Download pirates face being banned from the internet under Sarkozy law' (2008) *The Times*, 19 June, 39. Of course the facilitators have also been subjected to prosecutions and private claims when they were present in the State, see, e.g., decision against providers of peer-to-peer file sharing software used for copyright infringement: *Metro-Goldwyn-Mayer Studios Inc v Grokster Ltd* 545 US 125 (2005).

125 Including the US, France, New Zealand, Australia and the UK. See BBC, 'UK piracy warning letters delayed until 2015' (6 June 2013), available online at: http://www.bbc.co.uk/news/technology-22796723; Corinne Reichert, 'Piracy prevention vs policing: Industry debates piracy code, website blocking' (ZDNet, 27 August 2015), available online at: http://www.zdnet.com/article/piracy-prevention-vs-policing-industry-debates-piracy-code-website-blocking/

126 Unlawful Internet Gambling Enforcement Act 2006 (subject to certain exceptions); see also Hurt, above at n 57, 432ff.

127 Aiding and abetting violations of the Wire Act; see also Hurt, *ibid*, 435ff, and *People v World Interactive Gaming Corp* 714 NYS 2d 844, 851 (1999), relying *inter alia* on §225–05 of the New York Penal Code which prohibits the promotion of unlawful gambling activity.

128 Section 16(1) of the Gambling Act 2003.

Eastern states,[129] but also in the West. This becomes especially apparent if censorship is given a neutral meaning, i.e. a restriction on speech and thus extends to restrictions based on intellectual property rights, privacy, defamation or terrorist publications or child pornography.[130] This is not to argue that such censorship is illegitimate but simply to highlight that all states impose restrictions on speech; they simply vary in their judgment of what is and is not acceptable speech.

In repressive states, whole sections of the internet are regularly blocked via local ISPs to prevent access to unsuitable/illegal material.[131] In February 2008, the Pakistan Telecommunications Authority required all local ISPs to block access to YouTube because it had included disrespectful cartoons of the Prophet Muhammad that were initially published in Danish newspapers in 2005 and caused protests across the Muslim world.[132] During the 2008 Olympics China repeatedly defied the IOC by censoring online material via local ISPs initially even for foreign journalists; in August 2008 it blocked access to iTunes because Olympic athletes had downloaded a pro-Tibet album.[133] Clearly, such wholesale blocking often causes significant 'collateral damage' to the accessibility of online content more generally. The European Court of Human Rights in Case of Yildirim v Turkey (2013)[134] held that the wholesale blocking by Turkish ISPs of the Google Sites website (which had included material that violated Turkish law on the protection of Ataturk's memory) was inconsistent with the applicant's right to freedom of expression. Yildirim's site had been unrelated to the offending site and was entirely legal under Turkish law, but nonetheless inaccessible due to this general block. Turkey, however, insisted that blocking access to the whole of Google Sites was the only way to block the offending foreign site, although there had been no evidence that Google had been approached with the request to take down the specific offending sites.[135]

In the West, the involvement of intermediaries in upholding national legal standards is frequently incentivised through conditional legal immunity regimes. For example, under the EU Electronic Commerce Directive hosting intermediaries are given immunity from liability (for damages) for the illegal content of others (assuming potential control over the content of transmission) depending on their knowledge of the illegality and whether they act expeditiously upon obtaining that knowledge, e.g. through a takedown notice.[136] A notice-and-take-down approach has also been adopted in respect of terrorist publications under s 3 of the UK Terrorism Act 2006,[137] where the relevant notice comes from a constable who believes the publication to be a terrorist one. Whilst US law grants all online publishers an unconditional immunity from liability for the wrongdoing of others in s 230 of the Communications Decency Act 1996, that immunity is not extended to federal criminal law or intellectual property law.[138] In respect of copyright infringements, intermediaries are incentivised

---

129 BBC, 'Google censors itself for China' (BBC News, 25 January 2006), available online at: http://news.bbc.co.uk/1/hi/technology/4645596.stm

130 Jonathan Stempel and Dan Levin, 'Google ordered to remove anti-Islamic film from YouTube' (Reuters, 26 February 2014), available online at: http://www.reuters.com/article/us-google-youtube-film-idUSBREA1P1HK20140226, commenting on Garcia v Google Inc et al (9th US Circuit Court of Appeals, No 12–57302).

131 See Kristina M Reed, 'From the Great Firewall of China to the Berlin Firewall: The cost of content regulation on internet commerce' (2000) 13 Transnational Lawyer 451; Shanthi Kalathil and Taylor C Boas, 'The internet and state control in authoritarian regimes: China, Cuba and the Counterrevolution' (2001) Carnegie Endowment Working Papers, Global Policy Program No 21, available online at: http://www.carnegieendowment.org/files/21KalathilBoas.pdf; Zhen Feng, 'China to Introduce New Legislation to Deal with ISP Liability for Copyright Infringement' (2004) 5 World Internet Law Report 19.

132 Jeremy Page, 'YouTube is cut off over cartoons' (2008) The Times, 25 February, 30. Note Richard Owen, 'Comedian Sabina Guzzanti "insulted Pope" in "poofter devils" gag' (2008) The Times, 21 September, available online at: http://www.timesonline.co.uk/tol/news/world/europe/article4732048.ece

133 See Tania Branigan, 'China relaxes internet censorship for Olympics' (2008) The Guardian, 1 August, available online at: http://www.guardian.co.uk/world/2008/aug/01/china.olympics; and Hannah Fletcher, 'China blocks iTunes over all-star Tibet album free download' (2008) The Times, 22 August, available online at: http://technology.timesonline.co.uk/tol/news/tech_and_web/article4579783.ece

134 Case of Yildirim v Turkey No 3111/10 ECtHR (18 March 2013).

135 One question here is whether an expectation of self-censorship based on national legal requirements as was the case prior to the internet vis-à-vis communication bottlenecks, such as TV, radio and the press, is still legitimate vis-à-vis online intermediaries.

136 Arts 12–14 of the Electronic Commerce Directive 2000/31/EC.

137 See also regs 5–7 of the Electronic Commerce Directive (Terrorism Act 2006) Regulations 2007.

138 47 USC §§ 230(e)(1) and (2), but for copyright see the Digital Millennium Copyright Act.

to remove illegal material upon knowledge or notice of the infringement under the Digital Copyright Millennium Act (see Chapter 3 on Intermediaries within Online Regulation).

In addition to, or in conjunction with, these takedown obligations of intermediaries upon notices by private parties, censorship also occurs in the form of blocking orders by governmental agencies[139] and courts. For example, the English High Court in *Twentieth Century Fox Film Corp v British Telecommunications Plc* (2011)[140] ordered BT, one of the main ISPs in the UK, to prevent access to Newzbin, a piracy site that had moved its operations abroad after having been found guilty of copyright infringement under UK law. Finally, censorship occurs in the form of self-censorship by intermediaries which draft their Terms and Conditions on content partly in response to commercial considerations and partly to state law. So whilst they act partly in the shadow of national law, they often do not go to the permissible limits of those laws in order to create global standards for their platforms. For example, Facebook's 'Community Standards' do not fully exploit the legal limits, e.g. on obscenity or hate speech as understood in each national community where its platform is accessible.[141] Thus social networking sites or commercial intermediaries such (e.g. eBay or Amazon) may decide that it is more desirable to have a common policy to use across states and thus comply with the highest common legal denominator of major markets. Such policy deprives users of states with more lenient content standards of the benefit of those standards.

The examples highlight that internet blocking (either in respect of a territory or removing content altogether) is the 'natural' consequence of any law that imposes restrictions on communications and of those laws there are many different types with economic, political, moral, cultural or safety justifications. Regulators simply seek to extend their traditional law-and-order normativity to the internet which as a more egalitarian, empowering and control defying medium seems more violated by these efforts than traditional media. Yet, censorship has been commonplace for a long time. Media actors have been made to suppress defamatory, racist, violence inciting or terrorist material long before the internet. The profound Western disagreement with states such as China, Saudi Arabia or Pakistan relates to the content of the speech considered 'unworthy' rather than the practice of suppressing 'unworthy' speech *per se*. Otherwise, the difference in the practice of blocking is one of degree, and cannot be seen in isolation of other speech-chilling state activities, such as wide-spread surveillance.[142] Authoritarian states have resorted to blocking entire domains via closely monitored, often licensed ISPs.[143] In the West blocking is arguably more 'voluntary' and focuses on the specific material rather than entire domains, found to be illegal, coupled with a rejection of a TV-like licensing regime as a suitable regulatory model for internet content providers and intermediaries.

Although most of these avenues are not impervious to circumvention, one should not overestimate the proclivity of the ordinary internet users for seeking to undo blocking efforts, particularly when there is no awareness of that block in the first place. For example, as Google Search now accompanies most searches for people with a warning that some material may have been removed under the EU's right-to-be-forgotten, there is generally nothing to indicate that in the

---

139 See discussion on removal activities of UK Counter Terrorism Internet Referral Unit. For Google censorship based on notices by private and public parties, see Google's Transparency Report: http://www.google.com/transparencyreport/. See also the activities of the Internet Watch Foundation.

140 [2011] EWHC 1981. But such blocks are not always based on judicial authority, with the responsibility of censorship increasingly being shifted to intermediaries: Juliette Garside, 'Ministers will order ISPs to block terrorist and extremist websites' (2013) *The Guardian*, 29 November, available online at: http://www.theguardian.com/uk-news/2013/nov/27/ministers-order-isps-block-terrorist-websites

141 Stuart Dredge, 'Facebook clarifies policy on nudity, hate speech and other community standards' (2015) *The Guardian*, 16 March, available online at: http://www.theguardian.com/technology/2015/mar/16/facebook-policy-nudity-hate-speech-standards. See also, YouTube, 'YouTube Community Guidelines', available online at: http://www.youtube.com/t/community_guidelines

142 See Reporters without Borders, available online at: https://rsf.org/

143 Control over ISPs may be achieved through a licensing regime (as practised in Singapore) or routing all traffic through a government proxy server (as practiced in Saudi Arabia) which makes the state's entire net activities comparable to the intranet of a company.

particular case something has been removed.[144] However, in the case of copyright, state-based blocking has become increasing apparent.[145] Nonetheless, circumvention of any of these efforts is possible in different ways. First of all, there is the dark net which substantially falls below the radar of the law. Even on the open internet, avenues for accessing blocked material or sites or activities can be found. For example, Antiguan gambling providers may bill US punters through other companies to disguise payments as product purchases. Piracy sites may create mirror sites, as do political sites. IP-spoofing or VPN disguises a user's location and thus may allow him or her to access otherwise blocked material. Nonetheless, blocking measures create practical hurdles of varying severity to deter many would-be activities and transactions and in some instances circumvention is near impossible.[146] As the Antiguan complaint to the WTO shows, the US strategies made a significant dent in the number of Antiguan gambling providers. For states the temptation to make local intermediaries, especially ISPs, the gate-keepers of foreign content (or content more generally) is great,[147] but not unproblematic (see Chapter 3 on Intermediaries within Online Regulation).

There appears to be an increased recognition of the fact that the application of diverse national legal standards onto cyberspace cannot but lead to its territorial fragmentation. In 2003 the Council of Europe in its Declaration on Freedom of Communication on the Internet[148] declared with great confidence that: 'Member states should not subject content on the Internet to restrictions which go further than those applied to other means of content delivery' (Principle 1); yet it equally demanded that: 'Public authorities should not, through general blocking or filtering measures, deny access by the public to information and other communication on the Internet, regardless of frontiers' (Principle 3). The problem is that *merely* applying one's law to the internet means that online providers either comply or territorially restrict their site to avoid legal exposure in the first place, i.e. territorial fragmentation. Notably in 2015, the tone of the Council of Europe's Recommendation on the 'free, transboundary flow of information on the Internet'[149] is entirely different and appears to acknowledge that the application of existing national standards gives rise to a 'complex legal environment' and the need for a 'common international understanding, to consolidate norms' and makes 'the value of self-regulation' an express principle.[150]

## Transnational online civil disputes

The transnationality of the internet has triggered competence questions in civil disputes, particularly concerning defamation, contracts, intellectual property rights and privacy. Again, like in the criminal context, the broad competence question running through these disputes is: when can a state regulate the transnational dispute? In civil disputes this general inquiry is divided into two more specific questions: first, when does a national court have the right to adjudicate the dispute

---

144 See Google FAQs on the Right-to-be-Forgotten: https://www.google.co.uk/policies/faq/
145 Monica Horten, 'EU announces radical copyright overhaul for cross-border content (6 May 2015) IPTEGRITY.COM, available online at: http://www.iptegrity.com/index.php/european-union/998-eu-announces-radical-copyright-overhaul-for-cross-border-content; see also CRM Directive (Directive on collective management of copyright and related rights and multi-territorial licensing of rights in musical works for online use in the internal market (26 February 2014).
146 David Gilbert, 'Tiananmen Square 25th Anniversary: China Condemned for Blocking Google under "Strictest Censorship Ever"' (4 June 2014) *International Business Times*, available online at: http://www.ibtimes.co.uk/tiananmen-square-25th-anniversary-china-condemned-blocking-google-under-strictest-censorship-1451147
147 Ronald Deibert, John Palfray, Rafal Rohozinski and Jonathan Zittrain (eds), *Access Denied*, 2008, Cambridge, MA: MIT Press, esp. ch 5. They may also be useful for surveillance purposes, i.e. as data collectors.
148 Adopted by the Committee of Ministers on 28 May 2003. See Council of Europe, *Declaration on Freedom of Political Debate in the Media* (adopted by the Committee of Ministers on 12 February 2004) and Organization for Security and Co-operation in Europe (OSCE), *Amsterdam Recommendations on Freedom of the Media and the Internet* (2003); and Christian Ahlert, 'Technologies of Control: How Code Controls Communication' in OSCE Christiane Hardy and Christian Möller (eds), *Spreading the Word on the Internet*, 2003, Vienna: OSCE, 119.
149 Recommendation CM/Rec(2015)6 of the Committee of Ministers to Member States on the free, transboundary flow of information on the internet.
150 Recitals 4 and 5 and Principle 3 respectively.

(referred to as the 'jurisdiction' inquiry), and second, when is local law (or 'forum law') the appropriate substantive law to govern the dispute (known as the 'applicable law' or 'choice of law' inquiry). This latter inquiry is essentially asking how far does local civil law (either common law, e.g. defamation or legislation, e.g. copyright or data protection) reach to 'capture' conduct that is not entirely or even mainly local?[151] As noted above, in the criminal context these are not separate inquiries, as a court which has assumed the right to adjudicate a criminal matter would automatically apply forum law to the prosecution. That, however, is not necessarily the case in transnational civil matters. Despite this structural difference, many of the competence arguments raised in the criminal context find their counterparts in transnational online civil disputes. Again, states have tended to interpret their competence widely so as to regulate disputes arising out of foreign sites accessible in their territory (i.e. taking a country of destination/receipt approach) in order to guard against local legal standards and rights being undermined by foreign non-compliant sites. Again online providers have argued that this approach exposes them to too many compounding (and possibly conflicting) obligations and that they should only be subject to the laws of the state in which they are established (i.e. arguing for an exclusive country of origin approach).

Unlike in the criminal context, states have been more – though not always – ready to resolve the clash of interests between regulators and online content providers by a compromise in the form of the moderate destination approach (see above): online providers are exposed only to the legal systems of the states which they specifically target with their sites and not of all the states in which their sites can be accessed. This greater readiness in civil law to tolerate minor infiltrations of offending sites without any legal repercussions can be explained by reference to the nature of civil law. As it serves primarily individual private interests and only in the second instance the public good, those private interests may at times legitimately be compromised in the name of protecting online actors from overregulation.

The discussion below illustrates the competence approaches taken in civil law in the context of defamation, intellectual property and data protection disputes. Jurisdiction and choice of law questions in contractual disputes, including consumer contracts, are examined in Chapter 6. Finally, as a reminder, competence in transnational civil disputes is governed by domestic rather than international law, unless – as, for example, in the EU – there is a treaty harmonising national legal regimes.

## Personal jurisdiction

The first issue in any transnational civil dispute is whether the court in which the claim has been brought has the right to hear the claim and whether it should exercise that right. Courts assert that right if they have jurisdiction over the person of the defendant or what is known as personal jurisdiction or jurisdiction in personam. In common law legal systems personal jurisdiction exists if the defendant is 'present' in the territory of the court and can thus be served with the 'originating process'.[152] In civil law countries, the defendant's habitual residence creates jurisdiction in the courts of that place. Similarly, where Art 4(1) of the EC Regulation on Jurisdiction and the Recognition and Enforcement of Judgments in Civil and Commercial Matters (2012)[153] provides that 'persons domiciled in a Member State shall . . . be sued in the courts of that Member State.' The strength of this traditional focus on the location of the defendant is, first, that the defendant can easily be put on notice about the action that is brought against him or her (consistent with the idea of natural justice or due process) and, second, that any judgment against the defendant can easily be enforced against

---

151 Sometimes there is no connection at all, e.g. *Kuwait Airways Corp v Iraqi Airways Co* [2002] 3 All ER 209.
152 The service of the writ creates the jurisdiction of the court, and that service may occur within the jurisdiction even during a very temporary presence: *Colt Industries v Sarlie (No 1)* [1966] 1 WLR 440 (one night stay in a hotel).
153 EU Regulation on Jurisdiction and the Recognition and Enforcement of Judgments in Civil and Commercial Matters No 1215/ 2012, which replaces EU Regulation on Jurisdiction and the Recognition and Enforcement of Judgments in Civil and Commercial Matters, No 44/2001.

him or her without involving another state. It also seems *prima facie* fair that the claimant has to bring his case in the place of the defendant's location as it is the claimant who has the complaint against the potentially innocent defendant.

Despite its advantages, this basic default rule has long been subject to exceptions which allow claimants to bring actions in their home state.[154] These exceptions have expanded with the increase of international trade, travel and communications which would often make it unfair to require the claimant to instigate proceedings in the defendant's location, particularly when the defendant actually inflicted the damage in the claimant's jurisdiction. The question examined here is how these exceptions cover online disputes. More specifically, when do online content providers have to defend actions against them in foreign courts – based on the access and use of their sites abroad? As US jurisprudence on internet jurisdiction has until recently been the most comprehensive, the discussion below starts with it, followed by an examination of the EU.

## US – 'targeting'

Modern US jurisprudence on personal jurisdiction started with the Supreme Court decision in *International Shoe Co v Washington*[155] in 1945 when it abandoned the strict interpretation of the requirement that the defendant must be 'present' in the territory of the court and laid down what has become known as the 'minimum contacts' test. The court held that the constitutional guarantee of due process of law[156] required that 'in order to subject a defendant to a judgment *in personam*, if he be not present within the territory of the forum, he have certain *minimum contacts with it such that the maintenance of suit does not offend traditional notions of fair play and substantial justice.*'[157] The idea was that – rather relying on the often arbitrary question whether or not the defendant was present in the forum – legal accountability should hinge on defendant's contacts with the forum. The stronger these contacts, the fairer and more just it would be to require him to defend proceedings there. This rationale was made more explicit in the ruling of *Hanson v Deckla*[158] where the minimum contacts test was reformulated into the 'purposeful availment' test: a defendant may be sued in a state where he has purposefully availed himself of the privilege of conducting activities, thus invoking the benefits and protections of its laws.[159] In other words, if someone gains the commercial benefits of a foreign market and its legal protection, he must also carry the burden of being answerable to the courts in that place. Basically, here the law follows the market: the market boundaries are the legal boundaries.

The much debated issue has been whether the provider of a website can be said to avail himself of the privilege of conducting activities in *every* state where his site can be accessed. US courts have rejected that proposition. The mere accessibility of a site in a state does not expose the

---

154 For example, submission by the defendant to the court's jurisdiction.

155 326 US 310, 316 (1945). For a historic overview of the cases with special focus on online cases, see ABA, above n 81, 39ff. See also Sam Puathasnanon, 'Cyberspace and personal jurisdiction: The problem of using internet contacts to establish minimum contacts' (1998) 31 Loyola of Los Angeles Law Review 691; and Allan R Stein, 'The unexceptional problem of jurisdiction in cyberspace' (1998) 32 The International Lawyer 1167.

156 Fifth Amendment to the US Constitution (applicable to federal government) and 14th Amendment to the US Constitution (applicable to state governments).

157 *International Shoe Co v Washington* 326 US 310 (1945) [emphasis added]. US courts draw a distinction between general and specific personal jurisdiction of which only the latter has been used in internet related case. General personal jurisdiction arises where the out-of-state defendant has very strong connections with the forum (i.e. substantial or continuous and systematic contacts) which means he may be sued in relation to any dispute regardless of whether that the particular dispute arises out of the contacts with the forum state or not. On the other hand, specific personal jurisdiction arises where the contacts with the forum are relatively weak (i.e. isolated and sporadic contacts) and then there is the additional requirement that the dispute in question must be linked to those contacts.

158 357 US 235 (1958).

159 *Hanson v Deckla* 357 US 235, 253 (1958). In *World-Wide Volkswagen Corp v Woodson* 444 US 286 (1980), the US Supreme Court added a second strand to the purposeful availment test: even if minimum contacts were present, the court may decline to exercise personal jurisdiction if to do so would not be reasonable, taking into account the burden on the defendant, the forum state's interest in adjudicating the disputes, the claimant's interest in obtaining convenient and effective relief and the shared interest of states in furthering fundamental subjective social policies.

provider to legal accountability before its courts, essentially for two reasons. Practically, it would mean that 'every . . . court through the world, may assert jurisdiction over all information providers on the global World Wide Web . . . [which] would have a devastating impact on those who use this global service.'[160] Theoretically, it would 'eviscerate the personal jurisdictional requirement':[161] by saying that every online provider is potentially answerable to every court, courts no longer share adjudicative powers based on the relative strength of the connection of the defendant with the court's territory. Instead, US courts have generally taken a moderate destination approach by insisting that legal accountability shall only lie where the site was specifically targeted at the state. In such cases, of course, the defendant cannot reasonably complain about having to defend actions in the targeted market.

What evidence may indicate such 'targeting' varies and is to some extent dependent on the nature of the dispute. In trade mark disputes the commercial activity between the site and residents of the forum state shows an 'objective' intention to reach customers in that state. One well-accepted interpretation of the 'purposeful availment' test in the online context, especially in trade mark disputes, is the Zippo sliding scale interactivity test developed in *Zippo Manufacturing Co v Zippo Dot Com Inc* (1997).[162] In that case the world-famous Pennsylvanian producer of Zippo tobacco lighters and holder of the trade mark 'Zippo' brought an action in Pennsylvania for trade mark infringement against Zippo Dot Com Inc, a Californian corporation operating a website and internet news service using the domain names zippo.com, zippo.net and zipponews.com. The court reasoned that the likelihood of personal jurisdiction to be found was 'directly proportionate to the nature and quality of commercial activity that an entity conducts over the Internet'[163] and found that online activity fell along a spectrum in this respect:

> At one end of the spectrum are situations where a defendant clearly does business over the Internet. If the defendant enters into contracts with residents of a foreign jurisdiction that involve the knowing and repeated transmission of computer files over the Internet, personal jurisdiction is proper . . . At the opposite end are situations where a defendant has simply posted information on an Internet Web site which is accessible to users in foreign jurisdictions. A passive Web site that does little more than make information available to those who are interested in it is not grounds for the exercise of personal jurisdiction.[164]

The idea behind this test is that the owner of a site who regularly enters into contracts with residents of the forum state has knowing and intentional contacts with the forum, thus he cannot claim to have had no awareness with whom he is interacting: credit card details, invoice and delivery addresses allow sellers not just to know the location of their customers but also give them the opportunity to exclude customers from legally inhospitable states. The reverse applies to sites that simply post information online. The unsuspecting owner of such a site has prima facie neither knowledge of the location of those who access his site nor control in terms of preventing their access which in turn would make legal accountability in the states of those surfers unpredictable and unfair.[165] In short, knowing business contacts with forum residents via a site evidence that the forum was targeted and thus give rise to personal jurisdiction, but simply posting a passive

---

160 *Playboy Enterprises Inc v Chuckleberry Pub Inc* 939 F Supp 1032, 1039 (SDNY 1996).
161 *McDonough v Fallon McElligott Inc*, 40 USPQ 2d (BNA) 1826, 1829 (SD Cal 1996); see also *GTE New Media Servs Inc v BellSouth Corp* 199 F.3d 1343, 1350 (D.C.Cir.2000); and *ALS Scan Inc v Digital Service Consultants Inc* 293 F 3d 707, 712 (4th Cir, 2002).
162 *Zippo Manufacturing Co v Zippo Dot Com Inc* 952 F Supp 1119 (WD Pa 1997).
163 952 F Supp 119, 1123f (WD Pa 1997), relying in particular on *CompuServe Inc v Patterson* 89 F 3d 1257 (6th Cir 1996).
164 *Ibid*.
165 This argument is no longer quite as persuasive given the availability of geo-identification software (which allows site owners to establish the whereabouts of surfers and which has the potential to restrict the use of the site to certain jurisdictions). See Dan Jerker B Svantesson, 'Geo-location technologies and other means of placing borders on the 'borderless' internet' (2004) 23 John Marshall Journal of Computer and Information Law 101.

site (without more) does not. This test has been applied to many interstate US disputes[166] as well as transnational disputes.[167]

One such international case is *Euromarket Design Inc v Crate and Barrel Ltd* (2000)[168] where the well-known US retailer, selling house wares and furniture under the name of 'Crate & Barrel', wanted to sue the small Irish company, Crate & Barrel Ltd, selling similar goods for an infringement of its trade mark in Illinois in the US. The Irish company which had a shop in Ireland also advertised and sold its goods via a website. While it did not deliver goods to Illinois, the company had accepted online orders from Illinois customers (instigated by the claimant) with delivery in Ireland. The site, at least initially, stated its prices in US dollars and was formatted to accommodate US addresses for billing. While this may have been enough to show that the site was targeted at the US, including Illinois, other non-internet contacts strengthened the claimant's case in favour of the Illinois court's personal jurisdiction over the Irish defendant: the defendant used Illinois suppliers, attended trade shows in Illinois and advertised its business in UK and Irish magazines that were also circulated in the US. Under these circumstances the Illinois court felt that the defendant 'deliberately developed and maintained not only minimum, but significant, contacts with the forum'[169] and thus that personal jurisdiction is proper. Whether these contacts were indeed 'significant' and went much beyond 'minimum contacts' required is questionable.

In the factually not dissimilar case of *Toys 'R' Us Inc v Step Two* (2003)[170] the US Court of Appeals reached the opposite conclusion. Here the US retailer Toys 'R' Us brought a trade mark infringement action against the Spanish company, Step Two, that also sold toys. Both companies had registered, in their respective jurisdictions, trade marks relating to the name of 'Imaginarium' as well as domain names for their respective interactive websites, i.e. imaginarium.com and imaginarium.es. Although, as in *Euromarket Design*, the Spanish company had accepted two orders from New Jersey residents, which, like in *Euromarket Design*, had been initiated by the claimant to prove the willingness of the foreign defendant to accept orders from forum residents, the court dismissed these sales as orchestrated contacts that Step Two scarcely recognised as sales with US residents (presumably because the site did not require a billing address). Instead, the court focused on the fact that Step Two's site was in Spanish, payment in pesetas or Euros, merchandise could only be shipped to Spain and '[m]ost important, none of the portions of Step Two's websites are designed to accommodate addresses within the United States.'[171] Ultimately, the formatting of the site's address section made the critical difference between *Toys 'R' Us* and *Euromarket Design* and tipped the balance in either case. Not surprisingly the site's address section proves least ambiguous in revealing for whom the site was really created.

The sliding scale interactivity test has proved less useful in defamation or copyright claims,[172] when the offending site (e.g. online newspapers) is not essentially interactive and may classify as 'passive' under *Zippo*, but could still inflict serious damage in foreign states. In such cases an alternative avenue for establishing personal jurisdiction under the 'minimum contacts' test is provided by the intentional effects doctrine established in *Calder v Jones* (1984).[173] There the court held that

---

166 *Morantz Inc v Hang & Shine Ultrasonics Inc* 79 F Supp 2d 537 (ED Pa 1999); *ALS Scan v Digital Service Consultants Inc* 293 F 3d 707 (4th Cir 2002).

167 In international disputes there appear to be minor additions to the general jurisdiction test; in *Asahi Metal Industry Co v Superior Court* 480 US 102, 103 (1987) the Supreme Court noted that the 'procedural and substantive policies of other nations whose interests are affected by the forum State's assertion of jurisdiction over an alien defendant . . . as well as the Federal Government's interest in its foreign relations policies, will always be best served by a careful inquiry into the reasonableness of the particular assertion of jurisdiction.'

168 *Euromarket Design Inc v Crate and Barrel Ltd* 96 F Supp 2d 824 (ND Ill 2000).

169 *Euromarket Design Inc v Crate and Barrel Ltd* 96 F Supp 2d 824, 839 (ND Ill 2000).

170 *Toys 'R' Us Inc v Step Two* 318 F 3d 446 (3rd Cir 2003).

171 *Toys 'R' Us Inc v Step Two* 318 F 3d 446, 454 (3rd Cir 2003).

172 Similarly cybersquatting (trade mark) cases cannot be accommodated by the sliding scale test given the often inherent passivity of the site.

173 *Calder v Jones* 465 US 783 (1984).

personal jurisdiction over an out-of-state defendant is proper where there was an intentional tortious action that was expressly aimed at the forum state and in fact causes damage there to the claimant, i.e. a type of purposeful direction: While this test is framed slightly differently than *Zippo*, ultimately both seek to establish whether the acts by the out-of-state defendant were specifically aimed, directed or targeted at the forum state; they simply respond to different types of factual scenarios.

So in *Blumenthal v Drudge* (1998)[174] the issue was whether the Californian online publisher of the Drudge Report, which was alleged to be defamatory of Blumenthal, a White House employee, and his wife in Columbia, could be sued in Columbia. The Columbian court focused on the interactivity of the site (like many lower US courts at the time), when in fact 'a one line cite to Calder would have sufficed.'[175] Nevertheless, in substance the court did adopt the *Calder* approach: 'the subject matter of the Drudge Report primarily concerns political gossip and rumor in Washington . . . the subject matter of the Drudge Report is directly related to the political world of the Nation's capital . . . Drudge specifically targets readers in the District of Columbia by virtue of the subjects he covers . . . Drudge knew that *primary and most devastating effects* of the statements he made would be felt in the District of Columbia.'[176] In other words, the subject-matter of the report provided clues about the site's territorial target which in this case was Columbia. *Calder* was expressly relied upon in *Young v New Haven Advocate* (2002)[177] concerning two online Connecticut newspapers alleged to have defamed the claimant in Virginia. The court noted that the 'application of *Calder* in the Internet context requires proof that the out-of-state defendant's internet activity is expressly targeted at or directed to the forum state'[178] and reiterated that such targeting is not established by simply by posting matters online. Based on this, the Virginian court refused to hear the case, given that the 'newspapers maintain their websites to serve local readers in Connecticut, to expand the reach of their papers within their local markets, and to provide their local markets with a place for classified ads. The websites are not designed to attract or serve a Virginia audience.'[179]

Both the sliding scale interactivity test and the intentional effects test are examples of the moderate country of destination approach, discussed above, according to which only states specifically targeted by a site can regulate them.

## EU – 'location of the harmful event'

In contrast, the EU position under the Jurisdiction Regulation is far less moderate, claiming personal jurisdiction frequently based on the mere accessibility of a site. According to Art 6(1) the scope of the Regulation is, bar some exceptions,[180] limited to cases where the defendant is domiciled in a Member State; otherwise the national law on jurisdiction is applicable. For example, actions brought in England against, e.g. a US or Australian defendant, would generally be resolved by reference to the traditional English rules of private international law. When the Regulation is applicable, the default rule – that the defendant must be sued in his state of domicile – can in the defamation and intellectual property disputes be overridden by Art 7(2) which provides that a defendant can be sued 'in matters relating to tort, delict or quasi-delict, in the courts for the place where the harmful event occurred or may occur.' But where does the 'harmful event' occur on the internet? Considering a defamatory article, does the harm occur in the place where the article was uploaded (country of origin) or is it in the place or places where it was downloaded and where the claimant suffered the injury (country of destination)? And does it matter at all whether the site

---

174  *Blumenthal v Drudge* 992 F Supp 44 (DDC 1998).
175  ABA, above n 81, 51.
176  *Blumenthal v Drudge* 992 F Supp 44, 57 (1998) [internal marks omitted, emphasis added].
177  315 F3d 256 (4th Cir 2002); reversed 187 F Supp 2d 498 (WD Vir 2001); following *ALS Scan Inc v Digital Service Consultants Inc* 293 F 3d 707 (4th Cir, 2002).
178  *Young v New Haven Advocate* 315 F3d 256, 262f (4th Cir 2002).
179  Ibid, 263.
180  Subject to the exceptions in Arts 18(1), 21(2), 24 and 25.

is or is not targeted at the jurisdiction or can any site provider be sued wherever his or her site is accessible?

In the pre-internet case of *Shevill v Press Alliance SA* (1995)[181] the CJEU held that 'the harmful event' is either the place where the publisher is established or the place where the publication was distributed and the claimant suffered his injury. Thus, where a newspaper is distributed in a number of states, a defamed claimant can sue in the place of the origin of the damage, that is where the publisher is based, which comes close to the default rule and is often inconvenient for the claimant. The advantage is that the claimant can seek compensation for the entire damage suffered (including damage suffered in other states). Alternatively, he can sue in the state where the publication was distributed but only for the injury he suffered there. Should a site be considered to be distributed in every state in which it can be accessed? According to US jurisprudence that is not the case; intrinsically local publications are not transformed into transnational publication simply by being online. *Shevill* itself cannot provide the answer to that in the European context, but it could provide some guidance. In *Shevill* the allegedly defamatory French newspaper was distributed mainly in France (237,000 copies) but had a small circulation in other countries, including 230 copies in England and Wales. Even in relation to that small circulation, there was a knowing act by the defendant to bring about that distribution, which makes accountability before English courts appropriate. Thus it would be impossible for the defendant to claim that he or she had unwittingly distributed the newspapers in England. However, if the newspaper had only been published in France and a tourist had brought it back to England, the 'distribution' of the paper in England is beyond the control of the French publisher, and thus personal jurisdiction by the English courts would be unfair. Applying this to the internet (and considering the undesirability of holding that a provider is in principle subject to the law of every state where the site can be accessed), websites should only be treated as distributed in the places to which they are knowingly directed (consistent with Art 17(1)(c) applicable to consumer contracts, see Electronic Commerce Chapter). This would satisfy the notion that legal exposure must be both foreseeable and controllable. It would also be consistent with the 'no gain without pain' maxim, that is, if you seek to reap the benefits from foreign customs, you should also expect to carry the burden of being answerable to the laws of those states. However, this is not the interpretation adopted by the CJEU in numerous recent cases engaging Art 5(3), the identical predecessor of Art 7(2).

In the joint defamation/privacy cases of *eDate Advertising and Martinez* (2011)[182] the CJEU noted that the internet reduced the usefulness of the criterion relating to distribution given the universal accessibility of sites,[183] and then proceeded to adapt the *Shevill* holding. Accordingly, if personality rights are infringed online, an action can be brought for *all* the damage caused either where the publisher is established or where the victim has its centre of interests as, according to the court, the victim's personality rights can best be assessed there. Alternatively, an action also lies in each Member State where the 'content placed online is or has been accessible' but only in respect of the damage suffered in that Member State. In *Martinez* this meant that MGN could be sued by a French actor in a French court for an allegedly offending article on sundaymirror.co.uk, quite regardless of the fact that the main 'audience' was in Britain. Both the latter two tests do not at all examine the defendant's conduct and thus do not ask whether the assertion of jurisdiction is not just fair *vis-à-vis* the alleged victim, but also *vis-à-vis* the alleged wrongdoer.

Similarly, in the trade mark case of *Wintersteiger v Products 4U Sondermaschinenbau GmbH* (2012)[184] the issue was whether a German company could be sued in Austria for allegedly infringing the

181 C-68/93 [1995] 2 WLR 499, following *Bier v Mines de Potasse d'Alsace SA*, C-21/76 [1976] ECR 1735, para 24f which was decided under the almost identically worded Brussels Convention on Jurisdiction and the Enforcement of Judgments in Civil and Commercial Matters 1968, the predecessor of the Regulation.
182 Joined Cases *eDate Advertising and Martinez* C-509/09 and C-161/10 [2011] ECR I-10269.
183 Joined Cases *eDate Advertising and Martinez* C-509/09 and C-161/10 [2011] ECR I-10269, para 46.
184 *Wintersteiger v Products 4U Sondermaschinenbau GmbH* C-523/10 [2012] ECLI:EU:C:2012:220.

defendant's Austrian trade mark with advertising that had solely occurred on google.de, not google.at. The CJEU held that the Austrian court has jurisdiction to hear the claim because the trade mark was registered in Austria[185] and thus the place where the potential damage would occur. Again, the court in no way considered the defendant's activity and to what extent it was 'reaching out' beyond German borders; thus in principle the operator of any site from anywhere, which is accessible in Austria, could be sued in Austria for infringing an Austrian trade mark; and the same applies to any of the EU Member States. Notably, the Advocate General in the same case came to the same conclusion as the court, but applied a more moderate test that required an *a priori* potential for local harm, which depended on the *objective* focus of the foreign site:

> The fundamental factor or point is whether the information disseminated on the internet is really likely to have an effect in the territory where the trade mark is registered. It is not sufficient if the content of the information leads to a risk of infringement of the trade mark and instead it must be established that there are objective elements which enable *the identification of conduct which is in itself intended to have an extraterritorial dimension.* For those purposes, a number of criteria may be useful, such as the language in which the information is expressed, the accessibility of the information, and whether the defendant has a commercial presence on the market on which the national mark is protected.[186]

In the case of a site by a German company in German, Austria is not surprisingly also a natural market, and thus the Austrian court should have jurisdiction, even under the AG's Opinion. Thus the AG combined a focus on harm (as required by Art 7(2)) with sensitivity towards the defendant's activities.

In fact, there is a precedent for such an approach under the previous equivalent provisions in the Brussels Convention on Jurisdiction in the Scottish cybersquatting case of *Bonnier Media Ltd v Greg Lloyd Smith and Kestrel Trading Corporation* (2002).[187] Here the Greek defendant registered domain names very similar to the trade marks and domain names of the Scottish claimant. He then offered to sell them to the claimant under the threat of selling them elsewhere. The Scottish court assumed personal jurisdiction over the defendant but not simply because the sites were accessible in Scotland:

> In my opinion a website should not be regarded as having delictual consequences in any country where it is unlikely to be of significant interest. That result can readily be achieved by a vigorous application of the maxim *de minimis non curat praetor* [the law is not interested in trivial matters]; if the impact of a website is insignificant, it is appropriate in my opinion to look both at the content of the website itself and at the commercial or other context in which the website operates.[188]

Given this was a cybersquatting scenario, the defendant's act, i.e. the publication of the sites, was clearly aimed at the claimant's business in Scotland, and thus not within the *de minimis* maxim (see below) which is a result entirely consistent with the US approach in *Calder* (see above).

---

185  *Wintersteiger v Products 4U Sondermaschinenbau GmbH* C-523/10, [2012] ECLI:EU:C:2012:220, paras 21–29 at para 27: 'both the objective of foreseeability and that of sound administration of justice militate in favour of conferring jurisdiction, in respect of the damage occurred, on the courts of the Member State in which the right at issue is protected.'

186  *Wintersteiger v Products 4U Sondermaschinenbau GmbH* C-523/10 [2012] Opinion of the Advocate General [2012] ECLI:EU:C:2012:90, para 28 [internal marks omitted]; see also para 29: 'It is also necessary to establish the territorial scope of the market on which the defendant operates and from which the information was disseminated on the internet. For that purpose, an assessment must be made of facts such as, *inter alia*, the top-level domain, the address or other location data supplied on the website, and the place where the person responsible for the information has the place of business for his internet activities.' [internal marks omitted]

187  (Court of Sessions, Scotland, 1 July 2002).

188  *Bonnier Media Ltd v Greg Lloyd Smith and Kestrel Trading Corporation* (Court of Sessions, Scotland, 1 July 2002), para 19.

Yet, despite this evident way of combining the traditional test with the targeting approach, the CJEU again in *Pinckney v KDG Mediatech* (2013)[189] held that for personal jurisdiction to be present in a transnational copyright dispute it was not necessary 'that the activity concerned to be "directed to" the Member State in which the court seised is situated . . . [Jurisdiction is established] if the Member State in which that court is situated protects the copyrights relied on by the plaintiff and the harmful event alleged may occur within the jurisdiction of the court seised.'[190] And the latter possibility is established if an infringing reproduction, here infringing CDs, could be obtained from a 'site accessible within the jurisdiction of the court seised.'[191] This holding was further confirmed in *Pez Hejduk v EnergieAgentur.NRW GmbH* (2015)[192] which concerned the copyright infringement claim by an Austrian in respect of a German website with a German top-level domain. Again, the Austrian court could claim jurisdiction under Art 7(2) on the basis of the infringing site's accessibility in Austria. The CJEU held that it did not matter whether that site was or was not targeted at Austria.[193] This insistence by the CJEU on worldwide jurisdiction in respect of tort and tort-like disputes is unfortunate as well as surprising in light of its enlightened approach in respect of cross-border contractual consumer disputes (see Chapter 6 on Electronic Commerce).

## Traditional English law

If the defendant to a civil action is domiciled outside the EU, the jurisdiction of the court falls generally to be determined by the domestic law of the Member State rather than the EC Jurisdiction Regulation. Many of these actions have concerned transnational defamation, misuse of private information and data protection claims, often against US publishers. The English position on internet jurisdiction shows both elements of the US 'targeting' approach, particularly in relation to trade mark claims, as well as of the EU approach with its focus on local harm as a touchstone of legal exposure, especially in defamation claims. All in all, there appears to be a trend towards jurisdictional restraint. From a practical point of view such restraint appears not always justified or necessary considering that the defendants are often large online providers, e.g. Google, Amazon or Dow Jones, that are perfectly capable of defending suit in any court anywhere. This shines through judicial comments like: 'In any event, in the world in which Google Inc operates, the location of documents is likely to be insignificant, since they are likely to be in electronic form, accessible from anywhere in the world.'[194] However, worldwide legal accountability even in civil law also contributes towards the territorial fragmentation of the internet.

### (a) Gateways, e.g. 'damage within the jurisdiction'
Under English law on personal jurisdiction, a foreign defendant may be sued in England, even if not 'present' in England, where permission to serve the claim form out of the jurisdiction is granted. This in turn requires the claimant to show a 'good arguable case' in respect of one of the Gateways for such service. An important one in the cross-border internet context has been the one that permits service for 'a claim . . . in tort where the damage was sustained within the

---

189  *Peter Pinckney v KDG Mediatech AG* C-170/12 [2013] EUECJ (3 October 2013); see also *Donner* (*Free movement of goods*) C-5/11 [2012] EUECJ (21 June 2012) (taking the 'targeting' test with respect to the Copyright Directive 2001/29/EC, the CJEU took the targeting approach in a criminal copyright scenario, but note, in the circumstances the targeting approach was used to establish liability, rather than deny it, and thus required no regulatory forbearance).
190  *Peter Pinckney v KDG Mediatech AG* C-170/12 [2013] EUECJ (3 October 2013), paras 42 and 43.
191  *Peter Pinckney v KDG Mediatech AG* C-170/12 [2013] EUECJ (3 October 2013), para 44.
192  *Pez Hejduk v EnergieAgentur.NRW GmbH* C-441/13 EU:C:2015:28.
193  *Ibid*, para 34.
194  *Vidal-Hall v Google Inc* [2014] EWHC 13 (QB), para 132.

jurisdiction.'[195] That Gateway was contested in *Google v Vidal-Hall* (2015)[196] which concerned misuse of private information and data protection claims against Google Inc. Here Google, using cookies, had collected the claimants' private information about their internet usage via their Apple Safari browser without their knowledge and consent. It had then offered the browser-generated information to advertisers, which in turn tailored their advertising to the claimants' interests. Google's public position had in fact been that Safari users would only be subject to such 'surveillance' if they had expressly allowed it. Of course, browser-generated data can be of a very private nature. As the above Gateway for service out of jurisdiction is applicable to 'tort' claims, it was contested whether the 'misuse of private information' claim fell under it. The Court of Appeal rejected Google's argument that it was not a tort as it grew out of an *equitable* cause of action, i.e. breach of confidence, and thus was excluded from the Gateway. Whatever the history of that exclusion or the circumstances of the birth of 'misuse of private information' may have been, the 'natural classification' of the action was now a tort.[197] The court displayed a similar robustness to make the law fit the case in its treatment of 'moral damage' such as stress and distress in absence of any pecuniary damage. The lower court held this was sufficient for the claim of misuse of private information (which was not appealed)[198] and the Court of Appeal made the same happen for the data protection infringement, by disapplying s 13(2) of the Data Protection Act to bring it in line with Art 23 of the Data Protection Directive.[199] While the judiciary quite rightly stretched the law to penetrate the huge and economically very valuable world of digital data and its use and manipulation, in pure jurisdictional terms the case shows that the touchstone of legal accountability can be as little as causing 'distress' on foreign shores. That is not very much at all. Again, much like in respect of the EU jurisprudence on personal jurisdiction, focus on the defendant's activity and its territorial focus, rather the plaintiff's loss would appear to yield a more stable and substantial test and fair outcome.

### (b) Forum conveniens

Even if one of the Gateways is satisfied, the court has a discretion whether to exercise jurisdiction over the foreign defendant and that depends on whether it considered that in all the circumstances England is clearly the appropriate place to decide the case, considering the interests of all the parties and the ends of justice, commonly known as *forum conveniens* or, where an action has already started in the jurisdiction and a stay is sought, *forum non conveniens*.[200]

The leading case on this issue which set the stage for later internet defamation cases is the House of Lords' decision in *Berezovsky v Michaels* (2000)[201] concerning a traditional magazine. The claimant, a Russian businessman, wanted to sue the US publisher of *Forbes*, an influential American fortnightly magazine, in England on the basis of a few copies that were distributed in England and restricted his claim to those. They made up a meagre 0.2 per cent of the total circulation, the bulk of which had occurred in the US. Despite this tiny distribution, it would, according to the Lords, not be unfair that the foreign publisher should be sued in England, as 'all the constituent elements of the tort occurred in England.'[202] In other words, in legal terms the alleged wrong was a purely local wrong: there was a 'publication' in England which had damaged the reputation the

---

195 Rule 6.37(1)(a) of the Civil Procedure Rules (CPR) refers to para 3.1 of the Practice Direction 6B; para 3.1(9) states the claimant may serve a claim form out of the jurisdiction with the permission of the court where the claim is made in tort: where: (a) damage was sustained within the jurisdiction; or (b) the damage sustained resulted from an act committed within the jurisdiction.

196 *Google v Vidal-Hall* [2015] EWCA Civ 311, affirming *Vidal-Hall v Google Inc* [2014] EWHC 13 (QB).

197 *Google v Vidal-Hall* [2015] EWCA Civ 311, paras 43, 49. At the time of writing permission to appeal to the Supreme Court was granted (28 July 2015), UK Supreme Court, available online at: https://www.supremecourt.uk/news/index.html

198 Whether distress satisfies an action for misuse of private information was not appealed from the lower court.

199 *Google v Vidal-Hall* [2015] EWCA Civ 311, paras 52–105, relying on Art 47 of the European Charter of Fundamental Rights which guarantees an effective remedy if a right under EU law is violated and its holding in *Benkharbouche v Embassy of the Republic of Sudan (Rev 1)* [2015] EWCA Civ 33.

200 CPR r 6.37(3) and the leading authority in England and Wales is *Spiliada Maritime Corporation v Cansulex Ltd* [1987] AC 460.

201 [2000] 1 WLR 1004.

202 *Berezovsky v Michaels* [2000] 1 WLR 1004, 1013.

claimant enjoyed in England. And *prima facie* the 'natural forum' to adjudicate a tort is the place where it occurred.[203] Thus the competence of the English court was based on compartmentalising transnational activity into various national activities which in turn allowed for the easy application of national procedures and law. Such compartmentalisation seems already strained and distorts reality in the case of traditional newspapers, where the circulation in different countries at least presupposes a deliberate choice. In respect of online publications, a narrow focus on its purely local effects without any regard to the impact of the publication elsewhere seems like an exercise of blind faith in national law orthodoxy. And yet, this is exactly what happened.

*Berezovsky* was extended to online publications in *Harrods Ltd v Dow Jones Co Inc* (2003)[204] concerning Harrods Ltd's defamation claim against Dow Jones, the publisher of the *Wall Street Journal*. The offending article, which appeared only in the US, not the European, edition of the journal, had been sent to ten subscribers in the UK, in contrast to its US circulation of 1.8 million copies. Similarly, its online edition had a very small number of hits from the UK. In line with *Berezovsky* Harrods Ltd limited its claim to the damage suffered in the UK[205] and thus achieved that *technically* the only foreign element in the claim was the defendant; the tort itself occurred in England, the claimant lived in England and enjoyed a reputation there. Thus the court upheld Harrods' right to sue in England. Yet, *substantially* the case was quite 'foreign' indeed: the publication was produced in the US, predominantly for a US market; Harrods Ltd, although a UK company, has a global reputation and was ultimately concerned to vindicate its reputation not just in England but worldwide.

A year later in *Lewis v King* (2004)[206] the allegedly defamatory statements had been distributed exclusively via the internet. The statements in question were made by an attorney representing Lennox Lewis in litigation with boxing promoter Don King in the US, and published on fightnews. com and boxingtalk.com. These sites, although of US origin, were, unlike in the above cases, also popular elsewhere, including England. But also unlike in the above cases, both the defendant and the claimant were US residents.[207] In reaching its conclusion not to interfere with the decision of the first-instance judge to allow the claim to proceed, the Court of Appeal usefully isolated four strands emerging from existing jurisprudence on *forum conveniens* in transnational online defamation claims.[208] First, it said, there is a presumption that the natural and appropriate place to hear the case is where the tort occurred. In defamation, this is where the article is published, i.e. downloaded, and where the defendant has a reputation to protect. Second, the importance of the location of the tort diminishes, the more tenuous the claimant's connection with England and the more substantial the publication abroad. Third, the traditional defamation rule that each publication gives rise to a separate cause of action, as enunciated in *Duke of Brunswick v Harmer* (1849),[209] has survived the internet age; it has not been replaced by an assumption that an online publication gives rise only to one cause of action which would favour a hearing in the court of the foreign publisher where the bulk of the publication took place. Fourth, in deciding the appropriate forum in internet cases, the notion of 'targeting' makes little sense as in truth the defendant targets every jurisdiction where his site can be downloaded. This reasoning reflects traditional jurisprudence applied rigidly to the internet, leaving online publishers, small and large, in a virtually impossible legal position where they have to choose between compliance with the laws of all jurisdictions or restricting their sites to certain jurisdictions.

---

203 *The Albaforth* [1984] 2 Lloyd's Rep 91, 94.
204 [2003] EWHC 1162 (QB). In *Dow Jones & Co v Harrods Ltd* 237 F Supp 2d 394, the New York District Court refused to grant to Dow Jones a declaratory judgment and an injunction requiring Harrods Ltd to abstain from pursuing a defamation claim in the UK.
205 *Berezovsky v Michaels* [2000] 1 WLR 1004 at 1032, and also consistent with the European approach, see above n 175 and accompanying text.
206 [2004] EWCA Civ 1329, affirming *King v Lewis* [2004] EWHC 168 (QB).
207 As was the case in *Chadha v Dow Jones & Co* [1999] EMLR 724 where both parties were US residents and the UK number of subscribers to the publication in comparison to the US subscription was relatively small; there the English court declined to hear the case.
208 *Lewis v King* [2004] EWCA Civ 1329, paras 24–39.
209 *Duke of Brunswick v Harmer* (1849) 14 QB 184.

Similarly, the High Court of Australia in *Dow Jones & Co Inc v Gutnick* (2002)[210] took a very traditional approach in an online defamation case, declining to make any allowances for the intrinsically global nature of the internet and effectively held that the publication of a website was analogous to the worldwide circulation of a newspaper. Gutnick was given the go-ahead to sue Dow Jones, the US publisher of *Barrons Online*, in Victoria (Australia) despite the fact that the vast majority of subscribers to the site were from the US and tiny percentage from Australia. Relying on *Berezovsky*, the judges pointed to the fact that there was a small but perfectly formed defamation in Australia. Again, Gutnick had restricted his claim to the damage he had suffered in Victoria and thereby contrived what appeared to be an almost purely domestic claim , i.e. local publication, local damage and local claimant. Given that Dow Jones had very few subscribers in Australia, it might well have considered foreclosing access to its site in Australia in the future and when that is the case, we might ask, who is the real loser of those decisions?

Many of these defamation actions were brought in England for tactical reasons considering their unlikely success in the US given its publisher-friendly interpretation of free speech under the US Constitution. To prevent such forum-shopping in the future, the Defamation Act 2013 restricts the jurisdiction of English courts by requiring that 'of all the places in which the statement complained of has been published, England and Wales is clearly the most appropriate place in which to bring an action in respect of the statement.'[211] This provision suggests that compartmentalising a worldwide publication into a purely local one should no longer be so readily possible, as the provision invites a comparative analysis of the relative significance of different places of the publication.

### (c) 'A real and substantial tort'

Last but not least, a court will only allow service out of jurisdiction (i.e. exercise adjudicative jurisdiction) if the claimant can show that there is a 'serious issue to be tried on the merits of the claim,'[212] which in turn requires that there has to be a 'real and substantial tort' and this is a requirement which dates back to *Kroch v Rossell* (1937).[213] Here the Court of Appeal held that jurisdiction of the local court will only lie if the alleged tort committed in the jurisdiction was a 'real and substantial' one (analogous to the *de minimis* maxim referred to above in *Bonnier Media*):

> it would be ridiculous and fundamentally wrong to have these two cases tried in this country on a very small and technical publication, when the real grievance of the claimant is a grievance against the wide-spread publication of the two papers in the respective countries where they are published.[214]

The Belgium newspaper *Le Soir* had a circulation in England of fewer than 50 copies out of a total circulation of hundreds of thousands, and the French newspaper *Le Petit Parisien* with a total circulation of 1.5 million circulated 400 copies in England. Despite the publication not exactly being minute, the court saw no problems in setting aside service. Importantly the court did not just consider the local effect of the activity, but those effects in light of the totality of the activity. Effectively, the court held that the place where the 'bulk of the publication' occurred was the appropriate forum – a proposition expressly rejected by Lord Steyn in *Berezovsky*, on the basis that such a 'global theory runs

---

210 *Dow Jones & Co v Gutnick* [2002] HCA 56.
211 Section 9(2) of the Defamation Act 2013.
212 CPR r 6.37(1)(b). See, e.g., *Vidal-Hall v Google Inc* [2014] EWHC 13 (QB), paras 16, 105–128; *Metropolitan International Schools Ltd (t/a Skillstrain and/or Train2game) v Designtechnica Corp (t/a Digital Trends)* [2009] EWHC 1765 (QB), para 24.
213 [1937] 1 All ER 725; *Chadha v Dow Jones & Co Inc* [1999] EMLR 734.
214 *Kroch v Rossell* [1937] 1 All ER 725, 732.

counter to well established principles of libel law'[215] and that it would be unfair to the claimant if the publication in the forum was 'significant' and the claimant had a reputation in the forum.

Kroch was applied to an internet libel dispute in *Dow Jones & Co Inc v Jameel* (2005)[216] where the defendant successfully argued that no 'real and substantial' tort had been committed in the forum given that only five local subscribers had accessed the offending 'Golden Chain' list, and three of those were from the claimant's camp. In the words of the court: 'The game will not merely not have been worth the candle, it will not have been worth the wick.'[217] The court further held that Kroch was not just relevant to the *forum conveniens* inquiry, but also overlapped with the more general application to strike out a claim as an abuse of process (which may be relevant in purely domestic cases.) Consistently, it expressed doubts about the continued validity of *Brunswick v Harmer* (1849):

> Keeping a proper balance between the Article 10 right of freedom of expression and the protection of individual reputation must . . . require the court to bring to a stop an abuse of process defamation proceedings that are not serving the legitimate purpose of protecting the claimant's reputation . . . We do not believe that *Brunswick v Harmer* could today have survived an application to strike out for abuse of process. The Duke himself procured the republication to his agent of an article published many years before the sole purpose of bringing legal proceedings that that would not be met by a plea of limitation. If his agent reads the article he is unlikely to have thought the Duke much, if any, the worse for it . . . he acquired a technical cause of action but we would today condemn the entire exercise as an abuse of process.

Clearly, the judge softened the *Brunswick* stance by excluding self-induced publications and negligible ones. This is not quite the targeting approach as even in targeted jurisdictions there may not be any publications and in respect of non-targeted jurisdiction there may be more than negligible publications. Also the exclusive focus on *actual* publications, regardless of the objective intention of the publisher, does not square with the targeting analysis. Nevertheless, the move away from the dogmatic any-publication-counts-no-matter-how-small stance should provide some welcome relief for online publishers. It was endorsed in *Amoudi v Brisard* (2006)[218] where the court rejected an application for a summary judgment, as there is no presumption of law under English law that there is a substantial publication in a libel action concerning a freely accessible website. In other words, even if a website can be accessed, it must still be shown that it was in fact accessed.

Generally, the *Jameel* maxim applies where there is no prospect of obtaining any damages or other valuable relief proportionate to the parties' and court's resources likely to be expended on the trial. The test is: is the game worth the candle? However, in *Kaschke v Osler* (2010)[219] whilst striking out the claim concerning a defamatory blog, Eady J warned that 'the court must be vigilant to recognise the small minority of cases in which the legitimate object of vindication is not required or at least cannot be achieved without a wholly disproportionate interference with the rights of the defendants.'[220] The issue came up again in *McGrath v Dawkins* (Rev 1) (2012)[221] where McGrath tried to promote his own book in the disguise of a negative review of Dawkins' book on amazon.co.uk and then, under various aliases, created a fake discussion thread. When he was found out, he attracted abuse and accusation on amazon's site as well as on Richard Dawkins Foundation's US site by Mr Jones and others. Considering an application to strike out the claim for abuse of process, the court

215 *Berezovsky v Michaels* [2000] 1 WLR 1004, 1013, essentially relying on *Spiliada Maritime Corporation v Cansulex Ltd* [1987] AC 460. The *de minimis* maxim as well as *Kroch v Rossell* were expressly rejected in *Harrods Ltd v Dow Jones Co Inc* [2003] EWHC 1162 (QB), para 39: 'there is no *de minimis* principle when it comes to establishing publication', and para 44, distinguishing *Kroch v Rossell* on the facts.
216 *Dow Jones & Co Inc v Jameel* [2005] EWCA Civ 75.
217 *Dow Jones & Co Inc v Jameel* [2005] EWCA Civ 75, para 69.
218 *Amoudi v Brisard* [2006] EWHC 1062 (QB).
219 *Kaschke v Osler* [2010] EWHC 1075 (QB).
220 *Kaschke v Osler* [2010] EWHC 1075 (QB), para 22.
221 *McGrath v Dawkins* (Rev 1) [2012] EWHC B3 (QB), para 89f, affirmed in *McGrath v Dawkins* [2013] EWCA Civ 206.

found a small but not minimal readership, yet in combination with other factors (e.g. likely prospect of defences), the action for damages was too trivial to be justified.[222] The court also confirmed that the discussion board on the Foundation's US site would be considered 'published' for defamation purposes in the UK by virtue of being downloadable in the UK, but held that this did not automatically implicate the UK Foundation in the publication of its US sister corporation. However, in the particular case the UK Foundation was in principle implicated in the US site's wrongdoing as a simple click on its 'home' button took users to the US site.[223] Finally, in *Tamiz v Google Inc Google UK Ltd* (2012)[224] concerning defamatory comments on a blog called 'London Muslim' on Google's Blogger.com, Justice Eady held, on the issue of showing a 'real and substantial tort', that an allegation of a criminal offence 'cannot be discounted on the basis of a mere "numbers game"' but found that the period between notification and removal of the offending blog by Google was so short as to significantly limit Google's potential liability and thus make the action trivial.[225]

Finally, in *Google v Vidal-Hall* (2015) the Court of Appeal held that the *Jameel* maxim was not established, because even though the likely damages might be small, the case raised 'serious issues' arising out of the 'secret and blanket tracking and collation of information, often of an extremely private nature.'[226] In short, the wider implications of the case made it worth the candle.

## *In rem* jurisdiction

An alternative to personal jurisdiction to establish the adjudicative jurisdiction of the court is *in rem* jurisdiction (Latin, power against a thing). Here the court's competence is based upon the presence within the court's territory of an asset under dispute, rather than the defendant's presence.[227] Classically *in rem* jurisdiction has arisen in admiralty law where the presence of a ship within the court's jurisdiction provided the basis of the court's competence.[228] The presence of a ship within the court's enforcement power is used both as a lever against the defendant to defend the dispute (i.e. to submit to the court's jurisdiction) as well as an avenue to enforce a judgment against the defendant. Thus *in rem* jurisdiction does not entail the enforcement difficulties of other judgments against foreign wrongdoers. For this reason, it is surprising that it has not been exploited more frequently in the online context.

In the US *in rem* jurisdiction has proven useful in both online gambling and domain name disputes. The case of *US v $734,578.8 in US Currency*[229] concerns online gambling which, as discussed above, is severely restricted in the US. In this case the US government brought a civil *in rem* forfeiture action to indirectly enforce criminal restrictions on internet or telephone gambling. The action was brought against various US bank accounts used in the process of illegal gambling activity of the defendant English company, American Sports Ltd, which operated under a licence in England, solicited punters in the US via a website and finally facilitated the gambling via the telephone. As a New Jersey company had acted as an intermediary for the defendant to organise the financial side of the business, the court treated the case as a purely domestic case, seeing no need at all to engage with the transnationality of the underlying allegedly illegal transactions. All the US government had to show, to have the funds forfeited, was that there were reasonable grounds to believe that the New Jersey intermediary had violated US gambling prohibitions, which it did. The defendant's

---

222 *McGrath v Dawkins (Rev 1)* [2012] EWHC B3 (QB), para 90ff.
223 *McGrath v Dawkins (Rev 1)* [2012] EWHC B3 (QB), paras 16–26.
224 *Tamiz v Google Inc Google UK Ltd* [2012] EWHC 449, affirmed in *Tamiz v Google Inc* [2013] EWCA Civ 68.
225 *Tamiz v Google Inc Google UK Ltd* [2012] EWHC 449, paras 30 and 50 respectively.
226 *Google v Vidal-Hall* [2015] EWCA Civ 311, para 137.
227 Contrast in *rem* jurisdiction where the action is against a thing, with jurisdiction *in personam* which may also be based on the location of the subject-matter of the dispute (i.e. movable or immovable property) within the jurisdiction but where the action is still against the defendant.
228 See s 21 of the Supreme Court Act 1981; and *Republic of India v Indian Steamship Company Ltd* [1998] AC 878 where the House of Lords held that the owners of the ship are parties to an action in *rem*.
229 *US v $734,578.8 in US Currency* 286 F 3d 641 (NJ, 2002).

argument that the New Jersey intermediary dealt purely with the financial aspects of the gambling and all actual gambling took place beyond US borders in England where it was legal, was rejected by the court: 'the legality and/or licensure of the businesses in England is simply irrelevant to the issues raised in the instant forfeiture proceedings.'[230] Equally, even if 'British citizens and British companies will be affected by this in rem action in New Jersey'[231] that had no bearing on the action. The court could take such disinterested view of the foreign interests involved because it was in no way dependent upon the cooperation of the foreign state for the enforcement of its judgment – the in rem nature of the action guaranteed enforcement power.

In *Cable News Network LP v CNNews.com*[232] in rem jurisdiction was successfully relied upon in a trade mark dispute to catch a foreign defendant who would have fallen through the personal jurisdiction net. The dispute arose because a Chinese company registered cnnews.com with Network Solutions in Virginia in the US; the site provides news in Chinese to the Chinese market. As 'cn' is the country top-level domain for China and the name cnnews translates literally into 'Chinese news', it would appear to be an appropriate domain name for a Chinese news company. Nevertheless, the well-known US news corporation CNN took objection and alleged that cnnews.com infringed and diluted its CNN trade mark in the US. CNN would have had difficulties in having the case heard in the US relying on personal jurisdiction as the Chinese company had virtually no contacts with the US. As an alternative CNN relied upon the Anticybersquatting Consumer Protection Act (1999)[233] which applies to bad-faith domain name registration and allows claimants to recover the name (but no monetary awards). The Act provides for in rem jurisdiction in respect of domain name in the judicial district where its 'registrar, registry, or other domain name authority . . . is located.' As all .com names (the most popular name worldwide) are under the control of the US company VeriSign,[234] in rem jurisdiction over any dispute involving these names gives US courts wide powers over foreign registrants.[235] Indeed, in CNN the Virginian District Court held that the .com was an 'essentially American top-level domain name.'[236] As far as the in rem nature of the jurisdiction was concerned, the court held that there was no need either for the Chinese company to have had minimum contacts with the US,[237] nor was a showing of bad faith a jurisdictional requirement.[238] Thus it mattered not that the target audience of ccnews.com was almost exclusively located in China (99.5 per cent of the site's registered users were from China) and that the site did not sell any products or services to anyone outside China. The court then found that all the elements for a trade mark infringement claim under the Lanham Act under the Anitcybersquatting Consumer Protection Act were satisfied.[239] For the substantive claim, the 'bad faith' requirement was held to be satisfied on the basis that the Chinese company had not previously used the name nor a trade mark of that name.[240] It rejected that the application of US trade mark law would be extraterritorial. In its opinion, the dispute was a purely domestic dispute as

230 US v $734,578.82 in US Currency 286 F3d 641, 657 (3rd Cir 2002).
231 Ibid, 660.
232 In respect of the jurisdiction requirements see Cable News Network LP v CNNews.com 162 F Supp 2d 484 (ED Va 2001). On the substance of the claim, Cable News Network LP v CNNews.com 177 F Supp 2d 506 (ED Va 2001), affirmed in part and vacated in part on other grounds Cable News Network LP v CNNews.com 56 Fed Appx 599 (4th Cir 2003).
233 Codified in s 43(d) of the Lanham Act.
234 Until 2012 for the time being. BBC, 'Deal signed on .com domain future' (4 December 2006), available online at: http://news.bbc.co.uk/2/hi/technology/6199394.stm
235 Caesars World, Inc v Caesars-Palace.com 112 F Supp 2d 502 (ED Va, 2000); Hartog & Co, AS v Swix.com and Swix.net 2001 US Dist Lexis 3568 (ED Va, 2001); GlobalSantafe Corporation v GlobalSantafe.com 250 F Supp 2d 610 (ED Va, 2003); America Online, Inc v AOL.org 259 F Supp 2d 449 (ED Va, 2003); NBC Universal, Inc v NBCUniversal.com 378 F Supp 2d 715 (ED Va, 2005).
236 Cable News Network LP v CNNews.com 177 F Supp 2d 506, 517 (ED Va 2001).
237 Cable News Network LP v CNNews.com 162 F Supp 2d 484, 491 (ED Va 2001). In fact there was no need for the registrant of the domain name to be joined in the action under the ACPA: Cable News Network LP v CNNews.com 162 F Supp 2d 484, 493f (ED Va 2001).
238 Cable News Network LP v CNNews.com 162 F Supp 2d 484, 492f (ED Va 2001).
239 Cable News Network LP v CNNews.com 177 F Supp 2d 506 (ED Va 2001).
240 Cable News Network LP v CNNews.com 177 F Supp 2d 506, 524 (ED Va 2001).

the domain name was within the jurisdiction.[241] It then ordered that the domain name of cnnews. com be transferred to CNN.

In both of the above cases, the location of the property (i.e. the bank account and the domain name) within the US provided the basis of the court's right to hear the dispute in line with traditional in rem jurisdiction. Furthermore, on the basis of the location of the property the courts treated the disputes as purely domestic also in determining the application of the substantive law (even though, for example, the location of a domain name registration is entirely irrelevant to determining whether local trade mark law was applicable or infringed). The effect of treating in rem cases as purely domestic – regardless of the transnationality of the underlying transaction – is that safeguards normally in place to guard against exorbitant jurisdictional assertions are simply not called into play. The results are unfortunate insular decisions.

## Choice of law

Although the location of the court has in cross-border internet disputes been the main point of contention (given its huge practical as well as legal implications), once that is decided the court does not necessarily apply its own substantive law to the case, but chooses the one with the closest link, which often but, not always, is the local substantive law. Much like in respect of personal jurisdiction, there are different and competing tests to determine which law is most closely connected to a case, most of which have a territorial outlook. In the EU this question is resolved in non-contractual disputes by the EU Regulation on the Law Applicable to Non-Contractual Obligations (2007)[242] also known as 'Rome II' ('Rome I' governs the applicable law in contractual disputes, see Chapter 6 on Electronic Commerce), or at least provides the starting point of the inquiries. For tort cases, as understood in the broadest sense, Art 4 stipulates that the applicable law is 'the law of the country in which the damage occurs irrespective of the country in which the event giving rise to the damage occurred . . .' and this rule is only overridden where the 'tort/ delict is manifestly more closely connected with a[nother] country'.[243] Art 8(1) provides a more specific rule for intellectual property infringements, saying that the applicable law is 'the law of the country for which protection is claimed'. This is just another way of saying 'the law of the country in which the damage occurs' as one can only suffer damage (in a legal sense) in the place where one enjoys a legal protection. But how far, in territorial terms, does the 'legal protection' of intellectual property reach and how far should it reach? Ultimately both Art 4 for tort generally and Art 8 for intellectual property specifically require an analysis of the territorial reach of the substantive law on tort or trade mark or copyright.

Typically, in the early English case of *Euromarket Designs Inc v Peters and Crate & Barrel Ltd* (2000)[244] the US claimant alleged that the Irish defendant had infringed its UK and EC registered trade mark 'Crate & Barrell' by advertising its goods in a UK magazine with a UK and Irish circulation and on a website of the name crateandbarrel-ie.com. In a summary judgment, the court held that no trade mark infringement had occurred (in the UK) as the defendant had not 'used' the mark 'in the course of a trade' in the UK – applying a targeting analysis at this substantive stage. According to the

---

241 *Cable News Network LP v CNNews.com* 177 F Supp 2d 506, 527 (ED Va 2001). This approach also means that the test (concerning the extra-territorial reach of trade mark law) laid down in *McBee v Delica Co Ltd* 417 F3d 107 (1st Cir 2005) requiring that the extraterritorial activities of the foreigner under the offending name must have a substantial effect on US commerce, would not be called into play.

242 EC Regulation of the European Parliament and of the Council of 11 July 2007 on the law applicable to non-contractual obligations (Rome II) 864/2007, which excludes from its scope violations of privacy and defamation (see Art 1(2)(g)). K Lipstein, 'Intellectual Property: Jurisdiction or Choice of Law' (2002) 61(2) *Cambridge Law Journal* 294, 297; James J Fawcett and Paul Torremans, *Intellectual Property and Private International Law*, 1998, Oxford: OUP, 517–520; Mireille MM van Eechoud, *Choice of Law in Copyright and Related Rights: Alternative to the Lex Protectionis*, 2003, Kluwer Law International.

243 Art 4(1) and (3) respectively.

244 [2000] EWHC Ch 179.

court, neither the magazine advert nor the site constituted infringing use. In respect of the magazine (but also insightful for the online context) Jacob J held that:

> if the trader is merely carrying on business in X, and advertisement of his slips over the border into Y, no businessman would regard that fact as meaning that he was trading in Y. This would especially be so if the advertisement were for a local business such as a shop or a local service rather than for goods.

He continued that the website in this case merely allowed the surfer to look into the Irish shop, rather providing an active platform for trade itself:

> [in this case] the internet was more like the user focussing a super-telescope into the site concerned . . . you can look into the defendant's shop in Dublin . . . Other cases would be different – a well-known example, for instance, is Amazon.com. Based in the US it has actively gone out to seek world-wide trade, not just by use of the name on the internet but by advertising its business here, and offering and operating a real service of supply of books to this country. These defendants have done none of that.[245]

In coming to this conclusion Jacob J relied upon his earlier trade mark decision in *1–800 Flowers Inc v Phonenames Ltd* (2000)[246] where he said that the question whether a site is or is not 'used in the course of trade' in the place where it can be accessed depends on the objective intention of the owner in light of all the circumstances:

> the mere fact that websites can be accessed anywhere in the world does not mean, for trade mark purposes, that the law should regard them as being used everywhere in the world. It all depends upon the circumstances, particularly the intention of the website owner and what the reader will understand if he accesses the site.[247]

So, importantly, whilst moderation in form of the 'targeting' approach is absent at the personal jurisdiction stage in the EU (e.g. *Wintersteiger*) and to a lesser extent in England and Wales, it does enter the picture at the applicable law stage, at least in intellectual property disputes under Rome II, even if not expressly stated. This moderate approach has been confirmed by the CJEU in *L'Oréal SA and Others v eBay International AG* (2011)[248] where it held that the right of trade mark owners to offer goods under the sign for sale is infringed as 'as soon as it is clear that the offer for sale of a trade-marked product located in a third State is targeted at consumers in the territory covered by the trade mark.'[249]

> It must, however, be made clear that the mere fact that a website is accessible from the territory covered by the trade mark is not a sufficient basis for concluding that the offers for sale displayed there are targeted at consumers in that territory . . . Indeed, if the fact that an online marketplace is accessible from that territory were sufficient for the advertisements displayed there to be within the scope of . . . [EU trade mark law], websites and advertisements which, although obviously targeted solely at consumers in third States, are nevertheless technically accessible from EU territory would *wrongly* be subject to EU law.[250]

---

245 *Euromarket Designs Inc v Peters and Crate & Barrel Ltd* [2000] EWHC Ch 179, para 24.
246 [2000] ETMR 369.
247 *1–800 Flowers Inc v Phonenames Ltd* [2000] ETMR 369, para 12.
248 *L'Oréal SA v eBay International AG* C-324/09 (2011) ECR I-6011.
249 *L'Oréal SA v eBay International AG* C-324/09 (2011) ECR I-6011, para 61, under Art 5(3)(b) and (d) of Directive 89/104 (trade marks in EU Member States, now governed by EU Directive 2008/95/EC) or in Art 9(2)(b) and (d) of Regulation 40/94 (community trade marks).
250 *L'Oréal SA v eBay International AG* C-324/09 (2011) ECR I-6011, para 64 [emphasis added].

For a copyright case[251] to a similar effect (decided before Rome II[252]), see *Société Éditions du Seuil SAS v Société Google Inc, Société Google France* (2009)[253] where French publishers complained that Google infringed French copyright law because it 'made available to the French public' online excerpts of French books without the rights holders' authorisation. By now not surprisingly, the French court rejected the argument by Google that US copyright law, including its fair use doctrine, should govern the dispute. As this case concerned a 'complex' tort (the initiating act and the injury were in different countries), the *lex loci delicti* test was difficult to apply and the court looked for the law with which the dispute had the 'most significant relationship' which was French law: Google was delivering excerpts of French works to French users, on an .fr site, using the French language and one of the defendants was a French company. The court appears to have considered the acts to have been 'targeted' at France without analysing the case on such terms. Similarly in the US, the traditional approach for the extraterritorial reach of US anti-trust law was applied to trade marks, requiring that the extraterritorial activities of the foreigner must have a 'substantial effect' on US commerce before US trade mark law would be extended to such foreign activities.[254]

The disparity between the approaches to 'jurisdiction of the court' and 'choice of law' is illustrated by *Re the MARITIM Trade Mark* (2002)[255] a trade mark infringement action brought in Hamburg by the owner of a chain of hotels in Germany named MARITIM for which he had an EU and German trade mark. The Danish defendant ran a Bed & Breakfast in Copenhagen under the name HOTEL MARITIME (protected by a Danish trade mark). He advertised his B&B on his website hotel-maritime.dk in several languages, including German, which also allowed for online bookings. The German court took an expansive approach to Art 5(3) (now Art 7(2) of the Jurisdiction Regulation 2012, see above) saying that any site accessible in Germany would expose its owner to the jurisdiction of German courts, but then proceeded that on the substance no trade mark infringement had been committed. It held that that not every name used online should be subjected to German trade mark law; or put differently, German trade mark law will not be applicable/infringed simply because a foreign site is accessible in Germany – thus paving the road for the co-existence of national trade marks on the international online stage. German trade mark law extends extraterritorially only if the foreign site was commercially directed at Germany. In this case, the court found, this was not satisfied as the site advertised a service to be delivered entirely in Denmark, as the use of foreign languages was normal in this commercial sector and did not mean that the site was directed at consumers in Germany and, as the .dk domain suggested, the Danish market was the focal point of the site. It may be objected that the use of foreign languages was very much designed to attract foreigners, including Germans, to the site which is not undermined but rather reinforced by the fact that it is standard practice in the tourist industry. Thus Germany along with many other states was a target of the site. But regardless of this, the German court adopted the moderate destination approach at the second stage, whilst it would only seem fair to filter out unmeritorious cases at the earliest possible opportunity, which is at the point of personal jurisdiction.

Having said that, the courts in the defamation cases (see above) have not opted for the targeting approach at either stage; according to those decisions, the applicable law for an online defamation is the law of the place in which the defamatory material was published (*lex loci delicti*, as

251 For a case concerning Art 7 of the Database Directive 96/9/EC, see *Football Dataco Ltd v Sportradar GmbH* [2011] EWCA Civ 330.

252 Pekka Savola, 'The Ultimate Copyright Shopping Opportunity – Jurisdiction and Choice of law in Website Blocking Injunctions' (2014) 45 International Review of Intellectual Property and Competition Law 287.

253 *Société Éditions du Seuil SAS v Société Google Inc* (TGI Paris, 3eme, 2eme, 18 December 2009, n° 09/00540; see Jane C Ginsberg, Conflicts of Laws in the Google Book Search: A View from Abroad' (2 June 2010) *The Media Institute*, available online at: http://www.media institute.org/IPI/2010/060210_ConflictofLaws.php; and Jane C Ginsburg, 'International Issues: Which Country's Law Applies When Works are Made Available Over the Internet?' (2010) 34 Columbia Journal of Law & the Arts 49.

254 *McBee v Delica Co Ltd* 417 F3d 107 (1st Cir 2005).

255 *Re the MARITIM Trademark*, Hanteatisches Oberlandsgericht Hamburg, Urteil vom 2.5.2002, Internet-Zeitschrift für Rechtsinformatik und Informationsrecht, available online at: http://www.jurpc.de/rechtspr/20020317.pdf

defamation and privacy claims are excluded from Rome II) which on the internet means whenever a site can be downloaded rather than uploaded, or in short, wherever it is accessible

## Enforcement

The issue of enforceability is as prominent in relation to online civil disputes as it is in respect of criminal matters, and just like in criminal law the starting point for civil law is the strict territorial limit of enforcement jurisdiction of states. They cannot take any actions outside their own borders to enforce a judgment against a foreign defendant. However, unlike in criminal law, there is some cooperation in the form of the reciprocal enforcement of foreign judgments frequently enshrined in bilateral or multilateral treaties.

In England and Wales, the default position on the enforcement of foreign judgments is provided for under common law according to which a claimant can apply for a summary judgment on the foreign judgment. As the defendant has few defences to such claim and as the willingness of English courts to enforce foreign judgments is, rather generously, not dependent on reciprocity,[256] they are relatively easily enforceable. The common law position is replaced by statute in respect of foreign states which have entered into enforcement treaties with the UK, bringing either the Foreign Judgments (Reciprocal Enforcement) Act 1933 or the EC Regulation on Jurisdiction and the Recognition and Enforcement of Judgments in Civil and Commercial Matters (recast) (2012)[257] into play. The Regulation lays down a strong mutual recognition and enforcement regime in that any judgment (and not just money judgments) from another Member State is automatically recognised and, following compliance with some formal procedures, enforceable unless subsequently successfully challenged on one of five narrow grounds.[258]

One basis for challenging the enforceability of a foreign judgment – recognised under English common law or statute as well as in most other states – is 'public policy', i.e. the enforcement would be contrary to the 'public policy' of the enforcing state.[259] This exception to enforceability runs parallel to the exclusion of foreign law in locally adjudicated cases where the application of such foreign law would be inconsistent with public policy of the adjudicating state.[260] The effect of either exclusionary rule varies from state to state, being modestly applied in some and treated as catch-all escape route in others. In England, public policy has rarely been invoked to refuse enforcement or recognition of a foreign judgment[261] and in Canada the narrowness of the defence was recently affirmed in *Society of Lloyd's v Meinzer*[262] limiting it to cases affecting 'essential principles of justice' or 'moral interests' of the enforcing state.

The public policy exception is routinely used in the US, particularly to invoke US constitutional free speech standards, in order to deny the enforcement of foreign judgments, often concerning defamation claims. This has been the case even when the enforcement of the foreign judgment would take effect solely in the foreign state and not impact at all on any speech in the US.[263] The

256 *Adams v Cape Industries plc* [1990] Ch 433, 552.

257 1215/2012.

258 Arts 45 and 46 of the EC Regulation on Jurisdiction and the Recognition and Enforcement of Judgments in Civil and Commercial Matters, (recast) 1215/2012. Unlike common law, the Regulation does not allow for the review of the jurisdiction of the foreign court which pronounced the judgment and thus provides a more robust enforcement regime. Under the Regulation such review is not necessary as it harmonises jurisdiction rules and thus guards against exorbitant jurisdictional assertion by any Member State.

259 Under Art 45(1)(a) of the EC Regulation on Jurisdiction and the Recognition and Enforcement of Judgments in Civil and Commercial Matters, (recast) 1215/2012 the judgment must be 'manifestly' contrary to the public policy of the requested state for the exception to apply.

260 Lawrence Collins (ed), *Dicey, Morris & Collins on The Conflict of Laws*, 14th edn, 2006, London: Sweet & Maxwell, p 92.

261 *Ibid*, 629.

262 (2002) 210 DLR (4th) 519 (Ont CA).

263 Kyo Ho Yum, 'The Interaction between American and Foreign Libel Law: US Courts Refuse to Enforce English Libel Judgments' (2000) 49 International and Comparative Law Quarterly 132; Jeremy Maltby, 'Juggling Comity and Self-Government: The Enforcement of Foreign Libel Judgments in US Courts' (1994) 94 Columbian Law Review 1978.

SPEECH Act 2010 (Securing the Protection of our Enduring and Established Constitutional Heritage Act) consolidates this un-cooperation by prohibiting the recognition and enforcement of foreign defamation judgments against online providers, unless the defendant would have been liable under US law, including the US Constitution, its defamation law, its immunity for internet intermediaries and its due process requirement. Yet, this unwillingness does not necessarily stop claimants from bringing their actions, as the Australian and English defamation cases, discussed above, show. In *Gutnick*, the Australian High Court specifically acknowledged the likely unenforceability of any final order against the US-based publisher.[264] Especially in defamation action it is often more valuable to the claimant to have their reputation vindicated than the promise of a monetary award, and thus the unenforceability of the judgment is a secondary concern for these claimants.

A high-profile internet case where a US court in fact refused to enforce the foreign judgment is the French *Yahoo* case, discussed above. Here the Californian Supreme Court held that enforcement of the French order would be inconsistent with the First Amendment ostensibly because the enforcement of the foreign order would chill protected speech in the US.[265] This, however, was a result the French court had been at pains to avoid by ensuring that Yahoo! Inc had the technical means to restrict access to certain sites for French users only, but not others. The Californian court also asserted that the unenforceability of the French order on the basis of its unconstitutionality would not give the US First Amendment extraterritorial effect as it applied to Yahoo! Inc's 'actions in the United States, specifically [to] the ways in which it configures and operates its auction and Yahoo.com sites.'[266] The problem with this argument is that the very point of seeking the enforcement of a foreign judgment is to make the defendant do something in the enforcing state; in other words it is an argument which would require every foreign judgment to be compatible with the US constitution regardless of where the effects of the judgment would be felt. While the Californian judgment was on appeal reversed on other grounds, a majority of the US Court of Appeals agreed in *obiter* with its unenforceability.[267] The judges acknowledged that foreign laws need not be identical to US laws, but must not be repugnant to local laws and policies or, put more broadly, to fundamental principles of what is 'decent and just.'[268] Unfortunately, most judges decided that the US Constitution laid down what is decent and just, and anything inconsistent with it could not conceivably be so.[269]

## Case study

The most iconic internet case of recent times is the right-to-be-forgotten CJEU case of *Google Spain SL, Google Inc v Agencia Española de Protección de Datos (AEPD)* (2014)[270] and not just because it imposed on search engines a duty to respond to objections and erasure requests by users in respect of their search results (see Chapter 9). The foundational issue which had to be addressed first was whether the EU Data Protection Directive in fact extended to the processing of search results outside the EU when those results are on display within the EU – in short, the classic jurisdiction dilemma which has plagued courts worldwide since the 1990s.

---

264 *Dow Jones & Co v Gutnick* [2002] HCA 56, para 53.
265 *Yahoo! Inc v LICRA* 169 F Supp 2d 1181, 1192 (ND Cal, 2001).
266 *Ibid*, 1193.
267 As the issue of enforceability had not been appealed by LICRA, it was not within the remit of the court to decide it. Yet, six out of the 11 judges held that the order would not be enforceable either on public-policy grounds, being contrary to First Amendment, or, in Ferguson J's case, on the ground that the order was an act-of-state. Only Fletcher J, Schroeder CJ and Gould J left enforceability open as a possibility. Tashima J and O'Scannlain J expressed no opinion.
268 *Yahoo! Inc v LICRA & UEJF* 379 F 3d 1120, 1215 (9th Cir 2004).
269 *Ibid*, 1140.
270 *Google Inc. v Agencia Española de Protección de Datos, Mario Costeja González* C-131/12 (Grand Chamber, 13 May 2014); discussed in Brendan van Alsenoy, Marieke Koekkoek, 'Internet and jurisdiction after *Google Spain*: the extraterritorial reach of the 'right to be delisted' (2015) 5 International Data Privacy Law 105.

Before turning to how the CJEU resolved this question, it worth noting that the data protection scenario shows in many ways the artificiality of the public/criminal and private/civil law divide in that the case was both 'public' and 'private' at the same time. The action was initiated by Mr Gonzalez, whose professional reputation was haunted by the online publication of a newspaper archive from a decade earlier which included a public announcement of a compulsory real estate auction of his property to repay his social security debts. On Google Search this announcement ranked high on a search of his name. Under the Directive individuals are entitled to sue for a breach of their data protection rights (Art 22) and such claims would be characterised as a 'private' for jurisdictional purposes. Yet, at the same time, the case before the CJEU was supported by the Spanish Data Protection Authority (AEDP) which has separate enforcement powers as public supervisory authority (Art 28) and any of its activities would be characterised as 'public' and thus engage the jurisdictional rules under public international law. Whilst for data protection the jurisdictional scope was provided for by the Directive and thus the same rules apply regardless of the private or public nature of the claim, as shown above, this is not the case generally where very different legal regimes govern the private and public cross-border domain.

On the issue of the territorial scope of EU data protection law, the CJEU held that Art 4(1)(a) of the Directive captured Google's search processing and thus it was unnecessary to consider, in the alternative, Art 4(1)(c). Article (4)(1)(a) provides that the Directive applies where 'the processing is carried out in the context of the activities of an establishment of the controller on the territory of the Member State.' Google did not dispute that its Spanish subsidiary incorporated under Spanish law was an 'establishment' in Spain for the purposes of Art 4. However, it disputed that its processing activity of online data in response to search terms (which occurred on servers in the US) was carried out in the context of the activities of Google Spain which, like all its national subsidiaries, functions solely to promote and sell keyword advertising to clients within the national advertising market (Google's main source of income) and was not as such involved with the processing of search queries. The CJEU disagreed on the basis that:

> the activities of the operator of the search engine and those of its establishment situated in the Member State concerned are inextricably linked since the activities relating to the advertising space constitute the means of rendering the search engine at issue economically profitable and that engine is, at the same time, the means enabling those activities to be performed.[271]

Although the CJEU focused on the fact that Google used the local establishment that 'orientates' its activities towards the inhabitants of the particular Member State (i.e. a targeting approach), it also stressed that the broad territorial scope of the Directive was necessary to ensure the 'effective and complete protection' of persons in the EU under data protection law.[272] This then raised the question of whether Google's data protection obligation under the Directive only extended to Google's European domains, or whether other domains which do not target Europe (e.g. .com or .jp) are also subject to EU data protection law on the basis that they can be accessed in Europe. Should Mr Gonzalez's erasure request be extended to search on google.com as occasionally a Spanish user may use that site rather than google.es? The Article 29 Working Party in its advice on the implementation of the judgment made a recommendation in the affirmative as this would be the only way to provide for 'complete' protection.[273] But would such protection indeed be 'complete' as, of course, the information is not removed at its source. Also, does the law always guarantee or even aim for 'complete' protection? And what are the implications of such ruling for Google? In order not to

---

271 *Google Inc v Agencia Española de Protección de Datos, Mario Costeja González* C-131/12 (Grand Chamber, 13 May 2014), para 56.
272 Ibid, paras 60, 53–54 respectively.
273 Article 29 Data Protection Working Party, *Guidelines on the Implementation of the Court of Justice of the European Union Judgement on 'Google Spain and Inc v Agencia Española de Protección de Datos (AEPD) and Mario Costeja González'* C-131/12 (26 November 2014), para 7.

deprive other non-EU users of information to which they have an entitlement under their laws, Google could only comply with the holding by making Google.com or google.jp inaccessible in Europe, or tailoring even those sites to a European audience when they click on it.

When it comes to jurisdiction or competence rules in the broadest sense, one might be tempted to think, especially in the context of private international law, that these rules are merely technical rules that come to the aid of specific transnational cases and have no wider policy implications beyond these specific circumstances. Yet, the reality could not be further removed from this. Whilst undoubtedly many of these rules are indeed very technical, their repercussions for the online world go well beyond the specific cases in which they are raised. These rules require and certainly incentivise online providers to make their online offering territorially sensitive. By doing so, they encourage the creation of solid or porous cyberborders, as the case may be. In their cumulative effect, they lead to the gradual 'balkanisation' of cyberspace – a space which threatens to increasingly mirror the political and legal borders of the 'real' world. In fact, this is an inevitable outcome of trying to apply real world laws to cyberspace.

# Further reading

Hannah L Buxbaum, 'Territory, territoriality, and the resolution of jurisdiction conflict' (2009) 57 The American Journal of Comparative Law 631

Alex Mills, 'The private history of international law' (2006) 55 International and Comparative Law Quarterly 1

Alex Mills, 'Rethinking jurisdiction in international law' (2014) 84 The British Yearbook of International Law 187

Milton L Mueller, *Networks and States: the Global Politics of Internet Governance*, 2010, MIT Press

# Chapter 3

# Intermediaries within online regulation

## Chapter contents

# Introduction

In the 1990s – the early days of the commercial internet – the term 'disintermediation' played a significant part in academic discussions of the online world. The view was that the internet dispensed with the need for many of the traditional middlemen, allowing transactions and exchanges to occur directly between the primary actors. One commentator wrote, for example:

> Because of the capabilities of computer networks, the functions of central repository and archive are highly vulnerable to disintermediation. As applied to libraries, disintermediation means the diversion of information users from centralized physical repositories to alternate sources available directly through computers and computer networks. The Internet offers publishers a new way of reaching customers and offers users a new way of finding sources. Users no longer have to physically go to a library when the library is open. They can connect to the Internet anytime they want.[1]

Similar views were expressed about many other traditional commercial and non-commercial institutions, such as the press, newsagents, book and music shops, television companies, video stores, security brokers, estate and travel agents, and many other brick-and-mortar retailers. While some of these predictions have materialised – consider, for example, the dwindling number of music and bookshops, or the direct sale of flight tickets by airlines – the claim of disintermediation on the internet has still failed spectacularly. The online era has not only witnessed the replacement of many traditional intermediaries by online intermediaries (such as Virgin Megastores versus Apple iTunes), but also the emergence of new intermediaries that have no obvious brick-and-mortar equivalent, such as search engines or networking sites. In recent years these have in fact become major bottlenecks through which online content is now routinely accessed (and thereby centralised) – in contrast to the prior practice of site hopping via hyperlinks.[2] Alongside their greater factual importance, online intermediaries are also more and more integrated in the regulatory landscape, accompanied by much debate by academics, the judiciary and policy-makers about the rights and wrongs of making them regulatory gatekeepers.[3] Gatekeeping functions have been imposed by courts, as evidenced by a number of cases involving the online giants, such as Google, Facebook, eBay, Amazon etc, and by legislatures, as shown below. This Chapter makes no claim to comprehensiveness of coverage, but seeks to illustrate the range of regulatory involvement of intermediaries, the rationales behind it and the dangers and problems arising out of it.

Since the 2011 edition of this text, it seems now to be more appropriate to structure the discussion on intermediaries around their regulatory involvement, rather than their immunities – a trend that suggests that the internet is being absorbed by existing law. We have entered, what Debora Spar calls, the 'last phase' in the four-phase historical pattern which, she argues, accompanies major technological innovations in communication. The four phases are: (1) innovation; (2) commercialisation; (3) creative anarchy; and (4) rules.[4] Spar explains:

> If we view cyberspace from history . . . we see a more complex vision. Instead of a one-way scramble to a brave new world, it is a journey of twists and turns, a movement along a frontier

---

1 Robert Gellman, 'Disintermediation and the Internet' (1996) 13 Gov Inform Q 1.

2 Hossein Derakhshan, 'Iran's blogfather: Facebook, Instagram and Twitter are killing the web' (2015) *The Guardian*, 29 December.

3 Emily B Laidlaw, *Regulating Speech in Cyberspace: Gatekeepers, Human Rights and Corporate Responsibility*, 2015, CUP; European Commission, *Public consultation on the regulatory environment for platforms, online intermediaries, data and cloud computing and the collaborative economy*, 2015, 24 September; Rebecca MacKinnon, Elonnai Hickok, Allon Bar, Hae-in Lim/UNESCO, *Fostering Freedom Online – The Role of Internet Intermediaries*, 2013, UNESCO/ Internet Society; Karine Perset/OECD, *The Economic and Social Role of Internet Intermediaries*, 2010, Paris; European Commission, Information Society and Media Directorate General, *Legal analysis of a Single Market for the Information Society* (SMART 2007/0037) (30 May 2011), Chapter 6, available at: http://ec.europa.eu/digital-agenda/en/news/legal-analysis-single-market-information-society-smart-20070037.

4 Debora L Spar, *Ruling the Waves: Cycles of Discovery, Chaos, and Wealth from the Compass to the Internet*, 2001, London: Harcourt.

whose boundaries shift and stumble and collide. It is a view filled with the normal charac-ters of a frontier town: there are still the pirates and the pioneers, the inkers and the travel-ling salesmen. Only, in this view, the pirates and the pioneers aren't necessarily the winners. Instead, once the technological frontier has moved beyond a certain point, power and profits seem to shift away from those who break the rules and back to those who make them.[5]

Spar's thesis is that once the new technology has matured and been embraced commercially by pio-neers and pirates alike, they call for the help of government to protect their newly gained property interests, to coordinate the use of a limited resource, to intervene to limit dominance and ensure fair competition – in short, to regulate. This Chapter discusses how the main drivers for intermedi-ary liability – and thus effective online regulation – are not only the new entrepreneurs, but also pre-internet commercial establishments, the copyright and publishing industries, manufacturers of trade marked goods, national industries (such as the taxi and hotel), as well as existing national champions of moral and rights issues, e.g. for the protection of children. Typically, a UK organisa-tion representing commercial music producers responded in 2010 to a government consultation on intermediary liability/immunities:

Back in 2000 and in the years leading up to the adoption of e-Commerce Directive the objec-tive of legislative intervention was to limit the liability of Internet intermediaries in order to facilitate the development of the then nascent market for intermediaries. At this point in time, the potential of the internet was huge, although no one could foresee how the digital market would develop . . . The position in 2010 is very different: several intermediaries are now in an overwhelmingly strong economic position, particularly in comparison to individual composers/ performers and music publishers/ record companies who face significant challenges in pro-tecting and enforcing their rights in the online environment.[6]

Similarly, the majority in the US case of *Fair Housing Council of San Fernando Valley v Roommates.com* (2008)[7] when considering the liability of an online housing platform felt that the table had somewhat turned on intermediaries:

The Internet is no longer a fragile new means of communication that could easily be smoth-ered in the cradle by overzealous enforcement of laws and regulations applicable to brick-and-mortar businesses. Rather it has become a dominant – perhaps the preeminent – means through which commerce is conducted. And its vast reach into the lives of millions is exactly why we must be careful not to exceed the scope of the immunity provided by Congress and thus give online businesses an unfair advantage over their real-world counterpart, which must comply with the laws of general applicability.[8]

Whilst Spar's analysis is useful in historically contextualising the internet governance debate, demys-tifying cyberspace and debunking claims that it is an inherently unregulatable space, it should not be assumed that regulation of the internet is business-as-usual for state regulators – even with the help of intermediaries. As the discussion below shows, there are fundamental challenges that leave traditional state regulators no choice but to embrace 'private' allies in newly forged private-public

5 Ibid, 8.
6 UK Music, 'Response to: Consultation on the future of electronic commerce in the Internal market and the implementation of the Directive on electronic commerce' (November 2010), available online at: http://www.prsformusic.com/aboutus/policyand research/ourpolicyareas/Documents/UK%20Music%20Response%20to%20the%20Ecommerce%20Directive.pdf
7 521 F3d 1157 (9th Cir 2008).
8 Ibid, 1164.

partnerships that have no offline equivalents, which raise novel problems in themselves. Also, there are entirely new regulatory paradigms and institutions emerging that cannot easily be fitted within traditional state law and regulation at all, such as multistakeholderism in relation to ICANN, the global domain name authority.

A final preliminary comment concerns the effectiveness of disclaimers in the Terms and Conditions of intermediaries, such as the statement on the BBC website that 'the BBC is not responsible for the content of external websites' or disclaimers in relation to comment sections. Such contractual disclaimers are of limited effect because they can only bind those who agree to them – that is, users of the site – and thus are of limited value in non-contractual civil claims (for example, defamation or copyright claims) unless the injured party was also party to the contract;[9] even then, they may not be enforced for a number of reasons (see Chapter 6). Furthermore, these disclaimers would have little effect on obligation under criminal/regulatory law because private parties cannot generally contract out of such obligations, but they may go towards establishing the intermediary's intention or lack thereof in respect of any third-party conduct.

# Who is an 'intermediary'?

## Factual spectrum: Chronology of use

Intermediaries can be, and often are, classified according to where they fall on a 'chronological' spectrum, reflecting roughly the steps a user would take to retrieve online content.[10] This spectrum overlaps at least partly with a more significant spectrum for legal purposes, covering the relative level of editorial control by the intermediary, discussed below. The following identifies intermediaries in this rough chronological spectrum, but leaves out other more marginal players, e.g. the manufacturers of the PC, or software providers of the operating system or browsers, all of whom are also communication facilitators which have an impact on the display and structure of information and thus on the message itself.

- *Access/Connectivity* – At the most basic level, there are those intermediaries that provide or facilitate access to the internet, both in terms of providing connectivity for users. These intermediaries include the backbone telecommunications providers, including mobile telephone companies and cable companies, internet access providers (hereafter ISPs), e.g. BT, Sky, EE) and operators of WiFi networks, e.g. The Cloud service of Sky, in hotspots, such as shopping centres, cafes, libraries, airports or trains.
- *Navigation* – Another group of online intermediaries are those that facilitate navigation around the web by indexing online content and making it easily accessible to users, such as search engines, aggregation sites (that is, sites that collect links relevant to a certain topic), and all of those sites that provide hyperlinks to other related sites. Also within this category fall providers of sites implicated in the illegal downloading of music, films, games, and software, such as 'The Pirate Bay', which allows users to search for and download BitTorrent files necessary for peer-to-peer file sharing. Although peer-to-peer file sharing is a classic example of disintermediation, it ultimately cannot quite do without any intermediaries.
- *Content hosting (including online networking or commercial platforms)* – This group of online intermediaries are providers of online services, that allow for the storage of content, including the storage of websites, but also providing a platform for user-generated content, for commercial or social purposes. In the commercial context, examples are online auction houses, such as

---

9 See, e.g., the US case of *Grace v eBay Inc* 16 Cal Rptr 3d 192 (Cal App Ct 2004).
10 OECD, *OECD Internet Economy Outlook 2012*, 2012, OECD Publishing, 61ff.

eBay, or sites such as Amazon insofar as it connects buyers with marketplace sellers. In the social sphere, users may be connected with each other via social networking sites, such as Facebook, Twitter, Instagram, Skype, online messengers, dating or gaming sites, or sites the content of which is generated by and for users, such as YouTube, Wikipedia, blogs, and wikis – much of which falls within Web 2.0.

● *Providers of the sharing economy* (e.g. Airbnb or Uber) – This group of intermediaries is different from the above in that they do not support online services as such, but are exploiting the fact that many offline transactions, e.g. hotel reservations or taxi hire, ultimately rely upon communication between two distant parties and the provision of the services could tap into the 'unused' capacity of non-commercial providers. These services illustrate how deeply cyberspace can penetrate the 'real' world.

● *Traditional commercial facilitators* – These actors are in many ways the very opposite to those established for the sharing economy, in that they are traditional commercial intermediaries or their online equivalents, such as retailers (for example, play.com), financial institutions (for example, credit card providers or PayPal), advertisers (for example, Google), and agents of various descriptions (for example, lastminute.com or expedia.com), but their focus is to facilitate online transactions.

These different groups of intermediaries have been targeted by different stakeholders for different purposes. In particular, the intellectual property industry has tried to tackle piracy through a multi-pronged approach by focusing its efforts on almost all of them: access providers, search engines as well as online platforms. The same intermediaries have also been drawn into the regulatory agenda for child abuse images and, more recently, extremist content. What is certain is that internet access providers are in principle the most efficient gatekeepers as they have the most comprehensive coverage from a state-territorial perspective; yet they also have the least involvement with the content, which makes them *prima facie* less at fault and thus unlikely candidates for liability and also less suitable for evaluative judgments than content hosts.

## Legal spectrum: Active-passive/editorial control

This approximate chronological spectrum broadly overlaps with the active-passive spectrum that considers how much, if any, editorial control the intermediary has. From a legal perspective the more control there is or could be, the better the party is positioned to assume a more complex regulatory burden which could not easily be imposed on an actor who has no 'natural' knowledge of, and control over, the activity. Thus the precise shape of the regulatory burden takes into account who is in a position to assume what liability in light of any benefits received. These types of considerations are by no means new or limited to the online world. Offline, different responsibilities for a defamatory article in a newspaper would be borne by the journalist, the editor or the media company from those of the news agency or other distributor, or from those of the postal service. Whilst traditional law has settled this question in relation to traditional media, the online world raises issues of relative comparability: is Facebook more comparable to the traditional newspaper company or the newsagent?[11] At a more fundamental level, the issue is when an actor is in fact a primary actor rather than merely an intermediary or, alternatively, when is an actor's involvement so far removed from the communication as to not even amount to that of an intermediary? Both questions have been hotly contested in the online environment.

The first point of note here is that the term and concept of 'intermediary' is not as objective or politically neutral as one might assume. So one might assume that the concept simply points to

---

11 See also Michael Deturbide, 'Liability of Internet service providers for defamation in the US and Britain: Same competing interests, different responses' (2000) 3 JILT, available online at: http://www2.warwick.ac.uk/fac/soc/law/elj/jilt/2000_3/deturbide/

any organisation that facilitates communications between two or more primary actors. Consistently, the connotations especially in the online environment have been, first, an intermediary is an actor who is 'neutral' or 'passive' in the sense of simply facilitating communication without having any substantive impact on the communication itself; second, the automation of the mediating function reinforces that neutrality as 'machines', e.g. software, are value-neutral; and third, the intermediary has no preference between either of the primary actors.[12] So to label an actor as an 'intermediary' implies that the gist of the communication lies somewhere else – at its outer ends. But this may or may not be the case. For example, in the offline world, one would not consider the BBC an 'intermediary' even though it facilitates communications between the director of a programme or film or the reporter or journalist and the viewer; however, the 'intermediary' label would not do justice to the role played by the BBC itself in terms of selecting or de-selecting programmes and their order and ideological persuasion. In this context, the gist of the communication would be located not at the point of the reporter or the viewer, but rather in the BBC itself.

## Intermediary or content creator/co-creator?

For the same reason, the concept and label of 'intermediary' may not be particularly apt in relation to certain actors in the online communication chain, as it significantly underplays their input. Indeed, there are signs that this is being recognised. In *Google Spain SL, Google Inc v AEPD* (2014)[13] the question before the CJEU was whether Google as the provider of a search engine might have obligations under the European Data Protection Directive[14] in respect of search results. The court held that Google's search processing fell within the Directive and rejected *inter alia* the Greek government's submission that 'the activity in question constitutes such 'processing', but inasmuch as search engines serve *merely as intermediaries*, the undertakings which operate them cannot be regarded as 'controllers', except where they store data in an 'intermediate memory' or 'cache memory' for a period which exceeds that which is technically necessary.'[15] Even though the data 'have already been published on the internet and are not altered by the search engine,'[16] in deciding that Google was a 'data controller' which 'processed personal data', the CJEU was at pains to emphasise Google's effect on the communication in order to discard the idea of it being a 'mere intermediary':

> Moreover, it is undisputed that that activity of search engines *plays a decisive role in the overall dissemination* of those data in that it renders the latter accessible to any internet user making a search on the basis of the data subject's name, including to internet users who otherwise would not have found the web page on which those data are published. Also, the organisation and aggregation of information published on the internet that are effected by search engines with the aim of facilitating their users' access to that information may, when users carry out their search on the basis of an individual's name, result in them obtaining through the list of results a *structured overview of the information* relating to that individual that can be found on the internet enabling them to establish a more or less detailed profile of the data subject.[17]

Specifically on the question of whether Google's search activities are subject to a right-to-be-forgotten, even when the primary publisher has no such obligation, the CJEU again stressed the

---

12 Uta Kohl, 'Google: The rise and rise of intermediaries in the governance of the internet and beyond (Part 2)' (2013) 21 IJLIT 187.
13 *Google Inc v Agencia Española de Protección de Datos, Mario Costeja González* C-131/12 (CJEU, 13 May 2014); *Google Inc v Agencia Española de Protección de Datos, Mario Costeja González* C-131/12 (Opinion of Advocate General, 25 June 2013); K. O'Hara, 'The digital citizen: the right-to-be-forgotten: the good, the bad and the ugly' (2015) 19 IEEE Internet Computing 73.
14 95/46/EC.
15 *Google Spain* CJEU, [24].
16 *Google Spain* CJEU, [29] [emphasis added].
17 *Google Spain* CJEU, [36], [37] [emphasis added].

distinctiveness of search processing over and beyond the initial online publication.[18] In other words, the CJEU located the gist of relevant communication for the purposes of data protection within Google's activities rather than at the outer ends of the communication chain. That Google's processing is entirely automated was rightly neither here nor there, given that algorithms are man-made and not value free; and the court was well aware of Google's huge economic interest in its search engine.[19]

In this respect, the CJEU's reasoning has come a long way since its decision in the trade mark infringement case of *Google AdWords* (2010)[20] where it strongly distanced Google from any wrong-doing for the trade mark infringements of its AdWords clients (see below). Despite the parallels with *Google Spain* (2014), the court's approach there was to endorse Google as an intermediary only, by holding both that it had not 'used' the trade marks for the purposes of European trade mark law (and thus was not a joint primary wrongdoer), and that its possible contributory liability under national law might be immunised under the Electronic Commerce Directive (which is not applicable to data protection and thus was not considered in *Google Spain* (2014)[21]). In respect of the latter, the CJEU left it for national courts to determine whether Google's role in relation to the AdWords was of a mere 'technical, automatic and passive [nature], pointing to a lack of knowledge or control of the data which it stores.'[22] For this, the court was bound by the wording of Recital 42 of the Directive which defines 'intermediaries' in technological determinist terms, in contrast to the Data Protection Directive[23] which imposes obligations regardless of whether the process-ing is or is not automatic.[24] Nonetheless the *Google AdWords* (2010) court accepted the myth of the neutral value-free technology and added that it did not matter to the entitlement to the immunity, that Google financially benefited from the activity in question, including the wrongdoing, nor that it had knowledge of the 'concordance between the keyword selected and the search term entered by an internet user . . .'.[25] A different conclusion would have been possible, as illustrated by the opinion of the Advocate General, who had concluded that Google was not 'a neutral information vehicle' in relation to its AdWords, given its direct interest in users clicking on the AdWords and its relationship with the advertisers, and thus was outside the immunities regime.[26] In *L'Oréal SA v eBay International AG* (2011)[27] the CJEU, although endorsing *Google AdWords* (2010), was ready to contem-plate the possibility that eBay might be too 'active' in respect of third party offerings to be counted as an 'intermediary' for the purposes of the Electronic Commerce Directive; it held that:

> where the operator has provided assistance which entails, in particular, optimising the pre-sentation of the offers for sale in question or promoting those offers, it must be considered not to have taken a neutral position between the customer-seller concerned and potential buyers but to have played an active role of such a kind as to give it knowledge of, or control over, the data relating to those offers for sale.[28]

It would seem that Google in respect of its AdWords plays an equally active and maximis-ing role, as eBay does in terms of its market offering. In any event, in *Google Spain* (2014) the

---

18 *Google Spain* CJEU, [82]–[88].
19 *Google Spain* CJEU, [81], [97], [99].
20 *Google AdWords* C-236/08, C-237/08 and C-238/08 (CJEU, 23 March 2010); *Google AdWords* C-236/08, C-237/08 and C-238/08 (Advocate General, 22 September 2009).
21 Recital 14 of the Electronic Commerce Directive.
22 *Google AdWords* CJEU [114].
23 95/46/EC.
24 Art 2(b) of the Directive.
25 *Google AdWords* CJEU [116], [117], but see also [118].
26 *Google AdWords* AG [144], [145].
27 *L'Oréal SA and Others v eBay International AG* C-324/09 (CJEU, 12 July 2011).
28 Ibid, [116].

CJEU – albeit in a different context – went even further by imposing takedown obligations on Google over its 'natural' results and not merely its AdWords.

There have also been judgments by national courts that have identified online platforms as primary wrongdoers and not as mere intermediaries. This has generally occurred in the context of intellectual property infringements. For example, in the French case of *Lafesse v MySpace* (2007),[29] the Tribunal de Grande Instance de Paris ruled that MySpace had breached the copyright and personality rights of the French comedian Lafesse (in English 'butt') by allowing users to post unauthorised copies of the comedian's work on its networking site. The court treated MySpace as one of the publishers of the offending material because, according to the court, the information posted by MySpace members was published in a way strictly dictated and confined by MySpace's layout, and was accompanied by MySpace's advertisements: ' . . . by imposing such a specific, frame-based, structure for members to present their personal information and by displaying ads for each and every visit, [MySpace acted] as a publisher.'[30] So MySpace's control over the format of the information and financial benefit arising from each page was taken as indicative of MySpace's close association with, and implicit endorsement of, the substance of each page. Once an online actor is treated as having crossed the threshold from intermediary to primary actor/wrongdoer, it loses the benefit of the protective regime in the Electronic Commerce Directive,[31] and most importantly the prohibition of monitoring obligations (see more below). This was in fact, specifically, held in the French case of *Dailymotion* (2007),[32] in which Dailymotion, a French version of YouTube, was considered a contributor to the infringement of its users. The director and producer of the film *Joyeux Noel* sued Dailymotion for copyright infringement of the film illegally accessible on its site. The court held that Dailymotion had not caused the publication and therefore was not its publisher, but had forgone the immunities under the Directive, because the success of the website was largely predicated upon copyright infringements (that is, the broadcast of famous works that captured larger audiences and thus ensured greater advertising revenue). The court accommodated the fact that Dailymotion could only have found the specific infringing content through general monitoring of the site by noting that the prohibition of a general monitoring duty in Art 15 of Electronic Commerce Directive applied only to intermediaries that did not create or induce the offending activities. Arguably, the actor should, for the sake of clarity, not be labelled an intermediary at all.

## Intermediary or mere facilitator, tool or device?

At the other end of the spectrum, online actors have resisted the categorisation of intermediary to argue that they are even less than an 'intermediary' and comparable to mere tools in the communication chain, such as a pen and paper or hard or software, all of which facilitate communication but only at the most elementary level. These arguments have, for example, occurred in the context of Art 8(3) of the Information Society Directive and Art 11 of the Enforcement Directive,[33] which allow for injunctions against an intermediary whose services are used by third parties to infringe copyright or intellectual property more generally, which were under discussion in *Cartier International AG v British Sky Broadcasting Ltd* (2014)[34] in the context of blocking orders, discussed below. Article 8 of the Enforcement Directive also provides for orders against third parties to reveal 'the origin and distribution networks of the goods or services which infringe an intellectual property right'.

What makes these provisions special is that the availability of the injunction is not dependent on any wrongdoing by the intermediary and thus can be used against actors that have a relatively

29 *Lafesse v MySpace* (Tribunal de Grande Instance de Paris, Paris 13 July 2007); Nicolas Jondet, 'The silver lining in Dailymotion's copyright cloud' (19 April 2008) Juriscom.net. Consistent with *Lucky Comis v Tiscalis*, (Cour d'Appel de Paris, 7 June 2006).
30 Ibid.
31 2000/31/EC.
32 (Tribunal de Grande Instance de Paris, 24 October 2007).
33 2001/29/EC and 2004/48/EC respectively.
34 *Cartier International AG v British Sky Broadcasting Ltd* [2014] EWHC 3354.

marginal involvement in the communication, such as ISPs. So in *LSG-Gesellschaft zur Wahrnehmung von Leistungsschutzrechten GmbH v Tele2 Telecommunications GmbH* (2009),[35] the CJEU was asked whether Tele2, as an ISP, was an intermediary within Art 8(3) of the Information Society Directive and thus potentially subject to orders, sought by a copyright society, requiring the disclosure of identities of infringing subscribers in order to bring civil claims against them. Tele2 argued that it was not an 'intermediary' as it had no control, either *de iure* or *de facto*, over the services accessed by the user and thus no way of bringing any infringement to an end. But, according to the CJEU, they still provided 'a service capable of being used by a third party to infringe a copyright, inasmuch as those access providers supply the user with the connection enabling him to infringe such rights.'[36] In deciding so, it was strongly influenced by the fact that ISPs 'alone are in possession of data making it possible to identify the users who have infringed those rights.'[37] Going even further, in *UPC Telekabel Wien GmbH v Constantin Film Verleih GmbH* (2014)[38] the CJEU held that ISPs are equally intermediaries vis-à-vis any infringing website operator, i.e. piracy suppliers, regardless of whether the site is used by their subscribers. It further held that for Art 8(3) it did not matter that there was neither a contractual relationship between the ISP and the infringing website nor any other special relationship, nor whether any actual wrongdoing occurred via its service, i.e. that its subscribers actually used the website.[39] Again, the court's decision was supported by consequentialist reasoning that to hold otherwise 'would substantially diminish the protection of rightholders . . .'.[40] This decision stands in contrast to an earlier German case (2007),[41] where the claimant, a provider of online pornography, sought an injunction – based on an unfair competition claim – against an ISP seeking the blocking of access to pornography sites without age verification. The court refused to do so stressing that the ISP stood in no contractual relationship with the offending sites, did not profit from them in any way, and did not increase the danger of the distribution of illegal contents on the web by providing access to the web. Perhaps the decision would be different after *UPC* with ISPs being considered useful intermediaries, even in the absence of an equivalent Art 8(3) for competition purposes. So one might conclude that if other facilitators – e.g. the software providers of the browsers or operating system – could also offer 'remedies', they might equally be classified as 'intermediaries' for the purposes of enforcing intellectual property law. Indeed, the very players who would, for the purposes of intellectual property, be classified as 'intermediaries' (because of their sheer usefulness for blocking injunctions), are classified as mere tools in defamation claims and, in particular, in the context of the 'innocent dissemination' defence under s 1 of the Defamation Act 1996, expressed through the 'publisher versus facilitator' dichotomy, see below. (Neither law, however, imposes liability for wrongdoing in respect of these 'tools'.)

The term and concept of 'intermediary' is not referring to an objective reality ascertainable purely by examining facts, but is an elastic concept used by the intermediaries themselves and other interested parties to resist or assert regulatory burdens. That resistance or assertion is never justified simply by virtue of claiming or denying the status of an 'intermediary'. The political or policy dimension of identifying an online actor as an intermediary also shines through in the fact that even if an actor is identified as an intermediary for some legal purposes, and thus subject to some duties in respect of the communication, does not mean that that same status would also be granted in another area of law. For example, just because Google has minimal liability for defamatory content on its search results under English law (see below) does not mean that it is similarly immune under data protection law. So intermediary liability cannot be pinned down simply by reference

---

35 *LSG-Gesellschaft zur Wahrnehmung von Leistungsschutzrechten GmbH v Tele2 Telecommunications* C-557/07 [2009] ECR I-1227.
36 Ibid, [43].
37 Ibid, [45].
38 *UPC Telekabel Wien GmbH v Constantin Film Verleih GmbH* C-314/12 (CJEU, 27 March 2014).
39 Ibid, [33]–[39].
40 Ibid, [33].
41 *Haftung des Access-Providers* (LG Düsseldorf, 13 December 2007) 12 O 550/07.

to what an online actor actually does in the communication chain, but is a malleable concept responsive to economic and political conflicts of the time. Arguably since the last edition of this text, there has been a seismic shift in the distribution of power online with a few key players having consolidated their near monopolistic positions. This has affected their public image and had also an impact on their treatment by judiciaries and legislatures. Their claims of impotence and innocence ring increasingly hollow in light of their immense social and economic impact on cyberspace as well as real space.

# Intermediary involvement: Attractions and concerns

## Efficiency and circumvention

Traditionally actors with 'natural' gatekeeping roles,[42] such as shops or media companies, have had a role to play in the regulatory landscape of states. Their role as legal gatekeepers has had both a knowledge and an enforcement component. For example, an end-user can assume that a brick-and-mortar pharmacy only sells legal drugs and is thus relieved of the burden of finding out which drugs are and are not licenced. It is more efficient for a pharmacy to acquire this knowledge in the place of every end user. At the same time, the pharmacy also fulfils an enforcement function in that it acts as a gatekeeper for legal drugs and implicitly makes the acquisition of illegal drugs more difficult, albeit not impossible. Just because it is possible to circumvent that gatekeeping role played by pharmacies, e.g. by buying illegal drugs off known local dealers, does not mean that they are inefficient in their role as long as they make circumvention sufficiently difficult and thus discouraged widespread non-compliance. This offline example provides two main insights for online governance. First, in cyberspace intermediaries are sought after for the very same reason which has made them such attractive regulatory targets in the offline world, i.e. regulatory efficiency. On the internet the problem of regulatory inefficiency is severe, largely because the traditional intermediaries have been displaced; new choke points are being looked for. Second, pre-internet efficiency of many brick-and-mortar gatekeepers has been undermined by the decentralised internet which allows anyone with an internet connection to reach a mass audience, either as customers or user. To continue with the above example, it is relatively easy to buy illegal drugs online, and the easy circumvention of offline pharmacies online *does* undermine their regulatory efficiency. In other words, online rule breaking does not just undermine the efficiency of rules online, but also offline.

One of the questions with which courts have struggled is what projected level of efficiency is needed to legitimise the involvement of online intermediaries. For example, from the perspective of the copyright industry every little bit helps, but minimal efficiency gains would make the financial costs for intermediaries and the cost for the online community, e.g. inroads into freedom of expression and privacy, disproportionate. Occasionally, too, the law expressly requires for remedies to be 'effective' as a prerequisite for their imposition – as in the case of Art 3(2) of the Enforcement Directive. Courts have tackled the issue of effectiveness very differently. In the Dutch case of *Ziggo BV v Stichting Bescherming Rechten Entertainment Industrie Nederland (BREIN)* (2014)[43] concerning blocking orders of The Pirate Bay against ISPs, the Court of Appeal held that these orders were not proportionate considering that the *overall* level of infringement had not changed since the grant of such orders, even if traffic going to the particular blocked site had significantly reduced. Users had either circumvented the blocking software or, more commonly, gone to alternative BitTorrent sites.[44] This

---

42 Jonathan Zittrain, 'A history of online gatekeeping' (2006) 19 Harvard Journal of Law & Technology 253; and Emily B Laidlaw, 'A framework for identifying Internet information gatekeepers' (2010) 24 International Review of Law, Computers & Technology 263.
43 *Ziggo BV v Stichting Bescherming Rechten Entertainment Industrie Nederland (BREIN)* (Court of Appeal of The Hague, 28 January 2014).
44 *Cartier International AG v British Sky Broadcasting Ltd* [2014] EWHC 3354, [165]ff [emphasis added].

case was referred to the CJEU in November 2015.[45] In contrast in England and Wales, the court in Cartier (2014) decided that a blocking injunction against an ISP concerning websites selling counterfeit goods would not be disproportionate as long as it would 'at least seriously discourage users from accessing the target website.'[46] Rightholders do not have to show any reduction in the overall level of infringement, but 'blocking access to the target website is less likely to be proportionate if there is a large number of alternative websites which are likely to be equally accessible . . .'.[47] Justice Arnold thought this was consistent with the holding in UPC (2014) where the CJEU had rather more ambiguously held, in relation to 'effectiveness', that the order must 'have the effect of preventing unauthorised access to protected subject-matter, or, at least, of making it difficult to achieve and of seriously discouraging internet users who are using the services of the addressee of that injunction from accessing the subject-matter . . .'.[48] The court referred to the 'accessibility of the subject-matter' rather than of the blocked site and this suggests that it judged effectiveness by reference to overall accessibility. If that is the case, the case for any blocking injunctions against ISPs is damning, given that they have no measurable impact on the overall level of infringement.[49]

More generally, Justice Arnold in Cartier (2014) reasoned that the test on effectiveness should not be different online and offline. Given that in the offline world a rightholder need not show that an injunction would likely reduce the overall level of infringement of their trade marks, '[t]here is no reason to treat online infringers differently in this respect' – anything else would be inimical to the rule of law.[50] This type of reasoning is very common and seductive, but is it justified? Cyberspace differs in three significant aspects from the offline regulatory landscape which means that online intermediaries as quasi-regulators are both more in demand and more problematic. These three aspects, addressed in the following, suggest that online and offline regulatory equivalence ought to be treated with caution.

## Scale

The scale or quantity of communications online that potentially attract regulatory interest is significantly higher than pre-internet. Whilst the amount of communications may not have risen in absolute terms, what might previously have been 'private' communications at home, on the phone or in the pub and thus fallen below the regulatory radar, falls within that radar on the internet, if it is publicly accessible and thereby becomes a public communication, subject to laws governing the 'public space'. At the same time, the easy end-to-end connectivity in relative anonymity, without content bottlenecks, also means that deviant behaviour in respect of any activity that can be reduced to data has risen sharply. For example, in the UK the National Crime Agency estimated in 2014 that in UK alone 50,000 people regularly watched online indecent images of children or child abuse images,[51] which is well beyond the prosecutional capacity of the criminal justice system in the UK. The statistics for copyright infringement or different forms of hate speech are likely to be even higher. In other words, the traditional legal system, both for criminal and civil law, was set up for a smaller scale of wrongdoing. Traditional justice mechanisms are not designed for the scale of

45 Anthony Deutsch, 'Dutch Supreme Court seeks European clarification on Pirate Bay' (2015) The Reuter, 13 November, available online at: http://www.reuters.com/article/us-netherlands-piratebay-idUSKCN0T21M820151113
46 Cartier International AG v British Sky Broadcasting Ltd [2014] EWHC 3354, [175] [emphasis added].
47 Ibid, [176].
48 UPC Telekabel Wien GmbH v Constantin Film Verleih GmbH C-314/12 (CJEU, 27 March 2014), [63] [emphasis added].
49 Cartier International AG v British Sky Broadcasting Ltd [2014] EWHC 3354, [229]ff; as this evidence essentially showed the futility of his earlier orders, Justice Arnold sought to discredit the methodology of the studies.
50 Cartier International AG v British Sky Broadcasting Ltd [2014] EWHC 3354, [173].
51 Paul Peachey, National Crimes Agency says system realistically can't prosecute all 50,000 child sex offenders' (2014) The Independent, 22 October, available online at: http://www.independent.co.uk/news/uk/crime/national-crime-agency-says-that-realistically-the-system-cant-persecute-all-50000-child-sex-9806790.html. Note the existing prison population in the UK is around 85,000: Ministry of Justice, National Offender Management Service and HM Prison Service, Prison Population Figures: 2015 (November 2015).

online wrongdoing.[52] This makes private intermediaries indispensable as regulatory allies to share the implementation burden, with the promise of greater regulatory efficiency. The main attraction of intermediaries as targets for regulatory intervention lies in their relatively large size and small number:

> In considering legal regulation of the Internet, there is an important distinction between large players, which one might call 'elephants', and small, mobile actors called 'mice'. The style of regulation against elephants and mice differs substantially. Elephants are large, powerful, and practically impossible to hide. Consider a transnational corporation that has major operations in a country. If that country has strict regulations, the corporation's actions will be highly visible, and it may become an enforcement target if it flouts the law. At the same time, elephants are enormously strong and have all sorts of effects on the local ecosystem (potentially crushing trees, smaller animals, etc.). If a particular regulation angers an elephant, it may have the ability to change the rule. The situation is quite different for mice, which are small, nimble, and multiply annoyingly quickly . . . Would-be regulators can run around furiously with a broom, but with little chance of getting rid of all the mice.[53]

While not all intermediaries are 'elephants' and not all 'elephants' are intermediaries, the role of intermediation often triggers growth, for example, due to network effects.[54] Similarly if a business is more sizeable, it often becomes attractive as an intermediary because its size makes it more well known and trustworthy – matters upon which smaller players can piggyback as, for example, market players on Amazon.

The efficiency factor of intermediaries applies equally to civil actions and criminal prosecutions. Their easy identifiability and 'deeper pockets' are a practical advantage, but ultimately the main virtue of their regulatory involvement lies in the much wider ripple effects of any order against them. Thus for the music industry, it is much more efficient to sue the relatively few big intermediary operators, such as The Pirate Bay or YouTube or BT, for facilitating copyright infringement rather than the millions of the actual copyright infringers. If the regulator were to impose more proactive, rather than reactive, gatekeeping functions, the intermediary would then be much more like the offline pharmacy, sieving out unlawful content based upon its superior knowledge and advice on legal matters. Importantly, because the success of these large visible intermediaries, particularly in the online world, often depends on their perceived respectability, which entails not being a lawbreaker (although not always), there are commercial incentives for legal obedience even where the actual enforcement mechanisms by the state may be relatively weak.[55]

The large scale of online communication is in itself not a problem, but something that is also celebrated in terms of empowering the individual both in democratic and authoritarian states. When intermediaries are drawn into the regulatory sphere because of the non-scalability of traditional justice mechanisms, the danger is that their involvement has undesirable side-effects on that empowerment. Put differently, the empowerment of the individual through the internet has given rise to good and bad behaviour; by tackling deviant behaviour, there is a danger that the positive aspects will also suffer. This concern shines through some judgments and legislative developments, especially on regulation to enhance cybersecurity. In the copyright context, the CJEU in

---

52 Milton L Mueller, *Networks and States: the Global Politics of Internet Governance*, 2010, MIT Press, 4, 187f, 211f. See also Uta Kohl, *Jurisdiction and the Internet*, 2007, CUP, chapter 3.

53 Peter P Swire, 'Of elephants, mice, and privacy: international choice of law and the internet' (1998) 32 International Lawyer 991, 1019ff.

54 The network effect refers to the phenomenon that the value of some facilities goes up with an increasing number of users. So the more individuals use the telephone, Facebook or eBay, the more useful they become. Search engines also indirectly benefit from the network effect, as every search query is used to improve the search indexes to subsequent queries.

55 Kohl, above n 52, 207ff.

both *Productores de Música de España (Promusicae) v Telefónica de España SAU* (2008)[56] and *Scarlet Extended SA v SABAM – Société belge des auteurs, compositeurs et éditeurs* (2011)[57] made a point of asserting that measures designed to detect and ultimately prevent piracy must be balanced against the fundamental rights of all those individuals affected by the measures. In *Sabam* (2011), the court observed that a filtering and blocking system to be installed by the ISP to detect piracy by subscribers would monitor all incoming and outgoing traffic and thus affect all users' right to privacy; in addition there was the danger of over-blocking and thus infringements of users' freedom to receive or impart information.[58] Although such filter might stem the flood of piracy, it would also deprive online users of substantial benefits of the internet, and thus be disproportionate. Indeed, the empowerment of the individual through online communications might require profound rethinking of traditional balances of rights – rather than trying to replicate them online.

In addition to these strong human rights concerns, obligations imposed on private intermediaries to handle the scale of wrongdoing may also more indirectly affect otherwise desirable activity. As such obligations increase the running costs of intermediaries, smaller players might not be able to absorb them and thus create a less diverse market of service providers to the disadvantage of the online community generally.

## Territorial scope

Another aspect in which cyberspace has created entirely new challenges lies in its non-territoriality; all content and communications are, absent special limiting measures, as much inside a state as outside it. Whilst states have the power to attach their laws to activities that occur beyond their borders that have an effect within them, their enforcement power is strictly territorial (see Chapter 2). This means that foreign wrongdoers, with no presence or assets within the territory of a state, are beyond the state's enforcement reach. In civil litigation this is slightly alleviated, given the possibility of another state enforcing a foreign judgment. However, even in the civil law context, a suit against a local intermediary is much more practicable and the enforcement of an eventual judgment is more straightforward. Thus both in the criminal and civil context, intermediaries are attractive as local 'proxies' for law enforcement. These 'proxies' are either intermediaries that are locally established, such as BT or Virgin Media in the UK or local banks that process payments for illegal transactions, or foreign intermediaries that have a local presence. Typically, Google and Amazon have subsidiaries in most European states, Facebook's and eBay's European headquarters are Ireland and Microsoft's in Paris. These well-known brands have other reasons to comply with state regulatory demands than the threat of force; yet, still that threat remains a factor operating in the background.[59] A show of such enforcement potential occurred in 2015, when Uber Technologies Inc's offices in Amsterdam were raided by Dutch police to seize documents to support criminal proceedings. In the Netherlands, as in many other states, the UberPOP service, which allows for peer-to-peer ride sharing, is considered illegal under local transport laws, which require a special licence to provide a taxi service.[60] The extra-territorial aspect, coupled with the limited enforcement reach, shines through many cases seeking to obtain rights enforcement through intermediaries. Again, in *Cartier* (2014) the court legitimised blocking injunctions targeting counterfeit sites against local ISPs based on the ineffectiveness of alternative measures against other actors in the communication chain – due to their location abroad or their ability to move there. This futility

---

56 *Productores de Música de España (Promusicae) v Telefónica de España SAU* C-275/06 (CJEU, 29 January 2008).
57 *Scarlet Extended SA v SABAM – Société belge des auteurs, compositeurs et éditeurs SCRL* C-70/10 (CJEU, 24 November 2011).
58 Ibid, [50]–[53].
59 Kohl, above n 52, Ch 6.
60 Celeste Perri, Elco Van Groningen, 'Uber Offices in Amsterdam Raided for Third Time this Year' (2015) *BloombergBusiness*, 29 September.

affected actions against the primary wrongdoers, i.e. the operators of the target websites, and their hosts as well as attempts to seize the domain names.[61]

Much like in respect of 'scale', the involvement of local intermediaries in the implementation and enforcement of local law on the global internet carries the danger of throwing the baby out with the bathwater. The more successful the implementation of local legal standards on the internet via intermediaries, the more territorially fragmented the online environment will become and thereby undermine the value of cyberspace as a common global resource (see Chapter 2).

## A public communication space and 'private' judges

The internet allows for many of the same offline transactions and exchanges that have previously involved intermediaries, e.g. pharmacies, gun shops, supermarkets, and those intermediaries have always made decisions on right and wrong, legal and illegal, to pre-empt wrongdoing by the end user. Yet, the internet is not simply or even mainly a marketplace, but first and foremost a communicative place. It provides an unprecedented platform for the exercise of the right to receive and impart information and freedom of expression is a precious human right, protected for its essential role in the democratic process as well as in self-fulfilment.[62] In other words, online intermediaries are drawn into the regulatory process either as communication gatekeepers or 'mixed' gatekeepers that cover communication and commercial activity. This applies, for example, to search engines or social networking sites, as communication and commercial gateways financed through advertising; or Amazon or eBay which facilitate trade in communicative and non-communicative goods.

Prior to the internet, the public communicative space was full of speech bottlenecks, e.g. TV or newspapers, who acted as private censors of what speech should or should not reach a mass audience, partly for legal reasons and partly simply due to limited capacity. For the latter reason, these bottlenecks were non-deliberate in the sense that a selection between competing stories, programmes and viewpoints had to be made, although what the particular selection would be was and is, of course, deliberate. With the advent of the internet, the cost of reaching a mass audience has shrunk so much that this potential mass audience is now at the fingertips of most in the First World and an increasing number of people in the Third World.[63] Any freely accessible site, blog or even networking post is a public communication. Yet, even on the internet, intermediaries frequently engage and have to engage in prioritising content. For example, any search function whether on a search engine or on a particular content site, prioritises some content over other content (making the latter less visible and often almost invisible) and thus acts as private censors; equally social networking or news aggregations sites are in the business of making evaluative judgements about which content to make visible to the user from other users or news sources. Yet, whilst the internet much like the offline world has speech bottlenecks, there is a qualitative jump between the offline and online world, with the latter facilitating significantly more public communications from a bigger pool of sources. The point here is to stress the communicative, rather than merely transactional or commercial, nature of cyber activity and the continuity and discontinuity between the public communication space pre- and post-internet.[64] It is in light of this heightened sensitivity of the online world that the involvement of intermediaries as regulatory gatekeepers must be treated with heightened caution, in a number of ways.

61 *Cartier International AG v British Sky Broadcasting Ltd* [2014] EWHC 3354, paras [198], [201], [209] respectively.

62 Eric Barendt, *Freedom of Speech*, 2nd edn, 2007, OUP, pp 6–23.

63 Barney Wharf, 'Uneven geographies of the African internet: Growth, change, and implications (2010) 29 African Geographical Review 41.

64 On the legal challenges for traditional media regulation when transplanted to the online environment, see Jan Oster, *Media Freedom as a Fundamental Right*, 2015, CUP, esp 57ff.

First, analogising online intermediaries to apparent offline equivalents often underplays the former's role as communication vehicle. For example, it is doubtful whether ISPs – which provide internet connectivity for users who may then engage in illegal activity, or suffer or benefit from such activity, such as the sale of counterfeit goods-should be compared to market traders which sell goods, including counterfeit, and no more, as the court did in *Cartier* (2014) for the purpose of assessing the legitimacy of efficiency arguments.[65]

Second, the choice of the type of online intermediary as a regulatory vehicle has a profound impact on the level and extent of the speech restriction. For example, whilst a blocking order against a local ISP makes the blocked content *prima facie* inaccessible in the state where the order is granted, it allows for that same content still to be accessible elsewhere. This is important in relation to content regulation that varies from state to state (see Chapter 2). In contrast, if content is removed at its source, i.e. by the hosting intermediary, *prima facie* that content disappears from the online space. That may be highly appropriate for content that is universally condemned, such as child abuse images, but rather less so beyond the small core of universally condemned content. Where a hosting intermediary has different platforms for different territorial markets or regional filters, it may implement the takedown request only in respect of a particular state or region; see, for example, YouTube's common message: 'this video is not available in your country'. Whilst that message is unpopular, it is useful in highlighting that censorship has taken place in response to some legal requirement, and in allowing the existence of that online content where it is legal. Again in contrast, if content is deindexed by a search engine in response to a deindex notice, that content remains accessible online. In contrast to a blocking order on an ISP, inaccessibility is here limited to the domain of the search engine index, rather than to the territorial domain of a state. Deindexed content can be accessed from the particular territory but with much greater difficulty, and indeed may for that reason be considered invisible. So different intermediaries have varying communicative reaches and by implications their involvement as quasi-regulators must be sensitive to those reaches and their impact. More profoundly, communication regulation needs to be open to making a fundamentally fresh assessment of what is and is not legitimate censorship through these various new bottlenecks.

Third, the preciousness of cyberspace as a pubic communication space makes the large-scale involvement of private online intermediaries as judges of the legality of third party content and implementers of those 'judgements' problematic. This affects intermediaries that are closer to online content than access providers, such as hosts and 'navigators', through being subjected to notice-and-takedown and notice-and-deindex obligations. Typically, Google has had almost 70 million deindex requests of allegedly copyright infringing URLs from approximately 6,000 rightholders in November 2015 only.[66] In the 18 months after *Google Spain* (2014),[67] it also received 350,000 right-to-be-forgotten requests from European users.[68] In addition, there were government deindex notices (including from the judiciary) on a wide range of topics from defamation, harassment and bullying, national security, hate speech, violence and obscenity.[69] However, the vast majority of deindex notices comes from private parties. The vast scale of these requests and attendant decisions creates a demand for the privatisation of this essentially judicial task, but at the same time is of concern for various reasons underlying freedom of expression. The key concerns are the substantive fairness of the decisions, the procedural fairness of the process and the transparency and accountability surrounding those decisions. More specifically, it can be assumed that the interests of private intermediaries do not generally coincide with

---

65 *Cartier International AG v British Sky Broadcasting Ltd* [2014] EWHC 3354, [173].
66 Google, *Google Transparency Reports, Requests to remove content – Due to copyright* (December 2015).
67 *Google Inc v Agencia Española de Protección de Datos, Mario Costeja González* C-131/12 (CJEU 13 May 2014).
68 Google, *Google Transparency Reports, European Privacy Requests for Search Removals* (December 2015).
69 Google, *Google Transparency Reports, Requests to remove content – From governments: United Kingdom* (December 2015).

the public interest. Intermediaries may be overzealous police officers and remove controversial, but democratically important, content either for commercial reasons and to avoid the threat of sanctions.[70] This leads to greater censorship than is legally required, and for this reason, some content hosts have asserted that they will not remove any material or block access to it in the absence of a court order to that effect.[71] An interrelated question arises as to the accountability of these private 'judgements'. Google's decisions on the right-to-be-forgotten are appealable to national data protection authorities and so in theory subject to accountability, but so far only a small fraction of data subjects have appealed them.[72] At the same time, Google has been accused of a lack of transparency in respect of its implementation of the delisting requests.[73] This lack of transparency in fact and the lack of legal accountability mechanisms – otherwise applicable to public bodies, e.g. open justice, freedom of information and human rights more generally[74] – makes the large-scale outsourcing of law enforcement and censorship to private intermediaries a concern that has had no offline equivalent, and thus cannot easily be addressed with reference to traditional regulatory patterns.

# Regulatory involvement of intermediaries

Intermediaries have, in recent years, become the focal point of legal or regulatory activity in innumerable ways across a wide and expanding range of subject-matters – from defamation and data protection, intellectual property protection to obscenity, child abuse, surveillance and hate, extremist and terrorist speech and cybersecurity. The range of potentially 'useful' intermediaries is also extensive; according to the court in *Cartier* (2014) in addition to the ISPs, there are the various content hosts, the payment providers, the domain name registrars and search engines.[75] The following can do no more than give a flavour of the various quasi-regulatory roles intermediaries are now expected to play in internet governance. These roles are often not predicated on any wrongdoing by the intermediary, but simply on their positioning in the 'line of fire'. They are expected to help because they can. Yet, what becomes also clear is that in various respects, although intermediaries are ostensibly serving as vehicles for the enforcement of existing law by states, especially in relation to notice-and-takedown obligations, they are so extensively left to their own devices that they may increasingly be considered quasi-autonomous legal actors beyond state law.

## Gatekeeping abstention: Net neutrality and search neutrality

A concept that has been in the regulatory limelight for some time is net neutrality, according to which fixed and mobile internet access providers are prohibited from discriminating between different internet content. The network itself should be 'neutral' as to the content it carries and preserve the 'open internet' and its end-to-end network design. In the EU, net neutrality is now

---

70 For example, social networking sites are consensus orientated in their desire to retain as many participants as possible for as long as possible on their sites.
71 See, e.g., Jeremy Kirk, 'Irish ISP: We won't block the Pirate Bay' (2009) *PCWorld*, 24 February; see also on Google's position on defamatory postings on blogger.com in *Davison v Habeeb* [2011] EWHC 3031, [18].
72 For a discussion of some of these appeals, see M Peguera, 'In the aftermath of Google Spain': how the right-to-be-forgotten is being shaped in Spain by courts and the Data Protection Authority' (2015) 23 International Journal of Law and Information Technology 325.
73 J Kiss, 'Dear Google: open letter from 80 academics on 'right-to-be-forgotten' (2015) *The Guardian*, 14 May.
74 This is not to suggest that those mechanisms are particularly successful in making public bodies accountable. In *Richardson v Facebook* [2015] EWHC 3154, [60]ff, it was unsuccessfully argued that Facebook is a 'hybrid public authority'.
75 *Cartier International AG v British Sky Broadcasting Ltd* [2014] EWHC 3354, [197]ff.

legally enshrined in the Regulation on a European Single Market for Electronic Communications,[76] in force from 2016, which provides (in Art 3(3)):

> Providers of internet access services shall treat all traffic equally, when providing internet access services, without discrimination, restriction or interference, and irrespective of the sender and receiver, the content accessed or distributed, the applications or services used or provided, of the terminal equipment used.

The effect of this is that ISPs are no longer permitted to throttle internet speed for certain services for commercial reasons or even block them or ask for additional payments in return for priority. Mobile and broadband network providers have been known to block VoIP services, i.e. internet telephony, such as Skype or Facetime, given that it is in direct competition with their own services; or alternatively accepted payment for the promise to prioritise certain traffic.[77] Similarly, peer-to-peer networks have had traffic to and from their sites slowed down or even blocked. ISPs have justified their actions based, partly, on the basis of the security and the integrity of the network (e.g. hindering end user access to spam) and, partly, on the basis of limited network capacity and thus as a way to manage network traffic and deal with network congestion.[78] Nonetheless their discriminatory treatment has been considered problematic for: (1) being an unfair management practice; (2) weakening competition; (3) decreasing innovation; (4) being highly privacy-invasive, depending on the practice used; and (5) lacking transparency, as ISPs rarely publicise information regarding these practices.[79]

The concept of net neutrality seeks to differentiate between legitimate or reasonable and illegitimate traffic management or gatekeeping by ISPs. Illegitimate gatekeeping is carried out for anti-competitive, commercial reasons; in contrast reasonable traffic management encompasses 'day-to-day traffic management according to justified technical requirement, and which must be independent of the origin or destination of the traffic and of any commercial consideration.'[80] By definition, reasonable gatekeeping must also include complying with various legal obligations and executive or judicial orders, such as blocking orders, as discussed below. So the concept of 'net neutrality' is in many ways the antithesis to the involvement of intermediaries as regulatory vehicles: whilst the former forbids ISPs' gatekeeping for their own (commercial) purposes, the latter requires that gatekeeping by intermediaries for legal and regulatory purposes.

Before moving to these, it is worth mentioning that, in addition to network neutrality, the notion of 'search neutrality' has also figured in academic debates, in case law and in inquiries by competition authorities, including the European Commission.[81] Here it is not ISPs but search engines who are being accused of skewing internet traffic in their own favour. The context of 'search neutrality' differs from 'net neutrality' in that the very act of producing a search index in response to a search query is clearly an evaluative act, whereby an assessment has to be made – whether through an algorithm or otherwise – of the ranking of competing sites. Thus any such assessment

---

76 Regulation (EU) 2015 of the European Parliament and the Council laying down measures concerning open internet access and amending Directive 2002/22/EC on universal service and users' rights relating to electronic communications networks and services and Regulation (EU) No 531/2012 on roaming on public mobile communication networks within the Union (Brussels, 2 October 2015). For a critique, see James Vincent, 'European Parliament rejects amendments protecting net neutrality' (2015) The Verge, 27 October. For a general critique of 'net neutrality' esp in so far as it was promoted by Google, see Marcelo Thompson, 'In Search of Alterity: On Google, Neutrality, and Otherness' in Aurelio Lopez-Tarruella (ed), Google and the Law: Empirical Approaches to Legal Aspects of Knowledge-Economy Business Models, 2012, The Hague: TMC Asser Press, 355.

77 European Commission, Digital Agenda for Europe – A Europe 2020 Initiative: EU Actions (27 October 2015).

78 BEREC, A view of traffic management and other practices resulting in restrictions to the open Internet in Europe – Findings from BEREC's and the European Commission's joint investigation (29 May 2012, BoR(12) 30) 9.

79 European Commission, Digital Agenda for Europe – A Europe 2020 Initiative: Net Neutrality challenges (27 October 2015).

80 European Commission, Digital Agenda for Europe – A Europe 2020 Initiative: EU Actions (27 October 2015).

81 Kohl, above, n 12, 222. European Commission, 'Fact Sheet – Antitrust: Commission sends Statement of Objections to Google on comparison shopping service' (Brussels, 15 April 2015).

is of necessity an 'opinion', rather than a neutral, objective fact, as was recognised in the US case of *Search King Inc v Google Technology Inc* (2003)[82] where the claimant argued that Google had intentionally lowered the ranking of its websites which had an adverse impact on the sites' traffic. The court dismissed the complaint on the ground that Google's rankings are an expression of opinion and thus protected by the First Amendment to the US Constitution. The claimant had neither a right to be listed on Google's search engine nor have its page ranked at a particular place in response to search requests. And it made no difference that Google had 'corrected' the ranking manually, overriding its normal algorithms, allegedly because Search King's sale of advertising space on highly ranked sites, automatically, but wrongly, gave Search King a high rating under Google's PageRank system. Whilst the indispensable need for an evaluative decision-making by search engines makes the notion of 'search neutrality' somewhat of an oxymoron, there is undoubtedly still room for illegitimate gatekeeping by search engines for anti-competitive commercial reasons. This is the case, for example, when its favours its own sites over competing third party sites. In light of the empirical evidence showing that the majority of users click on one of the first three links,[83] search engines are very powerful online bottlenecks for speech and commerce,[84] that raise important questions about their accountability, particularly given the relative absence of competition in the search market.

## Identification of wrongdoers

Intermediaries, in particular ISPs but also networking providers, have been drawn into the regulatory framework through the possibility of requiring them to disclose the identity of primary wrongdoers, i.e. their subscribers or members, for the purposes of criminal prosecutions and civil litigation. Both Art 8(3) of the Information Society Directive and Art 11 of the Enforcement Directive,[85] as mentioned above, provide in very general terms that Member States must enable rights holders to obtain injunctions against an intermediary whose services are used by third parties to infringe their intellectual property. In addition, Art 8(1) of the Enforcement Directive also provides more specifically:

> Member States shall ensure that, in the context of proceedings concerning an infringement of an intellectual property right and in response to a justified and proportionate request of the claimant, the competent judicial authorities may order that information on the origin and distribution networks of the goods or services which infringe an intellectual property right be provided by the infringer and/or any other person who . . . was found to be providing on a commercial scale services used in infringing activities.

Yet, Art 8(3) of the same Directive proceeds by stipulating that the above applies 'without prejudice to other statutory provisions which . . . govern the protection of confidentiality of information sources or the processing of personal data.' The question thus raised is whether an order for the identification of wrongdoers would be inconsistent with data protection obligations of ISPs under the Data Protection Directive,[86] considering that the impact of such disclosure could not be restricted to the 'privacy' of the alleged wrongdoers, but extends to all subscribers even simply in terms showing that their general online activities are 'monitored' to the extent that infringing activity can be picked up.[87] In *Promusicae* (2008) concerning an ISP's possible duty to disclose to

---

82  No. Civ-02–1457-M (WD Okla, 13 January 2003).
83  Otify, *The Changing Face of SERPs: Organic Click Through Rate* (April 2011).
84  Notably, search algorithms that determine the ranking order are protected as 'trade secrets'.
85  2001/29/EC and 2004/48/EC respectively.
86  95/46/EC now replaced by the General Data Protection Regulation 2016/679.
87  Currently 'monitoring' for copyright infringement is done by the copyright industry, which records IP addresses and date and time stamps and sends these to ISPs to be matched to their records/customers, see Out-law.com, 'Digital Economy Act copyright regime shelved by UK government' (2014) Out-law.com 24 July.

rightholders the identity and addresses of infringing subscribers, the CJEU held that the exceptions to data protection obligations – as provided for in the ePrivacy Directive and the Data Protection Directive[88] – allow *inter alia* for measures which are 'for the protection of the rights and freedoms of others.' Thus Member States are not necessarily precluded from imposing an obligation to disclose personal data in the context of civil proceedings, but neither are they obliged to do so.[89] In other words, the court left it up to Member States to decide what to do, but warned that any adopted solution not only has to be consistent with the Directives, but national courts in particular have to observe the principle of proportionality and strike a fair balance between the protection of intellectual property rights and the protection of the fundamental rights of individuals who are affected by such measures, under the Charter of Fundamental Rights of the European Union.[90] The CJEU affirmed that decision in LSG (2009) which also concerned the disclosure of the identity of infringing subscribers, again with the warning that any copyright-protective measure has to strike a fair balance between the various fundamental rights at stake.[91] Given that there is now some evidence to suggest that online copyright infringement has not abated despite huge attempts by the intellectual property industry (see above) and considering the profound privacy invasions as a result of these orders, it seems at least questionable whether the disclosure of the identity of potentially infringing users could still be considered 'proportionate'.[92] Incidentally, in the UK the possibility of making such an order of disclosure in civil litigation against an innocent third party has been available since *Norwich Pharmacal Co v Customs and Excise Commissioners* (1974)[93] where the court was willing to facilitate litigation by rightholders by making such an order against 'a person mixed up, however unwittingly, in the tortuous wrongdoing of others.' Identification obligations are by no means restricted to copyright infringements or ISPs, even if they have assumed a particular prominence. For example, in *L'Oréal v eBay* (2011)[94] the CJEU observed in the context of trade mark infringements an online auction platform that:

> the operator of an online marketplace may be ordered to take measures to make it easier to identify its customer-sellers . . . [A]lthough it is certainly necessary to respect the protection of personal data, the fact remains that when the infringer is operating in the course of trade and not in a private matter, that person must be clearly identifiable.[95]

Finally, what has been a controversy in the intellectual property context from a data protection/privacy perspective, emerged as a much more low key affair in the field of defamation law vis-à-vis content hosts, largely because of the adoption of a less adversarial approach to online defamation disputes. In the UK, under s 5 of the Defamation Act 2013,[96] as elaborated by the Defamation (Operators of Websites) Regulations 2013,[97] the 'operator of a website' is immune from

88 Art 15(1) of the ePrivacy Directive 2002/58/EC and Art 13(1) of the Data Protection Directive 95/46/EC.
89 *Productores de Música de España (Promusicae) v Telefónica de España SAU* C-275/06 [2008] ECR I-271, [53]–[55].
90 *Productores de Música de España (Promusicae) v Telefónica de España SAU* C-275/06 [2008] ECR I-271, [70].
91 *LSG-Gesellschaft zur Wahrnehmung von Leistungsschutzrechten GmbH v Tele2 Telecommunications* C-557/07, ECR I-1227.
92 For an abusive practice in this context, see *Media CAT Limited v Adams* [2011] EWPCC 6, where ISPs had revealed to Media CAT the names and addresses of tens of thousands of subscribers based on allegations of copyright infringements of pornographic films. This information was then used by Media CAT, a company illegitimately purporting to be a copyright protection society, and its solicitors as a basis to make financial demands (£495 per person) against the alleged infringers, with no real intention and in fact no locus standi to bring legal actions.
93 *Norwich Pharmacal Co v Customs and Excise Commissioners* [1974] AC 133; as, for example, used in: *Totalise plc v Motley Fool Ltd* [2001] EMLR 29; and *G v Wikimedia Foundation Inc* [2009] EWHC 3148.
94 *L'Oréal SA v eBay International AG* C-324/09 (CJEU, 12 July 2011).
95 Ibid, [142].
96 The Act also establishes the 'single publication rule' in s 8, which abolishes the common law rule of *Duke of Brunswick v Harmer* [1849] 14 QB 154 that each publication of a defamation gives rise to a separate cause of action, which had been challenged before the ECtHR in *Times Newspapers Ltd (Nos 1 and 2) v the United Kingdom* – 3002/03 [2009] ECHR 451.
97 No 3028. In *Richardson v Facebook* [2015] EWHC 3154, [35], the court held that s 5 will only be of relevance if a site operator is in fact a 'publisher' at common law.

defamation liability if it can show that it did not post the statement, i.e. that it was not the actual wrongdoer. However, the intermediary loses that immunity if the person who posted the statement (the 'poster') cannot be identified for the purposes of civil proceedings and the intermediary received a notice from the complainant about the alleged defamatory statement and failed to respond to that notice, as provided for by the Regulation. (Note, there is a bewildering array of additional immunities: s 10 of the Defamation Act 2013; s 1 of the Defamation Act 1996; and Arts 12–14 of the Electronic Commerce Directive.[98]) In response to a notice, the intermediary can only disclose the identity of the poster to the complainant with the former's consent;[99] and only remove the statement by court order, or if the poster cannot be contacted by the intermediary, or does not respond to the notice by the intermediary or inadequately so, or consents to the removal.[100] Thus, first, the Act protects the poster's anonymity; a position which may at first appear unusual, until one considers the many circumstances when anonymity is needed to protect legitimate critical expression, e.g. corporate criticism, that may be attacked as being 'defamatory'.[101] Anonymity is not necessarily a cloak for wrongdoing. This explains also why 'real name' policies, e.g. by Facebook, have proven so controversial – they silence those that may otherwise have no voice in mainstream public discourse.[102] Second, the Defamation Act 2013 also takes a very different approach to 'normal' notice-and-takedown procedures as it requires the intermediary not to evaluate the merits of the allegations, but merely to play the role of a neutral 'mediator' between the disputing parties. One residual problem is that very occasionally a complainant may be left without a remedy where the poster refuses to take the statement down *and* to have his or her identity revealed and the intermediary has complied with all its notice obligations. In that case, a potentially valid defamation claim is sacrificed – in the name of protecting the intermediary's substantive non-involvement, the poster's privacy as well as online community's interest in freedom of expression. Of course, the intermediary may decide to remove the material voluntarily. Alternatively, the complainant might either go to the hosting ISP for a notice-and-takedown action (given that such ISPs do not 'operate' the website and appear to be outside s 5[103]) or, depending on the circumstances, frame his or her complaint as a data protection action, following *Google Spain* (2014).[104]

Apart from this unusually nuanced stance in the Defamation Act 2013, one might conclude that the role of intermediaries in the identification of wrongdoers is less innocuous than may appear at first sight, and the above has only considered disclosure in the civil law context. In the criminal law context, Art 15(2) of the Electronic Commerce Directive specifically envisages the potential cooperation by intermediaries with 'competent authorities' for the identification of users for the purposes (see below). Importantly, knowing the identity of users in cyberspace is key to governmental (and corporate) control. In the governmental context, the traceability of online activity accompanied by an awareness of such traceability goes towards the realisation of Bentham's concept of the Panopticon or Foucault's idea of the self-disciplining society. It is not surprising that France in the aftermath of the Paris shooting considered legislation for banning Tor and free public WiFi spots during a 'state of emergency', because these are the last bastions for

---

98 00/31/EC. Note s 5 of the Defamation Act 2013 would, as a *lex specialis*, be the law first to be applied to 'operator of websites'. Jan Oster, liability of internet intermediaries for defamatory speech – An inquiry into the concepts of "publication" and "innocent Dissemination"' (2013) *Society of Legal Scholars – Edinburgh Conference 2013*, available at: http://www.archive.legalscholars.ac.uk/edinburgh/restricted/download.cfm?id=336

99 Reg 8(2)(b)(ii) of the Schedule to the Regulations.

100 See regs 3(1), 5(2)(a), 6(2)(a) and 7(2)(a) respectively of the Schedule to the Regulations.

101 See, for example, *Martin Clark v TripAdvisor LLC for an Order under the Administration of Justice (Scotland) Act 1972 Section 1(1)(A)* [2014] ScotCS CSOH_20.

102 Lilian Edwards, 'From the fantasy to the reality: social media and real name policies' in *Festschrift for Jon Bing*, 2013, Oslo, 6.

103 See reg 1(2) of the Defamation (Operators of Websites) Regulations 2013, which defines 'operator' as 'the operator of the website on which the statement complained of in the notice of complaint is posted'.

104 *Google Inc v Agencia Española de Protección de Datos, Mario Costeja González* C-131/12 (CJEU 13 May 2014).

relatively anonymous online activity.[105] This is an instance, where the empowerment of individuals through anonymity is discarded in the name of containing the negative repercussions of that very empowerment.

## Blocking

It is only a small conceptual step from identifying online wrongdoing or wrongdoers to blocking online activity or actors, and again it is intermediaries, and in particular ISPs, who are at the sharp end of this regulatory measure. Blocking is intended to bring illegal activity to an end – much like notice-and-takedown procedures, discussed below. Yet, blocking has a very tainted reputation due its prevalence in authoritarian regimes and dictatorships; yet in fact it is also routinely used in the democratic liberal states, albeit for different substantive purposes.[106] Blocking may come in the form of website blocking (i.e. the content provider) or end user blocking (i.e. the receiver of information). The latter has been on the agenda, particularly vis-à-vis persistent copyright infringers. For example in the UK, the Digital Economy Act 2010 provided, in addition to the possibility of blocking sites, also for the power and obligation of ISPs to suspend subscriber accounts in certain circumstances.[107] This approach has since been abandoned in favour of self-regulation within which the suspension of internet access appears to no longer be considered an appropriate remedy.[108] This would, in any event, be contestable as the right to internet access is increasingly seen as a human right in itself or, at least, part and parcel of the right to freedom of expression and freedom to information.[109] Notably, an Australian court specifically rejected the removal of internet access as a reasonable remedy against persistent pirates in *Roadshow Films Pty ltd v iiNet Ltd (No 3)*.[110] The Federal Court of Australia found that iiNet, the third largest ISP in Australia, was not liable for the copyright infringements (peer-to-peer downloading) of its customers.[111] Even though the ISP had knowledge of the infringements and did not act to stop them, it did not thereby authorise them. It merely provided access to the internet and thereby the preconditions for infringement, which, according to the Court, was not the same as providing a 'means of infringement'; those 'means' were the BitTorrent system over which the ISP has no control. Following on from this, the ISP could not be treated as having intended for copyright infringements to occur, unlike providers such as Napster or Kazaa or The Pirate Bay, in which cases the site or software was deliberately structured to favour infringement.[112] Justice Cowdroy rejected that a scheme for notification followed by suspension and termination of customer accounts were *reasonable steps* to prevent infringements within Australia's copyright legislation, even where the ISP, as in this case, contractually reserved its right to do so.[113] Because the ISP was not providing the means of infringement, it was not incumbent upon it to stop them, considering that suspension would also lead to much non-infringing activity being suspended by the infringer and non-infringer, such as family members. In any event, the judge reasoned that any sanction for copyright infringement is not to be 'imposed until after a

---

105 James Cook, 'French police reportedly want to ban Tor and public WiFi in the wake of the Paris' (2015) *Business Insider UK*, 7 December.

106 OSCE, *Freedom of Expression on the Internet: A Study of Legal Provisions and Practices related to Freedom of Expression, the Free Flow of Information and Media Pluralism on the Internet in OSCE participating States* (15 December 2011).

107 Sections 17 and 18 (blocking sites) and 9 and 10 (suspending accounts). The Secretary of State had the power to impose technical obligations on ISPs to limit internet access to subscribers who have repeatedly infringed copyright. Such measures may be limiting the speed or capacity of the service, preventing the subscriber from accessing particular material, suspending the service, or limiting it in another way.

108 Out-law.com, 'Digital Economy Act copyright regime shelved by UK government' (2014) *Out-law.com*, 24 July

109 See, for example, *Case of Yildirim v Turkey* No 3111/10 ECtHR (18 March 2013), para 31; OSCE, above n 106.

110 [2010] FCA 24.

111 Thom Holwerda, 'Judge: Norwegian ISP does not have to block the Pirate Bay' (2009) *Osnews*, 7 November, available at: http://www.osnews.com/story/22456; contrast to District Court of Frederiksberg, Copenhagen (5 February 2008), aff'd Eastern High Court of Denmark (26 November 2008), requiring one of Denmark's largest ISPs to block access to The Pirate Bay.

112 *Roadshow Films Pty Ltd v iiNet Ltd (No 3)* [2010] FCA 24, point 14 of the summary.

113 Ibid, [430]–[442].

finding of infringement by a court. Such sanction is not imposed on anyone other than the person who infringed. Such sanction sounds in damages or, if criminal, possible fines and imprisonment, not removal of the provision of the internet.'[114]

Criticisms levelled against blocking of sites often appear to be more concerned with the merit of the substantive content blocked and the scale and extent of the blocking order, rather than its inherent vice as an enforcement mechanism. A key, more principled argument levelled against blocking is that it is a form of 'prior restraint' on expression which – as part of traditional media/ speech regulation – is to be treated with utmost caution to avoid undue censorship.[115] However, blocking does not necessarily occur 'prior' to a judgment by a court on the legality of the material to be blocked, although often it does, given that the wrongdoer is beyond the enforcement reach of the state in question. Also, the much more readily accepted notice-and-takedown procedure occurs, on the whole, with much less judicial oversight than blocking orders and to say that the former is a 'private voluntary action' in contrast to blocking being a 'state-based coercion'[116] misses the point that even notice-and-takedown obligations are backed by the threat of liability, which in turn is backed by the coercive power of the state. In any event, the inability or incapacity to pursue a case in court (due to issues of scale or territorial scope, see above) should hardly entail that nothing should be done with clearly illegal and highly harmful online material. Take, for example, the work of the Internet Watch Foundation which has, since 1996, provided a hotline for child-abuse images in the UK.[117] It operates a notice-and-takedown procedure for child abuse images hosted within the UK and notifies foreign counterparts of images hosted *outside* the UK. However, with regard to the latter it also operates a regularly updated blacklist of offending URLs sent to local ISPs for blocking to make these images inaccessible whilst the notice-and-takedown action is taken by the foreign counterpart. The objective is to protect the children within these images and discourage further abuses by disrupting the market for them. Assuming the sufficiency of accountability mechanisms for those decisions, it seems hardly persuasive to say that blocking of these images should be illegitimate, simply because it is a form of 'prior restraint'. Similar may arguably be said about the activities of the UK Counter Terrorism Internet Referral Unit[118] which has a mandate to identify and take down extreme graphic material, e.g. beheadings, and material that glorifies or incites terrorism and which has 'instigated the removal of over 55,000 pieces of online content, including 34,000 pieces'[119] from December 2013 to November 2014 based on s 3 of the Terrorism Act 2006.

This is not to assert that blocking is unproblematic, but whether it is or is not would appear to depend on the substantive merit of the material blocked, the decision-making procedure on the blocking, the scope of the order and the transparency accompanying all of this.[120] The European Court of Human Rights *Case of Yildirim v Turkey* (2013)[121] provides an example of a blocking order that arguably failed on most of these grounds, but most obviously on the issue of scope (see also Chapter 2). The case concerned an order by a Turkish court to have a site, hosted on Google Sites, blocked on the basis that it violated Turkish law on the protection of Ataturk's memory. This was a preventative measure in the context of possible criminal proceedings against the owner of the site who lived abroad, at some point in the future, i.e. it was a case of 'prior restraint'. As the Turkish telecommunications oversight body considered that blocking the particular site was not feasible without blocking access to Google Sites altogether (although there was no evidence

---

114 Ibid, [441].
115 Mueller, above n 52, 211
116 Mueller, above n 52, 201.
117 See http://www.iwf.org
118 See https://www.herts.police.uk/advice/counter_terrorism.aspx
119 Patrick Wintour, 'UK ISPs to introduce jihadi and terror content reporting button' (2014) *The Guardian*, 14 November; Mark Townsend, Toby Helm, 'Jihad in a social media age: how can the west win an online war?' (2014) *The Guardian*, 23 August.
120 Derek Bambauer, 'Cybersieves' (2009) 59 *Duke Law Journal* 377. See also Separate Concurring Opinion in *Case of Yildirim v Turkey* No 3111/10 ECtHR (18 March 2013), 27f.
121 *Case of Yildirim v Turkey* No 3111/10 ECtHR (18 March 2013).

that Google had been approached with the request to take down the specific offending sites), the Turkish court ordered the wholesale block of Google Sites. As a result, the applicant, Yildirim, was unable to access his academic site on Google Sites which was unrelated to the offending site and legal under Turkish law; indeed the collateral damage of this blocking order included necessarily all other sites on Google Sites. The ECtHR held that this blocking breached Art 10(1) of the European Convention on Human Rights and was not justified under Art 10(2) given that it was not 'prescribed by law': the particular Turkish law relied upon covered neither the applicant's site nor Google Sites (and were not considered by the court). The court had also failed to consider the possibility of less far reaching measures and the collateral effect of their order on the accessibility of large quantities of information. It had thus not acted with a 'framework establishing precise and specific rules regarding the application of preventative restrictions on freedom of expression,'[122] which the ECtHR felt was necessary to make any 'prior restraint' compatible with the Convention. The order therefore did not satisfy the 'foreseeability requirement under the Convention and did not afford the applicant the degree of protection to which he was entitled by the rule of law in a democratic society.'[123]

In addition to blocking of 'criminal' sites, blocking has also been adopted as a remedy for the breach of private interests, notably intellectual property interests, backed by civil litigation. Such blocking should be more controversial, given the lower position of civil claims in the general pecking order of regulatory priorities than criminalised activity. Yet, this does not appear to be the case. As mentioned above, in the EU Art 8(3) of the Information Society Directive provides for copyright infringement what Art 11 of the Enforcement Directive[124] does for intellectual property more generally; it requires Member States 'to ensure that rightholders are in a position to apply for an injunction against intermediaries whose services are used by a third party to infringe an intellectual property . . .'. Relying on the implementation of Art 8(3) in the UK through s 97A of the Copyright, Designs and Patents Act 1988, Justice Arnold in *Twentieth Century Fox Film Corp v British Telecommunications Plc* (2011)[125] granted the blocking injunction sought by film production companies and studios to be implemented by BT, being one of the key ISPs in the UK. The controversial site in question was Newzbin, which its operators had moved offshore after having been found guilty of copyright infringement in a previous judgment. The rightholders relied on the existence of BT's Cleanfeed filtering software,[126] designed to block child abuse images upon notification by the IWF (see above). The court held that that both the subscribers of BT and the operators of Newzbin used BT's services to infringe copyright. Although the grant of an injunction has, in the UK, also been made dependent on the intermediary's 'actual knowledge of another person using their service to infringe copyright', Justice Arnold rejected that the ISP has to have 'actual knowledge of a specific infringement of a specific copyright work by a specific individual'; all that was needed was a 'sufficiently detailed notice and a reasonable opportunity to investigate the position.'[127] This judgment has been followed by innumerable other blocking orders sought by different rightholders against various ISPs concerning a host of problematic sites.[128] In *Cartier* (2014)[129] Justice Arnold went further and held that similar blocking orders could also be granted to trade mark holders vis-à-vis counterfeiting sites, on the basis of Art 11 of the Enforcement Directive. According to Arnold J this Article is transposed into UK law though s 37(1) of the Senior Courts Act 1981 which provides

---

122  *Case of Yildirim v Turkey* No 3111/10 ECtHR (18 March 2013), [64].
123  Ibid, [67].
124  2001/29/EC and 2004/48/EC respectively.
125  *Twentieth Century Fox Film Corp v British Telecommunications Plc* [2011] EWHC 1981 (Ch).
126  For a description of the software operated by other ISPs, see *Cartier International AG v British Sky Broadcasting Ltd* [2014] EWHC 3354, [38]–[51]
127  *Twentieth Century Fox Film Corp v British Telecommunications Plc* [2011] EWHC 1981 (Ch), [148], [149].
128  For a list of these orders, see *Cartier International AG v British Sky Broadcasting Ltd* [2014] EWHC 3354, [3], [53].
129  *Cartier International AG v British Sky Broadcasting Ltd* [2014] EWHC 3354.

that the 'High Court may . . . grant an injunction . . . in all cases in which it appears to be just and convenient to do so.' He felt justified in making such an order, given that:

> the likely cost burden on the ISPs is justified by the likely efficacy of the blocking measures and the consequent benefit to . . . [the trade mark holders] having regard to the alternative measures which are available . . . and to the substitutability of the Target Websites . . . Accordingly the orders are proportionate and strike a fair balance between the respective rights that are engaged, including the rights of individuals who may be affected by the orders but who are not before the Court.[130]

As safeguards against possible abuses, he stipulated four safeguards: (1) ISPs can apply for a variation of the orders in the event of any material change of circumstances; (2) to protect the rights users, future orders should expressly permit affected subscribers to apply to the court to discharge or vary the order; (3) users who seek to access blocked sites should be presented with a notice that the site is blocked by court order and identify the parties who obtained the order and state that they have a right to apply to the court to discharge or vary the order; and (4) the orders should have a 'sunset clause' of two years after which they will cease to have effect, unless either the ISPs consent to their continuation or the court orders them to be continued.[131] Some of the points clearly go towards increasing the legitimacy of blocking orders along the lines mentioned above.

Justice Arnold had some reason to feel that his approach was the accepted one, given that in *UPC Telekabel Wien GmbH v Constantin Film Verleih GmbH* (2014)[132] the CJEU had just given its support in principle to blocking orders under Art 8(3) of the Information Society Directive. The case was brought by the owners of copyright in various films against an Austrian ISP and the site to be blocked was kino.to, one of the most popular sites for streaming and downloading copyrighted films and TV programmes. The court held that fundamental rights protection under the Charter of Fundamental Rights of the European Union did not preclude such order as long as: (1) the access provider can choose the specific measures how to implement the order and would not incur penalties for breach of the order if it had taken all reasonable measures (i.e. right to conduct business);[133] (2) the order is strictly targeted and does not prevent access to lawful content and users are able to challenge the order once implemented (i.e. the user right to freedom of information);[134] (3) the order would have the 'the effect of preventing unauthorised access to the protected subject-matter or, at least, of making it difficult to achieve and of seriously discouraging internet users who are using the services of the addressee of that injunction from accessing the subject-matter that has been made available to them in breach of the intellectual property right' (i.e. effectiveness).[135] It is the last point that will remain a bone of contention, particularly as more evidence emerges as to the overall effectiveness of these orders.

As a final comment, often the sites against which a blocking order is sought are themselves intermediaries that connect users with each other's, e.g. Newzbin or Google Sites, in contrast to sites that are the product of only one content provider. In the case of potential blocking of such intermediaries, the question of legitimacy is more difficult as the ripple effect of the blocking goes even further and affects more content providers and most of these intermediaries mediate or 'trade in' both legal and illegal content, and thus blocking would then also affect legal content. That difficulty tends to be resolved by reference to the relative proportions of legal and illegal content, as implicitly underpinned by an assessment of legal commitment or loyalty of the intermediary

---

130 *Cartier International AG v British Sky Broadcasting Ltd* [2014] EWHC 3354, [261].
131 *Cartier International AG v British Sky Broadcasting Ltd* [2014] EWHC 3354, [262]–[265].
132 *UPC Telekabel Wien GmbH v Constantin Film Verleih GmbH* C-314/12 (CJEU, 27 March 2014).
133 *UPC Telekabel Wien GmbH v Constantin Film Verleih GmbH* C-314/12 (CJEU, 27 March 2014), [51]–[54].
134 Ibid, [56]–[57].
135 Ibid, [62].

(see Chapter 4). Typically, in the German case of *Haftung des Access-Providers* (2008),[136] the court refused to grant a blocking injunction against an ISP, concerning google.de and google.com, for returning on searches for pornography results to sites that operated without the legally required access restrictions in unfair competition with the claimant's site.[137] One of the reasons for the refusal was that it would be disproportionate to block access to an important search engine, such as Google, just because a small percentage of the subscribers will come across the offending sites. By the same token, from a Western liberal democratic perspective, the blocking of sites like Newzbin (that provide content which is legal in most respects, other than copyright law) seems unexceptional. Perhaps from a non-Western perspective that same unexceptionality applies to sites like Google Sites or Google Search (that provide content that is equally illegal in a key aspect or simply unconcerned about that legality and thus overall intolerable).

## Monitoring (and reporting)

Given the scale of online communications and the ease with which anyone can reach a mass audience, a central regulatory question has been who could or should monitor online behaviour with the view to identifying illegality. Naturally, it is the bottlenecks or gateways which occupy ideal positions for such monitoring obligations. Yet, in the relatively early days of the internet the EU made the fundamental decision that online intermediaries should not be burdened with a general monitoring obligation; Article 15 of the Electronic Commerce Directive[138] provides that:

1.   Member States shall not impose a *general* obligation on information on providers, when providing the services covered by Articles 12, 13 and 14, to monitor the information which they transmit or store, nor a general obligation actively to seek facts or circumstances indicating illegal activity.

2.   Member States may establish obligations for information society service providers *promptly to inform* the competent public authorities of alleged illegal activities undertaken or information provided by recipients of their service or obligations to communicate to the competent authorities, at their request, information enabling the identification of recipients of their service with whom they have storage agreements. [emphasis added]

The first point of note is that Art 15(1) only prohibits the imposition of general monitoring obligations, but leaves Member States free to impose more specific monitoring obligations as provided for by Arts 12(3), 13(2) and 14(3) of the Directive (see below).[139] It must also be remembered that the prohibition on general monitoring duties only applies to matters covered by the Directive, not to those excluded by virtue of Art 1(4)–(6) of the Directive which specifically take out of the ambit of the Directive taxation, data protection and gambling regulation. In addition Art 15(2) also retains the possibility of Member States imposing reporting obligations on intermediaries, when they stumble across illegal content as well as the obligation to identify the wrongdoer (see above and also Chapter 10). Thus being applicable to criminalised activity, it provides the foundation for reporting obligations for the purposes of crime prevention and national security, such as those

---

136 *Haftung des Access-Providers* (OLG Frankfurt am Main, 22 January 2008, 6 W 10/08).

137 The court also found that while access to such sites may well create unfair competition, the ISP, as a mere conduit, is not responsible for the content of the site to which its subscribers may have access. The court refused to accept that an ISP is comparable to an online auction provider in terms of creating within its sphere of influence a 'danger zone' in which third parties may engage in wrongful conduct and for which it is responsible. When an ISP allows access to the Internet, the content on the internet is not within its sphere of influence.

138 2000/31/EC.

139 Recital 47 of the Electronic Commerce Directive: 'Member States are prevented from imposing a monitoring obligation on service providers only with respect to obligations of a general nature; this does not concern monitoring obligations in a specific case . . .'; Oster, above n 98, 2f.

agreed upon by the EU Parliament, in December 2015, in the EU's first cyber-security law, the Network and Information Security Directive.[140] This Directive applies *inter alia* to online intermediaries, i.e. 'digital service providers', such as search engines, online marketplaces and cloud providers, but not social networking providers, and imposes upon them security and reporting obligations, backed by the threat of sanctions.

In respect of civil law, it is the 'general monitoring' prohibition under Art 15(1) that has engendered much discussion. The controversy arises from the fact that, where intermediaries are obliged to stop illegal content passing through them, the issue is who should bear the technological and economic burden of identifying that illegal content in the first place. Rightholders have been keen to shift that burden to intermediaries as it would relieve them of the high-scale task;[141] and they certainly have made some modest inroads into the Art 15(1) prohibition, initially in German courts vis-à-vis online marketplaces. In *ROLEX v Ricardo.de* (2004),[142] and affirmed in *ROLEX v eBay* (2007),[143] concerning offers of counterfeits on Ricardo's online auction site, the Bundesgerichtshof held that, although Ricardo.de was neither a primary wrongdoer nor a participant of the wrongdoing, it could nevertheless be subject to a takedown duty as a *Störer* ('omittor'). The basis for this was that it had knowingly contributed to the infringement of the claimant's rights by omission. Importantly, this takedown duty extended beyond the particular infringing item of which the auction house was made aware. The auction provider must take all reasonably technically feasible measures to ensure that no further infringements occur – or, in short, monitor the site with a view to spotting similar infringements, although the court stressed that the site provider was under no general monitoring duty. The court elaborated on the reasonableness of any preventative measures being dependent upon:[144]

- a clear infringement being present;
- similar infringements being easily detectable; and
- the overall circumstances of each individual case, including the financial benefit received by the intermediary.

The ruling shows that the dividing line between any notice-and-takedown duty and monitoring obligations is not quite as clear and bright as one may assume; once on notice about a particular infringement, a monitoring burden in respect of repeat infringements moves to the platform operator. In *L'Oréal v eBay* (2011)[145] it was the CJEU that was presented with the question of future-oriented measures. The case concerned eBay's responsibility for the sales of goods via its platform in contravention of L'Oréal's trade marks as well as eBay's responsibility for having them advertised on Google's AdWords. Specifically, on the issue of 'general monitoring' with the view to picking up future infringements, the CJEU held that, first, 'it follows from Article 15(1) of Directive 2000/31 . . . that the measures required of the online service provider concerned cannot consist in an active monitoring of all the data of each of its customers in order to prevent any

---

140 European Commission, 'Network and Information Security Directive: co-legislators agree on the first EU-wide legislation on cybersecurity' (9 December 2015) European Commission – Digital Agenda for Europe, available online at: https://ec.europa.eu/digital-agenda/en/news/network-and-information-security-directive-co-legislators-agree-first-eu-wide-legislation; Julia Fioretti, 'EU lawmakers, countries agree on bloc's first cybersecurity law' (2015) *Reuters*, 8 December. See also, Antonio Segura-Serrano, 'Cybersecurity: Protection of critical information infrastructures and operators' obligations' (2015) 6 European Journal of Law and Technology, available online at: http://ejlt.org/article/view/396

141 For a description of the monitoring by IP rightholders, see 'Digital Economy Act copyright regime shelved by UK government' (2014) Out-law.com, 24 July.

142 *ROLEX v Ricardo.de* (BGH, 11 March 2004, Az I ZR 304/01).

143 *ROLEX v eBay* (BGH, 19 April 2007, Az I ZR 35/04), [33], [40] and [45], available online at: http://medien-internet-und-recht.de/pdf/VT_MIR_2007_246.pdf; see also *Haftung von Rapidshare* (OLG Hamburg, 2 July 2008, Az 5 U 73/07), it was also held where there have been a series of similar infringements, the host is obliged to carry out more proactive, preventive monitoring.

144 *ROLEX v Ricardo.de* (BGH, 11 March 2004, Az I ZR 304/01); *ROLEX v eBay* (BGH, 19 April 2007, Az I ZR 35/04); see above.

145 *L'Oréal SA v eBay International AG* C-324/09 (CJEU, 12 July 2011).

future infringement of intellectual property rights via that provider's website.'[146] Second, based on the right to legitimate trade, 'the injunction . . . cannot have as its object or effect a general and permanent prohibition on the selling, on that marketplace, of goods bearing those trade marks.'[147] Nonetheless, the platform operator may be ordered to suspend the perpetrator's account to 'prevent further infringements of that kind by the same seller in respect of the same trade marks' and make him or her identifiable[148] and, most importantly, the third sentence of Art 11 of the Enforcement Directive[149] which, as discussed above, allows for blocking orders, also requires:

> Member States to ensure that the national courts with jurisdiction in relation to the protection of intellectual property rights are able to order the operator of an online marketplace to take measures which contribute, not only to bringing to an end infringements of those rights by users of that marketplace, but also to preventing *further* infringements of that kind. Those injunctions must be effective, proportionate, dissuasive and must not create barriers to legitimate trade.[150]

Although this raises further questions as to what may or may not be sufficient to prevent further infringements, it is certain that the specific monitoring obligations must focus on the particular wrongdoer rather than the particular interests claimed by the rightholders, as the focus on the latter would ultimately involve scanning all files by all customers. The legality of such a filtering duty was in the spotlight in *SABAM – Société belge des auteurs, compositeurs et éditeurs v Scarlet Extended SA* (2011)[151] and subsequently in *SABAM – Société belge des auteurs, compositeurs et éditeurs SCRL v Netlog NV* (2012).[152] In both cases, SABAM, a Belgian society representing various copyright holders, sought to protect the rights of its members by requesting, in the case of Scarlet, an internet access provider, that it 'brings such infringements to an end by blocking, or making it impossible for its customers to send or receive in any way, files containing a musical work using peer-to-peer software'; and in the case of Netlog, an online social networking platform, to 'cease unlawfully making available musical or audio-visual works from SABAM's repertoire.' So it sought orders under Art 8(3) of the Information Society Directive[153] requiring the intermediaries to monitor for infringements of particular protected works and then prevent them. The CJEU in *Scarlet* found that for the ISP the implementation of the filtering system would involve '[p]reventive monitoring . . . [that would] require active observation of all electronic communications conducted on the network of the ISP concerned and, consequently, would encompass all information to be transmitted and all customers using that network.'[154] More specifically, it would require:

(1) that the ISP identify, within all of the electronic communications of all its customers, the files relating to peer-to-peer traffic;
(2) that it identify, within that traffic, the files containing works in respect of which holders of intellectual-property rights claim to hold rights;
(3) that it determine which of those files are being shared unlawfully; and
(4) that it block file sharing that it considers to be unlawful.[155]

---

146 Ibid, [139].
147 Ibid, [140].
148 Ibid, [141], [142].
149 2004/48.
150 Ibid, [144] [emphasis added], see also discussion at [128]–[134].
151 *SABAM – Société belge des auteurs, compositeurs et éditeurs SCRL v Scarlet Extended SA* C-70/10 (CJEU, 24 November 2011).
152 *SABAM – Société belge des auteurs, compositeurs et éditeurs SCRL v Netlog NV* C-360/10 (CJEU, 16 February 2012).
153 2001/29.
154 *Scarlet* [39].
155 *Scarlet* [38].

Such monitoring or surveillance falls squarely within the prohibition against general monitoring in Art 15(1).[156] Although this might have been the end of the judgment, the court continued by showing that such monitoring injunction could also not be granted as the filtering system in question would not strike a fair balance between the competing rights, 'the right to intellectual property, on the one hand, and the freedom to conduct business, the right to protection of personal data and the freedom to receive or impart information, on the other.'[157] The reasoning might be understood as explaining the rationale for the prohibition against general monitoring. First, intellectual property rights as secured by the Charter of Fundamental Rights of the European Union are not absolute rights, that must be protected at all cost (and this applies to almost any interests sought to be protected, and particularly 'private' interests). Second, such injunction would cause 'a serious infringement of the freedom of the ISP concerned to conduct its business since it would require that ISP to install a complicated, costly, permanent computer system'. Third, as such monitoring would 'involve a systematic analysis of all content and the collection and identification of users' IP addresses from which unlawful content on the network is sent', it would infringe data protection rights. Fourth and finally, it would affect the right to freedom of information as it 'could lead to the blocking of lawful communications', e.g. those allowed pursuant to copyright exemptions.[158] This holding was extended from access providers to networking platforms in Netlog.

## Voluntary monitoring?

Whether the notion of neutrality of the service provider requires that it does not voluntarily monitor the site's content is unclear, although it may be argued that monitoring is a form of exerting control over the site and thus places the provider outside the immunities. This would seem to be consistent with the opinion of the Advocate General in *Google AdWords* (2009):[159]

> I construe Article 15 of that directive not merely as imposing a negative obligation on Member States, but as the very expression of the principle that service providers which seek to benefit from a liability exemption should remain neutral as regards the information they carry or host.[160]

In his opinion, intermediaries that assert control over the third-party content through monitoring can no longer be considered neutral. This approach is problematic insofar as it creates a disincentive for intermediaries to monitor their content which they might want to do for commercial reasons, e.g. to brand themselves as a family-friendly site. In the USA, s 230 of the Communications Decency Act (1996) (discussed below) does not deprive online intermediaries of any immunity from civil liability on the basis of 'any action voluntarily taken in good faith to restrict access to or availability of material that the provider or user considers to be obscene, lewd, lascivious, filthy, excessively violent, harassing, or otherwise objectionable' (s 230(c)(2)). Indeed, the section was designed specifically 'to remove disincentives to self-regulation and encourage service providers to monitor the hosted material without the fear of incurring liability as a result of their trouble'[161] but, as shown below, even that statute fails to incentivise self-regulation.

---

156 *Scarlet* [40].
157 *Scarlet* [53].
158 *Scarlet* [43], [48], [51] and [52] respectively.
159 *Google AdWords* C-236/08, C-237/08 and C-238/08 (Advocate General, 22 September 2009).
160 *Ibid*, [143].
161 *Austin v CrystalTech Web Hosting* 125 P3d 389, 393 (Ariz App Div 1, 2005), citing *Zeran v America Online Inc* 129 F3d 327, 331 (4th Cir 1997) (internal marks omitted).

## Liability and notice-and-takedown duties

The avenues for intermediaries' involvement in the regulatory framework discussed above are not dependent on any wrongdoing by the intermediary and thus not based on establishing liability. This starting point reinforces their position as quasi-regulators (within private-public partnerships) as opposed to being part of 'the regulated'. Yet, at times, when the law imposes liabilities upon them, they also belong much more squarely to this latter category. These liabilities tend to take the form of notice-and-takedown duties, whereby liability arises only if the intermediary is on notice of the wrongdoing and fails to respond to the notice expeditiously. Notice-and-takedown duties are reactive in nature, and do not require the intermediary to engage in preventative monitoring (see above). The pervasiveness of this regulatory option within internet governance stands in marked contrast to the more proactive regulatory role of many traditional communication bottlenecks – which is due to the fact that the latter had to engage in 'editing' to fit their limited capacity. Given the decentralised nature of online communications this is no longer necessary, or less so. Thus any pre-emptive filtering on the internet would be much more a form of 'prior restraint' than unavoidable editing. From the perspective of the regulator, the notice-and-take down duty is attractive because of scale – it shifts the huge regulatory burden arising out of the huge number of online communications to private actors. Yet, for this very reason it is also democratically weak given the lack of accountability mechanisms attaching to these private actions; and as noted above, to argue that notice-and-takedown mechanisms are preferable to blocking because the former are voluntary rather than coerced actions glosses over the fact that notice-and-takedown obligations are very much backed by the threat of sanctions.

In the EU the notice-and-takedown mechanism is generally associated with the immunities regime for intermediaries under the Electronic Commerce Directive (see below). However, the notice-and-takedown duties have existed before and apart from the Directive, e.g. defamation or data protection. These separate regimes generally pre-empt the application of the immunities in the Directive, because the Directive does not of itself create liability but only immunities, assuming the prior existence of liability in substantive legal provisions. For example, an online intermediary – which is not an 'operator of a website' and thus outside the Defamation Act 2013 (see above) – would continue to take advantage of s 1(1) of the Defamation Act 1996 which provides:

(1)  In defamation proceedings a person has a defence if he shows that –

    (a)  he was not the author, editor or publisher of the statement complained of,

    (b)  he took reasonable care in relation to its publication, and

    (c)  he did not know, and had no reason to believe, that what he did caused or contributed to the publication of a defamatory statement.

This provision has long operated to protect 'distributors' in the communication chain from liability for defamation, provided they act expeditiously to stop the distribution of the defamatory material as soon as they obtain knowledge of it. The defence has also had a fair amount of online exposure and should remain relevant in the internet context to, for example, ISPs either in their role of providing access to the internet or hosting material, as in neither case would they appear to be 'operators of websites'. One of the earliest cases, in which it came into operation, is *Godfrey v Demon Internet Ltd* (1999),[162] in which the defendant ISP (carrying on business in England and Wales) stored on its news-server the posting of a newsgroup to which someone made a posting defamatory of the claimant. The court held that whilst Demon was clearly not the (primary) 'publisher' of the material in question within the meaning of s 1(2) and (3), it was a publisher/distributor

---

162  *Godfrey v Demon Internet Limited* [1999] EWHC QB 244.

within the wider common law meaning, of 'making known the defamatory matter after it has been written to some person other than the person of whom it is written'[163] as opposed to being a mere 'electronic device through which posting were transmitted', i.e. tool.[164] Whilst as a common law publisher/distributor it could in principle rely on s 1 of the Defamation Act 1996, here the 'innocent dissemination' defence was not available because Demon did not satisfy s 1(1)(b) and (c) given that it had not removed the posting from the newsgroup for some time after being notified of it by the claimant.

An example of when an online intermediary will be considered a mere 'tool' or 'facilitator' – not amounting to publisher/distributor in the wider common law sense – and thus need not rely on the 'innocent dissemination' defence is provided by the case of *Bunt v Tilley* (2006),[165] where John Bunt tried unsuccessfully to make the three ISPs of the primary defamers – AOL UK, Tiscali UK, and BT – liable simply on the basis of providing *access* to the internet, not hosting the material in question.[166] The judge held that for being a publisher at common law 'it is essential to demonstrate a degree of awareness or at least an assumption of general responsibility, such as has long been recognised in the context of editorial responsibility.'[167] This could not be said of ISPs as access providers:

> More generally, I am also prepared to hold as a matter of law that an ISP which performs no more than a passive role in facilitating postings on the internet cannot be deemed to a be publisher at common law . . . I would not . . . attribute liability at common law to a telephone company or other passive medium of communication, such as an ISP. It is not analogous to someone in the position of a distributor . . . There a defence is needed because the person is regarded as having 'published'. By contrast, persons who truly fulfil no more than the role of a passive medium for communication cannot be characterised as publishers: thus they do not need a defence.[168]

The holding that access providers are not publishers/distributors, but mere 'tools' for the purposes of defamation law and thus under no notice-and-takedown duty was extended to search engines in the English case of *Metropolitan International Schools Ltd v Designtechnica Corp* (2009),[169] which concerned Google's liability for defamatory comments on its search results. An English training business sued Google and the owner of a review website for publishing an allegedly defamatory review of its distance-learning course (calling it, *inter alia*, 'nothing more than a scam'), which appeared as snippets in Google's search results. Because Google Inc was based in California, the initiating process had to be served outside of England, and to do so the claimant had to show a 'reasonable prospect of success', which Google argued it had not (see Chapter 2). Thus Justice Eady had to consider Google's possible liability and concluded that Google was under common law not a publisher/distributor, as the concept of publication entails an awareness of the words to be published: '. . . it is not enough that a person merely plays a passive instrumental role in the process.'[170] It could not be a publisher, because its entire process was automated and it played no role in formulating the search terms that determine the 'snippets' displayed in response to the search; Google was a pure

163 *Pullman v Hill & Co* [1891] 1 QB 524, 527.
164 *Godfrey v Demon Internet Limited* [1999] EWHC QB 244, [19], [30] and [35] respectively.
165 [2006] EWHC 407.
166 But see ibid, [68], where BT is clearly characterised as a 'host'.
167 Ibid, [22], following *McLeod v St Aubyn* [1899] AC 549.
168 *Bunt v Tilley* [2006] EWHC 407, [36] and [37].
169 *Metropolitan International Schools Ltd (t/a Skillstrain and/or Train2game) v Designtechnica Corp (t/a Digital Trends)* [2009] EWHC 1765; Out-law. com, 'Google is not liable for defamatory snippets in search results, rules High Court' (2009) Out-law.com, 17 July.
170 *Metropolitan International Schools Ltd*, [49].

facilitator.[171] In the process of distinguishing *Godfrey*, Eady J asserted that search engines should be treated more generously than content hosts:

> A search engine, however, is a different kind of Internet intermediary. It is not possible to draw a complete analogy with a website host. One cannot merely press a button to ensure that the offending words will never reappear on a Google search snippet: there is no control over the search terms typed in by future users. If the words are thrown up in response to a future search, it would by no means follow that [Google] . . . has authorised or acquiesced in that process.[172]

Justice Eady held that as Google was not a publisher/distributor at common law, it was in no need of the defence in s 1.[173] Thus implicitly it was under no takedown duty even upon notice, i.e. the legal status of publisher/distributor translates into the notice-and-takedown duty. However, Google had in fact blocked specific URLs that it had been given by the claimants on google.co.uk (but not on other Google sites, nor the specific words complained of, which would have resulted in significant overblocking) and some of Eady J's remarks seem to suggest that Google has after all a limited takedown obligation disconnected from its status as a publisher at common law, even if it was practically impossible and disproportionate to expect Google to block *all* the offending snippets.[174] Generally, the judgment is very much in line with comparable holdings elsewhere. Google was found not liable for the defamatory sites linked to in its search results with snippets in the Spanish case of *Paloma v Google Inc* (2009)[175] in the Swiss case of *Subotic v Google Inc*,[176] the French case of *SARL Publison System v SARL Google France* (2009)[177] and the Dutch case of *Jensen v Google Netherlands* (2009).[178] Whilst defamation claims are *prima facie* within the ambit of the Electronic Commerce Directive, search engines and their 'natural' search results do not generally fall within the immunities; amongst the above states, only a few have extended the Directive's immunities to search engines.[179] Google's natural search facilities are protected under ordinary substantive law, at least for defamation purposes. Alternatively, search engines are protected from intermediary liability under the Defamation Act 2013.

In contrast, Google, as the owner of blogger.com, is more akin to a *hosting* ISP and thus would be more than a mere tool or facilitator, as Parkes J held in *Davison v Habeeb* (2011)[180] – although this case would now be caught by the Defamation Act 2013. However, at the time, Google as the platform operator was held to be 'a publisher at common law, [and thus] following notification it would be unable . . . to establish that it was ignorant of the existence of the defamatory material on Blogger.com, or to rely on the defence at s 1 Defamation Act 1996, exactly as the defendant was unable to rely on that defence in *Godfrey v Demon Internet* . . .'[181] This was also found to be the case in *Tamiz v Google Inc* (2013)[182] again concerning Google's blogger.com site where the Court of Appeal found that by not acting upon a takedown notice, Google 'might be inferred to have associated itself with, or to have made itself responsible for, the continued presence of that material on the

---

171 *Ibid*, [51].
172 *Metropolitan International Schools Ltd*, [55].
173 *Metropolitan International Schools Ltd*, [64].
174 *Metropolitan International Schools Ltd*, [55], [58], [59], [64], see also *Davison v Habeeb & Ors* [2011] EWHC 3031, [29], [46], but contrast to *Richardson v Facebook* [2015] EWHC 3154, [39].
175 (Court of First Instance, Madrid, 13 May 2009).
176 (Court of First Instance, Geneva).
177 (Court of Appeal, Paris, 19 March 2009).
178 (District Court of Amsterdam, 26 April 2007).
179 Spain, Portugal, Hungary, Romania, Bulgaria, Liechtenstein, see *Metropolitan International Schools Ltd v Designtechnica Corp* [2009] EWHC 1765, [98] ff.
180 [2011] EWHC 3031.
181 *Ibid*, [46].
182 [2013] EWCA Civ 68.

blog and thereby to have become a publisher of the material.'[183] Yet, the court ultimately did not allow the appeal because there was insufficient evidence that the blog had been accessed sufficiently between notification and removal to make the damage suffered by the claimant anything other than trivial (see Chapter 2).

Last but not least, in *Richardson v Facebook* (2015)[184] Warby J rejected a defamation claim against Facebook UK for comments on a fake profile page created by an impostor of the claimant. The judge found that it had not been established that Facebook UK (as opposed to Facebook Inc) had 'any form of control over any aspect of the content of the Facebook Service, let alone the Profile'; given the 'absence of an allegation that FBUK had the power or ability to control content, . . . [there was no] proper basis for the attribution of responsibility for publication on the basis of *Byrne v Deane* principles.'[185] Thus a notification of defamatory material to Facebook UK could not by itself create liability upon Facebook UK to remove the content. Importantly, Warby J found that the key to the concept of common law publisher was the power to act (upon gaining knowledge):

> The underlying rationale of the decision in *Byrne v Deane*, that the defendants were responsible for publication, was that they were in control of the notice board and had the power to act so as to remove a posting by a third party which was unauthorised and wrongful.[186]

*Byrne v Deane* (1937)[187] concerned the liability of a golf club for the anonymous defamatory posting on its notice board after it became aware of it; the court recognised responsibility for the publication based on the fact that 'they were entitled as proprietors to remove the trespassing article from the walls.'[188] Thus the emphasis in determining whether an intermediary is or is not a common law publisher and thus under a notice-and-takedown duty, rests on the intermediary's power to act to stop the publication once he or she knows about it. This question of power comes down to whether the intermediary has both the right and the ability to remove the content. Thus, much like in the case of blocking, intermediaries are being involved in the regulatory process based on practical considerations: they are obliged to takedown material, if and *because* they can.

Another important notice-and-takedown duty in the online environment independent of the Electronic Commerce Directive is created by the Data Protection Directive[189] and its interpretation in *Google Spain SL, Google Inc v AEPD* (2014).[190] As discussed elsewhere (see Chapter 2), in this case Mr González's professional activities were prejudiced by the fact that on a Google search of his name the top results referred to an online edition of a Spanish newspaper of more than a decade before, with a notice of the forced sale of his property in attachment proceedings for the recovery of his social security debts. The issue the CJEU was asked to settle was whether, given the information's lawfulness and truth at the source and the passive and automated nature of Google's search activity, Google should be dragged into this dispute. Certainly, in the defamation context, the automation of search queries and the absence of human input was critical in relieving Google of liability in *Metropolitan International Schools Ltd* (2009).[191] Yet, as noted above, the status of an intermediary for one legal purpose is by no means a once-and-for-all decision. For the purposes of data protection, the CJEU held that Google was indeed under an obligation to deindex certain search results in response to

183 *Ibid*, [34].
184 [2015] EWHC 3154.
185 *Ibid*, [39].
186 *Ibid*, [32].
187 [1937] 1 KB 818
188 *Ibid*, 837.
189 95/46/EC.
190 *Google Inc v Agencia Española de Protección de Datos, Mario Costeja González* C-131/12 (CJEU 13 May 2014); *Google Inc v Agencia Española de Protección de Datos, Mario Costeja González* C-131/12 (Opinion of Advocate General, 25 June 2013).
191 *Metropolitan International Schools Ltd (t/a Skillstrain and/or Train2game) v Designtechnica Corp (t/a Digital Trends)* [2009] EWHC 1765, [50].

a person name search.[192] In line with Art 6(1)(c) of the Directive, upon receiving a notice, Google has to take down results that are 'inadequate, irrelevant or no longer relevant, or excessive in relation to the purposes of the processing at issue carried out by the operator of the search engine.'[193] It did not matter that the information at the source was truthful, legal and remained otherwise accessible online. More specifically, the CJEU, first, decided that Google was a 'data controller' even though it does not control the data as *personal* data at the time of collecting it or responding to search queries,[194] with no reference at all to the principle of proportionality it had previously advocated in *Lindqvist* (2003).[195] It then proceeded to consider whether the processing of data was for *legitimate* purposes relative to the fundamental interests of the data subject;[196] and whether the data subject had a right to object 'on compelling *legitimate* grounds relating to his particular situation,'[197] both of which require a balancing of privacy/data protection with, for example, freedom of expression or the right to conduct business. Undeterred, the CJEU observed that search engines provide easy access to personal data and facilitate further dissemination, and then simply asserted that their economic interests could not trump data protection rights and that those data protection rights 'also override, as a general rule, that interest of internet users [in having access to information]'[198] subject to a public interest exception.[199] Indeed, if anything it was Google's ability to 'scale' the huge amount of primary data through its automated search engine that prompted the court to impose liability on it. Importantly, however, this liability is again retrospective, and thus not easily reconcilable with certain prospective duties of 'data controllers'.[200] Comparing the legal treatment of data protection with defamation, it may be argued that if Google can 'judge' personal data claims and take inadequate or irrelevant results down (which is not to say that this is a desirable position), there is no reason why it could not do the same for defamation allegation. Indeed as many defamation claims can be framed as data protection actions, this ruling certainly provides an attractive alternative to claimants whose defamation actions would be frustrated under common law or the Defamation Act 2013.[201] Moreover, from a wider regulatory perspective, it becomes clear that defamation is of a lower priority than data protection or intellectual property; it is one of the few causes of action from which various intermediaries have been almost fully exempted from liability, including a notice-and-takedown obligations, as well as other regulatory involvement regardless of any wrongdoing.

## 'Immunities' under the Electronic Commerce Directive

In light of the above discussion, it is clear that any immunities granted to online intermediaries play a residual role within the wider regulatory landscape: either they are pre-empted by substantive law (e.g. defamation), fall outside their specific ambit (e.g. blocking and other injunctions especially concerning intellectual property claims and criminal law) or are outside the general immunities

---

192 A Orlowski, 'Europe's shock Google privacy ruling: the end of history?' (2014) *The Register*, 14 May.

193 *Google Spain* CJEU, [94].

194 *Google Spain* AG [84]–[87].

195 *Lindqvist* C-101/01 [2003] ECR I-12971.

196 Art 7(f) of the Directive, as a basis for deciding whether the data subject has a right of rectification, erasure or blocking of data under Art 12(b). See also Art 7(e) which legitimises 'processing . . . carried out in the public interest'.

197 Art 14(a) of the Directive [emphasis added].

198 *Google Spain* CJEU, [81].

199 See *Google Spain* CJEU, [81] depending on 'the nature of the information in question and its sensitivity for the data subject's private life and on the interest of the public in having that information, an interest which may vary, in particular, according to the role played by the data subjected in public life.' Article 29 Working Party, *Guidelines on the Implementation of the CJEU Judgment on 'Google Spain v Agencia Española de Protección de Datos (AEPD) and Mario Costeja González'* C-131/12 (26 November 2014).

200 See *Google Spain* AG, [90], especially in relation to extra-sensitive personal data that are subject to Art 8.

201 Data protection or harassment claims may offer other strategic advantages: *Law Society v Rick Kordowski* [2011] EWHC 3185, discussed in Eddie Craven, 'Case Law: *Law Society v Kordowski*, "Solicitors from Hell" shut down' (2011) *Inforrm's Blog*, 20 December.

regime altogether (e.g. data protection). The EU immunities regime nonetheless helps in the creation of a more unified regulatory/regime (despite strong variation in its national implementation), if only because many of the cases concerning the large online actors come before the CJEU which contributes towards a more pan-European discourse on internet regulation.

Keeping this in mind, in the EU it is Arts 12–14 of the Electronic Commerce Directive[202] that create a staggered regime of immunities for 'intermediary service providers' corresponding to their relative involvement in the primary activities of others. The immunities regime is broadly conceived; it is not restricted to particular legal subject matters, also known as its 'horizontal effect', and thus overlaps with existing immunities (which are framed more narrowly in terms of subject-matter, e.g. defamation, but often more widely in terms of the type of intermediary, i.e. not being restricted to internet intermediaries[203]). In terms of subject-matter, the immunities apply to a wide range of concerns:

> from contractual liability, tortious/extra-contractual liability, penal liability, civil liability or any other type of liability, for all types of activities initiated by third parties, including copyright and trade mark infringements, defamation, misleading advertising, unfair commercial practices, unfair competition, publications of illegal content . . .[204]

So who exactly falls within the immunity of the Directive? At the time of the adoption of the Directive, the debate on intermediary liability centred mainly on ISPs and consequently these provide its main focus. However, the Directive is not confined to them. Although s 4 is titled 'Intermediary service providers', they are not as such defined in the Directive. 'Service providers' are defined as 'any natural or legal person providing an information society service' (Art 2(b)), which is 'any service *normally provided for remuneration*, at a distance, by electronic means and at the individual request of a recipient of services'.[205] Excluded are services not provided 'at distance', such as a consultation of an electronic catalogue on a shop terminal, services not 'by electronic means', such as offline services or non-electronic telephony services, and services not supplied 'at the individual request of a recipient', such as radio and television broadcasting services.[206] Included are activities such as the provision of services that are *not* remunerated by those who receive them (such as social networking sites), and those that provide tools allowing for search, access, and retrieval of data (such as search engines), as well as services consisting of the transmission of information via a communication network (such as telecommunication, cable, and mobile companies).[207] This still leaves a number of intermediaries outside the ambit of the Directive, such as those who provide services that are 'normally *not* for remuneration', such as educational institutions or charities, e.g. Wikipedia. In any event, 'normally' is a rather ambiguous term especially in the online world where entirely new business and non-business models are emerging. In the Cypriot case of *Papasavvas* (2014)[208] the CJEU clarified matters concerning the ambit of the immunities. It was asked whether a daily national newspaper, replicated on two online versions, could take advantage of the immunities for the purposes of a defamation claim. The court held that the immunities in the Directive covered online information services for which the service provider is remunerated, not by the recipient, but

---

202 00/31/EC.

203 For example, s 2(5) of the Obscene Publications Act 1959.

204 European Commission (2011), above n 3, Chapters 6 and 9.

205 Article 2(a) defining 'information society services' by reference to the definition of 'services' in Art 1(2) of Directive 98/34/EC, as amended by Directive 98/48/EC [emphasis added]. See also Recitals 17 and 18.

206 See Annex of the Directive 98/48/EC and Recital 18 of the Electronic Commerce Directive, as well as Art 1(5), which excludes from its scope taxation, data protection, cartel law, the activities of notaries and legal representation in court proceedings, and gambling activities.

207 Recital 18, see also *Papasavvas* C-291/13 (CJEU, 11 September 2014); *Bond van Adverteerders v the Netherlands* C-352/85 [1988] ECR 2085, [16]; *Davison v Habeeb* [2011] EWHC 3031, [55]; *Bunt v Tilley* [2006] EWHC 407, [41]; and *Metropolitan International Schools Ltd v Designtechnica Corp* [2009] EWHC 1765, [82]–[84].

208 C-291/13 (CJEU, 11 September 2014)

by income generated by advertisements posted on a website; and these immunities furthermore were by no means restricted to business – consumer transactions, and also applied to civil litigation, such as for libel. Nonetheless, it did not extend to the newspaper in question. Following *Google AdWords* (2010)[209] (see below) and in light of Recital 42, the Directive only covered information society service providers the activity of which 'is of a merely technical, automatic and passive nature, which implies that that service provider has neither knowledge of nor control over the information which is transmitted or stored.'[210] Consequently, a newspaper publishing company which 'has, in principle, knowledge about the information which it posts and exercises control over that information'[211] was outside the immunities of the Directive. Its focus is on 'technical' intermediaries, rather than those that create and provide content. For further discussion on the intermediaries included in the Directive (see below).

Furthermore, the absence-of-knowledge condition of the host immunity and, to a lesser extent, of the other immunities has also repercussions for the immunity's application and ambit. If an intermediary can only rely on the immunity when it does not know or is unaware of the activity in question, the section creates a mental element and is thereby relevant to strict liability offences/wrongs – that is, those that do not already have a mental element, such as defamation,[212] or contempt of court. It would appear to be superfluous for most criminal offences, because they require a *mens rea*. For example, the offence of inciting religious or homophobic hatred may be committed by an intermediary when it 'publishes or distributes written material which is threatening . . . if [it] *intends* thereby to stir up religious hatred or hatred on the grounds of sexual orientation'.[213] Where the intermediary has the state of mind to satisfy the element of intention, it would also have to have the knowledge to disentitle it from the immunity. Where, on the other hand, the intermediary is unaware of the illegal activity, it could not be liable for the offence and thus would not need the immunities. For this reason, the Electronic Commerce Directive (Hatred against Persons on Religious Grounds or the Grounds of Sexual Orientation) Regulations 2010,[214] which reaffirm the immunities of the Directive, would have been unnecessary. The same applies to the exemption in the Electronic Commerce Directive (Terrorism Act 2006) Regulations 2007[215] that neutralises ss 1 and 2 of the Terrorism Act 2006. Beyond strict liability wrongs, the Directive also captures negligence-based offences or wrongs, as any notice-and-takedown duty must be read in conjunction with the prohibition on monitoring in Art 15(1) which pre-empts any attempt to read the knowledge/awareness requirement in Art 14 as a constructive knowledge requirement. Thus the intermediary need not know whatever it could have known upon monitoring the hosted material, but negligently failed to do. Therefore any negligence-based offence or wrong based on a reasonable duty to keep an eye on hosted material is defused through Art 15.[216]

Finally, as foreshadowed in the discussion on the regulatory involvement of intermediaries, the Directive caters for the possibility – alongside the immunities – that a court or administrative authority may order an intermediary 'to terminate or prevent an infringement' and, in the case of hosting, also to disable access to the hosted content (Arts 12(3), 13(2), and 14(3)). For example, Art 14(3) reads:

> This Article shall not affect the *possibility* for a court or administrative authority, in accordance with Members States' legal systems, of requiring the service provider to *terminate* or *prevent*

---

209 *Google AdWords* C-236/08, C-237/08 and C-238/08 (CJEU, 23 March 2010), [113], discussed below.
210 *Papasavvas* C-291/13 (CJEU, 11 September 2014), [41].
211 *Ibid*, [45].
212 Note, many strict liability torts or offences incorporate a mental element in the defence. For example, s 1 of the Defamation Act 1996.
213 Section 29C(1) of the Public Order Act 1986, inserted by the Racial and Religious Hatred Act 2006 [emphasis added]. See also Obscene Publications Act 1959, s 2(5).
214 Still awaiting parliamentary approval.
215 SI 2007/1550.
216 For example, s 2(1)(c) of the Terrorism Act 2006 refers to recklessness as the sufficient *mens rea* for terrorist publications.

an infringement, nor does it affect the possibility for Members States of establishing procedures governing the removal or disabling of access to information.

[Emphasis added]

This explains why the above regulatory measures do not fall foul of the Directive, and courts have
been able to require intermediaries to identify wrongdoers, block access to identified illegal sites,
report on specified criminal activity and take down illegal content, but not to engage in general
monitoring. It must be stressed that the 'possibilities' referred to in Art 14(3) need to be grounded
in national legal provisions, as Arts 12–14 do not create the bases for such injunctive relief, but
simply allow for the retention of existing ones.

## Access providers

The first two immunities under the Directive for 'mere conduits' attach to those 'information society services' that consist only of the transmission of communications (and of 'caching' of data, via
proxy servers, for the purpose of making the transmission more efficient). These immunities run
roughly parallel to the immunities of traditional common carriers, such as telephone companies or
the postal service.[217] Article 12 deals with 'mere conduits' involved either in the 'transmission . . . of
information provided by a recipient of their service' (for example, an email sent by a subscriber)
or the 'provision of access to a communication network' (that is, internet access). Such conduits are
immune from any liability in civil or criminal law for the information transmitted – as long as they
neither initiate the transmission nor select the receiver of the transmission, nor select or modify
the information contained in the transmission (Art 12(1)). So as long as the conduit does not get
involved in the message, either its substance or the communicating parties, other than simply passing it on, the provider incurs no liability for damages. And this is so even if the transmission or the
provision of access requires 'the automatic, intermediate and transient storage of the information
transmitted' if such storage is solely for the purpose of transmission and not longer than reasonably necessary (Art 12(2)). Furthermore, under Art 12(3), the 'immunity' does 'not affect the possibility for a court or administrative authority, in accordance with Member States' legal systems, of
requiring the service provider to terminate or prevent an infringement'.

Article 13 also deals with the temporary storage by relieving intermediaries from liability
for cached data (that is, 'the automatic, intermediate and temporary storage of . . . information,
performed for the sole purpose of making more efficient the information's onward transmission'),
provided that:

(a)   the provider does not modify the information (i.e. no editorial input);
(b)   the provider complies with conditions on access to the information (e.g. age verification
      requirements for adult material, or other passwords);
(c)   the provider complies with rules regarding the updating of the information, specified in
      a manner widely recognised and used by industry (i.e. to prevent out-of-date cached
      information being passed on to end users when the information on the original site has
      been updated);
(d)   the provider does not interfere with the lawful use of technology, widely recognised and
      used by industry, to obtain data on the use of the information (e.g. data as to the number
      of hits on a site for determining advertising rates); and
(e)   the provider acts expeditiously to remove or to disable access to the information it has
      stored upon obtaining *actual knowledge* of the fact that the information at the initial source

---

217 For example, s 90 of the Postal Service Act 2000.

of the transmission has been removed from the network, or access to it has been disabled, or that a court or an administrative authority has ordered such removal or disablement. [Emphasis added]

So an intermediary forgoes its immunity if it either interferes with the cached data (other than what may legitimately occur as part of the process of storing it), or has knowledge of its removal or imminent removal at its source and fails to remove it expeditiously from the cached source. This is different from the notice-and-takedown duty applicable to hosts, because here a notice by the injured party of the alleged wrongfulness of the content cached does not, of itself, trigger the takedown duty,[218] but only notice of its removal at the source.

The primary targets of these two immunities are fixed and mobile ISPs (and backbone providers) in so far as they provide access to the internet, such as BT, Orange, Sky, TalkTalk, or Virgin Media in the UK, as well as WiFi providers. The underlying assumption of the immunities regime is that ISPs may otherwise be exposed to liability and certainly they create certainty in respect of the non-liability. However, the above discussions show that much regulatory involvement of ISPs is independent of pre-existing liability, particularly in the intellectual property context, and elsewhere, e.g. in defamation, ISPs are not liable. Furthermore other 'access' intermediaries that might incur liability are unlikely to be caught by the immunities as their involvement in the communication chain goes beyond the technical, automatic, passive nature, mentioned above.

One question that has arisen is whether a subscriber to a WiFi account may be liable for the illegal activities of those that use it – either on a commercial or private basis. For example, would a household or landlord internet subscriber be considered to have 'authorised' the copyright infringements of others within the household? According to German jurisprudence, the answer is yes, at least for the purposes of injunctive relief and the costs to cover any warning.[219] However, such cases would be outside Art 12 given that it is not a service the household subscriber would 'normally provide for remuneration,' as required by the Electronic Commerce Directive (see above). For a commercial example *Sony Music Entertainment (UK) Ltd v EasyInternet Cafe Ltd* (2003)[220] is instructive. Here a café called EasyInternet supplied customers with access to the internet and, at a cost of £5, made them copies of any recordings downloaded by them. The court rejected the cafe's argument that the illegal copying was involuntary: by copying the customers' files without checking the content, the cafe turned a blind eye to their infringement. Also, because copyright infringement imposes strict liability, there was no need to establish that the cafe knew that the source was copyrighted (see Chapter 4 on Copyright). Although this case arose before the Directive came into force, it is unlikely that EasyInternet would have fallen into the category of 'mere conduit' because its services went beyond internet access. Under Recital 44 of the Electronic Commerce Directive, a service provider 'who deliberately collaborates with one of the recipients of his service in order to undertake illegal acts goes beyond the activities of "mere conduit" or "caching" and as a result cannot benefit from the liability exemptions established for these activities.' Nonetheless, the question remains whether and under what conditions a WiFi provider may be considered a 'mere conduit' under Art 12. This issue is now before the CJEU in *McFadden* (2014)[221] which concerned McFadden's non-password-protected WiFi connection of his sound equipment and events lighting shop which allowed neighbours and passers-by to access the

---

218 This position is also more generous to ISPs than s 1 of the Defamation Act 1996. On the relationship of that defence with the Directive's immunities, see above at n 98.

219 *Haftung des Anschlusshabers für volljährige Tochter,* (LG Düsseldorf, 27 May 2009, 12 O 134/09); *Haftung für Ehemann und Kinder* (OLG Köln, 23 December 2009,Az 6 U 1001/09).

220 *Sony Music Entertainment (UK) Ltd, Sony Music Entertainment Inc, Polydor Ltd, UMG Recordings Inc and Virgin Records Ltd v EasyInternet Cafe Ltd* [2003] EWHC 62 (Ch).

221 C-484/14 (Third Chamber hearing, 9 December 2015). EU Law Radar, '*Case C-484/14, McFadden – a mere conduit?*' (24 November 2014), available online at: http://eulawradar.com/case-c-48414-mcfadden-a-mere-conduit/

internet. He offered this deliberately for free as a way of increasing people's awareness of the presence of his shop and visitors to his shop's home page – it was used to make an illegally copied, piece of music available to an unlimited number of internet users via a file sharing site. As a matter of background, McFadden is a representative of The Pirate Party which seeks to promote free and anonymous access to the internet. The questions referred to the CJEU are, amongst others, whether McFadden's service could qualify as a 'mere conduit' even though the service is not 'normally provided for remuneration': does this refer to the market generally or the particular service provider and if connected with the particular provider does it require some advertising? And more to the crux of the case, does Art 12(1) disallow 'any claims for injunctive relief, damages, and the recovery of warning costs and court fees, incurred in relation to the copyright infringement concerned, against the access provider'? Furthermore, must Art 12(3) (on the availability of injunctions) be read together with Art 12(1) and interpreted as preventing 'a national court from issuing an injunction in proceedings brought against the access provider, whereby the access provider must desist from enabling third parties access via a specific internet connection to a specific copyright-protected work made electronically available on demand on file sharing sites'?[222] Two initial points emerge from these questions: first, WiFi subscribers are prima facie within the scope of Art 12, and, second, even where the service provided is ostensibly 'technical, automatic and passive', this does not mean that the provider is neutral or unknowing in terms of the legality of the activity it facilitates.

## Hosting

The most controversial and potentially most useful of the immunities section under the Directive is Art 14, which deals with 'hosts' of online material. On the intermediary spectrum, this category comes closest to the boundary with content providers, because here the intermediary takes a greater part in the publishing process, which may undermine its status as a (neutral immunity-deserving) middleman, as opposed to a co-creator. Article 14(1) provides:

> (1) Where an information society service is provided that consists of the storage of information provided by a recipient of the service [third party], Member States shall ensure that the service provider [the intermediary] is not liable for the information stored at the request of a recipient of the service [third party], on condition that:
>
> > (a) the provider does not have actual knowledge of illegal activity or information and, *as regards claims for damages*, is not aware of facts or circumstances from which the illegal activity or information is apparent; or
> >
> > (b) the provider, upon obtaining such knowledge or awareness, acts *expeditiously* to remove or to disable access to the information.

This Article imposes a notice-and-takedown duty that requires that the host act *expeditiously* upon obtaining the relevant knowledge. Yet, how long is 'expeditious' and does it allow time for investigating the legitimacy of the takedown request? Under s 3(2) of the Terrorism Act 2006, it is two working days within which an intermediary must respond to a notice by a constable about a terrorist-related publication and block it before it is taken to have endorsed the publication. Yet, given the gravity of terrorist-related publications, it is likely that a longer time limit will be appropriate for less serious wrongs. In the defamation case of *Tamiz v Google Inc* (2013)[223] (discussed above), it took Google over a month after notification to remove the offending article,

---

222 Ibid.
223 [2013] EWCA Civ 68.

which meant that it had forgone its defamation defence. Apart from this, Art 14 creates two main areas of concern: who does it apply to and what level of knowledge is necessary to trigger the takedown obligation?

## Hosts?

Under Art 14(1), a hosting service 'consists of the storage of information provided by a recipient of the service' which means that the content or information is provided by another, not the host itself. Although this provision was also created with ISP hosting content on their servers in mind, it is of course potentially applicable to a wide variety of online intermediaries that store content on behalf of others, such as social networking sites, online marketplaces and cloud computing services, comments sections in online newspapers, blogging platforms, wikis or email service. The problem is that the dividing line between 'hosting' and 'creating' content is not necessarily a sharp one, particularly where content is shaped by the editing tools, structural lay-out and choices of the intermediary service. The problem of such 'co-creations' shines through Art 14(2) which disentitles an intermediary from the immunity, if 'the recipient of the service is acting under the authority or the control of the provider.' This applies to employers vis-à-vis content created by employees, but might arguably also cover all those platforms where the host retains the power to edit the content (e.g. Wikipedia, but see MB, PT and FD v Wikimedia Foundation Inc (2007)[224]) and/or has extensive Terms and Conditions governing the material that may or may not be put on the platform (e.g. Facebook's Community Standards). Such user-generated content is arguably created 'under the control' of the provider. Yet these arguments aside, Art 14 has in fact been applied to interactive sites, blogs, marketplaces and social networks,[225] but not to search engines.[226]

At the European level, some guidance on who may or may not be entitled to the 'host' immunity comes from the trade mark case of *Google AdWords* (2010)[227] joining the cases *Google France v Louis Vuitton Malletier, Google France v Vaiticum Luteciel,* and *Google France v CNRRH, Pierre-Alexis Thonet, Bruno Raboin Tiger*[228] which concerned Google's practice of auctioning – for its sponsored links (i.e. the advertising displayed above and next to the 'natural' results) – keywords identical to registered trade marks to interested parties regardless of their entitlement to use these marks. Not surprisingly, imitators and competitors of the registered owners bought these keywords, and then benefited from the goodwill and brand of the trade mark when, upon a search of the keyword, their Ads would show up. The trade mark owner wanted to stop Google from this selling practice and thereby effectively reserve the sale of those AdWords to themselves. For Google this would have had significant financial repercussions given that for these protected words it would eliminate the auction market. This in opinion of the Advocate General it would:

> create serious obstacles to any system for the delivery of information. Anyone creating or managing such a system would have to cripple it from the start in order to eliminate the mere possibility infringements by third parties . . . How many words would Google have to block from AdWords . . . It is no exaggeration to say that, if Google were to be placed under such an

---

224 (Tribunal de Grande Instance de Paris, 29 October 2007).

225 See Oster, above n 98, 7: *Kaschke v Gray* [2010] EWHC 690; *Tamiz v Google* [2012] EWHC 449; *L'Oréal SA v eBay International AG* C-324/09 (CJEU, 12 July 2011); and *SABAM – Société belge des auteurs, compositeurs et éditeurs SCRL v Netlog NV* C-360/10 (CJEU, 16 February 2012), respectively.

226 *Metropolitan International Schools Ltd (t/a Skillstrain and/or Train2game) v Designtechnica Corp (t/a Digital Trends)* [2009] EWHC 1765, [112].

227 *Google AdWords* C-236/08, C-237/08 and C-238/08 CJEU (23 March 2010). For an English case on the same issue, see *Interflora v Marks and Spencer* [2009] EWHC 1095 (Ch). See also *Rescuecom Corp v Google Inc* 562 F3d 123 (2d Cir April 3, 2009); Out-law.com, 'Rescuecom drops AdWords suit' (2010) Out-law.com, 8 March, available online at: http://www.out-law.com/page-10818

228 (Court of Paris, 4 February 2002); (Court of Appeal of Versailles, 10 March 2005); (Court of Appeal of Versailles, 23 March 2006) respectively.

unrestricted obligation, the nature of the internet and search engines as we know it would change.[229]

In the same spirit, the CJEU upheld the legality of Google's keyword system by finding Google had not itself 'used' the signs identical to the trade mark, which is necessary to show an infringement under Directive 89/104 and Regulation 40/94.[230] A search engine merely allows *its clients to use* signs in question, even where it creates, as Google had, 'the technical conditions necessary for the use of a sign and being paid for that service'.[231] Nonetheless, the CJEU left open the possibility that Google might incur contributory liability under national law, but for this Art 14 might come into play. This would be the case if a national court were to consider that 'the role played by that service provider is neutral, in the sense that its conduct is merely technical, automatic and passive, pointing to a lack of knowledge or control of the data which it stores.'[232] The 'mere facts that the referencing service is subject to payment, that Google sets the payment terms or that it provides general information to its clients' does not deprive it of the Art 14 immunity; but 'the role played by the provider in the drafting of the commercial message which accompanies the advertising link or in the establishment or selection of keywords' may undermine that neutrality.[233] As argued above, this holding is in spirit very different from the more recent *Google France* (2014) right-to-be-forgotten holding, where the court was quick to recognise Google's distinct and major contribution as an intermediary to the eventual harm suffered. Moreover that case concerned Google's 'natural' search results in relation to which it has arguably less and less to gain, at least directly. Following on from this, in *L'Oréal v eBay* (2011)[234] concerning the advertisement and sale of counterfeits on eBay, the CJEU was asked whether eBay might be able to take advantage of the 'hosting' immunity. EBay clearly stores data on behalf of its users but, according to the court, this is in itself not sufficient, if eBay otherwise plays an active role of such a kind as to give it knowledge of, or control over, the data:

> Where, by contrast, the operator has provided assistance which entails, in particular, optimis-
> ing the presentation of the offers for sale in question or promoting those offers, it must be
> considered not to have taken a neutral position between the customer-seller concerned and
> potential buyers but to have played an active role of such a kind as to give it knowledge of, or
> control over, the data relating to those offers for sale.[235]

In other words, where the operator more or less actively facilitates the wrongdoing through the presentation of the offers or their promotion, it is no longer neutral vis-à-vis the legality of the matter and thus outside the 'hosting' immunity. Yet, as the boundary between 'active' and 'passive' is as blurry and arbitrary as the boundary between intermediary and creator/primary actor (which relates to the same issue), the decisions in this area will invariably be strongly influenced by political/policy judgements about the relative economic strength of the competing economic actors and the repercussions of the rulings on the wider online and offline political economies.

---

229 *Google AdWords* C-236/08, C-237/08 and C-238/08 Opinion of Advocate General (22 September 2009), [121], [122]; for a critique, see Lilian Edwards, 'Stuck in "neutral"? Google, AdWords and the E-Commerce Directive Immunities' (2009–10) 20(5) Society for Computers and Law, available online at: http://www.scl.org/site.aspx?i=ed14010
230 Article 5(1)(a) of the Directive 89/104 and, in the case of Community trade marks; Art 9(1) of the Regulation 40/94. See also *Google AdWords* C-236/08, C-237/08 and C-238/08 (CJEU, 23 March 2010), [57]; and *Google AdWords* C-236/08, C-237/08 and C-238/08 Opinion of Advocate General (22 September 2009), [123].
231 Ibid, [57].
232 Ibid, [114].
233 Ibid, [116], [118]; see also *Papasavvas* C-291/13 (CJEU, 11 September 2014).
234 *L'Oréal SA v eBay International AG* C-324/09 (CJEU, 12 July 2011).
235 Ibid, [116].

## Knowledge?

The intermediary's level of prior knowledge about the content it 'mediates' goes towards establishing whether it is 'host' or more than that, i.e. a content creator. Where the required level of knowledge is not present, thus entitling the intermediary to the immunity, the immunity is lost if subsequently the intermediary gains the requisite knowledge and fails to act upon it, i.e. expeditiously remove or disable access to the information. Article 14(1)(a) provides two different levels of knowledge: either 'actual knowledge of illegal activity or information' or 'as regards claims for damages, awareness of facts or circumstances from which the illegal activity or information is apparent.' Whilst these levels of knowledge are broadly alternative heads, the latter head (being more onerous to the intermediary) is restricted to civil actions for damages and not, for example, available in the criminal context. Although both heads are at first sight straightforward, they have created a fair amount of difficulty.

To start with, what depth of knowledge concerning the illegal activity triggers the takedown duty: is it enough that the activity appears to be illegal on its facts or must it to appear illegal taking into account possible defences? The judge in *Bunt v Tilley* (2006) held that the host's takedown duty (or liability) is only triggered if it is in possession of information which would enable it to judge 'the strength or weakness of available defences.'[236] But even in possession of all the relevant information, it is still a hard call for the intermediary to make a final judgement, which, as argued, is also beset with various accountability problems. For example, under reg 7 of Electronic Commerce Directive (Terrorism Act 2006) Regulations 2007[237] the intermediary is required to judge whether the content is 'unlawfully terrorism-related information'. In light of this, Spain along with some other states,[238] insists on a legal declaration by a competent authority as the takedown trigger:

> The service provider shall be deemed to have the actual knowledge . . . when a competent body has declared that the information is unlawful or ordered that it be removed or that access to it be disabled.[239]

This means that intermediaries need not second-guess the illegality of the hosted content. Neither do they need to act overcautiously and remove the allegedly illegal content out of fear of liability – allegations which may be made by competitors of the alleged wrongdoer or by actors seeking to silence their legitimate critics.[240] In a study concerning the notice-and-takedown duty under US law, Google stated that 57 per cent of notices sent to it and demanding removal of links in the index were sent by competing businesses.[241] The downside of the Spanish interpretation is that it defeats the point of the notice-and-takedown duty – that is to get quick extrajudicial results and thereby minimise the damage caused. Also, the Spanish interpretation makes the condition of knowledge redundant because the intermediary's duty is effectively triggered by the competent body's order.

A further difficulty is caused by the 'awareness' head of knowledge: when could an intermediary be said to be 'aware of facts or circumstances from which the illegal activity or information is apparent'? Is this satisfied by a general awareness that illegal content is being hosted or does it require an awareness of the specific content that is said to be illegal? The answer cannot be a very general awareness of illegality as a trigger for the takedown action, as this would impose a general

---

236 *Bunt v Tilley* [2006] EWHC 407, [72]; but see also *CG v Facebook Ireland Ltd* [2015] NIQB 11, [96].
237 Terrorism Act 2006, s 3(7); and Electronic Commerce Directive (Terrorism Act 2006) Regulations 2007, SI 2007/1550.
238 European Commission (2011), above n 3, 19f.
239 Article 17 of Spanish Law 34/2002; discussed in *Metropolitan International Schools Ltd v Designtechnica Corp* [2009] EWHC 1765, [99]–[100].
240 Contrast with s 512(f) of the US Digital Millennium Copyright Act of 1998, which penalises frivolous and illegitimate takedown demands (discussed below).
241 Jennifer M Urban and Laura Quilter, *Efficient Process or 'Chilling Effects'? Takedown Notices under Section 512 of the Digital Millennium Copyright Act: Summary Report* (2005) Berkeley, CA: University of Southern California/University of California, available online at: https://www.law.berkeley.edu/files/Chilling_Effects_Report.pdf

monitoring duty on the intermediary as a defensive action to identify the specific wrongdoing, but neither can it be a very specific awareness as this would effectively amount to 'actual knowledge'. The question as to where on the general-specific spectrum Art 14 falls, was addressed in some detail by CJEU in *L'Oréal v eBay* (2011),[242] where it went as far as possible – considering the Art 15 prohibition on general monitoring duties – in pushing the onus on the intermediary to do its bit to identify wrongdoing. It imposed an expectation that, when short of actual knowledge but still aware of certain facts or circumstances, the intermediary has to act as a 'diligent economic operator' to identify the illegality:[243]

> Moreover, if the rules set out in Article 14(1)(a) of Directive 2000/31 are not to be rendered redundant, they must be interpreted as covering every situation in which the provider concerned becomes aware, in one way or another, of such facts or circumstances. The situations thus covered include, in particular, that in which the operator of an online marketplace uncovers, as the result of an investigation undertaken on its own initiative, an illegal activity or illegal information, as well as a situation in which the operator is notified of the existence of such an activity or such information. In the second case, although such a notification admittedly cannot automatically preclude the exemption from liability provided for in Article 14 of Directive 2000/31, given that notifications of allegedly illegal activities or information may turn out to be insufficiently precise or inadequately substantiated, the fact remains that such notification represents, as a general rule, a factor of which the national court must take account when determining, in the light of the information so transmitted to the operator, whether the latter was actually aware of facts or circumstances on the basis of which a diligent economic operator should have identified the illegality.[244]

By implication, the takedown obligation (or liability) is not dependent on the existence of a fully ledged notification, and the need for investigations by the host may be triggered even in the absence of a specific and substantiated notification, or even in its total absence. Despite this ruling, it would appear that when presented with inadequate notices, courts are reluctant to find in favour of the claimants on the basis that the intermediary should have done its own investigations. In *Davison v Habeeb* (2011) the court held that the defendant had not sufficient actual or constructive knowledge to trigger the takedown duty where, via the notification, it was 'faced with conflicting claims . . . between which it was in no position to adjudicate.'[245]

Although the Directive does not lay down any rules with respect to the notice, according to Recital 46 Member States are free to establish 'specific requirements which must be fulfilled expeditiously prior to the removal or disabling of information.' In the UK, reg 22 of the Electronic Commerce (EC Directive) Regulations 2002 provides that to determine whether the host had 'actual knowledge', the court must take into account all relevant matters, including:

(a)  whether a service provider has received a notice through a means of contact made available [by the intermediary] . . ., and

(b)  the extent to which any notice includes –

    (i)  the full name and address of the sender of the notice;

    (ii)  details of the location of the information in question; and

    (iii)  details of the unlawful nature of the activity or information in question.

---

242  *L'Oréal SA v eBay International AG* C-324/09 (CJEU, 12 July 2011), [118]–[124].
243  Ibid, [120].
244  Ibid, [121]–[122].
245  *Davison v Habeeb* [2011] EWHC 3031, [68]; see also *Kaschke v Gray* [2010] EWHC 690, [93]–[103].

One issue concerning the adequacy of the notice and the resultant extent of the takedown duty is whether the notice must specify the exact URL and, if so, whether the intermediary's duty extends only to that particular URL. As shown, in L'Oréal v eBay (2011)[246] the court held that the intermediary was under some prospective/preventative duty which, by implication, means that its duty is not discharged simply by responding to the specified URL. Similarly, in the Northern Ireland case of CG v Facebook Ireland (2015)[247] concerning the online harassment of a convicted sex offender, the court – in a harassment, negligence and data protection claim – held that Facebook's duty to take down the harassing material was not dependent on the claimant providing a specific URL for each offending post. It had requisite knowledge/awareness in three separate ways:

(1)   by virtue of related litigation;
(2)   by virtue of that litigation combined with letters sent to its solicitors; and
(3)   by virtue of those letters combined with some elementary investigation of the profile page and/or the internet.[248]

## Navigation

An important question on the extent of the above immunities is whether they also extend to online intermediaries that facilitate 'navigating' the internet, in particular search engines and, to a lesser extent today, hyperlinkers. Like the above intermediaries, they facilitate online communications and tend to have very limited interest in, or knowledge of, the actual place where they 'take' end-users. Equally, as shown above, they have been subjected to regulatory duties based on the fact that they produce results – with Google's data protection deindexing obligations since Google Spain (2014)[249] being the most high-profile example. As for the above immunities, there is a general consensus that none of them accommodate search engines easily or at all.[250] They are too active for being 'mere conduits' in Art 12, as they 'select . . . the information contained in the transmission' (i.e. it selects the search results) and also contribute towards 'select[ing] the receiver of the transmission' (i.e. top ranking are more likely to be the receivers).[251] Similarly, search engines make no easy fit for 'hosts' given that the information storage that occurs as part of providing the search facility does not occur 'at the request of a recipient of the service' (i.e. those who conduct the search). These difficulties are due to the fact that at the time the Directive was drafted search engines played a relatively minor role in cyberspace. Still some EU Member States, although not the UK, have specifically extended the immunities to them.[252] Also in Google AdWords (2010), discussed above, the CJEU held that a search engine may fall into the Art 14 immunity in respect of its AdWords, provided that a national court makes a finding of 'neutrality'. This means, first, that the liability position of search engines and hyperlinkers is more uncertain than in respect of other intermediary and definitely not unified across Europe; second, the answers to their liability entirely depend on the substantive law and any defences they may have under it; and third, those answers will vary not just from one state to state, but also from one legal area to another.

This is not the place to explore this liability for linking in-depth, but a few cases help to show that the themes discussed above are also relevant to 'navigators'. Issues of liability for navigation intermediaries have also been resolved by reference to their level of knowledge and control. What

---

246   L'Oréal SA v eBay International AG C-324/09 (CJEU, 12 July 2011), [118]–[124].
247   [2015] NIQB 11, [95].
248   Ibid, [94].
249   Google Inc v Agencia Española de Protección de Datos, Mario Costeja González C-131/12 (CJEU, 13 May 2014).
250   Metropolitan International Schools Ltd (t/a Skillstrain and/or Train2game) v Designtechnica Corp (t/a Digital Trends) [2009] EWHC 1765, [84], [92], [112].
251   Art 13 does not fit either search engines or hyperlinkers because the transmitted information is not provided by the recipient of the service, who would be the person using the search engine or clicking the hyperlink.
252   Member States have variously extended Arts 12, 13, or 14 to search engines and hyperlinkers.

is noticeable about judgments in this field, however, is how protective courts have been of hyperlinkers in the name of safeguarding a vital mechanism for the accessibility of cyberspace; and in many ways search engines are an automated and large-scale version of hyperlinkers which select links individually. The latter's legal treatment has often been more akin to 'mere conduits' than to 'hosts', with them being relieved of all liability, but often with the proviso that they were in no way engaged in encouraging third party wrongdoing.

An early example of hyperlinker liability for the content linked to is the French case of *Yahoo Inc v LICRA & UEJF* (2000)[253] in which the French subsidiary of Yahoo! Inc was found liable in a civil nuisance/public order action for providing a link to the US Yahoo page on which third parties had offered Nazi memorabilia contrary to French criminal law. The French subsidiary's failing consisted simply in linking to a site with illegal content, although in this case the external site was hardly 'external' because it belonged to the same Yahoo empire. Therefore, more knowledge and control over the linked page than would normally be present in the case of truly external links could be assumed. In the Canadian defamation case of *Crookes v Wikimedia Foundation Inc* (2008),[254] the lower court held that a provider of a hyperlink is not liable for the defamatory content of the linked *external* page. According to the court, a hyperlink does not constitute a 'republication' of the defamatory site and is comparable to a footnote:

> A hyperlink is like a footnote or a reference to a website in printed material such as a newsletter. The purpose of a hyperlink is to direct the reader to additional material from a different source. The only difference is the ease with which a hyperlink allows the reader, with a simple click of the mouse, to instantly access the additional material.[255]

The footnote analogy was qualified on appeal:

> I would not accept the footnote analogy to be a complete answer to the question of whether a hyperlink constitutes publication. More significant factors would include the prominence of the hyperlink, any words of invitation or recommendation to the reader associated with the hyperlink, the nature of the materials which it is suggested may be found at the hyperlink (for example, if the hyperlink obviously refers to a scandalous, or obscene publication), the apparent significance of the hyperlink in relation to the article as a whole, and a host of other factors dependent on the facts of a particular case.[256]

However, the Supreme Court of Canada in 2011 affirmed the ruling by being even more strongly defensive of hyperlinks as mere content-neutral conduits:

> Communicating something is very different from merely communicating that something exists or where it exists. The former involves dissemination of the content, and suggests control over both the content and whether the content will reach an audience at all, while the latter does not. Even where the goal of the person referring to a defamatory publication is to expand that publication's audience, his or her participation is merely ancillary to that of the initial publisher: with or without the reference, the allegedly defamatory information has already been made available to the public by the initial publisher or publishers' acts.[257]

---

253 *LICRA & UEJF v Yahoo! Inc & Yahoo France* Tribunal de Grande Instance de Paris (22 May 2000), aff'd in *LICRA & UEJF v Yahoo! Inc & Yahoo France* Tribunal de Grande Instance de Paris (20 November 2000).

254 [2008] BCSC 1424, aff'd in *Crookes v Newton* [2009] BCCA 392; and *Crookes v Newton* [2011] 3 SCR 269.

255 *Crookes v Wikimedia Foundation Inc* [2008] BCSC 1424, [29] also at [34]: 'It is not my decision that hyperlinking can never make a person liable for the contents of the remote site. For example, if Mr. Newton had written "the truth about Wayne Crookes is found *here*" and "here" is hyperlinked to the specific defamatory words, this might lead to a different conclusion.'

256 *Crookes v Newton* [2009] BCCA 392, [60].

257 *Crookes v Newton* [2011] 3 SCR 269, [26].

In response one may observe, first, that the court was highly cognisant of the central role played by hyperlinks on the internet: 'Without hyperlinks, the web would be like a library without a catalogue: full of information, but with no sure means of finding it.'[258] Second, the ruling is broadly in line with the position of search engines under English common law (see above). Finally, as also noted above, in *Google Spain* (2014)[259] concerning data protection duties of search engines, the fact that something was already accessible online did not stop the CJEU from recognising an intermediary's potential in significantly increasing the scale of that accessibility and from imposing responsibility based on this.

The discussion about hyperlinkers in defamation echoes some of the extensive and ongoing debate and reasoning of the same issue in the copyright context. For example, the CJEU in *Svensson* (2013)[260] held that providing a link to copyrighted material is *prima facie* a restricted act of 'communicating works to the public,'[261] but to incur liability it has to be shown that the links were directed to a 'new public', i.e. 'a public that was not taken into account by the copyright holders when they authorised the initial communication to the public.'[262] As in the particular case the protected articles were freely accessible to the public on the original site, the hyperlink could not in fact amount to a new act of communication to the public. However, this does not apply:

> where a clickable link makes it possible for users of the site on which that link appears to circumvent restrictions put in place by the site on which the protected work appears in order to restrict public access . . . [or] where the work is no longer available to the public on the site on which it was initially communicated or . . . only to a restricted public'.[263]

Whether the ruling applies to a hyperlinker who links to an infringing site and whether this depends on a hyperlinker's actual or constructive knowledge about the third party infringement, or on the scale of the facilitation, is still to be decided by the CJEU in *Sanoma Playboy v GS Media* (2015).[264] The Federal Court of Germany in *Heise Publishing* (2010)[265] decided that a hyperlink to a copyright infringing site (that provided access to circumvention software) was protected, as part of news reporting, by freedom of expression and the press, and it did not matter that Heise knew of the illegal nature of the linked-to site – in fact Heise had made it clear to the readers that the site was illegal. Importantly, the link was not simply designed to make access to the infringing site easier, but was an integral part of the journalistic coverage, i.e. providing its source and additional information. But for these justifying circumstances a link may well expose the hyperlinker to liability. Similarly, in an unfair competition claim, the same court in *Schöner Wetten* (2004)[266] held that an online newspaper was not exposed to liability for providing, in the course of reporting, a link to a foreign gambling site not licensed in Germany and therefore illegal. The link was provided in the

---

258 Ibid, [34], quoting Matthew Collins, *The Law of Defamation and the Internet*, 3rd edn, OUP, 2010, [5.42].

259 *Google Inc v Agencia Española de Protección de Datos, Mario Costeja González* C-131/12 (CJEU 13 May 2014).

260 C-466/12 (CJEU, 13 February 2013).

261 Art 3(1) of the Information Society Directive 2001/29.

262 *Svensson* C-466/12 (CJEU, 13 February 2013), [24]. 'Deep-linking' is another issue that has arisen here, see e.g. In *Verlagsgruppe Handelsblatt v Paperboy* (BGH, 17 July 2003, I ZR 259/00) where the German Federal Court exonerated the news search engine paperboy.de of all liability in respect of deep links to the claimant's articles, which deprived the claimant of advertising revenue from its front page. The court reasoned that it was up to the claimant to take up technical measures to prevent deep-linking or to structure its site in such a way that advertising was not limited to the front page, and was at pains to stress the importance of retaining the efficiency of the internet; in its opinion, the internet is all about finding information quickly and without detours – and search facilities to freely accessible material were at the heart of that.

263 Ibid, [31] and Arts 6 and 7 of the Information Society Directive 2001/29. See also, *C More Entertainment AB v Linus Sandberg* C-279/13 (26 March 2015) concerning the rights of broadcasters under Art 3(2) of the Information Services Directive 2001/29.

264 C-160/15 (reference by the Dutch Supreme Court, 3 April 2015).

265 (BGH, 14 October 2010, I ZR 191/08); see also the Norwegian case of *Phonefile v Startsiden* (District Court of Oslo, 29 October 2003), in which an internet portal was held not liable for the provision of links to file sharing programs on the basis that the sites could be found anyway and that it could be used for non-infringing purposes.

266 (BGH, 1 April 2004, I ZR 317/01).

course of an ordinary newspaper story and designed not to advertise or encourage such gambling, but to provide a complete story. Commenting on a takedown duty, the court held that it may arise on notice by a third party – taking into account whether the site is already easily accessible through other sources, as well as the more general public need for hyperlinks as an organisational tool in information wealth of the internet. The emphasis on the functions and motivations of the linker, other than encouraging wrongdoing, makes *Heise* and *Schöner Wetten* reconcilable with those judgments where the providers of links to piracy content were found to have 'authorised' or 'encouraged' copyright infringement via the provision of links as, for example, in *Twentieth Century Fox Film Corporation v Newzbin Ltd* (2010),[267] concerning Newzbin's activity of searching and indexing Usenet content and thereby providing its members with a facility that was used mainly for the unauthorised downloading of infringing copies of films. So the act of hyperlinking cannot be categorised, once and for all, as those of a 'mere conduit', but has to be scrutinised, much like the act of hosting third party content and even internet access provision, as to the relative 'neutrality' or involvement of the provider *vis-à-vis* the third party activity.

# US intermediary immunities

## Communications Decency Act of 1996

The USA takes a far more generous position towards online intermediaries than Europe, with the exception of some criminal law (federal criminal law) and intellectual property law. The intermediary friendly US position arises by virtue of the immunity in s 230 of the Communications Decency Act of 1996,[268] which was enacted to encourage self-regulation and monitoring of sites (consistent with the general US regulatory preference for the self-regulation of the internet and minimal government intervention). It was designed to neutralise the case of *Stratton Oakmont, Inc v Prodigy Services Co* (1995)[269] which imposed liability on an online intermediary on the basis of its self-regulatory monitoring efforts. Section 230(c), headed 'Protection for "Good Samaritan" blocking and screening of offensive material', states:

**(1)  Treatment of publisher or speaker**

*No provider or user* of an interactive computer service shall be *treated as the publisher or speaker of any information* provided by another information content provider.

[Emphasis added]

**(2)  Civil liability**

No provider or user of an interactive computer service shall be held liable on account of –

(A)   any action voluntarily taken in good faith to restrict access to or availability of material that the provider or user considers to be obscene, lewd, lascivious, filthy, excessively violent, harassing, or otherwise objectionable, whether or not such material is constitutionally protected; or

(B)   any action taken to enable or make available to information content providers or others the technical means to restrict access to material described in paragraph (1).

---

267  [2010] EWHC 608.
268  Title 47 of the US Code. See also Brandy Jennifer Glad, 'Determining what constitutes creation or development of content under the Communications Decency Act' (2004) 34 Sw U L Rev 258; Bryan J Davis, 'Untangling the "publisher" versus "information content provider" paradox of section 230: Toward a rational application of the Communications Decency Act in defamation suits against Internet service providers' (2002) 32 N M L Rev 75.
269  1995 WL 323710 (NY Sup Ct 1995).

Like the Electronic Commerce Directive, this immunity is 'horizontal' in that it applies across various legal subject-matters (e.g. defamation, negligence, harassment, but also the sale and distribution of child abuse images, privacy infringements or fraudulent information). Unlike the Directive it excludes from its scope liability under federal criminal law and intellectual property law.[270] Also importantly, unlike the Directive, the immunity is absolute in the sense that it is not coupled with a notice-and-takedown duty (see below).

Furthermore, courts have taken a very broad view of which intermediaries are entitled to the immunity and included 'hosting services, e-mail service providers, auction websites, general web shops, personal home pages, company websites, dating websites, chat rooms and internet access points . . . [being] allowed to make (minor) alterations to the [third party] information.'[271] It also extends to users of such services who may repost infringing content.[272] One challenge to the ambit of s 230 went to the heart of its self-regulatory agenda and concerned the question of whether s 230 relieves intermediaries of liability only as a publisher, or also of the lesser liability, at least for defamation law, as publisher/distributor. Put differently, do intermediaries have to remove objectionable content when put on notice of such content, which is a normal distributor's duty, or are they also exempt from that duty? Going further, should intermediaries that make no monitoring efforts at all also benefit from the exemption? In *Zeran v America Online Inc* (1997)[273] s 230 was interpreted widely: it protects intermediaries in respect of third-party defamatory content from the liability both as a publisher and distributor. The difference between the two is that a publisher is presumed to know what it is publishing and is therefore liable even in the absence of actual knowledge of the objectionable content, while a distributor's liability only arises upon specific notice. According to the court, everyone in the publishing process is a 'publisher', and this includes distributors; the legal distinction between the two merely 'signifies that different standards of liability may be applied within the larger publisher category.'[274] From a policy perspective, the court reasoned that s 230 immunity should extend to distributor liability because providers that monitor content are likely to be considered distributors and thus the threat of distributor liability might discourage such efforts. But as the case law shows, monitoring turns intermediaries legally into publishers, not distributors.[275] In any event, the court reasoned correctly that knowledge of the wrongdoing transforms the 'distributor' in law into the 'publisher' which is the very person to whom s 230 refers. Thus excluding distributors from the immunity if they have notice of the wrongdoing would lead to the paradoxical outcome of imposing liability on the intermediary for 'assuming the role for which § 230 specifically proscribes liability – the publisher role'.[276] This, however, is merely an issue of semantics: there is no need to hold that a 'distributor' becomes a 'publisher' upon notice, because one can simply say that a distributor becomes liable upon notice. The effect of *Zeran* is that the s 230 exemption is not coupled with a notice-and-takedown duty; the wider effect is that while monitoring turns the intermediary into an immune 'publisher', taking no action at all even where there is notice of wrongdoing means that the intermediary is an immune 'distributor' – thus self-regulatory monitoring is not encouraged:

> If this reading is sound, then § 230(c) as a whole makes ISPs indifferent to the content of information they host or transmit: whether they do . . . or do not . . . take precautions, there is no liability . . . As precautions are costly, not only in direct outlay but also in lost revenue from the

---

270 Section 230(e)(1) and (e)(2), respectively.
271 Europan Commission, above n 3, 32; see also H Holland, 'In defense of online intermediary immunity: facilitating communities of modified exceptionalism' (2007) 56 Kansas Law Review 101.
272 *Barrett v Roenthal* 146 P3d 510 (Cal 2006).
273 129 F3d 327 (4th Cir 1997).
274 *Ibid*, 332.
275 See above.
276 *Zeran* at 394.

filtered customers, ISPs may be expected to take the do-nothing option and enjoy immunity . . . Yet § 230(c) . . . bears the title 'Protection for "Good Samaritan" blocking and screening of offensive material', hardly an apt description if its principal effect is to induce ISPs to do nothing about the distribution of indecent and offensive materials via their services. Why should a law designed to eliminate ISPs' liability to the creators of offensive material end up defeating claims by the victims of tortious or criminal conduct?[277]

For this reason, in *Grace v eBay* (2004)[278] the court refused to follow *Zeran* given that doing so 'would eliminate potential liability for providers and users even if they made no effort to control objectionable content, and therefore would neither promote the development of technologies to accomplish that task nor remove disincentives to that development as Congress intended'.[279] So eBay was not protected by s 230 in respect of its failure to remove libellous feedback after notice. Ultimately, it avoided liability by virtue of its release of liability clause in its user agreement.[280] However, *Grace* was later 'depublished', and therefore could no longer be considered by later courts.[281] Despite its obvious deficiencies in argument and effect, *Zeran* has been followed in *Ben Ezra, Weinstein & Co Inc v America Online* (2000),[282] *Green v America Online* (2003)[283] and *Austin v Crystal Tech Web Hosting* (2005).[284]

A second challenge to the ambit of s 230 arises from the requirement that the wrongful information must have been provided 'by another information content provider', who is defined as 'any person or entity that is responsible, in whole or part, for the creation or development of information provided through the internet or any other interactive computer service' (s 230(f)(3)). Thus, an intermediary is liable for its own speech[285] (i.e. primary actor) and for third-party speech to which it made a material contribution (i.e. contributory actor). For example, in *Fair Housing Council of San Fernando Valley v Roommates.Com* (2008)[286] the Ninth Circuit court found that Roommates.com may be a contributory content creator – by virtue of the design and question in its questionnaires, which sought, for example, information about the preferred sexual orientation of the prospective roommate – and therefore not immunised under s 230 from liability for a discrimination claim under the Fair Housing Act of 1968. Although s 230 recognises the notion of a contributory wrongdoer who falls outside the immunity, it defines 'contributory' narrowly. The issue is framed in terms of when an intermediary 'helps to develop the unlawful content'.[287] This does not occur when, for example, a search engine allows a query for a 'white roommate' or a website operator edits user-generated content by correcting spelling, removing obscenity, or even shortening it,[288] but it does occur when an intermediary, such as Roommates.com, provides users with discriminatory choices on drop-down menus and checking-off boxes.[289] Having said that, in *Fair Housing*

---

277  *Doe v GTE Corp* 347 F3d 655, 660 (2003).

278  16 Cal Rptr 3d 192 (Cal App Ct 2004); see also *Barrett v Rosenthal* 9 Cal Rptr 3d 142 (App 2004).

279  *Ibid*, [3.c].

280  See also above. Notions of contracts can also work to the disadvantage of intermediaries and override s 230 immunity otherwise available. In *Barnes v Yahoo! Inc* 565 F3d 560 (9th Cir, 7 May 2009), amended by 570 F3d 1096 (9th Cir, 22 June 2009), Yahoo could not rely on the s 230 immunity because one of Yahoo's employees had promised the plaintiff to take down a false website profile and then failed to act upon that promise. Yahoo was thereby estopped from reliance on the immunity.

281  *Austin v Crystal Tech Web Hosting* 125 P3d 389 (2005), in which the court noted that because the Californian Supreme Court had granted review of the case, it was thereby 'depublished', which in turn meant that the decision could not be cited to the court and the court could not consider it.

282  206 F3d 980 (10th Cir 2000).

283  318 F3d 465 (3rd Cir 2003).

284  125 P3d 389 (Arz Crt App, 2005).

285  *Universal Communication System v Lycos* 478 F3d 413 (1st Cir 2007).

286  *Fair Housing Council of San Fernando Val. v Roommates.Com* 521 F3d 1157 (9th Cir 2008); following *Batzel v Smith* 333 F3d 1018 (9th Cir 2003); see also *Shiamili v Real Estate Group of New York Inc* 892 NYS 2d 52 (NY App Div 2009).

287  *Ibid*, 1167–1170.

288  *Ibid*, 1169.

289  *Ibid*, 1180–1186. For another US case on the issue of inducement of illegalities, see *Dart v Craigslist Inc* 665 F Supp 2d 961 (ND Ill 2009).

Council of San Fernando Valley v Roommates.com LLC (2012)[290] the same court held that the Fair Housing Act of 1968 did not actually cover shared living quarters, as facilitated by Roommates.com and thus on substance Roommates.com had not violated the law.

Thinking particularly about individual victims of online libel, abuse and harassment, the total immunisation of intermediary from any liability, including takedown duties, may leave those who have suffered significant harm because of online smear campaigns without any remedy in those cases where the primary wrongdoers cannot be identified or where the wrongful content has been 'multiplied' by many actors and across numerous sites.

## Intellectual property rights

The blanket immunity created in s 230 does not apply to liability under intellectual property law which in itself suggests the greater value attached to these property rights. Here both substantive law and, for copyright, the separate immunities regime of the Digital Millennium Copyright Act of 1998 create firm notice-and-takedown duties on intermediaries.

The position under the substantive law on trade marks and copyright is not dissimilar to that of Europe. For example, in *Tiffany (NJ) Inc v eBay Inc* (2010)[291] the Second Circuit court found that eBay was absolved of contributory trade mark infringements for the sale of counterfeit Tiffany goods on its site, in the absence of specific knowledge of the particular counterfeit listing; a generalised knowledge of infringing activity on its site was not sufficient to affix eBay with (constructive) knowledge, sufficient to implicate it in the third party wrongdoing. Thus, broadly in line with the CJEU judgment in *L'Oréal v eBay* (2011),[292] the onus is not on eBay to monitor its site for infringing copies; it is up to the trade mark holder to do so and then to put eBay on notice about any specific auction items to be delisted. The judgment occurred against the background that eBay had not turned a blind eye to the infringements and taken measures to discourage them and had responded to notices about specific infringements from Tiffany by pulling the relevant listings and suspending repeat offenders from its site. The CJEU went slightly further by holding that eBay's takedown duties would extend beyond the specific items listed in the takedown notices but any preventative policy does not extend to generally monitoring the site for infringements. Still on both sides of the Atlantic the wrangling is about who should bear the cost of the monitoring activity, at least in intellectual property law.

In copyright too very similar arguments and themes crop up. In *Perfect 10 Inc v Amazon.com Inc* (2007)[293] the Ninth Circuit court was asked to rule on the legality of Google's image search facility indexing unauthorised copies of Perfect 10's nude images. It was disputed whether Google had complied with specific takedown requests by Perfect 10. On the point of contributory liability, the court held Google would only be liable for intentionally encouraging (or inducing) copyright infringements through specific acts, where it had *actual* knowledge that *specific* infringing material is available using its system and could take simple measures to prevent further damage, but chose not to do so.[294] In so ruling, the court recognised the significance of the intermediary's magnifying effect (i.e. scale, see above) for the question of the imposition of liability:

> *Napster* and *Netcom* are consistent with the longstanding requirement that an actor's contribution to infringement must be material to warrant the imposition of contributory liability . . .

---

290 Fair Housing Council of San Fernando Valley v Roommates.com LLC 2012 WL 310849 (9th Cir 2 February 2012).

291 600 F3d 93 (2d Cir2010); see also Inwood Laboratories Inc v Ives Laboratories Inc 456 US 844 (1982).

292 L'Oréal SA v eBay International AG C-324/09 (CJEU, 12 July 2011).

293 Perfect 10 Inc v Amazon.com, Inc 508 F3d 1146 (9th Cir. 2007).

294 Ibid, [22].

[S]ervices or products that facilitate access to websites through the world can significantly magnify the effects of otherwise immaterial infringing activities.[295]

So under substantive trade mark and copyright law, intermediaries are – much like as in Europe – seen as important regulatory aids for enforcing these property interests. The burden of monitoring, however, is firmly placed on rightholders, and thus there is a sharing of responsibilities between these two economically powerful industries.

For copyright law that position is reinforced by the Digital Millennium Copyright Act of 1998 and which is, in a number of ways, comparable with the immunities regime under the European Electronic Commerce Directive:[296]

(a)     it offers an additional layer of protection over and above the substantive law;
(b)     it creates a staggered regime that differentiates between of data conduits, caching systems providers, hosts, and, unlike the Directive, also information location tools providers;
(c)     it imposes similar conditions for qualifying for each of the above categories;
(d)     it creates a notice-and-takedown duty for the latter three categories, with detailed provisions for the notice requirements;
(e)     the notice may be triggered by actual or constructive knowledge;
(f)     the immunities entail a complete bar on monetary damages and, unlike the Directive, also restrict injunctive relief;
(g)     there is no monitoring duty.

So while the broad approach and conception of DMCA and the Electronic Commerce Directive are the same, there are variations in the detail, partly arising simply because of the far more detailed provisions of the DMCA. For example, much like the Directive, the DMCA allows for injunctions against otherwise immune intermediaries, but spells out what sort of injunctions these may be in s 512(j) – such as restraining (or blocking) access to subscribers or an accountholder who is a repeat offender. Also whilst the Directive does not even mention any 'notice', the DMCA does not just lay down the specifications of any notice in s 512(c)(3), but also at least attempts to deal with the issue of illegitimate or contestable takedown requests, even if their effectiveness is disputed:[297]

- **s 512(f)** – any person who knowingly materially misrepresents that the material is infringing, or that it was removed or blocked through mistake or misidentification, is liable for any resulting damages incurred by the alleged wrongdoer, the copyright owner or its licensee, or the service provider
- **s 512(g)** – concerning hosted material, the host notifies the content provider that access to the material has been removed and, upon receipt of a counter notification by the allegedly infringing provider, reinstates access to the content within three weeks, unless it receives a notification from the initial complainant, that it has started court proceedings to seek an injunction.

In addition, there are also variations in nuance in how each statute defines its core concepts: how they define intermediaries as opposed to co-creators/wrongdoers and actual or constructive knowledge.[298] For example, the DMCA attaches, in respect of hosts, explicit importance to any

---

295 Ibid.
296 For an excellent comparison, see Brian McMahon, 'Different directions: The Digital Millennium Copyright Act and the Directive on Electronic Commerce offer similar protections to ISPs' (2014) 37 Los Angeles Lawyer 28.
297 European Commission (2011), above n 3, 29f.
298 MacMahon, above n 296.

financial benefit he or she receives, directly attributable to the infringing activity (s 512(c)(1)(B)). This has been interpreted to mean that an intermediary falls outside the immunity where the infringing activity hosted by the intermediary is of such an extent that it 'constitutes a draw for subscribers, not just an added benefit.'[299] No doubt, this test would deliver similar results in clear-cut cases to those based on the reasoning adopted by the CJEU on 'neutrality', but given the difference in emphasis may lead to divergent outcomes in borderline scenarios.

## Trends in intermediaries' regulatory roles

The topic of the involvement of intermediaries in internet governance goes to the heart of fundamental questions and concerns about the governance of cyberspace. For example, the continued viability of state-based law (and therefore of the state itself) depends largely on the extent to which states can enrol intermediaries as their regulatory aides. That states have realised the immense opportunities offered by intermediaries for government purposes has become clear since the Snowden revelations. Similarly, the efficiency and future of intellectual property is bound hand and foot with the (enforced) willingness of online gatekeepers to stop copyright and trade mark infringing traffic flowing through their arteries. At the same time, the more intermediaries on different levels are successfully engaged in various law enforcement activities by various states and stakeholders, the more pertinent are other core questions about the future of cyberspace as a space within which users can communicate with one other across national borders – free from corporate and state surveillance and law-based censorship by states implemented by intermediaries. Some of these wider concerns shine through some of the cases discussed above, yet the very nature of an individual dispute coming before, and being decided upon by, a national or regional court is that the wider picture is easily drowned out in by the particular interests claimed by the stakeholders. If nothing else, this chapter seeks to show the great variety of legal and regulatory demands made on internet intermediaries, without necessarily advocating a particular legal position, but with the intent of shining a light on the power and importance of intermediaries in online communications, activities and transactions and their enormous attractiveness as quasi-regulatory vehicles. In short, these various – seemingly disparate – decisions, statutes and arguments form a subject-matter with common themes flowing through them – and these require attention and debate.

The discussion was deliberately structured with an emphasis on the receding importance of establishing the intermediary's liability as a pre-requisite for getting them involved in regulatory activity, which is most pronounced in Europe vis-à-vis ISPs and intellectual property law. Furthermore, for intermediaries that are treated as more than mere 'tools' and thus potentially exposed to liability, the arguments systematically focus on whether the intermediaries should or should not be treated as a co-creator and co-wrongdoer and can therefore be legitimately placed under a monitoring/editing duty.

The table below does not purport to be exact science of intermediary liability because the legal areas of defamation, intellectual property law and data protection from either side of the Atlantic cannot easily be mapped onto each other. Not everything fits. For example, whilst Google – in the absence of any third party wrongdoing – was subjected to a form of primary liability under data protection law in *Google Spain* (2014),[300] that liability did not translate into proactive duties on the search engines, but only notice-and-takedown duties, which would normally be reserved for secondary/contributory wrongdoers. This in itself offers some commentary about the peculiar nature of online regulability. Furthermore, the new prevalence of reactive takedown obligations for

---

299 For example, *A&M Records Inc v Napster Inc* 239 F3d 1004 (9th Cir 2001). An example of when an intermediary was not held to benefit directly from the infringing activity, see *Ellison v Robertson* 357 F3d 1072 (9th Cir 2004).
300 *Google Inc v Agencia Española de Protección de Datos, Mario Costeja González* C-131/12 (CJEU, 13 May 2014).

## Table 3.1 Spectrum of Online Intermediaries and their Legal Positions

| **Mere facilitator/tool/device** (based on almost absolute passivity vis-à-vis content or substantive activity and remoteness from it) | **'Intermediary'** (based on relative lack of knowledge and control/power) | **Content creator/co-creator** (based on existence of knowledge and control/ power and involvement with content) |
| --- | --- | --- |
| **No liability** | **Secondary/contributory liability** (takedown duty upon notification and no monitoring duty) | **Primary liability** (generally proactive monitoring and preventative measures and editing duties) |
| e.g. Art 12 of the Electronic Commerce Directive; s 5 of the Defamation Act 2013; s 512(a) of the DMCA | e.g. s 1(1) of the Defamation Act 1996 (publisher/distributor); Arts 13 and 14 of the Electronic Commerce Directive; s 512(b), (c) and (d) of the DMCA | e.g. s 1(2) of the Defamation Act 1996 (author, editor, publisher) |
| **BUT: regulatory involvement regardless of liability,** e.g. Art 11 of the Enforcement Directive; Art 8(3) of the Information Society Directive | *Borderline cases* *Google Adwords and L'Oreal v eBay* (trade marks)*Google Spain* (Data Protection Act 1998) | |
| e.g. ISPs providing internet access; hyperlinkers and general search engines in the standard scenario | e.g. content hosts, such as networking sites and online marketplaces with limited editing control | e.g. certain hyperlinkers, search engines and hosts who knowingly encourage particular (illegal) content distribution or, Re hosts, who have overt editing responsibility such as Wikipedia |
| USA – no liability under s 230 of the Communication Decency Act (but not applicable to intellectual property law) | | |

internet regulation as well as their much more readily accepted legitimacy, as opposed to the highly contested legitimacy of blocking orders, raises fundamental questions about the accountability of these private law enforcers, their transparency and, ultimately, about the democratic nature of this form of governance.

And let us not confuse any ruling on the neutrality or passivity of these private actors for the purposes of their entitlement to the immunities with their nature more generally, and their role in these enforcement activities more specifically. To say that Google is neutral in respect of any trade mark infringements within its AdWords program is driven by the policy decision that it should not be burdened with monitoring duties, but this does not mean that it is neutral as a search engine provider: 'the modern Google is more than a match engine: it ranks search results, provides prompts beyond what the user enters, and answers questions.'[301] Equally, Google is not neutral in how it responds to takedown requests based on government demands or the private interests by rightholders or EU data protection subjects. The way it implements these duties is necessarily bound up with its commercial priorities.

One question arising particularly in respect of the EU immunities is whether – apart from Art 15 – they are in fact needed. This relates to the judicial attitude to the relationship between substantive liability and the immunities. The immunities regime pre-supposes that the intermediary would

---

301 Fair Housing Council of San Fernando Valley v Roommates.com 521 F3d 1157, 1183 (9th Cir 2008).

otherwise be exposed to liability. Yet, as shown, courts have often not relied on the immunities, but found the intermediary not liable under substantive law, making the immunity redundant. By the same token, there are also examples when judges have clearly wanted to avoid the effect of the immunity by, for example, constructing the intermediary as a co-creator/co-wrongdoer, making the immunity again redundant. This paradox is captured by the dissenting judges in the US case of Fair Housing Council of San Fernando Valley v Roommates.com (2008):

> Whether Roommate is entitled to immunity for publishing and sorting profiles is wholly distinct from whether Roommate may be liable for violations of the FHA [the Fair Housing Act of 1968]. Immunity has meaning only when there is something to be immune *from*, whether a disease or the violation of a law. It would be nonsense to claim to be immune only from the innocuous. But the majority's immunity analysis is built on substantive liability: to the majority, CDA immunity depends on whether a webhost materially contributed to the unlawfulness of the information. Whether the information at issue is unlawful and whether the webhost has contributed to its unlawfulness are issues analytically independent of the determination of immunity. Grasping at straws to distinguish Roommate from other interactive websites such as Google and Yahoo!, the majority repeatedly gestures to Roommate's potential substantive liability as sufficient reason to disturb its immunity.[302]

At least in Europe, one must question whether the immunities under the Electronic Commerce Directive are, in fact, needed and useful. If ultimately the 'substantive liability' trumps the immunity no matter what, then the answer is negative. This position is not necessarily regressive, because the various substantive laws have, over the years, developed defences that fairly reflect the relative fault or faultlessness of those who are not the primary source of the wrongdoing. And why should online intermediaries not simply be accommodated within these traditional substantive concepts, just like their offline counterparts? Or put differently, do we need a separate cyberlaw for intermediaries?

Otherwise, the variations in the judgments above may be explained with reference to the perceived usefulness of the intermediary in question, the relative importance of the substantive law infringed as well as national legal traditions and economic interests. First, the judge's and public perception on the relative usefulness of the particular intermediary may explain why Google, as a navigation intermediary, was treated more leniently for its role in trade mark-infringing AdWords, than eBay, as an online marketplace, for its quite comparable role in trade mark-infringing auction items. Web2.0 providers are considered as less essential to the use and functioning of the internet than search engines, which judges have described as essential building blocks of the internet. Even amongst Web2.0 providers, despite superficial similarities, there may be a hierarchy in their perceived value or contribution to society that can explain the different judicial attitudes towards them. The question is: are sites such as eBay, Facebook, YouTube, or Wikipedia one of a kind – for all to be subjected to the same liability/immunities regime? As a commercial facilitator, eBay may be rated more highly than Facebook as a social networking site, or YouTube, which is mainly used for entertainment. In contrast, Wikipedia, being non-profit and educational, is likely to be viewed with more favour by judges than Twitter, or Bebo. Despite the tendency of French courts to find online intermediaries liable, in MB, PT and FD v Wikimedia Foundation Inc (2007)[303] a judge found that Wikipedia was not liable for defamation and invasion of privacy, basing that finding on Art 14 of the Directive as an online host.

---

302  Ibid, 1182ff.
303  (Tribunal de Grande Instance de Paris, 29 October 2007).

Second, the different conclusions of liability of intermediaries may also be explained considering the perceived importance of the legal subject matter and the – often interrelated – scale of the wrongdoing. For example, the very fact that intellectual property rights are taken out of the very generous US immunities regime under s 230 suggests that these rights raise special interests. Similarly, it is clear that judges everywhere are more intermediary-friendly in defamation cases than in intellectual property cases, which may be partly a reflection of the varying scale of the wrongdoing, and its attendant effects on public and private interests.

Finally, the difference in judicial attitude towards online intermediaries is also reflective of different national values, legal traditions and economic interests, which make courts more predisposed towards or against intermediary liability. Given that most online intermediaries are based in the USA, with the vast proportion of their profits flowing back there, the strong immunities of the USA make perfect economic sense. Equally, as the music, film and publishing industry have strong footholds in the USA, it is not surprising that the immunities are weakened for the purposes of intellectual property. By the same token, many of the disputes in the EU – as, for example, *Google AdWords* (2010)[304] and *L'Oréal v eBay* (2011)[305] – were instigated by European, in particular French, commercial brands and it is hardly surprising that French courts have been at the forefront of imposing liability on these intermediaries. By the same token, the decision of the CJEU in *Google Spain* (2014)[306] is entirely consistent with Europe's stronger data protection and privacy legal culture, as well as by its economic interests in protecting its citizens' autonomy over their personal data as an economic asset.

# Further reading

Jonathan Zittrain, 'A history of online gatekeeping', (2006) 19 Harvard Journal of Law & Technology 253

Emily B Laidlaw, *Regulating Speech in Cyberspace: Gatekeepers, Human Rights and Corporate Responsibility*, 2015, CUP

Jan Oster, *Media Freedom as a Fundamental Right*, 2015, CUP Swiss Institute of Comparative Law, Comparative Study on Blocking, Filtering and Take-Down of Illegal Internet Content (20 December 2015) another reading: Council of Europe http://www.coe.int/en/web/freedom-expression/study-filtering-blocking-and-take-down-of-illegal-content-on-the-internet

---

304 *Google AdWords* C-236/08, C-237/08 and C-238/08 (CJEU, 23 March 2010).
305 *L'Oréal SA v eBay International AG* C-324/09 (CJEU, 12 July 2011).
306 *Google Inc v Agencia Española de Protección de Datos, Mario Costeja González* C-131/12 (CJEU, 13 May 2014).

# Chapter 4

# Copyright and the internet

# Introduction

The internet has created new methods of delivering and disseminating creative content online that have had a significant impact on the market in creative works; for example in 2014 the revenue generated for the music industry from digital channels matched that from physical format sales for the first time.[1] However, just as computer networks created new ways of committing traditional crime, so they provided new ways of infringing copyright. Some of these issues are the generic ones that have already been identified such as jurisdiction, detection, and enforcement, but others are specific to the law of copyright. Cornish and Llewellyn have referred to the internet and copyright as 'the most inflamed issue in current intellectual property',[2] and developing uses of this medium continue to challenge the traditional principles of copyright; as Ganley has commented, 'the internet has ruffled the feathers of copyright law'.[3] Indeed, the phrase 'digital copyright' is sometimes used misleadingly as an indication of another species of copyright with different rules, rather than an application of the existing rules to the digital environment, together with an attempt to draw an appropriate balance between authors' and users' rights in this context. This chapter will consider, in particular, some of the general issues relating to the application of copyright principles to a new medium, together with associated changes in the law in both Europe and the USA, using the practical examples of hypertext links, the operation of search engines and file sharing. Before considering how the law has responded to the issues, we will consider the origins of the problems that have been encountered.[4]

As every student knows, copying of material from the vast information source that is the internet is a trivial matter; similarly, the technology also makes it a trivial matter to make existing copyright works available on the internet. Examples of the latter range from individuals putting copyright works on YouTube, to major initiatives such as the Google Print Library Project,[5] but application of the law of copyright to these issues has not always proved to be straightforward and has frequently been controversial. The conundrum at the heart of traditional copyright law is how to balance the respective rights of the creator and user of copyright material. As noted in the Preamble to the Information Society Directive, 'a fair balance of rights and interests between the different categories of rightholders, as well as between the different categories of rightholders and users of protected subject matter must be safeguarded'.[6] It goes without saying that there is an inherent tension between these rights – that 'conflict is at the heart of copyright'.[7] How should this balance be struck on the internet?

There are those who suggest that the ethos and culture of the internet is radically different from previous media to the extent that copyright is no longer an appropriate vehicle for protecting the rights of authors and creators; because copyright originated and developed in a very different era, it may have outlived its usefulness.[8] One problem with this approach is that although the original culture of the internet may have been one of openness and inclusivity, the vast and diverse spectrum of both uses and users of the internet now makes identification of a prevailing ethos far more problematic. Others support a relaxation of traditional copyright rules for the

---

1 See www.ifpi.org/facts-and-stats.php

2 WR Cornish and D Llewellyn, *Intellectual Property*, 6th edn, 2007, London: Sweet and Maxwell, p 842.

3 Paul Ganley, 'Digital copyright and the new creative dynamics' (2004) 12 IJLIT 282.

4 For a more detailed review of the major issues relating to intellectual property on the internet, see, e.g., World Intellectual Property Organization (WIPO), *The Impact of the Internet on Intellectual Property Law*, 2002, Geneva: WIPO, available online at: http://www.wipo.int/edocs/pubdocs/en/intproperty/856/wipo_pub_856.pdf, ch 3 of which is devoted to copyright matters.

5 See further discussion on p 141.

6 Directive 2001/29/EC of the European Parliament and of the Council on the harmonisation of certain aspects of copyright and related rights in the information society: [2001] OJ L167/10, Recital 31.

7 Karla M O'Regan, 'Downloading personhood: A Hegelian theory of copyright law' (2009) 7 Can J L & Tech 1, 11.

8 For representative arguments, see, e.g., JP Barlow, 'Selling wine without bottles: The economy of mind on the global net' in P Bernt Hugenholtz (ed), *The Future of Copyright in a Digital Environment*, 1996, The Hague: Kluwer; and C Kergévant, 'Are copyright and droit d'auteur viable in the light of information technology?' (1996) 10 Int Rev LCT 55.

purely pragmatic reason that jurisdictional issues and problems of detection make copyright law difficult to enforce in practice. In contrast to this, others are of the view that copyright still has a role to play in encouraging imagination and originality in whatever medium is at issue, simply because material continues to be created that is the proper subject matter of copyright protection.[9] In other words, the concept of copyright is still a necessary one, albeit with a recognition that it may need modification or amendment if it is to be able to respond appropriately to contemporary challenges. Schønning[10] points out that the internet is no more likely to lead to a mass breakdown in the copyright system any more than happened when it had to deal with other forms of piracy and illicit copying of easy-to-copy media, such as videos, audiotapes, computer software, etc, and simply concludes thus: '. . . surely copyright will survive even this legal and technological challenge.' Wiese,[11] having reviewed the arguments on both sides, came to the conclusion that there are still reasons to rely on copyright law, that it should not be regarded as a threat to the internet society, and that an appropriate balance between competing interests was possible. He came to the conclusion that a concept that had been developed over decades should be adjusted to fit the new circumstances rather than abolished – 'the question is not so much whether copyright can adapt at all but rather how it should adapt'.[12]

The existence of copyright protection is assumed to stimulate the creative process and, in this vein, a clause was included in Art 1 of the US Constitution giving Congress the power 'to promote the progress of science and useful arts, by securing for limited times to authors and inventors the exclusive right to their respective writings and discoveries'. But it has always been the case that there is a wider public interest, not only in the creation of copyright works, but also in such works being available for the use and enjoyment of citizens at large. It is commonly stated that the purpose of intellectual property protection in general, and of copyright in particular, is to provide an incentive for creativity by ensuring that creators are justly rewarded for their creativity and that a remedy is available in cases of infringement. In providing creators with control over dissemination and reproduction, the resources that went into the creative process can be recompensed. At the same time, authorised acts and exceptions provide lawful users with certain rights to utilise the material. Taking such factors into account, the law of copyright seeks to balance the rights of the user and the rights of the creator in an optimum fashion. However, what is an appropriate balance in relation to traditional means of dissemination may not be appropriate for the digital environment, in which the distinction between users and creators has been blurred. Materials in a whole host of formats – text, audio, video etc – can now be distributed and copied 'with extraordinary ease and accuracy'.[13]

This chapter will concentrate on issues that have no straightforward parallel in traditional media, including the copyright issues generated by the use of hyperlinks, search engines, file sharing, and liability issues in relation to both individuals and ISPs. A number of these issues are interrelated and those specific to intermediary liability have been examined in the previous chapter. The discussion in this chapter focuses purely on the application and interpretation of copyright principles in the context of the internet – a fuller picture will be obtained by reading both chapters in conjunction. Disputes that have arisen include those between traditional newspapers and news websites involving linking to news reports, complaints relating to file sharing and complaints against search engines and ISPs for facilitating access to copyright material. The burgeoning

---

9 See, e.g., Ejan Mackaay, 'The economics of emergent property rights on the internet' in P Bernt Hugenholtz (ed), *The Future of Copyright in a Digital Environment*, 1996, The Hague: Kluwer, p 18.

10 Peter Schønning, 'Internet and the applicable copyright law: A Scandinavian perspective' [1999] EIPR 45. For a summary of the challenges facing copyright law, see also JAL Sterling, 'Philosophical and legal challenges in the context of copyright and digital technology' (2000) 31 IIC 508; and Simon Fitzpatrick 'Copyright imbalance: US and Australian responses to the WIPO Digital Copyright Treaty' [2000] EIPR 214, esp 214–18.

11 Henning Wiese, 'The justification of the information society in the digital age' [2002] EIPR 387.

12 *Ibid*, 393

13 Cornish and Llewelyn, above, p 842.

quantity of user-generated content on the internet on sites such as YouTube, social networking sites, and blogs includes the whole spectrum from content generated by the individuals themselves, which they make available for free, to copyright material, or modified copyright material, which is made available in breach of copyright, performing rights, etc. It is perhaps thus not surprising that many users perceive that the internet provides a repository of freely available material and pay scant attention to the rights of copyright holders, if indeed they are even aware that there are such rights holders.

How is an equitable balance of rights to be determined in an environment in which a dominant ethos is one of free, and freely shared, material, but also one that has become colonised by commercial operators and those whose living is made by creating and/or trading in copyright works? Digitisation of major collections of papers and books, etc, for example, may be in the interests of those who wish to access their contents, but may not always be in the interests of the copyright holders, especially if the ability to control dissemination would otherwise provide a significant part of their income.[14] Popular opinion may not sympathise with large record companies and publishing houses,[15] but may be more understanding of the plight of the struggling author or musician. The technology itself may provide a means of control and the use of copy protection devices has been enshrined in law in some jurisdictions although not without controversy.[16] Although there are a number of international treaties and conventions on copyright, copyright law is a matter for individual jurisdictions. This raises further questions of how copyright principles that are already enshrined in national laws should be applied and how any lack of global harmonisation is to be dealt with when the medium, itself, is a global one. Millé[17] indicates that the solution itself must necessarily be global; that copyright law needs to find answers to the questions posed by the presence of new modes of intellectual creation, of distribution to the public, and of use and enjoyment of the works; that there is a need to make the treatment given to intangible property uniform at world level; and that administration by an international organisation appears essential. However, some other commentators, having considered the various arguments, have sounded a note of caution about the consequences of being in too much haste to introduce new or amended legislative rules.[18]

# Hyperlinks

The phenomenon of hypertext linking, which allows the user to move from site to site, is now so familiar as to have lost all remaining vestiges of novelty, but is indisputably crucial to the existence and operation of the worldwide web. Linking provides the way in which information is retrieved via search engines and is the way in which users move from site to site. The web pioneer, Berners-Lee, suggested that it should be possible to link to any piece of information as 'universality is essential to the Web: it loses its power if there are certain types of things to which you can't link'.[19] At a practical level, a site with few links is less likely to be found by other users and its worth will also be diminished to the user if he or she cannot travel from that site to another. Conversely, many

---

14 Many major libraries have digitisation projects: see, e.g., details of the British Library digitisation project available online at: www.bl.uk/aboutus/stratpolprog/digi/digitisation/index.html. The National Library of Wales digitisation project caused some controversy: see, e.g., www.literaturewales.org/libraries-in-wales/i/134826/. See also the Google Books Project litigation discussed below at p 141.

15 See, e.g., Konstantinos Stylianou, 'ELSA Copyright Survey: What does the young generation believe about copyright?' [2009] IPQ 391.

16 See later discussion at pp 162–6.

17 Antonio Millé, 'Copyright in the cyberspace era' [1997] EIPR 570.

18 See, e.g., Lionel Bently and Robert Burrell, 'Copyright and the information society in Europe: A matter of timing as well as content' (1997) 34 CMLR 1197, 1208.

19 Tim Berners-Lee, 'Realising the full potential of the Web', Presentation at W3C meeting, 3 December 1997 (London), available online at: www.w3.org/1998/02/Potential.html

people will bookmark sites to compile a collection of links to sites relevant to their interests. The number of times different users arrive at a site (the number of 'hits') is a useful way of gauging the site's appeal and popularity, as well as the efficiency of its links; for commercial sites in particular, the number of hits may be an important way of raising advertising revenue. There has also been a significant growth in the number of sites which merely provide links to other material without hosting any substantive content; these might include, for example, news aggregation sites and lists of links to downloadable films and music. Allegations of copyright infringement have been directed at a number of these sites. Some of the resulting cases, such as *Reimerdes*, concern direct links to allegedly infringing material. Other disputes involve whether there is a right for third parties to link to a site, or whether the manner in which this is accomplished can infringe the copyright or other intellectual property rights of the host site. Typically, such cases involve so-called 'deep' linking, whereby the link bypasses the home page and directs the user to another page hosted by the site, or 'framing', in which the linked-to site opens within the 'frame' provided by the linking site and so, at first glance, can easily appear to be material created by or hosted on the original site. Few non-commercial sites and users seem to complain about links – probably because such sites are keen to take advantage of the intrinsic functionality of the web both to link and to be linked to in order to disseminate their information more efficiently and effectively. However, commercial actors, although obviously wishing to use the same functionality, are often equally concerned with exerting some control over how and in what circumstances links are created, resulting in a number of cases in which the manner in which links are made has been challenged. Deep links are often not popular with commercial sites for a number of reasons. Revenue may be generated by the number of 'hits' on adverts hosted on the home page that will be lost if the home page is bypassed. A number of cases have involved deep links to underlying databases – the commercial site may typically be trading in tickets for entertainment, flights, or whatever, which it sources via access to its database. Clearly, the contents of the database have significant commercial value that will be lost if other websites can link directly to the database, rather than deal with the business via its home page in the intended manner.[20]

## Conceptual views of hyperlinks

Various real-world analogies have been suggested for hypertext links. In *Universal City Studios v Reimerdes*,[21] it was said that 'links bear a relationship to the information superhighway comparable to the relationship that roadway signs bear to roads but they are more functional. Like roadway signs, they point out the direction'. An alternative analogy is that of the footnote or reference. Burk explains that 'the hypertext link is in essence an automated version of a scholarly footnote or bibliographic reference: it tells the reader where to find the referenced material'.[22] In a similar vein, a hyperlink has been judicially referred to as a 'cross-reference . . . appearing on one page that, when activated by the point-and-click of a mouse, brings onto the computer screen another web page'.[23] Deveci even made the categorical comment that 'a link is no different from a citation in hard copy'.[24] However, although a link may conceptually perform both of these apparently disparate purposes, in each case it goes beyond the functionality of the corresponding real-world analogy. As the court in *Reimerdes* went on to say, 'unlike roadway signs, [links] take one almost instantaneously to the desired destination with the mere click of an electronic mouse'. The same is clearly true for

---

20 Such information can also be extracted by 'bots', 'spiders', or 'webcrawlers': see, e.g., the facts of *eBay v Bidders Edge* 100 F Supp 2d 1058 (ND Cal 2000).
21 111 F Supp 2d 294 (SDNY 2000).
22 Dan L Burk, 'Proprietary rights in hypertext linkages' (1998) 2 JILT, available online at: www2.warwick.ac.uk/fac/soc/law/elj/jilt/1998_2/burk/
23 *Universal City Studios v Corley* 273 F 3d 429, 455 (2nd Cir 2001).
24 Hasan A Deveci, 'Hyperlinks oscillating at the crossroads' (2004) 10 CTLR 82, 84.

the citation/reference analogy as graphically explained by Burk: 'the user's browser . . . can then retrieve the material from its location, a process that is not only hidden from the user, but far more convenient than physically venturing into library stacks to retrieve hardcopy referenced in a plain footnote.' The adoption of such analogies could have a potential impact on the liability of the linkor. If a link is merely a pointer that the user may or may not choose to follow, the question is whether the linkor should be liable if the link provides access to unlawful material – specifically, in the context of this chapter, to material that infringes copyright. If a link is merely a reference, writers would not expect to find themselves liable for copyright infringement on the basis of an infringement in a work cited in a footnote; why should a different situation pertain in relation to links? To what extent should any additional functionality that links provide affect the potential liability of the linkor?

Given the fact that the worldwide web cannot function without links, does the fact of launching a website create an implied licence to link to it? Or could there be something akin to a right to link?[25] The discussion in this chapter will focus on potential liability for copyright infringement but, unsurprisingly, similar issues have arisen in relation to linking to other unlawful material.[26]

## Direct links and the right of communication to the public

A number of cases seem to suggest that the mere fact of providing a simple link without more is not sufficient in itself to constitute copyright infringement by the linkor.[27]

The case of *Reimerdes*[28] arose because the defendant had made available the decryption code for DVD recordings on his website. After removing this information, he continued to maintain links to other sites where the relevant code could be found. In the USA, trafficking in anti-circumvention technology is prohibited by the Digital Millennium Copyright Act of 1998 (DMCA) and the question for the district court was whether maintaining such links could be equated with trafficking. A significant factor in this case was that the linked-to sites contained no other material and, indeed, activating the link initiated an automatic download. In these circumstances, the court had no difficulty in finding liability for the links, although it conceded that the situation might not have been so simple if the linked-to sites had contained other material in addition to the infringing matter. Liability under the DMCA itself will be considered further below, but the court also discussed more general issues of linking noting that:

> Links are . . . often used in ways that do a great deal to promote the free exchange of ideas and information that is a central value of our nation. Anything that would impose strict liability on a web site operator for the entire contents of any web site to which the operator linked therefore would raise grave constitutional concerns, as web site operators would be inhibited from linking for fear of exposure to liability.[29]

Using the classic vocabulary of First Amendment discussion, the court found that imposing strict liability on website operators for links to sites containing infringing content could raise constitutional concerns about freedom of expression because of the potential 'chilling effects',[30] and, in

---

25 See comment from Berners-Lee, in an online article, that 'the ability to refer to a document . . . is in general a fundamental right of free speech to the same extent that speech is free. Making the reference with a hypertext link is more efficient but changes nothing else': 'Links and law: Myths' (1997), available online at: www.w3.org/DesignIssues/LinkMyths.html

26 In defamation cases for instance, the main issue is whether a link publishes or republishes the material in question see, e.g., Gary KY Chan, 'Defamation via hyperlinks – more than meets the eye' (2012) 128 LQR 346; and Matthew F Kelley and Steven D Zansberg 'A little birdie old me, "You're a crook": Libel in the Twittersphere and beyond' (2014)30-MAR Comm Lawyer 1, 37.

27 See, e.g., *Paperboy*, Case I ZR 259/00, 17 July 2003, 35 IIC 1097 (2004) referred to in *Paramount (No 1)*, [24]. It was also assumed to be the case in *Copipresse v Google* and in *Reimerdes*.

28 *Universal City Studios v Reimerdes* 111 F Supp 2d 294 (SDNY 2000) and see further discussion on p 165.

29 *Ibid*, 340.

30 But noted that this was unique to neither links nor to copyright.

consequence, ruled that, in the particular circumstances of the case, there should be no liability unless it could be shown that those responsible for the link:

(a)     know at the relevant time that the offending material is on the linked-to site;

(b)     know that it is circumvention technology that may not lawfully be offered; and

(c)     create or maintain the link for the purpose of disseminating that technology.[31]

It is arguably implicit in this test that, absent a known link to infringing material, the linkor would have had a 'right', or at least a freedom, to make the link. The question of whether or not there is the requisite knowledge is therefore crucial and such a test could, in principle, be extended to other cases of direct linking in which the linkor was both aware of the existence of unlawful content and was also, perhaps, making the link for that purpose. The decision in *Reimerdes* was subsequently affirmed by the Second Circuit in *Corley*, but the court stopped short of propounding a general test because 'it is not for us to resolve the issues of public policy implicated . . . Those issues are for Congress'.[32]

Notwithstanding the discussion on linking in *Reimerdes*, it is a case in which the functionality of the link was crucial to the outcome and the extent to which it can be applied to the more general case of a direct link is doubtful. Whether the knowledge test can be used if the linkor knows that the link may result in a breach of copyright ultimately depends on an adjudication of the function of links and whether legitimate restrictions on making links exist or whether there is something akin to a 'right to link'. On the latter, as evidenced by comments in cases such as *Kelly v Arriba*,[33] there is evidence that the courts may not wish to inhibit unduly the use and utility of the new technology. In addition, any knowledge test must necessarily be circumscribed if the linkor is not to run the risk of either being found liable for additional linked sites or liable at a future date because the content of the linked-to site has changed.

## The right of communication to the public

The WIPO Copyright Treaty (WCT) and WIPO Performances and Phonograms Treaty (WPPT) of 1996 added an additional right to the armoury for copyright holders which was intended to fill any lacuna in the Bern Treaty in relation to broadcast and transmitted material. This was the right of communication, and making available, to the public contained in Art 8 of the WCT. This gives the rightholder the exclusive right to authorise communication to the public which includes 'making available to the public of their works in such a way that members of the public may access these works from a place and at a time individually chosen by them.' In the EU this right was given effect by Art 3 of the Information Society (InfoSoc) Directive,[34] implemented in the UK by CDPA, s 20.

The CJEU were asked to consider the interpretation of this right in *Svensson*.[35] The complainants were journalists whose articles were published both in paper newspapers and on the web. As in a number of other linking cases, the defendant Retriever Sverige was an aggregation site which brought together lists of clickable links by which users could access news stories on a variety of other websites. The defendant's argument was that such links neither infringed the copyright in the underlying work nor provided actual transmission of the work. The CJEU noted that Art 3(1) of the InfoSoc Directive required that every act of communication be authorised by the

---

31  Ibid, 341.

32  *Universal City Studios v Corley* 273 F 3d 429, 458 (2nd Cir 2001).

33  336 F 3d 811 (9th Cir 2003), discussed further below.

34  Directive 2001/29/EC on the Harmonisation of Certain Aspects of Copyright and Related Rights in the Information Society [2001] OJ L167/10.

35  C-466/12 *Nils Svensson v Retriever Sverige AB* (CJEU 13 February 2014).

rightholder. In line with its earlier judgments,[36] the CJEU said that the right of communication must be interpreted broadly and involved a consideration of both the act of communication and the public to which it was communicated. As hyperlinks made the work available they clearly constituted an act of communication. Further, the harmonisation required by the Directive would be undermined if the concept of communication to the public could be given a different interpretation in different Member States. Arezzo is highly critical of the fact that there was no real explanation of why linking should be equated with transmission, especially in the light of the reasoning in cases such as *Paperboy* in which the Bundesgerichthof came to the opposite conclusion because a link 'refers to the work in a manner which facilitates the access already provided by others'.[37] Having decided there was a 'communication' the CJEU found it was to 'an indeterminate and fairly large number of recipients', i.e. a 'public'. However, as the material had already been placed on the internet and so was generally accessible, there was no communication to a *new* public: one which the authors did not have in contemplation when they first placed the material on the internet. The potential audience was the same whether the material was accessed via the original website or via Retriever's website. In these circumstances there was no infringement of the right of communication to the public.

The crucial matter in *Svensson* was that as the complainants' work was already freely available on the internet, they were deemed to have already authorised it being 'made available'. Are there situations in which hyperlinks might make a work available to a 'new public'? There appears to be an implication in *Svensson* that this could occur, for instance, if links facilitated access to an otherwise unavailable work.[38] Certainly, the factual matrix of a linking case is likely to be extremely significant to the outcome and if, for instance, a link enables access to content which would otherwise not be available to the user then the situation may be different.[39] In the UK, *Svensson* has subsequently been distinguished in the *Paramount v BskyB* cases.[40] Both cases involved applications for blocking injunctions against a service provider and as such the main consideration was the availability of this particular remedy.[41] However, there was inevitably some discussion on the question of copyright infringement and breach of the right of making available. The websites in question gave links to a large range of films and TV programmes; no actual content was hosted but the sites provided categorised, referenced and searchable links. In *Paramount (No 1)*,[42] prior to the *Svensson* judgment, Arnold J considered it 'arguable that the mere provision of a hyperlink is not enough to constitute a communication to the public' but that crucially what the infringer did went 'beyond the mere provision of hyperlinks ... they were intervening in a highly material way to make copyright works available to a new audience'.[43] The judgment in *Paramount (No 2)*[44] came after the *Svensson* decision and Henderson J did not take issue with the fact that the provision of a link was itself a 'making available'. However, he considered that the factors in *Svensson* 'could hardly be further removed from the facts of the present case'.[45] The films and TV programmes were copyright material, the website

36 See, e.g., C-403/08 and C-429/08 *Football Association Premier League Ltd v QC Leisure* [2011] ECDR 11 [186]. For a list of cases in which the CJEU has discussed communication to the public see *Paramount v BskyB (No 1)* [2013] EWHC 3479 (Ch), [11].

37 Emanuela Arezzo, 'Hyperlinks and making available right in the European Union – what future for the Internet after Svensson?' (2014) 45 IIC 524, 539.

38 Ibid, [31]. See also discussion in Toby Headdon, 'An epilogue to Svensson: the same old new public and the worms that didn't turn' (2014) 9 JIPLP 662.

39 *Svensson*, [31].

40 *Paramount Home Entertainment International Ltd v British Sky Broadcasting Ltd (No 2)* [2014] EWHC 937 (Ch).

41 See later discussion of blocking injunctions in the context of file sharing at p 154.

42 *Paramount Home Entertainment International Ltd v British Sky Broadcasting Ltd* [2013] EWHC 3479 (Ch). See also Julia Hörnle, 'Is linking communicating?' (2014) 30 CLSR 439.

43 Ibid, [32].

44 *Paramount Home Entertainment International Limited v British Sky Broadcasting Limited* [2014] EWHC 937 (Ch); and see discussion in Steven James, '*Paramount Home Entertainment International Ltd v British Sky Broadcasting Ltd* – another battle won in the UK in the war against online piracy' (2014) 25 Ent LR 319.

45 Ibid, [31].

operators had no authorisation to use them and he supported Arnold J's test that the website opera-tors were 'intervening in a highly material way'.[46]

More recently the matter has been discussed in the Netherlands in *GS Media BV v Sanoma Media Netherlands BV*. The material facts were that some photos of a Dutch TV personality which were to be published in *Playboy* magazine in the Netherlands were made available on the internet prior to publication in the magazine. The perpetrator who would have been guilty of copyright infringe-ment was unknown and so an action was brought against GS Media which had merely provided the links. The Supreme Court of the Netherlands (*Hoge Raad der Nederlanden*) found little help from the judgment in *Svensson* in which the material concerned had been placed on the internet with the rightholder's permission. This left open the question of whether a link should be properly con-strued as a communication to the public when the material was not authorised by the rightholder. The court therefore referred a number of questions on this issue to the CJEU.[47] In the opinion of AG Wathelet,[48] the posting of a hyperlink to a website which published photos without authorisation does not of itself constitute copyright infringement; neither was the knowledge of the person who made the hyperlink of relevance. The Advocate General was of the view that any other interpretation would both impede the functioning of the internet as well as the development of the Information Society which was an objective of the Copyright Directive. If the CJEU follows this reasoning the functioning of the internet as we know it will not be compromised. Whether this is the outcome remains to be seen when the CJEU gives its judgment; if it came to the opposite conclusion it would certainly not be the first time it had disagreed with the Advocate General on a matter crucial to the open use of the internet.[49]

## Browsing and downloading

Many of the cases on this issue concern the activities of so-called news aggregation websites which provide a one-stop shop for news allowing a user to access stories from a variety of sources. The Meltwater News Service provided a bespoke service for its clients which located articles of interest based on a client's search terms and created a 'monitoring report' consisting of a headline and brief text. The client can click on the headline to link to the full article on the original source website. Importantly, unlike some of the links discussed in the next section, this link did not bypass any paywall or other technical impediment. If registration or fee were required the client would be subject to the same requirements as other users. The monitoring report may be either emailed to the client or viewed on the Meltwater website. Meltwater had a licence from the Newspaper Licensing Agency (NLA); it was accepted that individual clients also needed a licence if they received email copies of the monitoring report but the NLA also maintained that such a licence was required even if the report was only read on the website, since this resulted in temporary copies of the copyright material being made in circumstances which fell outside the exemption for transient copies provided by Art 5 of the InfoSoc Directive, implemented in the UK by CDPA, s 28A.[50]

Both the High Court[51] and the Court of Appeal[52] concluded that the exemption did not apply in this situation. The Supreme Court[53] reviewed the CJEU's interpretation of the exemption in the

46 *Ibid*, [35].
47 Case C-160/15 *GS Media BV v Sanoma Media Netherlands BV*.
48 Given on 7 April 2016. Text not available at the time of writing but see CJEU press release at http://curia.europa.eu/jcms/upload/docs/application/pdf/2016-04/cp160037en.pdf. For discussion of the liability of intermediaries in these situations see Chapter 3.
49 See in particular the discussion on the 'right to be forgotten' in Chapter 9.
50 For details of the whole saga see, e.g., Michael Hart, 'The legality of internet browsing in the digital age' (2014) 36 EIPR 630.
51 *Newspaper Licensing Agency v Meltwater Holding BV* [2010] EWHC 3099 (Ch).
52 [2011] EWCA Civ 890.
53 *Public Relations Consultants Association Limited v The Newspaper Licensing Agency Limited* [2013] UKSC 18.

*Infopaq* cases and *FAPL v QC Leisure*.[54] It summarised this[55] as meaning that the exemption would apply if copies were made as an integral and necessary part of the 'technological process' and were temporary such that they were automatically deleted once the users terminated the relevant process and only lasted for the duration of that process. Importantly for this case, it concluded that the exemption was not limited to copies enabling transmission over a network but also applied to copies made to enable other lawful uses, including internet browsing. Further, a use would be lawful, whether or not with the authorisation of the copyright owner, it if was consistent with EU legislation governing the reproduction right. Overall, the Supreme Court found all these conditions to be satisfied when material was merely read on the screen and neither downloaded nor printed (for which there was no dispute that a licence was required). However, recognising that 'the issue has a transnational dimension and that the application of copyright law to internet use has important implications for many millions of people across the EU making use of what has become a basic technical facility', a reference was made to the CJEU for clarification of the relevant principles. For its part the CJEU arrived at the same conclusion; the relevant conditions were satisfied and the temporary copies produced as a result of the technological process could be made without the authorisation of the copyright holders.[56] Following the CJEU's earlier judgments, this outcome was perhaps not very surprising, it is an important one for, as James remarks, 'a decision otherwise would almost certainly have damaged Europe's attractiveness as a centre of commerce' and also avoids 'the unsatisfactory and impractical consequence that internet users would not be able to browse content on the internet without the copyright owner's consent.[57]

## Deep links

So-called 'deep links' have, however, proved to be rather more contentious, especially for commercial sites since bypassing the home page results in lost revenue from loss of advertising and/or access to or extraction of commercially valuable information. The first case to consider such matters was *Shetland Times v Wills*,[58] which, unsurprisingly, received substantial debate and comment despite being only an interlocutory hearing.[59] A web-based newspaper, the *Shetland News*, contained a selection of headlines on which the user could click to read the full story. Some of these headlines were reproduced verbatim from the *Shetland Times* website and, when these particular hyperlinks were followed, the reader would be taken directly to the story on the *Shetland Times* site, bypassing the *Shetland Times* home page, using a deep link. The *Shetland Times* alleged copyright infringement of both the headlines and the stories themselves. Using reasoning which is no longer current, an injunction was issued on the basis that the information could be deemed to be *sent* from the *Shetland Times* website, rather than waiting passively to be accessed.[60] Another early dispute, in which

---

54 Case C-5/08 *Infopaq International A/S v Danske Dagblades Forening* (*Infopaq I*) [2009] ECR I-6569; Case C-403/08 *Football Association Premier League Ltd v QC Leisure* [2010] ECR I-985; and Case C-302/10 *Infopaq International A/S v Danske Dagblades Forening* (*Infopaq II*), (CJEU 17 January 2012). Neither the judgment in *Infopaq II* nor the *FAPL* case had been given when the lower courts arrived at their decisions.
55 [2013] UKSC 18, [26].
56 Case C-360/13 *Public Relations Consultants Association Limited v The Newspaper Licensing Agency Limited* (CJEU 5 June 2014).
57 Steven James 'And breathe . . . you can continue browsing the internet, as the CJEU hands down its decision in *PRCA v NLA* (*Meltwater*)' (2014) 20 CTLR 169, 171.
58 1997 SLT 669; [1997] FSR 604.
59 See, e.g., KJ Campbell, 'Copyright on the internet: The view from Shetland' [1997] EIPR 255; James P Connolly and Scott Cameron, 'Fair dealing in webbed links of Shetland yarn' [1998] JILT, available online at: www2.warwick.ac.uk/fac/soc/law/elj/jilt/1998_2/connolly/; Hector L MacQueen, 'Copyright in cyberspace: *Shetland Times v Wills*' [1998] JBL 297. For comparison with other linking cases, see, e.g., Chris Reed, 'Controlling world wide web links: Property rights, access rights and unfair competition' (1998) 6 Indiana J Global LS 167; Mark Sableman, 'Link law revisited: Internet linking law at five years' (2001) 16 Berkeley Technology LJ 1273; Diane Rowland and Andrew Campbell, 'Content and access agreements: An analysis of some of the legal issues arising from linking and framing' (2002) 16 Int Rev LCT 171.
60 Much of the case concerns a discussion about whether or not the headlines themselves could be protected by copyright on which, see also Case C-5/08 *Infopaq International v Danske Dagblades Forening* [2009] ECR I-6569; and in the Belgian Court of First Instance in *Copiepresse SCRL v Google* [2007] ECDR 5.

Microsoft had created deep links that bypassed the Ticketmaster home page,[61] was apparently settled by agreeing a licence that required any links to be to the home page. A deep link may also access material for which a password or some form of registration would normally be required, but such technology can also be used to prevent links completely, other than to the home page. In the *Ticketmaster Corp v Tickets.com* litigation,[62] both parties provided information and sold tickets for a variety of entertainment and sporting events. For events for which it did not sell tickets itself, Tickets.com listed alternative vendors and often deep-linked to other similar sites, such as that of Ticketmaster. On the copyright issue, the court applied the decision of the Supreme Court in *Feist*[63] and reasoned that there was no copyright protection for facts or raw data. This limited the information that could be protected and, further, the four elements of the fair use doctrine[64] favoured Tickets.com. Tickets.com made temporary copies of the material from Ticketmaster's pages and the final webpage did not contain any infringing material. Ticketmaster thus gained very little assistance from the law of copyright in trying to prevent the deep links to its site.

Prior to *Svensson*, a number of cases from Europe did not seem to suggest that copyright law was a major tool in the regulation of deep links.[65] In *Algemen Dagblad BV v Eureka Internetdiensten*,[66] Eureka operated a website, www.kranten.com, containing a page of national newspapers that listed news reports and articles matching those provided on the papers' own websites. These were deep links taking the user straight to the story and bypassing the home page. In addition, Eureka also provided a daily email service with the latest news stories in the form of a list of these deep links. The court was unconcerned about the effect of deep-linking, noting that the home pages of the newspapers were not made inaccessible by the deep link, that kranten.com did not take over the function of these home pages, and nor did it prejudice the exploitation of the home pages. Its view was that, for the purposes of copyright law, adding a deep link could not be regarded as a reproduction of the works contained on the linked-to page. Although the complete taking of the list of stories might be afforded copyright protection, it would be subject to an exception for freedom of quotation for press surveys. On similar facts to those in *Kranten.com*, the Bundesgerichthof (Federal Court of Germany) did not find that copyright was infringed by deep links. In *Handelsblatt Publishers Group v Paperboy*,[67] Paperboy provided access to a large number of news sites, including those of newspapers, radio stations, political parties, etc, by means of deep links, together with a daily email service allowing users to create a personalised news service. As pointed out above, the court found that the links provided by Paperboy merely made access easier; they were not a prerequisite to access that could be obtained directly if the user knew the URL. Further, the court suggested that, given that there was no liability for the link if a URL was published as a footnote in a hardcopy publication, the situation should be no different if the URL was effectively made available via a deep link.

## Linking and framing

Slightly different issues arise when the links and references to other sites are made via the techniques of inline linking, in which images can appear as part of the viewed web page even though

---

61 No 97–3055 DDP (CD Cal 1997).

62 For discussion of the copyright issues, see 2003 WL 21406289 (CD Cal) and see discussion in Tarra Zynda, 'Ticketmaster corp v Tickets.com Inc: Preserving minimum requirements of contract on the internet' (2004) 19 Berkeley Tech LJ 495. Subsequent litigation focused on issues of unfair competition: see, e.g., 2003 WL 21397701 (CD Cal).

63 113 L Ed 2d 358 (1991). See also discussion in Chapter 11.

64 See below at p 139 n 84.

65 Although the focus of this discussion is the application of copyright law to linking, the majority of deep-linking cases base their actions on a number of claims. In Europe, these have usually been infringement of database rights and unfair competition, whereas in the USA, where there is at present no separate protection for databases, the more tortuous avenue of trespass has been attempted.

66 Case 139609/KGZA 00–846 (District Court of Rotterdam, 22 August 2000) ('the *Kranten.com* case') [2002] ECDR 1.

67 BGH, 17 July 2003, I ZR 259/00. See BC Müller, 'Case comment' (2003) 8 Comm L 375; also discussion in Susanne Klein, 'Search engines and copyright: An analysis of the Belgian *Copiepresse* decision in consideration of British and German copyright law' (2008) 39 IIC 451, 457ff.

they originate elsewhere, or framing, in which the viewed web page will appear divided into multiple, independently scrollable, windows, some of which may come from other sites although appearing within the frame of the first site. These avoid the issues of bypassing the home page seen in deep-linking cases, but instead give rise to other problems. Sableman suggests that this is 'a little bit like painting a picture of a gallery at the Louvre, simply by importing onto your canvas the Louvre's own digital reproductions of those drawings. At the very least, it seems sneaky'.[68] He refers to the case of *Washington Post Company v Total News Inc*,[69] in which a number of publishers objected to the way in which Total News used framing technology to set a news story from another site within the overall Total News frame – in particular by blocking banner advertisements and other distinguishing features. The objection here was not to the link per se, but to the way in which the link was accomplished and presented. In common with many linking cases, the issue was settled by agreement between the parties, originating the notion of the 'linking licence' whereby Total News agreed to link to other sites only in certain specified ways.

Aside from the potential loss of advertising, etc, the question in the *Total News* case was essentially whether framing led to the creation of derivative works. This same issue also arose in *Futuredontics Inc v Applied Anagramics Inc*.[70] Applied Anagramics linked to the Futuredontics website in such a way that Futuredontics material appeared within frames on the Anagramics site. Futuredontics claimed that this was a copyright infringement and sought an injunction to restrain the link. As no injunction was granted because Futuredontics had presented no real evidence of significant injury, the question of whether the material on the Anagramics site constituted a derivative work was not considered in any detail and no actual decision was made on this issue.

Questions were referred to the CJEU about the legality of framing in *BestWater International*.[71] BestWater had a video which was available on YouTube and which the defendants made available on their own websites by framing so that it was not obvious to the user that it originated from a third party. As the video was already freely available on YouTube, notwithstanding the fact that the content was framed, the CJEU considered that no different questions were raised than those which had already addressed in *Svensson* and issued an order which merely restates and applies those principles.[72]

## A licence to link?

There have been many cases filed in the USA and elsewhere on matters associated with linking and framing,[73] and the majority appear to have reached a settlement based on an agreement related to the manner of framing. However, framing is arguably a special case because of the ease of confusion as to the origin of the material. Nonetheless, a number of other cases have also settled by agreeing a licence to link, despite the fact that there does not appear to be a strong case that links are likely to be unlawful, other than in the comparatively rare cases in which the connection is made with knowledge, and indeed perhaps with intent, to connect the user to infringing material of some sort. Although an implied or actual licence to link may be a useful device that helps to ameliorate

---

68 Mark Sableman, 'Link law: The emerging law of internet hyperlinks' (1999) 4 Comm L & P 557.

69 97 Civ 1190 (PKL) (SDNY filed 20 February 1997).

70 45 USPQ 2d (BNA) 2005 (1998), affirmed 152 F 3d 925 (9th Cir 1998); see Robert L Tucker, 'Information superhighway robbery: The tortious misuse of links, frames, metatags and domain names' (1999) 4 Va JLT 8.

71 C-348/13 *BestWater International GmbH v Mebes and Potsch* (Order of 21 October 2014, CJEU).

72 See Laura Mazzola, 'BestWater practice for linking or framing content: BestWater International GmbH v Michael Mebes and Stefan Potsch' (2015) 26 Ent LR 56; and Pekka Savola 'Blocking injunctions and website operators' liability for copyright infringement for user-generated links' (2014) 36 EIPR 279, 282. Mazzola reports that BestWater alleged it had not given permission for its video to be on YouTube. Although this might provide a separate copyright action it has no bearing on the application of the *Svensson* principles to the particular facts.

73 See also the decision of the Landgericht (Cologne, 2 May 2001), in which a poetry website was framed by the defendant. This had the result of circumventing banner advertisements and was deemed to cause damage to the website owner: http://marketinglaw. osborneclarke.com/online-advertising/poetry-and-advertising-dont-mix-says-cologne-court/

any friction between the parties concerned, it is a moot point whether it is a necessary or essential device.[74] Afori suggests that, even where American courts allow linking without reference to an implied licence, 'their decisions are clearly motivated by it',[75] and that a rule presuming consent to link by virtue of posting material on the internet would infuse 'reasonableness into Internet activity'.[76] While it is difficult to argue with the latter point, the former seems debatable: if there is actually some hidden subtext, such decisions could equally be motivated by the existence of a general freedom to link provided that it did not adversely affect another's interests. Allgrove and Ganley point out that the implied licence device offers no more certainty to internet users since liability will still be dependent on the facts of the case. However, in their view, its utility could be to protect works for public policy reasons.[77] In contrast, the alternative view is that, far from requiring a licence from the linkee, the manner in which the internet and worldwide web have developed suggests that the linkor may have a right to link, which some have construed as part of the right of free expression.[78]

Whereas common law countries provide fair use or fair dealing exceptions to copyright, the majority of civil law countries instead list a number of public interest exceptions to copyright, which, in keeping with their status as exceptions, are generally construed quite strictly. This has meant that unless such jurisdictions are willing to invoke a right to link, the linkor can only feasibly rely on the presumption of the existence of an implied licence discussed earlier – a device that has also been invoked in relation to the operation of search engines, as discussed in the next section.

## Search engines

If links are an essential contributing factor to the universality of the internet, the user would not be able to enjoy the maximum benefit from their functionality without that other indispensable feature of internet technology – the search engine. Indeed, search engines are now recognised as 'essential sources of vital information for individuals, governments, non-profits, and businesses who seek to locate information'.[79] Links and search engines could be said to have a symbiotic relationship: while links create the vast web of information that is the worldwide web, search engines enable that web to be navigated more purposefully and, of course, they also rely on link technology to connect search engine users with the results of their searches. For this reason, some of the same issues arise in these cases as those on linking, such as whether or not there is a need to invoke an implied licence or whether freely available content can both be linked to and retrieved by search engines with impunity. Search engines are one of the most commonly used applications on the internet[80] and they have been described as 'managers of information, organizing and categorizing content in a coherent, accessible manner thereby shaping the Internet user's experience'.[81] Search engines basically rely on three processes: trawling the internet or worldwide web by means of an automated program (variously referred to as a 'spider', 'robot', or 'crawler'); analysing and prioritising the information returned; and then compiling a list of the information for the user.[82] Not

---

74 For further discussion on this point, see Rowland and Campbell, above, 59. On the use of implied licences generally in copyright law, see, e.g., Lionel Bently and Brad Sherman, *Intellectual Property Law*, 3rd edn, 2009, Oxford: Oxford University Press.
75 Orit Fischman Afori, 'Implied license: An emerging new standard in copyright law' (2009) 25 CHTLJ 275, 304.
76 Ibid, 305.
77 Ben Allgrove and Paul Ganley, 'Search engines, data aggregators and UK copyright law: a proposal' [2007] EIPR 227, 234.
78 See, e.g., Berners-Lee, 'Links and Laws: Myths', above n 25 and Monika Isia Jasiewicz 'Copyright Protection in an opt-out world: Implied License Doctrine and News Aggregators' (2012) 122 Yale LJ 837.
79 *Perfect 10 v Google* 416 F Supp 2d 828, 849 (CD Cal 2006).
80 See discussion in Eszter Hargittai, 'The social, political, economic, and cultural dimensions of search engines: An introduction' (2007) 12 Journal of Computer-Mediated Communication 769.
81 Emily B Laidlaw, 'Private power, public interest: An examination of search engine accountability' (2009) 17 IJLIT 113.
82 For further discussion of the technology, see, e.g., Allgrove and Ganley, above, and descriptions in the relevant case law, e.g., *Field v Google* 412 F Supp 2d 1109, 1110ff; *Perfect 10 v Google*, above, 832.

surprisingly, in view of their ubiquity and the extent of the information that they are able to make available by use of a variety of search technologies, they have also posed some questions for the application of the law of copyright.

A good example of this was found in the early case of *Kelly v Arriba Software*.[83] Kelly, a professional photographer, had uploaded original photographs to his website. Arriba operated an image search engine based on a database containing images copied from websites. The images were first copied at full size and were then converted to low-resolution 'thumbnails' for storage and retrieval, after which the first copies were deleted. The Court of Appeals for the Ninth Circuit considered the application of the four fair use factors in the US Copyright Act of 1976[84] to the creation and use of these thumbnails. It found that even though the images were reproduced exactly and entirely, it was for a completely different purpose. Although the search engine used exact replicas of the original image, they were much smaller, lower-resolution images, which could not be enlarged to the size of the original without significant loss of clarity.[85] The fact that Arriba was using the images commercially did not automatically negate a finding of fair use; instead, as part of the first factor, the court had to consider the extent to which the new use was 'transformative'.[86] In this case, it was not merely a question of retransmission of the work in a different form; rather, Arriba's use served a different function to that of Kelly. Arriba's use of the thumbnails was neither for artistic purposes, nor did it 'supplant the need for the originals', and, in addition, it also served the purpose of 'enhancing information-gathering techniques on the internet'.[87] Although the works at issue were entitled to strong copyright protection, there was no evidence that the use of the thumbnails would damage the market for the original works and it was found that, overall, the use was fair. *Kelly* first came to the District Court in 1999,[88] at a relatively early point in the history of the internet, but the court explicitly recognised the 'established importance of search engines'.[89] It suggested that, given the developing nature of the technology, the transformative nature of the use was the most important factor, commenting that where 'a new use and new technology are evolving, the broad transformative purpose of the use weighs more heavily than the inevitable flaws in its early stages of development'.[90]

In the early days of the internet, although there were a number of different search engines available, arguably none could really be said to dominate the market. This situation has changed over the years with the rise and rise of Google, which now has an overwhelming share of the available custom.[91] Google's domination has been accompanied by a number of legal challenges, including some concerning the way in which Google deals with the copyright works of others via its search methods and mechanisms. As mentioned, search engines glean their information via automated programs that crawl the web. Website owners can both optimise their websites so that they are more likely to be indexed by search engines, and therefore more likely to come to the attention of users, or, conversely, robot crawlers can also be instructed not to index sites.[92] In *Field v Google*,[93] the issue was not that Google's use of web crawlers to make copies of Field's documents infringed copyright, but that copyright was infringed by copying or distribution when a

83 336 F 3d 811 (9th Cir 2003).
84 17 USC § 107. The fair use factors are: the purpose and character of the use; the nature of the copyrighted work; the amount and substantiality of the portion used; and the effect on the potential market or value of the copyrighted work.
85 336 F 3d 811, 818 (9th Cir 2003).
86 See further *Campbell v Acuff-Rose* 510 US 569 (1994).
87 336 F 3d 811, 820 (9th Cir 2003).
88 77 F Supp 2d 1116 (CD Cal 1999).
89 *Ibid*, 1121.
90 *Ibid*.
91 See, e.g., ComScore, 'Global search market draws more than 100 billion searches per month', Press release, 31 August 2009, available online at: www.comscore.com/Press_Events/Press_Releases/2009/8/Global_Search_Market_Draws_More_than_100_Billion_Searches_per_Month. See also Chapter 3 for discussion of other litigation involving Google.
92 Typically by the use of metatags or a robots.txt file. For further information, see, e.g., www.robotstxt.org/
93 412 F Supp 2d 1106 (DC Nev 2006).

user clicked on the Google cache to view the documents in question. With respect to fair use, the court found that, as in *Kelly* above, Google's cache did not serve the same purpose as the original, but allowed users to access the document when the original source was, for whatever reason, inaccessible. It also enabled users to ascertain whether changes had been made to the document and to check why it was returned in response to their search. In other words, it was a transformative use; an explicit comparison was drawn with *Kelly* pointing out that the cache served 'multiple transformative and socially valuable purposes'.[94] Taking all of the relevant factors into account led to the decision that Google could rely on the fair use defence. In addition, there were further factors that had not appeared in *Kelly*: Field provided free access to all of his materials on the web, and had also used a robots.txt file to optimise his site for search engines and was thus well aware of technology that would inhibit search engines. Under these circumstances, Google was also entitled to rely on an implied licence to index Field's site.[95] As Kociubinski has commented, this decision, together with *Kelly*, 'establishes a seemingly broad sphere of protection around the activities of Internet search engines'.[96] However, the fact that search engines might not enjoy completely unfettered freedom of operation appeared to be illustrated subsequently by *Perfect 10 v Google*.[97]

*Perfect 10* concerned thumbnail images that had been copied from websites by a robot crawler and indexed for use as part of Google's popular image search. Distinctions between this and the situation in *Kelly* were that Perfect 10 was a subscription site and so the images were obtained from third-party sites, and that Google also used a program (AdSense), which allowed third parties to have advertising space and share any subsequent revenue based on the number of hits and 'click-throughs'. In addition, although, as with Arriba's thumbnails, there was a consequent resolution reduction as compared with the original, the thumbnails produced by Google's image search could also be downloaded to mobile phones. This practice effectively superseded Perfect 10's own licence with a company for sale and distribution of its images via mobile phones. These factors made Google's use both more commercial and less transformative than Arriba's, and were the major factors that tipped the balance in Perfect 10's favour and led to a finding that Google could not rely on fair use as a defence. In the light of the 'enormous public benefit that search engines such as Google provide',[98] the court expressed itself to be 'reluctant to issue a ruling that might impede the advance of internet technology',[99] but nevertheless was of the view that this should not be allowed to 'trump a reasoned analysis of the four fair use factors'.[100]

This apparent restriction on the operation of search engines was fairly short-lived, as the Ninth Circuit subsequently found that the use was fair using substantially the same reasoning as it had used in *Kelly*. In particular, it concluded that:

> the significantly transformative nature of Google's search engine, particularly in light of its public benefit, outweighs Google's superseding and commercial uses of the thumbnails in this case. In reaching this conclusion we note the importance of analyzing fair use flexibly in light of new circumstances.[101]

While it has been acknowledged that the decisions of the Ninth Circuit in *Kelly* and *Perfect 10* are practical outcomes for the technology, it has been pointed out that they rely on the fact that the new use is transformative rather than the subject of the copyright being transformed into a new

94 *Ibid*, 1121.
95 See also above discussion at p 137.
96 Ben Kociubinski, 'Copyright and the evolving law of internet search' (2006) BU J Sci & Tech L 372, 377.
97 416 F Supp 2d 828. (DC Cal 2008).
98 *Ibid*, 851.
99 *Ibid*.
100 *Ibid*.
101 *Perfect 10 v Amazon* 487 F 3d 701, 723 (9th Cir 2007).

creation.[102] It has also been suggested that a finding of fair use is problematic when the original work is copied in its entirety, although there are other areas in which copying of an entire work has not necessarily militated against fair use.[103] In addition, although paying lip service to policy reasons concerning the importance of search engines, the reasoning in both cases was 'based on a "micro" fair use calculus and not on "macro" policy grounds'.[104] On the other hand, other commentators are of the view that the copying that is a necessary part of search engine technology should be taken out of the discussion of copyright infringement and 'recognized as an orthogonal use, rather than being characterized as transformative'.[105]

In Europe, similar issues concerning the Google image search have been raised in the German courts, but with no conclusive outcome as to the reasoning. As in *Kelly*, the fact that thumbnails could not be enlarged without loss of quality was a relevant factor for the District Court of Erfurt in deciding that there was implied consent to the operation of search engines, because there was an actual benefit to the copyright holder in having the thumbnails retrieved by a visual search engine, which would help people to locate the works and make them available to a larger audience.[106] However, on appeal, the Thuringian Higher Regional Court did not follow this reasoning, but found that mere uploading of a work to a website should not be taken to imply consent to the indexing of the images by search engines. On the particular facts of the case, however, the site had been optimised for search engines and so the court found that the complainant was estopped from bringing a complaint about the manner in which search engines operated.[107] This decision was subsequently upheld by the Federal Supreme Court, the Bundesgerichtshof, which held that Google's image search does not amount to copyright infringement.[108]

## Digitisation and the Google Book Project

A number of the issues raised by search techniques, together with the more general problem of locating an appropriate balance of rights between author and user in the digital environment, were brought sharply into focus by the furore surrounding the Google Book Project launched at the end of 2004. Working with a number of major libraries, including some major university libraries, Google announced its intention to digitise all of the world's books to make them both accessible and searchable – in other words, those with internet access would potentially have the literary resources of the world available to them from their desks or wherever else they happened to be online. As Bracha has noted, 'digital technology has the potential of empowering many members of society by providing them access to gigantic quantities of information in highly retrievable and manipulable forms. Books are just the beginning'.[109] In brief, the project is in two parts: those books that Google has been given permission to copy (the 'Partner Program'); and the Library Project itself, which potentially includes all other books. Unless permission has been given for more material to be accessible, a search will typically provide users with 'snippets' – that is, a few sentences either side of the search term(s). In addition, Google provides an opt-out facility

---

102 See, e.g., Kathleen K Olson, 'Transforming fair use online: The Ninth Circuit's productive-use analysis of visual search engines' (2009) 14 Comm L & Pol'y 153.
103 See, e.g., *Sony v Universal Studios* 464 US 417, 78 Led 2d 574 (1984), discussed further below at pp 147–8.
104 Fischman Afori, above, 75.
105 Pamela Samuelson, 'Unbundling fair uses' (2009) 77 Fordham L Rev 2537.
106 Case No 3 O 1108/05, decision of 15 March 2007, full text available (in German) online at: www.linksandlaw.de/urteil171-bildersuche-thumbnails.htm
107 Case No 2 U 319/07, decision of 27 February 2008, full text available (in German) online at: www.linksandlaw.de/urteil228-olg-thumbnails-urteil.htm
108 *Vorschaubilder* Case I ZR 69/08 BGH, 29 April 2010; see Out-law.com, 'Google image search results do not infringe copyright, says German court' (2010) Out-law.com, 30 April, available online at: www.out-law.com/page-10980
109 Oren Bracha, 'Standing copyright law on its head? The googlization of everything and the many faces of property' (2007) 85 Tex L Rev 1799, 1803.

for copyright owners who do not wish their publications to be made available in this way.[110] This project was rapidly challenged as a copyright infringement by a number of authors and publishers.[111] Subsequent negotiations led to a settlement being agreed, which was given preliminary approval in 2009.[112] The Google books saga was finally concluded in 2013, when, after eight years of protracted litigation, the District Court ruled that Google had met all the requirements for fair use.[113]

Unsurprisingly, there was significant academic discussion about issues raised by the case. This included, amongst other things, assessment of the wider public benefit of increased accessibility, the practicability of obtaining consent from all copyright owners, and the question of whether the 'opt-out' turned copyright law on its head in that instead of copyright owners being asked to give an explicit permission, permission would be implied or assumed unless the copyright owner expressly opted out of the system. The most extensive academic scrutiny was about the potential application of the four fair use factors in the US Copyright Act of 1976 to these activities. It is beyond the scope of this work to provide a detailed analysis of this issue; arguably, the prevailing view was, as turned out to be the case, that Google might succeed in a fair use defence, but that opinion was by no means unanimous and neither did those who were in overall agreement necessarily agree about how each of the fair use factors should be applied or what weighting each should be given.[114] In brief, those supporting a finding of fair use tended to focus on the transformative nature of the use – namely, that Google was creating a tool that was not for reading books, but for finding them – and that the new use did not adversely affect the market for the originals, and might even stimulate and encourage it. In addition, most also mentioned the educational benefits of the Google Book Search facility, concluding that it had 'important social objectives that must be encouraged',[115] that it was 'an innovative contribution to the public's benefit by facilitating research and promoting scholarship',[116] and that there would, in consequence, be an immense benefit to both authors and the public.[117] Those who take a more circumspect stance focus particularly on Google's commercial activities and commercial use, and, instead of considering the project as a whole, often apply the fair use factors separately to the individual stages of the project, concluding overall that a finding of fair use could 'significantly diminish authors' and inventors' exclusive rights'.[118]

Even though academic opinion generally seems to suggest that Google may be able to rely on the fair use defence, the case-by-case approach to fair use, together with a lack of appropriate precedent, means that it is difficult to predict exactly how a court might weigh and balance the respective factors. A number of commentators have concluded that, because of the perceived public interest advantages, there is a case for legislative intervention to allow published works to

---

110 For further details and discussion of the project, see, e.g., Jonathan Band, 'Copyright owners v the Google Print Library Project' (2006) 17 Ent L Rev 21; and Joseph Savirimuthu, 'Legal reflections on the Google Print Library Project' (2006) 1 JIPL&P 801.

111 *The Authors Guild, Inc, et al v Google Inc*, Case No 05 CV 8136 (SDNY); see also http://fl1.findlaw.com/news.findlaw.com/nytimes/docs/google/aggoog92005cmp.pdf

112 This settlement had the effect that rightsholders would be compensated in return for Google indexing their books, displaying fragments and showing advertisements.

113 *Authors Guild Inc v Google Inc* 954 F Supp 2d 282 (SDNY 2013). See further Kelly Morris, '"Transforming" fair use: *Authors Guild Inc v Google Inc*' (2014) 15 NC JL & Tech On 170; and Jessie Woodhead, 'Digitisation after Google Books – is fair use fair dealing?' (2014) 25 Ent L Rev 129. In April 2016 the US Supreme Court refused leave for a further appeal.

114 For example, the following authors came to the conclusion that a finding of fair use could be supported: Nari Na, 'Testing the boundaries of copyright protection: The Google Books Library Project and the fair use doctrine' 16 Cornell JL & Pub Pol'y 417; Melanie Costantino, 'Fairly used: Why Google's Book Project should prevail under the fair use defense' 17 Fordham Intell Prop Media & Ent LJ 235; Kinan H Romman, 'The Google Book Search Library Project: A market analysis approach to fair use' 43 Hous L Rev 807; whereas the following were more circumspect: Aundrea Gamble, 'Google's Book Search Project: Searching for fair use or infringement' 9 Tul J Tech & Intell Prop 365; Steven Hetcher, 'The half-fairness of Google's plan to make the world's collection of books searchable' 13 Mich Telecomm & Tech L Rev 1; and Ari Okano, 'Digitized book search engines and copyright concerns' 3 Shidler JL Com & Tech 13.

115 Costantino, above, 114.

116 Na, above, 114.

117 See, e.g., Romman, above, 114.

118 Gamble, above, 114.

be available in this form.[119] Copyright law has two strands: the fact of unauthorised copying in the absence of permitted fair use or fair dealing provisions; and also more severe provisions for those who, as well as copying the work, distribute it to the public. Proskine suggests that copyright law should be revisited to focus solely on distributing to the public: in the Google Books context, this would presumably mean that a whole book scanned onto Google's database would not infringe because it was not available in that form for general consumption (in the absence of specific permission or for public domain material), but only as snippets, which would qualify as fair use.[120]

Overall there are many policy factors that could be used to make a case for a variation of copyright in this context based on the benefit to the public, including the fact that, although the whole of the work may be copied, the end user can never access it in this form, together with the ongoing issue of whether rules that have their origins in print and hard copy should continue to be applied without amendment in the digital age.[121]

In Europe, digitisation has been considered in a more general way in *Eugen Ulmer*.[122] A university had digitised a book published by Eugen Ulmer and it was available on dedicated terminals within the library where users could also print it and/or save it to a USB stick. The university declined to enter a licensing agreement or purchase it as an e-book and was accused of infringing copyright. Article 5(2)(c) of the InfoSoc Directive allows Member States to provide exceptions or limitations to the exclusive rights in relation to public libraries, educational establishments, etc and Art 5(3)(n) specifies that, at such establishments, this can include 'use by communication or making available, for the purpose of research or private study, to individual members of the public by dedicated terminals . . . of works and other subject-matter not subject to purchase or licensing terms which are contained in their collections.' The CJEU concluded that Art 5(3)(n) included an 'ancillary right of digitisation' in order to give full effect to the 'communication' referred to in that provision,[123] whilst pointing out that because Art 5 refers to specific acts of reproduction this precluded libraries from digitising their entire collection.[124] Despite this rider, Morgan suggests that the CJEU's 'creative' reasoning in establishing an indeterminate ancillary right 'may raise more than a few eyebrows among intellectual property right owners.'[125] The CJEU did, however, not extend this ancillary right to printing or saving to USB sticks although it left it open for Member States to make such provisions in national legislation.[126] There are clearly different issues at stake in relation to digitisation by libraries and research establishments than those raised by the Google litigation; Advocate General Sharpston pointed out for instance, that such digitisation could provide a way of protecting old, rare and fragile original documents,[127] but it remains to be seen whether further clarification of the scope of this ancillary right will be required.

# File sharing

Given the quality of the copies that can be obtained by digitisation, it is not surprising that ever-more-inventive ways have been found both to copy and to deal in copyright material, leading Helmer and Davies to remark that 'the staggering pace of development of the internet has fundamentally changed the rules of engagement with [intellectual property] infringers, who now

---

119 See, e.g., Okano, above.
120 Emily Anne Proskine, 'Google's technicolor dreamcoat: A copyright analysis of the Google Book Search Library Project' 21 Berkeley Tech LJ 213.
121 See also discussion in Savirimuthu, above.
122 Case C-117/13 *Technische Universität Darmstadt v Eugen Ulmer KG* (11 September 2014, CJEU).
123 *Ibid*, [43]
124 *Ibid*, [44]–[46].
125 Chris Morgan, 'On the digitisation of knowledge: copyright in the light of *Technische Universitat Darmstadt v Eugen Ulmer KG*' (2015) 37 EIPR 107, 110.
126 *Eugen Ulmer*, [54]–[55].
127 *Eugen Ulmer*, Opinion of Advocate General [37]

operate in a virtual world that cannot be policed using conventional means'.[128] There are many ways in which copyright can be infringed online, but the growth in both sophistication and usage of P2P file sharing software has arguably caused the greatest challenges for the application of traditional copyright principles. Historically, copyright infringement was rarely pursued against individual infringers not only because of difficulties of detection, but also because both the amount of copying and its economic impact were relatively insignificant.[129] The advent of the perfect copy that could be easily and simultaneously made available to multitudes of users has moved the focus of litigation onto both the individual infringer, and the means by which the infringement can occur – that is, those who facilitate individual copying and file sharing. Rights holders fear loss of significant revenue as a result of the activities of file sharers and copyright owners – notably the music recording industry – have taken action in a number of jurisdictions against not only those who make available various types of P2P file sharing software, but also individual infringers.

This litigation represents far more than merely a dispute over the application of copyright to new activities made possible by internet technology, but has been presented as a battle between corporate interests and those – usually individuals – who espouse the freedom to access information that the internet provides. As Cornish and Llewelyn remark, 'the *Napster* judgment in the US [see discussion below] has become a bleeding image much paraded in the campaigns to preserve the internet as an unfettered instrument of free exchange'.[130] In a similar vein, Sookman suggests that not only does the technology present a threat to rights holders, but that it also is 'changing philosophical views about the purpose and value of copyrights'.[131] Nevertheless, there is little evidence that any new model of regulation is being sought to respond to the challenges posed to copyright law by digital technology. It is certainly true that copyright law has proved able to evolve through its history to cope with technological change, and that its general ethos and provisions have not changed substantially during that time. On the other hand, one of the objectives of intellectual property law in general, and copyright law in particular, is popularly supposed to be the encouragement of creativity and innovation – yet the development of the technology that has produced P2P networks is more often viewed negatively for its perceived fostering of infringement, rather than celebrated for its innovatory qualities.[132] There seem to be no proposals for revision of the regulatory framework that would embrace the functionality of the technology; instead, as we shall see in the subsequent discussion, the response has been to preserve traditional copyright principles and to enhance enforcement against individual infringers. Although new business models that respond to the technology by diversifying the modes of delivery of copyright material are welcomed,[133] it seems that new regulatory modes are not on the agenda.[134] What has happened, whether or not as a result of litigation targeting file sharers, is a growth in the availability of legal downloads and streaming services which may have reduced the number of files which are shared unlawfully.[135] In addition, cloud computing services, digital storage lockers and other developments provide many other ways in which users can share files and other material. Even if unlawful file sharing via P2P

---

128 Stuart Helmer and Isabel Davies, 'File-sharing and downloading: Goldmine or minefield?' (2009) 4 JIPL 51.

129 See, e.g., Jane C Ginsburg, 'Putting cars on the information superhighway: Authors, exploiters and copyright in cyberspace' (1995) 95 Colum L Rev 1466, 1488–9; Tim Wu, 'When code isn't law' (2003) 89 Va L Rev 679, 711–16; Mark A Lemley and R Anthony Reese, 'Reducing digital copyright infringement without restricting innovation' (2004) 56 Stan L Rev 1345, 1373–9.

130 Cornish and Llewellyn, above, 851.

131 Barry B Sookman, 'Technological protection measures (TPMs) and copyright protection: The case for TPMs' (2005) 11 CTLR 143.

132 See, e.g., *Digital Britain*, above, ch 4, para 18; Mark Sweney, 'Lord Mandelson sets date for blocking filesharers' internet connections' (2009) *GuardianOnline*, 28 October, available online at: www.guardian.co.uk/technology/2009/oct/28/mandelson-date-blocking-filesharers-connections; Lord Mandelson, 'Keynote address', Cabinet Conference, 26–28 October 2009; see also Lord Mandelson, 'The future of the creative industries' (2009) 29 October.

133 In the final debates on the Digital Economy Bill, the Secretary of State reminded Parliament that 'we have stressed all along the importance of developing legitimate paid-for downloading models. The problem, however, is that those will become widespread and sustainable only if there is a proper legal framework to tackle unlawful downloading': HC Debs, vol 508, col 840 (6 April 2010); see also *Digital Britain*, above, ch 4, paras 13ff; European Commission, above.

134 For a quirky comment on this, see Lord Whitty, *Hansard HL*, vol 718, col 1725 (8 April 2010).

135 See, e.g., www.theguardian.com/arts/netmusic/page/0,13368,1127237,00.html

technology is reaching a plateau, recent estimates confirm that both the volume of such traffic and the number of users remains significant.[136] Neither is the appetite of copyright holders and their organisations for litigation diminishing. In 2015 it was reported that the Recording Industry Association of America took out a lawsuit against the music streaming app 'Aurous' only a matter of days after it had been launched.[137] While the RIAA compared the operation of Aurous to that of Grokster discussed further below, its creator has received the backing of the Electronic Frontier Foundation to defend the allegations and the outcome will be awaited with interest.

## File sharing technology

It is beyond the scope of this text to enter into a detailed explanation of the technology that has enabled file sharing over the internet, but some brief account of the modus operandi of the technology and the way in which it has developed over time will be of assistance. Readers who require more technical detail will find it in technical information,[138] commentary by legal scholars[139] and also in judicial discussion of some of the cases discussed below. Before the advent of P2P, different computers on a network could only communicate through a central server, but, in simple terms, P2P software now allows computers connected to a network to communicate both ways with other computers on the network without those communications necessarily being routed through a central server. Napster was one of the earliest examples of this in which, although the actual file transfers took place between individual users, there was an element of centralisation in that the requests for the files passed through a central server. Later applications, such as Grokster and Kazaa, were examples of the 'purest form of P2P network'[140] – that is, ones in which individual computers communicated without the need for a central server. Thus Grokster was an example of a P2P sharing network based on the 'supernode' model in which a number of select computers on the network are designated as indexing servers. The user initiating a file search connects with the most easily accessible supernode; this conducts the search of its index and supplies the user with the results. Any computer on the network could function as a supernode if it met the technical requirements, such as processing speed.[141]

There were limitations to these technologies; large files took a long time to download which meant that they were more likely to be used for downloading music tracks than films or TV programmes, for instance. Similarly, files which were in great demand might not be instantly available as transfer of files occurred between individual users. Some of these issues have disappeared with the use of the BitTorrent protocol. BitTorrent software enables users to download large files in smaller portions (bits) from multiple sources, thereby making economies on the required bandwidth. This makes it possible to share and swap much larger files than would be possible with earlier file sharing software. BitTorrent software was originally developed by Bram Cohen[142] and can now be downloaded from a number of sources. This software alone merely permits the requisite files to be downloaded; it does not itself provide search facilities

---

136 See, e.g., Richard Verrier 'Online piracy of entertainment content keeps soaring' (2013) *Los Angeles Times*, 17 September (www.latimes. com/entertainment/envelope/cotown/la-fi-ct-piracy-bandwith-20130917-story.html). The volume of internet traffic devoted to file sharing has been estimated at 6.803 petabytes per month for 2015, projected to rise to 6,875 petabytes per month in 2016 (www.statista.com/statistics/267182/forecast-for-global-internet-traffic-through-file-sharing/). It was reported that in 2014, there were 300 million users per month sharing files via BitTorrent (http://rt.com/news/162744-p2p-file-sharing-increase/).

137 Stuart Dredge, 'Music labels sue Aurous filesharing app for "copyright theft on a massive scale"' 14 October 2015, available online at: www.theguardian.com/technology/2015/oct/14/music-labels-sue-aurous-filesharing-copyright-theft. See also www.eff. org/deeplinks/2015/10/entertainment-distributors-push-site-blocking-power-get-more-extreme

138 See, e.g., http://computer.howstuffworks.com/bittorrent.htm

139 See, e.g., Richard Swope, 'Peer-to peer file sharing and copyright infringement: Danger ahead for individuals sharing files on the internet' (2004) 44 Santa Clara L Rev 861; *MGM v Grokster* 259 F Supp 2d 1029, 1032 (2003).

140 Maureen Daly, 'Life after *Grokster*: Analysis of US and European approaches to file-sharing' [2007] EIPR 319.

141 *MGM v Grokster* 380 F 3d 1154, 1159 (9th Cir 2004); see also the extensive explanation and discussion of the Kazaa file sharing application in *Universal Music Australia Pty Ltd v Sharman License Holdings Ltd* [2005] FCA 1242.

142 http://www.wired.com/2005/01/bittorrent-2/

and so, if it is to be used for illicit file sharing, needs to be used in conjunction with another file, the tracker. The tracker is often obtained from another website that allows users to search for the files they want, which can then be downloaded using BitTorrent.[143] The requisite parts of files are downloaded from multiple sources; in previous P2P systems, users often downloaded but without uploading but, in BitTorrent, as soon as a part of the file is on a user's computer it is instantly available for others. The more files are shared the faster the system becomes and, because the individual file size in each case is small, the application is much more effective for obtaining large files such as films. The process is completely decentralised and was the system used by the, now notorious, Pirate Bay.[144]

Although there are many entirely lawful ways for using this technology, it also facilitates the easy dissemination, distribution, and sharing of copyright material.[145] In the first instance, such applications spawned a number of cases of alleged copyright infringement against the providers of the P2P software that enabled materials – usually music files – to be shared between users. Those bringing the challenges were typically record companies and organisations, which protected the rights of the creators of copyright material.

## Actions against P2P network providers

### Napster

*Napster* was the first case of alleged copyright infringement by a P2P network provider.[146] Use of the Napster system had increased during the late-1990s, and, eventually, a number of record companies and music publishers brought various claims, including contributory and vicarious liability for copyright infringement under US law. Napster, for its part, responded that its users could avail themselves of the fair use defence, first on the basis of sampling the music before buying, and second, on the basis of space-shifting[147] – that is, using the Napster system to make a copy of an audio CD of which they were already the legitimate owner. The court considered the four fair use factors. In terms of the purpose and character of the use, the court found that a commercial use 'weighs against a finding of fair use but is not conclusive'. Although 'direct economic benefit was not required to demonstrate a commercial use', in relation to Napster, 'commercial use is demonstrated by a showing that repeated and exploitative unauthorized copies of copyrighted works were made to save the expense of purchasing authorized copies'.[148] In addition, merely retransmitting in a different format was not a 'transformative' use.[149] Given the creative nature of the works copied, the second fair use factor, 'nature of the use', militated against a finding of fair use. The third factor requires a consideration of the portion used. Copying a whole work generally militates against fair use. The final factor is the effect of the alleged fair use on the market. To assess this, the court considered a number of reports on the use of Napster and its effect on the sale of recorded music,

---

143 For more detailed explanation, see, e.g., Rhys Boyd-Farell, 'Legal analysis of the implications of *MGM v Grokster* for BitTorrent' (2006) 11 Intell Prop L Bull 77, 78; Okechukwu Benjamin Vincents, 'Secondary liability for copyright infringement in the Bit-Torrent platform: Placing the blame where it belongs' [2008] EIPR 4, 6; Mikko Manner, Topi Siniketo, and Ulrika Polland, 'The Pirate Bay ruling: When the fun and games end' (2009) 20 Ent L R 197, 198.
144 For further explanation see e.g. *Dramatico Entertainment Ltd v British Sky Broadcasting Ltd* [2012] EWHC 268 (Ch), [19]–[20].
145 This technique also facilitates the sharing of other illicit content; for discussion of file sharing and pornographic material see, e.g., Audrey Rogers 'From peer to peer networks to cloud computing: How technology is redefining child pornography laws' (2013) 87 St John's L Rev 1013, Mark O'Brien, 'The internet, child pornography and cloud computing: the dark side of the web?' (2014) 23 ICTL 238; and Jeremy Prichard, Paul A Waters and Caroline Spiranovic, 'Internet subcultures and pathways to the use of child pornography' (2011) 27 CLSR 585.
146 *A&M Records v Napster* 239 F 3d 1004 (9th Cir 2001).
147 By analogy with the seminal case of *Sony v Universal City Studios* 464 US 417, 78 LEd 2d 574 (1984), in relation to video recordings made for time-shifting purposes.
148 *Napster*, above, 1015.
149 Following the judgment of the Supreme Court in *Campbell v Acuff-Rose* 510 US 569, L Ed 2d 500 (1994).

and concluded that 'having digital downloads for free on the Napster system necessarily harms the copyright holders' attempts to charge for the same downloads'.[150]

The cumulative effect of these findings was that file sharing was not protected by the fair use provisions. Applying this reasoning to sampling, the court upheld the previous findings that 'sampling remains a commercial use even if some users eventually purchase the music . . . even authorized temporary downloading of individual songs for sampling purposes is commercial in nature'.[151] This was not affected by the fact that record companies themselves sometimes provide samples for users to try before purchase, because 'free downloads provided by record companies consist of thirty to sixty-second samples or are . . . programmed to . . . exist only for a short time on the downloader's computer'.[152] In comparison, Napster users download a full, free, and permanent copy of the recording. Overall, Napster was found to have 'an adverse impact on the audio CD and digital download markets'.[153] In relation to the space-shifting argument, the court noted that, in Sony, it was held that time-shifting was fair use, but the same argument was held not to be applicable to Napster because, in Sony, there was no question of also simultaneously making the copyright materials available to other members of the public: 'It is obvious that once a user lists a copy of music he already owns on the Napster system in order to access the music from another location, the song becomes available to millions of other individuals, not just the original CD owner.'[154]

Having ascertained that there was no fair use and that Napster users were directly infringing copyright, the court went on to consider whether Napster could be liable for contributory infringement; this required an assessment of whether it knew, or had reason to know, of the direct infringement. In Sony,[155] there had been no evidence of actual knowledge of specific cases of infringement, and neither did the Supreme Court assign constructive knowledge to Sony for infringing uses of its video recorders on the grounds that the equipment could be used for both infringing and 'substantial non-infringing' uses. The lower court in Napster had based liability on the fact that Napster had 'failed to demonstrate that its system is capable of commercially significant non-infringing uses', but the Court of Appeals departed from this reasoning, and instead found that Napster had 'actual knowledge that specific infringing material is available using its system, that it could block access to the system by suppliers of the infringing material, and that it failed to remove the material'.[156] Neither was it willing to countenance Napster's attempt to avail itself of the DMCA 'safe harbor' for ISPs.[157]

The outcome was that Napster, in its original incarnation, was closed down – although it has since been resurrected as a subscription service. The reason for Napster's demise was primarily due to its centralised architecture, and its consequent ability to both control and to block access. As Wu has commented: 'Napster taught peer network designers that both lack of control and general functionality had to be comprehensive and credible to avoid contributory liability.'[158]

## Subsequent developments

A decentralised system also failed to escape liability in the later case of Aimster.[159] Although there was no finding of direct infringement, the court was critical of the Ninth Circuit's interpretation of Sony, since the evidence showed that the technology was being used for both infringing and

---

150 Napster, above, 1017.
151 Ibid, 1018.
152 Ibid.
153 Ibid.
154 Ibid, 1019.
155 Sony v Universal City Studios 464 US 417.
156 Napster, above, 1022.
157 For consideration of the DMCA 'safe harbor' provisions for ISPs, see discussion below at p 341. and also further discussion in Chapter 3.
158 Wu, above, 730.
159 In Re Aimster Copyright Litigation 334 F 3d 643 (7th Cir 2003).

non-infringing uses, and the court did not wish to deny non-infringing users the benefit of the technology. It therefore disagreed with the suggestion that actual knowledge of specific infringing uses was a sufficient condition for a finding of contributory infringement. Instead, it took the view that 'when a supplier is offering a product or service that has non-infringing uses as well as infringing uses, some estimate of the respective magnitudes of these uses is necessary for a finding of contributory infringement'.[160] Although the Aimster system could, in principle, be used for entirely innocuous purposes, in fact the only examples given in the explanatory tutorial about Aimster involved the sharing of copyrighted material. As 'wilful blindness is knowledge in copyright law',[161] neither was the argument that encryption prevented the operators from knowing what was being copied persuasive and neither was there evidence that the service was ever used for non-infringing uses: 'its ostrich-like refusal to discover the extent to which its system was being used to infringe copyright is merely another piece of evidence that it was a contributory infringer.'[162] Further, even if it could be shown that there were substantial non-infringing uses, to avoid liability, it would still be necessary to show that preventing, or at least substantially reducing, the infringing uses would have been disproportionately costly.

At this point, it appeared that whether the system was centralised or decentralised, absent genuine evidence that a file sharing system both could have, and did have, non-infringing uses, the courts were likely to find liability for contributory infringement. This application of the law was criticised as having the potential to restrict innovation, especially in cases of dual-use technology,[163] but it appeared that this situation might be clarified when the Ninth Circuit gave a further judgment on file sharing in the Grokster case referred to above. The use of the Grokster 'supernode model' was described by the lower court as being 'novel in important respects', but nevertheless operating in 'a manner conceptually analogous to the Napster system'.[164] On appeal, the Ninth Circuit, referring to both its previous judgment in Napster and that of the Supreme Court in Sony, concluded that there was no liability for contributory infringement on the basis that it had been shown that not only could there be substantial non-infringing uses, but that those uses also had commercial viability. The technology employed in Grokster was specifically distinguished from that in Napster; it was pointed out that it had 'numerous other uses, significantly reducing the distribution costs of public domain and permissively shared art and speech, as well as reducing the centralized control of that distribution'.[165] The court went on to discuss the difficulties for the law in responding to fast-moving technologies, noting that 'we live in a quicksilver technological environment with courts ill-suited to fix the flow of internet innovation' and suggesting that although new technology might be 'disruptive to old markets . . . market forces often [provided] equilibrium in balancing interests, . . . it is prudent for courts to exercise caution before restructuring liability theories for the purposes of addressing specific market abuses, despite their apparent present magnitude'.[166] However, this was to prove a short-term victory for distributors of file sharing software, because the decision was overturned by the Supreme Court on the basis that Sony had been misapplied.[167] Instead, the Supreme Court said that the ruling in Sony meant that there would be no liability for the mere distribution of products that were capable of both infringing and non-infringing uses, but this did not mean that liability could not be found in cases in which 'there is no injustice in presuming or imputing an intention to infringe'.[168] It found that 'one who distributes a device with the object of promoting its use to infringe copyright, as shown by clear expression or other affirmative steps taken to foster

---

160  Ibid, 649.
161  Ibid, 650.
162  Ibid, 655.
163  Lemley and Reese, above, 1362.
164  MGM v Grokster 259 F Supp 2d 1029, 1032 (CD Cal, 2003).
165  MGM v Grokster 380 F 3d 1154, 1160 (9th Cir 2004).
166  Ibid, 1167.
167  MGM v Grokster 125 S Ct 2764 (2005).
168  Ibid, 2777.

infringement, is liable for the resulting acts of third parties'.[169] In the circumstances of *Grokster*, there was ample evidence that there had been both intent to promote, and actual promotion of, infringing use sufficient to find Grokster liable for contributory infringement.

## File sharing in other jurisdictions

The USA was not the only jurisdiction in which such cases were being heard, although not always with the same outcome. The supernode architecture, of which Grokster is an example, had been developed by a Dutch company, KaZaA, which itself distributed file sharing software via its website. This resulted in an action brought by the licensing organisation BUMA-STEMRA, in which the Amsterdam Appeal Court found that, although individual users might infringe copyright when file sharing, the distributor of the software, KaZaA, was not liable on the basis that, because there was no central server, there could be no control over the files that were shared once the software had been installed on a user's computer. As in *Grokster*, it was also the case that the software could be, and was being, used for legal purposes, including the exchange of both copyright material with the permission of the copyright owner and also non-copyright material. This reasoning was subsequently upheld by the Dutch Supreme Court in December 2003.[170]

The licence to distribute KaZaA was subsequently transferred to an Australian company[171] (and renamed 'Kazaa'), leading to further litigation. The US cases had been decided on the basis of secondary and contributory copyright infringement according to the provisions of the US Copyright Act. The differences between the operation of Kazaa and, say, Grokster, together with the differences in copyright law between the USA and Australia, meant that the US judgments were of little assistance to the Federal Court of Australian in *Universal Music Australia Pty Ltd v Sharman License Holdings Ltd*.[172] The Australian Court found that it could not be said that the owners of Kazaa themselves communicated the copyright works; instead, the more realistic argument was that they authorised individual users to infringe copyright in the sound recordings in question. Although acknowledging that the software could be used for non-infringing purposes, the court was not convinced that such use could account for more than a small proportion of the traffic on the Kazaa website.[173] In a long and detailed judgment, Wilcox J found that those in the company were well aware that Kazaa was widely used to share copyright files, that they had technical measures at their disposal that, had they been implemented, might have curtailed these activities, and that, although falling short of actual endorsement of file sharing, information on the Kazaa website was nevertheless critical of record companies that opposed it. However, Wilcox J was also anxious that any remedy would reflect the balance of rights at the heart of copyright law:

> I am anxious not to make an order which the respondents are not able to obey, except at the unacceptable cost of preventing the sharing even of files which do not infringe the applicants' copyright. There needs to be an opportunity for the relevant respondents to modify the Kazaa system in a targeted way, so as to protect the applicants' copyright interests (as far as possible) but without unnecessarily intruding on others' freedom of speech and communication.[174]

---

169 *Ibid*, 2780.
170 See Out-law.com, 'Kazaa is legal, says Dutch Supreme Court' (2004) *Outlaw.com*, 5 January, available online at: www.out-law.com/page-4169
171 The company, Sharman Networks Ltd, was originally organised in the Netherlands as Kazaa.com, but using software from Estonian companies. It was subsequently incorporated in Vanuatu, but had its headquarters in Australia. The first 'KaZaA' software was provided free of charge from a website in Estonia through internet servers located, at one time, in Denmark. The RIAA was apparently unsuccessful in pursuing Kazaa through the Estonian courts: Slyck News, 'US court loses case in Estonia over KaZaA' (2002) *Slyck News*, 21 December, available online at: www.slyck.com/story306_US_Court_Loses_Case_in_Estonia_Over_KaZaA
172 [2005] FCA 1242, [30].
173 *Ibid*, [184].
174 *Ibid*, [520].

Notwithstanding this attempt at balancing the rights of copyright holders and users, one critical issue that differentiates the legal framework in the USA from that in Australia is that, in the former, the *Sony* judgment provides a general defence for the distributor of technology that has 'substantial non-infringing uses', whereas the Australian decision focused more explicitly on the fact of the actual use of the software in question; the reasoning has thus the potential to be more far-reaching that that in *Grokster*.[175] There have, as yet, been no major cases taken against the distributors of file sharing software in the UK, although there has been speculation as to whether the courts would follow the approach in *Sharman* or whether they would use a *Sony*-type approach based on the case of *CBS Songs v Amstrad*,[176] in which the House of Lords held that Amstrad's production of twin-deck tape recorders did not, of itself, indicate that Amstrad authorised copyright infringement, because the devices could be used for both infringing and non-infringing purposes.[177]

## BitTorrent cases

What could be called the 'third generation' of file sharing technology, based on the use of Bit-Torrent software, raises some slightly different legal issues. There is no doubt that BitTorrent itself provides an extremely effective and efficient way of transferring files, and has substantial non-infringing uses. Because it also does not itself provide users with the tools to actually locate files, it is very likely that a *Sony*-type defence would succeed if any action were to be brought against sites that merely allow downloading of the BitTorrent software and on which there was no evidence of intent to induce users to breach copyright.[178] However, the situation regarding tracker websites is more complex. If litigation were to be pursued against a site that merely provided search facilities, it would arguably be difficult to support an argument that it had facilitated or authorised copyright infringement. It does not actually provide the wherewithal for the user to download the file; to take advantage of the pure tracker site as the user would have already had to have installed the BitTorrent application. On the other hand, some sites, of which the most famous is probably the Pirate Bay, not only provide search facilities, but also link to sites from which BitTorrent can be downloaded.[179] In the case of the Pirate Bay, it also made no secret of the fact that it supported illicit file sharing and had little respect for the rights of copyright holders.[180] On this basis, Touloumis, referring to the 'legal slipperiness' of BitTorrent technology, suggests that there is 'little doubt' that the Pirate Bay would be held liable for secondary infringement under US copyright law.[181]

The concept of secondary infringement discussed in the high-profile cases of *Napster* and *Grokster* does not feature in the majority of the civil law countries in Europe, and the Pirate Bay was, of course, not operating out of the USA, but out of Sweden. It had been founded in 2003 and had apparently become the most extensively used file sharing website. Files downloaded were not limited to music, but also included films, books, and TV programmes.[182] Under Swedish copyright law, it is a criminal offence to infringe copyright; further, the Swedish Criminal Code also criminalises any act that contributes to a criminal offence whether by words or actions.[183] So, although Swedish law contains no provisions that parallel secondary or contributory infringement, the possibility of criminal liability in this context arises if it can be established that those accused of contributing to, or

---

175 Jeffrey CJ Lee, 'The ongoing design duty in *Universal Music Australia Pty Ltd v Sharman License Holdings Ltd*: Casting the scope of copyright infringement even wider' (2007) 15 IJLIT 275.
176 [1988] AC 1013.
177 See also discussion in Haflidi Kristjan Larusson, 'Uncertainty in the scope of copyright: The case of illegal file-sharing in the UK' [2009] EIPR 124.
178 See, e.g., discussion in Boyd-Farell, above, 81ff.
179 For an overview of the operation of Pirate Bay, see, e.g., Jerker Edstrom and Henrik Nillson, 'The Pirate Bay: Predictable and yet . . .' [2009] EIPR 483.
180 See, e.g., Manner et al, above, 198.
181 Tara Touloumis, 'Buccaneers and bucks from the internet: Pirate Bay and the entertainment industry' (2009) 19 Seton Hall J Sports and Ent L 253, 262–6.
182 Henrik Wistam and Therese Andersson, 'The Pirate Bay trial' (2009) 15 CTLR 129.
183 Edstrom and Nillson, above.

facilitating, a copyright infringement had knowledge of the infringements, knew that their actions contributed to that infringement, and were doing so for financial gain.[184] On this basis, charges were brought against the three individuals operating the Pirate Bay website and its financier, together with a civil claim for damages on behalf of the copyright holders affected by their activities. The Stockholm District Court found that file sharing was an illicit communication to the public of copyright works and would be a criminal offence in Sweden, provided that it took place in that jurisdiction. This could clearly be established by the fact that the copyright materials were available to users in Sweden, the website was available in Swedish, and the servers were in Sweden. The primary offence was therefore deemed to have occurred in Sweden. Further, the defendants had contributed to the copyright infringement 'by providing a user-friendly interface and search engine, simple upload and download procedures and by administering contacts between users by its tracker or torrent files'.[185]

The eventual outcome attracted intense publicity when the court gave custodial sentences of one year to each of the defendants.[186] Although the custodial sentences were slightly reduced on appeal,[187] an important factor in the perceived severity of these sentences is likely to have been the attitude of the defendants to file sharing and copyright infringement evidenced by their comments on the website and their general attitude to the rights of copyright holders; they had 'made it clear that they were not going to put an end to such dissemination, even in cases where there could be no doubt that it was in violation of individual identified rights'.[188] Edstrom and Nillson refer to the decision as 'a minor milestone in society's quest to come to terms with the effects of digitalisation of products and the disruptive efficiency of the internet in the distribution of these digitalised products'.[189] In the Pirate Bay case, it was not at all difficult to infer intent from the surrounding circumstances, but a clearer exposition of what is required might be desirable for cases that are more equivocal. Two of the defendants unsuccessfully applied to the European Court of Human Rights claiming that the custodial sentences were a breach of their rights under Art 10 of the ECHR.[190] The court found the application to be 'manifestly ill-founded'. Although it acknowledged that the custodial sentences interfered with the right to freedom of expression, in the particular circumstances of the case, the Swedish courts were entitled to find that the applicants' conduct was criminal and required appropriate punishment and neither the prison sentence nor the award of damages was disproportionate.

The effect that this litigation has had on illicit file sharing activities is difficult to ascertain and evaluate. Since the Napster case, there have been an increasing number of sites providing lawful downloading services, such as Spotify and the resurrected Napster itself. Although, as noted above, figures continue to be quoted about the extent and effect of file sharing, Koempel reports that, following the Pirate Bay case, internet traffic in Sweden has reduced by 30 per cent compared to its value before April 2009, and further that 'the latest IFPI figures show that sales of recorded music rose 14 per cent with digital sales up 57 per cent',[191] which could be taken to suggest that the number of users who opt to download lawfully rather than to engage in illicit file sharing is increasing. However, these numbers may also be affected by the increasing use of another sanction – the website blocking injunction – discussed further below.

---

184  Manner et al, above, 198.
185  Wistam and Andersson, above, 130.
186  However, it was not the first case in Scandinavia in which criminal liability had been imposed on the administrators of a file sharing service. In June 2008, the Turku Court of Appeal in Finland upheld the decision against the 'Finreactor' BitTorrent-based P2P network. For further discussion, see Mikko Manner, 'A BitTorrent P2P network shut down and its operation deemed illegal in Finland' (2009) 20 Ent LR 21.
187  The Swedish Court of Appeal also increased the damages they were required to pay from €3.3 million to approximately €5 million and the Swedish Supreme Court subsequently refused leave to appeal, Neij and Sunde Kolmisoppi v Sweden (2013) 56 EHRR SE 19, [9]–[12].
188  Edstrom and Nillson, above, 487.
189  Ibid.
190  Neij v Sweden, above n 187. See also discussion in Joseph Jones, 'Internet pirates walk the plank with article 10 kept at bay: Neij and Sunde Kolmisoppi v Sweden' (2013) 35 EIPR 695.
191  Florian Koempel, 'Digital Economy Bill' (2010) 16 CTLR 39, 42.

## Actions against ISPs

The examples referred to above have been cases against those who make available file sharing software. In the bid to constrain unlawful file sharing, the music industry and associations representing the rights of copyright holders have not only pursued distributors of file sharing applications, but have also initiated actions against both ISPs that are perceived to allow access to file sharing applications via their networks and, as discussed below, individual file sharers. ISPs have been a popular target for those wishing to gain some recompense for violation of their rights in situations in which they cannot identify or cannot locate the offending parties, or in which there are other problems in bringing suit. ISPs, in contrast, are in line because they fulfil all of these criteria: being identifiable, locatable, and frequently situated in the same jurisdiction. There are some very different approaches to the question of the extent of ISPs' liability for copyright infringement, which, to a great extent, depends on whether they are acting merely as a communications carrier, providing the means of transmission between provider and user, or whether they have, or are capable of having, some input and control over at least some of the material to which they provide access. It has been fairly widely recognised that, when acting as a mere communications carrier, there is a very strong case for exemption 'from any type of copyright liability in respect of the provision of Internet infrastructure',[192] but that the situation may not be so clear-cut for ISPs that retain some control. The liability of ISPs for copyright infringement is governed in the USA by the DMCA, in the European Union (EU) by the provisions of the E-Commerce Directive[193] and the InfoSoc Directive,[194] implemented in the UK by the Copyright and Related Rights Regulations 2003.[195] Both the EU and US provisions purport to provide ISPs with immunity from suit (a 'safe harbor') provided that they are not acting as a content provider and have no involvement with the actual information transmitted via their networks – that is, that they are acting as a 'mere conduit'.[196] In both cases, immunity can be lost if there is evidence that the ISP had knowledge (actual or constructive) of the infringement. The provisions of the DMCA and the European Directives provide immunity from liability not only for transient and temporary copies, but also for the actual hosting of material that is in breach of copyright, provided that where there is knowledge of infringing material, that material is removed 'expeditiously'. The DMCA clarifies this duty with a very detailed 'takedown' procedure, whereas the parallel provision in Art 14(3) of the E-Commerce Directive allows Member States discretion to use such a procedure.

## Balancing rights

A frequent action by rights holders against ISPs is to attempt to require them to provide details of individual clients who are suspected of illicit file sharing in order that the rightholders – or, more usually, organisations acting on their behalf – can initiate action against the individuals concerned. Examples of this type of litigation can be found in a large number of jurisdictions, and have generated significant discussion over where the balance should be drawn between the right to uphold copyright, on the one hand, and, on the other, the individual user's right to privacy. The latter may ostensibly be protected by the contract with the ISP and/or specific data protection law, depending on the jurisdiction in question. In Europe, the issue had already arisen in a

---

192 See, e.g., F Macmillan and M Blakeney, 'The internet and communication carriers' liability' [1998] EIPR 52.
193 Directive 2000/31/EC of the European Parliament and of the Council of 8 June 2000 on certain legal aspects of information society services, in particular electronic commerce, in the Internal Market [2000] OJ L178/1.
194 Directive 2001/29/EC of the European Parliament and of the Council of 22 May 2001 on the harmonisation of certain aspects of copyright and related rights in the information society [2001] OJ L167/10.
195 SI 2003/2498.
196 See, in particular, E-Commerce Directive, Art 12, and DMCA § 512(a). ISPs can also take advantage of safe harbours in relation to the activities of caching and hosting.

number of jurisdictions[197] before being considered by the CJEU in *Promusicae*.[198] The facts of the case were not unusual: Promusicae, a non-profit-making association seeking to uphold the intellectual property rights of its members, was contesting the refusal of the ISP, Telefonica, to disclose names and addresses of certain of its customers. Promusicae was in possession of known IP addresses, data, and patterns of use that suggested file sharing using Kazaa, but did not have specific names and contact details. Questions were referred to the CJEU from the court in Madrid concerning the clash between, and the required balance of, intellectual property rights, specifically copyright, and the right to privacy in the form of data protection rights.[199] At the heart of these cases was the apparently simple question of whether data can be acquired without consent if it is needed to trace an intellectual property violation. The CJEU in *Promusicae* considered the provisions of a number of relevant directives on data protection, e-commerce, and intellectual rights.[200] Advocate General Kokott pointed out that, although rights of privacy were fundamental, the protection of copyright was also an interest of society the importance of which had been repeatedly emphasised by the Community,[201] so that, even though the interests of rights holders are private rather than public, they can still be categorised as a fundamental interest of society. However, the Advocate General was not certain that private file sharing threatened copyright protection to the extent that it should take precedence over data protection.[202]

The CJEU judgment itself raised the need to reconcile privacy with property rights,[203] but was very vague as to how this balance should be struck; having set out the overarching principle of reconciliation, it then left the matter for the national court to ensure that implementation of the relevant directives allowed a fair balance to be struck. No explicit guidance was provided on how this might be assessed, but, in the particular case, both the Advocate General and the ECJ found that the combination of the respective provisions did not require personal data to be divulged when the illegal act being pursued did not attract criminal sanctions in the home state. Nevertheless, the judgment leaves it open to Member States to make such provision, assuming that the balance between data protection and copyright is addressed in a proportional manner.

Attempts to pursue individual file sharers by obtaining their details from ISPs have continued in Europe and similar examples can be found in a number of other jurisdictions.[204] In all cases,

---

197 See, e.g., *SCPP v Anthony G* (Court of Appeal of Paris, 27 April 2007), available online at: www.legalis.net/jurisprudence-decision. php3?id_article=1954 (in French); *Peppermint Jam v Telecom Italia* discussed in Eugenio Prosperetti, 'The Peppermint "Jam": Peer to peer goes to court in Italy' (2007) 18 Ent LR 280; *KPN v Brein* (District Court of the Hague 2007) discussed in Diderik Stols, 'Brein v KPN Telecom and the Dutch Civil Code: ISPs under pressure' (2007) 18 Ent LR 147; see also (2007) 23 CLSR 317.

198 Case 275/06 *Productores de Musica de Espana v Telefonica de Espana* [2008] ECR I-271, and see discussion in Helmer and Davies, above and Marianna Rantou, 'The growing tension between copyright and personal data protection in an online environment: The position of Internet Service Providers according to the European Court of Justice' (2012) 3(2) EJLT, available online at: http://ejlt.org/article/view/103/241

199 For further discussion of data protection law in Europe, see Chapter 9.

200 Specifically, Directive 95/46 of the European Parliament and of the Council on the protection of individuals with regard to the processing of personal data [2005] OJ L281/31; Directive 2002/58/EC of the European Parliament and of the Council concerning the processing of personal data and the protection of privacy in the electronic communications sector [2002] OJ L 201/37; Directive 2000/31/EC of the European Parliament and of the Council on certain legal aspects of information society services, in particular electronic commerce, in the Internal Market [2000] OJ L178/1; Directive 2001/29/EC of the European Parliament and of the Council on the harmonisation of certain aspects of copyright and related rights in the information society [2001] OJ L167/10; and Directive 2004/48/EC of the European Parliament and of the Council on the enforcement of intellectual property rights [2004] OJ L 157/45.

201 [2008] ECR I-271, [105].

202 Ibid, [106].

203 Ibid, [65]

204 See, e.g., *Cinepoly Records Co Ltd v Hong Kong Broadband Network Ltd* HCMP002487/2005, available online at: http://legalref.judiciary.gov. hk/lrs/common/ju/ju_body.jsp?DIS=51414&AH=&QS=&FN=&currpage=, and discussed further in Jojo Mo, 'Cinepoly Records Co Ltd v Hong Kong Broadband Network Ltd' [2009] EIPR 48; *Odex Pte Ltd v Pacific Internet Ltd* [2007] SGDC 248 discussed in Susanna HS Leong, 'Pre-action discovery against a network service provider and unmasking the John Does of alleged online copyright infringements in Singapore' [2009] EIPR 185. See also John Leitner, 'A legal and cultural comparison of file-sharing disputes in Japan and the Republic of Korea and implications for future cyber-regulation' (2008) 2 Colum J Asian L 1; Matthew Starmer, 'Video game company hunts down individual gamers in clampdown on illicit peer to peer file sharing' (2009) Ent L Rev 20. For a more US-centred discussion, see, e.g., Weixiao Wei, 'ISP indirect copyright liability: Conflicts of rights on the internet' (2009) 15 CTLR 181.

though, courts seem to consider that file sharers should not be able to use privacy rights to prevent or inhibit them from being pursued for copyright infringement, even though the ethos of the technology is to foster and encourage the availability of such material. The prevailing legal response is encapsulated in the following comment of Poon J in the Hong Kong case of *Cinepoly Records Co Ltd v Hong Kong Broadband Network Ltd*:

> The Internet is invaluable and even indispensable, some would suggest, to the free commu-
> nication, dissemination and sharing of information in modern societies . . . I have no intention
> whatsoever to restrict, obstruct or otherwise frustrate the free flow of communication and
> information on the Internet . . . Users of the Internet, like any individuals, must abide by the
> law. And the law protects the users' rights as much as others' legitimate rights, including
> those of the copyright owners. Some online copyright infringers may well think that they will
> never be caught because of the cloak of anonymity created by the P2P programs. They are
> wrong . . . For protection of privacy is never and cannot be used as a shield to enable them to
> commit civil wrongs with impunity.[205]

Although, in Europe, the substantive provisions relating to ISPs are found in the E-Commerce Directive, Art 8(3) of the InfoSoc Directive requires Member States to ensure that injunctions are available against intermediaries whose services are used by a third party to infringe copyright. The use of such injunctions is discussed in more detail in the next section but the CJEU considered the balance of rights in such cases in *Scarlet Extended v SABAM*.[206] The case arose out of a decision of the Court of First Instance of Brussels both to grant such an injunction and to issue an order requiring the ISP to install filtering software to prevent users from accessing infringing downloaded files by means of P2P file sharing applications.[207] The Belgian Court of Appeal then referred questions to the CJEU about the scope of the ability to issue such an injunction, the requirement of filtering as a pre-ventive measure and the factors influencing the proportionality of such a measure. Unsurprisingly perhaps, the CJEU found that a general requirement to filter fell foul of Art 15 of the E-Commerce Directive and would, in any case, be overly burdensome on ISPs. A fair balance needed to be struck between copyright holders' interests and the interests of ISPs to conduct their business.[208] In the more recent case of *Telekabel*,[209] the CJEU held that injunctions requiring blocking access to specific sites could provide an appropriate balance between the intellectual property rights and the right of the ISP to conduct business as they left ISPs free to determine what measures they would take to comply with the order.[210]

## Blocking injunctions

As seen in *Promusicae* above, copyright holders cannot automatically require ISPs to provide the personal details of alleged file sharers and, as discussed below, attempts to legislate against file sharers have not provided a reliable alternative. Blocking injunctions can be used, not just to target sites facilitating file sharing but also against other sites which encourage copyright infringement

---

205 *Cinepoly Records*, above, [78].
206 Case C-70/10 *Scarlet Extended SA v Société belge des auteurs, compositeurs et éditeurs SCRL* (SABAM) [2011] ECR I-11959.
207 See also *Roadshow Films Pty Ltd v iiNet Ltd* [2009] FCA 332.
208 *Ibid*, [46]–[49]. See also discussion in e.g. Stefan Kulk and Frederik Zuiderveen Borgesius, 'Filtering for copyright enforcement after the Sabam cases' (2012) 34 EIPR 791; and Evangelia Psychogiopoulou, 'Copyright enforcement, human rights protection and the responsibilities of internet service providers after Scarlet' (2012) 34 EIPR 552.
209 Case C-314/12 *UPC Telekabel Wien GmbH v Constantin Film Verleih GmBH* (CJEU 27 March 2014).
210 See also discussion in Joel Smith, Andrew Moir and Rachel Montagnon, 'ISPs and blocking injunctions: *UPC Telekabel Wien GmbH v Constantin Film Verleih GmbH and Wega Filmproduktionsgesellschaft mbH* (C-314/12)' (2014) 36 EIPR 47; and Gemma Minero 'Case note on "UPC Telekabel Wien"' (2014) 45 IIC 848.

including digital storage lockers such as Kim Dotcom's now infamous Megaupload.[211] At first sight, it appears from cases such as *SABAM* and *Telekabel* that although general monitoring and filtering is precluded, injunctions couched in more precise terms are permitted. As a result, blocking injunctions seem to have become the copyright holder's remedy of choice and there have been numerous actions, especially in the UK, in which copyright holders have made an application for an injunction to require an ISP to block its subscribers' access to websites which facilitate file sharing or other copyright infringement.

## The legal basis

Article 8(3) of the InfoSoc Directive requires Member States to 'ensure that rightholders are in a position to apply for an injunction against intermediaries whose services are used by a third party to infringe a copyright or related right.' The CJEU has held in *Telekabel* that ISPs are intermediaries for this purpose; there was no need for a contractual relationship with the person who had infringed copyright, this was not required by the wording of Art 8(3) or any of the other provisions of the Directive.[212] This provision is implemented in the UK in s 97A of the CPDA which allows an injunction to be granted when a 'service provider has actual knowledge of another person using their service to infringe copyright.' Since the first cases involving the Usenet application NewzBin,[213] such orders have now become commonplace and they have been successfully used against streaming sites[214] and also against BitTorrent sites.[215] The principles now seem well established[216] and there have been no instances of ISPs appealing the orders, although the ISPs in *Twentieth Century Fox v BT* did unsuccessfully urge Arnold J to exercise discretion and refuse the order.[217] As a result, even though they might require access to be blocked to multiple different, unrelated and independent websites, they are often dealt with on paper without a full hearing as the issues are taken to be the same. Typically cases are presented in terms of any or all of communication to the public, authorisation and joint tortfeasance.[218]

In *Twentieth Century Fox v Sky*, however, the court opted not to deal with the matter on paper as the facts revealed new and different issues which should have been identified by the claimants; the situation was in fact 'much more complicated than it appeared to those seeking the s 97A order.'[219] On their face, the facts were unremarkable; the claimants held the copyright in a number of films and TV programmes and were making an application for website blocking orders which related to a number of different websites. Birss J observed that the websites in question included not only streaming sites and BitTorrent sites but also 'Popcorn Time' sites which raised new and different issues. Popcorn Time is an application which enables users to download films and TV programmes. It is based on a BitTorrent client but has additional features including media player software, indexing, images and descriptions. Whereas in the original BitTorrent all of the separate pieces of the file

211 MegaUpload was closed in January 2012 – see e.g., Larry McIntyre, 'Cybertakings: The war on crime moves into the cloud' (2014) 14 U Pitt J Tech L & Pol'y 333 Part IIIA, Joseph P Fishman, 'Copyright infringement and the separated powers of moral entrepreneurship' (2014) 51 Am Crim LRev 359, 382–385. Kim Dotcom is still wanted on criminal charges in the US but, at the time of writing is yet to be extradited from New Zealand. See, e.g., Cyrus Farivar, 'Why Kim Dotcom hasn't been extradited 3 years after the US smashed Megaupload' (2015) 18 Jan, available online at: http://arstechnica.com/tech-policy/2015/01/why-kim-dotcom-hasnt-been-extradited-3-years-after-the-us-smashed-megaupload/

212 *Telekabel*, above, [32]–[35].

213 *Twentieth Century Fox Film Corp v Newzbin Ltd (NewzBin 1)* [2010] EWHC 608 (Ch); and *Twentieth Century Fox Film Corp v British Telecommunications Plc (NewzBin 2)* [2011] EWHC 1981 (Ch).

214 See, e.g., *Football Association Premier League Limited v British Sky Broadcasting Limited* [2013] EWHC 2058 (Ch); and *Paramount Home Entertainment International Limited v British Sky Broadcasting Limited* [2013] EWHC 3479 (Ch).

215 See, e.g., *Dramatico Entertainment Ltd v British Sky Broadcasting* [2012] EWHC 268 (Ch).

216 *Twentieth Century Fox v Sky UK Ltd* [2015] EWHC 1082 (Ch), [5].

217 *Twentieth Century Fox Film Corporation v British Telecommunications plc* [2011] EWHC 1981 (Ch), [178]–[18].

218 See, e.g., extensive discussion of the s 97A procedure and the bases of liability in *Twentieth Century Fox v BT* and *Dramatico v BSkyB*, above.

219 *Ibid*, [15] and [60].

are assembled in an ad hoc manner so that the film, say, cannot be viewed until the download is complete, Popcorn Time applications allow sequential downloading of the pieces of the file so that a film can begin to be watched virtually as soon as the process is initiated. The user can thus choose whether to watch the film as a stream or download it to view later. Popcorn Time applications also appear to be able to circumvent any blocking measures that are already in place.

Birss J considered how communication to the public, authorisation and joint tortfeasance should be applied to this different method of viewing infringing material. He observed that in the previous cases, the target websites were not hosting content but were providing access to content hosted elsewhere and might be indexing and aggregating that content. In Popcorn Time applications, on the other hand, a user downloads the application from the target PTAS website but then never needs to reconnect to that site. As a result, Birss J did not think that the same reasoning could be used as with the other types of site. The PTAS itself did not communicate any copyright material to the public; from the users' perspective, all the cataloguing and indexing functions were provided with the application itself, whereas users needed to consciously visit a BitTorrent or streaming website each time they wished to access a film. He was therefore of the view that there was no breach of the right of communication to the public. Although there was an argument that the websites had authorised the infringement, this had not been made by the claimants. He was, however, satisfied that the suppliers of Popcorn Time applications were jointly liable with the operators of the host websites – they had a 'common design with the operators of the host website to secure the communication to the public of the claimants' protected works . . .' and they were using the services of the ISP to do this.[220]

## Are blocking injunctions appropriate and effective?

As mentioned already and discussed further below, actions against individual file sharers have not proved to be a particularly useful method for copyright holders seeking to uphold their rights. It is thus not surprising that they have seized upon the blocking injunction as a more reliable remedy. Nevertheless, a number of reservations have been expressed as to whether such injunctions are appropriate or effective, and there are conflicting views on the matter.

Although the CJEU has discussed the matter in terms of the rhetoric of balancing the competing rights and interests involved, this is not necessarily of practical assistance. As Angelopoulos has remarked in relation to the *Telekabel* decision, 'for all the crisp repetition of the vague maxim of "fair balance" no tools are provided to help identify where this balance should be or how to find it.'[221] In such cases, the CJEU leaves it to individual Member State courts to make the final adjudication of where the balance lies which is a recipe for inconsistency and lack of harmonisation. In *Twentieth Century Fox v BT*, Arnold J noted that the copyright of the claimants needed to be balanced against the freedom of expression of the ISP, the website operators and the users. As the order in question was 'narrow and targeted' and the cost of implementation was modest, he was satisfied that it was proportionate.[222] The Court of the Hague in *Ziggo*,[223] on the other hand, granted an appeal against a similar injunction, assessing that both the interference with freedom to conduct business and the likely ineffectiveness of the sanction in actually protecting copyright indicated a lack of proportionality.[224] However, in the German case of

220 *Ibid*, [55].
221 Christina Angelopoulos, 'Are blocking injunctions against ISPs allowed in Europe? Copyright enforcement in the post-Telekabel EU legal landscape' (2014) 9 JIPLP 812, 815.
222 *Twentieth Century Fox v BT*, above, [199]–[201]. He reached substantially the same conclusion in *EMI Records Limited v British Sky Broadcasting Limited* [2013] EWHC 379 (Ch).
223 *Ziggo & XS4ALL v BREIN* (28 January 2014).
224 See further discussion in Kevin T O'Sullivan, 'Enforcing copyright online: internet service provider obligations and the European Charter of Human Rights' (2014) 36 EIPR 577, 579.

*GEMA v RapidShare*,[225] the Bundesgerichthof has suggested that ISPs who gain financially by facilitating copyright infringement may attract more extensive monitoring obligations.[226]

The Court of the Hague was led to its conclusion that blocking injunctions might be ineffective by expert evidence from a study by University of Amsterdam researchers that showed that despite the existence of the injunction, BitTorrent traffic via the ISPs was undiminished.[227] In contrast, a report presented to the court in *Cartier* showed that, for the UK, there was 'a marked and sustained drop in traffic to the targeted websites after the date on which the blocking order was implemented' which was not present in the global traffic. Arnold J, who has given judgment in the vast majority of these cases, was critical of the methodology of the study relied upon in *Ziggo* and concluded that, in the UK, the 'blocking of targeted websites has proved reasonably effective in reducing use of those websites.'[228] He did however point out that there might be occasional problems of overblocking.[229] The UK Digital Economy Act 2010, discussed further below, included in ss 17 and 18 provisions granting powers to make blocking injunctions. A report by OFCOM reviewing these provisions suggested that website and URL blocking was neither desirable nor practical as a primary approach to copyright enforcement. This report (which was published prior to the explosion of blocking injunction cases) stated that copyright owners were reluctant to make use of s 97A and that it would, in any case, be unlikely to be suitable in streaming cases – which has clearly not proved to be the case.[230] The report suggested various features which would improve a site blocking scheme, most of which are now apparently implemented in s 97A orders.[231] The overall conclusion was that although site blocking might be able to play a useful role in tackling copyright infringement, the scheme proposed in DEA ss 17 and 18 was 'unlikely to give rise to a sufficient level of actions to have a material impact on copyright infringement' and further research was required as to what was a more suitable policy framework.[232] Section 17 was not called into question by the judicial review of the DEA,[233] but as a result of the OFCOM report, no regulations would be issued under ss 17 and 18[234] and these sections have now been repealed by s 56 of the Deregulation Act 2015. Meanwhile, whether or not they are the most effective or appropriate remedy, any residual reticence to make applications for s 97A orders appears to have evaporated.

## Actions against individual file sharers

Although there are many proponents of a freer exchange and dissemination of information via the internet, an increasingly hard line is also being taken against individual file sharers. Henslee reports that, in its attempts to stop unlawful file sharing, the RIAA has initiated suit against over 35,000

---

225  *GEMA v RapidShare AG* (I ZR 80/12, 15 August 2013). Discussed further in Anette Gärtner and Andreas Jauch, 'GEMA v RapidShare: German Federal Supreme Court extends monitoring obligations for online hosting providers' (2014) 36 EIPR 197 and case note (2014) 45 IIC 716.
226  For further discussion of approaches in other Member States see, e.g., Soren Sandfeld Jacobsen and Clement Salung Petersen, 'Injunctions against mere conduit of information protected by copyright: a Scandinavian perspective' (2011) 42 IIC 151.
227  O'Sullivan, above.
228  *Cartier International AG v British Sky Broadcasting Ltd* [2014] EWHC 3354 (Ch), [220]–[236]. This is actually a trade mark case so is not relevant here on the substance, but the use of s 97A orders is reviewed as part of the consideration of whether similar orders should be granted in trade mark cases.
229  Ibid, [67].
230  OFCOM, *Site Blocking to reduce online copyright infringement: A review of sections 17 and 18 of the Digital Economy Act* (May 2011) p 46, available online at: (http://stakeholders.ofcom.org.uk/binaries/internet/site-blocking.pdf
231  *Cartier*, above, [31].
232  OFCOM, above, p 50.
233  *R (on the application of British Telecommunications Plc) v Secretary of State for Business, Innovation and Skills* [2011] EWHC 1021 (Admin), discussed further below.
234  See Department of Culture, Media and Sport, *Next steps for implementation of the Digital Economy Act* (August 2011), p 7, available online at: www.gov.uk/government/publications/next-steps-for-implementation-of-the-digital-economy-act

individual file sharers since 2003.[235] In the first instance, RIAA and parallel institutions in other jurisdictions typically send 'cease and desist' letters to alleged file sharers, as a result of which most agree to settle for some agreed sum without formal action being taken.[236] The apparent intention is to try and reduce illicit file sharing and copyright infringement by making an example of those caught. The controversial, and potentially far-reaching, implications of a policy of aggressive pursuit of individual file sharers were highlighted by the action taken in the US case of *Capitol Records v Thomas-Rassett*. Although not brought by the RIAA itself, this case began in exactly the same way, but was the first such action to go to trial before a jury.

Damages payable in copyright cases in the US do not necessarily reflect the actual 'damage' suffered as the plaintiff can opt for statutory damages as provided by the US Copyright Act and which can be between US$750 and US$150,000 per work. Given that file sharers do not usually just download one work, this creates the likelihood of large awards. However, if the court views the total amount awarded as excessive, the common law doctrine of remittur allows the total amount to be reduced.[237] At the initial trial,[238] the jury was directed that the copyright holders' right to control distribution of their works was infringed merely by the act of 'making available' and she was ordered to pay US$9,250 for each of 24 songs; a total of US$222,000. A retrial was ordered on the basis that the instruction regarding 'making available' was erroneous and that, in any case, the damages were 'wholly disproportionate'.[239] However, the retrial returned the same verdict but the total damages payable was increased to US$1.92 million (US$800,000 per song) on the basis that the infringement was 'wilful'.[240]

The magnitude of this award led to specific criticism of the inequity of the use of statutory damages in such cases. As Samuelson and Wheatland's extensive analysis demonstrates,[241] statutory damages may be punitive in both intent and effect, and they proposed that reform was needed since such damages can be 'applied in a manner that often results in arbitrary, inconsistent, unprincipled, and grossly excessive awards'.[242] On the other hand, there were also those who believed that the deterrent value of making such awards against individual file sharers should not be overlooked and suggested that *Capitol Records v Thomas* served as 'an example of how well litigation works to spread the word that downloading is illegal'.[183]

But the litigation did not end there as the court, applying the doctrine of remittur, reassessed the amount and, after detailed consideration, concluded that 'US$2 million for stealing songs for personal use is simply shocking'.[243] The amount of damages was reassessed at US$2,250 per song, which is still not a trivial amount, but the plaintiffs chose not to accept it resulting in a further trial. On this occasion the jury award totalled US$1.5 million. The court intervened again but, as the plaintiffs had not previously been willing to accept remittur, instead reduced it back to the previous amount on the basis that the court had a duty to respond to a verdict which was 'unconstitutionally

235 William Henslee, 'Money for nothing and music for free? Why the RIAA should continue to sue illegal file-sharers' (2009) 9 J Marshall Rev Intell Prop L 1; see also http://recordingindustryvspeople.blogspot.com/. Such blanket action has now been abandoned by RIAA although it may still pursue persistent file sharers. See discussion in Brionna N Ned, 'Unenforceable Copyrights: the plight of the music industry in a P2P file-sharing world' (2014) 33 Rev Litig 397, 407.

236 See discussion in Ned, above, p 405; and Joshua A. Druckerman, 'The uncertifiable swarm: Why defendant class actions and mass bitTorrent copyright litigation don't mix' (2014) 58 NYL Sch L Rev 931, 939. In this context, see also the discussion of the practice and effect of volume litigation in Andrew Murray, 'Volume litigation: More harmful than helpful?' (2010) 20 Computers and Law 46.

237 For further explanation of the use of remittur in copyright cases see Casey Hultin, 'Remittur and Copyright' (2013) 28 Berkeley Tech LJ 715.

238 579 F Supp 2d 1210 (DC Minnesota 2008).

239 Ibid, 1227.

240 See Nate Anderson, 'Thomas verdict: Willful infringement, $1.92 million penalty' (2009) *arstechnica.com*, 18 June, available online at: http://arstechnica.com/tech-policy/news/2009/06/jammie-thomas-retrial-verdict.ars

241 Pamela Samuelson and Tara Wheatland, 'Statutory damages in copyright law: A remedy in need of reform' (2009) 51 Wm & Mary L Rev 439.

242 Ibid, 497.

243 *Capitol Records Inc v Thomas-Rasset* 680 F.Supp.2d 1045, 1054 (DC Minnesota 2010).

excessive.'[244] On appeal, the Eighth Circuit found that the damages awarded at the initial trial was not disproportionate, a denial of due process nor unconstitutional; copyright was not a private benefit but intended to 'achieve an important public interest.'[245] So, six years after the original trial and with leave to appeal to the Supreme Court denied,[246] the case was returned to the District Court with a direction to reinstate the original verdict together with an injunction prohibiting further file sharing. The protracted discussion in *Capitol v Thomas* related purely to the appropriate amount of compensation in file sharing cases; the decision left some confusion over whether or not merely 'making available' is sufficient to ground an action for infringement or whether there needs to be evidence of 'actual dissemination'. The Eighth Circuit declined to comment on this matter as 'important though the "making available" legal issue may be to the recording companies they are not entitled to an opinion on an issue of law that is unnecessary for the remedy sought . . . .'[247] Espousing the 'making available' approach would radically change the balance of copyright law, since rights holders would not even need to prove that any files had actually been transferred to establish a case of primary infringement. The reasoning on this point has been criticised by academic commentators and has not been uniformly accepted by all US court circuits.[248] The overall outcome was something of a pyrrhic victory for the record companies – the approach of the music industry in pursuing individuals who were, in any case, unlikely to be able to pay the amounts awarded, attracted considerable public opprobrium and consequent reputational damage and it appears that this aggressive stance has now ceased.[249] Instead, as discussed in the next section, bespoke legislation is now being used to target individual file sharers.

## Legislative developments

Legislation has now been enacted in a number of states which establishes a graduated response to copyright infringement. It is most frequently based on a 'three-strikes model' with escalating action up to the suspension of internet access.[250] The US has not passed legislation but has a voluntary self-regulatory 'six strikes' copyright alert scheme.[251] The graduated response approach has been controversial and has been criticised for interfering with rights of free expression and privacy as well as compliance with the rule of law and due process. But Giblin concludes that there is also 'no evidence demonstrating a causal connection between graduated response and reduced infringement'[252] and that 'regulators who have already enacted graduated response laws should take a close look at the evidence and consider whether it is desirable to maintain them in their current forms.'[253]

In June 2009, for example, France enacted the controversial Creation and Internet Law, with the objective of both providing sanctions for illegal downloading, and also encouraging the development of legal downloading. Amongst other things, the law established an administrative authority to deal with the protection of creative works online: *Haute Autorité pour la Diffusion des Oeuvres et la Protection des Droit sur Internet* (HADOPI – now usually adopted as the acronym for the law itself). The provisions of this law gave the authority the power to suspend internet access for up to a year on the third strike. However, the law, as originally enacted (HADOPI 1), was immediately challenged, and parts were ruled unconstitutional on the basis that there was an insufficient balance between

244 *Capitol Records, Inc v Thomas-Rasset* 799 F.Supp.2d 999, 1003 (DC Minnesota 2011).
245 *Capitol Records Inc v Thomas-Rasset* 629 F 3d 899, 908 (8th Cir 2012). There was a broadly similar outcome in *Sony BMG Music Entertainment v Tenenbaum* 719 F 3d 67 (1st Cir 2013).
246 *Thomas-Rasset v Capitol Records Inc* 133 S.Ct. 1584 (Mem) (2013).
247 Ibid, p 902.
248 See, eg, John Horsfield-Bradbury, 'Making available as distribution: File sharing and the Copyright Act' (2008) 22 Harv JL & Tech 273; Shana Dines, 'Actual interpretation yields actual dissemination: An analysis of the make available theory argued in peer-to-peer file sharing lawsuits and why courts ought to reject it' (2009) 32 Hastings Comm & Ent LJ 157.
249 See discussion in Druckerman, above, pp 407–8.
250 See, e.g., Rebecca Giblin, 'Evaluating Graduated Response' (2014) 37 Colum JL & Arts 147.
251 Administered by the Center for Copyright Information: www.copyrightinformation.org/
252 Giblin, above, 209.
253 Giblin, above, 210.

copyright and data protection rights,[254] that the sanctions were disproportionate to the user's freedom of expression, and that the burden of proof was placed on the user to show that he or she was not responsible for any alleged piracy. The consequent revisions resulted in the adoption of HADOPI 2, in which the function of the authority was reduced to monitoring illegal downloads and warning individuals when illegal downloads are detected. The power to impose sanctions, including suspension of internet accounts and custodial sentences in appropriate cases, was passed to judges,[255] but users could also be liable if third parties were to make illegal downloads from their accounts. HADOPI 2 was itself subject to a constitutional challenge, but the Constitutional Council, in a decision on 22 October 2009, upheld the law as it stood – a decision described by the lobbying group La Quadrature du Net as 'sad news for democracy and the rule of law'.[256] Given that the HADOPI law envisages custodial sentences, it may be that individual users will follow the path taken by the providers of file sharing software in the *Pirate Bay* case.

In 2006, in the UK, the *Gowers Review*, in its review of the current state of intellectual property law, recommended that the industry agreement of protocols for sharing data between ISPs and rights holders should be observed in order to remove and disbar users engaged in 'piracy', with the additional proviso that if this approach had not proved successful by the end of 2007, then the government should consider whether to legislate.[257] In the subsequent *Digital Britain* report, produced after extensive consultation, the government noted that 'unlawful downloading or uploading, whether via peer-to-peer sites or other means, is effectively a civil form of theft', together with its belief that a reduction of 70–80 per cent was needed in the incidence of unlawful file sharing.[258] In consequence, it set out the following intentions in relation to internet downloads:

> Firstly, to provide a framework that encourages the growth of legal markets for downloading that are inexpensive, convenient and easily accessible for consumers. Secondly, through encouraging suitable information and education initiatives, to ensure that consumers are fully aware of what is and is not lawful. And thirdly . . . to provide for a graduated response by rightsholders and ISPs so that they can use the civil law to the full to deter the hard core of users who wilfully continue unlawful activity.[259]

Legislative provisions dealing with the last of these points are now contained in the Digital Economy Act 2010 (DEA 2010), which, *inter alia*, inserts new ss 124A–124O into the Communications Act 2003 (CA 2003) providing for a 'graduated response' to illicit file sharing and copyright infringement on the internet. The Act, passed eventually in the 'wash-up' of Bills before Parliament was dissolved for the 2010 General Election, went further than *Digital Britain* and a number of its more controversial provisions were introduced at a later date. The Act was the subject of trenchant criticism both for its provisions relating to online copyright infringement and the manner of its enactment.[260] Indeed, the High Court allowed an application for judicial review of the statute on behalf of two ISPs, TalkTalk and BT, on the basis that there was insufficient scrutiny of the provisions dealing with file sharing discussed below, but the majority of claims were dismissed.[261] The provisions relevant to file sharing are both detailed and complex, but the following discussion provides

---

254 See also Case -275/06 *Productores de Musica de Espana v Telefonica de Espana* [2008] ECR I-271 (*Promusciae*).

255 This could include a fast-track procedure in which a single judge could issue a sanction without a hearing on an *ex parte* basis: see LinkLaters, 'France: The Hadopi Law and France's controversial fight against piracy' (1009) LinkLaters.com, 16 October, available online at: www.linklaters.com/Publications/Publication1403Newsletter/20091016/Pages/FranceTheHadopiLaw.aspx

256 La Quadrature du Net, 'HADOPI 2 validated: A defeat for the rule of law' (2009) *Laquadature.net*, 24 October, available online at: www.laquadrature.net/en/hadopi-2-validated-a-defeat-for-the-rule-of-law

257 *Gowers Review*, above, Recommendation 39.

258 *Digital Britain*, para 18.

259 *Ibid*, paras 45–46.

260 On the latter, see, e.g., Out-law.com, 'The legislative farce of the Digital Economy Bill' (2010) Out-law.com, 7 April, available online at: http://out-law.com/page-10900

261 *R (on the application of British Telecommunications Plc) v Secretary of State for Business, Innovation and Skills* [2011] EWHC 1021.

a summary. New ss 124A and 124B of the CA 2003 (ss 3 and 4 of the DEA 2010) provide details of the 'initial obligations' placed on ISPs, and provide certain rights for the copyright owner that the ISP must implement. These obligations are to be governed by an 'initial obligations code' (IOC), as provided for in new ss 124C and 124D (ss 5 and 6 of the DEA 2010). A new s 124E (s 7 of the DEA 2010) details the contents of such codes. In brief, s 124C allows UK communications regulator Ofcom to approve IOCs that have been drafted by specific ISPs, or the industry generally, to comply with their obligations under these new provisions. Section 124D further allows Ofcom to make a code to regulate the initial obligations in the event that there is no pre-existing approved IOC.

If an IOC is in force, then a copyright owner can make a copyright infringement report (s 124A(2)) to the ISP if it *appears* to a copyright owner that either a subscriber of an internet access service, or someone who he or she has allowed to use the service, has infringed the owner's copyright (s 124A(1)). 'Who [he or she has] allowed' has a potentially wide interpretation, and it has been speculated that this section could apply, for example, to businesses that provide WiFi as a service and also to domestic unsecured WiFi networks. Similarly, organisations (such as universities, pubs and cafes, for example), which provide access to the internet to large numbers of individuals, may also fall within the ambit of this section. Any such copyright infringement report must, *inter alia*, state that there appears to have been a copyright infringement, and offer both a description of that apparent infringement and evidence of it, including the subscriber's IP address and the time at which the evidence was gathered. Any ISP receiving such a notice must then, if required by the IOC, notify the subscriber in question within a month. These new provisions are based solely on the existence of an *apparent* infringement and contain no provisions that deal with reckless, negligent, speculative, malicious, or vexatious notifications. It has already been widely reported that subscribers have been mistakenly accused of file sharing, and it seems unlikely that this trend will be reduced by the enactment of this statute.[262]

The required contents of any such notification are detailed in s 124A(6). In addition to expected details, such as the description and evidence of the apparent infringement, the name of the copyright holder, etc, the notification must also include 'information about copyright and its purpose'. Given that the purpose of copyright can be a contentious topic and not infrequently features in essay topics for those studying the subject, it will be interesting to see what is included in the notification in this respect. Section 124A(6)(i) includes the catch-all that the notification must also include anything else that might be required by the IOC. Examples of what this could refer to are suggested in s 124A(8) and include, *inter alia*, that the copyright owner might apply to a court to both find out the subscriber's identity, and also bring proceedings for copyright infringement. Section 124B then further requires that, if requested, an ISP must supply a copyright owner with a copyright infringement list that 'sets out in relation to each relevant subscriber which of the copyright infringement reports relate to the subscriber but does not enable any subscriber to be identified'.[263]

The intention is that the notification process will itself deter online copyright infringement, but ss 124F–124J then make provision for subsequent action in the event that the desired reduction in online copyright infringement is not achieved. Ofcom is charged with the general oversight of the new regime and s 124F imposes a duty on Ofcom to prepare reports on the extent of infringement of copyright by internet users. Once an IOC has been in force for 12 months, 'technical obligations' may be imposed on ISPs to take 'technical measures' for the purpose of preventing or reducing infringement of copyright by means of the internet (ss 124G and 124H). A 'technical measure' in this context is something that may limit the speed of the internet connection, prevent access to particular sites, suspend the service, or otherwise limit what is provided to the subscriber.

---

262 Dan Sabbagh, 'Digital Economy Act likely to increase households targeted for piracy' (2010) *GuardianOnline*, 12 April, available online at: www.guardian.co.uk/media/2010/apr/12/digital-economy-bill-households-piracy; see also Murray, above.
263 Compare the CJEU discussion in *Promusicae*, above.

These provisions that allow for the introduction of punitive action with very little opportunity for external scrutiny, albeit subject to a code of practice (ss 124I and 124J) and an appeals process (s 124K), are probably the most controversial elements of the new regulatory framework, but there have been a number of delays in implementing the scheme and, at the time of writing, it seems unlikely that it will be operational before the end of 2015. It is thus too early to be able to state with any confidence exactly how it will operate in practice.

## Technological protection mechanisms and digital rights management

Digital technology allows the creation of multiple copies of works that are indistinguishable from the original and also copies of copies with no subsequent deterioration in quality. As Lemley and Reese comment, 'the great promise of digital dissemination – the virtual elimination of the costs of copy production and distribution – is a mixed blessing for copyright owners'.[264] It is hardly surprising, therefore, that as digital dissemination has increased, so have systems of digital rights management (DRM). DRM systems may be used both to prevent actual access to copyright works to prevent infringing copying, or to control the use of a copyright work, which the user has been authorised to access. In principle, therefore, they allow new methods of delivering content, while still maintaining protection for the rightholder's copyright and so, from a rightholder's perspective, look like an effective model for the control and dissemination of digital content. DRM systems have been made possible by the development of technological protection mechanisms (TPMs), which prevent copying, thereby providing an additional method of protection for an author's works that are disseminated online. The use of DRMs and TPMs has been paralleled by legal provisions supporting their use in both the EU and the USA, although these have proved to be a controversial addition to the law on copyright. In particular, these provisions proscribe anti-circumvention technologies, as required by Art 11 of the World Intellectual Property Organization (WIPO) Copyright Treaty 1996. Importantly, this Article implicitly allows circumvention of anti-copying measures for acts that would be permitted by law, but, in the nature of the Treaty provision, gives no practical guidance as to how this should or could be accomplished. The new approach targets the actual prevention of copying, together with those who provide the technology to circumvent this prevention. The circumvention of anti-copying devices raises specific issues in relation to the ability to, and the legality of, decompilation or disassembly of a computer program, but also has wider implications for the dissemination of copyright works on the internet.

In the EU, such provisions were introduced in the InfoSoc Directive. Although asserting in Recital 5 that 'no new concepts for the protection of intellectual property are needed', but that 'the current law on copyright and related rights should be adapted and supplemented to respond adequately to economic realities such as new forms of exploitation', the Preamble contains many references to the appropriate balance of rights that needs to be achieved. The need for incentives, and appropriate regard for creative and intellectual endeavour, is emphasised in Recitals 9–11. Recital 14 notes the simultaneous need to 'seek to promote learning and culture . . . while permitting exceptions or limitations in the public interest', and Recital 31 states explicitly that 'a fair balance of rights and interests between the different categories of rightholders, as well as between the different categories of rightholders and users of protected subject-matter must be safeguarded'. These provisos are then given legal effect in Art 6 of the Directive. The extent to which this provision is successful at balancing these competing interests is open to question, and the fact that the wording does not lend itself to easy apprehension is highlighted by the comment that 'the InfoSoc Directive's eventual provision on the subject, Art 6, became during the legislative process so twisted by conflicting

---

264 Lemley and Reese, above, 1375.

demands as to resemble Laocoon wrestling with the serpents. Legislation should never be so hideously contorted but here it writhes'.[265] Unfortunately, the effect of Art 6(4) in no way encompasses all possible exceptions and limitations to the exclusive rights granted to copyright holders, such as the right to use material for the purposes of criticism or review, for example, suggesting that for fair dealing rights not included in Art 6(4), the Directive does not assist in maintaining a fair balance between authors' and users' rights.[266] Foged, in particular, discusses a number of instances in which public user privileges may be diminished, including when anti-circumvention measures operate to prevent rights given by fair use provisions and the fact that access may, incidentally, be prevented to works that are not subject to copyright protection, such as ideas, facts, and scènes à faire.[267] Crucially, as pointed out by Favale, the TPMs are not themselves 'rights of the owners but the mere technical tools to enforce them' and so should not automatically be entitled to the broad and high level of protection accorded to the exclusive rights given to copyright owners.[268]

The provisions of Art 6 are very similar in essence to those of the US DMCA §1201, which has also been criticised both for its complexity and on a more general basis. Although the DMCA purports to leave the usual fair use exceptions in place, it is difficult to see how compatible fair use is with the DMCA. A number of commentators immediately expressed concern at this apparent disturbance of the traditional balance of copyright law.[269] Fair use is threatened because, even where DRM is used to control rights, it is the copyright holder's interpretation of what rights can be granted (particularly with regard to fair use) rather than any accepted legal interpretation. In particular, copyright owners might, by DRM, grant themselves more protection than copyright law allows them – as Lemley and Reese have remarked, 'copyright owners have a history of trying to enforce the law beyond its bounds'.[270] Given that fair use and fair dealing exceptions are a primary mechanism whereby copyright law balances the rights of the creator and the public interest, DRM has the capacity to cause fundamental changes in the application of copyright law in the digital environment; as Ottolia has suggested, DRM systems can be regarded as 'technical systems enforcing (il?)legal rules'.[271]

Samuelson suggests that, notwithstanding the US commitment to the WIPO Treaty that it had been instrumental in drafting, it might not have been necessary to create such elaborate statutory provisions to give effect to the Treaty's intentions, because the pre-existing law could be construed appropriately.[272] Further, she concluded that, although the way in which the USA implemented the WIPO Copyright Treaty generally conformed to the spirit of the Treaty, which provided a 'predictable, minimalist, consistent and simple legal environment', this could not be said of the anti-circumvention provisions, which were:

> unpredictable, overbroad, inconsistent, and complex. The many flaws in this legislation are likely to be harmful to innovation and competition in the digital economy sector, and harmful to the public's broader interests in being able to make fair and other non-infringing uses of copyrighted works.[273]

---

265 Cornish and Llewelyn, above, 857.
266 See also the more detailed discussion of this point in Terese Foged, 'US v EU anti-circumvention legislation: Preserving the public's privileges in the digital age' [2002] EIPR 525, 536–8; Michael Hart, 'The Copyright in the Information Society Directive: An overview' [2002] EIPR 58, 63–2.
267 Foged, above, 526.
268 Marcella Favale, 'A Wii too stretched? The ECJ extends to game consoles the protection of DRM – on tough conditions' (2015) 37 EIPR 101, 103.
269 See, e.g., Pamela Samuelson, 'Intellectual property and the digital economy: Why the anti-circumvention regulations need to be revised' (1999) 14 Berkeley Tech LJ 519; David Nimmer, 'A riff on fair use in the Digital Millennium Copyright Act' (2000) 148 U Pa L Rev 673.
270 Lemley and Reese, above, 1384.
271 Andrea Ottolia, 'Preserving users' rights in DRM: Dealing with juridical particularism in the information society' (2004) 35 IIC 491, 492.
272 Samuelson (1999), above, 530. For application of Art 11 to free software, see Chapter 12.
273 Ibid, 563.

The issues raised by this latter point have also been the subject of discussion by other commentators, who are concerned that such provisions have the potential to effect a drastic change on the traditional balance between copyright owners' rights and public user privileges in favour of the copyright owner.[274] The fact that such rules may provide blanket protection preventing not only infringing use, but also lawful use under fair use and fair dealing exemptions, has thus arguably reinvigorated the old debate about how copyright law should preserve the balance between the rights of the copyright holder and the public interest in the dissemination of copyright works.

A particular argument is that the overuse of TPM effectively 'locks up' the copyright work so that it is virtually removed from the public domain, notwithstanding provisions detailing permitted acts such as use in research, criticism review, etc. Technology has no way of divining the difference between copying that is an infringement of copyright and that which is not because, for example, it falls within one of the exceptions to copyright, such as fair use or fair dealing. Although they can be used in a permissive way, technological devices, on their face, thus have the potential to prevent copying in an indiscriminate way. This fact is probably the factor most capable of creating significant perturbations in the traditional balance that copyright law has tried to establish between the rights of the copyright holder and the public interest in providing and maintaining access to copyright works. From this perspective, the balance is too heavily in favour of the rightholder and neglects the rights given to users under copyright regimes. As Calandrillo and Davison remark, 'copyright scholars characterize the circumvention rule . . . as a "paradigm shift" away from a three century old focus on the activities of individuals who make unauthorized copies'.[275] On the other hand, proponents of TPM will suggest that there is no incentive to develop new methods of distributing content for the digital age without the use of reliable TPMs to prevent unauthorised downloads. Sookman, writing from a Canadian perspective, points out that 'the evidence is overwhelming that only a small portion of downloading does not involve infringement or illegal activity'[276] and that rights holders who try to establish legitimate payment-based digital delivery mechanisms are unable to compete with freely available content based on pirated copies. Sookman acknowledges that technological protection could potentially limit fair use, but suggests that the more significant issue is whether not providing sufficient protection for digital works will lead to a decline in innovation and creativity, and cites the DMCA provisions as demonstrating that the use and regulation of TPMs have not had a detrimental impact.[277] Overall, he concludes that TPMs are essential to counter the threat to rights holders from unauthorised downloading.

It is beyond the scope of this chapter to examine in detail the voluminous case law that there has now been on anti-circumvention provisions in the DMCA, but in their review of the history of the judicial interpretation of this case law, Calandrillo and Davison suggest that the approach has evolved from one in which the courts were 'blindly intent on preventing piracy and protecting copyright holders' through the nadir of an apparent abandonment of an accurate application of the *Sony* principle, to a more balanced approach in which courts have begun to recognise that 'a weak TPM does not outweigh the substantial public interest in information access'.[278] As well as the technical discussion about the relationship of the DMCA provisions with traditional copyright principles, the DMCA anti-circumvention measures have also been attacked as unconstitutional and constituting an unacceptable restriction on freedom of speech.[279] Mitchell, for example, points out that the goal of the copyright clause in the US Constitution is defined as promoting the 'progress of

---

274 See, e.g., Fitzpatrick, above, 219; Foged, above, 526.
275 Steve P Calandrillo and Ewa M Davison, 'The dangers of the Digital Millennium Copyright Act: Much ado about nothing?' (2008) 50 Wm & Mary L Rev 349, 363.
276 Sookman, above, 145.
277 Ibid, 152.
278 Calandrillo and Davison, above, 414–15.
279 TA Mitchell, 'Copyright, Congress and constitutionality: How the Digital Millennium Copyright Act goes too far' (2004) 79 Notre Dame L Rev 2115; GM Schley, 'The Digital Millennium Copyright Act and the First Amendment: How far should courts go to protect intellectual property rights?' (2004) 3 J High Tech L 115.

science and the useful arts', and that the widespread dissemination of information via the internet points is capable of fulfilling this objective by generally promoting learning. This issue of constitutionality was considered by the US courts in the case of *Reimerdes*.[280] The case arose because the defendant website owners, Reimerdes, Corley, and Kazan, had made available the decryption code for DVD recordings (DeCSS) on their websites. DeCSS was designed to circumvent the encryption technology (CSS) that prevented unauthorised viewing and copying of films. One of the arguments presented was that because computer code is protected speech, insofar as the DMCA prohibited the dissemination of DeCSS, it violated the First Amendment. It was held that computer code was not exempted from the protection of the First Amendment because it was 'abstract and, in many cases, arcane', and neither because the instructions within a program required a computer to execute them.[281] However, it was found that the provisions of the DMCA at issue were content-neutral and, because they were not intended to suppress the ideas of programmers, any impact of the dissemination of programmers' ideas was purely incidental. Congress can enact content-neutral regulation provided that there is a sufficiently important governmental interest; this need not involve the least restrictive means of achieving the desired objective as long as, in the process, it did not substantially overburden more speech than was necessary.[282] As a result, no violation of First Amendment rights was found.

Although the TPM provisions in the DMCA had been heavily litigated, the parallel provisions in Art 6 of the InfoSoc Directive have only been considered by the CJEU in *Nintendo v PC Box*, much more recently.[283] Article 6 requires Member States to provide adequate legal protection against both the circumvention of any effective technological measures and against the manufacture, import, distribution, etc of devices which are marketed and used primarily for such circumvention. Nintendo is a major producer of games consoles and videogames. The use of videogames has increased from 'niche to mainstream' and there has been a corresponding rise in the use and sale of devices which allow games not produced or licensed by Nintendo to be used on its consoles.[284] In particular, this has included the use of so-called 'modchips' and R4 type devices.[285] In the UK, Art 6 was implemented in ss 296ZA–296ZE of the CPDA and Nintendo was successful in preventing the import into the UK of such devices in *Nintendo v Playables*, in which the court described the devices in question as 'templates for infringement',[286] and *Nintendo v Console PC com*.[287]

Nintendo brought a number of other actions in EU states[288] and eventually questions were referred to the CJEU by an Italian court. The cases concerned the sale of 'modchips' and 'game copies' over the internet. The two questions were rather convoluted[289] but essentially the CJEU was being asked first, whether Art 6 applies to a system which includes a TPM within the hardware, even though this meant the device was not interoperable with non-proprietary products[290] and second, what importance should be attached to the uses of the circumventing device when assessing whether TPM should be protected.[291] One problem with video games is that they are difficult to classify for the purposes of copyright. Are they audio-visual works, computer programs, both, a hybrid or sui generis and in need of a new classification? The UK High Court took the stance

280 *Universal City Studios v Reimerdes et al* 111 F Supp 2d 294 (SDNY 2000), affirmed *Universal City Studios v Corley* 273 F 3d 429 (2nd Cir 2001), discussed above at p 131.
281 *Reimerdes*, 327; *Corley*, 447.
282 *Corley*, 454–5.
283 Case C-355/12 *Nintendo Co Ltd v PC Box Srl* (CJEU, 23 January 2014).
284 David Booton and Andre MacCulloch, 'Liability for the circumvention of technological protection measures applied to videogames: lessons from the United Kingdom's experience' [2012] JBL 165, 166–167.
285 See further explanation in *Nintendo Co Ltd v Playables Ltd* [2010] EWHC 1932 (Ch), [8]–[9].
286 Ibid, [48].
287 [2011] EWHC 1458 (Ch).
288 See Favale, above, fn 267.
289 See comment in Case C-355/12 (Opinion of AG Sharpston), [39].
290 Favale, above, p. 101.
291 Ibid, 103.

that they were both,[292] whereas it was apparently the view of a French court that a new category was required.[293] The point is not merely of academic significance as it will be the provisions of the Software Directive[294] and its implementation which will be applied to a computer program rather than Art 6.[295] This was the reason why the Italian court was concerned with questions of interoperability.[296] On the basis that the concept of technological protection measures was defined broadly in the Directive and was necessary for a high level of protection of copyright holders, the CJEU found that Art 6 was capable of covering technological measures comprised in hardware. In a conclusion heavily criticised by Rendas,[297] it decided that the Software Directive was not relevant as 'videogames . . . constitute complex matter comprising not only a computer program but also graphic and sound elements, which, although encrypted in computer language, have a unique creative value which cannot be reduced to that encryption. In so far as the parts of a videogame, in this case, the graphic and sound elements, are part of its originality, they are protected, together with the entire work, by copyright.'[298] It thus bypassed any discussion of interoperability. The proportionality issues were perhaps best set out by Advocate General Sharpston who used the classic proportionality criteria of whether there was a legitimate aim, whether the measure was suitable to achieve that aim and that it did not go beyond what was necessary to achieve that aim.[299] This suggested that TPMs should only prevent legitimate behaviour if there were no other methods suitable to protect copyright. The intended use of the device was not a relevant factor; the crucial fact was the ratio of infringing to legitimate use.[300] But as usual with proportionality issues the matter was left to the national court to consider all the relevant factors in the light of these guidelines.

The judgment effectively underlines the fact that TPMs are only intended to protect the exclusive rights of the copyright owner, and that their use is subject to a proportionality test. However, the conditions suggested for the legal protection of TPMs, namely that there are no less intrusive measures and that there are more non-infringing than infringing uses of the devices in question will prove difficult to assess in practice. Overall this could be good news for gamers but less so for games manufacturers.

## Conclusion

A pervasive theme throughout this chapter has been the need to balance the rights of the creators of copyright material with the rights of the users of that material. Whilst this is not a novel dilemma for copyright law, it may be that the balance requires rather different considerations online to offline. To what extent does copyright law need a root-and-branch reconfiguration for the digital age? Is copyright really so flexible a concept that it can accommodate the challenges of the digital age without contradicting the apparent precepts on which it was originally based? On the other hand, according to Deazley, copyright was initially based not on the rights of the individual, but on an intention to encourage and spread education, and to make information available to the reading public for the general benefit of society.[301] If, then, a digital copyright were to emerge in which the

292 [2011] EWHC 1458 (Ch), [31].
293 Sàrl Aakro Pure Tronic v Nintendo RG 10/1053 (26 September 2011). See Tito Rendas, 'Lex specialis(sima): videogames and technological protection measures in EU copyright law' (2015) 37 EIPR 39, fn 14.
294 The provisions of the Software Directive are discussed in Chapter 11.
295 For further discussion of these overlapping and sometimes conflicting provisions see, e.g., Petroula Vantsiouri, 'A legislation in bits and pieces: the overlapping anti-circumvention provisions of the Information Society Directive, the Software Directive and the Conditional Access Directive and their implementation in the UK' (2012) 34 EIPR 587.
296 See further discussion in Chapter 11.
297 Rendas above.
298 C-355/12, Judgment, [23].
299 C-355/12, Opinion of AG Sharpston, [56]–[63]
300 Ibid, [75].
301 Ronan Deazley, On the Origins of the Right to Copy, 2005, Oxford: Hart Publishing.

balance moved towards the user of copyright material, this could be viewed as returning copyright to its roots rather than a radical development. One solution may depend not on redrafting copyright law, but on continuing to create and accept new business models for the delivery of online content; this need not result in any modification of the copyright regime, but would take their place alongside it. Indeed, Turner and Callaghan have suggested that the growth of search tools, hyperlinkers, and content aggregators '[do] not necessitate a radical rewriting of current copyright laws', but propose instead that there should be rapid action at EU level to safeguard the providers of these tools by the provision of new mandatory exemptions.[302] The European Commission has noted that some rights holders prefer to protect existing revenue streams rather than actively to license their rights on new platforms, and that DRM and TPM have sometimes been perceived in a negative way, as technology used to restrict copying and competition.[303] Further, and more widely accepted, progress might occur if consensus and cooperation could be achieved on the development of both an appropriate rights regime and appropriate business models for the digital environment, rather than the apparent entrenchment favoured by some rights holder associations and user groups.

The fact that the technology produces such perfect copies may be the driving force behind the sometimes overzealous pursuit of copyright infringers. However, as Lemley and Reese remark, 'the content industries have never had or needed perfect control over infringement',[304] which suggests that the goal should be sufficient, rather than total, control of infringement. (It would be a rare area of law in which 100 per cent compliance was expected, much less achieved.) As Watson et al point out, 'it still remains to be seen how measures designed to protect rights holders, but seen by opponents as draconian, can be objectively justified as proportionate'.[305] Although this was written in the context of the case of *Scarlet v SABAM*, the same sentiment could equally be applied to the provisions of the DEA 2010. Powell's view is that the law is 'increasingly modified for the benefit of the major content holders'.[306] In this context, the outcome of *Scarlet v SABAM* itself will be important, because, notwithstanding the above, there often appears to be a quandary amongst rights holders as to whether to pursue those who infringe copyright or those who provide them with the wherewithal to do so, whether that is the P2P service itself or an ISP that provides access to that service. Rights holders may well prefer to target P2P network providers and ISPs, because they are easily identifiable, locatable, and (presumably) solvent. On the other hand, this could be seen as allowing those who infringe to escape liability. The abortive attempts at volume litigation underline some of the problems with pursuing individual infringers and, even with the assistance of measures such as those in the HADOPI law and the DEA 2010, individuals may be much less worth pursuing. Although commentators such as Lemley and Reese have suggested that the problems of enforcement against individuals, including issues of cost, could be reduced by introducing a cheap and speedy alternative dispute resolution (ADR) mechanism, rather than engaging the formalities of litigation,[307] this approach is not currently under serious consideration.

Other copyright modifications in the USA and Europe in response to the digital and online environment, including the US DMCA and the EU InfoSoc Directive, do not prevent standard copyright principles being applied to activities on the internet. The increasing use of blocking

---

302  Mark Turner and Dominic Callaghan, 'You can look but don't touch! The impact of the *Google v Copiepresse* decision on the future of the internet' [2008] EIPR 34, 38. During the passage of the Digital Economy Bill, Lord Lucas proposed an amendment that would have introduced new sections in the Copyright, Designs and Patents Act 1988, which would have provided search engines with immunity from copyright infringement in certain circumstances. Although not adopted, it demonstrates the concern in some quarters to protect the fundamental operation of the internet from excessive litigation. For details see Out-law.com, 'Peer proposes copyright exemption for search engines' (2010) Out-law.com, 12 January, available online at: www.out-law.com/page-10658; for the full text of the amendment, see www.publications.parliament.uk/pa/ld200910/ldbills/001/amend/ml001-iie.htm

303  COM(2007)836 final.

304  Lemley and Reese, above, 1394.

305  Watson et al, above.

306  Aaron Ross Powell, 'Creators, consumers and distributors: Understanding the moral structure of digital copyright' (2009) 5 ISJLP 383, 405.

307  Lemley and Reese, above, 1351–2.

injunctions provided for in Art 8(3) of the InfoSoc Directive has provided another tool for prevention of copyright infringement. Although provisions in both the US and EU provide ISPs with some immunity from liability, that does not necessarily result in a blanket immunity. In addition, if the amendments introduced by the DEA 2010 begin to bite, ISPs will become an essential component of the enforcement process against individual infringers rather than being the neutral entity suggested by the term 'mere conduit'.[308]

As yet, therefore, there is no emerging consensus on how digital copyright should develop and it is clear that, in addition to the debate over which direction should be taken in the future, there will be continuing debate over the developments so far: as concluded by Cornish and Llewelyn:

> How far the results have been effective in real terms, how far therefore they have been fair, is a debate for the moment that can only rage.[309]

## Further reading

Simon Stokes *Digital Copyright: Law and Practice* 4th ed. Hart Publishing (2014)
Department for Business, Innovation and Skills *Digital Britain* (2009) available online at www.gov.uk/government/uploads/system/uploads/attachment_data/file/228844/7650.pdf
Giuseppe Mazziotti *EU Digital Copyright Law and the End-User* Springer (2008)
Hector Postigo *The Digital Rights Movement: The Role of Technology in Subverting Digital Copyright* MIT Press (2012)

---

308 See also discussion of the role of ISPs in Chapter 3.
309 Cornish and Llewelyn, above, 805.

# Chapter 5

# Domain names

## Chapter contents

# Introduction

As new technologies develop, national intellectual property regimes designed to protect rights such as copyright and trade marks may struggle to fulfil their traditional roles. This may lead to reform of the scope of intellectual property rights, changes to the administrative processes for determining and defending such rights and, in the common law jurisdictions, new judicial interpretations of existing legislation and case law, to address usage in new environments or through new commercial practices.

Sometimes, however, the challenge to the existing regime may not be capable of being satisfactorily addressed by the law, in terms of practical application in particular dispute scenarios. Undertaking legal action via national courts to defend an intellectual property right can be costly, time-consuming, and difficult to enforce outside the jurisdiction in which the case is heard. These issues are compounded where the effort and cost of engaging in infringement is minimal for the infringer compared to the possible gains. The question then is whether there may be means, other than recourse to the courts, to protect the legitimate interests of intellectual property rightsholders, whilst also ensuring that they do not in turn abuse those rights. This chapter considers how this conundrum has played out in the area of domain name disputes and trade mark law, which has seen traditional forms of legal redress both augmented, and supplanted, by privately supplied administrative frameworks and alternative dispute resolution mechanisms.

## Domain names

A domain name can be likened to an address on the global computer network, which both identifies and gives other information about a specific internet site. A web domain name permits web users to use unique alphanumeric website addresses rather than to have to remember numeric IP addresses.[1] For example:

| | |
|---|---|
| **bris.ac.uk** | Registered domain name used by the University of Bristol |
| **http://www.bris.ac.uk** | Uniform resource locator (URL) that refers to the front page of the University of Bristol website |
| **137.222.10.86** | Internet protocol (IP) address of http://www.bris.ac.uk |

The domain name system (DNS) is overseen by a not-for-profit corporation, the Internet Corporation for Assigned Names and Numbers (ICANN), which was created in October 1998 and is based in California.[2] ICANN has, amongst other roles, policy responsibility for coordinating the

---

1 See further, Graham JH Smith, *Internet Law and Regulation*, 4th edn, 2007, London: Sweet & Maxwell, pp 148–58.
2 Internet Corporation for Assigned Names and Numbers (ICANN), online at: www.icann.org/

assignment of internet domain names.[3] The technical operation of the DNS is performed by the Internet Assigned Numbers Authority (IANA), which 'allocates and maintains the unique codes and numbering systems that are used in the technical standards ("protocols") that drive the Internet'.[4]

The term 'top-level domain' (TLD), or 'first-level domain', refers to the final segment of the domain name. In the example given above, the TLD is '.uk'. There were originally a limited number of TLDs, which pre-dated ICANN, and fell into three main categories.

| | |
|---|---|
| **Infrastructure top-level domains** | .arpa |
| **Country-code top-level domains (ccTLD)** | For example, .br (Brazil); .ca (Canada); .fr (France); .eu (European Union) |
| **Limited top-level domains** | .int; . gov; . mil; .edu |
| **Generic top-level domains (gTLD)** | .com; .net; .org |

However, there was no technical reason why the number of TLDs should be restricted, and it was envisaged when ICANN was established that one of its goals would be to 'collaborate on the design, development and testing of a plan for creating a process that will consider the possible expansion of the number of gTLDs'.[5] This process began in 2000 with the approval of seven new generic top-level domain names. Four of these – '.aero', '.coop', '.museum', and '.pro' – were restricted gTLDs where domain name holders were required to meet certain criteria, e.g. '.aero' was for use by members of the aviation industry and community. Three – '.aero', '.coop' and '.museum' – were also sponsored gTLDs, where a particular sponsoring organisation took responsibility for developing and implementing registry policies for the domain, e.g. the Société Internationale de Télécommunications Aéronautiques (SITA) sponsored '.aero'.

| | |
|---|---|
| **New generic top-level domains (2000 onwards)** | .aero, .biz, .coop, .info, .museum, .name, and .pro |

In 2003, a further seven sponsored TLDs were proposed. Six of the seven were approved by 2006, but the more contentious .xxx for pornographic websites only gained approval in 2011.

| | |
|---|---|
| **New sponsored top-level domains (2003 onwards)** | .asia, .xxx, .net, .cat, .mobi, .jobs, and .travel. |

By far the largest expansion of the DNS began in 2005, via ICANN's Generic Names Supporting Organization (GNSO),[6] the main policy-making body for generic top-level domains, which held consultations with governments, civil society, business and intellectual property stakeholders, and technologists. In 2007, it reported to the ICANN Board with a series of policy recommendations concerning the ongoing establishment of gTLDs.[7] In June 2008, ICANN accepted most of those recommendations and approved the introduction of a new range of gTLDs, with the initial

---

3 For a history of the role of ICANN in internet governance, see, e.g., Milton L Mueller, *Ruling the Root: Internet Governance and the Taming of Cyberspace*, 2002, Cambridge, MA: MIT Press; David Lindsay, *International Domain Name Law*, 2007, Oxford: Hart Publishing; A Michael Froomkin, 'ICANN and the Domain Name System after the "Affirmation of Commitments" in I. Brown (ed), *Research Handbook On Governance Of The Internet*, 2013, Cheltenham: Edward Elgar.

4 Internet Assigned Numbers Authority (IANA), online at: www.iana.org/about/

5 Memorandum of Understanding between the US Department of Commerce and the Internet Corporation for Assigned Names and Numbers, National Telecommunications & Information Administration, 1998, online at: www.ntia.doc.gov/page/1998/memorandum-understanding-between-us-department-commerce-and-internet-corporation-assigned-

6 ICANN, Generic Names Supporting Organisation, gnso.icann.org/en/

7 ICANN Generic Names Supporting Organisation, Final Report: Introduction of New Generic Top-Level Domains (1 & 8 August 2007), gnso.icann.org/en/issues/new-gtlds/pdp-dec05-fr-parta-08aug07.htm, gnso.icann.org/en/issues/new-gtlds/pdp-dec05-fr-partb-01aug07.htm

aim of accepting applications in mid-2009. ICANN stated that the new gTLDs would provide more innovation, choice, and competition on the internet, especially for non-English language domains. The new gTLDs would be anywhere from three to 63 characters in length, and could support Chinese, Arabic, and other scripts.

New internationalised country code TLDs (ccTLDs) were launched in June 2010, allowing the use of non-ASCII ccTLDs, such as one using Cyrillic, .рф (for Russia). However, concerns about the effects of DNS expansion in the gTLDs, in particular on the effective protection of intellectual property, community interests, consumer protection, and DNS stability, resulted in further review of the process through which ICANN introduced new gTLDs. What emerged from this review in 2011

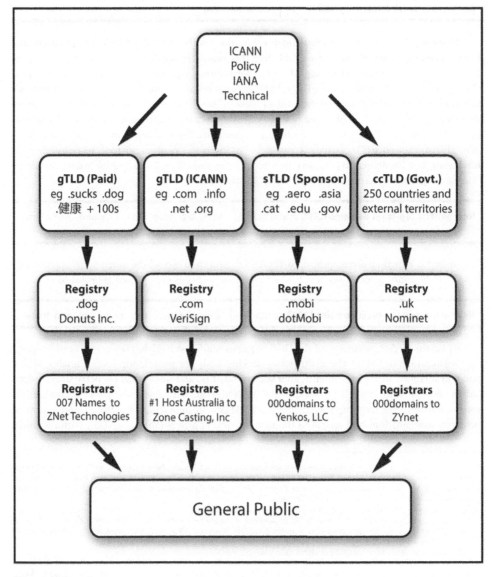

Figure 5.1

was ICANN's New gTLD Program which envisaged the introduction of a large number of new gTLDs, including both new ASCII and internationalised domain name (IDN) top-level domains.

ICANN began a new round of applications for new gTLDs in January 2012 and received 1,930 applications for 1,409 separate TLDs or 'strings' (e.g. '.amazon').[8] At the time of writing in 2015, close to 500 new TLDs from this process have been included in the DNS. Some of these are 'internationalised gTLDs' meaning that domain names can be displayed to users using non-ASCII characters such as those found in Chinese, Cyrillic, etc (see below).

The DNS gTLD expansion process could permit the creation of as many new gTLDs as there are presently domain names in the .com TLD. It allows, for example, Amazon.com Inc to own a gTLD '.amazon' with second-level domains such as '.uk.amazon' and '.france.amazon' instead of its current '.amazon.co.uk' and '.amazon.fr', or perhaps '.books.amazon' and '.cds.amazon'. In parallel with the development of IDNs, it could also permit '.中国.amazon' (or even '.中国.阿玛逊') instead of '.amazon.cn'. However, the proposal does not mean that anyone will be able to register a gTLD – there are two main barriers. The first is the cost. There is an evaluation fee (US$185,000 in the 2012 round) for registering a gTLD and then an annual charge of US$75,000 to maintain the registration (i.e. to keep that gTLD in the DNS root zone).[9] The second is the administrative process to which each new gTLD application is subjected (see below).

ICANN delegates control over each TLD to a domain name registry. It retains direct governance control over the generic top-level domains (gTLDs), and can thus define the terms and conditions to be applied by each gTLD registry. Organisations applying for a new gTLD are thus applying to run a registry business, and are responsible for all the domain names registered in their gTLD. For sTLDs, a sponsor representing the narrower community that is most affected by the TLD is responsible for appointing the domain name registry, and for establishing the terms and conditions to be applied, in conjunction with ICANN. For ccTLDs, the domain name registry is usually appointed or controlled by the government of the state or territory. ICANN does not control the terms and conditions applied by ccTLDs.

Within each TLD, the domain name registries manage the registration of domain names, administer the policies of domain name allocation, and control the technical operations. Some domain name registries are government departments; others are cooperatives of internet service providers or not-for-profit companies. Each registry may sell domain names directly, or via other organisations or registrars. A domain name registrar is a company accredited by ICANN, and/or by a national ccTLD authority or sTLD sponsor, to register internet domain names. Individuals cannot obtain domain names directly from ICANN, but must obtain them either through a registry, or a registrar, as applicable within the TLD in which the domain name is sought.

Under UK law, it appears still unresolved whether domain names are actually owned by the registrant. Nominet, the registry for the .uk TLD, states in its 'Terms and Conditions of Domain Name Registration' that:

10. A domain name is not an item of property and has no 'owner'. It is an entry on our register database reflected by our nameservers which we provide as part of this contract . . .[10]

This suggests that a domain name should be considered a licence from the registrar to use the domain name during the period of registration, and that title for the domain name thus ultimately belongs to the registrar. Bettinger suggests that this has little practical implication for the

---

8 ICANN, New generic top-level domains, newgtlds.icann.org/en/about/program

9 In the 2012 round there was a reduced evaluation fee of US $47,000 for applicants who could demonstrate financial need, provide a public interest benefit, and possess the necessary management and financial capabilities required to run a registry.

10 Nominet, 'Terms and conditions of domain name registration', available online at: www.nominet.org.uk/uk-domain-names/registering-uk-domain/legal-details/terms-and-conditions-domain-name-registration

commercial use of domain names, because, regardless of whether they are treated as items of property or simply as contractual rights, domain names can still be bought, sold, or licensed.[11]

In contrast, Abbot[12] notes that, in US state and federal case law, domain names have been categorised variously as contract rights,[13] tangible property[14] and intangible property.[15] He suggests that the fact that some US courts (notably the 9th Circuit Federal Court of Appeals) currently treat domain names as a form of 'intangible property' is not, in fact, without practical implication: it may, in some circumstances, lead to an unnecessary divergence in approach and outcomes between court cases brought under the US anti-cybersquatting legislation (see below) and arbitration proceedings before ICANN's UDRP panels (see below).

Moving from right to left, after the TLD comes a second-level domain name (SLD) which gives further information, which may be the name of the site in the case of the gTLD (for example, 'routledge.com') or further information about the type of site in the case of ccTLDs. In the ccTLD '.uk', until recently, there was a restricted list of SLDs available.[16]

| | |
|---|---|
| **ac.uk** | Higher and further education and research institutions |
| **co.uk** | Commercial entities and purposes |
| **gov.uk** | National, regional, and local government bodies and agencies |
| **ltd.uk** | Private limited companies |
| **me.uk** | Personal names |
| **mod.uk/mil.uk** | Military and related purposes |
| **net.uk** | ISPs' infrastructure |
| **nhs.uk** | National Health Service |
| **nic.uk** | Network use only |
| **org.uk** | Not-for-profit entities |
| **plc.uk** | Public limited companies |
| **police.uk** | Police forces |
| **sch.uk** | Schools |

However, in June 2014, in response to ICANN's expansion of the gTLDs, Nominet opened up its SLDs for .uk, thus permitting third parties to register 'short' .uk domain names, e.g. 'stephenfry.uk'.[17]

In cases in which the SLD is restricted, or provides another layer of general information, a further domain level will then identify the actual site (for example, 'bris.ac.uk'). Each domain name can identify only one site and is unique to that site, so that two companies who might trade under the same name quite successfully in the 'real world' cannot have exactly the same domain name in cyberspace.[18] There are many organisations that, for example, use the initials 'FSA'. Only one of these can have the domain name 'fsa.com', although there are, of course, other possible registrations and 'fsa.gov.uk', 'fsa.co.uk', 'fsa.org', and 'fsa.org.uk' have all been owned by different

11 Torsten Bettinger (ed), *Domain Name Law and Practice*, 2005, Oxford: Oxford University Press, p 871.
12 Frederick M Abbott, 'On the duality of internet domain names: Propertization and its discontents' (2013) 3(1) NYU J Intell Prop & Ent L 1; Daniel Hancock, 'You can have it, but can you hold it: Treating domain names as tangible property' (2010) 99(1) Ky LJ 185.
13 See, e.g., *Network Solutions, Inc v Umbro Int'l, Inc* 529 S.E.2d 80 (Va. 2000).
14 See, e.g., *In re Paige* 413 B.R. 882 (D. Utah 2009).
15 See, e.g., *Kremen v Cohen*, 337 F. 3d 1024 (9th Cir. 2003); *Office Depot v Zuccarini*, 596 F.3d 696, 701–02 (9th Cir. 2010); *GoPets v Hise*, 657 F.3d 1024 (9th Cir. 2011); *AIRFX.com v AirFX LLC* (2012) unreported (D.Ariz. 24 August).
16 Nominet, 'Rules of registration and use of domain names', available online at: www.nominet.org.uk/uk-domain-names/registering-uk-domain/choosing-domain-name/rules; www.nominet.org.uk/uk-domain-names/about-domain-names/uk-domain-family/second-level-domains
17 Nominet, Our Domains, available online at: agreatplacetobe.uk/our-domains/
18 The courts have provided agreed explanations of the operation of domain names in, e.g., *Pitman Training Ltd v Nominet UK* [1997] FSR 797; *Panavision International LP v Toeppen* 141 F 3d 1316 (9th Cir 1998). See also descriptions in, e.g., Bettinger, above; Lindsay, above.

concerns.[19] Conversely, it is common for the same company to register in more than one TLD: for example, a small fraction of Amazon.com Inc's (or its subsidiaries') registrations include the following.[20]

| | |
|---|---|
| **Main website** | amazon.com |
| **International subsidiaries** | amazon.com.br; amazon.ca; amazon.cn; amazon.de; amazon.es; amazon.fr; amazon.it; amazon.in; amazon.co.jp; amazon.com.mx; amazon.nl; amazon.co.uk |
| **Gateway/referring domain name** | amazon.eu; amazon.gr |
| **Redirect to Amazon main websites** | amazon.org; amazon.info; amazon.biz; amazon.cd |
| **Alternative spellings – redirect to Amazon main websites** | amaon.com; amazom.com; ajmazon.com; akazon.com; akmazon.com; amaozon.com; amamzon.com; wwamazon.com; smszon.com; zamazon.com, amazong.com |
| **Other – redirect to Amazon main websites** | amazonbooks.net; amazonbooks.org; amazonpic.com; amazonoutletstores.com; amazon-sales.com; amazon119.com |
| **Registered, but not in use** | amazon.us; amazon.tv; amazon.hk; amazon.pro; amazonfire.com; amazonisrael.com; amazon-order.com |

## Generic terms, trade marks and domain names

Paradoxically, it is both the uniqueness of individual domain names (there can be only one 'amazon.com') and the potentially unbounded opportunity for registration of domain names containing a trade mark ('amazon.ca', 'amazon.cc', etc) or similar to a trade mark ('amazom.com', 'amazom.ca') that have long posed problems for trade mark holders.[21] They would like to reduce costs by only registering and defending high-profile domain names containing their trade mark: for example, <their trade mark>.com, or <their trade mark>.co.uk. However, the nature of the internet means that unless they can control the use of their trade mark, and similar formulations, in domain names registered in all of the international registries, then a potential competitor or other third party may be able to register and use those names.

While it is possible to use trade mark law via traditional legal avenues to prevent abuses at the national level, that approach has proven difficult or impractical at the international level. This has led to the development of alternative methods of applying trade mark-like rules to the registration and use of domain names, usually through contractual mechanisms built into the registry system. As this chapter will demonstrate, while it still remains possible in certain circumstances for a third party to register a domain name that contains another's trade mark or 'well-known trade name',[22] the ability both to register and to use such domain names is increasingly subject to restriction, either under national law or, more commonly, via registry practices and procedures.

As trading and/or advertising on the web has become an integral part of many commercial enterprises' business strategies, some domain names can become highly valuable, either because

---

19 See Findlay Steele Associates (www.fsa.co.uk) and further discussion below at p 182. Findlay Steel Associates succeeded in retaining this registration in an acrimonious dispute with the then Financial Services Authority (www.fsa.gov.uk). The Financial Services Authority became the Financial Conduct Authority and Prudential Regulation Authority in April 2013. Compare the situation in *WWF-World Wide Fund for Nature v World Wrestling Federation Entertainment Inc* [2002] FSR 33.

20 'Bank of America owns more than 630 active, registered trade marks in the United States and approximately 700 trade mark registrations in other jurisdictions. In addition, the Corporation owns more than 11,500 domain name registrations. However, only http://www.bankofamerica.com provides access to Bank of America N.A.'s award-winning online banking services. Three other domains are authorized portals to other lines of business. All other domain names are defensively registered or were acquired through successful UDRP actions . . .': E Thomas Watson, Assistant General Counsel, Bank of America Corporation, Comment to ICANN on new gTLD Draft Applicant Handbook, 15 December 2008.

21 See, e.g., Dawn Osborne, 'Domain names, registration and dispute resolution and recent UK cases' (1997) EIPR 644.

22 At the time of writing, the domain name 'amazon.net' is not held by Amazon.com Inc (or its subsidiaries).

they contain trade marks or brand names; or because they contain a generic term that consumers are likely to seek out, either by direct search or via search engines.[23] Large corporations, such as Proctor and Gamble, will often register not only product names as domain names, but also the things for which its products may be used. It is thus the proud owner of 'diarrhea.com', which, when consumers type it into a browser, redirects them to 'pepto-bismol.com' – Proctor & Gamble's medicine for digestive complaints.

However, while some generic terms have caused major legal battles,[24] the primary triggers for dispute are domain names containing, or similar to, trade marks, brand names, and famous names. Whereas a large number of trade marks containing the same name can comfortably co-exist because they are associated with different products, belong to businesses in different jurisdictions, etc, the distinctive nature of the domain name in providing global exclusivity has been much sought after, with '.com' addresses in particular demand.[25] This has led to disputes between parties who wish to claim sole entitlement to use a particular domain name, but also to the emergence of activities such as 'cybersquatting', whereby domain names incorporating famous names are registered by third parties to either extract payments from the 'rightful owners', and/or to generate revenue by causing consumers to believe their website is linked with the trade mark.[26]

The introduction of new TLDs has often led to surges in disputes, as would-be domain name speculators attempt to obtain potentially high-value domain names.[27] As a result, new TLD registries have adopted a number of measures designed to limit disputes, often by giving trade mark holders and others the ability to reserve domain names in new TLDs before domain name registration is made more generally available (discussed further below). The mechanisms that ICANN has created to address the issues arising from the latest round of TLD expansion are the latest attempt to balance the interests of existing trade mark and domain name holders with wider public interests, such as fair competition and freedom of speech.

As disputes over the registration and use of domain names proliferated, litigants and potential litigants initially looked to the law for a suitable remedy. Many disputes in the commercial sector arose from the use of trade marks and trade names, and so answers were sought in the trade mark law, unfair competition, and passing off. Those cases that reached the courts can basically be divided into two types: those in which both parties have some legitimate interest in the name; and the more common 'cybersquatting' cases. The latter category includes those cases in which the defendant merely shelved the acquired domain names in order to block use by the 'rightful owner' and extract a high price for the transfer, and those in which the defendants used the name to maximise visits to their own sites, or to cause damage to the plaintiff as a result of the confusion created.[28]

In recent years, the alternative dispute resolution (ADR) procedures introduced by the registries, such as the Uniform Domain Name Dispute Resolution Policy (UDRP) that all registrars of the generic top-level domains must follow, have diverted most domain name disputes concerning trade marks away from national courts. Whilst this diversion may reflect the relative economy and efficiency

---

23 'Sex.com broke the eight-figure barrier in 2005 by nabbing $12 million, . . . Porn.com came in next, at $9.5 million last month, followed by Business.com ($7.5 million in 1999), Diamond.com ($7.5 million in 2006) and Beer.com (a reported $7 million in 1999)': Lisa LaMotta, 'The most expensive web addresses' (2007) *Forbes.com*, 29 June, available online at: www.forbes. com/2007/06/28/google-news-corp-ent-tech-cx_ll_0629webaddresses.html

24 Legal actions relating to the disputed ownership of the domain name 'sex.com' ran for over five years: see Kieren McCarthy, *Sex.Com: One Domain, Two Men, Twelve Years and the Brutal Battle for the Jewel in the Internet's Crown*, 2007, London: Quercus.

25 In 1998, there were 100,000 trade marks in the world that used the word 'Prince', but only one of these could have the domain name 'prince.com': see TW Krieger, 'Internet domain names and trade marks: Strategies for protecting brand names in cyberspace' (1998) 32(1) Suffolk UL Rev 47.

26 For further discussion of how such disputes arise, see, e.g., Bettinger, above; Lindsay, above.

27 See, e.g., CAC-4014/2007 *Game Group Plc v First Internet Technology Ltd* [2007] ETMR 78 (concerning game.eu), in which the respondent had registered 52 '.eu' domain names, including 'business.eu', 'computer.eu', 'hotels.eu', 'fashion.eu', 'finance.eu', and 'mortgage. eu'.

28 The issue of confusion has also been discussed in actions for trade mark infringement in relation to the unauthorised use of trade marks as metatags. For a consideration of the difference in the relevant factors suggesting confusion in metatag and domain name cases, see, e.g., *Brookfield Communications Inc v West Coast Entertainment Corp* 174 F 3d 1036 (9th Cir 1999).

of the ADR procedures, it has at the same time reduced the opportunities for significant development of legal precedents in this area, and limited the perceived need for legislative intervention.

## Internationalised domain names

The scope for trade mark-related disputes over domain names has been increased by the adoption of internationalised domain names (IDNs) which permit the use of non-English character sets. Because much of the initial development of internet services was carried out either by English speakers, or by formal or informal groups for whom the lingua franca was English, the character encoding scheme that was adopted for computer communications was the American Standard Code for Information Interchange (ASCII) based on the English alphabet. ASCII includes definitions for 94 printable characters; of these, a subset of 37 were adopted for use in the domain name system (26 letters of the Latin alphabet, ten digits, the hyphen, and the dot). Domain names are case-insensitive.

Since the original implementation, two factors have driven a demand for a wider range of characters to be available. The first is the fact that while English remains the largest single language in use on the internet, the percentage of internet users for whom English is a first language is estimated to be about 25–30 per cent of the general internet user population, with users for whom Chinese is their first language between 15–20 per cent. Thus, the greater proportion of internet users are non-native English speakers. The second factor is that using the original ASCII subset provides a limited number of viable domain names.

With this in mind, work was undertaken to develop a system capable of dealing with domain names containing non-ASCII characters. Making significant changes to the existing domain name system, including entirely reconfiguring how browsers and email packages handle domain names, was seen as impractical. The solution, adopted in 2003, is called 'Internationalizing Domain Names in Applications' (IDNA).[29] IDNA extends the number of characters that can be used in domain names to include Unicode characters (with some restrictions),[30] by using an ASCII representation of the non-ASCII elements of a domain name. An IDNA-enabled application can convert between the restricted-ASCII and non-ASCII representations of a domain, using the ASCII form in cases in which it is needed – such as for domain name server (DNS) lookup – but presenting the more readable non-ASCII form to users.[31] This allows a business that operates in a particular region (or wants to reach a community from that region) that does not use ASCII characters to represent its domain name on the internet using its native character set.

---

The domain name to be encoded is Zürich.com. This has two 'labels': 'Zürich' and 'com'. The second label is entirely ASCII and so is left unchanged. The first label is processed using the IDNA process to become 'zrich-kva', and then has 'xn – ' prepended to give 'xn—zrich-kva'. The final domain suitable for use with the DNS is therefore 'xn—zrich-kva.com'.

| Domain name input by user | Non-ASCII | zürich.com |
|---|---|---|
| IDNA-processed domain name | Restricted ASCII | xn—zrich-kva.com |
| Domain name input by user | Non-ASCII | tūdaliṇ.lv |
| IDNA-processed domain name | Restricted ASCII | xn—tdali-d8a8w.lv |
| Domain name input by user | Non-ASCII | 中国互联网络信息中心.cn |
| IDNA-processed domain name | Restricted ASCII | xn—fiqa61au8b7zsevnm8ak20mc4a87e.cn |

---

29 See further, FAQs.org, 'Internationalising domain names in applications (IDNA)', RFC3490, available online at: www.faqs.org/rfcs/rfc3490.html

30 Unicode contains more than 100,000 characters, and covers almost all writing systems in current use: see further, The Unicode Consortium, online at: http://unicode.org/

31 Punycode is a computer programming encoding syntax by which a Unicode string of characters can be translated into the more limited character set permitted in network host names. The encoding syntax is published on the internet in 'Request for Comments 3492', RFC 3492.

By early 2009, internationalised domain names (IDNs) were only available in some of the existing TLDs. Of those TLDs, many restricted the types of IDN available.[32] The establishment of new internationalised country code TLDs in 2010 has meant that IDNs have since become more prevalent.

As noted by several commentators,[33] IDNs can pose a number of potential legal problems, not least because several characters (glyphs) in non-Latin scripts are identical to glyphs in the Latin alphabet, but have a different Unicode character encodings, for example:

| Domain name (Latin) | Non-ASCII | microsoft.com |
| --- | --- | --- |
| IDNA-processed domain name | Restricted ASCII | microsoft.com |
| Domain name (Latin + *Cyrillic*) | Non-ASCII | microsoft.com |
| IDNA-processed domain name | Restricted ASCII | xn—mirsft-yqfbx.com |

The possibility of confusion between phonetically similar or visually similar IDNs may be used for spoofing or phishing (known as an 'IDN homograph attack'), as well as cybersquatting. However, to date, no cases appear to have come before UDRP panels.

Equally, registrants can register domain names in non-Latin alphabets that are identical to a famous name or trade mark. An example of this can be seen in *Citizen Watch (China) Co Ltd v Cheng Zhi Gang* in which a Chinese citizen registered the domain name 西铁城.com, the complainant having registered ' 西铁城'('CITIZEN' in simplified Chinese characters) and '西鉄城' ('CITIZEN' in normal Chinese characters) as a trade mark in China.[34] This means that trade mark holders may have to register yet more domain names to cover all possible language variations of their marks.

While the number of UDRP panel decisions involving IDNs remains relatively small at present, and almost entirely related to direct trade mark infringement, as more TLDs accept IDNs, or widen the range of character sets that they will accept, it is likely that such issues will become more common.

# National trade mark law, jurisdiction and domain names

It is understandable that companies that own trade marks in different jurisdictions will want to register the same name as a domain name. However, it has to be borne in mind that, when a word is used as a domain name, it is not performing the same function as when it is used as a trade mark. At the most basic level, a domain name is an address used to facilitate access to an internet site, whereas a trade mark is a jurisdictionally based intellectual property right that enables consumers to distinguish between different products and services. They should not, therefore, be regarded as serving the same purpose.

Nevertheless, given that many companies are closely associated with either their trade marks or products, it is unsurprising that there is some blurring of function. As Froomkin notes, 'a system that relies on geographic distance and sectoral differentiation maps badly to a borderless world in

---

32 The .com gTLD provides IDNs in 113 different languages, using the following character sets: Arabic; Armenian; Bengali; Bopomofo; Cherokee; Cyrillic; Devanagari; Ethiopic; Georgian; Greek; Gurmukhi; Han (Chinese, Japanese, and Korean ideographs); Hangul; Hebrew; Hiragana; Kannada; Katakana; Khmer; Lao; Latin; Malayalam; Mongolian; Myanmar; Oriya; Sinhala; Syriac; Tamil; Telugu; Thaana; Thai; Tibetan; Yi (Unicode 3.2). The .org gTLD provides IDNs in ten different languages. The .uk ccTLD does not currently register IDNs.

33 See Evgeniy Gabrilovich and Alex Gontmakher, 'The homograph attack' (2002) 45(2) Commun ACM 128; Caroline Wilson, 'Internationalised domain names: Problems and opportunities' (2004) 10(7) CTLR 174; and Oleksandr Pastukhov, 'Internationalised domain names: The window of opportunity for cybersquatters' (2006) 4 IPQ 421.

34 WIPO Case No D2001–1305.

which every participant on the global network needs a unique address'.[35] Generally, trade mark law can still be applied where a word used as a domain name is also used as a trade mark. If, then, a trade mark registered in one jurisdiction is incorporated into a website in another jurisdiction, can this constitute 'use' in the course of trade, so that the website owner becomes liable for trade mark infringement?

In theory, a website could be taken as an indication of trading in a worldwide market, whereas, in fact, for most undertakings, the actual market now is very little different geographically from how it was before the internet. In *Euromarket Designs Inc v Peters*,[36] the claimant had stores in the USA called 'Crate and Barrel', had a UK-registered trade mark from 1988 for household goods, and also held a (then) Community mark. Peters had a store in Dublin with the same name. Peters had created a website initially at 'crateandbarrel-ie.com' and then at 'createandbarrel.ie'. The dispute centred on whether the name 'Crate and Barrel' was used in the UK, although in substance neither of the parties traded in the UK. Jacob J was of the opinion that neither the domain name, nor the content of the site, would encourage the average person in the UK to assume that the site was directed at them.[37] He further reasoned that there was little evidence that the defendants were using the words 'Crate & Barrel' in the course of trade in goods that was specifically targeted at the UK consumer.[38] Thus, the mere accessibility of a site in the UK was insufficient for that site to be regarded as making 'use' of a trade mark in the UK. The website was effectively only visible to UK web-surfers because they had taken the initiative of reaching out to access it. As Edwards notes: 'in this view of the internet, websites are seen as essentially passive, and web-surfers (or consumers) as the active agents.'[39]

In *1-800-Flowers Inc v Phonenames*, also heard at first instance by Jacob J,[40] the key issue was the question of whether the name '800 FLOWERS', which, on an alphanumeric phone, connected to a service providing flowers, was sufficiently distinctive, as opposed to merely descriptive. However, there was also discussion of whether there had been use in the UK and, in particular, whether inclusion of the name on a website hosted in the USA would constitute 'use' in the UK if accessed from this jurisdiction. Jacob J, prefiguring his later judgment in *Euromarket Designs Inc v Peters*, suggested that, while there might be areas of law in which publication on a website could be considered to be a publication aimed at the world and thus trigger legal consequences (for example, defamation law), UK trade mark law required regard to particular circumstantial criteria, such as the intention of the website owner and the likely effect on the consumer, and that in this case examination of these did not suggest compelling evidence of 'use' in the UK.[41] The Court of Appeal was equally unconvinced that mere accessibility of a website automatically equated to trade mark 'use' despite the applicant's attempts to link trade mark 'use' on the internet with the jurisdictional rules then developing in defamation law.[42]

Since the *Euromarket* and *1-800-Flowers Inc* cases, the UK courts have had little opportunity to expand further upon the issue of 'use' as it pertains to the internet. In *Bonnier Media Ltd v Greg Lloyd Smith and Kestrel Trading Corp*,[43] a Scottish case concerning an appeal against an interdict (that is, injunction) preventing the defender from setting up websites using domain names containing the pursuer's trade marks, Lord Drummond Young held that although a business website established on

---

35 AM Froomkin, 'Semi-private international rule-making' in C Marsden (ed), *Regulating the Global Society*, 2000, London: Routledge.
36 [2001] FSR 20.
37 *Ibid*, [22].
38 *Ibid*, [23]–[24].
39 Lilian Edwards, 'The Scotsman, the Greek, the Mauritian company and the internet: Where on earth do things happen in cyber-space?' (2004) 8 Edin LR 99, 104. In the US litigation, *Euromarket Designs, Inc v Crate & Barrel Ltd* 96 F Supp 2d 824 (ND Ill, 2000), the District Court found that there was 'use in commerce' in Illinois for the purposes of the Lanham Act, that the Irish firm was operating an interactive website, and that, through both its internet and non-internet activities, had deliberately developed and maintained not only minimum, but significant, contacts with Illinois, thus grounding jurisdiction.
40 [2000] FSR 697.
41 [2000] IP&T 325, 332–3.
42 [2002] FSR 12, [136]–[138].
43 2003 SC 36, [18]–[19].

the internet was clearly intended for commercial communication and the form of such communication might create liability in countries in which the website was accessible, it should not be deemed to automatically do so; rather a judge should look to both the content and the context of the website in order to determine whether a legally significant impact was occurring.

While sparse, the existing UK case law appears consistent with holdings elsewhere in the world. In the USA, while there is no single USA-wide test for jurisdiction in cases involving trade mark infringement on the internet, the test arising from *Zippo Manufacturing Co v Zippo Dot Com Inc*[44] has been highly influential, if not always enthusiastically adopted. In *Zippo*, the Federal District Court of Pennsylvania recognised three categories of internet presence: active, passive, and interactive.

- An *active* site is clearly doing business over the internet in a jurisdiction by having an interactive website and making contracts with residents in that jurisdiction, involving the deliberate and repeated transmission of computer files over the internet – and it will clearly subject the defendant to personal jurisdiction.
- A *passive* site will do 'little more than make information available to those who are interested in it', and is not sufficient to justify the exercise of personal jurisdiction, even if the site is accessed frequently by residents of the forum state, in the absence of further 'minimum contacts'.[45]
- An *interactive* site is one through which the product or service being sold cannot be directly transmitted via the internet, but the site itself allows for the exchange of information between the visitor to the site and the site's owner. Here, 'the exercise of jurisdiction is determined by examining the level of interactivity and commercial nature of the exchange of information that occurs on the website'.[46]

It is arguable that the *Zippo* test is now dated, not least because technological advances since the 1990s have considerably altered our understandings of what website 'interactivity' may entail.[47] Courts are certainly less likely to see probative value in 'a mechanical assessment of the interactivity of the website'[48] alone. However, the underpinning rationale of examining both content and the context of the website, to evaluate the intent of the provider as regards impact in a particular forum, arguably remains unchanged.

An alternative test with similar effect can be seen in *Pebble Beach Co v Caddy*,[49] in which the US Court of Appeals for the Ninth Circuit applied the '*Calder* effects' test.[50] This test requires the defendant to have '(1) committed an intentional act which was (2) expressly aimed at the forum state, and (3) caused harm, the brunt of which is suffered and which the defendant knows is likely to be suffered in the forum state'.[51] Caddy, a citizen and resident of the UK, ran a bed and breakfast (B&B) in southern England, overlooking a pebbly beach, and used a website (www.pebblebeach-uk.com) to advertise the premises. The Californian golf course and resort, Pebble Beach, which had used 'Pebble Beach' as its trade name for 50 years and owned the website www.pebblebeach.com alleged that Caddy's domain name infringed and diluted its trade mark rights. However, the Court concluded that:

> Caddy did not expressly aim his conduct at California or the United States and therefore is not subject to the personal jurisdiction of the district court. A passive website and domain name

44 952 F Supp 1119 (WD Pa, 1997). See also discussion in Chapter 2.
45 See, e.g., *Bensusan Restaurant Corp v King* 126 F 3d 25 (2d Cir 1997).
46 See, e.g., *Maritz, Inc v Cybergold, Inc* 947 F Supp 1328 (ED Mo, 1996).
47 Dennis T Yokoyama, 'You can't always use the zippo code: The fallacy of a uniform theory of internet personal jurisdiction' (2005) 54 DePaul L Rev 1147; Saad Gul, 'Maryland personal jurisdiction law in the cyberspace context' (2014) 45 U Balt LF 1; Andrea M Matwyshyn, 'Of nodes and power laws: A network theory approach to internet jurisdiction through data privacy' (2004) 98 Nw U L Rev 493.
48 Saad Gul, *op.cit*, 11.
49 *Pebble Beach Co v Caddy* 453 F 3d 1151 (9th Cir 2006).
50 Derived from the US Supreme Court judgment in *Calder v Jones* 104 S Ct 1482 (1984).
51 *Bancroft & Masters, Inc v Augusta Nat. Inc* 223 F 3d 1082, 1088 (9th Cir 2000).

alone do not satisfy the *Calder* effects test, and there is no other action expressly aimed at California or the United States that would justify personal jurisdiction.[52]

# Domain name disputes in the courts
## UK

### Competing trade mark rights

*Pitman Training Ltd v Nominet UK Ltd*[53] concerned a dispute between Pitman Training and Pitman Publishing over the use of the name 'Pitman'. Pitman Publishing had been using the name 'Pitman' in association with publishing since 1849. The business had originally been a training business, which was sold in 1985 to Pitman Training Ltd. Pitman Publishing became one of the divisions of Pearson Professional Ltd, a wholly owned subsidiary of Pearson plc. By virtue of an agreement made when the businesses were divided, both Pitman Training and Pitman Publishing were allowed to use the name 'Pitman' in connection with their respective businesses, as long as Pitman Training used it only in connection with training and correspondence courses, and agreed not to publish books or engage in any other trade under that name.

The dispute arose when Pitman Publishing applied to Nominet, which administers registrations for the '.uk' domain, for use of the domain name 'pitman.co.uk', which was allocated to it on the usual 'first come, first served' basis in February 1996. It was intended that a website would be designed and constructed, but would not be ready for launch until December 1996. The domain name was not used in the interim except for advertising in connection with promotions. In March 1996, Pitman Training was told that 'pitman.co.uk' was still unallocated; its ISP therefore procured the name and began to use the email address 'enquiries@pitman.co.uk'. As noted by the court, the question of how this dual registration could have occurred was never resolved.[54]

Pitman Publishing became aware of the situation in December 1996 and requested immediate restoration of the domain name from Nominet, which acceded. Pitman Training commenced proceedings. Scott VC was not impressed by the argument that the actions of Pitman Publishing could constitute passing off:

> This strikes me as a strange proposition given that Pitman Publishing has traded under the style Pitman for nearly 150 years . . . The evidence does not even begin to support the contention that the public associates the domain name pitman.co.uk with PTC . . . That there may be some confusion by some members of the public is undoubtedly so. But that confusion results from the use by both companies . . . of the style 'Pitman' for their respective trading purposes.[55]

So, although the court appeared to accept that inappropriate use of a domain name might sometimes constitute passing off, that was not the case in these particular circumstances; any confusion that might have arisen had its origin in another source – namely, the agreement voluntarily entered into by both parties concerned.

Another case in which, as in *Pitman*, the dispute had arisen because both parties felt that they had a legitimate entitlement to the use of the domain name in question was *Prince plc v Prince Sportswear Group Inc.*[56] When the US firm, Prince Sports Group Inc, the owner of the trade mark 'Prince'

---

52 *Pebble Beach Co v Caddy* 453 F 3d 1151, 1160 (9th Cir 2006).
53 [1997] FSR 797.
54 Ibid, 804.
55 Ibid, 807.
56 [1998] FSR 21; Annette Orange, 'Developments in the domain name system: For better or for worse' (1999) (3) JILT, available online at: www2.warwick.ac.uk/fac/soc/law/elj/jilt/1999_3/orange

for sporting goods in the UK, tried to register the domain name 'prince.com', it found that it had already been registered by Prince plc, a UK computer services firm, which had also registered the domain name 'prince.co.uk'. The dispute led to proceedings being filed in both the USA and the UK. In the UK, Prince plc sought a ruling that the allegations of Prince Sports Groups that its registration of the domain name had resulted in trade mark dilution were unfounded and constituted groundless threats in relation to s 21 of the Trade Marks Act 1994. The High Court found for Prince plc and issued an injunction preventing Prince Sports from continuing with the threats, but there was no discussion of whether the UK trade marks held by Prince Sports were being infringed. The parties subsequently agreed a settlement in which Prince plc retained the domain name, and so the legal arguments went no further.

In most cases in which there is entitlement on both sides to use the name, the significant factor will be first use. It was for this reason that the dispute between Findlay Steele Associates and the Financial Services Authority was decided in favour of Findlay Steele.[57] Findlay Steele had registered the domain name 'fsa.co.uk' in 1997. A website was not launched until 2002, but the domain was used for email communications. The Financial Services Authority, which had the domain name 'fsa.gov.uk', was created six months after Findlay Steele's registration of its domain name. It subsequently sought to obtain 'fsa.co.uk' on the grounds that the similarity between the domain names might lead to confusion for the consumer who was trying to contact the Financial Services Authority.

Thus, in the absence of evidence of bad faith, the first-use principle will be the usual determinant. This principle has been adhered to in cases in which the choice of domain name registered was more dubious. An example of this is found in the case of *French Connection v Sutton*.[58] In 1997, French Connection began the advertising campaign that established the use of 'fcuk' as representing the company. Around the same time, Sutton registered the domain name 'fcuk.com'. He alleged that he intended to use it in connection with his IT consultancy business, First Consultants UK. His evidence was that he thought he would get more hits as a result of the use of this abbreviation. Subsequently, French Connection – which had registered the trade mark, but had overlooked registration of the domain name – sought to have the domain name transferred. Although the judge found the facts of the case from both parties 'unpalatable in the extreme', there was no evidence of bad faith. Sutton had not offered to sell fcuk.com to French Connection for significant financial gain and neither had he acquired any other domain names, which might have been indicative of cybersquatting (see below).

## Breach of registered trade mark rights and passing off

In cybersquatting cases, the typical behaviour is to register numerous domain names corresponding with well-known names and marks, and then attempt to sell them to the rightful owner.[59] On occasions, the names are merely shelved rather than used. Cases across a number of jurisdictions demonstrate that this behaviour is not viewed sympathetically by the courts. The first cybersquatting case in the UK was that of *Harrods plc v UK Network Services Ltd*.[60] The domain name 'harrods.com' was registered, but not used, by unrelated third parties, with the intention of selling the name to Harrods at an inflated price. Harrods sued for trade mark infringement, passing off, and conspiracy. In agreeing to issue an injunction, the legal arguments were not aired extensively, but Lightman J accepted the principle that the law relating to trade marks and passing off could be applied to domain names. He referred, by analogy, to the case of *Glaxo plc v Glaxowellcome Ltd*,[61] in which a

---

57 Adjudicated by Nominet under the Uniform Dispute Resolution Policy (UDRP).
58 (Ch D) December 1999 (unreported); also *MBNA America Bank v Freeman* (2000) unreported, July 2000 (Ch D).
59 See further, Abida Chaudri, 'Internet domain names and the interaction with intellectual property' (2008) 24(4) CLSR 360.
60 [1997] 4 EIPR D-106 discussed in, e.g., J Morton, 'opinion.com' (1997) 19(9) EIPR 496; Osborne, above.
61 [1996] FSR 388 (Ch D); see also *Direct Line Group Ltd v Direct Line Estate Agency Ltd* [1997] FSR 374 (Ch D).

company called 'Glaxowellcome' was registered in anticipation of the merger of Glaxo and Wellcome, and a sum of £100,000 was demanded for transfer of the name. Even though the company had not traded, the court in that case was not prepared to tolerate a price being demanded for a name in which another party had goodwill. In both cases, the court appeared to be heavily influenced by the perceived dishonest intentions of the defendants. In the *Harrods* case itself, the defendant had accumulated a range of domain names corresponding to famous names. Policy issues clearly play a part in these cases, since 'most would agree that some remedy should exist against a domain name pirate seeking to extract payment from the "rightful owner" in return for a domain name which the pirate possesses'.[62]

The issues were aired more extensively in the *One in a Million* case, which remains the leading case in the UK. One in a Million had registered domain names associated with a number of famous enterprises, including Marks & Spencer, Ladbrokes, Sainsbury, Virgin Enterprises, and British Telecommunications, for the apparent purpose of extracting a high price for transferring them. The domain names were not placed in use as active websites, but some were offered to the trade mark holders for significant sums of money. Actions were brought on behalf of all of the companies concerned, on the basis that the registration of the domain names was the equivalent of the creation of instruments of deception, and constituted actual or threatened passing off and trade mark infringement under s 10(3) of the Trade Marks Act 1994 (TMA 1994). In the High Court, Sumption J was faced with several important issues:

- the defendants claimed that trade mark infringement under TMA 1994, s 10(3), required use of the trade mark 'in the course of trade' and a likelihood of confusion on the part of the public, and that neither element was present;
- there was the question of whether mere creation of an 'instrument of deception' – that is, the registration of a trade mark – could constitute passing off, in the absence of a deceptive use, or the intent to supply it to someone else for deceptive use.

On the issue of trade mark infringement, the judge held that the use that the defendants were making of the trade marks in question – that is, of selling domain names containing the trade marks to the trade mark owner for a higher price than the cost of registration – was a use in the course of trade;[63] they did not have to be using the trade marks *qua* trade marks.[64] Regarding 'likelihood of confusion', he did not propose to decide whether s 10(3) of the TMA 1994 required a likelihood of confusion, but that if it was required, then the facts of the case – not least the defendants' own behaviour in registering the names – demonstrated its existence.

On the issue of passing off, the judge noted that the tort of passing off consisted of a misrepresentation to the public, intentional or otherwise, which would be likely to lead the public to assume that goods and services so denoted represented, or were, those of the plaintiff. The tort could also be committed by a party who provided, or authorised the provision of, an 'instrument of deception' to others. However, simply creating an 'instrument of deception' – for example, registering a domain name containing a third party's trade mark – did not involve deception, nor did it by itself constitute placing such an instrument in the hands of others, thus it could not be passing off.[65]

In this case, however, the judge held that it was clear that any party, other than the plaintiffs themselves, could only have one purpose for registering the domain names containing the plaintiff's trade mark – that being to pass off their website and/or products as the plaintiff's.[66] This fact,

62 R Meyer-Rochow, 'The application of passing off as a remedy against domain name piracy' (1998) EIPR 405.
63 *Marks & Spencer plc v One in a Million Ltd* [1998] FSR 265, 272.
64 Referring to *British Sugar Plc v James Robertson & Sons Ltd* [1996] RPC 281, 290–2
65 *Ibid*, 270–1.
66 *Ibid*.

taken in conjunction with the defendants' previous history of registering domain names similar to the names and marks of third parties with the intention of deception, meant that while there was no evidence as such that there had been any trading, or even any other activity via these domain names, the potential for passing off, rather than a demonstration of genuine threat, was sufficient to allow an injunction to be granted.[67] As in the *Harrods* case, there was clearly little judicial sympathy for the business practices adopted by the would-be cybersquatters.

In the Court of Appeal,[68] One in a Million sought to appeal the earlier decision and overturn the negative injunctions restraining it from engaging in passing off and infringement, and the mandatory injunctions requiring them to assign the disputed domain names to the plaintiffs. The Court, however, gave the company relatively short shrift, approving the reasoning of the first-instance judge with regard to TMA 1994, s 10(3), with little additional explanation. As regards the issue of passing off, Aldous LJ first reviewed the history of the action for passing off, noting the five familiar characteristics itemised by Lord Diplock in *Erven Warnink BV v J Townend and Sons (Hull) Ltd.*[69]

He then analysed the position with regard to distinctive names, such as 'Marks and Spencer' and non-distinctive names such as 'Virgin'. In the case of the former, he held that Marks and Spencer was clearly distinctive of Marks & Spencer plc. Thus, where a third party registered a domain name including the name 'Marks & Spencer', there was a clear misrepresentation that the third party was affiliated in some way with Marks & Spencer plc, which amounted to passing off. Neither One in a Million, nor any party to which it sold domain names comprising the name 'Marks & Spencer', could use those domain names without engaging in passing off, and therefore the domain names were fairly characterised as 'instruments of deception'. Thus an injunction preventing their use by One in a Million or their transfer to other third parties was justified.[70]

With regard to the non-distinctive names, Aldous LJ held that registering a domain name consisting of a well-known 'household name' that was not distinctive would not inevitably lead to passing off, and thus the domain name would not necessarily be an instrument of fraud. In the latter case, it would be up to the court to consider the circumstances surrounding registration of the domain name, including the intentions of the person registering the name, to determine whether the purpose of registration was to enable passing off; if it were so, then the domain name would become an instrument of fraud. If the circumstances led the court to believe that the domain name was intended to be used for passing off and was likely to be used fraudulently, then an injunction could legitimately be granted.[71]

As can be seen in *Tesco Stores Ltd v Elogicom Ltd*,[72] the *One in a Million* decision has been followed in a line of cases – primarily applications for summary judgment or interim injunction. In the *Tesco* case, the defendant registered 24 domain names, all of which included the word 'tesco' – for example, 'tesco2u.co.uk', 'tesco2u.com', 'tesco2you.co.uk' – for use in an internet affiliate program. Tesco had entered into a contractual arrangement with a firm called

---

67 Ibid, 273.
68 [1999] 1 WLR 903.
69 [1979] 2 All ER 927, 932: (1) There must be a misrepresentation. (2) The misrepresentation must have been made by a trader in course of trade. (3) The misrepresentation must have been made to the trader's prospective customers or to ultimate consumers of goods or services supplied by him or her. (4) The misrepresentation must be calculated to injure the business or goodwill of another trader ('calculated to injure' means, in this sense, that injury is a reasonably foreseeable consequence). (5) The misrepresentation must cause actual damage to a business or goodwill of the trader by whom the action is brought (or in the case of a *quia timet* action, it must be probable that the misrepresentation will cause damage to a business or goodwill of the trader by whom the action is brought).
70 [1999] 1 WLR 903, 924–5.
71 Ibid.
72 [2007] FSR 4; see also *Britannia Building Society v Prangley* (unreported) June 2000; *Metalrax Group Plc v Vanci* [2002] EWHC 167 (Ch D); *Easyjet Airline Co v Tim Dainty* [2002] FSR 6; *Easygroup IP Licensing Ltd v Sermbezis* [2003] All ER (D) 25; *Global Projects Management Ltd v Citigroup Inc* [2006] FSR 39; *Phones 4U Ltd v Phone4U.co.uk Internet Ltd* [2006] EWCA Civ 244 (CA); *Lifestyle Management Ltd v Frater* [2010] EWHC 3258. For similar results in another common law jurisdiction, see the New Zealand cases of *Oggi Advertising Ltd v McKenzie* [1999] 1 NZLR 631; and *Post v Leng* [1999] 3 NZLR 219. See also Clive Elliott and Breon Gravatt, 'Domain name disputes in a cross-border context' (1999) 21(8) EIPR 417.

TradeDoubler through which other website providers could become Tesco affiliates. Affiliates placed a link on their websites that, when clicked, took them to Tesco's website, and Tesco paid commission to the affiliate via TradeDoubler based on resulting sales. The defendant registered two general websites, 'Avon4me.co.uk' and 'Avonlady.co.uk', as affiliate sites with TradeDoubler after approval by a Tesco employee. However, TradeDoubler allowed the affiliates to group other domain names under the general websites, which also directed traffic to Tesco's website. These domain names were not visible to Tesco, but visitors entering those domain names into their browser would be taken directly to a website operated by Tesco without entering a website run by the defendant. The defendant grouped his 24 'Tesco-related' domain names under the 'Avon4me.co.uk' website, and TradeDoubler recorded traffic to Tesco's websites generated through these 'tesco'-related domain names and included it with the Avon4me website for commission payable by Tesco to the defendant. Tesco caught wind of the scam when its commission bill for Elogicom soared (from a monthly average of £60–70 to over £26,000). On investigation, Tesco discovered the registration and use of the domain names that incorporated the word 'tesco'. Tesco sought an injunction to restrain the defendants from infringing Tesco's registered trade marks and from passing off any goods or services as associated with Tesco by use of the sign 'Tesco' or similar, and an order that the defendants transfer to Tesco each of the domain names. The court, following the test in *One in a Million*, held in regard of the trade mark claim 'that the 'tesco'-related domain names registered by Elogicom were inherently fraudulent, like the 'Marksandspencer'-related name in *One in a Million* – but that even if this were not the case, then 'the relevant test in relation to the other names (such as "Sainsbury") considered in that case would also be satisfied in the circumstances of the present case, so that injunctive relief would be warranted on that basis'.[73] Equally, with regard to the passing-off claim, the court held:

> Elogicom, by its registration and use of the 'tesco' related domain names, has sought to associate itself with and trade upon the considerable goodwill which attaches to the name 'Tesco' for the benefit of Tesco. There is also no doubt that Elogicom continues to threaten to make use the Tesco name, so damaging Tesco's goodwill, both by retaining those domain names with the option of starting to use them again at some point in the future and by virtue of maintaining their registration against Elogicom's name in the register. Therefore, for the same reasons as I have given above in relation to Tesco's trade marks claim and by application of the principles in One in a Million, Tesco is entitled by way of summary judgment to the *quia timet* injunctive relief which it seeks . . .[74]

The result of the UK case law is that the practice of registering domain names that are the same as, or confusingly similar to, the distinctive name/trade mark of another party will, upon action by a claimant, inevitably result in the courts granting both injunctive relief and reassignment of the domain names. Registering domain names that are the same as, or confusingly similar to, a non-distinctive name/trade mark of another party may lead to the courts granting injunctive relief and reassignment of the domain names where it is clear from the context of the dispute that the party that registered the names did so with the clear intent of using them to appropriate the goodwill of the claimant, or to allow others to do so. While the ADR procedures introduced by the registries may now offer potential claimants a swifter and cheaper alternative to legal action, claimants are likely to still bring actions to the courts where they feel that the broader scope of protection afforded by injunctive relief is necessary to protect their future position.[75]

---

73 *Tesco Stores Ltd v Elogicom Ltd* [2007] FSR 4, 102.
74 Ibid, 102–3.
75 Ibid, 99.

## USA

The USA is one of the few jurisdictions to enact specific legislation regarding the registration and use of internet domain names, in the form of the federal Anti-cybersquatting Consumer Protection Act of 1999 (ACPA). The legislation is an addition to the federal legislation dealing with trade mark law, the Trade Mark Act of 1946 (known as 'the Lanham Act').[76] In the USA, trade marks may be protected both at the federal level, under the Lanham Act, and the state level, under states' statutory and/or common laws. This chapter will deal solely with the federal level.

The US legislation has particular significance, because the registries of the key .com, .org, and .net TLDs are based in the USA. Under the US ACPA legislation, legal actions may be taken against a registrant of a potentially infringing domain name (an *in personam* action) or, where the registrant is out of jurisdiction or is otherwise untraceable by the trade mark owner, against the domain name (an *in rem* action), when the action must be brought in the judicial district in which the domain name registrar is located, or in which the registry is located.[77] The registries for .com, .net (VeriSign Global Registry Services), .org (Public Interest Registry), and .biz (NeuLevel) are all based in a judicial district in Virginia. As a result, the reported cases from the federal courts connected to Virginia outnumber those from any other state.[78]

In the US federal courts, trade mark holders involved in domain name disputes have three main courses of action available to them:

- trade mark infringement litigation – in which the trade mark holder has to establish likelihood of confusion between its mark and a third party's domain name;
- trade mark dilution litigation – in which the trade mark holder has to establish that its mark is 'famous' and that the defendant's use of it in a domain name is devaluing the mark; or
- ACPA litigation – in which the trade mark holder has to show a bad faith intent to profit from use, registration, or trafficking in a domain name.

### The Lanham Act

Under the Lanham Act, the term 'trade mark' includes any word, name, symbol, or device, or any combination thereof that is: (1) used by a person; or (2) that a person has a bona fide intention to use in commerce and applies to register on the principal register established under the Act, to identify and distinguish his or her goods, including a unique product, from those manufactured or sold by others, and to indicate the source of the goods, even if that source is unknown.[79] Registered and non-registered trade marks are both eligible for protection.

### Trade mark infringement

Federal trade mark infringement actions require that there must be 'use in commerce' of the infringing mark.[80] However, the federal courts have often interpreted the meaning of 'use in com-

---

76 Codified within Title 15 of the US Code §§ 1051–1127.
77 See, e.g., *Standing Stone Media, Inc v Indiancountrytoday.com* 193 F Supp 2d 528 (NDNY 2002); *Cable Network News LP v Cnnews.com* 177 F Supp 2d 506 (ED Va, 2001).
78 When examining case law under the US Anti-Cybersquatting Consumer Protection Act of 1999 (ACPA), it is important to understand the structure of the US federal courts. The federal courts have jurisdiction to hear ACPA-based cases, because the ACPA is an Act of Congress. The lower federal courts, or district courts, are the federal trial courts for their particular districts. The judicial districts are organised into twelve regional circuits, each of which has a US Court of Appeals. A Court of Appeals will hear appeals from the district courts located within its circuit. It is important to remember that the judgments of a particular Court of Appeal are binding precedent only upon the courts within that circuit. It is possible, and indeed not uncommon, for different circuits to have conflicting precedents.
79 15 USC § 1127.
80 15 USC § 1114(1)(a).

merce' quite broadly.[81] If 'use in commerce' is found, a basic trade mark infringement suit will involve the court determining whether the use of an existing trade mark by a later party (a 'junior mark') will create a 'likelihood of confusion' with the goods provided by an existing party (a 'senior mark'). The federal circuit courts have come up with several similar, but not identical, tests in order to reach such determinations.[82] It appears, however, that there is less uniformity in opinion between the circuits as regards the appropriate test for 'likelihood of confusion' on the internet than there is in the off-line environment.[83]

Some federal circuits have examined the issue of likelihood of confusion as regards domain names by reference to the theory of 'initial interest confusion'. This theory suggests that, where a party lures potential customers away from a producer, by initially passing off its goods as those of the producer's, even if the confusion as to the source of the goods is dispelled by the time of a sale, this is sufficient to demonstrate actionable confusion. The primary consideration has been whether the mere fact that a user is drawn to a website that has used another party's trade mark should be the only criteria to be used. Early case law in the district courts suggested that it was. In those cases, the fact that the actual content of the website was clearly not related to the goods and services of the trade mark holder, and the fact that the website owner was clearly not seeking to profit from the mark, were held to be irrelevant.[84] On the other hand, in later case law, the appellate courts appear to require that there be some intention to capitalise financially on the misdirection of consumers.[85]

## Trade mark dilution

As well as bringing an action for infringement, owners of trade marks can also bring an action for trade mark dilution under federal law. Dilution essentially extends trade mark law to forbid the use of a trade mark, or a mark similar to it, in a way that would lessen the senior trade mark's effectiveness in functioning as a unique indication of the trade mark holder's goods or services.

The Trademark Dilution Revision Act of 2006 (TDRA), amending the Federal Trademark Dilution Act of 1996 (FTDA), provides remedies for trade mark dilution. It permits a dilution claim to be brought where the mark is 'famous', and the use made of the mark by a third party began after the senior mark became famous and was 'commercial use in commerce'. The TDRA defines a 'famous' mark as one that is 'widely recognized by the general consuming public of the United States as a designation of source of the goods or services of the mark's owner'.[86]

The TDRA permits owners of marks that are distinctive, either 'inherently or through acquired distinctiveness', to assert a claim. The Act also provides that it covers both 'dilution by blurring' and 'dilution by tarnishment', and defines the two distinct types of dilution:

- 'dilution by blurring' is defined as 'association arising from the similarity between a mark or trade name and a famous mark that impairs the distinctiveness of the famous mark'; and
- 'dilution by tarnishment' is defined as 'association arising from the similarity between a mark or trade name and a famous mark that harms the reputation of the famous mark'.

81 See, e.g., *Planned Parenthood Federation of America, Inc v Bucci* 42 USPQ 2d 1430 (SDNY 1997) (the registration of domain name 'planned-parenthood.com' and creation of website using that title, which contained information contrary to Planned Parenthood's views, was a use 'in connection with' commerce); cf *555–1212.com, Inc v Communication House Intern, Inc* 157 F Supp 2d 1084 (ND Cal, 2001) (simply reserving the domain name '5551212.com', without use in connection with any commercial enterprise, did not constitute use of allegedly infringing trade mark 'in commerce'); also *Bird v Parsons* 289 F 3d 865 (6th Cir 2002); *Taubman Co v Webfeats* 319 F 3d 770 (6th Cir 2003); *Bosley Medical Institute, Inc v Kremer* 403 F 3d 672 (9th Cir 2005).

82 See, e.g., *Polaroid Corp v Polarad Electronics Corp* 287 F 2d 492, 495 (2d Cir 1961); *AMF Inc v Sleekcraft Boats* 599 F 2d 341, 348–9 (9th Cir 1979); *Interpace Corp v Lapp, Inc* 721 F 2d 460, 463 (3d Cir 1983); *Eli Lilly & Co v Natural Answers, Inc* 233 F 3d 456, 462 (7th Cir 2000).

83 See, e.g., *Planned Parenthood*, above; *Brookfield Communications Inc v West Coast Entertainment Corp* 174 F 3d 1036 (9th Cir 1999).

84 See, e.g., *Planned Parenthood*, above; *Jews for Jesus v Brodsky* 993 F Supp 282 (DNJ 1998), affirmed 159 F 3d 1351 (3d Cir 1998).

85 See, e.g., *Lamparello v Falwell* 420 F 3d 309 (4th Cir 2005); *Interstellar Starship Servs, Ltd v Epix, Inc* 304 F 3d 936, 946 (9th Cir 2002); *PACCAR Inc v TeleScan Techs, LLC* 319 F 3d 243, 253 (6th Cir 2003).

86 15 USC § 1125(c)(2)(A).

The TDRA also clarifies those activities that are not actionable as dilution by blurring or dilution by tarnishment, including:

● fair use, such as comparative advertising or promotion of goods or services; or identifying and parodying, criticising, or commenting upon the famous mark owner or the goods or services of the famous mark owner;
● all forms of news reporting and news commentary; and
● any non-commercial use of a mark.

Prior to the enactment of the ACPA, the FTDA was used in a number of high-profile domain name cases.[87] In early case law, the courts applied a broad definition of whether a mark was 'famous', possibly because of the lack of other trade mark remedies for cybersquatting in the absence of obvious trade mark infringement.[88] Since the passage of the ACPA in 1999, the courts have taken a more restrictive approach towards the use of federal dilution law in domain name cases.[89] However, actions against holders of domain names for dilution where the trade mark incorporated in the domain name is 'famous' remain an option for trade mark holders.[90] As with trade mark infringement actions, federal dilution actions require a showing that the trade mark is being 'used in commerce'[91] and the statute explicitly states that the '[n]oncommercial use of a mark' is not actionable.[92]

## The Anti-cybersquatting Consumer Protection Act of 1999

The ACPA came into force in November 1999. Its application is solely to domain names.[93] It contains both trade mark-related provisions and non-trade mark provisions. The trade mark-related provisions are:

● outlawing of registration, with the bad faith intent to profit, of a domain name that is confusingly similar to a registered or unregistered mark or dilutive of a famous mark;[94] and
● limiting the liability of, and remedies against, domain name registrars for registering an infringing domain name and for refusing to register, cancelling, or transferring a domain name in furtherance of a dispute resolution policy.[95]

The non-trade mark provisions relate to protection against the use of non-trade marked personal names by cybersquatters.[96]

Under the Act,[97] a person is liable in a civil action by the owner of a mark (including a personal name protected as a mark) if, without regard to the goods or services of the parties, the defendant

87 See, e.g., *Hasbro, Inc v Internet Entertainment Group Ltd* 40 USPQ 2d 1479 (WD Wash, 1996), in which the use of 'candyland.com' as a domain name for a sexually explicit website diluted the value of the game company Hasbro's 'Candy Land' mark; and *Toys 'R' Us, Inc v Akkaoui* 40 USPQ 2d 1836 (ND Cal 1996); *Panavision International LP v Toeppen* 141 F 3d 1316 (9th Cir 1998).
88 See, e.g., *Teletech Customer Care Management, Inc v Tele-Tech Company, Inc* 977 F Supp 1407 (CD Cal 1997); cf *Washington Speakers Bureau, Inc v Leading Authorities, Inc* 33 F Supp 2d 488 (ED Va 1999).
89 See, e.g., *Avery Dennison Corp v Sumpton* 189 F 3d 868 (9th Cir 1999), in which it was held that to be 'famous', a mark must be truly prominent and renowned, and may not be merely distinctive (worldwide use of a non-famous trade mark does not establish fame); and *Hasbro, Inc v Clue Computing, Inc* 66 F Supp 2d 117 (D Mass, 1999).
90 See, e.g., *Ford Motor Co v Lapertosa* 126 F Supp 2d 463 (ED Mich 2000) (registration and use of the domain name 'fordrecalls.com' for selling pornography diluted the Ford trade mark).
91 15 USC § 1125(c)(1). See, e.g., *Bally Total Fitness Holding Corp v Faber* 29 F Supp 2d 1161 (CD Cal 1998).
92 15 USC § 1125(c)(4). See, e.g., *Northland Ins Companies v Blaylock* 115 F Supp 2d 1108 (D Minn 2000).
93 See, e.g., *Bihari v Gross* 119 F Supp 2d 309 (SDNY 2000).
94 15 USC § 1125(d).
95 15 USC § 1114(2)(D).
96 15 USC § 1129.
97 15 USC § 1125 (d)(1)(A)

has a bad faith intent to profit from that mark, and registers, traffics in, or uses a domain name that is:

- identical, or confusingly similar to, a mark that is distinctive at the time of registration of the domain name;
- identical, or confusingly similar to, or dilutive of, a famous mark that is famous at the time of registration of the domain name; or
- a trade mark, word, or name protected under 18 USC § 706 (the 'Red Cross', the 'American National Red Cross', or the 'Geneva Cross'), or 36 USC § 220506 (Olympic symbols, including the words 'Olympic', 'Olympiad', and 'Olympia').

The term 'mark' covers both registered and unregistered marks. The term 'confusingly similar' in this context means that the plaintiff's mark and the defendant's domain name are so similar in sight, sound, or meaning that the reasonable user would be confused. Thus, simply including some generic or descriptive term in the domain name along with the mark is unlikely to overcome this test.[98] Equally, misspellings of the plaintiff's marks are also likely to be held to be confusingly similar.[99]

The fact that confusion about a website's source could be overcome by visiting the website at the defendant's domain name will not necessarily sway a court.[100] This is in line with the ACPA's purpose of combating cybersquatting, in as much as cybersquatters may not actually use the domain name for a website, but may simply 'warehouse' it prior to sale to another party. The use of potentially negative terms (for example, 'sucks', 'fuck') in the domain name may persuade a court that there is little risk of confusion.[101] However, it appears that, in such cases, an 'unequivocal negative message' will be required.[102]

Because there has to be a 'use in commerce' for there to be trade mark infringement, courts have often rejected attempts by mark holders to prevent 'gripe sites' from using domain names that are very similar to their marks.[103] However, in *Bosley Medical Institute Inc v Kremer*, the Ninth Circuit held that the important test within the ACPA was the 'bad faith' test, and that:

> The non-commercial use exception . . . is in direct conflict with the language of the ACPA. The ACPA makes it clear that 'use' is only one possible way to violate the Act ('registers, traffics in, or uses'). Allowing a cybersquatter to register the domain name with bad faith intent to profit but get around the law by making noncommercial use of the mark would run counter to the purpose of the Act . . . Additionally, one of the nine factors listed in the statute that courts must consider is the registrant's 'bona fide noncommercial or fair use of the mark in a site accessible under the domain name' . . . This factor would be meaningless if the statute exempted all noncommercial uses of a trade mark within a domain name.[104]

---

98  See, e.g., *PACCAR Inc*, above, 252 (defendant's domain names, such as 'www.peterbiltnewtrucks.com', had the same appearance as plaintiff's domain name 'www.peterbilt.com'); *DaimlerChrysler v The Net Inc* 388 F 3d 201 (6th Cir 2004); and *Audi AG v D'Amato* 2006 WL 3392623 (6th Cir 2006).

99  See, e.g., *Shields v Zuccarini* 254 F 3d 476 (3d Cir 2001) (intentional registration of domain names that were misspellings of distinctive or famous names, causing an internet user who made a slight spelling or typing error to reach an unintended site, were confusingly similar).

100  See, e.g., *Coca-Cola Co v Purdy* 382 F 3d 774 (8th Cir 2004) (internet domain names for anti-abortion websites that differed from famous marks only by the addition of generic terms such as 'my', 'says', or 'drink' were confusingly similar to those marks).

101  *Ford Motor Co v 2600 Enterprises* 177 F Supp 2d 661 (ED Mich 2001).

102  See, e.g., *Sunlight Saunas Inc v Sundance Sauna Inc* 427 F Supp 2d 1032 (D Kan 2006) (use of 'www.sunlightsaunas-exposed.com', which contained the plaintiff's mark SUNLIGHT SAUNAS, did not send the same unequivocal negative message as 'sucks'; it might not immediately alert an internet user that he or she was entering a 'gripe site').

103  See, e.g., *Lamparello v Falwell* 420 F 3d 309 (4th Cir 2005) (registration of 'www.fallwell.com' domain name for website expressly critical of Reverend Jerry Falwell's views on homosexuality did not violate ACPA); see also *TMI Inc v Maxwell* 368 F 3d 433 (5th Cir 2004); and *Lucas Nursery & Landscaping* 359 F 3d 810 (6th Cir 2004).

104  *Bosley Medical Institute Inc v Kremer* 403 F 3d 672, 680–1 (9th Cir 2005).

The meaning of the terms 'distinctive', 'dilutive', and 'famous' are the same as those applied under the TDRA. Failure by a plaintiff to demonstrate that their mark is distinctive or famous will result in the rejection of the plaintiff's ACPA claims.[105]

### Bad faith under the ACPA

The Act lists nine non-exclusive, non-exhaustive factors for determining bad faith.[106] As the Second Circuit noted in an early judgment, often cited by other circuit courts, the most important grounds for finding bad faith 'are the unique circumstances of th[e] case which do not fit neatly into the specific factors enumerated by Congress, but may nevertheless be considered under the statute'.[107]

- *The trade mark or other intellectual property rights of the person, if any, in the domain name.* This recognises that, under trade mark law, there may be concurring uses of the same name that are non-infringing, due to their use in conjunction with different types of product or service, or in different national markets.[108]
- *The extent to which the domain name consists of the legal name of the person or a name that is otherwise commonly used to identify that person.* This recognises that a person should be permitted to register his or her legal name or widely recognised nickname as the domain name of his or her website.[109]
- *The person's prior use, if any, of the domain name in connection with the bona fide offering of any goods or services.* This recognises that the legitimate use of the domain name in commerce is a good indicator of good faith intent.[110]
- *The person's bona fide non-commercial or fair use of the mark in a site accessible under the domain name.* This recognises the line of case law developed prior to the ACPA that held that the non-confusing use of a company name or mark in a domain name on a website used solely to criticise the goods or policies of that company was a fair use and thus could not be infringement.[111] The courts are likely, however, to be unpersuaded by supposedly critical sites upon which criticism only appears after the domain name dispute arises.[112]
- *The person's intent to divert consumers from the mark owner's online location to a site accessible under the domain name that could harm the goodwill represented by the mark, either for commercial gain or with the intent to tarnish or disparage the mark, by creating a likelihood of confusion as to the source, sponsorship, affiliation, or endorsement of the site.* This recognises that cybersquatters who actually create a website under the domain names that they have registered using other parties' trade marks often intend to divert internet users to their own sites under false pretences.[113]
- *The person's offer to transfer, sell, or otherwise assign the domain name to the mark owner or any third party for financial gain without having used, or having an intent to use, the domain name in the bona fide offering of any goods or services, or the person's prior conduct indicating a pattern of such conduct.* This is premised on the

---

105 See, e.g., *Bavaro Palace, SA v Vacation Tours, Inc* 2006 WL 2847233 (11th Cir 2006).
106 15 USC § 1125(d)(1)(B).
107 *Sporty's Farm LLC v Sportsman's Market, Inc* 202 F 3d 489, 499 (2d Cir 2000).
108 See, as an example of 'bad faith', *Virtual Works, Inc v Network Solutions, Inc* 106 F Supp 2d 845 (ED Va, 2000), aff'd 238 F 3d 264 (4th Cir 2001) (defendant registered and used the domain name 'vw.net' for two years in its business, but never did business as VW nor identified itself as such and knew that it was registering a domain name bearing strong resemblance to a federally protected trade mark, and did so, at least in part, with the idea of selling the site 'for a lot of money' to the mark's owner).
109 See, e.g., *Nissan Motor Co v Nissan Computer Corp* 2002 WL 32006514 (CD Cal, 7 January 2002); and *Lewittes v Cohen* 2004 WL 1171261 (SDNY 2004).
110 See, e.g., *Sloan v Auditron Electronic Corp* 68 Fed Appx 386 (4th Cir 2003); cf *Sporty's Farm LLC*, above.
111 See, e.g., *Bally Total Fitness Holding Corp v Faber* 29 F Supp 2d 1161 (CD Cal 1998); *TMI, Inc v Maxwell* 368 F 3d 433 (5th Cir 2004); *Bosley Medical Institute, Inc v Kremer* 403 F 3d 672, 680–1 (9th Cir 2005).
112 See, e.g., *Shields v Zuccarini* 254 F 3d 476 (3d Cir 2001).
113 See, e.g., *Planned Parenthood Federation of America, Inc v Bucci* 42 USPQ 2d 1430 (SDNY 1997); *Jews for Jesus v Brodsky* 993 F Supp 282 (DNJ 1998), aff'd 159 F 3d 1351 (3d Cir 1998); *Coca-Cola Co v Purdy* 382 F 3d 774 (8th Cir 2004); *Faegre & Benson LLP v Purdy* 70 USPQ 2d 1315 (D Minn 2004); *March Madness Athletic Ass'n, LLC v Netfire, Inc* 310 F Supp 2d 786 (ND Tex 2003); *Venetian Casino Resort, LLC v Venetiangold.com* 380 F Supp 2d 737 (ED Va, 2005).

basis that cybersquatters often intend to trade on the value of trade mark owners' marks by engaging in the business of registering domain names consisting of or incorporating those marks and selling them to the rightful trade mark owners. However, Congress did not intend any offer to sell a domain name to a trade mark holder to be automatically indicative of bad faith.[114]

- *The person's provision of material and misleading false contact information when applying for the registration of the domain name, the person's intentional failure to maintain accurate contact information, or the person's prior conduct indicating a pattern of such conduct.* Cybersquatters will often take great pains to avoid contact with trade mark holders, particularly if they are using the relevant domain names to divert internet users to their own sites by creating confusion as to the source, sponsorship, affiliation, or enforcement of the site.[115]

- *The person's registration or acquisition of multiple domain names that the person knows are identical or confusingly similar to marks of others that are distinctive at the time of registration of such domain names, or dilutive of famous marks of others that are famous at the time of registration of such domain names, without regard to the goods or services of the parties.* This addresses the 'warehousing' of domain names whereby a cybersquatter has amassed hundreds of domain names identical or confusingly similar to the marks of others.[116] While the warehousing of many domain names, particularly where some of those domain names resemble well-known trade marks, tends to be viewed with suspicion by the courts,[117] 'warehousing' by itself (even including domain names that resemble well-known trade marks) is not definitive proof of bad faith.[118]

- *The extent to which the mark incorporated in the person's domain name registration is or is not distinctive and famous, as defined within the amended dilution section of the Lanham Act.* This provides that the court should have regard to the strength of the plaintiff's mark. The stronger the mark is, the more chance there is for the possibility of confusion, and the less likely it is that the defendant could have registered the domain name in good faith in the absence of knowledge of the mark.

The ACPA contains a 'safe harbour' provision that bad faith intent 'shall not be found in any case in which the court determines that the person believed and had reasonable grounds to believe that the use of the domain name was fair use or otherwise lawful'.[119] Some concerns have been expressed about its breadth.[120] However, while some defendants have successfully argued that they had reasonable grounds to believe that their use was lawful,[121] the courts have been quick to rule out such arguments in the light of actual fact situations.[122] Thus the safe harbour is a relatively narrow one, because it requires the registrant to have an objectively 'reasonable' basis for believing that he or she is making fair or lawful use of the domain name.

114 Contrast *VirtualWorks, Inc v Network Solutions, Inc* 106 F Supp 2d 845 (ED Va, 2000), aff'd 238 F 3d 264 (4th Cir 2001); and *Ford Motor Co v Catalanotte* 342 F 3d 543 (6th Cir 2003), with *Interstellar Starship Servs, Ltd v Epix, Inc* 304 F 3d 936, 946 (9th Cir 2002). However, the profoundly negative connotations that the courts often appear to attach to such offers, and the apparent willingness of plaintiffs to allege bad faith on the grounds of any offer to sell, means that it is probably unwise for a registrant of a domain name consisting of, or incorporating, a third party's mark to make such an offer or, potentially, even to enter into negotiations with the trade mark holder in a dispute scenario.

115 John Zuccarini appears routinely to have provided inaccurate or false contact information when registering websites for use in his 'mousetrapping' schemes: e.g., WIPO Case No D2002–0950 *Wal-Mart Stores, Inc v John Zuccarini d/b/a RaveClub Berlin.*

116 See, e.g., *Panavision Int'l LP v Toeppen* 945 F Supp 1296 (CD Cal 1996).

117 See, e.g., *E & J Gallo Winery v Spider Webs Ltd* 286 F 3d 270 (5th Cir 2002).

118 See, e.g., *Avery Dennison Corp v Sumpton* 189 F 3d 868 (9th Cir 1999).

119 15 USC S 1225(d)(1)(B)(ii).

120 *VirtualWorks, Inc v Volkswagen of America, Inc* 238 F 3d 264, 270 (4th Cir 2001).

121 See, e.g., *Cello Holdings, LLC v Lawrence-Dahl Companies* 89 F Supp 2d 464 (SDNY 2000); *Interstellar Starship Services Ltd,* above; *Mayflower Transit, LLC v Prince* 314 F Supp 2d 362 (DNJ 2004); *Rohr-Gurnee Motors, Inc v Patterson* 2004 WL 422525 (ND Ill, 9 February 2004).

122 See, e.g., *Shields v Zuccarini* 254 F 3d 476 (3d Cir 2001); *Coca-Cola Co v Purdy* 382 F 3d 774 (8th Cir 2004); *Audi AG v D'Amato* 2006 WL 3392623 (6th Cir 2006).

## In personam *and* in rem *actions*

Under normal circumstances, an action by a plaintiff under the ACPA would be an in personam action – that is, it would be against the domain name registrant, or his or her licensee. As already noted, in an in personam action, the defendant will be liable if he or she has a bad faith intent to profit from the mark, and register, traffic in, or use a domain name that is identical, confusingly similar, or dilutive to, or of, a distinctive or famous mark. When filing an in personam ACPA case, the normal rules of personal jurisdiction apply.[123]

Remedies in an in personam case under the ACPA can include both injunctive relief and monetary relief. Injunctive relief may simply be the transfer or cancellation of the domain name, but may also involve injunctions barring defendants from engaging in other action, such as registering any other plaintiff's other mark.[124] Monetary relief can be requested in the form of defendant's profits, plaintiff's damages, and, in exceptional cases, reasonable attorneys' fees.[125] In lieu of actual damages and profits, however, the plaintiff may elect, at any time before the trial court renders final judgment, an award of statutory damages ranging from US$1,000 to US$100,000 per domain name.[126]

The Fraudulent Online Identity Sanctions Act of 2004 (FOISA), part of the Intellectual Property Protection and Courts Amendments Act of 2004, creates a rebuttable presumption of wilfulness where a defendant knowingly provides materially false contact information in a domain name registration and then uses the website accessed by that domain name in infringing another party's copyright or trade mark. The presumption that the defendant committed wilful infringement can, at the court's discretion, lead to significantly increased damages – in trade mark cases, the statutory damages upper limit is increased to US$1 million in cases in which infringement is wilful.[127]

However, in a significant percentage of domain name cases, the trade mark owner may find itself unable to either identify, or serve notice of process upon, the owner of the domain name. This may be because the domain name registrant has registered domain names under aliases or otherwise provided false information in his or her registration applications. It may also be the case that personal jurisdiction cannot be established over the domain name registrant – for example, when a non-US resident has registered a domain name that infringes upon a US trade mark.

In such circumstances, the ACPA provides for in rem jurisdiction permitting the trade mark holder to file an in rem action against the name itself. The trade mark holder can only do this having first either:

- exercised due diligence in trying to locate the owner of the domain name, including publishing notice, but having been unable to do so, or been unable to effect service; or
- demonstrated that personal jurisdiction cannot be established over the domain name registrant because he or she is outside the USA.[128]

In other words, the plaintiff must show that he or she cannot obtain in personam jurisdiction over a person who would have been a defendant in an in personam action in any judicial district in the USA.[129] Both 'due diligence' and constitutional due process require that the plaintiff waits a 'reasonable time' after publishing notice; failure to do so may result in an in rem action being rejected due to the availability of an in personam defendant.[130]

---

123  See, e.g., *Alitalia-Linee Aeree Italiane SpA v Casinoalitalia.com* 128 F Supp 2d 340 (ED Va, 2001).

124  See, e.g., *Mattel, Inc v Internet Dimensions Inc* 2000 WL 973745 (SDNY 2000).

125  15 USC § 1117.

126  15 USC § 1117(a) and (d).

127  15 USC § 1117(e).

128  See, e.g., *Heathmount AE Corp v Technodome.com* 106 F Supp 2d 860 (ED Va, 2000) (no personal jurisdiction in the Eastern District of Virginia over Canadian citizen).

129  See, e.g., *Alitalia-Linee Aeree Italiane SpA*, above (in rem and in personam provisions are mutually exclusive avenues for cybersquatting relief).

130  See, e.g., *Lucent Technologies, Inc v Lucentsucks.com* 95 F Supp 2d 528 (ED Va, 2000).

In rem jurisdiction still requires a nexus based upon a US registry, or registrar, and jurisdiction does not extend to any domain name registries existing outside of the USA. An in rem action under the ACPA can be (and must be) filed in any district in which the domain name registrar, registry, or other domain name authority is located.[131]

Under an in rem action, the trade mark owner effectively has the following options:

- action for infringement of a registered mark;
- action for infringement of an unregistered mark;
- action for dilution of a famous mark; or
- action for cyberpiracy of a registered mark.[132]

While some district courts have required evidence of 'bad faith' under an in rem case, the Fourth Circuit has held that 'bad faith' is not always required.[133] The remedy in an in rem action is limited to a court order for forfeiture or cancellation and transfer of the domain name.

### Abuse of a dispute resolution procedure

If a registrar, registry, or other registration authority refuses to register, removes from registration, transfers, temporarily disables, or permanently cancels a domain name based on a knowing and material misrepresentation by any other person that a domain name is identical to, confusingly similar to, or dilutive of a mark, the person making the knowing and material misrepresentation shall be liable for any damages, including costs and attorney's fees, incurred by the domain name registrant as a result of such action.[134]

A court may also grant injunctive relief to the domain name registrant, including the reactivation of the domain name or the transfer of the domain name to the domain name registrant. This provision is designed to protect the rights of domain name registrants against overreaching trade mark owners; it is in essence a statutory reverse domain name hijacking provision.[135]

### The ACPA and domain name registrars

Prior to the ACPA, the US federal courts had already determined that Network Solutions, Inc (NSI) – at the time, the only domain name registrar – could not be held liable for registering domain names to alleged cybersquatters.[136] The ACPA provides domain name registrars with immunity from monetary and injunctive relief for the acts of:

- refusing to register, cancelling, or transferring a domain name in compliance with a court order pursuant to the ACPA; or
- in the implementation of a reasonable policy of the registrar, prohibiting the registration of a domain name that is identical to, confusingly similar to, or dilutive of another's mark.[137]

---

131 See, e.g., Fleetboston Financial Corp v Fleetbostonfinancial.com 2001 US Dist LEXIS 4797 (D Mass, 27 March 2001).
132 15 USC§ 1125(d)(2)(A)(i).
133 See, e.g., Harrods Ltd v Sixty Internet Domain Names 302 F 3d 214 (4th Cir 2002) (the in rem provision of the ACPA is not limited to claims of bad faith registration with the intent to profit under the ACPA, but also authorises in rem actions for certain federal infringement and dilution claims).
134 15 USCA § 1114(2)(D)(iv).
135 See Hawes v Network Solutions, Inc 337 F 3d 377 (4th Cir 2003); Barcelona.com, Inc v Excelentisimo Ayuntamiento De Barcelona 330 F 3d 617 (4th Cir 2003).
136 Panavision Int'l LP v Toeppen 945 F Supp 1296 (CD Cal 1996); Lockheed Martin Corp v Network Solutions, Inc 985 F Supp 949 (CD Cal 1997), aff'd, 194 F 3d 980 (9th Cir 1999).
137 USC § 1114 (2)(D)(i)(I).

The ICANN Uniform Dispute Resolution Procedure (UDRP) that has been adopted by the gTLD registrars is an example of a 'reasonable policy' for the purposes of the ACPA.[138] Thus, if a UDRP dispute resolution panel decides that a trade mark holder has good grounds to challenge the registration of a domain name as being identical or confusingly similar to a trade mark or service mark in which the trade mark holder has rights, that the respondent has no rights or legitimate interest in respect of the domain name, and that the domain name has been registered and is being used in bad faith, the panel may order the cancellation or transfer of the domain name. Under the ACPA, even where a court later decides that the respondent was entitled to the domain name and that the registrar should not have transferred or cancelled the domain name, the registrar will be immune from suit.

Registrars thus cannot be:

- liable for trade mark infringement, or dilution, or a violation of the ACPA for registering domain names that infringe trade marks;
- joined as a party to a lawsuit by a respondent/complainant who wishes to attack the result of a dispute resolution procedure; or
- liable for damages for the registration or maintenance of a domain name for another party in the absence of a showing of bad faith intent to profit from the domain on the registrar's part.

Registrars can be exposed to injunctions if they refuse to comply with their obligations in an in rem lawsuit – that is, if they:

- do not expeditiously deposit with a court such documents as are necessary to establish the court's control and authority over the domain name;
- transfer, suspend, or otherwise modify the domain name before an in rem action is decided; or
- wilfully fail to comply with a court order to do or not do the above acts.[139]

### The ACPA and personal names

Beyond US federal trade mark law, the ACPA also provides for civil liability for the registration of a domain name that consists of the name of another living person, or a name that is substantially and confusingly similar, without that person's consent, with the intent to profit by selling the domain name for financial gain to that person or any third party.[140]

A plaintiff must demonstrate that the defendant has:

- registered a domain name that consists of, or is confusingly similar to, the name of the plaintiff, who is a living person – there is no reference to 'traffics in or uses', as with the trade mark provisions;
- registered that domain name without the plaintiff's consent; and
- done so with the specific intent to profit from the plaintiff's name by selling the domain name for financial gain to the plaintiff or to a third party – 'bad faith intent' and the nine, non-exhaustive factors for determining bad faith under the trade mark provisions do not apply.

The Act does not define what is meant by a 'name', although the Congressional Record shows that it was intended to cover at least 'the registration of full names (e.g., 'johndoe.com'), appellations

---

138 Barcelona.com, Inc, above; Storey v Cello Holdings, LLC 347 F 3d 370 (2d Cir 2003).
139 USC § 1114(D)(i)(I). It appears likely that 'court' within this section of the ACPA refers only to US courts: Hawes, above.
140 15 USC § 1129.

(e.g., 'doe.com'), and variations thereon (e.g., 'john-doe.com' or 'jondoe.com') . . .'.[141] Other commentators have suggested that it may also 'include pen names, stage names or widely recognized nicknames . . . if they are widely used and understood as the identifier of a specific person'.[142]

The provision appears to be aimed at circumstances such as those in *Jeanette Winterson v Mark Hogarth*,[143] in which the respondent registered domain names consisting of about 130 famous writers' names, allegedly in order to develop websites devoted to them containing book extracts, reviews, biographies, signings, forthcoming works, and links to an e-book seller such as amazon. com, but offered at least some of the domain names for sale to the relevant writers or their agents. In such circumstances, the defendant in an ACPA personal name action whose name was different from the name contained in the domain name would clearly have a specific intent to profit from the name of another living person.

The use of a personal name in a domain name, where the defendant is using the website under the domain name to comment on the individual in question, is likely to fall outside the scope of the ACPA.[144] Equally, a domain name registrant whose name was 'Octavius Xavier' would not fall foul of the legislation if he were to register 'octaviusxavier.com', even if there were a famous person whose name was also 'Octavius Xavier' who wanted that domain name and the former party offered to sell it to the latter. Where a party has registered many common surnames as domain names and is offering them for sale, or is intending to use them for provision of services such as vanity email addresses, the fact that one of those domain names consists of, or is confusingly similar to, the name of another party, even a famous party, will be in itself insufficient to trigger the ACPA personal name provision in the absence of clear evidence of specific intent to profit from the plaintiff's name.

The ACPA exempts from its provisions regarding personal names (and only those provisions) a person who in good faith registers a domain name consisting of the name of another living person, or a confusingly similar name, if the domain name is used in, affiliated with, or related to, a work of authorship protected under Title 17 (the 'Copyright Act'), provided that:

- the person registering the domain name is the copyright owner or licensee of the work;
- the person intends to sell the domain name in conjunction with the lawful exploitation of the work; and
- the registration is not prohibited by a contract between the registrant and the named person.

The purpose of this exemption is to permit the registration of a domain name in good faith by an owner or licensee of a copyrighted work, such as an audiovisual work, a sound recording, a book, or other work of authorship, where the personal name is used in, affiliated with, or related to that work, where the person's intent in registering the domain is to sell the domain name as part of the lawful exploitation of the work – for example, 'the registration of a domain name containing a personal name by the author of a screenplay that bears the same name, with the intent to sell the domain name in conjunction with the sale or license of the screenplay to a production studio'.[145] A defendant to an action under this provision is entitled to any defence that is available to him or her under the Lanham Act, including any defence under s 43(c)(4) or relating to fair use, and to consideration of his or her right of free speech or expression under the First Amendment of the US Constitution.

141 Congressional Record (1999) 17 November, p S14715.
142 J Thomas McCarthy, *McCarthy on Trademarks and Unfair Competition*, 4th edn, 1998–2009 (looseleaf), Eagan, MN: West Publishing.
143 WIPO Case No D2000–0235.
144 See, e.g., *Ficker v Tuohy* 305 F Supp 2d 569 (D Md 2004).
145 Congressional Record (1999) 17 November, p S14715.

A successful plaintiff under this provision may obtain injunctive relief, including forfeiture, cancellation, or transfer of the offending domain name. There is no provision for monetary damages to either party beyond costs and attorney fees, and award of these is at the court's discretion.

Both US citizens and citizens of other nations have standing to invoke the ACPA provisions relating to personal names.[146] At least two UDRP dispute panels have made reference to the availability of the ACPA personal names provision to complainants with a connection to the USA, whilst denying them relief under the UDRP.[147]

## The Truth in Domain Names Act of 2003

While there are a range of trade mark-related actions that can be brought by a trade mark holder against a party who has registered a domain name that is identical to, or confusingly similar to, its own mark, neither those actions nor other non-trade mark legal approaches, such as the use of consumer protection legislation, may discourage the hardened cybersquatter.

The classic example is the case of US cybersquatter, John Zuccarini. Zuccarini was the subject of numerous World Intellectual Property Organization (WIPO) dispute resolution proceedings alleging cybersquatting or typosquatting,[148] and was successfully sued under the ACPA on two occasions.[149] He was also pursued by the US Federal Trade Commission (FTC) for violations of s 5 of the Federal Trade Commission Act of 1914 relating to unfair or deceptive acts or practices in or affecting commerce,[150] for redirecting consumers from their intended destinations on the internet to his own web pages, where he then obstructed them from leaving those pages using web pages displaying advertisements for goods and services for his financial gain (a process known as 'mousetrapping').[151] None of these legal setbacks dissuaded Zuccarini from engaging in his cybersquatting/typosquatting/mousetrapping activities, not least because the financial rewards from such activities were considerably greater than the costs of legal fees and damages.

In 2003, however, Congress passed the Truth in Domain Names Act of 2003 (TDNA).[152] This makes knowingly using a misleading domain name on the internet with the intent to deceive a person into viewing material constituting obscenity a criminal offence, punishable by a fine and/or imprisonment of up to two years. Where a party knowingly uses a misleading domain name on the internet with the intent to deceive a minor into viewing material that is harmful to minors on the internet, this is punishable by a fine and/or imprisonment of up to four years. In late 2003, Zuccarini was arrested and charged with offences under the Act relating to his use of domain names with spellings such as 'Dinseyland.com', 'Bobthebiulder.com', 'Teltubbies.com', and 'Britnyspears.com'. A person accessing Zuccarini's websites was presented with advertisements for free access to pornography, including numerous images of hardcore pornography. Zuccarini pled guilty to 49 counts of violating the TDNA and, in February 2004, was sentenced to 30 months' imprisonment.

---

146 See, e.g., *Schmidheiny v Weber* 146 F Supp 2d 701 (ED Pa, 2001).
147 See WIPO Case No D2002–0030 *Kathleen Kennedy Townsend v BG Birt*; WIPO Case No D2002–0184 *The Reverend Dr Jerry Falwell and The Liberty Alliance v Gary Cohn, Prolife.net, and God.info*.
148 WIPO Case No D2000–0330 *Encyclopaedia Britannica, Inc v Zuccarini*; WIPO Case No D2000–0996 *Diageo plc v Zuccarini*; WIPO Case No D2001–0489 *Disney Enterprises, Inc v Zuccarini*; WIPO Case No D2001–0700 *Lucasfilm Ltd and Lucas Licensing Ltd v Zuccarini*; WIPO Case No D2001–0654 *Backstreet Productions, Inc v Zuccarini*; WIPO Case No D2002–0666 *AT&T Corp v Zuccarini*; WIPO Case No D2002–0827 *AOL Time Warner Inc v Zuccarini*.
149 *Shields v Zuccarini* 254 F 3d 476 (3rd Cir 2001); *Electronics Boutique Holdings Corp v Zuccarini* 56 USPQ 2d 1705 (ED Pa, 2000).
150 15 USC § 45.
151 *FTC v Zuccarini* 2002 US Dist LEXIS 13324 (ED Pa, 10 April 2002).
152 18 USCA § 2252B. See further CG Clark, 'The Truth in Domain Names Act of 2003 and a preventative measure to combat typosquatting' (2004) 89 Cornell L Rev 1476.

# Dispute resolution and rights protection mechanisms

## All generic TLDs (gTLDs)

### The ICANN uniform dispute resolution policy (UDRP)

In the mid-to-late 1990s, as the commercialisation of the internet gathered pace, two key issues became apparent to those responsible for running the registry services for the domain name system. First, given the jurisdictional nature of trade marks, and the international nature of the web, there were likely to be a lot of trade mark-based disputes over domain names that the registries were not in a position to handle effectively. Second, in the absence of some form of legal immunity or other way of avoiding involvement, they were going to find themselves caught up as reluctant parties to trade mark litigation over decisions to allocate, reallocate, or put on hold domain names. A solution needed to be developed that would reduce the registries' exposure to such involvement. Initially, NSI (the forerunner to ICANN) [153] developed the NSI Domain Name Dispute Policy, which sought to provide clarity to the dispute process, but which still left NSI to make decisions under it – unfortunately, rather than preventing legal actions, this appears to have increased them. [154]

However, by 1998, the US government was in the process of devolving the administration of the domain name system to a wholly non-governmental entity, which would be a not-for-profit, US-based company. This process resulted in the creation of ICANN. As part of the process, the US government issued a White Paper, part of which stated that the WIPO was to conduct a consultative study on domain name/trade mark issues. The WIPO report was submitted to ICANN in early 1999 and recommended the establishment of a Uniform Domain Name Dispute Resolution Policy (UDRP) to be followed by all registrars in the .com, .net, and .org TLDs. The UDRP was agreed by late 1999, and the first proceeding under the UDRP took place in December 1999. [155] While it is difficult to obtain precise figures, WIPO's statistics suggest that its panels (which handle the lion's share of UDRP disputes) have decided in the region of 23,000 decisions since 1999. [156]

The UDRP [157] is used by ICANN-accredited registrars in all pre-2011 gTLDs (.aero, .asia, .biz., .cat, .com, .coop, .info, .jobs, .mobi, .museum, .name, .net, .org, .pro, .tel, .travel and .xxx), and will apply to all domain name registrations in ICANN-approved new gTLDs. The UDRP is a contractual policy between a registrar and its customers, and is included in registration agreements for all ICANN-accredited registrars. The UDRP provides that cancellation, transfer, or other changes to domain name registrations will only take place:

- where the registrar is instructed by the registrant or its authorised agent;
- on receipt of an order from a court or arbitral tribunal of competent jurisdiction, requiring such action;

153 The NSI was named as a defendant in several lawsuits during the period 1994–99, including *Knowledge-Net v Boone* No 1-94-CV-7195 (ND Ill, filed 2 December 1994); *Roadrunner Computer Systems, Inc v Network Solutions, Inc* No 96-413-A (ED Va, filed 26 March 1996); *Giacalone v Network Solutions, Inc* No C-96 20434 RPA/PVT, 1996 US Dist LEXIS 20807; *Network Solutions, Inc v Clue Computing, Inc* 946 F Supp 858 (D Colo 1996); *Panavision International v Toeppen* 945 F Supp (CD Cal 1996), aff'd 141 F 3d 1316 (9th Cir 1998); *Lockheed Martin Corp v Network Solutions, Inc* 985 F Supp 949 (CD Cal 1997); *Academy of Motion Picture Arts and Sciences v Network Solutions, Inc* 989 F Supp 1276 (CD Cal 1997); *Data Concepts Inc v Digital Consulting Inc* 150 F 3d 620 (6th Cir 1998). See further Sally M Abel, 'Trademark issues in cyberspace: The brave new frontier' (1999) 5 MTTLR 91.
154 Abel, *ibid*, 100.
155 WIPO Case No D1999–0001 *World Wrestling Federation Entertainment, Inc v Bosman*.
156 WIPO Domain Name Dispute Resolution Statistics, available online at: www.wipo.int/amc/en/domains/statistics/
157 ICANN 'Uniform Domain Name Dispute Resolution Policy' (UDRP), as approved by ICANN on 24 October 1999, available online at: www.icann.org/resources/pages/policy-2012-02-25-en

- on receipt of a decision of an administrative panel requiring such action in any administrative proceeding to which the registrant was a party and which was conducted under the UDRP; and
- in accordance with the terms of the registrant's registration agreement or other legal requirements.[158]

The UDRP is aimed squarely at the abusive registration of domain names; as such, it cannot provide a solution where both parties have legitimate claims to the domain name. In such circumstances, the 'first to register' rule will normally apply. Registrants agree that, in the event of a complaint by a third party that the domain name is identical or confusingly similar to a trade mark in which the complainant has rights, the respondent holder has no rights or legitimate interests in respect of the domain name, and the domain name has been registered and is being used in bad faith,[159] they will be subject to a mandatory administrative proceeding before one of ICANN's approved ADR service providers.[160]

At the administrative proceeding, the complainant has to prove each of the above elements in order to obtain ruling in his or her favour. It is worth noting that the UDRP does not operate on a strict doctrine of precedent. This means that different panels can come to different conclusions on similar fact scenarios. This can make definitive statements about what will happen in particular fact circumstances hazardous. The following points are derived from the WIPO 'Overview of WIPO Panel Views on Selected UDRP Questions'[161] and reflects trends in what is the largest of the UDRP providers.

- *The domain name is identical or confusingly similar to a trade mark in which the complainant has rights.* It appears well established that:

> The UDRP does not require that a complainant must hold rights specifically in a registered trademark or service mark. Instead, it provides only that there must be 'a trademark or service mark in which the complainant has rights,' without specifying how these rights are acquired.[162]

This can be seen in the *Jeanette Winterson v Mark Hogarth*[163] and *Julia Fiona Roberts v Russell Boyd*[164] panel decisions, in which the panel held that 'trade mark' includes unregistered marks recognised by the laws of unfair competition. Where the domain name is identical to the trade mark, there is no need to demonstrate likelihood of confusion; for this purpose, the gTLD suffix is ignored (for example, '.com').[165] Where there is a significant addition to the trade mark, the complainant is likely to have to prove likelihood of confusion; however, a domain name consisting of an entire trade mark with the addition of other terms, even derogatory ones, is likely to be found confusingly similar to the complainant's mark.[166] The content of a website (whether it is similar to or different from the business of a trade mark owner) will be considered irrelevant in the finding of confusing similarity.[167]

---

158 Ibid, para 3.
159 Ibid, para 4(a).
160 'Approved Providers for Uniform Domain-Name Dispute-Resolution Policy', available online at: www.icann.org/en/dndr/udrp/approved-providers.htm
161 'WIPO Overview of WIPO Panel Views on Selected UDRP Questions', 2nd edn, 2011, available online at: www.wipo.int/amc/en/domains/search/overview/index.html
162 Report of the Second WIPO Internet Domain Name Process, 3 September 2001, para 182.
163 WIPO Case No D2000–0235.
164 WIPO Case No D2000–0210.
165 See, e.g., WIPO Case No D2000–1838 *Celine Dion v Jeff Burgar.*
166 Hence the transfer to complainants of many domain names containing words such as 'suck'. However, the respondent may still prevail under the remaining two heads: see, e.g., WIPO Case No D2008–0647 *Sermo, Inc v CatalystMD, LLC*; WIPO Case No D2008–0430 *Southern California Regional Rail Authority v Robert Arkow.*
167 WIPO Case No D2000–1698 *Arthur Guinness Son & Co (Dublin) Ltd v Dejan Macesic.*

- *The respondent holder has no rights or legitimate interests in respect of the domain name.* The overall burden of proof rests with the complainant, but because this may, in some circumstances, effectively require the respondent to prove a negative, the general rule appears to be that the complainant is required to make out a *prima facie* case that the respondent lacks rights or legitimate interests, at which point the respondent assumes the burden of demonstrating rights or legitimate interests in the domain name.[168] If a domain name is being used for the purpose of a genuine non-commercial free speech website, there are two schools of thought exemplified in the panel decisions: first, the right to criticise does not extend to registering a domain name that is identical or confusingly similar to the owner's registered trade mark or conveys an association with the mark;[169] second, irrespective of whether the domain name as such connotes criticism, the respondent has a legitimate interest in using the trade mark as part of the domain name of a criticism site if the use is fair and non-commercial.[170] There are also two schools of thought exemplified in the panel decisions about 'fan sites': first, that an active and clearly non-commercial fan site may have rights and legitimate interests in the domain name that includes the complainant's trade mark, but it must be non-commercial and clearly distinctive from any official site;[171] second, a respondent does not have rights to express its view, even if positive, on an individual or entity by using a confusingly similar domain name, because the respondent is misrepresenting itself as being that individual or entity. In particular, where the domain name is identical to the trade mark, the respondent, in its actions, prevents the trade mark holder from exercising the rights to its mark and managing its presence on the internet.[172]
- *The domain name has been registered and is being used in bad faith.* If a domain name is registered before a trade mark right is established, the registration of the domain name is not in bad faith because the registrant could not have contemplated a non-existent right,[173] unless the respondent is clearly aware of the complainant, and it is clear that the aim of the registration was to take advantage of the confusion between the domain name and any potential complainant rights.[174] The lack of active use of the domain name does not as such prevent a finding of bad faith; a panel should examine all of the circumstances of the case to determine whether the respondent is acting in bad faith.[175] The existence of a disclaimer cannot cure bad faith, when bad faith has been established by other factors.[176] Evidence of offers to sell the domain name in settlement discussions can be used to show bad faith, because many cybersquatters wait until a trade mark owner launches a complaint before asking for payment. Panels can decide whether settlement discussions represent a good faith effort to compromise or a bad faith effort to extort.[177]

The UDRP provides specific, but non-exclusive, examples of evidence of the registration and use of a domain name in bad faith, including:

- circumstances indicating registration or acquisition of the domain name primarily for the purpose of selling, renting, or otherwise transferring the domain name registration to the complainant who is the owner of the trade mark or service mark, or to a competitor of

---

168  WIPO Case No D2001–0121 *Julian Barnes v Old Barn Studios*; WIPO Case No D2004–0110 *Belupo dd v WACHEM doo*.
169  WIPO Case No D2004–0136 *Kirkland & Ellis LLP v DefaultData.com, American Distribution Systems, Inc.*
170  WIPO Case No D2000–0536 *TMP Worldwide Inc v Jennifer L Potter*; WIPO Case No D2004–0014 *Howard Jarvis Taxpayers Association v Paul McCauley*.
171  WIPO Case No D2004–0001 *2001 White Castle Way, Inc v Glyn O Jacobs*.
172  WIPO Case No D2000–1459 *David Gilmour, David Gilmour Music Ltd and David Gilmour Music Overseas Ltd v Ermanno Cenicolla*.
173  WIPO Case No D2001–1182 *PrintForBusiness BV v LBS Horticulture*.
174  WIPO Case No D2003–0598 *Madrid 2012, SA v Scott Martin-MadridMan Websites*.
175  WIPO Case No D2002–0131 *Ladbroke Group Plc v Sonoma International LDC*.
176  WIPO Case No D2003–0316 *Pliva, Inc v Eric Kaiser*.
177  WIPO Case No D2004–0078 *McMullan Bros., Ltd, Maxol Ltd, Maxol Direct Ltd, Maxol Lubricants Ltd, Maxol Oil Ltd, Maxol Direct (NI) Ltd v Web Names Ltd*.

that complainant, for valuable consideration in excess of the documented out-of-pocket costs directly related to the domain name;

- registration of the domain name in order to prevent the owner of the trade mark or service mark from reflecting the mark in a corresponding domain name, where there is a pattern of such conduct;
- registration of the domain name primarily for the purpose of disrupting the business of a competitor; or
- using the domain name to attempt intentionally to attract, for commercial gain, internet users to a website or other online location, by creating a likelihood of confusion with the complainant's mark as to the source, sponsorship, affiliation, or endorsement of the website or location or of a product or service on the website or location.[178]

The UDRP also provides specific, but non-exclusive, examples of ways in which a respondent might demonstrate rights to or legitimate interests in a domain name, including that:

- before any notice to the respondent of the dispute, he or she used, or made demonstrable preparations to use, the domain name or a name corresponding to the domain name in connection with a bona fide offering of goods or services;
- he or she (as an individual, business, or other organisation) has been commonly known by the domain name, even if he or she has acquired no trade mark or service mark rights; or
- he or she is making a legitimate non-commercial or fair use of the domain name, without intent for commercial gain to misleadingly divert consumers, or to tarnish the trade mark or service mark at issue.[179]

Complaints will be heard by a panel consisting of one or three panellists. The default is a single panellist, but either party can request a three-person panel. The complainant pays the fee for the panel, except where the respondent requests a three-person panel, in which case the fee is split equally.[180] A panel normally accepts only written submissions; in-person hearings are at the sole discretion of the panel.[181] The panel decides complaints on the basis of the statements and documents submitted, and in accordance with the UDRP, UDRP Rules, and any rules and principles of law that it deems applicable.[182] This avoids charges of, for example, US-centricism, but has the disadvantage that different panels may decide similar cases under different national legal rules.

The panel's decision is a summary one; there is no appeal through the UDRP. The result of a successful complaint is limited to requiring the cancellation of the respondent's domain name, or the transfer of the domain name registration to the complainant. As noted earlier, complainants fearing damage in the short term, seeking a broader range of protection, or wanting compensation, may thus be inclined to seek injunctions or other remedies in the courts. The UDRP explicitly allows for recourse to the courts before, during, or after a UDRP panel hearing,[183] and a party who is unhappy with a panel decision can seek to overturn it in the courts. Cases have been brought in both the USA and UK to this end, although it appears that, in the UK courts, at least, losing respondents may find it difficult to identify a cause of action upon which the panel's decision can be challenged.

178  UDRP, para 4(b).
179  Ibid, para 4(c).
180  ICANN Rules for Uniform Domain Name Dispute Resolution Policy, as approved by ICANN on 30 October 2009, para 6, available online at: www.icann.org/resources/pages/rules-be-2012-02-25-en
181  Ibid, para 13.
182  Ibid, para 15(a).
183  UDRP, para 4(k).

In *Patel v Allos Therapeutics Inc*, the judge noted that the UDRP could not provide the court with a jurisdiction that it did not already have and that the court had no appellate or judicial review function with regard to the UDRP. Any claimant thus had to demonstrate a right of action that the court could consider. In the case of a UDRP complainant, he or she could clearly bring a trade mark infringement action before the court if the UDRP panel had rejected the complaint. In the case before the court, however, Mr Patel, as a registrant, had not identified a cause of action on which the court could adjudicate.[184]

In the USA, the position of losing respondents seems stronger, as the court in *Excelentisimo Ayuntamiento de Barcelona v Barcelona.com Inc* outlined:

> The ACPA recognizes the UDRP only insofar as it constitutes a part of a policy followed by registrars in administering domain names, and the UDRP is relevant to actions brought under the ACPA in two contexts. First, the ACPA limits the liability of a registrar in respect to registering, transferring, disabling, or cancelling a domain name if it is done in the 'implementation of a reasonable policy' (including the UDRP) that prohibits registration of a domain name 'identical to, confusingly similar to, or dilutive of another's mark.' . . . Second, the ACPA authorizes a suit by a domain name registrant whose domain name has been suspended, disabled or transferred under that reasonable policy (including the UDRP) to seek a declaration that the registrant's registration and use of the domain name involves no violation of the Lanham Act as well as an injunction returning the domain name.[185]

Opinion is divided on how successful ICANN and the UDRP have been to date. The UDRP has certainly proved popular with those seeking to resolve disputes over domain names and many more cases are decided by this mechanism than by national courts. There have, however, been criticisms of the procedural aspects of the policy,[186] and of the reasoning and outcomes of the panels.[187] However, as the process has 'bedded in' and an informal system of precedent has developed amongst the panels (albeit with some notable disagreements), leading to greater certainty, complaints appear to have diminished.

## Country code TLDs (ccTLDs)

The ccTLDs are not obliged to adopt the UDRP, or to agree to its recognition in binding form in customer contracts for domain registration, although some have done so.[188] Most ccTLDs have adopted their own ADR procedures,[189] although these often do not vary greatly from those of the UDRP,[190] and may often be heard by panels provided by the same dispute resolution providers as for the UDRP panels.[191] A key variation amongst ccTLDs is the expansion of the rights under which a

---

184 *Patel v Allos Therapeutics Inc* [2008] ETMR 75 (Ch D), [15].
185 330 F 3d 617, 625 (4th Cir 2003); see also *Sallen v Corinthians Licentiamentos LTDA* 273 F 3d 14, 28 (1st Cir 2001).
186 Christopher T Varas, 'Sealing the cracks: A proposal to update the anti-cybersquatting regime to combat advertising-based cybersquatting' (2008) 3(4) JIPLP 246.
187 See, e.g., O Armon, 'As good as it gets? An appraisal of the Uniform Domain Name Dispute Resolution Policy' (2003) 20(12) Computer & Internet Law 1; Juan Pablo Cortés Diéguez, 'An analysis of the UDRP experience: Is it time for reform?' (2008) 24(4) CLSR 349.
188 The UDRP is applied by the registrars of ccTLDs that have adopted the UDRP Policy on a voluntary basis, e.g. Uganda, Venezuela, Puerto Rico.
189 See, e.g., Nominet's Dispute Resolution Service, available online at: www.nominet.org.uk/disputes/resolving-domain-disputes
190 Nominet's DRS differs in some respects from the UDRP in both terms and procedure, for example, unlike the UDRP, it offers an appeal from its first level expert decision.
191 The ADR procedure for .eu domain name disputes is provided by the Prague-based Arbitration Court attached to the Economic Chamber of the Czech Republic and Agricultural Chamber of the Czech Republic (the 'Czech Arbitration Court', or 'CAC'), which is also a UDRP provider.

complainant can base a complaint.[192] However, the lack of uniformity in approach between different ccTLDs has been criticised for creating unnecessary complication, expense and uncertainty for both trade mark holders and would-be domain name registrants. Examples of problems include:

- **Lack of dispute resolution processes** – e.g. the .jo ccTLD (Hashemite Kingdom of Jordan), administered by the Jordanian National Information Technology Center has no dispute resolution policy or arbitration process to deal with domain name disputes: if there is a dispute, the NITC simply suspends the domain name until it receives official notification of settlement;[193]
- **Inefficient dispute resolution processes** – e.g. unlike the UDRP, the Dispute Resolution Policy for the .in ccTLD (India) requires a complainant to file a separate complaint for each disputed domain name, rather than permitting a consolidated complaint which, Anand and Kamath argue, can significantly raise the cost of enforcement for a complainant seeking to address cybersquatters who register multiple infringing domain names, and also increases the risk of inconsistent arbitration decisions relating to the same trade mark.[194]
- **Jurisdiction limitations** – e.g. unlike the UDRP, the Dispute Resolution Policy for the .ma ccTLD (Morocco) requires that the complainant must have rights protected in Morocco.[195]

## The new gTLDs

The WIPO has been heavily involved in the development of intellectual property policy in relation to domain names being influential in both the adoption of the UDRP[196] as well as advising on the protection of types of non-trade mark identifiers in the DNS. In 2005, it produced a report on the intellectual property issues raised by the proposed new gTLDs.[197] This report drew upon the experience gained from the first expansion of the DNS in 2000. Here, ICANN experimented with different trade mark protection mechanisms, including 'sunrise registration' where trade mark holders were able to register domain names before the general public during a 'Sunrise Registration Period'(.info);[198] and a 'Start-up Trademark Opposition Policy' (STOP) where trade mark owners could, for a fee, register IP claims in order to claim trade mark rights in relation to an alphanumeric string that was identical to their trade mark (.biz).[199] The report concluded that that a 'curative' mechanism like the URDP arbitration process would be insufficient to adequately protect intellectual property rights and that additional safeguards, including preventive trade mark protection, would be required.[200] It was suggested that such a mechanism should be uniform across new gTLDs in order that:

---

192  The .eu ADR Rules ('.eu ADRR') are not limited to trade marks in which the complainant has rights. Rights that can be relied upon are those recognised or established by the national law of a Member State or by EU law. These will include, but are not necessarily limited to: registered national and community trade marks, geographical indications or designations of origin, and, in as far as they are protected under national law in the Member State where they are held – unregistered trade marks, trade names, business identifiers, company names, family names, and distinctive titles of protected literary and artistic works. See ADRR para B11(d)(1)(i), based on Regulation EC/874/2004, Art 21(1).

193  Shereen Abu Ghazaleh, '.jo ccTLD domains protection' (2011) 17(5) CTLR 123.

194  Pravin Anand &Raunaq Kamath, 'Domain name dispute resolution: an Indian perspective', (2013) World Intellectual Property Review (1 April 2103), available online at: http://www.worldipreview.com/article/domain-name-dispute-resolution-an-indian-perspective

195  Règlement sur la Procédure alternative de résolution de litiges du .ma (1 août 2007), available online at: www.wipo.int/amc/fr/domains/rules/cctld/ma/index.html

196  Final Report of the First WIPO Internet Domain Name Process, 30 April 30 1999, available online at: http://www.wipo.int/amc/en/processes/process1/report/

197  WIPO, New Generic Top-Level Domains: Intellectual Property Considerations (2005 Report), available online at: www.wipo.int/amc/en/domains/reports/newgtld-ip/index.html

198  Ibid, at [57].

199  Ibid, [77].

200  Ibid, [113]-[141].

- 'Operators of new gTLDs would not be required to develop and implement their own IP protection mechanisms, a task for which they are not necessarily equipped;
- ICANN would not be required to monitor the correct implementation of multiple protection mechanisms applied by different gTLDs, but could concentrate its attention on one single mechanism;
- IP owners would not be required to devote significant resources to understanding multiple different IP protection mechanisms.'[201]

The report noted that given the trend towards Sunrise mechanisms, this might be the best uniform mechanism. New gTLDs could offer IP owners the option of registering their protected identifiers during a Sunrise period of a specified duration before they accepted registrations from the general public, or give them the option of obtaining defensive registrations during that period.

## 'Sunrise periods'

In 2005–2006, when the .eu ccTLD was created, a two-phase 'sunrise period' was established.[202] During this period, registration was limited to particular categories of applicant. Only after the expiry of the sunrise period did open registration – often referred to as the 'landrush period' – begin.

Phase 1 of the sunrise period began on 7 December 2005 and ran until 6 February 2006. During this phase, the following categories of applicant could register .eu domain names:

- anyone who met the EU eligibility criteria, and was:

   o   a public body; or
   o   a holder/licensee of a trade mark; or
   o   a holder of a geographical indication or denomination of origin.

Phase 2 began on 7 February 2006 and ran until 6 April 2006. During this phase, the following categories of applicant could register .eu domain names:

- anyone who met the EU eligibility criteria, and was:

   o   eligible to apply under Phase 1; or
   o   a holder of any other prior right protected under the national law of the Member State in which it was held.

All applications during the sunrise period were subject to prior validation by EURid's appointed validation agent – PricewaterhouseCoopers – and applicants were required to provide a range of mandatory information for this purpose. It was clear that, even within the sunrise period, there were likely to be multiple applicants for many domain names, because more than one party may hold an identical, or very similar, registered or unregistered mark due to their use of the mark in conjunction with different types of product or service, or in different national markets. Thus, within the sunrise period, legitimate applications were dealt with on a first-come, first-served basis: for example, if three parties claimed registered trade marks on the word 'merlin', the fastest one to apply would be given first chance to validate its right to the domain name 'merlin.eu'. In the event that the first applicant failed to present adequate documentation to authenticate its trade mark within a 40-day period, the second-fastest applicant's documentation would be examined, and so

---

201 *Ibid*, [139]
202 EC/874/2004, Art 10.

on, until an adequately authenticated registration was accepted. Once a registration was accepted, there was then a 40-day 'sunrise appeal period' during which other applicants were able to initiate an ADR procedure against the decision of EURid to effect registration. Therefore, a domain name, even when already applied for, remained open for continuing application by other parties until its actual activation.

During the sunrise period, a total of 346,218 applications were filed for 245,908 different domain names. It will be obvious, therefore, that, in many cases, two or more applicants were claiming a prior right in relation to the same domain name. Indeed, in some cases, the difference between a successful registration and failure could be measured in seconds under the first-come, first-served principle. The scope for disputes was obvious, even in the absence of attempts at cyber-squatting. Despite the use of the sunrise period, it is clear that the .eu registration process failed to prevent significant numbers of problematic registrations, even during the restricted registration periods. This was essentially due to the wide scope of prior rights that could be used to claim eligibility to register domain names during the period of phased registration,[203] and to textual ambiguities in Regulation EC/874/2004.

There was clear evidence of cybersquatting and warehousing by registrants of both generic domain names, and domain names identical to, or very similar to, names or marks in which a third party had rights recognised or established by the national law of a Member State and/or EU law. A large part of the problem arose from the expedited process for registration of a Benelux trade mark, available via the Benelux Trademark Office, which saw a flood of expedited 'bad faith' trade mark registrations at the end of 2005 in anticipation of the .eu launch. This process permitted would-be cybersquatters and warehousers to obtain Benelux trade marks in periods as short as 48 hours, and in full knowledge of the potential loopholes in the registration rules, either for the sunrise period, or generally.[204]

The lack of clarity in Regulation EC/874/2004, Art 11, regarding the registration of domain names based on trade marks that include special characters, spaces, or punctuations caused particular issues. It led to the registration, during the sunrise period, of hundreds of domain names such as barcelona.eu, frankfurt.eu, and petrom.eu, on the basis of Benelux word trade marks of, respectively, BARC & ELONA (trade mark applied for on 28 November 2005, granted on 30 November 2005), FRANKF & URT (trade mark applied for on 30 November 2005, granted on 2 December 2005), and PET & ROM (trade mark applied for 20 March 2006, granted 22 March 2006), in relation to which the holder of the Benelux mark claimed to have the right under Art 11 to decide whether the ampersand, as a special character, should be 'eliminated entirely from the corresponding domain name, replaced with hyphens, or, if possible, rewritten'. There can be little doubt as to the motives of some of the registrants in registering the Benelux trade marks, where hundreds of marks were registered and then almost immediately used to file applications for .eu domain names identical to the names of cities and existing famous brands. Many of these domain names have since been transferred via .eu ADR decisions to legitimate trade mark holders.[205]

---

203 Ibid, Art 10(2).

204 See, e.g., CAC-35/2006 *Leonie Vestering v EURid*.

205 A key difficulty in the .eu process was that the ADR process during the sunrise period (the sunrise appeal period) was restricted to challenges to decisions of EURid to register or not to register a domain name – actions could not be begun against registrants. The .eu ADR panels were not given direct jurisdiction to deal with obvious 'bad faith' applications and, where those applications had followed the letter of the registration requirements in EC/874/2004, it was hard for complainants to argue convincingly that EURid had unreasonably registered the relevant domain names. EURid claimed, not without some justification, that the Regulations did not oblige it, or its validation agent, to look behind the registration formalities for evidence of bad faith. Complainants thus had to wait until the sunrise appeal period ended to initiate an ADR proceeding against the registrant, based on violation of EC/874/2004, Art 21.

Later gTLDs appear to have learned from the .eu registration process, and taken steps to reduce the Benelux trade mark problem with respect to their sunrise periods. For example, in order for their holders to participate during the .mobi sunrise period, trade marks had to have been registered before 11 July 2005 (the date on which dotMobi signed its contract with ICANN), or have been applied for before that date, and registered by the time of domain name registration.

However, many trade mark holders remained dissatisfied with the protection that they were granted by the sunrise mechanism.

> . . . the 'sunrise' registration period employed by some registries is nothing more than an extremely expensive method of defensively registering brand names. Where a brand owner owns dozens of brands or more and there are hundreds of new gTLDs, sunrise registrations will be too expensive to even contemplate.[206]

Thus, during the next phase of preparation for DNS expansion, WIPO and ICANN revisited the issue of trade mark protection and, in addition to the application process for gTLDs, devised a further four mechanisms to supplement the use of 'sunrise periods' and the UDRP 'curative' process: Legal Rights Objections (LRO), the Trademark Clearinghouse (TMCH), the Uniform Rapid Suspension System (URS) and the Post-Delegation Dispute Resolution Procedure (PDDRP). Provision of all the Rights Protection Mechanisms is required of all new gTLD registries, who may also choose to provide further forms of protection.[207]

## The gTLD application process

Large-scale expansion of the gTLDs, with increasing numbers of gTLDs being privately owned and operated, means that there is now potential for disputes at both the top-level and second-level of a domain name. There may be disputes between parties:

- over the legitimate ownership of a new gTLD;
- over legitimate ownership of SLDs within a new gTLD, where both gTLD and all SLDs are owned by the same entity;
- over legitimate ownership of SLDs within a new gTLD, where the gTLD registry permits third parties to register SLDs;
- over the behaviour of a gTLD registry, where the registry does not take reasonable steps to ensure that third party misuse of SLDs within that gTLD is controlled.

The first level of dispute resolution for new gTLDs takes place during the application process. Each application for a new gTLD is first reviewed for administrative completeness, and then the gTLD 'string' (for example, '.amazon') is subjected to an initial evaluation process.[208] At the same time it is made available for public comment, where it is subject to a set of potential objections. A formal

---

206 E Thomas Watson, Assistant General Counsel, Bank of America Corporation, Comment to ICANN on new gTLD Draft Applicant Handbook, 15 December 2008.

207 See, e.g., Donuts' Domains Protected Marks List, available online at: www.donuts.co/dpml/

208 This process examines whether the string might cause security or stability problems in the DNS, including problems caused by similarity to existing TLDs or reserved names (string review); and whether the applicant is capable technically, operationally, and financially to run a registry (applicant review). If the application fails the initial evaluation, then the applicant can apply for the extended evaluation process, see ICANN, New gTLD Applicant Guidebook: Module 2, evaluation procedures (4 June 2012) at 27.

objection by a third party that falls within these categories will trigger a dispute resolution procedure.[209] The categories are:[210]

| Objection | Grounds for objection | Who has standing? | Possible outcomes |
| --- | --- | --- | --- |
| String Confusion Objection[211] | The string is confusingly similar to an existing TLD or to another applied-for gTLD string in the same round of applications | In general, an existing TLD operator or gTLD applicant in current round | Existing TLD operator successful – application rejected<br><br>If gTLD applicant successful – contention resolution procedure<br><br>If gTLD applicant unsuccessful – both applications move forward |
| Legal Rights Objection[212] | The string infringes the existing legal rights of the objector | Rightsholders (including registered or unregistered trade marks) | If rightsholder successful – application rejected |
| Limited Public Interest Objection[213] | The string is contrary to generally accepted legal norms of morality and public order under international law | No limitations. Objections subject to 'quick look' review to quickly weed out frivolous or abusive objections | If objector successful – application rejected<br><br>If objector unsuccessful – objection may be deemed an abuse of the right to object<br><br>If objection rejected at 'quick look' review, no hearing and refund of fees |
| Community Objection[214] | Substantial opposition to the application from a significant portion of the community to which the string may be explicitly/implicitly targeted | Any established institution associated with a clearly delineated community | If objector successful – application rejected |

Objections may also be filed against 'highly objectionable' gTLD applications, under the Limited Public Interest and Community Objection categories only, by an Independent Objector (IO) appointed by ICANN to act 'in the best interests of the public who use the global Internet.' The IO may not file against gTLD applications in which another objection in the same category has been filed, and cannot file an objection 'in the public interest'; unless at least one comment opposing the application is made in the public sphere.[215]

---

209 Not all public comments will be formal objections: general comments are considered in the initial evaluation. Formal objections are subject to dispute resolution and are not taken into account during the initial evaluation.
210 ICANN, New gTLD Applicant Guidebook: Module 3, Objection Procedures (4 June 2012) at 4. See also ICANN Generic Names Supporting Organisation, Final Report: Introduction of New Generic Top-Level Domains (1 and 8 August 2007), available online at: gnso.icann.org/en/issues/new-gtlds/pdp-dec05-fr-parta-08aug07.htm, gnso.icann.org/en/issues/new-gtlds/pdp-dec05-fr-partb-01aug07.htm
211 ICANN, New gTLD Applicant Guidebook: Module 3, Objection Procedures, ibid at 5.
212 Ibid, 6.
213 Ibid.
214 Ibid, 7.
215 Ibid, 9.

An applicant against whose application an objection has been filed has a range of options. They can:

- withdraw the application;
- seek a settlement with the objector, resulting in withdrawal of the objection;[216]
- file a response to the objection and enter the dispute resolution process;
- fail to respond to the objection, in which case the application will fail.

Formal objections must be filed directly with the appropriate Dispute Resolution Service Provider (DRSP) for each objection type, by the posted deadline date for each expansion round.[217] At the end of the objection filing period, ICANN posts on its website a notice of all objections filed. At that point the DRSP notifies the applicant, who has 30 days to respond to the objection(s). If both an objection and response are properly filed, the matter will proceed to an expert panel. Where there are multiple similar objections to an application, these may be consolidated into one objection by the DRSP for adjudication purposes.

Expert panels are selected by the DRSPs: their composition differs depending on the category of objection. Expert panels for adjudicating a string confusion objection or a community objection will have one member; panels considering a legal rights objection will have one member or,

| Objection | Grounds for objection | Criteria for standing | Key adjudication criteria |
|---|---|---|---|
| String Confusion Objection | The string is confusingly similar to an existing TLD or to another applied-for gTLD string in the same round of applications | Ownership of existing TLD or applicant in same TLD round | Does the string object so nearly resemble that owned or applied for by the objector that it is likely to deceive or cause confusion? Likelihood of confusion means it is probable, not merely possible, that confusion will arise in the mind of the average, reasonable internet user. Mere association by a user of one string with the other is insufficient.[218] |
| Legal Rights Objection | The string infringes the existing legal rights of the objector | Ownership of registered or unregistered trade mark or service mark (also IGO name or acronym recognised by treaty) | Will the potential use of the applicant's gTLD take unfair advantage of the distinctive character or the reputation of the objector's mark, unjustifiably impair the distinctive character or the reputation of the objector's mark, or otherwise create an impermissible likelihood of confusion with the objector's mark?[219] |

(Continued)

---

216 Ibid, 15. Mediation is encouraged by ICANN, but is not obligatory. Delay in the dispute resolution process for mediation must be jointly requested and should be no more than 30 days.

217 In the 2012 round, string confusion objection disputes are handled by The International Centre for Dispute Resolution; legal rights objection disputes are handled by The Arbitration and Mediation Center of the WIPO; Limited Public Interest and Community Objection disputes are handled by The International Center of Expertise of the International Chamber of Commerce. ICANN, New gTLD Applicant Guidebook: Module 3, Objection Procedures, ibid at 8. Details of the filing process can be found at 11–14.

218 See further, ICANN, New gTLD Applicant Guidebook: Module 3, Objection Procedures at 18.

219 Ibid.

| Objection | Grounds for objection | Criteria for standing | Key adjudication criteria |
|---|---|---|---|
| Limited Public Interest Objection | The string is contrary to generally accepted legal norms of morality and public order under international law | No limitation. Objection must not be an abuse of the right to object (e.g. manifestly unfounded or harassment) Independent Objector may object in absence of other parties | Is the string contrary to general principles of international law for morality and public order, including but not limited to, general principles contained in instruments such as The Universal Declaration of Human Rights (UDHR) and The International Covenant on Civil and Political Rights (ICCPR)?[220] |
| Community Objection | Substantial opposition to the application from a significant portion of the community to which the string may be explicitly/ implicitly targeted | The applicant is an established institution. Factors may include ability to demonstrate global recognition; existence for a significant period of time; a public history, e.g. a formal charter, national or international registration, validation by government, inter-governmental organisation, or treaty Independent Objector may object in absence of other parties | Is the community invoked by the objector a clearly delineated community? Is community opposition to the application substantial? Is there a strong association between the community invoked and the applied-for gTLD string? Does the application create a likelihood of material detriment to the rights or legitimate interests of a significant portion of the community to which the string may be explicitly or implicitly targeted?[221] |

if all parties agree, three members with relevant experience in intellectual property rights disputes; panels considering a Limited Public Interest objection will have three members recognised as eminent jurists of international reputation, with expertise in relevant fields. Adjudications will normally be made on the basis of the materials filed, although the panel may allow further written submissions, request further information and, exceptionally, allow an in-person hearing. Panels produce a written decision which will be published by the relevant DRSP on its website.

### The legal rights objections (LRO) process
For the 2012 round of gTLD applications, which ran from 12 January to 30 May 2012, the objection filing window opened on 13 June 2012 and closed on 13 March 2013. There were 1,930 applications for 1,409 separate strings, and 71 Legal Rights Objection filings were made to the WIPO, of which 69 were deemed administratively compliant and registered for processing,[222] and

220 Ibid, 20.
221 Ibid, 22.
222 Two LROs were dismissed for failure to assert relevant rights.

63 ended in a final expert determination.[223] Of those 63 expert determinations, 54 were by single-member expert panels, and nine by three-member expert panels. No proceedings were consolidated, no in-person hearings were held, and no joint requests for mediation were made. A majority of the objections (43/69) were filed by applicants against other applicants for the same gTLD string. The last of the LRO expert determinations was delivered in September 2013. The initial fee paid at the time of filing of an objection or response for a one-expert panel was US$10,000 ($2,000 DSRP fee + $8,000 panel fee).[224] The prevailing party in the dispute was entitled to a refund of the panel fee.

Unlike the UDRP, where complainants win a clear majority of panel decisions,[225] objectors fared relatively poorly in front of the LRO panels, with only four objections upheld (three with dissenting opinions) and 59 rejected. The WIPO's Report[226] on the process provides a brief over-view of some key factors in the panels' decision-making, which give some pointers as to the likely disposition of such determinations in the future:

- Objections by rightsholders whose trade marks appeared to have been obtained in order to make a new gTLD application or to bring a LRO, and which showed limited or no use, were unlikely to be upheld[227] – the few successful LROs were made on the basis of established rights or marks.[228] However, even having an established right or mark was by itself often insufficient.[229]
- Objections by rightsholders whose trade marks consisted of a common word in the English language faced an uphill struggle to demonstrate that a gTLD application which sought to use the word as a string taking advantage of the common meaning violated any of the key adjudication criteria.[230] However, an application that consisted of a common word in the English language and appeared, on the submissions made to a panel, to be targeting a trade mark would likely be seen as grounds for a successful objection.[231]
- Objections by rightsholders premised on the potential for misuse of their trade marks by third parties registering second-level domains under the disputed string were not likely to be upheld, especially where the applicant indicated that they intended to take measures to prevent abusive registrations.[232]

The WIPO suggests that the existence of the LRO mechanism may lie behind the relatively limited number of objectionable gTLD applications, in that it discouraged such applications being made.[233]

---

223 Six proceedings were terminated, three by withdrawal of the gTLD application. It is not specified why the other three proceedings were terminated, but it seems likely this was due to withdrawal of the complaint. All the expert determinations were in relation to trade marks – there were no IGO-related decisions, available online at: www.wipo.int/amc/en/domains/lro/

224 For a three-member panel the cost was $23,000.

225 WIPO statistics suggest that complainants succeed (e.g. domain name cancelled or transferred) in about 87% of its UDRP decisions.

226 WIPO Arbitration and Mediation Center, End Report on Legal Rights Objection Procedure 2013 (December 2013), available online at: www.wipo.int/export/sites/www/amc/en/docs/lroreport.pdf

227 *Defender Security Company v Baxter Pike LLC*, Case No LRO2013–0031 (.home); *Defender Security Company v .HOME REGISTRY INC* Case No. LRO2013–0039 (.home)

228 See, e.g., *Sina Corporation v Tencent Holdings Limited*, Case No LRO2013–0040 (.微博); *Sina Corporation v Tencent Holdings Limited*, Case No LRO2013–0041 (.weibo); *Del Monte Corporation v Del Monte International GmbH*, Case No LRO2013–0001. The successful Del Monte LRO complaint was challenged in a US legal action in *Del Monte Intern. GmbH v. Del Monte Corp* 995 F.Supp.2d 110. The applicant sought a declaration that it had bona fide rights in the mark, that it was not in violation of the Anti-cybersquatting Consumer Protection Act (ACPA), and that its gTLD registration would not create an impermissible likelihood of confusion. The court dismissed the case finding that plaintiff had failed to state a claim for which relief could be granted.

229 See, e.g., *Coach, Inc v Koko Island LLC*, Case No. LRO2013–0002 (.coach); *Limited Stores, LLC v Big Fest LLC*, Case No. LRO2013–0049 (.limited).

230 See, e.g., *Coach, Inc v Koko Island LLC*, Case No. LRO2013–0002 (.coach); *United States Postal Service v Charleston Road Registry Inc*, Case No.LRO2013–0045 (.mail).

231 See, e.g., *The DirecTV Group Inc v Dish DBS Corporation*, Case No. LRO2013–0005 (.direct).

232 See, e.g., *I-REGISTRY Ltd v Vipspace Enterprises LLC*, Case No. LRO 2013–0014 (.vip); *Express, LLC v Sea Sunset, LLC*, Case No. LRO 2013–0022 (.express); *Starbucks (HK) Limited v Grand Turn LLC*, Case No.LRO2013–0025 (.now).

233 WIPO Arbitration and Mediation Center, End Report on Legal Rights Objection Procedure 2013 (December 2013), at 13.

It is, however, equally plausible that both the cost of engaging with the gTLD process, and the cost of raising objections was a more dissuasive factor.[234]

## Trademark Clearinghouse

The Trademark Clearinghouse (TMCH) is a further mechanism designed to help trade mark holders defend their rights within the DNS.[235] It is a centralised global repository for data on trade marks that are registered, court-validated, or protected by statute/treaty, designed to support both the ICANN- mandated 30-day 'sunrise registration period' and later Trade Mark Claims processes, when new gTLDs open for registration. Trade mark owners register their trade marks (for a fee) with the TMCH and receive a unique authentication key, and access to the sunrise registration period of every new gTLD. The TMCH database is then used by the new gTLD registries and registrars as a source of authenticated information on trade mark authenticity and validity. During a 'sunrise registration period' the trade mark owners can more easily demonstrate that they have a priority right to register domain names corresponding to their marks. During general registration, when a third party seeks to register a domain name that corresponds to that of a trade mark holder registered in the TMCH, the would-be registrant is notified of the existence of the mark. If they continue with the registration of the domain name, the trade mark holder is then informed of that registration. It has been suggested that the TMCH would be more helpful to rightsholders if instead of after-the-fact notification, trade mark owners were to be given advance notice of a proposed registration, and a suitable mechanism for objecting to it. The TMCH may also be utilised in support of Uniform Rapid Suspension proceedings.

## Uniform Rapid Suspension System

Many of the proceedings before UDRP panels are relatively clear-cut cases of DNS abuse, such as cybersquatting. The Uniform Rapid Suspension System aims to address such cases whilst leaving more complex cases, e.g. those requiring decisions about questions of fact, to be handled by the UDRP panels. All new gTLDs must have the required processes in place prior to opening for registration.[236] The criteria used to determine the validity of a URS complaint are similar to those of the UDRP; however, URS complaints are designed to carry a higher burden of proof for complainants.[237]

> The standards that the qualified Examiner shall apply when rendering its Determination are whether:
>
> 8.1.2   The registered domain name is identical or confusingly similar to a word mark: (i) for which the Complainant holds a valid national or regional registration and that is in current use; or (ii) that has been validated through court proceedings; or (iii) that is specifically protected by a statute or treaty currently in effect and that was in effect at the time the URS Complaint is filed; and
>
> 8.1.2.1   Use can be shown by demonstrating that evidence of use – which can be a declaration and one specimen of current use – was submitted to, and validated by, the Trademark Clearinghouse.
>
> 8.1.2.2   Proof of use may also be submitted directly with the URS Complaint.

---

234  In *Coach, Inc v Koko Island LLC*, Case No. LRO2013–0002 (.coach), the applicant had made 307 gTLD applications and claimed to have over US$100 million in funds to acquire and administer those TLDs.

235  The Trademark Clearinghouse, trademark-clearinghouse.com/. See also ICANN, Understanding the Trademark Clearinghouse, see: newgtlds.icann.org/en/about/trademark-clearinghouse

236  Generally speaking, the URS does not apply to ccTLDs or to gTLDs established before 2012. However, some ccTLDs have adopted the URS, e.g. Palau.

237  ICANN, Uniform Rapid Suspension System Procedure (1 March 2013), available online at: newgtlds.icann.org/en/applicants/urs/procedure-01mar13-en.pdf

8.1.2   The Registrant has no legitimate right or interest to the domain name; and

8.1.3   The domain was registered and is being used in a bad faith.

8.2     The burden of proof shall be clear and convincing evidence.

When a complaint is received and validated by a URS provider, the relevant registry is informed and the domain name is 'locked'. This means that all changes to the registration data, including transfer and deletion of the domain names are barred, but the domain name itself will continue to work.[238]

The URS Examiner appointed by the URS Provider examines the submissions made by complainant and respondent to ensure that, firstly, the complainant has satisfactorily met the burden of proof for the three requirements, and secondly, that there is no material question of fact that needs to be decided. If the examiner decides that:

- the use of the domain name in question is a non-infringing use or fair use of the trade mark; or
- there is any genuine contestable issue as to whether a domain name registration and use of a trade mark are in bad faith;

then the URS complaint will be dismissed, although the complainant is still able to bring an appeal under the URS, begin a UDRP proceeding or start a legal action.[239]

If a complainant is successful under the URS, the disputed domain name is not transferred from the registrant to complainant but the registry is required to suspend the domain name, which remains suspended for the rest of the period for which it has been registered. The complainant can extend the suspension for an additional year by extending the registration period and paying the renewal registration fees; after that the domain name registration will expire and the domain may be re-registered by another party. Visitors to the domain name will be redirected to an informational web page provided by the URS Provider about the URS.[240]

If the registrant is successful, then the registry will unlock the domain name, thus restoring full control to the registrant.[241] Additionally, there may be penalties for the complainant, where the examiner believes that the complaint is abusive, i.e. that the complainant was seeking to harass, cause unnecessary delay to, or needlessly increase the cost of doing business for, the domain name holder, and their complaint was unwarranted by any existing law or the URS standards, or there was no evidence for the claims made, or their complaint contains a 'deliberate material falsehood'. In such circumstances, where the complainant has made two abusive complaints or one complaint containing a 'deliberate material falsehood' they can be banned for a year from using the URS. Making two complaints which contain a 'deliberate material falsehood' may lead to a permanent bar from using the URS.[242]

Both parties can seek an appeal of the Examiner's decision, including a determination that a complaint is abusive.[243] If a complainant does not believe the Registry Operator is properly complying with the URS process they may register a formal complaint with ICANN.

In the first year of URS operation, just over a hundred proceedings were brought, with mixed results for trade mark holders. It is clear that egregious cases of bad faith registration can be readily addressed by the URS process,[244] but equally trade mark holders may find it difficult in all

---

238 *Ibid*, section 4.

239 *Ibid*, section 8.

240 *Ibid*, section 10.1. See *Facebook Inc v Radoslav* Claim Number: FA1308001515825, NAF (respondent registered facebok.pw to host a web page listing links for popular search topics to generate click through fees. Respondent was engaged in an ongoing pattern of 'typosquatting' registrations).

241 *Ibid*, section 10.5

242 *Ibid*, section 11.

243 *Ibid*, section 12.

244 *Facebook Inc v Radoslav*, above; *Alibaba Group Holding Limited v Tian Shuping*, Case No. HKS-1400002 (ADNDRC 21 May 2014) (<alipay. technology>, <taobao.technology>, <alibaba.technology>).

circumstances (and given the limited word-length allotted for complaints) to prove that use of a domain name containing their mark is not fair use, particularly where the trade mark is also a generic term.[245] Trade mark holders also need to ensure that their complaint clearly demonstrates their rights to a mark.[246] The appeals process has seen relatively limited use, but appeals panels have clearly been willing to overturn initial decisions on the basis of further evidence filed on appeal.[247]

## Post-delegation dispute resolution procedure

There are several Dispute Resolution Procedures that target the behaviour of the gTLD registries themselves, rather than third parties utilising those registries, e.g. the Registry Restriction Dispute Resolution Procedure (RRDRP).[248] This addresses circumstances where a registry is in charge of a community-based gTLD, and a third party claimant which is an 'established institution' with 'an ongoing relationship with a defined community that consists of a restricted population that the gTLD supports' claims it has suffered harm because the gTLD registry operator is not complying with the registration restrictions set out in the Registry Agreement. Where the complainant has previously filed a claim through the Registry Restriction Problem Report System (RRPRS) it has standing to then file an RRDRP. If the administrative processes are completed satisfactorily by both complainant and respondent, the dispute is heard by a one or three person Expert Panel. To succeed the claimant must show:

- the community invoked by the objector is a defined community;
- there is a strong association between the community invoked and the gTLD label or string;
- the TLD operator violated the terms of the community-based restrictions in its agreement;
- there is a measureable harm to the complainant and the community named by the objector.[249]

The complainant bears the burden of proving its claim by a preponderance of the evidence.[250] If the claimant succeeds, the registry operator must pay all their administrative costs associated with the complaint. Failure to do so will be the subject of sanctions up to the termination of the registry agreement.[251] There can be no other financial sanctions.[252] The Expert Panel may also recommend that other enforcement measures be taken against the registry (taking into account the ongoing harm to the complainant, but also the harm the remedies might cause unrelated, good faith domain name registrants operating within the gTLD) by ICANN, including:

- remedial measures by the registry to prevent future registrations that do not comply with community-based limitations, where these are related to the names at issue in the RRDRP proceeding and are permitted under the Registry Agreement;
- suspension of new domain name registrations in the gTLD for a set period of time or until the issue in the complaint is satisfactorily addressed;
- where the registry operator can be shown to have acted maliciously, termination of a registry agreement.[253]

245 *Virgin Enterprises Limited v Lawrence Fain* (Claim No. FA1402001545807 (NAF 20 March 2014) (<branson.guru>)); *Finn.no AS v North Sound Names et al*, (Claim No. FA1405001558494 (NAF 25 May 2014) (<finn.sexy>)); *Nissan Motor Co Ltd v Domains By Proxy, LLC et al* FA1412001593524 (NAF 24 December 2014).

246 *Aeropostale Procurement Co Inc v Michael Kinsey* (Claim No. FA1403001550933 (NAF 10 April 2014) (<aeropostale.uno>)); *Wolfram Research Inc v Andrew Davis et al* (Claim No. FA1404001553139 (NAF 12 April 2014) (<mathematica.guru>, <wolfram.ceo>)).

247 *Stuart Weitzman IP, LLC v yoyo.email et al* (Claim No. FA1404001554808 (NAF 10 May 2014)).

248 ICANN, Registry Restriction Dispute Resolution Procedure (RRDRP), 4 June 2012, available online at: newgtlds.icann.org/en/applicants/agb/rrdrp-04jun12-en.pdf

249 Ibid, section 6.

250 Ibid, section 16.

251 Ibid, section 13.

252 Ibid, section 17.2.

253 Ibid, section 17.3.

All such penalties are at ICANN's discretion.[254] The Expert Determination can be appealed within the RRDRP process[255] and the subject of the complaint, including any liability imposed after such a determination, may also be appealed in the courts.[256] At the time of writing, no complaints appear to have been heard under this procedure.

The important procedure for trade mark holders is the Trademark Post-Delegation Dispute Resolution Procedure (TPDDRP).[257] This is designed to permit trade mark owners to protect their rights where a registry operator's operation, or use, of a domain leads to, or supports, trade mark infringement, either on the top level or second level. The process begins when a third party complainant files a complaint stating that it is a trade mark holder (including registered or unregistered marks) and that one or more of its marks have been infringed to its detriment by the registry operator's manner of operation or use of the gTLD.[258] Before the complaint moves forward, it is subject to both an administrative and threshold review. The former ensures that the procedural rules have been met, the latter that the complainant can demonstrate the following requirements:

- it holds a nationally or regionally registered word mark that is in current use; or has been validated through court proceedings; or is specifically protected by a statute or treaty at the time the complaint is filed (this may be shown by validation by the Trademark Clearinghouse);
- it has asserted material harm as a result of trade mark infringement;
- it has asserted with sufficient specificity facts which support a claim under the Top Level Standards, or a claim under the Second Level Standards;
- that 30 days or more prior to filing, it notified the registry operator in writing of the specific concerns and specific conduct it believes is resulting in infringement of its trade marks, and its willingness to meet to resolve the issue; whether the registry operator responded to this notice, and if it did, that the complainant attempted good faith discussions to resolve matters before initiating the TPDDRP.[259]

The registry operator is able to comment on the complainant's standing, and the complainant may then respond.[260] If the threshold review is not passed the complaint is dismissed without a full hearing.[261] If the threshold review is passed, the registry operator is asked for a response to the complaint, failure to respond leads to default and the matter goes to an expert hearing on the basis of the complaint alone.[262] The expert panel may consist of one or three panellists. Discovery prior to the hearing is expressly provided for in the procedure.[263] The complainant bears the burden of proving the allegations in the complaint by clear and convincing evidence.[264]

For a Top Level complaint to succeed, the complainant must show that:

- the registry operator's affirmative conduct in its operation or use of its gTLD string that is identical or confusingly similar to the complainant's mark, causes or materially contributes to the gTLD –
  - o taking unfair advantage of the distinctive character or the reputation of the complainant's mark; or

254 Ibid, section 18.5.
255 Ibid, section 19.
256 Ibid, section 21.
257 ICANN, Trademark Post-Delegation Dispute Resolution Procedure (RRDRP), 4 June 2012, available online at: newgtlds.icann.org/en/applicants/agb/pddrp-04jun12-en.pdf
258 Ibid, section 5.
259 Ibid, section 9.
260 Ibid, section 9.3.
261 Ibid, section 9.7.
262 Ibid, sections 11 and 12.
263 Ibid, section 15.
264 Ibid, section 17.

    o   impairing the distinctive character or the reputation of the complainant's mark; or

    o   creating a likelihood of confusion with the complainant's mark.[265]

For a Second Level complaint to succeed, the complainant must show that:

- through the registry operator's affirmative conduct –

    o   there is a substantial pattern or practice of specific bad faith intent by the registry operator to profit from the sale of trade mark infringing domain names; and

    o   the registry operator's bad faith intent to profit from the systematic registration of domain names within the gTLD that are identical or confusingly similar to the complainant's mark, which –

        - takes unfair advantage of the distinctive character or the reputation of the complainant's mark, or

        - impairs the distinctive character or the reputation of the complainant's mark, or

        - creates a likelihood of confusion with the complainant's mark.[266]

It is not enough for the complainant to demonstrate that the registry operator is aware of possible trade mark infringement through registrations in the gTLD. Examples of bad faith include the registry operator actively and systematically encouraging registrants to register second-level domain names and to take unfair advantage of the trade mark such that bad faith is apparent, or acting as the registrant or beneficial user of infringing registrations to monetise and profit in bad faith.

If the complainant succeeds, the registry operator has to pay their administrative costs associated with the complaint.[267] The Expert Panel can also recommend penalties similar to those for breach of the RRPRS, which ICANN will take into account when making their decision.[268] Unlike the RRPR, if the complainant in the TPDDRP fails to make its case, the Expert Panel may recommend that their compliant was 'without merit' and that ICANN should impose sanctions, including:

- temporary bans from filing complaints;
- making the complainant pay the registry operator's costs, including reasonable attorney fees; and
- if the complainant makes repeated 'without merit' complaints, a permanent ban from filing complaints.[269]

The Expert Determination can be appealed with the TPDDRP process[270] and the subject of the complaint, including any liability imposed after such a determination, may be appealed in the courts.[271]

# Protecting trade marks in domain names: Which remedy?

As can be seen from the foregoing discussion, trade mark holders do not lack for options when it comes to mechanisms for protecting their rights. The key question for a rightsholder is thus which

---

265 *Ibid*, section 6.1.
266 *Ibid*, section 6.2.
267 *Ibid*, section 14.3.
268 *Ibid*, section 18.
269 *Ibid*, section 18.5.
270 *Ibid*, section 20.
271 *Ibid*, section 22.

of the remedies will be most effective in terms of achieving the level of protection required, in a reasonable time, and at a reasonable cost. Arnot suggests that there are seven key criteria that should be considered: standing in the forum, jurisdiction, time constraints, cost, desired remedies, enforceability of judgment, and possibility of appeal.[272]

The starting point for many rightsholders will be the sending of a 'cease and desist' letter to a domain name holder. This will usually assert trade mark rights, outline how the trade mark holder believes the domain name infringes on those rights, require that the domain name holder cease using the domain name, and usually demand that the domain name holder turn over ownership of the domain name to the trade mark holder within a set period of time. While this may resolve some potential disputes rapidly and cheaply either by causing the domain name holder to change their use of the domain name or to transfer it to the trade mark holder, there are a number of potential pitfalls.

Contacting the domain name holder may prove problematic, because the necessary details are either missing from the WHOIS database (which is supposed to identify who holds a domain name registration),[273] or that data is inaccurate.[274] While ICANN has imposed new rules on registrars via its 2013 Registrar Accreditation Agreement[275] requiring them to verify the information supplied by registrants, and is currently in the process of redesigning the registration directory service,[276] a significant percentage of WHOIS entries are flawed. Actual cybersquatters will have little interest in providing valid details, or responding to correspondence from a trade mark holder. Arnot notes that the very act of sending a 'cease and desist' letter may cause a cybersquatter to transfer owner-ship of the domain name to another party, or its registration to another registry, a process known as 'cyberflying'.[277] To tackle this issue, ICANN amended the notification rules under the Uniform Domain Name Dispute Resolution Policy (UDRP). From July 2015, registrars will place a lock on a domain name within two business days of receiving notice of a UDRP action – and before notify-ing the domain owner of the action. Additionally, complainants will no longer have to send a copy of their complaint to respondents in advance, preventing them transferring the disputed domain name.[278] So it may, in fact, be best not to send a 'cease and desist' letter, particularly if dealing with a known cybersquatter.

'Cease and desist' letters can also cause public relation nightmares for trade mark holders (and/ or their legal representatives) if they are over-used or poorly targeted. There have been numerous cases where 'cease and desist' letters have been sent to domain name holders who are clearly not infringing on the trade mark at issue. This is often perceived as misuse of trade mark rights and bullying – in such circumstances the domain name holder's response will often be to go straight to the media, usually leading to an embarrassing climb-down by the trade mark holder. Consider, for example, the 'cease and desist' letter sent by the international Copthorne hotel chain's 'brand protection' agents to the Copthorne Village Resident's Association claiming they had registered without permission or authorisation, the domain name <copthornevillage.org>, which 'includes a protected trade mark'.[279]

---

272 Jordan A Arnot, 'Navigating cybersquatting enforcement in the expanding internet' (2014) 13 J. Marshall Rev. Intell. Prop. L. 321 at 337.
273 ICANN, About Whois, available online at: whois.icann.org/en/about-whois
274 See, e.g., NPL, *A Study of Whois Privacy and Proxy Service Abuse – Final Report*, 7 March 2014, available online at: whois.icann.org/sites/default/files/files/pp-abuse-study-final-07mar14-en.pdf
275 ICANN 2013 Registrar Accreditation Agreement, available online at: www.icann.org/resources/pages/approved-with-specs-2013-09-17-en
276 ICANN, Final Report from the Expert Working Group on gTLD Directory Services, 9 June 2014, available online at: www.icann.org/en/system/files/files/final-report-06jun14-en.pdf
277 Arnot, above, p 329.
278 ICANN, Policy Implementation Update, 17 November 2014, available online at: www.icann.org/news/announcement-2014-11-17-en
279 Anon, 'Village fights . . . to use its own name' (2015) *Daily Mail Online*, 28 April, available online at: www.dailymail.co.uk/news/article-3059658/

If a 'cease and desist' letter is not sufficient to resolve the issue, or would be tactically unhelpful, then the trade mark holder will need to consider whether to resort to a legal action or to an appropriate dispute resolution process.

Consider a scenario where trade mark holder A is a UK-based entity, and domain name holder B is a non-UK resident who has registered a domain name that is the same as or confusingly similar to the trade mark in question, with C, a US-based registry of a new gTLD. The domain name is used to host a simple website containing click-through advertising links to the websites of A's UK competitors. B receives a payment when a user visits the website and clicks through to one of A's competitors. A could potentially:

- Bring a trade mark infringement action against B in the UK courts, seeking a range of remedies, including transfer of the domain name, damages, and an injunction against B to stop B registering other domain names containing A's trade mark. In practice, depending upon where B is located (if that can be ascertained), even if a legal action could be successfully brought, only the transfer of the domain name is likely to occur – as and when C receives notice of A's successful legal challenge to the registration. Legal action is likely to be costly, relatively slow, and in this case unlikely to offer significant additional remedies to the dispute resolution processes.
- Raise a Uniform Rapid Suspension (URS) complaint resulting initially in the locking of the domain name, and if A is successful the domain name will be suspended for the rest of the registration period + 1 year if A is willing to extend the registration period and pay the renewal registration fees. A may be able to acquire the domain name when the registration lapses to prevent further use by third parties. Failure of the URS complaint does not preclude either a UDRP complaint or legal action. If A is suffering losses as a result of B's activity then the speed of the URS process may limit those losses. There is nothing to stop B registering another domain name that is the same as, or confusingly similar to, the trade mark in question, with C or with another registrar.
- Raise a Uniform Dispute Resolution Policy (UDRP) complaint, if A is uncertain whether the stricter requirements of the URS process can be met, or if A wishes the domain name to be transferred to it, rather than temporarily suspended. The process will be somewhat slower than the URS, but quicker and cheaper than legal action. However the only remedy if A is successful is transfer of the domain name. As with the URS, there is nothing to stop B registering another domain name that is the same as, or confusingly similar to, the trade mark in question, with C or with another registrar. However, UDRP panels will usually take patterns of 'bad faith' behaviour by B into account in deciding future UDRP hearings.
- Raise a Trademark Post-Delegation Dispute Resolution Procedure (TPDDRP) complaint against C, claiming that C's operation, or use, of its gTLD leads to, or supports, trade mark infringement. This might be the case if C has allowed B and other registrants to systematically register domain names within the gTLD that are identical or confusingly similar to A's trade mark. Proving this is likely to be a heavy burden for a lone or small trade mark holder. If successful, A could get its costs back and C would be open to a range of ICANN penalties, up to and including termination of their right to run the gTLD registry.

## The future of domain name disputes

Both ICANN's decision to establish internationalised country code TLDs in 2010, and its decision to move ahead with the expansion of the gTLDs in 2012, have proved controversial. Significant numbers of high-profile companies expressed major concerns about the implications of those expansions in the number and variety of gTLDs – for example:

We do not believe there is significant demand from businesses or consumers for additional gTLDs to host commercial sites . . . Additional top level domains, will, however, offer unprecedented opportunities for the registration of new second level domain names that are deliberately confusingly similar to existing second level registrations or to legally protected brand names, without offering any countervailing benefits . . . Brand owners have found it necessary to 'defensively' register their brands, common misspellings and variations of their brands in existing gTLDs in order to prevent consumer confusion between sites legitimately associated with their products and services and those that are not. As pointed out in our introduction, we currently own a portfolio of over 11,500 essentially useless domain names. For the most part, their existence benefits only the registrars that maintain them and the registries that host them.[280]

This controversy deepened when Canadian company Vox Populi was granted the right to run a '.sucks' gTLD in 2014. The sunrise registration period for '.sucks' started in March 2015 and general availability began in June 2015. During that time, any company registered with the Trademark Clearinghouse (TMCH) had to pay $2,500 to register a domain name, and will have to pay the same amount for each future annual renewal – a cost significantly higher than sunrise pricing seen in most other new gTLDs. This has been viewed by trade mark holders and other commentators as 'little more than a predatory shakedown scheme' raising 'fears that the purpose of gTLD expansion is to enrich the domain name industry rather than benefit the broader community of Internet users'.[281] Certainly the expansion of the gTLDS and the creation of internationalised domain names has opened up a new frontier for those seeking to take advantage of others' trade marks. Outside the US, with its existing domain name-specific legislation, it seems likely that future developments in this area are more likely to centre upon the perceived effectiveness of the administrative measures taken by ICANN and the gTLD registries in keeping cybersquatting and other abuses at a level that can be tolerated by commerce, than upon the application and development of trade mark law by national courts.

## Further reading

Milton L Mueller, *Ruling the Root: Internet Governance and the Taming of Cyberspace*, 2002, Cambridge, MA: MIT Press

David G Post and Danielle Kehl, *Controlling Internet Infrastructure The 'IANA Transition' and Why It Matters for the Future of the Internet, Part I* (April 2015) Open Technology Institute

Jordan A Arnot, 'Navigating cybersquatting enforcement in the expanding internet' (2014) 13 J. Marshall Rev. Intell. Prop. L. 321

Mairead Moore, 'Cybersquatting: prevention better than cure?' (2009) 17(2) IJLIT 220

Leanne Wood, 'A name of thrones – why domain names should now be a separate intellectual property right' (2014) 36(7) EIPR 452

---

280  E Thomas Watson, Assistant General Counsel, Bank of America Corporation, Comment to ICANN on new gTLD Draft Applicant Handbook, 15 December 2008.
281  See, e.g., Letter from Senator Jay Rockefeller, Chairman, Senate Commerce Committee to ICANN, 12 March 2014, available online at: www.commerce.senate.gov/public/?a=Files.Serve&File_id=3da71cc8-9baa-4aaa-a8b4-3e159a3335bc

# Chapter 6

# Electronic commerce

## Chapter contents

\* Many thanks to Edward Ditchfield, PhD student at Aberystwyth University, for his work as a research assistant.

# Introduction

Electronic commerce, or commerce taking place via electronic communication media, ranges from the traditional electronic data interchanges on closed networks and commerce via fax or telex, to the modern forms of online commerce via the web, email, and mobile phones. The focus of this chapter is on the latter, and in particular the online selling and buying of goods and services, as opposed to the provision of ancillary services to enable internet access, retrieve data, or host material. The spectrum of the goods or services sold online is wide, encompassing goods and services delivered physically, as well as the new digital intangible goods, such as films, music, software, books, news, financial data, and pornography; and services, such as online banking, internet telephony, or the provision of recreational activities, such as gambling and gaming in virtual worlds. In these latter instances, the contract is not only made, but also performed, electronically. The vast majority of these online transactions are relatively low-value business-to-consumer (B2C) or consumer-to-consumer (C2C) transactions (for example, eBay transactions) rather than business-to-business (B2B) transactions, and so the legal protection of consumers forms a central part of the regulatory landscape.

There is no single legal definition of 'electronic commerce' and indeed, in most legal contexts, none is needed; when electronic transactions are treated the same as comparable offline transactions, there is no need to define electronic commerce. Such a legal position accords perfectly with the notion of 'technological neutrality'[1] according to which legal rights and obligations ought to be dependent solely on the substance of the transaction and not on the underlying technology used to carry it out – whether the 'technology' is the voice, paper, fax, telephone or electronic channels. In some ways, the discussion in this chapter (and indeed book) focuses on the areas of law that cannot be applied to the online environment in a straightforward fashion and, by definition, this is because the law is or was not sufficiently technologically neutral. However, the notion of technological neutrality – which has figured prominently in the regulatory debate on electronic commerce in the European Union (EU) – tends to be understood more narrowly than described above. For example, in the lead-up to the 2002 ePrivacy Directive, the Commission stated that '[t]he aim is to cover *all electronic* communication services in a technology neutral fashion'.[2] In other words, technological neutrality becomes relevant only after a decision has been made that 'electronic communication services' require special regulation. But once within the electronic sphere, it ought not to matter legally whether a film or music file is downloaded onto a computer, a TV set, a mobile phone, or

---

1 Chris Reed, 'Taking sides on technology neutrality' (2007) 4:3 SCRIPTed 263, available online at: http://www2.law.ed.ac.uk/ahrc/script-ed/vol4-3/reed.asp
2 Proposal for a Directive of the European Parliament and of the Council Concerning the Processing of Personal Data and the Protection of Privacy in the Electronic Communication Sector, COM(2000)385 final, 12 July 2000, Brussels, p 29.

one's coffee machine. This approach then requires a definition of 'electronic commerce', but it also begs the question whether electronic communications indeed require such special regulation and, if so, why. The discussion below shows that much of the special regulation created for electronic commerce is designed to create no more than a level playing field for online and offline transactions, to fill gaps created by the characteristics of the electronic communications. These characteristics of the electronic networked environment may, depending on the context, be the speed and ease of transacting, its low cost, its anonymity, or its irreverence for national boundaries. However, in the final analysis, the rationale for special electronic commerce regulation is substantive technological neutrality: consumers or businesses ought not to prefer one medium over another for transacting on the basis of fearing its increased risks and inadequate remedies. And this aim of substantive neutrality ultimately provides the yardstick for assessing the wisdom or otherwise of the particular regulatory approaches taken to electronic commerce.

Much of this book, not only this chapter, is concerned with the regulation of electronic commerce, given that online trading potentially triggers a multitude of regulation of both civil and criminal nature. On the civil law front, electronic trading often raises implications under intellectual property laws or tort, such as negligence, defamation, or privacy. In the criminal sphere, electronic commerce may be affected by laws regulating data protection or laws regulating certain industries, such as pharmaceutical products, gambling, or banking activities, as well as by consumer protection laws or anti-terrorist, racism or obscenity regulation. This chapter does not deal with these regulatory concerns. Its focus is broadly contract law in domestic and transnational electronic contracts,[3] as well as laws that affect contractual rights and obligations or are integral to the contractual process, such as electronic signatures.

A fundamental canon underlying contract law is contractual autonomy – that is, that individuals are free to decide whether to contract or on what terms. The flipside of the freedom to contract on terms mutually agreed is the freedom from state interference with those terms.[4] In practice, however, contractual autonomy never amounts to a total freedom from the state even when it is treated with utmost sanctity. Contractual autonomy interacts with the laws of the land in two fundamental ways. First, it is not a principle that exists over and above the regulatory sphere of a state; its very existence is dependent upon its recognition by the relevant legal order, and in cases of disputes reliant upon the state's enforcement mechanisms. States invariably recognise contractual autonomy, albeit subject to certain limitations, often to protect the consumer, which vary from state to state. For example, under Islamic law, a contract that provides for the payment of interest on a loan is void, and in most legal systems, contracts entered into with minors are not enforceable. Second, contractual parties cannot contract out of the criminal laws or public regulation of a state. This reflects the 'superiority' of public regulation and criminal laws over any terms agreed by private parties, and foreshadows the not infrequent legitimate interferences of public regulation in private bargains. The above points deserve a special mention in the context of online contracts, given that online Terms and Conditions often have the appearance of standing over and above any state law. Sometimes they purport to apply to everyone and not just to the contracting parties, see, for example, Facebook's Term 16(1) which states:

> We strive to create a global community with consistent standards for everyone, but we also strive to respect local laws. The following provisions apply to users and *non-users* who interact with Facebook outside the United States: You consent to having your personal data transferred to and processed in the United States. . .'.[5]

---

3 For a critical overview of contract law, see Scottish Law Commission, *Review of Contract Law, Discussion Paper on Formation of Contract* [2012] SLC 154 (DP) (March 2012), available online at: http://www.bailii.org/scot/other/SLC/DP/2012/154.html. For a systematic overview of legal rules in transnational contracts, see Faye Fangfei Wang, *Internet Jurisdiction and Choice of Law*, 2010, CUP.

4 As an often-forgotten adjunct, party autonomy also entails personal responsibility for one's own decision and thus no protection against unwise decisions.

5 [Emphasis added].

This term is paradoxical in a number of ways, but first of all in terms of purporting to bind those who have no connection with Facebook whatsoever. This perception of the overreach of online T&Cs (beyond state law and beyond the contracting/subscribing users) may partly be explained by the view of cyberspace as separate space from the 'real' world, and partly by the over-regional dimension of online transactions and interactions. Certainly, from a national-law perspective this is an entirely mistaken perception.

# Online contracting

## Online advertising: spam emails and behavioural targeting

The internet provides an ideal platform for advertising as marketing is fast, relatively cheap, far reaching and potentially highly accurate and thus effective. Such advertising occurs in numerous ways – as commercial bulk emails, commonly known spam or junk, as web banners, as sponsored (targeted) advertising on search engines and social networking sites. Indeed advertising plays a crucial role in the business model of many core online providers that finance their 'free' services, e.g. search, through related highly profitable marketing activities.[6] Whilst online advertising is subject to the same rules and regulations governing traditional advertising, e.g. against misleading behaviour, it also raises additional security and privacy concerns that have prompted regulation.

In the EU that regulation has shown a strong preference for seeking to empower users through the adoption of an opt-in approach. For example, initially regulatory efforts were focused on spam email which continues to make up a large proportion of all email traffic: it was estimated that in 2014, 54 billion spam emails were sent every day.[7] Apart from the obvious harm arising out of fraudulent and unsavoury messages, even 'innocent' unsolicited commercial email clogs up networks, slows down other traffic and requires time and expense from businesses and consumers to deal with these unwanted messages.[8] Thus in response, Art 13 of the ePrivacy Directive (2002)[9] requires that the subscriber gives *prior* consent to such marketing, unless he or she is an existing customer of a business and is 'clearly and distinctly . . . given the opportunity to object, free of charge and in an easy manner, to such use of electronic contact details when they are collected and on the occasion of each message in case the customer has not initially refused such use'[10] – the 'opt-in approach'. In contrast, in the USA the Controlling the Assault of Non-Solicited Pornography and Marketing Act of 2003 (CAN-SPAM Act) does not prohibit unsolicited email *per se*, but the receiver must have an opportunity to opt out of receiving advertising messages – the 'opt-out approach'.[11] As with most internet regulation, differences in national law are highly problematic for the effectiveness of the stricter standard, here that of the EU, as the more lenient standard is liable to undermine it (see Chapter 2). So in order to achieve compliance with varying national standards, online businesses could territorially segregate their marketing depending on the customer's (known) location or comply with the more restrictive approach (here the opt-in approach) to comply with both EU and US law.

In recent years the EU's focus has turned on the increasing use of cookies for behavioural targeting through monitoring a person's online activities and then using the data collected to tailor advertising, search results or social media posts to align with the person's perceived likes, dislikes, concerns, political affiliations, sexual preferences, etc in order to increase the likely success of the

6 Internet Advertising Bureau, 'U.S. Internet Ad Revenues Reach Historic $13.3 Billion in Q1 2015' (11 June 2015).
7 MarketWatch, 'CYREN Internet Trend Report Shows 73 Percent Increase in Phishing URLS Related to PayPal' (27 May 2014), available online at: http://ir.cyren.com/releasedetail.cfm?releaseid=850478
8 European Commission, *Measures to counter unsolicited commercial communications* ('spam') (22 January 2004) COM(2004) 28.final.
9 Directive 2002/58/EC, implemented in the UK in Privacy and Electronic Communications (EC Directive) Regulations 2003.
10 Article 13(2). Australia adopts much the same approach in the Spam Act 2003 (Cth), see esp s.16.
11 Section 5(a)(4).

advert. The privacy implications of this are significant, as the judge in *Vidal-Hall v Google Inc* (2014) observed:

> if the targeted advertisements apparently reveal other information about the users, whether about their personalities, or their immediate plans or ambitions, then if these matters are sensitive, or relate to protected characteristics (e.g. beliefs), or to secret wishes or ambitions, then the fear that others who see the screen may find out those matters, and act upon what they have seen, may well be worrying and distressing.'[12]

In response to the pervasiveness of such personalised advertising and the high sensitivity of much of the collected data,[13] the EU adopted the same opt-in approach explicitly for the use of cookies and similar technology in Directive 2009/136/EC which amends the ePrivacy Directive (2002) and requires that the user has given 'his or her consent, having been provided with clear and comprehensive information . . . about the purposes' of the cookie,[14] which spells out in detail what is already more generally provided in the Data Protection Directive (see Chapter 9).

It is difficult to gauge the relative effect or effectiveness of the above regulation given the continued pervasiveness of spam and behavioural targeting. Enforcement activity of both the Data Protection Directive and the ePrivacy Directive remains fairly low-key. Part of the problem is the dispersion of very minor and mainly non-pecuniary harm amongst a large number of internet users which makes it very unlikely that victims bring an action for a judicial remedy, i.e. an injunction and/or compensation, and thereby enforce the Directives. However, *Google Inc v Vidal-Hall* (2015)[15] which concerned Google's surreptitious tracking of Apple Safari users, has eased the way for such enforcement actions in the UK, by allowing 'moral damage' by itself, even in the absence of any pecuniary loss, to found a data protection claim[16] (see further Chapter 2 and Chapter 9). In the case of spam, online intermediaries are often more strongly incentivised to bring enforcement actions, given the cost of spam for them. In *Microsoft Corporation v McDonald* (2006)[17] Microsoft obtained a summary judgment against Mr McDonald for instigating spam email through his website that offered email addresses for sale. The damage suffered by Microsoft was, on the one hand, the damage to its goodwill *vis-à-vis* its subscribers for failing to protect them from spam and, on the other hand, the money expended on coping with the volume of spam and on fighting spam, for example, via decoy accounts specifically created to catch spammers. In fact, in the USA, the CAN-SPAM Act makes ISPs (which are widely defined) the only private parties that can take advantage of the civil cause of action for damages.[18] In addition, in the EU, penal enforcement actions – taken in the UK by the Information Commissioner – are an alternative sanction against

---

12 *Vidal-Hall v Google Inc* [2014] EWHC 13 (QB), para [24].
13 For online profiling generally, see The Psychometrics Centre, Cambridge; or G Park, M Kosinski, D Stillwell, J Eichstaedt, A Schwartz, P Kern, L Ungar and M Seligman, 'Automatic Personality Assessment through Social Media Language' (2015) 108(6) Journal of Personality and Social Psychology 934.
14 Art 5(3) of Directive 2002/58/EC. See Information Commissioner's Office, *Guidance on the rules on use of cookies and similar technologies* (May 2012), available online at: https://ico.org.uk/media/for-organisations/documents/1545/cookies_guidance.pdf
15 *Google Inc v Vidal-Hall* [2015] EWCA Civ 311.
16 *Google Inc v Vidal-Hall* [2015] EWCA Civ 311, paras 52–101.
17 *Microsoft Corporation v McDonald (Also Known As Gary A Webb)* (t/a *Bizads and Bizads UK*) [2006] EWHC 3410 (Ch).
18 Successfully applied in *MySpace Inc v Wallace* 498 F Supp 2d 1293 (CD Cal, 2007), in which the defendant had created 11,000 MySpace profiles to disseminate spam to other MySpace.com users. See also *America Online, Inc v IMS* 24 F Supp 2d 548 (ED Va, 1998); *America Online, Inc v LCGM, Inc* 46 F Supp 2d 444 (ED Va, 1998); and *America Online v Prime Data Systems* [1998] US Dist LEXIS 20226. In the US trespass to chattel has also been used to tackle spam, see, e.g., *CompuServe v Cyber Promotions Inc* 962 F Supp 1015 (SD Ohio, 1997) where the court dealt with the requirement for physical contact with the chattel by stating that that 'electronic signals generated and sent by computer [are] . . . sufficiently physically tangible to support a trespass cause of action' (at 1021) and then consider the damage suffered by the defendant: 'the defendants' multitudinous electronic mailings demand the disk space and drain the processing power of plaintiff's computer equipment, those resources are not available to serve CompuServe subscribers. Therefore, the value of that equipment to CompuServe is diminished even though it is not physically damaged by defendants' conduct' (at 1022). See also *Cyber Promotions Inc v American Online Inc* 948 F Supp 436 (ED Pa, 1996); *America Online Inc v IMS* 24 F Supp 2d 548 (ED Va, 1998); and Mark D Robins, 'Electronic trespass: An old theory in a new context' (1998) 15 Computer Law 1.

spammers, but from a regulatory perspective they are more onerous considering the number of spammers, and the fact that such actions only effectively lie against domestic offenders.[19]

## Clickwrap and browsewrap agreements

Under English law, a valid contract requires an offer, an acceptance, consideration, and an intention to create legal relations. Whether these elements are satisfied depends to some extent on the type of the online contract. The main types of online contract are clickwrap and browsewrap agreements, and rather more rarely contracts by exchange of emails. In a clickwrap agreement, the customer clicks on an 'I agree' or 'I accept' button close to the terms of the agreement, or a link to them to indicate his or her assent to them. A 'browsewrap', or 'click-free', agreement is one of which most internet users are not aware, or only vaguely so. These agreements are generally found behind links such as 'Terms of use' or 'Legal' at the top or bottom of the web page, to which users agree by virtue of their conduct, such as browsing or downloading or using software. For example, Huffington Post UK Terms of Service state: 'By using AOL Web Services as a casual visitor, or by completing the registration process to obtain and use a Screen Name or User Name, you signify that you agree to this Agreement.'[20] So, Huffington Post's 'casual visitors' would certainly enter into a browsewrap agreement with AOL (UK) Ltd, assuming these agreements are held to be binding contracts. Similarly, anyone conducting a search on Google agrees, according to Google, to its terms by virtue of this term: 'By using our Services, you are agreeing to these terms'[21] although again the question is whether these terms are in fact binding (see below).

Although clickwrap agreements are legally 'safer', many sites still opt for browsewrap agreements, because they are visually and practically less intrusive and as rarely products or money changes hands in these cases, disputes are less likely. Ultimately, as shown below, the difference between clickwrap and browsewrap agreements is one of degree given that the 'click' on a button does not always show as unambiguously as a signature, contractual intention or consent to the contract and its terms, and then the question for both clickwrap and browsewrap agreements turns to the general one of reasonable notice and objective intention in all the circumstances.

## Offer and acceptance

For a contract to be formed, there has to be an offer and an acceptance of that offer. Internet contracts have raised the questions, first, whether a website is an offer or merely an 'invitation to treat'; and second, whether an acceptance via email or web-based communication occurs upon sending it or only upon its actual communication to the offeror. Neither of these questions is problematic in browsewrap agreements, because here the acceptance by the user/offeree occurs at the time and place of his or her use, as stipulated by the terms of the agreement.

In relation to clickwrap agreements, both of these questions appear to be answered by Art 11(1) of the Electronic Commerce Directive:[22]

> Member States shall ensure . . . that in cases where the recipient of the service places his order through technological means the following principles apply:
>
> - the service provider has to acknowledge the receipt of the recipient's order without undue delay and by electronic means;
> - the order and the acknowledgement of receipt are deemed to be received when the parties to whom they are addressed are able to access them.

---

19 Article 15(2), which refers to Ch III of the Data Protection Directive 95/46/EC. Note that, in the UK, it is only the Information Commissioner that can ask for an injunction.
20 http://www.huffingtonpost.co.uk/p/huffingtonpostcouk-terms-of-service.html
21 https://www.google.co.uk/intl/en/policies/terms/regional.html
22 Directive 2000/31/EC.

The first paragraph seems to suggest that the supplier of online services *accepts* the customer's *offer* when he *acknowledges* the costumer's *order*. This assumes that the term 'order' equates with the legal concept of 'offer' and the term 'acknowledgement' with the legal concept of 'acceptance'. In the UK, reg 12 of the Electronic Commerce (EC Directive) Regulations 2002 validates such an assumption only with respect to the second paragraph and only in relation to the 'order'.[23] Thus, even in respect of the second paragraph above, it cannot be assumed that the acknowledgement of the order is an acceptance. Although such assumption would be helpful in providing answers to the online contracting analysis, they are not justified. First, the language of the Article and its meaning in plain English does not support such an interpretation: an 'acknowledgement' of an order does not convey whether the supplier is willing to accept it or not. Second, the provisions are, on their face, intended to give additional safeguards (in the form of confirmations of messages) to online contractual parties in view of the perceived unreliability of cyberspace – consistent with the other provisions in the Directive.[24] So, quite regardless of whether the order is, in legal terms, an offer or an acceptance, under the Article the receipt of the order must still be acknowledged. So the Directive does not offer any guidance as to the proper contractual analysis of offers and acceptances online.

Of some help is Art 10 of the Electronic Commerce Directive, which requires that the service provider must, at least in consumer contracts, give the recipient of the service prior notice of the 'different technical steps to follow to conclude the contract'.[25] Thus, under Art 10, the service provider must make it clear when the deal is struck. Unfortunately, this requirement does not apply to contracts concluded 'via electronic mail or by equivalent individual communications'[26] and not at all to providers outside the ambit of the Directive – that is, non-EU providers.

## Offer or invitation to treat

The issue of whether a website offering goods or services is legally an offer or a mere invitation to treat is significant because it determines whether and, if so, when a contract was concluded, preventing the parties from withdrawing from the bargain. If a website constitutes an offer, the order by the customer concludes the contract and the supplier cannot reject it. If, however, the site is a mere invitation to treat, the customer's order constitutes the offer that he or she can withdraw until the provider accepts it.

Whether a communication constitutes an offer or a mere invitation to treat is a question of the intention of the offeror as communicated to the offeree and as objectively ascertainable from all of the circumstances (hereafter 'objective intention'): did he or she intend to be bound by it, *or* did he or she merely intend to elicit an offer or negotiations with the view to an offer?[27] Although, ultimately, this is a question of fact to be decided in the particular circumstances of the case, traditionally, shop-window displays, supermarket shelves, and advertisements have been treated as invitations to treat,[28] while automatic vending and ticket machines make offers that the customer accepts by putting money in the machine.[29] So far, there has been no judicial pronouncement by an English court on online contracts, but academia on the whole supports the shop-window analogy for two reasons:[30]

- In the case of non-digital goods, the online business may have a finite supply of those goods and would not want to be exposed to a situation in which the acceptances outstrip the

---

23 SI 2002/2013. Regulation 12 states: 'Except in relation to regulation 9(1)(c) and regulation 11(1)(b) where "order" shall be the contractual offer, "order" may be but need not be the contractual offer for the purposes of regulations 9 and 11.'

24 Articles 5 ('General Information to be Provided') and 6 ('Information to be Provided').

25 Article 10(1)(a), which is also applicable to non-consumer contracts unless agreed otherwise.

26 Article 10(4).

27 See, e.g., *Gibson v Manchester CC* [1979] 1 WLR 294.

28 *Fisher v Bell* [1961] 1 QB 394; *Pharmaceutical Society of GB v Boots Cash Chemists* [1953] 1 QB 401; *Partridge v Crittenden* [1968] 2 All ER 421.

29 *Thornton v Shoe Lane Parking* [1971] 2 QB 163.

30 For example, Christoph Glatt, 'Comparative issues in contract formation' (1998) 6 Int JLIT 34, 49ff.

number of goods in its possession.[31] (Note that this argument is generally inapplicable to digital goods, although a business may have a licence to supply only a limited number of them.[32] In any event, the limited supply concern can generally be addressed by making the offer subject to availability.)

● An online business may want to be able to weed out certain customers – for example, customers from legally inhospitable jurisdictions or customers below a certain age.

Although these arguments are persuasive *prima facie*, they cannot by themselves be decisive, if they are not consistent with the objective intention of both parties as ascertainable by the circumstances of the case.

In clickwrap agreements, in which the costumer has to click a 'Proceed', 'Place your order', 'Confirm', or 'Purchase' button after ticking a box with the terms and conditions, it would be reasonable for him or her to expect that this act constitutes the acceptance, not the offer – contrary to academic opinion.[33] The wording and the contractual process of compiling all of the relevant data (such as the name, delivery address, and the payment details), the core/essential terms (i.e. price, product and delivery date) as well as displaying to the customers the other terms of the contract before his or her final click, all suggest that this click is the last act needed to conclude the contract once and for all. Most people would assume, and arguably reasonably so, that they have now entered into a contract; or put differently that they could not easily 'undo' their actions. For them, any subsequent web notice or email notification merely confirms the details of that contract. From the customer's perspective, because the whole order is on the supplier's terms, why would the supplier need to consent to it? Noteworthy, under German law (interpreting § 145 of the German Civil Code), a declaration is an offer if it is clear and complete as far as all of the essential terms of the contract are concerned, so that the other party simply needs to say 'yes' to conclude the contract.[34] That 'yes', it would seem, comes from the online customer after being presented with all of the essential (and non-essential) terms of the agreement. While an online business may analyse orders with a view to rejecting unsuitable ones, if that is not obvious to the customer, it cannot alter his or her reasonable expectation of finality. In that sense, many online contract formation scenarios are comparable to those with traditional vending machines, in which the machine makes the offer and the customer accepts by putting money into it. As Lord Denning stated in *Thornton v Shoe Lane Parking*: 'The offer is made when the proprietor of the machine holds it out as being ready to receive the money. The acceptance takes place when the customer puts his money into the slot.'[35] So even if there are business considerations that support a different conclusion, these will be irrelevant if the (reasonable) customer has no awareness of them.

Because it is in the interest of suppliers to have the power of finally concluding the contract, online businesses may expressly alter what would otherwise be the customer's reasonable expectations, and indeed many do. Typically amazon.co.uk's 'Conditions of sale' state in Term 1:

> Your order is an offer to Amazon to buy the product(s) in your order. When you place an order to purchase a product from Amazon, we will send you a message confirming receipt of your order and containing the details of your order (the 'Order Confirmation') . . . The Order Confirmation is acknowledgement that we have received your order, and does not confirm acceptance of

---

31 *Grainger & Son v Gough* [1896] AC 325. For a recent online case, see *Kevin Khoa Nguyen v Barnes & Noble Inc* US App LEXIS 15868 (9th Cir 2014).

32 Glatt, above, 50.

33 Most academic treaties argue for the opposite, but note, in the typical software licence agreements: Andres Guadamuz-González, 'The licence/contract dichotomy in open licenses: A comparative analysis' (2009) 30 U La Verne L Rev 296, 301; Lawrence E Rosen, *Open Source Licensing: Software Freedom and Intellectual Property Law*, 2004, London: Prentice Hall, p 60.

34 Peer Zumbansen, 'Contracting in the Internet: German contract law and Internet auctions' (2001) 2 German Law Journal, available online at: germanlawjournal.com/index.php?pageID=11&artID=65

35 [1971] 2 QB 163, 169.

your offer to buy the product(s) or the services ordered. We only accept your offer, and conclude the contract of sale for a product ordered by you, when we dispatch the product to you
and send e-mail or post a message on the Message Centre of the website confirming to you
that we've dispatched the product to you (the 'Dispatch Confirmation').

In short, Amazon expressly provides that the customer makes the offer, and the acceptance by
Amazon occurs upon the dispatch of the product. So it is the business that accepts and thereby concludes the contract.[36] Such contractual classification is likely to be upheld provided that the parties
enjoy the rights that are consistent with the classification:[37] the customer is an offeror only if he or
she is able to withdraw the offer at any time *after* clicking the 'Confirm' or 'Accept' button, but *before*
the acceptance, and the seller is the offeree provided that he or she is not, by the terms of the contract, bound to accept the offer regardless of his or her wish to do so (as is often the case in online
auctions). As Amazon allows customers to cancel orders (albeit not without requiring a reason for
the cancellation), this contractual provision in its terms is in line with its actual contractual process.
If that was not the case, the 'labels' in the contractual terms must be taken as wrong in light of the
objective intention of the parties.[38]

The above clause is particularly important to avoid contracts based on pricing errors that have
often made headlines. If, in addition, a vendor uses software to pick up unusual buying patterns,
it may be able to pick up pricing errors before its acceptance. Once this acceptance has occurred,
the situation becomes trickier. For example, in the Singaporean case of *Chwee King Keong v Digilandmall.
com Pte Ltd*,[39] the online seller of laser printers worth $3,854, mistakenly priced at $66, tried to get
out of 1,600 orders made by six buyers. At the trial stage, the vendor unsuccessfully argued that
no contracts came into existence given that the placing of the order was followed by an automated
message and email confirming the 'successful transaction'.[40] He succeeded on a different ground:
namely, that the orders were void under the common law doctrine of unilateral mistake. On appeal,
the court rejected the lower court's reasoning that constructive, and not only actual, knowledge
of the mistake by the non-mistaken party is sufficient for the common law doctrine of unilateral
mistake, but held that, in equity, constructive knowledge plus an impropriety would suffice to allow
the vendor to avoid the contract:

> constructive knowledge [of the mistake by the non-mistaken party] alone should not suffice to
> invoke equity. There must be an additional element of impropriety. The conduct of deliberately
> not bringing the suspicion of a possible mistake to the attention of the mistaken party could
> constitute such impropriety.[41]

The holding clearly depended on the price being very obviously erroneous. In scenarios in which
the mistake is of a lesser order, it would be much more difficult to prove some form of bad faith.

---

36 For a discussion (in the context of shrink-wrap licences) on why the acceptance of the contract can occur long after the payment
   was accepted, see *ProCD Inc v Zeidenberg* 86 F 3d 1447 (7th Cir, 1996).
37 For other form-versus-substance debates in contract law, see, e.g., (employee or independent contractor) *Autoclenz Ltd v Belcher* [2009]
   EWCA Civ 1046; (condition or warranty in insurance contracts) *Kler Knitwear Ltd v Lombard General Insurance Co Ltd* [2000] Lloyd's Rep IR
   47; (fixed or floating charge in debentures) *National Westminster Bank plc v Spectrum Plus Ltd* [2005] UKHL 41, [119]: 'Its right to do so
   was inconsistent with the charge being a fixed charge and the label placed on the charge by the debenture cannot, in my opinion,
   be prayed-in-aid to detract from that right.'
38 By the same token, regardless of whether the parties label a communication an acceptance, it will not be an acceptance (but a
   counteroffer), if it is not on the same terms as the offer, because this is a fundamental aspect of an acceptance: *Hyde v Wrench* (1840)
   3 Beav 334. On the use of the word 'offer', see also *Spencer v Harding* (1870) LR 5 CP 561.
39 [2005] 1 SLR 502 (CA); aff'd *Chwee King Keong v Digilandmall.com Pte Ltd* [2004] 2 SLR 594. See also German cases in which price errors
   were not binding on vendors: *Anfechtung wegen Übermittlungsfehlers* (OLG Hamm, 12 January, 2004, 13 U 165/03); *Irrtumsanfechtung bei
   falscher Preisangabe* (AG Lahr, 21 December 2004, 5 C 245/04).
40 *Chwee King Keong v Digilandmall.com Pte Ltd* [2005] 1 SLR 502, [29] and [104].
41 *Ibid*, [80].

Delaying acceptance via the terms of the contract and using software to detect errors by unusual buying patterns, as well as addressing pricing errors in the terms and conditions, should go a long way towards minimising the risk of pricing accidents.

## Offer or invitation to treat in online auctions

Contract formation is complicated in auction scenarios, given the presence of a third party, the auctioneer, and the competing bidders. According to ordinary contract law on auctions (partly codified in s 57 of the Sale of Goods Act 1979, which is presumptive, not mandatory), offers are made by the bidding parties;[42] each offer lapses if overtaken by a higher offer and can be withdrawn any time before the hammer falls, which indicates the seller's acceptance. The auctioneer (as an agent for the seller) is free to accept or reject the final bid. However, in auctions without a reserve price there is a collateral contract between the highest bidder and the auctioneer pursuant to which the auctioneer promises to sell to the highest bidder no matter how low the bid is. If the auctioneer fails to honour the highest bid, there is no contract between the bidder and the seller, but the bidder can sue the auctioneer for the difference in market value and the value of the bid.[43]

How does this apply to online auctions? First, the providers of online auctions, such as eBay, are unlikely to be seen to step into the shoes of the traditional auctioneer. In contrast to traditional auctioneers, eBay, according to its User Agreement, merely provides an auctions platform:

> eBay does not have possession of anything listed or sold through eBay, and is not involved in the actual transaction between buyers and sellers. The contract for the sale is directly between buyer and seller. eBay is not a traditional auctioneer.

So instead of the triangular relationship of traditional auctions, there appears to be only a two-way relationship between the buyer and the seller in online auctions. Does this mean that online auctions fall outside the traditional rules for auctions? The answer to this question must depend on the legal issue at stake and to what extent the presence of a third party auctioneer is critical in that context. As argued below, it should not matter to the right of withdrawal (see below), but the different contracting process is likely to impact on the contract formation analysis.

Returning to the issue of offer and acceptance, although s 57 of the Sale of Goods Act 1979 seems prima facie applicable to online auctions, eBay's terms largely override it.[44] According to those terms – and in contrast to the default auction rules – bidders cannot, or only very exceptionally, retract their 'offers' (not used in the legal sense). In its terms relating to 'Changing or retracting your bid',[45] eBay states:

> As a general rule, you can't retract or cancel a bid. Once you place a bid, you agree to pay for the item if you're the winning bidder . . . You can [only] retract a bid for the following reasons: . . . The item's description changed significantly after you entered your last bid.

Sellers can end their listings early without much ado, in which case, all bids are cancelled automatically ('Ending your listing early'), but once the time is up, the seller's 'acceptance' occurs automatically and he or she cannot refuse to honour the highest bid; thus unlike in a traditional auction, the final fall of the 'hammer' is not discretionary.

---

42 *Payne v Cave* (1789) 3 Term Rep 148; *British Car Auctions Ltd v Wright* [1972] 1 WLR 1519.

43 *Barry v Heathcote Ball & Co (Commercial Auctions) Ltd* [2001] 1 All ER 944; *Warlow v Harrison* (1859) 1 E & E 309. This rule would presumably extend to auctions with a publicly known reserve.

44 These terms imposed by eBay on the participants affect the contract between sellers and buyers vis-à-vis each other by informing their reasonable expectations towards each other; under English law, these terms would be implied terms of the contract between the seller and the highest bidder.

45 http://pages.ebay.co.uk/help/buy/bidding-overview.html#change

Both German and Australian courts have had the opportunity to consider the contract formation of online auctions. In the German *Ricardo.de* (2001) case[46] the seller was unhappy with the highest bid that he got for a new VW-Passat (about half the list price) and sought to reject it on the basis that it was up to him to accept or reject the highest bid. This indeed seemed consistent with the terms and conditions of the online auction site (ricardo.de), which all participants had to accept during the registration process, and which stated that posting merchandise on the site served as an invitation to treat. Yet these terms also required the seller to accept the highest bid and required his express declaration to that effect when he uploaded his post to the site. The court at first instance[47] agreed with the seller's argument that no acceptance had taken place; in fact, according to the court, his protest proved his non-acceptance – consistent with the German (and English) default position, which does not require the auctioneer to accept the highest bid.[48] The automatic mail sent to the buyer by the auction site at the end of the auction did not bind the seller, despite the standard term of the auction site. According to the court, these terms were 'too abstract' to qualify as the seller's specific contractual intent. The parties could not possibly have intended to enter into an agreement for the sale of a car so substantially below the list price. On appeal, the court overturned this decision,[49] and upheld the standard terms of the auction site as the basis for the creation of a binding contract between the parties. The court viewed the initial offering by the seller as the offer (and not an invitation to treat or a pre-offer acceptance, as stipulated in the auction house's terms) and the highest bid at the end of the auction as the acceptance. Given the completeness of the initial offering – in terms of stating all of the essential terms – and the lack of any danger of over-acceptances, the contract was concluded by the highest bidder at the time when the auction ended. The court also reasoned that even in disregard of the auction terms, considering all of the surrounding circumstances, including the nature of the auction, one would still have to conclude that the seller intended to sell at any price whatsoever. On appeal, the German Federal Supreme Court[50] again upheld the contract, but left open – because it made practically no difference – whether the acceptance was made by the highest bidder or came in the form of a pre-offer acceptance by the seller made via his declaration to the system at the time of uploading his posting. Consistently, other German cases have held that for the seller/auctioneer not to make a binding offer, he or she must have made that clear: for example, a request not to bid and take the stated price as a basis for negotiations only, or a statement inviting expression of interests only and not bids.[51]

Virtually the same scenario was the basis of the Australian dispute in *Peter Smythe v Vincent Thomas* (2007).[52] In this case, the seller wanted to get out of a finished eBay transaction for a WWII aircraft (for AU$150,000) for which he had received a significantly better offer offline after the end of the auction. The court, referring to the German judgment, adopted the same contractual analysis of the posting being the offer and the highest bid the acceptance, and refused to allow the seller to weasel out of the deal.[53] Understanding the seller's post as the offer and not only an invitation to treat, and the highest bid at the end of the auction as the acceptance, would appear to be in line with the objective intention of the parties in an ordinary eBay transaction, as informed by the site's standard terms. It would explain why the seller can withdraw his or her post, but the bidder cannot generally retract his or her bid, and why the seller is not at liberty to reject the highest bid.

---

46 *Ricardo.de* (BGH, 7 November 2001, Az VIII ZR 13/01); Peer Zumbansen, 'Contracting in the Internet: German contracting law and Internet auctions' (2001) 2(7) NJW, available online at: http://www.germanlawjournal.com/article.php?id=65; Jan-Malte Niemann, 'Online auctions: Germany – Online auctions under German contract' (2001) 17(2) CLSR 114.

47 *Ricardo.de* (LG Münster, 21 January 2000, 4 O 429/99), (2000) Juristen Zeitung 730.

48 German Civil Code, § 156.

49 *Ricardo.de* (OLG Hamm, 14 December 2000, 2 U 58/00, (2001) Juristen Zeitung 764; (2001) NJW 1142.

50 *Ricardo.de* (BGH, 7 November 2001, Az VIII ZR 13/01).

51 *Preisangabe in Internetauktion als Verhandlungsbasis* (AG Kerpen, 25 May 2001, 21 C 53/01); *Umfrage statt Verkauf auf Internet-Auktionsplattform* (LG Darmstadt, 24 January 2002, 3 O 289/01).

52 [2007] NSWSC 844.

53 *Peter Smythe v Vincent Thomas* [2007] NSWSC 844, [39].

## Receipt or postal rule

Another contract formation issue is whether the internet contract is concluded upon the receipt of the acceptance by the offeror or already upon the sending of it by the offeree. The answer to this question is important because, first, it again determines the point of no return for the parties, and is likely to be a bone of contention where the acceptance was lost or damaged. Second, the timing of the conclusion of the contract may also have implications on *where* the contract is considered to be concluded – an issue that is of great importance in the online environment where many contracts, including consumer contracts, are of a transnational nature (see below).

The traditional standard rule is the receipt rule – that is, the contract is concluded when the acceptance is communicated to the offeror.[54] The receipt rule is straightforward in face-to-face transactions in which the acceptance being spoken by the offeree coincides perfectly with it being heard by the offeror – freak circumstances apart. Yet, in distance contracts, there is always the risk of a break in the communications. And then it needs to be decided which party should bear the risk of loss. In contracts formed using the post, the main rule was displaced in favour of the 'postal rule', according to which a posted acceptance is already effective upon posting.[55] Thus, provided that the letter was properly addressed and posted, the risk of it going astray lies with the offeror.[56] The question much debated in the internet context is whether online contracts should be governed by the standard or the postal rule.[57]

First of all, contractual parties may avoid uncertainties by addressing this issue in their terms, as some online businesses seek to do. For example, Easyjet.com adopts the postal rule in its Terms and Conditions (Term 3.1.3) insofar as the contract is concluded regardless of the communication of the acceptance to the customer:

> If We accept Your offer Our internal reservations system will create a Booking (including a Booking Reference) which is then sent to You as a Confirmation Document via an email or via post for Your records. Once the Booking has been made in Our reservations systems (whether a Confirmation Document has been sent or not), there is a binding contract in place . . .

If there is no such express provision,[58] the question remains whether the standard or the postal rule govern the contract. According to traditional common law rules, the answer is as good as cut-and-dried given that courts have shown a strong reluctance to extend the postal rule to other modern forms of communications. The postal rule has been applied to telegrams,[59] but not to acceptances by telex,[60] telephone[61] or email[62] in respect of which the receipt rules reigns. Equally clickwrap contracts are likely to fall within the receipt rule.

The reasons for this reluctance are not entirely clear, which is not surprising given the disagreements about the rationale for the postal rule and, by implication, for the standard receipt rule. In *Entores Ltd v Miles Far Eastern Corp* (1955)[63] Lord Denning favoured the standard rule for an acceptance by telex because, according to him, in these scenarios, 'the man who sends the message

54 *Entores v Miles Far East Corp* [1955] 2 QB 327 (CA).
55 *Adams v Lindsell* (1818) 1 B & Ald 681.
56 *Household Fire Insurance v Grant* (1879) 4 Ex D 216.
57 Valerie Watnick, 'The electronic formation of contracts and the common law "mailbox rule"' (2004) 56 Baylor L Rev 175; Marwan Al Ibrahim, Al'eldin Ababneh, and Hisham Tahat, 'The postal acceptance rule in the digital age' (2007) 2 JICLT 47.
58 In most online consumer contracts, such express provisions are required under Art 10 of the Electronic Commerce Directive.
59 *Cowan v O'Connor* (1888) 20 QBD 640.
60 *Entores v Miles Far East Corp* [1955] 2 QB 327 (CA); app'd in *Brinkibon Ltd v Stahag Stahl* [1983] 2 AC 34 (HL).
61 *Apple Corps Ltd v Apple Computer Inc* [2004] EWHC 768.
62 *Surrey (UK) Ltd v Mazandaran Wood & Paper Industries* [2014] EWHC 3165, [20] where contractual communications were exchanged by email but it was not clear what constituted the offer and acceptance; see also *Bernuth Lines Ltd v High Seas Shipping Ltd, The Eastern Navigator* [2005] EWHC 3020, [29]–[31], per Clarke J , discussing when service of process by email under the CPR (Civil Procedures Rules) may be effective.
63 *Entores v Miles Far East Corp* [1955] 2 QB 327 (CA).

of acceptance knows that it has not been received or he has reason to know it'.[64] His reasoning suggests that, unlike in the case of the post, the instantaneity of the media helps to alert the sender to any malfunction in the media. So if a line goes dead, the telephone conversation will be interrupted and the teleprinter motor will stop working – and these are matters obvious to the offeree and thereby within his or her control. By the same token, where the offeror is at fault for knowing that the acceptance was in some ways compromised and failed to alert the offeree of that fact, he or she 'is clearly bound, because he will be estopped from saying that he did not receive the message of acceptance'.[65] Along similar lines, Lord Denning's reasoning was reformulated by Lord Fraser in the House of Lords' decision in *Brinkibon Ltd v Stahag Stahl* (1983):[66]

> a party (the acceptor) who tries to send a message by telex can generally tell if his message has been received on the other party's (the offeror's) machine, whereas the offeror, of course, will not know if an unsuccessful attempt has been made . . . It is therefore convenient that the acceptor, being in the better position, should have the responsibility for ensuring that his message is received.[67]

So in the postal context, the problem is not so much that control is surrendered to a third party or the lack of instantaneity *per se*, but rather that the post as a communication channel does not give feedback on its operability, unlike the telephone or telex.[68] However, email would in this respect be more like the post, as there is no necessary feedback mechanism: an email writer is not always alerted to the failed delivery. In the case of a clickwrap agreement, a click is generally followed by some confirmation of its success, but again sometimes the processing of an order may appear unsuccessful when in fact it is not, as directly averted to by Easyjet's terms (see above). In both cases, neither party appears to be more obviously at fault than the other. So going back to basics, the idea behind the standard receipt rule is the contractual notion of a 'meeting of two minds' which occurs only upon the offeror receiving the offeree's acceptance. In addition, one might justify the receipt rule on the basis that the effectiveness of a communication should *prima facie* rest with the communicator himself or herself, unless there are strong reasons to set aside that general position, e.g. delays in the case of postal transmissions. Finally, the reluctance of the courts to extend the postal rule may be explained by the pragmatic reason, that where an acceptance is lost or delayed in transport, the postal rule suffers from the flaw that the offeror is contractually bound without his or her knowledge. This position is less desirable than that created by the standard receipt rule which is that the offeree is not bound by a contract by which he or she believes he or she is bound.

Finally on the issue of acceptance, an effective communication does not require that the offeror has actually read it as long as he or she is capable of doing so – consistent with Lord Fraser's statement in *Brinkibon* that it is the offeror's 'responsibility to arrange for the prompt handling of messages in his own office'.[69] This would also be consistent with the spirit of Art 11(1) of the Electronic Commerce Directive ('the order and the acknowledgement of receipt are deemed to be received when the parties to whom they are addressed are able to access them'), although, as explained above, the Article only deals to a very limited extent with the legal concepts of offer and acceptance. So in terms of timing, the acceptance is effectively communicated when it can be accessed, assuming access within ordinary business hours.[70]

---

64  *Ibid*, 333.
65  *Ibid*.
66  [1983] 2 AC 34 (HL).
67  *Ibid*, 43.
68  *Ibid*, 43.
69  *Brinkibon Ltd v Stahag Stahl*, 43.
70  *Schelde Delta Shipping BV v Astare Shipping Ltd (The Pamela)* [1995] 2 Lloyd's Rep 249, in which receipt of the telex received at midnight on a Friday was held to be effective Monday morning.

# Intention to contract

## Automated contracting

A contract is a bargain that is *voluntarily* entered into between two or more persons with legal capacity. In the technological age, one question raised by the notion of volition (implicit in the requirement of the intention to create legal relations) is whether a contract can be struck by computers programmed to make offers or acceptances without any further human intervention or the possibility thereof in the particular contract (that is, electronic agents). In other words, is automation compatible with the notion of a *voluntary* agreement? The answer is 'yes'.

Even before the advent of computer technology, courts have accepted automated responses by machines as valid contractual communications. In *Thornton v Shoe Lane Parking*,[71] Lord Denning held that a user of a vending machine accepts the offer made by the machine 'at the very moment that he puts his money in the machine. The contract is concluded at that time'.[72] By the same token, and more importantly, the proprietor of the machine is also bound by the offer made by his or her machine even if – had he or she known the particular circumstances of the intended transaction – he or she would not have made the offer.[73] The arguments in favour of accepting the contractual validity of automated responses by machines, computers, websites, etc, are, first, that it gives legal recognition to an ever more pervasive commercial reality that favours the efficiency and convenience of automated transacting, and second, that machines – whether they are relatively simple vending machines or highly sophisticated computer systems (capable of making 'intelligent' decisions on behalf of their owners) – are only tools in the hands of their owners or users. Their actions and 'intentions' are no more than the prior intention of their human or corporate owners put into a programmed form. The owners or users have legal responsibility for their actions and are bound by them.[74] Thus sellers on auction sites are bound by the site's automatic acceptance of the highest bid even if it is not to their liking, because that is what everyone agreed upon registration (see above). Similarly, bidders in such auctions are committed by the acts of any automated bidding agent that they employ.[75] In the USA, search engines have been held bound by the browsewrap agreements of the sites that their electronic agents access while gathering information.[76] Similarly, the automated practice of screen scraping has not exempted the scrapers from being bound by the terms of the scraped sites as, e.g. in the Canadian case of *Century 21 Canada Limited Partnership v Rogers Communications Inc* (2011)[77] or in the Irish cases of *Ryanair Ltd v Billingfluege.de GmbH* (2010) and *Ryanair Ltd v On the Beach Ltd* (2013);[78] the latter two cases concerned automated use of Ryanair's site and automated use and clicking of its sites, respectively.[79] The message is clear, you cannot hide behind your electronic agent. The debate on automation will have to be revisited if, or when, true artificial intelligence is invented.

## Contractual intention

Whether, in clickwrap or browsewrap agreements, the required contractual '*mens rea*' – that is, the intention to create legal relations – must be present. With respect to browsewrap agreements especially, it may come as a surprise to many surfers that their act of surfing should be legally significant

---

71 [1971] 2 QB 163 (CA).
72 Ibid.
73 For a discussion of liability for pricing errors, see above.
74 Guide to Enactment of the UNCITRAL Model Law on Electronic Commerce, para 35: 'Data messages that are generated automatically by computers without human intervention should be regarded as "originating" from the legal entity on behalf of which the computer is operated.'
75 *Einsatz eines Bietagenten* (AG Hannover, 7 September 2001, Az 501 C 1510/01).
76 *Cairo Inc v Crossmedia Services Inc* WL 756610 (ND Cal, 1 April 2005); see also *Register.com Inc v Verio Inc* 356 F3d 393 (2d Cir 2004), discussed below.
77 [2011] BCSC 1196.
78 [2010] IEHC 47 and [2013] IEHC 124, both affirmed by the Irish Supreme Court in *Ryanair Ltd v Billingfluege De GmbH/Ticket Point Reiseburo GmbH; Ryanair Ltd v On the Beach Limited* [2015] IESC 11.
79 *Ryanair Ltd v Billigfluege De GmbH/Ticket Point Reiseburo GmbH; Ryanair Ltd v On the Beach Limited* [2015] IESC 11, [8]–[15].

and make them parties to the site's user agreements.[80] The question is whether, despite the user's ignorance of the offer made in the site's terms, his or her conduct – either in the form of browsing or clicking on an apparently legally neutral button, e.g. 'print' or 'download' – amounts to an acceptance (in the browsewrap context) or an 'offer' (in the clickwrap context, depending on how it is constructed). This issue is often of no more than academic interest, given that even if one were to assume a contractual intent and thus *prima facie*, the existence of a contract, the terms of such contracts may after all not be enforceable for lack of reasonably sufficient notice of them (see below). Trying to challenge the enforceability of the site's T&Cs on the basis of lack of contractual intention would offer an advantage, if the test for intention was subjective, unlike the objective test adopted in relation to notice. McDonald has argued that the law in England and Wales on the question of subjective or objective intention for contract formation is ambiguous, but generally favours the objective test even if it is uncomfortable with subjecting wholly unaware actors to contractual obligations simply on the basis of doing a particular act, e.g. surfing a site.[81] In the EU, Art 8(2) of the Consumer Rights Directive[82] requires that the trader ensures:

> the consumer, when placing his order, explicitly acknowledges that the order implies an obligation to pay. If placing an order entails activating a button or a similar function, the button or similar function shall be labelled in an easily legible manner only with the words 'order with obligation to pay' or a corresponding unambiguous formulation . . .

So, at least for B2C non-gratuitous clickwrap agreements unambiguity of the contractual nature of the click is necessary.

More generally, the case law on the issue of intention for online contracting is still relatively meagre, as these disputes are mostly decided under 'notice'.[83] In the automated cases mentioned above, courts have found contracts to be in existence even in the case of browsewrap agreements, where the terms that were simply triggered by the use of the site, e.g. screen scraping. Laffoy J in *Ryanair Ltd v On the Beach Ltd* (2013) ruled that the defendant was bound by the jurisdiction clause 'by its use, either through the medium of an automaton or a manual operator or a third party data provider.'[84] However, these rulings concerned businesses exploiting the data of other online businesses, as specifically mentioned by Hanna J in *Ryanair Ltd v Billingfluege.de GmbH* (2010),[85] and may not be extended to consumers.

In the USA, there have been some judicial pronouncements touching on intention in cases that are half-way between click- and browsewrap agreements: they involve a click by the user, but that click is not obviously legally significant and the term/offer making it significant is inconspicuous, e.g. at the bottom of the page. Whilst the courts here have not specifically addressed the issue of subjective or objective knowledge, both tests would likely have been satisfied, but the reasoning tends to be couched in objective terms, consistent with the notice inquiry. For example, in *Specht v Netscape Communications Corp* (2002)[86] Netscape tried to enforce an arbitration clause contained in its software licence agreement applicable to the free software that Netscape encouraged users to download via a 'Download' button. As the T&Cs could have only been found if users had scrolled

---

80  Note exceptionally that the business itself may not want the terms to have binding effect: *Re JetBlue Airways Corp Privacy Litigation* 379 F Supp 2d 299 (EDNY, 2005).

81  Elizabeth McDonald, 'When is a contract formed by the browse-wrap process?' (2011) 19 International Journal of Law and Information Technology 285. See also *Tinn v Hoffman & Co* (1873) 29 LT 271 (concerning identical cross-offers).

82  2011/83/EC, implemented in the UK by the Consumer Contracts (Information, Cancellation and Additional Charges) Regulations 2013 (SI 2013/3134).

83  American Bar Association (ABA) Joint Working Group on Electronic Contracting Practices, 'Browse-wrap agreements: Validity of implied assent in electronic form agreements' (2003) 59 Business Lawyer 279.

84  [2013] IEHC 124, [43], aff'd by the Irish Supreme Court in *Ryanair Ltd v Billigfluege De GmbH/Ticket Point Reiseburo GmbH; Ryanair Ltd v On the Beach Limited* [2015] IESC 11.

85  [2010] IEHC 47, as aff'd by the Irish Supreme Court in *Ryanair Ltd v Billigfluege De GmbH/Ticket Point Reiseburo GmbH; Ryanair Ltd v On the Beach Limited* [2015] IESC 11.

86  306 F3d 17 (2d Cir 2002), aff'ing 150 F Supp 2d 585 (SDNY 2001); see also below.

down right to the bottom of the site. According to the court, 'plaintiffs' *bare act of downloading the software did not unambiguously manifest assent* to the arbitration provision contained in the license terms.'[87] So while the consumer undoubtedly intended to click on 'Download', a reasonable consumer would have had no awareness of the legal significance of that act. Thus consumers could not be bound by the agreement because the 'consumer's clicking on a download button does not communicate assent to contractual terms if the offer did not make clear to the consumer that clicking on the download button would signify assent.'[88] In *Feldman v United Parcel Service Inc* (2008)[89] United Parcel sought to rely upon a limitation-of-liability clause contained in its terms behind a hyperlink immediately below a 'Print' button with the following instructions: 'Review everything carefully and then click "Print" to print your shipping request.' According to the court, this statement did not make it sufficiently clear that 'Print' – unlike 'I Agree' – would amount to an acceptance of the terms; '[r]ather, for example, one might interpret the directions to mean that the shipper is being asked to confirm and carefully review the addresses before printing the shipping label.'[90] In these cases, the consumers engaged in an act (subjectively and objectively) unaware of its legal consequences. The latter case also shows that very rarely, users may have reasonable notice of terms, but no knowledge or awareness of the legal significance of the critical act as 'acceptance'. This indeed may be the case for many browsewrap scenarios, where users of a site may well know about the existence of T&Cs on the site, but have no reasonable knowledge that browsing itself could trigger a binding contract. In such circumstances, it would be unlikely that a court would find that a contract has been formed. For a contrasting, but legally consistent case on online contractual intention, see *Druyan v Jagger* (2007)[91] where a Rolling Stones fan brought a class action against Ticketmaster, an online ticket agency, and Mick Jagger for breach of contract for failing to provide timely notice of the postponement of a concert, which caused the plaintiffs to incur travel, food and other costs. Because, under its agency's terms of use, Ticketmaster was relieved from any liability for the cost incurred on postponement of an event, the question was whether these terms were binding. To purchase her ticket, the plaintiff had to click on a 'Look for tickets' button supported by the statement: 'By clicking on the "Look for Tickets" button or otherwise using this web site, you agree to the Terms of Use [hyperlinked] . . .'. Whilst a 'Look for Tickets' button by itself would be legally neutral, the accompanying sentence did not only put the plaintiff on notice of the terms, but put beyond doubt the contractual effect of clicking on the button as acceptance.

## Notice of contractual terms

A basic rule of contract law is that contractual parties are only subject to those terms and conditions of which they had notice. Such notice can be established either by showing a signature under the relevant terms or by proving 'reasonably sufficient notice'[92] of them before the contract was concluded. There has been much debate how the traditional law on incorporation of terms should be transplanted to online contracts, and in particular whether an 'I Agree' click is the equivalent to the concept of a signature on a contract or, alternatively, should fall under the reasonable sufficient notice doctrine. Whilst the Law Commission favours the former position, it has also been argued that the 'reasonable sufficient notice' would potentially be less harsh on consumers,[93] but perhaps that harshness is better addressed by consumer protection legislation.

---

87  *Specht v Netscape Communications Corp* 306 F3d 17, 19 (2d Cir 2002) [emphasis added].
88  *Specht v Netscape Communications Corp* 306 F3d 17, 29f (2d Cir 2002), relying on § 2204(1) of the Californian Commercial Code: 'A contract for sale of goods may be made in any manner sufficient to show agreement, including conduct by both parties which recognizes the existence of such a contract'.
89  WL 800989 (SDNY, 24 March 2008).
90  *Feldman v United Parcel Service Inc* WL 800989, 16 (SDNY, 24 March 2008).
91  508 F Supp 2d 228 (SYNY 2007).
92  *Parker v South Eastern Railway Co* (1877) 2 CPD 416 (CA); *Thornton v Shoe Lane Parking Ltd* [1971] 2 QB 163 (CA); *Interfoto Picture Library Ltd v Stiletto Visual Programmes Ltd* [1989] QB 433 (CA).
93  Elizabeth Macdonald, 'Incorporation of standard terms in website contracting – clicking "I Agree"' (2011) 27 Journal of Contract Law 198.

Whatever the answer to that issue may be, what is clear is that terms agreed to via a click-wrap agreement are generally effectively incorporated into the contract and, as shown below, more effectively incorporated than through a browsewrap agreement. A fairly unusual case where the effectiveness of the T&Cs was raised is the US case of *John Doe v SexSearch.com* (2007),[94] where the plaintiff sued the owner of SexSearch.com, amongst other things, for breach of contract for allowing him to establish contact and then have sex with a minor, Jane Roe, for which he was subsequently arrested. Jane had been 14 years of age but had claimed to be 18 when going onto the site, which was limited to those over 18. He unsuccessfully sued SexSearch for its failure to prevent minors from becoming members purportedly contrary to its contract. In *obiter* the court held that SexSearch's term in its clickwrap agreement disclaiming responsibility for verifying its members' age would have been effective, if it had not already been immune from liability as an intermediary (see Chapter 3).

## Incorporation by signature[95]

The traditional position is that a signature under the terms of the contract means that these terms are incorporated into the contract. In *L'Estrange v F Graucob Ltd* (1934)[96] it was held that '[w]hen a document containing contractual terms is signed, then, in the absence of fraud, or . . . misrepresentation, the party signing it is bound, and it is wholly immaterial whether he has read the document or not'.[97] The first question in the internet context is whether clicking on an 'I Agree' or 'Place your Order' button, as in a typical clickwrap agreement, is the equivalent to the traditional signature for the purposes of showing intention to contract and acceptance of the terms provided. Although such a click does not satisfy the requirements of an 'advanced electronic signature' (discussed below), it is still sufficient to show the contractual intention and acceptance of terms. According to the Law Commission, 'it satisfies the principal function of a signature: namely demonstrating an authenticating intention. We suggest that the click can reasonably be regarded as the technological equivalent of a manuscript "X" signature,'[98] which has long been accepted as valid for that function.

Provided that the title of the button is unambiguous, e.g. 'I Agree', a click demonstrates the intention of the signer to be bound by the contract. But because a click is, like the 'X' or a stamp, a non-personalised signature,[99] it cannot reliably establish who the signer was, which may give it very little evidentiary weight where the clickor's identity is disputed and there is no extrinsic evidence to establish it.[100] Arguably, however, the password-protected use of a site ensures that the click is reasonably reliably linked to the owner of the password and thus 'personalises' the click. As English law takes a functional approach to signatures, a mark or act may or may not be recognised as a valid signature depending on the legal requirements and circumstances of the case. The validity of the click as the functional equivalent of a signature to show contractual intention or notice of terms has been assumed in a number of cases, one of which is *Midasplayer.com Ltd v Watkins* (2006).[101] Here the High Court upheld what appeared to be a clickwrap agreement between King.com and the defendant who had been a registered user of the site and used it in contravention of the term that forbade 'unfair methods'.

In the US it is settled law that when online users click on 'I Agree' or equivalent icons, the contractual terms behind a hyperlink near the icon are incorporated into the contract. One of

---

94 502 F Supp 2d 719 (ND Ohio, 22 August 2007).
95 See also discussion below.
96 *L'Estrange v F Graucob Ltd* [1934] 2 KB 394; see also *Levison v Patent Steam Carpet Cleaning Co Ltd* [1978] QB 69 (CA).
97 *Ibid*, 403.
98 Law Commission, *Electronic Commerce: Formal Requirements in Commercial Transactions*, 2001, London: HMSO, paras 3.36ff.
99 *Goodman v J Eban Ltd* [1954] 1 QB 550 (rubber stamp); *Brydges (Town Clerk of Cheltenham) v Dix* (1891) 7 TLR 215 (printed signature).
100 German cases: *Internet-Versteigerung* (AG Erfurt, 14 September 2001, 28 C 2354/01); *Auktion durch Trojaner* (LG Konstanz, 19 April 2002, 2 O 141/01); *Beweisfragen bei Vertragsschluss in der Internet-Auktion* (OLG Köln, 6 September 2002, 19 U 16/02).
101 [2006] EWHC 1551 (Ch).

the first cases to establish this was *Caspi v Microsoft Network LLC* (1999)[102] where the court upheld an exclusive jurisdiction clause contained in an online subscriber agreement of Microsoft against the subscribers who had agreed to Microsoft's term by clicking on 'I Accept'. In *AV v iParadigms LLC* (2008)[103] the defendants owned a software system that checked essays for plagiarism and archived them for comparison with later submissions. The plaintiffs were students and required by their university to submit their work to the defendant's system to confirm its originality. Before submitting their work, they had to click the 'I Agree' icon that appeared directly below the contractual terms of the defendant's site. Because the plaintiffs did not want their essays to be archived, they put a disclaimer to that effect on their essays. When the defendant then still archived the plaintiffs' work, they brought an action for copyright infringement. The court found that, under Virginian law, the students' disclaimer was ineffective, because by clicking the 'I Agree' button, they had given their consent to the full terms of use, including the very first term – according to which the defendant's offer was 'conditioned on your acceptance, without modification of the terms . . . contained therein.' The students had been given a clear choice of either accepting the terms or not accepting them; modifying them was not an option, and their click confirmed the choice they had made. On a critical note, it is not clear why the students' submission was not treated as a counter-offer (rather than an acceptance, given that they disagreed with one of the proposed terms), which in turn was impliedly accepted by the site operator by retaining the essays and checking them for plagiarism. Clickwrap agreements have also been validated in Canada. In *Rudder v Microsoft Corp* (1999)[104] two law school graduates attempted to bring a class action (the class consisted of the 89,000 Canadian MSN members) against Microsoft, claiming damages for breach of contract, breach of fiduciary duty, misappropriation and punitive damages, totalling $75 million. They tried to bring the claim in Canada, despite a forum selection clause – pointing to the law and courts of the state of Washington – in the membership agreement to which they had indicated their consent by clicking on an 'I Agree' button. The judge held that this 'Membership Agreement must be afforded the sanctity that must be given to any agreement in writing'.[105]

What is noteworthy about the above decisions is that the judges do not attach magical weight to the click-come-signature issue,[106] but treat the issue of incorporation of the terms within the broader question as to whether and to what extent users were given the opportunity to familiarise themselves with the terms. So, in *Rudder*, Justice Winkler notes that, during the sign-up process, users were given twice the chance to view and accept or reject the terms, the terms themselves were in plain English and the agreement was viewable much like 'a multi-page written document which requires a party to turn the pages.'[107] The explanation for this approach is either that a click is not treated as the equivalent of a signature or, even if it is, incorporation by signature is treated as part of the broader incorporation-by-reasonable-notice inquiry.[108] This general approach is particularly helpful in scenarios in which the click is not unambiguously the functional equivalent of a signature as, for example, where the button said 'Look for Tickets'[109] or 'Print' (rather than 'I Agree' or 'I Accept'), or where the terms are not unambiguously linked to the click in borderline clickwrap/browsewrap agreements,[110] or where the terms in browsewrap seek to make visiting a site the

---

102  732 A2d 528 (NJ Super Ct App Div 1999).
103  544 F Supp 2d 473 (ED VA 2008).
104  2 CPR (4th) 474 (1999).
105  *Rudder v Microsoft Corp* (1999) 2 CPR (4th) 474, [17] (Ont SC).
106  Juliet M Moringiello and William L Reynolds, 'Survey of the law of cyberspace: Electronic contracting cases 2006–2007' (2007) 63 Business Lawyer 219; Juliet M Moringiello and William L Reynolds, 'Survey of the law of cyberspace: Electronic contracting cases 2007–2008' (2008) 64 Business Lawyer 199.
107  *Rudder v Microsoft Corp*, [14].
108  The traditional strict division of incorporation by notice and incorporation by signature has also shown some cracks in England and Wales: see dicta in *McCutcheon v David MacBrayne* [1964] 1 WLR 125, 133; *Ocean Chemical Transport Inc v Exnor Craggs Ltd* [2000] 1 All ER 519, 530.
109  *Druyan v Jagger* 508 F Supp 2d 228 (SYNY 2007).
110  *Specht v Netscape Communications Corp* 306 F3d 17 (2d Cir 2002).

legal equivalent of a signed written contract (see below). In such scenarios, the broader and more helpful question would have to be whether the user had reasonable notice of the terms, and not whether the contract was signed or not.

## Incorporation by 'reasonable notice'

Under English law, terms in unsigned contracts are incorporated provided that reasonable steps were taken to bring them to the attention of the other party before the conclusion of the contract.[111] Again, this inquiry comes down to the facts of each case. In the past, it has been held that a reference to the terms on the front of a ticket provides reasonable notice of them.[112] Conversely, a notice at the back of a document with no further reference at the front, or one made illegible by a stamp, does not satisfy the 'reasonable notice' test.[113] Furthermore, the more onerous or unusual the term, the more effort must be made to bring it to the attention of the other party: '. . . if one condition . . . is particularly onerous or unusual, the party seeking to enforce it, must show that particular condition was fairly brought to the attention of the other party.'[114] And last but not least, notice of the terms may be provided by the regular and consistent course of dealing between the parties, or any 'common understanding' derived from the custom in a particular trade – a basis that is generally confined to B2B transactions.[115]

There is no doubt that these rulings can be applied to online contracts of various types, whether by email click or browsewrap agreements or mixed methods. Especially the latter type may create pitfalls for contracting in otherwise ordinary commercial relationships. For example, in *Transformers & Rectifiers Ltd v Needs Ltd* (2015)[116] the purchase orders had variously been sent by post, fax or email and in the case of email or fax communications the terms on the back of the physical documents were not sent. In a 'battle of forms' dispute the English High Court held that neither party, for different reasons, had done what was necessary to incorporate their terms into the contract. In the similarly mix-media US case of *Fadal Machining Centers LLC v Compumachine Inc* (2011)[117] concerning a distributorship agreement, there was a conflict between the terms of the plaintiff's hard copy contract and its online T&Cs; the court found the latter were successfully incorporated into the contract through referencing them in the defendant's invoices.

In pure online contracts, browsewrap agreements in particular present problems for notice/incorporation of terms. In the USA there is a spectrum of cases in terms of the enforceability of T&Cs in such contracts.[118] At one end of the spectrum are cases such as *Register.com Inc v Verio Inc* (2004)[119] – often concerning competing businesses – in which browsewrap agreements have been upheld. Register.com, an internet domain name registrar, sought an injunction against Verio enjoining it from using its search robot to access and collect information of registrants from Register.com's online interactive WHOIS database contrary to Register.com's terms of use posted on its site. Verio used this information for marketing its services to those registrants (in direct competition with Register.com). To add insult to injury, Register.com had refrained from marketing its services to the registrants who had opted out of receiving sales and marketing communications during the registration process, and who now complained to Register.com about the spam and telemarketing by Verio. Verio argued, *inter alia*, that it was not bound by the terms of use, because it had not clicked on an 'I Accept' icon. In rejecting this submission, the New York court reasoned that because the terms stated that,

---

111  *Parker v South Eastern Railway Co* (1877) 2 CPD 416 (CA); in relation to timing, see *Thornton v Shoe Lane Parking* [1971] 1 All ER 686 (CA); and *Beta Computers (Europe) Ltd v Adobe Systems (Europe) Ltd* [1996] FSR 37.
112  *Thompson v London, Midland and Scottish Railway Co* [1930] 1 KB 41.
113  *Henderson v Stevenson* (1875) 1 All ER 172; and *Sugar v London, Midland and Scottish Railway Co* [1941] 1 All ER 172, respectively.
114  *Interfoto Picture Library Ltd v Stiletto Visual Programmes Ltd* [1989] QB 433, 439 (CA).
115  *British Crane Hire Corp v Ipswich Plant Hire Ltd* [1975] QB 303.
116  [2015] EWHC 269 (TCC).
117  WL 6254979 (9th Cir 4 December 2011).
118  For excellent case summaries, see Moringiello and Reynolds, above.
119  356 F3d 393 (2d Cir 2004). See also discussion above on 'Automated Contracting'.

by using the site, the user agrees to abide by the terms, by using the site, Verio 'manifested its assent to be bound by Register.com's terms of use'.[120] These cases are very similar to the Irish decisions on screen-scraping (see above) that have equally upheld the terms of the targeted site.

At the other end of the spectrum are consumer actions against online businesses in which browsewrap agreements are not upheld. For example, in *Specht v Netscape Communications Corp* (2002)[121] the consumers brought a class action against Netscape on the basis that the free software down-loaded from Netscape violated their right to privacy because, unbeknown to them, it enabled Netscape to carry out electronic surveillance of their online activities through cookies. The court found that the arbitration clause in the licence agreement far below the 'Download' button was not enforceable: 'an offeree . . . is not bound by inconspicuous contractual provisions of which he is unaware, contained in a document whose contractual nature is not obvious.'[122] The consumers were not put on inquiry or constructive notice of those terms.[123] *Specht* was followed in *Defontes v Dell Computers Corp* (2004),[124] in which it was held that 'the terms via a hyperlink, inconspicuously located at the bottom of the webpage' could not bind the consumer. This was affirmed in *Kevin Khoa Nguyen v Barnes & Noble Inc* (2014),[125] where the court refused to bind a consumer to an arbitration clause contained in Barnes & Noble's T&Cs at the bottom of each page which users did not have to affirmatively accept through a click. In the court's view the users had neither actual nor constructive knowledge of those terms. The general position in the USA is that the terms must not be hidden or be so inconspicuous that a reasonably prudent user would not become aware of them.[126] The common practice adopted by many online businesses of inserting a small link to its terms at the bottom of the screen is by itself unlikely to provide adequate notice.[127]

In a number of cases,[128] courts have considered as a point in favour of the existence of notice that the plaintiff was a long-term user of the site – comparable to the English concept of notice through a regular and consistent course of dealing between the parties. This argument is dubious, because an inconspicuous notice would not become any more conspicuous simply through a user's regular access of the site. Having said that, a growing familiarity with the internet and the universal custom of site providers to have terms of use makes it now more difficult to argue that a reference to the terms at the bottom of the screen is inconspicuous.[129]

A variation of the notice problem occurs when the terms of use or of the service contract get changed after the initial contract conclusion – for example, where users have entered into a long-term relationship with the site provider, such as on social networking or email account sites. In contractual terms, this scenario presents essentially the same notice issue as the one at the formation stage: a variation of the terms by one contractual party amounts to an offer that the other party may or may not accept, and again acceptance is premised on reasonable notice of the varied terms. Thus, in the US case of *Douglas v District Court, ex rel Talk America Inc* (2007)[130] even a conspicuous notice of the change of terms on the website was held to be insufficient to put the plaintiff on notice of the change of terms of his agreement with his telephone service provider, because he simply had no reason to visit the site in the meantime. An English court would have to come to the same conclusion.

---

120  *Register.com Inc v Verio Inc* 356 F3d 393 (2d Cir 2004).
121  306 F3d 17 (2d Cir 2002).
122  *Specht v Netscape Communications Corp* 306 F3d 17, 29 (2d Cir 2002).
123  Ibid, 32.
124  WL 253560 (RI Super, 29 January 2004).
125  *Kevin Khoa Nguyen v Barnes & Noble Inc* US App LEXIS 15868 (9th Cir 2014).
126  See also *AV v iParadigms LLC* 544 FSupp 2d 473 (ED Va, 2008), in which the usage policy, unlike the clickwrap agreement, was not binding on the student users of the plagiarism service.
127  US case on the matter: *Defontes v Dell Computers Corp* WL 253560 (RI, 29 January 2004).
128  *Druyan v Jagger* 508 F Supp 2d 228 (SDNY, 2007); *Southwest Airlines Co v BoardFirst LLC* LEXIS 96230 (ND Tex, 12 September 2007); *Register.com Inc v Verio Inc* (above); *Cairo Inc v Crossmedia Services Inc* WL 756610 (ND Cal, 1 April 2005).
129  *Alexander v Railway Executive* [1951] 2 KB 882, 886, noting inter alia: 'After all, most people nowadays know that railway companies have conditions subject to which they take articles into their cloakrooms.'
130  495 F3d 1062 (9th Cir, 2007).

It is perhaps self-evident that, even if a user is on notice about the existence of the terms of the agreement in notice-by-reference cases, for those terms to be binding, they must also be relatively easily accessible. But what does that actually mean? Again, there are US cases illustrating this notion of accessibility. In *Greer v 1–800-Flowers.com Inc* (2007)[131] it was held that if a contract concluded via one means of communications, such as telephone, makes an express reference to the terms of the agreement accessible via another communication medium, such as the internet, the terms are easily enough accessible to be incorporated. Ultimately, whether this is the case or not depends on the peculiar facts of the case. In *Trujillo v Apple Computer Inc, and AT&T Mobility LLC* (2008)[132] it was not enough that, prior to buying an iPhone, the purchaser was told in an Apple store that the AT&T mobility service agreement could be accessed on the internet. Similarly, in *Feldman v United Parcel Service Inc* (2008)[133] there was no evidence that the I-Ship kiosk, which the plaintiff used to conclude the shipping agreement with UPS, was connected to the internet, when in fact the terms of the agreement were accessible online. Thus those terms were not incorporated into the contract. Thus, accessibility is a matter of degree, depending on what is reasonable and feasible in the circumstances – and this would equally be the case in the UK.

## Consideration in gratuitous agreements

Under English common law a binding contract requires consideration, which distinguishes contracts from *prima facie* unenforceable gifts. The requirement of consideration has remained intact despite various criticisms[134] and its discrepancy with civil law systems. Although consideration can come in all forms and sizes, ultimately something of value must be exchanged.[135] This raises the question of whether there is any value being exchanged in most browsewrap agreements or in those clickwrap agreements in which the user gets a free product or service, such as free software downloads, or access to email, social networking, or auction sites. The less controversial question of whether the owner of the site provides the user with consideration was raised in *Ryanair Ltd v Billigfluege.de GMBH* (2010),[136] where Billigfluege, a price comparison website, screen-scraped Ryanair's site in order to provide the information for a fee to its users. Billigfluege argued, rather counter-intuitively, that Ryanair had not provided it with consideration, which the Irish court rightly rejected:

> Consideration must be provided by the party who seeks to enforce the contract. Here, Ryanair are seeking to enforce their Terms of Use. Ryanair, therefore, must satisfy the Court that they have provided the defendant with consideration. It seems to me that the plaintiff, through their website, offer information for use, subject at all times to their Terms of Use policy, to the users of their website, including the defendants. Although the defendants deny that they use the plaintiff's website and claim that it is the customer or the consumer who does so, it again seems to be that the defendants accept the offer of information made by the plaintiff when they systematically access the Ryanair website though the screen-scraping mechanism. In my view, the provision of information as to flights and prices of flights by Ryanair on their site, subject at all times to their Terms and Conditions, constitutes a sufficient act of consideration for the purposes of making the contract legally binding.[137]

131 *Greer v 1–800-Flowers.com Inc* LEXIS 73961 (SD Tex, 3 October 2007).
132 No 07 C 4946 (ND Ill, 18 April 2008).
133 WL 800989 (SDNY, 24 March 2008); see also *Treiber & Straub v United Parcel Service Inc* 474 F3d 379 (7th Cir 2007).
134 *Johnson v Gore Wood & Co* [2001] 1 All ER 481, 507.
135 *Thomas v Thomas* (1842) 2 QB 851, 859.
136 [2010] IEHC 47.
137 *Ryanair Ltd v Billigfluege.de GMBH* [2010] IEHC 47. Note the Supreme Court of Ireland later overruled that the existence of a valid choice of law clause depends on the validity of the existence of a contract: *Ryanair Ltd v Billigfluege De GmbH / Ticket Point Reiseburo GmbH; Ryanair Ltd v On the Beach Limited* [2015] IESC 11, [18] and [25].

However, the simple provision of an online platform by itself may not be sufficient consideration to make its T&Cs binding. In *Spreadex Ltd v Cochrane* (2012)[138] concerning an online bookmaker (see further below), the court held that prior to each trade the bookmaker did not provide the subscribers with any consideration as it did not have any obligation to enter into any trade and, at any time, could withdraw access to the platform or the account:

> The consideration necessary to support a contract can of course be found in conduct alone . . . That test is, however, in my view not satisfied by arrangements which merely facilitate the making by the two parties of ad hoc contracts in the form of the individual trades. The provision of an on-line interactive platform is in effect simply a more modern equivalent of the expressed readiness of a potential contracting party (also covered in the Consumer Agreement) to enter into contracts . . . .'[139]

An even more borderline issue is whether the user of a free site or product passes a benefit to the provider that would amount to 'valuable consideration'? That question may not arise often, as generally the provider seeks to enforce its T&Cs against the user and thus has to prove that it provided consideration, but occasionally it may also be the user who wants to enforce the provider's T&Cs, e.g. in respect of data protection commitments. Then the user needs to show that he or she provided the provider with consideration. Many providers of free sites and services benefit from users by delivering them advertisements of third parties' products, e.g. Google's search or Facebook. Yet in direct monetary terms that benefit generally only materialises if the user clicks on one of the advertisements.[140] Is simply suffering the exposure to advertisements sufficient to count as consideration? Also, not all free sites live off advertising revenue, such as Wikipedia, which relies on donations, and these would not appear to gain any particular benefit from any particular user accessing the site. Yet, even those latter sites benefit in more distant ways from the cumulative effect of a high number of users as, for example, it would improve their search ranking and further their popularity and thus their chance of donations. Equally, (big) data gathered from users is increasingly recognised as one of the most valuable resources within the information economy,[141] but again the benefit derived from any individual user would be rather negligible. Despite the academic difficulties concerning consideration in gratuitous online agreements, its absence has not proven a stumbling block for the validity of click or browsewrap agreements in the USA or England and Wales (see above cases) even if the enforcement claims are on the whole made by the providers rather than the users.[142] Yet, even in the case of user claims, the non-recognition of online agreements would be out of sync with the pragmatism of common law judges to follow and facilitate commercial practice; in Lord Steyn's words, judges have shown a 'readiness to hold that the rigidity of the doctrine of consideration must yield to practical justice and the needs of modern commerce.'[143] Given that the providers of a host 'free' online services, such as eBay, free email providers, social networking sites, search engines, indirectly derive significant financial benefits from their non-paying customers, it is highly unlikely that a court would deny the existence of binding T&Cs equally enforceable by either party, for lack of consideration.

---

138 [2012] EWHC 1290.
139 Ibid, [15]. For another instance where 'discretionary' consideration was discussed, see *eBay International AG v Creative Festival Entertainment Pty Limited (ACN 098 183 281)* [2006] FCA 1768, [79].
140 Under the pay-per-click advertising model e.g. https://www.google.co.uk/adwords/
141 Viktor Mayer-Schönberger, Kenneth Cukier, *Big Data: a Revolution that will Transform how we Live, Work, and Think* (Eamon Dolan/Mariner Books, 2014) where the authors describe the data as a valuable resource, comparable to a gold mine.
142 But see e.g. *Spreadex Ltd v Cochrane* [2012] EWHC 1290, para 14–15, where the court pointed to the possible lack of consideration prior to individual betting contracts.
143 Lord Johan Steyn, 'Contract law: Fulfilling the reasonable expectations of honest men' (1997) 113 LQR 433, 437.

## Goods or services

For most legal purposes, it is irrelevant whether the subject matter of the contract is one for goods or services. However, it matters when it comes to quality control, where traditionally the law imposed more onerous implied terms into contracts for goods than for services: goods must be of 'satisfactory quality' under the Sale of Goods Act 1979,[144] whilst for services the Supply of Goods and Services Act 1982 simply requires that the provider must have exercised reasonable care and skill to the degree expected of a professional man of ordinary competence and experience[145] – so what matters is effort and not outcome. These two categories have proven problematic for many digital products, such as software, films, books, news, financial data, etc, which are not easily categorised as either goods or services. So it is a welcome development that under the Consumer Rights Act 2015 a new third category of 'digital content'[146] does away with these artificial divisions, but of course only with respect to the material scope of the Act, covering business-to-consumer contracts. The above Acts and their categories will remain relevant to business-to-business contracts as well as consumer-to-consumer contracts, and thus the goods-versus-services debate remains alive, as further as discussed in relation to contracts for the supply of software elsewhere in this book. See Chapter 12.

## Consumer protection

### Unfair contract terms

An issue that follows the question to what extent the terms are accessible in a practical sense, is the issue to what extent they are accessible in a substantive way. The problem concerning the unreadability and unreality of standard-form contracts is, of course, far from peculiar to the internet. However, the internet exacerbates the artificiality of standard-form agreements given that almost every site purports to create contractual relations with lengthy convoluted terms. While this has again been acknowledged in various US cases, judges have predictably shied away from declaring them non-binding, which would have had major ramifications for the vast majority of online providers. For example, *Scarcella v America Online* (2004)[147] concerned AOL's sign-up process, which involved viewing 91 computer screens and which was described by the court as lulling customers 'into a trance of lethargy and inattentiveness from the seemingly endless presentment of useful and inconsequential information'.[148] Yet it still upheld the maxim that a signatory to a contract is presumed to know its content, but left open the possibility that the consent was procured by deceit, because, according to the plaintiffs, AOL, like many other online businesses, 'encourages its customers to skip the [member agreement] with no expectation that you will actually go back and read it, yet comforted in their knowledge that you clicked the correct box in order for them to cloak themselves in the protection of the contract they drafted'.[149] In the end, the court found the agreement unenforceable for other reasons.

In the EU with a strong consumer protection tradition, unfair terms in consumer contracts are dealt with by the Unfair Terms in Consumer Contracts Directive (1993).[150] Article 3(1) provides that a 'contractual term which has not been individually negotiated shall be regarded as unfair if, contrary to the requirement of good faith, it causes a significant imbalance in the parties' rights and

---

144 Section 14 of the Act, as amended by the Sale and Supply of Goods Act 1994.
145 Contrast the approach taken in *St Albans City and District Council v International Computers Ltd* [1996] 4 All ER 481 (CA) (requiring 'goods' to be tangible and thereby excluding digital products).
146 Section 33-47 of the Act.
147 WL 2093429 (NY City Civ Ct 2004); see also *Novak v Overture Services Inc* 309 F Supp 2d 446 (EDNY 2004).
148 *Scarcella v America Online* WL 2093429 (NY City Civ Ct, 8 September 2004), 1.
149 Ibid, 2.
150 Council Directive 93/13/EEC on Unfair Terms in Consumer Contracts, which was implemented in the UK by the Unfair Terms in Consumer Contract Regulations 1999 (SI 1999/2083), which have been revoked by the Consumer Rights Act 2015.

obligations arising under the contract, to the detriment of the consumer' and, by virtue of Art 6(1), such term is then not binding on the consumer whilst leaving the remainder of the contract, if possible, intact. In the UK this is now implemented in Part 2 of the Consumer Rights Act 2015 which revokes the Unfair Terms in Consumer Contract Regulations 1999. Despite the huge prevalence of T&Cs online and their routine acceptance by users, there is an astounding lack of cases challenging some of them which is partly, but not entirely, explicable by the low value of many online transactions.[151] Part of the dearth of cases in the UK is probably also due to the restrictive approach taken to 'good faith' by the House of Lords in *Director General of Fair Trading v First National plc* (2001).[152] The Lords rejected that a term that would take a consumer by surprise – that is, assuming a normal lazy consumer who had not read the terms – would be contrary to 'good faith'. According to the Lords, a term is in 'good faith' as long as that term was 'expressed fully, clearly and legibly, containing no concealed pitfalls or traps'[153] – irrespective of its substance. The emphasis is on the wording of the terms, rather than their length or existence of the terms *per se*.

Such interpretation gives fairly little room for claims based on the terms listed in Sch 2 Pt 1 of the Consumer Rights Act 2015 as potentially unfair. Of particular relevance for online contracts would be Term 10 in Schedule 2: 'A term which has the object or effect of irrevocably binding the consumer to terms with which the consumer has had no real opportunity of becoming acquainted before the conclusion of the contract.' On a wide interpretation, and taking into account the length and language of most online terms and conditions, and the frequency of being required to read them and the low risk associated with not reading them, it would seem that the opportunity to become acquainted with any particular set of online terms is *unreal* indeed. Whilst in light of the Lords' decision, such a wide reading would appear unlikely; the court in *Spreadex Ltd v Cochrane* (2012)[154] was keenly astute to the unreality of consent of online T&Cs. Here an online bookmaker sought to enforce a £50,000 debt against Mr Cochrane who denied having authorised the relevant trades. According to him, it was his girlfriend's child who had placed the trades in his absence. Whether true or otherwise,[155] Spreadex argued that Cochrane had agreed to its T&Cs including Clause 10(3): 'Your password must be declared, together with your account number, when you wish to access your account. You will be deemed to have authorised all trading under your account number . . .'. In addition to finding that the term was not binding for lack of consideration in respect of the pre-trade platform contract (see above), the court held that the term was 'unfair' because it landed the customer with liability for any unauthorised trade made on his account, regardless of his negligence, whilst the provider assumed no obligations of any sort.[156] This should be a warning to platform providers in respect of the balance of obligations imposed via their T&Cs. Finally, the court in deciding on the unfairness of the term also took into account the method of incorporations:

> A further, and compounding, factor to be taken into account is the manner in which the clause was incorporated into any contract (if there was one). As I described earlier, the potential customer was told that four documents, including the Customer Agreement, could be viewed elsewhere on-line by clicking 'View'. Many, one might suspect most, would have passed up on that invitation and proceeded directly to click on 'Agree', even though it was suggested that they should do so only when they had read and understood the documents. Even if, exceptionally, the defendant in fact chose to look at the documents, he would have been faced in the

---

151 Nick Trend, 'Thomson case could spell end of "unfair" holiday cancellation charges' (2014) *The Telegraph*, 26 February.
152 [2001] UKHL 52.
153 *Ibid*, [17].
154 [2012] EWHC 1290.
155 Note, in the application for summary judgment, Spreadex accepted the accuracy of this and argued that even if the description of the events was accurate, the defendant was liable to pay for the trades.
156 *Ibid*, [17]–[20].

Customer Agreement alone with 49 pages containing the same number of closely printed and complex paragraphs. It would have come close to a miracle if he had read the second sentence of Clause 10(3), let alone appreciated its purport or implications, and it would have been quite irrational for the claimant to assume that he had. This was an entirely inadequate way to seek to make the customer liable for any potential trades which he did not authorise, and is a further factor rendering the second sentence of Clause 10(3) an unfair term.[157]

With this holding, the court did not just throw doubt on browsewrap agreements, but also on clickwrap agreements, particularly lengthy ones, emphasising the need to bring onerous terms to the actual attention of users. Whether this judgment is consistent with the Lords' decision is questionable, but for the time being providers may be slightly less tempted to create terms that strongly favour them and to incorporate them in the almost certainty that the vast majority of users will not familiarise themselves with them. Still, the problem remains that too few unfair terms are tested in the courts and so unfair practices persist and are not challenged. In the US the consumer class action has been an avenue to overcome the low stakes involved in individual consumer claims.[158] For example, in *Meguerian v Apple Inc* (2011)[159] parents brought a class action against Apple for allowing their children to play games that encouraged them to make in-app purchases from the Apple store as part of the game, often without password protection. The claim against Apple, which took a cut from each purchase from the third party game developer, alleged that it had inadequately brought the existence of child-targeted games to the attention of its subscribers and, much like in *Spreadex*, the court would have had to rule on the incorporation and fairness of Apple's terms. As it is, Apple settled the case before it reached trial in 2013.[160]

In so far as the Consumer Rights Act 2015 seeks to comprehensively deal with unfairness in consumer transactions, these are no longer within the scope of the Unfair Contract Terms Act 1977.[161] This Act is now confined to business-to-business and consumer-to-consumer transactions (e.g. on eBay or Gumtree). In respect of these it provides for the ineffectiveness of exemption clauses based on unreasonableness,[162] taking into account, for example, 'whether the customer knew or ought reasonably to have known of the existence and the extent of the term (having regard, among other things, to any custom of the trade and any previous dealing between the parties).'[163] And to judge what is reasonable 'it is necessary . . . to consider to what extent the party has actually consented to the clause'.[164] While it is debatable whether it is indeed actual, rather than constructive, knowledge of the terms that should be decisive, even taking the test of a reasonable person, it would often be possible to argue that a lack of knowledge of the online terms of browsewrap agreements is well within the realms of reasonableness.

## Additional transparency requirements

While traditional contract law expects internet businesses, just like any other business, to put their customers on reasonable notice of the contractual terms, various EU Directives[165] impose additional pre-contractual requirements in long-distance and/or electronic transactions. These informational

---

157 *Ibid*, [21] [internal marks omitted].
158 In the UK, the problem is that the class action relies on an opting-in, rather than opting-out mechanism used in the US. For a technological solution to this see: 'The law and the internet: Mass action' (2015) *The Economist*, 7 March, available online at: http://www.economist.com/news/britain/21645732-how-technology-might-make-english-law-more-american-mass-action
159 Case number 5:2011-cv-01758, US District Court for the Northern District of California.
160 BBC, 'Apple offers compensation for kids' in-app purchases' (23 February 2013).
161 See Sch 4.
162 Reasonableness (s 11) is required under ss 2(2), 3, 6(3) and 7(3), but is not required to trigger the ineffectiveness of the exemption, see, e.g., s 2(1).
163 Unfair Contract Terms Act 1977, Sch 2(c).
164 *AEG (UK) Ltd v Logic Resources Ltd* [1996] CLC 265, 279.
165 Electronic Commerce Directive 2000/31/EC; Services Directive 2006/123/EC and the Consumer Rights Directive 2011/83/EC.

obligations are designed to give consumers more leverage against distant/online businesses that might otherwise be difficult to trace and hold accountable, and thus inspire more confidence in them. For example, Art 6 of the Consumer Rights Directive[166] (which is applicable to most electronic transactions other than, for example, financial services or gambling contracts)[167] provides that in distance contracts the trader must provide the consumer with information concerning, for example:

(a)   the main characteristics of the goods or services;
(b)   the identity of the trader, such as his trading name;
(c)   the geographic address of the trader, as well as telephone, fax or email (where available);
(e)   the price of the goods or services, including taxes and delivery cost;
(g)   the arrangements for payment, delivery or performance;
(h)   the right of withdrawal;
(o)   the duration of the contract, where applicable.

The information must be provided prior to the conclusion of any distance contract or made 'available to the consumer in a way appropriate to the means of distance communication used in plain and intelligible language.'[168] This requirement came under the spotlight in the German case in which the court held that the provision of the required information via a 'Contact' link was insufficient to bring it to the attention of the user.[169]

The Electronic Commerce Directive[170] imposes overlapping informational requirements in Arts 5–7, 10, and 11 – all broadly designed to put online consumers on a level playing field with consumers in a face-to-face or other long-distance transaction.[171] They add to the distance selling obligations by focusing more strongly on the intangible and ephemeral nature of electronic communications. So, for example, under Art 5, service providers have to give users information about their geographical address; under Art 10, information on the technical means of identifying and rectifying input errors;[172] and under Art 11, service providers have to confirm transactional communications.

Despite, or perhaps because of, the wide range of the transparency requirements, the European Commission found in a Europe-wide survey of online electronics retailers in 2009[173] that 55 per cent of the surveyed sites showed irregularities particularly relating to consumer information; of those, two-thirds completely failed to inform consumers of their rights, such as the 'right of withdrawal' (discussed below); 45 per cent gave misleading information about the total price; and 33 per cent gave incomplete or no contact details of the trader. The survey focused on the biggest websites selling consumer electronics. Following the survey, national authorities will have to take enforcement actions, first, by contacting the relevant sites and requiring corrections, and second, in

---

166  2011/83/EC (previously Art 4 of the Distance Selling Directive 97/7/EC), implemented in the UK by the Consumer Contracts (Information, Cancellation and Additional Charges) Regulations 2013 (SI2013/2014). For critiques of the Consumer Rights Directive, see Stephen Weatherill, 'The Consumer Rights Directive: How and why a quest for "coherence" has (largely) failed' (2012) 49 Common Market Law Review 1279; and Alexandre Duterque, 'Do we really want a "Ius Commune" for EU consumer protection?' (2012) 35 Dublin University Law Journal 73.
167  On the scope of the Directive, see Art 3.
168  Article 8(1).
169  *Wetten über Internet-Lottospielgemeinschaft als Fernabsatzgeschäft* (OLG Karlsruhe, 27 March 2002, 6 U 200/01).
170  Directive 2000/31/EC.
171  For a case interpreting Art 5(1)(c) of the Directive, see *DIV C-298/07* (CJEU, 16 October 2008).
172  This is the only section in the Directive that allows the customer to rescind the contract.
173  European Commission, *Consumer: EU Crackdown on Websites Selling Consumer Electronic Goods*, IP/09/1292, 9 September 2009, Brussels: European Commission.

case of failure, by bringing legal actions leading to fines and possible closure of the site.[174] The low compliance level with both Directives may at least partly be due to the fact that non-compliance does not affect the contracts made, and gives users at the most a statutory right to seek compliance or damages.[175]

## Rights of withdrawal

In the EU, traditional contract law has been changed quite dramatically with the creation of the right of withdrawal in distance selling contracts. This right presents a major departure from English contract law and the sanctity of contract, as it allows one party, i.e. the consumer, to pull out of the contract within a certain time after its conclusion, for no particular reason. This right is a classic instance of where the law treats distance contracts[176] more favourably than face-to-face contracts in order to ultimately achieve a level playing field. The inability to inspect the goods,[177] the lack of advice from the trader's shop and the physical ease with which contracts can be entered into online mean that hasty and ill-informed contracts come into being; the right of withdrawal provides a cooling-off period within which the consumer may make good his or her haste. The right of withdrawal was previously provided for by the Distance Selling Directive, but is now governed in some detail by Arts 9–16 of the Consumer Rights Directive (and increased a number of consumer entitlements). Most notably Art 9(1) extends the cooling-off period to two weeks:

> Save where the exceptions provided for in Article 16 apply, the consumer shall have a period of 14 days to withdraw from a distance or off-premises contract, without giving any reason, and without incurring any costs other than those provided for in Article 13(2) and Article 14.

The right of withdrawal starts ticking when the goods are received or, in the case of services, either when the contract is concluded.[178] The two-week withdrawal period may extend up to 12 months, if the trader does not provide the consumer with the information about the right as required by Art 6(1) (see above).[179] Generally, the only cost that has to be borne by the consumer is the cost of returning the goods assuming the trader had informed the consumer to that effect.[180]

The right of withdrawal is excluded in circumstances where a benefit has been irrevocably passed to the consumer and the contract cannot be 'undone' without prejudicing the trader as, for example, in respect of a service contract where the service has been fully performed or in the case of a contract for the supply of goods made to the consumer's specifications or where the goods were personalised, or are liable to deteriorate quickly.[181] One disputed area of application of the right of withdrawal are contracts concluded at auctions. Previously, the Distance Selling Directive expressly excluded 'auctions' from its entire scope,[182] but the Consumer Rights Directive *prima facie* applies to auctions, but excludes 'contracts concluded at a public auction' from the right of withdrawal.[183] As 'public auction' is defined as 'a method of sale where goods or services are offered by

---

174 For example, Arts 18 and 20 of the Electronic Commerce Directive 2000/31/EC, dealing respectively with legal actions and sanctions; see also the Injunction for the Protection of Consumers' Interests (Codified Version) Directive 2009/22/EC.

175 For example, Electronic Commerce (EC Directive) Regulations 2002, SI 2002/2013, reg 13.

176 For a definition see Art 2(7) of the Consumer Rights Directive.

177 Recital 37 of the Consumer Rights Directive.

178 Article 9(2) of the Consumer Rights Directive.

179 Article 10 of the Consumer Rights Directive.

180 Article 14(1) of the Consumer Rights Directive, see also Art 13; and *Verbraucherzentrale Nordrhein-Westfalen eV v Handelsgesellschaft Heinrich Heine GmbH* C511/08 (ECJ, 15 April 2010) concerning the validity of German law allowing online sellers not to refund delivery costs incurred by the consumer when excising the right of withdrawal. See also *Messner v Firma Stefan Kruger* C-489/07 (CJEU, 3 September 2009); and *Voraussetzungen des Wertersatzanspruchs bei Widerruf im Fernabsatzkauf* (BGH, 3 November 2010, VIII ZR 337/09) concerning the seller's right to claim compensation for the value of their use before the right of withdrawal was excised.

181 See Art 16 for the full list of exceptions.

182 See Art 3 of the Distance Selling Directive 97/7/EC.

183 See Art 16(d) of the Consumer Rights Directive.

the trader to consumers, *who attend or are given the possibility to attend the auction in person*, through a transparent, competitive bidding procedure run by an auctioneer and where the successful bidder is bound to purchase the goods or services,'[184] this exception appears to be applicable only to traditional 'presence' auctions where the bidder chooses to bid through distant means. Pure distance auctions, as those on online platforms, such as eBay, are squarely within the new Directive, including its right to withdrawal: thus *commercial* sellers on eBay must grant their customers the right of withdrawal.

The rationale for an auction exception to the cooling-off period lies in the nature of auctions. Given their speculative character, the finality of the highest bid adds to the tension of the bidding process and is critical for its success: 'If buyers are enabled to revoke their contracts after the end of an auction there would be no risk for a buyer in making the highest possible bid, thus rendering the auction a farce.'[185] Thus a right of withdrawal – that is, a *cooling-off* period – would sit uncomfortably with auction transactions, the essence of which is the *heated* competition between the buyers. Also, '[t]he seller would lose all advantages if a bidder could revoke his or her contract freely. The situation of the auction before the final bid cannot be reinstalled; the seller cannot take resort to the next highest bid because the auction has already been terminated.'[186] Thus auctions are much like those other contracts that cannot be 'undone' without prejudicing the traders and are therefore excluded from the withdrawal right. So why then are online auctions (between businesses and consumers) not excluded? The answer to this must lie in the same rationale for the cooling-off period more generally; protecting consumers from hasty ill-judged bargains with online businesses is so powerful a concern that, even in the online auction context, it trumps the 'heat-of-the-moment' argument. Ultimately the availability of this right will also work as a moderating force, preventing or undoing very unfair bargains. Finally, online auctions are fairly easily repeated and thus do not suffer the non-repeatability of presence auctions.

## Transnational online contracting

The internet has opened up transnational trade to the ordinary consumer. The incidence of cross-border B2C transactions has drastically increased and, in practical terms, it often makes little difference whether you buy something from someone in your own jurisdiction or from abroad. However, legally this cross-border element is certainly a complicating factor, particularly when a dispute arises[187] (see Chapter 2). So prior to dealing with this contractual dispute, the transnational element needs to be accounted for. Here the first issue is which court has the right to hear the dispute (the jurisdictional inquiry); the second, which law applies to the dispute (the applicable law inquiry); and the third, whether the judgment can be enforced against the foreign defendant (that is, enforcement jurisdiction) (see Chapter 2). What sets a transnational contractual dispute apart from other civil disputes is that the parties have frequently contractually agreed the answer to the first two questions in the form of a 'choice of forum' and 'choice of law' clause. For example, Term 15 of Facebook's Terms of Service state:

> You will resolve any claim, cause of action or dispute (claim) you have with us arising out of or relating to this Statement or Facebook exclusively in the U.S. District Court for the Northern District of California or a state court located in San Mateo County, and you agree to submit to the personal jurisdiction of such courts for the purpose of litigating all such claims. The laws

---

184 See Art 2(13) of the Consumer Rights Directive.
185 Gerald Spindler, 'Internet-auctions versus consumer protection: The case of the Distant Selling Directive' (2005) 6(3) German Law Journal, available online at: http://www.germanlawjournal.com/article.php?id=585
186 Ibid.
187 This is not necessarily the case, because it may turn out that the contract is simply governed by the terms agreed by the parties or that the dispute is resolved entirely by reference to local laws and procedures.

> of the State of California will govern this Statement, as well as any claim that might arise
> between you and us, without regard to conflict of law provisions.

The question is: when would such a term be enforceable and what happens if the parties have
not agreed on such a clause? For online businesses, particularly with a worldwide clientele, such
clauses provide significant protection and certainty; not enforcing them is said to discourage online
activity of commercial and non-commercial nature. Yet, for users and consumers, such clauses are
highly troublesome, because they effectively deprive them of a realistic chance of a remedy. Thus,
enforcing them also undermines user and consumer confidence in the safety and regulability of the
online sphere through domestic law.

## Jurisdiction

The enforceability of jurisdiction clauses and, more generally, the issue of which court settles the
dispute are significant both in practical and substantive terms. In practical terms, it means the difference between being able to bring or defend proceedings in your home jurisdiction, on the one
hand, and having to go abroad, on the other hand, and thus face the cost of travelling and unfamiliarity with the foreign legal system, customs, and possibly the language. Substantively, the choice of
the court is also likely to have an impact on the substantive outcome of the case because the court
deciding the case always applies its own procedural law to the matter,[188] will generally favour local
substantive law as the applicable law, and will not allow the exclusion of local mandatory rules even
where foreign substantive law is otherwise applicable. For these reasons, the choice of the court is
often a hotly disputed issue.

## Jurisdiction in EU law

### Contractual choice

In the EU, choice-of-forum clauses are principally validated by Art 25(1) of the EC Regulation on
Jurisdiction and the Recognition and Enforcement of Judgments in Civil and Commercial Matters
(recast):[189]

> If the parties, *regardless of their domicile*, have agreed that a court or the courts of a Member
> State are to have jurisdiction to settle any disputes which have arisen or which may arise in
> connection with a particular legal relationship, that court or those courts shall have juris-
> diction, *unless the agreement is null and void as to its substantive validity under the law of that
> Member State*. Such jurisdiction shall be exclusive unless the parties have agreed otherwise.[190]

Whilst previously at least one of the parties had to be domiciled in a Member State, now both can
come from outside the EU – as an exception to Art 6, which otherwise extends the Regulation
regime only to cases where the defendant is domiciled in the EU. The effect of this new provision
is that traditional national law on validating choice of law clauses will only very rarely come into
play, e.g. when the court specified in the choice-of-forum clause is not the court of a Member State.
In the UK this means that in the vast majority of cases with a contractual choice-of-forum clause,

---

188 That may include matters such as discovery or the quantification of damages.
189 1215/2012, which replaces the earlier Regulation on Jurisdiction and the Recognition and Enforcement of Judgments in Civil
   and Commercial Matters 44/2001/EC. For a still useful commentary of the earlier Regulation, see Ulrich Magnus and Peter
   Mankowski (eds), *Brussels I Regulation*, 2007, Brussels: Sellier European Law Publishers. See also Arts 1 and 2 of the Hague Conference on Private International Law's Convention on Choice of Court Agreements (2005), which, by virtue of Art 2(1), does not
   apply to consumer contracts and thus is not applicable to most online clickwrap agreements.
190 Emphasis of the amendments added.

service of the initiating process can be effected outside the jurisdiction without the permission of the court (see further below). Also under the recast Regulation, 'an agreement conferring jurisdiction which forms part of a contract shall be treated as an agreement independent of the other terms of the contract' (Art 25(5)). This means that even where the claim alleges that the contract is invalid, the choice-of-forum clause can be separated and upheld; this provides much needed certainty with respect to the jurisdiction in which the substantive case should be battled out.

What remains unchanged are the exceptions on party autonomy, in particular consumer contracts, and the fact that the agreement must be either in writing (Art 25(1)(a))[191] or in another form consistent with the practices of the parties or usage within the industry (Art 25(1)(b) and (c)). In *Ryanair Ltd v Billigfluege De GmbH/Ticket Point Reiseburo GmbH; Ryanair Ltd v On the Beach Limited* (2015)[192] the Irish Supreme Court upheld Laffoy J's ruling affirming the validity of Ryanair's jurisdiction clause in its browsewrap and clickwrap agreements on the basis of Art 25(1)(c) looking for conformity with common usage in the case of international trade or commerce:

> The second question is whether a practice exists in the branch of trade or commerce in which the parties are operating. The evidence clearly establishes that in the airline business and in the travel agency online business the practice is that the website user becomes contractually bound by means of clicking, or ticking a box, whereby he demonstrates his assent or agreement to terms which the website owner has displayed. Moreover, in accordance with the standard internet practice in that business, the Terms of Use of a particular website are available throughout by way of hyperlink with the objective that, by utilising a provision such as Clause 1 of the plaintiff's Terms of Use, the use of the website, browsing or viewing the website, binds the user to the Terms of Use . . . [A] range of screen shots from websites, focusing in particular on websites of airlines, which bear this out. Accordingly, in my view, the evidence does establish that there is a practice in the airline and online travel agency sectors of contractually binding web users by click wrapping or browse wrapping, which practice is generally and regularly followed by the operators in those sectors. In reality, it is difficult to see how online trade could be carried on in the absence of those devices.[193]

Also in respect of both travel sites that screen-scraped Ryanair's site, the Supreme Court observed that the very business of screen scraping to feed the comparison site required a system that paid attention to the detail of data and from that one may 'reasonably infer . . . a close scrutiny of not only the data that needed to be captured from the sites of airlines such as Ryanair in order for these comparison and purchase online sites to work, but also the other aspects of the airlines' requirements for use of their online material . . .'.[194] This made it unlikely that the travel site were unaware of the jurisdiction clause and, by implication, difficult to argue that there was 'no consensus between the parties on jurisdiction'.

### In the absence of contractual choice

Where the parties to a contract have not agreed on the court that should be the venue for their dispute resolution, the general rules in Arts 4 and 7 would come into play. Article 4(1) provides the default position: the defendant must be sued where he or she is domiciled. This rule accords with notions of fairness and practicalities: it is fair, all things being equal, that the plaintiff has to bring the complaint to the so-far 'innocent' defendant, and it is practical, because if the defendant

---

191 Electronic communications are covered in Art 25(2), which provides that 'any communication by electronic means which provides a durable record of the agreement shall be the equivalent to "writing"'. See further below.
192 [2015] IESC 11. See also *Ryanair Ltd v Bravofly and Travelfusion Ltd* [2009] IEHC 41.
193 *Ryanair Ltd v Billigfluege De GmbH/Ticket Point Reiseburo GmbH; Ryanair Ltd v On the Beach Limited* [2015] IESC 11, [34]–[35].
194 *Ibid*, [18].

is found liable, the judgment is more easily enforceable against him or her in his or her home jurisdiction.

Article 7 provides rules of 'special' jurisdiction basing jurisdiction on the close connection between the dispute and a particular court. Pursuant to Art 7(1), the defendants in a contractual dispute may be sued in the place in which the contract was or should have been performed – that is (unless the parties agreed otherwise), where the goods or services were or should have been delivered, or performed, respectively.[195] Although there may be difficulty in categorising an electronic contractual subject matter as either 'goods' or 'services', such categorisation would not appear to be critical in this context given the focus of the Article on the place of the performance of the contract. Again, the term 'place' is ambiguous where a digital good or service is involved, because it may or may not be said to be delivered or performed in any particular physical place. Yet, as the terms 'delivery' and 'performance' focus on the receipt of the goods or services, it would appear reasonable that, in most cases, the place of business or domicile of the buyer is the place of performance. In the internet context, these rules are of very limited relevance given the prevalence of online T&Cs which generally include a choice-of-forum clause, in favour of the seller's jurisdiction, and/or fall within the following consumer contract exceptions.

### Consumer protection provisions

Consumer contracts are governed by Arts 17–19 of the Regulation,[196] which have been modified to the consumer's advantage in the recast Regulation. Article 18 states what the exceptions are, whilst Art 17 determines to which consumer contracts they apply. So not all consumer contracts fall within the protective regime, but for those that do, Art 18 on the one hand, allows consumers to sue either at home or in the court of the Member State in which the other party is domiciled and, on the other hand, it requires the business to sue the consumer only in the court of the Member State where the consumer is domiciled. Thus the consumer gets a choice, but the business does not. In either event, Art 18 displaces any forum selection clause (although not necessarily other contractual clauses) as well as of the default position in Art 4.

In the recast Regulation, Art 18(1) opens up the possibility of consumers suing traders from outside the EU at home, when it states that a consumer may sue the trader 'regardless of the [trader's] domicile in the courts for the place where the consumer is domiciled.' This significantly expands the ambit of these provisions especially in the online context, where many online businesses are established in the US. Previously, those non-EU traders were outside the Regulation in general (but for Art 25) and the consumer provisions in particular, unless they had a 'branch, agency or establishment' within a Member State and the consumer dispute arose out of the activities of that EU establishment.[197] Whilst many of the large online operators (e.g. Facebook, Google, Amazon) have European headquarters, the transactions they enter into with European consumers are not necessarily connected to their European headquarters and thus would have fallen outside the protective provisions. Although the expanded domicile rule has been retained in Art 17(2) of the recast Regulation, it appears of little importance now that the consumer's right to sue at home is extended to any trader, regardless of the domicile within the EU or elsewhere.

That in turn means that the discussion of what may or may not amount to an 'establishment' in the electronic environment within Art 17(2) is also of relatively minor significance. There has been

---

195 See also Art 7(5): '. . . a person domiciled in a Member State may be sued, in another Member State, as regards a dispute arising out of the operations of a branch, agency or other establishment in the court for the place in which the branch, agency or other establishment is situated.'

196 For a critical discussion of the need or otherwise of consumer protection provisions online, see Arnold Roosendaal and Simone Van Esch, 'Commercial websites: Consumer protection and power shifts' (2007) 6(1) JITLP 13.

197 See Arts 4(1) and 15(2) of the Regulation 44/2001. Note the difference between Arts 15(5) and Art 5(5) (now Art 7(5)) which also deals with the right to sue in the place of a business's branch, agency, or other establishment, is that the latter is only applicable if the business itself is domiciled in a Member State.

some debate over whether the mere presence of a local server hosting a site or a local electronic agent amounts to an 'establishment'.[198] Such a position is expressly rejected in the Electronic Commerce Directive, which defines an 'established service provider' as:

> a service provider who effectively pursues an economic activity using a fixed establishment for an indefinite period. The presence and use of the technical means and technologies required to provide the service do not, in themselves, constitute an establishment of the provider.[199]

A comparable position is likely to be applicable under the Regulation to avoid a position where the 'establishment' may easily be manipulated by the parties through the location of the server and thus create legal connections that do not at all reflect the real connection of the parties or the dispute with the forum. Also traditional CJEU jurisprudence on 'agency, branch or other establishment'[200] focuses both on the actuality and the perception of a real place of business:

> a *place* of business which has the *appearance* of permanency, such as the extension of a parent body, has a *management and* is materially equipped to *negotiate* businesses with the third parties so that the latter, although *knowing* that there will if necessary be a legal link with the parent body . . . abroad, do not have to deal directly with such parent body but may transact business at the place of . . . the extension.[201]

It may be arguable that business transacted via a local server, using an electronic agent, 'negotiates' business and is thus an 'establishment'. However, the above definition is also concerned with the perception of the extension through the eyes of the customer. Where the business of a foreign provider is simply transacted via a local server, this would not create any expectations in the mind of the customer that there is a local extension of the foreign business given that the location of the server would be invisible to all but the most computer-savvy clients. This situation may be different where the local server hosts a country-specific website of an international well-known company, such as amazon.fr or ebay.fr, which then might create the expectation of a locally supported corporate base, and thus would seem to satisfy the appearance test. Some academics have gone further and argued that 'place of business' does not necessarily refer to a physical place, and would thus include even country-specific websites not supported by local servers.[202] Certainly, such a wide interpretation of 'establishment' would accord with the consumer's or customer's legitimate expectations, the above test also requires local personnel as a necessary requirement of any 'establishment' (note the reference to 'management'). It thereby appears to exclude lonely servers hosting sites and electronic agents of any kind which makes good sense in practical terms. One rationale for the 'establishment' exception is to serve the interest of the due administration of justice. The personnel of a local establishment are likely to have knowledge of the dispute and can thus be called before a local court without unduly inconveniencing the defendant.[203] But, as argued above, at least for the consumer protection provisions, the precise ambit of 'agency, branch or other

---

198 Joakim ST Øren, 'Electronic agents and the notion of establishment' (2001) 9 Int JLIT 249; M Foss and L Bygrave, 'International consumer purchases through the Internet: Jurisdictional issues pursuant to European law' (2000) 8 Int JLIT 99.

199 See Art 2(c) (and also Recital 19) of the Regulation.

200 Most of the jurisprudence concerns Art 7(5) of the Regulation or its identically worded predecessor. See, e.g., *Wolfgang Brenner and Peter Noller v Dean Witter Reynolds Inc* C-318/93 [1994] ECR I-4275.

201 *Somafer v Saar-Ferngas* C-33/78 [1978] ECR 2183, [12] (emphasis added); *Lloyd's Register of Shipping v Société Campenon Bernard* [1995] ECR I-961. In certain circumstances, establishment may not even be an extension of the foreign company, but a legally independent business entity: *SAR Schotte GmbH v Parfums Rothschild Sarl*, C-218/86 [1987] ECR4905, [15]. See also Magnus and Mankowski, above, pp 224ff.

202 Øren, above, 258ff.

203 Foss and Bygrave, above, 132

establishment' is not rather academic, considering that these provisions now prima facie apply to defendants that have no territorial seat of any kind at all in the EU.

But which are the consumer contracts that benefit from this protective regime? This is determined by Art 17 which, first of all, defines a consumer contract as one that is 'concluded by a person . . . for a purpose which can be regarded as being outside his trade or profession'.[204] The Article is silent on the status of the other party to the contract; it is, however, unlikely that C2C transactions, such as via online auctions, are within the Article's ambit given its underlying idea of protecting the vulnerable party in an unequal bargaining scenario.[205] Beyond that Art 17 sets out two types of consumer contracts that fall within the protective regime.[206] A consumer may sue, and must be sued by, a foreign business in the consumer's domicile,[207] regardless of any 'choice of forum' clause,[208] provided that the conditions in Art 17(1)(c) are satisfied:

- the contract has been concluded with a person who pursues commercial or professional activities in the Member State of the consumer's domicile, or
- by any means, directs such activities to that Member State or to several states including that Member State,

and the contract falls within the scope of such activities.

In relation to the first point, the question is whether an online business that advertises and sells its products via its site in the consumer's state would thereby 'pursue commercial activities' there. While the phrase by itself would appear to allow for that possibility, the very scenario is already and more neatly covered by the second exception (see below). Thus it seems that 'pursues commercial or professional activities in the Member State' suggests more substantial activities in the state than mere web presence, probably requiring the physical presence of the trader in the state.[209]

The second exception was specifically drafted with e-commerce in mind. It gives a consumer the benefit of litigating at home, whenever the foreign trader specifically directed its products at the consumer's state and the consumer entered into a contract on the basis of those activities. The rationale underlying it is the same as that endorsed by its predecessor – namely, that businesses cannot expect to take the benefit of the custom of foreign markets that they specifically seek out (previously, for example, through mail order catalogues or doorstep selling) and then not take the burden of defending suits in those markets.[210] The controversial question is when an online business should be held to have 'directed' its online activities to a Member State. Perhaps every website is directed to every state? To avoid this position, as well as any uncertainty, the European Parliament proposed amending Art 17 (previously Art 15):

> [t]he expression 'directing such activities' shall be taken to mean that the trader must have purposefully directed his activity in a substantial way to that other Member State or to several countries including that Member State. In determining whether a trader has directed his activities in such a way, the courts shall have regard to all the circumstances of the case,

---

204 See *Johann Gruber v BayWa AG* Case C-464/01 (ECR 2005 p I-00439).

205 Magnus and Mankowski, above, pp 312ff. See also the wording of Art 17(1)(c) ('who pursues commercial or professional activities in the Member State'); and *Rudolf Gabriel* Case C-96/00 [2002] ECR I-6367, [39].

206 Joakim ST Øren, 'International jurisdiction over consumer contracts in e-Europe' (2003) 52 ICLQ 665.

207 See also Arts 18(1) and (2) and 19 of the Regulation.

208 See Art 19 of the Regulation.

209 Øren (2003), above, 677.

210 This was not satisfied in *Rayner v Davies* [2003] 1 All ER 394, but was satisfied in *Gabriel v Schlank & Schick GmbH* C96/00 [2002] ECR I-6367 on the basis of a number of personalised letters being sent to the consumer inviting him to enter into the contract. Both cases were decided under Art 13(3) of the Brussels Convention on the Enforcement of Judgments in Civil and Commercial Matters (1968). There are clear parallels to the US 'purposeful availment' test generally adopted in civil matters: see Chapter 2.

including any attempts by the trader to ring-fence his trading operation against transactions with consumers domiciled in particular Member States.[211]

So just because a trader has an isolated contact with a resident in a Member State does not mean that he or she is subject to the court processes of that Member State. However, the European Commission rejected this amendment, which, in its opinion:

> runs counter to the philosophy of the provision. The definition is based on the essentially American concept of business activity as a general connecting factor determining jurisdiction, whereas that concept is quite foreign to the approach taken by the Regulation. Moreover, the existence of a consumer dispute requiring court action presupposes a consumer contract. Yet the very existence of such a contract would seem to be clear indication that the supplier of the goods or services has directed his activities towards the state where the consumer is domiciled.[212]

The Commission also noted that 'the language or currency which a website uses does not constitute a relevant factor'[213] in determining whether the activities were directed at the state or not. According to the Commission, if there is a contract with a consumer, then the business is presumed to have targeted the state's residents. This interpretation by the Commission is not reconcilable with the existence of Art 17.[214] Article 17 can only ever be invoked if there is a consumer contract, but then it limits the privilege of the consumer to litigate at home to certain consumer contracts; otherwise it could simply have stated that, whenever there is a consumer contract, the consumer can sue the foreign defendant in his or her home jurisdiction. In short, it envisages the possibility that sometimes, despite there being a consumer contract, the consumer will fall outside the privileged exceptions – contrary to the position of the Commission.

The better approach to 'directing' was adopted by the CJEU in *Peter Pammer v Reederei Karl Schlüter GmbH & Co KG and Hotel Alpenhof GesmbH v Oliver Heller* (2010)[215] where the court held that the mere use of a website by a trader in order to engage trade does not by itself mean that the site is 'directed to' other Member States, but other evidence is needed to show the trader's manifested intention to establish commercial relations with those foreign consumers. Such evidence may come in the form of an express mentioning of the targeted Member State(s), or paying search engines to advertise the goods and services there, or through more indirect and subtle factors, such as:

- the international nature of the activity at issue, e.g. tourism;
- the use of telephone numbers with the international code;
- the use of a top-level domain name other than that of the Member State in which the trader is established, e.g. .de or .fr, or the use of neutral top-level domain names, e.g. .com or .eu;
- the description of itineraries from one or more other Member States to the place where the service is provided;

211 Amendment 37 (OJ C 146/98, 2001) to the Proposal for a Council Regulation on Jurisdiction and the Recognition and Enforcement of Judgments in Civil and Commercial Matters (OJ C 376/17, 1999).
212 Amended Proposal for a Council Regulation on Jurisdiction and the Recognition and Enforcement of Judgments in Civil and Commercial Matters (OJ 062 E, 27.2.2001 P.0243–0275), para 2.2.2.
213 Joint Council and the Commission Statements (14 December 2000), 5.
214 Frederic Debusseré, 'International jurisdiction over e-consumer contracts in the European Union: *Quid novi sub sole?*' (2002) 10 Int JLIT 344. See also Magnus and Mankowski, above, p 317.
215 *Peter Pammer v Reederei Karl Schlüter GmbH & Co KG and Hotel Alpenhof GmbH v Oliver Heller* (Joined Cases C-585/08, C-144/09) ECLI:EU:C:2010:740.

- the mention of an international clientele composed of customers domiciled in various Member States, in particular by presentation of accounts written by such customers;
- the use of a language or a currency, other than that generally used in in the trader's Member State, and the possibility of translations.

In short, the ECJ quite rightly adopted the holistic approach, looking at the overall business activity, which the European Commission had rejected as 'too American'. This approach also means that an isolated contract with a consumer from a Member State will not in itself be sufficient to amount to 'directing'.

Finally, even if a choice-of-forum clause survives these protective consumer provisions, it may still be invalidated under the Unfair Terms in Consumer Contracts Directive,[216] which has priority over the Regulation.[217] In a preliminary ruling, the ECJ decided in *Océana Grupo Editorial SA v Roció Murciano Quintero, Salvat Editores SA v José M Sánchez Alcón Prades et al* (2000)[218] that choice-of-forum clauses in consumer contracts are unfair under Art 3 of the Directive if the clause was not individually negotiated and confers exclusive jurisdiction on the court where the seller or supplier is established, as is usually the case.[219] Consistently, the Guidelines by the UK's former Office of Fair Trading (now subsumed by the Competition and Markets Authority) treat jurisdiction clauses unfavourable to the consumer as unfair almost as a matter of presumption.[220]

## Jurisdiction under national law

The traditional rules of jurisdiction under the national law of the Member States now only have a very residual role to play in governing electronic contracts – as even contractual disputes with defendants from outside the EU are now almost always captured by the EU Jurisdiction Regulation (i.e. whenever there is a choice of forum which refers to a court within the EU) or where there is a consumer contract (that satisfies the 'directing' test).[221] In England and Wales, the relevant jurisdictional gateways can be found in the Civil Procedure Rules. The main difference with the EU regime is that bringing a claim against a foreign defendant (and being entitled to service out of jurisdiction) requires the permission of the court; so it is discretionary and needs to satisfy the forum *conveniens* test[222] in addition to one of the following five gateways:[223]

> The claimant may serve a claim form out of the jurisdiction with the permission of the court under rule 6.36 [CPR] where –
> Claims in relation to contracts
>
> (6)   A claim is made in respect of a contract where the contract –
>
>    (a)   was made within the jurisdiction;
>    (b)   was made by or through an agent trading or residing within the jurisdiction;

---

216  93/13/EEC, now implemented in the UK by the Consumer Rights Act 2015, Sch 2 lists the terms 'that may be regarded as unfair'; see Term 10: 'a term which has the object or effect of irrevocably binding the consumer to terms with which he had no real opportunity of becoming acquainted before the conclusion of the contract'; and Term 20: 'a term which has the object or effect of excluding or hindering the consumer's right to take legal action or exercise any other legal remedy.'

217  See Art 67 of the Jurisdiction Regulation, and discussion in Magnus and Mankowski, above, pp 322ff.

218  *Océana Grupo Editorial SA v Roció Murciano Quintero, Salvat Editores SA v José M Sánchez Alcón Prades, José Luis Copano Badillo, Mohammed Berroane and Emilio Viñas Feliù*, Joined Cases C-240/98, C-241/98, C-242/98, C-243/98, C-240/98 [2000] ECR I-4941, I-4971, and I-4973, [24].

219  See also Art 6 and Annex 1(q) of the Unfair Terms in Consumer Contracts Directive 93/13/EEC.

220  Office of Fair Trading (OFT), *Unfair Contract Terms Guidance*, OFT 311, 2008, London: HMSO, pp 67ff.

221  See Arts 18 and 25, discussed above. See generally Lorna E Giles, *Electronic Commerce and Private International Law*, 2008, Aldershot: Ashgate, ch 6. In Scotland, the rules are provided in Sch 8 to the Civil Jurisdiction and Judgments Act 1982.

222  See Civil Procedure Rules rr 6.32–6.36. *Spiliada Maritime Corp v Cansulex Ltd* [1987] AC 460. For an application of these principles, see *Apple Corps Ltd v Apple Computer Inc* [2004] EWHC 768. See also Chapter 2.

223  CPR r. 6.36, Practice Direction 6B, 3.1(6) and (7). For their interpretation, see Lawrence Collins (ed), *Dicey, Morris and Collins on the Conflicts of Laws: Vol 1*, 14th edn, 2006, London: Sweet and Maxwell, pp 375ff.

(c) is governed by English law; or

(d) contains a term to the effect that the court shall have jurisdiction to determine any claim in respect of the contract.

(7) A claim is made in respect of a breach of contract committed within the jurisdiction.

Given the very residual role of these jurisdictional gateways in disputes concerning transnational (electronic) contracts, they only require a few comments here. Much like the EU jurisdictional rules, under these rules a forum selection clause is *prima facie* respected as a matter of contractual autonomy,[224] but is likely to be struck down as 'unfair' in consumer contracts where it is favourable to the foreign business. Striking down a forum selection clause that refers the dispute to a foreign court may also be necessary to override a parallel choice-of-law clause that purports to exclude local mandatory rules, given that a foreign tribunal is unlikely to apply those mandatory rules (see below).[225] In the absence of a valid choice-of-law clause, the other four gateways become relevant.

The first one requires a decision on *where* an electronic contract is concluded. A contract is concluded where the last act necessary for its conclusion has occurred. Assuming the applicability of the receipt rule to online contracts (see above),[226] this would be where the electronic acceptance is received by the offeror – or, more specifically, where he or she is capable of accessing it (assuming the receipt is adopted for electronic contracts), as argued but rejected in a contract allegedly concluded by email in the case of *Surrey (UK) Ltd v Mazandaran Wood & Paper Industries* (2014).[227] In this context, it should neither matter where the offeror's mail is stored nor where he or she happens to check it as these are fickle indicators. A more stable criterion for fixing the contract's location is the offeror's place of business or residence, with one proviso: when the offeror's actual residence or place of business is different from that reasonably communicated to the offeree, the parties must be considered to have objectively intended to conclude the contract in the second location.[228] For example, if someone were to buy a book through amazon.fr using a French credit card and providing a French delivery address, it would be concluded that the parties have objectively intended to conclude the contract in France, even if the person was resident in the UK and entered into the online contract from the UK.[229] In respect of the above analysis it has rightly been argued that 'locating' a transnational contract in a particular jurisdiction is highly artificial and arbitrary. Mann J in *Apple Corps Ltd v Apple Computer Inc* (2004)[230] went as far as holding that the contract in dispute was concluded both in England and California, and thus fell into the above gateway. He reasoned:

> I confess that I can detect no conceptual barriers to the notion of a contract being treated as having been made in two places, and some not inconsiderable attractions. In a case where the two parties to a contract are not in the same location at the time of contracting, the notion of where the contract is made is essentially a lawyer's construct. It seldom matters of course, but where it does matter (principally for the purposes of jurisdiction under English law) the law has to provide some answers where an application of the experience of everyday life does

224 *Attock Cement Co v Romanian Bank for Foreign Trade* [1989] 1 WLR 1147. It is within the discretion of the court to grant a stay of proceedings on forum *conveniens* grounds: *Donohue v Armco Inc* [2001] UKHL 64.
225 This would fall with *The Eleftheria* [1970] P 94, in which the court laid down the factors that may be taken into account in its discretionary exercise whether to override a jurisdictional clause, including the law governing the contract.
226 *Entores v Miles Far East Corp* [1955] 2 QB 327 (CA); *Brinkibon Ltd v Stahag Stahl* [1983] 2 AC 34 (HL); see above.
227 [2014] EWHC 3165, [20].
228 For similar reasoning, see above discussion on the interpretation of 'branch, agency or establishment' and the relevance of any (reasonable) perception.
229 Comparable to the approach taken in Art 4 of Regulation on the Law Applicable to Contractual Obligations 593/2008, discussed below.
230 [2004] EWHC 768.

not enable one to provide them . . . [W]here oral telephone communications are even more common, and where such communications can involve three or more participants in three or more different jurisdictions, and where parties might even conclude a written contract by each signing, and observing each other signing, over a video-link, the law may have to move on and to recognise that there is nothing inherently wrong or heretical in allowing the notion of a contract made in two (or more) jurisdictions at the same time. This is not merely a way of avoiding an unfortunate, and perhaps difficult, evidential enquiry. It may well reflect the reality of the situation.[231]

This reasoning, whilst entirely understandable, makes the jurisdictional gateway a less legitimate means for assuming personal jurisdiction over the foreign contracting party. The whole point of these gateways is to find the forum most strongly connected with the dispute and thus a gateway that acknowledges each forum as equally connected is not particularly helpful.

The second jurisdiction gateway, focusing on agents trading or residing within the jurisdiction, is not particularly relevant to the online contracting environment, as what is so novel about the internet is that it facilitates transnational contracting without any physical presence within the state of the consumer. In any event, this gateway broadly overlaps with 'agency, branch or other establishment' head of jurisdiction in Arts 7(5) and 17(2) of the Jurisdiction Regulation (see above); so localised technology supporting online services should not by itself be treated as an 'agent'.

The third jurisdiction gateway that permits service out of jurisdiction is based on the fact that the contract is governed by English law and addressed below on 'applicable law'. Suffice to say here that while a finding in favour of English law is not a conclusive factor in favour of an English court hearing the dispute,[232] it carries weight where the foreign law is significantly different from English law or not bringing the case before a local court would defeat a valid claim under English law, such as where the foreign court would not apply local mandatory consumer protection provisions.[233]

Last but not least, the 'location of the breach' gateways is perhaps the most ambivalent basis for the court's jurisdiction, both in offline and electronic contracts. To start with, whether a contract is breached within the jurisdiction depends on the type of breach. If the breach occurs by an anticipatory breach/repudiation (for example, an email in which one party informs the other that he or she does not intend to perform the contract), then, according to traditional case law, the repudiation occurs from where the communication was sent and not where it was received.[234] Where, on the other hand, the breach takes the form of a failure to perform the contract, the focus is on the location where the performance ought to have occurred.[235] Again, in the electronic context, it might be tempting to look at the location of the technology involved in the transaction, but traditional rules support more stable factors, such as the place of business or residence of the parties as the default position.[236] In respect of non-payment, *The Eider* (1893)[237] established long ago that '[t]he general rule is where no place is specified, either expressly or by implication, the debtor must seek out his creditor'.[238] In most electronic contracts, the buyer is expressly required to pay the outstanding

---

231  Ibid, [37], see also [43].
232  *Amin Rasheed Shipping Corp v Kuwait Insurance Co* [1984] AC 50.
233  Collins, above.
234  *Cherry v Thompson* 918720 LR 7 QB 573; *Holland v Bennett* [1902] 1KB 867 (CA); *Martin v Stout* [1925] AC 359 (PC); *Atlantic Underwriting Agencies Ltd v Compagnia di Assicurazione di Milano* [1979] 2 Lloyd's Rep 240; *Stanley Kerr Holdings Pty Ltd v Gibor Textile Enterprises Ltd* [1967] 2 NSWLR 372.
235  This is reminiscent of Art 7(1) of the Jurisdiction Regulation which provides for jurisdiction over a foreign defendant 'in matters relating to a contract, in the courts for the place of performance of the obligation in question'. The difference is that in the Jurisdiction Regulation, the focus is only on the substantive obligation concerning the delivery of the goods or the performance of the service, not on the monetary obligation.
236  *Thompson v Palmer* [1893] 2 QB 80 (CA); *Bremer Öltransport GmbH v Drewy* [1933] 1 KB 753.
237  [1893] P 119.
238  Ibid, 136.

sum into the seller's account, often via intermediaries such as PayPal. While that account could be anywhere, in the absence of any contrary indication, it would be inferred that the account is where the place of business or residence of the seller is located. Conversely, when the breach of an electronic contract consists of a non-delivery of the promised goods or services, the place of the performance should generally be the buyer's place of business or residence. Whilst this appears contrary to s 29(2) of the Sale of Goods Act 1979, which provides that – bar any *express or implied contractual provision to the contrary* – 'the place of delivery is the seller's place of business if he has one, and if not, his residence', the Act clearly belongs to the pre-internet era. In a more contemporary vein, s 39 of the Consumer Rights Act implies that 'digital content' is delivered at the place of either the consumer's device or at the place of a third party trader chosen to supply digital content to the consumer. Even in the electronic context, most contracts would have an implied or express term providing for the delivery of the goods to the buyer.[239]

## Jurisdiction in the USA

The greater US deference for party autonomy means that choice-of-forum clauses are upheld not only in B2B contracts, but also frequently in B2C contracts. In *Carnival Cruise Lines Inc v Shute* (1991)[240] the US Supreme Court held that even in adhesion contracts – that is, standard-form contracts – such clauses are enforceable unless there is a finding of unfairness or unconscionability. While this appears to echo the European position under the Unfair Terms in Consumer Contracts Directive,[241] the devil is in the detail. According to the Supreme Court, a clause is not simply unfair because it is onerous to the consumer and it will stand provided that it serves legitimate reasons (rather than simply trying to discourage legitimate claims by customers), such as protecting the business from being exposed to proceedings in the innumerable locations of its customer, wishing to bring proceedings in a place to which the business has a link, eliminating *ex ante* uncertainty and argument as to the forum, and thus saving costs that may even have been passed onto the consumers. Apply this to the online world, most choice-of-forum clauses would withstand US judicial scrutiny. Having said that, *Carnival Cruise* concerned an intra-national case and, in an international scenario, US courts might be more sympathetic to its local consumers' plight. Where the parties to the electronic contract have not agreed on a choice-of-forum clause, the US default rules on jurisdiction come to bear. See Chapter 2.

## The applicable law

The rules determining the law applicable to contractual disputes have, in the Member States of the EU, only one provenance (unlike the dual system in place for jurisdictional questions): the EC Regulation on the Law Applicable to Contractual Obligations,[242] commonly referred to as 'Rome I'. The Regulation applies regardless of the connection of the parties with any Member States, and may well lead to the application of the law of a non-Member State to the dispute (Art 2). Although the Regulation is thus broader in its catchment area than the Jurisdiction Regulation, it generally mirrors the contractual provisions in the latter Regulation.

Another point worth noting is that different aspects of a contract may be governed by different laws, e.g. if so agreed by the parties (Art 3(1)). While the contractual dispute may be governed by Greek law, the validity of a party's consent may be determined by reference to Spanish law, if that is

---

239 Generally, if the buyer is expected to collect the goods from the seller, this would be expressly stated given its exceptional nature.
240 499 US 585 (1991).
241 Directive 93/13/EEC, discussed above.
242 Regulation 593/2008/EC, replacing the Rome Convention on the Law Applicable to Contractual Obligations (1980); see Nils Willem Vernooij, 'Rome I: An update on the law applicable to contractual obligations in Europe' (2009) 15 Colum J Eur L 71. There is no room for the residual application of the national choice of law rules. Article 1(1) provides that the 'Regulation shall apply, in situations involving a conflict of laws, to contractual obligations in civil and commercial matters'.

the law of the country in which he or she is habitually resident (Art 10(2)). While the court may uphold the parties' choice of law for most purposes, it may not do so for all purposes (for example, Art 3(3)). Certainly, parties cannot exclude any public, criminal, or other mandatory laws of any state, which – if the contract falls within their scope – will take priority over the 'applicable law' (Art 9, discussed below).

## Contractual choice and its limits

The starting point of Rome I for determining the applicable law is the contract between the parties. Article 3(1) upholds contractual autonomy:

> A contract shall be governed by the law chosen by the parties. The choice shall be made expressly or clearly demonstrated by the terms of the contract or the circumstances of the case. By their choice the parties can select the law applicable to the whole or to part only of the contract.

Most frequently, online businesses include an express choice-of-law clause that, according to the above provision, binds the parties – a matter of utmost importance for online businesses that may otherwise potentially be exposed to the multiple sets of contract law of the countries of their customers. Where the existence or validity of the contract or any of its terms (such as the choice-of-law clause) is in dispute, the validity issue is decided by reference to the law that would be applicable if the contract or term were valid (Art 10(1)). Article 3 itself already creates a significant inroad into the sanctity of choice-of-law clauses. Article 3(3) of Rome I provides that parties cannot avoid mandatory provisions of a state with which a contract is closely connected by choosing the laws of another state:

> Where all other elements relevant to the situation at the time of the choice are located in a country other than the country whose law has been chosen, the choice of the parties shall not prejudice the application of provisions of the law of that other country which cannot be derogated from by agreement.

This provision prevents the evasion of regulation often protective of the weaker contractual party and stops contractual parties from a wholesale buying out of regulatory requirements of a state by choosing the laws of another state. Both the Unfair Contract Terms Act 1977 and the Consumer Rights Act 2015 provide examples of laws that may not be derogated from by agreement. For example, according to s 27(2)(a) of the Unfair Contract Terms Act 1977 (now only applicable to B2B and C2C contracts):

> This Act has effect notwithstanding any contract term which applies or purports to apply the law of some country outside the United Kingdom where . . . the terms appear to the court or arbitrator or arbiter to have been imposed wholly or mainly for the purpose of enabling the party imposing it to *evade* the operation of the Act. [emphasis added]

Similarly, s 74(1) of the Consumer Rights Act 2015 which transposes the EC Directive on Unfair Terms in Consumer Contracts into UK law, provides that where parties have chosen as applicable law the law of a state from other than an EEA state,[243] the Act's 'unfair terms' regime applies regardless of the parties' choice, provided the consumer contract has a close connection with the UK.

---

243 Referring to the European Economic Area, which refers to EU Member States plus Iceland, Liechtenstein and Norway which allows them to participate in the EU single market. Note, where the law chosen is the law of an EEA state, the substantive rules are those under the Directive.

So in B2C transactions, it does not matter whether there was any attempt to deliberately evade the local regulatory provisions.

Article 9 of Rome I makes further inroads into party autonomy with respect to choosing the substantive law that governs their contractual relationship. It affirms the superiority of regulatory law – such as rules on cartels, competition, restrictive practices, and rules regulating certain industries, such as the banking, insurance, and investment sectors – which is unaffected by the applicable contract law. By the same token, states also retain a residual power to refuse to enforce the otherwise applicable law of another state 'if such application is manifestly incompatible with the public policy . . . of the forum' (Art 21).

So although choice-of-law clauses are a valuable tool for online businesses to reduce their exposure to unwanted laws, their ambit is limited in two significant respects: first, these clauses are only enforceable against those who consented to them – not strangers to the contract, such as those alleging violations of intellectual property rights or defamation; second, their effectiveness is also circumscribed by not preventing the application of certain non-derogatory or mandatory laws of the states affected. See Chapter 2.

## In the absence of contractual choice

Where the parties have failed to agree on the law applicable to their contract, which is very infrequent in the online environment, Art 4 of Rome I provides for rules that move from specific default rules to more general rules as fall-back options where the default rules prove inappropriate. Starting with the very specific tests, Art 4(1)[244] provides that, for example,

(a) a contract for the sale of goods shall be governed by the law of the country where the seller has his habitual residence;

(b) a contract for the provision of services shall be governed by the law of the country where the service provider has his habitual residence; . . .

(g) a contract for the sale of goods by auction shall be governed by the law of the country where the auction takes place, if such a place can be determined; . . .

It is then followed by two wider tests that are intended to catch ambiguous cases – that is, those that are covered by more than one of the above heads, or by none. In those cases, the law governing the contract is 'the law of the country where the party required to effect the characteristic performance of the contract has his habitual residence' (Art 4(2)). Because the 'characteristic performance' is the non-monetary consideration, again this rule leads to the law of the place of habitual residence of the seller or service provider.[245] Again Mann J in *Apple Corps Ltd v Apple Computer Inc* (2004)[246] reflected on the difficulty associated with localising the 'performance' in the case of de-materialised contracts with mutual negative obligations:

> The concept of 'performance' is an easier concept to deal with where what is required is positive acts. Although there will always be cases of difficulty, one can see how the concept applies where one can see what positive acts have to be done under the contract, identify one act or set of acts as lying at the heart of it, and identify the party that has to do those acts. That is not the case for much of the Trademark Agreement. At the heart of the agreement are, in effect, negative

---

244 Article 4 reverses the approach taken under its predecessor, the Rome Convention on the Law Applicable to Contractual Obligations (1980), by opting for specific rules supplemented by more general default tests, rather than, as previously, providing for a very general test as the main rule, which was then given substance by more specific presumptions: see Vernooij, above, 73ff.

245 For operation of similar, but not identical, rules under Rome I's predecessor see *Surrey (UK) Ltd v Mazandaran Wood & Paper Industries* [2014] EWHC 3165, [21]–[29].

246 [2004] EWHC 768.

provisions . . . However, I am prepared to assume that a negative obligation can amount to 'performance' . . . Nonetheless, in relation to the present contract, it seems to me that the mutuality of the obligations means that the central performance elements (I deliberately avoid the expression 'characteristic performance' at this point of the argument) are shared between the parties.[247]

Where that rule fails to yield a suitable applicable law, then it is the law of the country that is most closely connected to the contract that shall prevail (Art 4(3) and (4)) which also is not without difficulty in particular in relation to contracts between two companies in two different jurisdictions governing their global activities and relationship.[248] In these cases, private international law effectively operates at the margin of the possible by applying national law to intrinsically global activity.

Rome I makes the 'habitual residence' of one of the parties the reference point for fixing the applicable law which – as everybody has to be resident somewhere – is *prima facie* less affected by the non-geography of cyberspace. 'Habitual residence' means, in the case of companies, the place of its central administration,[249] in the case of natural persons acting in the course of business, their principal place of business, and finally, in the case of operations of a branch, agency, or any other establishment, the place of that branch, agency, or establishment (Art 19). As in respect of the Regulation's predecessor, the 1980 Rome Convention on the Law Applicable to Contractual Obligations, there may be some who argue that a web server by itself may amount to a 'place of business'.[250] Given the fortuitous nature of the location of servers, such arguments should meet as much resistance as arguments that a web server may be treated as an agent or an establishment in the jurisdiction enquiry (see above).

## Consumer protection provisions

Finally, Art 6 of Rome I deals specifically with consumer contracts and thus has a narrower ambit than Arts 3 and 9 in terms of the contracts to which it applies. However, in respect of these contracts – provided that certain preconditions are satisfied – it confers wider benefits: it applies the law of the country of the consumer's habitual residence and not only the mandatory laws (Art 6(1)). However, where there is a choice-of-law clause, Art 6(2) states that the choice will stand in so far as it does not have 'the result of depriving the consumer of the protection afforded to him by provisions that cannot be derogated from by agreement by virtue of the law which, in the absence of choice, would have been applicable on the basis of paragraph 1'. In other words, the court will examine the law of the consumer's residence and see whether the chosen law would be less beneficial than the mandatory provisions of the consumer's home law. The preconditions that must be satisfied before the consumer exception in the Regulation kicks into place are spelled out in Art 6(1):

[A] contract concluded by a natural person for a purpose which can be regarded as being outside his trade or profession (the consumer) with another person acting in the exercise of his trade or profession (the professional) shall be governed by the law of the country where the consumer has his habitual residence, provided that the professional:

    (a)   pursues his commercial or professional activities in the country where the consumer has his habitual residence, or

    (b)   by any means, directs such activities to that country or to several countries including that country.

---

247  *Ibid*, [52]–[53].
248  *Ibid*, [61], [64].
249  Contrast Art 60(1) of the Jurisdiction Regulation, which provides for a choice of three criteria to determine a company's domicile; see also below.
250  Michael Chissick and Alistair Kelman, *Electronic Commerce: Law and Practice*, 3rd edn, 2000, London: Sweet & Maxwell, p 120.

Because this Article is virtually identical to Art 17(1)(c) of the Jurisdiction Regulation,[251] it means that if the court of the consumer's habitual residence has the power to hear the dispute, then that court can also apply the substantive law of the forum to the dispute. This creates consistency and simplicity that is advantageous to both consumers and businesses, particularly in the online world. Regarding the interpretation of Art 6(1)(a) and (b) in the online context, especially of the 'directing' test, the arguments are the same as those discussed above. See also Chapter 2. This approach is by no means new; it simply applies to the internet what previously applied to offline communications:

> Thus the trader must have done certain acts such as advertising in the press, or on radio or television, or in the cinema or by catalogues aimed specifically at that country, or he must have made business proposals individually through a middleman or by canvassing. If, for example a German makes a contract in response to an advertisement published by a French company in a German publication, the contract is covered by the special rule. If, on the other hand, the German replies to an advertisement in American publications, even if they are sold in Germany, the rule does not apply unless the advertisement appeared in special editions of the publication intended for European countries. In the latter case the seller will have made a special advertisement intended for the country of the purchaser.[252]

Although the targeting or directing approach is not new in principle, its application to the internet is likely to produce many boundary cases in which it will not be clear – on the basis of the site's language, currency, names or products or services – who exactly is the site's intended clientele. While a willingness to deliver products to a particular country is likely to be taken as a confirmation that the country is part of the site's target, this indicator is hardly significant in respect of digital content (see above).

## The origin rule under the Electronic Commerce Directive?

Within the EU, transnational electronic commerce is substantially affected by the allocation principle of the Electronic Commerce Directive.[253] This Directive provides – within the sphere of the EU – the origin principle[254] as a basis for sharing out certain regulatory space over electronic commerce between the Member States; online providers are only subject to the law of their state of origin. Article 3 of the Directive provides:

1.  Each Member State shall ensure that the information society services provided by a service provider established on its territory comply with the national provisions applicable in the Member State in question which fall within the coordinated field.
2.  Member States may not, for reasons falling within the coordinated field, restrict the freedom to provide information society services from another Member State. [emphasis added]

The duty of Member States to refrain from restricting services by providers from other Member States (regulatory forbearance) in Art 3(2) goes hand-in-hand with their duty to regulate online

---

251 The Rome Regulation uses the concept of 'habitual residence' rather than 'domicile' used in the Jurisdiction Regulation. On the difference of those terms, see Pippa Rogerson, 'Habitual residence: The new domicile?' (2000) 49 ICLQ 86.
252 Mario Giuliano and Paul Lagarde, 'Council report on the Convention on the Law Applicable to Contractual Obligations' (1980) OJ C282, 24.
253 Directive 2000/31/EC, implemented in the UK by the Electronic Commerce (EC Directive) Regulations 2002, SI 2002/2013. See Lokke Moerel, 'The country-of-origin principle in the E-Commerce Directive: The expected one-stop shop' (2001) 7 CTLR 184; Mark Turner, Mary Traynor and Herbert Smith, 'E-Commerce Directive: UK implementation – Electronic Commerce (EC Directive) Regulations 2002: Worth the wait?' (2002) 18(6) CLSR 396.
254 For the reasons behind the acceptability of the origin approach in the EU, see Chapter 2 above.

providers established on their territory (duty to regulate) in Art 3(1).[255] That latter duty is designed to ensure that there is no regulatory vacuum, and thus is taken seriously. Thus, in situations such as in the CJEU case of *Cornelius de Visser* (2012)[256] where the place of establishment of the service provider was unknown, Art 3(1) cannot be fulfilled and thus neither will Art 3(2) apply. Overall the idea appears to be to expose service providers only to one set of rules (the rules of their state of origin), rather than the multiple sets of rules from all of the states in which they offer their online services. This approach to transnational regulation is desirable for online businesses and rather exceptional. See Chapter 2. But is this really the effect of Art 3(2): what is the scope of this origin rule under the Electronic Commerce Directive? The answer to this question is found: (1) in the material scope of the rule; and (2) in its relationship to competence rules (esp. the rule of private international law, discussed above.)

Coming to the first point, the Directive is ground-breaking in that it does not limit Art 3(2) to the substantive law dealt with and harmonised by the Directive. This makes for a very broad starting point and explains the resulting complexity on its scope. Having said that, there are some significant areas of law that are excluded from the scope of the entire Directive (i.e. in respect of which states were not prepared to surrender control): taxation; data protection; cartel law; activities of notaries; legal representation before the court; gambling, lotteries, and betting.[257] Also, under Art 3(3) certain legal areas are excluded specifically from the scope of the origin rules, such as copyright, electronic money or spam email; and under Art 3(4), Member States can derogate from it, where it is perceived to be necessary for reason of public policy, in particular the prevention, investigation, detection, and prosecution of criminal offences; the protection of public health; public security; and the protection of consumers.[258] Having regard to the area excluded or restricted from the origin, it is clear that it is *prima facie* designed to operate across both civil and criminal/regulatory law.[259] Furthermore the origin rule applies to all 'information society services' and legal requirements 'within the coordinated fields' – both of which are broadly defined concepts. 'Information society service' is defined as 'any service normally provided for remuneration at a distance, by electronic means, and at the individual request of a recipient of services'[260] – covering any commercial activity by online actors and facilitators, such as ISPs, including free services, such as search engines, which are financed by third parties, such as advertisers, as confirmed by the CJEU in *Papasavvas* (2014).[261] The 'coordinated fields' relate to any requirements concerning:

- the taking up of the activity of an information society service, such as requirements concerning qualifications, authorisation, or notification; or
- the pursuit of the activity of an information society service, such as requirements concerning the behaviour of the service provider, requirements regarding the quality or content of the service, including those applicable to advertising and contracts, or requirements concerning the liability of the service provider.[262]

---

255 See Art 2(c) of the Directive, which defines 'established service provider' as 'a service provider who effectively pursues an economic activity using a fixed establishment for an indefinite period. The presence and use of the technical means and technologies required to provide the service do not, in themselves, constitute an establishment of the provider.'

256 C-292/10 (CJEU, 15 March 2012).

257 Article 1(5) of the Directive.

258 Other conditions for the justified derogation are that: the information society service against which it is directed prejudiced, or was highly likely to prejudice, the above objectives; the measure taken must be proportionate to the objective; the origin state failed to take the required measures after being asked to do so; and the Commission was informed of the Member State's intention to take such measures.

259 Department of Trade and Industry, *A Guide for Business to the Electronic Commerce (EC Directive) Regulations 2002* (SI 2002/2013), London: HMSO, para 4.8.

260 *Ibid*, Art 2(a), which refers to the definition in Art 1(2) of Directive 98/34/EC (as amended by Directive 98/84/EC).

261 C-291/13 (CJEU, 11 September 2014).

262 *Ibid*, Art 2(h)(i).

The 'coordinated fields' do not include requirements applicable to goods, to the delivery of goods or those applicable to services not provided by electronic means.[263] Recital 21 of the Directive in fact clarifies that 'the coordinated field covers only requirements relating to on-line activities such as on-line information, on-line advertising, on-line shopping, on-line contracting and does not concern Member States' legal requirements relating to goods such as safety standards, labelling obligations, or liability for goods . . .'. In other words, the origin rule deals with matters that are peculiar to electronic commerce and does not seek to regulate commercial activities that happen to have some incidental electronic aspect. For example, while legal or medical advice provided online triggers the origin rule (concerning qualification requirements), any such advice provided offline following an online advert would be outside its scope – although the online advert would again be within its scope. Similarly, when it comes to 'goods', any legal requirement relating to advertising and selling them online falls within the coordinated fields, but any requirements relating to the tangible good itself (for example, its legality, safety standards, labelling requirements, or liability for it) or to its delivery (for example, medicine with or without prescription) are outside the origin rule. In *Ker-Optika* (2010)[264] the CJEU held that the duty of regulatory forbearance under the Directive covered the national rules on the selling of contact lenses online, but not those covering the physical supply of such lenses. This aim of separating the offline aspects of electronic commerce from its true electronic core makes sense to some extent, because otherwise the Directive would apply far beyond its intended electronic sphere. Nevertheless, such separation is also problematic in the borderline scenarios and overlapping areas. In the final analysis, it illustrates the difficulties created by regulation that is not technologically neutral. For example, does it make sense to apply a different set of rules to an electronic book than to its paper variant? Similarly, labelling requirements of medicine are outside the origin rule, but rules on advertising of medicine online are within it: how are these positions reconcilable when the online advert reproduces the label?

Second, further complexity is created by the appearance of Art 3(2) as a type of competence rule, such as those provided by private international law determining which court can hear a dispute or which national law applies to it (see above and Chapter 2). Yet, Art 1(4) states categorically: 'This Directive does not establish additional rules on private international law nor does it deal with the jurisdiction of Courts;'[265] and Art 3(3) specifically provides that the origin rule shall *not* apply, amongst other things, to, 'the contractual freedom to choose the law applicable to a contract' and 'contractual obligations concerning consumer contracts'.[266] Having said that Recital 23 provides that 'provisions of the applicable law designated by rules of private international law must not restrict the freedom to provide information society services as established in this Directive,' which suggests that Art 3(2) may operate as a type of check on choice-of-law rules. This issue was addressed in *eDate* (2011),[267] where the CJEU held that Art 3(2) did not furnish a choice of law rule and thus service providers could, even in relation to matters falling with the coordinated fields, be subjected to foreign law: 'Member States must ensure that, subject to the derogations authorised in accordance with the conditions set out in Article 3(4) of Directive 2000/31, the provider of an electronic commerce service is not made subject to stricter requirements than those provided for by the substantive law applicable in the Member State in which that service provider is established.' So Art 3(2) provides a cap on foreign law (and thus is only a limited type of origin rule). Whether it is always possible to determine whether a rule is more or less 'strict' than another rule, rather than simply different and thereby an additional regulatory burden, is another question.

---

263 *Ibid*, Art 2(h)(ii).
264 C-108/09 (CJEU, 2 December 2010). Member States are also not entitled to insist on the sale of contact lenses through physical shops.
265 This statement is misleading in so far as rules governing the jurisdiction of the courts are part of private international law.
266 *Ibid*, Art 3(3) and Annex.
267 C-500/09 (CJEU, 25 October 2011).

# Formalities and signatures

## Requirement of writing and durability

Although there are few contracts that, under English law, must be in writing in order to be binding,[268] a written contract is desirable, and thus frequently adopted, because it provides parties with greater certainty as to their rights and obligations, and it gives them a reliable record of the transaction useful for evidentiary purposes. The law implicitly acknowledges these benefits by frequently requiring, or entitling the parties to, a written record of the agreement.[269] There are also wide-reaching statutory requirements concerning instruments, documents, notices, and records – which were invariably assumed to be paper-based.[270] The shift from paper-based communications to electronic communications has raised two interrelated issues in respect of all of these requirements, as follows.

(1) Does an electronic record satisfy the legal requirements of writing – that is, is the law technologically neutral?

(2) What are the characteristics that an electronic record must have to be functionally equivalent to a paper-based record?

In relation to the first question, one of the earliest international attempts to facilitate electronic commerce by validating electronic records is the United Nations Commission on International Trade Law (UNCITRAL) Model Law on Electronic Commerce (1996), which provides in Art 5 that '[i]nformation shall not be denied legal effect, validity or enforceability solely on the ground that it is in the form of a data message'. This general axiom is then spelled out more explicitly with reference to the requirement of writing in Art 6:

1. Where the law requires information to be in writing, that requirement is met by a data message if the information contained therein is accessible so as to be usable for subsequent reference.

2. Paragraph 1 applies whether the requirement therein is in the form of an obligation or whether the law simply provides consequences for the information not being in writing.

Where the law requires the 'original' document, according to Art 8, data messages are valid as long as there is 'a reliable assurance as to the integrity of the information': has the information remained complete and unaltered? The standard of reliability varies depending on the purpose for which the information was generated, but would often require encryption of the message (discussed below). The effect of these provisions for evidential purposes is governed by Art 9, according to which a data message cannot be denied admissibility solely because it is a data message, and the evidentiary weight attached to any such message varies depending on its reliability, such as how it was created, stored, communicated, or maintained.

Of a mandatory character in the UK[271] are the provisions of the Electronic Commerce Directive and, in particular, Art 9, which requires Member States to ensure the legal effectiveness and validity of electronic contracts, and to remove any obstacles to the use of such contracts. Such obstacles

---

268 For example, contracts for the sale or transfer of land must be in writing, according to s 2 of the Law of Property (Miscellaneous Provisions) Act 1989, and guarantees under s 4 of the Statute of Frauds 1677.

269 For example, Art 13 of Commercial Agents Directive 86/653/EEC, Art 6(3) of the Consumer Sales Directive 1999/44/EC, or Art 25 of the Jurisdiction Regulation.

270 Such as communications of individuals and companies with government departments, such as Companies House.

271 A Model Law, unlike a Convention, creates no binding legal obligations. It is designed to provide useful guidance on the area of law covered. In incorporating a Model Law into national law, states may make any modifications that they like, and thus it is inherently more flexible, but less harmonising, than a Convention.

would be '[r]equirements that a contract (or any steps required to be taken under or in relation to a contract) be in writing, evidences in writing, or signed . . .'.[272] Unlike the Model Law, the requirement is restricted to electronic contracts (with some exceptions, such as real estate transactions).

How then are these requirements implemented in UK law? On a very general level, they are implemented via the definition of 'writing' in Sch 1 to the Interpretation Act 1978: '"Writing" includes typing, printing, lithography, photography and other modes of representing or reproducing words in a visible form, and expressions referring to writing are construed accordingly.' Although there was some early disagreement whether electronic writing that relies on a series of electronic impulses is in essence visible, the general consensus now is that if electronic writing is visible on a computer screen, it satisfies the above definition and, by implication, most legislative writing requirements.[273]

Nevertheless, to forestall any arguments, the Electronic Communications Act 2000 was enacted. Section 8 of the Act allows for the 'appropriate Minister' to modify (via Orders) existing law 'in such manner as he may think fit for the purposes of authorising or facilitating the use of electronic communications or electronic storage' for a multitude of specified purposes (s 8(1) and (2)) – going far beyond the contractual context, in line with the Model Law. To do so, the Minister must be satisfied that the records based on electronic communications and storage will be no less satisfactory than previous records (s 8(3)) – in other words, the section does not support the wholesale conversion of traditional records into electronic records, but requires the comparability of the electronic communications with paper-based communications in the circumstances. Such comparability may be achieved by the conditions that the Minister can put on the form or use of the electronic communication or storage under s 8(4). In respect of the use of electronic communications in court proceedings, conditions may be imposed for determining and proving whether an electronic communication has taken place and, if so, when, by whom, and its content (s 8(4) (g) and (5)). Although s 8 potentially provides for the wide-ranging incorporation of electronic communications into existing law, in fact it requires further actions by the appropriate Ministers in the form of Orders, of which there have been around 40 so far.[274] There has so far been no Order that implements Art 9 of the Electronic Commerce Directive (dealing with electronic contracts generally).[275] This may partly be explained by reference to the fact that writing requirements are 'very rare in English Law [and i]n those rare cases . . . the form requirements are . . . capable of being satisfied by email or website trading'.[276]

Finally, a number of recent EU instruments address either how the term 'writing' should be understood in the electronic era or, more generally, how information must be disseminated. For example, Art 25(2) of the Jurisdiction Regulation states that 'any communication by electronic means which provides a durable record of the agreement shall be the equivalent to "writing"'. Similarly, Art 7(1) of the Consumer Rights Directive stipulates that 'with respect to off-premises contracts, the trader shall give the information provided for in Article 6(1) to the consumer on paper or, if the consumer agrees, on another durable medium. That information shall be legible and in plain, intelligible language.'[277] A term that reappears in these definitions is 'durable' which is defined in Art 2(10) of the Consumer Rights Directive:

---

272 Law Commission, above, para 3.48.
273 *Ibid*, para 3.8. For a general early discussion on the writing requirement, see also DTI, *Building Confidence in Electronic Commerce: A Consultation Document*, URN 99/642, 1999, London: HMSO; and Chris Reed, *Digital Information Law: Electronic Documents and Requirements of Form*, 1996, London: Centre for Commercial Law Studies, Queen Mary and Westfield College, University of London.
274 An early example was the Companies Act 1985 (Electronic Communications) Order 2000, SI 2000/3373. A more recent one is the Companies (Striking Off) (Electronic Communications) Order 2014 (SI 2014/1602).
275 The Electronic Communication (EC Directive) Regulations 2002, SI 2002/2013, which implement much of the Electronic Commerce Directive 2000/31/EC, do not cover Art 9.
276 Law Commission, above, para 3.48.
277 See also Art 6(3) of the Consumer Sales Directive 1999/44/EC; Art 10(3) of the Electronic Commerce Directive 2000/31/EC; Art 2(3) of the Financial Collateral Arrangements Directive 2002/47/EC.

> 'durable medium' means any instrument which enables the consumer or the trader to store information addressed personally to him in a way accessible for future reference for a period of time adequate for the purposes of the information and which allows the unchanged reproduction of the information stored.[278]

Recital 23 of the same Directive provides examples of what such durable medium may be: 'paper, USB sticks, CD-ROMs, DVDs, memory cards or the hard disks of computers as well as e-mails.' From this, it seems clear that 'durable' is not a term of art that requires encryption to guarantee absolutely the inalterability of the information in question – in tune with the facilitative, rather than restrictive, objective of EU ecommerce policy. Yet, on the other hand, the term 'durable' itself, as well as the reference to 'future reference', suggests a certain reliability of the record over time – a notion confirmed by the requirement of the 'unchanged reproduction of the information stored'. Thus T&Cs of internet providers would prima facie not be durable, because they can easily be changed by the provider – unless users are given access to relevant historic versions, or are specifically encouraged to print and/or retain an electronic copy of these online sources, or are sent a copy of them by email.[279] This interpretation would also be in line with Art 10(3) of the Electronic Commerce Directive, which simply provides that '[c]ontract terms and general conditions provided to the recipient must be made available in a way that allows him to store and reproduce them'.

## The significance of signatures[280]

Although signatures (like writing) are not a legal requirement for the vast majority of commercial transactions,[281] they are nevertheless commonplace, because they unequivocally indicate (or are in law taken to do so) that that the signer adopts or approves the content of the document, which is its acceptability or its veracity. The purpose of a signature is broadly three-fold:

(1) *Identification and authentication of signatory:* A signature identifies a person and confirms that he or she is who he or she claims to be. So a signature establishes a person's association and personal involvement with the document at a particular time and place with certainty – that is, it provides certainty as to the personal involvement of a person in the act of signing the document.

(2) *Acceptance of the content as it is by the signatory:* A signature confirms that the signer accepts, adopts, or endorses the document as it stands – that is, it is an accurate reflection of what is/was agreed.

Integrity/authenticity of the document/data – It is in this way that the signatory authenticates the data: '. . . the document is the "original" support of the information it contains, in the form it was recorded and without any alteration.'[282] This function relies upon the relative difficulty of altering a document without detection.

---

278 See also Art 4(25) of the Payment Services Directive 2007/64/EC; Art 2(f) of the Distance Marketing Financial Services Directive 2002/65/EC; and Art 2(12) of the Insurance Mediation Directive 2002/92/EC.

279 See also OFT/DTI, *A Guide for Businesses on Distance Selling*, OFT698, 2006, London: HMSO, para 3.10.

280 On electronic signatures, see: UN Commission on International Trade Law (UNCITRAL), *Promoting Confidence in Electronic Commerce: Legal Issues on International Use of Electronic Authentication and Signature Methods*, 2009, Vienna: United Nations; UNCITRAL, *UNCITRAL Model Law on Electronic Signatures with Guide to Enactment*, 2001, Vienna: United Nations, available online at: http://www.uncitral.org/pdf/english/texts/electcom/ml-elecsig-e.pdf; Chris Reed, 'What is a signature?' 2000 (3) JILT, available online at: http://www2.warwick.ac.uk/fac/soc/law/elj/jilt/2000_3/reed/; Law Commission, above; Attorney General of Australia, *Electronic Commerce: Building the Legal Framework – Report of the Electronic Commerce Expert Group to the Attorney-General*, 1998, Canberra: Government of Australia.

281 Exceptions, such as s 4 of the Statute of Frauds 1677, which makes guarantee unenforceable in the absence of writing and signature: see *Mehta v J Pereira Fernandes SA* [2006] EWHC 813 (Ch).

282 UNCITRAL, 2009, above, p 5.

[3]  *Legal intention of signatory:* Finally, because signatures are known to be legally significant,[283] a signature shows the signer's intention to engage in a legally significant act: the signer does not sign unless he or she really means it. A signature thereby also encourages reflection before the act of signing.

These three aspects of a signature bolster the reliability and security of contracts, which makes them useful in the commercial world. As will be seen, these three functions of a signature, fulfilled to varying degrees by different types of signature, also go towards defining them.

## Electronic signatures under common law

What constitutes a signature generally in law? They are defined neither in the statutes that require a signature, nor in the Interpretation Act 1978. Under common law, the paradigm signature would be a person writing by hand his or her full name, that is, a handwritten or manuscript signature. However, 'lesser' signatures have long been accepted, such as an 'X' or a person's initials, as well as non-personalised marks in the form of stamps, or printed or typed names.[284] Common law courts have taken a pragmatic approach to signatures by examining whether the particular mark fulfilled the function of the signature under the particular legislation or contractual provision in question. Thus the legal validity of a signature has not been set in stone, but has been made dependent on the circumstances of the case and the reason for its requirement. An 'X' or stamp would often be a valid signature as long as there was evidence that identified the signatory and showed that he or she intended for the writing or mark to be his or her signature. Broadly, a signature is 'any name or symbol used by a party with the intention of constituting it his signature'.[285]

In light of the functional definition of signatures at common law, various electronic ways of indicating assent seem to satisfy the traditional test of signing. The modern electronic equivalent of 'X' is the click on the 'I Agree', 'I Accept', or similar icon in clickwrap agreements (see above); a printed name at the end of an email or an instant message is no different from a printed or typed name at the end of a paper document, and a scanned manuscript signature at the end of an electronic message is comparable to the traditional stamp.

This is borne out by the case law on the subject. In the employment case of *Hall v Cognos Ltd*,[286] it was held that a term in an employment contract was effectively varied – in accordance with a term requiring a variation to be in writing and signed by the parties – by an email exchange between Hall and his line manager, Keith Schroeder, and Sarah McGoun from personnel. When the latter two signed their emails 'Keith' and 'Sarah', respectively, the signature requirement under the contractual term was satisfied. By the same token, a personal guarantee provided by email in *Mehta v J Pereira Fernandes SA* (2006)[287] was not signed for the purpose of s 4 of the Statute of Frauds 1677, because the sender's name only appeared in the email address and not at the bottom of the text:

> [T]he inclusion of an e mail address in such circumstances is a clear example of the inclusion of a name which is incidental in the sense identified by Lord Westbury in the absence of evidence of a contrary intention. Its appearance divorced from the main body of the text of the message

---

283  Where a signed document is not intended to be legally binding (e.g., a book signed by the author or a signed mediation agreement), the lack of the legal intention arises by virtue of the substance of the document or the transaction, rather than by virtue of the signature.

284  *Phillimore v Barry* (1818) 1 Camp 513 (initals); *Ex p Dryden* (1893) 14 NSWR 77; *Goodman v J Eban LD* [1954] 1 QB 550; *British Estate Investment Society Ltd v Jackson* (HM Inspector of Taxes) [1956] TR 397 (stamping); *Brydges (Town Clerk of Cheltenham) v Dix* (1891) 7 TLR 215 (printing); *Newborne v Sensolid (Great Britain) LD* [1954] 1 QB 45; *Evans v Hoare* [1892] 1 QB 593; and *Leeman v Stocks* [1951] Ch 941 (typewriting).

285  *Alfred E Weber v Dante de Cecco* 1 NY Super 353, 358 (1948).

286  Hull Industrial Tribunal 1803325/97; discussed in Stephen Mason, 'Lawyers and electronic signatures' (2005) July/Aug Internet Newsletter for Lawyers, available online at: http://www.venables.co.uk/n0507signatures.htm

287  [2006] EWHC 813 (Ch); see also *Firstpost Homes Ltd v Johnson* [1995] 1 WLR 1567.

emphasises this to be so. Absent evidence to the contrary, in my view it is not possible to hold that the automatic insertion of an e mail address is, to use Cave J's language, '. . . *intended for a signature* . . .'. To conclude that the automatic insertion of an e mail address in the circumstances I have described constituted a signature for the purposes of Section 4 would I think undermine or potentially undermine what I understand to be the Act's purpose . . .[288]

Similarly, it is questionable whether the automatic inclusion of a signature line in every email should be taken to mean that these emails are signed, rather than to provide contact details for the addressee.[289] These examples highlight that although the functional approach to signatures allows for a range of marks and acts (for example, clicks) to amount to signatures, it is certainly always critical that the signatory is conscious of the mark's or act's symbolic legal significance – as a signature. In that sense, the legal intention function is a necessary attribute – a *sine qua non* – of any signature.[290] Such awareness would not normally be present in respect of browsewrap agreements, which purport to make the act of browsing the equivalence of a signature:

> By using the Services, you, the User, indicate that you understand these Terms and Conditions and intend them to be the legal equivalent of a *signed*, written contract and equally binding, and that you accept such Terms and Conditions and agree to be legally bound by them. If you do not agree to these Terms and Conditions, please discontinue your use of the Services.[291]

Unless the user has knowledge of the symbolic legal effect of visiting the site, his or her conduct in the form of visiting the site lacks the legal intentionality that, by definition, accompanies a signature. In any event, the argument to support the binding effect of the above term is circular: the term is only binding if it is incorporated into the contract and it is only incorporated if it is binding. In any event, asserting that the simple use of a site is equivalent to signing the terms and conditions stretches the ordinary meaning of signature beyond recognition. Certainly, in neither clickwrap nor browsewrap agreements is there any 'mark' or 'marking' to speak of, comparable to stamps, printed, typed, or manuscript signatures,[292] but the same would also apply to digital signatures (discussed below). For many statutory provisions, in which a signature goes hand-in-hand with the requirement of writing or visible equivalent, such as s 4 of the Statute of Frauds 1677, it is doubtful whether these signatures that are neither visible nor personal would be sufficient. And for all of those instances in which a signature is not a legal requirement, little is gained by arguing that the conduct in question equates with a signature rather than what the signature is designed to signify – that is, generally, notice or acceptance of the Terms.

The weakness of the above non-personalised signatures is their failure to authenticate along the lines of a hand-written signature, which provides assurances as to the identity of the signatory and the reliability of the document. In *Bergin v Walsh* (2015)[293] the authenticity of emails was successfully challenged as fraud. Where the authentication functionality of an online contracting method is weak and the alleged signatory's identity is disputed (for example, in cases of identity

---

288 Ibid, [29], emphasis added.
289 Alan L Tyree, 'Electronic signatures' (2008), available online at: http://austlii.edu.au/~alan/electronic-signatures.html
290 See *Jenkins v Gaisford & Thring, In the Goods of Jenkins* (1863) 3 Sw & Tr 93, 164 ER 1208: 'Now whether the mark is made by pen or by some other instrument cannot make any difference . . . [it] was intended to stand for and represent the signature of the testator.' An exception to this rule (driven by pragmatic considerations) was the 'authenticated signature fiction', which allowed unsigned documents to be considered signed if the name appeared in the document prepared by the 'non-signer' and there was evidence that he or she considered it a complete and final document that becomes binding upon the signature of the other party: *Leeman v Stocks* [1951] 1 Ch 941; cf *Firstpost Homes Ltd v Johnson* [1995] 1 WLR 1567.
291 [Emphasis added], available online at: http://www.ecfmg.org/annc/terms.html
292 For references to a mark, see, e.g., *Jenkins*, above, and *Re a Debtor (No 2021 of 1995)* [1996] 2 All ER 345.
293 [2015] IEHC 594; see also *BSkyb Ltd & Anor v HP Enterprise Services UK Ltd (Rev 1)* [2010] EWHC 86.

theft), extrinsic evidence is required to prove it.[294] The equivalence of a handwritten signature that fulfils all three of the above functions of a signature would be satisfied by more sophisticated electronic signatures, such as digital signatures (discussed below), or the much more common forms of online signatures, such as pin numbers or passwords used for online or ATM banking, shopping, or utility or e-government transactions. Other less-prevalent personalised signatures that further minimise the risk of forgeries are biometric signatures based, for example, on fingerprints or retinal patterns, or biodynamic signatures that measure and analyse the physical activity of signing, the pressure applied, the speed, and the stroke order.

That these personalised electronic signatures are prima facie validated like handwritten signatures is implicit in the judgment of *Standard Bank London Ltd v Bank of Tokyo Ltd* (1995)[295] concerning a forerunner of today's sophisticated electronic signatures. In this case, Standard Bank received from the Bank of Tokyo three letters of credit issued by 'tested telexes' (which contain a secret code confirming the authenticity of letters of credit) with a total face value of US$19.8 million. When it later transpired that those telexes had been sent by a fraudster, it was held that Standard Bank was entitled to rely on the telexes, as it in fact had. The Bank of Tokyo was liable for negligent misrepresentation, because the fraud could only have occurred if the Bank was negligent. So, here, the law of negligence tempered the default legal position that a forged signature is a nullity and thus a risk placed on the recipient.[296] Negligence, particularly on the part of the signer, is likely to play a greater role in electronic signatures, such as pin numbers and passwords, because these can be more easily misappropriated than handwritten signatures and, once used by the fraudster, cannot easily be detected by the recipient.[297]

Ultimately, contracting parties who use electronic signatures are free to allocate the risk of any fraudulent or unauthorised use amongst themselves, as they often do. So where, as in the case of digital signatures, the use of the electronic signature between two parties entails reliance on the assurances of a third party, this third party could contractually shift the risk of forgery to the signer and/or the recipient of the signature[298] – subject to the rules discussed in the following section. Also in consumer contracts, as in the case of *Spreadex Ltd v Cochrane* (2012)[299] (discussed above) any terms that seek to shift all liability for unauthorised transactions to the consumer, regardless of his or her negligence, may well be struck down as unfair.[300]

## Electronic signatures and other 'trust services' within the EU

The wide and flexible common law position is, in the context of electronic signatures, complemented by the EU Regulation on Electronic Identification and Trust Services for Electronic Transactions in the Internal Market, known as 'the eIDAS Regulation',[301] which repeals the Electronic Signature Directive.[302] Unlike the latter, the eIDAS Regulation does not just deal with electronic signatures, but also with other forms of so-called 'trust services' (such as electronic seals, electronic time stamping, electronic delivery service, electronic documents admissibility, and website

---

294 There are German cases: *Internet-Versteigerung* (AG Erfurt, 14 September 2001, 28 C 2354/01); *Auktion durch Trojaner* (LG Konstanz, 19 April 2002, 2 O 141/01); *Beweisfragen bei Vertragsschluss in der Internet-Auktion* (OLG Köln, 6 September 2002, 19 U 16/02). Note that the authenticity of a signature is in the offline world rarely routinely checked; cheques and cheque guarantee cards are an example.
295 [1995] CLC 496; [1996] 1 CTLR T-17, discussed in Stephen Mason, 'Electronic signatures explained' (2002) Jan/Feb Internet Newsletter for Lawyers, available online at: http://www.venables.co.uk/n0201signatures.htm
296 *Brook v Hook* (1871) LR 6 Exch 89.
297 See, e.g., pin number case *Job v Halifax plc* (unreported), 4 June 2009, applying s 24 of the Bill of Exchange Act 1882; cf Payment Services Regulations 2009, SI 2009/209, reg 60, implementing Art 59 of the Payment Services Directive 2007/64/EC.
298 For an analogy with cheque guarantee cards, see *First Sport Ltd v Barclays Bank plc* [1993] 3 All ER 789.
299 [2012] EWHC 1290.
300 Ibid, [17]–[20].
301 910/2014. Department for Business, Innovation & Skills, *Electronic Signatures* (September 2014), available online at: https://www.gov.uk/government/uploads/system/uploads/attachment_data/file/356786/bis-14-1072-electronic-signatures-guide.pdf
302 1999/93/EC.

authentication) in Chapter III and with 'electronic identification' systems in Chapter II. The latter systems especially are not just aimed at the commercial world (e.g. banks or the sharing economy, such as Airbnb or Uber), but are also directed at the public sector, catering for the increasing provision of online government services, through the use of e-ID providers, e.g. the Open Identity Exchange UK (OIX UK).[303] These services are invariably advertised as necessary to 'build trust' and address security concerns, such as identity theft and fraud more generally. The focus on the function of the services and system is reflective of the general aim of the Regulation to be 'technology-neutral.'[304]

With respect to both 'trust services' and 'e-IDs', the eIDAS Regulation seeks to set up a framework that facilitates a better functioning internal market in cross-border online services, including public services, and electronic commerce, such as cross-border banking, in the EU. To achieve this, the Regulation takes a two-prong approach: one, encourage technical interoperability[305] and, two, legal mutual recognition of national 'trust services' and 'e-ID' systems. For example, in respect of the latter approach, Art 4 of the Regulation establishes an 'origin rule' similar to that adopted under the Electronic Commerce Directive (discussed above), whereby a trust service provider established in one Member State and compliant with the Regulation, cannot be restricted by another Member State and must 'be permitted to circulate freely in the internal market'.[306] The differences to the Electronic Commerce Directive are, on the one hand, that the principle of regulatory forbearance only extends to the substantive matters covered by the Regulation and, on the other hand, that the Regulation does not impose any obligations on Member States to create qualified 'trust services' in the first place. In that sense, the eIDAS Regulation is facilitatory.

Having said that, considering that it deals with electronic IDs and other methods that generate authenticated personal data and digital footprints, a legitimate concern is that what is currently of a purely facilitatory nature may later be transformed from optional to obligatory usage and then be used for more restrictive purposes (at most extreme, eIDs as a legal pre-requisite for internet usage *per se*). The Regulation shows some recognition of the sensitivity of the matters covered in it in Art 5 which provides that all data processing must be done in the conformity with the Data Protection Directive,[307] and that the use of pseudonyms in electronic transactions must not be prohibited[308] (see Data Protection Chapter). Does this mean that eIDs in electronic transactions, albeit under a pseudonym, can be legally mandated? Recital 33 suggests that identification may indeed be required: 'Provisions on the use of pseudonyms in certificates should not prevent Member States from requiring identification of persons pursuant to Union or national law.' At the moment most commercial providers have authentication systems in place as a matter of commercial expedience, rather than to comply with a legal requirement.[309]

The Regulation deals with electronic signatures in Arts 25 to 34, and distinguishes between two types by reference to their varying legal effect. First, there is the ordinary type – an electronic signature which is defined as 'data in electronic form which is attached to or logically associated with other data in electronic form and which is used by the signatory to sign;'[310]

---

303  http://openidentityexchange.org/. See also, for example, Art 27 which deals with electronic signatures in public services.
304  Recital 27: 'This Regulation should be technology-neutral. The legal effects it grants should be achievable by any technical means provided that the requirements of this Regulation are met.'
305  For example, Art 12.
306  But see also Arts 6, 14, 18 or 25(3).
307  95/46/EC.
308  See also Arts 20(2) and 24(1)(j).
309  But see, e.g., financial institutions which are under 'Know your customer' obligations by virtue of the Money Laundering Regulations 2007.
310  See Art 3(10).

and this type 'shall not be denied legal effect and admissibility as evidence in legal proceedings solely on the grounds that it is in an electronic form or that it does not meet the requirements for qualified electronic signature.'[311] The eIDAS Regulation focuses on the signatory's intention to sign rather than, as the previous Directive, on its authentication functionality.[312] This position is comparable to the common law position and its treatment of stamps, printed signature and the like that do not authenticate the identity of the signatory, but fulfil other functions, most importantly to express legal intentionality. Within this type would appear to be many different forms of electronic actions, including clicking on an Accept button, signing an email message or using a PIN code.

The second type is a 'qualified electronic signature' which is defined as an '*advanced electronic signature that is created by a qualified electronic signature creation device, and which is based on a qualified certificate for electronic signatures*'[313] and legal effect of this type is two-fold: it is treated as the legal equivalent of a handwritten signature (i.e. it authenticates the signatory plus all the other functions) and it attracts mutual recognition in all other Member States.[314] Thus it is for these signatures that the Regulation creates value over and above the existing common law, discussed above. As qualified signatures are defined by reference to 'advanced electronic signatures' the question is what amounts to one of these? Article 26 of the eIDAS Regulation adopts a definition very similar to that of its predecessor and broadly spells out the functions it has to fulfil (which helps to make it technology-neutral and thus future proof):

An advanced electronic signature shall meet the following requirements:

(a)  it is uniquely linked to the signatory;
(b)  it is capable of identifying the signatory;
(c)  it is created using electronic signature creation data that the signatory can, with a high level of confidence, use under his sole control; and
(d)  it is linked to the data signed therewith in such a way that any subsequent change in the data is detectable.

The first three points broadly focus on the signatory to ensure that he or she is who he or she purports to be, the last one addresses the integrity of the data with which the signature is associated.[315] Of course, as the Regulation effectively creates an accreditation regime for electronic signatures, it is not enough that the 'advance electronic signature' has the above functionality but this must be accredited in a specified way. Only once they have gone through the accreditation process, are they treated as manuscript signatures and fall within the mutual recognition regime. The hurdles which are created in a rather convoluted way are that the signature must be created using a '*qualified electronic signature creation device*' (Annex II),[316] be supported by a '*qualified certificate for electronic signatures*' and issued by a '*qualified trust service provider*' (Annex I). Without going into the detail of these requirements, broadly they are designed to ensure the usefulness, accuracy and security of the data in order to protect both the signatory and those relying upon it as backed by the liability regime which the Regulation creates. Under Art 13 liability for damage arising out of a defective signature rests with the (qualified) trust service provider,

---

311  See Art 25(1).
312  European Commission, *Report on the Operation of Directive 1999/93/EC on a Community Framework for Electronic Signatures*, COM(2006)120final, 2006, Brussels: European Commission, para 2.3.2 [emphasis added].
313  See Art 3(12).
314  See Art 25(2) and (3).
315  Note that the Directive explicitly excludes from its scope the 'legal intention function' discussed above.
316  Art 3(22): 'electronic signature creation device' means configured software or hardware used to create an electronic signature.

unless the trust service provider can show that the defect was due to a limitation of its service of which he had his customer duly informed in advance and which would be recognisable by third parties:

Art 13(1)  Without prejudice to paragraph 2, trust service providers shall be liable for damage caused intentionally or negligently to any natural or legal person due to a failure to comply with the obligations under this Regulation.

The burden of proving intention or negligence of a non-qualified trust service provider shall lie with the natural or legal person claiming the damage referred to in the first subparagraph.

The intention or negligence of a qualified trust service provider shall be presumed unless that qualified trust service provider proves that the damage referred to in the first subparagraph occurred without the intention or negligence of that qualified trust service provider.

(2)  Where trust service providers duly inform their customers in advance of the limitations on the use of the services they provide and where those limitations are recognisable to third parties, trust service providers shall not be liable for damages arising from the use of services exceeding the indicated limitations.

## Further reading

Elizabeth Macdonald, 'Incorporation of standard terms in website contracting – clicking 'I Agree'' (2011) 27 Journal of Contract Law 198

Christine Riefa, *Consumer Protection and Online Auction Platforms*, 2015, Ashgate

Chris Reed, 'What is a signature?' 2000 (3) Journal of Information Law and Technology, available online at: http://www2.warwick.ac.uk/fac/soc/law/elj/jilt/2000_3/reed/

Jos Dumortier, Niels Vandezande, 'Critical observations on the proposed Regulation for Electronic Identification and Trust Services for Electronic Transactions in the Internal Market' (26 September 2012) Interdisciplinary Centre for Law and ICT Research Paper 9

# Chapter 7

# Cybercrime
## Fraud and computer misuse

## Introduction

It has been estimated that 3 billion people will be using the internet by 2016 for business, education, pleasure and also crime.[1] The continuing developments in digital technology both in terms of the proliferation of devices and the increased connectivity epitomised by the 'internet of things' is challenging in security terms[2] and so brings advantages not only to the law-abiding but also to criminals; it has been remarked that 'Cybercrime is a growth industry. The returns are great, and the risks are low.'[3] As discussed below there is a wide variety of types of cybercrime – perpetrators may be lone hackers or organised gangs and victims range from the ordinary consumer to large organisations. In November 2014, Sony Pictures Entertainment was the victim of a cyber attack in which a skull appeared on computer screens along with a message threatening to release data 'secrets' if undisclosed demands were not met and which resulted in its entire system being shut down.[4] Other branches of the organisation had previously been targeted and Sony PlayStation has proved particularly vulnerable.[5] These instances were particularly newsworthy, but it is not difficult to find other examples of hacks into the computer systems of large commercial and government organisations with results which can include the theft of large quantities of personal identifying information and/or significant damage to the computer systems involved. At the other end of the scale there can be few computer users who have never been affected by a computer virus. Although hacking and virus attacks continue to occur and cause damage, disruption, and financial loss, the range of subversive activity is far wider than this. Those wishing to cause disruption to computers and computer systems are just as likely to instigate a denial-of-service (DoS) attack or distributed denial-of-service (DDoS) attack, in which the perpetrator sets up a system that will generate a high volume of traffic to the target site, severely impeding normal communications with the site or preventing them altogether. While hacking and virus attacks are unlikely to be confused with legitimate use, the same effects as those produced by DoS attacks can occur quite innocently, making criminalisation more problematic.[6] Unfortunately, cybercrime is clearly very much part of the internet environment and this chapter and the following one will examine the extent to which the law has been able to respond to the issue.

## What is cybercrime?

Given the increased connectivity of us all, many crimes committed rely on internet technology at some level, even if only for communication. Indeed the police in the UK apparently define cybercrime as the use of any computer network for crime,[7] but despite this apparently wide approach, until recently, only offences under the Computer Misuse Act (CMA) were actually recorded as cybercrime for statistical purposes. It may be, however, that more accurate figures will be available in the future as, in 2015, the Office for National Statistics reported that it would be attempting to

---

1 National Audit Office *The UK Cyber Security Strategy: Landscape Review* HC 890 (2013) p 4.

2 See, e.g., Nicole Perlroth, 'Hackers Lurking in Vents and Soda Machines' (2014) *New York Times*, 8 April, p A1, available online at: www.nytimes.com/2014/04/08/technology/the-spy-in-the-soda-machine.html and the comment on this article at http://motherboard.vice.com/read/the-sheer-difficulty-of-securing-the-internet-of-things

3 Center for Strategic and Economic Studies *Net Losses: Estimating the Global Cost of Cybercrime* (Economic impact of cybercrime II), July 2014.

4 www.bbc.co.uk/news/technology-30189029 and for subsequent discussion see, e.g., David E Sanger and Martin Fackler, 'N.S.A. Breached North Korean Networks Before Sony Attack, Officials Say', available online at: www.nytimes.com/2015/01/19/world/asia/nsa-tapped-into-north-korean-networks-before-sony-attack-officials-say.html

5 See, e.g., www.bbc.co.uk/news/technology-13169518; www.bbc.co.uk/news/technology-28925052; www.cnet.com/uk/news/sony-hacked-again-this-time-the-playstation-store/; and www.theguardian.com/technology/2014/dec/26/xbox-live-and-psn-attack-christmas-ruined-for-millions-of-gamers

6 See, e.g., Lilian Edwards, 'Dawn of the death of distributed denial of service: How to kill zombies' (2006) 24 Cardozo Arts & Ent LJ 23, and further discussion at pp 125–127.

7 Home Affairs Committee E-Crime (2013–2014, 70-I) para 6.

include online fraud and other cybercrime incidents in the official crime statistics in order to try and provide a better understanding of the problem. Certainly, as we shall see, CMA offences are only the tip of the iceberg in relation to the totality of cyber criminal activity. Although cybercrime may have become accepted terminology, specific and workable definitions of what it includes have proved notoriously difficult to draft. Although one school of thought might suggest that it is not necessary to delineate a specific category, as we shall see, cybercrime can display some different characteristics from 'traditional' crime and so attempting to define its scope may not be a completely futile exercise. Categorisations could be made in a number of ways. The US Department of Justice describes computer crime as 'any violations of criminal law that involve a knowledge of computer technology and their perpetration, investigation and prosecution'.[8] It suggests that computer crime can be subdivided into three categories in which the computer is the object of the crime, the subject of the crime, or the instrument of the crime.[9] The first of these refers to the theft of the hardware itself and will not be considered further here. The second category refers to criminal activity directed at the integrity of the computer itself or at a computer network, including the internet, and encompasses a range of behaviour that may have no exact parallel outside the computer context. Examples include: hacking; the introduction of malicious software (so-called malware), such as viruses and other damaging software; DoS attacks; and botnets that facilitate the sending of spam and phishing emails, etc. The third category covers those instances in which the computer is used as a tool to facilitate other crimes, such as fraud, identity theft, and also content-based crimes, such as child pornography.[10] In the UK, the Home Office and the Cyber Threat Reduction Board[11] divide cybercrime into three categories; 'pure' online crimes where a digital system is the target as well as the means of attack; 'existing' crimes that have been transformed in scale or form by their use of the internet; and use of the internet to facilitate other traditional crimes such as drug smuggling and people trafficking. An alternative approach divides cybercrime into cyber-dependent and cyber-enabled categories.[12] The former includes offences which can only be committed by using a computer or other ICT while the latter encompasses traditional crimes which can be committed more easily and/or on a wide scale using computers. A further categorisation separates those crimes that can be committed both offline and online, those that deal with content rather than the integrity of the computer systems themselves, and those that have no clear parallel in the offline world.[13]

Despite different methods of classification, references to cybercrime usually indicate some specific, albeit disparate, activities. These include a number of 'traditional' crimes that may be facilitated by the use of computer systems, such as: offences of theft, deception, and fraud; offences related to obscenity and indecency; criminal breaches of copyright arising from intentional distribution and commercial exploitation of copyright works; and criminal damage aimed at the computer system itself. The diverse nature of the criminal activities relating to computer use and misuse was reflected in the Cybercrime Convention,[14] which made provision for acts based on illegal access, illegal interception, data interference, system interference, misuse of devices, computer-related fraud, computer-related forgery, offences related to child pornography, and offences related

---

8 National Institute of Justice, Computer Crime: Criminal Justice Resource Manual 2, 1989, Washington, DC: US Department of Justice; and see also H Marshall Jarrett, Michael W Bailie and Ed Hagan, Prosecuting Computer Crimes, 2015, Washington, DC: Office of Legal Education, available online at: www.justice.gov/sites/default/files/criminal-ccips/legacy/2015/01/14/ccmanual.pdf
9 For an alternative formulation based on the computer as tool, storage device, and victim, see Richard W Downing, 'Shoring up the weakest link: What lawmakers around the world need to consider in developing comprehensive laws to combat cybercrime' (2005) 43 Colum J Transnat'l Law 705.
10 See further discussion in Chapter 8.
11 Part of the Serious Organised Crime Agency (SOCA).
12 See, e.g., Mike McGuire and Samantha Dowling, *Cyber crime: A review of the evidence*, Home Office Research Report 75, Summary of key findings and implications (October 2013), pp 6–12.
13 For another approach, see Anne Flanagan, 'The law and computer crime: Reading the script of reform' (2005) 13 IJLIT 98, 100.
14 Convention on Cybercrime, CETS No 185, available online at: http://conventions.coe.int/Treaty/en/Treaties/Html/185.htm; and see further discussion in Chapter 8.

to copyright and related rights. That these are different in kind, both from each other and from the 'new' offences related to or relying on computer hacking, goes without saying, but together they make up a body that has come to be referred to, however inaccurately, as 'cybercrime' or 'computer crime', and which, in varying degrees, has caused problems for the interpretation and development of the law in this area. This chapter will focus on crimes in which the damage can be measured as economic loss, including computer fraud and hacking while the following chapter will consider content crimes such as the dissemination of obscene and indecent material which present a threat to the social order.

## Victims and perpetrators

Although many different criminal acts might fall within a definition of cybercrime, ascertaining the total extent of such activity and its effect on its victims is no trivial matter. Examples such as those referred to in the introductory paragraph are merely the tip of the iceberg and, in addition, for a variety of reasons, many cybercrimes are never reported. Organisations may not wish to appear vulnerable and fear loss of consumer confidence so, other than in high-profile cases, may prefer to view cyber losses as an inevitable part of the 21st-century business environment. Consumers may be reimbursed by banks and credit card companies and much low level loss is rarely reported, much less investigated. It may thus be necessary 'to aggregate thousands of individually small crimes to build up a picture of the true scale of criminality'.[15]

The costs of recovering from cybercrime can be substantial and include not just any direct financial loss from fraud or theft but also the recovery costs including upgrading cyber security, removing malware and generally restoring the *status quo*. Businesses may suffer losses when systems are down as well as loss of consumer confidence when they are restored. Despite these difficulties, estimates of the extent of cybercrime and the resultant economic loss are attempted. The amounts vary in magnitude but are by no means insignificant. The National Audit Office has suggested that there were 44 million cyber attacks in the UK in 2011 and estimated the annual cost to be between £18 billion and £27 billion.[16] Successive editions of the Norton Report estimated the number of victims of cybercrime at 556 million in 2012 and 378 million in 2013. But this apparent decrease in the number of victims was accompanied by an increase in financial losses; the total estimated cost was US$113 billion in 2013 compared to US$110 in the previous year.[17] In two consecutive reports, the Center for Strategic and Economic Studies estimated that the 'likely annual cost to the global economy from cybercrime is more than $400 billion. A conservative estimate would be $375 billion in losses, while the maximum could be as much as $575 billion. Even the smallest of these figures is more than the national income of most countries . . . '.[18] One UK company apparently lost £800m from a single attack[19] but, despite such losses, few of the biggest cybercriminals have been caught or even identified.

---

15 House of Lords Science and Technology Committee, Fifth Report of Session 2006–07: Personal Internet Security, 2007, London: HMSO, para 7.19, and see also discussion in the preceding paragraphs in the section entitled 'High-volume, Low-denomination Crime'.
16 Ibid, n.1.
17 The Norton Report is an annual research study commissioned by Symantec. See Norton Cybercrime Report (September 2012) available online at: http://now-static.norton.com/now/en/pu/images/Promotions/2012/cybercrimeReport/2012_Norton_ Cybercrime_Report_Master_FINAL_050912.pdf; and Norton Cybercrime Report October 2013 available from www.symantec. com/en/uk/about/news/resources/press_kits/detail.jsp?pkid=norton-report-2013
18 Center for Strategic and Economic Studies, Net Losses: Estimating the Global Cost of Cybercrime (Economic impact of cybercrime II), July 2014. See also James Lewis and Stewart Baker, Center for Strategic and Economic Studies, The Economic Impact of Cybercrime and Cyber-espionage (July 2013).
19 See Tom Whitehead, 'Cyber Crime A Global Threat, MI5 Head Warns' (2012) The Telegraph, June 6, available online at: www.telegraph. co.uk/news/uknews/terrorism-in-the-uk/9354373/Cyber-crimea-global-threat-MI5-head-warns.html

Overall criminal activity appears to be increasing in proportion to the development of computer technology and computer networks and as their use has become ever more ubiquitous. Attacks on computers with a view to mere malicious damage may be less frequent, perhaps because criminals realise that there may be more to gain by more subtle means such as introducing malware that does not actually impair the operation of the computer or network, but instead compromises or removes data stored on it. Card fraud and online identity theft are now arguably two of the fastest-growing computer crimes, facilitated by a combination of phishing and malware.[20] Indeed, the growth and development of the internet and worldwide web has facilitated the transition from computer crime to cybercrime assisted by the growth of peer-to-peer and social networking, organised crime groups on the internet and new types of 'malware'.[21] Whatever form the activity takes, it can be extremely costly for victims both as a result of remedying the disruption caused by damage and loss of data, and because of direct pecuniary loss due to fraud.

## Who are the victims?

The characteristics of victims are probably more heterogeneous than those of offenders and surveys apparently demonstrate that 'individual cyber crime victimization is significantly higher than for "conventional" crime forms'.[22] Both individuals and organisations, large and small, public and private, can be victims of cybercrime. In principle, anyone who uses the internet, i.e. several billion of us, can be at risk from destructive malware; large organisations may be more frequent targets for hacking but individual users are not immune. Although there is significant underreporting of cybercrime, reports of all types of negative online incidents by individuals suggest that those in younger age brackets are more likely to be victims, or at least report that fact, and that men are more likely to be affected than women.[23] Many users may now be alert to the huge variety of online scams and frauds, but in response perpetrators have become ever more sophisticated. Refined techniques such as 'spear phishing' which targets the users or members of specific organisations are far more plausible to the recipient and such emails often appear *bona fide*, even to the most vigilant, and are thus more successful at duping the victim than mass phishing ventures.

There is some evidence that users of social media sites are more likely to fall victim to scams disseminated in those mediums as they are lulled into a false sense of security by the 'feel' of a supportive online community of 'friends'. Users of mobile devices and unsecured or public WiFi are also more vulnerable to cybercrime.[24] Fairly elementary security measures including the use of up-to-date anti-virus software and secure payment sites can protect against certain types of cybercrime, but although this may be fairly standard for users of PCs and laptops, the evidence is that the same tools are less frequently used by owners of smartphones and tablets[25] – often, of course, the same people.

## Who are the perpetrators?

An explanation for the continued increase in cyber criminality is difficult not only because of the problems in defining appropriate offences, but also because of a lack of homogeneity coupled with continued transmutation.[26] As early as 1990, Wasik pointed out that such factors made 'any

---

20 For a summary of the latest malicious activity, see, e.g., Symantec, 2016 *Internet Security Report* available online at: https://www.symantec.com/security-center/threat-report

21 See Terence Berg, 'The changing face of cybercrime' (2007) 86 Mich BJ 18.

22 Home Affairs Committee E-Crime (2013–2014, 70-I).

23 See HORR 75, p 17–8; and the 2013 Norton Report, p 3.

24 2013 Norton Report.

25 See HORR75, p 19 and the 2013 Norton Report, p 4.

26 See also Charlotte Decker, 'Cyber Crime 2.0: An argument to update the United States Criminal Code to reflect the changing nature of cyber crime' (2008) 81 S Cal L Rev 959.

monolithic explanation of this phenomenon quite implausible'.[27] No significantly different explanations have been advanced subsequently; indeed the current diversification of criminal activities relating to computers and computer networks suggests that a 'monolithic explanation' may be even less feasible now than it was then. A coherent explanation is also made elusive by the under-reporting already mentioned and the fact that computer crime statistics are not comprehensive. There appears to have been relatively little discussion amongst criminologists about the nature of any differences between patterns of offending and the characteristics of offenders on and offline, and commentary thus far has been inconclusive. There has been rather more discussion about the nature of the computer hacker than the characteristics of the computer criminal. Although 'hacking' might be equated with illicit behaviour in common parlance, this is neither the sense in which it originated, nor the way in which it is commonly understood in the computing fraternity.[28] Nonetheless the characteristics that are popularly supposed to define computer hackers[29] have also been identified by Rogers as those that most often attach to computer criminals: namely, male, young, and unattached.[30] A further study also suggested that introversion might be more common amongst those engaging in unlawful behaviour on computer networks.[31] The extent to which this assists in the analysis is uncertain since these characteristics are also frequently shared by perpetrators of street crime, but one aspect that differentiates the two, at least anecdotally, is that it appears that, in a number of cases, convicted hackers not only eventually become law-abiding citizens, but also actually use their knowledge and expertise to improve computer security systems or even to assist with law enforcement.[32]

Yar points out that the media and popular fiction frequently portray hackers as having abnormal intelligence and skill and can thus use 'knowledge and techniques far beyond the comprehension of normal people to achieve the most awe-inspiring control over computerized systems.'[33] Although there may have originally been a grain of truth in this perception, such technical skills are no longer a prerequisite for the successful cybercriminal. As software applications have become more used-friendly, and more and more people are computer literate, so it has become easier to engage in criminal activity. Tools to hack and crack, launch DoS attacks and create viruses and worms are readily available to download. In common with other computer applications, these apparently come with Windows-style interfaces, drop down menus and help guides so that they can be used not just by the computer elite, but by any average computer user.[34] Cybercrime is thus no longer restricted to the technologically savvy.

It should not however be thought that cybercrime is always perpetrated by a lone offender. Although many hackers operate alone, hackers have also collaborated and colluded and hacker groups and organisations may either share knowledge or act in concert.[35] Similarly frauds and

---

27 M Wasik, *Crime and the Computer*, 1990, Oxford: Clarendon, p 33.

28 See, e.g., http://encyclopedia2.thefreedictionary.com/Computer+hacking

29 See, e.g., Debora Halbert, 'Discourses of danger and the computer hacker' (1997) 13 The Information Society 361, 363.

30 See Marcus K Rogers, 'A social learning theory and moral disengagement analysis of criminal computer behavior: An exploratory study' (2001), Unpublished PhD Thesis, Winnipeg, MB: University of Manitoba, Table 1, p 86. But see also Tim Jordan and Paul Taylor, 'A sociology of hackers' (1998) 46 Sociological Review 758, suggesting that, notwithstanding such characteristics, hackers do associate within specific social groups and communities.

31 See Marcus K Rogers, Kathryn Seigfried, and Kirti Tidkea, 'Self-reported computer criminal behavior: A psychological analysis' (2006) 3S Digital Investigation S 116.

32 Probably the best example in the UK is Robert Schifreen. See the discussion of *R v Gold and Schifreen* [1988] AC 1063, [1988] Crim LR 437 (HL) below, and compare Robert Schifreen, 'The internet: Where did IT all go wrong?' (2008) 5(2) ScriptEd 419. Gary McKinnon, whose case is discussed on p 297 also now apparently uses his skills in pursuit of a legitimate business, see www.theguardian.com/world/2014/jul/31/gary-mckinnon-hacking-ill-father-glasgow-extradition-us

33 Majid Yar, *Cybercrime and Society*, 2nd edn, 2013, Sage, p 32.

34 *Ibid*, p 33. See, also, the facts of *DPP v Lennon* (2005) unreported, 2 November, Wimbledon Youth Court, discussed below at 295 Byron Acohido, 'DIY cybercrime kits power growth in net phishing attacks' (2010) *USA Today*, 18 January, available online at: http://usatoday30.usatoday.com/tech/news/computersecurity/2010-01-17-internet-scams-phishing_N.htm; and the facts of *Wellman* [2007] EWCA Crim 2874 who ran a website dealing in software to facilitate phishing. For further discussion of markets in illicit software see, e.g., TJ Holt, 'Examining the forces shaping cybercrime markets online' (2013) 31 Soc Sci Comp Rev 165.

35 See, e.g., the facts of *Bedworth* discussed below at p 297 for an early example.

scams may be perpetrated by individuals acting alone but, in addition, there are extensive opportunities for white collar and financial crime because the internet 'allows anonymous contact with a large pool of victims without incurring significant costs.'[36] Organised crime groups on the internet have apparently created a thriving 'underground economy' with a turnover of millions of dollars.[37]

## Rationales for cybercrime

The impossibility of a 'monolithic' explanation for cybercrime extends also to a discussion of the rationales and reasons for offending. While it may be easy to identify the motivation for scams and frauds, there are many different motivations for hacking and these may have a bearing on the perceived deviancy of the behaviour. At one level hackers, whether as individuals or in groups, may want to prove that they can circumvent security measures, treating the process as akin to solving a puzzle. Others may do this in order to damage computer systems,[38] either as an act of apparent vandalism or as an insider with a grudge against the organisation and others may have a political motive, the so-called 'hactivists' and, of course, at the top of the pyramid[39] are the ones most feared by governments, the cyberterrorists.[40] A number of hacking groups self-identify as 'hactivists' and see themselves as part of a long tradition of political protest and civil disobedience, predicated on the view that 'the internet can enable mass, participatory, possibly illegal action in a way the world has never seen before'.[41] An example is the hacking group 'Anonymous', whose members appear in public wearing Guy Fawkes masks, and whose activities are well publicised both by themselves and by reporting in the media.[42] Although they allege themselves to be motivated by political and even altruistic ideals, those affected may not see it in that way and for governments, as is sometimes the case offline, there may be a fine line between protest and more serious and even terrorist acts.[43] Other groups do not profess to occupy any moral high ground. An example is the 'Lizard Squad' which claimed responsibility for the Sony Playstation hack referred to in the introduction.[44] The actions of these different groups have resulted, not only in damage to their victims but also, because of their different motivations, in clashes between them – at the time of writing, Anonymous is reported as having launched a DDoS attack on the Lizard Squad.[45]

In terms of explanations for such criminal behaviour, Capeller, for example, remarks that 'a revision of criminological patterns is necessary as the criminological universe is incapable of explaining the new forms of criminality and deviance which make up cybercrime',[46] whereas Grabosky takes the opposite line and suggests that '[criminological theories] derived initially to explain conventional "street" crime [are] equally applicable to crime in cyberspace'.[47] Capeller's analysis of deviant behaviour made possible on the internet to an extent parallels the analysis above in that she distinguishes between computers as a 'support' for criminal activity – that is, as providing a tool to engage in deviant behaviour – and also as an 'environment' in which criminal activity is increasing. She identifies the evolution, noted above, from 'an occasionally provocative deviance,

---

36 Gerald Cliff and Christian Desilets, 'White Collar Crime: What is it and where is it going?' (2014) Notre Dame J L Ethics & Pub Pol'y 481, 505.
37 See also Rob Thomas and Jerry Martin, 'The underground economy: Priceless' (2006), available online at: www.team-cymru.org/ReadingRoom/Articles/
38 So-called cyberpunks in the nomenclature set out in HORR75, p 24.
39 See discussion in HORR75, pp 24–5.
40 See further Yar, above, p 50ff.
41 See www.theguardian.com/technology/2012/sep/08/anonymous-behind-masks-cyber-insurgents
42 See further, www.cbc.ca/news/canada/from-anonymous-to-shuttered-websites-the-evolution-of-online-protest-1.1134948; and www.newyorker.com/magazine/2014/09/08/masked-avengers
43 See www.theguardian.com/us-news/2015/feb/02/fbi-anonymous-hacktivist-jeremy-hammond-terrorism-watchlist
44 See www.bbc.co.uk/newsbeat/30306319. For further illustrations of the activities of hacking groups see, e.g., Sally Ramage and Edward Stefan Wheeler, 'The criminal offence of computer hacking' (2011) 203 Crim. Law. 3.
45 See www.techworm.net/2015/01/anonymous-vs-lizard-squad-anonymous-down-lizard-squad-website-twitter.html
46 See Wanda Capeller, 'Not such a neat net: Some comments on virtual criminality' (2001) 10 Social and Legal Studies 230.
47 See Peter Grabosky, 'Virtual criminality: Old wine in new bottles?' (2001) 10 Social and Legal Studies 243, 248.

committed within the electronic computer system, towards a more and more sophisticated virtual criminality',[48] and suggests that this marks a move from behaviour that could be termed merely 'problematic' to that which is genuinely criminal. This parallels the observation that computer crime is no longer the sole prerogative of the lone computer criminal, if indeed it ever was, but that such behaviour is now eclipsed by criminality, whether organised or not, which is motivated by the promise of financial gain. Grabosky agrees that computer crime is proliferating in both variety and extent, but is of the view that the human motivation to criminal activity remains the same and is independent of the technology: '. . . the thrill of deception characterized the insertion of the original Trojan Horse no less than did the creation of its digital descendants.'[49]

Debate and theorising from both a legal and a criminological perspective will clearly continue as to the causes and explanations of computer crime and cybercrime,[50] but in whatever way the debate evolves, it is clear that global computer networks have created an environment that provides fertile ground for criminal behaviour both old and new, and the phenomenon of cybercrime has become a permanent feature of the internet. Whatever the origin and type of behaviour at issue, it is clear that the law has had to respond to these activities, and it has done so with varying degrees of consistency and success. This chapter, and the following one, will consider the response of the law and will draw conclusions as to its effectiveness.

## Computer fraud

Consumer fraud in all its manifestations is the most prevalent of cybercrimes[51] and online frauds and scams may have cost consumers in the UK over £670 million in 2013/14.[52] As long ago as 1985, the Audit Commission defined computer fraud as 'Any fraudulent behaviour connected with computerisation by which someone intends to gain dishonest advantage'.[53] As computer technology has advanced, the number of ways of defrauding consumers as well as stealing from large organisations has increased and has become an extremely lucrative activity; the financial rewards are great whereas the likelihood of being apprehended is remote as it has been suggested that although 'fraud and e-crime is going up, the capability of the country to address it is going down'.[54] In the UK, recommendations in the Attorney General's *Fraud Review*[55] culminated in the establishment of a National Fraud Strategic Authority on 1 October 2008, which was followed by publication of the first *National Fraud Strategy*[56] which acknowledges the power of the technology both to exploit large numbers of victims at low cost and to operate within sophisticated global markets that cross national borders.[57]

Fraudulent schemes are intended to create some pecuniary benefit for the perpetrators or to relieve them of a financial burden and there are now a variety of ways in which consumers can be defrauded.[58] These include online banking and credit card frauds, fraudulent sales via legitimate retail sites and online auctions or completely bogus websites, mass scams to raise money in

---

48 Capeller, above, p 235.

49 Grabosky, above, p 248.

50 See, e.g., Choi, Kyung-Schick, *Risk factors in Computer Crime Victimisation*, 2010, LFB Scholarly Publishing, ch 2.

51 See, e.g., 'British Crime Survey reveals extent of fraud and cyber crime in England and Wales' available online at: http://www.actionfraud.police.uk/news/british-crime-survey-reveals-extent-of-fraud-and-cyber-crime-in-sngland-and-wales-oct15

52 See, e.g., www.thisismoney.co.uk/money/news/article-2801328/top-ten-online-scams-fraudsters-stole-victim-s-money-conned-facebook-friends-too.html

53 Audit Commission, Computer Fraud Survey, 1985, London: HMSO, p 9.

54 Home Affairs Committee E-Crime (2013–2014, 70-I), para 24.

55 Office of the Attorney General, *Fraud Review: Final Report*, 2006, London: HMSO.

56 National Fraud Strategic Authority, *The National Fraud Strategy: A New Approach to Combating Fraud*, 2009, London: HMSO.

57 Ibid, p 29.

58 For greater detail than is possible here see, e.g., Ibid Home Office Research Report 75, ch 2. See also Neil MacEwan, 'A tricky situation: deception in cyberspace' (2013) 77 J Crim L 417, 418–425.

response to various 'sob stories' in which individuals are targeted by email or on social networking sites. A typical phishing scam involves setting up a website that has the appearance of a legitimate website, usually a bank or other financial institution. Phishing emails are then sent to recipients advising them of some security issue with their account and requiring them to visit the spoof website to confirm their account details, provide passwords, etc. Pharming, on the other hand, redirects users from the legitimate site that they were intending to access to a spoof site, which may appear identical to the intended site.[59] Both of these are very efficient ways of harvesting personal identifying information and security information including passwords and account information. Many phishing and pharming emails are sent automatically using a botnet; a network of thousands or even millions of computers, often ordinary home PCs, set up by installing malware on the target computers. The resultant network is controlled by a 'master computer' and provides a very efficient method of disseminating phishing and pharming emails, launching DoS attacks and distributing damaging malware. They can install 'scareware' which can lead to consumers parting with money in order to rid their PCs of non-existent viruses and facilitate many other scams. As an example, MacEwan reports that as a result of a court order obtained by Microsoft, a botnet was closed down which obtained US\$1 m per year.[60] In 2015 it was reported that the Dridex virus could be responsible for worldwide losses of US\$100m from personal bank accounts. Computers become infected with the virus by opening an attachment in an email. The virus then recorded login and password details used to access internet banking services allowing the perpetrators to take money from the accounts.[61] Many of these activities are particularly insidious both because individuals may not be immediately aware that the security of their computer has been compromised, and also because many of these scams arise from what may appear to be legitimate messages at first sight.

## Computer fraud: The legal response

How has the law responded to the issue of computer fraud? In its first consideration of the problem, the Law Commission concluded that, although the nature of computer technology might complicate matters, existing offences were capable, in principle, of application to cases of computer fraud.[62] There were, however, problems with offences which relied on proof of deception, such as the provisions of s 15 of the Theft Act 1968.[63]

As summarised by Buckley J in *Re London and Globe Finance Corp Ltd*,[64] deception relates to the state of a person's mind. In early cases of fraud facilitated by computer such as *R v Thompson*,[65] the court was able to find a human mind that was deceived but it was clear that in cases where the fraud was carried out without any direct communication or intervention by humans, the application of certain offences under the Theft Act 1968 would inevitably, at some point, require wrestling with the thorny question of whether a machine (that is, a computer) could be deceived. Although this lacuna was recognised by the Law Commission Reports of both Scotland and England and Wales,[66] the view was that such occasions would be rare. Consequently no action was taken until amendments were eventually made to the Theft Act as a result of the decision of the House of Lords in *R v Preddy*.[67] This case arose as a result of false statements made to obtain mortgage advances that were credited electronically, leading to a charge of obtaining property by deception. Although the

---

59 For more information about phishing and pharming see, e.g., Scot M Graydon, 'Phishing and pharming: The new evolution of identity theft' (2006) 60 Consumer Fin LQR 335.

60 MacEwan, above, p 419.

61 Vikram Dodd, 'Cyber-attack warning after millions stolen from UK bank accounts' 13 October 2015, available online at: www. theguardian.com/technology/2015/oct/13/nca-in-safety-warning-after-millions-stolen-from-uk-bank-accounts

62 Law Commission, Report on Computer Misuse, Cm 819, 1989, London: HMSO.

63 Now repealed by the Fraud Act 2006.

64 [1903] 1 Ch 728, 732.

65 [1984] 1 WLR 962.

66 Law Commission, Reforming the Present Law: Hacking, Working Paper No 110, 1988, London: HMSO, paras 2.2–2.7.

67 [1996] AC 815.

Theft (Amendment) Act 1996, introduced new ss 15A and 24A into the Theft Act 1968, creating offences of obtaining a money transfer by deception and dishonestly obtaining a wrongful credit, there was no comprehensive overhaul of the legislation, which could have taken into account the difficulties with the concept of deception and computerised accounting methods. The result was that there still appeared likely to be a range of conduct that could result in an acquittal on a charge based on deception, and which might not fit comfortably into any of the other offences in the Theft Act 1968.

As more and more transactions could be, and were being, instigated without human input or intervention, the time was clearly ripe for a change in the law. As Chapman had pointed out: 'If it is essential that criminal offences attach liability to the wrong conduct itself, rather than to some peripheral activity associated with the same, then it is equally important to identify accurately the conduct that attracts moral obloquy.'[68] This was the situation when the Law Commission returned to the issue of computer fraud as part of a more general consideration of the law of fraud at the end of the 1990s.[69] The consequent report[70] summed up the difficulties surrounding the issues related to deceiving a machine, pointing out that, as the use of the internet expanded, the 'gap in the law will be increasingly indefensible'.[71] The report concluded that the problem should be tackled 'head on'[72] and new offences created that did not depend on deception, but instead on dishonesty.[73] This proposal was qualified by two provisos that 'it should not be possible to commit the offence by omission alone'[74] and that 'the offence could be committed only where the dishonesty lies in an intent not to pay for the service'.[75]

As a response to the Law Commission's proposals, the Home Office responded by issuing a Consultation Paper seeking views on the proposal to 'create a general offence of fraud with [three] different ways of committing it'.[76] The outcome was the Fraud Act 2006, which has made significant changes to this area of the law including repealing the amendments introduced as a result of the decision in Preddy.[77]

Although, for the purposes of this discussion, we shall be concentrating only on those changes in the law that are relevant to computer fraud, the Fraud Act 2006 has made sweeping changes to the law of fraud in its entirety. It completely repeals the offences based on deception in the Theft Acts of 1968 and 1978 and replaces them with a single fraud offence that can be committed in three specific ways – namely: fraud by false representation (s 2); fraud by failing to disclose information (s 3); and fraud by abuse of position (s 5). As Ormerod has pointed out, 'it is worth emphasising how dramatic is the shift from a result-based deception to a conduct-based representation offence'.[78]

The 2006 Act was generally very well received; Lord Lloyd described the Bill as 'one of the best Bills to come out of the Home Office for many a long year',[79] and Spencer suggested that it had been 'drafted with admirable clarity'.[80] Unlike cases based on deception in which a crucial

---

68 M Chapman, 'Can a computer be deceived? Dishonesty offences and electronic transfer of funds' (2000) 64 J Crim L 89, 96.
69 Law Commission, Legislating the Criminal Code: Fraud and Deception, Consultation Paper No 155, 1999, London: HMSO.
70 Law Commission, Fraud, Law Com No 276, Cm 5560, 2002, London: HMSO.
71 Ibid, para 3.35.
72 Ibid, para 8.4.
73 Ibid, para 8.8.
74 Ibid, para 8.11.
75 Ibid, para 8.12.
76 Home Office, Fraud Law Reform: Consultation on Proposals for Legislation, 2004, London: HMSO. See also discussion in GR Sullivan, 'Fraud: The latest Law Commission proposals' (2003) J Crim L 139.
77 After the Law Commission report, but before legislative action, it was reiterated in Re Holmes [2004] EWHC 2020, [12], in relation to the new s 15A, that it remained the position that it was not possible in law to deceive a machine.
78 David Ormerod, 'The Fraud Act 2006: Criminalising lying' [2007] Crim L Rev 193, 196. This article provides a general assessment of the provisions of the Fraud Act; see also Carol Withey, 'The Fraud Act 2006: Some early observations and comparisons with the former law' (2007) 71 J Crim L 220.
79 Hansard, 22 June 2005, col 1664.
80 JR Spencer, 'The drafting of criminal legislation: Need it be so impenetrable?' (2008) 67 CLJ 585.

part of the case rested on the state of mind of the victim, fraud under the new s 2 is complete on making the false representation, independently of whether or not anyone is actually taken in by the scam. This section therefore should allow phishers to be prosecuted even if there is no identifiable victim, and it was certainly the intention that s 2 was drafted sufficiently widely to deal with cases of phishing.[81] In the absence of this provision, it is not clear that the mere act of phishing would be caught under existing provisions. The original Computer Misuse Act 1990 (CMA) made it an offence to cause an unauthorised modification to computer material[82] – but it is a moot point whether the receipt of a phishing email could be categorised in this way. The High Court in Re Yarimaka was of the view that a 'spoofing' email, which, like a phishing email, purports to come from one source, but actually comes from another, could be a breach of the CMA because 'if a computer is caused to record information which shows that it came from one person, when it in fact came from someone else, that manifestly affects its reliability'.[83] However, the Court of Appeal in Lennon was not entirely persuaded that this would always be the case.[84]

Section 2, together with s 7 of the Act, which makes it an offence to make, adapt, supply, or offer to supply any article, including software,[85] knowing that it is designed or adapted for use in connection with fraud, or intending for it to be used in this way, certainly seems to augment the prosecutor's armoury in relation to cybercrime. It remains to be seen how juries will react to prosecutions in which actual victims are not identified, or how this fact might be reflected in sentencing. As yet, no cases have reached the higher courts on the substantive issues relating to phishing and similar frauds, but appeals against sentence provide details of some of the situations in which these provisions have been applied.[86] Although overall, it probably makes more sense to cover actions which are widely perceived to be fraudulent in the Fraud Act rather than in the Computer Misuse Act; if a general view is to be obtained as to the efficacy of the legal provisions in dealing with this type of cybercrime it would be useful if cases involving phishing for example were recorded not just as breaches of the Fraud Act but as having a 'cyber' element. In contrast, in the USA, a number of states have passed specific legislation to deal with the problem of phishing,[87] although it is also possible to use the generic offences of wire fraud and mail fraud.[88] Although the cases are not numerous, some have resulted in significant sentences; in 2011 the head of an international phishing scheme was sentenced by the District Court of California to 11 years' imprisonment on charges of bank and wire fraud, computer fraud identity theft and money laundering.[89]

Notwithstanding that s 2 of the Fraud Act removes the uncertainties which might arise in prosecuting fraud cases in which it was difficult to identify a human mind which had been deceived, the fact remains that deception of internet users is still a significant part of the operation of online fraud and scams. Few of the examples of the scams listed above would succeed if those on the receiving end did not believe that the messages and the instructions contained within them were genuine. Although there may be clever technology involved, much of this is aimed at exploiting the human

---

81 Fraud Act 2006, Explanatory Notes, para 16, and see discussion in Section 2 of Anne Savirimuthu and Joseph Savirimuthu, 'Identity theft and systems theory: The Fraud Act 2006 in perspective' (2007) 4(4) SCRIPTed 436, available online at: http://www2.law.ed.ac.uk/ahrc/script-ed/vol4-4/savirimuthu.asp

82 See discussion below at p 290.

83 [2002] EWHC 589 Admin, [2002] Crim LR 648, [18]. See also discussion in Maureen Johnson and Kevin M Rogers, 'The Fraud Act 2006: The e-crime prosecutor's champion or the creator of a new inchoate offence?' (2007) 21 Int Rev LCT 295.

84 [2006] EWHC 1201 (Admin), [12].

85 Fraud Act 2006, s 8.

86 See, e.g., R v Wellman [2007] EWCA Crim 2874; R v Jabeth and Babatunde [2014] EWCA Crim 476; and R v Agrigoroaie (2015), unreported, 21 January, CA Crim.

87 See, e.g., discussion in Jasmine E McNealy, 'Angling for phishers: Legislative responses to deceptive e-mail' (2008) 13 Comm L & Pol'y 275.

88 These offences are also used in cases of internet auction fraud as discussed below at p 282.

89 US v Lucas 539 Fed.Appx. 826 (9th Cir 2013) where Lucas was one of those apprehended following the FBI operation 'Phish Phry'; see www.fbi.gov/news/stories/2009/october/phishphry_100709. For further details of the apparent outcomes see, e.g., www.forbes.com/sites/billsinger/2012/05/15/feds-catch-their-illegal-limit-in-operation-phish-phry/; and http://garwarner.blogspot.co.uk/2012/05/nichole-michelle-merzi-of-operation.html

mind.[90] This apparent gullibility has led some to suggest that there should be a greater focus on placing at least some of the responsibility on the individuals who are affected by these activities. Depending on the precise circumstances, banks and credit card companies will reimburse or compensate victims of banking and card fraud and strict conditions governing this procedure are, arguably, best compared with homeowners who are denied insurance if they leave their homes insecure and are burgled. The reality online, as well as offline, is that both approaches may be necessary and will have a part to play if the level of computer fraud and other cybercrime is to be reduced.

## A specific example – internet auction fraud

The online auction phenomenon began in 1995 with the establishment of ebay.com, and has since expanded dramatically. Although eBay is by far the most high-profile internet auction site and, according to its website, the total worth of goods sold on eBay was US$255 billion in 2014,[91] it is not the only such site and the number of providers has proliferated, as a simple web search will confirm.[92] Although there are many satisfied users of internet auction sites, they also provide an environment in which fraudulent activities can flourish and provide some of the most frequent complaints of monetary loss via computer networks. As Gray J remarked in *Anderson and Rice*: 'Internet fraud, and more particularly eBay internet fraud, is relatively easy to commit. It can, and in this case did, affect a large number of individuals.'[93]

Most internet auction sites distance themselves from the actual transaction process and explicitly state that they should not be treated as traditional auctions.[94] The validity of such statements has been doubted by Harvey and Meisel, who suggest that it is at least arguable that they act as auctioneers in some ways if, for example, they charge a fee and/or commission on sales, provide advice to buyers and sellers, and offer dispute resolution procedures, etc.[95] Certainly, to an outsider, a typical internet auction has obvious similarities with a traditional auction, in which the items are offered for sale and potential buyers make bids, the sale being concluded with the person who has offered the highest bid at the predetermined time when bidding is concluded (analogous to the fall of the hammer). The website can therefore be likened to the sale room, but without providing the chance to see or examine the goods; the bidder must act purely in response to the details and description provided on the website. With the exception of the case in which the website operates as a business providing the merchandise, the auction site will facilitate consumer-to-consumer (C2C) transactions so that, when the auction is over and a bid has been accepted, the seller deals directly with the buyer in relation to payment and delivery. Such a system provides much scope for the less-than-honest buyer or seller.[96] There is considerable scope for fraudulent activity, which may include auctioning of intentionally substandard goods,[97] or even fictitious goods,[98] or operating illicit bidding arrangements.

What is the best method of regulating these activities? Can the existing law be applied satisfactorily? A number of the problem issues are more accurately and appropriately analysed in contractual terms, but the discussion in this chapter will be confined to those areas in which the criminal

---

90  See, e.g., Neil MacEwan, 'A trick situation: deception in cyberspace' (2013) 77 J Crim L 417.

91  See www.ebayinc.com/in_the_news/story/ebay-inc-reports-fourth-quarter-and-full-year-results

92  See, e.g., www.auctionlotwatch.co.uk/auction.html

93  See *R v Anderson and Rice* [2005] EWCA Crim 3581, [21].

94  See eBay's current user agreement, valid from 15 September 2014, contains the following text: 'eBay is a marketplace that allows users to offer, sell and buy just about anything . . . The contract for the sale is directly between buyer and seller. eBay is not a traditional auctioneer.'.

95  Brian Harvey and Franklin Meisel, *Auctions Law and Practice*, 3rd edn, 2006, Oxford: Oxford University Press, p 17.

96  For a comprehensive summary of the possibilities, see, e.g., MR Albert, 'E-buyer beware: Why online auction fraud should be regulated' (2002) 39 Am Bus LJ 575; Dara Chevlin, 'Schemes and scams: Auction fraud and the culpability of host auction web sites' (2005) 18 Loy Consumer L Rev 223; Mary M Calkins, Alexei Nikitov, and Vernon Richardson, 'Mineshafts on Treasure Island: A relief map of the eBay fraud landscape' (2007) 8 U Pitt J Tech L & Pol'y 1.

97  See, e.g., the facts of *US v ajdik* 292 F 3d 555 (7th Cir 2002).

98  See, e.g., the facts of *R v Anderson and Rice* [2005] EWCA Crim 3581.

law does, may have, or perhaps should have, a role to play. Many jurisdictions already have laws that govern the conduct of auctions and/or which create offences in certain situations of fraudulent dealing. Can these be applied directly or by analogy? In a study focused mainly on business auctions online, rather than the consumer interactions that are the subject of this section, Ramberg points out, with some specific examples, that jurisdictional difficulties make the regulation of internet marketplaces by national legislatures problematic, and that this is just as much an issue in relation to illicit and fraudulent behaviour as to more general commercial activities.[99]

However, that is not to say that there is no pre-existing law[100] that might be capable of application. Conventional auctions are an old, established method for the sale of goods, and as such are the subject of a well-developed body of law, in addition to the generic offences now provided in the Fraud Act 2006. The first issue to consider is the extent to which this existing law might be applicable and suitable to online and internet auctions. There is no authoritative or comprehensive definition of an 'auction' in English law, but the essential element is generally agreed to be sale to the highest bidder in a public competition.[101] There are a number of different types of auction. Arguably, the most common model is the so-called 'English', or 'ascending bid' auction, but there are a number of other possible variants;[102] the one that most closely represents the online situation is a now-obsolete form in conventional auction houses in which a time limit is placed on the bidding, traditionally by the burning of a candle or the use of another timing device. One notable difference between an internet auction and a traditional auction is the absence of an auctioneer. This is a significant distinguishing feature because, in a conventional auction, the role of the auctioneer is subject to a number of legal controls.[103] The auctioneer is technically an agent of the seller, but will have duties and responsibilities in relation to both parties to the sale; these could provide some form of legal remedy if similar improper actions to those that are possible on online auction sites were to occur in a conventional auction.

The very nature of a sale by auction lends itself to fraudulent activity by rigging the bidding. Sellers can arrange to inflate the bidding artificially either alone, or in collusion with others, making bids on their own items. This is sometimes referred to, especially in the USA, as 'shill bidding'. Unscrupulous buyers, on the other hand, either alone or in collusion with others, can place multiple bids of differing values for an item, some of which will be high to deter other potential purchasers – a practice sometimes referred to as 'bid shielding'. In the final minutes of the auction, the buyer then removes all of the high bids leaving only their own low bid at which the item must be sold. Engaging in such activities can be much easier on internet auction sites than in a traditional sales room. A detailed consideration of the law relating to bidding is beyond the scope of this chapter, but, in many jurisdictions, criminal sanctions can be invoked in relation to certain illicit bidding arrangements. In commercial terms in the UK, the Sale of Goods Act 1979, s 57(4), generally proscribes bidding on behalf of the seller and s 57(5) goes on to provide that any such sale may be treated as fraudulent by the buyer. Further, certain types of collusion between bidders are regulated by the Auctions (Bidding Agreements) Act 1927, as amended by the Auctions (Bidding Agreements) Act 1969. The 1927 Act, as amended, is generally aimed at dealers who contrive to obtain goods on a low bid by offering a consideration, in some form, to a bidder in return for abstention from bidding. In particular, s 1(1) creates an offence in the case that 'any dealer agrees to give, or gives, or offers any

---

99 Christina Ramberg, *Internet Marketplaces: The Law of Auctions and Exchanges Online*, 2002, Oxford: Oxford University Press, p 27.
100 In relevant cases the provisions of the Fraud Act 2006 discussed above can be applied, see e.g., www.theguardian.com/money/2007/aug/22/crime.scamsandfraud; and R v Curren [2013] EWCA Crim 1477.
101 See, e.g., Harvey and Meisel, above.
102 See, e.g., *ibid*, p 3; and Ramberg, above.
103 In the UK, for example, the activities of the auctioneer are governed by the Auctioneers Act 1845, s 7 of which requires that the name and place of residence of the auctioneer should be displayed prominently to all those attending the auction. In some jurisdictions, auctioneers still require a licence to operate, but in the UK, this provision in the 1845 Act was repealed by the Finance Act 1949.

gift or consideration to any other person as an inducement or reward for abstaining, or for having abstained, from bidding at a sale by auction either generally or for any particular lot, or if any person agrees to accept, or accepts, or attempts to obtain from any dealer any such gift or consideration'. As a result of s 2, any resultant sale can be regarded as having been induced by fraud.[104]

There are thus some pre-existing offences related to fraudulent activity in conventional auctions.[105] A crucial issue for application of existing provisions may be the definition of an auction. As noted previously, despite fulfilling the requirements of sale to the highest bidder in a competitive sale, most C2C auction sites are at pains to point out in their conditions of use that they are not true auctions, but merely provide a 'venue' within which the buying and selling of goods to the highest bidder can be facilitated – that is, the better analogy is with a bazaar rather than a conventional auction.[106] The question is then not so much whether the site is an 'auction' as such, but whether it can be held to have played any part in the perpetration of the fraud. This issue has not yet been directly addressed by the courts, but there may be some circumstances in which they could operate in similar ways. In the French case of *Chambre Nationale des Commissaires Priseurs v Nart SAS*,[107] the defendants, who operated an online auction site, argued that sales via its website could not be considered as a public auction and neither could the internet be construed as an auction house in Paris. In addition, it was suggested that 'the sales should not be treated as auctions because they do not create the pressure to bid more provoked by the heat of the auction and the simultaneity of the bidding'.[108] In contrast, the court was of the view that, although it might achieve the end result in a different way from its real-world counterpart, an online auction could present all of the characteristics of a public auction, including the 'same atmosphere and heat in the bidding';[109] the court described the internet as 'a vast auction room extending to infinity and able to change in order to take account of the changes in physical space in which the offers of auctions are distributed'.[110] Although the Tribunale de Grande Instance de Paris found that the French law on auctions could be applied in this case, the internet auction site in question was operated by a conventional auction house. In other words, there was both control and management of the auction process, and it would perhaps be dangerous to extend this view directly to some other forms of online auctions. On the other hand, for all online auctions, it seems clear that the primary characteristics of competitive bidding and sale to the highest bidder are fulfilled, and the points about the need for identification of bidders in ways that are appropriate to the situation are also relevant in making the parallel between the two activities.

An alternative view is that, in considering the volume of transactions on online auction sites, there is more similarity with an ISP for which the liability issues have been well rehearsed by both courts and academics, and have also been the subject of legislative intervention in some jurisdictions. There is an argument that, given that the major role of auction sites is one of facilitation rather than active interaction, there should be no liability, especially in relation to the potential imposition of criminal sanctions, in the absence of actual knowledge of fraudulent activity or collusion in the same.[111]

---

104 The Auctions (Bidding Agreements) Act 1969, s 3, provides further rights for the seller of goods by auction where an agreement subsists that some person shall abstain from bidding for the goods, but these are basically confined to the provision of contractual remedies and relate to the situation in which one of the parties to the collusion is a dealer, as defined in the 1927 Act. However, this statute has been so rarely used that it has been suggested that its lack of application must be a deliberate policy: see discussion of *R v Jordan* [1981] CLY 131, cited in Harvey and Meisel, above, p 209.

105 Although the civil actions which may be available against a traditional auctioneer could not be used by a purchaser from an online auction.

106 See, e.g., the eBay user agreement, noted above at n 94.

107 [2001] ECC 24.

108 *Ibid*, [21].

109 *Ibid*, [27].

110 *Ibid*, [25].

111 Note also that if these websites were auctions as defined in the UK, there would also be criminal liability under the Trade Descriptions Act 1968, s 1, for any false or misleading descriptions of the goods: see, e.g., *May v Vincent* (1990) 154 JP 997. It should also be noted that auction sites such as eBay are cognisant of the potential fraud problems and do operate procedures that are intended to minimise any such damage: see http://resolutioncenter.ebay.com/

As mentioned above, one scam that is used by the unscrupulous vendor is to instigate fictitious bids in order to artificially inflate the price that the eventual buyer has to pay to secure the desired item. In the old case of *Heatley v Newton*,[112] a property was being sold by auction. The prospective buyer believed that it was about to be sold to a *bona fide* bidder for £12,950 and so offered £13,000 to clinch the sale. The reality was far different and the nearest *bona fide* bid was some £5,000 below that. The immediately preceding bids, which led to the offer of £13,000 being made, were made by the vendors or their agents, or were entirely fictitious, because the auctioneer was also a party to the collusion and, in many of the instances in which he intimated that he had received a bid, in fact he had not. Murdoch discusses the view of the Court of Appeal in the action for recovery and goes on to analyse the reasons for the illegality on the basis of the law as it stood at that time.[113] He noted that if offers that constitute misrepresentations are done knowingly, then this activity can be classified as fraud. Even where such bids are below the reserve price, they can still influence the bidding above that figure and, as long as dishonesty can be established, there seems no reason not to regard this as obtaining by deception. In addition, at least, prior to the Fraud Act 2006, such collusion might feasibly be sufficient to establish the common law offence of criminal conspiracy. Although the Law Commission report that preceded the Act recommended the abolition of this offence, this did not occur, because consultation showed widespread support for its retention. Although in principle, therefore, prosecution for this offence remains a possibility, the expectation is that it will become less relevant following the Fraud Act.[114] Similar arguments can be applied to damping the bids for fraudulent reasons. By analogy with the situation above, it might be expected that it would also be a criminal conspiracy for bidders to collude to depress the hammer price – by bid shielding, for example, as referred to above – but it appears that this is not the case.[115]

In the USA, the operation of auctions is governed by the Uniform Commercial Code (UCC) §2-328, and para 4 is a parallel provision to that in the Sale of Goods Act 1979, s 57(4), which merely provides contractual remedies. Any criminal activity that may have taken place is left to be dealt with by, for example, generic fraud offences. Because they focus on the communication method by which the fraud is perpetrated, the provisions on 'mail fraud' and 'wire fraud', in 18 USC §§ 1341 and 1342, have proved to be easily adaptable to situations of online auction fraud.[116] Both provisions are similar in essence. They require that: there be a scheme or plan for obtaining money or property by the use of false statements that would reasonably influence someone to part with the money or property; the statements were known to be false; and there was an intention to defraud. For mail fraud, the offence is complete when the statements are made via the mail, and for wire fraud by the transmission of wire, radio, etc. Charges under these sections have been used successfully in a number of cases in which the relevant medium was an online auction, and in which the prospective vendors either did not possess, or did not intend to deliver, the items for which bidders had offered payment.[117]

112 (1881) 19 ChD 326.
113 John Murdoch, *Law of Estate Agency and Auctions*, 4th edn, 2003, London: Estates Gazette, p 187.
114 See Office of the Attorney General, *Guidance on the Use of the Common Law Offence of Conspiracy to Defraud*, 2007, London: HMSO. This document also points out that whether a need for this offence remains will be considered when the Home Office reviews the implementation of the Fraud Act.
115 Murdoch, above, p 196.
116 See, e.g., Decker, above.
117 See, e.g., *US v Hartman* 74 Fed Appx 159 (3rd Cir (Pa) 2003); *US v Jackson* 61 Fed Appx 851 (4th Cir (Va) 2003); *US v Blanchett* 41 Fed Appx 181 (10th Cir 2002). More recently, see Dan Goodin, 'eBay scammer gets four years in slammer' (2009) *The Register*, 28 April, available online at: www.theregister.co.uk/2009/04/28/ebay_scammer_sentenced/. Custodial sentences have also been imposed for convictions for, *inter alia*, mail fraud and wire fraud on a number of defendants in a bidding ring involving shill bidding: see Brian Melley, 'California eBay scam artist sent to federal prison' (2004) *USA Today*, 27 May, available online at: http://usatoday30.usatoday.com/tech/news/2004-05-27-ebay-art-fraud_x.htm

## Computer 'hacking'

### Before the Computer Misuse Act 1990

Although the above discussion shows that, in the case of fraud, the same offences can be used both online and offline, some other behaviour provided rather greater challenges for the criminal law. During the 1980s, a number of cases came to court in a number of jurisdictions that could, perhaps, be regarded purely as examples of antisocial behaviour, but which caused problems for the law in trying to locate the behaviour within existing legal provisions. A number of these were cases of computer hacking and the outcomes were often inconsistent, even in relation to ostensibly similar facts. In some cases, there might be an acquittal because the charge chosen was deemed to be inappropriate or, alternatively, the law was interpreted in novel ways in order to found a conviction.[118] In the UK some of these issues came to a head in R v Gold and Schifreen.[119]

Gold and Schifreen were hackers who had obtained the password used by BT engineers to gain access to its Prestel System. Their activities aroused suspicion and they were tracked down by monitoring their telephone usage. A prosecution was brought under s 1 of the Forgery and Counterfeiting Act 1981, which provides that:

> A person is guilty of forgery if he makes a false instrument with the intention that he or another shall use it to induce somebody to accept it as genuine and by reason of so accepting it do or not do some act to his own or any other person's prejudice.[120]

Gold and Schifreen were convicted at first instance, but appealed on the basis that no false instrument had been made. 'Instrument' is defined in s 8 of the Act and includes disks, tapes, etc, on which the material is stored by electronic means. The prosecution argument relied on the assertion that the dishonestly obtained password could constitute such an instrument, because it generated and was transmitted in the form of electrical impulses. This contention was rejected for two reasons. First, it was felt that any instrument for the purposes of this Act had to be *ejusdem generis* with the other examples in the statutory definition, which were all physical objects, and because the electrical impulses in question were only transient; this did not correspond well with the idea of the creation of an instrument. In addition to the difficulties with the definition of the instrument, the inapplicability of the charge was held to be due to the nature of the offence of forgery. In this case, the password was not false – it was genuine – but there was no entitlement to use it. As a result, the Court of Appeal was of the view that the use of the statute was inappropriate; it was not intended to apply to this type of activity. Lord Lane summed up these views as follows:

> The Procrustean attempt to force these facts into the language of an Act not designed to fit them produced grave difficulties for both judge and jury which we would not wish to see repeated. The appellants' conduct amounted in essence, as already stated, to dishonestly gaining access to the relevant Prestel data bank by a trick. That is not a criminal offence. If it is thought desirable to make it so, that is a matter for the legislature rather than the courts.[121]

The wholehearted and unanimous endorsement of this approach by the House of Lords shows the disdain with which the attempt to squeeze the activity of computer hacking into the framework of

---

118 Compare, e.g., the contested behaviour and the reasoning in R v Gold and Schifreen [1988] AC 1063, [1988] Crim LR 437 (HL), Cox v Riley (1986) 83 Cr App R 54; and R v Whiteley (1991) 93 Cr App R 25, discussed subsequently in this section.
119 [1988] AC 1063, [1988] Crim LR 437 (HL). See also FJ Kwiatkowski, 'Hacking and the criminal law revisited' (1987) 4 CL & P 15.
120 Note that, for offences under this section, the problems identified in relation to the deception of a machine are overcome by express provision in the Act.
121 [1987] QB 1116, 1124.

an inappropriate statute was treated. The clear message was that although it might be appropriate in some areas of the law to expand and develop the interpretation of existing legal provisions to take account of advances in technology, such provision had to be consonant with the alleged 'offence', in order not to stretch the law beyond its breaking point.[122]

Other attempts to find suitable offences to pursue cases where computers had been modified without authority, including hacking, used the Criminal Damage Act 1971. The first of these found a conviction based on a meaning of damage as 'injury impairing value or usefulness.'[123] Although this was arguably a laudable attempt to find a proscribed actus reus in a situation where the defendant clearly possessed the mens rea, the reasoning was subsequently criticised by the Law Commission as it was based on an old precedent which did not conform to the definition of damage in the 1971 statute.[124] The reasoning in the later case of R v Whiteley[125] might have provided a more suitable avenue for the use of the Criminal Damage Act in hacking cases, particularly those which are not limited to mere browsing of files but in which material is deliberately modified or deleted. By the time this decision was reached, however, the Computer Misuse Act 1990 had been passed which, as a result of the above criticism, effectively removed such cases from the ambit of the Criminal Damage Act 1971.

## The Computer Misuse Act 1990

Because of situations such as those that gave rise to the cases above, the Law Commissions for both Scotland, and England and Wales, reviewed the existing criminal law and its relation both to hacking and to computer misuse more generally. The Scottish Law Commission reported first[126] and recommended that the problem could be tackled by the creation of an unauthorised access offence. The Herculean task of drafting such legislation was noted by Tapper, who commented that 'the encapsulation of the burgeoning technology within the strait jacket of the ordinary language and comprehensible structure ideally characterising Acts of Parliament constitutes a formidable task'.[127] He considered the three separate alternative approaches to computer misuse – relying on the judiciary to interpret existing rules; amending existing rules to facilitate judicial interpretation; and enacting new offences – and concluded that there was no clear choice as to which of these was preferable, or likely to be most effective.

Despite some adverse criticisms of the Scottish Law Commission's proposal, it was clearly quite influential when the Law Commission for England and Wales came to consider the problems created by this new species of 'computer crime'. The first exploration of the issues considered whether or not it was in the public interest that the type of activity in question should be regarded as criminal.[128] It concluded that there were the following arguments for the use of criminal offences: the overall importance of computers to society as a whole and a consequent need to maintain their integrity; the need to signal society's disapproval of deliberate hacking, especially as this might cause damage to the computer system itself; and the fact that prohibition of hacking might also reduce other conduct, such as computer fraud, etc. On the other hand, it also noted that there were a number of arguments against criminalisation: the fact that although obtaining

---

122  This should, however, be distinguished from the situation in R v Governor of Brixton Prison, ex p Levin [1997] 1 Cr App R 355, in which it was held that the word 'disk' was within the definition of 'instrument' in the Forgery and Counterfeiting Act 1981, s 8(1)(d), and embraced the information stored, as well as the medium on which it was stored. By entering false instructions on the disk, it was, in the court's opinion, falsified, and the applicant had thereby created a false instrument.
123  Cox v Riley (1986) 83 Cr App R 54.
124  Law Commission, Report on Computer Misuse, Cm 819, 1989, London: HMSO, para 2.30.
125  (1991) 93 Cr App R 25.
126  Scottish Law Commission, Report on Computer Crime, Cmnd 174, 1987, London: HMSO.
127  Colin Tapper, 'Computer crime: scotch mist' [1987] Crim L Rev 4, 8.
128  Law Commission, Reforming the Present Law: Hacking, Working Paper No 110, 1988, London: HMSO, Pt VI.

unauthorised access might breach privacy it was not, of itself, a matter for the criminal law, and that enforcement was likely to cause a number of problems.

When the Law Commission finally reported on the matter,[129] it concluded that the existing criminal remedies were inadequate to deal with many instances of computer crime and misuse, although it conceded that a number of charges under the Theft Act 1968 might be appropriate in cases of computer fraud. Taking all of the issues into account and the outcome of the consultations, two new criminal offences were proposed,[130] and it was noted that 'the main argument . . . does not turn on the protection of information but rather springs from the need to protect the integrity and security of computer systems'. The new offences were to have a broad and a narrow ambit, respectively: the first created an offence for all types of unauthorised access to computer access; and the second imposed more severe penalties on those who obtained unauthorised access to computer systems for the purpose of committing more serious crimes.

Despite the Law Commission's report, the government did not implement the recommendations and, in the end, the CMA was the result of a private member's Bill introduced by Michael Colvin. This Bill did, however, follow fairly closely the Law Commission's proposals. In particular, it took a two-tier approach: the first section contains a basic hacking offence; and the second, an ulterior intent offence designed to cover situations in which there is unauthorised access with the intent to commit a further crime. These sections are hierarchical and when charges are brought under s 2, it is still possible to convict under s 1, even where the necessary intent for a s 2 offence is not proved. Certain activities, however, do not fall within the ambit of the statute – in particular, reading of the contents of files non-interactively, for example, unauthorised reading after printing out in cases in which the print operation had been performed by an authorised user, or mere reading of information on a computer screen. Depending on the nature of the material, such acts could fall within the scope of the Data Protection Act 1998. Section 3 then went on to create an offence of unauthorised modification of computer material. This was a response to the Law Commission's criticism, referred to above, of the use of the Criminal Damage Act 1971 in such cases and, to put the matter beyond doubt, s 3(6) excluded the use of the 1971 Act in cases of computer misuse unless the effect of the misuse was to impair the physical condition of the computer, or computer-storage medium.[131] In common with statutes in other jurisdictions, the Act does not define the word 'computer',[132] nor does it use the word 'hacking', but a lengthy interpretation section demonstrates the wide-reaching scope of some of the other crucial concepts in the Act.[133]

## The 'hacking' offence

Section 1(1)(a) of the Act provides that:

> a person is guilty of an offence if—(a) he causes a computer to perform any function with intent to secure access to any program or data held in any computer; (b) the access he intends to secure is unauthorised; and (c) he knows at the time when he causes the computer to perform the function that that is the case.

Although s 1 has popularly been referred to as proscribing hacking the requirement of 'unauthorised access' is much wider than hacking; any sort of activity will suffice other than merely reading

---

129  Law Commission, *Report on Computer Misuse*, Cm 819, 1989, London: HMSO.

130  Whether this outcome is desirable has been questioned: see, e.g., M Wasik, 'Misuse of information technology: What should the role of the criminal law be?' (1991) 5 LC & T Yearbook 158.

131  The original s 3 has now been repealed and replaced as a result of the amendments introduced in the Police and Justice Act 2006: see discussion at p 292.

132  One exception is the legislation in Singapore: see, e.g., A Endeshaw, 'Computer misuse law in Singapore' (1999) 8 ICTL 5; I Mahalingham Carr and KS Williams, 'A step too far in controlling computers? The Singapore Computer Misuse (Amendment) Act 1998' (2000) 8 Int JLIT 48.

133  Computer Misuse Act 1990, s 17.

a screen and it extends also to access to the contents of portable storage devices, such as disks and memory sticks, if this occurs while they are in any computer. The very first case under the Act, *R v Cropp*,[134] underlined the fact that this section did not just criminalise hacking. Cropp had used his knowledge of his ex-employer's computer system to give himself a 70 per cent discount on goods. He was charged with the ulterior intent offence in s 2(1) and a submission of 'no case to answer' was made, on the grounds that, in order to contravene s 1(1) (and, therefore, s 2(1)), it had to be established that the accused had used one computer with intent to secure unauthorised access i.e. to hack into another computer. This argument succeeded at trial, but the Court of Appeal gave it short shrift and, referring to the 'plain and natural meaning' of the section, found that there were 'no grounds whatsoever for implying such an interpretation'.[135] The Act had been drafted so as to deal not only with the situation in which indirect access to a computer system is gained by using another computer, but also with the situation in which a person misuses a computer to which he or she has direct (but unauthorised) access. Without such an interpretation the potential useful-ness of the CMA could have been severely curtailed, resulting in what was described at the time as 'total emasculation'.[136] The dramatic effect that this might have had is particularly apparent with hindsight, as a number of prosecutions have been brought that have far more in common with the situation in *Cropp* than with hacking.

## Unauthorised modifications and malware

The term 'malware', an abbreviation of 'malicious software', has been coined to denote any soft-ware that is intended to cause damage, disruption, and annoyance to users. It includes viruses, worms, Trojans,[137] keystroke loggers, botnets, and any other programs of a potentially destructive nature. Such software can spread rapidly across networks and may do anything from destroying the contents of a hard disk, to generating facetious messages. Purely destructive malware is perhaps less common than it once was, as there can be more for criminals to gain by malware which is rather more sophisticated in its operation, but there have been some high-profile examples. The ILOVEYOU virus, which was estimated to have infected some 45 million computers in 2000 and caused billions of dollars' worth of damage, has even been described as 'the most devastating crime in history'.[138] The Conficker worm, whose unidentified creator was described as 'a criminal mas-termind worthy of a James Bond thriller',[139] was first reported to Microsoft in November 2008[140] and by January 2009 had apparently infected up to 15 million computers.[141] As already mentioned, the activities of botnets and keystroke loggers can be controlled from external sites and be used to steal data – often personal details, and especially bank and credit card details – and can be used

---

134 (1991) unreported, but see case note at (1991) 7 CLSR 168.
135 *AG's Reference* (No 1 of 1991) [1992] WLR 432, 437.
136 EA Dumbill, 'Computer Misuse Act 1990: Recent developments' (1992) 8 CLSR 105.
137 These, and similar terms, are sometimes used interchangeably in non-technical parlance and even from a technical perspective the differences between them are now of diminishing importance. A virus is a self-replicating program that may not be immediately apparent on examination of a system, but which copies itself into the computer memory and, from there, to any disks that are subsequently loaded and/or in the memory of other computers attached to the same network as data is exchanged. The type of program commonly referred to as a 'worm' is an example of a program that was developed for exploring the capabilities of computer systems and networks, and may adversely affect systems on which it is unwanted by consuming resources. A 'Trojan' is a program that appears to be a program performing an innocuous function, but which hides the fact that it also has another, usually more sinister, function. For general definitions, see, e.g., Joseph Audal, Quincy Lu, and Peter Roman, 'Computer crimes' (2008) 45 Am Crim L Rev 233. The word 'virus' is itself often used as a generic term for many types of malware: for a history of viruses, see, e.g., M Klang, 'A critical look at the regulation of computer viruses' (2003) 11 IJLIT 162, 163–7.
138 NK Katyal, 'Criminal law in cyberspace' (2001) 149 U Pa L Rev 1003; see also, e.g., SC Sprinkel, 'Global internet regulation: The residual effects of the "iloveyou" computer virus and the Draft Convention on Cyber-Crime' (2002) 25 Suffolk Transnat'l L Rev 491; and K Cesare, 'Prosecuting computer virus authors: The need for an adequate and immediate international solution' (2001) 14 Transnat'l Law 135, 145.
139 Paul Thurrott, 'April Fools: World preps for Conficker attack' (2010) Paul Thurrott's Supersite for Windows, 6 October, available online at: www.winsupersite.com/article/windows-server/april-fools-world-preps-for-conficker-attack
140 See www.microsoft.com/en-us/safety/pc-security/conficker.aspx, which also includes an explanation of how the worm works.
141 Duncan B Hollis, 'An E-SOS for Cyberspace' (2011) 52 Harv Int'l LJ 373, 428.

to propagate spam, phishing, and pharming emails.[142] The targets of this activity will vary – business and government sites are most likely to be the victims of DoS and DDoS, and well-respected and frequently visited sites also provide fertile ground for harvesting data from visitors to these sites for subsequent targeting. However, domestic users are not immune: they may be less likely to be targeted directly by hackers, but they may be extremely vulnerable to malware, which can be spread by apparently innocuous activities including sending emails or visiting websites.

The first worm to be released onto the embryonic internet was created in 1988 by a Cornell University student, Robert Morris, who was subsequently successfully prosecuted under the US Computer Fraud and Abuse Act of 1986 (CFAA 18 USC § 1030) on what was basically a hacking charge. This decision was upheld by the US Court of Appeals for the Second Circuit,[143] which found that Morris had both exceeded the authorisation for those computers that he was allowed to access and, because the program was designed to spread to other machines, had also accessed computers that he had no authority to access.[144] A short while later, not long before the CMA was passed in the UK, the strange case of Dr Lewis Popp hit the headlines. A large number of people associated with computer use received disks through the post purporting to contain important information about the AIDS virus. If, in fact, the disks were used, although they did reveal information on that subject, they also contained a Trojan that was programmed to destroy the contents of the hard disk after the computer had been used about a hundred times. At that time, there would have been little legal action that an affected user could have taken unless the courts would have been happy to use the reasoning in *Whiteley* discussed above.[145] The Law Commission had found no evidence that such activities should not be criminalised and was also of the view that the existing law on criminal damage was unsuitable.[146] The Popp incident was referred to in the parliamentary debates on the Computer Misuse Bill and it was evident that the new legislation was intended to cover such activities: '. . . circulation of an infected disk, such as this is not an offence. However, the Bill will make it one.'[147]

The original s 3(1) of the CMA thus created an offence of doing any act that caused the unauthorised modification of the contents of any computer with the requisite intent and knowledge:

(1)   A person is guilty of an offence if –

(a)   he does any act which causes an unauthorised modification of the contents of any computer; and

(b)   at the time when he does the act he has the requisite intent and the requisite knowledge.

(2)   . . . the requisite intent is an intent to cause a modification of the contents of any computer and by so doing –

(a)   to impair the operation of any computer;

(b)   to prevent or hinder access to any program or data held in any computer; or

(c)   to impair the operation of any such program or the reliability of any such data.

---

142  For details of the latest such activity, see, e.g., Symantec, 2016 *Internet Security Report*, above. For further discussion of the legal response to spam, see Chapters 6 and 9.

143  *US v Morris* 928 F 2d 504 (2nd Cir 1991).

144  See also later discussion on questions of authorisation.

145  See, e.g., Y Akdeniz, 'Section 3 of the Computer Misuse Act 1990: An antidote for computer viruses!' [1996] 3 Web JCLI, available online at: http://www.bailii.org/uk/other/journals/WebJCLI/1996/issue3/akdeniz3.html. In fact, Dr Popp was eventually arrested in Ohio and charged with extorting money with menaces, because those affected were also directed to transfer sums of money to a bank account in Panama. In the event, there was evidence that Popp's mental condition had deteriorated to such an extent that he was pronounced unfit to plead.

146  Law Commission, Cm 819, 1989, paras 2.27–2.29, note that this was before the judgment in *R v Whiteley* (1991) 93 Cr App R 25, discussed above.

147  Michael Colvin, *Hansard*, vol 166, col 1139, 1990.

Section 3, even as first drafted, appeared to be capable of catching a wide variety of types of activity, including not only the type of modification and erasure seen in *Cox v Riley*,[148] but also the intentional introduction of viruses, worms, Trojans, and other programs of a potentially destructive nature. Since the intent did not need to be directed at any particular computer (s 3(3)), the liability of the person who originated the virus or worm would be unaffected if, in the event, a virus was introduced to a system by means of an infected disk innocently acquired by a third party. On the other hand, it was clear that anyone knowingly introducing an infected disk had an intent to modify the contents of a computer. Despite some comment to the contrary,[149] the fact that s 3 was applicable to malware was put beyond doubt in the case of *R v Pile*.[150] Pile, who referred to himself as the 'Black Baron', developed two particular viruses – Queeg and Pathogen – and also Smeg, a guide to writing viruses. These viruses were capable of masquerading as other, innocent programs, and he was even successful in incorporating a virus into an anti-virus scan program. This was the first time that a person had appeared in court as a result of intentionally introducing computer viruses to a system and the court had no problems in finding a breach of s 3.

While a computer user rapidly becomes aware that their machine has been infected by a virus, Trojan programs can apparently be installed on a computer without the user's knowledge and provide a common vehicle for the introduction of other types of malware. A range of different actions can then be initiated that may or may not come to the notice of the user. As an example, the Sinowal Trojan was able to install itself on the computers of those who visited infected websites, and was then able to collect personal and financial data undetected by the user. It was estimated that many thousands of bank accounts, credit cards, and debit cards had been compromised in this way.[151] As discussed above this could result in fraud charges but could this offence of unauthorised modification also be used? The operation of Trojans was a central feature in three separate cases in the UK: those of *Green* (2002), *Caffrey* (2003), and *Schofield* (2003).[152] The common feature in all of these cases was that the defendant alleged that the acts complained about resulted from the installation of a Trojan on their computers of which they were unaware. Both Green and Schofield were charged with possession of indecent images of children, but succeeded in bringing evidence that the presence of the images on their computers was due to them having been infected with Trojans that then, without their knowledge, downloaded the images whenever the internet was accessed. *Caffrey*, on the other hand, was a prosecution under s 3 of the CMA, in which Caffrey was acquitted for a DoS attack on the Port of Houston computer network. The result of the attack was to impair the operation of the network to such an extent that necessary navigation data was inaccessible. There was no dispute that Caffrey's computer was not the source of the attack, but the prosecution case was that it was initiated by Caffrey as a misdirected attack on a fellow chatroom user, whereas the defence argument was that the attack was the result of the activity of a Trojan, which had infected Caffrey's machine and over which he had no control. No trace of the Trojan was found, but evidence was accepted that the Trojan had self-deleted after launching the attack, despite the prosecution's view that such technology did not exist. These cases all demonstrate the evidential difficulties for both sides when it is possible that the acts, harm, or damage complained of could have originated from a Trojan. Certainly, a browse through a virus library shows that there are Trojan programs that exhibit some of the properties alleged in the above cases,[153] meaning that

---

148 (1986) 83 Cr App R 54.

149 See, e.g., M Wasik, 'Introduction' (1995) 9 LC & T Yearbook, ix; and cf Michael Colvin, *Hansard*, vol 166, col 1139 (1990). More recently, see APIG, below, para 23.

150 (1995) unreported. For further details, see, e.g., S Jones, 'Computer terrorist or mad boffin?' (1996) 146 NLJ 46; Akdeniz, above.

151 See Maggie Shiels, 'Trojan virus steals banking info' (2008) BBC News, 21 October, available online at: http://news.bbc.co.uk/1/hi/technology/7701227.stm

152 All unreported, but see discussion in S Hill, 'Driving a Trojan horse and cart through the Computer Misuse Act' (2003) 14(5) C&L 31; and SW Brenner, B Carrier, and J Henninger, 'The Trojan horse defense in cybercrime cases' (2004) 21 CHTLJ 1.

153 Troj/Newsflood, for example, is a Trojan horse that continually posts messages about child pornography to Usenet newsgroups, see: https://www.sophos.com/en-us/threat-center/threat-analyses/viruses-and-spyware/Troj~Newsflood/detailed-analysis.aspx

the mere facts of the case may not provide any indication of whether or not the act complained of occurred with or without the user's knowledge or consent.

## DoS attacks and the Police and Justice Act 2006

Trojans are used to install and disseminate many types of malware but, in particular, are often used to launch DoS and DDoS attacks. This created two major issues for application of the original provisions of the CMA. The first was the question of authorisation, but as was demonstrated by the reasoning of the appeal court in *Lennon*, discussed below, this need not be fatal to a charge under s 3. More fatal, however, is the fact that data may not actually be modified. Although the DoS attack initiated by Caffrey's PC, referred to above, may have arisen as the result of infection by a Trojan, which could bring it within the ambit of the original s 3, it is clear that many DoS and DDoS attacks will not modify computer material as such, but instead will merely clog up the victim's computer system and be generally disruptive.[154] Similar effects can be seen when websites crash because of an unusual amount of traffic attempting to access the site; more sophisticated attacks exploit known and/or foreseeable vulnerabilities in the software, and, especially if a DDoS harnesses a network of other computers, the effect of a deliberately targeted attack can be on a radically different scale. Nevertheless, if there is no actual modification of the data, then whether or not the actions of the attacker are deemed to be authorised or unauthorised, it is difficult to see how s 3 can be applied. Neither is it easy for victims to take adequate precautions, as pointed out by Wyatt:

> Providing protection against some types of DOS and especially DDOS attacks can be technically challenging. It is often hard to distinguish legitimate from illegitimate activity, which means that genuine traffic can be discarded through protective measures.[155]

The undesirability of the legality of DoS and DDoS depending of the precise mode of execution was one of the issues discussed by the All Party Internet Group (APIG) in its public inquiry into the operation of the CMA in 2004, noting that 'it is the particular circumstances of each attack that makes it obvious whether the CMA wording applies'.[156] Although it was perhaps more likely that the CMA would be applicable to instances of DDoS attacks because software, such as the disputed Trojan in *Caffrey*, would need to be installed, to put the matter beyond doubt, a specific recommendation was made to enact an 'explicit "denial-of service" offence of impairing access to data'.[157] It was intended that this would cover all instances of deliberate DoS whether or not they would currently fall within s 3, and thus remedy both actual and perceived deficiencies in CMA, s 3. The EU Council Framework Decision on attacks against information systems of the following year then required Member States to criminalise illegal interference with both systems and data.[158] The Police and Justice Act 2006, s 36, which creates a new s 3 of the CMA, eventually gave effect to both the requirements of this Decision and the recommendation of the APIG report. The new section 3 creates an offence where anyone does an unauthorised act in relation to any computer with the knowledge that the act is unauthorised and the act is done with the intent to impair the computer's operation,

---

154 It has been suggested that they should therefore be categorised as 'unauthorised disruptions': see Katyal, above, 1023–7.
155 Derek Wyatt, HC Debs, 5 April 2005, col 1294; and APIG, below, para 58.
156 *Revision of the Computer Misuse Act*: Report of an Inquiry by the All Party Internet Group (June 2004), para 2, available online at: www. cl.cam.ac.uk/~rnc1/APIG-report-cma.pdf
157 *Ibid*, para 75. Some of the other issues raised in the report are discussed in subsequent sections. A similar gap was identified in the German legislation relating to unauthorised modification of data: see Julia Hörnle, 'Germany: Denial of service attack – Case review' (2006) 8 EBL 11, 15.
158 Council Framework Decision 2005/222/JHA of 24 February 2005 [2005] OJ L/69, 67.

to prevent or hinder access to a program or data, to impair the operation of a program or the reliability of data, or to enable any of these things:

(1)    A person is guilty of an offence if –

    (a)    he does any unauthorised act in relation to a computer;

    (b)    at the time when he does the act he knows that it is unauthorised; and

    (c)    either subsection (2) or subsection (3) below applies.

(2)    This subsection applies if the person intends by doing the act –

    (a)    to impair the operation of any computer;

    (b)    to prevent or hinder access to any program or data held in any computer;

    (c)    to impair the operation of any such program or the reliability of any such data; or

    (d)    to enable any of the things mentioned in paragraphs (a) to (c) above to be done.

In addition, s 3(3) now specifically allows that the offence will also be committed if these acts are done recklessly as to whether they will have any of the above effects.

A number of points can be made about the new section. First, it is clear that the scope of the new section is far wider than the old, and the fact that the need for actual modification of computer material has been removed suggests that the section is clearly capable of encompassing both DoS and DDoS attacks. As is frequently the case, however, it may be that the solution to one problem has resulted in the creation of new ones. Most obvious is the replacement of the objective criterion of 'modification' with the more subjective requirement of 'impairment': an act could be done with the requisite intent to impair the operation of the computer, but the actual effect be unnoticed by the user. It is not clear what would be a better word. Fafinski suggests that 'a meaningful legal definition of impairment . . . might be "deterioration in performance that is noticeable by the senses"',[159] which has the advantage of excluding technical, but *de minimis* impairment, but it could still be a matter of debate at what point an alleged impairment became noticeable – it seems likely that computer experts would be more likely to notice an impairment before the average user, for example. This issue may, of course, be resolved by the question of when it might be in the public interest to prosecute on occasions on which all of the other elements of the offence appear to be in place. The new section retains the requirement for the act to be unauthorised, and for the perpetrator to have the knowledge that that is the case, so any residual problems with the concept of authorisation have not been resolved. The old s 3(6) required that any modification should not be regarded as damage for the purpose of the Criminal Damage Act 1971 unless it resulted in physical damage to the computer or computer system. Because the whole of the original section has been repealed, this could, in theory at least, allow the courts to resurrect the reasoning in *Whiteley*.[160]

## Questions of authorisation

Authorisation, or the lack of it, is of central importance not only to the provisions of the CMA, but also to the legal protection offered to computer systems by similar provisions in other jurisdictions.[161] In relation to the CMA, it has been described as the 'keystone'.[162] Section 1 requires access to the computer in question to be unauthorised and although impairment has now replaced modification in the amended s 3, lack of authorisation is still a key requirement. The issue of authorisation is

159   Stefan Fafinski, 'Computer misuse: The implications of the Police and Justice Act 2006' (2008) 72 JCL 53; see also S Fafinski, 'Access denied: Computer misuse in an era of technological change' (2006) 70 JCL 424.
160   See above p 287 and see also LH Leigh, 'Some observations on the Police and Justice Act 2006' (2007) 171 JPN 28, 31.
161   See, e.g., Peter A Winn, 'The guilty eye: Unauthorized access, trespass and privacy' (2007) 62 Bus Law 1395.
162   Neil MacEwan, 'The Computer Misuse Act 1990: Lessons from its past and predictions for its future' [2008] Crim L Rev 955, 957.

less likely to be controversial in relation to a remote hacker with no connection to the hacked site, but has proved to be an issue in cases of 'inside hacking' such as where the alleged unauthorised access occurs in employment. On this specific issue, the Law Commission suggested that:

> an employer should only have the support of the hacking offence if he has clearly defined the limits of authorisation applicable to each employee, and if he is able to prove that the employee had knowingly and recklessly exceeded that level of authority.[163]

It was made clear in Ellis v DPP[164] that a person's subjective belief that he or she should have access to a computer network was not sufficient to provide the requisite authorisation. Ellis was an alumnus of a university and had thus previously been authorised to use the university's computer network. Several years after graduating, he continued to use the system via terminals that had been left logged on by a previous user. It was concluded that although he thought that he should have such access, he neither had authorisation nor believed that he was so authorised. The question of authorisation was returned to in DPP v Bignell,[165] in which no criminal liability was found on the basis of lack of authorisation, even though the consequent access was then exploited in an unauthorised manner. The reasoning in this decision, although not the outcome as such, was subsequently criticised by the House of Lords in R v Bow Street Magistrates Court and Allison, ex p United States,[166] because, in attempting to distinguish the control of access from the authority to access, it introduced 'a number of glosses which are not present in the Act'.[167] Lord Hobhouse suggested that the words of s 1 in relation to authorisation were 'clear and unambiguous',[168] but that problems had arisen in the reasoning of the court in Bignell, and also in the Court of Appeal in Allison itself, because of confusion between s 1 and the definition of authorisation set out in s 17(5):

> Access of any kind by any person to any program or data held in the computer is unauthorised if –
>
> (a)  he is not himself entitled to control access of the kind in question to the program or data; and
> (b)  he does not have consent to access by him of the kind in question to the program or data from any person who is so entitled.

Lord Hobhouse pointed out that it was, for example, possible for individuals to have authority to view data, but not to do anything further with it, and set out a detailed explanation of how the various issues relating to access and authorisation should work together. In identifying the two ways in which authority could be acquired, the meaning of s 17(5) was clear, but also subsidiary to the requirements of s 1. In particular, he made it clear that 'the authority must relate not simply to the data or programme but also to the actual kind of access secured',[169] and summarised the matter by suggesting: 'These plain words leave no room for any suggestion that the relevant person may say: "Yes, I know that I was not authorised to access that data but I was authorised to access other data of the same kind".'[170]

As mentioned above, s 3 also originally made it an offence to make an unauthorised modification. There was little difficulty in applying this concept to virus attacks,[171] but as the use and

163 Law Commission, 1989, above, para 3.37.
164 [2001] EWHC Admin 362.
165 [1998] Crim LR 53, [1998] 1 Cr App R 1.
166 [2000] 2 AC 216.
167 Ibid, 225.
168 Ibid, 226.
169 Ibid, 224.
170 Ibid.
171 See, e.g., the discussion of R v Pile (1995) unreported and similar cases at p 291.

functionality of the internet developed, so did other ways of causing problems for users of computer networks.[172] A particular example is provided by the initiation of DoS attacks and DDoS attacks, in which the perpetrator sets up a system that will generate a high volume of traffic to the target site. They also raise both separate and related questions about whether or not there was authorisation to send the traffic to the site. In *Caffrey*, discussed in more detail above, the issue was raised as to whether or not the CMA, s 3, covered DoS attacks. Insofar as the requirements of s 3 hinge on unauthorised modification, the natural conclusion might be that those attacks that result in data or program modification would fall within the Act, but those that merely clog up the system with excessive traffic would not. The relevant matters were further underlined by the case of *DPP v Lennon*.[173] Lennon had been dismissed from his job and, in retaliation, he sent emails to his former employer using a 'mail bombing' program that he had downloaded from the internet. The majority of the emails received purported to come from the firm's HR manager. Estimates as to the number of emails sent vary (para 2 of the official transcript of the case suggests 5 million, whereas paras 5 and 9 refer to half a million), but the volume was certainly sufficient to cause significant disruption to the firm's communications. At first instance, the defence pleaded that, because the function of the firm's servers was to receive emails, potential senders were authorised to modify the contents of the server by sending them. This argument succeeded and it was held that there was no case to answer because any modifications could not be shown to be unauthorised.

This decision was compared unfavourably at the time with the case of *Cuthbert*, in which a software tester was convicted of unauthorised access to a charity website.[174] His intention was to donate money to the tsunami appeal, but, when he received no acknowledgement, he became suspicious about a number of factors about the website and concerned that, having given his name address and credit card details, he had been the victim of a phishing scam. Accordingly, he used his technical expertise to test the security settings and was relieved to find there was no problem. However, this attempt was logged by the site as a potential intrusion and he was eventually charged with breach of s 1 of the CMA. There were detailed logs of his web activity, which showed that there were no attempted frauds or other illicit activity; in addition, although he had considerable technical expertise that could have caused widespread disruption to computer networks, he clearly had not done so. Nevertheless, he was found guilty of unauthorised access to the website and fined £400. Although the judge apparently reached this outcome 'with some considerable regret',[175] in comparison with other CMA cases, this could be viewed as a harsh outcome – the alternative of a conditional discharge would presumably have been a possibility.[176]

However, *Lennon* was subsequently appealed by way of case stated.[177] With regard to authorisation, the court was of the view that implying authorisation via consent to receive emails could not be without limit and that the behaviour complained of had to be considered as a whole. Whereas consent for the sending of one email might be granted, it was unlikely that permission would be given for the sending of half a million emails. It was therefore held that there was a case to answer, but in the event Lennon pleaded guilty and so there was no further legal discussion of the matter. Authorisation thus remains a slippery concept.

Neither is this issue confined to the CMA; authorisation, or the lack of it, has also proved problematic in other jurisdictions as the majority of 'hacking' offences are based on unauthorised access. A specific difficulty is the extent to which authorised users of computers who intentionally

---

172 See, e.g., Bill Goodwin, 'The law must be changed to redefine criminal activities' (2002) *Computer Weekly*, 14 March, available online at: www.computerweekly.com/Articles/2002/03/14/185735/the-law-must-be-changed-to-redefine-criminal-activities.htm
173 (2005) unreported, 2 November, Wimbledon Youth Court. For details, see [2006] EWHC 1201 (Admin).
174 See Peter Sommer, 'Computer misuse prosecutions' (2006) 16(5) Computers and Law 24.
175 See John Oates, 'Tsunami hacker convicted' (2005) *The Register*, 6 October, available online at: www.theregister.co.uk/2005/10/06/tsunami_hacker_convicted/
176 See further discussion on prosecutions and penalties below.
177 [2006] EWHC 1201 (Admin).

exceed their authorisation should be guilty of a criminal offence. In the US, for instance, Kargiannopoulos has suggested that 'the concept of authorization is creating more problems and controversy than solutions for computer crime' and suggests that a radical change is required given that the notion of exceeding unauthorised access has been given a number of interpretations in the courts.[178]

## Prosecutions and penalties

Significant problems of detection have bedevilled apprehension of computer criminals throughout the history of the enforcement of the CMA and the statute does not appear to have had conspicuous success in deterring or apprehending computer criminals. Although there have been some high-profile cases, the total number of prosecutions under the Act has been relatively small.[179] There may be many reasons for this; prosecution of computer crime may not be a priority; police forces may lack relevant expertise; it can be difficult to track down and locate the alleged offenders; the offenders can easily be in a different jurisdiction. Even where there have been prosecutions, in the UK, at least, these have not often attracted severe penalties although it appears that s 3 offences are possibly treated more seriously than s 1 'hacking' offences – the criminal 'intent' and the damage in the former presumably being more obvious in relation to the introduction of malware than in cases of hacking.

In Pile, the first case using CMA, s 3 following its introduction, a custodial sentence of 18 months was imposed. Many virulent virus programs have since been unleashed on the world's computer networks causing damage estimated at many billions of dollars. The originators of some of the more high-profile attacks have been detected, although not necessarily apprehended. The creator of the 'Melissa' virus, the major effect of which was to cause infected computers to send emails containing an infected attachment to the first 50 names in the user's computer address book, was prosecuted in the USA under 18 USC § 1030 and sentenced to 20 months' imprisonment, together with a fine of US$5,000.[180] On the other hand, although Filipino ex-computer science student Onel de Guzman was identified as the creator of the ILOVEYOU virus referred to at the beginning of this section, there were no appropriate charges that could be brought against him in the Philippines[181] and, as there was no Filipino computer crime statute at the time, neither could he be extradited to stand trial elsewhere.[182] The writer of the Anna Kournikova virus voluntarily confessed, and was charged and convicted in the Netherlands; two people have appeared in court in connection with the Blaster worm;[183] and in the UK, a man was jailed for two years for releasing viruses onto the internet. In the unsuccessful appeal against sentence in the latter case, Penry-Davey remarked that 'criminal conduct of this kind has the capacity to cause disruption, consternation and even economic loss on an unimagined scale',[184] showing that courts were becoming aware of the potential severity of such activities.

---

178 Vasileios Kargiannopoulos 'From Morris to Nosal: the history of exceeding authorization and the need for a change' (2014) 20 J Info Tech & Privacy L 465.
179 See HORR75, ch 1 and for latest figures see: www.parliament.uk/business/publications/written-questions-answers-statements/written-question/Commons/2015–01–27/222192/
180 US v Smith DNJ 2 May 2002, see: https://www.justice.gov/archive/criminal/cybercrime/press-releases/2002/melissaSent.htm
181 New law has since been enacted in the Philippines, but it does not have retrospective effect. For further discussion, see, e.g., Sprinkel, above; MD Goodman and SW Brenner, 'The emerging consensus on criminal conduct in cyberspace' (2002) UCLA J L & Tech 3, which also contains details of the new law in the Appendix.
182 See also discussion of the Gary McKinnon case below.
183 US v An Unnamed Juvenile WD Washington 26/9/2003; US v Parson WD Washington 29/8/2003; see: https://www.justice.gov/archive/criminal/cybercrime/press-releases/2003/parsonArrest.htm
184 R v Vallor [2004] 1 Cr App R (S) 54, [7].

An early case of hacking, that of *Bedworth*,[185] achieved a certain amount of notoriety. Bedworth was a teenager whose hacking activities started when he was given a computer for his 14th birthday in 1987. By the time he was arrested in 1991, together with fellow hackers who had all communicated under pseudonyms via an electronic bulletin board, he had hacked into an impressively long list of computer systems, including the *Financial Times*, a cancer research institute in Brussels, the European Commission offices in Luxembourg, and many others, resulting in significant financial losses being incurred by the institutions involved. At his trial, he made no attempt to deny that he had done the acts of which he was accused. His defence was that he was obsessed: he was subject to compulsive behaviour, so that although he knew that what he was doing was unlawful, his obsession denied him the freedom to stop – in other words, he was addicted to hacking.

For addiction to be a sufficient defence to a criminal charge, the individual should be affected to such an extent that the affliction may be viewed as a 'disease of the mind', sufficient to prevent the formation of the requisite *mens rea*. This would then effectively equate with a defence of insanity. Whether or not there is clinical evidence to support any finding of addiction to computer hacking is not a subject that can be debated here, although supporting evidence was produced during the trial. It is certainly the case that, at the trial, Bedworth gave repeated assertions not only that he had committed the acts at issue, but also that he was aware that these acts were wrong and would not be repeated. If he were truly addicted, would he be able to make this latter promise? Charlesworth,[186] citing the case of *Lawrence*,[187] points out that courts are unlikely even to take addiction into account in mitigation. *Lawrence* was, of course, a case in which the offence (of burglary) was committed to feed the addiction rather than being directly related to that addiction. Whilst it can be problematic to draw analogies between such cases and those, such as *Bedworth*, in which the addiction is to the criminal behaviour itself, there is also confirmation for the absence of a general defence of addiction in *Kopsch*:[188] 'The defence of uncontrollable impulse is unknown in English law.' Nevertheless, despite the judge's summing-up, the defence of addiction apparently persuaded the jury and Bedworth was acquitted. At the time, there was concern that this outcome might drive the proverbial 'coach and horses' through the enforcement of the CMA. However, notwithstanding the success of Bedworth's defence, there appears to have been no further attempt to plead such a defence despite anecdotal references to addiction to computers. On the other hand, his co-defendants, Strickland and Woods, were sentenced to six months' imprisonment – a recognition, perhaps, of the fact that the behaviour in question resulted in significant financial loss, can cause serious damage to the systems affected, and should be viewed seriously.

## Case study: The attempted extradition of Gary McKinnon

Some of the issues associated with the treatment of hackers by the legal system and the public perception of such activities and those who are involved are vividly illustrated by the case of Gary McKinnon. McKinnon was accused of, and generally admitted to, hacking into a number of computer systems in the US including those of the US military and NASA. When he had gained access to a computer system he then used it to locate further victims. He did not just browse but also, amongst other things, extracted passwords, installed unauthorised software including remote administration and hacker tools and deleted files including critical system files.[189] Nearly 100 computers in total were affected, but he was able to scan over 73,000, with an estimated

---

185 (1993) unreported. See further A Charlesworth, 'Addiction and hacking' (1993a) 143 NLJ 540 and 'Legislating against computer misuse: The trials and tribulations of the UK Computer Misuse Act 1990' (1993b) J L & IS 80; C Christian, 'Down and out in cyberspace' (1993) 90 Law Soc Gazette 2; D Fisch Nigri, 'Computer crime: Why should we still care' (1993) 9 CLSR 274.
186 A Charlesworth, 'Between flesh and sand: Rethinking the Computer Misuse Act 1990' (1995) 9 LC & T Yearbook 31.
187 [1989] Crim LR 309.
188 (1925) 19 Cr App R 50.
189 For details see: https://www.justice.gov/archive/criminal/cybercrime/press-releases/2002/mckinnonIndict2.htm; and *McKinnon v Government of USA* [2008] UKHL 59, [11]–[16].

monetary loss to the organisations affected of US$900,000 together with the damage consequent on around 2,000 users being without access to the internet for three days.[190] These activities are crimes in both the US and the UK and so the US sought his extradition to stand trial in the US.

A detailed discussion on the law of extradition is beyond the scope of this work but in brief, extradition between the UK and US is governed by the Extradition Act 2003 and the United Kingdom–United States Extradition Treaty 2003. The main rationale for extradition is to attempt to address serious international and transnational crime and 'should provide a quick and effective framework to extradite a person to the country where he is accused or has been convicted of a serious crime, provided that this does not breach his fundamental human rights.'[191] There has been discussion about the fact that extradition between the US and the UK is not evenly balanced; as a result of the requirements of the US constitution, requests to extradite offenders from the US to the UK must be based on 'probable cause' that the offence was committed while in the reverse case as in the McKinnon situation what is required 'reasonable suspicion'. Although there have been attempts to show that this favours extradition to the US, the Baker Review on extradition, which was set up in part as a response to a number of controversial extraditions including that of McKinnon, concluded that the Treaty did not 'operate in an unbalanced manner' and that there was no significant difference between the two tests.[192] In any event, it was not a relevant factor in the McKinnon case as he did not deny the majority of the charges against him. Neither is there evidence for the view that the US is the dominant partner with respect to extradition; the figures show that since the 2003 Treaty the US has not refused any requests for extradition from the UK whereas the UK has denied ten such requests from the US.[193]

McKinnon was offered a plea bargain which if he pleaded guilty and did not contest the extradition would have resulted in a shorter sentence (around four years) most of which could be served in the UK. If he contested the extradition and was subsequently extradited and convicted he could expect a sentence of between eight and ten years with no repatriation although some remission was possible.[194] His appeal was based on this being an abuse of process in the UK but the House of Lords was not persuaded this was different in substance from prosecution bargains in this country to charge for a lesser offence in exchange for a guilty plea and his appeal was unsuccessful. Whilst the legal proceedings were ongoing he was diagnosed with Asperger's syndrome and the argument began to be presented that the pressure of trial and imprisonment in the US could result in him committing suicide and that extradition would breach his human rights. However, the European Court of Human Rights (ECtHR) subsequently rejected his application that extradition would infringe his rights under the European Convention on Human Rights (ECHR).[195] Because the fact that he suffers from Asperger's syndrome came to light fairly late in the proceedings, he was granted a judicial review of both the Home Secretary's decision to extradite and permission to review the Director of Public Prosecution's refusal to prosecute in the UK; but these actions were also unsuccessful.[196]

---

190 Ibid.

191 Extradition Act 2003, Explanatory notes para 7.

192 *A Review of the United Kingdom's Extradition Arrangements* September 2011 paras 1.20 and 1.21, and more detailed consideration at paras 7.35–7.45. See also discussion in Paul Arnell, 'The law of extradition' [2012] 3 SLT 13.

193 See https://uk.usembassy.gov/our-relationship/policy-history/the-u-s-uk-extradition-treaty/frequently-asked-questions-on-the-us-uk-extradition-relationship/. See also discussion in Katherine Higgins, 'Extradition arrangements between the UK and the US' (2012) 10 Arch Rev 6.

194 *McKinnon v Government of USA* [2008] UKHL 59, [2008] 1 WLR 1739, [18]–[20].

195 [2009] EWHC 2021, [16]; see also case comment by Nick W Taylor, 'R (on the application of McKinnon) v DPP' [2010] Crim L Rev 422.

196 Ibid. For a useful timeline of events, see also 'Gary McKinnon: Timeline of the computer hacker's case' (2009) The Telegraph, 31 July, available online at: www.telegraph.co.uk/news/worldnews/northamerica/usa/5945693/Gary-McKinnon-timeline-of-the-computer-hackers-case.html

While the legal process was slowly unfolding, a media campaign against his extradition, spearheaded by this mother, Janis Sharp, was gaining momentum. Against the tacit assumption that hacking was not really a serious criminal activity, McKinnon was increasingly portrayed as a vulnerable individual, a 'harmless oddball',[197] who had committed the crimes almost unwittingly, and was being persecuted by a strong-arm government. It was reported in the courts that he had:

> admitted leaving a note on one army computer reading: 'US foreign policy is akin to government-sponsored terrorism these days . . . It was not a mistake that there was a huge security stand down on 11 September last year . . . I am SOLO. I will continue to disrupt at the highest levels . . .'.[198]

This appears to have been ignored in popular media reports. He was reported as being in search of evidence of UFOs, anti-gravity technology and the 'suppression of free energy'.[199] As well as supportive articles in many newspapers, the campaign gained the support of politicians including David Cameron and Nick Clegg and the organisation Liberty whose director Shami Chakrabati referred to 'The shoddy treatment of this vulnerable man'.[200] The eminent human rights lawyer Geoffrey Robertson was even quoted as saying that McKinnon would be unlikely to receive any custodial sentence if tried in this country,[201] although there seems no particular basis for that view; as evidenced by the discussion in this chapter, custodial sentences are allowed for[202] and have been imposed for breach of the CMA, albeit perhaps not comparable in length to those imposed in the US. However, he was certainly not likely to face anything like 60 years in a US jail; despite the impression given by many of newspaper reports.[203] The *Daily Mail*, in particular, mounted a particularly vociferous campaign on his behalf and the overall publicity generated led a new Home Secretary, Theresa May, to suspend the decision to extradite on the receipt of new medical evidence. This led her to conclude that McKinnon's extradition would give rise to such a high risk of him ending his life that a decision to extradite would be incompatible with his human rights.[204] This decision was trumpeted by the *Daily Mail* as 'a timely reminder of the vital role of a free Press in holding politicians to account, and giving a voice to the powerless, when nobody else will stand up for our ancient liberties'[205] although Alan Johnson, the Home Secretary who had following the legal arguments made the initial decision to extradite remarked that a Home Secretary should put justice before popularity and that justice should not depend on whether you have a feisty mother, an effective campaign or even the backing of a major national newspaper.[206]

## Review and reform

On a first examination, it appears that the bespoke provisions of the CMA have not had any more conspicuous success at deterring or apprehending computer misuse than the hotchpotch of offences

197 See www.telegraph.co.uk/comment/columnists/allison-pearson/9615113/Gary-McKinnon-a-harmless-oddballs-triumph-over-torment.html
198 [2008] UKHL 59, [16].
199 See, e.g., www.telegraph.co.uk/news/uknews/law-and-order/9622065/Gary-McKinnon-humanity-wins-out-over-spooks.html. In addition, the website freegary.com is still active and now provides a vehicle for McKinnon to market his computer skills.
200 Quoted in Azmina Gulamhusein, 'Gary McKinnon case is acid test of coalition government's integrity' (2010) *Law Society Gazette*, 7 June, available online at: www.lawgazette.co.uk/55767.article
201 See www.theguardian.com/world/2009/nov/26/computer-hacker-gary-mckinnon-extradition
202 The maximum custodial term which can be imposed on indictment is now two years for s 1, five years for the aggravated offence in s 2, and ten years for s 3. See later discussion at p 301.
203 See, e.g., www.dailymail.co.uk/news/article-2248209/Gary-McKinnon-face-charges-hacking.html
204 See https://www.gov.uk/government/news/theresa-may-statement-on-gary-mckinnon-extradition
205 See www.dailymail.co.uk/debate/article-2218757/A-triumph-Gary-McKinnon-British-justice.html
206 See www.telegraph.co.uk/news/uknews/law-and-order/9618928/Alan-Johnson-Home-Secretary-Theresa-May-took-the-easy-way-out.html

in use prior to its enactment. The absence of homogeneity of subject matter already evident in the discussion in this chapter and which will be continued in the next has meant that a coherent legal response to 'computer crime' and 'cybercrime' has proved to be problematic.

Prior to the amendments to s 3 as a result of the APIG report, there had been many calls for a review to establish whether the provisions of the Act were still appropriate in the light of new technological advances. The pressure was intensified by observations that the CMA had not originally been designed to deal with the internet and that, in that respect, its 'premature birth' had left it 'weak and vulnerable'.[207] Interestingly, in the light of all of the criticisms and the perception that the statute had passed its sell-by date, the general impression from the report was one of satisfaction with the way in which the CMA was perceived to have stood the test of time and a finding that some of the expressed dissatisfaction with the statute was due to misapprehension about its provisions – a fact described by the report as 'an entirely undesirable state of affairs'.[208] A number of respondents, for example, had asked for the statute to be extended to deal with hacking and viruses, despite the fact that ss 1 and 3 had been used successfully with respect to both activities. The report also concluded that the absence of definitions had not been shown to be an impediment to application of the Act by the courts, because the relevant terms had been understood to 'have the appropriate contemporary meaning'.[209] Given the clear evidence of ignorance about the nature and application of the provisions, there was a need for the Home Office to 'prioritise the provision of website material about the CMA because it is directly relevant to internet users and because it is clearly widely misunderstood'.[210]

## Problems of enforcement

Further criticisms related to the apparently small number of prosecutions even though, as discussed at the beginning of this chapter, the apparent incidence of computer misuse is both large and increasing. Prosecution cannot be commenced unless the crime is detected and the offender identified and it seems to be not much easier to catch cybercriminals now than it was in the 1990s. It has been commented in the US that 'computer crimes are notoriously difficult to prosecute due to both the nature of the technology itself and law enforcement's relative unfamiliarity with technology'[211] and this comment could probably be applied just as easily to other jurisdictions. Without doubt the nature of the technology itself creates many problems for enforcement and new developments are happening all the time, but the internet has been with us now for many years and for much of that time has been readily recognised as facilitating many types of criminal activity so perhaps it is time law enforcement stopped hiding behind the shield of general unfamiliarity. It has been suggested that consumers should be provided with 'an authoritative policing voice on current cyber crime issues'; that cybercrime should be included in the Strategic Policing Requirement; that there should be sufficient resources for local forces to respond to cybercrime and that it should be made easier for the public to report cybercrime.[212] Implementation of any of these initiatives might lead to improvements in detection.

A major obstacle to a realistic assessment of both the magnitude of the problem and the law's response to it is the difficulty in collecting accurate data. Crime statistics do not separate cybercrime from the equivalent crime committed offline – neither is the cyber element recorded. As pointed out by the House of Lords Science and Technology Committee,[213] for some offences, it can often be difficult to extricate computer crime from the same crime committed by more traditional methods, but nevertheless the Committee recommended that a more coordinated approach to data collection

---

207 MacEwan, above, 956.
208 APIG, above, para 23.
209 Ibid, para 17.
210 Ibid, para 25.
211 Alexander Galicki, Drew Haven and Alden Pelker, 'Computer Crimes' (2014) 51 Am Crim L Rev 875, 913.
212 House of Commons Science and Technology Committee, Twelfth Report of Session 2010–12: Malware and Cyber Crime, 2012, Conclusions paras 13–16.
213 Ibid, para 2.29

should be introduced, including a classification scheme for recording the incidence of all forms of e-crime.[214] However, at the time of writing, there are, as yet, no more accurate estimates of cyber-crime. From the numbers that are available, it certainly appears to be the case that there have been very few prosecutions although 55 defendants were proceeded against in 2013 which is more than double the number in any previous year.[215] This information was published as a response to ques-tions asked in Parliament about convictions for computer misuse, misuse of social media and cyber-stalking. Only convictions for CMA offences were given and the assertion that it was 'not possible to separately identify . . . convictions and sentences involving the use or misuse of social media, or cybercrime'[216] underlines that identifying the extent of such activities remains a problem.

## Penalties

Further amendments having their origins in the APIG report included a revision of the penalties for the s 1 offence. It was felt that this would allow a more realistic reflection of the damage that might be done, s 35 of the Police and Justice Act 2006, thus amended s 1 of the CMA both to make the offence triable either way and to increase the maximum penalties. The maximum penalties on indictment now include custodial sentences of two years for the s 1 offence, five years for the s 2 offence, and ten years for the s 3 offence. As it appears even more difficult to get accurate infor-mation on sentencing than on convictions, it is not easy to assess how these penalties are employed. As was clear from comments made in relation to the McKinnon case, there is certainly a perception that custodial sentences are not frequently imposed in response to breaches of CMA.[217]

Anderson et al note that robbery generally appears to attract larger penalties than burglary, even though the average financial loss tends to be greater in the latter and suggests this is because of the 'disproportionate social costs' in cases of robbery.[218] They suggest that the typically lighter sentences imposed in CMA cases may be because the offences are perceived as less vindictive and evoke less resentment. In contrast to some other views that the individual user should take more responsibility for their own cyber security;[219] and suggestions that resources should be directed more in response to those who commit cybercrime that is 'on the prosaic business of hunting down cyber-criminals and throwing them in jail';[220] and that their analysis of the increasing inci-dence of cybercrime indicates that 'the case for more vigorous policing is stronger than ever.'[221] There is also support for the need to ensure that the CMA sentences should better reflect the dam-age done by cybercrime from the Home Affairs Committee:

> We were surprised by the fact Anonymous hackers who cost Paypal over £3.5m were given sentences of 7 and 18 months and do not believe they would have received such sentences had they physically robbed a bank of £3.5 million. The DPP should review the sentencing guidance and ensure e-criminals receive the same sentences as if they had stolen that amount of money or data offline.[222]

Even if the maximum penalties under CMA do send out 'a clear message that society now takes hacking offences rather more seriously than in 1990',[223] an important aspect of sentencing is not

---

214 Ibid, para 2.42.
215 See www.parliament.uk/business/publications/written-questions-answers-statements/written-question/Commons/2015–01–27/222192/
216 Ibid. But see also discussion on p 319 with respect to social media cases.
217 See comment of Geoffrey Robertson discussed on p 299.
218 Ross Anderson et al, 'Measuring the Cost of Cybercrime', 11th Annual Workshop on the Economics of the Information Society (Berlin 2012), available online at: http://weis2012.econinfosec.org/papers/Anderson_WEIS2012.pdf (see p 26).
219 See e.g. Robert LaRose, Nora J. Rifon, and Richard Enbody 'Promoting personal responsibility for internet safety' (2008) 51 Com-munications of the ACM 71.
220 Anderson et al, above, p 1.
221 Ibid, p 26.
222 Home Affairs Committee, E-Crime (2013–2014, 70-I) [56].
223 APIG, above, paras 98 and 99.

only the robustness of the penalties and the perceived deterrent effect, but also that they actually fit the crime. For technology-specific crimes such as the basic hacking offence in s 1 of the CMA, penalties are defined in statute, and the 2006 amendments have begun to address any perceived shortfall, a process which is set to continue as discussed below. However, for other computer crime – particularly offences involving fraud – the problem of high-volume, low-denomination crime may mean that large scams go unpunished.[224]

## Investigations and international cooperation

There is a demonstrable lack of consensus both in the definition of, and in the severity of, the offences, and also in identifying the jurisdiction in which the offence occurred. This means that an international approach is desirable if measures to combat cybercrime are to have any chance of success, but as demonstrated by the facts surrounding the cases of McKinnon and Guzman,[225] this is not always a straightforward matter. Provisions aimed at facilitating international cooperation and mutual assistance were included in Arts 23–35 of the Council of Europe Cybercrime Convention.[226] In addition to the usual Council of Europe states, participation in the treaty also included USA, Canada, Japan, and South Africa. There have been a number of criticisms of its provisions on various bases, as will be explored further in the next chapter, but the mutual assistance provisions were a particular issue for many US civil liberties organisations such as the Electronic Privacy Information Center (EPIC), ACLU, etc. This objection was largely predicated on a distrust of other states to provide a basic level of human rights protection. Thus, although Keyser suggested that 'it seems very important for an international regime to be set up to combat these types of crimes in a growing and integrated global society which is becoming ever more vulnerable to cyber attacks',[227] nevertheless he still espoused the view that 'although it may not be such a big deal to have the US government wield greater power, the same new powers will also be given to member countries that may not have a strong tradition of checks and balances on police power'.[228] The ACLU was even stronger in its opposition to the mutual assistance provisions, stating that 'ratification of the Council of Europe's Convention on Cybercrime will put the United States in the morally repugnant position of supporting the actions of politically corrupt and evil regimes',[229] and, in its submission to the Senate Foreign Relations Committee considering the ratification, the ACLU suggested that 'the Senate should carefully consider what it means to agree to provide mutual legal assistance to countries whose substantive laws and procedures do not comport with American understandings of justice'.[230]

A further criticism was that the Convention did not satisfactorily provide a balance between the objectives of investigating cybercrime, and the privacy of those who use the internet and worldwide web. Such critics highlighted the data preservation requirements in the Convention and their potential to infringe the privacy of innocent internet users, and, in addition, Aldesco suggested that the data preservation requirements could also infringe freedom of expression by exerting a chilling effect on anonymous online speech.[231] Since 11 September 2001 ('9/11'), many countries have passed laws that allow data preservation or data retention in an attempt not to lose

---

224 See House of Lords Science and Technology Committee, above, para 7.70, and discussion above at p 274.
225 Discussed above at p 296.
226 The substantive provisions of this Convention are discussed in more detail in Chapter 8.
227 M Keyser, 'The Council of Europe Convention on Cybercrime' (2003) 12 J Transnat'l L & Pol'y 287, 296.
228 Ibid, 316.
229 American Civil Liberties Union (ACLU), 'Memo on the Council of Europe Convention on Cybercrime' (2004) 16 June, available online at: www.aclu.org/technology-and-liberty/aclu-memo-council-europe-convention-cybercrime
230 American Civil Liberties Union (ACLU), 'Letter to the Senate Foreign Relations Committee on the Council of Europe Convention on Cybercrime' (2004) 16 June, available online at: www.aclu.org/technology-and-liberty/aclu-letter-senate-foreign-relations-committee-council-europe-convention-cybe
231 Albert I Aldesco, 'The demise of anonymity: A constitutional challenge to the Convention on Cybercrime' (2002) 23 Loy LA Ent L Rev 81, 110. See also discussion on freedom of speech in relation to content crime in Chapter 8.

data that might be relevant to the investigation of international terrorism. Interestingly, in response to such fears, the USA has favoured data preservation over the mandatory retention of data that has received favour in many European states.[232] Both techniques have the propensity to infringe privacy, but, arguably, expeditious preservation is more likely to meet the proportionality requirement in Art 15(1), to which all of the provisions on expedited preservation of stored computer data are expressly subject, than the data retention regimes being introduced in Europe, including the UK.[233] Arguably, it is difficult in an international convention to be anything other than aspirational, and to rely on the will of the individual participants to translate and implement the provisions appropriately. Nevertheless, Taylor remarked that a 'vague reference to proportionality will not be adequate to ensure that civil liberties are protected'[234] and Jarvie suggested that 'the European Cybercrime Convention is regrettably silent on the appropriate safeguards'.[235]

## Directive 2013/40/EU – the 'Botnet Directive'
There has also now been further recognition of the need for a coordinated international approach by the European Union. The EU Council Framework Decision of 2005[236] has been replaced by a directive[237] which effectively requires Member States to harmonise their criminal law in relation to attacks on information systems given that 'the approximation of law was considered to be the only way of ensuring that the victims of computer crime were provided with a minimum level of protection.'[238] It is aimed particularly at large-scale cyber attacks which threaten the critical infrastructure of Member States or the EU.[239] It establishes minimum rules regarding the definition of offences and that these offences should be punishable by 'effective, proportionate and dissuasive criminal penalties.' At the time of the Framework Decision this would not have been possible as criminal competence at the EU level was not recognised until the Lisbon Treaty which came into force in 2009. Article 83(2) of the TFEU now provides that directives can establish minimum rules for definitions offences and penalties in situations where the approximation of criminal laws is necessary to implement an EU policy. The EU strategy on cybersecurity was subsequently published in 2013 as a part of the Common Foreign and Security Policy.[240]

The Directive includes provisions that outlaw the use of botnets and malicious software, as well as illegally obtained passwords. As discussed above botnets can be used to control many different types of cybercrime and cyber attacks and their control is a particular objective of the Directive.[241] In particular, the Directive requires Member States to criminalise illegal access to information systems (Article 3), illegal system interference (Article 4), illegal data interference (Article 5) and illegal interception (Article 6). In all of these cases, the conduct will be criminal when it is done 'intentionally and without right.' 'Without right' is defined in Art 2(d) to mean conduct which is 'not authorised by the owner or by another right holder . . . or not permitted under national law.' From this wording it seems likely that there may still be issues regarding authorisation in borderline cases. In support of the above provisions, Art 7 requires Member States to criminalise the use, production, sale etc of computer programs, passwords and access codes with the intention to commit one of the specified offences.

232  For further discussion on data retention, see Chapter 10.
233  See, e.g., the Anti-terrorism, Crime and Security Act 2001 and the associated Code of Practice on Data Retention 2003.
234  G Taylor, 'The Council of Europe Cybercrime Convention: A civil liberties perspective' (2002), available online at: www.crime-research.org/library/CoE_Cybercrime.html
235  N Jarvie, 'Control of cybercrime: Is an end to our privacy on the internet a price worth paying?' (2003) 9 CTLR 110, 115.
236  See above p. 292.
237  Directive 2013/40/EU of the European Parliament and of the Council of 12 August 2013 on attacks against information systems and replacing Council Framework Decision 2005/222/JHA, [2013] OJ L218/8.
238  Sarah Summers, Christian Schwarzenegger, Gian Ege and Finlay Young, *The Emergence of EU Criminal Law: Cybercrime and the Regulation of the Information Society*, 2014, Hart, p 100.
239  Recitals 1–6.
240  Joint Communication to the European Parliament, the Council, the European Economic and Social Committee and the Committee of the Regions, *Cybersecurity Strategy of the European Union: An Open, Safe and Secure Cyberspace* JOIN(2013) 1 final, 7 Feb 2013.
241  Recital 5.

The Directive requires Member States to provide sanctions that are 'effective, proportionate and dissuasive' and, in particular, mandates minimum and maximum penalties of between two and five years' imprisonment. The more severe penalties should be used when organised groups attack information systems or in cases of significant damage or damage to key information infrastructures.[242] The cross-jurisdictional nature of cybercrime is recognised by provisions establishing when Member States can exert jurisdiction and which aim to improve co-operation between judicial and other competent authorities.[243] In recognition that better data is needed to 'gain a more complete picture of the problem of cybercrime . . . at Union level and thereby to contribute to a more effective response',[244] Art 14 requires Member States to instigate systems for recording statistical data relating to the offences defined by the Directive. Such action has already been recommended[245] and it will be interesting to see if the need to comply with this Directive precipitates action.

## Cybercrime and the Serious Crime Act

Directive 2013/40/EU will be implemented in the UK by certain provisions of the Serious Crime Act 2015 which amend the CMA. The main one of these is to create a new offence of impairing a computer such as to cause serious damage. As noted above, the existing s 3 offence carries a maximum penalty of ten years' imprisonment which is already well in excess of the minimum required by the Directive. However this penalty was not considered sufficient where 'the impact of the action is to cause serious damage, for example to the critical national infrastructure'[246] and the offence in the new s 3ZA, which was brought into force in May 2015, will carry a maximum penalty of life imprisonment where the damage is to national security or involves threat to life or loss of life. In cases of damage to the economy or the environment, the maximum penalty will be 14 years.

(1)  A person is guilty of an offence if –

    (a)  the person does any unauthorised act in relation to a computer;

    (b)  at the time of doing the act the person knows that it is unauthorised; and

    (c)  the act causes, or creates a significant risk of, serious damage of a material kind; and

    (d)  the person intends by doing the act to cause serious damage of a material kind or is reckless as to whether such damage is caused.

(2)  Damage is of a 'material kind' for the purposes of this section if it is –

    (a)  damage to human welfare in any place;

    (b)  damage to the environment of any place;

    (c)  damage to the economy of any country; or

    (d)  damage to the national security of any country.

Further subsections expand on what constitutes damage to human welfare and other ancillary matters. Although the concept of 'serious damage' is crucial to the new section there appears to be no guidance on the meaning of 'serious'. Although in many cases it may be clear that the damage is 'serious', there is likely to be dispute in more borderline cases as to whether or not the new section is applicable.

Other minor amendments to CMA ss 3A and 4 also ensure conformity with the Directive which had to be implemented by September 2015.

---

242 Article 9.
243 Articles 12 and 13 and see also Recitals 22, 23, 26 and 27.
244 Recital 24.
245 House of Commons Science and Technology Committee, above, para 2.42.
246 Serious Crime Bill, Explanatory Notes [126].

## Conclusions

Cybercrime has become endemic within the environment created by ICT. The Home Affairs Select Committee on e-crime (HC 70) has remarked that the UK is losing the war against online criminal activity and that the government is too complacent about the issue. Although bespoke legislation may have been drafted and amended appropriately, the most significant issue is arguably not the legislation itself but its application and enforcement. The existence of the legal provisions of themselves will do little to deter crime; it should not come as a surprise that perpetrators flout the law and it seems unlikely that much will change unless more people are caught and prosecuted and, on conviction, are handed appropriate sentences. Further, given the global dimension, supportive international cooperation will often be an important prerequisite to successful apprehension of cybercriminals.

There is little reason to suppose that this will be changed by the amendments introduced to give effect to Directive 2013/40/EU. The cyber attacks which are of most concern to governments and the supranational EU are those which either threaten national security or compromise the critical IT infrastructure and these are a particular target of the Directive and its implementation. But, as we have seen, other cyber criminal activity can have a devastating effect on its victims, whether individuals or organisations and the new amendments will have little impact on that. It is therefore unlikely that there will be any significant reduction in the damage inflicted by cybercrime unless users of ICT increase practical security measures which can be taken to deter cyber criminals. In recognition of this both the UK and the EU have developed cyber security strategies but uptake of relevant recommendations needs to be widespread if cybercrime is not to continue to be a growth industry.

## Further reading

Majid Yar, *Cybercrime and Society*, 2nd edn, 2013, Sage
David S Wall, *Cybercrime: The Transformation of Crime in the Information Age*, 2007, Polity
Mike McGuire and Samantha Dowling, *Cybercrime: A review of the evidence*, 2013, Home Office Research Report 75, available online at: www.gov.uk/government/publications/cyber-crime-a-review-of-the-evidence
J Clough, *Principles of Cybercrime*, 2010, Cambridge University Press

# Chapter 8

# Content crimes

## Chapter contents

# Introduction

The previous chapter focused on crimes which either caused damage to computers or computer networks or which resulted in pecuniary loss to individuals or organisations. In such cases, the loss can be measured in financial terms. The discussion in this chapter will focus on another type of activity which has been made significantly easier by the increase in size and capability of computer networks and which is damaging in a different way: the propagation and dissemination of criminal content.

Although there are clearly great benefits to be gained from the use of global computer networks, regulating the type of content available has proved challenging in a number of ways. Computer networks facilitate communications between both individuals and groups, as well as provide the means to access and retrieve extensive information from a variety of sources across the globe. Not surprisingly, this not only includes educational and informative material, but also includes information that might, at the least, be undesirable or antisocial, but might also be defamatory, obscene or pornographic, racist, malicious, threatening or abusive, or may constitute undesirable religious or political propaganda. Much of this information might attract the application of the criminal law in a number of jurisdictions, but it may be that the existing law in a jurisdiction is not tailored appropriately for application to computer networks. The CMA and similar statutes in other jurisdictions are a particular example of the law's response to some of these activities, which, despite the differences between the jurisdictions, in many respects shows a remarkable consistency of philosophy and approach. There is, however, unlikely to be such consensus over the standard of content that is made available through this medium. Certain governments may be sensitive about the expression of some political or religious views, and it is also evident that acceptable standards and definitions of obscene or pornographic material will vary from place to place. Although, in line with international instruments, many states now guarantee a constitutionally protected right to freedom of expression, there is no consistency about the extent to which content deemed undesirable may fall outside the scope of such a right. Exceptions to the right of freedom of expression are heavily dependent on historical, cultural, and political factors, as well as general social mores within a jurisdiction. Some jurisdictions may concur on one type of speech, but have widely divergent views on others. Thus Germany and the USA both protect freedom of expression in their respective constitutions, but, as noted by Delacourt, although they are 'at least on the same page with regard to pornography . . . their treatment of divisive political propaganda differs dramatically'.[1]

Given the ease of accessing information that originates in another jurisdiction, is it possible to control the propagation of such material or to enforce national laws on a medium that does not recognise national boundaries? What factors should determine the acceptability of content on global networks? Should the same standards be applied as are applied to publishing of hard copy, or to television and radio broadcasts? The fundamental difference between the internet or worldwide web and these other forms of communication is that the global network is capable of fulfilling all of these functions simultaneously; thus, in some circumstances, it may be appropriate to utilise similar rules as are used for traditional publication, but at other times, such an attempt may be felt to be a violation of the right to free speech, or even the right to privacy. This chapter will consider some of the issues raised by the publication of criminal content, using the legal response to pornographic material as a specific example, although other content will be referred to as appropriate.[2] Although the legal responses to what content is or is not acceptable depends on

---

1 JT Delacourt, 'The international impact of internet regulation' (1997) 38 Harv Int LJ 207, 214. See also, in this context, JF McGuire, 'When speech is heard around the world: Internet content regulation in the United States and Germany' (1999) 74 NYUL Rev 750, and the *Yahoo! v LICRA* litigation discussed in Chapter 3.

2 For a discussion of other extreme content, see, e.g., A Roversi, *Hate on the Net, Extremist Sites, Neo-fascism On-line, Electronic Jihad*, 2008, Farnham: Ashgate.

local legal traditions and mores, as discussed below, most jurisdictions have either applied existing legislation, sometimes with amendments, or enacted bespoke legislation to respond to criminal content on the internet.

## Content regulation in the US

The USA has a strongly embedded commitment to free speech enshrined in the First Amendment, but this has does not mean that there has not been significant legal activity surrounding the question of regulation of content on the internet. In the 1990s, the use of the internet as a medium for the circulation of various types of pornography, together with the fact that such material could then easily be accessed by minors, caused both concern and controversy amongst both politicians and the public. An examination of the legislative and judicial response to this issue provides a useful illustration of some of the difficulties encountered when attempting to regulate content on the internet.

### The Communications Decency Act of 1996

The US Communications Decency Act (CDA), passed in 1996, was aimed at preventing young people from accessing indecent material via computer networks. It made it a criminal offence to engage in communication on computer networks that was either 'indecent' or 'patently offensive' if the contents of that communication could be viewed by a minor. Neglecting the not-inconsiderable difficulty of ascertaining the age of those accessing the material, although the motive behind the legislation was generally recognised as benevolent, the wide scope of the provisions was regarded by many as an unacceptable intrusion into the right to free speech, and consequently a potential breach of the First Amendment. This led to the American Civil Liberties Union (ACLU) immediately challenging the constitutionality of the statute, and beginning what turned out to be lengthy saga of litigation and legislation.

The primary issue was, of course, that some forms of pornography were entirely legal for distribution and consumption by an adult audience. Given the nature of the medium, it was likely that action to prevent viewing by minors would also prevent legitimate viewing by adults. A further feature of the challenge to the CDA was the assertion that the provisions were not only unnecessarily broad, but also vague. 'Obscenity' had a well-accepted definition derived from *Miller v California*,[3] which was based on an application of contemporary community standards. The CDA, however, referred not to 'obscene', but to 'indecent', material – indecent speech, as well as obscene speech, could permissibly be regulated on broadcast media, but the former had a rather wider scope, merely referring to 'nonconformance with accepted standards of morality'.[4]

At first instance, the court considered extensively the characteristics of the medium, and the distinctions between it and other methods of mass communication – particularly the broadcast media – and noted that:

> Four related characteristics of Internet communication have a transcendent importance to our shared holding that the CDA is unconstitutional on its face . . . First, the Internet presents very low barriers to entry. Second, these barriers to entry are identical for both speakers and listeners. Third, as a result of these low barriers, astoundingly diverse content is available on the Internet. Fourth, the Internet provides significant access to all who wish to speak in the medium, and even creates a relative parity among speakers . . . [5]

---

3 413 US 15 (1973).
4 See discussion in *FCC v Pacifica Foundation* 438 US 726 (1978).
5 *ACLU v Reno I* 929 F Supp 824, 872 (ED Pa 1996).

Further, the court noted that, unlike broadcast media, which had the potential to be particularly invasive,[6] locating information on the internet required deliberate, affirmative acts. The court found evidence that communication on the internet had more in common with a telephone conversation than with broadcasting and that, based on this reasoning, the government had little pretext for regulating its content. Although it was well established that First Amendment guarantees would be lost in cases of obscenity and child pornography, the court was of the view that the existing law that proscribed this type of content could equally be applied to the internet. But in any case, the target of the CDA was not obscene material, but that which was 'indecent' or 'patently offensive'. 'Obscene' might have a recognised meaning, but that was not the case with regard to 'indecent' and neither was it defined by the statute. Given the criminal penalties attached to breach of the Act, and the difficulties in ascertaining what material would be covered and the range of defendants, the court was unanimously of the opinion that the statute was unconstitutional for reasons of vagueness.

This decision was upheld by the Supreme Court, which discussed what it saw as the impossibility of applying the community standards test for obscenity to the propagation of material on the internet, because it would inevitably mean that the standard applied would have to be that of the community most likely to be offended by the material. This would reduce the constitutionally protected material available to adults to 'only what is fit for children'.[7] Justice Stevens drew particular attention to factors already underlined in the lower court, such as the democratising effect on speech, the growth and acceptance of internet communication, and the important issue of proportionality, noting that the CDA could not be constitutional if its objectives could be achieved by 'a more carefully drafted statute'.[8]

## The Child Online Protection Act of 1998

A further attempt at legislative intervention followed immediately[9] in the form of the Child Online Protection Act of 1998 (COPA), in which Congress intended to rectify the specific concerns raised in the CDA litigation. The provisions of COPA made it a federal crime to propagate material online that was 'harmful to minors' for 'commercial purposes' (47 USC § 231(1)). By virtue of 47 USC § 231(e)(2)(A), it would only be inferred that the communication was for commercial purposes if the person were 'engaged in the business of making such communication'. The phrase 'engaged in the business of communication' was defined in 47 USC §231(c)(2)(B) and 'harmful to minors' was defined in 47 USC §231(e)(6) in terms of obscenity, appearing to or pandering to the prurient interest, as recognised by 'contemporary community standards'. This statute was again challenged by ACLU on the basis that it was invalid, both because it violated the First Amendment rights of both adults and minors (on the grounds that what might be inappropriate for a six-year-old might be permissible for someone aged 16), and because it was constitutionally vague. The government's view that the statute was aimed purely at commercial pornographers received short shrift from the court, which pointed out that there was nothing in the text that suggested that the statute's provisions were limited in this way. Like its predecessor, the CDA, the court was of the view that COPA infringed the right of adults to freedom of speech and expression, concluding, albeit somewhat reluctantly, that 'the protection of children from access to harmful to minors materials on the web, the compelling interest sought to be furthered by Congress in COPA, particularly resonates with the court', and that its decision to allow an injunction against enforcement would 'delay

6 See FCC v Pacifica, above
7 521 US 844, 888.
8 Ibid, 874.
9 Blanks Hindman reports that this statute passed through Congress quickly with limited debate and that the House of Representatives only devoted about half an hour to its discussion: Elizabeth Blanks Hindman, 'Protection childhood: Rights, social goals and the First Amendment in the context of the Child Online Protection Act (2010) 15 Comm L Pol'y 1.

once again the careful protection of our children'. However, the court was 'acutely cognizant of its charge under the law of this country not to protect the majoritarian will at the expense of stifling the rights embodied in the Constitution', and so the injunction was granted.

On appeal, the Court of Appeals for the Third Circuit[10] focused specifically on the application of contemporary community standards in cyberspace and came to the conclusion that the overbreadth of the definition 'harmful to minors' consequent on using this standard must lead inexorably to a holding of unconstitutionality of the whole statute. The court thus arrived at the conclusion that the concept of community standards derived from Miller was not applicable in this situation, although it remained a 'useful and viable tool in contexts other than the internet and the Web'[11] and this was the primary basis on which the court upheld the decision that COPA was unconstitutional. The Supreme Court, however, disagreed on this point. It specifically considered the rejection of the Miller test, disagreeing with the finding that it was inappropriate for computer networks, and concluded that this of itself did not result in COPA being overbroad.[12] Given that the legal argument on appeal had only focused on this one aspect of unconstitutionality, the case was remanded to the Third Circuit for further consideration. On this occasion, the court considered all of the issues relating to whether COPA could withstand strict scrutiny, whether the statute served a compelling governmental interest, and whether it was narrowly tailored to achieve that interest and was the least restrictive means of advancing that interest, as well as whether it was overbroad.[13] Although accepting that there was a compelling interest, the court found a number of the provisions not to be narrowly tailored, including the definitions of 'material harmful to minors' and 'commercial purposes'. In addition, in considering less restrictive means of achieving the same objective, there was significant discussion of the use of technological devices in place of legislation to control content. The conclusion was reached that 'the various blocking and filtering techniques . . . may be substantially less restrictive than COPA'.[14] The use of filtering and blocking mechanisms for undesirable content provides a method of self-regulation of content in line with the view that 'at the heart of the First Amendment lies the principle that each person should decide for himself or herself the ideas and beliefs deserving of expression consideration and adherence'.[15] This in turn is also in line with the judgment in Pacifica[16] that regulatory intervention could be supported for broadcast media because listeners were not always able to control what they received; this was one of the bases for the distinction made between the internet and broadcast media in ACLU v Reno I, discussed earlier.

Although the case had still not been subjected to the rigours of a full trial, this decision of the Third Circuit led to the case once more being considered by the Supreme Court.[17] On this occasion, the Supreme Court supported the imposition of the injunction. It noted that 'content-based prohibitions, enforced by severe criminal penalties, have the constant potential to be a repressive force in the lives and thoughts of a free people',[18] and so focused particularly on the use of filtering software as a method of regulating content, which was, in its view, both less restrictive and more effective than COPA. As a result, the case was then remanded for full trial to determine whether a permanent injunction should be issued – a decision that led to acid comments from Breyer J, who had given a dissenting judgment: '. . . after eight years of legislative effort, two statutes and three Supreme Court cases the Court sends this case back to the District Court for further proceedings.

---

10 *ACLU v Reno II* 217 F 3d 162 (3rd Cir 2000).
11 Ibid, 180.
12 *Ashcroft v ACLU* 535 US 564 (2002) (renamed following a change in Attorney General).
13 322 F 3d 240 (3rd Cir 2003).
14 Ibid, 265.
15 *Turner Broad Sys Inc v FCC* 512 US 622, 641 (1994).
16 *FCC v Pacifica Foundation* 438 US 726 (1978); see also John B Morris Jr and Cynthia M Wong, 'Revisiting user control: The emergence and success of a First Amendment theory for the internet age' (2009) 8 First Amend L Rev 109.
17 *Ashcroft v ACLU* 542 US 656 (2004).
18 Ibid, 660.

What proceedings? I have found no offer by either party to present more relevant evidence. What remains to be litigated?'[19] Cognisant, perhaps, of the strong lobbies on both sides of the debate, the Court made it clear that it was not deciding that it was not possible to draft suitable legislation relating to minors' access to the internet, and that its decision did not therefore 'foreclose the District Court from concluding, upon a proper showing by the Government, . . . that COPA is the least restrictive alternative available to accomplish Congress' goal'.[20] However, this was not to be the outcome. In 2008, the Third Circuit Court of Appeals upheld the decision of the District Court[21] to issue a permanent injunction and, by using substantially the same reasoning that had been employed previously, effectively affirmed Breyer J's contention that there was little else to be litigated. The overall conclusion was that COPA 'could not withstand strict scrutiny, vagueness or overbreadth analysis and thus is unconstitutional'.[22] Nevertheless, the US government remained undeterred and made a further appeal to the Supreme Court, but its refusal to hold a further hearing[23] finally terminated the long cycle of litigation.

This saga of judicial and legislative debate provides a vivid demonstration of the almost-irreconcilable tension between different interests even within one jurisdiction. Notwithstanding the US courts continuing to maintain strong judicial protection for free speech, the persistence of the US government attempts to get COPA onto the statute book highlights the strength of the lobby on the other side of the argument, which views the internet as an anarchic mode of communication justifying legislative intervention to regulate content and forming the 'compelling interest' recognised by the courts. As we have seen, the original litigation dates back to 1996, and the COPA litigation alone was of ten years' duration as it worked its way 'through three levels of the court system (some of them three times), four attorneys general and through all or part of the terms of three presidents'.[24]

On the one hand excessive regulation has a chilling effect on free expression but on the other there are genuine societal concerns over what is acceptable content and the fulcrum between the two can vary considerably. Given the difficulty in achieving any consensus on either an appropriate standard, or an appropriate regulatory method, finding a global solution seems extremely remote. The evidence shows that, as might be expected, there is a plethora of approaches to these issues, reflecting a variety of cultural and legal traditions. An early example of the effect of a mismatch between acceptable standards arose at the end of 1995 as a result of the difference in approach between Germany and the USA. It was found that customers of the ISP, CompuServe Germany, could access certain pornographic sites. In order to comply with the resultant court order, the parent company, CompuServe USA, blocked access to sites that the police had designated unsuitable because they contained representations of violent, child, or animal pornography. As a result, for a short period, no customers of CompuServe worldwide could access the sites in question, showing the potential for the actions of only one jurisdiction to have a global effect. Following the global block, general access was restored, but customers in Germany were offered free blocking software, although this did not prevent the offending sites being accessed by German customers and, eventually, the local manager of CompuServe Germany, Felix Somm, was charged with assisting in the dissemination of pornographic writings contrary to s 184 of

---

19 Ibid, 668.

20 Ibid, 673. For discussion of the proposition that a combination of regulatory techniques might be a more viable way forward, see Douglas Husack, 'The criminal law as last resort' [2004] OJLS 207.

21 ACLU v Gonzales 478 F Supp 2d 775 (ED Pa 2007).

22 ACLU v Mukasey 534 F3d 181, 207 (3rd Cir 2008).

23 129 SCt 1032 (2009).

24 Blanks Hindman, above. For discussion of First Amendment philosophies with respect to the protection of children, see also Samuel D Castor, 'Internet Child Protection Registry Acts: Protection children, parents and . . . pornographers? Allowing states to balance the First Amendment with parents' rights to privacy and sovereignty in the home' (2009) 59 Cath U L Rev 231.

the German Penal Code, although he was eventually acquitted on appeal.[25] There continue to be attempts made to block users in one country from accessing material which may be unlawful there but which may have been lawfully produced (or not) in the jurisdiction of origin. Despite international initiatives such as the Cybercrime Convention discussed further below, there remains no generally accepted consensus on what is or is not deemed to be acceptable content and even on issues such as child pornography where agreement is more likely, different approaches are still possible.[26]

## Other approaches to content regulation

Many other jurisdictions have also introduced legislation purporting to regulate the content and use of information on the internet, or have applied existing legislation to regulate undesirable content on computer networks. Only a sample of that activity is discussed here, but there are a number of sources that can be accessed for an overview of legislative activity on this topic in many more states.[27] Reaction to the legislative activity in different parts of the world has been mixed, and although there may be more severe restrictions in some other states which have been impugned as restrictions on free speech, none seems to have precipitated the volume of litigation that has been seen in the USA.

Whereas some extreme measures, for example those employed in China, discussed below, are frequently labelled as censorship, the majority of states attempt to exert some modicum of control over content on the internet.[28] Coroneos points out that there are three forces, the interaction of which feed into the way in which new internet content regulation is likely to be promulgated:[29]

(i) cultural values and institutions within a country. Institutions in this sense could include the traditional media;
(ii) the ease with which political debate can actually be translated into new legislation;
(iii) the existence of constitutional guarantees such as freedom of expression and the extent to which new laws can be enacted which will survive a constitutional challenge.

## Australia

Applying the above criteria to the situation in Australia, Coroneos observed that they created fertile ground for the creation of a strict regime regulating content and access to the internet. The traditional media had been active in pointing out the 'dangers' of the internet and these views then became espoused as a political cause of importance to the public: Bills were able to become law sometimes with 'only perfunctory scrutiny and debate'; and there was no explicit protection

---

25 For full details, see Lothar Determann, 'Case update: German Compuserve director acquitted on appeal' (1999) 23 Hastings Int'l & Comp L Rev 109. The current situation in Germany is that effective age verification systems must be in place to ensure that only adults can access pornographic sites. This is an onerous requirement and the Bundesgerichtshof has ruled that such systems will not be considered to be effective unless steps have been taken to prevent obvious circumvention methods: see Mark Turner, 'European national news' (2010) 26 CLSR 237, 239.

26 See, e.g., discussion below at p 327 on 'virtual child pornography'. For a discussion of some of the practical issues involved in implementing such blocking see, e.g., Dan Jerker B Svantesson, 'Delineating the reach of Internet intermediaries' content blocking – "ccTLD Blocking", "Strict Geo-location Blocking" or a "Country Lens Approach"?' (2014) 11 SCRIPTed 153.

27 See e.g., William H Dutton, Anna Dopatka, Michael Hills, Ginette Law and Victoria Nash, 'The changing legal and regulatory ecology shaping the Internet' UNESCO (2011) available online at: http://unesdoc.unesco.org/images/0019/001915/191594e.pdf; and Freedom on the Net 2015 available online at: https://freedomhouse.org/sites/default/files/FH_FOTN_2015Report.pdf

28 For more detailed consideration of censorship and control see, e.g., Jeffrey (Chien-Fei) Li, 'Internet control or Internet censorship? Comparing the control models of China, Singapore and the United States to guide Taiwan's choice' (2013) U Pitt J Tech L & Pol'y 1.

29 Peter Coroneos, 'Internet content policy and regulation in Australia' in Brian Fitzgerald, Fuping Gao, Damien O'Brien, and Sampsung Xiaoxiang Shi (eds), *Copyright Law, Digital Content and the Internet in the Asia-Pacific*, 2008, Sydney: Sydney University Press, ch 4, p 49.

for freedom of expression. The enabling statute in question is the Broadcasting Services Act 1992, as amended, which is now administered by the Australian Communications and Media Authority (ACMA).[30] Even prior to action at the federal level, a number of states in Australia had introduced legislation aimed both at restricting access to certain material on the internet and controlling content, but with little opportunity for public debate on the issue.[31] The 1992 Act was subsequently amended by the Broadcasting Services Amendment (Online Services) Act 1999 (the 'Online Services Act') in the belief that 'responsible online content regulation will help to create an environment in which the internet's positive opportunities and advantages are able to be nurtured, developed and accessed by a growing number of citizens, while allowing the proper concerns of current and future users to be addressed'.[32] The amendments were aimed at restricting content that 'is likely to cause offence to a reasonable adult' and at protecting children from exposure to 'internet content that is unsuitable for children'.[33] These amendments came into force at the beginning of 2000, and basically apply the same level of censorship to the internet as is applied to films and videos by using the same classification system.

The system operates primarily in a reactive way and action under the statute is mainly initiated as a result of complaints. The rules have had a mixed reception; criticism has been based on a questioning of the underlying rationale,[34] of the difficulties of ensuring compliance,[35] and on wider concerns about restrictions on freedom of expression.[36] On the other hand, some have taken the pragmatic approach that, whatever the imperfections of the new regime, it should be welcomed because 'the internet's power and (potential) persuasiveness make it crucial to immediately begin trying to develop an effective and usable system for extending classification to it . . . the "Online Services Act" represents a useful first step in that direction'.[37] Further, there has also been the suggestion that although there appear to be more and more restrictions in place, this is a result of the degree of politicisation of the issue and, in reality, 'most Australians can access the same range of content that they always could'.[38] Indeed, Kortlander reports that the legislation has had little effect because even if content is removed as the result of a takedown notice in Australia it can easily be hosted elsewhere and still be accessible in Australia.[39]

There were also plans to require ISPs to filter proscribed websites;[40] initially, the targets were intended to be sites associated with child pornography and the abuse of children, although the scheme could easily have been extended further. The belief of the government was that filtering at the ISP level would be more effective at achieving the objective of protecting children than filters on individual PCs, and steps had been taken for ISPs to trial the filtering software. However, the mandatory filtering proposals were shelved in 2012 and the

---

30 See www.acma.gov.au/. ACMA was formed in 2005 as a result of the merger of the Australian Broadcasting Authority and the Australian Communications Authority.

31 See, e.g., G Greenleaf, 'Law in cyberspace' (1996) 70 Aust LJ 33.

32 See J Corker, S Nugent, and J Porter, 'Regulating internet content: A co-regulatory approach' (2000) 23 UNSWLJ 5.

33 Australian Broadcasting Services Act 1992, s 3(1), as amended.

34 See, e.g., P Chen, 'Pornography, protection, prevarication: The politics of internet censorship' (2000) 23 UNSWLJ 4, suggesting that 'from the outset the premise on which the legislation was proposed was highly questionable'; see also K See, Chen, above; N Arasaratnam, 'Brave new (online) world' (2000) 23 UNSWLJ 205; P Argy, 'Internet content regulation: An Australian Computer Society perspective' (2000) 23 UNSWLJ 126; and Heitman, 'Vapours and mirrors' (2000) 23 UNSWLJ 10, expressing the view that drawing an analogy with television and film was a tragic fallacy.

35 See, e.g., Chen, above; N Arasaratnam, 'Brave new (online) world' (2000) 23 UNSWLJ 205; and P Argy, 'Internet content regulation: An Australian Computer Society perspective' (2000) 23 UNSWLJ 126.

36 See, e.g., T Voon, 'Online pornography in Australia: Lessons from the First Amendment' (2001) 24 UNSWLJ 141; R Trager and S Turner, 'The internet down under: Can free speech be protected in a democracy without a Bill of Rights?' (2000) 23 U Ark Little Rock L Rev 123.

37 E Handsley and B Biggins, 'The sheriff rides into town: A day of rejoicing for innocent westerners' (2000) 23 UNSWLJ 13.

38 Coroneos, above, p 66.

39 Jenny Kortlander, 'Is Filtering the new silver bullet in the fight against child pornography on the internet? A legal study into the experiences of Australia and Germany' (2011) 17 CTLR 199, 202.

40 For further details, see, e.g., Alana Maurashat and Renée Watt, 'Clean feed: Australia's internet filtering proposal' (2009) 12 Internet Law Bulletin [2009] UNSWLRS 60.

current approach is to make optional filtering software available together with a programme of education and information.[41]

## Singapore

In Singapore, the broad definitions of broadcasting, programme, etc, in the Broadcasting Act 1994 and the Broadcasting Authority Act 1994, as amended, which do not refer to a specific medium of communication, have the result that all content, including that on the internet, can be regulated under the umbrella of these statutes. Under these auspices, a licence scheme has been applied to ISPs and content providers since 1996.[42] The scheme is administered by the Singapore Media Development Authority (MDA), which describes itself as being 'mindful of the dynamic and bor-derless nature of the Internet' and adopting 'a practical and light-touch approach in regulating the Internet'.[43] All ISPs are subject to a class licence and must, *inter alia*, block access to any site that is considered against the public interest, public order, or national harmony, offends against public decency, or violates the Singapore Internet Code of Practice.[44] Although these sound quite broad, further detail in the Code of Practice suggests that the primary concerns are obscenity, violence, child pornography, or hate speech. These class licences are automatically applicable, but, in addi-tion, ISPs and certain types of content provider, such as political parties and religious groups, are also required to register with the MDA.

Seng has criticised the regulatory model used in Singapore on the basis that it is predicated on a 1990s conception of the internet that does not so readily adapt to more recent develop-ments such as Web 2.0 and the growth of user-generated content.[45] He points out that this type of regulation depends on the nature of the communication rather than the type of parties that are communicating. Although private communications are excepted from the regulatory ambit, cur-rent technology means that something that may have been initiated as a private communication can readily be transmitted to a much more public forum, thus blurring the edges between what can be regarded as private or public. The MDA itself describes the approach as 'co-regulation' with industry, meaning that the MDA does not actively censor content, but provides guidelines and codes of practice for content providers.[46] In practice, although internet content providers have to exercise their judgement and not place anything on the internet that is prohibited under the code of practice, it is clear from the MDA's Internet Industry Guidelines that the main con-cerns are with pornography, violence, and incitement of racial or religious hatred.[47] Although there appear to be few sanctions available for failure to comply with the terms of the licensing scheme,[48] there have also been reports that censorship also takes the place of sites that are critical of the government.[49]

41 Paula Pyburne and Rhonda Jolly, 'Australian Governments and dilemmas in filtering the Internet: juggling freedoms against potential for harm', 8 August 2014, available online at: www.aph.gov.au/About_Parliament/Parliamentary_Departments/Parliamentary_Library/pubs/rp/rp1415/InternetFiltering#_Toc395250040

42 See Geoffrey Pereira, 'Internet regulation to start on Monday' (1996) *Straits Times*, 13 July. For details of the scheme, see http://www.mda.gov.sg/RegulationsAndLicensing/Licences/Pages/InternetServiceAndContentProviderClassLicence.aspx; and discussion in Malobika Banerji, 'Internet Regulation in Singapore' (2013) 17(4) J Internet L 3.

43 See http://www.mda.gov.sg/RegulationsAndLicensing/ContentStandardsAndClassification/Pages/Internet.aspx

44 Ibid.

45 Daniel Seng, 'Regulation of the interactive digital media industry in Singapore' in Brian Fitzgerald, Fuping Gao, Damien O'Brien, and Sampsung Xiaoxiang Shi (eds), *Copyright Law, Digital Content and the Internet in the Asia-Pacific*, 2008, Sydney: Sydney University Press, ch 5, p 67.

46 See http://www.mda.gov.sg/RegulationsAndLicensing/ActsCodesOfPracticeAndGuidelines/Pages/ActsCodesofPracticeand-Guidelines.aspx

47 See http://www.mda.gov.sg/RegulationsAndLicensing/ActsCodesOfPracticeAndGuidelines/Documents/Acts,%20Codes%20of%20Practice%20and%20Guidelines/PoliciesandContentGuidelines_Internet_InterneCodeOfPractice.pdf

48 See, e.g., Li, above, pp 26–28.

49 See, e.g., Reporters without Borders, 'Singapore' (2007) 1 February, available online at: https://rsf.org/en/singapore

# China

In a number of other jurisdictions, the regulation of the internet has not only been about the content that might objectively be seen as against a societal interest, such as pornography or hate speech, but has also been focused on the harsh suppression of dissenting political views. China has now more than twice as many internet users as the US and makes up more than 20% of the total number of users globally.[50] Internet regulation in China began in 1994,[51] focusing on maintaining the internet merely as a tool to assist the economic development of the country, and new regulations continue to be added. A complex mixture of legislation, technical measures and corporate cooperation has had the effect of isolating the Chinese internet and allows its use and content to be closely monitored and controlled.[52] ISPs are required to obtain licences which require them to implement filtering hardware and software. They are liable for all illegal content and must report criminal activity and assist in investigations of offenders. Internet users themselves are required to register with the police. In contrast to Singapore, the legal basis of the regulatory framework is both vague and general and can thus be interpreted as including anything which apparently conflicts with communist social values. Consequently, formal regulation is augmented by many users over self-regulating as they are unsure of the boundaries of what is and is not permissible.[53] The whole system is reinforced by the so-called 'great firewall of China'; a 'massive, sophisticated national censorship system' which uses a number of filtering and blocking techniques to prevent access to foreign websites.[54] It appears that:

> The Chinese government has created a closed, national Intranet that it protects with a censorious architecture of information technology, regulatory offences, Internet Service Providers and an Internet police squad.[55]

In the rest of the world, this has often been most apparent when sites from outside China, such as Google, have been blocked, but there are also examples of the strict enforcement of the relevant laws that has been directed at both ISPs and also individual computer users.[56] However, there are also reports that there is some small progress with regard to legal reform in this regard and, in addition, a plan to require approved filtering software on all PCs sold in China has been indefinitely delayed.[57]

# Regulation of obscenity and offensive material in the UK

In the UK, there has been debate about the extent to which existing laws were adequate to deal with the distribution of pornography on the internet;[58] this included the extent to which they were

---

50 See www.internetlivestats.com/internet-users-by-country/
51 See Assafa Endeshaw, 'Internet regulation in China: the never-ending cat and mouse game' (2004) 13 ICTL 41.
52 For a more detailed discussion than is possible here see, e.g., Vasileios Karagiannopoulos, 'China and the Internet: Expanding on Lessig's regulation nightmares' (2012) 9 SCRIPTed 150; Jyh-An Lee, Ching-Yi Liu and Weiping Li, 'Searching for internet freedom in China: A case study on Google's China experience' (2013) 31 Cardozo Arts & Ent. L.J. 405, 419–424; Li, above, pp 21–26.
53 Karagiannopoulos, p 164.
54 For an explanation of the operation of the firewall in non-specialist terms see, e.g., John Naughton, 'The fascinating truth behind all those 'great firewall of China' headlines' (2015) The Guardian, 14 February; and 'How does China censor the internet?' (2013) The Economist, 21 April.
55 Lyombe Eko, Anup Kumar and Qingjiang Yao, 'Google this: The great firewall of China, the IT wheel of India, Google Inc and Internet regulation' (2011) 15(3) J. Internet L. 3.
56 See, e.g., Reporters without Borders, 'A "journey to the heart of internet censorship" on eve of party congress' (2007) 10 October, available online at: https://rsf.org/en/china; Wentao Sha and Difei Yu, 'Internet content provider licences in the People's Republic of China internet industry: A practical perspective' in Brian Fitzgerald, Fuping Gao, Damien O'Brien and Sampsung Xiaoxiang Shi (eds), Copyright Law, Digital Content and the Internet in the Asia-Pacific, 2008, Sydney: Sydney University Press, ch 7, p 143; Justine Nolan, 'The China dilemma: Internet censorship and corporate responsibility' (2009) 4 Asian J Comp Law Article 3; Diane Rowland, 'Virtual worlds, real rights?' in Marco Odello and Sofia Cavandoli (eds), Emerging Areas of Human Rights in the 21st Century: The Role of the Universal Declaration of Human Rights, 2011, London: Routledge, ch 1.
57 See Human Rights Watch, above, pp 285–8.
58 See, e.g., C Manchester, 'Computer pornography' [1995] Crim LR 546; T Gibbons, 'Computer-generated pornography' (1995) 9 IC & T Yearbook 83.

capable of dealing with instances in which children are exposed to material intended only for an adult audience, as well as instances in which the internet was used to propagate child pornography. In response to the widespread concern surrounding the perceived proliferation of 'indecent' material available via the internet, a Home Affairs Committee was given a wide brief to examine and assess the extent of the problems caused by the use of information technology (IT) to disseminate such material and the likelihood of additional problems arising as a result of the development of the relevant technologies, and, in particular, to ascertain whether any changes in legislation were required to deal with existing and potential concerns relating to computer pornography.[59] Although the possibility of dedicated legislation at some future date was not ruled out, the Committee decided that it was possible to deal with the matter by amending the existing legislation to make it clear that it applied equally to the dissemination of material via computer networks. Its recommendations were given effect in the Criminal Justice and Public Order Act 1994, which amended certain sections of the Obscene Publications Act 1959 and the Protection of Children Act 1978.

Section 1(1) of the Obscene Publications Act 1959 makes it a criminal offence to publish any obscene article. Publication still takes place even if there is only one recipient as, for instance may be the case on internet relay chat.[60] 'Article' is defined as 'any description containing or embodying matter to be read or looked at or both, any sound record, any film etc'. Unlike the standard in the USA, which allows for different standards in different communities, such matter will be obscene if, taken as a whole, it is such as to 'tend to deprave and corrupt persons likely to read, see or hear matter contained or embodied in it'. To avoid any possibility that 'article' could be construed as not including information on a computer, this section was amended by the Criminal Justice and Public Order Act 1994 to include the transmission of electronically stored data that, on resolution into user-viewable form, is obscene. Because the definition of 'publication' includes distribution, circulation, etc, this could have the effect of making a network provider liable for obscene material, as well as the originator of that information. One issue with general availability on the internet is that it is impossible to predict what section of the public is 'likely' to be exposed to it, but no specific recommendation was made on this point. This point was considered in R v Perrin when it was suggested that all that the section requires is that there is a likelihood that vulnerable people may see the material, not that any actually did.[61] Such a condition will easily be met by publication on open-access web pages, which was what was under consideration in the appeal in Perrin.[62]

In addition, there may be more specific offences applicable to particular types of material, such as offences under the Children and Young Persons (Harmful Publications) Act 1955, which applies to any book, magazine, or other like work that is of a kind likely to fall into the hands of children and young persons. Such publications have to be pictorial in the main to attract the provisions of this Act and include stories portraying 'the commission of crimes, acts of violence or cruelty or incidents of a repulsive or horrible nature in such a way that the work as a whole would tend to corrupt a child or young person'. In the absence of specific amendments, the application of this statute will rest on whether an interpretation of 'other like work' includes material available on computer.

## Child pornography

The Protection of Children Act 1978 creates offences relating to the display and distribution of indecent photographs of children. These provisions have also been amended by the Criminal Justice and Public Order Act 1994 to include both photographs and 'pseudo-photographs', the latter referring to computer-generated or partially computer-generated images of children. Data stored

59 Home Affairs Committee, Computer Pornography, HC No 126, 1993–94, London: HMSO.
60 R v Smith [2012] EWCA Crim 398, [21] and [22].
61 [2002] EWCA Crim 747, [22].
62 See also discussion in Jacob Rowbottom, 'Obscenity laws and the internet: Targeting the supply and demand' [2006] Crim L Rev 97, 99.

on a computer disk or other electronic means that is capable of conversion into a photograph or 'pseudo-photograph' is also included.[63] In addition, there have been other amendments and enhancements of the law relating to child pornography and, more generally, in relation to sexual offences involving children in the Sexual Offences Act 2003 that will apply to the internet, just as much as they do to other methods of creation and dissemination. As a result of these changes, the upper age limit for a 'child' in the Protection of Children Act 1978 has been changed from 16 to 18, new offences relating to child pornography have been introduced,[64] and new defences in respect of indecent images have been provided.[65] A further offence introduced by s 15 of the 2003 Act is directed at the conduct known as 'grooming', in which adults gain the confidence of children on prior occasions with the intention of committing a sexual offence at a later date.[66] This prepara-tory behaviour often takes place in internet chatrooms and so this new provision is expected to close the previous loophole in the law in this respect.[67]

The interpretation of the relevant sections of the Protection of Children Act 1978 has been discussed in R v Fellows and Arnold,[68] in which the Court of Appeal dismissed an appeal against convic-tions for possessing indecent photographs of a child, having an obscene article for publication, and distributing indecent photographs, the material in question being available over a computer net-work. The defendants had contended that such computer data did not constitute a photograph for the purposes of s 1 of the 1978 Act and that the data were not, in any event, distributed or shown merely by reason of being made available for downloading. In contrast, Evans LJ decided that the data 'was a form of copy which made the original photograph, or a copy of it, available for viewing by a person with access to the disk'.[69]

In the case of R v Bowden, the question was whether downloading such images from the internet should be construed as 'making' or 'possessing',[70] both of which are offences under this statute, in contrast to the Obscene Publications Act 1959, which has no offence of possession. Further, 'mak-ing' a pseudo-photograph is considered a more heinous offence and is subject to a more severe sentence than mere possession. It could be argued that downloading images is more analogous to possession, since, if the material were acquired by traditional means, there would be no suggestion of 'making' of an image.[71] However, because of the nature of the technology and the objective of the statute, the court inclined to the view that downloading and printing of images is more akin to 'making' them. The court agreed that the 'Act is not only concerned with the original creation of images but also their proliferation'. Further, if the images in question were to originate outside of the UK, such activities would have the effect of creating new material that was not previously in this jurisdiction:[72] '. . . a person who either downloads images onto a disk or who prints them off is making them.'

Atkins v DPP,[73] an appeal by way of case stated, concerned not only downloading from the internet, but also the question of whether images stored in the computer's cache were either 'made' or 'possessed'. It was submitted in this case that Bowden was wrongly decided, but although the divisional court declined to follow this, it did decide that this could not be extended to the

---

63 Protection of Children Act 1978, s 7(4)(b). For a comprehensive discussion of issues relating to child pornography on the internet, see, e.g., Yaman Akdeniz, *Internet Child Pornography and the Law: National and International Responses*, 2008, London: Ashgate.
64 Sections 48–50.
65 Sections 45 and 46, and see discussion in A Gillespie, 'The Sexual Offences Act 2003: (3) Tinkering with "child pornography"' [2004] Crim LR 361, 363.
66 For a review of this provision, see JR Spencer, 'The Sexual Offences Act 2003: (2) Child and family offences' [2003] Crim LR 347, 351.
67 See, e.g., A Gillespie, 'Children, chatrooms and the law' [2001] Crim LR 435.
68 [1997] 2 All ER 548, and see case note by C Colby (1997) 2 Comm L 30; T Palfrey, 'Pornography and the possible criminal liability of internet service providers under the Obscene Publication(s) and Protection of Children Act' (1997) 6 ICTL 187.
69 [1997] 2 All ER 548, 557.
70 [2000] 2 All ER 418.
71 See also A Gillespie, 'Sentences for offences involving child pornography' [2003] Crim LR 81.
72 [2000] 2 All ER 418, 423.
73 [2000] 1 WLR 1427.

inadvertent storing or unintentional making of images in the cache – an issue that had not been raised in *Bowden*; neither could the storage in the cache constitute possession in the absence of the knowledge of the defendant.[74] Whether the defendant had the requisite knowledge will thus be a matter of fact to be decided in every case. Both *Bowden* and *Atkins* were considered in the later joined appeal cases of *Smith* and *Jayson*. This appeal considered two separate cases, both involving the alleged making of indecent pseudo-photographs of a child: one by opening an email attachment; the other by downloading directly from the internet. In each case, temporary copies were also made in the computer cache. The judgment underlined how important the factual matrix is in such cases, since it was shown that the defendant, Smith, had good reason to believe that the attachment in question contained illicit images. However, in the absence of such a belief, it appears that the very fact of opening such an attachment will not inevitably criminalise the unsuspecting and the unwary.[75] In other words, to be guilty of the 'making' offence, there has to be a deliberate and intentional act. This point was returned to in the later case of *R v Harrison*,[76] in which it was decided that the offence would also be made out when illegal material was encountered in unsolicited internet 'pop-ups' that appeared on the user's PC when accessing pornographic, but otherwise legal, sites.

The above cases suggest that downloading of images and copying onto disk or other storage medium will be regarded as the more serious offence of making a pseudo-photograph, notwithstanding analogies that could be made with activities using traditional media.[77] However, the scope of the meaning of 'possession' has also caused some problems in respect of images on computer networks. In *R v Porter*, it was suggested that, to establish possession, 'it may seem superficially attractive to say that all that is required . . . is that, to the knowledge of the defendant, the images were on the defendant's hard disk drive within the computer which was in his custody and control at the material time'.[78] However, in this particular case, the defendant had deleted the images in question and had then emptied the 'recycle bin'. Although he could have recovered the images with forensic software, he neither had such software, nor had he attempted to obtain any, such that, in reality, he could not have retrieved the images. The court therefore reasoned that, 'in the special case of deleted computer images, if a person cannot retrieve or gain access to an image, in our view he no longer has custody or control of it'.[79] In other words, defendants are not automatically in possession of an image merely because they possess the hard disk and the image could be retrieved by forensic techniques, unless they have the wherewithal to do this. Again, this will depend on the particular factual matrix of the case in question.

## Extreme pornography

Notwithstanding the applicability of these offences to material made available over computer networks, a problem may still arise where the source of the material is outside the UK jurisdiction. If the offence is one in which mere possession of the offending material is sufficient, there may be still a defendant who can be apprehended in the UK courts, but this may not be the case where the offence is one of 'publication'. These factors were significant in more recent changes to the law relating to obscene publications. The issues raised by the availability of pornographic content on the internet, its potential link to violent and abusive behaviour, and the difficulties in controlling material created outside the jurisdiction led to recommendations to establish an offence of possessing 'extreme' pornographic material to parallel the possession offence in relation to child

---

74 See also Criminal Justice Act 1988, s 160(2)(b), and compare also the situation in the Trojan horse cases discussed in Chapter 7 at p 291.
75 [2003] 1 Cr App R 13, [19].
76 [2007] EWCA Crim 2976.
77 For further discussion of the meaning of 'possession' in relation to digital images, see, e.g., Jonathan Clough, 'Now you see it, now you don't: Digital images and the meaning of possession' (2008) 19 Crim LF 205.
78 [2006] EWCA Crim 560, [16].
79 Ibid, [21].

pornography.[80] The proposals for new offences were aimed at specific types of prohibited content rather than the effect that the content might have on the viewer. The latter approach, as embodied in the Obscene Publications Act 1959, has proved notoriously difficult to apply, and McGlynn and Rackley have even commented that 'no one really knows what constitutes obscene material'.[81] One possible advantage to the approach under the 1959 Act is that it is able to reflect the fact that what is or is not acceptable is likely to change over time, as evidenced by the fact that material at issue in early successful prosecutions under the Act might legitimately no longer be viewed in the same light. The new offence is contained in s 63 of the Criminal Justice and Immigration Act 2008, which provides that it is an offence for a person to be in possession of an extreme pornographic image. As Rowbottom remarks, 'for a possession offence, clarity is crucial', and the statute defines the key concepts of 'pornographic' and 'extreme'. However, 'possession' remains undefined and similar problems to those arising in determining possession of images on computer in relation to child pornography[82] may continue to be encountered in the implementation of the new offence.

## Case study: Social media and the criminal law

As all users of the internet will know, there is a broad spectrum of material available on websites and also as user-generated content propagated via social media sites.[83] While much of this could not be defined as discourse which was in the public interest, however broadly defined, it is hard to draw a line between what should or should not be criminalised and to what extent. Criminalising content creates a clear restriction on freedom of expression; as has been made clear by the ECtHR, Art 10 of the ECHR is protective of speech which some may find offensive, shocking or disturbing.[84] Whilst it may be easy to find consensus as to what is or is not acceptable at the outer ends of the speech spectrum, this is not such an easy task in other cases.

The use of social media sites is now commonplace[85] and has created a space within which there is both the opportunity to speak freely and also, potentially, to reach a much wider audience than using traditional means of communication. Much of the content on Twitter is freely available even to those without a Twitter account and, depending on settings, communications on, e.g. Facebook may be read by 'friends' and also by 'friends of friends' which can mean that the content can be accessed by a very large number of people. Although this may have had an even greater democratising effect on speech than that described in the seminal case of *ACLU v Reno* discussed earlier, it also creates a potential for harmful effects ranging from 'the rapid spread of gossip, the decline of privacy, the growth in cyberstalking, bullying, hate speech, the echo chamber effect and the persistence of falsities and conspiracies.'[86] Although for reasons outlined in Chapter 7,[87] statistics on the use of the criminal law relating to social media are very difficult to obtain, it has been suggested that in 2011 there were almost 2,500 investigations following complaints about posts on social media[88] so the situations discussed here merely represent the tip of the iceberg.

---

80 Home Office, *On the Possession of Extreme Pornographic Material*, Consultation Paper, 2005, London: HMSO.
81 Clare McGlynn and Erika Rackley, 'Criminalising extreme pornography: A lost opportunity' [2009] Crim L Rev 245, 246.
82 See, e.g., R v Porter [2006] EWCA Crim 560, above, and see also the discussion in McGlynn and Rackley, above.
83 For the purposes of this discussion the focus will be on Twitter and Facebook but the same issues and principles are relevant to other social media sites.
84 See, e.g., *Handyside v UK* (A24) (1979–80) 1 EHRR 737, [49]; *Sunday Times v UK* (No 2) (A 217) (1992) 14 EHRR 229, [50].
85 At the end of 2014, Facebook was recorded as having 890 million daily active users and nearly 1.4 billion monthly active users – for latest statistics see: http://newsroom.fb.com/company-info/. Twitter has approximately 288 million monthly active users who send around 500 million tweets each day – see: https://about.twitter.com/company
86 Jacob Rowbottom, 'To rant, vent and converse: protecting low level digital speech' (2012) 71 CLJ 355, 356.
87 See p 272.
88 See Laura Scaife, 'The DPP and social media: a new approach coming out of the Woods?' (2013) 18 Comms L 5, 6. In contrast it has been reported in answer to a written question in Parliament that it is not possible to separate out social media cases from other cybercrime, see discussion at p 301.

## Using the criminal law

The fact that social networking sites can be potent tools in the wrong hands is graphically illustrated by the appeals against sentence arising out of convictions following the riots in London and other UK towns and cities in early August 2011.[89] The case involved ten appellants, two of which, Blackshaw and Sutcliffe, had not been directly involved in violent activities but had independently used Facebook in an attempt to instigate rioting in Northwich and Warrington respectively. They were charged with offences under the Serious Crimes Act 2007 and were each given a custodial sentence of four years. The posts on Facebook were not intended to be a joke and the appellants believed the events would occur. In reviewing the sentences the court was unimpressed by the fact that they had not personally committed any violent acts. Although no actual harm resulted it was not 'accurate to suggest that neither crime had any adverse consequences';[90] people had clearly been put in fear, exacerbated by the general unrest in many parts of the country. Neither was it relevant that Blackshaw and Sutcliffe had not personally contacted anyone: 'modern technology has done away with the need for . . . direct personal communication . . . the abuse of modern technology for criminal purposes extends to and includes incitement of very many people by a single step.'[91] The deterrent sentences were upheld.

Although some disquiet was expressed at the time about the draconian application of the law, it is not with such extreme cases that the discussion here is primarily concerned. Rather the focus is on more mundane interchanges which perhaps spiral out of control or have an effect on the recipient which is augmented, sometimes excessively so, by the effect of the mode of communication. There is, arguably, a difference in effect between an ill-judged or heat-of-the-moment remark made orally and one which is disseminated via social media. As an example of what was submitted in the case to be a demonstration of the dangers of social media, consider what happened in *MacDonald v Dunn*.[92] MacDonald, a supporter of Rangers Football Club, used Twitter to post the following comment about the chief executive of Celtic Football Club 'Lawwell needs a bullet. Simples' Having realised that this was irresponsible, he deleted it the next day but was subsequently charged and pleaded guilty to breach of the peace. He said that he was 'just being an idiot' – should such behaviour be prosecuted?

Freedom of expression always has to be balanced against any harmful effects or breaches of other rights, such as privacy. It is well established, for instance, that the laws of defamation apply to internet communications[93] but what of provisions which are used to criminalise content in other situations? Examples in the UK include the Public Order Act 1986, the Malicious Communications Act 1988, the Protection from Harassment Act 1997, and the Communications Act 2003. Such statutes were introduced in response to very different situations than that under consideration here; are they useful for dealing with inappropriate comments on social media?

## Public order offences

The Public Order Act 1986 (POA) is aimed at regulating behaviour in public and has to accommodate the freedom to protest and the rights of people sharing the same space. It contains provisions dealing specifically with expression which incites hatred on the grounds of race, religion and sexual orientation[94] but s 4A and s 5 are of more general application. Section 5 requires that the expression has to be made within the hearing or sight of the victim and it seems unlikely that this

---

89 *R v Blackshaw* [2011] EWCA Crim 2312.
90 *Ibid*, [72].
91 *Ibid*, [73].
92 [2013] SLT 128.
93 See, e.g., *Dow Jones v Gutnick*, etc and also discussion in Chapter 2.
94 For an example of the use of the statute in relation to racially inflammatory information on the internet, see *R v Sheppard and Whittle* [2010] EWCA Crim 65.

would apply in an internet case.[95] Section 4A, however, has already been applied to speech on the internet on the basis that 'any person who posts material on the Internet puts that material within the public ambit.'[96]

Section 4A makes it an offence for a person to use 'threatening, abusive or insulting words or behaviour' or display 'any writing, sign or other visible representation which is threatening, abusive or insulting' which causes 'that or another person harassment, alarm or distress' and which the speaker intends to have that effect. The issue in S v CPS was whether the posting of the material in question had actually *caused* the harassment, alarm or distress, given that, although the victim was aware in general terms that the material was on the internet, they did not actually see it until shown a hard copy by the police some five months later by which time it was no longer available on the internet. It was held to be sufficient that the defendant had the requisite intent at the time of posting, as there would then be the chance that it would cause the intended harassment, alarm or distress.

This certainly suggests that Public Order Act offences could be used when material is generally accessible on the internet which will include many messages on Twitter for example.[97] What then are the options for communications on social networking sites such as Facebook, most of which are not available to the public at large?

## Communications offences

There are two main statutory provisions which have been applied to social media communications; the Malicious Communications Act 1988 (MCA), s 1 and the Communications Act 2003 (CA), s 127. The rationale for these statutes is different; the MCA being aimed at those who send 'poison pen' letters while the CA provision is a descendant of similar provisions originating in the Post Office (Amendment) Act 1985 designed to proscribe the use of communications systems for the sending of menacing and offensive messages.[98] Although the provisions appear not dissimilar at first sight, there are differences between them. MCA, s 1 creates an offence of sending a letter, electronic communication or article conveying a message which is indecent or grossly offensive, a threat or false and known to the sender to be false. The offence created by CA, s 127 is sending by a public electronic communications network a message which is grossly offensive or of an indecent, obscene or menacing character or causing such a message to be sent. There is a further offence of sending or causing to be sent a false message for the purpose of causing annoyance, inconvenience or needless anxiety.

The distinctions between these two provisions were outlined by the House of Lords in DPP v Collins.[99] Essentially, for MCA, s 1 to apply, the sender of the grossly offensive message must intend it to cause distress or anxiety to its immediate or eventual recipient.[100] In contrast, an offence will be committed under CA, s 127 by merely sending such a message via a public communication network,[101] the rationale for the offence being to 'prohibit the use of a service provided and funded by the public for the benefit of the public for the transmission of communications which contravene the basic standards of our society.'[102] Many messages which might be tested under one of

---

95 S v CPS [2008] EWHC 438, [12] and [15].
96 Ibid, [13], per Maurice Kay LJ supporting the reasoning of the District Judge.
97 See, e.g., R v Stacey Appeal No A20120033 against a sentence for posting racist and offensive comments on Twitter – see discussion in, e.g. Sarosh Khan, 'Can the trolls be put back under the bridge? (2013) 19 CTLR 9, 11; and Jennifer Agate and Jocelyn Ledward, 'Social media: how the net is closing in on cyber bullies' (2013) 24 Ent L Rev 263, 264. Agate and Ledward (p 267) also report that Stacey might not have been prosecuted under the new CPS guidelines (discussed below at p 322).
98 See, e.g., Chambers v DPP [2012] EWHC 2157 (Admin).
99 [2006] UKHL 40.
100 Ibid, [26].
101 Ibid.
102 Ibid, [7]

these sections involve offensive or obscene content[103] but in *Chambers v DPP*,[104] a case which attracted considerable attention for a number of reasons, the issue was whether or not the message was of a 'menacing character.' In brief, Chambers was on his way to see his girlfriend in Belfast when Doncaster airport was closed because of adverse weather. In his frustration at the situation he posted a number of tweets suggesting that in that event he 'would have to resort to terrorism' and when it did close, culminating in the following 'Crap! Robin Hood Airport is closed. You've got a week and a bit to get your shit together otherwise I am blowing the airport sky high!' The tweet was sent from his personal account on which he was clearly identifiable. It could be read by his followers but was not directed at the airport itself; unlike the situation in *Blackshaw*, there was no evidence that anyone who read it found it 'even minimally alarming.'[105] However, the comment was subsequently seen five days later by the airport duty manager when casually searching for any mention of Robin Hood airport. It was then passed to his manager, the airport police and South Yorkshire Police. It appears that none of these really thought this was a genuine threat to the airport, the police commenting that it appeared to be 'a foolish comment posted on "Twitter" as a joke for only his close friends to see.' Despite this, it was referred to the CPS and Chambers was charged with using a public electronic communications network to send a message of a menacing character. He was convicted in the magistrates' court; this was upheld on appeal to the Crown Court but a case was stated for consideration by the High Court concerning various elements of the offence in CA, s 127.

The court noted that the Communications Act 2003 created no new interference with freedom of expression and that:

> satirical, or iconoclastic, or rude comment, the expression of unpopular or unfashionable opinion about serious or trivial matters, banter or humour, even if distasteful to some or painful to those subjected to it should and no doubt will continue at their customary level, quite undiminished by this legislation.[106]

Regarding the tweets in question, it was 'unsurprising, but not irrelevant' that none of his followers had reported this message, neither had the airport staff evinced any urgency in responding or introduced additional security and so on. The court had little difficulty in finding that, taken in context, the comments could not be regarded as being menacing. Foster has suggested that this decision is 'a victory for common sense and pragmatic statutory interpretation rather than freedom of expression';[107] whether this is the case or not, it was to lead to a consideration of the factors which should influence the decision whether or not to prosecute in social media cases with particular reference to the importance of preserving freedom of expression. This does not require a change to the overall approach to free expression, nor demand blanket protection, but rather a consideration of the overall context and a proportionate response.[108]

## Speech on social media and the CPS guidelines

Without doubt speech on social media can be both alarming and extremely distressing; even if subsequently retracted, messages may already have been circulated to a wide audience. In *Smith v ADVFN*, Eady J observed, in the context of an internet bulletin board, that such speech was analogous to bar room banter, 'often uninhibited, casual and ill thought out; those who participate know this and

---

103 See, e.g., the cases of Woods who received a custodial sentence for breach of CA, s 127 for making offensive comments on Facebook about the disappearance of April Jones, discussed in Agate and Ledward, above, p 264; Scaife, above, p 5; and Dominic McGoldrick, 'The limits of free expression on *Facebook* and social networking sites: A UK Perspective' (2013) 13 HR L Rev 125, 133.

104 [2012] EWHC 2157 (Admin).

105 *Ibid*, [13].

106 *Ibid*, [28].

107 Steve Foster, 'Freedom of expression; is there a human right to make a joke?' (2012) 17 Cov LJ, 97, 101.

108 Rowbottom, above, p 383.

expect a certain amount of repartee or "give and take"'.[109] This clearly advocates a generally tolerant approach. But in contrast to conversation in the bar, speech on social media is both searchable and persistent. So how should the law treat it? Rowbottom observes that although perpetrators may not get much public sympathy, they are not necessarily deserving of criminal penalties.[110] Many comments might be in appalling taste, very sick jokes and offensive to some but should we be 'sentencing people for bad jokes, poor taste and terrible manners?'[111] The comments made by Matthew Woods in the wake of the disappearance and subsequent murder of April Jones resulted in some 50 people surrounding his house, clearly outraged at his actions. But should this have led to his conviction and imprisonment?[112] Rozenberg suggests that while society should shun and shame those who behave in such a way, prosecution and imprisonment should focus on those who 'make credible threats to kill or maim others, putting their victims in genuine fear for their safety.'[113]

Cases such as those mentioned above together with the associated concerns raised, led to the CPS considering the various offences which could be used in such cases and stating the factors which should be taken into account when considering a prosecution for a comment on social media.[114] Essentially the guidelines create a two stage process; the first is to consider whether the evidence indicates that the comments at issue fall within the relevant statutory provisions and, if it does, the second part requires a consideration of whether it is in the public interest to prosecute.

Given the potentially chilling effect, the need to preserve freedom of expression is a major focus of the guidelines which require a 'high threshold'[115] at the evidential stage and, following Art 10 of the ECHR, any restriction must be both necessary and proportionate.[116] In addition, the guidelines emphasise the overwhelming importance of the *context* of the communication.[117] In sum, this stage will only be passed if the comments at issue are *more* than:

- offensive, shocking or disturbing; or
- satirical, iconoclastic or rude comment; or
- the expression of unpopular or unfashionable opinion about serious or trivial matters, or banter or humour, even if distasteful to some or painful to those subjected to it.[118]

The guidelines go on to suggest that it is unlikely to be in the public interest to prosecute where:

- the suspect has expressed genuine remorse;
- swift and effective action has been taken . . . to remove the communication in question or otherwise block access to it;
- the communication was not intended for a wide audience . . . ; or
- the content of the communication did not obviously go beyond what could conceivably be tolerable or acceptable in an open and diverse society which upholds and respects freedom of expression.[119]

---

109 [2008] EWHC 1797 (QB) [14].
110 *Ibid*, p 382.
111 John Kampfner, 'Joking' about April Jones on Facebook is sick not criminal' (2012) *The Guardian*, 9 Oct.
112 See above n 103.
113 Joshua Rozenberg, 'April Jones Facebook Comments: Should Matthew Woods be in prison?' (2012) *The Guardian*, 9 Oct. See also: http://ukhumanrightsblog.com/2012/10/09/twelve-weeks-in-prison-for-sick-jokes-really/; and Agate and Ledward, above, p 264.
114 *Guidelines on prosecuting cases involving communications sent via social media* (in effect 30 June 2013), available online at: www.cps.gov.uk/legal/a_to_c/communications_sent_via_social_media/. For more detailed discussion than is possible here see, e.g., McGoldrick, above, p 135ff; Alasdair Gillespie, 'Obscene conversations, the internet and the criminal law' [2014] Crim L Rev 350, 359.
115 *Ibid*, [34].
116 *Ibid*, [37].
117 *Ibid*, [40].
118 *Ibid*, [41].
119 *Ibid*, [48].

But these factors have to be carefully balanced against harm to a specifically targeted victim and evidence of intention to cause distress and anxiety.[120] The approach advocated in the guidelines can be described as a 'light touch' which may serve to ameliorate any heavy handed application of statutory provisions which were never drafted with social media in mind.[121] If they had been in effect at the time, it seems certain that Chambers would never have been prosecuted and, it has been suggested, neither would Woods.[122]

### 'Revenge porn'

The distribution of sexually explicit images without the subject's consent, colloquially referred to as 'revenge porn' is apparently becoming more frequent on social media.[123] In the majority of such cases, those involved apparently consented to the production of the image but not to its publication and dissemination. Distribution of such images often occurs in the aftermath of the breakdown of a relationship; at the very least it is unpleasant for the victim but can also result in significant psychological and emotional harm.[124] As Barmore has commented (with respect to the US situation):

> harm exists independent of the speaker's motivation, opinion, or idea, and it justifies restricting revenge porn as patently offensive speech for which the rights of the speaker must yield to the rights of third parties.[125]

In other words, in the UK context,[126] this is a situation where, applying the guidelines above, it would be likely to be in the public interest to prosecute. In particular, the context of the distribution of such images suggests that there would be no problem in passing the evidential stage as it violates the generally accepted standard of privacy in sexual relationships, thus militating against any free speech considerations. To put the matter beyond doubt, the Criminal Justice and Courts Act 2015 s 33 now expressly proscribes the disclosure of private sexual photographs and films with intent to cause distress and further interpretation is included in ss 34 and 35.[127] This provision was the result of a Lords Amendment during the passage of the Bill in response to widespread public concern about the practice.[128] A large number of US states have also passed legislation criminalising revenge porn.[129]

## Cybercrime convention

A more intransigent problem at the international level is providing suitable procedures for policing global criminal activity and even allowing for a degree of harmonisation of criminal law. Aside from a number of particularly heinous acts over which there is consensus – such as murder and other violent crime, for example – criminal offences may vary between states, and reflect the particular cultures and mores of the society that caused them to be enacted. As we have seen in the discussion so far, certain jurisdictionally based laws have been used, or attempted to be used, to apprehend the perpetrators of 'cybercrime'. Unlike the scope of the jurisdictionally based laws that

---

120 *Ibid*, [49].
121 See, e.g., discussion in Rowbottom, above, p 365.
122 Agate and Ledward, above, p 364.
123 Cynthia Barmore, 'Criminalization in context: Involuntariness, obscenity and the first amendment' (2015) 67 Stan. L. Rev. 447.
124 See, e.g., Danielle Keats Citron and Mary Ann Franks 'Criminalizing Revenge Porn' (2014) 49 Wake Forest L Rev 345, 350ff.
125 Barmore, above, p 465.
126 For discussion of the legal background in the UK see, e.g., Justine Mitchell, 'Censorship in cyberspace: closing the net on "revenge porn"' (2014) 25 Ent LR 283.
127 Not yet in force at the time of writing.
128 *Hansard* HL Vol, 755, Col 969 (2014).
129 For a comprehensive list and discussion, see e.g., Cynthia Barmore, 'Criminalisation in context: Involuntariness, obscenity and the First Amendment' (2015) 67 Stan L Rev 447.

are pressed into service, the criminal acts that are committed in or via cyberspace cannot always be confined within convenient jurisdictional boundaries. The territoriality of many criminal provisions, together with the global reach and spread of the technology, provides an almost perfect environment for the perpetrator to be situated in one jurisdiction, but the effect of their acts to be felt in another or others.[130] This can hamper enforcement efforts quite dramatically, since 'while the Internet is borderless for criminals, law enforcement agencies must respect the sovereignty of other nations'.[131] To the extent that cybercrime and cybercriminals have scant regard for national borders, then, arguably, the appropriate legal response should be one that also transcends these boundaries. Unless there are in place agreements with respect to cooperation, bilateral or multilateral enforcement, and/or extradition, it will be practically difficult, if not impossible, to apprehend those responsible, and many writers have testified, in principle at least, to the desirability of an international regime that could address and hopefully begin to combat cybercrime on a global scale.

The Council of Europe has been active in this area since the second half of the 1980s, and issued recommendations in both 1989 and 1995. This work continued and culminated in the Cybercrime Convention, which was opened for signature on 23 November 2001.[132] Although it has been suggested that 'the inherent difficulties of formulating satisfactory global internet regulation result in model treaties taking years to approve',[133] in fact, the Convention was drafted in a relatively short time in international agreement terms, and was completed in four years and 27 drafts.[134] The Explanatory Report on the Convention refers to this earlier work, but expresses the view that 'only a binding international instrument can ensure the necessary efficiency in the fight against these new phenomena'.[135] The report concludes that the need and rationale for international action to combat cybercrime is due to a number of factors, but that crucial ones are the accessibility and searchability of information, the emergence of new types of crime, as well as the incidence of traditional crime, and that both of these may have consequences that are not easily restricted by national boundaries, and the inability of domestic laws to rise to those challenges.[136]

Participation in this Convention was not confined to the Member States of the Council of Europe itself: the USA, Canada, Japan, and South Africa were also parties to the negotiations. In one sense, the Convention can be viewed as ground-breaking and pioneering, in that it was and remains the only binding international treaty on this subject.[137] The Convention is also wider in scope than Directive 2013/40/EU (discussed in the previous chapter) because it also applies to crimes where a computer is used to commit the crime, e.g. fraud and content crimes. It adopts a three-pronged approach and contains provisions relating to the harmonisation of substantive criminal law,[138] the necessary domestic procedural powers for investigation and prosecution,[139] and, as discussed in Chapter 7, also provisions aimed at facilitating international cooperation and mutual assistance.[140] The list of substantive offences is not exhaustive or comprehensive, and follows a fairly conventional classification scheme in being divided into sections relating to: the integrity of computer systems, such as access, interception etc;[141] 'computer-related' crimes, such as computer-related forgery and computer-related fraud;[142] content-related offences (although these relate exclusively

130 As already discussed in Chapter 7 at p 302.
131 M Keyser, 'The Council of Europe Convention on Cybercrime' (2003) 12 J Transnat'l L & Pol'y 287, 326.
132 Convention on Cybercrime, CETS No 185, available online at: http://conventions.coe.int/Treaty/en/Treaties/Html/185.htm
133 SC Sprinkel, 'Global internet regulation: The residual effects of the "iloveyou" computer virus and the Draft Convention on Cyber-Crime' (2002) 25 Suffolk Transnat'l L Rev 49, 509.
134 See further Keyser, above, 296.
135 See http://conventions.coe.int/Treaty/en/Reports/Html/185.htm
136 Ibid, paras 4–6.
137 See http://conventions.coe.int/Treaty/en/Treaties/Html/185.htm
138 Articles 2–13.
139 Articles 14–22.
140 Articles 23–35.
141 Articles 2–6.
142 Articles 7 and 8.

to child pornography);[143] and copyright crime subject to the provisions of the Bern Convention, the Trade-related Aspects of Intellectual Property Rights (TRIPS) Agreement, the World Intellectual Property Organization (WIPO) Copyright Treaty, etc.[144] In addition, there are provisions covering aiding and abetting,[145] corporate liability,[146] and sanctions,[147] which should be 'effective, proportionate and dissuasive', and include the possibility of 'deprivation of liberty'. To assist the implementation of the substantive provisions, the procedural provisions include, *inter alia*, provisions allowing 'expeditious preservation of specified computer data, including traffic data',[148] together with a number of Articles providing powers to require production of such data, and empowerment to search and seize relevant data, to collect data in real time, and to intercept data.[149] Some of these provisions necessarily require the cooperation and participation of third parties and private organisations, such as ISPs. Significantly for the subsequent discussion, these provisions are expressed to be subject to the provisions of Art 14, detailing the overall scope of the provisions, and Art 15, which, *inter alia*, requires implementation to recognise general rights under, for example, the ECHR and to incorporate the principle of proportionality. The Preamble to the Convention also makes reference to the international human rights instruments referred to in Art 15(1) and in addition reaffirms 'the right of everyone to hold opinions without interference, as well as the right to freedom of expression, including the freedom to seek, receive, and impart information and ideas of all kinds, regardless of frontiers, and the rights concerning the respect for privacy'. Despite the fact that earlier drafts were modified to take into account the concerns of a number of lobby groups,[150] and notwithstanding both the ideals expressed in the Preamble and the content of Art 15 above, much of the early criticism of the Convention centred on the extent to which it preserved an appropriate balance of rights, and was compatible with the general protection of human rights and civil liberties guaranteed by other international treaties or national constitutions.

In particular, major concerns were voiced in the USA in relation to a perceived clash with protected First Amendment rights in that jurisdiction. The apparent problems related both to the substantive provisions on content, the associated procedural provisions, and also to the requirement of cooperation and mutual assistance discussed in Chapter 7. Keyser[151] suggested that the criticisms of the Convention could be categorised as follows:

- it curtailed freedom of expression;
- it overextended the powers of the enforcement agencies;
- it required private persons and organisations to provide and retain much further information than previously; and
- it infringed civil liberties.

To what extent are these criticisms legitimate and well founded? It is certainly the case that the First Amendment of the US Constitution offers substantial protection to free expression. Indeed, although the USA originally participated in the subsequent Protocol of the Cybercrime Convention concerning the criminalisation of acts of a racist and xenophobic nature committed through computer systems,[152] it did not become a party to the final version, believing that it was inconsistent with First Amendment guarantees of free expression.

---

143 Article 9.
144 Article 10.
145 Article 11.
146 Article 12.
147 Article 13.
148 Article 16.
149 Articles 17–20. See also discussion in Chapter 7 at p 302.
150 See further Sprinkel, above, p 510.
151 Keyser, above, 324.
152 See http://conventions.coe.int/Treaty/en/Treaties/Html/189.htm; see also Yaman Akdeniz, 'Governing racist content on the internet: National and international responses' (2007) 56 UNB LJ 103.

## Consensus and 'virtual child pornography'

It is notable that, despite actions in a number of jurisdictions to address the distribution of pornography on the internet, restrictions on content under the Convention itself are limited to child pornography – presumably because it was not possible to obtain a consensus between negotiating states on other content-based offences. Child pornography was already illegal in the USA by virtue of the provisions of 18 USC §§ 2252 and 2252A (the Protection of Children from Sexual Predators Act of 1998), but the definitions in Art 9(2) of the Cybercrime Convention proscribe not only child pornography as such, but also 'virtual child pornography' – that is, material that has not been created by the use of actual children, but by computer manipulation of images of adult actors, or by altering innocent pictures of children.[153] Earlier attempts in the USA to outlaw such virtual child pornography in the Child Pornography Protection Act of 1996 were struck down as unconstitutional by the Supreme Court in *Ashcroft v Free Speech Coalition*,[154] which found that the law as it stood was unacceptably broad. Virtual child pornography could be distinguished from actual child pornography in that it was not 'intrinsically related to the sexual abuse of children',[155] but this law attempted to outlaw images that were produced without the involvement of actual children, together with images that might pass the community standards test for obscenity. It was in consequence an unacceptable restriction on free expression.

Following this decision, Congress attempted to address the deficiencies in the Prosecutorial Remedies and Tools against the Exploitation of Children Today (PROTECT) Act of 2003. This statute outlawed morphed child pornography, provided that it could be proved beyond reasonable doubt that there was an intention to make others believe that the children depicted were genuine. It also contained an amendment introduced by the Child Obscenity and Pornography Protection Act of 2003 proscribing any solicitation to buy or sell child pornography whatever its origin. The PROTECT Act was itself subject to constitutional challenges, but was eventually upheld by the Supreme Court.[156] However, the ability of the US Congress to outlaw virtual child pornography while still satisfying the stringent requirements of First Amendment jurisprudence should not really have any bearing on whether or not to ratify the Cybercrime Convention. Although, as shown, the Convention contains provisions dealing with virtual child pornography, Art 9(4) also provides that states can reserve the right not to apply in whole or in part these particular provisions, suggesting that this should, in any case, not be a bar to ratification if there were serious First Amendment concerns.

## Ratification

The Convention came into force in July 2004 and, at the time of writing, has been ratified by 45 states, including the USA – although, as discussed below, the ratification process itself was not without controversy.[157] The original decision of the US government to participate in the drafting of the Cybercrime Convention was made in the belief that such a Treaty would assist in the international investigation of computer-related crime and that it was generally in line with US law. However, although President Bush pressed for its ratification in 2003,[158] the opposition to ratification arising out of the issues outlined above delayed its ratification by Senate until 2006.[159]

In contrast, there was little controversy over the UK's plans for ratification of the Cybercrime Convention as indicated in the comment in the APIG report that the inquiry 'received very few

---

153 Proscribed in the UK by Protection of Children Act, s 7(4)(b) discussed above at p 317.
154 535 US 234 (2002).
155 Ibid, 250.
156 *US v Williams* 553 US 285 (2008).
157 See http://conventions.coe.int/Treaty/Commun/ChercheSig.asp?NT=185&CL=ENG
158 Declan McCullagh, 'Bush pushes for cybercrime treaty' (2003) *cnet News*, 18 November, available online at: http://www.cnet.com/uk/news/bush-pushes-for-cybercrime-treaty/
159 John R Crook, 'Senate approves UK Extradition Treaty and other bilateral and multilateral treaties, attaches reservations and understandings' (2007) 101 Am J Int'l Law 199, 200.

comments on the implications of the CMA of ratifying the Convention on Cybercrime, suggesting that this is not widely seen as a contentious issue'.[160] Some of the provisions of the Cybercrime Convention were likely to be covered by the existing CMA,[161] but, in the event, despite the matter being apparently uncontroversial, the UK did not actually ratify the convention until May 2011, almost five years after the US.[162] Although there are certainly concerns that could arise if the Cybercrime Convention were transposed into the national law of any of the contracting parties without appropriate safeguards for individual rights and liberties, this is not necessarily something that is confined to this international convention.

## Concluding remarks

The inherently jurisdictionally based nature of criminal law meets its greatest challenges in relation to content-based offences. There is little prospect of global consensus on a number of relevant concepts and definitions of offending behaviour, and it is significant that, for this type of conduct, the Cybercrime Convention contains only provisions relating to child pornography. Further, it is perhaps ironic that, in an area that stands to benefit most from international cooperation, it has been these very provisions that created the greatest stumbling block to ratification.

## Further reading

Richard Wortley and Stephen Smallbone, *Internet Child Pornography: Causes, Investigation, and Prevention* 2012, ABC-CLIO

A Roversi, *Hate on the Net, Extremist Sites, Neo-fascism On-line, Electronic Jihad,* 2008, Farnham: Ashgate

Yaman Akdeniz, *Internet Child Pornography and the Law: National and International Responses,* 2008, London: Ashgate

Dominic McGoldrick, 'The limits of free expression on *Facebook* and Social Networking sites: A UK Perspective' (2013) 13 HR L Rev 125

Jacob Rowbottom, 'To rant, vent and converse: protecting low level digital speech' (2012) 71 CLJ 355

---

160 *Revision of the Computer Misuse Act*: Report of an Inquiry by the All Party Internet Group June 2004 para. 82 available online at: www.cl.cam.ac.uk/~rnc1/APIG-report-cma.pdf
161 *Ibid*, para 77.
162 See http://www.coe.int/en/web/conventions/full-list/-/conventions/treaty/185/signatures

# Chapter 9

# Privacy and data protection

## Chapter contents

# Introduction

Since time immemorial, information has been collected and exchanged about individuals. More than 25 ago Earl Ferrers remarked that: 'The collection of personal data is as old as society itself. It may not be the oldest profession but it is one of the oldest habits.'[1] Unsurprisingly nothing has happened to break this habit. It is not an overstatement to say that the internet has revolutionised

---

1 Earl Ferrers, *Hansard* HL, vol 549, col 37 (11 October 1993).

the storage, exchange and availability of information, some of which will inevitably be about individuals. Such information may be generated by any internet user whether on behalf of government departments, commercial entities, charitable organisations, educational institutions or private individuals – anyone who has access to the internet. This is potentially a worldwide activity. When the existing Data Protection Directive was adopted in 1995 less than 1 per cent of the world population had access to the internet – the current figure is 40 per cent and a total of approximately 3 billion users.[2]

This chapter is devoted to a consideration of the way in which the law is able to deal with abuses of the global information infrastructure in so far as this relates to information about individuals, whether true or false. This will involve a study of whether, and in what manner, the use of computers and computer networks to process and transfer increasing quantities of personal data can compromise an individual's privacy, or facilitate acts that threaten the individual's reputation or integrity, together with an analysis of the legal response to these issues.

## Data protection: The nature of the problem

Prior to the so-called 'information revolution', information and data held on individuals would only be kept in traditional filing cabinets or their equivalent. Not only might these be accessed only relatively infrequently, perhaps by the holder of the data, but it would also be difficult for other users of similar information or information about the same individual to gain access. The ease with which even the first generation of computers was able to store and manipulate data caused a dramatic change in this respect, and made it a simple matter for information about particular individuals held in a number of places to be correlated. Indeed, a whole industry arose out of the operation referred to as 'data matching', in which a profile of a particular individual is assembled from data held at a number of sources. Such profiles are now a familiar part of marketing activities: lists of those with similar profiles form a commodity that, itself, can be traded to businesses to enable selective targeting of a particular sector of the market. Neither is this process confined to business use, as pointed out succinctly by Browne-Wilkinson VC:

> If the information obtained by the police, the Inland Revenue, the social security services, the health service and other agencies were to be gathered together in one file, the freedom of the individual would be greatly at risk. The dossier of private information is the badge of the totalitarian State.[3]

This highlights the potential dangers of data matching to individual rights and liberties, and is indicative of some of the fears that surround the storage of personal data on computer systems. These fears have been voiced since the advent of widespread computerisation[4] and, even as far back as 1975, a significant amount of information about identifiable individuals was already kept on computer by central government.[5] Such anxieties were exacerbated as industry and commerce also began to rely on the use of computers to such an extent that it is today impossible to imagine

---

2 See www.internetlivestats.com/internet-users/ – this growth is also illustrated by the fact that the number of internet users has increased by around 1 billion since the last edition of this book.
3 *Marcel v Metropolitan Police Comr* [1992] Ch 225, 240.
4 See, e.g., P Ashdown, *Hansard*, col 86 (30 January 1984); Data Protection Registrar, Eighth Report of the Data Protection Registrar, 1992, London: HMSO, Appendix 1, quoting the above comment of Browne-Wilkinson VC.
5 For details, see Secretary of State for the Home Department, Computers: Safeguards for Privacy, Cmnd 6354, 1975, London: HMSO, Tables 1 and 2, further updated in Secretary of State for the Home Department, Report of the Committee on Data Protection, Cmnd 7341, 1978, London: HMSO, Appendix 6.

business being possible without them; the words of Perri 6, that 'personal information has become the basic fuel on which modern business and government run', remain an accurate description.[6]

In 1972, despite the fact that computerisation was then still at an embryonic stage, the Younger Committee on Privacy identified characteristics that distinguished storage of information on computer from more traditional methods. The Committee noted in particular three specific areas of concern: the use of computers to compile personal profiles; their capacity to correlate information; and the ease with which unauthorised access to data could be obtained, often from remote sites.[7] There was no recommendation for action at that time, because the Committee found insufficient evidence that there had been any abuse of the above capabilities, and so regulatory intervention was, at that time, unwarranted; nevertheless some of these fears had already been recognised as a reality in the USA.[8] Even as such issues were under discussion, the nature of the threat was undergoing a subtle change as the technology continued to progress. In the 1970s and early 1980s, the focus was on the development of large, centralised databases held on mainframe computers. Technological advancement then changed direction and, instead of even larger machines being developed, the advent of the microcomputer resulted in computers rapidly becoming a common tool, both at work and in the home, rather than being confined to large institutions. Further, the creation of computer networks on a global scale moved the emphasis from centralised systems to increasingly decentralised systems, typified by the internet and worldwide web.[9] These give rise to qualitatively different problems. In the early days, only large public and private organisations operated computers, giving them the exclusive ability to accumulate and correlate information about individuals from multiple sources. The advent of networked PCs and the later development of Web 2.0, which further blurs the difference between the user and the subject of the personal data, have meant that personal profiling is no longer the exclusive prerogative of the large organisation.

As computer networks – specifically the internet – developed, the task of aggregating personal data became much more widespread, facilitated by the technology. As a user surfs the net, transactional data are created and, 'with each click in the internet, your browser leaves a piece of information about you behind. As these pieces of information accumulate, a roadmap of personal, private information emerges'.[10] This is by no means a new phenomenon: similar warnings have been made for almost 20 years.[11] The development of Web 2.0,[12] which further blurred the difference between the user and subject of the personal data, meant that personal profiling was no longer the exclusive prerogative of the large organisation, as illustrated by Zittrain's remark that 'the Net puts private individuals in a position to do more to compromise privacy than the government and commercial institutions traditionally targeted for scrutiny and regulation'.[13] Such

---

6 Perri 6, *The Future of Privacy Volume 1: Private Life and Public Policy*, 1998, London: Demos, p 23.

7 Secretary of State for the Home Department, Report of the Committee on Privacy, Cmnd 5012, 1972, London: HMSO, para 581.

8 AR Miller, The Assault on Privacy: Computers, Databanks and Dossiers, 1971, Ann Arbor, MI: Michigan University Press, ch 2.

9 Some describe the communication between two computers in the same laboratory in 2 September 2009 as the birth of the internet: see National Geographic, 'Internet's 40th "birthday" marked' (2009) 31 August, available online at: http://news.nation-algeographic.com/news/2009/08/090831-internet-40th-video-ap.html. Others have pointed out that it is 'impossible to say for certain when the internet began', but nevertheless marked the occasion on 29 October 2009, the apparent anniversary of the first communication between two computers at remote sites: see Oliver Burkeman, 'Forty years of the internet: How the world changed forever' (2009) *The Guardian*, 23 October, available online at: www.guardian.co.uk/technology/2009/oct/23/internet-40-history-arpanet. Whenever the internet, as we now know it, was invented, it was not until the mid-1980s that it began to be used on a regular, day-to-day basis outside the research community.

10 Brian Kane and Brett T Delange, 'A tale of two internets: Web 2.0 slices, dices, and is privacy resistant' (2009) 45 Idaho L Rev 317, 318.

11 See, e.g., Article 29 Working Party, Recommendation 3/97, above; Article 29 Working Party, Recommendation 1/99, above; Electronic Privacy Information Center (EPIC), Surfer Beware III: Privacy Policies without Privacy Protection, 1999, available online at: www.epic.org/reports/surfer-beware3.html; Federal Trade Commission, Privacy Online: Fair Information Practices in the Electronic Marketplace, 2000, available online at: www.ftc.gov/reports/privacy2000/privacy2000text.pdf (p 9).

12 So-called Web 2.0 does not reflect any new technical features of the internet, but instead refers to the use of applications that foster and facilitate interactive information-sharing and user-generated content. Well-known examples are Wikipedia, social networking sites such as Facebook, and video sharing sites such as YouTube, etc.

13 Jonathan Zittrain, 'Privacy 2.0' (2008) U Chi Legal F 65.

developments have resulted in an increased potential for privacy invasion rather than a suggestion that large commercial or government databases are no longer of concern. In respect of the latter, there continue to be examples of organisations both public and private losing or mishandling personal data, often because of poor security and carelessness, rather than any sophisticated technical reason.[14] Further, powerful search engines now provide the tools for retrieving all of the available data about a person that might be held on completely unrelated sites and might be no longer either current or accurate, and this, together with the longevity of information circulating on the internet has fuelled calls for a 'right to be forgotten'[15] to supplement existing informational privacy rights. Fears about the power of computer technology to compromise the privacies of its users have thus not abated and there continues to be a debate about the appropriate way to regulate the accessibility and availability of personal data.

Despite the fact that users may recognise, at least in principle, the potential threat to their privacy from these invasive technologies, it clearly does not deter use of the internet; indeed, as Kane and Delange have observed, it appears as if the internet 'inspires a trust factor that otherwise does not exist outside of the online world', and although the internet might have originated as 'a one or two-dimensional system of information and transactions', it has subsequently 'morphed into a three dimensional platform through which we participate through online shopping, email and social networking sites . . . '.[16] Unfortunately, this level of trust means that either users do not recognise any potential threat to their privacy, or, if they do, are unconcerned about it,[17] or do not always take appropriate steps to protect their own privacy until they find that privacy unacceptably compromised. Although there have been significant legal initiatives – notably the law on data protection – the rapid development of the internet and Web 2.0 applications in particular has meant that the law has not kept pace; in particular, as we shall see later, the European Data Protection Directive 95/46/EC was drafted and implemented when the internet was still in its infancy and the extent to which its provisions can be easily applied to the circulation of personal data on the internet remains controversial. For this and other reasons, a new General Data Protection Regulation (GDPR)[18] was adopted by the European Parliament on 14 April 2016 and came into force on 24 May 2016.

# Data protection and privacy

Despite privacy and 'privacy-invading features' being discussed in the context of data protection, it has not always been easy to reconcile the terms 'data protection', on the one hand, and 'privacy', on the other. This is not helped by the fact that an agreed definition of privacy remains elusive. Although privacy issues have probably been in existence ever since walls were invented, the legal academic discussion only began in earnest at the end of the nineteenth century, when Warren and Brandeis penned their seminal article in response to developments in a different technology – photography.[19] The analysis of the multifaceted and slippery concept of privacy continues to the present, but with no agreed conclusion or consensus, much less the emergence of any workable legal definition. Westin suggested that 'Privacy is the claim of individuals, groups or institutions

---

14 See, e.g., the Information Commissioner's reports of enforcement action online at: https://ico.org.uk/action-weve-taken/data-security-incident-trends/. Many of these relate to the theft of unencrypted laptops or the loss of USB sticks resulting in the loss of personal data. Zittrain refers to similar examples in the USA, including, for example, the loss of 1.2 million Bank of America customer records in 2005: above, 70–1.

15 See further discussion at p 361.

16 Zittrain, above.

17 See, e.g., Zittrain, above, p 68.

18 Regulation (EU) 2016/679 of the European Parliament and of the Council of 27 April 2016 on the protection of natural persons with regard to the processing of personal data and on the free movement of such data and repealing Directive 95/46/EC. [2016] OJ L119/1. See later discussion at p 387.

19 S Warren and L Brandeis, 'The right to privacy' (1890) 4 Harv L Rev 193.

to determine for themselves when, how and to what extent information about them is communicated to others', a definition based on the right of self-determination, which may be placed at particular risk by the practice of data matching made so simple by modern information technology (IT).[20] This notion was supported by Miller,[21] in the specific context of this technology, who considered privacy to be 'the individual's ability to control the circulation of information relating to him'. Gavison, on the other hand, is critical of the ability to control personal information as being a determinant of the definition of privacy precisely because a dependence on subjective choice makes both a realisation of the scope of the concept and the provision of legal protection problematic.[22] The definitional difficulties are exacerbated by the fact that whether or not privacy is considered to have been invaded is a very subjective issue, which will depend not only on the view of the person whose privacy is being invaded, but also on who is the invader and what information he or she is uncovering. Even using the apparently neutral approach of Gavison, based on the three components of secrecy, anonymity and solitude, the question of whether there has, in fact, been an invasion of privacy is likely to remain a subjective one. Perri 6 has submitted that the reason why there is no consensus over definition is that 'as a society we do not and cannot agree on what it is about private life and privacy that we value',[23] while Feldman comments that 'The problem is that privacy is controversial. The very breadth of the idea and its tendency to merge with the idea of liberty itself produces a lack of definition which weakens its force in moral and political discourse'.[24] More recently, Richards and Solove, having explored the conceptual and doctrinal differences relating to the protection of privacy in both the USA and the UK, conclude that 'privacy cannot be reduced to a single essence; it is a multiplicity of different yet related things'.[25]

Whether or not there is an accepted and acceptable definition of 'privacy', it is usually recognised as a fundamental human right, and accorded specific protection under human rights conventions and national constitutions. In contrast, data protection is often viewed as a technical term relating to specific information management practices – the preferred stance of those who would see data protection primarily as an aspect of business regulation. Even if the precise nature of the relationship between data protection and privacy is elusive, one approach to the undeniable tension between the rights of all those who would seek to exert control over personal information can be found in the terminology of risk and risk assessment, concepts that are, perhaps, more familiar in a business environment. Three risk factors can be identified that could be considered to be elements of privacy.[26] The first of these is the risk of injustice due to significant inaccuracy in personal data, unjust inference, 'function creep' (the gradual use of data for purposes other than those for which it was collected), or reversal of the presumption of innocence, as seen in data matching when correlation of information from disparate sources may produce an impression that is greater than the sum of the parts. The second risk is to one's personal control over the collection of personal information as a result of excessive and unjustified surveillance (which would presumably include monitoring the use of particular websites), collection of data without the data subject's consent, and also the prohibition or active discouragement of the means to remedy these risks, such as the use of encryption and anonymising software. Finally, there is a risk to dignity as a result of exposure or embarrassment due to an absence of transparency in information procedures, physical intrusion into private spaces, unnecessary identification or absence of anonymity, or unnecessary or unjustified disclosure of personal information without consent. Although these have been described in

---

20 AF Westin, *Privacy and Freedom*, 1967, London: Bodley Head, London; see also Yves Poullet, 'Data protection between property and liberties' in HWK Kaspersen and A Oskamp (eds), *Amongst Friends in Computers and Law*, 1990, The Hague: Kluwer, p 161.
21 Miller, above.
22 R Gavison, 'Privacy and the limits of law' (1980) 89 Yale LJ 421.
23 Perri 6, above, p 21.
24 D Feldman, 'Secrecy, dignity or autonomy? Views of privacy as a civil liberty' (1994) 10 CL & P 41.
25 Neil M Richards and Daniel J Solove, 'Privacy's other path: Recovering the law of confidentiality' (2007) 96 Geo LJ 123.
26 See Perri 6, above, p 40.

the terminology of privacy, there are echoes of data protection issues and, in the technical sense, data protection measures may be considered as risk management devices that need to balance the risk to the individual from unnecessary invasion of privacy with the measures necessary to control that risk.[27] It may be that such differences in terminology are not so disparate as they might appear at first sight.

The precise relationship between privacy and data protection remains unresolved, and it is possible to continue to find conflicting views. Art 1 of the Data Protection Directive explicitly protects the privacy of an individual with respect to the processing of data; on the other hand, there is no mention of the word 'privacy' in the Data Protection Act 1998 intended to implement the Directive. In contrast, a parallel provision has not been included in the General Data Protection Regulation which makes very little mention of privacy at all. Although this could be viewed as a move away from a focus on privacy Costa and Poullet believe that 'it is certain that affirming the autonomy of the right to protection of personal data does not imply denying privacy as its fundament.'[28] In the USA, a tort of privacy has been developed by the courts, but this focuses primarily on physical intrusion and there is no general law on data protection or information privacy – although there are sector-specific rules for data acknowledged to be particularly sensitive, such as that pertaining to medical or health records. How has the unresolved relationship between privacy and data protection affected the development of the legal provisions? As mentioned above, Gavison defines three components of privacy – that is, secrecy, anonymity, and solitude – while Feldman uses the words 'secrecy, dignity, autonomy'. In both of these formulations, the word 'secrecy' is used to encompass the idea of informational privacy, reflecting the desire of individuals to be able to place checks on what is known about them not only in the sense of data released, but also in terms of control over its subsequent use and reuse. Does this concept of informational privacy equate with data protection or overlap with it? In 1978, the Lindop Committee was established to look exclusively at the issue of data protection in the UK. The Lindop Report referred to the definitions of both Westin and Miller, quoted above, but was at pains to distinguish 'privacy' and 'data protection'. It noted that the physical aspects of privacy were unrelated to data protection and also that aspects of data protection were not connected with privacy.[29] It conceded, however, that there was an overlap between the two concepts, which could be termed 'informational' or 'data' privacy.[30] But the report also stressed that the subjective nature of privacy meant that there was a wide variation in what might, or might not, be regarded as private, and that 'such variations exist between an individual and another, between different sections of society, between societies in different countries and between different periods of time in the same society'.[31] This also served to indicate that 'privateness' could not be considered to be directly related to the data themselves, nor could it be used as a synonym for secrecy.

Notwithstanding any attempt at semantic differentiation, other sources and commentators have often used the words 'data protection' and 'privacy' interchangeably or appear to assume some link between the two. Gellman, for example, refers to 'the slice of privacy known as "data protection"', and goes on to refer to it as a 'useful European term referring to rules about the collection, use and dissemination of personal information' and an 'important subset of privacy law'. He further suggests that a 'major policy objective of data protection is the application of fair information practices, an organized set of values and standards about personal information defining the rights

---

27 See also C Raab, 'The governance of data protection' in J Kooiman (ed), *Modern Governance*, 1993, London: Sage, pp 89–103; F Bott, A Coleman, J Eaton, and D Rowland, *Professional Issues in Software Engineering*, 3rd edn, 2000, London: Taylor & Francis, p 323.
28 Luiz Costa and Yves Poullet, 'Privacy and the regulation of 2012' (2012) 28 CLSR 254, 255.
29 Secretary of State for the Home Department, Cmnd 7341, above, para 2.03.
30 *Ibid*, para 2.04.
31 *Ibid*, para 2.05.

of record subjects and the responsibilities of record keepers'.[32] It is arguably this entrenchment of good records management practice in law that is the salient characteristic of data protection law. As acknowledged by Gellman, the term 'data protection' originated in Europe, but few would dispute the contention that it has become a globally recognised term. However, it could be argued that the coining of this specific term has itself been the root of the problem – suggesting or being indicative of separate strands of meaning where perhaps none exist.[33] Although recent initiatives seem more likely to stress the link between data protection and privacy, even in 1980, both the Organisation for Economic Co-operation and Development (OECD) and the Council of Europe were in no doubt that data protection was a facet of privacy. In the context of the automatic processing of personal data, the Council of Europe considered that 'it is desirable to extend the safeguards for everyone's rights and fundamental freedoms, and in particular the right to the respect for privacy',[34] while the OECD commented that 'privacy protection laws have been introduced . . . to prevent what are considered to be violations of fundamental human rights such as the unlawful storage of personal data or the abuse or unauthorised disclosure of such data'.[35] The now ubiquitous term 'data protection' was reserved for the explanatory memorandum accompanying the Guidelines.

Even in the UK, with its historic reluctance to acknowledge an explicit law of privacy, the link between data protection and privacy has increasingly been recognised. In 1994, the then Data Protection Registrar said, in his Final Report, that 'data protection legislation is about the protection of individuals rather than the regulation of industry. It is civil rights legislation rather than technical business legislation'.[36] Even though the Data Protection Act 1984 never used the word 'privacy', Lord Hoffmann, in R v Brown, remarked: 'English common law does not know a general right of privacy and Parliament has been reluctant to enact one. But there has been some legislation to deal with particular aspects of the problem. The Data Protection Act 1984 . . . is one such statute.'[37] The decision of the then Data Protection Tribunal in British Gas Trading Ltd v Data Protection Registrar was more specific, stating that 'an underlying purpose of the data protection principles is to protect privacy with respect to the processing of personal data',[38] a view that looks both back to the Council of Europe Convention and forward to Directive 95/46/EC. Following implementation of this Directive, the Deputy Data Protection Registrar asserted that although data protection legislation could not be regarded as 'comprehensive privacy legislation' it could not be doubted that 'as a matter of law, data protection is a form of privacy protection.'[39]

Notwithstanding that such comments and pronouncements originate from a variety of sources, the historic lack of legal protection for privacy per se in the UK has meant that there is still resistance, and even suspicion in some quarters, towards any legislation that purports to protect, or that could be regarded as protecting, privacy. Proponents of such views seek to divorce the concepts of data protection and privacy. This has resulted in warnings against data protection law bringing in privacy law surreptitiously by the 'back door'. Those who espouse such views concentrate, instead, on the business regulation aspects of data protection and its role in promoting the free flow of personal data. Thus Viscount Astor stated that 'the Bill which implements the Directive is designed

---

32 Robert Gellman, 'Does privacy law work?' in PE Agre and M Rotenberg (eds), Technology and Privacy: The New Landscape, 1998, Cambridge, MA: MIT Press, p 194.
33 But see also Juliane Kokott and Christoph Sobatta, 'The distinction between privacy and data protection in the jurisprudence of the CJEU and ECtHR' (2013) 3 IDPL 222; and Orly Lynskey, 'Deconstructing data protection: the "added-value" of a right to data protection in the EU legal order' (2014) 63 ICLQ 569.
34 Recitals to Council of Europe Convention No 108.
35 OECD Guidelines on the Protection of Privacy and Transborder Flows of Personal Data 1908, available online at: www.oecd.org/sti/ieconomy/oecdguidelinesontheprotectionofprivacyandtransborderflowsofpersonaldata.htm. The OECD guidelines have now been updated to respond to technological change and user expectations. See now www.oecd.org/sti/ieconomy/2013-oecd-privacy-guidelines.pdf
36 Data Protection Registrar, Tenth Annual Report of the Data Protection Registrar, 1994, London: HMSO.
37 [1996] 1 All ER 545, 555.
38 British Gas Trading Ltd v Data Protection Registrar (1998), available online at: www.informationtribunal.gov.uk/DBFiles/Decision/i162/british_gas.pdf (p 11).
39 Francis GB Aldhouse, 'Data protection, privacy and the media' (1999) 4 Comm L 8, 11.

to improve the free movement of personal data throughout the Community . . . we need to protect the rights of individuals but we do not want a back door privacy law'.[40] In the same debate, Lord Wakeham was to suggest that the Data Protection Bill (now the Data Protection Act 1998, implementing Directive 95/46/EC) was 'an excellent piece of legislation which avoids all the perils of a privacy law. It is entirely in line with the Government's stated commitment to self-regulation and their opposition to a privacy law'.

Both sides of this debate have always recognised that the reliance by business on the increased use of computers and computer networks, both internally and externally to the enterprise, enhances any disparity between business needs and individuals' right of privacy. There is a fundamental conflict at the heart of informational privacy or data protection between the individual whose data is at issue and the person who is collecting or otherwise processing it. Some might suggest that personal information should be under the control of the person to whom it refers. On the other hand, a case can be made out that, in so far as personal data arises from information provided by one person to another that is then recorded or processed in a particular way, the latter should be able to exert at least some rights over its use. This inevitably creates a tension between the two parties. The Lindop Report noted that 'a balance must be found between the interests of the individual and the interests of the rest of society, which include the efficient conduct of industry, commerce and administration'. It also suggested that the balance might need to be 'established differently in different cases. It may also be settled differently in different societies, and may shift within the same society'.[41] Competing interests, although often a reflection of the conflict between the individual and the state, may equally well refer to a balancing of the right of individuals to privacy and control over the use of their own information with the right of other individuals or organisations to use that same information, which they may have compiled and processed, to the best commercial effect. Whilst, in upholding a general right to privacy, civil libertarians might tip this balance in favour of the right of individuals to control data concerning themselves, this may not be an automatic or obvious result.[42] Whereas it is accepted that civil liberties and human rights cannot be absolute and unfettered, it is clearly difficult to achieve an acceptable balance between the competing rights of those involved. It is the Herculean task of data protection regulation to achieve that balance.

# Regulatory approaches and initiatives

Recognition of the competing needs raised by the collection and processing, together with consequent pressure from a variety of intergovernmental organisations such as the OECD and the Council of Europe, eventually led to regulation in a number of jurisdictions. However, this has not been accompanied by any global consensus on either the most appropriate way of achieving and maintaining the balance between the competing objectives or the provision of a suitable regulatory framework. If it is accepted that data protection regulation is necessary to respond to the threat to individual privacy from the use of computers and computer networks, it might be supposed that the central issue is merely the problem of reaching agreement on the method of achieving this result. But the counter-argument is that data protection laws impede the free flow of data, stifle rapid innovation and generally restrict the free market. There is also a considerable compliance burden related to the cost of implementation. On this argument, only minimal external regulation is likely to be tolerated and the advantages of market-driven, self-regulatory practices espoused. In other words, strong data protection will, inevitably, hinder commercial activity. Moderating this view, some legal and economic analyses have apparently demonstrated that the reality may not be

---

40  *Hansard* HL, vol 585, col 445 (2 February 1998).
41  Secretary of State for the Home Department, Cmnd 7341, above, para 2.09.
42  See further, Yves Poullet, 'Data protection legislation: What is at stake for our society and our democracy?' (2009) 25 CLSR 211.

so simple and that a strong legal infrastructure may actually encourage commerce. Whichever side of the argument is supported, it does seem to be generally recognised that privacy regulation may be more apt and relevant in relation to business-to-consumer (B2C) transactions than for business-to-business (B2B) ones.

If it is taken as a given that some regulation is necessary for the protection of individuals, what is the most suitable method? A clear division in approach is evident between the USA, on the one hand, which favours a sectoral, self-regulatory system, and Europe, on the other, which has a long history of legislative intervention.[43] Indeed, as already pointed out, the very concept of data protection appears to be a European creation. In order to be able to appreciate the nature of the debate that has unfolded surrounding the regulation of data protection in different jurisdictions, especially in the USA and Europe, it is prudent to examine some of the advantages and disadvantages of these apparently opposing philosophies.

As already discussed, 'self-regulation' is arguably a much maligned and frequently misunderstood term. It should not be confused with 'non-regulation',[44] but can reasonably be equated with 'non-governmental regulation', although a number of self-regulatory regimes do, in fact, operate within a statutory framework. At its most reduced form, it suggests the propensity of individuals to provide rules for themselves, although these may include, of course, compliance with external, central regulation. Within the business and commercial sector, the term is usually used to denote a much more formal regulatory framework, which may be established by the industries, trade, and professional associations themselves in response to the need to be accountable for their members' activities or in response to a statutory framework, imposed for the control of a particular activity, as noted above. This last system is sometimes referred to as 'enforced self-regulation'. Self-regulatory schemes of this nature have become an increasingly familiar aspect of the regulation of commercial activity in many jurisdictions, and it is in reference to such schemes that the majority of academic scrutiny and comment has occurred.[45] Thus, self-regulation provides a particular type of regulatory regime, the flexibility and relative informality of which is often appreciated by the business community. Although frequently the subject of criticism by both lawyers and economists, particularly in relation to apparent inadequacies of enforcement, it nevertheless may be seen as advantageous by businesses. Self-regulatory agencies often have specific technical and sector-specific expertise, the regulatory process is less formal, and there are significant savings that can be made on monitoring activity, updating and revising standards, as well as more general administration of such schemes.[46] In practice, it may be difficult to assess how well the regime has been implemented or performs its functions, but this is a criticism that can also be directed at some statutory regimes. For the purposes of the present discussion, the major question is whether it can be as effective in protecting individual rights as a statutory scheme (see Chapter 1).

## The origins of data protection legislation

In Europe, there has been little consideration of the use of self-regulatory regimes as the primary method of regulation. In the UK, the origins of data protection legislation can be traced back to the Younger Committee on Privacy,[47] which was established in response to growing concerns during the 1960s about the amount of personal information kept by various organisations to which the individuals concerned had no right of access. Its terms of reference were 'to consider whether legislation is needed to give further protection to the individual citizen and to commercial and

---

43 See also Andrew Charlesworth, 'Clash of the data titans? US and EU data privacy regulation' (2000) 6 EPL 253.
44 See further, AC Page, 'Self-regulation: The constitutional dimension' (1986) 49 MLR 141.
45 See, generally, Robert Baldwin, Martin Cave, and Martin Lodge (eds), The Oxford Handbook of Regulation, 2010, Oxford: Oxford University Press; Anthony I Ogus, Regulation: Legal Form and Economic Theory, 1994, Oxford: Clarendon.
46 Anthony I Ogus, 'Rethinking self-regulation' (1995) 15 OJLS 97, 98.
47 Secretary of State for the Home Department, Cmnd 5012, above.

industrial interests against intrusion into privacy by private persons and organisations or by companies', suggesting that a statutory framework was what was in contemplation. Although, at this time, the use of computers was still comparatively novel, and was largely confined to big commercial and educational institutions, the potential for the problems identified earlier in the use of computer systems for these purposes had already been identified, and Chapter 20 of the Younger Report focused specifically on this perceived threat to privacy. Although, as already noted, there was no recommendation to legislate at that time, the Report formulated ten principles of good data management, which were suggested to provide a guide for the use of computers that manipulated personal data.[48] They included: collecting and holding information for a specific purpose and not using it for other purposes; collecting only the minimum information necessary; not holding it longer than was necessary; ensuring its accuracy; informing the subject of the information held on them; and taking appropriate security measures. Similar principles enunciating fair information practices have since formed the backbone of legal instruments for the regulation of data protection, at both the national and international levels. The OECD Guidelines of 1980 covered essentially the same ground, referring to its data management principles as covering: collection limitation; data quality; purpose specification; use limitation; security safeguards; openness, individual participation; and accountability. Again, a statutory regime was envisaged, the OECD recommending that these Guidelines be taken into account in the member countries' domestic legislation on privacy. Around the same time, the Council of Europe adopted the Convention for the Protection of Individuals with regard to Automatic Processing of Personal Data, based on similar principles.[49] Article 4(1) of this Convention also seemed to envisage an approach that would be primarily legislative, providing that 'Each Party shall take the necessary measures in its domestic law to give effect to the basic principles for data protection'. It was international activity of this type that was to lead many of the signatories to these agreements to produce legislation for the regulation of this area, recognising that not only did these international instruments provide a benchmark for the appropriate standard, but also that transnational data flows might be compromised without the adoption of a common standard. Amongst such jurisdictions was the UK, the first data protection legislation of which, the Data Protection Act 1984, was enacted as a direct result of the perceived need to ratify the Council of Europe Convention.[50]

Both the OECD and Council of Europe documents were thus instrumental in precipitating legislative action in many European states. Indeed, Mayer-Schönberger has commented that, in Europe, 'almost all the national norms enacted after 1981 reflected the spirit if not the text of the OECD Guidelines'. However, notwithstanding the central influence of the various principles of good data management, this has not had the result that the statutory regulatory regimes adopted have had uniformity of provisions. There is clearly room for variation in the scope and emphasis of the protection provided – and neither has the legislative approach remained static. Mayer-Schönberger has further traced this development in terms of a succession of generations of data protection legislation. Of these, he suggests that the first generation represents those laws passed in the early 1970s that reacted to the onset of large databanks and the overall phenomenon of data processing. The second generation, which emerged in the late 1970s, began to focus more explicitly on the individual rights of citizens. This was further developed by the third generation of regulation in the 1980s, which emphasised informational participation and self-determination.[51]

---

48 Ibid, paras 592–600.
49 Convention for the Protection of Individuals with regard to Automatic Processing of Personal Data, CETS No 108, Ch II (Basic Principles for Data Protection); full text available online at: http://conventions.coe.int/Treaty/en/Treaties/Html/108.htm. Modernisation of Convention 108 was approved in December 2014, see details at: www.coe.int/t/dghl/standardsetting/DataProtection/default_en.asp
50 See, e.g., William Whitelaw (Home Secretary), Hansard HC, vol 40, col 554 (11 April 1983).
51 For a discussion suggesting that it is a fallacy that data protection can provide informational self-determination, see Bert-Jaap Koops, 'The Trouble with European Data Protection Law' (2014) 4 IDPL 250, 251ff.

The fourth generation, which Mayer-Schönberger suggests focuses more on holistic and sectoral perspectives, is exemplified by Directive 95/46/EC and emerged in the 1990s.[52] However, despite the categorisation into generations, not all jurisdictions within Europe necessarily embraced the later generations of norms to the fullest extent. In addition, all of these developments in the regulatory landscape still tended to focus on the tension between individual informational rights and the use of personal data by large organisations, and, as we shall see, more recent regulatory activity has attempted to respond to the more diffuse and amorphous threat to individual privacy resulting from the use of computer networks.

## Different approaches compared

Although regulation of this area within Europe is primarily dependent on legislative rules embodying the above principles of good data management, this approach is not confined to legislation and such principles are also a feature of the primarily self-regulatory regime in use in the USA. Business regulation in the USA is much more market-led and there is far less intervention in the private sector than there is in Europe. There are, however, informational privacy rules with legislative force at both federal and state levels that focus on specific issues such as health care, financial details, and so on,[53] but data protection in the private sector remains 'decentralized, fragmented, ad hoc and narrowly tailored to target specific sectors'.[54] This can create a very complex situation, which has resulted in 'a myriad of overlapping, and at times conflicting, state and federal laws'.[55] The differences in ethos and approach between the USA and Europe on this topic can be related to a number of things, including the contrasting approach to personal data privacy in the respective jurisdictions. In the USA, as implied above, this is regulated by a mixture of the Constitution, and federal and state laws, as well as the common law of tort. In Europe, on the other hand, data protection has been allied much more explicitly with fundamental human rights and is now incorporated in the Treaty on the Functioning of the European Union (TFEU) as a result of the coming into force of the Lisbon Treaty at the beginning of December 2009.[56]

At a basic level, it could appear that, notwithstanding the conceptual and philosophical differences, the fundamental principles do not differ dramatically. The 1998 report of the US Federal Trade Commission (FTC)[57] discussed five core principles of privacy protection by reference to the corresponding OECD guidelines – namely: notice/awareness; choice/consent; access/participation; integrity/security; and enforcement/redress. Beyond this apparent similarity, however, the regulatory regimes in Europe and the USA diverge markedly, and, as might be expected, the emphasis on individual rights in Europe appears to have been the prime catalyst to the legislative approach to data protection, whereas business needs have been set much more centre stage in the USA. Although acknowledging some of the deficiencies of a self-regulatory approach, in its 1998 report, the FTC felt that consumer concerns about privacy could be resolved by the encouragement of self-regulation.[58] This approach was confirmed in a further report in July 1999 which stated that 'self-regulation is the least intrusive and most efficient means to ensure fair information

---

52 Viktor Mayer-Schönberger, 'Generational development of data protection in Europe' in PE Agre and Marc Rotenberg (eds), *Technology and Privacy: The New Landscape*, 1998, Cambridge, MA: MIT Press, ch 8.

53 For more precise details, see, e.g., Liz Harding, 'Oceans apart: Overview of the US legal framework' (2010) 21(2) Computers and Law 27.

54 Tracie B Loring, 'An analysis of the informational privacy protection afforded by the European Union and the United States' (2002) 37 Tex Int'l LJ 421.

55 Susan Mann, 'Oceans apart: Data transfers between the EEA and USA' (2010) 21(2) Computers and Law 22, 23.

56 Treaty on the Functioning of the European Union (TFEU), Art 16(1), amending Art 286, EC Treaty: Everyone has the right to the protection of personal data concerning them. See also Loring, above, and Mann, above.

57 Federal Trade Commission (FTC), Privacy Online: A Report to Congress, 1998, available online at: https://www.ftc.gov/sites/default/files/documents/reports/privacy-online-report-congress/priv-23a.pdf

58 Ibid.

practice, given the rapidly evolving nature of the internet and computer technology'.[59] It noted that, although there were still observable problems with compliance, there had been significant developments reflecting 'industry leaders' substantial effort and commitment to fair information practices'. The approach has remained substantially the same in the interim albeit with a stricter emphasis on enforcement, together with specific legislative response in a number of states to loss of personal data and other security breaches.[60] In an apparent change of direction, a Consumer Bill of Rights, described as 'a blueprint for privacy in the information age', was released by the Obama administration in February 2012 on the basis that there was a need to provide greater privacy for individuals online.[61] This is built round similar principles to those in data protection legislation, but it has not yet been enacted and reports suggest it has been 'largely ignored by Congress'[62] and that progress has been at 'a glacial pace'.[63] So, whether or not a greater consensus on a suitable regulatory approach emerges between the US and the EU on this issue remains to be seen.

These brief details of the contrasting approaches to regulation of data protection in Europe and the USA illustrate some of the points of conflict, but it would be misleading to imagine that these apparently opposing mechanisms are entirely mutually exclusive. The view is expressed in the recitals of the OECD's 1998 *Ministerial Declaration on the Protection of Privacy on Global Networks* that, although there are different approaches to privacy in member countries, these methods can, nevertheless, 'work together to achieve effective privacy protection on global networks'.[64] Although self-regulatory mechanisms are frequently invoked as a substitute for, or an avoidance of, legislation, they may also play a valuable role in both implementing and supplementing framework legislation by providing particular rules for specific sectors and/or purposes. Consider, for example, how a general framework for maintaining privacy might be put into effect in relation to direct marketing as opposed to the management of health records. In each of these cases, the risks and consequences of inappropriate processing are very different. Codes of practice (a common form of self-regulation) can be very effective at filling in the necessary detail to enable the framework requirements and guidance to be complied with in specific cases. The disadvantage, of course, is that too great a reliance on self-regulatory codes may result in divergence between the sectors, which, in turn, can lead to fragmentation at the implementation level.

Despite the possibilities for reconciliation, at the moment, the two conflicting approaches in the USA and Europe appear entrenched within the existing regulatory frameworks. With the adoption and implementation of Directive 95/46/EC, with its provisions requiring the adequacy of data protection in third countries to be assessed before transborder data flows will be allowed it became imperative to negotiate an accommodation between the two.[65] In May 2000, the European Union (EU) Member States approved an agreement with the USA concerning arrangements to safeguard individual privacy in transborder data flow that, in effect, attempt to reconcile the self-regulatory regime in the USA with the legislative approach in the EU (the so-called 'Safe Harbor Agreement', discussed in more detail below). Surprisingly, perhaps, in view of the content of the previous reports and the sometimes acrimonious nature of the Safe Harbor discussions, a further report from the FTC suggested that statutory intervention might be necessary in order to safeguard

---

59 Federal Trade Commission (FTC), Self-Regulation and Privacy Online, 1999, available online at: https://www.ftc.gov/system/files/documents/reports/self-regulation-privacy-onlinea-federal-trade-commission-report-congress/1999self-regulationreport.pdf
60 See, e.g., Christopher Wolf, 'New directions in enforcement and policy at the FTC and the impact on businesses' (2010) 1005 PLI/Pat 421.
61 Consumer Data Privacy in a Networked World: A Framework for Protecting Privacy and Promoting innovation in the Global Digital Economy. February 2012, available online at: www.whitehouse.gov/sites/default/files/privacy-final.pdf
62 See https://www.washingtonpost.com/politics/consumer-privacy-rights-need-urgent-protection-in-washington-activists-say/2014/02/24/1764ba22-9cb7-11e3-975d-107dfef7b668_story.html
63 Rob Corbet, 'EU v US data protection – exploring the similarities' (2013) 13(6) P & DP 3, 4.
64 OECD Working Party on Information Security and Privacy, Ministerial Declaration on the Protection of Privacy on Global Networks, DSTI/ICCP/REG(98)10/FINAL, 1998, Ottawa, ON: OECD, available online at: www.oecd.org/dataoecd/39/13/1840065.pdf
65 See the discussion on Arts 25 and 26 below at p 368.

individual privacy in the USA;[66] however, there has been no follow-up activity in this respect and that the regulatory mismatch between the two jurisdictions is still in evidence has now been brought sharply into focus by the decision of the CJEU in *Schrems v Data Protection Commissioner*.[67]

# The Data Protection Directive 95/46/EC and its UK implementation

## The need for a directive

Notwithstanding the fact that all of the EU Member States are also members of the Council of Europe, by the end of the 1980s, some Member States still had no data protection legislation and there were sufficient discrepancies between those that had to warrant further harmonisation. A further concern was that any differences in the protection afforded to data in each Member State might lead to restrictions on transborder data flow from those countries with a higher level of protection. This would obviously impede the functioning of the internal market – a crucial factor in the wake of the date of 31 December 1991 set by the Single European Act 1986 for the completion of the single European market. Accordingly, in 1990, a proposal for a Directive on the Protection of Individuals with regard to the Processing of Personal Data and on the Free Movement of such Data was published.[68]

The centrality of the single market might suggest that a primary reason for harmonisation was business efficacy and the facilitation of free movement of data, but the competing interests endemic in this area are strongly represented in the Preamble to the original proposal, which refers not only to transborder data flows, but also to the importance of protecting the right of privacy. In the event, the final version was to be a long time in gestation – one problem was to devise legislation that would both ensure a high level of protection and yet not compromise that already in place in some Member States. In view of the different interpretations put on the various concepts in the different jurisdictions, the Economic and Social Committee was particularly concerned as to whether the proposal actually increased the level of protection or merely accentuated the differences between Member States.[69] An amended proposal was published in 1992,[70] but although this was debated by the European Parliament and approved subject to amendments,[71] progress then seemed to come to a halt. Action was eventually precipitated by the Bangemann Report, which was produced for the Corfu Summit of 1994 and looked at all facets of the 'information society', but, in particular, noted that although Europe was a world leader in data protection, 'without the legal security of a Union-wide approach, lack of consumer confidence [would] undermine the rapid development of the information society', recommending that 'a fast decision' was required on the proposed Directive. This recommendation, from such an eminent source, proved the necessary boost to revive the proposed Directive and the final version of the Directive was agreed using the codecision procedure in 1995.[72] The final version was a much-amended and augmented version of the original 1990 proposal, and contains a total of 72 Recitals in the Preamble. However, the fact that the final text only differs in very minor ways from the common position can probably be taken as an indication of the general agreement between Parliament and the Council on this issue.

---

66 FTC, 2000, above, p 44.
67 Case C-362/14 *Schrems v Data Protection Commissioner* (CJEU 6 October 2015). See discussion below.
68 COM(1990)314 final, SYN 287 [1990]; [1990] OJ C 277/3.
69 This is actually one of the reasons why the new Regulation has been drafted – see later discussion on p 387.
70 COM(1992)422 final, SYN 287 [1992]; [1992] OJ C 311/30.
71 [1992] OJ C 94/198.
72 European Parliament and Council Directive 95/46/EC on the Protection of Individuals with regard to the Processing of Personal Data and on the Free Movement of Such Data, 24 October 1995, [1995] OJ L 281/31.

## Provisions of Directive 95/46/EC

Article 1 sets out the objectives of the Directive. First, and fundamentally, this Article refers to the protection of privacy with respect to the processing of personal data, signalling that, even though limited, data protection is part of the fundamental right of privacy. However, the provision also includes an important counterbalancing provision that requires Member States not to restrict or prohibit the free flow of data between them. Thus, as far as EU Member States are concerned, the free flow of personal data is envisaged for whatever purpose and this flow cannot be restricted, assuming that there is compliance with the provisions of the Directive. This is, of course, a necessary consequence of the harmonisation of data protection law throughout the EU and the situation is, as we shall see below, rather different for transborder data flow to third countries. Further, Arts 2 and 3 demonstrate that the scope of the Directive is independent of the mode of storage of the personal data. Although the discussion in the earlier part of this chapter focuses on the technological threat to privacy, so-called 'manual data' are also covered by the Directive as long as they are stored in a structured filing system.[73] The provisions of the Directive extend only to the processing of data for purposes that fall within the areas of business, economic, and social activity that are within the EU competences set out in Art 6 of the TFEU. It will then be a question for individual Member States to decide whether or not to include other activities within the scope of the domestic legislation. Some of the first-generation data protection statutes were based on a concept of universal registration, but this had been criticised as unnecessarily bureaucratic and cumbersome to administer. Instead, the Directive requires notification of processing, which is intended to ensure transparency, rather than to create a method of control.[74]

## UK implementation

The Data Protection Directive was implemented in the UK by the Data Protection Act 1998 (DPA 1998). The structure of this statute is similar to that of its predecessor, the Data Protection Act 1984, but both are rather different from most other UK statutes. In relation to the 1984 Act, Stallworthy suggests that this arose because the main provisions follow the Council of Europe Convention and were therefore influenced by principles of statutory draftsmanship that are more usually associated with civil law systems.[75] The view of Aldhouse is that 'the Data Protection Act is unprecedented. Even the black letter criminal provisions make use of new concepts'.[76] Although both statutes are based on the premise of compliance with principles of good data management, the 'data protection principles' – which, as well as implementing the Directive, arguably have their origins in the Younger Report and can be discerned in the relevant international instruments on data protection – are not to be found in the body of the statute, but are contained in a Schedule appended to the Act. The earlier statute was based on the notion of universal registration, but, unfortunately, the manner of drafting meant that these principles could only be enforced against those registered. Registration has now been superseded by notification as required by the Directive and the principles can be enforced against all users regardless of whether notification has, in fact, taken place. Enforcement is the task of the Information Commissioner[77] and a number of criminal offences, together with individual rights and remedies, are also created in the body of the statute.

---

73 See also Recital 27.
74 See Arts 18–20.
75 Mark Stallworthy, 'Data protection: Regulation in a deregulatory state' [1990] Statute L Rev 130.
76 Francis GB Aldhouse, 'UK data protection: Where are we in 1991?' (1991) 5 LCT Yearbook 180, 184.
77 The role of the Data Protection Commissioner created by the 1998 Act having been subsumed in the Office of Information Commissioner following the Freedom of Information Act 2000.

## Key definitions and concepts

'Personal data' and 'processing' are crucial concepts and the interpretation of these will be considered in more detail below. The definitions also distinguish the 'controller' and the 'processor' of data. Article 2(d) defines the 'controller' as the person who (alone or in conjunction with others) determines 'the purposes and means of processing personal data'; in DPA 98, s 1(1)(e) this has been implemented as 'the purposes for which and the manner in which any personal data are, or are to be, processed'. The concept of data controller is a crucial one since it is the controller who has the duty to comply with data protection rules and respond to the rights of the data subject. A 'data processor', on the other hand, merely processes such data on behalf of the data controller; given the responsibilities placed on the controller it is important to be able to both identify the controller and distinguish that person from a data processor. The distinction can be important, because the central responsibilities for complying with the data protection principles, discussed below, fall on the data controller. The Article 29 Working Party has pointed out that the controller should be identified by a factual rather than a formal analysis.[78] While a contract purporting to be between a controller and processor may be useful in this respect, it is what happens in practice which is definitive. Whoever determines the purposes and means of processing is the controller; while the means in the sense of the requisite technical and organisational arrangements could be delegated, ascertaining who determines the purpose of processing is a significant part of locating the controller. Thus a liquidator of a company did not become the data controller in relation to the personal data held by the company in liquidation and so was not responsible for complying with data subject access requests made prior to the liquidation.[79]

### Personal data

Personal data is defined in Art 2(a) of the Directive as 'any information relating to an identified or identifiable natural person. This person is known as the 'data subject' and is someone who can be 'identified , directly or indirectly, in particular by reference to an identification number or to one or more factors specific to his physical, physiological, mental, economic, cultural or social identity'. In contrast, DPA 98, s 1(1) defines personal data as data relating to a living individual who can be identified from those data, or from a combination of those data and other information in the possession of the data controller. This specifically includes 'any expression of opinion about the individual and any indication of the intentions of the data controller or any other person in respect of the individual.' In Art 8 the Directive identifies certain 'special categories' of data namely that relating to 'racial or ethnic origin, political opinions, religious or philosophical beliefs, trade-union membership, and the processing of data concerning health or sex life', the processing of which is prohibited unless certain conditions are met as discussed below. DPA 98 refers to this as 'sensitive data' and, in addition to the above list, the definition in s 2 includes data relating to criminal offences or related proceedings.

### Durant v Financial Services Authority

These statutory definitions of both 'personal data' and 'relevant filing system' were the subject of judicial discussion in *Durant v Financial Services Authority*.[80]

Durant's case arose out of a dispute with Barclays Bank that eventually led to him making a subject access request (see later discussion) in order to obtain personal data about him held by the Financial Services Authority (FSA), which had been adjudicating his complaint with the bank.

---

78 Opinion 1/2010 on the concepts of 'controller' and 'processor' (adopted 16 February 2010) (WP169 264/10/EN) which contains a number of practical examples.
79 *Re Southern Pacific Personal Loans Ltd, Oakley Smith v Information Commissioner* [2013] EWHC 2485, [32]–[35].
80 [2003] EWCA Civ 1746, [2004] FSR 28.

The FSA refused to provide all of the information to which Durant believed he was entitled, on the basis that it did not all constitute 'personal data' as defined or that, if it did, it was not contained within a 'relevant filing system'.[81] The argument for Durant was that both definitions suggested a 'wide and inclusive definition of "personal data"' and one that 'covered any information retrieved as a result of a search under his name, anything on file which had his name on it or from which he could be identified or from which it was possible to discern a connection with him'.[82] Although the Court of Appeal acknowledged the importance of interpreting the provisions of the Act in the light of the definition of personal data in Art 2 of the Directive, it came to the conclusion that the definition was not as wide as postulated by Durant. The fact that data might be retrieved from a search of a name was not sufficient to make it personal. Two further factors were needed: the first was whether the 'information is biographical in a significant sense'; the second was one of focus – that is, the data should not merely incidentally include reference to the data subject. In sum, it needed to be 'information that affects his privacy, whether in his personal or family life, business or professional capacity'.[83]

Auld LJ went on to distinguish information about Durant and information about his complaints, and, in effect, said that the data Durant was trying to retrieve was not data about himself – that is, personal data – but data about his complaint and that this did not fall within the definition. He was also of the view that this narrow interpretation of personal data went 'hand in hand with a narrow meaning of "relevant filing system"'.[84] Having considered the provisions and objectives of the Act, and also of both the Directive and the Council of Europe Convention that preceded them, he was extremely influenced by the fact that, notwithstanding the Convention's provision permitting extension to manual data, the provisions of all of the instruments were substantially focused on computerised data and that the statutory provisions were only intended to be extended to manual records 'of sufficient sophistication to provide the same or similar ready accessibility as a computerised filing system'.[85] He therefore concluded that the term 'relevant filing system' referred to a system:

(1) in which the files forming part of it are structured or referenced in such a way as clearly to indicate at the outset of the search whether specific information capable of amounting to personal data of an individual requesting it under s 7 is held within the system and, if so, in which file or files it is held; and

(2) which has, as part of its own structure or referencing mechanism, a sufficiently sophisticated and detailed means of readily indicating whether and where in an individual file or files specific criteria or information about the applicant can be readily located.[86]

The definition of 'personal data' in Art 2 of the Directive does not seem to be limited in this way. Nevertheless it could be said that the protection of privacy required by Art 1 of the Directive does not necessarily imply an unlimited right to control or retrieve every single mention of the data subject's name.[87] Auld LJ preferred to equate the 'personal data' with 'information that affects his privacy'. This decision has the propensity to remove a number of references to data subjects from the ambit of 'personal data', although the subjectivity of the concept of privacy would inevitably create ambiguity and uncertainty in some cases. Certainly this could be construed as being in line with the view of the Article 29 Working Party on the subject, which pointed out that the data

---

81 As defined in DPA 98, s 1(1)(e). DPD uses the term 'personal data filing system' in Art 2(d).
82 Ibid, [24].
83 Ibid, [28].
84 Ibid, [27].
85 Ibid, [48].
86 Ibid, [50].
87 But see later discussion of *Google Spain* on p 361 and also of the definition of personal data in the GDPR Art 4(1).

protection rules were designed to deal with situations in which the rights of individuals were at risk, and suggested that a balance should be achieved in which the data protection rules were not overstretched, but neither were they unduly restricted.[88]

## Application of the decision in *Durant*

The Court of Appeal's interpretation of personal data and relevant filing system were subsequently applied in both *Johnson v Medical Defence Union*[89] and *Smith v Lloyds TSB Bank plc*.[90] Both Johnson and Smith argued in their individual cases that, because there was information that had been processed in the past on computer, it should be made available in response to the subject access request although it was no longer available in that format. Johnson, in particular, argued that even though the documentation in question no longer existed, it had been both recorded 'with the intention that it is processed' and 'in a relevant filing system', and so fell within the definition of data in the DPA 1998.[91] Similarly, in *Smith*, the information sought had originally been kept on computer, but was no longer in that format when the request was made. In both cases, Laddie J declined to hold that this was personal data within the meaning of the 1998 Act[92] or that, on the facts, it was held in a 'relevant filing system'. For either claimant to succeed, it would have been necessary to show both that the information was personal data within the ruling in *Durant* and also that it was held in a relevant filing system at the time of the request.[93]

The House of Lords did, however, return to the issue of personal data in *Common Services Agency v Scottish Information Commissioner*,[94] a case under the Freedom of Information Act (Scotland) 2002. In this case, the Common Services Agency (CSA) refused to release information concerning the extent of childhood leukaemia, on the grounds that this might identify particular individuals, and that the data would therefore be personal data under the DPA 1998 and so would fall within the exemption in s 38 of the Act. In response, the Scottish Information Commissioner required the CSA to 'barnadise' the data – a technique used to manipulate statistics prior to publication in order to reduce the possibility that any particular individual can be identified. As far as the Act was concerned, the question that had to be answered was whether or not the barnadised data was 'personal data' for the purposes of the Act so that the exemption in s 38 would be engaged. This could have been an opportunity to review the decision in *Durant*, but this was not to be. The Inner House of the Court of Session, using Auld LJ's two-factor approach, concluded that the effect of barnardisation was to move the focus of the information away from individual children so that it thus fell outside the definition of 'personal data'. In the House of Lords, however, Lord Hope said that although it may have that effect, that did not resolve the question, which required instead a consideration of the definition in DPA 1998, s 1(1), in the light of the provisions of the Data Protection Directive. In particular, this required a consideration of whether or not it was possible for the data controller or anyone else in possession of the barnadised data to identify a specific individual from either the data itself or in conjunction with other information. If not, then it was not information from which an individual could be identified, was therefore not personal data, and so fell outside the ambit of the Act. Which of these was the case was a question of fact for the Scottish Information

88 Article 29 Working Party, Opinion 4/2007 on the concept of personal data.
89 [2004] EWHC 347.
90 [2005] EWHC 246 (Ch).
91 [2004] EWHC 347, [30].
92 See also discussion in Case EA/2007/0058 *Harcup v Information Commissioner and Yorkshire Forward*, available online at: www.information-tribunal.gov.uk/DBFiles/Decision/i37/harcupFinalDecision_050208.pdf
93 See also discussion in Usha Jagessar and Vicky Sedgwick, 'When is personal data not "personal data"? The impact of *Durant v FSA*' [2005] 21 CLSR 505.
94 [2008] 1 WLR 1550.

Commissioner.[95] Lord Rodger further stated that there was no need to consider the kinds of issue addressed by the Court of Appeal in *Durant*; the significant issue was purely whether or not any individual was identifiable from the data.[96] The case thus leaves the *Durant* precedent in place, but without any review of the reasoning on which it is based.[97]

The dangers which could follow from an unthinking application of *Durant* are well illustrated by the reasoning of the First Tier Tribunal in *Edem v Information Commissioner*.[98] Edem had made a Freedom of Information request to the then Financial Services Authority (FSA) for all the information held about him and his complaint concerning Egg Plc. The issue which led to the appeal was whether the names of FSA employees who had worked on the response to his request, but who were not directly corresponding with him or in any position of authority, should be withheld on the basis that these names were personal data and, as such were exempted from disclosure under the exception in s 40(2) of the Freedom of Information Act 2000. It might seem only common sense that an individual's name should be classed as personal data, and indeed the Information Commissioner declined to divulge the names on this basis. In *Durant*, however, Auld LJ had set out what he referred to as two 'notions' intended to assist in determining whether information was personal data but not to limit or define the scope of that concept.[99] Applying these notions the First Tier Tribunal concluded that the names were not in fact personal data; they were not 'biographical in any significant sense' and the individuals were 'in no way the focus of the information', the focus being the investigation of Edem's complaint. Overturning the decision of the First Tier Tribunal, the Higher Tier Tribunal described this reasoning as either or both a misdirection and a misapplication of the principles set out by Auld LJ in *Durant*.[100] Its decision was upheld by the Court of Appeal which commented that Auld LJ's 'notions' were an 'explanation as to why the information and documents in which Mr Durant's name appeared were not personal data relating to him', however in Edem's case, 'questions of whether the information is biographical or sufficiently focussed upon a particular named individual are of no relevance whatever. They have nothing to do with the question whether disclosure of a person's name is disclosure of personal data. A name is personal data unless it is so common that without further information, such as its use in a work context, a person would remain unidentifiable despite its disclosure.'[101]

Although there were suggestions after *Durant* that the CA's interpretation of personal data was more restrictive than required by the Directive, the CJEU has subsequently given a judgment which is also restrictive of the definition of personal data. In *YS v Minister voor Immigratie, Integratie en Asiel*,[102] YS and M and S had all applied for residence status in the Netherlands. YS's application was refused and those of the others were accepted for a fixed period only. They all tried to use the subject access provisions[103] to obtain a copy of the document containing the preliminary legal analysis relevant to their cases. This analysis could be accepted or rejected by the case officer making the final decision and did not itself form part of the final decision. The evidence was that there was no template for this document,[104] but it would typically include the applicant's personal details, supporting information

95 *Ibid*, [17]ff. The Scottish Information Commissioner subsequently concluded that, on the particular facts in question, the barnadised data were indeed personal data for the purposes of the DPA: Decision 021/2005, *Mr Michael Collie and the Common Services Agency for the Scottish Health Service* (26 May 2010), available online at: www.itspublicknowledge.info/ApplicationsandDecisions/Decisions/2005/200500298.asp

96 *Ibid*, [74].

97 See also discussion in Richard Cumbley and Peter Church, 'What is personal data? The House of Lords identifies the issues – *Common Services Agency v Scottish Information Commissioner*' [2008] UKHL 47, [2008] 24 CLSR 565; Renate Gertz, 'Mr Collie Goes to London: The House of Lords decision in *Common Services Agency vs. The Scottish Information Commissioner*' (2009) 3(1) Studies in Ethics, Law, and Technology 4, available online at: www.bepress.com/selt/vol3/iss1/art4

98 [2014] EWCA Civ 92.

99 [2003] EWCA Civ 1746, [28].

100 *Information Commissioner v FSA & Edem* [2012] UKUT 464 (AAC), [37]–[41].

101 [2014] EWCA Civ 92, [20] and compare GDPR Art 4(1).

102 Joined cases C-141/12 and C-372/12.

103 See later discussion at p 358.

104 C-141/12 *YS v Minister voor Immigratie, Integratie en Asiel* Opinion of Advocate General Sharpston, [17].

etc together with the legal analysis which could be brief or more lengthy depending on the complexity of the case. When YS applied for access to this document, a summary of the data and its origins, together with details of those who had access to it, was provided but the document itself was withheld as the policy was not to release the relevant legal analysis.[105] Could this legal analysis of the case constitute personal data?

The facts on which it was based were clearly personal data and these had been provided to the data subject, but both the Advocate General and the CJEU were in agreement that the legal analysis should not be classified as personal data. Although facts which were personal data were 'inputs to the process', the legal analysis itself was not information relating to an identified individual,[106] and, as pointed out by the CJEU the purpose of Directive 95/46 was to protect privacy with respect to the processing of personal data. Providing the legal analysis itself 'would not in fact serve the directive's purpose . . . but would serve the purpose of guaranteeing . . . a right to administrative documents, which is not . . . covered by Directive 95/46.'[107] There seems no reason why this reasoning should not be extended to cover any assessment of facts leading to a decision on a data subject by any organisation. A decision or opinion expressed as a result of that assessment could still be classified as personal data, but the judgment in YS would suggest that the reasoning itself could be withheld. This does not, of itself, interfere with any duty placed on an authority or organisation to explain the reasons for its decision, an issue which was not raised in these cases as discussed by the Advocate General.[108]

## How much information can identify the data subject?

The definition in Art 2(a) refers to both direct and indirect identification. In the DPA 1998, the definition of personal data includes data which is capable of identifying the data subject when combined with other information possessed by the data controller. This was one of the issues which arose in *Google Inc v Vidal-Hall*.[109] The complaints in the case arose out of targeted advertising based on Google's collection of browser generated information from Apple's Safari web browser.[110] As the claimants lived in England and Google is an American company, the hearing was to determine whether there was a sufficiently serious issue to be tried to permit service of the proceedings out of the jurisdiction.[111] The evidence was that Google obtained and collated a wide variety of information relating to users ranging from general browsing habits to more specific information, some of which might be sensitive. Could this browser generated information (BGI) be construed as personal data? The CA decided that there was an argument that it could. Referring to the opinion of the Art 29 Working Party on personal data which specifically discussed IP addresses[112] and the decision of the CJEU in *Lindqvist*,[113] it concluded that 'identification for the purposes of data protection is about data that "individuates" the individual, in the sense that they are singled out and distinguished from all others. It is immaterial that the BGI does not name the user. The BGI singles them out and therefore directly identifies them for the purposes of section 1(1)(a) of the DPA . . .'.[114] The BGI contained two relevant elements; a detailed browsing history and also a unique identifier from the double-click advertising cookie which together

105 Interestingly the NL had originally had a policy of making this information available on request but this had been reversed as it had apparently created a heavy workload: ibid, [19].
106 Ibid, [59].
107 C-141/12 YS v Minister voor Immigratie, Integratie en Asiel, [46].
108 C-141/12 YS v Minister voor Immigratie, Integratie en Asiel, Opinion of Advocate General Sharpston, [31]–[38].
109 [2015] EWCA Civ 311.
110 For further discussion of how much personal data is processed by Google, see, e.g., Caitlin Dewey, 'Everything Google knows about you (and how it knows it)' available online at: www.washingtonpost.com/news/the-intersect/wp/2014/11/19/everything-google-knows-about-you-and-how-it-knows-it/
111 For discussion on the claim for compensation under s 13 see below.
112 Above [88]
113 Case C-101/01 Lindqvist [2003] ECR I-12971. See also discussion below.
114 [2015] EWCA Civ 311 at [115].

enabled a link to be made to a specific device or user. It was irrelevant whether in practice this information was kept separate or aggregated – the relevant fact was whether the data subject could be identified from the data in question or as a result of combination with other information in possession of the data controller.

## Processing

The definition of 'processing' in Art 2(b) and implemented by DPA 98, s 1(1) is of central importance as it is a prerequisite for the application of the data protection principles discussed below. The definition is wide, encompassing the majority of acts that could be done during the life cycle of the data, starting with the initial obtaining, through to the final destruction. Indeed the use of the words 'such as' in Art 2(b) and 'including' in DPA 98, s 1(1) indicated that the lists are indicative and not exhaustive. One question that arose was whether anonymising data – and, presumably therefore the barnadising referred to above in *CSA v Scottish Information Commissioner* – constituted processing and would therefore be subject to the requirements of data protection principles. This matter arose in *R v Department of Health, ex p Source Informatics*,[115] a case which occurred before the implementation of the Directive and was primarily based on breach of confidence. Nevertheless, the Court of Appeal considered the likely impact of the implementation of the Directive and, specifically, whether the anonymising of data could be considered processing. Simon Brown LJ, having considered the arguments for and against including anonymisation within the definition of processing, concluded that 'common sense and justice alike' favoured the proposition that it should not be included, and that such a finding would be 'unobjectionable'.[116]

Anonymisation is an important tool in safeguarding the privacy of individuals. It is also useful for organisations since, once data has been anonymised then it is no longer personal data and so the data protection principles do not apply. However the process is not entirely risk free and there remains a possibility that an individual could be identified or re-identified even after anonymising has occurred. This possibility was actually discussed by Latham J at first instance in *Ex parte Source Informatics*. This led him to suggest, in contrast to the Court of Appeal, that, given these risks, data subjects should have some control over whether their data was included in any anonymisation process. Such an approach would mean that anonymising was a type of processing and so the data protection provisions would apply. This is now the generally accepted position.[117]

The scope of processing has also been considered in a further case concerning Johnson's dispute with the Medical Defence Union (MDU).[118] Johnson was a consultant orthopaedic surgeon, whose professional indemnity cover was terminated by the MDU. In deciding both whether to provide, refuse, or withdraw such cover, the MDU used risk assessment procedures based on the number of incidents or complaints on file about a subject, regardless of their severity or outcome. The number of such incidents relating to Johnson was such that a decision was made to terminate cover and this led to his litigation. In this second round, he sought compensation under the DPA 1998, s 13 (see later), on the grounds that, although the risk assessment had been carried out entirely according to the agreed rules, the policy of not taking into account whether any complaints had actually been substantiated led to unfair processing – in other words, that the Act effectively created a quasi-contractual right to a particular type of processing. At first instance, it was held that

115 [2000] 1 All ER 786; see discussion in H Rowe, *Data Protection Act 1998: A Practical Guide*, 2000, Croydon: Tolley, pp 248ff.
116 [2000] 1 All ER 786, 798.
117 See further, the ICO's Code of Practice, *Anonymisation: Managing Data Protection Risks* November 2012, available online at: http://ico.org.uk/for_organisations/data_protection/topic_guides/anonymisation – discussed in Marion Oswald 'Data anonymisation and managing risk – the ICO's new code' (2012) 13 P. & D.P. 3; *Handbook of European Data Protection Law*, ch 2; European Union Agency for Fundamental Rights and Council of Europe (2013), available online at: www.coe.int/t/dghl/standardsetting/dataprotection/TPD_documents/Handbook.pdf. For a different perspective see Paul Ohm, 'Broken promises of privacy: responding to the surprising failure of anonymization' (2010) 57 UCLA Law Rev 1701.
118 *Johnson v Medical Defence Union* (No 2) [2007] EWCA Civ 262.

the procedure for reviewing his records that led to the adverse decision did not amount to actual processing of the data, but that even if it did, it had been carried out according to the agreed rules, of which Johnson was aware when he joined the MDU, and so could not be regarded as unfair.

Buxton LJ noted that the case raised issues that, in his view, had 'nothing or almost nothing to do with the protection of privacy and integrity of a person'.[119] In a lengthy decision, the majority found that a case officer had reviewed Johnson's records (that is, a human, not an automatic, judgment) and that her subsequent decision to make a recommendation to the risk assessment group that his cover should be withdrawn did not constitute processing of the data. This was so even though the case officer had downloaded the relevant files prior to review, which did constitute processing, and had then recorded her recommendation on computer. The act complained of was a human judgment based on the information extracted – something that the majority distinguished from 'processing' within the meaning of the Act. The dissenting judgment of Arden LJ carefully considered the definition of processing in the DPA 1998 in the light of the Directive and concluded that all stages in the process, including the selection and judgment of the records, constituted processing. Buxton LJ had also considered the Directive's provisions, but had given particular weight to the Recitals at the expense of the actual provisions of the Directive, whereas Arden LJ's analysis arguably shows a greater understanding of the interpretation of European directives and also avoids the artificiality of dissecting the decision-making process. However, despite this difference in relation to processing, the judges were unanimous that Johnson's appeal failed, because, in any event, the 'processing' could not be regarded as unfair.[120]

## The data protection principles

The Directive sets out to protect the privacy of data subjects with respect to the processing of their personal data by embedding principles of good data management within the legislative framework. Five of these principles are listed in Art 6:

- personal data should be processed fairly and accurately;
- personal data should be collected for specific purposes and not further processed for other purposes;
- personal data processed should be relevant and not excessive;
- personal data should be accurate and kept up to date; and
- personal data should be kept no longer than is necessary.

The DPA 98 sets out eight data protection principles in Pt I of Sch 1 to the 1998 Act. These include those listed in Article 6 together with processing in accordance with the rights of the data subject, security and transborder data flow which are dealt with elsewhere in the Directive. Some guidance as to the interpretation of the Data Protection Principles in contained in Pt II of DPA 98 Sch 1.

## First data protection principle – fair and lawful processing

### Fairness

Article 6 and the first data protection principle in DPA both impose a general requirement of fairness in relation to processing. An essential aspect of fairness is that the data subject should know how his or her data is being processed and so should be informed of the fact of processing, the identity of the data controller, the type of data held, the purposes of processing, the likely recipients and so on.[121]

---

119 *Ibid*, [1].
120 *Ibid*, [63], per Buxton LJ, and [149], per Arden LJ.
121 See further, DPD Art 10 and DPA 98 Sch 1 Pt II paras 1–4.

In addition to this, any assessment of whether processing is fair will need to take into account the purposes of processing, the type of processing, and the consequences to the data subject. Fair processing has always been a central feature of data protection law and some of the issues are illustrated by a number of appeals under the Data Protection Act 1984 against enforcement notices served against certain credit reference agencies. In each case, the important fact was that the method of processing was too wide – typically by address rather than by name, resulting in persons being judged to be bad credit risks on the basis of another person's record. CCN Systems Ltd and CCN Credit Systems Ltd v Data Protection Registrar was agreed to be a representative complaint.[122] J had bought a house from W. Three years later, J applied for a cheque guarantee card, but was refused and was told that CCN had provided the credit reference. A copy of his file (obtained under s 158 of the Consumer Credit Act 1974) showed a judgment against W. The only connection between J and W was that they had, at separate times, lived at the same address. Two important points were made in the Tribunal's decision that unfairness had been made out: first, that the purpose of the legislation is to protect the rights of the individual; and second, that the standard required is one of objective fairness. It is therefore irrelevant whether or not the data user had the motive or intention to process the data unfairly.

A further case, Infolink Ltd v Data Protection Registrar,[123] discussed the 'extraction of information constituting the data'; although this is no longer part of the statutory definition, it is arguably the process that was at issue in Johnson v MDU (No 2). In addition, it clarified the position in relation to balancing the competing interests of the individual and the processor. It was noted that the fact that, in CCN, the needs of the individual had been referred to as paramount did not mean that the applicant's interests prevailed over all other interests; it was necessary to balance various considerations in relation to both subject and user, but, in so doing, the Tribunal was entitled to give more weight to the interests of the individual, in line with the objectives of the legislation. The DPA 1998 subsequently increased the emphasis on individual rights which will have a bearing on this balance and some of the problems inherent in adjudicating the balance of rights and interests in data protection cases are discussed further below.[124]

## Lawful processing

Article 7 of the Directive lays down the basic criteria for the lawful processing of non-sensitive data. Compliance with this provision requires the data controller to comply with one of a number of options that will legitimise processing. These include where the data subject has 'unambiguously given consent' or where processing is for one of a list of reasons that include the performance of a contract to which the data subject is a party and the protection of the vital interests of the data subject. Article 8 then prohibits the processing of sensitive data – that is, that which reveals racial or ethnic origin, political opinions, religious or philosophical beliefs, trade union membership, and health or sex life – unless one of a list of more stringent requirements applies. In comparison with the more general legitimising provisions in Art 7, the provisos in relation to sensitive data are mostly targeted at very specific situations in which there are other legitimate objectives to be attained by the processing of the data in question. Overall the constraints on processing are thus based on a requirement of consent, unless the processing falls within one of the listed categories for which the process or its purpose is deemed necessary.

## Consent

Consent is defined in Art 2(h) as 'any freely given specific and informed indication of his wishes by which the data subject signifies his agreement to personal data relating to him being processed'.

---

122 Case DA/90 25/49/9, available online at: www.informationtribunal.gov.uk/DBFiles/Decision/i166/ccn_systems.pdf
123 Case DA/90 25/49/6, available online at: www.informationtribunal.gov.uk/DBFiles/Decision/i233/infolink.pdf
124 See also the assessment of fairness in Cases EA/2007/0096, 98, 99, 108, 127, Chief Constables of Humberside, Staffordshire, Northumbria, West Midlands and Greater Manchester v Information Commissioner, [161]–[166], available online at: www.informationtribunal.gov.uk/DBFiles/Decision/i200/Chief_Constables_v_IC_final_decision_2007081_web_entry[1].pdf

The requirement for the processing of sensitive data in Art 8 is that any consent given by the data subject must be 'explicit' rather than 'unambiguous', as required under Art 7. What is the significance of the different qualifications placed on consent in these two Articles? Clearly, if consent is to be construed as unambiguous, then there must be no room for doubt, but explicit consent suggests a higher standard of proof, in that the consent is distinctly stated and cannot be implied, however unequivocal the implication. Before the adoption of the Directive, it was common to construe consent from the absence of objection, but, even for non-sensitive data, the Directive requires more positive action to legitimise processing of personal data. The presumption is thus changed from one under which further processing is permitted unless a contrary indication is notified to one under which it is not permitted unless there is definite evidence of consent. At a minimum, it would appear that even the qualification 'unambiguous' 'strengthens the argument that the consent must entail a clear indication of the agreement of the individual', whereas the use of the qualification 'explicit' suggests that the fact that consent has been given must be established beyond doubt.[125]

Surprisingly, perhaps, there is no definition of the meaning of consent in DPA 98, but general approaches to statutory interpretation would suggest that the Directive provision would provide the definitive standard. Although there are different approaches to consent in different areas of law,[126] as discussed above, the extent to which implied consent might be effective is a moot point. Shaw LJ, in *Bell v Alfred Franks & Bartlett Co Ltd*,[127] distinguished 'consent' from mere acquiescence, suggesting that the former required an active rather than a passive step – an action of a 'positive affirmative kind'. Such distinctions, and cases such as *Linguaphone v DPR*[128] and particularly *British Gas Trading Ltd v Data Protection Registrar*,[129] have resulted in a change from the use of opt-out boxes to opt-in boxes by which data subjects can notify their consent for their data to be passed on to other data controllers.

## Other criteria which legitimate processing

The other criteria which can legitimate processing are listed in Art 7 as follows:[130]

(b)    processing is necessary for the performance of a contract to which the data subject is party or in order to take steps at the request of the data subject prior to entering into a contract; or

(c)    processing is necessary for compliance with a legal obligation to which the controller is subject; or

(d)    processing is necessary in order to protect the vital interests of the data subject; or

(e)    processing is necessary for the performance of a task carried out in the public interest or in the exercise of official authority vested in the controller or in a third party to whom the data are disclosed; or

(f)    processing is necessary for the purposes of the legitimate interests pursued by the controller or by the third party or parties to whom the data are disclosed, except where such interests are overridden by the interests for fundamental rights and freedoms of the data subject . . .

These alternative criteria to the consent of the data subject are all qualified by the use of the word 'necessary', which imports a strict construction and an objective standard beyond mere convenience and desirability for the data controller. In Case C-465/00 *Rechnungshof v Österreichischer*

---

125 For a trenchant critique of the use of consent to legitimise processing, see Bert-Jaap Koops, 'The Trouble with European Data Protection Law' (2014) 4 IDPL 250, 251; and see also Peter Blume, 'The inherent contradictions in data protection law' (2012) 2 IDPL 26, 29. See now GDPR Art 4(11) and Art 7.

126 See discussion in Rosemary Jay, *Data Protection Law and Practice*, 3rd edn, 2007, London: Sweet & Maxwell, pp 150–2.

127 [1980] 1 All ER 356.

128 Case DA/94 31/49/1, available online at: www.informationtribunal.gov.uk/DBFiles/Decision/i164/Linguaphone_Institute.pdf

129 Case DA98 3/49/2, available online at: www.informationtribunal.gov.uk/DBFiles/Decision/i162/british_gas.pdf

130 For UK implementation see DPA 1998 Sch 2 paras 2–6.

*Rundfunk*,[131] the European Court of Justice (ECJ) considered the nature of the obligations in Arts 6 and 7 – specifically, Art 6(1)(c), which requires that personal data must be relevant and not excessive in relation to the purpose for which it was collected, and Art 7(c) and (e), which legitimise processing that is necessary for compliance with a legal obligation and for the performance of a task in the public interest or the exercise of official authority. The ECJ concluded that all of these provisions were directly effective, because they were sufficiently precise and unconditional to be relied upon by individuals in their national courts.[132] Because the other provisions of Arts 6 and 7 are couched in similar language, this decision suggests that they will also be directly effective.

## The legitimate interests of the data controller

The criterion for law processing in Art 7(f) is that the processing is in the legitimate interests of the data controller except where such interests are overridden by the interests or fundamental rights and freedoms of the data subject.[133] The scope and intention of this requirement are not at all clear. At first glance it could be assumed that all the usual activities associated with an organisation, such as processing of student data in a university, for instance, could be construed to be in furtherance of its legitimate interests and would not necessarily conflict with the rights and freedoms of the data subject. This wide interpretation would appear to render the previous criteria redundant and so clearly cannot be what was intended.

The matter was touched upon in *ASNEF v Administración del Estado*[134] in which the CJEU noted that Art 7(f) sets out two cumulative conditions and that the balancing of the interests needed to be considered within the context of the circumstances at issue. In particular, in the context of the circumstances of that case, the seriousness of the infringement of individual rights was likely to depend on whether or not the information concerned had been made public. The CJEU found that nothing in the Directive prevented Member States from providing guidelines on adjudicating the balance of rights, but the uncertainty created by the need to determine that balance did not of itself 'cast doubt on the unconditional nature of that provision'.[135] Article 7(f) was therefore sufficiently precise and unconditional to be directly effective.

Article 6(1)(f) of the new General Data Protection Regulation[136] amplifies the original wording a little, but without providing general guidelines on the balance of rights, by requiring that processing will be lawful if it is 'necessary for the purposes of the legitimate interests pursued by a controller, except where such interests are overridden by the interests or fundamental rights and freedoms of the data subject which require protection of personal data, in particular where the data subject is a child.' Where the data controller purported to legitimise processing under Art 7(f), Art 14(a) of the Directive gave data subjects the right to object 'on compelling legitimate grounds relating to his particular situation'. Article 21(1) of the GDPR again amplifies the previous provision by giving a right to object 'unless the controller demonstrates compelling legitimate grounds for the processing which override the interests or fundamental rights and freedoms of the data subject' and places the burden of proof on the data controller.[137] It is underlined in Recital 47 of the GDPR that the balance between the respective interests will require 'careful assessment'. These provisions clearly provide little practical guidance for the data controller.

131 [2003] ECR I-4989.
132 *Ibid*, [100]–[101]. The GDPR is directly applicable, see later discussion at p 385.
133 Schedule 2 para 6(1) of the DPA 1998 translates this as 'except where the processing is unwarranted in any particular case by reason of prejudice to the rights and freedoms or legitimate interests of the data subject.'
134 Joined cases C-468 and C-469/10 *ASNEF and FECEMD v Administración del Estado* [2011] ECR I-12181.
135 *Ibid*, [53].
136 Regulation (EU) 2016/279 [2016] OJ 119/1. For a more general discussion see below p 385.
137 See Recital 69 GDPR.

Against this background, the Article 29 Working Party has issued a lengthy opinion on the topic.[138] This opinion notes that Art 7(f) can sometimes be seen, erroneously, as an 'open door' to legitimise any data processing which does not fit in one of the other legal grounds' but stresses that it should be neither a last resort for rare or unexpected situations, nor an automatic choice as being less constraining than the other criteria.

Article 7(f) can 'play a very useful role as a ground for lawful processing, provided that a number of key conditions are fulfilled'. Whereas the other criteria in Art 7 cover specific situations, Art 7(f) provides a specific test which can be applied to more general situations. The fact that it has more general application is exactly the reason why there has to be an assessment of the rights and interests of both data controller and data subject and a consequent balance found between them. As always when a balance has to be struck between the rights and interests of different parties, there is the propensity for uncertainty and a lack of consistency, although it does, of course, allow the circumstances of the particular case to be taken into account. Further complexity is introduced as it is not usually a matter of merely weighing up two competing factors; there may be a myriad of factors which need to be taken into account. The Article 29 Working Party was therefore of the view that it would be useful to provide guidelines on the application of Art 7(f) to ensure both that relevant issues are taken into account, and to maintain harmonisation and avoid differences in implementation between Member States. Its Opinion thus lists a number of criteria to assist in determining where this balance lies including; the nature and source of the legitimate interest; the impact on the data subject; and any safeguards which could assist in minimising that impact. In broad terms, the Working Party is of the view that 'an interest can be considered as legitimate as long as the controller can pursue this interest in a way that is in accordance with data protection and other laws.'[139] In other words, if a data controller wishes to rely on Art 7(f) its 'legitimate interest' must be lawful, sufficiently specific to allow the balancing test to be carried out and be a real and present interest rather than one which is merely speculative.[140] On the opposing side of the balance, a broad approach should be taken to the rights and interests of the data subject in relation to informational privacy. Once the factors on either side have been identified, the balancing act becomes akin to an assessment of proportionality – major interests of the data controller will trump those of the data subject and vice versa. The challenging part for data controllers will be the more common one of judging interests which are fairly evenly matched.[141]

## Second data protection principle – purpose specification and limitation

Although all of the data protection principles are clearly important, arguably the first and second ones encapsulate the most important facets of good data management. The second data protection principle contains two strands. First, personal data should only be collected for specified purposes and second, it should not then be processed in a way that is incompatible with those purposes. Compliance with this principle, coupled with communicating the purpose or purposes of processing provides assurance to the data subject about how his or her data will be used. A violation of this principle is illustrated by the facts of *Macgregor v Procurator Fiscal of Kilmarnock*, a case under the 1984 Act.[142] The neighbour of a police officer was concerned about the man with whom his 18-year-old daughter was living and asked the police officer if he could find out any information for him.

---

138 Opinion 06/2014 on the notion of legitimate interests of the data controller under Article 7(f) Directive 95/46/EC (adopted 9 April 2014) (WP217 844/14/EN).
139 *Ibid*, p.25
140 *Ibid*.
141 For some useful cases studies and guidance on how this balance could be assessed in practical situations see, *ibid*, pp 31–33 and Annexes 1 and 2.
142 (1993), unreported, 23 June.

Certain information about the man in question was obtained from both the Police National Computer and the Scottish Criminal Records Computer, and the police officer communicated some of this to the daughter in a telephone call, with the intention of trying to persuade her to return to her father. Although it was accepted that he had good motives, his actions could not be equated with policing purposes, and he was found to have used the information for another purpose.

It is important to note that not all further processing is prohibited – only that which is incompatible with the initial purpose and, conversely, further processing does not automatically imply incompatibility. A key issue is therefore the assessment of what additional processing is or is not compatible with the original purpose of collection. The Article 29 Working Party has suggested that regard should be had to (a) the relationship between the original purpose and the further purpose, in other words whether the further purpose could be seen as a logical progression from the original or completely disparate; (b) the context of the collection and the reasonable expectations of the data subject about future use, which may well be related to (a); (c) the nature of the personal data and the potential impact of further processing on data subjects; and (d) any safeguards which might be adopted by the data controller to ensure fair processing and prevent any such adverse impact.[143] These criteria do not give the impression of being unreasonable on their face, especially in view of the overall objective of protecting the privacy of individual data subjects.

### Purpose limitation and the 'internet of things'

However, one challenge is to be able to determine when a purpose is actually new and cannot just be seen as an extension of the original. In particular, new technological developments, including the use of 'big data', discussed further below, and the increased connectivity of devices termed the 'internet of things', create particular challenges with regard to ongoing compliance with the purpose limitation principle. Potentially any object which can be assigned an IP address and can transfer data can be connected. Not all such devices will process personal data but there are three broad areas where this is likely or inevitable; wearable computing such as watches; 'quantified self', meaning devices which monitor individual performance or vital signs such as pedometers and so on; home automation or 'domotics', including thermostats, smoke alarms and any household appliance which can be controlled remotely over the internet.[144] Although, in principle, any personal data transferred between devices must be processed according to data protection principles, as pointed out by Treacy and Bapat:[145] 'the difficulty with the application of the purpose limitation principle to the Internet of Things is the infinite number of activities that potentially may be linked'.[146]

## Third data protection principle – adequate, relevant and not excessive

Having dealt with the processing and purpose of the personal data collected, the third principle imposes a requirement of proportionality; that the data must be no more than the data controller needs for the purpose or purposes in question. It must be adequate, relevant and not excessive in relation to the purpose of collection. The interpretation of the equivalent principle in the 1984 Act was discussed in a number of tribunal decisions prior to the implementation

---

143 Opinion 03/2013 on purpose limitation (adopted 2 April 2013) (WP203 569/13/EN). See also discussion of this opinion in Ellis Parry, 'Purpose limitation: from "original intent" to "social economic realism"' (2013) 10 DPL&P 12.
144 Opinion 08/2014 on recent developments on the internet of things (adopted 16 September 2014) (WP223 569/14/EN).
145 Bridget Treacy and Anita Bapat, 'The "internet of things" – already in a home near you' (2013) 13 P&DP 11.
146 Purpose limitation is not the only data protection issue in relation to the internet of things – there may also be issues of fairness, lack of consent and transparency, security and so on. See further discussion in Opinion 08/2014 and also the case study 'Big Data and the Data Protection Principles' below.

of the Directive. During the existence of the short-lived Community Charge, or 'Poll Tax', a number of complaints were received that information required by those administering the tax was in excess of that needed. The task of compiling and maintaining the register of those who were subject to the charge was the duty of the Community Charge registration officers (CCROs) in each area, who were provided with guidance by the then Data Protection Registrar about the minimum amount of information that they could hold that was compatible with their intended purposes. However, a number of CCROs continued to gather information about the type of property inhabited – a factor that was argued to have no relevance to the levying of a per capita tax and was found to breach this principle.[147] Another case arrived at the same conclusion in relation to the gathering of information regarding dates of birth, which could be relevant to certain categories of individual whose eligibility to pay the Community Charge was related to their age, but in other cases was far in excess of what was required to administer the Community Charge.[148]

## Fourth data protection principle – accurate and, where necessary, kept up to date

How extensive is the duty to ensure data is accurate? In *Lyon v House*[149] the Outer House, Court of Session rejected the contention that the duty required a data controller to investigate the accuracy of data it had collected. Subsequently the Inner House[150] found no breach of the fourth data protection principle but without any further discussion on this point. The guidance in Sch 2 to the DPA 98 also provides that the principle will not be contravened where the data controller has taken reasonable steps to ensure the accuracy of the data. This was one of the issues discussed in *Smeaton v Equifax Plc*.[151]

Smeaton was made bankrupt in 2001 and the details placed by the Official Receiver on the Register of Bankruptcy orders (now the Individual Insolvency Register) and published in the London Gazette as required by the Insolvency Rules 1986. Smeaton appealed and the order was subsequently rescinded. There was no equivalent duty on the Official Receiver to publish details of the rescission and neither did Smeaton take any steps to publicise the fact. In 2006, Smeaton's application to open a bank account and obtain a loan was refused as a result of an adverse credit rating from Equifax based on the information published in the London Gazette as, at that time, credit reference agencies had no direct access to the Register of Bankruptcy orders. Smeaton alleged, amongst other things, that the adverse credit rating was a consequence of Equifax not keeping its data accurate and up to date in breach of the fourth data protection principle. At first instance,[152] it was held that Equifax should have done more to ensure that its records were updated to take account of rescission orders (which there was no duty to publicise) given the damage that can be caused to a data subject by inaccurate data. But on appeal, Tomlinson LJ, although acknowledging the importance of the fourth principle, pointed out that a sense of proportion had to be retained in determining the scope of the duty to ensure accuracy.[153] On the facts Tomlinson LJ found this would not be feasible as the number of rescission orders was small and, in addition, the advice at the time placed the onus on those who were the subject of a rescission order to inform the credit reference agencies of this fact. The Court of Appeal ruled that, taking into account the context and

---

147 Cases DA/90 24/49/3–5, *Community Charge Registration Officers of Runnymede BC, South Northamptonshire DC and Harrow BC v Data Protection Registrar*, available online at: www.informationtribunal.gov.uk/DBFiles/Decision/i167/CCRO.pdf
148 Case DA/90 25/49/2 *Community Charge Registration Officer of Rhondda BC v Data Protection Registrar*, available online at: www.information-tribunal.gov.uk/DBFiles/Decision/i168/CCRO2.pdf
149 [2012] CSOH 45; see also discussion in 'Police intelligence, regulatory bodies and libel': (2012) 17 Comms L [138].
150 [2013] CSIH 46.
151 [2013] EWCA Civ 108.
152 [2012] EWHC 2088.
153 [2013] EWCA Civ 108, [59].

circumstances; that rescission orders were uncommon and, at the time, there was no easy way for credit reference agencies to locate this information, Equifax had taken reasonable steps to ensure that its data were accurate and up to date.[154]

## Fifth data protection principle – not kept longer than necessary

The objective of this principle is to encourage data to be reviewed and destroyed at appropriate intervals, removing the possible temptation to process for further purposes, which might also fall foul of principles 1 and 2. However, how long is longer than necessary is still a question akin to 'how long is a piece of string'. University lecturers and tutors will frequently be asked to provide references for students and graduates for which they will need to rely on personal data recorded while the subject was a student. At what point can much of that personal data (other than results etc) be deleted? Requests will obviously be more frequent in the early life of the data, but it is nevertheless clear that the fifth data protection principle does not support keeping personal data just in case it may be required subsequently. In general, there is no definitive answer to the question how long should data be kept,[155] it will depend on the context and circumstances in each case.

One of the complaints in *Pal v General Medical Council*[156] was that personal data had been kept longer than was justified. The case arose out of complaints made by Dr Pal to the General Medical Council (GMC) in the spring of 2000 about the treatment of elderly patients. Although the complaint was closed in October 2000, correspondence continued between the defendants in which were expressed personal views about Dr Pal's actions. There was no complaint about her from either colleagues or patients, but nevertheless, despite the GMC's retention policy, which required documentation in such cases to be destroyed after six months, relevant material was still available four years later. At a preliminary hearing, the argument that this was because the GMC was reconsidering its policy on document retention received little sympathy from the court, which concluded that the chances of Pal succeeding at trial were 'promising', because 'either [the GMC] is acting in compliance with the legislation or it is not. The fact that it may be spending several years deciding when, whether and how to comply cannot excuse or justify non-compliance'.[157]

A number of cases arose out of various complaints that criminal convictions frequently remained on the Police National Computer (PNC) even after more than 20 years of non-offending and when the offences themselves were not of a serious nature. While it was accepted that it was a police purpose to disclose conviction data held on the PNC to bodies such as the Criminal Records Bureau and Independent Safeguarding Agency for the carrying out of their statutory duties, this did not mean that there was a duty to retain data for this purpose when it was no longer required for core policing purposes. However, the Court of Appeal, in allowing appeals from the decision of the Information Tribunal that the data in question had been kept for longer than necessary, held that whether or not particular records could be regarded as still relevant was not a question for the Information Commissioner, but for the police themselves, taking all of the relevant circumstances into account.[158] In other words, it is for a data controller such as the university in the earlier

---

154 For discussion of the wider issues raised in the case; see also Helen Morrison, 'Credit reference agencies and the accuracy of personal data' (2013) 29 PN 195; and Lee Mason, 'Personal data and credit reference agencies: UK statutory obligations owed to consumers and the means of redress' (2014) 29 JIBLR 411.

155 For provisions on the retention of data in some specific situations see Directive 2006/24/EC of the European Parliament and of the Council of 15 March 2006 on the retention of data generated or processed in connection with the provision of publicly available electronic communications services or of public communications networks and amending Directive 2002/58/EC discussed further in Chapter 10.

156 [2004] EWHC 1485.

157 Ibid, [31].

158 *Chief Constable of Humberside Police v Information Commissioner (Secretary of State for the Home Department intervening)* [2010] 1 WLR 1136.

example to determine at what point the data are no longer necessary and it is good practice for data controllers to set appropriate retention policies for the various types of data which they hold.

In re *Southern Pacific Person Loans Ltd, Oakley Smith v Information Commissioner*[159] concerned a company in liquidation. What should happen to any personal data when the company had ceased trading? It was held that the fifth data protection principle required that it should be disposed of as soon as possible. It was held that, in general all the personal data held by the company should be destroyed after liquidation, the only exceptions were likely to be for any data needed to respond to subject access requests received prior to liquidation or to respond to claims made afterwards.[160]

## Processed in accordance with the rights of the data subject

Given the commitment to individual rights to privacy with respect to the processing of data that is embedded in Art 1 of the Directive, it is not surprising that a number of its other provisions relate to specific rights to be enjoyed by the data subject. These rights can be divided loosely into the right to information about the nature of the personal data held and the type of processing,[161] the right of access to data held by the data controller,[162] and the right to object to processing in certain situations.[163] However, there is no general right to object to data processing because this would be likely to be disproportionate to the internal market objective of maintaining the free flow of personal data.

### The right of access to personal data

DPD Art 12(a) contains the subject access right, the essential elements of which are the confirmation that personal data is being processed, information about the purposes of processing, categories of data and recipients etc and the communication of that data to the data subject in an intelligible form, together with any information about the source. The subject access right found in DPA 1998, s 7, is an amplified and detailed implementation of the provisions of DPD, Art 12(a) but, despite its length and detail, compliance with this section is not necessarily a straightforward matter. The first issue is the definition of personal data, since it is only that to which the data subject has a right of access. As discussed above, the potentially wide ambit of the definition has been restricted by the Court of Appeal in *Durant v FSA*,[164] and also by the CJEU in Joined Cases C-141/12 and C-372/12, *YS v Minister voor Immigratie. Integratie en Asiel*. In *Durant*, Auld LJ pointed out that the purpose of s 7 was to allow a data subject to ascertain that any processing being carried out by the data controller was not unlawfully infringing his or her privacy, but that it was 'not an automatic key to any information readily accessible or not of matters in which he may be named or informed',[165] and this view was also taken by the CJEU in *YS*. The right in Art 12(a) is to be provided with the information in 'intelligible form'. In *YS*, the CJEU ruled that this provision does not require the provision of the actual document(s) in question. In support of their right of privacy with respect to the processing of their data, this right is intended to allow data subjects to check the accuracy of the data held and that it is being processed in accordance with the provisions of the Directive. Any such communication must be 'intelligible' but the right can be satisfied without any duty to provide a copy of the original documentation.[166]

---

159 [2013] EWHC 2485.
160 *Ibid*, [38]–[41].
161 Articles 10 and 11.
162 Article 12.
163 Articles 14 and 15.
164 [2003] EWCA Civ 1746.
165 *Ibid*, [27].
166 Joined Cases C-141/12 and C-372/12, CJEU judgment [56]–[58]. But cf now GDPR Art 15(3).

Subject access requests may be quite burdensome for the data controller, especially in cases in which, as is not uncommon, the data subject requests all information that is held on him or her and/or has other motives for obtaining the information. This was the situation in *Ezsias v Welsh Ministers*,[167] in which Ezsias, who was in an employment dispute with the North Glamorgan NHS Trust, made a succession of data subject access requests to the National Assembly for Wales. He had been involved in voluminous correspondence about the issues raised in his dispute with a number of departments and the evidence was that there was extensive documentation, which had to be assessed to ascertain whether or not it could be released in response to the request. The facts and procedural history of the case are complex, but the judgment in the case points out that the wording of s 7 merely gives a right to know about whether personal data are being processed, for what purposes, and to what recipients disclosure is made. Although there was a requirement to communicate the information constituting the personal data that could be complied with by providing the actual document, the right itself was not 'coterminous with a right to disclosure of documents'.[168] The decision also considered the problems encountered by data controllers to voluminous requests such as this, and concluded that the duty on controllers was to make a 'reasonable and proportionate search'.

A number of commentators believe this to be somewhat controversial.[169] Carey suggests that 'the judgment in this case seems to make assumptions about data protection law which are not immediately obvious from the wording of the relevant legal provisions',[170] although Rodway and Church find that the 'reasonable and proportionate search' requirement was 'clearly signposted by earlier decisions'.[171] It is true that there was some discussion of proportionality in *Durant*, although this was in the context of relevant filing systems rather than s 7.[172] Section 8(2) of the DPA 1998 also makes it possible for the data controller not to provide a copy of the data sought in permanent form if this would involve disproportionate effort, but this does not refer to the search to locate the personal data, which was one of the main issues in *Ezsias*. However, because this statute implements the Data Protection Directive, the concept of proportionality should perhaps suffuse its more general interpretation – proportionality being one of the fundamental doctrines of EU law; as Brooks concludes, it would also be 'illogical for proportionality to only apply to the supply of a copy of the data, when the real difficulty and expense is in locating, retrieving and collating the information in the first place'.[173] There is, though, another approach allowed for in the statute to assist in locating data in response to a subject access request: s 7(3) provides that where data controllers reasonably require further information to locate the information sought by the data subject, then they are not obliged to comply unless provided with that further information. This envisages a dialogue between the data subject and data controller to assist in the retrieval of the relevant information, which could go some way towards alleviating the problems associated with large-scale searches of documents and data.

Beyond this, s 7(4)–(6) potentially raise considerable uncertainty for the controller regarding the circumstances in which personal data can be revealed when to do so might reveal data about a third party. Although such disclosure can clearly be legitimised by the consent of the third party, uncertainty arises when such consent cannot be obtained. Section 7(6) requires, amongst other things, the controller to have particular regard to any duty of confidentiality owed to the other

---

167  [2007] EWHC 815 (QB).
168  *Ibid*, [53]–[54]. GDPR Art 15(3) now requires controllers to provide a copy of the data.
169  See, e.g., Suzanne Rodway and Peter Church, 'Wanting it all: Unreasonable subject access requests' (2008) 19(2) Comp & L 24, 25; Gary Brooks, 'Implications of Ezsias' Case for subject access: Proportionality may apply to searches of data' (2008) 8 PDP 5(3). The Court of Appeal granted leave to appeal on this point: [2008] EWCA Civ 874, [13]; but there have been no subsequent proceedings.
170  Peter Carey, *Data Protection: A Practical Guide to UK and EU Law*, 2009, Oxford: Oxford University Press.
171  Rodway and Church, above.
172  [2003] EWCA Civ 1746, [45]–[50].
173  Rodway and Church, above.

individual, any steps taken to seek the consent of the other individual, whether the individual is capable of giving consent, and any express refusal of consent. Overall, though, an assessment has to be made as to whether, in the words of s 7(4)(b), it is nevertheless 'reasonable in all the circumstances' to comply with the subject access request. The balancing of interests that this entails was discussed in *Durant*. Auld LJ pointed out that the question was whether it was reasonable for the data controller to comply with the request rather than reasonable to refuse to comply, and that 'reasonableness' in the circumstances did not mean there was an explicit requirement to seek the third party's consent. It was also important to consider the legitimate interests of such third parties, including their right to privacy in making the decision. In conclusion, he suggested that:

> it all depends on the circumstances whether it would be reasonable to disclose to a data sub-
> ject the name of another person figuring in his personal data, whether that person is a source,
> or a recipient or likely recipient of that information, or has a part in the matter the subject of
> the personal data . . . I believe that the courts should be wary of attempting to devise any prin-
> ciples of general application one way or the other.[174]

Rather than laying down any guidelines for the anxious data controller, this judgment serves only to underline the potential difficulties in deciding whether it is 'reasonable in all the circumstances' to disclose the information.

A further problem could arise with the potential clash between a putative duty of confidentiality and the data subject's right of access. This is illustrated most clearly by the issue of when a reference given in 'confidence' nevertheless may be disclosed to the data subject. References given by a data controller 'in confidence' are exempt from the subject access provisions by virtue of the miscellaneous exemption in s 7(1), but this appears to have no effect on the exercise of the subject access right to the data controller who receives such a reference. Can such references remain confidential? Briefly, the general requirement at common law is that an obligation of confidence will arise if the information is confidential in the sense that it is not known to others and is given in circumstances in which the receiver is made aware that there is an expectation of confidentiality. A party to whom information is given in confidence may not divulge it unless there are specific grounds for doing so; these are the consent of the confider, legal compulsion, or overriding public interest. The only relevant one here would be consent, which, as in s 7(4), will obviously legitimise disclosure. Where third party data might be revealed, what role does this obligation play in the balancing act required by s 7(4)–(6)? One construction of the requirement in s 7(6) to have regard to any duty of confidentiality could be that a confidence is not overridden merely by the right of subject access. On the other hand, s 27(5), which provides that, but for the provisions on exemptions, the 'subject information provisions shall have effect notwithstanding any enactment or rule of law prohibiting or restricting the disclosure, or authorising the withholding, of information', could be construed as suggesting the opposite. In summary, consent will always validate the disclosure of third party information, but in other cases, data controllers may be faced with a complex balancing exercise.[175]

## Other rights of the data subject

In line with the other provisions of the Directive relating to the rights of the data subject (see Arts 12(b), 14 and 15), the 1998 Act now includes specific rights to prevent processing likely to cause damage or distress (s 10), to prevent processing for purposes of direct marketing (s 11), and

---

174 [2003] EWCA Civ 1746, [66].
175 Note that there are certain cases in which consent is deemed to be given by virtue of the third party's professional status: see, e.g., Data Protection (Subject Access Modification) (Health) Order 2000, SI 2000/413; Data Protection (Subject Access Modification) (Education) Order 2000, SI 2000/414; Data Protection (Subject Access Modification) (Social Work) Order 2000, SI 2000/415.

in relation to automated decision-making (s 12). The right in s 11 was a central issue in *Robertson v Wakefield Metropolitan District Council*.[176] Robertson wished to have his name withheld from the electoral register because he objected to the practice of selling the register for use for direct marketing purposes. The electoral registration officer refused on the grounds that it was a legal requirement for electors to complete the requisite form and be included in the register. The court considered the provisions in Art 14(b) of the Directive and its implementation in DPA 1998, s 11, and found that s 11 implemented the requirement in Art 14(b) and that, even if it did not, Art 14(b) had direct effect, so that it could be relied on by an individual. It was therefore held that the legal rules concerning representation of the people must be construed 'in a manner which is Directive-compliant and consistent with the Data Protection Act 1998'. As a result, the electoral register is now in two parts: the full version lists the details of all those entitled to vote and cannot be used for direct marketing purposes; the edited version includes the details of those people who are willing for their data to be made available for other purposes.

## The 'right to be forgotten'

A significant and controversial decision was made by the CJEU in May 2014 in a case involving Google and the Spanish Data Protection Authority which has established the so-called 'right to be forgotten.'[177] In brief, the proceedings arose because Costeja González was concerned about the fact that his name was mentioned in both the printed edition and searchable online edition of the newspaper *La Vanguardia* as being the owner of property which was for sale by auction in order to pay off social security debts. Despite the fact that this matter dated back to 1998 and the issue had been resolved, if his name was entered into Google (or presumably any other search engine) it continued to list links to the online articles in question. Initially Costeja González asked the newspaper to erase his personal data on the basis that the proceedings concerning his debts were concluded and so no longer of contemporary relevance. The newspaper refused as publication of the details had been by order of the Ministry of Labour and Social Affairs. He then sent a request to Google asking that links to the newspaper articles should not be displayed if anyone used his name as a search term. A complaint then ensued to the Spanish Data Protection authority (AEPD) in which he requested that AEPD should require the publisher to remove his personal data or ensure that it was not retrieved by the actions of search engines, and that Google should ensure that search results based on his name did not provide links to the newspaper articles containing his name. AEPD rejected the complaint with respect to the newspaper on the basis that publication was legally justified, but upheld the complaint against Google. Google then sought an order for an annulment of this decision in the Spanish High Court (Audienca Nacional).

The Spanish court referred a number of questions to the CJEU concerning both the territorial and material scope of the provisions of Directive 95/46. The latter including *inter alia* whether the locating, retrieving, listing etc of search results containing personal data should be classified as 'processing' within the meaning of the Directive and, if so, whether search engines should be classified as 'data controllers' which would, of course, mean that they were responsible for ensuring that any processing was lawful. Further questions related to the data subject's rights of rectification, erasure and blocking in Art 12 of the Directive and whether the right to object in Art 14 should be construed as imposing a duty on Google (in this case) to remove links to articles containing personal data published by third parties from its search results and whether or not that obligation would be affected by the fact that the information was lawfully published by such third parties.

In relation to the questions on territorial application, as might be expected, the CJEU found that the provisions of the Directive would apply when there was a subsidiary of a search engine in

---

176 [2002] QB 1095.
177 Case C-131/12 *Google Spain SL and Google Inc v Agencia Española de Protección de Datos (AEPD) and Mario Costeja González.*

a Member State (in this case Google Spain) which targeted its activities at that Member State. So the fact that the search process itself was operated by Google.com which was established in the US did not prevent Google searches being subject to the provisions of the Directive through its subsidiary Google Spain. More interesting and controversial was the fact that Advocate General Jääskinen and the CJEU came to dramatically opposing conclusions on the substantive questions relating to the material scope of the Directive.

## The Advocate General's opinion and the balancing of rights

The Advocate General noted in particular the fact that, at the time of drafting, the current technological environment could not have been foreseen and that 'the internet magnifies and facilitates in an unprecedented manner the dissemination of information'[178] which, of course, includes personal data, resulting in the potential scope of Directive 95/46 becoming 'surprisingly wide'[179] He warned against using a literal, or even teleological interpretation of the provisions of the Directive since that 'completely ignores the fact that when the Directive was drafted it was not possible to take into account the emergence of the internet and the various new phenomena.'[180] He pointed out a number of times that almost anyone with a smartphone, tablet or laptop could potentially be processing data within the meaning of the Directive. Against this background he considered the importance of applying the principle of proportionality to 'avoid unreasonable and excessive legal consequences'[181] and placed an emphasis on the balance between the conflicting rights of those involved, namely the right of privacy of the individual, the right of freedom of expression of the press and other publishers as well as the economic rights of the businesses involved, including Google. He observed the central role of search engines and ISPs in the development of the information society and overall called for a 'correct, reasonable and proportionate balance between the protection of personal data, the coherent interpretation of the objectives of the information society and legitimate interests of economic operators and internet users at large.'[182]

On the crucial question of whether Google was a data controller in relation to the data retrieved in response to a user's search, he made a distinction between determining the purposes and means of processing 'personal data' and processing other data. In his view the focus should be on where the responsibility for processing personal data lies in the sense that the controller knows of the existence and character of personal data and processes it with this in mind.[183] At the time of the search the search engine cannot distinguish personal data from other data, it does not control personal data on third party webpages and it is not aware of the existence of personal data on these pages other than as a statistical fact. This led him to the conclusion that the search engine could not be considered to be a data controller in relation to data retrieved from searches.[184] Underlining this view he suggested that any other conclusion could mean that search engines were incompatible with EU law which would be an 'absurd' outcome.[185] Further, he suggested that, even if the search engine were to be construed as a data controller in this context, the processing would be legitimised as pursuing its legitimate interests. He concluded that neither could a 'right to be forgotten' be founded on Arts 12(b) and 14(a) of the Directive, a deduction supported, in his view, by the fact that the draft right in Art 17 of the GDPR was intended to be a legal innovation and not a codification of the existing law.[186]

---

178 Ibid, Opinion of the Advocate General, [28].
179 Ibid, [29].
180 Ibid, [77].
181 Ibid, [30].
182 Ibid, [31].
183 Ibid, [82]. In passing he noted that this also accords with the view of the Article 29 Working Party that 'the concept of controller is a functional concept, intended to allocate responsibilities where the factual influence is, and thus based on a factual rather than a formal analysis': ibid, [83].
184 There is no question that a search engine is a data controller when obtaining and retaining the personal data of its users: ibid, [50].
185 Ibid, [90].
186 Ibid, [110].

## The judgment of the CJEU and the protection of the individual

In complete contrast, the CJEU decided that search engines were data controllers in relation to search results in that they did 'determine the purposes and means of processing', but gave no real indication of the rationale for this conclusion.[187] Whereas the Advocate General had warned of the dangers of a wide interpretation of the provisions of Directive 95/46, in the CJEU's view a broad definition was required; any other finding would not only be contrary to the literal meaning of the provision but to its objective. A broad definition was required to 'ensure effective and complete protection of the data subject.'[188] In this respect it is difficult to see how a data subject can ever be *completely* protected; this is explicitly recognised in the directive itself in the balancing of rights of free expression with data protection rights required in the special purposes exemption as well as the balance which needs to be struck when processing in pursuit of the legitimate interests of the data controller.[189] That there are grounds for lawful processing other than the consent of the data subject, is also implicitly suggestive of the fact that there may be processing which the data subject has not actually consented to, but yet is lawful for certain overriding reasons and subject to certain safeguards. The CJEU makes the valid point that using names as search terms enables personal profiling and that the activities of search engines thus impact on the privacy of individuals in a different way than the initial publication. Neither could search engines be absolved from their responsibility by the fact that the original sites could use technical means to prevent indexing; it was still the case that 'the purposes and means of . . . processing are determined by the operator of the search engine'.[190]

The discussion with regard to human rights focuses primarily on privacy rather than any other competing rights which may be held by the parties who are involved or may be affected. Whilst it is reasonable to suggest that the economic interests of the search engine should not be a determinative factor when assessing whether processing is legitimised by Art 7(f), there is no explicit consideration of the freedom of expression of the original publisher. Interestingly, if the personal data in question happen to be 'sensitive' then there is no lawful basis for processing as Art 7(f) can only be used to legitimise the processing of non-sensitive data.[191] The CJEU's decision seems to have been most influenced by the fact that internet searches make access to the personal data in question, and possible further dissemination, extremely easy and so can have a dramatic interference in the data subject's right to privacy, even though the original information has been published lawfully. The CJEU's final summary[192] again makes no reference to freedom of expression; neither is there any suggestion of a general public interest exception. Although in a technical sense the CJEU only had to respond to the questions referred to it, this was perhaps a missed opportunity to take a rather wider view of the application of these provisions and their intersection with other rights in relation to the use of the internet. In the words of Koutrakos 'the judgment approaches a critically important issue relating to a fiendishly complex and rapidly evolving policy areas by making a number of general statements about only an aspect of the dispute namely the significance of the protection of personal data.'[193] As it stands, the only chink in the armour of the new right appears to be if the data subject 'plays a prominent role in public life' although how prominent a role and how public the life is a discussion for another time.

187 Case C-131/12 *Google Spain SL v González*, [33].
188 Ibid, [34].
189 Relevant factors affecting this balance have been discussed extensively by the Article 29 Working Party in Opinion 6/2014 on the notion of legitimate interests of the data controller under Art 7 of Directive 95/46/EC (WP217) as discussed earlier at p 353.
190 Case C-131/12 *Google Spain SL v González*, [40].
191 Case C-131/12 *Google Spain SL v González*, Opinion of the Advocate General, [90]; see also Simon Stokes, 'A decision to quickly forget: Google Spain and Google on the right to be forgotten' (2014) 25 Ent L Rev 233.
192 Case C-131/12 *Google Spain SL v González*, [99].
193 Panos Koutrakos, 'To strive, to seek, to Google, to forget' (2014) 39 EL Rev 293, 294.

### The impact and implementation of the 'right to be forgotten'

The judgment has been welcomed by a number of data protection practitioners but other reaction has been very mixed. First, although many, including Advocate General Jääskinen, have suggested that Directive 95/46/EC is no longer fit for purpose in relation to its application to the widespread circulation of personal data on the internet, the CJEU certainly appears to have demonstrated that it can be used to regulate both the availability of such data and the activities of search engines in retrieving it. Far from taking a lenient approach to search engines in recognition of their pivotal role in internet use 'the CJEU almost moulded the Directive . . . to catch Google.'[194] The effect of the CJEU ruling 'makes search engines responsible for the vast amount of information published on the internet even though it was not their decision to publish it, they have no means of modifying it and they are not aware of the content . . . '.[195] Apart from raising the spectre of private censorship, the practical reality is that the initial burden of determining legality falls to the search engine which will have to adjudicate potentially complex matters of balancing individual rights with wider issues of the public interest. Not only is this an onerous burden in terms of the volume of such adjudications which may have to be made, it could be a recipe for inconsistency and unfairness, which would be something of an irony given that an existing lack of harmonisation is one of the rationales for the introduction of the General Data Protection Regulation. In an attempt to ameliorate this situation the Article 20 Working Party has issued guidelines on the implementation of the 'right to be forgotten ruling'.[196] One potentially controversial aspect of these guidelines is the suggestion that delisting of links should also be extended to .com websites to ensure that EU law cannot be circumvented. However, any adjudication made may not achieve the desired outcome for the data subject as the information will almost certainly still be able to be located by an assiduous researcher. As the action required of search engines is neither appropriate nor necessary and there are less severe ways of achieving the same outcome, in Prieto's view this clearly demonstrates that the judgment has failed to take proportionality into account appropriately.[197]

The magnitude of the task imposed on search engines is illustrated by the fact that Google apparently received 40,000 requests in the first four days that the online form which it created in response to the ruling was in place, which increased to 91,000 involving 328,000 URLs in the following two months.[198] This has led the House of Lords European Committee in its response to the ruling to question how easy compliance will be in practice.[199] A request to Google does not stop the information being available by using other search engines, the individual will need to make the same request to all search engines and, notwithstanding the guidelines, there is always the propensity for them to assess the request differently leading to inconsistency in implementation of the right. The HL Report also notes that the CJEU's ruling leads to 'further absurdities', in particular that if 'search engines are data controllers so logically are users of search engines'.[200] Such an outcome was referred to by Advocate General Jääskinen as an illustration of 'the irrational nature of the blind literal interpretation of the Directive',[201] although he could not, at the time, have been aware of how critical that would turn out to be of the final decision of the CJEU. An undesirable consequence may be to close down 'access to information in the EU that is open to the rest of the world',[202] which

---

194 Steven James, 'The right to privacy catches up with search engine: the unforgettable decision in *Google Spain v AEPD*' (2014) 20 CTLR 130, 132.

195 Paula Herrero Prieto, 'Search engines: interplay of fundamental rights and the principle of proportionality' (2014) 20 CTLR 213.

196 Guidelines on the Implementation of the Court of Justice of the European Union Judgment on '*Google Spain v. Agencia Española de Protección de Datos (AEPD) and Mario Costeja González*' C-131/12 (adopted 26 November 2014) (WP 225/14/EN).

197 Prieto, above, p 220.

198 *EU Data Protection law: a 'right to be forgotten'?*, HL Paper 40 (July 2014), p 14; and Bert-Jaap Koops, 'The trouble with European data protection law' (2014) 4 IDPL 250, 253.

199 Ibid, p 5.

200 Ibid, p 16.

201 Case C-131/12 *Google Spain SL v González*, Opinion of the Advocate General, [81].

202 HL Paper 40, p 20. See also Stokes, above, p 235.

would do little to promote the development of the objectives of the information society in the EU. It thus does little to achieve the second of the objectives in Art 1 which the CJEU had treated as an equally important purpose of the Directive in Lindqvist.[203]

There have also been a number of semantic criticisms. The term 'right to be forgotten' is perhaps something of a misnomer; it has even been said that 'the use of the word 'forgotten' is stretching language to a degree which would make the most liberal of English teachers blush'.[204] Given that information cannot be deliberately forgotten, it could perhaps more accurately be described as placing a 'duty to be forgetful'[205] on search engines. No general right to have lawfully published material containing personal data permanently removed from records is created, merely that it should not be retrievable by using the name as a search term. On the actual facts of the case, the article in La Vanguardia can still apparently be accessed by searching on the co-owner's name or other relevant keywords or by using a different search engine including google.com which is not affected by the ruling. The information may also be held by the Spanish courts and government authorities. At best it can only make the information less easily accessible and may achieve the opposite – as with all privacy actions the paradoxical outcome is that far from being forgotten, the old debts of Costeja González will now be 'remembered' by many more people than those in a similar situation.

## Remedies for the data subject

Directive 95/46 requires Member States to provide judicial remedies for breach of the data protection rights (Art 22) and that also that anyone who suffers damage as a result of unlawful processing should be eligible for compensation from the data controller (Art 23). In the UK, this right to obtain compensation is contained in DPA 98 s 13. Section 13(1) and (2) distinguish compensation for damage for distress. Section 13(2) limits compensation for distress to situations where there is also compensation for 'damage' under s 13(1) or where the personal data is processed for the special purposes. Whereas Art 23 appears to place no qualification on 'damage', other than for the special purposes, the Act thus makes damage a prerequisite for compensation for distress. Damage is taken to mean pecuniary loss without which no compensation for distress is apparently available as discussed in, e.g. Johnson v MDU,[206] although this narrow view was doubted by the CA in Murray v Express Newspapers.[207] However, in appropriate cases, courts seemed willing to award a nominal amount for 'damage' in order to facilitate a claim for 'distress' under s 13(2). Halliday v Creation Consumer Finance Ltd,[208] in particular, was a case where H had not suffered any actual financial loss as a result of an inaccurate credit rating but was awarded nominal damages under s 13(1) thus allowing an award to be made for distress under s 13(2) of £750.

Although subsequent cases used the Halliday approach to provide damages for distress,[209] in retrospect this case perhaps paved the way for the decision in Vidal-Hall.[210] In this case, the claimants did not claim for pecuniary loss but rather for acute distress and anxiety as a result of the apprehension that third parties might find out personal and sensitive things about them as a result of Google's collection and collation of BGI. In a hearing to establish whether to serve proceedings out of the jurisdiction, it was noted at first instance that a reasoned opinion in 2010 had apparently suggested that provision of compensation only for financial loss did not accord with the provisions of Art 23

203 C-101/01 Lindqvist [2003] ECR I-12971 at [79]–[80] and Opinion of Advocate General Tizzano, [6]–[8]. See also Peter Blume, 'The inherent contradictions in data protection law' (2012) 2 IDPL 26, 27.
204 Ashley Roughton, 'Google and the "right to be forgotten" – setting the record straight' (2014) 14 P&DP 6.
205 Dan Jerker, B Svantesson, 'Limiting borderless forgetfulness? Limiting the geographical reach of the "Right to be Forgotten"' [2015] Oslo Law Review 116, 137 available online at: www.journals.uio.no/index.php/oslawreview/article/view/2567
206 [2004] EWHC 347. See discussion above.
207 [2008] EWCA Civ 446 at [63].
208 [2013] EWCA Civ 333.
209 See, e.g., A B v Ministry of Justice [2014] EWHC 1847 (QB).
210 Google Inc v Vidal-Hall [2015] EWCA Civ 311. See also discussion above.

of Directive 95/46 which DPA s 13 is intended to implement and which merely refers to compensation for 'damage' without further qualification.[211] For its part, the Court of Appeal observed that a term that was used in an EU instrument, in this case 'damage', did not depend for its meaning on its construction in individual Member States. In a different context, the AG, subsequently supported by the CJEU, said that damage should 'be interpreted widely, that is to say in favour of the argument that, at least in principle, the scope of the Directive was intended to cover all types of damage . . .'.[212] This is particularly important as Directives are harmonising measures and any differences in interpretation which arise out of particular Member State legal concepts would work against this. In *Vidal-Hall*, the Court of Appeal concluded that 'the same approach to construction leads to the conclusion that Art 23 of the Directive must be given its natural and wide meaning so as to include both material and non-material damage.'[213] As the Directive purported to protect privacy, the 'distressing invasion of privacy . . . must be taken to be the primary form of damage'[214] for which the data subject should be able to be compensated. Compensation for distress was available for a breach of Art 8 ECHR and it would be irrational to restrict the meaning of damage with regard to a breach of data protection principles when these were also intended to protect the right to privacy, albeit with respect to data processing; the court could not accept that damage could include distress where convention rights were engaged but not otherwise. In the light also of the protection of personal data in Art 8 of the EU Charter, it was unlikely that the Member States intended that a data subject could only recover when there had been financial loss. Neither was it relevant that the compensation if available might not be significant – 'the damages may be small, but the issues of principle are large.'[215]

How could such a conclusion be reconciled with s 13(2)? S 13(2) in most situations prohibits compensation for distress absent damage and was clearly what Parliament originally intended even though there was no evidence as to why this should be. In the case of conflict between EU law and domestic law, Member State courts are required to interpret the domestic law in the light of the relevant EU law. In this case s 13(2) and Art 23 were completely incompatible so a reconciling interpretation could not be found. However, as Art 8 of the EU Charter provided the right to the protection of personal data and Art 47 required a domestic court to ensure an effective remedy for violation of Charter rights, together these could be complied with by disapplying the conflicting provision, s 13(2), without any 'legislative choices'[216] having to be made by the court. 'The consequence of this would be that compensation would be recoverable under section 13(1) for any damage suffered as a result of a contravention by a data controller of any of the requirements of the DPA'[217] and s 13(2) would effectively be excised from the statute. The Supreme Court has given Google leave to appeal on whether s 13(2) is incompatible with Art 23 and whether the CA was correct to disapply s 13(2) so this is not yet the end of the matter.[218]

In cases of inaccuracy, s 14 also gives the court the power to order rectification, blocking, erasure, and destruction of the relevant data. In *Hegglin v Persons Unknown and Google*,[219] a banker had been subject to abusive and defamatory anonymous internet posts and was seeking to use the provisions of ss 10 and 14 and Directive 95/46 to obtain an injunction to prevent these appearing in Google searches on the grounds that they were inaccurate and causing him distress. At the initial hearing, it was found that his cause of action under the DPA 1998 was 'clearly established in principle and there is at least a good arguable case for the grant of some form of injunction'.[220] In *Google Spain*,

---

211 [2014] EWHC 13 (QB) at [94].
212 Case C-168/00 *Leitner v TUI Deutschland GmbhH & Co KG* [2002] ECR 1-1631, AG's Opinion [29].
213 [2015] EWCA Civ 311 at [76].
214 Ibid, [77].
215 Ibid, [139].
216 Ibid, [105].
217 Ibid.
218 www.supremecourt.uk/news/permission-to-appeal-decisions-28-july-2015.html.
219 [2014] EWHC 2808 (QB).
220 Ibid, [16].

discussed above, the CJEU found search engines to be data controllers in relation to personal data retrieved in response to searches and established the 'right to be forgotten'. *Hegglin* had the potential to provide further consideration of the data protection duties and responsibilities of search engines not only in relation to information which a data subject wishes to 'forget', but in relation to the inaccurate and distressing information which forms the content of a typical trolling campaign. In the event though, this discussion will have to wait as, in this case, a settlement was agreed on the eve of the full trial.[221]

## Security issues

Safeguarding the privacy of individuals with respect to the processing of their data is not just a matter of appropriate processing and compliance with the principles mentioned thus far. The effect of all these provisions could be rendered nugatory if insufficient care is taken to keep the personal data safe. Lack of security appears to create the greatest likelihood of loss of personal data as illustrated by the fact that in the UK, for example, there have been more monetary penalties imposed[222] for breaches of data security than all the other principles put together. Article 17 of the Directive requires that the 'controller must implement appropriate technical and organizational measures to protect personal data against accidental or unlawful destruction or accidental loss, alteration, unauthorized disclosure or access . . . ' and this has been implemented as the sixth data protection principle in the DPA 1998. The guidance on this principle in Pt II of the Schedule suggests that what is an appropriate level of security depends on the state of technological development and the nature of the data to be protected. The data controller must also take reasonable steps to ensure the reliability of any employees who have access to the personal data. There are also specific security requirements in Art 17(2)–(4) to cover the situation where a data processor processes data on behalf of the controller.

The specific reference to the state of technological development is an interesting one; to what extent can technical solutions to privacy protection, such as the use of encryption, be specifically required by the law on data protection? Where personal data is particularly sensitive or confidential, it may be that the seventh data protection principle will not be deemed to be complied with without the use of cryptography or other technical mechanism. Certainly applying the doctrine of proportionality would suggest that the higher the risk of loss or misuse of data, and/or of significant damage or distress to the data subject, the greater the security provisions should be. In the UK, the ICO has issued guidelines on when encryption should be used to safeguard personal data[223] and has taken enforcement action when the lack of encryption jeopardised the security of personal data as well as causing potential distress to data subjects. Examples include a £120,000 fine imposed on Stoke-on-Trent City Council for sending unencrypted emails containing highly sensitive data to an incorrect recipient,[224] and an enforcement notice issued against Marks and Spencer following the theft of a laptop containing details of 26,000 employees.[225] The overriding duty to ensure the security of the data is placed on data controllers even when there is outsourcing to a data processor.

221 See, e.g., www.theguardian.com/technology/2014/nov/24/google-settles-online-abuse-court-case-daniel-hegglin
222 See ICO webpages at https://ico.org.uk/action-weve-taken/enforcement/. Penalties and enforcement are discussed further below.
223 See https://ico.org.uk/for-organisations/encryption/
224 See www.out-law.com/articles/2012/october/ico-reiterates-warning-over-encryption-as-it-fines-council-120k-over-second-data-protection-breach/. See also the details of the action taken by the ICO against North East Lincolnshire County Council, available online at: https://ico.org.uk/enforcement/~/media/documents/library/Data_Protection/Notices/north-east-lincs-council%20-monetary-penalty-notice.pdf
225 See www.ico.gov.uk/upload/documents/library/data_protection/notices/m_and_s_sanitiseden.pdf. For further discussion of the role of cryptography in data protection, see, e.g., SA Price, 'Understanding contemporary cryptography and its wider impact upon the general law' (1999) 13 Int Rev LC & T 95, 108ff. See further discussion of encryption in Chapter 10.

A topic related to the provisions on security is that of data breach notifications such as the Marks and Spencer example above. This is by no means an isolated example and such data security breaches are frequently in the news in apparently ever-increasing numbers and in many jurisdictions.[226] How should data controllers respond when loss or widespread misuse of personal data occurs? As a result of these occurrences there has now been legislative action in many jurisdictions making it mandatory to provide notice of personal data breaches. These laws incorporate 'elements of privacy regulation, consumer protection and corporate governance mechanisms'.[227] Europe has been no exception and Directive 2009/136/EC[228] introduced new provisions relating to personal data breaches into Directive 2002/58/EC.[229] The Preamble notes that such breaches can result in both economic loss and social harm, as well as adversely affect privacy – especially where they lead to identity theft, for example.[230] 'Personal data breach' is defined as a breach of security leading to the accidental or unlawful destruction, loss, alteration, unauthorised disclosure of, or access to, personal data transmitted, stored, or otherwise processed in connection with the provision of a publicly available electronic communications service. On the occasion of such a breach, the new provisions require notification to the national data protection authority, together with notification of individuals concerned where the personal data breach is likely to adversely affect personal data or privacy, which should explain the nature of the breach and explain any steps to mitigate it. There is no need to do this if sufficient technological measures, such as the use of encryption as discussed above, have been implemented to make the data unintelligible to a third party, but where the controller has not notified the individual, the authority can require it to do so if there are likely adverse effects.[231]

## Transborder data flow

In the discussion of individual rights, it must not be forgotten that the Directive, in common with other data protection regulation, has the dual objective of both safeguarding privacy in relation to processing of personal data and facilitating transborder data flow, as illustrated by Art 1.[232] The importance of the free flow of such data is further underlined by part of the first sentence of Recital 56: '. . . cross-border flows of personal data are necessary for the expansion of international trade.' Thus, there are no grounds for restricting the free flow of data, provided that the appropriate safeguards are in place. Indeed, it is the very necessity referred to in Recital 56 that makes protection of the individual so vital. In principle, given the expected harmonisation of protection created by the Directive, crossborder data flow between individual Member States would not be expected to create an additional threat to the privacy of individuals. The situation could be very different, though, in relation to the transfer of data to third countries that may not have data protection to the same extent, or at all and, as noted by the Commission, the 'importance of efficient protection in case of

---

226 See n 14 above and see discussion in, e.g., Mark Burdon, Bill Lane, and Paul von Nessen, 'The mandatory notification of data breaches: Issues arising for Australian and EU legal developments' (2010) 26 CSLR 115.

227 Ibid.

228 Directive 2009/136/EC of the European Parliament and of the Council of 25 November 2009, amending Directive 2002/22/EC on universal service and users' rights relating to electronic communications networks and services, Directive 2002/58/EC concerning the processing of personal data and the protection of privacy in the electronic communications sector, and Regulation (EC) No 2006/2004 on cooperation between national authorities responsible for the enforcement of consumer protection laws, [2009] OJ L 337/11.

229 The e-privacy Directive discussed further below. Now supplemented by Commission Regulation (EU) No 611/2013 of 24 June 2013 on the measures applicable to the notification of personal data breaches under Directive 2002/58/EC of the European Parliament and of the Council on privacy and electronic communications: [2013] OJ L173/21.

230 Recital 61.

231 New Art 4(3) inserted in Directive 2002/58.

232 Compare, e.g., the Council of Europe Convention, which attempts, inter alia, to reconcile the notion of effective data protection with the ideal of free flow of information, as set out in the European Convention on Human Rights, Art 10. In pursuance of this, Art 12 of the Convention, on automatic processing of data, contains provisions allowing restriction of transborder data flows 'except where the regulations of the other Party provide an equivalent protection [for the personal data]'.

transfers of personal data has increased due to the exponential increase in data flows central to the digital economy and the very significant developments in data collection, processing and use'.[233] For this reason, Art 25,[234] which proscribes the transfer of personal data to a third country unless that country ensures 'an adequate level of protection', is of extreme importance and its inclusion within the Directive led many commentators to speculate on the potentially wide-reaching effect that its provisions may have. Thus Bennett suggested that the 'Data Protection Directive now constitutes the rules of the road for the increasingly global character of data processing operations'[235] and Mayer-Schönberger predicted that the Directive will assist the drive to homogeneity of approach on a global scale.[236] These early comments on the potentially global reach of the provisions of the Directive have now arguably been ratified by the judgment in Schrems discussed further below.

## Has data been transferred?

We are now accustomed to the wide availability of data on the internet but how easy is it to draw a line between data flow out of the EU and data flow within its borders? The question of whether or not personal data had actually been transferred to a third country was considered by the ECJ in Case C-101/01 Bodil Lindqvist.[237] Mrs Lindqvist had developed an internet home page as part of a course that she was following. She published on this site the personal data of a number of people who worked with her on a voluntary basis in a parish of the Swedish Protestant church for which she was a catechist. This included not only names and addresses, but also family circumstances, health issues, and other comments. Her colleagues were not informed of this and neither did she notify the relevant supervisory authority. She was subsequently charged with a number of offences relating to breaches of data processing rules and, as a result, a number of questions were referred to the ECJ. One of these asked:

> whether there is any transfer [of data] to a third country . . . where an individual loads personal data onto an internet page which is stored on an internet site on which the page can be consulted and which is hosted by a natural or legal person . . . thereby making those data accessible to anyone who connects to the internet, including people in a third country.

The question also went on to ask whether it made any difference to the answer if no one from a third country actually accessed the page.

As already noted and discussed further below, the Directive was not drafted with the transmission of personal data via the internet in mind and the ECJ noted that it could not be presumed that the provisions in question had been intended to apply to the loading of data onto an internet page, even if that process then made the data accessible to individuals in other jurisdictions.[238] It further pointed out that if there were a finding that there was a transborder data flow every time a website was accessed in another country, then the Directive would have global application and, further, even if only one of the countries were to fail to provide adequate protection (which would, of course, be very likely), the result would be that no personal data could lawfully be placed on the internet or web pages. With regard to the access to specific data such as that posted by Lindqvist in particular, the ECJ concluded that, to obtain that data, a user would have to take all of the necessary technical actions to locate and access the data – in other words, 'the internet pages did not contain the

---

233 Communication from the Commission to the European Parliament and the Council on the Functioning of the Safe Harbour from the Perspective of EU Citizens and Companies Established in the EU COM(2013) 847 final p 17 [8].

234 Implemented in the DPA 98 as the eighth data protection principle.

235 C Bennett, 'Convergence revisited' in PE Agre and M Rotenberg (eds), Technology and Privacy: The New Landscape, 1998, Cambridge, MA: MIT Press, p 111.

236 Mayer-Schönberger, above, p 223.

237 [2003] ECR I-12971.

238 Ibid, [68].

technical means to send that information automatically to people who did not intentionally seek access to those pages'.[239] The court's overall conclusion with regard to transborder data flow was that when data was accessed on a website, that data was not directly transferred between those who had posted the information and those reading it, and that, in consequence, there was no transfer of data to a third country as a result of information posted on a web page being available for access in third countries.

This is perhaps not a surprising judgment given the potential impact, noted at para [69] of the judgment, that a contrary finding could have.[240] Conceptually, it can be likened to a finding that, in the virtual world, individuals accessing an internet page containing personal data 'visit' that page rather than that the data is sent to them. This is not dissimilar to the approach taken by Jacob J in *Euromarket Designs Inc v Peters*,[241] in relation to trade mark infringement, in which he likened browsing on commercial sites on the internet to looking into a shop or 'visiting' it. On the other hand, the approach taken in some defamation cases[242] equates publication on the internet with publication to the world – that is, something rather more active. Given the patchy development of the law in this respect, it is difficult to assess whether these apparently opposing approaches can be reconciled or whether it matters in either the practical or conceptual sense.[243]

## What is an adequate level of protection?

Assuming that, in a particular case, there has actually been a transfer of personal data, the more difficult issue raised by Art 25 is the interpretation of 'adequate'. Should 'adequate' mean 'in conformity with the Directive'? Or 'functional similarity'? Or some lesser standard? How should, or can, this be assessed? The subsequent paragraphs of Art 25 attempt to provide guidance on this issue and give details of relevant factors including the nature of the data, and the purpose and duration of the processing, as well as the relevant legal, security, and professional rules in the country in question. However, this is of little help in providing any indication of clear priority amongst the criteria to be applied in assessment of adequacy and does not explicitly create a reference point by which adequacy may, or should, be determined.[244] It was envisaged that there would be practical problems encountered in the assessment of adequacy and a number of possible methodologies were explored. One report prepared for the Commission used the concept of 'functional similarity', noting that Europe should not seek the direct transposition of its own principles and systems of protection into other countries.[245] Instead, adequacy might be determined in the presence of any element in the regulation of a third country providing the relevant requirements, even if this was accomplished in a completely different way. Such an approach permits better respect for local legal structures than the requirement for equivalent protection inherent in complete juristic similarity. The particular technique employed was to reduce the elements of data protection to 'risk factors' – namely, loss of control, reuse, non-proportionality, and inaccuracy – and assess the way in which they were protected. A further report referred to the problem of 'cultural and institutional non-equivalence', pointing out that a judgment of adequacy must appreciate and remain sensitive to

---

239 Ibid, [60].
240 But the potential impact of such a decision does not seem to have been an issue for the CJEU in *Google Spain* discussed above, albeit the Advocate General took a rather more circumspect view.
241 [2001] FSR 20. See discussion above at p 179.
242 See, e.g., *Dow Jones & Co v Gutnick* [2002] HCA 56.
243 For an alternative view of where actual publication takes place, see also *Moberg v 33T LLC* 666 F Supp 2d 415 (2009), discussed online at http://jolt.law.harvard.edu/digest/copyright/moberg-v-33t-llc. In a different context, the Court of Appeal has referred questions to the ECJ about whether publication on the internet takes place where it is uploaded or where it is accessed: *Football Dataco Ltd v Sportradar GmbH* [2011] EWCA Civ 330; now pending Case C-604/10, [2011] OJ C 89/14.
244 But see now Case C-362/14 *Schrems* [70]–[73] discussed further below.
245 Yves Poullet et al, *Preparation of a Methodology for Evaluating the Adequacy of the Level of Protection of Individuals with Regard to the Processing of Personal Data*, 1998, Luxembourg: OOPEC.

important cultural differences.[246] Despite the apparent convergence of data protection rules, privacy is still a variable concept, and different legal traditions still place different emphasis on protection and apportionment of rights. The report also submitted that 'assessment of adequacy will be incomplete to the extent that it cannot assess actual practices and the realities of compliance', and that 'a more empirical analysis of policies and practices, as well as rules, serves both to advance the debate and to anticipate the specific problems that will be encountered in the implementation of the Directive'.

The Article 29 Working Party,[247] which has produced a large number of opinions and recommendations, has considered the concept of 'adequate protection' in the context of Art 25.[248] It suggested that, as noted earlier in this chapter, a 'core' of data protection principles and methods of application could be determined from a consideration of the provisions of both the Data Protection Directive and other international instruments on data protection, and that these could be used to formulate an appropriate minimum requirement for 'adequate protection'. It was pointed out that this was not the same as suggesting that 'adequate' in this context meant complete equivalence and that there would not be insistence on complete conformity with the Directive. However, both the Advocate General and the CJEU in *Schrems*,[249] discussed further below, have now agreed that adequacy basically means that the protection in the third country must be virtually identical to that under Directive 95/46 if it is to be deemed adequate. Article 25(6) gives the Commission powers to determine the 'adequacy' of the protection for personal data in third countries and a number of decisions have been issued under this provision.[250] The majority of these are not controversial but this has not been true of the discussion on transborder data flow between the EU and the USA.

## The 'safe harbour'

In practice, one of the greatest transfers of personal data out of the EU is to organisations based in the US. As discussed earlier the adoption of Directive 95/46/EC led to discussions between the two jurisdictions as to how to create a bridge between the EU legislative approach and the primarily self-regulatory approach in the USA. Building such a bridge, referred to by Leathers as 'an ambitious project',[251] was never likely to be simple and straightforward; in the event, it took two years to build, and involved discussions that were at times both heated and acrimonious. The, at times, turbulent history of the 'Safe Harbor' negotiations can be charted by an examination of successive documents of the Working Party,[252] which exposed the tension between the objectives of the various players involved. This included not only tension between the USA and EU, but also between the various EU bodies involved in the negotiations. Given the commercial power of the USA, there were clearly political motivations driving those who were directly participating in the discussions to work towards a negotiated, albeit inevitably compromised, settlement. On the other hand, the Working Party, with its independent yet only advisory status, showed itself keen to uphold standards, suggesting a potential criticism that it was actively trying to equate the term 'adequate' with the protection afforded under the Directive.

The starting point was the perceived inadequacy from the European perspective of the patchwork of narrowly focused sectoral laws and voluntary self-regulation that characterised the

---

246 Charles Raab et al, *Application of a Methodology Designed to Assess the Adequacy of the Level of Protection of Individuals with Regard to Processing Personal Data*, 1998, Luxembourg: OOPEC.

247 For constitution and remit, see further Arts 29 and 31.

248 Article 29 Working Party, *Transfers of Personal Data to Third Countries*, Opinion 12/98.

249 Case C-362/14 *Maximillian Schrems v Data Protection Commissioner* (CJEU, 6 October 2015).

250 See http://ec.europa.eu/justice/data-protection/international-transfers/adequacy/index_en.htm for the current list.

251 Daniel R Leathers, 'Giving bite to the EU–US data privacy safe harbor: Model solutions for effective enforcement' (2009) 41 Case W Res J Int'l L 193, 194.

252 Six separate Opinions and a Working Document on this topic were published from the beginning of 1999. These documents can be accessed via http://ec.europa.eu/justice/policies/privacy/workinggroup/wpdocs/1999_en.htm; and http://ec.europa.eu/justice/policies/privacy/workinggroup/wpdocs/2000_en.htm

regulatory framework in the USA. In addition, the fact that the USA had ostensibly adopted the OECD Guidelines of 1980 was suggestive that an agreement on minimum requirements ought to be feasible. However, as already mentioned, stormy waters were encountered in the search for the safe harbour and it was some time before a mutually acceptable outcome was reached.

So that the USA would not be seen as a 'data haven', the adopted approach was to attempt to define a 'safe harbor' for personal data – a set of principles to which US companies would sign up on a voluntary basis, but to which they would then be bound. Expanding on the metaphor, it has been suggested that 'the safe harbor is, figuratively, a place where US companies can find shelter from potentially damaging crosswinds caused by different privacy regimes in the US and EU'.[253] The advantage of this approach in principle is that, whilst respecting the different regulatory cultures on both sides of the Atlantic, it is able to provide legal certainty for EU data controllers exporting data to 'safe harbor' participants, it does not impose too onerous an administrative burden, and it provides guidance to US companies and other organisations that wish to meet the 'adequate protection' standard specified in the Directive. An agreement was eventually reached in the summer of 2000 and confirmed by a Commission Decision.[254] The rationale of the Safe Harbor is that organisations wishing to accept personal data from EU or European Economic Area (EEA) countries can agree to comply with the Safe Harbor principles by a self-certification method,[255] and the level of protection offered to that data will then be deemed to be adequate for the purposes of Arts 25 and 26. The Safe Harbor requirements consist of seven principles issued by the US Department of Commerce and contained in Annex 1 to Decision 2000/520, which give provisions relating to notice, choice, onward transfer, security, data integrity, access, and enforcement. As might be expected from the previous discussion, these principles broadly conform to those articulated in the Council of Europe Convention and the OECD Guidelines, although not to the more detailed requirements of the Directive.[256] To begin with, US companies did not rush to join and the uptake was very slow – although membership of the Safe Harbor has now become much more widespread.[257]

The Safe Harbor principles are enforced by the Federal Trade Commission (FTC), but although that body could be said to be in 'an ideal position to create a stronger regulatory program for online privacy',[258] as yet there has been little evidence of significant activity in this respect. Although the FTC has the power to seek several remedies for consumers whose data have been compromised,[259] action by the FTC is the final stage in a multilayer approach to enforcement, which means that many complaints may never reach this final stage whether or not they have been satisfactorily resolved at an earlier stage. Although the FTC seems now to be prepared to take more formal action, this is a relatively recent development and comes some ten years after the inception of the 'Safe Harbor' agreement.[260] It is therefore not surprising that there has been 'growing concern among some data protection authorities in the EU about data transfers under the current Safe Harbour scheme' and criticism of the 'very general formulation of the principles and the high

---

253 See E-Policy News, 'Privacy & data protection: Safe Harbor agreement approved by EU Member States' (2000) June, available online at: http://clinton3.nara.gov/WH/New/Europe-0005/factsheets/data-privacy-accord-with-eu.html; White House, 'Data Privacy Accord with EU (Safe Harbor)', Press release, 31 May 2000, available online at: http://clinton4.nara.gov/WH/New/Europe-0005/factsheets/data-privacy-accord-with-eu.html

254 Decision 2000/520/EC of 26 July 2000 [2000] OJ L215/7.

255 For further details, see www.export.gov/safeharbor/

256 See also M Ewing, 'The perfect storm: The Safe Harbor and the Directive on data protection' (2002) 24 Hous J Int'l L 315, 339.

257 Schriver reports that, after six months, only 12 companies had signed up; this number increased very slowly, so that there were still only 168 organisations in the Safe Harbor in March 2002: RR Schriver, 'You cheated, you lied: The Safe Harbor agreement and its enforcement by the Federal Trade Commission' (2002) 70 Fordham L Rev 2777, 2793. The current list is available online at: https://safeharbor.export.gov/list.aspx, although because there is a requirement to renew notification every twelve months, not all of those on the list are actually currently members.

258 Ibid, 575.

259 See Leathers, above, 207.

260 For examples of FTC action in this area, see FTC, 'FTC approves final settlement order with Dave & Busters; FTC rejects COPPA Safe Harbor application' (2010) 6 August, available online at: www.ftc.gov/opa/2010/06/davecoppa.shtm

reliance on self-certification and self-regulation.'[261] Since 2009 the FTC has brought ten enforce-ment actions relating to the Safe Harbour, including against MySpace, Google and Facebook for deceptive practices,[262] and has reiterated its apparent commitment to enforcement of the safe har-bour principles.[263] Nevertheless, the need for effective and efficient enforcement of the Safe Har-bour principles is underlined by the fact that the current transfer of personal data from the EU to the US is now on a scale which has been described as 'inconceivable'[264] when the Safe Harbour negotiations began, Given the quantity of data involved, ten enforcement actions in five years can surely only represent the tip of the iceberg.

Overall, the 'Safe Harbor' has had a mixed reception – particularly in relation to the perceived lack of redress for individuals and weak enforcement mechanisms. As pointed out by Palekar, the lack of effective enforcement mechanisms in particular resulted in the Safe Harbor principles creat-ing privacy protection 'more in form than function',[265] because the self-regulatory system in the USA provides little scope either for uniform enforcement or for the provision of effective remedies. More recently Kuner has also noted that enforcement and compliance are poor and have not kept pace with technological change, neither has there been any general consensus or oversight. He suggests that this is due to the fact that 'national governance is too parochial, international gov-ernance would not provide for sufficient public involvement, and technological or private sector solutions could lack democratic legitimacy'.[266] He suggests that a better solution might not be to have a separate legal regime but to include risks in transborder data flow in the more general risk assessment approach required of organisations which process data. This debate has now arguably been rendered nugatory by the decision of the CJEU in *Schrems* that the Commission Decision estab-lishing the Safe Harbour is invalid.

## The Snowden revelations and *Schrems*

The Snowden disclosures of files from the US National Security Agency in May 2013 showed wide-scale interception and surveillance of internet communications including personal data and immediately raised issues as to whether the Safe Harbour could provide adequate protection for personal data which had been transferred from Europe. Following these revelations, concern was soon expressed by the German data protection authorities that there was a 'substantial likelihood that the principles in the Commission's decision are being violated'.[267] Two Communications from the Commission in November that year[268] concluded that 'a robust Safe Harbour scheme is in the interests of EU and US citizens and companies' and that better supervision and monitoring of com-pliance with the Safe Harbour principles by self-certified companies was needed by the US authori-ties. Importantly in this context, the Safe Harbour Privacy Principles provide that adherence to these Principles may be limited: (a) to the extent necessary to meet national security, public interest, or law enforcement requirements; (b) by statute, government regulation, or case law that create conflicting obligations or explicit authorizations . . . '.[269] The Commission also concluded that any

---

261 COM(2013) 847 final, above, p 5.
262 See https://www.ftc.gov/sites/default/files/documents/public_statements/privacy-enforcement-safe-harbor-comments-ftc-staff-european-commission-review-u.s.eu-safe-harbor-framework/131112europeancommissionsafeharbor.pdf
263 See, e.g., Julie Brill, 'Data Protection, Privacy and Security: Re-Establishing Trust Between Europe and the United States' Open-ing Panel Remarks, European Institute 29 October 2013, available online at: www.ftc.gov/public-statements/2013/10/data-protection-privacy-security-re-establishing-trust-between-europe
264 COM(2013) 847 final.
265 Nikhil S Palekar, 'Privacy protection: When is "adequate" actually adequate?' (2008) 18 Duke J Comp & Int'l L 549, 550.
266 Christopher Kuner, *Transborder Data Flows and Data Privacy Laws*, 2013, OUP, p 160. Such comments could, of course, be applied equally to many of the other areas discussed in this book.
267 Quoted in COM (2013) 847 final.
268 COM (2013) 846 final Communication from the Commission to the European Parliament and the Council 'Rebuilding Trust in EU-US Data Flows' and COM (2013) 847 final Communication from the Commission to the European Parliament and the Council on the Functioning of the Safe Harbour from the Perspective of EU Citizens and Companies Established in the EU.
269 Commission Decision 2000/520, Annex 1.

such exceptions should only be used to the extent that they are strictly necessary and proportionate. Echoing the general problems that have been encountered in applying data protection rules to processing of personal data on the internet, the Commission observed that 'web companies such as Google, Facebook, Microsoft, Apple, Yahoo have hundreds of millions of clients in Europe and transfer personal data to the US on a scale inconceivable . . . when the Safe Harbour was created'. Although various shortcomings of the Safe Harbour were identified, it was concluded that revoking Decision 2000/520 would have adverse effects and so the Commission would discuss the matter further with the US. These events formed the background to the CJEU decision in *Schrems*. Some of the interception and surveillance was of personal data held by Facebook. Facebook is a US organisation, its European headquarters are in Dublin and all Facebook users in Europe enter an agreement with Facebook Ireland which is then the *de facto* data controller for European Facebook users. Data held by Facebook in Dublin is subject to the Irish Data Protection Act 1988 but personal data was also transferred and held on servers in the US. Schrems was an Austrian user of Facebook. He alleged that the fact of the Snowden disclosures showed that there was no effective data protection regime in the United States and requested the Irish Data Protection Commissioner to exercise his statutory powers to stop the transfer of personal data from Facebook Ireland to its US parent company. As Facebook had signed up to the Safe Harbour Privacy Principles, the Irish Data Protection Commissioner considered that he was obliged to find that the US system provided adequate protection. A judicial review of this decision concluded that whether or not Schrems' own personal data had actually been revealed he was 'entitled to object to a state of affairs where his data are transferred to a jurisdiction which, to all intents and purposes, appears to provide only a limited protection against any interference with that private data by the US security authorities'[270] and that 'the Snowden revelations demonstrate a massive overreach on the part of the security authorities, with an almost studied indifference to the privacy interests of ordinary citizens'.[271]

The court reviewed privacy protection under national and EU law, including that provided by Art 8 of the EU Charter which had not been in existence when the Safe Harbour principles were laid down. Irish law precludes the transfer of personal data outside national territory save where the third country ensures an adequate level of protection for privacy and fundamental rights and freedoms. Any interference with the privacy rights granted by the Irish constitution must be both proportionate and in accordance with the law. Mass and undifferentiated accessing and interception of personal data violates proportionality unless it can be shown that it is targeted, that the surveillance of certain persons or groups of persons is objectively justified in the interests of national security or the suppression of crime and that there are appropriate and verifiable safeguards. Purely on the basis of Irish law, therefore, the court found that there was not adequate protection for the personal data on transfer to the US. However, given that it was also necessary to take into account EU law and specifically the effect of the Safe Harbour principles the Irish High Court decided to refer to the CJEU. The questions essentially asked whether, when it was claimed that a third country did not provide adequate protection for personal data whether a Member State was bound to follow a Commission finding of adequacy or whether it was open to it to conduct its own assessment in the light of developments since the publication of the Commission's Decision.

The CJEU[272] reviewed the relevant legal provisions noting in particular that it could be legitimate for certified companies not to comply with the principles if this was necessary to meet other conflicting legislative obligations to which they were subject by US law, such as those introduced with the objective of combatting terrorism. Directive 95/46 had to be interpreted in the light of other protections of rights and freedoms. Articles 25 and 26 were complementary to the general regime on lawful processing in the rest of the Directive; data could only be transferred to third

---

270  *Schrems v Data Protection Commissioner* [2014] IEHC 310 at [45].
271  *Ibid*, [4]
272  Case C-362/14 *Maximillian Schrems v Data Protection Commissioner* (CJEU, 6 October 2015).

countries if the protection is deemed adequate and Art 25(1) prohibits transfers of personal data to countries without adequate protection. Decision 2000/520, like other Decisions, is binding on those to whom it is addressed and measures of EU institutions are presumed lawful and create legal effects until proved otherwise. Member States therefore cannot adopt measures contrary to the decision. But this does not preclude claimants from bringing actions concerning the protection of their rights and freedoms. Further National Supervisory Authorities (NSAs), such as the Irish Data Protection Commissioner, are given powers by Art 28 to investigate complaints relating to any processing of personal data including transborder data flow. This meant that NSAs can examine 'with complete independence whether the transfer of that data complies with the requirements of the Directive'.[273] If this were not the case, the provisions of the EU Charter would be contravened. Taken together, NSAs are not prevented by Commission decisions regarding the adequacy of protection in third countries from examining a claim as to whether an individual's rights and freedoms with respect to the processing of personal data have been infringed by data transfer. National courts may consider the validity of an EU measure but cannot themselves declare it invalid. Article 25(6) of Directive 95/46 requires the Commission to assess the adequacy of the data protection rules in a third country; however Decision 2000/520 does not actually do this and so fails to comply with Art 25(6) read in the light of the Charter. The CJEU therefore held it was invalid. Article 3 of Decision 2000/520 was also held to be invalid as it effectively denied NSAs the power derived from Art 28. Given that these provisions were effectively inseparable from Arts 2 and 4, the CJEU found the whole Decision to be invalid. The CJEU arrived at this decision without actually making any assessment of the adequacy of the substantive contents of the Safe Harbour privacy principles or the lack of it. It is clear from the judgment though that a third country must maintain a high standard of protection for personal data if it is to be deemed adequate for the purposes of Art 25 which is intended to ensure that a high level of protection is maintained when data is transferred to a third country:

> The word 'adequate' in Article 25(6) of Directive 95/46 admittedly signifies that a third country cannot be required to ensure a level of protection identical to that guaranteed in the EU legal order. However . . . the term 'adequate level of protection' must be understood as requiring the third country to ensure, by reason of its domestic law or its international commitments, a level of protection of fundamental rights and freedoms that is essentially equivalent to that guaranteed within the European Union by virtue of Directive 95/46 read in the light of the Charter . . . [274]

In reality, this is tantamount to suggesting that the Directive should be the *de facto* standard for data protection globally or the 'rule of the road' to use Bennett's phrase.[275] At the time of writing it is too early to predict what will be the next stage in the saga of the Safe Harbour.

## Derogations from Article 25

For whichever country to which data are to be exported, the detailed rules in Art 25 can be ameliorated to a certain extent by derogations provided in Art 26(1), which are based primarily on the data subject's consent, the data subject's interest, or where transfer is from publicly available registers or documents. In addition, Art 26(2) provides for a contractual route to the assurance of adequate protection. This provision resulted in a further Commission Decision on standard contractual clauses

273 *Ibid*, [57].
274 *Ibid*, [73].
275 Above note 235.

for the transfer of personal data to third countries.[276] This decision sets out, in Annex 1, standard clauses for the protection of personal data that will conform to the requirements of the Directive. Further guidance has now been published by the Commission to take into account the expansion of data processing activities; these are also applicable to the increasingly common situation in which there is further outsourcing of processing to sub-processors.[277] Although the new rules leave the initial Decision in place, the new model clauses will apply to new transfers and to modifications of existing data processing operations. In addition, adequate protection may also be ensured by the use of 'binding corporate rules' (BCR). This is a system proposed and developed by the Article 29 Working Party[278] and requires organisations to develop a code of practice, which then has to be approved by every data protection authority in the jurisdictions in which they will be relied upon. Binding corporate rules might seem to be a more appropriate way of dealing with the practical issues that arise in relation to global data transfers and, especially for large multinational organisations, this system may prove to be an attractive alternative route to compliance with data protection rules.[279]

## Exemptions

As already mentioned, the Directive does not extend to personal data processed for purposes that fall outside of the competence of the EU to legislate and, in addition, Art 3(2) also provides that the Directive does not apply to processing of personal data 'by a natural person in the course of a purely personal or household activity'. It remains an open question exactly how far the latter extends. The decision in *Lindqvist* would suggest that if personal data are originally collected for purely personal or domestic use the immunity from the provisions of the Directive will be lost when that data is subsequently placed on the internet. By extension it seems that this ruling could be applied to sharing personal data on social media sites such as Facebook. Article 13 contains a number of other areas that may attract exemption from some or all of the provisions in recognition of the fact that there may be overriding reasons that will mitigate against disclosing what would otherwise be public information, or allowing access to what would otherwise be protected as personal. The list includes, amongst other things, national security, defence, public security, and the prevention, investigation and prosecution of crime. This means that on occasions, the strict data protection rules will be relaxed if necessary to achieve an appropriate balance of interests: it may be that, at times, the public interest favours the data subject, whilst at others it favours the purpose of the processing. But in all cases, exemptions should be applied in a proportionate manner and should only go as far as is required to address the legitimate public interest at issue. As well as the exemptions expressly referred to above, there are other limitations on the application of the Directive. These include the permissible derogations from the obligation to notify. It also appears, from Recital 29 and Art 6(1)(e), that it is expected that, under appropriate conditions, there should be

---

276 Commission Decision 2001/497/EC of 15 June 2001 on standard contractual clauses for the transfer of personal data to third countries: [2001] OJ L181/19.

277 Commission Decision 2010/87 of 5 February 2010 on standard contractual clauses for the transfer of personal data to processors established in third countries: [2010] OJ L39/5; see discussion in Rohan Massey, 'Outsourcing: New standard contractual clauses for the transfer of personal data outside the EU': [2010] 16 CTLR 88.

278 See Article 29 Working Party, *Setting Forth a Co-operation Procedure for Issuing Common Opinions on Adequate Safeguards Resulting From 'Binding Corporate Rules'*, Working Document WP 107; and *Establishing a Model Checklist Application for Approval of Binding Corporate Rules*, Working Document WP 108, both available online at: http://ec.europa.eu/justice/policies/privacy/workinggroup/wpdocs/2005_en.htm. The Working Party has subsequently published details of the operation of binding corporate rules (BCR) in *Setting up a Table with the Elements and Principles to be Found in Binding Corporate Rules*, Working Document WP 153; and *Setting up a Framework for the Structure of Binding Corporate Rules*, Working Document WP 154, both available online at: http://ec.europa.eu/justice/policies/privacy/workinggroup/wpdocs/2008_en.htm

279 For further details of the operation of BCR, see Information Commissioner's Office (ICO), 'Binding Corporate Rules', available online at: https://ico.org.uk/for-organisations/binding-corporate-rules/; see also the discussion in Lingjie Kong, 'Data protection and transborder data flow in the European and global context' (2010) 21 EJIL 441.

an exemption provided for storage of personal data used for historical and statistical purposes, so that it can be kept for a sufficiently long time or perhaps indefinitely.

A significant exemption is also contained in Art 9 regarding the potential tension between the processing of personal data and freedom of expression, particularly in the context of journalism and artistic or literary expression (the so-called 'special purposes'). There is no indication of the scope of the meaning of 'journalism' but the CJEU in Case C-73/07 *Satamedia* has said that in order to give effect to the provisions of the Directive it is necessary to interpret the concept broadly.[280] Further, the provisions apply not just to the media but to 'every person engaged in journalism'[281] and neither was the mode of dissemination a determining factor, suggesting that the lone citizen journalist has the same duty to comply as established media enterprises.[282] Whatever the definition, there appears to be a tacit assumption behind Art 9 that the media should be treated differently, although on what basis is not explicitly stated. Whether or not the media are a special case, it is axiomatic that upholding a right of privacy may at the same time be breaching the right to freedom of expression, and vice versa. Where the protection of one fundamental right may impinge on the enjoyment of another right, the problem of achieving a satisfactory balance is never amenable to an easy solution. The Directive leaves it to Member States to achieve an appropriate balance in this context – a process that needs to be viewed within the wider debate of press freedom and privacy,[283] but which will, inevitably, be influenced by the distinctive cultures and legal traditions of the individual Member States.[284]

The DPA 98 contains a long list of exemptions from some or all of the requirements of the Act. The so-called 'primary exemptions', broadly corresponding to those in the Directive, are to be found in ss 28–36. In addition, Sch 7 contains the 'miscellaneous exemptions', specific to the DPA 1998, which include provisions relating to: preparation of confidential references (referred to above); armed forces; judicial appointments; Crown employment; management forecasts; negotiations; corporate finance; examination scripts and marks; legal professional privilege; and self-incrimination. The fact that a topic is apparently covered by an exemption does not necessarily imply that the exemption is from the requirements of the Act in *toto* and the precise terms of the exemption will need to be studied in each case; some examples are considered below.

## Examples of application of the exemptions

### Crime and national security

The 'crime' exemption in DPA 98, s 29 exempts only from the first data protection principle (except to the extent that it requires compliance with the conditions in Schs 2 and 3) and s 7, the right of subject access. Further, this exemption only applies to the extent that the application of those provisions would be likely to prejudice the prevention or detection of crime. So, in many cases, the full force of the Act will apply, and, in all cases, the police will be required to process personal data in conformity with the majority of the principles; remedies are also available to those whose rights have been compromised.[285] In contrast, the exemption on the grounds of

280 Case C-73/07 *Tietosuojavaltuutettu v Satakunnan Markkinapörssi Oy and Satamedia Oy*, [56]. For further discussion on the scope of the term 'journalism' in the context of freedom of information and data protection see *Sugar v BBC* [2012] UKSC 4. For a consideration of whether the 'special purposes' should be applied to academic publishing, see David Erdos, 'Freedom of expression turned on its head? Academic social research and journalism in the European privacy framework' [2013] PL 52.

281 Ibid, [58].

282 Ibid, [60]. See also *Law Society v Kordowski* [2011] EWHC 3185 (QB) [99].

283 See, e.g., Department of National Heritage, *Review of Press Regulation*, Cm 2135, 1993, London: HMSO; Lord Chancellor's Department, *Infringement of Privacy*, Consultation Paper, 1993, London: Scottish Office; R Wacks, *Privacy and Press Freedom*, 1995, London: Blackstone; House of Commons Culture, Media and Sport Committee, *Press Standards, Privacy and Libel: Second Report of Session 2009–10*, 2010, London: HMSO.

284 See the discussion below on the application of this exemption in the UK.

285 For application of the data protection principles to policing and crime data, see also Cases EA/2007/0096, 98, 99, 108, 127 *Chief Constables of Humberside, Staffordshire, Northumbria, West Midlands and Greater Manchester v Information Commissioner*, available online at: www.informationtribunal.gov.uk/DBFiles/Decision/i200/Chief_Constables_v_IC_final_decision_2007081_web_entry[1].pdf

national security found in s 28 has the potential to exclude from data protection law all processing of personal data that could be construed to come under this head. The ambit of s 28 is very wide: it exempts from compliance with the data protection principles as well as the provisions on the rights of the data subject, notification of processing and enforcement procedures. Given the non-applicability of the data protection principles to personal data processed for national security purposes, there can be no assurance that the processing will be fair or that other guarantees will be provided related, for example, to adequacy and relevancy. Removing the need to comply with the principles allows users to be cavalier with the personal data of others and, accepting that there might be corresponding problems with enforcement and the provision of remedies, it is difficult to see what would be lost by requiring adherence to the principles, especially those relating to fair and lawful processing for the purposes for which the data were collected. However, the precise wording of the exemption does suggest that exemption should not be granted if compliance with the Act is possible without prejudicing national security. In theory, therefore, there is no automatic blanket exemption.

Although s 28 only applies to data processed 'for the purpose of safeguarding national security', s 28(2) provides that a certificate signed by a relevant Minister is all that is required as 'conclusive evidence' of this fact. Sections 28(4) and (5) then give a person 'directly affected' by such a certificate the right to appeal to the Information Tribunal, which may allow the certificate to be quashed if it is satisfied that the Minister did not have reasonable grounds for issuing it. The scope and effect of these provisions was considered in *Norman Baker MP v Secretary of State for the Home Department*.[286] The case arose out of a subject access request by the Member of Parliament (MP) Norman Baker for all of the information held on him by the security services. A certificate, as detailed in s 28(2), had been issued by the Home Secretary, which was both 'detailed and carefully drafted'.[287] Although there were differences between the treatment of personal data in different categories, the overall effect of the certificate could 'fairly be described as a blanket exemption for "any personal data that is processed by the Security Service" in the performance of its statutory functions'.[288] In particular, this meant that there was an exemption from s 7(1)(a) relating to subject access, which supported the use of a 'neither confirm nor deny' policy whereby data subjects would not be informed whether or not data was, in fact, held. Accordingly, Baker was informed that the security services would notify of processing of personal data for staff administration, building security CCTV, and commercial agreements, but that it held no information on him in those categories and that all other processing was exempt from the requirements of the DPA 1998. Baker subsequently appealed against this decision and, in its consideration of the matter, the Tribunal itemised a number of general considerations that applied to the work of the security services and the need for some of its work to remain secret. In particular, there was agreement that it was a necessary policy objective that some of this work should remain secret, even to the extent of not revealing that files existed, and that – in some cases at least – a 'neither confirm nor deny' policy was justifiable.[289] However, the point was made that the blanket exemption absolved the security services from any need to consider individual cases on either their particular merits or whether they actually do pose any threat to national security.

In its decision, the Tribunal, accepting that national security was obviously a legitimate aim, nevertheless considered that proportionality was of central importance – especially where individual rights were at stake and there was discretion in the review process. Having considered the relevant case law – notably, the decisions of the Privy Council in *De Freitas v Permanent Secretary of Ministry*

---

286 See www.informationtribunal.gov.uk/Documents/nsap/baker.pdf
287 *Ibid*, [25].
288 *Ibid*.
289 *Ibid*, [35].

of *Agriculture, Fisheries, Land and Housing*,[290] and the House of Lords in R (*Daly*) v *Secretary of State for the Home Department*[291] – the Tribunal concluded that 'where convention rights are engaged, judicial review principles may require a more intrusive judicial attitude' and that this would always be sensitive to the context of the subject matter of the review. In the context of national security matters in particular, there was no area in which 'judges have traditionally deferred more to the executive view than that of national security; and for good and sufficient reason'.[292] Taking all of these issues into account, the Tribunal concluded, amongst other things, that the blanket exemption was wider than was necessary to protection national security and resulted in individual requests not being considered on their merits, and also that some personal data could be released without endangering national security and that the burden of responding to such requests would not be unduly onerous. The certificate issued under s 28(2) was quashed, but the Tribunal pointed out that this did not inevitably mean that all s 7 requests would need to be responded to, because a new certificate could be issued, provided that it took into account the points made in the decision.[293]

## The 'special purposes'

The other exemption that has received judicial consideration in the UK is that relating to the special purposes contained in DPA 1998, s 32, which implements Art 9 of the Data Protection Directive relating to data protection and freedom of expression. To the extent that data protection is a facet of privacy, there is always going to be a tension between the rights guaranteed under the data protection legislation and the right to freedom of expression, insofar as that might involve discussion of an individual's personal details. Section 32 provides that where processing is for the publication of journalistic, artistic, or literary material and that the data controller reasonably believes that publication is in the public interest, then the processing is exempt from the provisions relating to the rights of the data subject in so far as these might be incompatible with that publication.

The application of this exemption was considered in *Campbell* v *MGN*. The case arose as a result of photographs published by the *Daily Mirror* of the model, Naomi Campbell, arriving at meetings of Narcotics Anonymous. The ensuing litigation was based on breach of confidence, privacy, and also the right in DPA 1998, s 13, to receive compensation for processing likely to cause damage or distress. Whether or not the publication was in the public interest was thus central to the adjudication. In the High Court,[294] Morland J found publication not to be in the public interest. In relation to the claim under the Act, he held that the published information constituted 'sensitive personal information' and that the newspaper had therefore failed to comply with the first data protection principle, because none of the relevant conditions in Schs 2 and 3 had been satisfied; neither could the newspaper rely on the exemption in s 32, because he held that this exemption applied up to – but not on or after – publication.

The Court of Appeal approached the application of the exemption in a different manner. It considered three specific questions: whether the Act applied to the publication of newspapers and other hard copies that had been subject to data processing; whether s 32 applied up to the moment of publication; and whether s 32 applied to the publication itself. In answer to the first question, an examination of the objectives of the legislation and the Directive that it implemented, the competing balance between the rights of privacy and freedom of expression given in the European Convention on Human Rights (ECHR) and referred to in the Recitals to the Directive, and the general scope of both the Directive and the Act resulted in the finding that 'the publication forms part of

290 [1999] 1 AC 69.
291 [2001] 2 WLR 1622.
292 *Baker v Home Secretary*, [69]–[76].
293 *Ibid*, [113]–[116].
294 [2002] EWHC 499.

the processing and falls within the scope of the Act'.[295] An assessment of the relevant provisions did not, however, lead to the conclusion that s 32 only applied pre-publication. Indeed, the reverse was the case, for 'if these provisions apply only up to the moment of publication it is impossible to see what purpose they serve'.[296] In addition:

> it would seem totally illogical to exempt the data controller from the obligation, prior to publication, to comply with provisions which he reasonably believes are incompatible with journalism, but to leave him exposed to a claim for compensation under section 13 the moment that the data have been published.[297]

Having decided unequivocally that s 32 could, in general, be relied on at all stages of the publication process, the Court went on to consider whether or not the provisos in s 32(1) could be relied on in this particular case. In the High Court, Morland J had accepted the editor of the *Daily Mirror*'s evidence regarding why he had decided to publish. This was deemed sufficient to satisfy the public interest test in s 32(2), based on the fact that Campbell was a role model for young people; she had nevertheless been involved in the use of drugs over a period of time despite public denials and had now 'admitted to drug addiction, chosen to seek help for it, and had demonstrated real commitment to tackling her problem by regular attendance at Narcotics Anonymous over a prolonged period'. The reason why it was not possible to comply with the data protection legislation was that Campbell had 'made it plain that there was no consent to the publication'. On this basis, the Court of Appeal decided that the public interest justified the publication of the article without Campbell's consent.[298]

This decision was referred to with favour by the High Court in *Douglas v Hello (No 5)* as making 'an understanding of the Act easier than do the unvarnished provisions of the Act itself'.[299] This much-publicised case concerned the unauthorised publication of the wedding of Michael Douglas and Catherine Zeta-Jones by *Hello!* magazine when exclusive coverage had been granted to a rival publication. In that case, *Hello!* was not able to rely on the s 32 exemption, because there was 'no credible evidence' that the publication of the photographs could be in the public interest. However, the decision in favour of publication in *Campbell* was subsequently reversed by a divided House of Lords, which considered the balance between the rights guaranteed in Arts 8 and 10 of the ECHR, and concluded that:

> . . . looking at the publication as a whole and taking account of all the circumstances the claimant's right pursuant to [A]rticle 8 to respect for her private life outweighed the newspaper's right pursuant to [A]rticle 10 to freedom of expression; and that, accordingly, publication of the additional information and the accompanying photographs constituted an unjustified infringement of the claimant's right to privacy.[300]

However, there was no discussion of the interpretation of the DPA 1998 as such, and it seems reasonable to assume therefore that the judgment of the Court of Appeal with respect to the application of s 32 to all stages of the publication process remains authoritative. In fact, despite the existence of the 'special purposes' exemption, in common with the House of Lords in *Campbell*, s 32 is rarely discussed in cases concerning alleged privacy intrusions. Indeed, Black has remarked, with 'disappointment' in respect of *Ferdinand v MGN Ltd*,[301] that 'there now appears to be a fairly consistent approach in privacy

---

295 [2003] QB 633, [96]–[106].
296 Ibid, [117].
297 Ibid, [119].
298 Ibid, [132].
299 [2003] EMLR 31, [230].
300 [2004] 2 AC 457.
301 [2011] EWHC 2454 (QB).

cases that data protection considerations are sidelined, and treated either as an "insurance policy" in case the privacy action fails or as an unnecessary extra where the privacy action succeeds.'[302]

## The Leveson recommendations

It may be though, that there are changes ahead for the 'special purposes' exemption. The year 2012 saw the publication of the four volumes of the Leveson report on the inquiry into press practices,[303] instigated as a result of allegations of phone hacking by a number of journalists. This report goes into some depth into the application of the DPA 98 and specifically s 32 to the media and makes a significant number of recommendations both for amendments to the Act and also for a more robust approach to the industry from the ICO.[304] With regard to s 32, the Leveson report recommended that it be amended to reduce both its availability and its scope. It should only be available when:

(a) the processing of data is necessary for publication, rather than simply being in fact undertaken with a view to publication;

(b) the data controller reasonably believes that the relevant publication would be or is in the public interest, with no special weighting of the balance between the public interest in freedom of expression and in privacy; and

(c) objectively, that the likely interference with privacy resulting from the processing of the data is outweighed by the public interest in publication.

Further, the scope of the section should be reduced so that it could not, of itself, exempt from the requirements of most of the first data protection principle, the second, fourth, sixth and eighth data protection principles and also the right of subject access, although the importance of preserving the confidentiality of sources was recognised. A number of suggestions and recommendations were directed at the administration of the ICO[305] including a requirement that the ICO 'prepare and issue comprehensive good practice guidelines and advice on appropriate principles and standards to be observed by the press in the processing of personal data.' This was to be done in consultation with the industry and be produced within six months of the publication of the report. In the event the guidelines were two years in preparation and essentially summarise how the current law applies to the process of journalism.[306] At the time of writing it remains to be seen to what extent the legislative and other recommendations will be acted upon. Interestingly, although s 32 implements Art 9 of Directive 95/46/EC, the Leveson recommendations, both the original version and the proposed amended versions, could be construed as in conformity with the Directive which appears to leave the form of any such exemption to individual Member States to 'provide for exemptions or derogations . . . for the processing of personal data carried out solely for journalistic purposes or the purpose of artistic or literary expression only if they are necessary to reconcile the right to privacy with the rules governing freedom of expression.' Arguably, though, the proposed amendments accord more closely with what is *necessary* for this purpose than the existing s 32. Neither is the

---

302 Gillian Black, 'Privacy considered and jurisprudence consolidated: *Ferdinand v MGN Ltd*' (2012) 34 EIPR 64, 68 referring to Eady J in *Quinlon v Peirce* [2009] EWHC 912, [3] and Baroness Hale in *Campbell* [2004] UKHL 22, [130].

303 Leveson *An Inquiry into the culture, practices and ethics of the press* HC 780 (2012), available online at: www.gov.uk/government/publications/leveson-inquiry-report-into-the-culture-practices-and-ethics-of-the-press

304 See ibid, Vol 3 Part H ch 5 for a detailed discussion. The recommendations with respect to data protection are summarised in Part H ch 7. See also GDPR Art 85.

305 See ibid, p 1113.

306 *Data Protection and Journalism: A Guide for the Media*, ICO, September 2014, available online at: http://ico.org.uk/for_the_public/topic_specific_guides/~/media/documents/library/Data_Protection/Detailed_specialist_guides/data-protection-and-journalism-media-guidance.pdf. For general discussion on the ICO's response to the Leveson recommendations see, e.g., Jane Regan and Ruth Larkin, 'ICO Response to the Leveson Report' (2013) 24 Ent L Rev 172 and for further discussion on the media guidelines see, e.g., Howard Johnson, 'Principles and standards to be observed by the media when processing personal data' (2014) 19 Comms L 27.

situation likely to be changed substantially by the adoption of GDPR, Art 85 of which is couched in similar terms.

## Administration and enforcement

The Data Protection Directive refers to a 'supervisory authority', but is not prescriptive about the way in which its requirements should be enforced and administered. Most Member States have set up a specific commission and commissioner for this purpose.[307] In the UK, the role of Data Protection Commissioner established in the 1998 Act, which continued the role of Data Protection Registrar under the 1984 Act, has now been subsumed within the role of Information Commissioner. The functions and duties of this office are detailed in Pt VI of the Act and include: promoting good practice and observance of the Act by data controllers; producing codes of practice; reporting to Parliament; providing assistance to individuals who are bringing proceedings under certain sections of the Act; and participating in international cooperation. The Commissioner also has a role in enforcement and, *inter alia*, is empowered by s 40 to issue enforcement notices where he or she 'is satisfied that a data controller has contravened or is contravening any of the data protection principles'. However, the enforcement of the data protection principles has recently been enhanced by new ss 55A and 55B,[308] which give the Commissioner the power to impose monetary penalties for serious breaches. There are clearly potential conflicts of interest when the roles of policeman, judge, and jury – as well as sometimes lawgiver – are combined in the one office, but the original rationale was the need for best use of resources, together with consistency of approach.[309] This combination of responsibilities at the primary enforcement level is common to a number of other regulatory regimes; however, it is rare to have one individual responsible for such a range of activities. Whatever the conflicts between the varying roles of the Commissioner, the enforcement function is, arguably, of central importance, with other duties, such as dissemination of information, being ancillary to this. This is in contrast with data protection commissioners in some other jurisdictions, whose role can be likened more to that of an ombudsman.[310]

The Information Commissioner also has powers to bring criminal proceedings in relation to the commission of the offences created by the legislation. Most of these are regulatory offences of strict liability, all of which are qualified by a defence of due diligence. Thus, s 21 of the 1998 Act makes it an offence not to register particulars with the Commissioner or to fail to notify any changes in these particulars, and s 47 creates an offence for failure to comply with a notice. Section 55, on the other hand, creates a number of other offences relating to the unauthorised obtaining of personal data. The offences created by this section are all based on obtaining, disclosing, or procuring disclosure 'knowingly or recklessly' – a phrase that also qualified similar offences in s 5(5) of the 1984 Act. In *Data Protection Registrar v Amnesty International (British Section)*,[311] Amnesty was charged under both s 5(2)(b) and (d) of the 1984 Act in relation to two offences of trading in and disclosure of personal information for purposes and to persons not described in the Register. At first instance, Amnesty was acquitted, on the basis that the relevant factor was foreseeability of harm, rather than whether or not the user had been reckless as to the management of the data in a manner incompatible with the registration. Using this test, because the outcome of the action was merely an unsolicited mailing, it was held that Amnesty had not been reckless. On appeal to the divisional court by way of case stated, it was held that the seriousness of the consequences of the breach had been confused with the breach itself. In ruling that the appropriate definition of

---

307 See http://ec.europa.eu/justice/data-protection/article-29/structure/data-protection-authorities/index_en.htm
308 Inserted by the Criminal Justice and Immigration Act 2008 and brought into force on 6 April 2010.
309 William Whitelaw, *Hansard* HC, vol 46, col 556 (11 April 1983).
310 See, e.g., Aldhouse (1991), above.
311 (1994) *The Times*, 23 November, [1995] Crim L R 633.

'recklessness' for s 5 was an objective definition,[312] it had to be shown both that the circumstances were such that the ordinary prudent individual would realise that his or her act was capable of causing the kind of damage that the section was designed to prevent, that the risk could not justifiably be treated as negligible, and that the defendant had either given no thought to the possibility of that risk or had nevertheless continued with the act in question – in other words, the recklessness required was foresight of serious harmful consequences. This decision was criticised on the basis that the need for such foresight 'seems entirely inappropriate in the context' and that to 'insist on the foresee-ability of serious consequences to constitute recklessness would be to make out the more serious form of the offence' – that is, more serious than knowingly disclosing personal data in contravention of the legislation.[313] How the issue of recklessness – or, indeed, inadvertence – will be approached in this context following the subsequent overruling of Caldwell by the House of Lords in R v G remains to be seen.[314] However, the new powers to exact monetary penalties for breach of the data protection principles specifically provide (s 55A(3)) that the Commissioner must be satisfied that either the controller knew, or ought to have known, that there was a risk of a contravention likely to cause substantial damage or distress, and yet failed to take reasonable steps to prevent it. 'Ought to have known' clearly imports an element of objectivity that is consonant with the approach to what are now breaches of s 55 in DPR v Amnesty.

The later case of Information Commissioner v Islington London Borough Council[315] also related to events that occurred when the 1984 Act was in force. Islington Borough Council had been registered in respect of a number of purposes for the use of personal data, but had let some of these registrations lapse without renewal. Reminders had been issued, which had not been acted upon, and personal data had continued to be processed in connection with purposes for which there was no longer a current registration. The Council was charged with the unauthorised use of personal data contrary to s 5 of the Data Protection Act 1984, and, as in the Amnesty case above, it had to be established that the Council had been reckless. One difficulty was that it was the Council that was the 'data controller', but the use of the personal data was by individual employees. In the statement of the case, one of the questions asked was how, in applying the test of recklessness, the 'actions and inferred responsibilities of the Council as a body through its servants or agents past and present' should have been approached, and whether an omission to ensure registration was enough to constitute recklessness. In essence, the decision suggested that, in order to find the requisite recklessness in the use of the data, it was possible to aggregate the acts of employees in using the data with the recklessness of the Council in failing to renew the registration. Although both of the above cases were brought under the 1984 Act, it seems unlikely that the approach under the 1998 Act would be any different.[316]

Section 55(2) of the DPA 1998 provides defences in a number of situations when the person who obtains the data has a reasonable belief that either he or she had a lawful right or duty to disclose the data or that the data controller would have consented to the disclosure.[317] This defence could not be relied on in R v Rooney,[318] in which an employee in a human resources department, who was authorised to access the human resources databases for work purposes, gave information to her

312 Often referred to as Caldwell or Lawrence recklessness: see R v Caldwell [1982] AC 341; R v Lawrence [1982] AC 510.
313 [1995] Crim LR 633, 634.
314 [2003] UKHL 50; see also discussion in Amirthalingam Kumaralingam, 'Caldwell recklessness is dead, long live mens rea's recklessness cases' (2004) 67 MLR 491.
315 [2002] EWHC 1036.
316 See also Jay, above, pp 598 and 606.
317 The Criminal Justice and Immigration Act 2008 introduced a further head of defence (s 55(2)(ca)) specifically covering the situation in which a person reasonably believes that the data is subject to the special purposes exemption, but as yet this provision has not been brought into force. Arguably, a number of such circumstances might, in any case, be covered by the existing s 55(2)(b) and/or (d).
318 [2006] EWCA Crim 1841.

sister about the new address of her ex-partner and the person with whom he was living, who were also employed by the same organisation.

## Data protection and the internet

In *Google Spain*, Advocate General Jääskinen commented that, at the time Directive 95/46/EC was drafted, 'nobody could foresee how profoundly [the internet] would revolutionise the world.'[319] This is true both generally and for the processing of personal data and yet neither the approach nor the substance of the Directive has been amended. This chapter has already contained a number of comments about the difficulties of applying the provisions of the Directive to the internet despite the fact that it is now probably the most common way in which personal data are communicated and transferred. Although the original Directive might be fairly successful at responding to the issues caused by large-scale databanks, it is much less appropriate for application to the more diffuse use of personal data on global computer networks. Such problems have been brought sharply into focus in a number of cases but particularly in the debate surrounding *Google Spain* and the 'right to be forgotten.' The original fears expressed about the potential for the abuse of personal data were based on the existence of separate computer networks a fraction of the size of the internet. Although quantification of such matters cannot be exact, it is not an unreasonable presumption that the magnitude of this risk might increase supralinearly with the size of the network. The growth of the internet and worldwide web, together with the functionality made possible by advances such as Web 2.0, has provided many more opportunities for the capture, retention, and subsequent processing of personal data. How should the original data protection legislation designed to deal with a much more static situation be applied to the dynamic environment of the internet? How could, for example, the restriction on transborder data flows be applied? Can there be any guarantees of appropriate safeguards? How can the originator of the material know in which jurisdiction the resultant data might be used? If the information is made available by an individual, on, for example, a social networking site, does that mean that the processing attracts an exemption on the grounds of personal and domestic use? In short, can the original legislation on data protection cope with this phenomenon? Even if the capability is there, does enforcement and supervision become such a gargantuan task that it becomes impossible, for all practical purposes, to locate and deal with contraventions? As we have already seen, many of these issues have now been debated in the courts with not always harmonious and sometimes even contradictory results.[320]

### Directive 2002/58/EC

Broadly speaking there are two strands of problems. The first is the application of Directive 95/46/EC to the processing of personal data in internet applications as exemplified by *Google Spain*. The second still necessarily involves the processing of personal data but in a much less overt sense. As individuals use the internet and the web, they leave a trail everywhere they go on their journey through cyberspace. There are a variety of ways in which personal data can be harvested as a user surfs the internet and thus compromise privacy, including browsing trails, clickstream data and cookies, 'sniffers' (which can be used to capture data in transit on a network), 'intelligent agents' (which can be used to retrieve required information), and also spyware and adware.[321] Indeed, it

---

319 Case C-131/12 *Google Spain v AEPD and Gonzáles* Opinion of Advocate General, [10].
320 Compare, e.g., the approach of the CJEU in *Bodil Lindqvist* and *Google Spain*.
321 For more details on the technicalities, see, e.g., Brian Keith Groemminger, 'Personal privacy on the internet: Should it be a cyberspace entitlement?' (2003) 36 Ind L Rev 827; PM Schwarz, 'Property, privacy and personal data' (2004) 117 Harv L Rev 2055; and Frederic Debusseré, 'The EU E-Privacy Directive: A monstrous attempt to starve the cookie monster?' (2005) 13 IJLIT 70, 73–6.

has been suggested that this gathering of data is an essential part of the survival of the web in its current form, albeit that it can 'ride roughshod over the whole idea of consent'.[322] Notwithstanding the inevitable difficulties, these more insidious and secretive ways of collecting personal data should not be immune from application of accepted legal rules and principles merely because they take place on global networks. When first adopted, the 1995 Directive could have reasonably been regarded as the 'state of the art' as far as data protection legislation was concerned, but the technology has developed considerably since then and, unsurprisingly, it has not proved a panacea to all privacy concerns raised by the use of computers and, especially, computer networks; neither has it provided a completely suitable privacy protection framework for e-commerce. The difficult issues are not so much the cases in which the data subject is aware that data has been collected and used, or even those in which this information is made available on the internet, since this is, arguably, the type of activity for which data protection law was designed; rather, the problems arising as a consequence of the traceability of operations online will be in situations in which the potential data subject may not be aware that data is being collected and retained.

How should the Directive and implementing legislation be applied in such cases? As already discussed, central to the requirements of Directive 95/46/EC is the need for the consent of the data subject, except in a restricted number of specific situations. A valid consent needs more than an affirmative response: it necessitates the data subject being made aware, at the time that the consent is given, of the intended purposes of processing, likely use of the data, possible disclosures, etc. Even where the collected data can be correlated with a specific identifiable individual, the invisibility of the collection leaves little opportunity for informed consent. An attempt to address some of these issues was made in Directive 2002/58/EC.[323] This Directive supplements the Data Protection Directive and attempts to clarify how the provisions of that Directive can be applied to later developments. Its provisions are intended to be as technology-neutral as possible, so that it is applicable to a wide range of communications technologies. However, this means that commonly recognised terms such as 'cookies' and spyware, for example, are not referred to in the body of the Directive, although it is made clear in the Preamble that these are a specific focus of its provisions.[324] It is possible for cookies, in particular, to be of benefit to the user: they can be used to verify identity and make certain applications more user-friendly. Some cookies automatically delete when the browser is closed ('session' cookies), whiles others are stored permanently. The Directive does not distinguish the two types and although the latter may, in principle, give rise to more privacy concerns, both can be used for legitimate purposes; this is recognised in Recital 24. Article 5, which refers to 'the use of electronic communications networks to store information or to gain access to information stored in the terminal equipment of a subscriber', can clearly be applied to cookies. However, Garrie and Wong point out that this provision may not apply to more general clickstream data that do not involve storage, as it is 'device specific'.[325] Such processing would presumable fall under the general provisions on data protection, although it is perhaps ironic that it was to remedy perceived deficiencies with the general regime that Directive 2002/58/EC was introduced. The original requirement in Art 5(3) was premised on the need for information about the purpose of storing or accessing information, together with an opportunity to refuse such processing but was amended so that, having been provided with clear and comprehensive information about the purposes of processing, a user then had to give his or her consent to the use of cookies. Nevertheless cookies remain legitimate where they are 'for the sole purpose of carrying out the transmission

---

322 Paul Bernal, 'Collaborative consent: Harnessing the strengths of the internet for consent in the online environment' (2010) 24 Int Rev LCT 287.

323 Directive 2002/58/EC of 12 July 2002 concerning the processing of personal data and the protection of privacy in the electronic communications sector: [2002] OJ L201/37. The Directive has been implemented in the UK in the Privacy and Electronic Communications (EC Directive) Regulations 2003, SI 2003/2426.

324 See Recitals 24 and 25.

325 Daniel B Garrie and Rebecca Wong, 'The future of consumer web data: A European/US perspective' (2007) 15 Int Rev LTC 129.

of a communication over an electronic communications network, or as strictly necessary in order for the provider of an information society service explicitly requested by the subscriber or user to provide the service'.

Although Directive 2002/58/EC responded to a number of concerns about the tracking of online users, some problems remain. One particular activity that has caused some difficulties is behavioural advertising, which allows advertisers to build up a profile of users' interests from their online journeys and so allows targeted advertising. The Article 29 Working Party published an extensive opinion in June 2010 about the application of both Directive 95/46/EC and Directive 2002/58/EC to this activity.[326] Although conceding the economic benefits of behavioural advertising, the opinion notes that such operators are bound by Art 5(3) and that, currently, browsers can only provide the capability for consent in limited situations. The opinion concludes that 'the nature of the practice of behavioural advertising, transparency requirements are a key condition for individuals to be able to consent to the collection and processing of their personal data and exercise effective choice', and recommends that, given the duty to comply with the regulatory regime, a dialogue should be initiated between the industry and the Working Party with a view to developing both technical and other means to ensure compliance. However, in the UK at least, the issues raised by this practice had already been brought to a head by the Phorm case. Phorm's system was more detailed than its predecessors, and, as a result, led to a number of protests from consumers and privacy groups – especially when it was revealed that BT had trialled the system without users' consent. The Article 29 Working Party opinion is of general application, but, with regard to the Phorm case, even before this opinion, the European Commission had begun action against the UK for failure to implement Directive 2002/58/EC properly in a way that would respond appropriately to this situation; as a result, the matter is to be referred to the ECJ.[327] The view of the Information Commissioner's Office (ICO) is that behavioural advertising is not 'intrinsically unfair', but that nevertheless website users should have the option to use website services without their personal details being recorded.[328]

The regulation of unsolicited commercial emails (UCE) – more popularly referred to as 'spam' – is also reliant on the provision of information and consent. Unsolicited email communications are dealt with generally by Art 13, which requires that these may only be sent for direct marketing purposes if the recipient has given consent and, further, proscribes any such emails that obscure the identity of the sender.[329] Spam has proved to be something of an intractable problem for internet users all over the globe. It has been described as one of the 'killer applications' that can prejudice security and reliability, and create a climate of distrust.[330] The problems caused by spam have led to legislative activity not only in the EU, but in a number of other jurisdictions. In the USA, the CAN-SPAM Act[331] was passed at the end of 2003. In contrast to the perceived relationship between UCEs, direct marketing, and intrusions into personal privacy evident in Directive 2002/58/EC,[332] this statute arose in response to the perceived threat to the convenience and efficiency of electronic mail, additional costs, etc, together with concerns about, for example, the increasing use of misleading subject headers and the nature of the content of some UCEs. The statute makes it an offence, inter alia, not to give recipients information about how not to receive further communications; it nevertheless puts the onus on the recipient to opt out before any

---

326 Article 29 Working Party, Opinion 2/2010 on online behavioural advertising.
327 European Commission, 'The European Commission refers UK to Court over privacy and personal data protection', Press release, 30 September 2010, available online at: http://europa.eu/rapid/press-release_IP-10-1215_en.htm
328 See Information Commissioner's Office, *Personal Information Online: Code of Practice*, 2010, available online at: https://ico.org.uk/media/for-organisations/documents/1591/personal_information_online_cop.pdf
329 Spam is further regulated by Directive 2002/31 (the E-Commerce Directive), Art 7, implemented in the UK by the Electronic Commerce (EC Directive) Regulations 2002, SI 2002/2013, reg 8.
330 Abu Bakir Munir, 'Unsolicited commercial e-mail: Implementing the EU Directive' (2004) 10 CTLR 105.
331 Controlling the Assault of Non-solicited Pornography and Marketing Act of 2003, 15 USC §§ 7701–7713 and 18 USC § 1037.
332 See, e.g., Recital 40.

cause of action arises. The use of an opt-out rather than an opt-in approach,[333] together with the fact that the enterprise that adheres carefully to the statute can still lawfully send out unsolicited emails until an objection is received, has been severely criticised.[334] It may be that a technological solution to the problem of spam is likely to be both more effective and more appropriate, or that a combination of techniques is required,[335] whether the objective is the protection of privacy or wider concerns about the effects of spam.

The internet, and particularly, the development of user-generated and shared content which began with Web 2.0, has created a completely different environment for personal data – one in which anyone with a smartphone, tablet or laptop could potentially be processing data within the meaning of the Directive.[336] Lack of comprehensive updating has meant that the Directive has failed to 'keep pace with globalization, the relentless improvement and expansion of technological capabilities and the changing ways in which individuals create, share and use personal data.'[337]

Although a new data protection regime is being introduced in the EU, surprisingly perhaps, despite these profound changes since the first Directive was adopted, they were arguably not the main impetus for the proposed reforms.

## The proposal for a General Data Protection Regulation

A Directive is meant to be a harmonising measure such that there is uniformity over the effect which the legal instrument achieves but which leaves it to Member States to choose the precise method and form. In principle this allows Member States to utilise existing provisions which conform to the requirements of the Directive and also take into account the particular legal culture within that jurisdiction. However, in practice there are considerable differences in the way the states had implemented Directive 95/46 which generally give rise to inconsistency and 'hampers the functioning of the internal market and cooperation between public authorities in relation to EU policies, creates confusion and uncertainties for data controllers and provokes a loss of trust for citizens.'[338] In practice this means that both data controllers and data subjects may have to get to grips with 28 different national rules and requirements. Not only does this create unequal protection for data subjects, but it also imposes unnecessary costs and administrative burdens on data controllers.[339]

The resulting lack of harmonisation led the Commission to suggest the use of a General Data Protection Regulation (GDPR), rather than a Directive for the proposed new regulatory framework.[340] As a regulation is directly applicable in all Member States without the need for implementing legislation (TFEU Art 288), the intention was that it would 'reduce legal fragmentation, provide greater legal certainty, improve the protection of individuals and contribute to the free flow of personal data within the Union.' Blume suggests that use of a regulation emphasises that data protection law is EU law and so reduces the importance of the Member States and presumably

333 Compare Directive 2002/58, Art 13, and also the Australian Spam Act 2003, which contains a much clearer prohibition on UCEs together with strict rules concerning those commercial emails that are permitted.

334 See, e.g., JD Sullivan and MB De Leeuw, 'Spam after CAN-SPAM: How inconsistent thinking has made a hash out of unsolicited commercial email policy' (2004) 20 CHTLJ 887; EA Alongi, 'Has the US canned spam?' (2004) 46 Ariz L Rev 263.

335 See, e.g., Sullivan and De Leeuw, above, 931; cf A Mossoff, 'Spam: Oy, what a nuisance' (2004) 19 Berkeley Tech LJ 625.

336 Cf Case C-131/12 *Google Spain v AEPD and González*, Opinion of Advocate General, [10], [27], [29] and [81].

337 Ira S Rubinstein, 'Big Data: The end of privacy or a new beginning' (2013) 3 IDPL 74.

338 Luiz Costa and Yves Poullet, 'Privacy and the regulation of 2012' (2012) 28 CLSR 254.

339 Viviane Reding, 'The European data protection framework for the 21st century' (2012) 2 IDPL 119, 121.

340 Regulation (EU) 2016/679 of the European Parliament and of the Council of 27 April 2016 on the protection of natural persons with regard to the processing of personal data and on the free movement of such data and repealing Directive 95/46/EC [2016] OJ L119/1. It was accompanied by Directive (EU) 2016/680 of the European Parliament and of the Council on the protection of natural persons with regard to the processing of personal data by competent authorities for the purposes of prevention, detection, investigation or prosecution of criminal offences or the execution of criminal penalties, and the free movement of such data [2016] OJ L119/89. Further discussion of this proposal is outside the scope of this chapter but see e.g. Paul de Hert and Vagelis Papakonstantinou 'The new Police and Criminal Justice Data Protection Directive: a first analysis' (2016) 7 NJECL 7.

therefore any societal and cultural differences relating to privacy.[341] On the other hand, however, the nature of an EU regulation means that the current data protection provisions in the individual Member States will cease to have effect and it may 'take a great effort to explain to citizens and probably also national parliaments that data protection has been improved even though there is no longer a data protection act.'[342]

The Regulation, adopted on 24 May 2016, is a long and complex measure containing 173 recitals and 99 articles and it is not possible to analyse its provisions in any detail in the limited space available here. But amongst other things it is intended to clarify the definition and conditions relating to consent,[343] enhance the data breach requirements,[344] introduce a 'right to be forgotten',[345] provide a right of access and data portability,[346] enhance administrative and judicial remedies,[347] enhance the responsibilities of data controllers and data processors,[348] facilitate international transfers[349] and provide for independent and consistent enforcement.[350] Although no domestic legislation is needed (or indeed generally allowed) to transpose a regulation, there are some areas where Member States will still need to create their own rules. These include the difficult area of balancing data protection with the right of freedom of expression[351] and also the regulation of data processing in the employment context.[352] Whilst this might be understandable as these are topics where individual legal, political and social cultures have particular relevance, it does open up the spectre of lack of harmonisation which the Regulation was designed to remove. In addition, the Article 29 Working Party will be abolished and replaced with a European Data Protection Board with authority with respect to more than one Member State.[353]

Although Reding is of the view that the new Regulation will 'strengthen individual rights by improving individuals' ability to control their data and by giving data subjects efficient and operational means to make sure they are fully informed about what happens to their personal data and to enable them to exercise their rights more effectively',[354] others are rather more circumspect. Although De Hert and Papakonstantinou generally welcome the updated provisions they are concerned that there will still be inconsistencies in applying the provisions uniformly in 28 Member States with different legal systems.[355] In an instrument which is intended to provide benefits for citizens it is particularly important that the legal rules should be accessible. Blume has particular concerns that the measure is both more complex and more opaque than its predecessor which also suffered from these problems. It is 'in all respects an extremely complicated legal text and it seems obvious that it has not been the ambition to keep it simple.'[356] Such complexity is of course much more of a problem in a Regulation than a Directive since there is no possibility of reducing the opacity of the provisions in the implementing legislation. It does appear that the proposed Regulation is still based on essentially the same premise as the original and essentially gives us more of the same: a very detailed and complex set of rules which does not take a more holistic view of the

---

341  Peter Blume, 'Will it be a better world? The proposed EU Data Protection Regulation' (2012) 2 IDPL 130, 131.
342  Ibid, 134.
343  Art 4(11) and Art 7.
344  Arts 33 and 34.
345  Art 17. Possibly in response to the semantic quibbles following the *Google Spain* judgment discussed above at p 362 the European Parliament has suggested that this should just be called the right of erasure. See http://www.europarl.europa.eu/sides/getDoc.do?type=TA&reference=P7-TA-2014-0212&format=XML&language=EN
346  Art 20.
347  Arts 77–85.
348  See Arts 5, 11, 12, 14, 17 and Chapter IV (Arts 22–34).
349  Chapter V.
350  Chapter VI.
351  Art 85.
352  Art 88.
353  Arts 68–76.
354  Above, p 124.
355  Paul de Hert and Vagelis Papakonstantinou, 'The proposed data protection Regulation replacing Directive 95/46/EC: a sound system for the protection of individuals' (2012) 28 CLSR 130, 142.
356  Blume, above, p. 134.

effect on individuals and their personal data of the technological changes which have taken place since Directive 95/46 was drafted. As summed up by Koops, 'the direction of the data protection reform is fundamentally flawed. It focuses too narrowly on solving too many ICT-related challenges to legal protection within a single general framework of data protection law, and by doing so diverges from the reality of the 21st century data-processing practices.'[357] This is particularly the case in relation the application of data protection rules to processing of 'big data' discussed further below. At the time of writing the proposal is still under debate and consideration and the time scale for adoption does not appear to be set in stone so it remains to be seen whether the final version resolves any of these tricky issues.

## Case study: 'Big data'

It should be clear by now that the provisions of the Data Protection Directive and the Data Protection Act were not really drafted with the internet in mind. But it is not just the method of transfer of data which may cause problems in the application of the data protection rules. In the 21st century there is both a much greater volume and variety of data which is being transferred at greater and greater velocities. Laney is widely attributed as first identifying the three characteristics, volume, variety and velocity, frequently seen as key attributes of what is referred to as 'big data'.[358] The term itself seems to have gradually become an easy label to attach to the rapid growth of data collection, storage and transference consequent on increased processing power and the multiplicity of connected devices in the so-called 'internet of things'. Indeed, big is perhaps something of an underestimate as it has been suggested that the annual data traffic will pass the zettabyte[359] threshold by the end of 2016. Rubinstein sets out the issues as 'Big Data refers to novel ways in which organizations including government and businesses, combine diverse digital datasets and then use statistics and other data mining techniques to extract from them both hidden information and surprising correlations.'[360]

In whatever way it is described, we are clearly now living in a world of big data. What consequences does that have for informational privacy and data protection? Although the precise definition of this term may vary depending on the context in which it is used, as far as informational privacy is concerned, the issues are not so much what it can do, although this is important in assessing the proportionality of any measures taken which might fetter its use, but how it can be misused. As intimated above, the analysis of big data can deliver unprecedented and unexpected results in a diversity of areas such as medicine, marketing, monitoring and surveillance to name just a few.[361] This not only potentially creates a large and valuable market in personal data but the 'newly discovered information is not only unintuitive and unpredictable, but also results from a fairly opaque process.'[362] The extent to which the results from big data analysis produce a general societal benefit may range from the definite to the debatable, but the sheer quantity of personal data collected and processed has the propensity to be both more invasive and more insidious as it is frequently occurring without any knowledge or awareness on the part of the data subject. The data is typically loosely structured and may be both incomplete and inaccessible. This means that

---

357 Bert-Jaap Koops, 'The trouble with European data protection law' (2014) 4 IDPL 250.
358 Douglas Laney, '3D Data Management: Controlling Volume, Velocity and Variety', available online at: http://blogs.gartner.com/doug-laney/deja-vvvue-others-claiming-gartners-volume-velocity-variety-construct-for-big-data/. For an interesting look at the origins of the term 'big data' see http://bits.blogs.nytimes.com/2013/02/01/the-origins-of-big-data-an-etymological-detective-story/?_php=true&_type=blogs&_r=0
359 $10^{21}$ bytes.
360 Ira S Rubinstein, 'Big Data: The end of privacy or a new beginning' (2013) 3 IDPL 74.
361 For basic practical information about big data see, e.g., www.sas.com/en_us/insights/big-data/what-is-big-data.html. For more information about what big data can do see, e.g., Jonathan Shaw, 'Why "big data" is a big deal' Harvard Magazine (March/April 2014), 30–35 and 74–75, available online at http://harvardmagazine.com/2014/03/why-big-data-is-a-big-deal
362 Rubinstein, above, p 76.

there is little opportunity for the individual to assess the quantity and type of personal data available or determine whether it is accurate or how it might be used. Whereas in the past, the problem might have been one of unexpected data matching, the current issue is data fusion from a variety of sources and devices. All of this 'raises crucial questions about whether our legal, ethical and social norms are sufficient to protect privacy and other values in a big data world.'[363] The challenge, as ever, is to be able to utilise the benefits whilst at the same time minimising any adverse properties.

## The privacy challenges of big data

The internet of things, together with the development of wearable or portable technology which is always on, creates a trend towards constant and ubiquitous collection of personal data which may reveal identity, location and other aspects of a person's private life. Given the ever increasing value of the data market, it is not surprising that organisations are reluctant to destroy data which may turn out to be useful either by itself or combined with other data, notwithstanding rules on fair collection or purpose limitation. This propensity is underlined by the fact that 'collective investment in the capability to fuse data is many times greater than investment in technologies that will enhance privacy'.[364] Put simply, data has value on the market, privacy doesn't. It has further been suggested by PCAST[365] that the 'positive benefits of technology are (or can be) greater than any new harms.'[366] They further conclude that strict adherence to traditional data protection principles could negate the potential benefits of big data analysis, and that 'in particular notice and consent is defeated by exactly the positive benefits that big data enables: new, non-obvious, unexpectedly powerful uses of data'.[367] While PCAST is firm about the perceived 'positive benefits' outweighing any privacy problems it is clear that not everyone will view the balancing exercise in this way. The value placed on privacy is mediated by both cultural and social perspectives as well as by the subjective view of the data subject and, perhaps depending on the precise uses of big data in question, many will question whether the benefits are indeed positive or outweigh either the perceived or actual threat to individual privacy. In particular the view expressed by PCAST in the US may not be so well accepted in the EU where cultural and legal expectations of privacy protection are generally very different and the data protection legislative framework is far more extensive than that in the US. Whereas the balance in practice may be a very nuanced one, views on both sides can be extremely polarised:

> It seems that for privacy hawks, no benefit, no matter how compelling, is large enough to offset privacy costs, while for data enthusiasts, privacy risks are no more than an afterthought in the pursuit of complete information.[368]

## Big data and the data protection principles

How can the existing data protection principles be applied to 'big data' analytics? And will any problems be resolved by the new provisions of the GDPR? As envisaged in the Directive 95/46/EC, and there is apparently little change in this respect in the GDPR, data collection and use is a simple relationship between data controller and data subject. The situation becomes far more complicated as large datasets are combined and further analysed. Cate and Mayer-Schönberger report on the

---

363 *Big Data: Seizing Opportunities, Preserving Values*, Executive Office of the President, May 2014 p 3 available online at: www.whitehouse.gov/sites/default/files/docs/big_data_privacy_report_may_1_2014.pdf

364 *Ibid*, p 54.

365 US President's Council of Advisors on Science and Technology.

366 PCAST Report to the President: *Big Data and Privacy: A Technological Perspective* (May 2014), p 7 available online at: www.whitehouse.gov/sites/default/files/microsites/ostp/PCAST/pcast_big_data_and_privacy_-_may_2014.pdf

367 *Ibid*, p 38.

368 Jules Polnetsky and Omer Tene, 'Privacy and Big Data: Making Ends Meet' (2013) 66 Stan L Rev Online 25, available online at: www.stanfordlawreview.org/online/privacy-and-big-data/privacy-and-big-data

global privacy summit which considered the application of some of the common data protection principles to the use of big data concluding that in a world of big data there was 'an urgent need to adjust information privacy regulations and the principles that underlie them to meet the needs of a new era' and that there was a need to 'revisit the balance between privacy and information flows in a world of not only vastly more data but also more rapidly changing, valuable uses of that data.'[369]

As demonstrated above, although consent is merely one method espoused by the Directive for legitimising processing, it seems to have become or to have been perceived to be the dominant method, especially for personal data on the internet. Intuitively informed consent seems to make sense as a method of ensuring individuals have control over their personal data. A concept of 'informed' consent may have limitations in the context of big data as may limiting the use to that envisaged at the time of collection. Many useful results obtained from analysis of big data have been unexpected such that it would have been impossible to have given notice to the data subject at the time of collection since that purpose was not yet in existence. When data is processed in this way, obtaining the consent required may prove impracticable and, in any case, could make the research too costly. In any case, when data subjects have no knowledge of the data use then they cannot provide a valid consent. In addition, consent may not have been sought if the data was not 'personal' (perhaps because it had been anonymised for instance), but big data analytics can potentially lead to the reidentification of individuals from non-personal data. Whether consent could or should be incorporated into this process may depend on views as to the likely social benefits of the outcome of the processing which may well be unknown at that stage. It also raises questions about the extent to which anonymisation can remain a useful privacy tool.

By definition the amount of data involved in big data processing is large – it is its very magnitude which enables the results and predictions based on its analysis. In this context is it realistic to restrict the collection of data to the minimum, namely only that which is relevant, etc.? If big data processing is capable of blurring the boundaries between non-personal and personal data then this distinction which is at the heart of current data protection provisions may need rethinking. How this would or could be achieved and on what basis is a moot point since 'applying the collection limitation principle to all data seems unworkably broad but to limit it to data already recognized as "personal" seems too narrow.'[370] This is not to say that there should be the freedom to collect unlimited amounts of data, just that it may need a different type of regulatory framework to ensure the appropriate protection for the data subject.

Kerr and Earle[371] point out that much of the discussion of the impact of big data on privacy has centred on the details of the data itself whereas an equal threat comes from the ability of big data analysis to make preemptive predictions which can be used to influence decision making in ways that make 'individuals unable to observe, understand, participate in, or respond to information gathered or assumptions made about them'.[372] How satisfactorily can the existing legal regimes be applied in this context? Polnetsky and Tene suggest that 'finding the right balance between privacy risks and big data rewards may very well be the biggest public policy challenge of our time.'[373] 'It requires deciding whether efforts to cure fatal disease or eviscerate terrorism are worth subjecting human individuality to omniscient surveillance and algorithmic decision making.'[374]

The big question is should we tear up data protection law in the face of big data or should we attempt to apply it? Without doubt there are important benefits which have accrued as a result of

369 Fred H Cate and Viktor Mayer-Schönberger, 'Notice and Consent in a world of big data' (2013) 3 IDPL 67, 73.
370 Ibid, p 71. See also Ira S Rubinstein, 'Big data: The end of privacy or a new beginning?' (2013) 3 IDPL 74.
371 Ian Kerr and Jessica Earle, 'Prediction, Preemption, Presumption: How big picture threatens big picture privacy' (2013) 66 Stan L Rev Online 65.
372 Ibid, p 71.
373 Jules Polonetsky and Omer Tene, 'Privacy and big data: Making ends meet' (2013) 66 Stan L Rev Online 25, available online at: www.stanfordlawreview.org/online/privacy-and-big-data/privacy-and-big-data
374 Ibid, p 26

big data analytics but these should surely not be realised without some regard for the privacy of those whose data is processed. There have been various suggestions as to how the accountability of those who conduct big data analytics can be ensured if both the existing regulatory regime and the proposed reforms prove unfit for purpose. The use of internal review boards within organisations have been suggested as 'a proactive response to concerns regarding data misuse' which would consider the balance between the likely benefits of the big data analysis and the privacy risks to the individual.[375] It seems unlikely that this would be successful without an extensive education programme on the issues to be taken into account being launched in tandem or, perhaps, to the appointment of privacy or data protection officers, something which is envisaged in the GDPR. Other proposals respond to the issues by suggesting the development of more complex and innovative business models.[376]

As has been evident in the earlier discussion in this chapter, data protection law has not kept pace with technological changes in modes of communication and it seems unlikely that it will do any better in responding to the challenges of big data which can produce decisions about individuals which challenge both their personal autonomy and their capacity for informational self-determination.

## Further reading

Rosemary Jay Data Protection Law and Practice 4th ed. Sweet and Maxwell (2014)
Viktor Mayer-Schonberger Delete: the Virtue of Forgetting in the Digital Age Princeton University Press (2011)
Christopher Kuner Transborder Data Flows and Data Privacy Laws Oxford University Press (2013)
Kenneth Cukier and Viktor Mayer-Schönberger Big Data: A Revolution that will transform how we live, work and think John Murray (2013)
Serge Gutwirth, Ronald E. Leenes, Paul De Hert and Yves Poullet (eds) European Data Protection: Coming of Age Springer (2013)
Information Commissioner's Office Big Data and Data Protection (2014) available online at https://ico. org.uk/media/for-organisations/documents/1541/big-data-and-data-protection.pdf

---

375 Christopher Wolf, 'Technological advances and privacy challenges' (2014) Aspatore 1. See also Polonetsky and Tene, above, p 95.
376 See, e.g., Rubinstein, above.

# Chapter 10

# Surveillance, data retention, and encryption

## Chapter contents

# Introduction

In contrast to the laws relating to the protection of privacy and personal data are those laws that justify, formalise, and regulate state and private party actions likely to impact upon individuals' normal expectations of privacy, in the pursuit of other legitimate social, political, and economic goals. These include laws that influence the use of information technologies, such as telecommunications and the internet, by:

- facilitating the tracing of links between individuals – for example, permitting collection of 'traffic data' identifying when and with whom technology users communicate;
- facilitating the collection of information about the detail of individuals' interactions – for example, permitting interception of the content of their communications; or
- preventing the effective employment of surveillance countermeasures – for example, forbidding, or limiting the utility of, the use of encryption technologies.

In the digital information environment, the primary aim of UK state surveillance has been to ensure that law enforcement and national security agencies have suitable access and powers to maintain effective investigatory practices across the diverse range of public communications options. A secondary aim, motivated largely by external pressures – notably European Court of Human Rights (ECtHR) rulings – has been to place both access and investigatory powers within a legal framework. Such a framework, in theory, allows oversight of their lawful use, meaningful penalties for their abuse, and greater public transparency about their operation, without unduly compromising their effectiveness. While, on paper, considerable advances have been made toward this second aim, achieving and maintaining a proportionate balance between efficiency and legitimacy in an area in which technology is in a state of constant flux is far from a simple task. As a result, both legislators and judiciary have struggled to keep pace with developments.

A complicating factor is that powers granted to state agencies to access and collect digital information generated by the public often produce, or permit the production of, datasets relevant to commercial organisations. For example, internet traffic data can be valuable to content providers wishing to monitor potential infringements of their intellectual property, or to advertising companies seeking to deploy 'behavioural advertising'.[1] This can lead to pressure from commercial organisations for greater access to such datasets, or for the wider grant of access and investigatory powers to the private sector. Here, too, there is a delicate balancing act for legislature and judiciary to consider – that is, the extent to which the business interests of commercial organisations can be accommodated, without undue impact upon either the public interest, or the perceived legitimacy of state access and investigatory powers. Thus the requirement of a legal framework for the legitimate exercise of access and investigatory powers by state agencies is mirrored by the need for a similar framework for private entities – a need that, in the UK, is again being addressed mainly following adverse rulings from the ECtHR.

As the UK regulatory framework for surveillance has developed in a piecemeal fashion, its legislative foundation is currently spread across a range of Acts, including:

- Regulation of Investigatory Powers Act 2000 (RIPA 2000);
- Regulation of Investigatory Powers (Scotland) Act 2000 (RIPSA 2000);
- Data Retention and Investigatory Powers Act 2014 (DRIPA 2014);
- Intelligence Services Act 1994 (ISA 1994);
- Part III Police Act 1997 (PA 1997);

---

1 For example, behavioural advertising uses information about an individual's web-browsing behaviour, such as pages that he or she has visited, or searches that he or she has made, to determine which advertisements he or she is offered.

- Data Protection Act 1998 (DPA 1998);
- Protection of Freedoms Act 2012 (PoFA 2012);
- Human Rights Act 1998 (HRA).

In addition numerous regulatory/oversight bodies have been created, the primary bodies being:

- Information Commissioner's Office;
- Investigatory Powers Tribunal;
- Surveillance Camera Commissioner;
- Office of the Surveillance Commissioner;
- Interception of Communications Commissioner;
- Intelligence Services Commissioner;
- Commissioner for the Retention and Use of Biometric Material.

These bodies have varying roles and responsibilities in overseeing surveillance-related legislation. The complexity of the situation is such that the bodies themselves have compiled a publicly accessible document to outline their particular responsibilities, and to ensure that where overlaps exist between their roles/powers, those responsibilities are clear.[2]

The key pieces of legislation considered in this chapter are the Regulation of Investigatory Powers Act 2000 (RIPA 2000) and related statutory instruments, and the Data Retention and Investigatory Powers Act 2014 (DRIPA 2014). The chapter will examine the three key elements of the current regime for surveilling the digital environment:

- the legal framework for the interception of content in transit between parties – that is, the interception of communications;
- the requirement upon public telecommunications providers, including internet service providers (ISPs), to retain communications traffic data – that is, data retention; and
- the requirements placed on users of encryption technologies to make their communications accessible to the authorities upon demand – that is, decryption powers.[3]

It will also examine possible future developments, including the extent to which public concerns over the use of information technologies to surveil consumers may require further consideration of the regulatory framework with regard to the private sector.

# The Regulation of Investigatory Powers Act 2000

In 1997 the ECtHR's decision in the *Halford* case[4] identified key omissions in the UK's statutory regime for interceptions as contained in the Interception of Communications Act 1985 (IOCA 1985). Chief amongst those omissions was the fact that while the IOCA regime provided a regime for the lawful interception of communications on public telecommunications networks, it was silent on interception of communications on private telecommunications networks. This meant that an individual who, absent a warning about monitoring, had a legitimate expectation of privacy

---

2 *Surveillance Road Map: A shared approach to the regulation of surveillance in the United Kingdom*, Version 3.2, 7 August 2014, available online at: ico. org.uk/media/for-organisations/documents/1042035/surveillance-road-map.pdf

3 This chapter does not consider broader issues of electronic surveillance, such as bugging. For a broader survey, see Laura K Donohue, *The Cost of Counterterrorism: Power, Politics, and Liberty*, 2008, Cambridge: Cambridge University Press; Simon McKay, *Covert Policing: Law and Practice*, 2nd edn, 2015, Oxford: Oxford University Press.

4 *Halford v United Kingdom* (1997) 24 EHRR 523.

(under Art 8 of the ECHR) in calls made on a private telecommunications network had no redress (under Art 13 of the ECHR) in the event that their telephone calls were intercepted.

The *Halford* case thus required the UK government to reconsider the statutory regime for interceptions under ICOA 1985. Even absent the *Halford* decision, the IOCA regime was increasingly unfit for purpose by the late 1990s, because both the economic and technical environments had changed so significantly since 1985. The government thus wanted to adopt wide-ranging new legislation. This would not only address the issue of interception of communications on private telecommunications, but also bring all communications within a statutory interception framework, alongside other forms of surveillance:

> The intention is to provide a single legal framework which deals with all interception of communications in the United Kingdom, regardless of the means of communication, how it is licensed or at which point on the route of the communication it is intercepted . . .
>
> The Government believes that it should not make any difference how a communication is sent, whether by a public or non-public telecommunications or mail system, by wireless telegraphy or any other communication system. Nor should the form of the communication make any difference; all interception which would breach Article 8 rights, whether by telephone, fax, e-mail or letter, should all be treated the same way in law. A single authorising framework for all forms of lawful interception of communications will mean that each application will follow the same laid down procedure and will be judged against a single set of criteria.[5]

The new legislation would be part of the ongoing strategy for bringing state surveillance powers, and other elements of national security and law enforcement, onto a more harmonised statutory footing, alongside statutes such as the Security Service Act 1989, Intelligence Services Act 1994, Security Service Act 1996, Criminal Investigations and Procedure Act 1996 and Police Act 1997.

The result of the government's consultation and deliberations post-*Halford* was the Regulation of Investigatory Powers Act 2000 (RIPA 2000). This repealed the Interception of Communications Act 1985, but still maintained much of the pre-existing public telecommunications interception regime, including the oversight mechanisms. The Act itself is split into seven parts covering the following:

- 'Communications';
- 'Interception';
- 'Acquisition and disclosure of communications data';
- 'Surveillance and covert human intelligence sources';
- 'Investigation of electronic data protected by encryption etc';
- 'Scrutiny etc of investigatory powers and of the functions of the intelligence services'; and
- 'Miscellaneous and supplemental'.

The remainder of this section will consider the interception provisions: the following two sections will consider acquisition and disclosure of communications data, and the investigation of electronic data protected by encryption. Surveillance and covert human intelligence sources are outside the scope of this chapter.

## Interception: basic principles

Under RIPA 2000, it is a criminal offence, punishable by up to two years' imprisonment, for a person 'without lawful authority' to knowingly intercept communications by post, or through

---

5 Home Office, Interception of Communications in the United Kingdom, paras 4.1 and 4.5.

a public telecommunications system.[6] It is also a criminal offence, punishable by up to two years' imprisonment, for a person without the express or implied consent of a person having the right to control the operation or the use of that system, and 'without lawful authority', to intercept communications through a private telecommunications system.[7]

Where communications are intercepted on a private telecommunications system, with the express or implied consent of a person having the right to control the operation or the use of that system, but without 'lawful authority', parties to the communication may bring a civil action. For example, if an employee believes that his or her employer has unlawfully intercepted their telephone conversation with a third party, either the employee or the third party may sue the employer.[8] The individual authorising, or carrying out, the interception in such circumstances would not, however, be guilty of a criminal offence.[9]

Interception takes place with 'lawful authority' where:

- all parties to the communication have consented to it[10]
- one party has consented to it, and the interception is authorised under Pt II of the RIPA 2000 as surveillance, rather than an interception;[11]
- it is necessary for the purposes of providing the telecommunications service, and carried out by the provider of that service, or on its behalf;[12]
- it is permitted under s 48 of the Wireless Telegraphy Act 2006;[13]
- it is permitted under an international mutual assistance agreement;[14]
- it is permitted under regulations made by the Secretary of State to permit certain kinds of interception in the course of lawful business practice;[15]
- it is permitted under prison rules, in hospital premises in which high security psychiatric services are provided, and in state hospitals in Scotland;[16]
- it is carried out under any statutory power that permits the obtaining of information or of taking possession of any document, or other property;[17] and
- an interception warrant has been issued by the Secretary of State.[18]

RIPA 2000, as drafted, did not address the issue of interceptions that were made unlawfully, but where there was no criminal intent. This became relevant in 2007–2008 when major internet service providers in the UK, such as BT, TalkTalk, and Virgin Media, were considered adopting, via a third-party service supplier, a technique called 'deep-packet inspection' to inspect and sort their users' data as it travelled through their systems, and to use the data gathered (web pages visited, etc) to send targeted advertising based on their users' web activity.

The suppliers of the ISP-based behavioural targeting technology, notably a company called Phorm, claimed that their systems did not allow them to know exactly where an individually identifiable user had been or what they had done. As a result, it was claimed that such systems did not

---

6 RIPA 2000, s 1(1).
7 Ibid, s 1(2).
8 Ibid, s 1(3).
9 Ibid, s 1(6).
10 Ibid, s 3(1).
11 Ibid, s 3(2).
12 Ibid, s 3(3).
13 As per Wireless Telegraphy Act 2006, Sch 7, paras 21–24.
14 RIPA 2000, s 4(1).
15 Ibid, s 4(2).
16 Ibid, s 4(3)–(6).
17 Ibid, s 1(5)(c); see, e.g., s 9 and Sch 1 to the Police and Criminal Evidence Act 1984 (PACE); see R (on the application of NTL Group Ltd) v Ipswich Crown Court [2002] EWHC 1585.
18 RIPA 2000, s 1(5)(b).

breach data privacy laws such as the DPA 1998.[19] Campaigners against the use of the technology argued instead that such deep-packet inspection would be caught by the interception provisions of RIPA 2000.[20] However, in 2008, the City of London police declined to act on complaints about the Phorm service under RIPA 2000 because it was unclear that a crime had been committed. Later, in 2009, the Home Office released a document (the precise legal status of which is unclear) in response to a request from Phorm, which suggested that 'targeted online advertising' would not be considered to be performing an illegal interception under RIPA 2000.[21]

## Interception under warrant

The Secretary of State may issue an interception warrant for the interception and disclosure of communications where the scope of the warrant is proportionate to the aim to be achieved, the information required could not reasonably be obtained by other means, and the purpose of obtaining the information is necessary to:

- protect the interests of national security; or
- prevent or detect serious crime in the UK, or in the context of any international mutual assistance agreement; or
- safeguard the economic well-being of the UK.[22]

Interception warrants may only be applied for by, or on behalf of, specific senior members of the intelligence services, police forces, and Commissioners for HM Revenue and Customs (HMRC); they may only be issued by the Secretary of State, except in limited circumstances.[23]

Warrants essentially fall into two categories: warrants for interception of domestic communications; and warrants for interception of telecommunications with an element external to the UK. Internal warrants (or 'targeted' warrants) are required to be limited in scope, in as much as they must refer to one person, or specific premises, as the subject of the interception, and must provide suitable information to be used for identifying the communications that may be, or are, to be intercepted.[24] External telecommunication warrants (often referred to as 'untargeted', 'strategic' or 'certificated' warrants[25]) are considerably broader in scope. The Secretary of State may authorise intercepts on an external communications link (for example, commercial submarine cables having one terminal in the UK and carrying external commercial communications to Europe) on the basis of a certificate that sets out the categories of information to be extracted from the total volume of communications intercepted under a particular warrant, and the reason for the intercept, such as 'national security', 'preventing or detecting serious crime', or 'safeguarding the economic well-being of the United Kingdom'.[26]

The Act sets out limits for the duration of warrants, as well as their renewal and cancellation,[27] and provides a process for their modification.[28] The initial duration is three months, with renewals

19  Richard Clayton, 'The Phorm "Webwise" system' (2008) 18 May, available online at: www.cl.cam.ac.uk/~rnc1/080518-phorm.pdf
20  Nicholas Bohm, 'The Phorm "Webwise" system: A legal analysis' (2008) 23 April, available online at: www.fipr.org/080423 phormlegal.pdf
21  See Home Office, 'Targeted online advertising', FOI Release 9187, 29 April 2009.
22  Ibid, s 5.
23  Ibid, ss 6–7. Emergency warrants of up to five days' duration can be issued by a senior official, e.g. a senior civil servant.
24  Ibid, s 8(1)–(2). Note, however, that s 81 defines 'person' as including 'any organisation and any association or combination of persons'.
25  See, e.g., Liberty v Secretary of State for Foreign and Commonwealth Affairs [2014] UKIPTrib 13_77-H, [65].
26  Ibid, s 8(4)–(5); originally contained in IOCA 1985, s 3(2).
27  Ibid, s 9.
28  Ibid, s 10.

for preventing or detecting serious crime for three months.[29] There is no limit on the number of renewals if the perceived need for the warrant under s 5 remains.

Material obtained under general warranted interception, including communications data, must be held in accordance with specific safeguards. These are that:

- the number of people to whom the material/data is disclosed, the amount of data that is disclosed, and the amount of copying permitted are limited to the minimum required to meet the stated purpose of the interception;
- the material/data is destroyed as soon as there are no longer any grounds for retaining it to meet the stated purpose of the interception;
- the above points are overridden where the Secretary of State, the Interception of Communications Commissioner, or the Tribunal require the material/data to be retained/disclosed/copied to fulfil their functions under RIPA 2000, or a person conducting a criminal prosecution requires it to meet his or her duty to secure the fairness of the prosecution.[30]

Material obtained under certificated warranted interception:

- must be certified as necessary to be examined in the interests of national security for the purpose of preventing or detecting serious crime, or for the purpose of safeguarding the economic well-being of the UK; and
- cannot be intended to identify material contained in communications sent by, or intended for, an individual who is presently in the British Islands, and has not been selected by reference to such an individual.[31]

Anything to do with the existence or implementation of a warranted interception, including the content of the intercepted material and related communications data, must be kept secret by those to whom the warrant is addressed (for example, the applicant for an interception warrant), by those involved in the interception process (for example, civil servants, police officers), and by those undertaking the interception (for example, public telecommunications service providers and their employees, ISPs, anyone controlling part of a UK telecommunications system). Disclosure, unless specifically permitted under the Act, is a criminal offence.[32]

The bar on the use of evidence, or questioning or assertion, in legal proceedings likely to reveal the existence or absence of a warrant under s 9 of the IOCA 1985, which caused so much judicial confusion, is retained in s 17 of the RIPA 2000. However, the Act attempts to clarify both when that bar does not apply, and when material may or may not be disclosed.

The bar is removed where:

- there is a 'relevant offence', including offences under IOCA 1985, RIPA 2000, the Wireless Telegraphy Act 2006, and the Official Secrets Acts 1911 and 1989, etc;[33]
- there are civil proceedings initiated by the Secretary of State under s 11(8) of the RIPA 2000, to require a person to give effect to a warrant;[34]
- there are proceedings before the Tribunal, or an appeal from the Tribunal permitted by order of the Secretary of State;[35]

---

29 Ibid, s 9(6). Under IOCA 1985, the initial duration of warrants was two months, and renewals lasted for one month for the police, and up to six months for the security and intelligence services.
30 Ibid, s 15.
31 Ibid, s 16.
32 Ibid, s 19.
33 Ibid, s 18(1).
34 Ibid, s 18(1)(b).
35 Ibid, s 18(1)(c)–(d).

- there are proceedings before, or arising out of proceedings before, the Special Immigration Appeals Commission or Proscribed Organisations Appeal Commission;[36] or
- anything is done in, for the purposes of, or in connection with, so much of any legal proceedings as relates to the fairness or unfairness of a dismissal on the grounds of any conduct breaching ss 1(1) or (2), 11(7), or 19 of the RIPA 2000 or s 1 of the IOCA 1985.[37]

Disclosure can be made:

- generally, where there is a lawful interception without a warrant under RIPA 2000 ss 1(5)(c), 3 or 4, including any disclosure needed to prove that this was the case;[38]
- generally, about the conduct of a person convicted of an offence under RIPA 2000 ss 1(1) or (2), 11(7) or 19, or IOCA 1985, s 1;[39]
- to a prosecutor, about the facts of and materials (where not destroyed) relating to an interception, to ensure that a prosecution is conducted fairly;[40]
- to a judge, in a case in which he or she has ordered the disclosure to be made to him or her alone on the ground that it is essential in the interests of justice;[41]
- in exceptional circumstances, following a disclosure to a judge, of such limited facts derived from interception by the prosecution as he or she thinks essential in the interests of justice, except for facts disclosing that an interception has taken place, where this is barred by RIPA 2000, s 17(1).[42]

In terms of providing oversight, RIPA 2000 provides for an Interception of Communications Commissioner who holds, or has held, a high judicial office.[43] The Commissioner's role is, first, to review the processes for provision of interception warrants, acquisition of communications data, and decryption notices, and second, to review arrangements for the protection of intercepted material and encryption keys.[44] The Commissioner makes an annual report to the Prime Minister, and may additionally report on breaches of the Act within his or her remit, and failures in the protection of intercepted material and encryption keys. The Prime Minister must lay the annual report before each House of Parliament, but can redact material that is contrary to the public interest, or prejudicial to national security, or that relates to the prevention or detection of serious crime, the economic well-being of the UK, or the operations of certain public authorities.[45]

The Act further provides for a Tribunal, the Investigatory Powers Tribunal (IPT), which, amongst other tasks, considers complaints made with regard to the interception of communications – notably:

- proceedings concerning interception of communications in the course of their transmission that are incompatible with ECHR rights; and
- complaints by a person who believes that his or her communications have been intercepted in challengeable circumstances, or carried out by or on behalf of the intelligence services.[46]

---

36 Ibid, s 18(1)(e)–(f); SIAC and POAC can see the intercept material in order to make their decision, but it cannot be disclosed to an organisation or individual in question, or to their legal advisers (s 18(2)).
37 Ibid, s 18(3).
38 Ibid, s 18(4)–(5).
39 Ibid, s 18(6).
40 Ibid, s 18(7)(a).
41 Ibid, s 18(7)(b); see R v Gibbs [2004] EWCA Crim 3431.
42 Ibid, s 18(8)–(10); see R v Khachik [2006] EWCA Crim 1272.
43 Ibid, s 57.
44 Ibid, s 57(2).
45 Ibid, s 58(2)–(7).
46 Ibid, s 65.

The IPT is restricted to application of the principles that would be applied by a court on an application for judicial review, although since the Human Rights Act 1998, this will include violations of an individual's human rights, including the principle of proportionality.[47] The Secretary of State is empowered to create Rules regarding the exercise of the Tribunal's jurisdiction and hearings or consideration of complaints, under powers granted by RIPA 2000.[48] The IPT has the power to award compensation, quash or cancel any warrant or authorisation, and require the destruction of records of information. Where proceedings, complaints, or references are brought before the Tribunal, its public decision on the matter is confined to making a statement to the complainant that it has found in his or her favour, or not. No reasons will be given for the decision.[49] Decisions of the Tribunal cannot be appealed or questioned in any court.[50]

The Act also provides for the making of codes of practice in relation to the powers and duties in RIPA 2000. The Secretary of State is required to consult on any codes of practice, lay the drafts before Parliament, and bring them into force through an order. This requirement is largely designed to overcome criticisms that there was both a lack of clarity in, and public information about, the interceptions regime under IOCA 1985. The Home Office published a Code of Practice on Interception of Communications in 2002,[51] and further Codes of Practice on Investigation of Protected Electronic Information,[52] and Acquisition and Disclosure of Communications Data in 2007.[53] The Codes have no binding force, and there are no direct consequences for breaching them. However, by providing the public with general information about the workings of the UK interceptions regime they play an important part in ensuring that the regime is broadly in compliance with the requirements of the European Convention on Human Rights, notably Art 8.

Following the passage of RIPA 2000, the Telecommunications (Lawful Business Practice) (Interception of Communications) Regulations 2000 (LBPR) were laid before Parliament under s 4(2). The aim of the Regulations was to authorise a range of interceptions of communications on private telecommunications systems (including those run by government departments and public authorities) that would otherwise be prohibited by RIPA 2000, s 1. Lawful interceptions must be carried out by, or with the consent of a person carrying on a business, for purposes relevant to that person's business, and using that business's own telecommunication system; the Regulations do not authorise private interceptions on public telecommunications systems. The controller of the telecommunications system must also have made all reasonable efforts to inform potential users that interceptions may be made.[54]

Where these criteria are met, interceptions are authorised for monitoring or recording communications:

- to establish the existence of facts, to ascertain compliance with regulatory or self-regulatory practices or procedures, or to ascertain or demonstrate standards that are or ought to be achieved (for example, quality control and training);[55]
- in the interests of national security;[56]

---

47 Ibid, s 67(2).
48 Ibid, s 69. See *The Investigatory Powers Tribunal Rules 2000* (SI 2000/2665).
49 Ibid, s 67(7).
50 Ibid, s 67(8).
51 Home Office, *Interception of Communications: Code of Practice*, 2002, London: HMSO.
52 Home Office, *Investigation of Protected Electronic Information: Code of Practice*, 2007, London: HMSO.
53 Home Office, *Acquisition and Disclosure of Communications Data: Code of Practice*, 2007, London: HMSO, revised in 2015 following the passage of the Data Retention and Investigatory Powers Act 2014.
54 The Regulations do not define 'users'. However, the government's intention is fairly clear: 'The persons who use a system are the people who make direct use of it. Someone who calls from outside, or who receives a call outside, using another system is not a user of the system on which the interception is made': see Department of Trade and Industry, *Notes for Business: Lawful Business Practice Regulations Information*, URN 06/1481, London: HMSO, p 15.
55 LBPR 2000, SI 2000/2699, reg 3(1)(a)(i).
56 Ibid, reg 3(1)(a)(ii). Interception for this purpose can only be carried out by, or on behalf of, specific persons named in the RIPA 2000, s 6(2)(a)–(i), such as the Director-General of the Security Service: Ibid, reg 3(2)(d)(i).

- to prevent or detect crime;[57]
- to investigate or detect unauthorised use of telecommunication systems;[58] or
- to secure, or as an inherent part of, effective systems operation.[59]

They are also authorised for monitoring, but not recording:

- received communications to determine whether they are business or personal communications;[60] or
- communications made to anonymous telephone helplines.[61]

## Interception post-RIPA 2000

RIPA 2000 was designed to harmonise the interception of communications across public and private telecommunications systems, to provide a technology-neutral approach to interception, to address some of the more problematic aspects of IOCA 1985, and to be ECHR-compliant.[62] Subsequent case law and debate suggests that the Act's approach to these issues has met with mixed results, not least because of its complexity and the lack of clarity in key definitions.[63]

### Interception

The issue of when an 'interception' took place was initially at issue, because the definition in s 2(2) was felt to be unclear:

> a person intercepts a communication in the course of its transmission by means of a telecommunication system if, and only if, he –
>
> (a) so modifies or interferes with the system, or its operation,
> (b) so monitors transmissions made by means of the system, or
> (c) so monitors transmissions made by wireless telegraphy to or from apparatus comprised in the system,
>
> as to make some or all of the contents of the communication available, while being transmitted, to a person other than the sender or intended recipient of the communication.

In *Hardy*,[64] it was argued that tape recordings of a telephone conversation made by an undercover police officer who was a party to the call were interceptions. The court disagreed, holding that the recording was not an interception under RIPA 2000, s 1(5)(b), for which an interception

---

57 Ibid, reg 3(1)(a)(iii).
58 Ibid, reg 3(1)(a)(iv).
59 Ibid, reg 3(1)(a)(v).
60 Ibid, reg 3(1)(b).
61 Ibid, reg 3(1)(c).
62 It was also designed to implement Art 5 of the *Telecommunications Data Protection Directive* (Directive 97/66/EC), which required Member States to safeguard the confidentiality of communications. This has since been replaced by the *Privacy and Electronic Communications Directive* (Directive 2002/58/EC) as amended by Directive 2009/136/EC.
63 See also Gillian Ferguson and John Wadham, 'Privacy and surveillance: A review of the Regulation of the Investigatory Powers Act 2000' (2003) Special edn EHRLR 101; David C Ormerod and Simon McKay, 'Telephone intercepts and their admissibility' [2004] Crim LR 15; Hiral Bhatt, 'RIPA 2000: A human rights examination' (2006) 10(3) Int J Hum Right 285; Okechukwu B Vincents, 'Interception of internet communications and the right to privacy: An evaluation of some provisions of the Regulation of Investigatory Powers Act against the jurisprudence of the European Court of Human Rights' [2007] EHRLR 637; John R Spencer, 'Telephone-tap evidence and administrative detention in the UK' in M Wade and A Maljevic (eds), *A War on Terror? The European Stance on a New Threat: Changing Laws and Human Rights Implications*, 2009, Guildford: Springer.
64 R v Hardy [2002] EWCA Crim 3012 (CA). The Court relied upon the judgment in R v Hammond, McIntosh & Gray [2002] EWCA Crim 1243, decided under the IOCA 1985, for the proposition that interception did not include the recording of a telephone conversation by one party to the call. See also R v M [2003] EWCA Crim 3764; R v MacDonald (2002) unreported, 23 April (Woolwich Crown Court).

warrant would be required (and from which any evidence would be inadmissible under s 17(1)). If it had been an interception, it would fall under s 3(2), and would thus be authorised if one of the parties to the telephone call (the police officer) had consented and the surveillance/interception was authorised under Pt II of the Act (and the evidence would be admissible under s 18(4) as an unwarranted interception). However, the court held that, because the contents of the calls were not made available, whilst being transmitted, to any third party, there was no interception at all.[65]

In R v E,[66] police installed a surveillance device in the defendant's car, which recorded his conversation with people in the car, as well as his side of conversations on his mobile phone. E sought to have the audio evidence collected excluded on the basis that it was an interception of his phone calls, that this required an interception warrant or was otherwise an unlawful interception by police officers, and that s 17(1) meant the evidence was inadmissible. He referred to the RIPA 2000 Code on Covert Surveillance, which stated that:

> The use of a surveillance device should not be ruled out simply because it may incidentally pick up one or both ends of a telephone conversation, and any such product can be treated as having been lawfully obtained. However, its use would not be appropriate where the sole purpose is to overhear speech, which at the time of monitoring is being transmitted by a tele-communications system. In such cases an application should be made for an interception of communication warrant under s. 5 of the 2000 Act.[67]

The Court was unpersuaded by this, or by the argument that compliance with Directive 97/66/EC and Art 8 of the ECHR required the interpretation of 'interception' to be considered much more broadly, stating that EU Member States must issue national regulations to protect the confidentiality of telecommunications. In particular, they must prohibit listening, tapping, storage, or other kinds of interception of communications by others without prior consent, except when legally authorised in accordance with Art 14(1).

It held that the Code of Practice went further than RIPA 2000 required, and that, while the Directive clearly called for protection against infringement of confidentiality of communications by means other than simple interception, this did not justify the interpretation that E sought to place on the term 'interception' in RIPA 2000. Rather, the court felt that:

> The present case, in which nothing was recorded which had passed through any telecommunication system, even if the words did simultaneously go into it is, if anything, a clearer case of the absence of interception than are those cases of participant monitoring.[68]

It appears that the courts have adopted a strict technical test for interception under RIPA 2000, relating to considerations around securing the integrity of particular technologies (that is, the transmission mode is protected), rather than on the confidentiality of private communications (that is, the content is protected).[69]

---

65 See Ormerod and McKay, above, 25–7, for discussion of this point.
66 R v E [2004] EWCA Crim 1243. See also R v Allsopp [2005] EWCA Crim 703; R v Kennedy [2005] EWCA Crim 2859.
67 Home Office, Covert Surveillance: Code of Practice, 2002, London: HMSO, para 4.32, adopted under RIPA 2000, s 71(5). Since replaced by Home Office, Covert Surveillance and Property Interference: Revised Code of Practice, 2014, London: TSO, which states that: 'If one or both ends of a telephone conversation held in that car are recorded during the course of the operation, this will not constitute unlawful intercep-tion provided the device obtains the product from the sound waves in the vehicle and not by interference with, or modification of, any part of the telecommunications system', para 2.10.
68 R v E, [30]. See also R v Smart and Beard [2002] EWCA Crim 772 (under IOCA 1985); R v Allsopp [2005] EWCA Crim 703 (under RIPA 2000).
69 Both Ormerod and McKay, above, 24–7; and Ian Walden, 'Communication service providers: Forensic source and investigatory tool' (2006) 11(1) Inform Secur Tech Rep 10, 13, suggest that this is too narrow an interpretation to provide the privacy protec-tions required under the ECHR, which are premised on the suspect's ability to foresee, with a reasonable degree of certainty, the consequences of his or her actions.

## Control

The question of the meaning of '"control" of the operation, or the use of, a private telecommunications system' under s 1(6)(a)–(b) was addressed in *Stanford*,[70] in which the defendant had either personally intercepted emails, or had had emails intercepted on his behalf, via a mirroring service set up on a mail server owned by a company of which he had been deputy chairman.

1. ...

(6) The circumstances in which a person makes an interception of a communication in the course of its transmission by means of a private telecommunication system are such that his conduct is excluded from criminal liability under subsection (2) if –

(a) he is a person with a right to control the operation or the use of the system; or

(b) he has the express or implied consent of such a person to make the interception.

Stanford's argument was that a third party, X, an employee of the company, had been given and permitted to use an administrator username and password for the company server by Y, who was authorised to use an administrator username and password on that system. X was not given any limits to his use of the system, but was not expressly permitted to set up the mirroring processes that he then used to divert email messages to a server operated by himself and Stanford. Because X had been given the administrator username and password, Stanford suggested, either X was a person who had a right to control the operation or use of the system (s 1(6)(a)), or X had the express or implied consent of such a person to make the interception (s 1(6)(b)).

The judge at first instance rejected this line of argument, holding that 'right to control' for the purposes of s 1(6) meant 'more than merely "the right to access or to operate the system". It meant the right to authorise or forbid the operation or the use of the system'. Even if X had a general authorisation to operate or use the system, this would not include authorisation to 'make the interception' for the purposes of s 1(6)(b), which would only apply if X had authority to make the specific interceptions. The judge drew the reasoning for this from the House of Lords' judgment in *Allison*,[71] in which the court addressed s 17 of the Computer Misuse Act 1990:

Access of any kind by any person to any program or data held in a computer is unauthorised if –

(a) he is not himself entitled to control access of the kind in question to the program or data.

In *Allison*, Lord Hobhouse stated that 'the word "control" in this context clearly means authorise and forbid ... it is plain that [the subsection] is not using the word "control" in a physical sense of the ability to operate or manipulate the computer'.

---

70 *R v Stanford* [2006] EWCA Crim 258. See also David C Ormerod, 'Interception of communications: Meaning of "control" of the operation or the use of a private telecommunications system' [2006] Crim LR 1069; Clive Walker, 'Email interception and RIPA: The Court of Appeal rules on the "right to control" defence' (2006) 11(1) Communications Law 22; Fiona Mares, 'The Regulation of Investigatory Powers Act 2000: Overview of the case of *R v Clifford Stanford* (CA (Crim Div) 1 February 2006) and the offence of unlawfully intercepting telecommunications on a private system (section 1(2) offence)' (2006) 22(3) CLSR 254.

71 *R v Bow Street Metropolitan Stipendiary Magistrate and Allison, ex p Govt of the United States of America* [2000] 2 AC 216; cf *Bignell v DPP* [1998] 1 Cr App R 1. See also discussion in Chapter 7.

Faced with this interpretation, the defendant pleaded guilty, but sought leave to appeal on the ground that the judge had misinterpreted the meaning of 'control'. This was refused by the Court of Appeal, which held that:

- the purpose of RIPA 2000 was to protect the privacy of private telecommunications;
- this purpose was primarily to be achieved by the criminal sanctions in s 1;
- if anyone with unrestricted physical ability to operate and use a telecommunications system were to be exempt from criminal liability for intercepting communications, this would wholly undermine s 1;
- s 1(6)(b) made provision for the grant of express authority to make intercepts; and
- the grant of express authority to make intercepts must come from a person with a right to control the operation or the use of the system (for example, a senior manager), but such persons would not necessarily have the ability physically to operate and use a telecommunications system.

Thus, for s 1(6)(b) to make sense, 'control' had to mean 'authorise and forbid', not 'the ability physically to operate and use a telecommunications system'.

## Admissibility of intercept evidence

Despite the attention paid in RIPA 2000, ss 17 and 18, to the question of the admissibility of intercept evidence, several issues remained unclear. In *Scotting*,[72] the appellant was a serving prisoner. His telephone calls from prison were monitored and recorded by the prison authorities, as was general practice. He telephoned his girlfriend and arranged for her to smuggle drugs into the prison. Following the interception of these calls, they were arrested and charged. At trial, it was argued that the interceptions were inadmissible under s 17(1) and did not fall under any of the s 18(4) exceptions. The court held that:

- s 17(1) was not relevant, because there was no interception falling within s 17(2) – that is, an interception under warrant, or an interception that should have been under warrant;
- s 18(4) permitted the disclosure of the contents of a communication if the interception of that communication was lawful by virtue of ss 1(5)(c), 3, or 4.

Under RIPA 2000, s 4(4), interceptions taking place in prisons are authorised if they are in conformity with the Prison Rules made under s 47 of the Prison Act 1952, and r 35(a)(iv) of Prison (Amendment)(No 2) Rules 2000 (SI 2000/2641), permitting interceptions of telecommunications from prison for the prevention, detection, investigation, or prosecution of crime. If disclosure was not statutorily barred, then interceptions were admissible under the ordinary rules of evidence.

Harder questions were raised in *Attorney General's Reference (No 5 of 2002)*,[73] in which the Attorney General requested an opinion as to whether – and, if so, to what extent – a criminal court might investigate whether intercept material relied on by the Crown was obtained by tapping a private, as opposed to a public, telecommunications system. The questions arose from a case in which police officers were believed to be supplying confidential and sensitive information to a known criminal, and to journalists. Authorisation was given by the chief constable to intercept communications on several telephone extensions used by the officers. The interceptions were

---

72 *R v Scotting* [2004] EWCA Crim 197; see also *R v Abiodun* [2005] EWCA Crim 9.
73 *Attorney General's Reference (No 5 of 2003)*; *Re R v W* [2003] EWCA Crim 1632 – a reference under Criminal Justice Act 1972, s 36(1); [2004] UKHL 40 – a reference under Criminal Justice Act 1972, s 36(3).

made on a telecommunications system, which linked several police stations. This was made up of several private automated branch exchanges (PABX) linked by telecommunications lines, which were part of a public telecommunications system. A telephone call received on, or made from, the relevant telephones activated the interception equipment, which created a duplicate call. This was relayed through a BT telephone line to another police station, where recording equipment had been installed. Evidence was gathered confirming the supply of confidential information to unauthorised persons, and the police officers and another person were prosecuted on the basis of it.

The prosecution claimed that the interceptions had occurred within a private telecommunications system and it served evidence on the defence pre-trial to prove that fact. The defence countered that the interceptions had taken place on a public telecommunications system and, before presenting its evidence, argued that RIPA 2000, s 17, prevented any investigation into the circumstances of the interception, including its claim that the interceptions took place on the public side of the telecommunications system. The judge agreed that this was so, and also that, under RIPA 2000, the prosecution could present evidence that the interception had occurred on the private side. This, the defence argued, was unfair and all of the interception evidence should thus be excluded under s 78 of the Police and Criminal Evidence Act 1984 (PACE 1984). The judge agreed. Because the prosecution's case was based on the interception material, it collapsed, and the defendants were acquitted.

The Attorney General sought answers to the following questions.

- Does RIPA 2000, s (1), prevent, in criminal proceedings, any evidence being adduced, question asked, assertion or disclosure made, or other thing done in order to ascertain whether a telecommunications system is a public or a private telecommunications system?
- Where interception of a communication takes place on a private telecommunications system, is it permissible in criminal proceedings to ask questions or adduce evidence, etc, to establish that the interception has been carried out by, or on behalf of, the person with the right to control the operation or use of the system?[74]

In its opinion, the Court of Appeal distinguished the previous case law in *Preston* (decided under IOCA 1985, s 9), and stated that its answers to these questions would be, respectively, 'No' and 'Yes', but referred the questions to the House of Lords for further consideration. Both the Court of Appeal's and Lords' rationales for reaching their judgments are compelling testimony to the complexity of the RIPA 2000 exclusionary rule.

After examining the statutory provisions at length, their Lordships concluded that:

> Given the obvious public interest in admitting probative evidence . . . and the absence of any public interest in excluding it, I am satisfied that a court may properly enquire whether the interception was of a public or private system and, if the latter, whether the interception was lawful. If the court concludes that it was public, that is the end of the enquiry. If the court concludes that it was private but unlawful, that also will be the end of the enquiry. If it was private but lawful, the court may (subject to any other argument there may be) admit the evidence . . .[75]
>
> Before the statute of 2000 was enacted the clear understanding was that a court may examine whether an interception was made within a public or private system . . . Neither the text of the 2000 Act, nor any of the external aids to its construction, give any indication that such a radical change of policy was intended.[76]

---

74 The AG asked these questions with regard to interceptions that took place before and after the coming into force of RIPA 2000, because the events in the case took place under the IOCA 1995 regime. This discussion only covers the post-RIPA questions.

75 [2004] UKHL 40, [20], per Lord Bingham.

76 Ibid, [30], per Lord Steyn.

Two government reviews published in 2005 and 2008 disagreed on the possibility of changing the current position. The report of the former led the government to conclude that the risks of using intercept evidence outweighed the benefits of doing so,[77] while the latter review, headed by Sir John Chilcot, felt that 'it would be possible to provide for the use of intercept as evidence in criminal trials in England and Wales by developing a robust legal model, based in statute and compatible with [the] ECHR'.[78] While the government broadly accepted the Chilcot Review's findings in early 2008, actual law reform has proved elusive.[79]

In 2009, the government set up a programme overseen by a cross-party Advisory Group of Privy Counsellors to examine if it was possible to enable intercept material to be used as evidence in criminal trials, whilst continuing to meet the operational requirements necessary for public protection and national security.[80] The programme created a model for how intercept material could be used as evidence, based on the Chilcot Review's 'Public Interest Immunity Plus' scenario.[81] This model was then reviewed against three criteria: would it increase the availability of incriminating evidence, was it legally viable, and would it affect the operational capability of law enforcement and intelligence agencies. The programme report concluded that implementing such a model in law would bring useful gains, albeit at a significant financial cost, as introduction of intercept material would increase the complexity of trials,[82] and also that these gains could be obtained without significantly harming operational requirements.[83] However, it was felt that the model was not legally viable, in that there were serious risks to fairness at trial.[84] The government thus decided to continue working on implementation without setting a target for completion.

There have been at least three attempts in 2005,[85] 2007[86] and 2012[87] to introduce legislation by means of a Private Member's Bill (PMB) (beginning in the House of Lords), all introduced by Lord Lloyd of Berwick, an ardent campaigner for the admission of intercept material as evidence, who has also sought to address the issue through amendments to a number of other government Bills relating to crime and terrorism. None of the PMBs appear to have progressed further than a second Reading in the Lords, all having been opposed by the government.[88]

Thus the position with regard to admissibility of evidence obtained by interception under RIPA 2000 currently remains that it is broadly inadmissible, except in limited statutorily defined circumstances, or where it is necessary to determine whether an interception took place on a public or private telecommunications system.

## Use of internal warrants

### The Kennedy case

The compliance of the arrangements for internal warrants under RIPA 2000, s 8(1)–(2) with the ECHR was challenged in *Kennedy v UK*.[89] Kennedy had been imprisoned for manslaughter in the early 1990s amidst controversy concerning the veracity of the police evidence against him.[90] Upon his

77 Statement by Home Secretary, HL Deb, vol 668, cols 52–3WS (26 January 2005). The report was not made public.
78 Home Office, *Privy Council Review of Intercept as Evidence*, Cmnd 7324, 2008, London: HMSO.
79 Letter from Sir John Chilcot to the Prime Minister, 9 February 2009.
80 Home Department, *Intercept as Evidence: A Report* Cm 7760, 2009, The Stationery Office Limited.
81 *Ibid*, Annex C: The Intercept as Evidence model, 18.
82 *Ibid*, 7.
83 *Ibid*.
84 *Ibid*, 8.
85 Interception of Communications (Admissibility of Evidence) Bill, *Hansard*, HL Deb, vol 675, cols 1301–1336 (18 November 2005).
86 Interception of Communications (Admissibility of Evidence) Bill, *Hansard*, HL Deb, vol 692, cols 966–994 (16 May 2007).
87 Interception of Communications (Admissibility of Evidence) Bill, *Hansard*, HL Deb, vol 737 col 389 (16 May 2012).
88 Baroness Scotland of Asthal's statement in Hansard, referring to the 2007 iteration of the Bill, betrays a certain weary resignation at having to rehearse the government position for the 5th time in two years: above, col. 990.
89 *Kennedy v United Kingdom* (2011) 52 EHRR 4.
90 See further, *Kennedy v United Kingdom* (1999) 27 EHRR CD266.

release in 1996, he set up a small business, whilst also becoming a high-profile campaigner against miscarriages of justice. The business ran into difficulties, which the applicant alleged were at least partially the result of telephone calls from his customers not being connected, and a large number of hoax calls. These problems, he claimed, came about because his communications by mail, telephone and email were being intercepted by the police and security services who were continually and unlawfully renewing an interception warrant, originally authorised for the criminal proceedings against him, with the aim of damaging his business and intimidating him.

Kennedy initially sought to discover whether his suspicions were well founded, by making subject access requests, under the Data Protection Act 1998, to MI5 and GCHQ to discover whether information about him was being processed by them. Unsurprisingly, these applications were refused on grounds of national security.[91] He then made a complaint to the Investigatory Powers Tribunal (IPT) that his communications were being interfered with in 'challengeable circumstances', as per s.65(7) of RIPA 2000, i.e. that the interference was taking place under a warrant, but without judicial authorisation;[92] and that under ss 6(1) and 7(1) of the Human Rights Act 1998 (HRA 1998) and s 65(2)(a) of RIPA 2000 there was an unlawful interference with his rights under Art 8 of the ECHR.

As part of his application to the IPT, Kennedy sought also to challenge key elements of the IPT's Rules regarding the exercise of its jurisdiction and hearings or consideration of complaints. As noted above, these Rules are made by the Secretary of State under s 69 of RIPA 2000. In particular, he sought to challenge the:

- restrictions on the disclosure of information and documents;[93]
- holding of hearings in private;[94]
- departures from the adversarial procedure in having separate hearings without the attendance of the other party;[95]
- absence of cross examination and the power to compel witnesses;[96]
- restrictions on the content of the determinations notified to the parties.[97]

Kennedy requested that there be an oral hearing conducted in public, with mutual disclosure and inspection by both parties, and with a reasoned determination of claim/complaint, even if his claim was unsuccessful.

The IPT noted that oral hearings (*inter partes* or separate) were at its discretion, and that it believed this discretion was compatible with rights under Arts 6, 8 and 10 of the ECHR. It also noted that the Rules made by the Secretary of State stated that: 'The Tribunal's proceedings, including any oral hearings, shall be conducted in private.'[98] However, the IPT held this to be *ultra vires* the powers granted to the Secretary of State under s 69 of RIPA 2000, stating that 'the public, as well as the parties to the complaint, has a right to know that there is a dispute about the interpretation and validity of the law.' Thus, subject to the general duty imposed to prevent the disclosure of sensitive information,[99] the Tribunal could exercise its discretion and hold open *inter partes* hearings.

It was, however, unconvinced that the Rules' departure from normal adversarial procedures resulted in an 'inequality of arms' incompatible with Convention rights, holding that these were

---

91 The information requested was exempt from the disclosure requirements of the DPA 1998 on the grounds of national security under certificates issued by the Secretary of State on 22 July 2000 (MI5) and 30 July 2000 (GCHQ).
92 *Kennedy*, IPT/01/62 & 77, 23 January 2003. See also *Kennedy v Security Services, GCHQ and The Met*, IPT/01/62, 9 December 2004.
93 The Investigatory Powers Tribunal Rules 2000 (SI 2000/2665), r 6(2)-(5).
94 Ibid, r 9(6).
95 Ibid, r 9(4).
96 Ibid, r 11(3).
97 Ibid, r 13.
98 Ibid, r 9(6).
99 Ibid, r 6(1).

*intra vires* the power conferred on the Secretary of State.[100] They were also compatible with Arts 8 and 10 of the ECHR, given the public interest and national security exceptions in Arts 8(2) and 10(2), being required for the effective operation of the legitimate 'Neither Confirm nor Deny' Policy (NCND) applying to the use of investigatory powers.[101] The IPT was also unpersuaded that the limitations placed by the Rules on the right to a reasoned determination of a claim or a complaint given in public,[102] was incompatible with the Convention right to a fair trial, indicating that the distinction between information given to the successful complainants and that given to unsuccessful complainants (to protect the NCND policy) was necessary and justifiable.

Having thus determined in a preliminary hearing that, with the exception of the outright bar on public hearings, the Rules were valid and binding on the IPT, the Tribunal then addressed Mr Kennedy's complaint in private. It held that no determination had been made in his favour in respect of his complaints, meaning that there had been no interception, or if there had been any interception it was undertaken lawfully. Mr Kennedy then took his case to Strasbourg claiming that his communications had been unlawfully intercepted in violation of Art 8 of the ECHR, that his allegations did not receive a fair hearing by a tribunal, contrary to Art 6(1) of the ECHR, and that he was denied an effective remedy for those claims, contrary to Art 13 of the ECHR.

The Court noted that, Kennedy's suspicions notwithstanding, there was insufficient evidence on which to support a reasonable likelihood that his communications were being intercepted. However, following its previous case law,[103] which noted that a complainant might not be able to provide concrete evidence on interception by the very nature of the secrecy surrounding the practices of surveillance, the court indicated that, insofar as it was not out of the question that secret surveillance measures might be applied to Kennedy, or that he was potentially at risk of being subjected to such measures, that he could complain about interference in his Art 8 rights. As that was the case, it was appropriate for the Court to assess the compatibility of the RIPA regime with Art 8(2) in terms of the proportionality of the legislation and the safeguards built into the system.[104] To do so, the court undertook its established three-stage test:[105]

- Did the UK's interception regime have some basis in domestic law?
- Was that domestic law compatible with the rule of law and accessible to the person concerned?
- Was the person affected in a position to foresee the consequences of the domestic law for him?

The court noted that it was accepted by the parties that the surveillance measures permitted by RIPA 2000 pursued the legitimate aims of the protection of national security, the prevention

---

100 Section 69(1), as limited by RIPA 2000, s 69(6).
101 The 'Neither Confirm nor Deny' Policy (NCND) operates in circumstances where to confirm or deny the existence of information would itself communicate sensitive and potentially damaging information, to the detriment of the public good. It means that the IPT may decline to say whether complainants have ever been targeted, whether lawfully or not. It is based on the premise that if allegations of interception or surveillance are made, but not denied, a complainant is likely to infer that such acts have occurred or are occurring, particularly if other complainants are being told that they have no cause for complaint, because no such acts are, or have been, occurring in relation to them.
102 The Investigatory Powers Tribunal Rules 2000 (SI 2000/2665), r 13 and RIPA 2000, s 68(4).
103 *Klass v Germany* (1979–80) 2 EHRR 214; *Malone v United Kingdom* (1985) 7 EHRR 14; *Esbester v United Kingdom* (18601/91) (1994) 18 EHRR CD72 – The court's 'task is not normally to review the relevant law and practice in *abstracto*, but to determine whether the manner in which they were applied to, or affected, the applicant gave rise to a violation of the Convention . . . but an individual may, under certain conditions, claim to be the victim of a violation occasioned by the mere existence of secret measures or of legislation permitting secret measures, without having to allege that such measures were in fact applied to him. The relevant conditions are to be determined in each case according to the Convention right or rights alleged to have been infringed, the secret character of the measures objected to, and the connection between the applicant and those measures.'
104 *Kennedy v United Kingdom* (2011) 52 EHRR 4, [155].
105 See, e.g., *Rotaru v Romania* (2000) 8 BHRC 449, [52].

of crime and the protection of the economic well-being of the country.[106] It also stated that the provisions of the RIPA Code of Practice,[107] which had been subject to parliamentary scrutiny, could be taken into account by courts and tribunals, and were contained in a public document available via the internet, should be taken into account in assessing the foreseeability of the RIPA regime.[108] Following its caselaw in *Weber* on foreseeability, it then scrutinised the RIPA regime to determine whether it met the minimum safeguards required:

- the nature of the offences which may give rise to an interception order;
- a definition of the categories of people liable to have their telephones tapped;
- a limit on the duration of telephone tapping;
- the procedure to be followed for examining, using and storing the data obtained;
- the precautions to be taken when communicating the data to other parties; and
- the circumstances in which recordings may or must be erased or the tapes destroyed.[109]

It found that the Act and the Code of Practice indicated with sufficient clarity the procedures for the authorisation and processing of interception warrants as well as the processing, communicating and destruction of intercept material collected.[110] In terms of potential for abuse of the regime, the court examined the role of the Interception Commissioner and of the IPT, and found that the safeguards against abuse in the procedures in tandem with the general safeguards offered by the supervision of the Commissioner and the review of the IPT suggested that there was 'no evidence of any significant shortcomings in the application and operation of the surveillance regime' under RIPA 2000.[111] As such, there was no breach of Art 8(2) of the ECHR.

Examining Kennedy's claim that the manner in which the proceedings before the IPT were conducted resulted in a violation of his right to a fair hearing under Art 6 of the ECHR, the court concluded that the need to keep sensitive and confidential information about surveillance measures out of the public view could justify the restrictions in the IPT proceedings, if those restrictions taken as a whole were not disproportionate and did not operate to impair the applicant's right to a fair trial. It stated that neither the entitlement to disclosure of relevant evidence, nor the obligation to hold a hearing were absolute rights, and that in both cases the interests of national security or the need to keep surveillance methods secret could justify restrictions. It also noted that the IPT had discretion in both cases, limited only by its duty to prevent the potentially harmful disclosure of sensitive information. As such, insofar as Art 6(1) applied to the proceedings, there was no violation.[112]

Turning to Kennedy's claim that he had no effective remedy for complaints in breach of Art 13 of the ECHR, the court noted that, given its conclusions in respect of the Art 8 and Art 6(1) claims, it was clear that the IPT provided an effective remedy for Kennedy's specific complaints about the alleged interception of his communications. In terms of a broader Art 8 complaint about the RIPA regime, the court reiterated that Art 13 did not go so far as to guarantee a remedy allowing a general challenge, unlimited in application to any particular factual or legal context, to primary legislation before a national authority on the ground of being contrary to the Convention or to equivalent domestic legal norms.

The decision in *Kennedy* was regarded in many quarters as indicating that the UK had finally developed a robust legal framework for internal warranted interceptions that met the requirements of the ECHR. Some commentators, however, have suggested that there may still be scope for further

---

106 *Kennedy*, above, [155].
107 Home Office, *Interception of Communications: Code of Practice*, 2002, London: HMSO.
108 *Kennedy*, above, [156]–[157].
109 *Weber and Saravia v Germany* (2008) 46 EHRR SE5, [93]–[95]
110 *Kennedy*, above, [159]–[164].
111 *Ibid*, [169].
112 *Ibid*, [184]–[191].

improvement, pointing to the court's comment that 'in a field where abuse is potentially so easy in individual cases and could have such harmful consequences for democratic society as a whole, it is in principle desirable to entrust supervisory control to a judge'.[113] Given that the RIPA regime still permits the exercise of significant powers by 'designated persons' who are not judges, e.g. senior police officers, there may still be room for further future challenges under Art 8(2).[114]

### The Belhadj case

The difficulty that individuals may have in utilising the IPT to determine whether their ECHR, Art 8 rights have been breached by interceptions under the RIPA 2000 regime is demonstrated in the proceedings in Belhadj.[115] Here, the claimants, who had been subject to illegal rendition to Libya in 2004, and who had brought civil claims against the Security Service and UK Government in 2012,[116] brought a claim before the IPT in 2013, under s 65(2)(a) of the RIPA 2000 alleging breaches of Arts 6, 8 and 14 of the ECHR arising from the alleged interception of their legally privileged communications. The government initially claimed that their policies on interception and use of LPP material could not be disclosed because to do so would damage 'national security'. However, shortly before a hearing to determine whether the government might be ordered to disclose these policies, it released extracts from MI5, MI6, and GCHQ's policies on use of LPP material. These disclosures acknowledged that from January 2010 the regime for the interception/obtaining, analysis, use, disclosure and destruction of legally privileged material contravened Art 8 of the ECHR and was unlawful. As a result, privileged information between the claimants and their legal advisers might have been made available to lawyers or government advisers in the civil claims.

Having determined that the policies on use of LPP material at the time of the civil actions breached their Art 8 rights, the claimants requested that if the IPT found during its closed hearing that there had been any interception or obtaining of LPP material, that it should make a determination in favour of any claimant affected, and that a summary of the Tribunal's determination, including reasons for the determination, should be provided to such claimant(s).[117] The claimants also sought compensation; delivery up of any LPP material intercepted or obtained; and injunctions.[118]

By contrast, the government argued that even if the IPT considered that there had been a contravention of Arts 8 or 10 (or a non-compliance with RIPA) it should still make no determination, and that if it did, either no reasons or summary should be provided, or any reasons or summary provided should be as abbreviated as possible to accord with r 6(1).[119] It also claimed that no injunctions were required as the faulty policies in question were already the subject of emergency review.[120]

After holding a closed hearing, the IPT made a determination in favour of only one of the nine claimants. Despite the determination in favour of the claimant, the IPT decided it would state only the essential elements of its determination, as its requirement under r 13(2) to provide a successful claimant with a summary of that determination including any findings of fact was subject, under r 13(4), to the general duty imposed on the Tribunal by r 6(1) to:

> not provide any information by way of findings of fact that raise any substantial risk of damaging national security interests by, *inter alia*, revealing or indicating the methods of operation of the intelligence agencies in carrying out surveillance or interception functions.[121]

---

113 Ibid, [167].
114 Andrew Ashworth, Kennedy v United Kingdom (Case Comment) (2010) 11 Crim LR 868.
115 Belhadj v Security Service [2015] UKIPTrib 13_132-H (judgment).
116 See, e.g., Belhaj v Straw [2013] EWHC 4111 (QB).
117 Belhadj [2015] (judgment) at [6].
118 Ibid, [9].
119 Ibid, [7].
120 Ibid, [10].
121 Belhadj v Security Service [2015] UKIPTrib 13_132-H (determination) at [5].

It held that there was an infringement of Art 8 of the ECHR, relating to two documents containing material subject to legal professional privilege which were held by GCHQ, noting that although the information was covered by privilege, it did not disclose nor refer to any legal advice.[122] It also decided there was no use or disclosure of the privileged information for the purpose of defending the civil claim brought by that claimant and others, and there was thus no breach of ECHR, Art 6.[123] The IPT refused to grant compensation to the claimant stating that there was no evidence the claimant had suffered any detriment or damage, because the information was of no significant value and was not disclosed nor used to his prejudice, and thus 'just satisfaction' by virtue of the finding in favour of the claimant was sufficient.[124] It refused to accept a need for injunctions. It also denied the request for delivery up of any LPP material intercepted or obtained, on the grounds that this

> would in effect be a disclosure of information which might give an indication of the means by which the information was obtained by the Intelligence Agency, or enable a person who is legitimately subject to surveillance or interception to take measures to make such surveillance or interception more difficult to achieve in the future.[125]

It required instead that that the parts of the two documents containing legally privileged information should be destroyed or deleted so as to render such information inaccessible, and that GCHQ should provide a closed report confirming that the destruction and deletion of the two documents had been effectively carried out.

The decision in *Belhadj* was hailed as a landmark, inasmuch as it was the first time the IPT had upheld a complaint against the security services, and required an intelligence agency to destroy surveillance material. Yet the decision was not received uncritically, with Alistair MacDonald QC, Chairman of the Bar Council noting that:

> Though it is encouraging that the IPT found . . . communications were unlawfully intercepted as a direct result of the inadequate policies relating to LPP material, there remains a major concern about the wider implications of the Tribunal's decision not to give injunctive relief . . . Currently, the public has to take the government's word that it is not unlawfully intercepting that material. As things stand, intelligence agencies will be able to intercept LPP material freely without being held to account . . . Even when the new draft codes and policies are put in place, they will not be robust enough to give that kind of protection to the public. LPP needs proper parliamentary and judicial oversight to be sufficiently protected.[126]

## Use of external warrants

### *The* Liberty *case*

The compliance of the arrangements for external warrants under both IOCA 1985 (s 3(2)) and RIPA 2000 (s 8(4)–(5)) with the ECHR was challenged in Liberty v UK.[127] During the 1990s, the Ministry of Defence routinely intercepted all telephone, facsimile, and email communications transmitted between BT's radio stations at Clwyd and Chester, including the majority of electronic communications between Ireland and England and Wales. The interception system could intercept

---

122 Ibid, [8].
123 Ibid, [9].
124 Ibid, [12].
125 Ibid, [14].
126 Reported in 'Bar Council response to Belhaj tribunal decision on LPP' (1 May 2015) Politics Home, available online at: www.politicshome.com/document/press-release/bar-council/bar-council-response-belhaj-tribunal-decision-lpp
127 Liberty v United Kingdom (2009) 48 EHRR 1. See Benjamin Goold, 'Liberty and others v The United Kingdom: A new chance for another missed opportunity' [2009] Public Law 5.

10,000 simultaneous telephone channels and operated from 1990 until 1997. The claimants, Liberty, British Irish Rights Watch, and the Irish Council for Civil Liberties, noted that, during this period, they were in regular telephone contact with each other and also provided legal advice, via telephone, to those who sought their assistance. Many of their communications would have passed between the BT radio stations and would thus have been intercepted.

Interception was, it was alleged, a five-stage process, as follows.

(1) A broad warrant would be issued, specifying an external communications link, or links, to be physically intercepted.

(2) The Secretary of State would issue a certificate, describing the categories of information that could be extracted from all of the communications intercepted under a particular warrant. These would be based on the broad classes of information specified in IOCA 1985, such as 'national security', 'preventing or detecting serious crime', or 'safeguarding the economic well-being of the United Kingdom'. The combination of a certificate and a warrant formed a 'certified warrant'. All communications falling within the specified category would be physically intercepted.

(3) Once communications were intercepted, they would be filtered using an automated process operating under human control, looking for specific search terms. Search terms and filtering criteria were not specified in certificates, but were selected and administered by state officials without judicial scrutiny or ministerial oversight.

(4) Communications intelligence reports were then reviewed to remove names or material identifying individuals or organisations, where their inclusion in the final report was not proportionate or necessary for the lawful purpose of the warranted interception.

(5) Information obtained by an interception would then be disseminated to recipients whose purpose(s) for receiving the information was proportionate and necessary in the circumstances.[128]

This process, the organisations claimed, breached Art 8 of the ECHR, because it constituted an interference with their rights under Art 8(1), and was not 'in accordance with the law' under Art 8(2), because it did not have a basis in domestic law that was adequately accessible and formulated with sufficient precision as to be foreseeable.

The claimants had initially sought to investigate the lawfulness of any warrants that had been issued in respect of their communications between England and Wales and Ireland, via the Interception of Communications Tribunal (under IOCA 1985, s 7) in September 1999. The Tribunal investigated their complaint and, in December 1999, ruled that there was no contravention of IOCA 1985, ss 2–5, in relation to a relevant warrant or certificate. The problem that claimants faced was that the Tribunal's ruling, whilst meeting the statutory criteria for a response under IOCA 1985, left them without any definitive statements as to whether a warrant had been issued or, if it had, whether it had been complied with. The claimants also complained to the Director of Public Prosecutions (DPP) about an unlawful interception and requested that those responsible be prosecuted. The DPP passed the matter to the Metropolitan Police for investigation. In April 2000, the police reported that their enquiries had not revealed an offence contrary to IOCA 1985, s 1.

In December 2000, IOCA 1985 was replaced by RIPA 2000, and the Investigatory Powers Tribunal was created, incorporating the former functions of the Interception of Communications Tribunal. In August 2001, the complainants began proceedings in the Investigatory Powers Tribunal

---

128 Before the ECtHR, the UK government refused to confirm or deny that this was the process, but conceded that, in principle, any person who sent or received any form of telecommunication outside the British Islands during the period in question could have had it physically intercepted under an s 3(2) (IOCA 1985) warrant. It insisted, however, that if interception of the applicants' communications occurred, it was lawfully sanctioned by an appropriate warrant.

complaining of interferences with their rights to privacy for their telephone and other communications from 2 October 2000 onwards.[129] During the proceedings, the key question became whether the interception of communications between the UK and an external source, captured under a warrant under IOCA 1985, s 3(2), or later RIPA 2000, s 8(4), in order to filter them for intelligence data was 'in accordance with the law'. In December 2004, the Investigatory Powers Tribunal ruled on the issue of accordance with the law, stating that:

> The selection criteria in relation to accessing a large quantity of as yet unexamined material obtained pursuant to a s8(4) RIPA 2000 warrant . . . are those set out in s 5(3) RIPA 2000. The Complainants' Counsel complains that there is no 'publicly stated material indicating that a relevant person is satisfied that the [accessing] of a particular individual's telephone call is proportionate'. But the Respondents submit that there is indeed such publicly stated material, namely the provisions of s 6(1) of the Human Rights Act which requires a public authority to act compatibly with Convention rights, and thus, it is submitted, imposes a duty to act proportionately in applying to the material the s 5(3) criteria.
>
> To that duty there is added the existence of seven safeguards listed by the Respondents' Counsel, namely (1) the criminal prohibition on unlawful interception (2) the involvement of the Secretary of State (3) the guiding role of the Joint Intelligence Committee ('JIC') (4) the Code of Practice (5) the oversight by the Interception of Communication Commissioner (whose powers are set out in Part IV of the Act) (6) the availability of proceedings before this Tribunal and (7) the oversight by the Intelligence and Security Committee, an all-party body of nine Parliamentarians created by the Intelligence Services Act 1994 . . .
>
> It is plain that, although in fact the existence of all these safeguards is publicly known, it is not part of the requirements for accessibility or foreseeability that the precise details of those safeguards should be published . . .
>
> . . . [F]oreseeability is only expected to a degree that is reasonable in the circumstances, and the circumstances here are those of national security . . . In this case the legislation is adequate and the guidelines are clear. Foreseeability does not require that a person who telephones abroad knows that his conversation is going to be intercepted because of the existence of a valid s 8(4) warrant . . .
>
> The provisions, in this case the right to intercept and access material covered by a s 8(4) warrant, and the criteria by reference to which it is exercised, are in our judgment sufficiently accessible and foreseeable to be in accordance with law . . . In this difficult and perilous area of national security, taking into account both the necessary narrow approach to Article 8(2) and the fact that the burden is placed upon the Respondent, we are satisfied that the balance is properly struck.[130]

However, the ECtHR was unconvinced by this reasoning and the UK government's arguments. In its ruling in 2008, which assessed the IOCA 1985 external warrant system, the court reiterated that:

> the mere existence of legislation which allows a system for the secret monitoring of communications entails a threat of surveillance for all those to whom the legislation may be applied. This threat necessarily strikes at freedom of communication between users of the telecommunications services and thereby amounts in itself to an interference with the exercise of the applicants' rights under Article 8, irrespective of any measures actually taken against them.[131]

---

129 British-Irish Rights Watch v The Security Service, IPT/01/62/CH.
130 Cited in Liberty v United Kingdom, above, [15].
131 Ibid, [56], citing Weber and Saravia v Germany (2008) 46 EHRR SE5.

With regard to IOCA 1985, the court noted that:

> 66.   Under s 6 . . . the Secretary of State, when issuing a warrant for the interception of exter-
> nal communications, was called upon to 'make such arrangements as he consider[ed] neces-
> sary' to ensure that material not covered by the certificate was not examined and that material
> that was certified as requiring examination was disclosed and reproduced only to the extent
> necessary. The applicants contend that material was selected for examination by an electronic
> search engine, and that search terms, falling within the broad categories covered by the cer-
> tificates, were selected and operated by officials . . . According to the Government . . . , there
> were at the relevant time internal regulations, manuals and instructions applying to the pro-
> cesses of selection for examination, dissemination and storage of intercepted material, which
> provided a safeguard against abuse of power . . . however, details of these 'arrangements'
> made under s 6 were not contained in legislation or otherwise made available to the public.
>
> 67.   The fact that the Commissioner in his annual reports concluded that the Secretary
> of State's 'arrangements' had been complied with . . . , while an important safeguard against
> abuse of power, did not contribute towards the accessibility and clarity of the scheme, since he
> was not able to reveal what the 'arrangements' were . . .
>
> 68.   The Court notes the Government's concern that the publication of information regard-
> ing the arrangements made by the Secretary of State for the examination, use, storage, com-
> munication and destruction of intercepted material during the period in question might have
> damaged the efficacy of the intelligence-gathering system or given rise to a security risk.
> However, . . . the German authorities considered it safe to include in the G10 Act, as examined
> in *Weber and Saravia* . . . express provisions about the treatment of material derived from stra-
> tegic interception as applied to non-German telephone connections . . . The G10 Act further set
> out detailed provisions governing the transmission, retention and use of data obtained through
> the interception of external communications . . . In the United Kingdom, extensive extracts
> from the Code of Practice issued under s 71 [RIPA 2000] are now in the public domain . . . which
> suggests that it is possible for a State to make public certain details about the operation of a
> scheme of external surveillance without compromising national security.

This led the court to conclude that IOCA 1985 failed to indicate sufficiently clearly to individuals
the scope of the powers available under the external warrant process, or the degree of discretion
available over the ways in which they could be exercised. In particular, it failed to follow ECtHR case
law in providing, in a publicly accessible form, an overview of the procedures used when selecting
intercepted material for examination, sharing, storage, and destruction. This meant that the interference with the claimants' rights under Art 8(1) could not be justified as being 'in accordance with
the law', as required by Art 8(2).

The judgment clearly had implications for the RIPA 2000 external warrant system, because
that is based on the IOCA 1985 system. It appeared that, to meet the ECtHR's test for acceptability,
further amendments to the existing system would be required, with the ECtHR having given clear
indication of the types of safeguard that it expected, in its reference to the German G10 Act.[132] The
G10 Act provides a clearly defined set of legal checks and balances, including the following.

● There are different rules for individual targeted interceptions and 'strategic' interceptions,
the latter of which can be conducted only for specific types of criminal offence (for example,

---

132 Law on the restriction of the privacy of posts and telecommunications, Gesetz zu Artikel 10 Grundgesetz v 26 June 2001 (BGBl
I S 1254), as amended 9 January 2002 (BGBl I S 361).

drug trafficking or international terrorism), and when authorised by the Parliamentary Control Panel and G10 Commission.

- The nine-member Parliamentary Control Panel (PCP), with general oversight of postal and telecommunications monitoring, receives six-monthly reports from the Federal Minister and appoints G10 Commission members. The PCP can request intelligence service documents and files, question staff, and conduct on-site visits to the intelligence services. It can receive information from intelligence service members and ordinary citizens. It reports to the Bundestag and provides information to the general public.
- The four-member G10 Commission examines requests by the intelligence services for specific surveillance operations to ensure that they are legal, necessary, and proportionate. Where filtering of intercepted communications is used, it approves the search terms. Its decisions to permit or deny authorisation are binding. The Commission's staff can demand information, inspect government documents, and conduct on-site visits, and can receive complaints from the public.[133] The Commission is also responsible for notifying subjects of monitoring once the purpose of the monitoring, or use of the data obtained, has ended.[134]

While the G10 Act framework has itself been criticised as too secretive, and the G10 Commission is said to be too overstretched to undertake intensive investigations into the activities of the intelligence services,[135] it appears more open and democratically robust than the current RIPA 2000 regime.

### The Snowden affair, the IPT and PRISM/TEMPORA

Since *Liberty* and *Kennedy*, the nature and scale of public communications technology has continued to develop apace, as the bulk of our communications, and a significant proportion of our accessing of information has migrated to electronic platforms. At the same time, as was revealed in 2013 by the leaking of classified information to *The Guardian* newspaper by US intelligence contractor, Edward Snowden, UK state agencies engaging in interception have made significant advances in their systems for collection, processing and analysis of intercepted communications traffic, and increasingly share data with, and receive data from, other foreign state agencies.

Amongst other revelations, Snowden released information relating to a number of international communications interception programmes, Including PRISM/UPSTREAM and TEMPORA. In brief, PRISM/UPSTREAM are programs via which the US National Security Agency collects foreign intelligence information from electronic communication service providers and intercepts from fibre optic cables owned by US communications services, under US court supervision.[136] This includes emails, chat, video, images, documents, links and other files and metadata. Information gathered in this way may then be shared by the US authorities with the UK intelligence services. TEMPORA is a UK GCHQ operation for mass communications surveillance designed to obtain data from traffic passing through UK-US fibre-optic undersea cables.[137] This comprises both internet and telephone communications, including the content of emails, Facebook entries and website histories, and metadata. The use of the two programs raised significant questions about the extent to

---

133 See further, Christian Heyer, 'Parliamentary oversight of intelligence: The German approach' in S Yui-Sang Tsang (ed), *Intelligence and Human Rights in the Era of Global Terrorism*, 2007, Westport CN: Praeger, pp 67–77.

134 Goold, above, p 10.

135 Heyer, above, p 77. A number of scandals suggest that those critics may have a point: see e.g. 'German spies caught reading journalist's e-mails' (2008) *Deutsche Welle*, 21 April.

136 See further, Privacy and Civil Liberties Oversight Board, *Report on the Surveillance Program Operated Pursuant to Section 702 of the Foreign Intelligence Surveillance Act*, 2 July 2014, available online at: www.pclob.gov/library/702-Report.pdf

137 See further, Ewen MacAskill et al, 'GCHQ taps fibre-optic cables for secret access to world's communications' (2013) *The Guardian*, 21 June, available online at: www.theguardian.com/uk/2013/jun/21/gchq-cables-secret-world-communications-nsa

which the activities of the UK agencies were adequately regulated via the existing UK interception regime under RIPA 2000, and in accordance with the requirements of ECHR, Art 8.

In 2014, these questions were raised in front of the Investigatory Powers Tribunal by a group of claimants, including Liberty, Privacy International and Amnesty International who argued that the activities breached Arts 8 and 10 of the ECHR, the latter by virtue of the 'chilling effect' on the speech of bodies that believe their communications are likely to be monitored.[138] It is worth noting that the IPT dealt with the issue of the legality of the regimes largely by references to assumed rather than established facts about the PRISM and TEMPORA processes, as the UK government has consistently applied the 'neither confirm nor deny' (NCND) principle to the activities of the intelligence and security services.

With regard to the operation of PRISM/UPSTREAM, the issue was whether by gaining access to foreign intercept material held by the US NSA, including communications made by UK citizens which were routed via US servers, the UK intelligence agencies might be circumventing the warranting process for interception of domestic communications required under s 8(1) of the RIPA 2000 – in effect using the US authorities as a 'backdoor' to access information that would need to be warranted under RIPA if collected by the UK intelligence agencies. As the RIPA mechanisms were not applicable to information accessed in that fashion, it was argued that the UK legal framework was thus inadequate to comply with the 'in accordance with the law' requirement under Art 8(2) (the *Weber* requirements).[139] A declaration was thus sought that the government had unlawfully failed to ensure that there was an Art 8 (and Art 10) compliant regime in place to govern the soliciting, receiving, storing and transmitting by UK authorities of private communications of individuals located in the UK, which had been obtained by US authorities. The claimants also asked for a declaration that the soliciting, receipt, storage and transmission of such information by the UK intelligence agencies was unlawful, and for an order that those agencies would not solicit, receive, store or transmit such information unless and until such activities were governed by an appropriate legal regime, and should destroy any material unlawfully obtained.

In assessing the legal regime applying to access and use of PRISM/UPSTREAM data, the IPT held that the *Weber* requirements should be seen as part of the ECHR's special emphasis on interception. Insofar as the UK intelligence agencies were not engaged in interception, a lower standard of 'prescribed by law' than that set out in *Weber* should apply, namely:

> in order for interference with Article 8 to be in accordance with the law:
>
> (i) there must not be an unfettered discretion for executive action. There must be controls on the arbitrariness of that action.
> (ii) the nature of the rules must be clear and the ambit of them must be in the public domain so far as possible, an 'adequate indication' given . . . so that the existence of interference with privacy may in general terms be foreseeable.[140]

and that this standard could be met where:

> (i) Appropriate rules or arrangements exist and are publicly known and confirmed to exist, with their content sufficiently signposted, such as to give an adequate indication of it . . .
> (ii) They are subject to proper oversight.

---

138 *Liberty v Secretary of State for Foreign and Commonwealth Affairs* [2014] UKIPTrib 13_77-H.
139 *Weber and Saravia v Germany* (2008) 46 EHRR SE5.
140 *Liberty* [2014], [37], citing *Bykov v Russia* (4378/02) ECHR, 21 January 2009; *Leander v Sweden* [1987] 9 EHRR 433; *Esbester v UK* [1994] 18 EHRR CD 72.

Having laid out this 'Weber-lite' test, the IPT determined that the appropriate rules or arrangements could be derived from the range of legislation placing specific statutory limits on the information that each of the Intelligence Services could obtain, and on the information that each could disclose, including the Security Service Act 1989, Intelligence Services Act 1994 and the Counter-terrorism Act 2008, as well as general legislation including the Data Protection Act 1998, the Official Secrets Act 1989 and the Human Rights Act 1998.[141] There were also 'arrangements below the waterline' within the agencies (i.e. those not publicly explained) but which were disclosed to the tribunal in closed hearing.[142] The oversight element was satisfied by the UK Parliament's Intelligence and Security Committee (ISC) and the Interception of Communications Commissioner (ICC), as well as the IPT itself.[143]

In sum, while the obtaining of intercept material within from the NSA via PRISM triggered an interference with Art 8 of the ECHR, there was an appropriate legal framework in place, and adequate arrangements in place for the purpose of ensuring compliance with it. The arrangements were sufficiently accessible to the public, by virtue of the visible statutory framework, via statements by the ISC and ICC, and through the disclosures made by the government and reported in the IPT judgment itself.[144] Therefore, the requirements of Art 8(2) of the ECHR were met, and there was no breach of either Arts 8 or 10 of the ECHR.

In the case of TEMPORA, the issue was whether, given the massively expanded capacity and processing power of its interception facilities, the use of broad external communications warrants under s 8(4) of the RIPA 2000 permitting the capture of vast amounts of communication, meant that the UK regulatory structure for interceptions (including the safeguards in ss 15 and 16 of the RIPA 2000) no longer made adequate legal provision for ascertainable checks against its arbitrary use.[145] A particular concern was that while RIPA 2000, s 8(4) permitted UK agencies to intercept 'external communications', i.e. communications sent or received outside the British Islands, as internal and external communications were commingled in the communications medium targeted by TEMPORA for bulk collection, it was inevitable that interception of internal communications would also occur. Once collected the intercepted communications and communications data would be retained and automatically searched through the use of a large number of search terms. The claimants queried whether:

- the difficulty of determining the difference between external and internal communications, whether as a theoretical or practical matter, was such as to cause the RIPA 2000, s 8(4) regime not to be in accordance with law contrary to Art 8(2) of the ECHR;
- RIPA 2000, s 16 was a sufficient safeguard in order to render the interference with Art 8 of the ECHR in accordance with law;
- the interception regime, whether with or without the s 16 safeguards, was sufficiently compliant with the Weber requirements.[146]

In essence, this revisited some of the issues raised before the IPT in the 2004 British-Irish Rights Watch case where the IPT had concluded that the s 8(4) regime was in accordance with law.[147]

The IPT acknowledged that the RIPA 2000, s 8(4) interception process would trigger an interference with Art 8 of the ECHR. However, it rejected the contention that the developments

---

141 Liberty [2014], [18]–[19].
142 Ibid, [47] and [54]. Some of these 'below the waterline' internal intelligence agency arrangements appear to also have been publicly disclosed in the course of Belhadj v Security Service [2015] UKIPTrib 13_132-H, discussed above.
143 Ibid, [22]–[24].
144 Ibid, [55],
145 Ibid, [80].
146 Ibid, [80]. There was a fourth question relating to whether s 16(2) was indirectly discriminatory contrary to Art 14 of the ECHR. The IPT gave this short shrift.
147 British-Irish Rights Watch and ors v The Security Service and ors, IPT/01/62/CH (discussed above).

in technology and volume of communications had made the difference between external and internal communications more difficult to determine at the point of interception (as opposed to processing);[148] or that these developments meant that the RIPA 2000, s 8(4) regime was being expected to cope with issues not present, foreseeable or foreseen at the time of the passage of RIPA 2000 by Parliament in 2000.[149] It also rejected the claims that RIPA 2000, s 16 was an insufficient safeguard because the hurdle for determining when a communication was an internal communication and thus outside the scope of a s 8(4) warrant was set too low; or that the section did not cover the use of communications data (data about the message, or 'metadata'), but only the communications content.[150] Finally, based on a similar analysis to that undertaken for the PRISM/UPSTREAM collection, it held that the interception regime met the *Weber* requirements, even though some of the administrative arrangements within the agencies were undisclosed because this might reveal sensitive and specific details relating to methods of obtaining and dealing with information, and reveal the precise capacity and capabilities of the agencies.[151] Therefore, the requirements of Art 8(2) of the ECHR were met, and there was no breach of either Arts 8 or 10 of the ECHR.

This was not quite the end of the issue, for after a closed hearing which sought to elucidate whether the government had in fact met the requirements of the 'Weber-lite' as regards the PRISM/UPSTREAM process the IPT then released a second judgment.[152] This judgment held that, prior to the government disclosure of two paragraphs that related to internal agency arrangements, made and referred to in the IPT's judgment of 5 December 2014,[153] there was insufficient information in the public domain to satisfy the 'in accordance with/prescribed by law' requirement in Arts 8 and 10 of the ECHR. This meant there was a breach.[154] However, the IPT concluded, as the government had made that disclosure, and the IPT considered it to provide 'an adequate indication' of the nature and content of the 'arrangements in place', the PRISM/UPSTREAM process was in compliance with Arts 8 and 10 of the ECHR from 5 December 2014.[155]

Commentary on the decision has cast doubt upon the appropriateness of the IPT's acceptance that the government's limited disclosure was sufficient to repair the breach. Simonsen notes that:

> . . . the IPT's view, [that] the 'prescribed by law' requirement in Arts 8 and 10 of the European Convention can be satisfied by GCHQ's disclosure of two paragraphs from an internal policy document; little more than a promise that the agencies will not, and do not, 'deliberately circumvent RIPA' . . . is an extraordinary result, particularly given the recent revelations in the *Belhaj* case . . . to the effect that MI5 and MI6 deliberately intercepted privileged communications between lawyers and clients, in at least one case passing on intercepted communications to the legal team defending the intelligence agencies against Mr Belhaj's claim. Despite this evidence of past infractions, the IPT was prepared to accept . . . that the duties undertaken by the intelligence services were 'underpinned . . . by a culture of compliance'.[156]

It appears unlikely that the issues raised by the PRISM/UPSTREAM and TEMPORA processes will rest here, as Liberty has indicated it will mount a further challenge against the IPT's decision at the European Court of Human Rights.

---

148 Liberty & Ors [2014], [93]-[102].
149 Ibid.
150 Ibid, [104]-[114].
151 Ibid, [117]-[140].
152 Liberty v Secretary of State for Foreign and Commonwealth Affairs [2015] UKIPTrib 13 77-H.
153 Liberty, (2014), [47].
154 Liberty, (2015), [23].
155 Ibid, [32].
156 Natasha Simonsen, *The Investigatory Powers Tribunal and the rule of law*, 16 February 2015, available online at: ukhumanrightsblog. com/2015/02/16/the-investigatory-powers-tribunal-and-the-rule-of-law-natasha-simonsen/

## Communications data, traffic data, and data retention

As was argued by the claimants in the TEMPORA proceedings before the IPT, even where the content of messages is not intercepted and accessed, a considerable amount of information can be gathered, or extrapolated, from communications data. Communications data can be broadly divided into three main types:

- *traffic data* – information about a communication, such as the location of a person when using his or her mobile phone;
- *service use data* – information about the use of a communications service, such as itemised telephone call records showing the numbers called; and
- *subscriber information* – information about the user of a communications service, such as the identity of the subscriber to a particular telephone number.[157]

However, the line dividing what is 'content data' and what is 'communication data' is not always clear-cut, because modern communications systems, such as internet services, have rarely been developed with monitoring in mind. Consider, for example, a URL such as www.bristol.ac.uk/

- Click on a link containing that URL on a third-party web page and the browser will access the computer at that location – this is *communication data* (Computer A accessed www.bristol. ac.uk/ at Computer B).
- Visit the Google search engine and key in the search 'University of Bristol'; the search engine will return a list of websites including URLs, one of which will be (the University of Bristol webmaster hopes) www.bristol.ac.uk/ – this is *content data* (Computer A asked Computer B for information relating to the University of Bristol).

Both content data and communication data may be capable of being analysed to permit identification of the individual involved in the communication, as well as to provide information about the social group with which the individual communicates (for example, by social network analysis/ subject-based data mining), and the individual's behaviour (for example, by pattern-based data mining).

A key difference between 'content data' and 'communication data', both in technological operation and practical use, is that content data is rarely retained by the operator of the communications system in routine operations. A telephone company does not keep a recording of the content of a conversation and an ISP does not keep a copy of an email (although an email may be temporarily stored at various points in the ISP's email system – not so that the ISP can access and read it, and the user and not the ISP has control over its retention). Communications data is usually collected and stored for a period of time to allow the communications provider to provide services (for example, location-based services, personalised phone tariffs), to record transactions for billing purposes (for example, itemised phone or text bills), and to identify individuals using their services (for example, to ensure authorised use). It may also be used by providers to identify further marketing opportunities through behavioural analysis (for example, personalised advertisements on web pages based on browsing history).

---

157 It is worth noting that there does not appear to be a widely agreed terminology: e.g., OECD Convention on Cybercrime, Ch 1, Art 1(d), defines 'traffic data' as 'any computer data relating to a communication by means of a computer system, generated by a computer system that formed a part in the chain of communication, indicating the communication's origin, destination, route, time, date, size, duration, or type of underlying service'. See further on this point Lilian Mitrou, 'Communications data retention: A Pandora's Box for rights and liberties?' in A Acquisti and S Gritzalis (eds), *Digital Privacy: Theory, Technologies, and Practices*, 2007, Abingdon: CRC Press, pp 412–13.

Thus there is an expectation that communication data will be collected, held, and used for a limited period of time, and for specific purposes, by communications providers. There is also an expectation that content data will not be treated in that fashion. This has been reflected in the legal frameworks relating to each type of data, in which communication data has, until recently, received significantly less protection than content data. However, as modern communications technology has developed, it is clear that the significance of communications data for individual privacy has increased:

> Traffic data is directly linked to our identity and can be automatically processed and evaluated. Whom we know, where we go and what we do on the Internet reflects our personalities, our preferences and our weaknesses in unprecedented detail.[158]

This change was recognised in the EU Directive on Privacy and Electronic Communications,[159] which extended privacy protection beyond the content of the communication to include associated traffic and location data.[160] The Directive required that:

- traffic data relating to subscribers and users be erased or made anonymous when it was no longer needed for the purpose of the transmission of a communication;[161]
- processing of traffic data for the purposes of subscriber billing and interconnection payments could only take place in the period during which the bill could lawfully be challenged or payment pursued;[162]
- traffic data could only be processed for marketing electronic communications services or for the provision of value added services with the subscriber or user's prior consent, which could be withdrawn at any time;[163]
- subscribers or users had to be informed of the types of traffic data processed, the purpose of the processing, and its duration;[164] and
- processing of traffic data must be carried out by authorised persons handling billing or traffic management, customer enquiries, fraud detection, marketing electronic communications services, or providing a value-added service, and must be restricted to what is necessary for the purposes of such activities.[165]

The Directive prohibited Member States from permitting the listening, tapping, storage, or other kinds of interception or surveillance of communications and the related traffic data by persons other than users, without the consent of the users concerned, except where these actions are permitted by domestic law.[166] Any such law had to be a necessary, appropriate, and proportionate measure within a democratic society to safeguard national security, defence, and public security, and for the prevention, investigation, detection, and prosecution of criminal offences or of

---

158 Working Group on Data Retention, 'Position on the processing of traffic data for "security purposes"' (2009) 21 March, available online at: www.statewatch.org/news/2009/mar/eu-dat-ret-wg-e-security-position-paper.pdf
159 Directive 2002/58/EC of the European Parliament and of the Council of 12 July 2002 concerning the processing of personal data and the protection of privacy in the electronic communications sector, [2002] OJ L201/37, as amended by Directive 2009/140/EC of 25 November 2009.
160 Article 2(b): '"traffic data" means any data processed for the purpose of the conveyance of a communication on an electronic communications network or for the billing thereof'; Art 2(c): '"location data" means any data processed in an electronic communications network, indicating the geographic position of the terminal equipment of a user of a publicly available electronic communications service'.
161 Directive 2002/58/EC, Art 6(1).
162 Ibid, Art 6(2).
163 Ibid, Art 6(3), as amended.
164 Ibid, Art 6(4).
165 Ibid, Art 6(5).
166 Ibid, Art 5.

unauthorised use of the electronic communication system.[167] The Directive also permitted Member States to adopt legislative measures providing for the retention of data for a limited period for those purposes.[168]

The political environment after the Madrid bombings in 2004 and the London subway bombings in 2005 led to a reassessment of the data retention provisions in the EU, and a new Data Retention Directive was proposed as part of a package of measures during the UK presidency of the EU, at the end of 2005.[169] The EU adopted the Data Retention Directive[170] in March 2006, requiring its transposition by Member States by 15 September 2007.

While the terrorist attacks were a key motivator, the stated purpose of the Directive was to achieve EU-wide harmonisation of national requirements for mandatory retention of communications data. It aimed to prevent Member States from, accidentally or deliberately, creating barriers to the cross-border supply of electronic communications services via legal and technical differences in national provisions for data retention designed to aid the prevention, investigation, detection, and prosecution of criminal offences. For example, prior to the Directive, a mobile phone service provider might find that, in order to provide services to customers in multiple Member States, it would be legally required to retain different types of communications traffic data, under different conditions, and for different time periods in each of those Member States. This would be a potential disincentive to entering other Member State markets, and thus protect existing national providers from external competition.

The UK implemented the Directive via secondary legislation in two stages. The first piece of legislation, the Data Retention (EC Directive) Regulations 2007, covered fixed network telephony and mobile telephony communications providers.[171] The Data Retention Directive permitted Member States to postpone application of that Directive to the retention of communications data relating to internet access, internet telephony, and internet email,[172] and the UK delayed implementation in those areas until the Data Retention (EC Directive) Regulations 2009, which then replaced and repealed the 2007 Regulations.[173]

## Access to retained communications data in the UK

In the UK, since 2004, access to communications data has been largely controlled by Ch II of Pt I of RIPA 2000.[174] Prior to this, access by a range of agencies was premised on the basis of powers derived from the common law and various legislation.

The Act permits access to communications data[175] in the form of traffic data,[176] service use information,[177] and subscriber information.[178] The Home Office gives examples of these in its Code

---

167 Ibid, Art 15(1).
168 Ibid.
169 A draft framework Decision on Data Retention had been proposed in 2004, suggesting retention periods of one to three years, but this was rejected by the European Parliament.
170 Directive 2006/24/EC of the European Parliament and of the Council of 15 March 2006 on the retention of data generated or processed in connection with the provision of publicly available electronic communications services or of public communications networks and amending Directive 2002/58/EC, [2006] OJ L105/54.
171 SI 2007/2199. See Richard Jones, 'UK Data Retention Regulations' (2008) 24(2) CLSR 147.
172 Directive 2006/24/EC, Art 15(3).
173 SI 2009/9780. See Claire Walker, 'Data retention in the UK: Pragmatic and proportionate, or a step too far?' (2009) 25(4) CLSR 325.
174 Relevant public authorities for the purposes of Ch II of Pt I of the Act may only use other statutory powers to obtain communications data from a postal or telecommunications operator if that power provides explicitly for obtaining communications data, or is conferred by a warrant or order issued by the Secretary of State or a person holding judicial office: Home Office, 2007, above, p 5.
175 RIPA 2000, s 21(4).
176 Ibid, s 21(6).
177 Ibid, s 21(4)(b).
178 Ibid, s 21(4)(c).

of Practice. Communications data can be accessed if a public authority can demonstrate that it is necessary and proportionate, and required:

- in the interests of national security;
- for the purpose of preventing or detecting crime or of preventing disorder;
- in the interests of the economic well-being of the UK;
- in the interests of public safety;
- for the purpose of protecting public health;
- for the purpose of assessing or collecting any tax, duty, levy or other imposition, contribution or charge payable to a government department;
- for the purpose, in an emergency, of preventing death or injury or any damage to a person's physical or mental health, or of mitigating any injury or damage to a person's physical or mental health; or
- for any purpose, not already covered, which is specified for the purposes of this subsection by an order made by the Secretary of State.[179]

A wide range of public authorities can lawfully obtain communications data, including:

- intelligence and law enforcement agencies – such as the security services, police, the Serious Organised Crime Agency (SOCA), and HMRC;
- emergency services – such as ambulance services, fire authorities, and HM Coastguard; and
- other public authorities – such as the Financial Services Authority (FSA), local councils, and the Home Office UK Border Agency.[180]

'Authorisations' to obtain communications data are granted by a 'designated person' within each of these authorities.[181] A formal authorisation or notice must be completed by the relevant senior official of that authority, stating the necessity and proportionality of obtaining specific information about a given individual.[182] This notice or authorisation has an authorisation period of one month, unless renewed.[183] These powers are self-authorised by the body concerned, with no direct external or judicial oversight, although the Interception of Communications Commissioner maintains general oversight, notably by a system of periodic inspection.[184] A Code of Practice on the Acquisition and Disclosure of Communications Data was published by the Home Office in 2007, and provides guidance for public authorities on how to meet the requirements for acquisition of data. While the Code is not legally binding, it is likely to be taken as a benchmark by the courts for deciding whether authorisations and notices by public authorities are lawful. In 2007, there were 519,260 requisitions of communications data from telephone companies and ISPs; this dropped slightly to 504,073 in 2008.[185]

---

179  Ibid, s 22(2). See the Regulation of Investigatory Powers (Communications Data) Order 2010, SI 2010/480, which adds 'to assist investigations into alleged miscarriages of justice; and for the purpose of assisting in identifying any person who has died as a result of a crime or who is unable to identify himself because of a physical or mental condition, other than one resulting from crime, or obtaining information about the next of kin or other connected persons of such a person or about the reason for his death or condition'.
180  In 2009, the Interception Commissioner noted that 52 police forces, the three security agencies, 474 local authorities, and 110 other authorities were able to request communications data: Interception of Communications Commissioner (ICC), Report of the Interception of Communications Commissioner for 2008, 2009, London: HMSO.
181  See SI 2010/480.
182  RIPA 2000, s 23.
183  Ibid, s 23(5).
184  Ibid, s 57(b). The Commissioner carried out only one inspection of a large local authority in 2008, and only eight inspections of local authorities in total, due to 'a temporary shortage of staff': ICC, above, p 18.
185  ICC, Report of the Interception of Communications Commissioner for 2007, 2008, London: HMSO; ICC, 2009, above.

### The UK code of practice for voluntary retention of communications

When the Data Retention Directive was adopted, the UK was already operating a voluntary system of data retention of communications traffic data via the Code of Practice for Voluntary Retention of Communications.[186] The Code was provided for in Pt 11 of the Anti-terrorism, Crime and Security Act 2001 (ATCSA 2001), and came into force in January 2004. Although the Code was, in principle, a voluntary system, there was considerable pressure from government on the telecommunications industry to accede to it, with the threat of a mandatory scheme being imposed via statutory instrument. The Code was unpopular with communications providers, partly because of industry concern that compliance with a voluntary code – as opposed to a legal obligation – could breach human rights and data protection legislation, and partly because of concerns about the expense attached to developing permanent retention processes.

The Code only applied to communication service providers who provided a public telecommunications service in the UK, as defined in RIPA 2000, s 2, and who retained communications data in line with the provisions of the ATCSA 2001. It did not apply to individuals and organisations that did not provide a public service (for example, corporate telecommunications and computer networks).

The Code did not require telecommunications service providers and ISPs to retain communications data, but it was designed to suggest agreed time periods for the retention of certain types of communications data, and to provide a basis for the retention of communications data beyond normal business operations for national security purposes, and the prevention or detection of crime, or the prosecution of offenders relating to the national security. The Code did not require that service providers collect information that they would not have collected in their business activities. The maximum retention period for communications data held under the Code was 12 months. However, if the communication service provider's business practices required a longer retention period, the Code did not prevent this.

The voluntary Code was replaced for fixed network telephony and mobile telephony communications providers in 2007, and for internet access, internet email, or internet telephony in 2009, by secondary legislation, based on the Data Retention Directive.

### The EU Data Retention Directive

Like the Code, the Data Retention Directive was only concerned with the traffic and location data of legal entities and natural persons, and any related data necessary to identify a subscriber or registered user. It explicitly stated that the retention of the content of electronic communications, including information consulted using an electronic communications network, was outside its scope – but while it did not require such retention, it did not explicitly bar it.

The Directive applied to a limited subset of communications networks, requiring that certain data were to be retained where those data were generated or processed by providers of publicly available electronic communications services, or by providers of a public communications network, in the process of supplying the communications services concerned. Determining what activities would cause an organisation to be deemed to be a 'provider of publicly available electronic communications services' or 'a provider of a public communications network' was left to the Member States. There was no requirement in the Directive for communications service providers to create new data for retention purposes; merely a requirement to retain existing data generated or produced in the course of their service provision.[187]

---

186 See further, Edgar A Whitley and Ian Hosein, 'Policy discourse and data retention: The technology politics of surveillance in the United Kingdom' (2005) 29(11) Telecommunications Policy 857.
187 Eleni Kosta and Peggy Valcke, 'Retaining the Data Retention Directive' (2006) 22(5) CLSR 370, 374.

The Directive set out several categories of data to be retained. These were data necessary to:

- trace and identify the source of a communication, such as the telephone number and sub-scriber name and address (telecoms), or user ID and name and address of the subscriber or registered user (internet);
- identify the destination of a communication, such as the number called, any number to which a call is rerouted, name and address of subscriber/user (telecoms), or user ID or telephone number of the intended recipient(s) of an internet telephony call, and name and address of subscriber/user (internet);
- identify the date, time, and duration of a communication;
- identify the type of communication, such as the telephone or internet service used;
- identify users' communication equipment, or what purports to be their equipment; and
- identify the location of mobile communication equipment, such as cell ID and the geographic location of cell.

The Directive also required the retention of data relating to unsuccessful call attempts where those data were generated or processed, and stored (for example, telephony data) or logged (for example, internet data). This was not data that would normally be held, for example, by telecommunications companies for billing purposes.[188] The Directive permitted Member States to set a retention period of not less than six months and not more than two years from the date of the communication, but gave Member States the ability, in limited circumstances and for a limited period of time, to extend the maximum period where they informed the other Member States and the Commission that they had done so, and of their reason for doing so.

The Directive required that data retained had to be kept subject to appropriate technical and organisational measures to ensure that they could be accessed by specially authorised personnel only; except for data accessed and preserved (presumably for the purposes specified under the Directive), retained data had to be destroyed at the end of the period of retention.

The Directive provided that data retained under the Directive had to be provided only to 'the competent national authorities in specific cases and in accordance with national law'. It did not specify any criteria for 'competent authorities' – which allowed Member States to widen access beyond law enforcement agencies – nor did it provide guidance as to the reasons for which retained data might be accessed – again leaving this to the discretion of the Member States.[189]

The Data Retention Directive was controversial from its inception. The first legal opposition came by way of a legal basis challenge brought by Ireland and Slovakia, which argued unsuccess-fully that the Directive's purpose was not ensuring the functioning of the internal market (Art 95 EC), but the investigation, detection and prosecution of crime (Title VI TEU – in particular Arts 30, 31(1)(c), and 34(2)(b)).[190]

Member States were often slow to implement the Directive,[191] and when they did, implementations were often subject to successful national legal challenges, as in Romania, Germany, Cyprus,

---

188 Gareth Davies and Gayle Trigg, 'Being data retentive: A knee jerk reaction' (2006) 11(1) Communications Law 18.

189 See Gerrit Hornung and Christoph Schnabel, 'Data protection in Germany II: Recent decisions on online-searching of computers, automatic number plate recognition and data retention' (2009) 25(2) CLSR 115.

190 Case C–301/06, *Ireland v Council and Parliament*, [2009] ECR I-593. See Monica Vilasau, 'Traffic data retention v data protection: The New European Framework' (2007) 13(2) CTLR 52; Lukas Feiler, The legality of the Data Retention Directive in light of the fundamental rights to privacy and data protection (2010) European Journal of Law and Technology, 1(3), available online at: ejlt. org//article/view/29/75#_edn9

191 The Commission brought several infringement actions for non-transposition, see Case C-211/09, *Commission v Greece* (2009); Case C-192/09, *Commission v Netherlands* (2009); Case C-185/09, *Commission v Sweden* (2010); Case C-189/09, *Commission v Austria* (2010).

Bulgaria, Czech Republic and the Netherlands.[192] National courts tended to focus on similar issues with the Directive and national implementing measures:

- blanket data retention measures were viewed as acceptable only in exceptional circumstances and then only if operated within a framework of clear and robust safeguards;
- national transpositions were seen as too imprecise, particularly concerning which bodies or agencies could access data retained under the law and for what purposes;
- measures which sought to retain data about all electronic communications without a specific cause did not appear to adequately weigh the need for such retention against the potential for breach of individual rights and were thus disproportionate.

The controversies in the Member States led courts in Ireland and Austria, hearing challenges to national implementations under the Directive, to make preliminary references to the CJEU, which the CJEU interpreted as a request to consider the validity of the Data Retention Directive in the light of Arts 7, 8 and 11 of the EU Charter of Fundamental Rights (CFR).[193] The court held that the requirements of the Directive that communications data be retained, in order that competent national authorities might have access to them, directly and specifically affected private life and, thus, the rights guaranteed by Art 7 of the CFR (respect for private and family life). It was unimportant whether the information was sensitive or whether the persons concerned were inconvenienced in any way.[194]

> [The] data make it possible . . . to know the identity of the person with whom a subscriber or registered user has communicated and by what means, and to identify the time of the communication as well as the place from which that communication took place. They also make it possible to know the frequency of the communications of the subscriber or registered user with certain persons during a given period . . . Those data, taken as a whole, may allow very precise conclusions to be drawn concerning the private lives of the persons whose data has been retained, such as the habits of everyday life, permanent or temporary places of residence, daily or other movements, the activities carried out, the social relationships of those persons and the social environments frequented by them.[195]

It further held that data retention constituted the processing of personal data within the meaning of Art 8 of the CFR (protection of personal data), and that the data retention process thus had to demonstrate compliance with data protection requirements.[196] Thus, given that data retention interfered with the rights granted by Arts 7 and 8 of the CFR, it was necessary under Art 52(1) of the CFR (scope of guaranteed rights) to demonstrate that this interference with Charter rights and freedoms was provided for by law, respected the essence of those rights and freedoms, was necessary, and genuinely met objectives of general interest recognised by the Union, or the need to protect the rights and freedoms of others.[197] The court concluded that the harmonisation of Member State data retention law in order to facilitate the use of modern investigation techniques in the

---

192 See Romanian Constitutional Court Decision No 1258, 8 October 2009, Romanian Constitutional Court Decision No 440, 8 July 2014; German Federal Constitutional Court 2 March 2010, 1 BvR 256/08; Czech Constitutional Court, 22 March 2011, Pl. ÚS 24/10; Supreme Court of Cyprus, Decision of 1 February 2011; *Stichting Privacy First et al v de Staat der Nederlanden*, Case No C/09/480009/KG ZA 14/1575 (11 March 2015); Bulgarian Supreme Administrative Court, Decision No 13627, 11 December 2008, Bulgarian Constitutional Court, Decision of 12 March 2015.

193 Joined Cases C-293/12 and C-594/12, *Digital Rights Ireland Ltd* [2014] (Grand Chamber, 8 April 2014).

194 *Ibid*, [33]–[34].

195 *Ibid*, [26]–[27].

196 *Ibid*, [35]–[36].

197 *Ibid*, [38].

fight against serious crime and to public security satisfied an objective of general interest.[198] It was not convinced, however, means by which this was to be achieved was proportionate, i.e. that the measures in the Directive did not exceed the limits of what was appropriate and necessary in order to achieve that objective. In particular, the Directive:

- was too general in scope, covering '. . . in a generalised manner, all persons and all means of electronic communication as well as all traffic data without any differentiation, limitation or exception being made in the light of the objective of fighting against serious crime'.[199]
- applied to individuals whose conduct was not linked by any evidence to serious crime, and provided none of the exceptions that might be expected, i.e. communications subject to an obligation of professional secrecy.[200]
- failed to provide any means of determining the limits of the access of the competent national authorities to the data and their subsequent use for the purposes of prevention, detection or criminal prosecutions, referring only to 'serious crime', as defined by Member States' national laws.[201]
- did not contain substantive and procedural conditions to ensure that access to and subsequent use of retained data should be strictly restricted to preventing and detecting precisely defined serious offences or conducting criminal prosecutions, thus leaving Member States to decide what mechanisms and safeguards should be required to ensure that access to retained data addressed the requirements of necessity and proportionality.[202]
- set a data retention period without making any distinction between categories of data, based on either their potential value for the purposes pursued or on the basis of the type of person involved, and gave an unfettered discretion to Member States to pick a retention period without requiring objective criteria demonstrating necessity of time period.[203]

Having so decided, the CJEU then held the Data Retention Directive to be invalid. This meant that Member States that had passed implementing legislation on the basis of the Directive were left with a dilemma. They could maintain their existing legislation, by arguing that their implementation was capable of meeting the requirements that the Directive itself could not,[204] in the face of national legal challenges arguing that, if the Directive was invalid, then it was probably the case that national implementing legislation based on it was similarly flawed. Alternatively, they could pass new national data retention legislation, independent of the Directive, which addressed the issues that the CJEU indicated would render EU legislation to be invalid.

## UK Data Retention (EC Directive) Regulations 2009

The 2009 Regulations required any public communications provider generating or processing communications data in the UK to retain the specific categories of data pertaining to its type of network or service[205] for up to 12 months.[206] Public communications providers included fixed network telephony communications providers, mobile telephony communications providers, and

---

198 *Ibid*, [41]–[44].
199 *Ibid*, [57].
200 *Ibid*, [58]–[59].
201 *Ibid*, [60].
202 *Ibid*, [61]–[62].
203 *Ibid*, [63].
204 As Member States retain competence to adopt their own national data retention laws under Art 15(1) of the Directive on Privacy and Electronic Communications (2002/58/EC) provided that those laws comply with the fundamental rights principles that form part of EU law. See European Commission, *Frequently Asked Questions: The Data Retention Directive*, Brussels, 8 April 2014.
205 Data Retention (EC Directive) Regulations 2009, reg 4.
206 *Ibid*, reg 5.

internet access, email, and internet telephony providers. Where a communications provider failed to cooperate with this requirement, the Secretary of State was authorised to take civil action to seek an injunction, or specific performance of a statutory duty under s 45 of the Court of Session Act 1988, or other appropriate relief.[207] The data retained had to be stored so that it could be transmitted without undue delay in response to requests.[208] However, the storage had to comply with the requirements of the Data Protection Act 1998 (and was subject to review by the Information Commissioner),[209] and the data retained could only be released for a specific purpose permitted or required by law, such as a properly constituted request under RIPA 2000, s 22.[210] The government was able to reimburse any expenses incurred by a public communications provider in complying with the Regulations that were agreed in advance.[211]

When the Data Retention Directive was held to be invalid, the initial position of the UK government was that the Regulations would remain in force and that organisations in receipt of a notice under the Regulations should continue to observe their obligations as outlined in that notice.[212] When it became clear this position was likely to be untenable in the longer term,[213] it was decided to replace the 2009 Regulations with new emergency legislation to fill the gap until alternative EU legislation was produced. The Data Retention and Investigatory Powers Act 2014 (DRIPA 2014) was introduced as an emergency bill on 14 July 2014, and came into force on 17 July 2014.[214] The legislation is temporary and is intended to only remain in force until 31 December 2016.[215]

## Data Retention and Investigatory Powers Act 2014

The justification for the Data Retention and Investigatory Powers Act 2014 (DRIPA 2014) was to ensure continuity of legal data retention in the UK by maintaining the *status quo* under the 2009 Regulations, as the government claimed that the stringent controls and safeguards provided by domestic laws (e.g. RIPA 2000) provided many of the safeguards that the European Court of Justice said were missing from the Data Retention Directive.[216] To this end, the Secretary of State is authorised to require providers of telecommunications services, by notice, to retain certain types of communications data generated or processed by them in the course of supplying their services, if the Secretary of State believes it is necessary and proportionate to do so for one or more of the purposes set out in s 22(2) of RIPA 2000, e.g. national security, prevention or detection of crime, etc.[217]

However, the Act alters the way in which public telecommunications systems and services are defined. Under the 2009 Regulations, the definitions were drawn from s 151 of the Communications Act 2003, which in turn derived from definitions of publicly available electronic communications

---

207  Ibid, reg 10(6).
208  Ibid, reg 8.
209  Ibid, reg 6.
210  Ibid, reg 7. This was not necessarily a very restrictive definition, as Parliament (and possibly the courts, through disclosure orders such as *Norwich Pharmacal* orders) could permit or require that further public and private bodies be granted access to retained data.
211  Ibid, reg 11.
212  *Hansard* HC Deb, 16 June 2014, c445W.
213  The 2009 Regulations were secondary legislation made under s 2(2) of the European Communities Act 1972 to implement a EU Treaty obligation in the form of implementation of a Directive. Given that the Directive was now held to be invalid, the ground for the making of the Regulations was undercut.
214  A judicial review challenge to DRIPA 2014, brought by the MPs David Davis and Tom Watson, claiming that the law is in breach of EU law and human rights law as it intrudes disproportionately into the private lives of members of the public, was heard in June 2015. At the time of writing a judgment has not been rendered.
215  As per the 'sunset' clause in DRIPA 2014, s 8(3).
216  Home Secretary's oral statement about the use of communications data and interception: *Hansard* HC Vol 582 cols 456–459, 10 July 2014.
217  DRIPA 2014, s 1(1).

services and networks contained in the EU Communications Framework Directive.[218] By contrast, DRIPA 2014 uses definitions of 'telecommunications service provider' and 'communications data' as set out in RIPA 2000, Pt 1[219] whilst inserting a new subsection 2(8A) into RIPA 2000 to ensure the definition of 'telecommunications service' includes internet-based services, such as webmail.[220] It has been suggested that this change may widen the scope of services caught by the provision.[221]

Under DRIPA 2014, a data retention notice may:

- apply to a specific telecommunications service provider, or to a described category of providers;
- require the retention of all data or any description of data;
- only require the retention of data types permitted by the 2009 Regulations, or a subset of these;
- specify the period or periods for which data is to be retained;
- include requirements and restrictions in relation to data retention, e.g. keeping data retained under a notice in a separate store from data retained for other purposes;
- make different data types subject to different provisions, e.g. different types of data might be required to be retained during different periods of time;
- apply to data whether or not the data is in existence at the time of the notice.[222]

The Secretary of State is empowered by DRIPA 2014 to make further provision concerning the retention of relevant communications data by means of regulations.[223] The current Data Retention Regulations 2014 repeal and replace the 2009 Regulations.[224] The 2014 Regulations:

- indicate what a retention notice must contain;[225]
- specify the issues the Secretary of State must take into account before giving a notice;[226]
- require that a notice must be kept under review;[227]
- place obligations on public telecommunications operators to take appropriate measures to ensure the integrity and security of data held, and that it is disposed of appropriately when no longer required;[228]
- provide for oversight by the Information Commissioner of the integrity, security and destruction of retained data requirements;[229]
- make provision for a statutory code of practice on the retention of data;[230]
- provide for variation or revocation of retention notices;[231]

---

218 Directive 2002/21/EC of the European Parliament and of the Council on a common regulatory framework for electronic communications networks and services, OJ L 108, 24.4.2002, p 33–50.
219 DRIPA 2014, s 2(1), as amended by s 21 of the Counter-terrorism and Security Act 2015 (CTSA 2015).
220 Ibid, s 5.
221 See, e.g., Graham Smith, *Mandatory communications data retention lives on in the UK — or does it?*, 22 July 2014, available online at: www.twobirds.com/en/news/articles/2014/uk/mandatory-communications-data-retention-lives-on-in-the-uk
222 DRIPA 2014, s 1(2).
223 Ibid, s 1(3).
224 Data Retention Regulations 2014, reg 14.
225 Ibid, reg 4.
226 Ibid, reg 5.
227 Ibid, reg 6.
228 Ibid, regs 7 and 8.
229 Ibid, reg 9.
230 Ibid, reg 10. See Home Office, *Retention of Communications Data: Code of Practice*, March 2015, London: TSO. The Code covers the issue, review, variation and revocation of data retention notices; the CSPs' ability to recover their costs; data security; oversight by the Information Commissioner; and safeguards on the disclosure and use of retained data by CSPs. It also outlines the scope and definitions of relevant communications data, including data that may be retained following provisions in CTSA 2015. See also Home Office, *Acquisition and Disclosure of Communications Data: Code of Practice*, March 2015, London: TSO.
231 Ibid, reg 11.

- impose a civil duty on public telecommunications operators to comply with retention notices and the data security integrity and non-disclosure requirements;[232] and
- provide for reimbursement by the Secretary of State of expenses incurred by telecommunications providers under DRIPA 2014 and the Regulations.

Where the 2009 Regulations mandated a fixed 12-month retention period from the date of a communication, applicable across the board,[233] under DRIPA 2014 the retention period for data in existence may vary, with a maximum retention period of 12 months.[234]

The types of data to be retained are those as set out in the Schedule to the 2009 Regulations. Fixed network telephony communications providers have to provide the:

- calling telephone number;
- name and address of the subscriber or registered user of any such telephone;
- telephone number dialled and any telephone number to which the call is forwarded or transferred;
- name and address of the subscriber or registered user of any such telephone;
- date and time of the start and end of the call; and
- telephone service used.[235]

Mobile telephony communications providers must provide the:

- calling telephone number;
- name and address of the subscriber or registered user of any such telephone;
- telephone number dialled and any telephone number to which the call is forwarded or transferred;
- name and address of the subscriber or registered user of any such telephone;
- date and time of the start and end of the call;
- telephone service used;
- international mobile subscriber identity (IMSI) and the international mobile equipment identity (IMEI) of the telephone from which a telephone call is made;
- IMSI and the IMEI of the telephone dialled;
- the date and time of the initial activation of the service and the cell ID from which the service was activated, for prepaid anonymous services;
- cell ID at the start of the communication; and
- data identifying the geographic location of cells by reference to their cell ID.[236]

Internet access, email, and telephony providers must provide the:

- user ID allocated;
- user ID and telephone number allocated to the communication entering the public telephone network;
- name and address of the subscriber or registered user to whom an internet protocol (IP) address, user ID, or telephone number was allocated at the time of the communication;
- user ID or telephone number of the intended recipient of the call (internet telephony);

---

232 *Ibid*, reg 12.
233 Data Retention (EC Directive) Regulations 2009, reg 5.
234 DRIPA 2014, s 1(5).
235 Data Retention (EC Directive) Regulations 2009, Sch 1.
236 *Ibid*, Sch 2.

- name and address of the subscriber or registered user and the user ID of the intended recipient of the communication (internet email or internet telephony);
- date and time of the log in to and log off from the internet access service, based on a specified time zone (internet access);
- IP address, whether dynamic or static, allocated by the service provider to the communication (internet access);
- user ID of the subscriber or registered user of the service (internet access);
- date and time of the log in to and log off from the service, based on a specified time zone (internet email or internet telephony);
- internet service used (internet email or internet telephony);
- calling telephone number (dial-up access); and
- digital subscriber line (DSL) or other end point of the originator of the communication.[237]

As well as attempting, temporarily at least, to place the UK data retention regime on a sound national legal footing, the government also used DRIPA 2014 to explicitly state that RIPA 2000 has extra-territorial effect.[238] The rationale for this was that, while the government has maintained that RIPA 2000 implicitly applies to communications providers based outside the UK which provide communication services to consumers in the UK, several overseas communications providers had argued that RIPA interception capability notices, interception warrants and communications data acquisition notices did not apply to them. As well as clarifying this point, and indicating that such duties are enforceable by civil proceedings,[239] DRIPA 2014 also sets out procedures for serving warrants or notices within the UK on communications providers located outside the UK.[240]

While DRIPA 2014 indicates the UK government's commitment to maintaining what it sees as an essential component of law enforcement and intelligence agency investigative capabilities, the question remains whether the Act and associated secondary legislation goes far enough to fully address the grounds upon which the CJEU found the Data Retention Directive to be invalid, and indeed whether it is necessary for it to do so. A number of points may be raised here. The CJEU's judgment in *Digital Rights Ireland* related to whether a piece of EU legislation was in compliance with the Charter of Fundamental Rights (CFR), not a free-standing piece of national legislation. That said, several commentators suggest that following Case C-390/12 *Pfleger*,[241] national measures which impede a fundamental freedom must be interpreted in line with the general principles of EU law including fundamental rights enshrined in the Charter – DRIPA 2014 itself being an exception to the Privacy in Electronic Communications Directive.[242] It also remains to be seen how well the jurisprudence of the CJEU and ECHR, as regards the necessity of measures that interfere with Convention or Charter rights, match up – it is not beyond the bounds of possibility that national legislation might be plausibly argued to be in compliance with the requirements of the ECHR whilst falling short of meeting the CJEU's requirements in *Digital Rights Ireland*.

The UK government's own Legislative Impact Assessment makes it clear that while there has been a concerted attempt to address some of the key criticisms that the CJEU levelled at the Directive, the UK government does not necessarily agree with the scope of those criticisms, stating that it would ensure 'that there is a functioning data retention regime with a clear basis in law that also addresses, *to the extent practicable*, the points raised in the ECJ judgment'. Other

---

237 Ibid, Sch 3.
238 DRIPA 2014, s 4(1)–(3).
239 Ibid, s 4(5) and (10).
240 Ibid, s 4(6)–(8).
241 CJEU (Third Chamber), 30 April 2014.
242 See, e.g., Franziska Boehm & Mark D. Cole, *Data Retention after the Judgement of the Court of Justice of the European Union*, 30 June 2014, available online at: www.janalbrecht.eu/fileadmin/material/Dokumente/Boehm_Cole_-_Data_Retention_Study_-_June_2014.pdf

government documents note that DRIPA 2014 and the 2014 Regulations provide a range of safeguards, including:

- the requirement for Ministers to consider necessity and proportionality before issuing retention notices, as well as the impact of the notice on the provider;
- the maximum, rather than absolute, retention period of 12 months – data may be retained for less time if it is not necessary or proportionate to keep it for longer;
- the requirement for the Secretary of State to keep notices under review;
- the limitation of data retention notices to a strict list of data types;
- the more specific content of data retention notices, setting out the data categories and services the retention applies to;
- access to data retained is limited to requests under RIPA and court orders;
- communications providers' data security requirements are set out in data retention notices and are enforceable;
- the Information Commissioner will oversee all relevant aspects of data retention;
- there is a Code of Practice on Data Retention, putting best-practice guidance on a statutory footing;
- amendments have been made to existing Codes of Practice ensuring that where privileged information is retained, law enforcement should give additional consideration of the level of intrusion; and emphasising that officers authorising access to data should be independent of the investigation.[243]

This list of safeguards suggests that that the government has drawn a number of lessons from its sojourns over the years before the ECHR, as to the likely requirements of a data retention mechanism that will pass muster under Art 8 of the ECHR. However, the problems with this approach are laid out in the written intervention made by the Open Rights Group and Privacy International during the judicial review of DRIPA 2014.[244]

> there is nothing in the relevant provisions that requires a retention notice issued by the Secretary of State:
>
> (a) to be person- or crime- specific. Indeed there is no obligation on the S/S to satisfy herself that there is any connection (even indirect) between the person whose data is being collected and a situation which is liable to give rise to criminal prosecutions. The data retention obligation in the notice not only can but, having regard to the stated purpose behind the legislation, is likely to capture the data of persons for whom there is no evidence capable of suggesting their conduct might have a link, even an indirect or remote one, with a serious crime, . . .
> (b) to exclude persons whose communications are subject to professional secrecy obligations . . .
> (c) to be confined to the minimum period 'strictly necessary' . . .
> (d) to ensure that the data is retained within the EU . . .
>
> Finally, rules governing restrictions on access to retained data are insufficient. Under Part II of RIPA a wide range of public authorities can obtain access and do so for purposes

---

243 Home Office, *Factsheet: communications data*, 10 July 2014, available online at: www.gov.uk/government/uploads/system/uploads/attachment_data/file/330510/Factsheet_Data_Retention.pdf
244 *R (on the application of David Davis MP and Tom Watson MP) v Secretary of State for the Home Department* (unreported).

not confined to safeguarding national security or the prevention, detection or prosecution of defined, sufficiently serious crimes . . .

Presently, then, there is something of an impasse. On the one side, the government maintains that it is vital in certain circumstances to engage in bulk collection of communications data that can then be automatically processed, in order to protect national security and prevent serious crime, and that suitable safeguards can be put in place to ensure that innocent parties are not subject to unnecessary encroachment on their rights. On the other, a broad-based opposition argues that such bulk collection cannot ever be justified, and that limiting collection of communication data to a pre-determined set of tightly circumscribed circumstances is the only acceptable means of protecting individual rights, even if this impacts on the effectiveness of law enforcement and national security agencies.

At their base, these arguments boil down to the issue of trust. To permit the state to engage in bulk collection of content or communications data, is to allow state agencies greater power over citizens, and citizens have to trust that such power will be used fairly, proportionately and transparently. Unfortunately, the recent history of surveillance offers up a diverse range of abuses of power and failures to protect fundamental rights. It is perhaps unsurprising then that, while the public are increasingly aware of the problems which developing communications technologies bring for law enforcement and national security, many remain unpersuaded that the way forward lies in bulk data collection and retention mechanisms hedged around with putative safeguards. This is especially the case where the safeguards are difficult to comprehend or access, or where the authorities providing the safeguarding are themselves opaque or secretive. Simply refusing to permit such collection may thus appear a beguilingly simple solution: if the data is not collected there is no requirement to trust in those agencies and safeguards. In the real world, however, non-collection is unlikely to be a realistic option, rather the courts must determine the veracity of the promises made by governments, scrutinise the plausibility of safeguards, and understand the day-to-day practicalities of organisational practices and operational requirements, with the aim of encouraging and reinforcing attitudes and behaviours in state agencies and actors that are supportive of increased social trust. While the history of state surveillance in the UK may not always make for edifying reading, what it does demonstrate is that it is possible, with time and oversight, to change both individual and institutional behaviour, such that encroachments on individual rights come to be increasingly viewed as unacceptable aberrations and not as normal practice.

Ultimately, given the steady development of the jurisprudence surrounding surveillance in the UK, it seems likely that the regime for data retention will come to resemble that for interception of content. In other words, it will be accepted that bulk collection and automated processing of communication data is a potential interference with rights of privacy and data protection, but that this interference can have legitimate goals, and can be undertaken in a proportionate and appropriately transparent fashion. There will undoubtedly be more negotiation on the best mechanisms for ensuring fair and lawful processing of such data, and this negotiation will continue to take place in both the legislature and the courts.

## Encryption

Encryption involves turning ordinary information (or plaintext), such as letters or emails, into apparent random strings of characters (or ciphertext). Decryption is the reversal of this process. Both encryption and decryption require the use of specific algorithms and a 'key'. Symmetric-key cryptography refers to encryption in which both the sender and receiver share the same key; asymmetric key cryptography refers to encryption in which two different but mathematically related keys are used – a public key and a private key. In asymmetric systems, the public key is typically used for encryption, while the private key is used for decryption. Thus if Alice wants to send Bob a secret message, she uses her private key to generate a public key, which she passes to Bob. Bob uses the public key to encrypt the message to send to Alice, who decrypts it with her private key. Even if a third party, Eve, intercepts the public key, she cannot decrypt the message from Bob to Alice, because the private key cannot be generated from the public key.[245]

The use of encryption is not a new phenomenon. Long before the development of computers, various groups, including the military, spies, diplomats, and powerful elites, were using encryption techniques to try to protect individual and group secrets in communications. Equally, other parties were constantly seeking to decrypt their ciphers. The trial and execution of Mary Queen of Scots in 1587 were, in part, precipitated by the interception and decryption, by cryptographers in the employ of Elizabeth I, of Mary's encrypted communications with the members of the Babington Plot. During the Second World War, the ability of Polish and UK cryptographers to decrypt messages enciphered using the Enigma machines conferred a significant advantage on the Allied forces.[246] However, the widespread availability of strong encryption for personal privacy protection is a relatively recent phenomenon, driven by the rise of ubiquitous access to personal computing facilities.

Since the development of significant open academic/commercial research into encryption in the 1970s, the problem that has faced national governments has been how to ensure a balance between public access to, and use of, strong encryption, whilst maintaining the ability of national security and law enforcement agencies to access private communications.[247] Initially, this tended to take the form of direct or indirect prohibitions on public access to encryption. In the USA and UK, for example, public research into the development and use of encryption technologies was not barred, but was subject to national security restrictions, such as patent secrecy orders and classification of research. In France, the use of encryption in communication was prohibited without authorisation by the government.

However, there were a number of problems with these approaches. The primary problem was that as information technologies were taken up by the commercial sector, the need for widespread access to strong encryption to provide adequate security for the use of those technologies – notably in sectors such as banking and online services – became increasingly obvious. Additionally, some countries, such as the USA, found it difficult, on constitutional grounds, to justify barring their citizens from securing their communications, should they wish to do so. Indeed, arguments based on the US First Amendment played a significant role not only in the spread of strong encryption technology to the American public, but also in the export of such technology overseas.

Even as national governments were losing the battle to restrain the use of encryption technologies by their own citizens, they were also discovering that it was difficult to prevent the spread of such technologies outside their borders. An international arrangement, negotiated amongst Western countries led by the USA, during the period immediately after the Second World War, and which remained in place throughout the Cold War, sought to limit the spread of strong encryption. Initially, this was because it was seen to be of purely military application, then because it was a 'dual-use' technology, in that it had legitimate civilian uses, but also still had military applications. However, by the 1990s, with the effective end of the Cold War, the united position began to fragment and, despite attempts led by the USA to build a new consensus on restriction of encryption technologies, many countries began openly selling strong encryption products into the international marketplace.[248] This led to increased pressure on the US government to relax its export posi-

---

245  For a detailed discussion of cryptography, see HX Mel and Doris M Baker, *Cryptography Decrypted*, 5th edn, 2002, Indianapolis, IN: Addison-Wesley Professional; Friedrich L Bauer, *Decrypted Secrets: Methods and Maxims of Cryptology*, 4th edn, 2006, Berlin: Springer.

246  For a definitive history of cryptography, see David Kahn, *The Codebreakers: The Comprehensive History of Secret Communication from Ancient Times to the Internet*, 1996, New York: Scribner.

247  See further, Andrew Charlesworth, 'Munitions, wiretaps and MP3s: The changing interface between privacy and encryption policy in the information society' in K De Leeuw and JA Bergstra (eds), *The History of Information Security*, 2007 Amsterdam: Elsevier; Aaron Perkins, 'Encryption use: Law and anarchy on the digital frontier' (2005) 41 Hous L Rev 1625.

248  Charlesworth, above, pp 782–8.

tion, as US companies complained that they were losing significant competitive advantage by only being able to sell products with weak encryption.

The economic pressures to permit public use of strong encryption in support of widening public take-up of internet technologies, including email communication, web-browsing, and e-commerce, left governments looking for a viable fallback position. It was no longer economically tenable (particularly in laissez-faire Western economies) to use legal measures to directly ban or inhibit such uses of encryption. Equally, it was politically problematic to be seen to be permitting the widespread use of a technology that could potentially damage national security or hinder law enforcement. How could this circle be squared?

One possible avenue that suggested itself was to mandate a government-approved encryption standard under which national security agencies and law enforcement bodies were provided with a back door, or with access via 'escrowed' encryption keys. Attempts to implement this approach dominated government encryption policy and lawmaking in the USA and Europe through the late 1990s. Such a policy approach, however, provided the potential for future wholesale public surveillance by government bodies and law enforcement agencies. This possibility, combined in many jurisdictions with the proposed provision of relatively weak protections to deter abuse, was to provoke a furious backlash from privacy organisations and the commercial sector alike.[249]

By the early 2000s, it was clear that, at the international level, even states such as France, which had fought a long rearguard action alongside the USA to prevent strong encryption gaining a foothold amongst the general public, had been largely defeated. Although they might not have totally liberalised their policies on encryption, they had been forced by market pressures to accept that the use of regulatory tools, such as export controls and the various iterations of key escrow, were no longer effective means of controlling the use of encryption technologies by the public.[250] The Cold War national security arguments that had held sway for half a century were unpersuasive in a globalised commercial marketplace that was increasingly dependent upon secure telecommunication and computer network services. However, if the requirements of national security were diminishing as a justification for government intervention in the public use of encryption, their place was being rapidly overtaken by the perceived requirements of law enforcement. The 'Red Menace' was replaced in the rhetoric of those promoting greater powers for law enforcement agencies to combat criminal use of encryption by the 'Three Horsemen of the Internet' – that is, child pornographers, drug dealers, and terrorists.

## UK encryption controls

The UK government tested the water with regard to internal encryption controls (as opposed to export restrictions) in the late 1990s, when it sought to garner support for key escrow in the form of a system of trusted third parties (TTPs).[251] The Labour Party in opposition had been opposed to encryption controls, including key escrow.[252] In power, the new Labour government largely continued the policy approach that the Department of Trade and Industry (DTI) had adopted prior to the 1997 General Election.[253] This envisaged the introduction of licensing arrangements for TTPs, possibly modelled on the licensing of telecommunications providers, and specifying the competence criteria that TTPs (offering services to the public) would have to

---

249 *Ibid*, 794–7.

250 It is worth noting, however, that certain types of cryptographic product still remain subject to export controls: see Department for Business, Enterprise and Regulatory Reform (BERR), *UK Strategic Export Control Lists*, 2009, London: HMSO.

251 See further, Yaman Akdeniz and Clive Walker, 'UK government policy on encryption: Trust is the key' (1998) 3 *Journal of Civil Liberties* 110.

252 Labour Party, *Communicating Britain's Future: Labour Party Policy on the Superhighway*, 1995, London: Labour Party.

253 Department of Trade and Industry (DTI), *Paper on Regulatory Intent concerning Use of Encryption on Public Networks*, 1996, London: HMSO; DTI, *Licensing of Trusted Third Parties for the Provision of Encryption Services: Public Consultation Paper on Detailed Proposals for Legislation*, 1997, London: HMSO.

meet, as well as what legal access arrangements (to client's encryption keys) would be required by law enforcement agencies. In April 1998, the DTI announced, in its secure Electronic Commerce Statement, that it would introduce legislation to license those bodies providing, or facilitating the provision of, cryptography services and to enable law enforcement agencies to obtain a warrant for lawful access to information necessary to decrypt the content of communications or stored data

The government did, indeed, pass legislation providing for the registration and requirements of cryptography service providers in ss 1–6 of the Electronic Communications Act 2000 (ECA 2000). However, these required a further statutory instrument to be made by the Secretary of State to bring them into force,[254] and when this did not occur, they were repealed on 25 May 2005 under a 'sunrise provision'.[255]

## National security and criminal investigations

This left the issue of law enforcement and national security-related access to encrypted materials, and that was duly addressed in RIPA 2000, Pt III, headed 'Investigation of Electronic Data Protected by Encryption'.[256]

The Act applies where any encryption-protected information:

- comes into the possession of any person (or is likely to do so)–

  o via a statutory power to seize, detain, inspect, search, or otherwise to interfere with documents or other property;
  o by means of the exercise of any statutory power to intercept communications;
  o as a result of having been provided or disclosed in pursuance of any statutory duty; or

- has, by any other lawful means not involving the exercise of statutory powers, come into the possession of any of the intelligence services, the police, or HMRC.[257]

In such circumstances, where permission is granted by court order, by warrant, by statute, or (in certain circumstances) by the Secretary of State,[258] that person can require a third party in possession of an encryption key to disclose that key where it is necessary:

- for the exercise or proper performance by any public authority of any statutory power or statutory duty;
- in the interests of national security;
- for the purpose of preventing or detecting crime; or
- in the interests of the economic well-being of the UK.[259]

The disclosure requirement must be proportionate to the aims to be achieved, and the protected information must not be reasonably accessible by other means.[260] No public authority may serve any notice under RIPA 2000, s 49, or, when the authority considers it necessary, seek to obtain appropriate permission without the prior written approval of the National Technical

254 ECA 2000, s 16(2).
255 Ibid, s 16(4).
256 See further Alan S Reid and Nicholas Ryder, 'For whose eyes only? A critique of the United Kingdom's Regulation of Investigatory Powers Act 2000' (2001) 10(2) ICTL 179; Yaman Akdeniz and Clive Walker, 'Whisper who dares: Encryption, privacy rights and the new world disorder' in Y Akdeniz, C Walker, and D Wall (eds), The Internet, Law and Society, 2000, London: Longman.
257 RIPA 2000, s 49(1)(a)–(e).
258 Ibid, Sch 2.
259 Ibid, s 49(2)(b) and (3).
260 Ibid, s 49(2)(c)–(d).

Assistance Centre (NTAC) to do so. The NTAC provides technical support to public authorities, particularly law enforcement agencies and the intelligence services. It may grant approval in specific cases, or it may give approval generally to a public authority if it assesses that authority as competent to exercise the powers in RIPA 2000, Pt III.[261]

Where a disclosure notice is made, it must:

- be in writing, or in some other permanent record;
- describe the protected information, state the grounds for disclosure, specify the office, rank, or position held by the person making it, specify the office, rank, or position of the person who gave permission for it, and specify a reasonable time period in which it must be complied with; and
- set out the disclosure that is required by the notice, and the form and manner in which it is to be made.[262]

Where a disclosure notice is given to an officer or employee of a corporation, it must, unless impracticable, be given to the most senior employee or officer available, unless this would defeat the purpose of the notice.[263]

When a disclosure notice is issued, if the person receiving it holds both the protected information and a means of obtaining access to the unencrypted information, he or she may use any key in his or her possession to obtain access to the information and make a disclosure of the information in an intelligible form, or he or she may disclose the key to the issuer of the notice. If he or she holds only the key, he or she must disclose that. If he or she no longer holds the key, he or she must disclose all information that would facilitate the obtaining or discovery of the key, or the putting of the protected information into an intelligible form.[264] Failure to make necessary disclosures is a criminal offence carrying a penalty of up to two years' imprisonment and the burden of proof is on the individual to demonstrate that he or she no longer had access to the encryption keys when the notice was given.[265]

In certain circumstances, a disclosure notice may require the person to whom the notice is given and any other person who becomes aware of it, or of its contents, and who knows, or has reasonable grounds for suspecting, that the notice contains a secrecy requirement to keep secret the giving of the notice, its contents, and any actions taken under it. Breaching this requirement (that is, 'tipping off') is also a criminal offence, carrying a penalty of up to five years' imprisonment.[266]

The Act also requires that:

- those who issue disclosure notices and those who operate on their behalf only use disclosed keys for obtaining access to, or putting into an intelligible form, the protected information covered by the notice;
- the uses to which the keys are put are reasonable and proportionate in the context of the case; and
- the keys are stored in a secure manner and that all records of the key are destroyed when no longer required.[267]

---

261 Home Office, 2007, above, paras 3.09–3.11.
262 RIPA 2000, s 49(4).
263 Ibid, s 49(5)–(6).
264 Ibid, s 50.
265 Ibid, s 53.
266 Ibid, s 54.
267 Ibid, s 55; see further Nicko van Someren, 'RIPA Part III: The intricacies of decryption' (2007) 4(3–4) Digital Investigation 113.

Persons making disclosures under the RIPA 2000 can be compensated by the government for any costs incurred in complying with a disclosure order.[268] The Home Office has provided a Code of Practice for the Investigation of Protected Electronic Information. This provides guidance to be followed when requiring the disclosure of protected electronic information in an intelligible form, or acquiring the means by which protected electronic information may be accessed or put into an intelligible form.[269]

The disclosure powers under RIPA 2000, s 49, did not come into force at the same time as the main RIPA 2000 provisions, and their implementation was delayed until October 2007. Relatively few disclosure orders were initially sought,[270] although the number has increased over time.[271] The requirement to disclose was challenged in R v S & A,[272] in which the defendants, having been served notices under s 49 of the Act by the police and refused to comply with them, were each charged with an offence under s 53(1). The defendants claimed that the requirement to provide information to the police under ss 49 and 53 was an infringement of the privilege against self-incrimination and contravened Art 6 of the ECHR. The Court of Appeal, in rejecting their claim, noted that the principle that evidence existing 'independent of the will of the subject' does not normally engage the privilege against self-incrimination is clearly established in domestic law[273] and, comparing the encryption key to the key to a locked drawer, concluded that the encryption key was 'independent of the will of the subject'. The court further noted that if the encrypted item did prove to contain incriminating evidence, then the fact that the defendant knows the encryption key is itself incriminating, and this might trigger the privilege against self-incrimination. However, even were the privilege to be triggered, it was not an absolute privilege, and could be legitimately overridden by a statutory provision, without breaching Art 6 of the ECHR, where the purpose for doing so was legitimate and proportionate.[274] Since R v S & A, the issue of enforced disclosure of encryption keys and the possibility of self-incrimination has rarely troubled the courts.[275]

While it is clear that some offenders do routinely make use of encryption,[276] and that this can hinder law enforcement investigations,[277] it is also the case that the UK courts have been willing to draw adverse conclusions from a refusal to supply encryption keys subject to RIPA 2000, s 49.[278] It

---

268 Ibid, s 52.
269 Home Office, 2007, above.
270 Between April 2008 and March 2009, NTAC approved 26 applications for service of a notice under s 49, RIPA 2000. Seventeen notices were then judicially authorised (no notice placed before a judge was refused) and 15 notices were served. Eleven individuals failed to comply, resulting in seven charges and two convictions: Office of Surveillance Commissioners, *Annual Report of the Chief Surveillance Commissioner to the Prime Minister and to Scottish Ministers for 2008–2009*, 2009, HC 704 SG/2009/94, London: HMSO, 12.
271 Between April 2013 and March 2014, NTAC approved 76 applications for service of a notice under s 49, RIPA 2000. Permission was not sought in six cases after NTAC approval. Permission was granted by a Circuit Judge in 37 cases, and 33 notices were served. Of these, seven complied with and 17 were not (the remainder still being processed). Offences for which notices were sought included importation of controlled substances, possession of indecent images, domestic extremism, terrorism, insider dealing, fraud, evasion of excise duty, drug trafficking, people trafficking and drug possession with intent to supply: Office of Surveillance Commissioners, *Annual Report of the Chief Surveillance Commissioner to the Prime Minister and to Scottish Ministers for 2013–2014*, 2014, HC 343 SG/2014/92, London HMSO, 14.
272 R v S(F) and A(S) [2008] EWCA Crim 2177; R Pattenden, 'Privilege against self-incrimination' (2009) 13(1) IJEP 69; Andrew J Roberts, 'Evidence: privilege against self-incrimination: Key to encrypted material' [2009] Crim L Rev 191.
273 Citing *Attorney-General's Reference (No 7 of 2000)* [2001] EWCA Crim 888; R v Kearns [2002] EWCA Crim 748; and R v Hundall and Dhaliwal [2004] EWCA Crim 389.
274 Brown v Stott [2001] 2 WLR 817.
275 See, e.g., *Greater Manchester Police v Andrews* [2011] EWHC 1966 (Admin).
276 See, e.g., R v G [2013] EWCA Crim 1027 (indecent images); R v Lewys Martin [2013] EWCA Crim 1420 (hacking); *Harlan Laboratories UK Limited v Stop Huntingdon Animal Cruelty* [2012] EWHC 3408 (QB) (harassment); *Hamza v Secretary of State for the Home Department* [2012] EWHC 2736 (Admin) (terror offences); *Eli Lilly & Company Limited v Stop Huntingdon Animal Cruelty* [2011] EWHC 3527 (QB) (harassment); R v Delucca, R v Murray, R v Stubbings [2010] EWCA Crim 710 (indecent images).
277 See, e.g., R v Lewys Martin [2013] EWCA Crim. 1420 (hacking); R v Cutler (Barry George) [2011] EWCA Crim 2781 (indecent images).
278 See, e.g., R v Pierre Padellec [2012] EWCA Crim 1956. The appellant appealed against a sentence of 30 months' imprisonment imposed following his plea of guilty to failing to disclose a key to protected information contrary to RIPA 2000, s 53. He pleaded guilty on the basis that he had not provided the passwords because he had used wiping software to remove a small number of indecent images accessed during internet browsing. Held that: it was entirely wrong for a basis of plea to be accepted in such cases. It enabled the defendant to identify, to his advantage, what was or was not on the computer and benefit from a lesser sentence than otherwise might be appropriate. The whole point of requiring access was so that it could be seen what was in fact there; see also R v Cutler (Barry George) [2011] EWCA Crim 2781 (indecent images).

also appears that use of encryption by offenders is by no means ubiquitous,[279] and that even where encryption is used, it may not be used effectively.[280] Courts are also willing to restrict or prevent the use of encryption technologies by convicted offenders via conditions in serious crime prevention orders (SCPO) under Pt 1 of the Serious Crime Act 2007,[281] or in sexual harm prevention orders (SHPO) under s 104 of the Sexual Offences Act 2003.[282]

Other states have adopted a similar approach to obtaining access to encrypted materials.[283] The Council of Europe's Cybercrime Convention requires that all parties to it 'adopt such legislative and other measures as may be necessary to empower its competent authorities to order any person who has knowledge about the functioning of the computer system or measures applied to protect the computer data therein to provide, as is reasonable, the necessary information' to permit search or access to computer systems and computer storage media in their jurisdiction. Citing the Cybercrime Convention as a model, the Australian government introduced a new federal law, the Cybercrimes Act 2001 (Cth), which as one of its measures amended the federal Crimes Act 1914 (Cth), inserting a new section allowing law enforcement agencies to compel individuals to reveal private encryption keys, ID numbers, or passwords for the purpose of prosecuting computer-related offences. Failure to comply is a criminal offence.[284]

# The future of interception, data retention and encryption in the UK

The changes in the UK legal framework surrounding the collection of information by interception and data retention, and the control of methods by which the public might seek to obscure communication content, have tended to reflect two main objectives. The first is to preserve the legitimate need of government and law enforcement agencies to retain and enhance access to such information in a changing technological environment, to fulfil mandates such as preserving national security and fighting crime. The second is the requirement, in a democratic society, to ensure that the scope of the powers – and the extent of political and administrative discretion in undertaking such collection – is clearly known to the public, that the uses of such powers are necessary, proportionate, and subject to meaningful oversight, and that any abuses of those powers are exposed and appropriately remedied.

---

279 See, e.g., *R v Grant Youlden Hockey* [2012] EWCA Crim 3242 (indecent images), [9]: 'It was clear from the programs that had been deleted that the appellant had tried to use other methods of downloading images such as subscribing to newsgroups. He had tried, unsuccessfully, to use encryption and deletion software'.

280 For example, in the US a total of 3,576 wiretaps were reported as judicially authorised in 2013. The number of wiretaps in which encryption was encountered was 41. In nine of these wiretaps, officials were unable to decipher the plain text of the messages. Encryption was also reported for 52 wiretaps that were conducted during previous years, but reported in 2013. Officials were able to decipher the plain text of the communications in all 52 intercepts. See US Courts *Wiretap Report* 2013, available online at: www.uscourts.gov/statistics-reports/wiretap-report-2013#sa9

281 See, e.g., *R v Glen Steven Mangham* [2012] EWCA Crim 973. Here, however, the SCPO was struck down as disproportionate in the circumstances of the case. A breach of a SCPO without reasonable excuse is a criminal offence. The maximum penalty on a summary conviction is 12 months imprisonment and a prison sentence of five years on conviction on indictment (SCA 2007, s 25).

282 Formerly sexual offences prevention orders (SOPO), as amended by the Anti-social Behaviour, Crime and Policing Act 2014. See, e.g., *R. v Cutler (Barry George)* [2011] EWCA Crim 2781 where the SOPO prohibited 'Installing any encryption-only software; for example: Jetico Best Crypt or Pretty Good Privacy'; and *R v Grant Youlden Hockey* [2012] EWCA Crim 3242 where the SOPO prohibited 'using or possessing any form of programme designed to encrypt high or securely delete data.' The content of such orders must be proportionate to the risk the offender poses to society, see *R v Grant Youlden Hockey; R v Mortimer (Jason Christopher)* [2010] EWCA Crim 1303. A breach of a SHPO without reasonable excuse is a criminal offence. The maximum penalty on a summary conviction is six months' imprisonment and a prison sentence of five years on conviction on indictment (SOA 2003, s 113). A breach of the prohibitions can only be committed within the UK.

283 See further, Stephen Mason, 'Electronic evidence: dealing with encrypted data and understanding software, logic and proof' (2014) 15(1) *ERA Forum* 25.

284 Nickolas J James, 'Handing over the keys: Contingency, power and resistance in the context of section 3LA of the Australian Crimes Act 1914' (2004) 23 *U Queensland LJ* 10.

There will always be a tension between these two objectives, influenced by ongoing political, social, and technological developments. As a result, the balance between the power of the state to engage in communications surveillance and the ability of the citizen to prevent, or exert influence to control, excessive use or abuse of those powers is in constant flux. It is a measure of the importance of both objectives that, when it comes to drafting laws, granting administrative powers, and designing practical processes, rational analysis of that balance can easily be lost amidst polemic. Measured assessment and appropriate balancing often comes only later.

The UK's data surveillance framework, across its provisions on interception powers, access to retained data, or control of public use of encryption, provides a salutary example of this. Criticisms of the use of RIPA 2000 powers, including access to communications data by public authorities, led to a consultation of which public authorities should have those powers and the level of authorisation required to employ their use in local authorities.[285] Perhaps unsurprisingly, this resulted in little change.[286] Even the limited use of the RIPA 2000 decryption powers has also led to criticism that they are being used for purposes that are disproportionate to the original goal of the legislation in tackling serious crime and threats to national security.[287]

## The Communications Data Bill 2012

In 2012, the Conservative-Liberal Democrat coalition government proposed to update and expand the data surveillance framework via the Communications Data Bill.[288] This would have required ISPs and mobile telecommunications companies to retain records of their users' internet browsing activities (including social media), email correspondence, voice calls, internet gaming, and mobile phone messaging services for 12 months.[289] As with other communications data, under the then Data Retention (EC Directive) Regulations 2009, the retained data would then be capable of access by authorised bodies, where authorised by a designated senior officer of a relevant public authority, subject to tests of necessity and proportionality.[290] The Communications Data Bill's scope, and the perceived weaknesses in its safeguards proved controversial, and it was swiftly dubbed 'the Snoopers Charter' by the media. In April 2013, the Liberal Democrats withdrew their support for the Bill, and effectively blocked its introduction during the Parliamentary sessions in 2012–2014.

The nature of the existing framework and the legislative changes being proposed raise important questions. What impact will developing and future technologies have on the communications surveillance framework in the UK? To what extent should the state or private organisations be able to deploy them in circumstances that may impact negatively on individual citizens? What safeguards should be required in order that the balance between state interests and individual rights is maintained? And are such safeguards appropriate in circumstances in which private interests and individual rights are in the balance?

---

285 Home Office, *Regulation of Investigatory Powers Act 2000: Consolidating Orders and Codes of Practice – A Consultation Paper*, 2009, London: HMSO; Home Office, *Regulation of Investigatory Powers Act 2000: Consolidating Orders and Codes of Practice – Summary of Responses to the 2009 Consultation Paper*, 2009, London: HMSO.

286 The Regulation of Investigatory Powers (Communications Data) Order 2010 (SI 2010/480), made adjustments to some public authorities' powers, but did not significantly reduce the number of authorised public authorities. More recently, the Regulation of Investigatory Powers (Communications Data) (Amendment) Order 2015 (SI 2015/228) removed 13 public authorities from the lists of those in the 2010 Order. It also adds a new statutory purpose to RIPA to allow for the Financial Conduct Authority and Prudential Regulation Authority to access communications data under RIPA for the purpose of non-criminal enforcement of financial services regulation.

287 For example, RIPA, s 49 notices used against animal rights activists: Mark Ward, 'Campaigners hit by decryption law' (2007) BBC *News*, 20 November, available online at: news.bbc.co.uk/1/hi/technology/7102180.stm

288 Home Office, *Draft Communications Data Bill*, June 2012, Cm 8359, available online at: www.parliament.uk/draft-communications-bill/

289 Ibid, Pt 1.

290 Ibid, Pt 2.

## The Investigatory Powers Review Report 2015

These questions were addressed in the independent review of the investigatory powers regime that was mandated by the Data Retention and Investigatory Powers Act 2014.[291] The Review report, published in June 2015,[292] considered the existing position, and made 124 recommendations for reform. The review took as its starting point, the need to build trust, noting that discussion about the proper scope of investigatory powers was "characterised by exaggerated rhetoric and by a lack of trust between participants".[293] Its recommendations, therefore, were premised on five key principles:

- *minimising 'no-go' areas*: in other words, that there should be an absolute minimum of spheres of activity, either physical or digital, in which the state should be forbidden to exercise investigatory powers. In some spheres, such exercise should be available in only exceptional and occasional circumstances, and in some circumstances such exercise might be impracticable. However, the defining issue was when it should be lawful for the state to exercise such powers, under what tightly defined circumstances, and with what safeguards; not whether such powers should exist at all.[294]
- *ensuring state powers are limited to protect privacy*: current and developing technologies permit the use of investigatory techniques in the digital sphere that are both wide-ranging and low cost, allowing the collection of data even where there is no particular suspicion of wrongdoing (in contrast to physical surveillance where costs often limit the data collected and require targeting of resources). Limits on the acceptable uses of those state powers cannot be left to the discretion of its agents, to counter-measures or to technical limitations: clearly defined limits, and not just safeguards, must be enshrined in law.[295]
- *ensuring the state complies with internationally guaranteed rights and freedoms*: intrusions into the privacy of communications should be expressly provided for by accessible and foreseeable laws; the exercise of state power should be restricted to when it is necessary to fulfil a legally prescribed mandate; measures adopted should be proportionate to the objective to be achieved; there should be a clear and comprehensive system for the authorisation, monitoring and oversight of measures that interfere with privacy rights.[296]
- *ensuring that laws relating to investigatory powers are both readily comprehensible and transparent*: the fact that the law deals with a technical subject is no reason for it to be only comprehensible to an expert; what is required is a series of limited powers, safeguards and review mechanisms presented with a high degree of clarity and without technical jargon.[297]
- *providing a unified approach to interception and communications data powers*: the interplay between, and interoperability of, the UK security and intelligence agencies and police forces (and between the various branches of the intelligence services) is such that there should be one law to govern all their uses of interception and communications data powers.[298]

The Report's key recommendations began with the proposal that the existing patchwork of legislation should be swept away and replaced with comprehensive and comprehensible new legislation defining the intrusive powers available to state agencies, and setting clear limits and safeguards on those powers.[299] It further suggested the need to clarify and update key definitions,

---

291  DRIPA 2014, s 7.
292  David Anderson, *A Question of Trust: Report of the Investigatory Powers Review*, 2015, London: HMSO, available online at: terrorismlegislationreviewer.independent.gov.uk/wp-content/uploads/2015/06/IPR-Report-Print-Version.pdf
293  *Ibid*, [13.2].
294  *Ibid*, [13.7]–[13.14].
295  *Ibid*, [13.15]–[13.24].
296  *Ibid*, [13.25]–[13.30].
297  *Ibid*, [13.31]–[13.34].
298  *Ibid*, [13.35]–[13.44].
299  *Ibid*, [14.3]–[14.7].

including 'content' and 'communications data'.[300] The existing Commissioners (Interception of Communications Commissioner's Office (IOCCO), the Office of Surveillance Commissioners (OSC) and the Intelligence Services Commissioner (ISCommr)) should also be replaced by a new Independent Surveillance and Intelligence Commission (ISIC),[301] with the oversight and auditing functions of its predecessors,[302] as well as authorisation and approval functions.[303]

It supported the case for communications data retention where this was compliant with the ECHR and EU CFR,[304] including developing a clear case for retention of particular kinds of data, such as user/device interaction logs and third party data, before moving to legislation.[305] Acquisition of communications data by appropriate state agencies should be authorised by a designated person at the agency, independent of the operation or investigation for which the authorisation was sought.[306] Communications data relating to privileged or confidential matters or to persons handling privileged or confidential information should be subject to special and more stringent protections.[307] The Report also supported the bulk collection of intercept material and communications data, under a new bulk communications data warrant, but indicated that such collection required more stringent authorisation and other safeguards.[308] It argued that all interception warrants should be judicially authorised via a Judicial Commissioner (a serving or retired senior judge) at the ISCl, and the warrant process clarified and streamlined.[309] It also called for the jurisdiction of the Investigatory Powers Tribunal (IPT) to be expanded, for it to have the capacity to make declarations of incompatibility, and for its rulings to be subject to appeal on points of law.[310]

It remains to be seen whether the recommendations of the Review report are taken on board by the government in full or in part. Following the 2015 General Election, in which the Conservative Party won a narrow majority, the barrier posed by the Liberal-Democrat opposition to legislation similar to the 2012 Communications Data Bill has been removed (although there remains limited opposition amongst Conservative MPs). In the Queen's Speech in May 2015, the Conservative government reaffirmed its commitment to a new Investigatory Powers Bill.[311] Given that the DRIPA 2014 legislation will expire at the end of 2016, it is to be expected that new legislation will be in place at that point.

## Further reading

Simon McKay, *Covert Policing: Law and Practice*, 2nd edn, 2015, Oxford: Oxford University Press
David Anderson, *A Question of Trust: Report of the Investigatory Powers Review*, 2015, London: HMSO
Andrew Charlesworth, 'Munitions, wiretaps and MP3s: The changing interface between privacy and encryption policy in the information society' in K De Leeuw and JA Bergstra (eds), *The History of Information Security*, 2007, Amsterdam: Elsevier
Bela Bonita Chatterjee, 'New but not improved: a critical examination of revisions to the Regulation of Investigatory Powers Act 2000 encryption provisions' (2011) 19(3) IJL&IT 264
Marie-Pierre Granger and Kristina Irion, 'The Court of Justice and the Data Retention Directive in Digital Rights Ireland: telling off the EU legislator and teaching a lesson in privacy and data protection.' (2014) 39(4) *European Law Review* 835

---

300 *Ibid*, [14.10]–[14.12].
301 *Ibid*, [14.94]–[14.100].
302 *Ibid*, [14.95]–[14.96].
303 *Ibid*, [14.95].
304 *Ibid*, [14.14]–[14.22].
305 *Ibid*, [14.32]–[14.45].
306 *Ibid*, [14.80].
307 *Ibid*, [14.85a]–[14.85b].
308 *Ibid*, [14.73] and [14.77].
309 *Ibid*, [14.47]–[14.57].
310 *Ibid*, [14.101]–[14.108].
311 Cabinet Office, *Queen's Speech 2015: background briefing notes*, 27 May 2015, available online at: www.gov.uk/government/publications/queens-speech-2015-background-briefing-notes

# Chapter 11

# Intellectual property rights in software

## Chapter contents

# Introduction

The first computers were large custom-built machines and were found primarily in large organisations and the intellectual property in the software and programs could be protected adequately by contract, supplemented by actions for breach of confidence if appropriate.[1] The advent of microcomputers together with the accompanying trend towards general applications programs, rather than specific bespoke software, meant that it rapidly became impossible to rely purely on contract and confidence to protect any intellectual property rights in computer programs. A property of computer software, and a significant difference from other forms of intellectual property, is its extreme vulnerability to copying. This is a direct consequence of the nature of the technology – the actual functioning of a computer is dependent on copying code backwards and forwards. It is a trivial matter therefore to make copies of software and widespread piracy is easy. As Petersen J remarked in *University of London Press Ltd v University Tutorial Press Ltd*, what is worth copying is *prima facie* worth protecting;[2] as a considerable amount of research and development time and money may be devoted to the creation of new computer software, it is not surprising that those engaged in this activity look for assurance that their intellectual property rights are protected. However, application of the traditional intellectual property regimes of copyright and patents to software and computer programs has not proved an easy task. This chapter will consider the way in which these intellectual property rights in computer programs have developed and the scope of the legal protection which they provide.

# Choice of intellectual property protection

## Copyright

In principle, copyright appears to be a suitable method of protection given that a program can be expressed in written form and copyright protects the form or expression of an idea rather than the idea itself. This should have the advantage of protecting the form of the program rather than

---

1 These methods may still provide a useful remedy in certain cases. As an example, *Ibcos Computers Ltd v Barclays Mercantile Highland Finance Ltd* [1994] FSR 275 (discussed below) concerned an action for breach of confidence, as well as an action for copyright infringement.
2 [1916] 2 Ch 601, 610, per Petersen J.

the ideas that lie behind it, thus leaving it open to another programmer to write an independent program performing the same function without infringing copyright in the first program. In addition, copyright protection arises automatically on creation of the work and generally requires no fundamental creativity or originality as long as it is the author's own individual handiwork – albeit that the need for some minimal creativity/originality can create difficulties in respect of some utilitarian or functional works.[3] When a work is subject to copyright protection, the law gives a copyright owner certain rights to control the dissemination and use of the material that is subject to the copyright, including, of course, the rights to allow or prevent copying. This is intended to be balanced by certain rights for users that allow a certain amount of copying for certain specified reasons and under certain specified conditions, referred to as 'fair dealing' in UK law and 'fair use' in the USA. Copyright is long-lasting. The term of copyright protection under Art 7 of the Berne Convention is the life of the author plus 50 years, and this has been extended in many jurisdictions.[4] Computer programs can become obsolete in very short times and so could equally well be protected by a shorter term, but neither is the longer term available under current copyright law particularly detrimental. Overall, therefore, copyright could clearly be a suitable method of protection as long as any issues arising out of the functional or utilitarian nature of computer programs can be accommodated.

## Patents

While copyright is the principal method of protecting creative works, in contrast, patent protection is usually considered the appropriate method of protecting intellectual property rights in functional works. Whereas copyright only protects form and expression, patents also protect the underlying ideas. Unlike copyright, patents do not arise automatically, but must be applied for and examined for compliance with the essential attributes of the patent – that is, novelty, inventiveness, and industrial application. Once a patent has been granted, it confers a monopoly on the holder for a limited period of time; this may appear to be more suitable for computer technology. On the other hand, it would, of course, mean that an independently produced program based on the same idea would violate the patent – the opposite situation to that pertaining to copyright protection. The application of patent law to computer programs will be considered in much more detail later in the chapter, but for now it should be pointed out there are two major obstacles to granting patent protection to computer programs. The first is the requirement of inventiveness: as pointed out by Karjala, 'most programs are simply an application of well-known techniques to a well-defined problem'.[5] The majority of programs are incremental changes to existing programs and do not exhibit the inventive step that is an essential prerequisite for patent protection. Second, in the UK and Europe at least, computer programs have been the subject of statutory exclusions from patent protection, as detailed in European Patent Convention (EPC), Art 52(2), and the UK Patents Act 1977, s 1. Although other jurisdictions have developed a more relaxed approach to patenting software, as discussed later in the chapter, this exclusion is still a controversial one in Europe.

## Making the choice

As early as the beginning of the 1970s, well before the use of computers was as ubiquitous as it is today, the World Intellectual Property Organization (WIPO) considered the above issues, and

---

3 See, e.g., *Baker v Selden* 101 US 99 (1879), discussed later.

4 In Europe, the standard copyright duration for literary works was harmonised in the 1990s. The relevant provisions are now to be found in Directive 2006/116/EC of the European Parliament and of the Council of 12 December 2006 on the term of protection of copyright and certain related rights (codified version) [2006] OJ L 372/12.

5 Dennis S Karjala, 'Copyright protection of computer software in the United States and Japan: Part 1' [1991] EIPR 195.

reviewed the most appropriate and effective method of protecting the intellectual property rights in computer software and programs.[6] It identified with accuracy a number of issues that were to trouble the courts. In particular, it noted the legal difficulties in patenting software and estimated that perhaps only 1 per cent of computer programs would exhibit the necessary inventiveness to qualify for patent protection. In contrast, copyright protection was, on balance, considered to be far more appropriate, taking into account the fact that a computer program could be regarded as a form of expression of the ideas behind it. The problems that some jurisdictions would encounter with according copyright protection to such a utilitarian work were noted, but, overall, copyright was thought to have more advantages than disadvantages. This initial study proved to be very influential and the approach that has been taken subsequently, both in individual jurisdictions and by global consensus, is to protect computer programs 'as literary works' and, on the whole, absorb the protection of intellectual property rights in computer programs into existing copyright principles.

In many ways, this appeared to be a sensible and pragmatic response. The copyright system was already well established and internationally recognised; copyright arises automatically on creation of a work and clearly provides protection against the more blatant forms of line-by-line copying and piracy. But in relation to both the philosophical and pragmatic objectives, the choice of copyright can, at times, seem to raise as many problems as it solves. What is it about computer programs and computer technology that might cause problems for traditional copyright law? In simple terms, there are two broad areas that need to be considered. The first, and simplest in conceptual terms, if not in solution, is the mode of operation of computers and the ease of copying. Computer programs were made to be copied. It is impossible to run a computer program and avail oneself of its useful effects without copies being made, however transient, within the depths of the computer. Also, because programs may be corrupted or inadvertently erased, it is good computing practice to take and keep a back-up copy of each computer program. Whilst even this level of copying could constitute a technical breach of copyright unless express provision is made, such copying does not, on the whole, threaten the commercial exploitation of that program. However, it is precisely the fact that the success of computer technology relies heavily on the ease with which programs can be copied that also makes it a trivial matter to produce multiple illicit copies, whether for private use, use within a commercial organisation, or for selling on the open market. This is not an issue as far as the actual application of copyright law is concerned, but causes significant problems for the enforcement of such law in relation to straight disk-to-disk copying and piracy of computer programs.[7] No special equipment is needed to make copies, and multiple copies can be made quickly and for minimal capital outlay. These can then be marketed at much lower prices than the authentic version. Even the widespread copying of software within an organisation can also have a severely prejudicial effect on the rights of the copyright owner. This problem of enforcement in relation to direct copying has been further exacerbated by the growth of the internet and the consequent ease with which software can be downloaded from remote sites.

The second general difficulty is that application of traditional copyright rules to the process of copying at the stage at which the computer program is written by the programmer has not been straightforward. Copyright was originally developed to protect the authors of literary, artistic, and other works from those who might copy the way in which their ideas had been expressed, especially where this was done for commercial gain. On the face of it, therefore, protecting computer programs as literary works would seem to be an appropriate method. However, as discussed in the next section, computer programs differ from conventional literary works in a number of important and fundamental ways, bringing into question the suitability of copyright for this purpose.

---

6 World Intellectual Property Organization (WIPO), *Model Provisions for the Protection of Intellectual Property Rights in Computer Software*, 1978.

7 In an early note, now of only historical significance, it was nevertheless recognised that widespread piracy was likely to be a problem in the industry, even in an age in which *only those large enough to own computers are well established businesses*: see John Banzhaf, 'Copyright protection for computer software' (1964) 64 Colum L Rev 1274.

A number of commentators are still of the view that, given the differences between computer programs and traditional literary works, a *sui generis* scheme would be more appropriate, tailored to take into account the particular properties of computer programs.[8] In such a global market as that for computer programs, one further benefit of the copyright system is the level of international consensus; it is debatable whether such consensus could be achieved on the form of a *sui generis* protection for computer software. There have been *sui generis* schemes in place for some time to protect the topography of semiconductor chips, although in this context, the USA was the dominant actor in the market and easily able to enforce its standards on other jurisdictions, and so global consensus proved not to be a major issue.[9] In contrast, the European Database Directive provides for a *sui generis* database right for databases that do not qualify for copyright protection,[10] but this is controversial in the USA, which continues to make no such provision.

# Copyright protection

## Computer programs as literary works

Given that computer programs have now 'joined books, poems and plays as full members of the literary work club',[11] they should be subject to the usual copyright regime. But even on a cursory examination it is apparent that there are significant differences between computer programs and more traditional literary works. Indeed, Karjala goes as far as to suggest that the 'decision to protect computer programs under copyright was in fact a radical departure from traditional intellectual property principles . . . Software is not art, music or even literature'.[12] Neither can programs, in their 'literary form', be readily understood other than by a person skilled in the particular programming language employed. Indeed, end users of the program will often have no knowledge of the underlying program that is causing their computer to perform a particular task or function, nor will they have any need for such knowledge. Such characteristics are not shared by other literary works, even those of a utilitarian nature. This section will examine the extent of the similarities and differences, and begin to consider whether or not any differences are legally significant.

### Expressed in writing

The choice of copyright may seem obvious at first sight because of the fact that programs can be represented in 'writing'. In written form, computer programs can be expressed as both *source code* and *object code*. The former is the program as written by the programmer and may be in any one of a host of different languages. Many of these are the so-called *high-level languages* (HLL) that bear a certain resemblance to literary language, and have their own rules of syntax and grammar. It is rare to be given the actual source code when acquiring software, whether off-the-shelf or bespoke – the usual situation is that the end user has neither knowledge of, nor need for knowledge of, the underlying program that causes the computer to perform the particular function.

The computer cannot respond to the source code in HLL as it can only recognise a stream of electrical pulses. So, in order for the computer to perform the intended function, the source code, as written by the programmer, has to be translated, or *compiled*, into a version that can be 'understood' by the computer. This version of the program is referred to as the 'object code' and can be

---

8  Lawrence Diver, 'Would the current ambiguities with the legal protection of software be solved by the creation of a *sui generis* property right for computer software?' (2008) 3 JIPLP 125.

9  See, e.g., US Semiconductor Chip Protection Act of 1984 (SCPA) 17 USC §§ 901–914; European Council Directive 87/54/EEC of 16 December 1986 on the legal protection of topographies of semiconductor products [1987] OJ L 24/36.

10  See later discussion below at pp 476–482.

11  Pheh Hoon Lim and Louise Longdin, 'Fresh lessons for first movers in software copyright disputes: A cross-jurisdictional convergence' (2009) 40 IIC 374, 376.

12  Karjala, above.

represented on paper by a list of binary instructions – a series of '0's and '1's reflecting the presence or absence of an electrical pulse. This conversion is normally carried out by another program referred to as the 'compiler'. As with literary languages, HLLs will only be understood by those conversant in the language in question:

> If someone chose to write a novel entirely in computer object code by using strings of 1's and 0's for each letter of each word, the resulting work would be no different for constitutional purposes than if it had been written in English. The 'object code' version would be incomprehensible to readers outside the programming community (and tedious to read even for most within the community), but it would be no more incomprehensible than a work written in Sanskrit for those unversed in that language. The undisputed evidence reveals that even pure object code can be, and often is, read and understood by experienced programmers. And source code (in any of its various levels of complexity) can be read by many more.[13]

Notwithstanding these comments from *Corley*,[14] although the source code may be intelligible to a programmer, even experienced programmers often find difficulty in reading and following object code; however, some of the simpler programming languages, such as machine and assembly code, do approach simple binary form and are favoured by some programmers.[15]

Already, it can be seen that computer programs exhibit a number of differences from traditional literary works. Programs in their literary form are not readily understood other than by a person skilled in that programming language, but the program cannot achieve its ultimate objective unless it can be understood by the computer. Such characteristics are not shared by other literary works, even those of a utilitarian nature, as succinctly expressed by the High Court in *Navitaire v EasyJet*:

> Computer programs are curious literary works in that they are the prescriptive expression of the manner in which a completely deterministic machine is required to operate. Something more different from an imaginative work of fiction which attracts exactly the same protection it is difficult to imagine.[16]

Although it has been accepted for a long time that copyright can subsist in code,[17] there was discussion in early software copyright cases in a number of jurisdictions as to whether both source code and object code could be protected by copyright. US copyright law, for example, required the subject of copyright protection to be a 'writing' and also denied copyright protection to works of a utilitarian nature. This led to the suggestion that, although there might be copyright in the source code, this could not be true of the object code, which could not be construed as a 'writing'. Further credence was given to this view by the argument that object code was created not by a person, but by a machine, referring to the process of compilation described above. On the other hand, computer programs are contained within the definition of 'literary work' in the US Copyright Act of 1976, and amendments introduced in 1980 included the definition 'a set of statements or instructions to be used directly or indirectly in a computer in order to bring about a certain result' and, in cases such as *Apple Computer Inc v Franklin Computer Corp*,[18] the US courts began to recognise that object code was subject to copyright protection.

13 *Universal City Studies v Corley* 273 F 3d 429, 446 (2nd Cir 2001).
14 *Ibid.*
15 This was true in the case of *John Richardson Computers Ltd v Flanders* [1993] FSR 497, which will be discussed in more detail later in the chapter.
16 [2004] EWHC 3487(Ch), [13].
17 *DP Anderson & Co v Lieber Code Co* [1917] 2 KB 469.
18 714 F 2d 1240 (3rd Cir 1983).

These developments were mirrored in other jurisdictions, as, for example, in the UK in *SEGA Enterprises v Richards*.[19] Whilst the court was happy to accept in principle that computer programs could be the subject of copyright, there was some discussion as to whether copyright could subsist in both the source code and the object code. At the heart of this discussion was the supposition that copyright protection could be extended to software either because of the writing requirement or because a computer program is a form of 'literary work', as opposed to any other type of creation attracting copyright protection. However, even this view was challenged in the Australian case of *Apple Computer v Computer Edge Pty Ltd*.[20] The initial decision declined to extend copyright protection to computer programs because the purpose of literary works was for enjoyment and, in the view of the court, this was not the function of computer programs.[21] The Federal Court reversed this decision, holding that the source programs were protected by copyright as new and original literary works, and that the object programs were protected in consequence as adaptations of the source programs.[22] On a further appeal, the High Court of Australia[23] concluded, albeit not without difficulty, that the source programs could be protected as literary works. There was, however, a division of opinion as to whether there was any basis for affording protection to the object code. Gibbs J, for example, found that nothing had persuaded him that 'a sequence of electrical impulses in a silicon chip, not capable itself of communicating anything directly to a human recipient, and designed only to operate a computer, is itself a literary work, or is the translation of a literary work'.[24] Brennan J suggested that although these electrical impulses could be represented in writing, 'the written representation must not be confused with what is represented not written'.[25] Since the object codes could neither be detected by, nor had any meaning for, humans, they could not, in the view of the majority, be construed as literary works. Neither, again in the view of the majority, could the object code be protected as an adaptation of the source program. This decision led to some consternation in the common law world based on both the theoretical and conceptual issues raised, and also the practical issue of whether object code could be protected by copyright. This led directly to statutory action being taken in the UK: the Copyright (Computer Software) Amendment Act was passed in 1985 and its provisions have now been re-enacted in the Copyright, Designs and Patents Act 1988 (CDPA 1988), putting the matter beyond doubt for all practical purposes.[26] Since then, a number of international instruments have made it clear that computer programs are protected as literary works within the meaning of the Berne Convention.[27]

## The boundary between idea and expression

The general concept of copyright and the application of copyright law in particular is bedevilled by the 'nothing new under the sun' problem. Even the most creative mind often borrows from, reworks, adapts, or is inspired by the ideas and work of others. Prohibiting such processes would be to stifle the very innovation and creativity that intellectual property protection is said to encourage. But this, of course, results in a conundrum: how to distinguish what is acceptable use of the ideas and work of others from copyright infringements. One approach to this is reflected in the fact that copyright protects the form in which authors or artists create their work rather than the idea itself.

---

19 [1983] FSR 73.
20 (1983) 50 ALR 581, [1984] FSR 246.
21 A view that echoes the dictum of Davey LJ in *Hollinrake v Truswell* [1894] 3 Ch 420, 428.
22 (1984) 53 ALR 225.
23 (1986) 161 CLR 171.
24 *Ibid*, [18].
25 *Ibid*, 201.
26 Nevertheless the arguments about the relevance of the 'literary' differences between source and object code have not disappeared: see, e.g., Susan Corbett, 'What if object code had been excluded from protection as a literary work in copyright law? A New Zealand perspective' (2008) Mich St L Rev 173.
27 See, e.g., Art 10(1) of the Trade-related Aspects of Intellectual Property Rights (TRIPS) Agreement; Art 4 of the WIPO Copyright Treaty; Art 1(1) of the Software Directive (discussed below at p 460).

This explanation has its advocates and its opponents, but the premise recognises that different creators and authors may well have the same or similar ideas, but that these are likely to be expressed in very different ways; thus it is the particular expression that should be protected. Although, as we shall see, approaches to this distinction have varied between both courts and jurisdictions, some of the issues raised have been in the context of the scope of software copyright protection and so a brief discussion is pertinent here.

The 'idea' of a work includes, most obviously, the original notion behind the work, but can also encompass the subject matter or the general style of the composition.[28] This has two broad consequences. The most obvious is that the underlying idea is not protected, and so other authors and creators can incorporate and build upon ideas behind existing copyright works within their own works. Additionally, or alternatively, many works may be based on well-recognised general themes. Both *Romeo and Juliet* and *West Side Story* tell similar tragic tales of star-crossed lovers. But although *West Side Story* clearly borrows from *Romeo and Juliet*, there the similarity ends. The general idea of feuding gangs and forbidden love might be the same, but the expression and detailed development of that idea is dramatically different. However, the more detailed an idea becomes, the more difficult it is to distinguish between idea and protectable expression.

In *Ibcos v Barclays*,[29] Jacob J suggested that the distinction had no real relevance in English law although he was later to describe it as being well known to copyright lawyers all over the world.[30] Whether or not it is specifically articulated as such, the distinction certainly exists in the UK.[31] The problems of separating idea and expression were discussed in the high-profile case, *Baigent v The Random House Group*.[32] Baigent and his co-authors were alleging copyright infringement in their work *The Holy Blood and the Holy Grail* by Dan Brown in his now-famous book, *The Da Vinci Code*. Although the claimants' work was referred to and recognised explicitly in Brown's book, the claimants' submission was that their work had been appropriated to such an extent as to constitute copyright infringement. The case is complex, but is concerned with the extent to which both general themes and more specific, well-documented detail can be the subject of copyright protection. After some examination, the court found that what had been taken were general themes and ideas that were either at too high a level of abstraction or were already sufficiently well known that they did not qualify for protection. Although *The Holy Blood and the Holy Grail* was clearly one of the sources for *The Da Vinci Code*, as indeed was acknowledged within the work, there were also many ideas and themes within *The Da Vinci Code* that did not originate in *The Holy Blood and the Holy Grail*. For a combination of these reasons, no infringement was found, but the court found itself unable to lay down any general principle to distinguish ideas and expression:

> What is said to have been copied is a theme of the copyright work. Copyright does not subsist in ideas; it protects the expression of ideas, not the ideas themselves. No clear principle is or could be laid down in the cases in order to tell whether what is sought to be protected is on the ideas side of the dividing line, or on the expression side.[33]

*Baigent v Random House* is a case involving many ideas and many ways of expressing of those ideas. What of the situation in which there are only a few ways, or perhaps only one way, of expressing a particular idea? Arguably, this is not very likely in creative and artistic works, but is much more feasible in relation to factual works or computer programs. The function that the computer

---

28 See further Lionel Bently and Brad Sherman, *Intellectual Property Law*, 3rd edn, 2007, Oxford: Oxford University Press, pp 181ff.
29 [1994] FSR 275 discussed in more detail below.
30 *Nova v Mazooma Games* [2007] EWCA Civ 219, [2007] RPC 25 [31].
31 See, e.g., *Donoghue v Allied Newspapers Ltd* [1938] Ch 106, 109, 110; *LB Plastics Ltd v Swish Products Ltd* [1979] FSR 145, 160; and *Total Information Processing Systems Ltd v Daman Ltd* [1992] FSR 171, 181.
32 [2007] EWCA Civ 247.
33 *Ibid*, [5].

program is required to perform may restrict the way in which it can be written to the extent that, if two programmers independently both create programs for the same purpose, they may have a number of, or even many, similar features. If there is only one way in which the program or part of the program can be written, can this reasonably be treated as the expression of an idea, or has the expression merged with the idea, so that the whole cannot be protected by copyright? The issue of when ideas merge with actual expression has caused particular problems in determining the scope of copyright protection for computer programs, which will be explored in more detail below.

There are thus a number of difficulties in distinguishing idea and expression, which have led to some criticism of the concept, particularly in the UK. Cornish and Llewelyn refer to it as a 'distinction with an ill-defined boundary',[34] while Laddie et al, in a discussion of what they refer to as the idea/expression fallacy, comment that 'a moment's thought will reveal that the maxim is obscure, or in its broadest sense suspect'.[35]

The expression/idea distinction is more specifically entrenched in the copyright law of the USA, where the issue was first examined in the now-famous case of *Baker v Selden*.[36] It has subsequently been enshrined in s 102 of the US Copyright Act of 1976, which sets out the categories of work to which copyright can be applied and then goes on to state explicitly that copyright protection does not extend to 'any idea . . .'. That is not to say that the US courts have always found the distinction an easy one to identify. In *Nichols v Universal Pictures Ltd*, Learned Hand J enunciated his frequently quoted 'levels of abstraction' test in an attempt to elucidate the demarcation between idea and expression,[37] but nevertheless went on to conclude that: 'Nobody has ever been able to fix that boundary, and nobody ever can.'

Nonetheless, the distinction between idea and expression has been recognised internationally in both the Trade-related Aspects of Intellectual Property Rights (TRIPS) Agreement[38] in Art 9(2) ('Copyright protection shall extend to expressions and not to ideas . . . as such') and also in the European Software Directive.[39] The original version of this Directive purported to be implemented into UK law by the Copyright (Computer Programs) Regulations 1992,[40] amending the CDPA 1988, but has no express provision that reflects Art 1(2), which provides that the expression in any form of computer program is protected by copyright, but not the ideas and principles underlying any elements of it. However, notwithstanding the implicit acceptance of the idea/expression distinction in these provisions, neither instrument gives any guidance on its practical implementation.

The idea/expression distinction is thus both controversial in some quarters and also difficult to apply. As Ginsburg has succinctly pointed out, separating idea from expression is 'one of the hardest tasks in traditional copyright analysis. It remains difficult, but not necessarily more so, when computer programs are at issue'.[41] However, it should be remembered that the reason it is invoked is to identify what elements of a work qualify for protection or to ascertain whether an alleged copyright infringement actually involved copying part of an author's work that was protected by copyright. Such an adjudication will always have to be made by some means and it may be that invoking the idea/expression distinction is helpful in some cases, but not in others. As we shall explore further later in the chapter, identification of the particular idea behind a computer

---

34 William Cornish and David Llewelyn, *Intellectual Property Law*, 6th edn, 2007, London: Sweet and Maxwell, p 455.
35 Hugh Laddie, Peter Prescott, Mary Vitoria, Adrian Speck, and Lindsay Lane, *The Modern Law of Copyright and Designs: Vol 1*, 2000, London: Butterworths, pp 97ff.
36 101 US 99 (1879).
37 *Nichols v Universal Pictures* 45 F 2d 119, 121 (2nd Cir 1930).
38 TRIPS Agreement: see www.wto.org/english/tratop_e/trips_e/t_agm0_e.htm
39 Directive 2009/24/EC of the European Parliament and of the Council of 23 April 2009 on the legal protection of computer programs: [2009] OJ l111/16. This Directive repeals and codifies Council Directive 91/250/EEC [1991] OJ L 122/42; references to the repealed Directive are to be construed as references to Directive 2009/24. On this point, see also *Nova Productions Ltd v Mazooma Games Ltd* [2007] EWCA Civ 219, [31]ff, and further discussion of the provisions of the Directive below at p 460.
40 SI 1992/3233.
41 Jane C Ginsburg, 'Four reasons and a paradox: The manifest superiority of copyright over *sui generis* protection of computer software' (1994) 94 Colum L Rev 2559, 2569.

program has provided particular challenges, as has, on occasions, extricating the expression from the idea.

## Structure, sequence, and organisation

The basic explanation given above of the design of a computer program in terms of source and object code oversimplifies the task of creating a workable computer program. In practice, many computer programs are constructed in a modular fashion by using standard instructions (code) obtained from libraries of tried-and-tested software. Generally, a program is not created in a linear fashion, but has a particular structure at the level at which the computer operates. In addition to this, it will also have a certain structure at the higher level – that is, the level at which the user interacts with the program via the user interface. It is this higher-level structure that creates the so-called 'look and feel'[42] of the program. The 'look' includes the screen display and the 'feel' refers to the way in which it is used. The familiar dropdown menus used by Microsoft are part of the 'feel' of Microsoft office. The generic term 'look and feel' recognises that these concepts may frequently overlap or be interdependent. The 'look and feel' of a program is often the factor that may give a particular program a competitive edge over its rivals, and therefore may be the element that the originators of the program most want to protect and competitors most want to emulate.[43] The extent to which the non-literal elements of a program – the structure, sequence, and organisation (SSO) – can be protected by copyright has, arguably, caused the most difficulties for the application of copyright principles, accentuated by the issues raised in identifying the boundary between idea and expression referred to above. Does, or could, the particular structure of a computer program represent the idea behind the program – or is it merely part of the expression? The consideration of the extent to which non-literal elements of a computer program can be protected by copyright law, together with the formulation of a suitable test for ascertaining whether non-literal copying has actually occurred, have arguably been the aspects of software copyright that have caused the most challenges for the courts and for which there are few parallels in more traditional literary works.

## Functionality and behaviour

Notwithstanding the fact that computer programs can be expressed in a written form, one important difference between computer programs and other literary works is that the program is written not for its own sake, but in order to make the computer perform some task or function either within the computer system itself or in the real world. In other words, the literary is combined with the technical, causing technology to operate to produce a defined result. In Karjala's words: '. . . computer programs are literary works only in form . . . In operation, they are pure works of function, that is, of technology.'[44] Samuelson et al[45] explain this characteristic in terms of the 'behaviour' of software, a property that, they suggest, means that programs cannot be regarded merely as texts: '. . . a crucially

---

42 A concept that originated in relation to greetings cards and children's books, and entered the analysis of copyright infringement of computer programs in cases involving video games: see, e.g., JWL Ogilvie, 'Defining computer program parts under Learned Hand's abstractions tests in software copyright infringement cases' (1992) 91 Mich L Rev 526; J Velasco, 'The copyrightability of non-literal elements of computer programs' (1994) 94 Col L Rev 242.

43 A number of the court decisions discussed in this chapter provide more detailed explanations of the design and construction of computer programs, which have the advantage for legal analysis that they have usually been accepted by both sides. In particular, useful basic explanations are provided in the following: *John Richardson Computers Ltd v Flanders* [1993] FSR 497, 503–4, per Ferris J; *Ibcos v Barclays Bank* [1994] FSR 275, 285–8, per Jacob J; *Computer Edge v Apple Ltd* (1986) 161 CLR 171, 178–9, per Gibbs CJ, and 199, per Brennan J. A more recent, but rather more technical, explanation can be found in *Cantor Fitzgerald v Tradition Ltd* [2000] RPC 95, 145, Appendix A: 'An introduction to computers and programming languages'. For a discussion of the significance of this for the application of copyright concepts, see, e.g., Steven R Englund, 'Idea, process or protected expression? Determining the scope of copyright protection of the structure of computer programs' (1990) 88 Mich L Rev 866, 867–72; more recently, Daniel B Garrie, 'The legal status of software' (2005) 23 J Marshall J Computer & Info Law 711.

44 Karjala, above, 198.

45 P Samuelson, R Davis, MD Kapor, and JH Reichman, 'A manifesto concerning the legal protection of computer programs' (1994) 94 Colum L Rev 2308.

important characteristic of programs is that they behave; programs exist to make computers perform tasks.' Since this attribute is central to the essential nature of programs, it gives them a 'dual character': they can be regarded simultaneously as both 'writings and machines'. This means that, in Samuelson et al's view, neither copyright nor patent law is suitable for protecting software innovation. Other commentators have, however, pointed out that computer programs are not the only works that are protected by copyright that can be said to exhibit 'behaviour'; this is also true of a range of creative and more functional works, ranging from music manuscripts, to architectural drawings. If there are a number of ways of achieving the ultimate purpose of a work, then it can be afforded copyright protection without subsequent creativity of innovation being stifled.[46]

## Interoperability requirements

One feature that may be desirable in a computer program, but which has no clear parallel in relation to more conventional literary works, is the need for interoperability – that is, the capacity of the computer program to be compatible with other computer programs or hardware elements in a system, such as a printer, for example. The copyright in a more traditional work does not depend on the medium in which it is stored; neither does a traditional work have to interact with other works.[47] In contrast, compatibility between different programs – and particularly between applications and systems software – is of central importance to the software market. It would be no good purchasing the latest games software produced by one manufacturer only to find that it would not operate on a PC produced by another manufacturer. However, if a computer program is to be interoperable with another, it will need to contain some of the same features, at least at the interface between the two. If the code of the other program is not available, one way of producing a computer program that is interoperable with other programs is by decompiling (that is, compiling in reverse), or reverse engineering, the object code of the program with which interoperability is desired, to obtain the source code in an HLL. The features that are required to ensure interoperability are then duplicated – that is, copied – in order to create the interface between the existing and the new or proposed program. Where the creator of the new program does not have the copyright in the other program, this can lead to allegations of copyright infringement as a result of the decompilation and subsequent development of the new program.[48] There is no exact parallel to this process for other works that are eligible for copyright protection and so, inevitably, questions have arisen as to the extent to which copyright law allows decompilation for these purposes.

## Scope of protection

Many aspects of a computer program can be copied from straight line-to-line copying of both source and object code – so-called 'literal' copying – to copying of the structure of the program – often referred to as 'non-literal' copying, although 'non-textual' copying might be a more accurate description. Should all of these aspects of copying be protected by the law of copyright, or only those that correspond to literal copying of the work, by analogy with a literary work? How far can computer programmers use the work done by others in their own creation of new programs without infringing the original developer's rights? How can compatibility with another program be ensured without infringing copyright? At what point does the code for a commonly used routine enter the public domain? These, and other issues, have resulted in discussion in many jurisdictions regarding the extent of the scope of copyright protection for computer programs and the literature on the subject is now voluminous.

---

46 See further Ginsburg, above, 2566.
47 See further Dennis S Karjala, 'Copyright protection of computer software in the United States and Japan: Part 2' [1991] EIPR 231, 233.
48 See, e.g., the facts of *SAS Institute Inc v World Programming Ltd* [2010] EWHC 1829.

How much needs to be copied before an infringement occurs is defined differently in different jurisdictions. In the UK, the concept is one of taking a substantial part, whilst the law in the USA considers the amount and substantiality of the portion used, often interpreted by the courts in terms of substantial similarity.[49] While the detail of these may differ, they both require some assessment of what and how much has been copied in comparison with the whole. However, the US test for substantial similarity requires much more wrestling with the idea/expression dichotomy than the UK test of establishing whether there has been copying of a substantial part. A consideration of the manner of constructing computer programs, to which reference has already been made, will reveal that many aspects of a program can be copied, from straight, line-by-line copying of the source or object code (literal copying), to copying of the SSO of the program (non-literal copying). Whereas line-by-line copying is both easy to identify and fits within the framework of copyright protection, the formulation of a suitable test for non-literal copying has not been quite so amenable to accepted and acceptable solutions. It has been established, in relation to other areas of copyright law, that the test of substantial taking may be either quantitative or qualitative.[50] Thus, if part of a work is copied that is small in quantity, but highly significant in terms of its overall contribution to the work, then an action will lie.[51] Copying can be detected if, for example, spurious lines of code are included that are not essential to the execution of the program. Other evidence may also raise a strong presumption of literal copying. Thus, in *MS Associates v Power*,[52] it was noted that there were a number of similarities in the names of the variables in the defendants' and plaintiffs' programs and also that the function 'vtprs' appeared in both the defendants' and the plaintiffs' list of variables even though the function was not actually used in the defendants' program.

If there are similar errors in two programs, this can raise a strong presumption of copying. However, this may be capable of rebuttal because of another difference between computer programs and other forms of literary work. Whereas it is statistically improbable that, if two authors independently have the same idea for a novel, they will write it in the same words and sentence construction, this is not necessarily such a remote possibility in the case of a computer program. If two programmers independently write a program to perform the same task, especially if this is a relatively simple task or subroutine, it may be very likely that they will write the same, or a similar, program. It is also equally possible that they may make the same errors. If such programs contain the same errors, then, although this may provide persuasive evidence, copying will not be a foregone conclusion, because some errors are more frequent and obvious than others. Illustrations of these issues are again to be found in *MS Associates v Power*, in which the same errors were noted in one part of the program, but, in relation to another part, it was perhaps possible to explain the observed similarities. Such factors have not really caused major headaches for the courts in contrast with the challenges created by, for instance, the attempts to accommodate non-literal copying and decompilation within the existing copyright regime. The following sections will examine some of the case law on this topic primarily from US and UK perspectives.

## Copyright and non-literal copying in the USA

### The *Whelan* test

The first case to consider the issue of both non-literal copying and issues surrounding the idea/expression boundary was *Whelan Associates v Jaslow Dental Laboratory Inc*.[53] The case concerned two computer programs for the organisation of dental laboratory records created by the same programmer

49 CDPA 1988, s 16(3); 17 USC § 107(3).
50 See, e.g., *Hawkes & Son (London) Ltd v Paramount Film Services Ltd* [1934] Ch 593; *Ladbroke (Football) Ltd v William Hill (Football) Ltd* [1964] 1 WLR 273, in which Lord Pearce said: 'Whether a part is substantial must be decided by its quality rather than its quantity.' This latter case was relied upon by Ferris J in *John Richardson Computers v Flanders* [1993] FSR 497 (see below).
51 See, e.g., the cases reviewed in Nancy J Mertzel, 'Copying 0.03% of software code base was not *de minimis*' (2008) 3 JIPLP 547.
52 [1987] FSR 242.
53 797 F 2d 1222 (3rd Cir 1987), [1987] FSR 1.

whilst in different employment. It was accepted that the functionality of both programs was the same, but the coding was different and internal similarities were absent. Given that the programs had similar structures, the defendant's argument was that the structure was the idea, rather than the expression, of the programs and was thus beyond the scope of copyright protection. The judgment considered various copyright precedents, including the much-quoted authority *Baker v Selden*,[54] and concluded that 'the purpose or function of a utilitarian work would be the work's idea, and everything that is not necessary to that purpose or function would be part of the expression of the idea'.[55] The necessary corollary was that if there were only limited ways in which to express the function, then these would be construed as part of the idea. The judgment refers to Learned Hand's dicta on the delineation of idea and expression, but does not build on his famous abstractions test; instead, it relies on another line of case law and also on statute to show that the SSO of the program, the non-literal elements, should be afforded copyright protection. In brief, the court found that the purpose of the program at issue was the organisation of the dental laboratory records, and that the structure of the program was not necessary to that purpose and so was entitled to copyright protection.

Velasco makes the point that the ideal test would be one that is both simple and accurate,[56] and one significant aspect of the test in *Whelan* is that it is both straightforward and easy to apply.[57] However, in such a technically complex area as computer software, it has proved difficult to pursue either of these aims without compromising the other and it is unsurprising, therefore, that certain inadequacies have been identified in the straightforward test enunciated in *Whelan*. One criticism is that it is an oversimplification to suggest that a single purpose can be defined and isolated for a particular program. An obvious consequence of this is that if programmers are to be able to devise other programs that perform the same function, but do not infringe copyright, then there has to be a number of other possible structures for the program that could, reasonably and efficiently, fulfil that same purpose. If not, the *Whelan* formulation is capable of conferring an almost patent-like protection on the first programmer to develop a suitable structure. Given that 'many aspects of application code are dictated by basic principles of software engineering',[58] this is a very real consequence of adherence to the test in *Whelan*. Also, it is difficult, if not impossible, to identify a single purpose behind many, if not most, commercially important programs, because the reality is that they usually consist of a number of subroutines and modules, each of which could, validly, be considered as an idea. It thus has the propensity to stifle, rather than stimulate, innovation by giving preferential protection to the first comer on the market.[59]

## Abstraction, filtration, comparison

The US Court of Appeals Second Circuit recognised some of these problems in the later case of *Computer Associates v Altai*,[60] noting that the decision in *Whelan* had received a 'mixed reception' in the courts and that '*Whelan* has fared ... poorly in the academic community where its standard ... has been widely criticised for being overbroad',[61] and going on to use rather different reasoning. Again, the case concerned a programmer developing similar software for two different employers. In the first program produced for Altai, there had been literal copying of 30 per cent of Computer Associates' code. Another program was produced using new programmers, but Computer Associates then alleged that this version still made use of the non-literal elements of the original program. This led

54 101 US 99 (1879).
55 797 F 2d 1222, 1236.
56 Velasco, above.
57 See further Englund, above.
58 PS Menell, 'An analysis of the scope of copyright protection for application programs' (1989) 41 Stan L Rev 1045, 1082.
59 *Ibid*.
60 982 F 2d 693 (2nd Cir 1992).
61 *Ibid*, 705.

to the Second Circuit formulating what has become known as the 'abstraction–filtration–comparison' test as it struggled to articulate a suitable method for determining the extent to which the non-literal elements of a computer program could be protected by copyright and, in particular, how 'substantial similarity' could be adjudicated. It was accepted in the case that copyright protection of computer programs extends beyond literal similarities in code and also includes similarities in structure. In contrast to the decision in *Whelan*, the judgment of the Second Circuit utilised Learned Hand's famous abstractions approach, at least for the first part of the test, and the *Whelan* formulation, that the overall purpose of the program can be equated with its idea, was roundly criticised on the basis already mentioned that the majority of programs do not consist of a single 'idea', but are more accurately described as composites.

The new three-stage test comprises breaking down the work into its constituent parts, separating out the elements that are not protected by copyright, and then comparing what remains (the 'kernel' of creative expression) with the allegedly infringing program.[62] The first step – the *abstraction* – essentially replicates Learned Hand's levels of abstractions approach in *Nichols v Universal Pictures*. The second stage – *filtration* – involves identifying, at each level of abstraction, the constituent elements and, in particular, whether they are dictated by efficiency, external factors, or are taken from the public domain. The first of these reflects the fact that, as discussed above, there may be only one way of accomplishing a given task, so that the only efficient way in which to construct the program is to replicate these elements. The court suggested that, 'since evidence of similarly efficient structure is not particularly probative of copying, it should be disregarded in the overall substantial similarity analysis'.[63] The second category of element to be filtered out is those that are dictated by external constraints, such as the specification of the system on which the program has to run, necessary compatibility with other programs, etc. Finally, this stage of the test requires any material already in the public domain to be disregarded in assessing substantial similarity. The result of the filtration stage is to leave behind what the court referred to as 'a core of protectable expression. In terms of a work's copyright value, this is the golden nugget . . .'.[64] It is only at this stage that there is a comparison with an alleged infringing program to ascertain whether or not there is 'substantial similarity' between the two.

The court recognised that the decision narrowed the scope of protection and so was more favourable to the defendant than *Whelan*, but asserted that it was merely the outcome of applying standard copyright principles to computer programs.[65] The judgment was generally well received as demonstrating a good understanding of the way in which computer programs are designed and written. It was acknowledged by some writers that the decision was also able to deal with constraints of interoperability and compatibility.[66] On the other hand, some reservations were expressed that it would leave non-literal elements underprotected, and it was also suggested that 'the court was unduly constrained by a uniquely literary view of the creative process and thus failed to recognise its own ability to "keep pace" with technological change within the traditional copyright framework', even though, despite its imperfections, the test was 'arguably a "practical necessity" in the computer program context'.[67] A practical example of a situation in which there could be said to be underprotection occurred in *Apple Computer Inc v Microsoft Corp*.[68] In this case, applying the abstraction–filtration–comparison test resulted in there being little to compare, because the program had been constructed from existing subroutines already in the public domain or dictated by

62 *Ibid*, 706.
63 *Ibid*, 709.
64 *Ibid*, 701.
65 *Ibid*, 712.
66 See, e.g., TS Teter, 'Merger and the machines: An analysis of the pro-compatibility trend in computer software copyright cases' (1993) 45 Stan L Rev 1061, 1084. Interoperability issues are explored in more detail below at pp 463–6.
67 'Case note on *Computer Associates v Altai*' (1992) 106 Harv L Rev 510.
68 35 F 3d 1435 (9th Cir 1994); see also Steve S Moutsatsos and John CR Cummings, '*Apple v Microsoft*: Has the pendulum swung too far?' (1993) 9 CL & P 162.

efficiency requirements, with a consequent denial of copyright protection. In such cases, whether or not there is any copyright protection will depend on an assessment of the way in which the sub-routines have been assembled and interlinked. In these situations, another strand of case law – that on the copyright of compilations – may become very relevant.[69]

## The impact of *Whelan* and *Altai*

In different ways, both *Whelan* and *Altai* have been influential, have generated much debate, and have subsequently been referred to in cases in the UK and other jurisdictions. In some ways, they can be viewed as two ends of the spectrum of copyright protection for computer programs, because 'both approaches are rooted in and use the language and legal precedent of copyright law but with vastly differing results'.[70] *Whelan*, with its almost patent-like protection, operates in favour of the original developer of the program, whereas application of the test in *Altai* changes the balance considerably. Where the balance lies may be significant for certain sectors of the industry, depending on whether they produce primarily systems or applications software. Different commentators have both supported and opposed the decision in *Altai*, but Miller suggests that the differences between the two have been overstated because the decisions can be reconciled by viewing *Altai* as a further refinement of the approach begun in *Whelan*.[71]

Whatever view is taken of the relationship between the decisions in these two cases, the situation in the US courts has been more complex than the analysis above might suggest. As we have seen, both *Whelan* and *Altai* were decided in different circuits of the US Court of Appeals and, despite the criticisms of *Whelan* contained in the court's judgment in *Altai*, it was certainly not the case that the test in *Altai* immediately eclipsed that in *Whelan*. In addition, other tests were devised sometimes based in part on either of these tests. This resulted, at times, in certain contradictions and confusions, and, in the words of the court in *Altai*, 'many of the decisions in this area reflect the courts' attempt to fit the proverbial square peg in a round hole'.[72] The Ninth Circuit, for example, developed its own test (the intrinsic/extrinsic test) for copyrightability of computer programs in *Brown Bag Software v Symantec Corp*.[73] The proliferation of such tests and their subsequent modification led one commentator to state: 'The "look and feel" cases . . . can fairly be characterised as a mess.'[74] Thus the situation with regard to copyrightability of computer software in the US courts has been more confused than is sometimes presented,[75] although the *Altai* test now appears to be generally accepted.[76]

## Developing a test for non-literal copying in the UK

*John Richardson Computers Ltd v Flanders*[77] was the first case in the UK to consider these issues. The facts of the case are complex, but, in brief, both parties developed and marketed programs to print labels for prescriptions at pharmacists, and to keep details of the stock of drugs; the same programmer, Flanders, was involved in each. There was no evidence of substantial taking of literal parts of the code; rather what was alleged was that parts of the general 'scheme' of the program,

69 In the USA, see *Feist Publications Inc v Rural Telephone Service Co* 113 L Ed 2d 358 (1991), cited in *Altai*, and discussed in the context of databases below at p 475. In the UK, see the discussion of *Richardson v Flanders* [1993] FSR 497, below.
70 Moutsatsos and Cummings, above.
71 AR Miller, 'Copyright protection for computer programs, databases and computer-generated works: Is anything new since CONTU?' (1993) 106 Harv L Rev 977.
72 982 F 2d 693, 712 (2nd Cir 1992).
73 960 F 2d 1465 (9th Cir 1992).
74 DL Hayes, 'What's left of look and feel? A current analysis' (1993) 10 CL 1.
75 A more detailed analysis is beyond the scope of this publication: see, e.g., ibid; Miller, above; Velasco, above; Karjala, '. . . Part 2', above; J Drexl, 'What is protected in a computer program? Copyright protection in the US and Europe' (1994) 15 IIC.
76 S Lai, *The Copyright Protection of Computer Software in the United Kingdom*, 2000, Oxford: Hart Publishing, ch 2.
77 [1993] FSR 497.

including some rather idiosyncratic subroutines, had been copied. Ferris J noted that the *Altai* approach had already been adopted in two federal circuits in the USA and that there was nothing to suggest that the *Whelan* approach should be preferred.[78] However, Ferris J did not adopt the *Altai* approach verbatim, but instead first assessed whether or not under English copyright law the program in question was, as a whole, entitled to copyright protection by considering it as a compilation by analogy with the *William Hill* case.[79] Only after establishing that the non-literal elements were protectable as a compilation did Ferris J go on to apply the *Altai* test, concluding that the copyright infringement was minor and limited. The steps in his analysis can perhaps be summarised by the following:

(1)    Is the claimant's program as a whole entitled to copyright protection?
(2)    Are there similarities to the claimant's program in the defendant's program?
(3)    Is any similarity attributable to copying?
(4)    Do any such similarities amount to the copying of a substantial part of the claimant's program assessed by application of the abstraction–filtration–comparison test of *Computer Associates v Altai*?

Whether or not this is an appropriate approach,[80] it is difficult to apply – a fact that was recognised in the judgment itself.

## General and 'detailed' ideas

*Richardson v Flanders* was soon followed by another case, that of *Ibcos Computers Ltd v Barclays Finance Ltd*.[81] Again, the facts are rather complex, but basically centred on an ex-employee continuing to develop and rewrite software on which he had been working during employment. Copyright infringement was claimed in the individual programs and subroutines, the general structure, and certain general features of the system. Jacob J first considered whether the work in question attracted copyright protection. He found it generally unhelpful to focus on the idea/expression distinction, but did suggest that '[t]he true position is that where an "idea" is sufficiently general, then even if an original work embodies it, the mere taking of that idea will not infringe. But if the "idea" is detailed, then there may be infringement. It is a question of degree'.[82]

Jacob's notion of a detailed idea that might be protected by copyright is, presumably, in the context of computer programs, that are found when a number of subroutines are put together to form one program. This would be the result of the intellectual effort, skill, and judgment of the software writer, as opposed to a general idea, which would not be protected by copyright, and presumably might equate with the 'function' in the *Whelan* sense. He was generally dismissive of reliance on US copyright cases, particularly in the light of the fact that the idea/expression distinction is treated differently in the two jurisdictions, and held that the question of judging a substantial part was a matter of applying the standard principles of copyright law in the UK. Although the decision suggests that non-literal elements can be protected by copyright, this was a case in which there was evidence of literal copying of the code and so an assessment of what might constitute a substantial part of the non-literal elements was not a critical part of the decision.

78  General references had been made to the *Whelan* judgment in the interlocutory hearings in both *Computer Aided Design v Bolwell* (1989), unreported, 23 August; and *Total Information Processing Systems Ltd v Daman Ltd* [1992] FSR 171.
79  *Ladbroke (Football) Ltd v William Hill (Football) Ltd* [1964] 1 WLR 273.
80  See further, Richard Arnold, 'Infringement of copyright in computer software by non-textual copying: First decision at trial by an English court' [1993] EIPR 250.
81  [1994] FSR 275.
82  Ibid, 291.

## Moving on from *Flanders* and *Ibcos*

In *Cantor Fitzgerald v Tradition*,[83] Pumfrey J agreed with the general approach in *Ibcos*. Although not actually concerned with the copying of non-literal aspects of a program, he considered 'the inter-relationship of the originality of the work (the prerequisite for the subsistence of copyright) and substantiality of the part of the work copied (the prerequisite for infringement)'. He pointed out that the correct approach to substantiality was straightforward: there would be a copyright infringement if a part of a work were appropriated 'upon which a substantial part of the author's skill and labour were expended'. Using the analogy of a novel or a play, he concluded that the 'architecture'[84] of a computer program could be protected by copyright if it resulted from the expenditure of a substantial part of the programmer's skill, labour, and judgment.[85]

Pumfrey J returned to the issue of software copyright in *Navitaire v Easyjet*.[86] The claimant alleged copying of the overall 'look and feel' of software for an airline booking system, detailed copying of individual commands, and copying of certain screen displays showing the results. This software had been created by observing and studying the original and as he explained:

> . . . two completely different computer programs can produce an identical result: not a result identical at some level of abstraction but identical at any level of abstraction. This is so even if the author of one has no access at all to the other but only to its results.[87]

In a lengthy discussion of the problems of trying to protect functional elements of computer programs by copyright,[88] no assistance was found from the decisions in *Flanders* and *Ibcos*, and overall it was held that the claim failed for both a lack of substantiality and the nature of the skill and labour to be protected, and that neither was any of the code read or copied by the defendants. Thus copyright protection could not be relied on to prevent the creation of a competing product. However, this is not necessarily an unusual position and, although the US authorities were not relied upon, it seems likely that, on these facts, a similar result would be obtained by applying the *Altai* test.[89] In other words, in the absence of access to the original code, if a programmer writes a program that is based on the general idea of a program written by another person, that will be insufficient to establish copyright infringement. This was subsequently confirmed by the Court of Appeal in *Nova v Mazooma Games*,[90] upholding the reasoning in *Navitaire*, which has since been referred to as the 'leading case on the copyright protection of computer programs'.[91] The decision seems to have been generally welcomed as providing a coherent approach to the application of copyright principles to the production of similar programs[92] that has 'blown away the fog of technical obfuscation'.[93]

# The Software Directive and its implementation

Around the time that *Flanders* was under consideration, legislative action was also being taken in the EU with respect to intellectual property rights in computer programs in the form of the Software Directive. This Directive was a recognition of the issues that had caused debate in relation

---

83 [2000] RPC 95.
84 *Ibid*, [73].
85 *Ibid*, [76].
86 [2004] EWHC 1725 (Ch).
87 [2004] EWHC 1725 (Ch), [2006] RPC 3 [125].
88 *Ibid*, [118]ff.
89 See also discussion in R Marchini, '*Navitaire v easyJet*: What now for look and feel?' (2005) 15(6) Comp and Law 31.
90 [2007] EWCA Civ 219
91 *SAS v World Programming* [2010] EWHC 1829 (Ch), [174], in which Arnold J also lists the reasons why Pumfrey J was in a good position to decide the case.
92 See, e.g., Simon Miles and Emma Stoker, '*Nova Productions Ltd v Mazooma Games Ltd*' (2006) 17 Ent L Rev 181; Andrew Clay, '*Nova Productions Ltd v Mazooma Games Ltd*: Game over for Nova' (2007) 18 Ent L Rev 187.
93 Lim and Longdin, above, 375

to the protection of intellectual property rights in computer programs, and also of the fact that, without harmonisation of these provisions, the completion and operation of the single European market in goods and services might be compromised. This was particularly necessary in view of the fact that different Member States had adopted quite different attitudes to the legal protection of computer programs. Thus, notwithstanding that many other jurisdictions, both inside and outside Europe, were basing their protection on copyright principles, this was not possible in Germany, for example, where computer programs were viewed as technical and scientific products, rather than literary works.[94] The fact that such states might be signatories to the Berne Convention was of little relevance, because the issue was one of the categorisation of computer programs as copyright material. The Directive was adopted in 1991, with an implementation date of 1 January 1993, and its provisions seem to have stood the test of time. A subsequent report from the European Commission on its implementation found that overall implementation by Member States was satisfactory and that the effects of the implementation were beneficial. It therefore concluded that 'experience to date does not lead to the view that the substantive copyright provisions of the Directive should be revisited at this time'.[95] This view was effectively endorsed by the fact that no amendments to this Directive were included in the later Copyright Directive, which notes that it is 'based on principles and rules already laid down in the directives currently in force in this area, in particular Directive 91/250/EEC . . .'.[96] In 2009, the provisions of the original Directive were codified in Directive 2009/24/EC, but the substantive requirements remain unchanged.[97]

## Scope of the Directive

Article 1(1) protects computer programs as literary works and this is deemed to extend to any preparatory design material; however, the protection only extends to the expression and does not include any underlying ideas (Art 1(2)). *Bezpečnostní softwarová asociace – Svaz softwarové ochrany v Ministerstvo Kultury* (BSA)[98] raised the question of whether the graphical user interface was an expression of the underlying computer program within the meaning of Art 1(2). Advocate General Bot explained that, in the absence of a definition of 'computer program' within the Directive this effectively required an exploration of the scope of the Directive.[99] He concluded that the concept of any form of expression of computer program referred to forms of expression which enable the computer program to perform the task for which it was created.[100] As the GUI alone could not give that result it could not be viewed as part of the expression of the program; also as different computer programs with different source and object code can share the same GUI, deciding differently would create practical difficulties.[101] Although the GUI is outside the scope of the Directive, this is not to say that it cannot be protected by the normal rules of copyright in appropriate cases, a point that was made clear by both the AG and the CJEU in agreeing with this construction of the Directive.

Article 1(3) further requires that the program must be original in the sense of 'the author's own intellectual creation'. This requirement hides a potential clash between the civil law and common law approach to originality. The former looks for some innovative or creative quality specific to the author, whereas the latter merely uses a test based on the author's own endeavours. As would be expected, cases on computer programs in Germany, France, Belgium, and the Netherlands prior

---

94 See, e.g., Andreas Wiebe, 'European copyright protection of software from a German perspective' (1993) 9 CL & P 79.
95 Report from the Commission to the Council, the European Parliament and the Economic and Social Committee, COM(2000) 1999 final.
96 Directive 2001/29/EC of the European Parliament and of the Council of 22 May 2001 on the harmonisation of certain aspects of copyright and related rights in the information society: [2001] OJ L 167/10, Recital 20.
97 Directive 2009/24/EC of the European Parliament and of the Council of 23 April 2009 on the legal protection of computer programs (Codified version): [2009] OJ L 111/16.
98 Case C-393/09 [2011] ECR I-3787 (CJEU).
99 Opinion of AG, [42] and [43].
100 *Ibid*, [64].
101 *Ibid*, [65].

to the Directive looked for evidence of some aspect of the author's personality to sustain a finding of originality.[102] The Directive sought to harmonise this 'mosaic of originality interpretations',[103] but the conflict between the approaches persists because the phrase 'own intellectual creation' can be interpreted in conformity with either approach. Given this possibility, and in the light of case law in Belgium, Deene calls for referrals also to be made to the CJEU to establish a uniform interpretation of originality with respect to computer programs.[104] Assessment of originality in some of the recent copyright litigation in the CJEU, including the BSA case referred to above, certainly appears to be moving away from the definition of originality in English law as merely being something which is the product of the author's own skill and labour – the so-called 'sweat of the brow' test. However Rahmatian has suggested that any such departure is more imaginary than real and, in practice, courts in different legal traditions are approaching such cases in broadly similar ways creating a 'non-legislative harmonisation through judicial convergence, based on different protection philosophies as their starting point.'[105]

## Restricted acts and their exceptions

The Directive reserves the usual rights to copyright holders. An application of traditional copyright principles would suggest that non-infringing use is then possible with express authorisation of the copyright holder or within one of the general 'fair use' exceptions. The 1991 Software Directive introduced for the first time a new category of acts that, rather than being generally available, are reserved for a person with a 'right to use the program' – that is, introducing a concept of a 'lawful user'. The substance of these exceptions reflects some of the differences between computer programs and traditional literary works. They are contained in Art 5 and include anything necessary for the use of the computer program by the lawful acquirer for its intended purpose, including: error correction; the making of a back-up copy; and a right for the lawful user to 'observe, study or test the functioning of a program in order to determine the ideas and principles underlying any element of the program', as long as this is done whilst performing acts that are otherwise permitted by copyright law. Further, most of these exceptions to the restricted acts are obligatory and cannot be excluded by contract.[106] It has been suggested that these new exceptions 'mark the advent of a more active approach to copyright exceptions', which creates 'rights' that are 'legal hybrids between exceptions and rights'.[107] Section 50C of the CDPA 1988, giving effect to Art 5(1), speaks in terms of 'lawful use'. There is no definition of either lawful use or the 'lawful user', but it seems clear that it does not equate with all people who use the program, but is more akin to the term 'lawful acquirer' that is used in Art 5(1).[108]

## Case study – software emulation

The market in applications software is a lucrative and highly competitive one and many software developers try to gain a share of the market in a successful application by emulating an existing program produced by another developer. That is not to say that they make a pirated copy of the program but that they are able to reproduce its functionality by observing its operation so that the

---

102 Discussed in Joris Deene, 'Originality in software law: Belgian doctrine and jurisprudence remain divided' (2007) 2 JIPLP 692, 693.
103 Ibid.
104 Ibid, 698.
105 Andreas Rahmatian, 'Originality in UK copyright law: the old 'skill and labour' doctrine under pressure' (2013) 44 IIC 4, 29. See also discussion of originality in relation to databases below at p 475 and 482.
106 Directive 91/250, Art 9; now Directive 2009/24, Art 8. The provisions have been implemented in the UK by introducing new ss 50A, 50BA, 50C and 296A into the Copyright, Designs and Patents Act 1988 (CDPA 1988). These should be read in conjunction with the new s 21(3)(ab), which introduces a new element into the definition of 'adaptation' – namely, 'an arrangement or altered version of the program or a translation of it'.
107 Tatiana-Eleni Synodinou, 'The lawful user and a balancing of interests in European copyright law' (2010) 41 IIC 819, 826.
108 For discussion of the requirements of Art 5(1) and (2) see p 506.

new program operates in the same way as the original program. This process is also able to produce low cost alternatives to proprietary products. Not surprisingly perhaps, the creators of the original program are often not very happy about this process, but given that it is not produced by copying the code of the original or indeed having access to the original code, does it violate copyright law? The courts in *Navitaire* and *Nova v Mazooma Games* referred to above, found that this practice did not breach copyright. Nevertheless, disputes continue to arise in this type of situation.

As already mentioned the Software Directive only protects the expression not the idea and Art 5(3) allows for observing, studying or testing of the functionality of a program in order to ascertain the underlying ideas and principles. This latter provision was not explicitly referred to in either *Navitaire* or *Nova* but came to the fore in *SAS v World Programming*.[109] SAS had developed various statistical applications programs written in SAS language – a proprietary language created for this purpose. World Programming (WP) created alternative programs that had similar functionality to the SAS applications programs and could support application programs written in the SAS language. The WP Language effectively emulated the functionality of SAS so that its customers' applications programs performed the same with both WP and SAS applications. It was agreed that WP intended this outcome and that neither had it copied or had access to SAS source code. As Onslow and Jamal have observed, 'the facts were perfect for a test case because the fidelity of the emulation was nearly perfect.'[110]

At first instance, Arnold J reviewed the arguments on both sides.[111] These included: whether or not Art 5(3) complied with the Berne Convention 'three-step test'; whether it was an 'avoidance of doubt' provision; the effect of any licence provisions; and the effect of the legislative history and relevant recitals. His provisional view was that, as an exception, Art 5(3) should be interpreted as a positive defence not an avoidance of doubt measure; that it was significant that it could not be overridden by contract – that is, by standard licence terms – and that its provisions should be interpreted broadly. Nevertheless, he concluded that the issue was not free from doubt and that this was a matter, along with questions relating to the distinction between idea and expression in Art 1(2), that should be referred to the CJEU.[112]

Advocate General Bot viewed Art 5(3) as an extension of Art 1(2) effectively reasoning that since only the expression is protected, it follows that non-invasive methods of ascertaining the underlying ideas and principles does not breach copyright in the first program.[113] This is further supported by the fact that the right in Art 5(3) cannot be excluded by contract so that a first creator cannot protect ideas indirectly by licence terms.[114] The CJEU was in broad agreement with the fact that Art 5(3) was consistent with Art 1(2)[115] and concluded that 'copyright in a computer program cannot be infringed . . . where the lawful acquirer . . . did not have access to the source code . . . but merely studied, observed and tested that program in order to reproduce its functionality in a second program' provided the acts of the alleged infringer do not breach the exclusive rights of the copyrightholder.[116]

It had been argued that WP had breached the terms of the SAS licence and so had lost the protection of Art 5(3). But when the case returned to the High Court, Arnold J, in a lengthy analysis of the CJEU's decision on this point, concluded that any breaches that occurred did not have this effect

109 Case C–406/10, [2010] OJ C 346/26.
110 Robert Onslow and Isabel Jamal, 'Copyright infringement and software emulation – *SAS Inc v World Programming Limited*' (2013) 35 E.I.P.R. 352, 353.
111 [2010] EWHC 1829 (Ch), [291]–[315].
112 A number of other questions were also referred – see Case C–406/10, *SAS Institute v World Programming Ltd*, [28].
113 Ibid, Opinion of the Advocate General, [92].
114 Ibid, [93].
115 Judgment of CJEU, [52].
116 For further discussion see, e.g., Paul Przemyslaw Polanski, 'Some reflections on the duality of regime for software protection in the European Union' (2013) 29 CLSRev 282; and Daniel Gervais and Esgtelle Derclaye, 'The scope of computer program protection after SAS: are we closer to answers?' (2012) 34 EIPR 565.

as these breaches did not impinge on the fact that there was no access to the source code and that WP merely studied, observed and tested the program.[117] A subsequent appeal by SAS was unsuccessful and on this particular point Lewison LJ found that there had been no breach of the terms of use and left no room for doubt that WPL could benefit from the protection of Art 5(3).[118] Although this may not be the answer that original software developers had been hoping for, it seems clear that this was what was intended to be the effect of the provisions of the Software Directive.

Samuelson et al suggest that the approach to SAS in the CJEU brings EU and US software copyright law more closely in alignment.[119] However, there have been further developments in the US in relation to protection of functionality in *Oracle Inc v Google Inc*[120] and the debate continues. Google was accused of copying parts of the JAVA applications program interface (an Oracle product) in the development of its Android operating system. In order to emulate the functionality Google had replicated a number of names and functions but had used different source code. At first instance the District court engaged in a lengthy review of the US cases on functionality and copyright protection for the SSO of a computer program. This led to the dismissal of Oracle's claim; the reasoning included the fact that copyright law gave no monopoly over how a particular functionality could be implemented and that Google (and anyone else) was therefore free to create its own program with the same functionality. Whether or not the SSO qualified for copyright protection depended on the particular facts of the case and could be ascertained by, for instance, using the abstraction – filtration – comparison test.

If this had been the last word then the similarity in approach to the CJEU would be clear. But the Federal Circuit has now overturned this decision.[121] The focus of the discussion on appeal was not so much on the method of creating a program with the same functionality but rather with the fact that the SSO was both original and creative and that there were a number of ways in which the code could have been written which would have produced the same effect. It was therefore entirely possible for Google to have infringed the copyright in the JAVA API. Whether it had or not, depended not on the reasoning employed in the lower court but on whether Google's actions could be categorised as 'fair use'. Because the jury at first instance had not been able to arrive at a decision on this point the case was remanded for reconsideration of the fair use criteria.

While this outcome could appear to give some satisfaction to original software developers, it is unlikely that this will be the last word on this. As Hansen et al point out,[122] the apparently broad copyright protection for functional aspects of programs given by the Federal Circuit does not sit well with the other decisions reviewed by the District Court. So it may be premature to suggest that the EU and the US are not in harmony on this issue. The development of software copyright law may well be proving more favourable to those who seek to increase both innovation and competition by building on existing programs and applications.

## Decompilation and fair use

One feature that may be desirable in a computer program, but which has no clear parallel in relation to more conventional literary works, is the need for interoperability – that is, the capacity of the computer program to be compatible with other computer programs or hardware elements in a system, such as a printer. This means that the interoperable program will need to contain some of

---

117 [2013] EWHC 69 (Ch) [56]–[73].
118 [2013] EWCA Civ 1482 [91]–[110]. See also discussion in Iona Silverman, 'SAS: major software copyright ruling upheld' (2014) 9 JIPLP 179.
119 Pamela Samuelson, Thomas Vinje and William Cornish, 'Does copyright protection under the EU Software Directive extend to computer program behaviour, languages and interfaces?' (2012) 34 EIPR 158, 161.
120 *Oracle Inc v Google Inc* 872 F.Supp.2d 974 (ND Cal, 2012).
121 *Oracle Inc v Google Inc* 750 F.3d 1339 (Fed Cir, 2014).
122 David W Hansen, Stuart D Levi, James F Brelsford, Jose A Esteves and Anthony J Dreyer, 'Federal Circuit overturns Oracle v Google and potentially widens debate over copyright protections' 26 No. 9 Intell. Prop & Tech LJ 13.

the same features as the original, at least at the interface between the two. One way of accomplishing this is to decompile (that is, to compile in reverse), or reverse engineer, the object code of the program with which interoperability is desired, to obtain the source code. This can then be used in the creation of the interface between the existing and the new or proposed program. Unlike the programs discussed in the previous section, this requires access to part of the code of the original program. Until the advent of the Software Directive, such activity was likely to breach copyright unless it could be brought within the fair use or fair dealing exceptions, and this led to much discussion about how these provisions could be applied to reverse engineering and decompilation, but with no unanimity of opinion.[123]

The court in *Atari Games Corp v Nintendo of America Inc* concluded that reverse engineering object codes to discern the unprotectable ideas in a computer program was 'fair use'.[124] In *SEGA Enterprises v Accolade*,[125] the Court of Appeals for the Ninth Circuit, reversing the decision of the district court, seemed to suggest that decompilation may be permissible in certain circumstances and found its reasoning to be compatible with that in *Atari*. In particular, there was likely to be fair use where the end product did not contain copyright material and the copying was necessary to obtain access to the functional elements of the program. The application of the fair use factors to acts of decompilation was considered again in *Sony v Connectix*.[126] Connectix created 'emulator software' that allowed Sony games to be used not only on the proprietary Playstation console, but also on a standard PC. During the development process, Sony was contacted for 'technical assistance', but the request was declined; Connectix then decompiled Sony's software in order to ensure compatibility, but the final product contained none of the original code. The Ninth Circuit, applying the fair use provisions, found that decompilation was necessary to provide access to the unprotected functional elements; although the whole of Sony's software had been copied, there was no infringing material in the final product and so this factor could be accorded little weight. Connectix's use was 'modestly transformative' in that a wholly new product had been produced and the new product was a 'legitimate competitor'. The decompilation was thus protected by the fair use provisions.

Further developments in the USA have centred around the extent to which decompilation and reverse engineering of software can be controlled or precluded by contractual provisions. The Digital Millennium Copyright Act of 2000 (DMCA 2000) introduced a new s 1201 into the US Copyright Act of 1976, which generally prohibits the circumvention of copyright protection systems. Section 1201(f) appears to allow reverse engineering along similar lines to that developed by the judiciary, but it still appears to be the case in the USA that decompilation or reverse engineering can be prohibited by contractual terms. Indeed, this situation appears to have been underlined in *Davidson & Assocs v Jung*.[127] Despite such decisions, the official comment to s 105 of the proposed Uniform Computer Information Transactions Act (UCITA) noted recognition of 'a policy not to

123 Compare, e.g., the views expressed in Susan A Dunn, 'Defining the scope of copyright protection for computer software' (1986) 38 Stan L Rev 497, 518, and Miller, above, 1026.

124 975 F2d 832, 843 (Fed Cir 1992).

125 977 F 2d 1510 (9th Cir 1992). Compare the views of Miller, above, 1014ff; RH Stern, 'An ill-conceived analysis of reverse engineering of software as copyright infringement: *Sega Enterprises v Accolade*' [1992] EIPR 107, discussing the district court's decision; RH Stern, 'Reverse engineering of software as copyright infringement: An update – *Sega Enterprises v Accolade*' [1993] EIPR 34, following the judgment of the Court of Appeals. Hunter notes that the Australian courts would not arrive at the same conclusion: 'Reverse engineering computer software: Australia parts company with the world' (1993) 9 CL & P 122. See also P Waters and PG Leonard, 'The lessons of recent EC and US developments for protection of computer software under Australian law' [1991] EIPR 125.

126 203 F3d 596 (9th Cir 2000); see also discussion in D Prestin, 'Where to draw the line between reverse engineering and infringement: *Sony Computer Entertainment Inc v Connectix Corp*' (2002) 3 Minn Intell Prop Rev 137.

127 422 F 3d 630 (8th Cir 2005); see also discussion in Benjamin I Narodick, 'Smothered by judicial love: How *Jacobsen v Katzer* could bring open source software development to a standstill' (2010) 16 BU J Sci & Tech L 264.

prohibit some reverse engineering where it is needed to obtain interoperability',[128] but this enactment, which was intended to modify the Uniform Commercial Code in relation to contracts for, for example, software, remains controversial and has not been implemented in most states.

The issue of decompilation has not been discussed by the UK courts in the context of the fair dealing provisions in s 29 of the CDPA 1988. Indeed, the exception for research and private study in s 29(1) now only applies to non-commercial research, so, without the decompilation provisions of the Software Directive discussed below, it seems unlikely that the fair dealing provisions would 'save' decompilation.[129] Similar fair dealing provisions in the Singapore Copyright Act of 1988 were discussed in *Aztech Systems Pty Ltd v Creative Technology Ltd*. The case concerned the development of computer sound cards that would be interoperable with the 'Sound Blaster' card – the market leader. On the evidence, there had actually been no decompilation, because the new application had been created by non-invasive methods, together with trial and error, until the new product was compatible with the 'Sound Blaster' card. Research for industrial purposes or by companies was expressly excluded by s 35 of the Singapore Copyright Act of 1988 and so Aztech sought to rely on fair dealing for private study. Although this argument succeeded at first instance,[130] this was reversed by the Singapore Court of Appeal,[131] which held that extending the meaning of 'private study' would 'render otiose the specific exclusion of commercial research under s 35(5)'.[132] The High Court of Australia also found reverse engineering of software not to be legitimised by the fair dealing provisions in the case of *Data Access v Powerflex Services*.[133] The Court noted the potential effect this interpretation could have on the software market, but felt that this was something that had to be addressed by the legislature rather than the judiciary. In Europe, this was effectively what happened with the adoption of the Software Directive.

Difficulty in delineating the circumstances in which decompilation would be acceptable to all sectors of the industry was one of the main reasons for the protracted gestation of the Directive.[134] Those sections of the industry that create software primarily for running on operating systems created by others clearly have a vested interest in allowing decompilation to the maximum extent without fear of infringement, whereas other sectors of the industry, such as those that produce complete systems, are less likely to wish to permit decompilation, or any other form of reverse engineering or analysis. Article 6(1) provides that, subject to certain conditions, decompilation is permissible where it is 'indispensable to obtain the information necessary to achieve the interoperability of an independently created computer program with other programs'. As for the exceptions in Art 5, this right is reserved for the 'lawful user'; it cannot be used if the relevant information has already been made available, and it only extends to those parts of the program necessary to ensure compatibility, not to the program in total. Article 6(2) further provides that any information

---

128 Further discussion of this point is beyond the scope of this chapter, but for a more complete consideration, see, e.g., E Douma, 'The Uniform Computer Information Transactions Act and the issue of preemption of contractual provisions prohibiting reverse engineering, disassembly or decompilation' (2001) 11 Alb LJ Sci & Tech 249; *Bowers v Baystate Technologies* 320 F 3d 1317 (Fed Cir 2003); DL Kwong, 'The copyright–contract intersection: *Softman Products Co v Adobe Systems Inc & Bowers v Baystate Technologies Inc*' (2003) 18 Berkeley Tech LJ 349; JA Andrews, 'Reversing copyright misuse: Enforcing contractual prohibitions on software reverse engineering' (2004) 41 Hous L Rev 975; S Son, 'Can black dot (shrinkwrap) licenses override federal reverse engineering rights?: The relationship between copyright, contract and antitrust laws' (2004) 6 Tul J Tech & Intell Prop 63.

129 For a discussion of how the UK fair dealing provisions might be applied to copyright of computer programs in the absence of specific provisions, see Chris Reed, 'Reverse engineering computer programs without infringing copyright' [1991] EIPR 47.

130 [1996] FSR 54.

131 [1997] FSR 491.

132 *Ibid*, 505.

133 [1999] HCA 49, available online at: www.austlii.edu.au/au/cases/cth/HCA/1999/49.html

134 For details of the discussions both before and after the adoption of the Directive see, e.g., the debate between Cornish, Lake et al, and Colombe and Meyer in [1989] EIPR 391, [1989] EIPR 43, [1990] EIPR 79, [1990] EIPR 129, [1990] EIPR 325; Jerome Huet and Jane Ginsburg, 'Computer programs in Europe: A comparative analysis of the 1991 EC Software Directive' (1992) 30 Col J Transnat L 327; J Haaf, 'The EC Directive on the Legal Protection of Computer Programs: Decompilation and security for confidential programming techniques' (1992) 30 Col J Transnat L 401; PG Hidalgo, 'Copyright protection of computer software in the European Community: Current protection and the effect of the adopted Directive' (1993) 27 Int Lawyer 113; and David Bainbridge, 'Computer programs and copyright: More exceptions to infringement' (1993) 56 MLR 591.

obtained in this way cannot be used for other purposes, given to others unless for the purposes of making an interoperable program, or used to create a computer program that is substantially similar in its actual expression. This provision is a compromise that tries to reconcile the needs and interests of the various sectors in the industry. It appears to be aimed at allowing products to be developed that are compatible with the original, rather than those that might be viewed as being in direct competition with the original.[135] This is a fine line to draw.

This right was implemented in the UK by removing decompilation from the ambit of the fair dealing provisions relating to research and private study contained in s 29 of the CDPA, and introducing it as a new permitted act in s 50B. In these provisions, 'decompilation' refers to the conversion of a computer program in a low-level language to one in an HLL. It is by no means clear that this definition coincides with the one in the Directive.[136] The Directive refers to decompilation as 'reproduction of the code and translation of its form', which appears to represent a much wider view of its scope. The new s 50B(2) provides that decompilation will be allowed where it is 'necessary to create an independent program which can be operated with the program decompiled or another program'. This, taken together with s 50B(3), suggests that it may be lawful to create a competing program, provided that it is not substantially similar to the original program, but that it would be impermissible to devise modifications to an existing program to make it interoperable with another. This latter act would, apparently, be permitted under the Directive, which allows decompilation where it is 'indispensable to obtain the information necessary to achieve the interoperability of an independently created computer program with other programs'.

## Patents and computer related inventions

Whereas copyright has evolved primarily as a device for protecting the literary and the creative, patents are associated with inventions and technical products. While the aim of copyright is to stimulate creativity while respecting the rights of the creator, patents are intended to encourage innovation, while also providing rights to the inventor or developer. Unlike copyright, a patent does not arise spontaneously on creation, but a claim has to be made[137] and important criteria fulfilled – namely, that the invention is new, involves an inventive step, and is capable of industrial application.[138] Once granted, a patent is valid for a shorter period (up to a maximum of 20 years) than copyright, but, during the term of its validity, it gives the owner of the patent the exclusive right to control the production and use of the invention. Although many programmers have relied on copyright protection for software, that in no way means that patents have not also been employed in this respect. As we have seen above, the protection that copyright can afford to the functional elements of computer programs is both limited and uncertain. Patent law, on the other hand, is able to protect ideas, and therefore the functional aspects of a program, provided that the other criteria for the grant of a patent are met. The exclusive rights granted mean that patent protection is far stronger than copyright and can prevent the development of a similar independently produced product.[139] A patent can be extremely valuable in providing the opportunity to those

---

135 For a discussion of the balance of rights in the Directive specifically in relation to decompilation, see ER Krocker, 'The Computer Directive and the balance of rights' [1997] EIPR 247.
136 See also criticism in COM(2000)199 final, pp 13–14.
137 To the relevant awarding body. In the UK, this is the Intellectual Property Office, online at: www.ipo.gov.uk. The European Patent Office (EPO), online at www.epo.org, administers the European Patent Convention and provides a uniform application process for obtaining patents in up to 40 countries in Europe. Further streamlining of the process will take place when the European Unitary Patent comes into effect. See Regulation (EU) No 1257/2012 of the European Parliament and of the Council of 17 December 2012 implementing enhanced cooperation in the area of the creation of unitary patent protection [2012] OJ L361/1, and discussion in, e.g., Angelos Dimopoulos and Petroula Vantsiouri, 'Of TRIPs and traps: the interpretative jurisdiction of the Court of Justice of the EU over patent law' (2014) 39 E.L. Rev. 210–233.
138 See European Patent Convention, Art 52(1); Patents Act 1977, s 1(1).
139 See further Daehwan Koo, 'Patent and copyright protection of computer programs' [2002] IPQ 172, 199ff.

developing the programs to recoup their research and development costs, and in facilitating control over exploitation of the patented matter, especially in the early stages of the product. This value is demonstrated by the extent of the lobby from software producers, although this is matched by an equally vociferous lobby from programmers and users who believe that patent protection will, amongst other things, stifle the technology.[140] Guadamuz, on the other hand, has remarked that, if the arguments for the use of patents are accepted, 'society can only benefit from the patentability of some software inventions'.[141]

## The 'as such' exclusion

But the above does not tell the whole story: under the European Patent Convention (EPC), and therefore under the law of those states that are signatories to that convention, there are a number of exclusions from patentability. So, although Art 52(1) of the EPC allows patents to be granted subject to the criteria above for 'any inventions, in all fields of technology', Art 52(2) subsequently lists things that are not deemed to be inventions for these purposes and so are excluded from patentability in so far as the claim relates to any of these 'as such'. The list includes, amongst other things, mathematical methods, business methods, and computer programs.[142]

A crucial question is thus whether the claim for a patent for an invention involving a computer program can be regarded as an application for a patent for a program 'as such' – that is, does the inventiveness and non-obviousness lie solely in the computer program itself, or, rather, is the effect to create an entirely new product or process within which the computer program can merely be regarded in the same light as any other component might be? Some of the perceived difficulties appear to have arisen from definitional difficulties. Since the statutory exclusion is for a computer program as such, a uniform interpretation of the exclusion is very dependent on an accepted and acceptable definition, and yet this is not something that has ever been decisively defined in law. What is a computer program? Since computer programs can be expressed in the form of algorithms, the origin of the exclusion appears to derive from the same source as the exclusion for mathematical methods.[143] For some time, there have been arguments that such an exclusion is unnecessary, and that any bar to patentability should rest merely on the basic requirements of novelty and non-obviousness. Article 27 of the TRIPS Agreement, for example, although allowing exclusions in order to restrict the exploitation of, for example, human and animal tissue, seems to envisage no other exclusions and merely requires that 'patents shall be available for any inventions, whether products or processes, in all fields of technology'. Many have expressed the view that claims for patents involving computer software should be treated in the same way as those concerning computer hardware; others advocate the opposite view on the basis that software technology is significantly different from that which applies to hardware.[144]

Chisum poses the question: 'Why are new and useful developments in mathematics with direct industrial applications per se excluded from the patent system when developments in all other areas of applied technological knowledge are included?'[145] In his view, the confusion over patentability in the USA was entirely due to the decision of the Supreme Court in *Gottschalk v Benson*, which had held that a mathematical algorithm could not be patented, no matter how new and useful, and that 'policy considerations' indicated that patent protection was as appropriate for

---

140  Andres Grosche, 'Software patents: Boon or bane for Europe' (2006) 14 IJLIT 257, 259.

141  Andrés Guadamuz Gonzáles, 'The software patent debate' (2006) 1 JIPLP 196, 202.

142  In the UK, these provisions are given effect by the Patents Act 1977, s 1.

143  But cf the view of the High Court of Australia in *Data Access v Powerflex* [1999] HCA 49, [20] that 'the definition of a computer program seems to have more in common with the subject matter of a patent than a copyright'.

144  For a more conceptual discussion of the nature of technology, and the purpose and application of both patents and exclusion from patentability, see, e.g., A Von Helfeld, 'Protection of inventions comprising computer programs by the European and German Patent Offices: A confrontation' (1986) 3 CL & P 182.

145  DS Chisum, 'The patentability of computer algorithms' (1986) 47 Pitt UL Rev 959, 1007, following *Re Pardo* 684 F 2d 912 (1982).

mathematical algorithms that are useful in computer programming as for other technical innovations.[146] Harrington has suggested that the crux of the problem lies in different approaches to the meaning of 'computer program' between lawyers and electronic or electrical engineers. Whereas lawyers tend to define a computer program in terms of instructions, creating a *prima facie* impression of non-patentability, electrical engineers are more likely to think in terms of 'a process for performing a specific function or a means for creating circuitry in a block of silicon'.[147] This carries echoes of the bifurcated nature of software noted by Samuelson et al,[148] and sounds much more like the substance of a patent claim. He cites with approval *Re Alappat*,[149] in which Judge Rich said that it was 'inaccurate and confusing to speak in terms of a mathematical algorithm as excluded subject matter when assessing the patentability of a computer related invention' and used an approach that was much more in accordance with engineering definitions of 'computer program'. In Harrington's view, this approach 'recognises the reality of what actually occurs when a program is run on a computer and the utility of the mathematical sciences as a powerful vehicle for applied technology'.

In the USA, by virtue of 35 USC §101, patents are available for 'any new and useful process, machine manufacture, or composition of matter or any new and useful improvement thereof'. The exclusion of algorithms from patentability in *Gottschalk v Benson*, referred to earlier in the chapter, originally ruled out computer program claims. But a turning point came in 1981, with the case of *Diamond v Diehr*;[150] as long as the whole system could be considered the subject matter of the claim, tests for the patentability of software could be based on the overall functioning of the system. The reasoning was relaxed further in *Re Alappat*, in which the approach taken was to consider the computer as a machine so that a program could be construed as a 'new and useful improvement thereof' within the meaning of §101. In later cases such as *State Street Bank v Signature*[151] and *AT & T Corp v Excel Communications*,[152] the US courts enunciated a test that is based on the identification of a 'useful concrete and tangible result' which resulted in a consequent liberalisation of the criteria for patentability of computer software in the USA.[153] It appeared that a further relaxation might result from the ruling of the Supreme Court in *Bilski v Kappos*[154] which although relating primarily to business methods, is capable of wider application.[155] However, this apparent generosity towards software patents may have come to an end with the decision in *Alice Corporation Pty Ltd v CLS Bank*, bringing the general approach much closer to that in Europe, discussed below. In this case the US Supreme Court ruled that a number of software patents were invalid on the basis that they gave protection to the abstract ideas behind the software and so would prevent other developers from using the same concepts. Although there was no explicit statutory exclusion, abstract ideas and principles were implicitly non-patentable under §101 and 'the mere recitation of a generic computer cannot transform a patent-ineligible abstract idea into a patent-eligible invention.'[156] The decision in *Alice*

---

146  409 US 63 (1972). But note the comment on the nature of algorithms in response to Chisum's article in A Newell, 'The models are broken, the models are broken' (1986) 47 Pitt UL Rev 1023.

147  D Harrington, 'The engineers have it! Patenting computer programs in the USA' (1996) 1 Comm L 232.

148  Above.

149  33 F 3d 1526 (Fed Cir 1994); see also AD Lowrie, 'Developments in US case law' (1997) 28 IIC 868.

150  450 US 175 (1981).

151  149 F 3d 1368 (Fed Cir 1998).

152  172 F 3d 1352 (Fed Cir 1999).

153  For further discussion, see, e.g., J Fellas, 'The patentability of software-related inventions in the US' [1999] EIPR 330; DM Attridge, 'Challenging claims! Patenting computer programs in Europe and the United States' [2001] IPQ 22; Koo, above; Jack George Abid, 'Software patents on both sides of the Atlantic' (2005) 23 J Marshall J Computer & Info L 815.

154  130 S Ct 3218 (2010).

155  See, e.g., 'Patent-eligible subject matter' (2010) 124 Harv L Rev 370.

156  134 S.Ct. 2347, 2358 (2014). See also discussion in Brendon Beheshti, 'Getting beyond abstract confusion; How the United Kingdom's jurisprudence can aid in developing an analytic framework for patent-eligibility in light of *Alice v CLS Bank*' (2014) 10 Wash J L Tech & Arts 137, Richard H Stern 'Alice v CLS Bank: US business method and software patents marching toward oblivion?' (2014) 36 EIPR 619; and Dan Burk, 'The inventive concept in *Alice Corp Pty Ltd v CLS Bank International*' (2014) 45 IIC 865.

has led to a readjustment of the approach to patents for computer-related inventions in the US and may also have an impact on the granting of software patents in other jurisdictions.[157]

The explicit exclusions from patentability in Europe have led to an ongoing debate over their interpretation. Unsurprisingly, it has proved a relatively simple task to identify cases that fall at either end of the spectrum: no patent will be granted, for example, where the application relates merely to the operation of the computer under the control of the program. However, there is no bright line between what is, or what is not, within the exclusions and the border between the two has proved difficult to delineate. Given that the statutory exclusions are well known, there have been many attempts to associate the patent claim with some technical effect made possible by the novelty of the invention as a whole. The fact that, subject to these provisos and the general requirements for patentability, patents are available for computer-implemented inventions has led to a steady increase in the number of patent applications relating to computer-implemented inventions. This has only exacerbated the difficulties in drawing a line between what is, and is not, patentable subject matter and the subsequent outcomes have been neither straightforward nor uncontroversial. A key issue for both the Technical Board of Appeal (TBA) of the European Patent Office (EPO) and the courts in contracting states of the EPC has been to attempt to clarify the criteria governing the interpretation and application of the exclusions in Art 52(2) of the EPC – in particular, whether or not the invention exhibits any technical effect outside of the operation of the computer.

## The approach of the European Patent Office

The original strict test for patentability of computer-related inventions set out by the TBA was in *Vicom*.[158] A decisive point was that the application was susceptible of industrial application and the requisite technical effect was found in the operation of the program rather than in the actual program. The test was what 'technical contribution the invention . . . when considered as a whole makes to the known art.'[159] Criticisms of this interpretation developed for a number of reasons. First was that it did not represent a true picture of the technology, because the 'description of computer programs as non-technical sits uncomfortably with the reality that many programs are of technical "real world" significance'.[160] Second, and arguably more significant, was the argument that, during the 1990s, the European practice on computer-implemented inventions diverged from that of two major trading partners, the USA and Japan, both of which had become more flexible over the grant of 'software patents'.[161] The third issue was the lack of a similar exclusion in Art 27 of the TRIPS Agreement.

Whether or not as a response to these factors, two decisions of the TBA – the so-called IBM 'Twins',[162] in which the applicant referred to both the TRIPS Agreement, and the situation in the USA and Japan – were to provide the opportunity for a review of the approach to the 'as such' exclusion. With regard to TRIPS, the TBA, in T1173/97, was not convinced that it applied to the EPC, but even so it was 'appropriate to take it into consideration'. With regard to the comparison with the USA and Japan, it emphasised the difference in the respective legal systems, but pointed out that 'nevertheless . . . these developments represent a useful indication of modern trends'. Having pointed out that the only applicable law that the Board could be bound to consider was the EPC, it continued in its review of the interpretation of the exclusions, noting that the main problem was

---

157 See further Ravinda Chingale, '*Alice* and software patents: implications for India' (2015) 10 JIPLP 353.
158 T208/84 [1987] EPOR 74.
159 *Ibid*, [16].
160 J Newman, 'The patentability of computer-related inventions in Europe' [1997] EIPR 701.
161 S Davies, 'Computer program claims' [1998] EIPR 429.
162 T935/97, [1999] EPOR 301; T1173/97 [2000] EPOR 219.

the definition of 'technical character'. Having considered this in some detail, it reached the overall conclusion that:

> a computer program claimed by itself is not excluded from patentability if the program, when running on a computer or loaded into a computer, brings about, or is capable of bringing about, a technical effect which goes beyond the 'normal' physical interactions between the program (software) and the computer (hardware) on which it is run.[163]

The TBA acknowledged that its decision was 'based on a slightly different approach in thinking and reasoning' from previous case law, but did not feel that there was any real inconsistency.[164] Although the decision had been reached 'in the light of developments in information technology', it had 'not gone beyond the ordinary meaning given to the terms of the EPC'.[165] An essentially similar judgment and outcome occurred in T935/97. The wording of Art 52 of the EPC was subsequently amended in 2000 and now, in common with Art 27 of the TRIPS, includes the phrase 'in all fields of technology'.

Following these decisions, the TBA again revisited the nature of technicality in T931/95 *Pension Benefit Systems Partnership*. T931/95 contained a claim for a process for managing and controlling a pension benefits program, and also for an apparatus for performing this process. The former was rejected as being purely a claim for a business method. In relation to the latter, the TBA decided that 'a computer system suitably programmed for use in a particular field, even if that is the field of business and economy' could be an invention because it 'has the character of a concrete apparatus in the sense of a physical entity, manmade for a utilitarian purpose'.[166] It was critical of the 'contribution approach' to technicality that had been used in a number of previous cases, since if this contribution were not of a technical character, then, on the previous reasoning, there would be no invention. Referring to both of the IBM cases, the TBA concluded that possession of technical character was an implicit requirement of an invention, and there was no basis for distinguishing between 'new features' of an invention and features of that invention that are known from the prior art. This approach, which has subsequently been dubbed the 'any hardware' approach, appears to focus less on the exclusion of a computer program and more on whether or not the claim in question relates to an invention.[167] The focus, therefore, is on the identification of the inventive step. Likhovski has remarked that this decision 'elevates the form of the claim over its substance' and 'sanctions what seem to be almost automatic findings of technicality for apparatus claims',[168] while Laakkonen and Whaite suggest that the ruling was intended to 'end the discussion on the patentability of programs for computers' and that it 'appears to remove practically all restrictions derived from patentability of programs as such'.[169]

The reasoning in T931/95 was developed further in T258/03 *Hitachi/Auction Method*. Noting that the term 'invention' was to be construed as 'subject matter having technical character', the TBA appeared to respond to some of the criticism by deciding that, where there was a mix of technical and non-technical features, 'a compelling reason' for not engaging Art 52(2) was that the 'technical features may in themselves turn out to fulfil all the requirements of Article 52(1) EPC'.[170] Although, on the facts, Hitachi's claim failed for lack of inventive step, the TBA nevertheless extended the

163 T1173/97, [11.5].
164 Ibid.
165 Ibid, [10.2].
166 [2002] EPOR 52, [5].
167 For further discussion see, e.g., Anna Feros, 'A comprehensive analysis of the approach to patentable subject matter in the UK and EPO' (2010) 5 JIPLP 577.
168 M Likhovski, 'Fighting the patent wars' [2001] EIPR 267, 270; see comments in *Hutchins' Application* [2002] RPC 8, [33] and [34], discussed below at p 472.
169 A Laakkonen and R Whaite, 'The EPO leads the way, but where to?' [2001] EIPR 244.
170 [2004] EPOR 55, [3.5].

application of technicality in T931/95 to methods, as well as to systems, claims noting that 'this reasoning is independent of the category of claim'. In focusing again on the inventive aspects of the claim, the TBA acknowledged that it was now using a comparatively broad interpretation of the term 'invention', but argued that this did not lead inexorably to the conclusion that all methods involving technical means would be granted patents; they still had to satisfy the standard criteria of novelty, inventiveness, and industrial application.

This line of decisions saw further development in the *Microsoft* (*Clipboard format*) cases.[171] The claim provided an additional functionality for an existing computer that was both new and involved an inventive step. This 'trio' of decisions has been followed in subsequent EPO cases such as *Sharp/Graphical user interface*, in which it was said that the exclusion would be unlikely to be engaged where the 'technical effect relates to functional features rather than cognitive aesthetic content'.[172] The above cases represent a significant move away from the test in *Vicom* and have proved to be controversial in the UK.

## The European Patent Convention and national courts

The EPC was implemented in the UK by the Patents Act 1977, s 130(7) of which declares that a number of its provisions, including the criteria for patentability and the exclusions in s 1 are 'so framed as to have, as nearly as practicable, the same effects in the United Kingdom as the corresponding provisions of the European Patent Convention'. Further, s 91(1)(c) requires 'judicial notice' to be taken of 'any decision of, or expression of opinion by, the relevant convention court on any question arising under or in connection with the relevant convention'. In addition, the EPC is a multilateral international treaty and so should be construed in the light of the corresponding international law – in particular, Art 31(1) of the Vienna Convention, which requires the provisions of a treaty to be interpreted in good faith, taking into account the meaning of the words in context, and having regard to the object and purpose of the provisions in question. Evidence of such a purposive construction can perhaps be identified in some of the decisions made under the EPC. The discussion of the decisions in UK courts needs to be set against this background. Notwithstanding Aldous LJ's remark in *Fujitsu's Application* that 'the intention of Parliament was that there should be uniformity in this regard and that any substantial divergence would be disastrous',[173] as we shall see, there has indeed been a divergence between the UK courts and the TBA. This appears to have resulted partly from a less purposive interpretation of 'as such' and also from a perceived need for strict adherence to previous precedents.[174]

## The UK situation

An early case to reach the Court of Appeal was that of *Merrill Lynch's Application*. The original examiner had declined to grant a patent on the basis that the 'as such' exclusion meant that excluded matter could not be considered to contribute to either novelty or inventive step. The Court of Appeal noted that it was required to take 'judicial notice' of *Vicom* and thus ruled that matter excluded from patentability could, nevertheless, contribute to the inventive step required to make an invention patentable. However, it could not be permissible to patent an item excluded by s 1(2) under the

---

171 T424/03 and T411/03, [2006] EPOR 39 and 40.
172 T 1188/04, [2008] EPOR 32, [14].
173 [1997] RPC 608, 611.
174 Although the discussion in this chapter focuses on the situation in the UK, other jurisdictions have struggled with the same issues – notably Germany (the majority of software patents in Europe are claimed in the UK or Germany): see, e.g., Re IBM's *Patent Application* ('search for incorrect strings') [2003] ENPR 2; Bundesgerichtshof X ZR 27/07 *Windows-Dateiverwaltung*, 20 April 2010; Bundesgerichtshof Xa ZB 20/08 '*Dynamische Dokumentengenerierung*', 22 April 2010. The last two are discussed in Phillip Ess, 'Bundesgerichtshof clarifies software patentability prerequisites: First step towards legal certainty in Europe?' (2010) 5 JIPIL 827.

guise of a claim for an article that included it; there had to be something more – and that something, applying *Vicom*, was 'a technical advance on the prior art in the form of a new result'.[175]

However, this test proved difficult to apply. As Nicholls LJ succinctly put it in *Re Gales' Application*: 'I confess to having difficulty in identifying clearly the boundary between what is and what is not a technical problem.'[176] Even so, the centrality of this basic test was subsequently affirmed in *Fujitsu Ltd's Application*, in which Laddie J summarised the requirements for patentability of computer programs.[177] The effect of these cases was to allow claims where the advance on the prior art was achieved in software. What mattered was what the computer control was accomplishing: as long as it was not performing one of the activities in s 1(2), then it could still be eligible for patent protection. However, these cases gave no real clarification of the meaning of technical contribution; on appeal, Aldous LJ found little help from *Vicom* and declared that he had 'difficulty in identifying clearly the boundary line between what is and what is not a technical contribution'.[178]

The later case of *Hutchins' Application* was heard after the evolving reasoning in the IBM 'Twins' and *Pensions Benefit*. These decisions were criticised on the basis that the new 'any hardware' approach conflicted with the 'long established practice of the United Kingdom courts originating from the *Merrill Lynch* judgment' and suggesting that the TBA was 'adopting an approach that was accepted as erroneous' in *Merrill Lynch*.[179] The court concluded that it was bound to follow the UK decisions, but that, in any case, their approach was preferable. Subsequent cases have all had to get to grips with this divergence of approach. In *CFPH LLC's Application*, Prescott QC observed that the jurisprudence of the EPO was not constant, but that the UK courts were bound by earlier decisions, even though they might follow decisions of the EPO that the EPO itself no longer applied. However, he observed that it was not good that the law should be applied differently and suggested that 'in practice it may not be useful to consider whether something is an invention without considering whether it is new and non-obvious',[180] and went on to suggest the 'little man' test:

> The question to ask should be: is it (the artefact or process) new and non-obvious merely because there is a computer program? Or would it still be new and non-obvious in principle even if the same decisions and commands could somehow be taken and issued by a little man at a control panel, operating under the same rules? For if the answer to the latter question is 'Yes' it becomes apparent that the computer program is merely a tool, and the invention is not about computer programming at all.[181]

This decision led to an immediate change in approach to the examination of computer-implemented inventions that acknowledged the usefulness of the 'little man' test and stated that, 'in identifying the advance in the art that is said to be new and non obvious, examiners will look at the claim as a whole, including aspects that might fall within s 1(2)'.[182]

## The *Aerotel* test and its application

The most significant influence on the patenting of computer-implemented inventions in the UK is now *Aerotel Ltd v Telco Holdings Ltd, Macrossan's Patent Application*.[183] In this case, the Court of Appeal noted that a number of contradictory approaches had been used in both the EPO and national courts.

---

175 [1989] RPC 561, 569.
176 [1991] RPC 305, 327.
177 [1996] RPC 511,530.
178 [1997] RPC 608, 616.
179 [2002] RPC 8, [25] and [28].
180 [2006] RPC 5, [94].
181 Ibid, [104].
182 Practice Note [2006] RPC 6, [9] and [10].
183 [2006] EWCA Civ 1371, [2007] RPC 1.

These were referred to as the 'contribution' approach, the 'technical effect' approach, and the 'any hardware' approach, the last of which had three variants displayed in *Pensions Benefit*, *Hitachi*, and *Microsoft* (the 'trio'). Having decided that the reasoning in *Pensions Benefit* and *Hitachi* was 'not intellectually honest',[184] Jacob LJ reformulated the statutory test in a way that effectively required answers to the following questions.

(1)  What is the proper construction of the claim?
(2)  What is the actual contribution?
(3)  Does it fall solely within the excluded subject matter?
(4)  Is the actual or alleged contribution actually technical in nature?[185]

The UK Intellectual Property Office (UKIPO) subsequently declared that this four-step test must be treated as a definitive statement, and that it should rarely be necessary to refer back to previous UK and EPO case law. Nonetheless, although it severely limited the occasions on which computer-implemented inventions would be patentable, the decision was not believed to make any major changes to the boundaries of patentability. Although the reasoning was undoubtedly different to that of the EPO, it was suggested that, in most cases, the actual outcome would be the same.[186]

Cases following *Aerotel*, including *Raytheon*,[187] *Astron Clinica Ltd v Comptroller General of Patents, Designs and Trade Marks*,[188] and *Autonomy Corporation Ltd's Patent Application*,[189] have all applied the four-step test. In *Astron Clinica*, Kitchin J expressed the view that it was 'highly undesirable that provisions of the EPC are construed differently in the EPO from the way they are construed in the national courts of a Contracting State'.[190] Although he felt obliged to follow the *Aerotel* four-step test, he thought that a consistent result could be produced despite the apparent disparity in approach and concluded overall that 'claims to computer programs are not necessarily excluded by Article 52'.[191] Recognising a range of different nuances on the basic test, the court in *Autonomy* set out in great detail how the tests from the various cases should be applied.[192] In *Symbian Ltd v Comptroller General of Patents*, it was agreed that 'it was manifestly difficult to formulate a precise test . . . and it would also be dangerous to suggest that there was a clear rule available to determine whether or not a program was excluded by Art 52(2)'.[193] This was important because the claim in *Symbian* was effectively for a computer program that improved the performance of a computer. If it were to have improved the performance of any other apparatus or device, the whole would clearly be patentable, and Symbian's main point was that it should not be excluded merely because that device was a computer and not something else. In this case, a differently constituted Court of Appeal produced a more conciliatory judgment than *Aerotel*, attempting to find common ground between earlier Court of Appeal judgments and the current EPO approach rather than accentuating differences. Interestingly, the *Symbian* appeal was heard after the EPO's decision in T 154/04 *Duns Licensing Associates LP*, in which the TBA, while appreciating that the *Aerotel* decision might be understandable given the previous case law, found it not to be consistent 'with good faith interpretation of the EPC'.[194] *Symbian* was applied in the subsequent

184  *Ibid*, [27].
185  *Ibid*, [40].
186  Practice Direction [2007] RPC 8. The Aerotel patent was litigated again in *Aerotel Ltd v Wavecrest Group Enterprises* [2008] EWHC 1180 (Pat) and upheld by the Court of Appeal in [2009] EWCA Civ 400; however, these infringement proceedings have no bearing on the four-step test and its application.
187  [2007] EWHC 1230 (Pat), [2008] RPC 3.
188  [2008] EWHC 85 (Pat), [2008] RPC 14.
189  [2008] EWHC 146 (Pat), [2008] RPC 16.
190  [2008] EWHC 85 (Pat), [2008] RPC 14, [50].
191  *Ibid*, [51].
192  [2008] EWHC 146 (Pat), [2008] RPC 16, [29].
193  [2008] EWCA Civ 106, [2009] RPC 1, [52].
194  [2007] EPOR 349, [12].

cases of *AT&T KnowledgeVentures LP*[195] and *Gemstar-TV Guide International v Virgin Media Ltd*.[196] The former sets out what it believed to be useful 'signposts' to assist with the meaning of 'technical effect',[197] but both use the *Aerotel* four-step test as the starting point.

## Resolving the conflict?

Despite the concerns expressed in some of the UK decisions and in the EPO, there has still been no resolution of the divergence of approach to patentability of computer-implemented inventions even if, in practical terms at least, the outcome might be similar. But is the Court of Appeal as strictly bound by its own rulings as these cases would have us believe? As is well known, the rule on Court of Appeal precedents and the permissible exceptions was set out in *Young v Bristol Aeroplane*.[198] In a patent dispute in a different area of claim, the Court of Appeal in *Actavis UK Ltd v Merck & Co Inc* considered this issue in great detail and noted that, because that court created the rules in the first place, it could also rule on whether there should be further exceptions.[199] Overall, it concluded that, given the developing nature of new technologies and the importance of patents to the economy, there 'ought to be, and is, a specialist and very limited exception to the rule'.[200] The real problem may be, not that the Court of Appeal is not at liberty to follow the EPO rulings, but that it just does not agree with the reasoning in computer-related invention cases.[201]

For its part, the President of the EPO referred questions on the issue to the Enlarged Board of Appeal (EBA).[202] These were ruled inadmissible on the grounds that the EPO jurisprudence on the matter was clear, did not contain any significant inconsistencies on the substance, and exhibited a legitimate development of the case law.[203] Nevertheless, on the substance, the EBA did concede that although there was no actual divergence, there was 'at least the potential for confusion, arising from the assumption that any technical considerations are sufficient to confer technical character on claimed subject-matter'.[204]

Had more definitive guidance emerged from the EPA, then perhaps some reconciliation might have occurred but, in its absence, the Court of Appeal has seen no reason to abandon the approach set out in *Aerotel*[205] and the salient question remains whether the invention makes a technical contribution to the known art. There has been some further development of the 'signposts' for assessing technical effect[206] and, overall, an invention which is patentable in accordance with conventional patentability criteria does not become unpatentable because a computer program is used to implement it.[207] Whether or not the tests in the Court of Appeal and TBA arrive at the same destination by a different route and are merely a 'difference without a difference', no reconciliation appears to be on the horizon. Lewison LJ suggests the problem is rooted in the opacity of the small phrase 'as such' and that it is 'regrettable that because these apparently simple words have no clear meaning both our courts and the Technical Boards of Appeal at the EPO have stopped even trying

---

195 [2009] EWHC 343 (Pat), [2009] FSR 19.
196 [2009] EWHC 3068 (Ch), [2010] RPC 10.
197 [2009] EWHC 343 (Pat), [2009] FSR 19, [40].
198 [1944] KB 718, 729–30.
199 [2008] EWCA Civ 444, [2009] 1 WLR 1186, [92].
200 *Ibid*, [107].
201 *Symbian*, [36].
202 G03/08 *President's Reference/Computer program exclusion* [2009] EPOR 9.
203 [2010] EPOR 36.
204 *Ibid*, [13.5]. See also discussion in Justine Pila, 'Software patents, separation of powers and failed syllogisms: a cornucopia from the Enlarged Board of Appeal of the European Patent Office' (2011) 70 CLJ 203.
205 *HTC Europe Ltd v Apple Inc* [2013] EWCA Civ 451 [44]. See also Nicholas Fox and William Corbett, 'UK and EPO approaches to excluded subject-matter and inventive step: are *Aerotel* and *Pozzoli* heading for the rocks?' (2014) 36 E.I.P.R. 569.
206 See *ibid*, [45]–[49] together with the summary in *Lantana Ltd v The Comptroller-General of Patents, Designs and Trade Marks* [2013] EWHC 2673 (Pat), [11]–[13] and their application discussed further in *Lantana* [2014] EWCA Civ 1463.
207 *HTC v Apple* [57].

to understand them . . . Instead of arguing about what the legislation means, we argue about what the gloss means.'[208]

# Intellectual property rights in databases

Computer technology revolutionised information storage and retrieval and facilitated the creation and commercial exploitation of databases, providing ready access to information on a wide range of subject matter. Collections and compilations are not new, but the ease of search and correlation made possible by computerisation of such products has had a dramatic effect on both their ease of use and their ultimate usefulness. The value of the database often lies, not in the individual entries per se, since, depending on the nature of the database, these may be obtained from public domain material, or may be brief facts that are not individually subject to copyright protection; rather, the value lies in the way in which this material is available for retrieval, the sheer volume and comprehensive nature of the material that may be accessed, and the manner in which it is presented to the user. Electronic databases are important tools for users in many segments of the economy and the fact that they can be readily copied suggests that some consideration of the way in which intellectual property rights in databases can be protected is essential.[209]

Even prior to the burgeoning of the market in databases, many jurisdictions had found difficulty in extending copyright protection to collections, compilations, and directories.[210] There was a marked division also between the common law and civil law approaches to copyright, based on a different view of originality and its role in imparting copyrightability.[211] The acceptable standard of originality in the civil law *droit d'auteur* reflects the fact that the material should exhibit something of the author's personality and creativity, or demonstrate original – in the sense of novel – intellectual activity. Such a standard will, inevitably, exclude many databases from being protectable by copyright.[212]

The common law approach, on the other hand, is based on a literal 'copyright' – a legal method of safeguarding work against commercial exploitation arising as a result of copying by a third party. This requires only a low threshold of originality. It may be sufficient merely that the work is the author's independent creation and not copied from elsewhere, rather than the necessity of a finding of particular novelty. Instead of novelty, the common law courts tended to look for a 'sweat of the brow' test for the subsistence of copyright in which if a work needed skill or expense to create it then it was entitled to be protected against copying.[213] However, in *Feist Publications Inc v Rural Telephone Service Company Inc*, the US Supreme Court did not extend copyright protection to a telephone directory.[214] Despite earlier decisions that had found copyrightability in a 'sweat of the brow' or 'industrious collection test', the Court held that originality was the only standard for deciding whether or not a factual compilation is protectable by copyright. Factual compilations could be protected by copyright, but only if the selections 'are made independently by the compiler and

208 *Ibid*, [143].
209 See further, P Cerina, 'The originality requirement in the protection of databases in Europe and the United States' (1993) 24 IIC 579; Neeta Thakur, 'Database protection in the European Union and the United States: The European Database Directive as an optimum global model' [2001] IPQ 100.
210 For a review of the situation in a number of jurisdictions at the beginning of the 1990s, see EJ Dommering and PB Hugenholtz (eds), *Protecting Works of Fact: Copyright, Freedom of Expression and Information Law*, 1991, The Hague: Kluwer.
211 See also Diane Rowland, 'The EC Database Directive: An original solution to an unoriginal problem?' [1997] Web JCLI, available online at: www.bailii.org/uk/other/journals/WebJCLI/1997/issue5/rowland5.html
212 See, also Cerina, above. For a review of the treatment of originality in relation to fact-based compilations in a number of jurisdictions, see, e.g., Hasan A Devici, 'Databases: Is *sui generis* a stronger bet than copyright?' (2004) 12 Int'l JL & Info Tech 178.
213 See, e.g., *Macmillan & Co Ltd v Cooper* (1924) 40 TLR 186, 188; and *Ladbroke (Football) Ltd v William Hill (Football) Ltd* [1964] 1 WLR 273, 291. For a comprehensive review of the relevant cases, see *Desktop Marketing Systems Pty Ltd v Telstra Service Company Inc* [2002] FCAFC 112, [20]–[160].
214 113 L Ed 2d 358 (1991).

entail a minimal degree of creativity' and 'are sufficiently original that Congress may protect such compilations through the copyright laws'.[215] *Feist* makes it clear though that this standard of originality is somewhat lower than the civil law standard and is related purely to independent creativity.

According to Thakur, '*Feist* caused ripples of alarm in Europe',[216] and it was against this general background of inconsistency and doubt over both the existence and scope of copyright protection for databases and factual and other compilations that the EC Database Directive was drafted and adopted. The main impetus was a desire to harmonise the legal protection provided for databases and, as an adjunct, to ensure that there was no impediment to the free market in both information products and information services. Even before the judgment in *Feist*, some commentators[217] had expressed concern that insistence on a high threshold of originality for copyright protection would cause problems for modern informational works and that copyright, at least in its common law manifestation, had always needed to balance creative aspects of the work with commercial demands. Ginsburg's suggested solution was to recognise a differential between works of 'high' and 'low' authorship, and to provide corresponding protection.[218] In essence, this could be said to be what the Database Directive does by extending conventional copyright protection to those works that satisfy the requisite originality requirement and also by providing a *sui generis* right for those databases that do not satisfy this test, but are, nevertheless, the result of considerable investment.

## The Database Directive[219]

The Directive applies to both electronic and non-electronic databases, but not to the underlying computer programs. It defines 'database' in Art 1(2) as 'a collection of independent works, data or other materials arranged in a systematic or methodical way and individually accessible by electronic or other means'. It retains copyright protection for those databases that reach the requisite standard of originality (Art 3), but also provides a *sui generis* database right for those databases that fall short of this standard. The *sui generis* right is independent of copyright eligibility; its scope is delineated in Arts 7–9, together with the rights and obligations of lawful users and exceptions to the right. Databases qualify for the *sui generis* right if the maker of the database can show that 'there has been qualitatively and/or quantitatively a substantial investment in either the obtaining, verification or presentation of the contents to prevent extraction and/or re-utilization of the whole or of a substantial part, evaluated qualitatively and/or quantitatively, of the contents of that database'. The terms 'extraction' and 'reutilization' are themselves defined in Art 7(2). Article 9 provides exceptions to the *sui generis* right in respect of use for private purposes, for teaching and scientific research, and for the purposes of public security or an administrative or judicial procedure. However, 'the repeated and systematic extraction and/or re-utilization of insubstantial parts of the contents of the database implying acts which conflict with a normal exploitation of that database or which unreasonably prejudice the legitimate interests of the maker of the database' is not permitted (Art 7(5)).

In many European jurisdictions, databases that satisfy the requirements of Art 3(1) with regard to eligibility for copyright protection would, in any case, be likely to be protected by the law of copyright even in the absence of the Directive, but, in the UK in particular, there are likely to be many databases that would have qualified for copyright protection under the old 'sweat of the brow' test that will now be denied that protection. However, as long as these fulfil the requirement

---

215  Ibid, 370.
216  Above, 110.
217  See, e.g., Jane Ginsburg, 'Creation and commercial value: copyright protection of works of information' (1990) 90 Col L Rev 1865.
218  Ibid.
219  Directive 96/9/EC of the European Parliament and of the Council of 11 March 1996 on the legal protection of databases: [1996] OJ L77/20.

of 'substantial investment', which is not defined in the Directive, they will still qualify for the *sui generis* database right in Art 7, although this has a duration of only 15 years (Art 10) compared with the standard term for copyright protection of 70 years. This approach has been criticised on the basis that a 'two-tier' system has implicit connotations of a higher and lower mode of protection, and there have also been expressions of doubt as to whether the compromise solution of the combination of a traditional copyright with a new form of right is the correct model.[220] It may be misguided, though, to view the protection afforded by the *sui generis* right as second rate. A major threat to large databases is that of piracy and a 15-year term of protection against copying is, in most cases, likely to be sufficiently extensive to accommodate the shelf life of even the most enduring database. This should not be divorced from the fact that any further substantial investment, such as might be required by necessary revision and updating, will generate a further term of protection. It can thus be said that the two-tier system, rather than providing a superior and an inferior protection, instead maintains the necessary balance between creativity and investment.

That is not to say, however, that the line between creative and non-creative databases will be an easy one to draw. Smith Ekstrand's consideration of the similar problem confronting the US courts post-*Feist* revealed judicial analysis that 'bordered on hair-splitting, infinitesimal detail, as courts attempted to peel back each layer of the work, attempting to find its creativity or lack thereof'. She concludes that a flexible test is needed to determine when a compilation is sufficiently creative, because 'a creative database may be comprised of creative parts but uncreative selection, arrangement or coordination; or it may be comprised of creative selection, coordination and arrangement with uncreative parts. Databases may lie anywhere along the continuum'.[221]

The Database Directive was implemented in the UK by the Copyright and Rights in Databases Regulations 1997 (the Database Regulations),[222] amending the CDPA 1988 in relation to copyright, by inserting definitions of 'database' and 'originality in databases' (new s 3A), making relevant amendments to ss 29 (fair dealing) and 50 (permitted acts), and also inserting a new s 296B, which provides that acts permitted by virtue of the amended s 50 cannot be excluded by contract. The new database right contained in Pt III of the Regulations, not being a copyright as such, has not been subsumed within the text of the 1988 Act, although certain of the available rights and remedies are, nevertheless, those contained in that statute (see reg 23).

Although the Directive only provides a definition of 'extraction and re-utilisation', the Regulations provide explicit definitions of both 'substantial' and 'investment'. 'Substantial', the meaning of which is implicit within the Directive with regard to extraction and reutilisation, includes substantial in respect of both quality and quantity or a combination. Any use of financial, human, or technical resources can qualify as 'investment'.

## The scope of the database right

The Directive creates a *sui generis* database right for those databases which have been created as the result of substantial investment protecting the right owner against unauthorised acts of extraction and re-utilisation. There is room for argument as to where such acts of extraction and reutilisation take place when databases are accessed over the internet and given that no specific provisions on this issue were included in the Directive, any questions of jurisdiction fall to be considered under the usual rules and the particular facts of the case.[223] The overall purpose was not to create a

---

220 There have also been criticisms based on the fact that a 'neighbouring rights' regime would have provided a suitable solution without necessitating the creation of a specific *sui generis* right: see, e.g., CC Garrigues, 'Databases: A subject matter for copyright or for a neighboring rights regime?' [1997] EIPR 3. Cornish, on the other hand, suggests that the *sui generis* right is to take account of the fact that there is no harmonised law of fair competition in the EU: Cornish and Llewelyn, above, p 833.

221 V Smith Ekstrand, 'Drawing swords after *Feist*: Efforts to legislate the database pirate' (2002) 7 Comm L & Pol'y 317.

222 SI 1997/3032.

223 See Case C-173/11 *Football Dataco Ltd v Sportradar GmbH* (CJEU, 18 October 2012; and discussion in Perttu Virtanen, 'Football Dataco v Sportradar: Second half and home field for database makers' (2013) 10 SCRIPT-ed 278.

uniform *sui generis* right in the EU but to harmonise national law in line with the provisions of the Directive.[224]

## Substantial investment and the 'spin-off' doctrine

The interpretation of 'substantial investment' has, perhaps predictably, been a key issue in much of the litigation, especially in relation to so-called 'spin-off' databases – those in which compilations of data arise incidentally to the main activities of the database owner. Typical examples include travel timetables, television programme listings, details of sports fixtures, etc. In such cases, the primary investment is in the activities, rather than the database that catalogues those activities, or their results or outcomes. There is a school of thought – sometimes referred to as the 'spin-off' theory – that suggests that the database right should not protect such databases. The relevant arguments include the fact that the database right is based on utilitarian reasoning in order to promote investment in databases. On this basis, there would be no need to extend protection to databases that were the (inevitable) by-product of other activities. This also makes it difficult to establish a direct link between the investment and the database at issue. An alternative argument is that investment costs should be recouped from primary, rather than incidental, activities – that is, from the television programmes, sports fixtures, etc, themselves. Laddie J, in the first-instance decision in *British Horseracing Board v William Hill*,[225] distinguishes 'creating' and obtaining', the latter implying an object with a prior existence. Whereas 'creating' implies at the least labour and effort, 'obtaining' can arise much more easily – in some cases, even automatically.

The spin-off doctrine is unlikely to be popular with database producers because it severely restricts the scope of protection, but the obverse of this argument is that it fosters a 'broader public domain'.[226] Given that the doctrine apparently originated in the Netherlands, it was entirely foreseeable that it should be referred to in decisions in that jurisdiction and, in *NV Holdingmaatschappij de Telegraaf v Nederlandse Omroep Stichting*,[227] the court found that there was no evidence of substantial investment when information about television programmes was gathered merely as a spin-off of broadcasting activity. Similar reasons have been used in other courts in the Netherlands. In *Algemeen Dagblad v Eureka Interntdiensten* (the *Kranten.com* case), for example, the District Court of Rotterdam declined to offer the protection of the database right to a list of headlines from newspapers,[228] but other Member States have not embraced the theory so readily. In *Danske Dagblades Forening* (DDF) *v Newsbooster*, the Copenhagen City Court, on similar facts to those in *Kranten.com*, did extend protection to a collection of headlines and articles.[229]

A number of cases in which the spin-off theory could be deemed to be relevant involved Fixtures Marketing Ltd, and concerned a database created by the English and Scottish Football leagues and containing lists of football fixtures. The information on football fixtures in this database was used, *inter alia*, by companies in Sweden, Finland, and Greece, which organised pools games or other gambling activities based on forecasting the results of these matches. Applying the spin-off theory, it could be concluded that the lists were a mere by-product of the Football Leagues' main activity, but all three disputes led to questions being referred to the CJEU concerning the nature of the substantial investment required. The Advocate General, in C-444/02 *Fixtures Marketing Ltd v Organismos prognostikon agonon podosfairou AE*, considered the spin-off theory, but, after analysing the factors

---

224 C-127/11, [24]–[27].
225 [2001] 2 CMLR 12.
226 Estelle Derclaye, 'Databases *sui generis* right: Should we adopt the spin-off theory?' [2004] EIPR 402.
227 [2002] ECDR 8.
228 [2002] ECDR 1.
229 [2003] ECDR 5. Both of these cases also involved the legality of hypertext links to the websites containing the lists of headlines and articles: see Chapter 4.

relevant to obtaining, concluded that it did not apply. Databases could also be protected where 'the obtaining was initially for an activity other than the creation of a database'.[230] The CJEU itself, in C-338/02 *Fixtures Marketing v Svenska Spel*,[231] paid lip service to the fact that such databases could involve substantial investment – that is, there could be no automatic conclusion that a spin-off database could not be protected by the database right. However, in these particular cases, no additional investment was required to constitute the database and so the database could not benefit from that protection. In other words, the same result was obtained as if the spin-off doctrine had been applied. As the judgment allows for the possibility of such databases to be subject to the database right, each case has to be considered on its merits; in the cases above, it is a fairly simple matter to distinguish creating and obtaining, but this may not always be so.[232]

At the same time as the *Fixtures Ltd* cases, the CJEU also gave judgment in a similar, albeit rather more complex, case – C-203/02 *British Horseracing Board v William Hill*.[233] BHB operated a database of various facts related to horse racing. The size of this database was significant and the estimated annual cost of keeping the 20 million records up to date was £4 million. The information was made available to other interested organisations and was licensed to a number of bookmakers, including William Hill. William Hill also provided online betting services and BHB alleged that this process used information derived from the BHB database without the requisite licence. Laddie J, at first instance, gave a wide interpretation to the Directive, leading to questions being referred by the Court of Appeal to the CJEU.[234] The CJEU reiterated its view in the *Fixtures* cases that, in this case, there was no substantial investment in the obtaining or verifying the contents of a database.[235] None of these cases, however, provide any real guidance on the *quantum* that would be considered 'substantial' in terms of investment, because, in all of the cases, the investment was judged to be minimal.

## Substantial part

The *sui generis* right is the right to prevent extraction and reutilisation of a 'substantial part'. In the *William Hill* case, the CJEU concluded that 'substantial part, evaluated quantitatively', referred to the volume of data involved, whereas 'substantial part, evaluated qualitatively', referred to the scale of investment in obtaining the contents. The intrinsic value of the contents was irrelevant to this assessment; anything that did not fall within it could be regarded as insubstantial. The rejection of the notion that 'substantial part' bears any relation to the intrinsic value of the data[236] is especially significant. Holding otherwise would be to afford a very wide protection to database owners, who could presumably usually argue that the data was valuable to them. The judgment then goes on to discuss the interpretation of 'repeated and systematic extractions of insubstantial parts', and concludes that these will only infringe if they are sufficient to allow the alleged infringer to reconstitute the whole, or a substantial part, of the database.[237] In this case, given the size of the BHB database, there was 'no possibility that, through the cumulative effect of its acts, William Hill might reconstitute and make available to the public the whole or a substantial part of the contents of the BHB database'.[238]

---

230 Case C–444/02, [2004] ECR I–10549, [2005] 1 CMLR 16, [AG73].
231 Case C–338/02, [2004] ECR I–10497; see also Case C–46/02 *Fixtures Marketing Ltd v Oy Veikkaus AB* [2004] ECR I–10365.
232 See examples in Mark J Davison and P Bernt Hugenholtz, 'Football fixtures, horseraces and spinoffs: The ECJ domesticates the database right' [2005] EIPR 113, 115.
233 Case C–203/02 [2004] ECR I–10415.
234 [2001] 2 CMLR 12 (High Ct), [2002] ECC 24 (CA).
235 [2004] ECR I–10415, [29]–[41].
236 Ibid, [78].
237 Ibid, [86] and [87].
238 Ibid, [91].

## Term of protection

As noted above, the term of protection provided for the database right in Art 10 is 15 years and Art 10(3) further provides that any substantial change in a database will itself qualify for protection. A final point in the *William Hill* case was the extent of the term of protection in relation to dynamic databases. Very few databases remain static, but are regularly updated in an incremental fashion: what effect does this have on the term of protection? Does each amendment effectively create a new database, so that a new term of protection is initiated? If so, that may have the effect of extending the protection for dynamic databases in perpetuity – an ironic result given that the original philosophy behind the database right is to provide a weaker protection for those databases that do not qualify for full copyright protection. This had been referred as a question by the Court of Appeal, but remains unresolved by the CJEU decision. Given that the CJEU's decision had the effect of depriving BHB of the benefit of the database right, it did not feel it necessary to answer this question. The matter had been discussed in the Advocate General's opinion, who concluded that, having brought a database up to date, the whole database must be the object of new investment. The consequence was that a new term of protection must commence with each update – that is, Art 10(3) of the Directive did indeed provided for a 'rolling' *sui generis* right. Although the logic behind this argument cannot be denied, how easily it sits with the CJEU's generally restrictive interpretation to other provisions of the Directive is difficult to assess.

## The meaning of 'extraction'

The CJEU considered the scope of 'extraction' in C-304/07 *Directmedia Publishing GmbH v Albert-Ludwigs-Universitat Freiburg*.[239] The case concerned a project at the University in Freiburg that involved the creation of a database of 1,100 poetry titles intended to represent the most important poems in Germany from the period 1730–1900. The list, which was selected from around 20,000 titles in a variety of German anthologies, had taken two-and-a-half years to compile and received funding of €34,900 from the university. Directmedia marketed a CD of '1,000 poems everyone should have', of which 856 were from the university list. Directmedia admitted using the database, but denied simply copying, asserting that it had performed a critical examination of the contents in order to decide on the selection. In addition, the CD contained full text, whereas the university list contained only author, date of publication, opening line, and details of citations in anthologies. The university's claim for copyright infringement was rejected by the German courts, but, in relation to the database right, questions were referred about whether extraction required physical copying, or whether it was sufficient to consult, assess, and then select some material. Unlike the spin-off cases, it was clear that the substantial investment in creating the database qualified it for the protection of the database right. Having considered the Directive and its Recitals, the CJEU concluded that 'extraction' should not be narrowly construed and limited to technical criteria; neither did addition of other material preclude a finding that parts of the first database had been extracted. It was also held that the intention of Directmedia was irrelevant; it made no difference that the new product would not be in competition with the original one.

The CJEU returned to the scope of 'extraction' in C-545/07 *Apis-Hristovich EOOD v Lakorda AD*, a case from Bulgaria involving a database of legal materials.[240] The Court reiterated that the objective of transfer (that is, whether a competing product was intended) was immaterial, and that the Directive covered both temporary and permanent transfer of data within the concept of extraction. In this case, the database in question consisted of official legal data that were publicly

---

239 [2008] ECR I–7565; see also Anne Christopher and Kate Freeman, '*Directmedia Publishing GmbH v Albert-Ludwigs-Universitat Freiburg*' (2009) 31 EIPR 151.
240 [2009] ECR I–1627; see also Stephen Vousden, 'Apis, databases and EU law' [2011] IPQ 215.

accessible, but the CJEU held that as long as the criteria regarding investment, etc, were met, this did not preclude it from being protected by the database right.

## Reutilisation and 'screen scraping'

'Screen scraping' or more accurately 'content scraping' is a process in which data is extracted from a third party's website by means of automated systems or software.[241] A common way of achieving this is by the use of a meta search engine which uses search engines provided by other websites to retrieve results. Many websites use such techniques; they can provide the user looking for a specific product or service with a one stop site which accesses many other sources for them and returns a composite result. To the user, the meta search engine will appear to resemble a database of the information of the type which they are looking for without actually holding the data. In the absence of appropriate licence agreements to legitimate such activities, these techniques are clearly capable of diverting customers from databases which may have required considerable resources to produce.

In *Innoweb v Wegener*,[242] Wegener provided a searchable database of adverts for second hand cars some of which were only available there. Innoweb used a meta search engine dedicated to search for car sales. When users made a query it initiated a search of various online car advertisers including Wegener. The user then received a list of results obtained from the various sites. The evidence was that there were some 100,000 searches of Wegener's database each day as a result of queries on the Innoweb site, but which resulted in only a small part of the database contents being actually displayed to the user. The CJEU found that, given that there were an indeterminate number of users, the dedicated meta search engine made the information from the database available to the public for the purposes of Art 7(2)(a) and the operator of the search engine reutilised the contents of the database. Although the result displayed was itself only a very small part of the data in the database, the reutilisation was of a substantial part as it involved a search of the entire contents. Referring to its decisions in *British Horseracing Board* and *Football Dataco v Sportradar*, it said that in order to give effect to the purpose behind the Database Directive it was necessary to give a broad meaning to the concept of reutilisation.

This decision appears effectively to proscribe screen scraping[243] and is protective of creators of databases which are protected under Art 7 and suggests that it behoves websites which make data available from other databases to ensure that they have appropriate licence agreements in place. A further twist occurred in the recent case of *Ryanair v PR Aviation BV*.[244] PR Aviation extracted the data from Ryanair's database for use on its own booking website by 'screen scraping'. Ryanair did not make its data generally available to other agents and the terms of use of its database included a clause which prohibited the use of automated systems or software to extract data for commercial purposes without a written licence agreement. In *Innoweb*, in the absence of discussion on the issue, it appears that the Wegener database qualified for the Art 7 right. However in Ryanair's case, the CJEU found that its database did not qualify for the *sui generis* right; there had not been substantial investment and it was insufficiently original to qualify for copyright protection. In other words it was a database which qualified for neither of the rights in the Directive. In these circumstances it was appropriate for Ryanair to protect its database contractually, assuming this did not contravene national law. Paradoxically, this perhaps suggests that Ryanair may actually be better placed to

---

241 See, e.g., Mark Ward, 'Screen scraping: How to profit from your rival's data' (2013) BBC News, 30 September, available online at: www.bbc.co.uk/news/technology-23988890

242 Case C-202/12 *Innoweb BV v Wegener ICT Media BV* (CJEU, 19 December 2013), see also discussion in Tatiana Eleni Synodinou, 'Database *sui generis* right and meta search engines: what's new and what's next?' (2014) 36 EIPR 755.

243 See further, Emma Cartwright and Tughan Thuraisingam, 'CJEU condemns the "scraping" of databases: *Innoweb v Wegener*' (2014) 25 Ent LR 195.

244 Case C-30/14 *Ryanair Ltd v PR Aviation Ltd* (CJEU, 15 January 2015).

protect its database from screen scraping than if it had qualified for protection under the Directive. It seems unlikely that this type of situation will not result in further litigation.

## Copyright in databases

As mentioned above, the Directive makes provision in Art 3 for copyright protection of databases that is entirely independent of the *sui generis* database right.[245] Article 3(1) has been implemented in the UK by amendment to the CPDA 1988, s 3(1), which now includes databases as literary works, distinct from tables and compilation. A new s 3A provides that for a database to qualify for copyright protection, it must be original, meaning that the database constitutes the author's own intellectual creation by virtue of the selection or arrangement of the contents of the database. As already mentioned the traditional standard of 'originality' in English law has been determined by a 'sweat of the brow' test; is this sufficient to accord copyright protection to suitable databases?

This matter has been considered in other litigation about the compilation of football fixtures and the resulting databases. In *Football Dataco Ltd v Brittens Pools Ltd*,[246] the database in question computed the dates of football fixtures, taking into account a number of complex and interrelating factors relating to the number of times each team played each other, when and where. The fixtures could not be determined purely mechanically, because some of these factors might clash, and so a judgment had to be made as to which rule should prevail in any particular instance. The effect was that the claimant's main effort was in creating the fixtures and that the further process of compiling a database of the fixture lists was trivial, in other words in line with the spin-off theory it did not qualify for the *sui generis* right. Floyd J, following the *Fixtures Marketing* cases discussed above, thus had no difficulty in finding that the database did not qualify for the database right. But, as he found that creating the database involved considerable skill and judgment which went beyond mere 'sweat of the brow', it therefore qualified for protection under Art 3.

This issue was explored further in the Court of Appeal which referred questions to the CJEU including whether more than significant labour and skill was need to meet the originality requirement and whether the intellectual effort and skill should be excluded.[247] The CJEU found that Art 3 was focused on protecting originality in the structure and selection of the database and so any effort in creating the actual data was not relevant. Originality would be satisfied if creative ability was demonstrated in the original selection and arrangement of the data in the database, but not when creation of the database was dictated by technical considerations, rules or constraints.[248] In other words, the type of database at issue in the case could not be protected by the Art 3 copyright protection. Handig describes *Football Dataco* as Europe's *Feist*, and it certainly appears that it requires a higher standard of originality than has traditionally been required in the UK.[249] Rahmatian, however, suggests that it still falls short of harmonising the originality in line with that in civil law countries and that the standard of originality as described by the CJEU in *Football Dataco* is not as far from that in the UK as it might appear at first sight.[250] There have been decisions by the CJEU on this matter in other areas of copyright law so this may not be the last word on this issue.[251]

---

245 See Case C-604/10 *Football Dataco v Yahoo! UK* [27] (CJEU, 1 March 2012).
246 [2010] EWHC 841 (Ch); see also Mark Rodgers, 'Football fixture lists and the Database Directive: *Football Dataco Ltd v Brittens Pools Ltd*' (2010) 32 EIPR 593; Colin Sawdy, 'High Court decision revisits protection of databases in the United Kingdom: *Football Dataco Ltd v Brittens Pools Ltd*' (2010) 21 Ent LR 221.
247 *Football Dataco v Yahoo! UK* [2010] EWCA Civ 1380.
248 Case C-604/10 *Football Dataco v Yahoo! UK* [38] [39] (CJEU, 1 March 2012).
249 Christian Handig, 'The "sweat of the brow" is not enough! – more than a blueprint of the European copyright term "work"' (2013) 35 EIPR 334.
250 Andreas Rahmatian, 'Originality in UK copyright law: the old "skill and labour" doctrine under pressure' (2013) 44 IIC 2013 4.
251 For a range of approaches to the more general issue see, e.g., Rahmatian, above, Estelle Derclaye, 'The Court of Justice copyright law: quo vadis?' (2014) 36 EIPR 716; Deming Liu, 'Of originality: originality in English copyright law, past and present' (2014) 36 EIPR 376; Eleanor Rosati, 'Originality in a work or a work of originality: the effects of the *Infopaq* decision' (2011) 36 EIPR 746.

## Database protection outside Europe

At present, the creation and harmonisation of database rights in the EU is specific to that jurisdiction and, despite attempts in the US Congress, similar modifications have not yet been adopted elsewhere. Following *Feist*, Lavenue noted that it was paradoxical that even though the USA might be the world leader in the database market, database content was not provided with specific intellectual property protection.[252] Nevertheless, cases in the USA continue to use the Feist reasoning although Bitton suggests that the US courts' application of the principles in *Feist* often seems to demonstrate a misunderstanding of that approach with the result that it is possible to find cases which are factually indistinguishable but which have been decided in different ways.[253] In particular, there have been difficulties with applying the creativity threshold in *Feist* and the problem of separating idea from expression.[254] As case law in the CJEU demonstrates, however, the existence of a sui generis right would not necessarily guarantee any greater consistency of approach.[255] There have been a number of attempts to legislate in the USA but none has succeeded.[256] There are powerful lobby groups on both sides of the debate and academic opinion over the need for, and suggested form of, a database right is divided. Thus Thakur concludes that 'a robust global model with an international *sui generis* regime is, undoubtedly, a necessity so as to bring the United States database industry also under the protective umbrella for an effective stimulation of databases in the global community'[257] and Johnson suggests that both the US and Canada should consider introducing a database right especially given the lucrative market in sports data.[258] Greenbaum, on the other hand, warns that 'the United States should not be pressured by the European Union to follow in its unproven protectionist policies' and Bitton suggests that neither is there empirical evidence that a bespoke right is actually necessary.[259]

A completely different approach was first taken in Australia where, notwithstanding the apparent impact of *Feist* in the common law world, it appeared that the 'sweat of the brow' test had certainly not been rejected. In *Desktop Marketing Systems Pty Ltd v Telstra Corp Ltd*,[260] the Federal Court of Australia allowed copyright protection to a database on the basis of 'industrious collection'. The database in question was a purely factual compilation being, as in *Feist*, a public telephone directory produced by Telstra. After an extensive review of relevant case law and a consideration of a number of issues related to originality, the decision was that the overriding concern was whether the work originated with the creator, even if the amount of effort in arranging and compiling the information might be rather minimal. The case referred to the differing situation in the UK as a result of the Database Directive, but concluded that any parallel action was for the legislature in Australia rather than the courts. After *Desktop*, it appeared that very little effort was needed for databases to be protected by copyright as compilations in Australia. The principle on which it was based appeared to be 'simple, certain and close to immutable',[261] and were followed in a number of cases. Recently

252 LM Lavenue, 'Database rights and technical data rights: The expansion of intellectual property for the protection of databases' (1997) 38 Santa Clara L Rev 1.
253 Miriam Bitton, 'Protection for Informational Works after *Feist Publications Inc v Rural Telephone Service Inc*' (2011) 21 Fordham Intell Prop Media Ent LJ 611, 632.
254 Ibid, 641.
255 See, e.g., Stephen Vousden, 'Innoweb, search-engines and engineering legitimacy in EU law' (2014) 4 I.P.Q. 280.
256 Examples include the Collections of Information Antipiracy Act and the Consumer and Investor Access to Information Act at the end of the 1990s, and the Database and Collections of Information Misappropriation Act in 2003. For details and discussion see, e.g., J Gibson, 'Re-reifying data' (2004) 80 Notre Dame L Rev 163; JA Loy, 'Database and Collections of Information Misappropriation Act of 2003: Unconstitutionally expanding copyright law?' 7 NYUJ Legis & Pub Pol'y 449.
257 Thakur, above, 130.
258 Julia Johnson 'Database protection a reality? How the professional and fantasy sporting world could benefit from a sui generis intellectual property right' (2015) 27 I.P.J. 237, 262.
259 Bitton, above, p 669.
260 [2002] FCAFC 112, available online at: www.austlii.edu.au/au/cases/cth/FCAFC/2002/112.html; see also SE Strasser, 'Industrious effort is enough' [2002] EIPR 599.
261 Mark Davison, 'Nine Network Australia Pty Ltd v IceTV Pty Ltd and Telstra Corp Ltd v Phone Directories Co Pty Ltd: Copyright protection for compilations – Australia does a U-turn' (2010) 32 EIPR 457, 458.

however, the situation has apparently undergone a transformation following the High Court of Australia's decision in *Nine Network Australia Pty Ltd v IceTV Pty Ltd*.[262] A detailed analysis of what is a complex case is beyond the scope of this chapter, but, in brief, it questioned the assessment of originality in *Desktop* and appeared to abandon the 'sweat of the brow' standard, although without making clear what standard should replace it. Generally, though, the earlier decision was subjected to considerable criticism, it being suggested that the reasoning in *Desktop Marketing* with respect to compilations might be 'out of line with the understanding of copyright law over many years', and that the emphasis in that case on 'labour and expense' per se should be treated with caution.[263]

The *Ice* decision was subsequently applied in *Telstra Corp Ltd v Phone Directories Co Pty Ltd*, which again considered the subsistence of copyright in telephone directories.[264] Following the decision in *IceTV*, these were no longer found to be protected by copyright on the basis that the 'sweat of the brow' test had now been abandoned. This decision was subsequently upheld on appeal, the Full Federal Court concluding that 'the reasons of the High Court in *IceTV* authoritatively establish that the focus of attention in relation to the subsistence of copyright is not upon a general concern to prevent misappropriation of skill and labour but upon the protection of copyright in literary works which originate from individuals.'[265] As the directories in question were generated automatically, they could not be protected by copyright. The court also pointed out that the creation of a right akin to the EU database right was a matter for the legislature. However, as pointed out by Davison,[266] who advocates caution in respect of introducing a *sui generis* right in Australia, the court failed to mention that other jurisdictions that reject the 'sweat of the brow' test – notably the USA – have nevertheless not provided a standalone right. This discussion shows that there is a considerable polarisation between Europe and other jurisdictions in the intellectual property protection accorded to databases. Although the *sui generis* database right was introduced to promote investment in, and development of, the market, there is no real evidence of the actual effect that the existence of the right has had on the market in Europe; neither do those jurisdictions without such a right appear to be at any major disadvantage.

## Concluding remarks

The beginning of this chapter contained a discussion about the appropriate intellectual property protection for computer programs. As we have seen, the law in a number of jurisdictions has, on occasions, struggled to accommodate the particular properties of software and has sometimes needed to modify traditional copyright principles in order to apply them satisfactorily to computer programs. In Europe, a *sui generis* right for computer programs was rejected under the influence of the observed case law trend towards copyright already formulated by the courts in a number of jurisdictions. Nonetheless, it could be argued that some of the modifications that were negotiated for inclusion in the Software Directive and which have led to new derogations with respect to decompilation rights, for example, modify traditional copyright principles to such an extent that the resulting protection is, more accurately, described as a *sui generis* right.[267] Because copyright emphasises the literal, a copyright-type protection might be seen as the appropriate form of protection for the expression and writing of computer programs. Patents, on the other hand, emphasise the functional, but in this respect too there has been no agreed solution. Campbell-Kelly discusses

262 [2009] HCA 14, available online at: www.austlii.edu.au/au/cases/cth/HCA/2009/14.html; see also Davison, above.
263 *Ibid*, [188].
264 [2010] FCA 44, available online at: www.austlii.edu.au/au/cases/cth/FCA/2010/44.html
265 *Telstra Corporation Limited v Phone Directories Company Pty Ltd* [2010] FCAFC 149; and see discussion in Sam Ricketson, 'The need for human authorship – Australian developments: *Telstra Corp Ltd v Phone Directories Co Pty Ltd*' (2012) 34 EIPR 54.
266 Above.
267 See, e.g., the views expressed by Wiebe, above. See also discussion in P Goldstein, 'The EC Software Directive: A view from the USA' in M Lehmann and CF Tapper (eds), *Handbook of European Software Law: Pt 1*, 1993, Oxford: Clarendon.

the divided debate over software patentability, observing that members of the open source community are often hostile to software patents, whereas the academic discussion encompasses all shades of opinion. He concludes, however, that patents have the propensity to encourage more investment in reinvention and software components, while in contrast 'trade secrecy is antithetical to cooperation' and 'copyright is wholly inadequate in this context'.[268] Nonetheless, software patents remain controversial; some commentators assert that 'computer programs are texts, not machines as some lawyers have confused themselves into believing, and thus they may be copyrighted . . . but they are not patentable as machines'.[269]

It is perhaps not surprising either, that the European patent system has been stricter over the computer program claims than its counterparts in the USA (at least before *Alice v CLS Bank*) and Japan, given the focus and activity on copyright, as evidenced by the Software Directive. An attempt to harmonise the patentability of computer programs in the European Union (which includes most of the contracting states to the EPC), and to bring it more into line with US and Japanese trading partners, had a stormy ride through the various stages of the codecision procedure. The text finally adopted ignored most of the European Parliament's amendments, which, not surprisingly perhaps, led to its rejection by that institution. So we see that neither copyright nor patents have provided a perfectly tailored solution. As Onslow and Jamal have remarked:

> There has never been a systematic economic investigation into whether intellectual property rights are needed to protect investment in research and development in the field of computer programming, and if so, whether copyright or patents should fulfil that role.[270]

It is thus not surprising that the debate over the appropriate form of protection for software continues to ebb and flow.

Would a bespoke *sui generis* solution have been an improvement? Could this take into account the dual nature of software – namely, that it can be regarded as both writing and machine?[271] Opponents of *sui generis* protection stress both the unknown and potentially unpredictable effects of new provisions, and the fact that intellectual property law has, in the past, often proved flexible in adapting to changing technological environments. Indeed, this very evolution has been likened to a type of *sui generis* protection in the way that it allows a new approach to the intellectual property in software. Guarda appears to conclude that a *sui generis* right might be more appropriate but is silent as to what form it might take other than being 'somewhere between' the existing regimes.[272] On the other hand, more than 20 years ago, Stern remarked that:

> We need a system that borrows appropriately from copyright law, patent law, and utility model law – perhaps slavish imitation law as well – and combines selected features of each, and new features where the nature of software dictates it, to provide a form of legal protection congruent to the subject matter, the commercial needs of industry, software professionals, and software users, and the interests of the public.[273]

Arguably, we are no closer to this utopian vision. In an area where *sui generis* rights have been created, namely the database right in the EU, there has been no more conspicuous success in establishing a coherent and consistent level of protection. Some decisions have had the effect of apparently

---

268  Martin Campbell-Kelly, 'Not all bad: An historical perspective on software patents' 11 Mich Telecomm & Tech L Rev 191, 248.
269  Peter D Junger, 'You can't patent software: Patenting software is wrong' 58 Case W Res L Rev 333, 481.
270  Onslow and Jamal, above, 356.
271  See, e.g., Samuelson et al, above; Diver, above.
272  Paolo Guarda, 'Looking for a feasible form of software protection: copyright or patent is that the question?' (2015) 35 EIPR 445, 453.
273  Richard H Stern, 'Is the centre beginning to hold in US copyright law?' [1993] 2 EIPR 39, 40.

curbing what had been seen as the wider excesses of the Directive, which had the potential to harm the public domain of information and ideas.[274] Although they might not have been welcomed by certain database owners, they probably represented a more realistic approach to the position of the database right in the general hierarchy of intellectual property rights. However, some other cases have appeared rather more generous in their approach.[275] A bespoke *sui generis* right does not inevitably resolve the problems of applying existing regimes to new technological developments.

The discussion in this chapter has demonstrated that the unique nature of computer software, and the particular products and inventions that it makes possible, have created a considerable challenge for intellectual property law. Despite the individual protagonists who champion copyright, patents, or *sui generis* rights, it is apparent that, in appropriate situations, all of these mechanisms have been, and are being, used to foster and protect exploitation of computer software and products relying on it. Globalisation is a significant feature of the software market and this has forced different jurisdictions, even in the absence of suitable international treaties, to take account of the legal and regulatory activity in other jurisdictions to an unprecedented degree. It should perhaps be no surprise that the needs and requirements of a worldwide market may operate as a more potent force for international harmonisation than intergovernmental cooperation.

## Further reading

Elad Harison *Intellectual Property Rights, Innovation and Software Technologies: The Economics of Monopoly Rights and Knowledge Disclosure* Edward Elgar (2008)
Ashwin van Rooijen *The Software Interface Between Copyright and Competition Law; A Legal Analysis of Interoperability in Computer Programs* Wolters Kluwer (2010)
Philip Leith *Software and Patents in Europe* Cambridge University Press (2007)
Emanuela Arezzo and Gustovo Ghidini *Biotechnology and Software Patent Law: A Comparative Review of New Developments* Edward Elgar (2011)
Estelle Derclaye *The Legal Protection of Databases: A Comparative Analysis* Edward Elgar (2008)

---

274 See, e.g., C-203/02 *British Horseracing Board v William Hill* [2004] ECR I-10415; C-338/02 *Fixtures Marketing v Svenska Spel*, [2004] ECR I-10497; and discussion in J Lipton, 'Databases as intellectual property: New legal approaches' [2003] EIPR 139, 144.
275 See, e.g., C-545/07 *Apis-Hristovich EOOD v Lakorda AD* [2009] ECR I–1627 and discussion in Vousden, above.

# Chapter 12

# Software licences, free and open source licensing (F/OSS), and 'software as a service' (SaaS)

## Chapter contents

# Introduction

## Scope of the chapter

A chapter in a book on IT law cannot deal in depth with all aspects of contract law; instead, the discussion here will focus on some aspects of contract law that are particularly relevant in the context of software transactions. As the title implies, this chapter deals with the licensing of software and related issues.

## Types of contract

There are a wide range of contracts that can relate to computer hardware and software, including: contracts for the sale or lease of hardware, or of a hardware and software package; contracts licensing software; contracts for the maintenance of hardware or software (or support contracts); distribution agreements between manufacturers and distributors of software or hardware; and bureau services contracts, under which one party that has computer hardware and software supplies computer services or facilities to a party that does not have its own hardware or software. Detailed discussion of each of these would (and does) merit a separate book.[1] Thus, this chapter is concerned primarily with the key issues that may arise in relation to contracts concerned with computer software.

The reason for this narrow choice of topic is simple: hardware clearly constitutes goods, and contracts dealing with goods are familiar from other contexts; it is software that poses the significantly different questions. Although the term 'software' can be used to mean anything that is not hardware, it will be used here to mean computer programs, unless otherwise indicated. This is the type of software that raises significant issues for information technology law.

---

1 See, e.g., Richard Morgan and Kit Burden, *Morgan and Burden on Computer Contracts*, 9th edn, 2013, London: Sweet & Maxwell.

## Bespoke and standard software

Discussion of contracts dealing with software requires a distinction to be made between different basic types of software. At one end of the spectrum is 'bespoke' software – that is, software written by a supplier for a particular user, often for a user-specific task.[2] At the other end is mass-produced software, which is simply bought 'off the shelf' by many users. Somewhere in between will be modified standard software, for which the basic program will be the same in each case, but will then be modified to some extent to meet the needs of the individual user.[3] This division may be relevant, for example, in considering whether a contract for the supply of software should be regarded as a contract for the sale of goods or the supply of services (or something else).[4]

With the recognition that copyright can exist in software,[5] the licence has become the vehicle by which the acquirer is given rights to use the software. In so doing, it provides the means by which those who develop software can recoup the large costs of that development, make a profit, and encourage further development. There are difficulties in licensing software when the developer does not deal directly with the end-user and, with the trend away from bespoke to off-the-shelf software, this has become a common situation.

If the end-user does not deal with the developer, how is his or her use to be licensed? The answer is that there may be a chain of contracts. The end-user may be a sublicensee of a distributor who obtained a licence from the developer – the distributor's licence, including the right to create sublicenses. However, the mass production of standard software has posed its own legal difficulties. How are licences to be 'mass produced' when someone can acquire software simply by walking into a shop, selecting software from a display, and paying for it at a till? The attempt to create licences in this type of case, by means of what has been called the 'shrink-wrap' licence, will be returned to below.

# Goods or services or something else?

One problem that has been of particular conceptual and practical significance is the legal nature of software. As discussed in the previous chapter, the nature of computer programs has raised issues in relation to the choice of intellectual property protection. At one level, a program is basically information, hence the use of copyright to protect the intellectual property rights. But does this prevent software also being regarded as 'goods'? Or should the supply of software be regarded as a service? On a practical level, these questions have arisen in the context of the applicability of legislation such as the Sale of Goods Act 1979 (SoGA 1979), the Supply of Goods and Services Act 1982, and the Commercial Agents (Council Directive) Regulations 1993.[6]

However, two initial points should be made. First, even if a software contract is not seen to fit within one of the statutory regimes, software may well be found to be subject to the same type of implied terms at common law – particularly the requirement of reasonable fitness for the acquirer's particular purpose. Second, it would seem that a contract for the supply of a system involving both hardware and software will be categorised as one for the supply of goods (unless the services element dominates the particular contract).[7] These two points mean that the content of the implied terms should be considered even if software itself cannot be categorised as goods.

---

2 See, e.g., *St Albans City and District Council v International Computers Ltd* [1997] FSR 251.
3 See, e.g., *Watford Electronics Ltd v Sanderson Cfl Ltd* [2002] FSR 19.
4 See further Ken Moon, 'The nature of computer programs: Tangible? Goods? Personal property? Intellectual property?' (2009) 31(8) EIPR 396.
5 See CDPA 1988, ss 1 and 3.
6 SI 1993/3053.
7 *Toby Constructions Products Pty Ltd v Computa Bar (Sales) Pty Ltd* [1983] NSWLR 48; *St Albans*, above.

The discussion in this area has been complicated somewhat by the Consumer Rights Act 2015 (CRA 2015) which came into force in October 2015.[8] Part 1 of the CRA 2015 treats consumer contracts for digital content as a separate category of content with its own statutory rights and remedies. The CRA 2015 uses the definition of 'digital content' found in the Consumer Rights Directive,[9] 'data which are produced and supplied in digital form' resulting in a broad range of products being classified as digital content including mobile apps, computer programs and software. However, the CRA 2015 applies to business to consumer (B2C) contracts only[10] – it does not apply to business to business (B2B) or consumer to consumer (C2C) contracts, to which existing legislation, including the Unfair Contract Terms Act 1977, Sale of Goods Act 1979 and Supply of Goods and Services Act 1982, will continue to apply. Its possible implications for the debate surrounding the categorisation of software will be considered below.

## Goods: Definition and arguments

The starting point for considering whether software can be goods should be the statutory definition of 'goods'. Section 61 of the SoGA 1979 states: '"Goods" includes all personal chattels other than things in action and money . . .' One argument thus raised is that a computer program cannot be goods, because it is, in nature, information and not a 'personal chattel'. Another is that it is intellectual property and so is covered by the exclusion from the definition of 'things in action'.

### Software as information

It is clear that software consists of information in the form of the particular arrangement of source code. Following the line of reasoning in *Oxford v Moss*[11] (in which confidential information was held not to be 'property' within the meaning of s 4 of the Theft Act 1968), it seems plausible that, despite its having clear value, which is recognised in law via the medium of intellectual property rights, software should therefore not be considered as goods in the context of sale of goods.[12] However, when a program is embodied on a computer disk or other such medium, the argument that it is simply information has been open to challenge from two perspectives: the physical; and the functional.

(a) *Physical/tangible:* There has been relatively little discussion of the physical or tangible nature of software in the UK case law compared, in particular, to the USA.[13] The physical argument – that the program has physical form on the disk or other such medium – was recognised indirectly in Sir Iain Glidewell's obiter comments in the *St Albans* case.[14] It was also employed in the criminal case of *R v Whiteley*,[15] in which the question was whether the alteration and deletion of computer files by a 'hacker' could constitute criminal damage

8 The CRA 2015 consolidates a large proportion of existing consumer law, including provisions of the Sale of Goods Act 1979, the Supply of Goods and Services Act 1982 and the Unfair Contract Terms Act 1977. It also revokes and replaces the existing Unfair Terms in Consumer Contracts Regulations 1999. Under s 2 of the CRA 2015, 'consumer' means 'an individual acting for purposes that are *wholly or mainly* outside that individual's trade, business, craft or profession' – a broadening of the definition in the Consumer Rights Directive which refers to 'natural persons who are acting *outside* their trade, business, craft or profession'. 'Goods' refers primarily to tangible moveable items.

9 Directive 2011/83/EU of the European Parliament and of the Council of 25 October 2011 on consumer rights, amending Council Directive 93/13/EEC and Directive 1999/44/EC and repealing Council Directive 85/577/EEC and Directive 97/7/EC OJ L 304, 22.11.2011, p 64–88.

10 CRA 2015, s 1.

11 *Oxford v Moss* [1978] 68 Cr App R 183.

12 See further Andrew Scott, 'Software as goods: Nullum simile est idem' (1987) 4 CL & P 133.

13 Moon, above, 398–400.

14 *St Albans*, above.

15 *R v Whiteley* (1991) 93 Cr App R 25, per Lord Lane LCJ; see also *Cox v Riley* [1986] CLR 460. The type of situation that was considered in *Whiteley* was taken outside the scope of the Criminal Damage Act 1971 by the Computer Misuse Act 1990. See further discussion in Chapter 7.

within s 1(1) of the Criminal Damage Act 1971. The court held that deletion or alteration of computer data imposed a physical change in the nature of the disks (the rearrangement of magnetic particles), and this change could be considered 'damage' for the purpose of the Act. This reasoning suggests that software could be considered to have a physical manifestation in the media in which it is stored.

However, neither case provides convincing support for the idea that software itself has a physical or tangible form, and the concept is further undermined by the ability to acquire software across a network, such as the internet, with no obvious storage mechanism. The *coup de grâce* must surely be delivered to such notions by the wireless network, in which not only the software, but also the very transfer mechanism by which it is acquired is intangible.

(b) Functional: The second point to be raised against the argument that software cannot be goods because it is information, is that based on its functional aspect. It should be asked whether a program, embodied on a disk and ready to be fed into a computer, is merely information. Is it distinguishable from the exam paper in *Oxford v Moss*,[16] which was referred to by Scott? If a program is likened to a literary work, which is the categorisation applied to it to provide it with the protection of copyright, then it is most like an instruction manual or 'how to' book, which was the analogy made by Sir Iain Glidewell in *St Albans*. Certainly, software is not like a novel! However, a program differs from even an instruction manual. It does not simply tell the individual what to do; the software interacts directly, with the hardware. In *St Albans*, at first instance, Scott Baker J was of the opinion that software 'is not simply abstract information like information passed by word of mouth. Entering software alters the contents of the hardware'.[17] This may not be an entirely accurate view of the effect of software on hardware, but the general idea is clear enough: software is not mere information; rather it has a direct effect on hardware. Another point can also be made, following on from this. If there is a defect in software, there may well not be a point at which an individual has an opportunity to exercise judgment, assess what is occurring, and intervene to prevent some unexpected, and unwanted, result. Software may be information, but it is not simply information.

An analogy can be made here with the US case of *Winter v G P Puttnam & Sons* decided in the Court of Appeals for the Ninth Circuit.[18] In that case, the question arose as to the applicability of product liability laws to a book on collecting and cooking mushrooms. It was held that the information contained in the book was not a product. What is of interest here is that, in coming to that conclusion, the court contrasted the situation before it with one involving software. It was indicated that software would be a product. The software was seen as something more than only information.[19] It could thus be contended that the functional aspect of software strengthens the case for the 'goods' categorisation to cover both a disk and the program embodied on it. On the other hand, as commentators have pointed out, despite wide coverage at the time, *Winter* has had little influence in the USA, probably due to its unusual fact circumstances, the paucity of argument in the judgment surrounding the suggestion that software was more than only information, and the

---

16 *Oxford v Moss*, above.
17 *St Albans*, above, 699.
18 *Winter v G P Puttnam & Sons* 938 F 2d 1033 (9th Cir 1991). See further, Michael R Maule, 'Applying strict products liability to computer software' (1992) 27(4) *Tulsa LJ* 735, 737; Lori A Weber, 'Bad bytes: The application of strict products liability to computer software' (1992) 66(2) *St John's L Rev* 469, 470; Patrick T Miyaki, 'Computer software defects: Should computer software manufacturers be held strictly liable for computer software defects?' (1992) 8(1) CHTLJ 121.
19 In fact, this type of distinction has been made in relation to US product liability laws in a way that might be used to argue that a program supplied as a written source code could constitute goods: see *Saloomey v Jeppesen* 707 F 2d 671 (1983).

disinclination of either the Ninth Circuit or any other US court to pursue and expand upon that line of reasoning.[20]

## Software as intellectual property

As we have seen, the definition of 'goods' in the 1979 Act excludes 'things in action', and it might be argued that programs are covered by this exclusion and therefore are not goods. However, the program is not itself copyright; it is protected by copyright. This was recognised by Steyn J in *Eurodynamics Systems v General Automation Ltd*:[21] 'Although the ideas and concepts involved in software remained [the defendants'] intellectual property, the reality of the transaction is that there has been the transfer of a product.'

When there is a contract for the supply of a program, it is not simply an assignment of intellectual property rights. In fact, as has been indicated, in most cases, there will not be an assignment of the copyright in a program, although licences are normally granted. Properly identified, the problem is whether, when intellectual property rights are in question, they dominate the transaction to prevent the disk, with the program embodied in it, from being regarded as goods. Copyright restrictions are not seen as preventing a book, video tape, or CD from being goods, but such items do not have a functional use in the way that software does, and that difference in use is not only noteworthy in itself, but also makes a considerable difference to the impact of intellectual property rights. Intellectual property rights impact upon the enjoyment of books and videos to a very much more limited extent than upon the enjoyment of software.[22] A book can be read or a video watched without any need for the purchaser to obtain a licence to avoid being in breach of copyright.[23] In contrast, the use of software will entail copying it onto hardware, which, in the absence of a licence, would *prima facie* be in breach of copyright,[24] absent Art 5 of the EC Software Directive.[25] In other words, the basic purpose for which a book or video is purchased can be fulfilled without any need for the purchaser to consider intellectual property rights; the same is not true of software. Indeed, the view has been taken that software cannot be likened to books or other such goods, but must be regarded as *sui generis*.[26]

However, the argument that software cannot be goods because of the intellectual property rights involved was considered by the US Court of Appeals for the Third Circuit in *Advent Systems Ltd v Unisys Corp*.[27] The Court had to determine the applicability of Art 2 of the Uniform Commercial Code to a contract under which Advent agreed to supply hardware and 'license software' to Unisys.[28] Weiss L, delivering the opinion of the court, said that 'a computer program may be copyrightable as intellectual property does not alter the fact that once in the form of a floppy disk or other medium, the program is tangible, movable and available in the marketplace'.[29] The court emphasised the physical embodiment of the program in a disk or other such medium in concluding that it was goods, and not merely intellectual property, and fell within Art 2. This same approach could be taken to indicate that a program embodied on a disk would be goods under the SoGA 1979. However, there is a further argument, based on the significance of the intellectual property rights

---

20 Seldon J Childers, 'Don't stop the music: No strict products liability for embedded software' (2008) 19(1) U Fla JL & Pub Pol'y 125, 143.

21 *Eurodynamics Systems v General Automation Ltd* (1988) unreported, 6 September.

22 See *Beta Computers (Europe) Ltd v Adobe Systems (Europe) Ltd* [1996] FSR 387.

23 See, e.g., Jessica Litman, 'Fetishizing copies', (2014) U of Michigan Public Law Research Paper No 422, available online at: ssrn.com/abstract=2506867

24 CDPA 1988, s 17(1).

25 That is, Directive 2009/24/EC *on the legal protection of computer programs* (codifying Directive 91/250/EEC) (the 'Software Directive').

26 *Beta Computers*, above, 396, per Lord Penrose.

27 *Advent Systems Ltd v Unisys Corp* 925 F 2d 670 (1991); cf *Conopco Inc v McCreadie* 826 F Supp 855 (1991). The argument was not considered, as such, in *Beta Computers*, but some support for it may be found in the approach taken there.

28 Article 2 applies to goods and intellectual property is outside the Uniform Commercial Code: see, generally, Andrew Rodau, 'Computer software: Does Article 2 of the Uniform Commercial Code apply?' (1986) Emory LJ 853.

29 *Advent*, above, 145.

in software, as to whether a contract for the provision of software is capable of being a contract for the sale of goods.

Section 2(1) of the SoGA 1979 states that a contract for sale of goods is 'a contract by which the seller transfers or agrees to transfer the property in goods to the buyer for a money consideration called the price'. The 'property in goods' is not the physical object, but, basically, the ownership of the goods. The person to whom a disk is supplied will take it subject to the restrictions of copyright and a licence will normally be involved. The question is whether those restrictions are sufficient to prevent that person acquiring the 'property' in the goods. Certainly, copyright restrictions are not seen as preventing there from being a sale of a book, video tape, or CD, but, as has been indicated, such restrictions impact rather differently on books from their effect on software. However, if a disk with a program on it were to be classified as 'goods', it may be doubted whether this type of argument would prevail.

Of course, if there is clearly no transfer of the ownership, even of the disk or other such medium (which may well occur where non-standard software is in question), but a mere supply under an agreement that the disk will be returned when the program licence terminates, then the contract will not fall within the 1979 Act. However, it should be remembered that similar terms to those implied by the SoGA 1979 are implied into contracts for the hire of goods by the SGSA 1982.

## Pragmatism vs appropriateness

In the St Albans case, both Scott Baker J and Sir Iain Glidewell indicated that a program supplied on a disk or other such medium, but without any hardware, should be treated as 'goods'. Scott Baker J's reasoning was basically pragmatic. He took the view that, otherwise, no statutory regime would apply and the recipient would be unprotected in the absence of express terms. This type of pragmatic argument was positively received by early commentators.[30]

However, even though there are undoubted attractions in finding software to be included in a well-established legal category, it must be considered whether that is appropriate. The law may say that, henceforth, elephants are to be called 'mice', but the law cannot say that elephants *are* mice. Is software too unlike other things that are categorised as 'goods' for the label to be appropriate? The goods to which software is most akin are books, music CDs, and video tapes, but one of the factors used to indicate that software is not only information, its functional aspect, also makes it very different from those types of good. Additionally, despite the comment of Scott Baker J in the St Albans case,[31] it should be noted that programs are decreasingly transferred using a disk or some other such medium. Could a program transferred across a network constitute goods? That seems unlikely,[32] but, if it cannot, then a problem with the pragmatic argument arises. The 'goods' categorisation might provide an existing legal framework for consideration of some transactions involving computer programs, but certainly not all. Would categorising as goods a program embodied, and transferred, on a disk or other such medium inappropriately divorce its legal categorisation from that of programs transferred without the use of such a medium?[33] In *Beta Computers (Europe) Ltd v Adobe Systems (Europe) Ltd*, a Scottish case that dealt with the question of the effectiveness of a 'shrinkwrap' licence, Lord Penrose, obiter, considered the contention that software should be regarded as goods. He said:

> This reasoning [that software is goods] appears to me to be unattractive, at least, in the context with which this case is concerned. It appears to emphasise the role of the physical medium

---

30 Brian Napier, 'The future of information technology law' (1992) 51(1) CLJ 46.

31 St Albans, above, 699.

32 Such a categorisation would seem contrary to an approach that emphasises the importance of the embodiment of the program in a disk or other such medium.

33 And of some cases in which such a medium was used, but not delivered to the recipient of the program, as in St Albans, above.

and to relate the transaction in the medium to sale or hire of goods. It would have the somewhat odd result that the dominant characteristic of the complex product, in terms of value or the significant interests of the parties, would be subordinated to the medium by which it was transmitted to the user in analysing the true nature and effect of the contract.[34]

### Common law considerations

It is worth noting Scott Baker J's concerns, in the *St Albans* case, that if the supply of software was not a supply of goods, it would be 'something to which no statutory rules apply, thus leaving the recipient unprotected in the absence of express agreement'.[35] The SoGA 1979 is largely based on the Sale of Goods Act 1893 of the same name. Legislation covering other contracts dealing with goods occurred much later (for example, the SGSA 1982). However, prior to the existence of wider legislation, the common law often proved capable of implying the same, or similar, terms into contracts dealing with goods that did not fall within the Sale of Goods Acts.[36] Similarly, it would not be impossible for the court to find that the common law implied terms that programs should be of 'satisfactory quality' and 'reasonably fit' for the purchaser's 'particular purpose', even if, in all cases or some cases, software is not categorised as goods. When the Court of Appeal considered the St Albans case, Sir Iain Glidewell thought that, in the absence of an express term requiring the program to be fit for its purpose, one could have been implied at common law.[37]

As will be seen, when consideration is given to the terms implied by s 14 of the SoGA 1979, those terms requiring the goods to be of 'satisfactory quality' and 'reasonable fitness' for the buyer's 'particular purpose' are flexible in their content, and similar terms dealing with the functioning of the program may be appropriate, generally, in contracts for the supply of programs. It is worthwhile considering the terms implied by the SoGA 1979 not only because software may be categorised as goods in some cases, but also because, even if that is not seen as appropriate in any case, the common law may imply the same or similar terms. In any event, they should be addressed, because it would seem that a system involving both hardware and software will be treated as goods.[38]

## Services

Even if software can be goods and ownership of the disk passes, it may still be argued that it is inappropriate that its supply should be categorised as a sale of goods. It may be argued that the transaction should be regarded as a contract for work and materials (or, more broadly, for 'services'), rather than for goods. Of course, there may well be found to be a contract for services if no goods are in question. However, what is of particular note here is the distinction between a contract for services, which also involves goods, and one that is simply for the sale of goods. The line between such contracts for services and contracts for the sale of goods has been one that the courts have attempted to draw in many different contexts, and it has never proved an easy categorisation to make.[39] Nevertheless, it may be a very important distinction. If a contract for the supply of software is one for the sale of goods, then, subject to the possibility of their inapplicability, or of the effectiveness of an exemption clause, the software will have to comply with the statutorily implied terms as to description (s 13 of the SoGA 1979), satisfactory quality (s 14(2)), and reasonable fitness for the buyer's particular purpose (s 14(3)). Whilst the terms implied by s 14 set standards by reference to the 'reasonable person' (s 14(2)) or require 'reasonable fitness' (s 14(3)), they are

---

34 *Beta Computers*, above, 376.
35 *St Albans*, above. Here, there was an express term that the computer system would be reasonably fit for the buyer's purpose.
36 For example, *Dodd v Wilson* [1946] 2 All ER 691.
37 *St Albans*, above, 494. The implication envisaged would appear to have been one made 'in fact', but such an implied term might be found more generally 'in law'.
38 *Toby Constructions*, above; *St Albans*, above.
39 See, e.g., Robert A Samek, 'Contracts for work and materials' (1962) 36 ALJ 66.

all nevertheless strict. The seller cannot escape liability for his or her breach by proving that the problem with the goods was not due to any fault on his or her part.[40] In contrast, if what is in question is the provision of a service, then the relevant implied term stems from s 13 of the SGSA 1982, which merely requires that, where the supplier of a service acts in the course of a business, he or she should do so with due care. The strict terms, requiring goods to be, inter alia, of satisfactory quality would apply only to goods supplied incidentally to the service.[41]

Two basic approaches to distinguishing contracts for the sale of goods and contracts for the supply of services can be found. These can be seen in the cases of Lee v Griffin[42] and Robinson v Graves.[43] Lee v Griffin was concerned with a contract made by a dentist to supply a set of false teeth, made to fit the individual patient. On appeal, that was concluded to be a contract for the sale of goods, on the basis that if the services produced goods, the ownership of which the supplier transferred to the other party, there was a contract for the sale of goods, save only where the transfer of ownership of any goods could be regarded as relatively insignificant, as in the example of the solicitor drawing up the deed. In Robinson v Graves, a contract was made with an artist for a portrait of a particular individual and the Court of Appeal looked to the dominant element in the contract – the end product or the skill and expertise of the person providing the services – and concluded that it was a contract for the services of the artist, rather than one for the sale of goods.

In the context of contracts concerned with software and the statutory regimes, the impact of a contract being for services rather than goods can be illustrated. If there is a contract to write a bespoke program, which is categorised as a contract for services, then the strict liability would seem only to apply to the fabric of the disk.[44] The content of the program would be the outcome of the services and the relevant statutorily implied term would simply be that requiring the services to be performed with due care. In other words, the strict liability terms would not apply to the product of the services; they would apply only to goods transferred to the other party incidentally to those services. A more complex problem might arise where the contract is for the supply and installation into the purchaser's system of an 'off the shelf' program. If such a contract were characterised as being one for services, because of the work involved in the installation, then it would seem that any aspect of the program adapted by that installation would only be covered by the requirement that the work should be carried out with due care. However, if the 'off the shelf' software were to be characterised as goods, then any defect in the program that was not caused by the installation would seem to be subject to the strict requirements of the statutorily implied terms as to fitness for purpose and satisfactory quality.

## The supply of software

Obviously, the acquisition of bespoke software provides the strongest case for arguing that a contract for the supply of software must be regarded as one for services rather than goods. However, even then, the categorisation should not be assumed in every case. Two particular examples can be suggested in which a contract for bespoke software might nevertheless be characterised as one for goods. The first example relates to the case in which, although the software is being written because it was requested by one particular company, the suppliers realise that there will be a market to supply it to other companies and intend to do so.[45] It might be argued that the intent to 'mass

---

40  Kendall v Lillico [1969] 2 AC 31; Frost v Aylesbury Dairy Co [1905] 1 KB 685.
41  In Dodd v Wilson, above, the contract was for the services of a vet. He was strictly liable when a vaccine with which he inoculated a cow was not reasonably fit for its purpose. Of course, had the problem been with, e.g., the way in which the injection was given, he would only have been liable in the absence of due care.
42  Lee v Griffin (1861) 1 B & S 272. See also, e.g., J Marcel (Furriers) Ltd v Tapper [1953] 1 WLR 49.
43  Robinson v Graves [1935] 1 KB 579.
44  But see the assumption in Saphena, above, 652, per Staughton LJ, that it made no difference to the applicability of the strict liability terms as to quality whether the contract was characterised as being for goods or services.
45  This was the fact situation in Saphena Computing, which led to a dispute as to the ownership of copyright.

supply' the software subsequently could affect the characterisation of a contract to supply what was, at that stage, bespoke software, making it appropriate to characterise it as being for goods, rather than services. The other example concerns the 'turnkey contract'. Even where goods are to be manufactured by a seller, it is possible for that seller to contract simply in relation to a result (the goods), rather than the manufacture and delivery of the goods. The former case may be argued to be one for the sale of goods rather than the supply of services and this argument would seem to apply to the so-called turnkey contract – that is, the type of contract in which a complete system is installed and then simply handed over to the party to whom it is being supplied. In such contracts, the way in which the supplier arrives at the completed product seems to be irrelevant to the other party. It is a contract purely concerned with results and a 'goods' rather than 'services' categorisation may be appropriate, even where what is in question is bespoke software.

After considering bespoke software, modified standard (or modified 'off the shelf') software should be looked at. The approach taken in *Robinson v Graves*[46] could provide a strong argument in favour of the services classification where some modified standard software is in question, depending upon the extent and novelty of the modification.

At the other end of the spectrum from bespoke software is standard, or 'off the shelf', software. There seems to be little scope for an argument that, even if such software is goods, a contract for its supply must nevertheless be characterised as one for services.[47] In *Toby Constructions Products Ltd v Computer Bar Sales Pty Ltd*, in which the contract was for the supply of a computer system composed of hardware and 'off the shelf' software, Rogers J concluded that he was dealing with a contract for goods and dismissed the argument that it was services that were in question. He said:

> Whilst representing the fruits of much research work, [the software] was in current jargon, off the shelf, in a sense, mass produced. There can be no comparison with a one-off painting. Rather is the comparison with a mass-produced print of a painting.[48]

## Another fine intangible mess . . .

When one considers the state of play today in relation to software and its uncertain place in the existing statutory framework governing contracts, it is perhaps hard to comprehend how UK law has so signally failed to address the issue. On the part of the courts, it is at least partially attributable to the fact that the judiciary can only address the issues placed before them and that, on the whole, questions going to the nature of software do not seem to have arisen very often. That having been said, when such issues have arisen, as in *Eurodynamics*, *St Albans*, and *Beta*, the courts seem disinclined to address them directly.

There appears to have been a similar reluctance to address the issue by the legislature. It is interesting to speculate why that might be so. In New Zealand, the perceived solution has been to amend the definition of 'goods' in the Sale of Goods Act 1908 to include 'software', howsoever it is delivered.[49] This has been criticised as 'statutory fantasy',[50] on the grounds that there are no other 'goods' that can be 'converted to electromagnetic signals which are then transmitted from one geographical location to another to emerge as goods again at the other end'.[51] Thus the New Zealand law achieves the aim of providing a clear statutory regime for software, but only at the cost of doing some violence to the traditional meaning of the word 'goods'. In the USA, where the issue seems equally unresolved, a proposed legislative standard in the form of the Uniform Computer

---

46 *Robinson v Graves*, above.
47 But see *James Ashley v London Borough of Sutton* [1995] Tr LRep 350.
48 *Toby Constructions*, above, 51.
49 New Zealand Sale of Goods Amendment Act 2003.
50 Moon, above, 402.
51 Ibid.

Information Transactions Act (UCITA), designed to standardise the law and provide the default rules for licensing and contracting of software and all other forms of digital information, as the US Uniform Commercial Code does for the sale of goods, failed to find much support.[52] Drawing upon those examples, one might surmise that the UK Parliament has been unwilling to involve itself in an issue in which there:

- has been relatively little concerted pressure from either the software industry or other interested parties for a 'root and branch' reformulation of the ad hoc contract paradigm for software;
- is the possibility of simply increasing the current uncertainty or complexity in contract law, without necessarily reaching a satisfactory solution, because of the need to address different types of software contract (off-the-shelf, bespoke, customisable) being sold to different types of acquirer (general public, small-to-medium-sized enterprises [SMEs], corporations, etc) through different media (tangible medium, network) in a marketplace that is constantly evolving ('open source software', SaaS, etc).

Whatever the reason, what appears to have developed has been, as Moon notes, an environment in which a highly important sector of the economy is governed by laws that are currently failing to 'understand intangibles in general and to evolve to properly recognise them without the use of anachronistic legal fictions which pretend that they are tangibles in situations which have diminishing applicability in modern (electronic) commerce'.[53] This issue will be discussed further below, in the context of the resale or 'reuse' of computer software licences for software delivered primarily via the internet.

## A third way

For consumers engaging in B2C transactions, the Consumer Rights Act 2015 (CRA 2015), appears to cut through the Gordian knot of whether software is a good or a service by effectively declaring it to be neither. This approach was adopted following research commissioned by the UK Department for Business, Innovation and Skills, which noted that:

> that to be effective consumer law must be clear, accessible and comprehensible. The law relating to digital products currently satisfies none of these criteria. The law is uncertain, and is found in reports of decided cases, which are difficult enough to access and even more difficult – in some cases impossible – to reconcile.[54]

It suggested that a solution to this issue was unlikely to be achieved via the courts, in the light of the precedential inertia arising from established case law following St Albans, and also due to the lack of likely opportunities for the issue to come before the High Court or Court of Appeal to even permit them to readdress the issue.

The report itself identified a solution along the lines of that adopted by New Zealand, noting that there was 'no existing legal constraint which would prevent the extension of the definition of "goods" to make it explicit that digital content such as computer software is goods,' but conceding that in practical terms the key element of the supply of software was not a transfer of property,

---

52 Although the American Law Institute's *Principles of the Law of Software Contracts* (3rd edn, 2015) covers much of the same ground. However, the Principles are designed to be persuasive rather than to provide a model basis for legislation.
53 Moon, above, 407. See also Reto M. Hilty and Kaya Koklu, 'Software agreements: stocktaking and outlook – lessons from the *UsedSoft v Oracle* Case from a comparative law perspective' (2013) International Review of Intellectual Property and Competition Law 44(3): 263–292.
54 R Bradgate, *Consumer Rights in Digital Products*, 2010, Department for Business, Innovation and Skills at [21].

but the grant of a copyright licence, and that this would make it impossible simply to expand the definition of 'goods' to include digital products.

It suggested a number of ways this might be achieved, including extending the Sale of Goods Act to digital products 'regardless of their status as goods or otherwise, simply confirming that the provisions of the SGA shall apply to software and or digital products and/or to contracts for the supply of software and/or digital products'. Ultimately, following a consultation procedure in 2013,[55] the government's preferred solution was a variant of this suggestion, linked to the transposition of the Consumer Protection Directive. As noted above, software falls under the Act's definition of 'digital content', regardless of whether the code is supplied over a network, or on a tangible medium such as a DVD or USB datastick.

The CRA 2015 then provides digital content sold in the B2C environment with its own statutory regime of rights and remedies, separate from those for goods and services. This sets out, amongst other issues, a number of rights which will be implied into a contract for digital content if not dealt with expressly. These include that digital content, such as software, sold to consumers must be:

- of satisfactory quality according to the expectations of a reasonable person, e.g. a reasonable expectation of quality for a 99p app would not be as high as for software costing £150;
- fit for the purposes for which the type of digital content in question is usually supplied, i.e. safe and durable, and meets reasonable expectations as to quality, e.g. a complex game or piece of software will often contain some bugs on release so a reasonable person might not expect that type of digital content to be free from minor defects;
- where the consumer specifies that the digital content will be used for a particular purpose, fit for that particular purpose.

On its face, the legislation appears to provide a sensible approach to the sale of 'off-the shelf' (or perhaps more accurately today, 'across-a-network') software, whilst leaving the issue of how best to classify often highly customised bespoke software supplied under B2B contracts to a case-by-case analysis in the courts. However, given that that the CRA 2015 defines a 'consumer' as 'an individual acting for purposes that are wholly or mainly outside that individual's trade, business, craft or profession' – a broadening of the definition in the *Consumer Rights Directive* which refers to 'natural persons who are acting outside their trade, business, craft or profession' – it is not outside the bounds of possibility that, over time, acceptance of the requirements for software set out in the legislation for the B2C marketplace may begin to infiltrate into the small-medium enterprise (SME) environment and beyond.

## The software licence

When computers first began to be sold, the software was merely something that came with them; it simply was not seen as something to be separately exploited. The focus was on the hardware. It was in the early 1970s that serious consideration began to be given to software as a resource to be protected and exploited, and the practice grew up of using licences to do so. The licence would set out what the acquirer could, and could not, do with the software. Despite initial uncertainty, it became clear that licensing does, indeed, provide an appropriate approach to the exploitation of software.

---

55 Consumer Rights Bill: Policy papers > Consumer Rights Bill: government response to consultations on consumer rights (June 2013) available online at: www.gov.uk/government/publications/consumer-rights-bill

## Terms

When software is in question, some of the most significant terms will be those licensing its use – these will be considered below. First, we should briefly consider sources of contractual terms, although pre-contractual statements becoming terms will be looked at below in relation to the quality/functionality of the software.

If the relevant party signed a contractual document, its contents will provide contractual terms, whether he or she has any knowledge of them or not.[56] If such a document is not signed, then, in the absence of actual knowledge of its contents, its effectiveness to import terms into the contract will depend upon whether there has been reasonably sufficient notice of it.[57] This is an objective test, requiring sufficient notice for the reasonable person, rather than the particular individual concerned.[58] Even if clauses have not been appropriately introduced into a particular transaction, they may be imported if there has previously been a consistent course of dealings between the parties involving those terms.[59] There is a considerable degree of artificiality in the way in which clauses can become terms of a contract. It means that written contractual terms – particularly standard terms – may be seen as having very little to do with the agreement of the parties in any subjective sense.

Contract terms may be implied,[60] as well as express. They may be implied by statute, such as the terms implied by ss 13–15 of the SoGA 1979. Otherwise, at common law, they may be implied in fact, in law, or by custom. Terms are implied in fact on the basis of the parties' intention, but within very narrow confines. A range of tests have been applied, including whether it is necessary to imply the term to give the contract 'business efficacy',[61] and also the 'officious bystander' test – that is, whether the term was so obvious that, had an officious bystander approached the contracting parties and suggested it, they would have said that of course the term in question was included.[62]

In *BP Refinery (Westernport) Pty Ltd v Shire of Hasting*,[63] Lord Simon of Glaisdale stated that it was 'not . . . necessary to review exhaustively the authorities on the implication of a term in a contract', but that the following conditions ('which may overlap') must be satisfied:

(1)   it must be reasonable and equitable;
(2)   it must be necessary to give business efficacy to the contract, so that no term will be implied if the contract is effective without it;
(3)   it must be so obvious that 'it goes without saying';
(4)   it must be capable of clear expression;
(5)   it must not contradict any express term of the contract.[64]

However, in *Attorney General of Belize v Belize Telecom Ltd*, Lord Hoffmann ruled that such tests were, in fact, simply variations on a single theme and that the fundamental question was what 'the instrument,

---

56  *L'Estrange v F Graucob Ltd* [1934] 2 KB 394. There are limited exceptions, including fraud, misrepresentation (*Curtis v Chemical Cleaning and Dyeing Co* [1951] 1 KB 805) and non est factum (*Lloyds Bank Plc v Waterhouse* [1993] 2 FLR 97, in which the fundamental basis of the signed contract was completely different from what the party intended).

57  *Parker v South Eastern Rly Co Ltd* (1877) 2 CPD 416. See, generally, Elizabeth Macdonald and Ruth Atkins, *Koffman & Macdonald's Law of Contract*, 8th edn, 2014, Oxford: Oxford University Press, 135–6.

58  *Thompson v LM & S Rly* [1930] 1 KB 41.

59  See, e.g., *Circle Freight International v Medeast Gulf Exports* [1988] 2 Lloyd's Rep 427; see, generally, MacDonald & Atkins, above, 149–150.

60  See, generally, Macdonald & Atkins, ibid, 96–109.

61  *The Moorcock* (1889) LR 14 PD 64.

62  *Shirlaw v Southern Foundries Ltd* [1939] 2 KB 206, 227, per Mackinnon LJ.

63  *BP Refinery (Westernport) Pty Ltd v Shire of Hastings* (1977) 180 CLR 266 (PC).

64  Ibid, 282–3.

read as a whole against the relevant background, would reasonably be understood to mean'.[65] In his view, Lord Simon's list was to be regarded:

> ... not as a series of independent tests which must each be surmounted, but rather as a collection of different ways in which judges have tried to express the central idea that the proposed implied term must spell out what the contract actually means, or in which they have explained why they did not think that it did so.[66]

The implication of terms in law is not based on the intention of the parties, but upon necessity and the type of contract[67] – that is, the term must be one that it is 'necessary' to imply into the type of contract in question. Intention is relevant only to the extent that a term will not be implied in the face of a contrary term.[68]

The final issue to be addressed here is the question of the interpretation, or construction, of the contract. Obviously, once the terms have been established, the interpretation of the contract has to be ascertained. The objective when construing or interpreting a contract is that of determining the parties' intention, objectively ascertained. Traditionally, there has been an overwhelming emphasis upon the written words used and a restrictive approach to what further evidence of the parties' intention could be considered. However, in *Investors Compensation Scheme Ltd v West Bromwich Building Society*,[69] the House of Lords took the view that a 'fundamental change ... has overtaken this branch of the law', the result of which has largely been to discard the previous 'intellectual baggage of interpretation' and to give such documents the meaning obtained from 'the common sense principles by which any serious utterance would be interpreted in ordinary life'.[70]

In this case, Lord Hoffmann provided a summary of principles that are now frequently referred to by the courts.[71] These principles require the interpretation to take account of what the document would mean to a reasonable person with all of the requisite background knowledge. Other than information about the parties' previous negotiations and declarations of subjective intent, this knowledge is taken to included everything that was available to the parties at the time of contracting and anything that might affect the manner in which the reasonable man would understand the document. Lord Hoffmann, went on to explain that the background information was important, because it allowed the reasonable man to resolve any ambiguities or even, referring to *Mannai Investments Co Ltd v Eagle Star Life Ass Co Ltd*,[72] to decide that the wrong words or syntax had been used. Although it should not easily be assumed that the meaning of the formal documents departed from the 'natural and ordinary meaning' of the words, this should be a permissible conclusion in cases in which the background information showed that the words did not, in fact, convey the intention of the parties.

## Copyright ownership

When software is acquired under a commission, the copyright interest in it is unlikely to be acquired as well; rather there will be a right to use it under the terms of a licence. However, there will be some cases in which the acquirer also acquires the copyright. This might happen in relation

65 *Attorney General of Belize v Belize Telecom Ltd* [2009] UKPC 10, [21]. See further, KFK Low and KCF Loi, 'The many "tests" for terms implied in fact: Welcome clarity' (2009) 125(Oct) LQR 561.
66 Ibid, [27].
67 *Liverpool CC v Irwin* [1976] 2 All ER 39.
68 *Johnstone v Bloomsbury HA* [1991] 2 All ER 293, in which the Court of Appeal indicated that an express contrary term might be treated as an exclusion clause falling within UCTA 1977 in appropriate circumstances.
69 *Investors Compensation Scheme Ltd v West Bromwich Building Society* [1998] 1 All ER 98.
70 Ibid, 114.
71 Ibid.
72 [1997] 3 All ER 352.

to software that the acquirer commissioned the developer to devise for him or her. In such cases, it is advantageous to both parties to own the copyright. Chappatte[73] notes, in particular, that the end-user acquires substantial benefits from copyright ownership including the avoidance of all restrictions on use, the possibility of gaining royalties for subsequent reuse, and (what is often the most important benefit vis-à-vis competitors) obtaining control over the software. He contrasts this with the disadvantages for the software house, which relate not only to the loss of the above rights, but also include the consequent administrative burdens of maintaining a register of proprietary interests together with the problem of ensuring that its software designers do not inadvertently use software developed for one user in a project for another customer. Given the nature of the software development process, this last issue is a very real problem and many of the copyright infringement cases discussed earlier are based on related scenarios.

As Lord Hoffmann has pointed out, terms will be implied only when no express provision has been made. This is usually the end of the matter, since 'if the parties had intended something to happen, the instrument would have said so'.[74] So, in cases in which acquirers seek to obtain the copyright in the software, it is crucial that they do so by means of express contract terms, for while the courts have the power to imply an assignment of copyright, they are often disinclined to use it. Disputes are most likely to arise in relation to commissioned works and there have been occasions on which the courts have found it necessary to imply a term to give effect to the parties' apparent intentions concerning copyright. In such cases, the law will imply either an equitable copyright assignment or a licence, depending on the particular circumstances. In the absence of an express term, a licence rather than an assignment was implied in *Robin Ray v Classic FM*.[75] In arriving at this decision, Lightman J considered in detail the relevant law on implied terms and set out a list of nine propositions summarising the situations in which a contractor was entitled to retain copyright. These were subsequently described as 'masterful' by Jacob LJ in *Griggs Group Ltd v Evans*.[76] In brief, Lightman J concluded that if the contract makes provision for entitlement, that will be given effect, but in the absence of any contractual terms to the contrary, whether express or implied, the contractor retains copyright. There is, however, no entitlement to copyright merely because the work has been commissioned. Any terms that are implied must do no more than is necessary in the circumstances and must not conflict with any express terms. Specifically in relation to copyright, this means that a licence will usually be implied rather than an assignment, as this will be the least term that will achieve what the parties are deemed to have intended at the date of the agreement. Nevertheless, an assignment can be implied if the surrounding circumstances demonstrate that the client needs actually to own the copyright.[77]

The nature of software development – in which programmers will frequently seek to reuse source code that they have created for previous projects – means, however, that the UK courts are unwilling to imply terms assigning copyright from developer to acquirer. This is, first, because the likely need to be able to reuse source code without infringing the assigned copyright would mean that it was unlikely that a developer would intend to make such an assignment, and that if it did intend to do so, it would be a sufficiently unusual business step as to merit clear express terms in the contract. Second, when implying a term into a contract, the courts will usually examine whether the document, considered in the light of the background to it, could reasonably be understood to have meant to have achieved an assignment. In as much as the software would still

73 Philip Chappatte, 'Specific problems in the licensing of software' (1995) 11 CL &P 16.
74 *Attorney General of Belize*, above, [17].
75 [1998] FSR 622.
76 [2005] EWCA (Civ) 11, [14].
77 See also discussion in Peter Groves, 'Copyright in commissioned work: Court of Appeal put the boot in' (2005) 16(3) Ent L Rev 56; Rebecca Baines, 'Copyright in commissioned works: A cause for uncertainty' [2005] EIPR 122.

be usable by the acquirer without an assignment of the copyright and the impact on the developer of implying such a term would be significant, it is hard to see a court reaching that conclusion.[78]

A rare victory for an acquirer came in *Cyprotex Discovery Ltd v University of Sheffield*,[79] in which a highly convoluted set of facts arising from a seriously defective research contract led both the High Court and Court of Appeal to explore means of reaching a conclusion that supported what they saw as the underlying factual basis and commercial purpose of the contract. The facts clearly showed that an employee of Cyprotex had created the software code that was the subject of the dispute and that, in the absence of any agreement to the contrary, Cyprotex owned the copyright. However, the University of Sheffield was the focal point of the research collaboration, carried the responsibility for the research being financed, and had agreed to license the software to the other parties to the research contract. If Cyprotex were to retain the copyright, there would be no such obligation to license. In these circumstances, both courts found for the university: the High Court on what the judge admitted was a 'strained interpretation' of the contract that aimed to avoid making 'commercial nonsense of the Research Agreement';[80] and the Court of Appeal on an argument (rejected by the lower court) based on a side agreement between the parties that the Court held meant that Cyprotex's employee was actually an agent of the university.[81] The judge at first instance additionally noted that if the 'strained interpretation' were wrong, then because there was a clear intention that Sheffield should own the copyright in the program, it would be appropriate to imply a term assigning the copyright to Sheffield.[82]

However, the best that an acquirer can usually hope for in such circumstances is likely to be a licence sufficient to make the arrangement between acquirer and developer commercially workable. Thus, in *Clearsprings Management Ltd v Businesslinx Ltd*,[83] Clearsprings and Businesslinx, a small software development company, entered into a software development contract under which Businesslinx was to provide the necessary software to Clearsprings to enable it to operate a web-based database system. The contract was silent on the ownership of the software to be developed. Shortly after the contract had started, Clearsprings sent an email stating that it wanted to have the copyright so that it could, if it wanted to, sell it to third parties – at which point a dispute arose between the two companies as to the ownership.

Both parties accepted that Businesslinx was the first owner of the copyright. However, Clearsprings asserted that it was an implied term of the contract between it and the Businesslinx that Clearsprings would own by assignment, or at least have an exclusive licence under, all existing and future copyrights in the software. Failing that, Clearsprings maintained that there should be implied terms to the effect that it had a licence to use the software, and that this was to be perpetual, irrevocable, exclusive, and royalty-free. The implied licence would allow it to repair, maintain, and upgrade the software to meet its business requirements, and to distribute and sublicense software to third parties on its own terms. Businesslinx, on the other hand, argued that to imply an assignment of copyright or an exclusive licence to Clearsprings would prevent Businesslinx from making use of generic code incorporated in the software. It stated it had told Clearsprings that it would be using its pre-existing code in developing the new software, and that it was common practice amongst software developers to reuse quantities of code written for one client in one application when writing a similar or related application for another client.

In his judgment, Christopher Floyd QC noted that, although it was not established that Businesslinx had expressly told Clearsprings that it would use pre-existing software in developing the

---

78 See *Meridian International Services Ltd v Richardson* [2008] EWCA Civ 609; *Infection Control Enterprises Ltd v Virrage Industries Ltd* [2009] EWHC 2602.

79 *Cyprotex Discovery Ltd v University of Sheffield* [2003] EWHC 760 (TCC); [2004] EWCA Civ 380.

80 [2003] EWHC 760 (TCC), [135].

81 [2004] EWCA Civ 380, [71].

82 [2003] EWHC 760 (TCC), [136].

83 *Clearsprings Management Ltd v Businesslinx Ltd* [2005] EWHC 1487.

new software, it was an accepted practice that pre-existing code would be used to create bespoke software. Absent specific instruction from Clearsprings that the software had to be entirely bespoke, it was thus to be expected that Businesslinx would import pre-existing code into the code for Clearsprings and use it in other projects, and seek to continue to develop it. In such circumstances, there was little to support Clearsprings' claim for an exclusive licence.[84] All that was necessary to give business efficacy to the contract was an implied licence for Clearsprings to use the software for the purposes of its business and an implied restriction on Businesslinx's use of information about Clearsprings' business practices.[85] If there were insufficient grounds to grant an exclusive implied licence, then there were clearly insufficient grounds for granting an assignment of copyright.[86]

In sum, Clearsprings was thus entitled to an implied non-exclusive, personal copyright licence, which would be perpetual, irrevocable, and royalty-free, and would permit Clearsprings to repair, maintain, and upgrade the system in accordance with its business requirements. However, it would not entitle it to sublicense the software.[87]

# The licence

## Licence terms

The software licence will deal with such matters as:

- to whom the licence is granted;
- the equipment on which, and location at which, it may be used;
- the use to which the software can be put[88] (for example, sublicensing is usually forbidden);
- whether the source code or object code is supplied (normally, the acquirer only receives the object code);
- whether the licence is exclusive or non-exclusive (normally, it will be non-exclusive, unless it is being granted to a distributor who is to exploit the software through sublicensing it);
- whether the licensee can transfer the licence;[89]
- the duration of the licence, which may be for a fixed or indefinite period (it will normally state that it is to terminate on the occurrence of certain breaches by the licensee or on the licensee's insolvency);[90]
- confidentiality (the licence may state that the 'software' is confidential information that should not be disclosed, if the licensor is attempting to gain the protection afforded to such information);
- exemption clauses (the licensor will insert an exemption clause in an attempt to exclude or restrict any liability that he or she might incur to the licensee).

The effectiveness of exemption clauses must be considered in the light of the Unfair Contract Terms Act 1977 (UCTA 1977), which is considered in the website materials. In addition, the Unfair Terms in Consumer Contracts Regulations 1999[91] will subject to a test of 'fairness' many non-individually

---

84 *Ibid*, [39]–[48].
85 *Ibid*, [48].
86 *Ibid*, [49].
87 See also *Wrenn v Landamore* [2007] EWHC 1833 (Ch), [2008] EWCA Civ 496, in which the acquirer was held to be entitled to an implied exclusive licence and an entitlement to access the source code.
88 Defining the use rendered 'lawful' by the licence may be particularly important in the light of the CDPA 1988, s 50C, which bases its limited right to, e.g., copy, adapt, or correct errors in software on what is necessary for the software's 'lawful' use.
89 The copyright holder may wish to prevent a licence from being transferred to a rival.
90 Such termination has serious potential consequences for a licensee whose business is organised around the use of the software. The purchaser of such a business may require a check to see that the relevant software licences have not been infringed.
91 SI 1999/2083.

negotiated terms in contracts between sellers or suppliers and consumers. Here, some further consideration should be given to the importance of the source code and the recognition of its significance by the courts.

## Source code

The difference between source code and object code has already been discussed, but, in this context, some further consideration should be given to the difference between them, the significance of these differences to the licensee, and the courts' recognition of the importance of source code under certain circumstances. Most off-the-shelf software programs are received by the consumer in their machine-language format. This means that the user can run the program directly, but cannot easily read or modify it.

As noted in the last chapter, the object code is rarely intelligible to human beings. The source code is used to write the program and, as a result, it is needed if any bugs are to be corrected or improvements made. Obviously, the licensee of the program would prefer to have a licence that extends not only to the object code, but also to the source code, but the licensor will want to maintain control of the source code to prevent the program information from becoming known. The most likely form of arrangement through which the licensee might achieve access to the source code in limited circumstances is an escrow arrangement.

A simple escrow agreement consists of a three-way contractual arrangement entered into by the licensor, the licensee, and an independent third party – the escrow agent. Under the arrangement, the licensor agrees to deposit the source code of the software with the escrow agent, and the parties agree the conditions under which the source code will be released by the escrow agent to the licensee to enable ongoing maintenance. Common reasons for such release will include the licensor going into liquidation, cancelling further development of the software, being acquired by a competitor of the licensee, or failing to maintain and update the software under its contractual maintenance obligations.

A source code escrow agreement will usually include terms that:

● identify the subject of the escrow – usually the source code of a particular program – and such documentation, software tools or libraries, and hardware as is required for the licensee to maintain the software;
● require that the source code in escrow be updated within a short period of time after new releases and updates;
● specify the conditions that will trigger release of the source code to the licensee and those that will not, such as removal of support for a product that is to be succeeded by an equivalent upgrade or replacement product from the licensor;
● specify the rights of the licensee with regard to the use of the released source code, such as permitting general maintenance or error correction; and
● identify the fees payable to, and responsibilities of, the escrow agent, which may include verification of the source code's authenticity.

Software escrow is clearly not suited to all types of software licence agreement. A large company such as Microsoft, with significant market share in particular applications, is unlikely to agree to such an arrangement, even if its many off-the-shelf licensees desire it to do so.[92] It is most likely to

---

92 For example, Microsoft announced in June 2009 that it was no longer going to support its popular Money personal finance software, and that support for the software would end in January 2011. Users of the US versions of Money were provided with a free, but unsupported, product, Microsoft Money Plus Sunset, so as to access and maintain existing Microsoft money files. Users outside the US were not.

be used in the commercial bespoke software sector, in which the interest of the licensor in attracting and keeping clients justifies the costs and risks of escrow. This will be particularly true for small software developers who want to persuade companies to take on their software in mission-critical business areas, or who are seeking to attract large client licensees without having to risk making their source code immediately available.

While, as noted above, the English courts have been loath to assign copyright in source code to acquirers of commissioned software, they have nonetheless recognised the importance of access to source code by licensees under particular circumstances. As a result, they have shown some willingness to interpret the contract, or to imply terms, in such a way as to allow the acquirer to use the source code in circumstances in which it is necessary to make the contract commercially viable.[93]

In *Saphena Computing Ltd v Allied Collection Agencies*,[94] the availability and use of source codes for error correction was considered. The case was concerned with an attempt to provide an 'online' computer system for a debt collecting agency. The plaintiff supplier experienced difficulties in trying to make the software function as required. The time that it spent in attempting to deal with the problems eventually led the defendant acquirer to agree to a termination of the contract. It then called in a third party to deal with the problems. The particular point that needs to be considered here is the question of whether the defendant was entitled to possession of the source code, and in order to remedy the defects in the software. Havery QC (the Official Receiver) considered the question in general terms under the original supply agreement, and in the more specific situation of the agreement to terminate an incomplete supply contract. He noted that the source code remained the property of the plaintiff, but that unlike more tangible products, a purchaser was not in a position either to repair or improve the program. It could not, he decided, have been the intention of the parties that, when the business relationship ended, the software should remain in a state that was not entirely fit for purpose. On this basis, although he concluded there was no right to the source code, he was prepared to imply a term to give business efficacy to the termination agreement and allow copying of the source code to the extent necessary to ensure fitness for the intended purpose. Once the source program has been made available to the acquirer, s 50C(2) of the Copyright, Designs and Patents Act 1988 (CDPA 1988) will now be relevant to the question of whether it can be copied in order to correct errors and will be discussed further below.

There are indications of willingness to go somewhat further to make the contract workable in *Psychometric Services v Merant*,[95] in which what was in question was the ordering of the supply of the source code to the acquirer. The case was again concerned with a problem caused by uncompleted software. The acquirer was arguing that the supplier was in breach and that it wanted to have the software completed by someone else. Laddie J only had to consider whether, as a matter of interim relief, to order the supply of the source code to the acquirer (the dire financial situation of the acquirer if the program was not swiftly made to function pointed to such relief). However, what is of interest are the indications of his willingness to interpret the contract so as to find an entitlement to the source code by the acquirer. He found an express term that 'strongly supports PSL's claim to the source code',[96] and he had already pointed out that, in any event, had everything happened as it should have done under the contract, the 'loyalty period' of maintenance by the supplier needed to last for only two years (and might even have been shorter in some circumstances). At the end of that period, if the acquirer was not entitled to the source code, 'none of the inevitable bugs would be able to be fixed. No development [would] be possible'.[97] Laddie J made the point that the suppliers did not 'dissent strongly' from the proposition and that, if it was correct, 'the agreement

---

93 But see *Mars UK v Teknowledge Ltd* [2000] FSR 138.
94 *Saphena Computing Ltd v Allied Collection Agencies* [1995] FSR 616.
95 *Psychometric Services v Merant* [2002] FSR 8.
96 Ibid, [37].
97 Ibid, [36].

made no commercial sense at all'.[98] There is an impetus to interpret contract terms in a way that makes good commercial sense[99] and against a construction that achieves an unreasonable result. The 'more unreasonable the result the more unlikely it is that the parties can have intended it, and if they do intend it the more necessary it is that they [should] make that intention abundantly clear'.[100]

# The EC Software Directive

## Basic use of software

It is generally said that using software will be in breach of copyright unless the user has a licence. This is because its use almost inevitably requires it to be copied onto hardware and, in the absence of a licence, such copying has generally been said to entail a breach of copyright.[101] However, what must be considered is the effect on this of Art 5(1) of the Software Directive.[102] This might be seen as providing the acquirer with a right to make the copy required for the basic use of software.

Article 5(1) states:

> In the absence of specific contractual provisions, the acts referred to in Article 4(a) and (b) shall not require authorisation by the rightholder where they are necessary for the use of the computer program by the lawful acquirer in accordance with its intended purpose, including for error correction.

The 'acts' referred to in Art 4(a) and (b) are, inter alia, the 'permanent or temporary reproduction of computer programs', and 'the translation, adaptation, arrangement and any other alteration of a computer program and the reproduction thereof'. This means that the Directive might be seen as providing the right to make the copy of software that its basic use requires. However, any such right would be limited and it would seem that the copyright owner could prevent any such right from being acquired by including an express contrary term.

Article 5(1) has been implemented in what is now s 50C of the CDPA 1988, which states:

> (1) It is not an infringement of copyright for the lawful user of a copy of a computer program to copy or adapt it, provided that the copying or adapting–
>
> (a) is necessary for his lawful use; and
>
> (b) is not prohibited under any term or condition of an agreement under which his use is lawful.
>
> (2) It may, in particular be necessary for the lawful use of a computer program to copy or adapt it for the purpose of correcting errors in it . . .[103]

This section seems generally restrictive of any notion of a right to make basic use of software. There is an important difference between the Directive's references to 'lawful acquirer' and use of the

98 Ibid.
99 *Antaios Cia Naviera SA v Salen Rederierna AB* [1985] AC 191, 221.
100 *L Schuler AG v Wickman Machine Tool Sales Ltd* [1974] AC 235, 251.
101 See CDPA 1988, s 17(1), (2), and (6).
102 Directive 2009/24/EC of the European Parliament and of the Council of 23 April 2009 on the legal protection of computer programs (Codified version) [2009] OJ l111/16.
103 It should be noted that s 50C would require a contrary contract term. If the Directive is construed so that there is no right under Art 5(1) where there is a contrary agreement, it does not seem to require any such agreement to be contractual.

software in accordance with its 'intended purpose', and the statutory references to 'lawful user' and 'lawful use'. It would seem that someone might well be argued to be a 'lawful acquirer' although he or she lacks the rights to make him or her a 'lawful user'; the same point can be made in relation to 'lawful use' and 'intended purpose' ('lawful user' is defined in s 50A(2)). *Prima facie*, the person who purchases software in a shop should be regarded as a 'lawful acquirer', but, on any natural meaning of the words, it seems doubtful that he or she can be registered as a 'lawful user' unless he or she has an effective licence. However, whatever the natural meaning of the words, because the provision is intended to give effect to a provision of a Directive, it should be construed in a way so as to achieve that implementation. 'Lawful user' may thus be understood here as 'lawful acquirer'.

## Back-up copies

Making back-up copies of software is commonly regarded as sound practice. A disk can be affected, and the program corrupted, by a number of factors, such as a faulty disk drive, heat, or an electromagnetic field. Some copyright holders even put instructions in the manual that, before the software is put to any other use, it should be copied and a copy put in a safe place, to be used in the event of the other becoming corrupted. However, some copyright holders do not want any copies of this type made, perhaps for security reasons. Consideration should now be given to s 50A of the 1988 Act, which states that it is not an infringement of copyright for a 'lawful user' of a copy of a computer program to make any back-up copy of it 'which it is necessary for him to have for the purposes of his lawful use' (s 50A(I)). This right to make a necessary back-up copy cannot be removed by any contrary agreement. Section 50A(3) states that, where an act is permitted by the section, 'it is irrelevant whether or not there exists any term or condition in an agreement which purports to prohibit or restrict the act'. Any such term is void under s 296A. Section 50A is based on Art 5(2). Both are of limited scope. The right to make a back-up copy, irrespective of contrary agreement, is limited to cases in which it is 'necessary' to make such a copy. If 'necessary' is strictly construed, this would be of very limited application. In most cases, a back-up copy will be highly desirable, but not strictly necessary, in the sense of 'essential to' the actual use of the program. However, 'necessary' may be understood in its context. In a commercial context, it might be taken to mean 'necessary' for the commercial use of the software. It might then be found that having a readily accessible back-up copy would often be necessary for its commercial use, the business user effectively being unable to use it if it could become unavailable to him or her for a time, through corruption of the disk, for example. This last approach was envisaged by Singleton. She suggested that, where licensors did not want to allow users to make back-up copies for reasons of security, for example, then compliance with this section could be achieved by providing a 24-hour duplication service (or alternatively depositing a copy in a bank or other secure place) to deal with those occasions on which the program had been deleted or corrupted. The availability and use of this service could be reflected in the terms of the licence and it would remove the 'necessity' for the user to make a back-up copy.[104]

## Error correction

Error correction will normally require the use of the source code, rather than merely the object code. It will not normally be undertaken by the acquirer of software. In particular, a maintenance agreement will often be made in relation to software, coming into effect once acceptance has occurred and encompassing error correction.[105] The question may arise as to whether the error in

104 Susan Singleton, 'Computer software agreements and the implementation of the EC Directive' (1993) 9 CL & P 50.
105 There will be difficulties for the acquirer of software if access to the source code for necessary error correction is denied because the copyright holder becomes insolvent or otherwise ceases to function. To deal with these situations, source code 'escrow' (see above) can be used. There may, however, be difficulties with this under insolvency law.

question amounts to a breach of the supply contract, and that will depend upon the express and implied terms of that contract.

However, the point on which to focus here is whether the acquirer can correct errors in the software. Article 5 of the Directive includes 'error correction' within the acts that are not in breach of copyright when they are necessary for the intended purpose of a program.[106] Similarly, s 50C of the CPDA 1988 states that, subject to contrary agreement, the copying or adapting that is necessary for the lawful use of a program is not a breach of copyright. Section 50C(2) makes it clear that 'it may, in particular, be necessary for the lawful use of a computer program to copy or adapt it for the purpose of correcting errors in it'. Some of the difficulties in interpreting these provisions were outlined above. It should be noted that, whatever the extent of the 'right' conferred by the Directive, it is not the acquirer's 'right' to have errors corrected; he or she can merely correct them without being in breach of copyright. In addition, it would seem that there is no obligation, in these provisions, on the seller to supply the source code, which is generally needed for error correction. The contractual obligation is normally only to supply the object code, but it may provide for the supply of the source code. The Directive and the legislation would not seem to make the source code, as such, available to any greater extent to the acquirer.

## 'Shrink-wrap' licences[107]

Software may be acquired via the web, directly from the copyright holder. In such a situation, there is obviously no difficulty in creating a contractual licence for the acquirer of the software – all that is required is that the licence terms appear appropriately on the website for them to be incorporated.[108] However, the more common situation is for the end-user to acquire the software from a supplier who is not the copyright holder. This raises the issue of the creation of the licence, which has been termed the 'shrink-wrap' licence problem.

The problem of the effectiveness of the shrink-wrap licence can be epitomised by the purchase of software 'off the shelf' from a shop. The purchaser will take his or her newly acquired software home, open the box, and discover that it is contained in an envelope, on which it is stated that opening the envelope constitutes acceptance of the copyright holder's licence terms. (These are also included in the box.) Alternatively, on starting to use the software, the acquirer may discover an on-screen message stating that the software cannot be used unless there is an agreement to licence terms by 'clicking' on a button (if the acquirer is online, which may generate a message to the copyright holder). This is referred to as 'click wrap'. Whatever form it takes, the statement on-screen or on the box may also include that if the purchaser does not want to accept the licence terms, the software may be returned to the shop from which it was purchased for a full refund.[109]

---

106 It has been argued to the contrary that, on its wording, Art 5(1) does not only encompass the error correction that is necessary for the intended purpose of the program, but rather treats error correction as an intended purpose: M Sherwood-Edwards, 'Seven degrees of separation: The Software Directive and UK implementation' (1993) 9(55) CL & P 169.

107 See, generally, Clive Gringras, 'The validity of shrink-wrap licences' (1996) 4(2) Int JLIT 77; Diane Rowland and Andrew Campbell, 'Supply of software: Copyright and contract issues' (2002) 10(1) Int JLIT 23; Phillip Johnson, 'All wrapped up? A review of the enforceability of "shrink-wrap" and "click-wrap" licences in the United Kingdom and the United States' (2003) 25(2) EIPR 98.

108 Such licences are often termed 'click-wrap' licences. As has been the case with 'shrink-wrap' licences, these have not been the subject of particular scrutiny by the courts in England and Wales. Their effectiveness has been more widely explored in the USA, where such 'agreements are generally enforceable provided that the user has the opportunity to review the contractual terms prior to clicking': Nancy S Kim, 'The software licensing dilemma' [2008] BYU L Rev 1103, 1125, citing *Davidson & Assoc v Jung* 422 F 3d 630, 638–39 (8th Cir 2005); *Forrest v Verizon Commc'n, Inc* 805 A 2d 1007, 1010 (DC 2002), and *Caspi v Microsoft Network, LLC* 732 A 2d 528, 532 (NJ Super Ct App Div 1999) as positive rulings; *Specht v Netscape Commc'n, Corp* 306 F 3d 17, 28–30 (2nd Cir 2002) and *Comb v Paypal, Inc* 218 F Supp 2d 1165, 1172–3 (ND Cal 2002) as negative rulings.

109 There may be difficulties in finding that the supplier is under an obligation to the acquirer to take back the software and return the price paid, particularly where the software packaging has been opened.

There are numerous variations on the fact situation indicated above. The packaging arrangements may vary, but all raise the same type of issues. It may also be that the software is not acquired from a shop, but by mail or telephone order. The software may also be downloaded from the web, from a supplier's website, and a form of 'click wrap' will then be in question. Again, many of the same issues arise as under the above fact situation. Primary consideration will be given to the purchase in a shop, with comments on other situations in which that is required. The basic question in each situation is whether the shrink-wrap licence is effective, and there are two basic possibilities to consider in relation to this:[110] it might be argued that it is part of the contract made between the supplier, S, and the acquirer, A, for the acquisition of the software (that is, the supply in the shop); alternatively, it might be considered part of a contract formed between A and the copyright holder, C, when the envelope is opened.

## Acquisition contract

In considering the acquisition of software from a shop, the first point to consider is with whom the acquirer, A, contracts. *Prima facie*, at that stage, there is simply a contract between the shop, S, and A. The transaction certainly looks like a simple sale of the software by S to A. On this basis, two issues need to be addressed: first, the timing of the introduction of the licence terms; and, second, the fact that the copyright holder, C, is a third party to the acquisition contract.

The first point to be made is simply that new terms cannot be introduced into a contract once it has been made.[111] If the licence terms are not introduced into the transaction until after the contract in the shop has been made, they cannot be part of the contract between A and S.

Contract formation is normally analysed in terms of offer and acceptance. An offer expresses a willingness to be contractually bound by certain terms,[112] if the other party accepts them. An acceptance occurs when the other party agrees to the same terms.[113] In a shop, the offer is normally made by the customer when the goods are taken to the till, and it is accepted by the assistant.[114] If the existence of licence terms does not become apparent until after the box has been opened, and that does not take place before offer and acceptance have occurred, obviously, they have been introduced after the contract was made and cannot be part of it. This was recognised in the Scottish case of *Beta Computers (Europe) Ltd v Adobe Systems (Europe) Ltd*.[115] The same point can also be made in relation to the mail order or telephone order of software. In those cases, the contract will normally be made when the acquirer's order (the offer) is accepted by dispatch of the goods (in the case of mail order) or by express acceptance on the telephone, in the case of a telephone order. If not even the existence of the licence was indicated prior to A's opening of the box, it cannot form part of the contract terms, and a similar point can be made in relation to web-based order and delivery.

The situation also has to be considered in which the licence terms are referred to on the outside of the box[116] (or on the website, when that is from where the software is acquired). Clauses may be incorporated into contracts from unsigned documents on the basis of reasonably sufficient notice.[117] It should also be noted that incorporation by reference is possible – that is, the document

---

110 A third possibility, combining elements of the two considered, was arrived at in the Scottish court in *Beta Computers (Europe) Ltd v Adobe Systems (Europe) Ltd* [1996] FSR 367.

111 *Olley v Marlborough Court Hotel* [1949] 1 KB 532; *Thornton v Shoe Lane Parking* [1971] 2 QB 163.

112 See, e.g., *Gibson v Manchester CC* [1979] 1 WLR 294.

113 *Jones v Daniel* [1894] 2 Ch 332.

114 *Pharmaceutical Society of Great Britain v Boots Cash Chemists* [1953] 1 QB 401.

115 [1996] FSR 367; see below, p 512.

116 This fact seems to have been emphasised by the US court in *ProCD, Inc v Zeidenberg* 86 F 3d 1447 (7th Cir 1996).

117 *Parker v South Eastern Rly Co* (1877) 2 CPD 416. The 'red hand rule' has been added to this, so that the more unreasonable or unusual a clause, the greater the degree of notice required to provide reasonably sufficient notice: *Thornton v Shoe Lane Parking* [1971] 1 QB 163; *Interfoto Picture Library v Stiletto Visual Programmes* [1988] 1 All ER 348. The name of the rule stems from a famous dictum of Denning LJ, as he then was, in *Spurling v Bradshaw* [1956] 1 WLR 461, 461: 'The more unreasonable a clause is, the greater the notice which must be given of it. Some clauses which I have seen would need to be printed in red ink on the face of the document with a red hand pointing to [them] before the notice could be held to be sufficient'. On incorporation more generally, see Macdonald & Atkins, above, 130–150.

providing notice does not have to contain the terms, but can merely refer to where they can be found.[118] The test is objective[119] and whether incorporation by notice occurs is basically[120] a question of fact in each case,[121] dependent upon such matters as the legibility and prominence of the relevant writing. One factor that has been seen as relevant to the test generally is whether the place in which the notice is to be found is the type of place in which the reasonable person would expect to find a contractual term. One reason why the clause on the deckchair ticket in *Chapelton v Barry UDC*[122] did not provide reasonably sufficient notice of an exemption clause was that the ticket was seen as something that the reasonable person would view merely as a method of proving that the deckchair hire charge had been paid, rather than as a document containing contract terms. One question is whether people normally expect to find contract terms referred to on the back of a box containing software. The size and position of any such notice on the box would also be relevant, and it would, for example, be ineffective if the shop were to have stuck a price tag, or some other label, over it.[123] It should be easier for such incorporation to take place as acquirers, in general, begin to assume that the acquisition of software will involve licence terms.[124]

However, if the licence is incorporated into the contract between S and A, the fact that C is a third party to that agreement must now be considered. Traditionally, the response in English law would have been that incorporation of the licence into the contract between A and S could not assist C. Traditionally, the doctrine of privity of contract would not have allowed a third party, C, to enforce contract terms, even if they were for the third party's benefit. However, privity has now been considerably modified by the Contracts (Rights of Third Parties) Act 1999. Basically, a third party may now enforce a term of the contract if either:

(a)  'the contract expressly provides that he may'; or
(b)  'the term purports to confer a benefit on him' and it does not appear that the parties did not intend the term to be enforceable by the third party.[125]

The overall effect of this would seem to be that if the licence terms are appropriately drafted (and they are drafted by C), then A will indirectly acquire a licence to use the software (through a chain from C, via S, to A) and C will have a right to enforce the licence terms, which can be regarded as providing him or her with a benefit. (The benefit of the protection of an exemption clause is expressly recognised as falling within the 1999 Act.)[126] An analogy might be made with the Scottish case of *Beta v Adobe*,[127] in which, under Scottish law, the court did not have to contend with the privity rule and a third party could gain the benefit of a contract under the doctrine of *ius quaesitum tertio*.

## Opening the envelope

The second possibility to consider is that of a second contract, separate from the acquisition contract, made when A opens the packet or clicks on the button on screen. The argument would be

---

118  *Thompson v LM & S Rly* [1930] 1 KB 41. It would seem that a copy of the terms should be accessible before a contract.
119  In *Thompson*, ibid, it was indicated that it was irrelevant that the passenger in question was illiterate. The reasonable person was to be presumed to be able to read English. The situation would be otherwise where the party seeking to incorporate the terms knew, or should, as a reasonable person, have known that the other party, or the group to which he or she belongs, was in some way less able to read or understand the notice: *Richardson, Spence & Co v Rowntree* [1894] AC 217; *Geier v Kujawa, Weston and Warne Bros (Transport)* [1970] 1 Lloyd's Rep 364.
120  But note the 'red hand rule' (above).
121  *Hood v Anchor Line* [1918] AC 837, 834.
122  *Chapelton v Barry UDC* [1940] 1 KB 532.
123  *Sugar v LM & S Rly* [1941] 1 All ER 172.
124  *Alexander v Rly Executive* [1951] 2 KB 882, 886.
125  Contracts (Rights of Third Parties) Act 1999, s 1.
126  Ibid, s 1(6).
127  [1996] FSR 371.

that the offer is made by C and A accepts by performing the stated act of opening the envelope. Acceptance of an offer normally requires communication and communication may occur in the click-wrap situation if the acquirer is online, but it is possible to have acceptance by conduct.[128] However, that conduct would have to be unequivocal and another explanation of the opening of the envelope may be possible. It could be argued that A may not be responding to C's offer of a licence, but, rather, that he or she is exercising a right already acquired. The contention would be that, at the time that the software was acquired from S, A also acquired certain basic rights to use it. Such rights might stem from the legislation implementing the Software Directive, from a common law licence, or from terms implied into the contract between S and A.

As was indicated above, Art 5(1) of the Software Directive provides the lawful acquirer of software with a right to, *inter alia*, copy it where such copying is necessary for its use in accordance with its 'intended purpose'. The reference to 'lawful acquirer' might well be seen as encompassing the person who buys software in a shop and as providing him or her with a right, which would explain the opening of the software packet as something other than an acceptance of the licence. However, as has already been indicated, s 50C of the CDPA 1988, the provision intended as an implementation of Art 5(1), does not refer to the 'lawful acquirer' of software, but rather to its 'lawful user', and also refers to 'lawful use' rather than 'intended purpose'. It seems doubtful whether, without using an implied term (considered below) or some such device, the acquirer of the software in the shop can be seen as a 'lawful user' unless the licence is effective. Certainly, that would seem to be the case in any natural construction of 'lawful user', but the point should be made that something other than a natural construction of the section may be required if it is to be seen as a proper implementation of the Directive. In addition, as it stands, any natural interpretation of the reference to 'lawful user' in s 50C is open to the criticism of circularity.[129]

Another possible explanation for the opening of the envelope is that the common law provides a limited licence for the acquirer of software so that the acquisition is not rendered pointless. An analogy with patent law might lead to such a conclusion.[130]

The point must be made, however, that it is, in any event, now unclear to what extent this analogy is still possible in the face of Art 5(1) of the Software Directive. That Article provides for the basic use of software in the absence of contractual provision. Certainly, it would seem that a non-contractual[131] implied licence should not provide a means to reduce an acquirer's rights below the level provided for by Art 5, and the impetus for non-contractual rights to be implied may not survive the Directive at all.

The final possibility to be considered here is that the opening of the software envelope was based not on acceptance of the licence, but on a right to use the software derived from an implied term in the contract under which the software was acquired (that is, the contract made in the shop with S, in our primary example). Certainly, in *Saphena Computing Ltd v Allied Collection Agencies Ltd*,[132] in which software was supplied to the defendants for the purposes of their business as a debt-collecting agency, the court regarded it as 'perfectly clear' that there had to be an implied term 'that the defendants should have a copyright licence to enable them to use the software for that purpose'.[133] Courts may well be reluctant to find that a supply of software is quite pointless because the acquirer has no right to use the software. They may be willing to imply a term in law giving a basic right to use the software on the basis that such a term is necessary in that type[134]

---

128 *Brogden v Metropolitan Rly Co* (1877) 2 App Cas 666.
129 'Lawful user' is defined in s 50A(2). For criticism of the phrase, see Sherwood-Edwards, above.
130 Graham P Smith, 'Shrinkwrap licensing in the Scottish courts' (1996) 4(2) Int JLIT 131, 140–1.
131 But note that s 50C, 'implementing Article 5(1)', merely refers to contrary agreement, without specifying that it must be contractual.
132 *Saphena Computing Ltd v Allied Collection Agencies Ltd* [1995] FSR 617.
133 *Ibid*, 637, Havery QC (Off Ref).
134 The argument here would seem to apply whether the transaction is a sale of the disk or merely a hiring of it (as may sometimes be argued to be the case). In either situation, its acquisition is completely undermined if it cannot be used.

of contract. Of course, there are difficulties with the idea of an implied term conferring rights to do what would otherwise be a breach of copyright if the contract is not between the acquirer and the copyright holder. A chain of implied terms might be suggested, although such a chain would be vulnerable to the insertion of an express contrary term in the first contractual link between the copyright holder and the person to whom he or she supplies.[135]

Obviously, there are considerable hurdles in the way of finding that there were two effective contracts – the supply contract and the licence. It should also be noted that the two-contract analysis was considered, and rejected, by the Scottish court in *Beta v Adobe*,[136] because of the difficulties that might ensue. If the situation was construed as one that could give rise to two distinct contracts, with S, the supplier, not being a party to any second licence or contract, Lord Penrose was concerned that A, the acquirer, might not be able to recover the purchase price of the software, or might refuse to pay it, if he or she did not wish to accept the licence terms. Any statement on the packaging that A can recover the purchase price if the licence is unacceptable will not be contractually enforceable by A against S, unless it has been properly incorporated into the contract between A and S. However, A might be able to claim that S's supply was in breach of contract.[137] It might be argued that the supply of software that, without further agreement with C, could not be used without infringing C's copyright would be in breach of the term implied by s 12 of the SoGA 1979[138] that the seller has a right to sell the goods. In *Niblett Ltd v Confectioner's Materials Co Ltd*,[139] a breach of that implied term was found when the sellers supplied tins of condensed milk that were labelled in such a way as to infringe a third party's trade mark.

The problem considered by Lord Penrose, outlined above, obviously arises if the view is taken that A cannot use the software without accepting the licence terms. However, Lord Penrose's other concern with the two contract analysis was in relation to the possibility that C's attempt to create a licence with A would be ineffective, but A would nevertheless be able to use the software. He was concerned that S might be liable to C, through a breach of the contract under which C supplied the software to S, and, more significantly, that the position of C, as the copyright owner, would be undermined.

## Pragmatism

The desire of the Scottish court in *Beta v Adobe* not to undermine the position of the holder of the copyright was noted above, together with Lord Penrose's view that it was generally in the interests of both the industry and the general management of transactions that effect should be given to the provisions of a licence. There may thus be an impetus to find shrink-wrap licences to be effective because that result is viewed as being of practical benefit.[140]

Something of this approach is also to be found in the US case of *ProCD Inc v Mathew Zeidenberg*.[141] In that case, unlike the earlier *Step-Saver* case,[142] the licence was held to be effective against a background of the court's view of the benefits of such a conclusion. In *ProCD v Zeidenberg*, ProCD used different licence terms to differentiate between consumer and commercial purchases of its database. The consumer was charged US$150 for the purchase, which was much less than the commercial

---

135 Even a term that would otherwise be implied in law will not be implied in the face of an express contrary term, although sometimes the express contrary term might be rendered ineffective and the implication therefore allowed, under UCTA 1977: *Johnstone v Bloomsbury HA* [1991] 2 All ER 293; see also UCTA 1977, s 3; Elizabeth Macdonald, 'Exclusion clauses: The ambit of s 13(1) of the Unfair Contract Terms Act 1977' (1992) 12 LS 277.
136 *Beta v Adobe* [1996] FSR 371.
137 A restitutionary claim might also be made, but it would prove problematic to argue that a total failure of consideration had occurred when A had, technically, received title to the disk: see the approach taken in *Rowland v Divall* [1923] 2 KB 500.
138 If the contract is not one for the sale of goods, then it can be argued that an analogous term has been breached.
139 *Niblett Ltd v Confectioner's Materials Co Ltd* [1921] 3 KB 387.
140 *Beta v Adobe* [1996] FSR 371, 379.
141 *ProCD Inc v Mathew Zeidenberg* 86 F 3d 1447 (7th Cir 1996); but see Smith, above, 140–1.
142 *Step-Saver Data Systems Inc v Wyse Technology and Software Link Inc* 939 F 2d 91 (3rd Cir 1991).

buyer, but was also authorised to do much less with the database than the commercial buyer. The court took the view that it was beneficial to both consumers and commercial buyers that ProCD should take such an approach, which was obviously dependent on the effectiveness of the licence terms.

Since the ProCD case, despite considerable US academic debate over the validity of shrink-wrap licences and the rationales for finding them enforceable (or not), it appears that courts have generally been inclined to find them to be enforceable.[143] A move to create a statutory means of ensuring the validity of shrink-wrap licences in the USA was made with the Uniform Computer Information Transactions Act of 1999 (UCITA).[144] This was a draft state contract law designed to standardise the law, and to provide the default rules for licensing software and all other forms of digital information, as the US Uniform Commercial Code does for the sale of goods.[145] Despite strong support from major industry players, UCITA was seen as too heavily weighted in favour of large software vendors[146] and was only passed into law by two states, Virginia and Maryland. Four states — West Virginia, North Carolina, Vermont, and Iowa — were sufficiently concerned about the impact of UCITA on consumers' rights that they adopted laws ('bomb shelters') that made UCITA-based contracts unenforceable in those states. In 2003, UCITA was effectively abandoned by its sponsor, the US National Conference of Commissioners on Uniform State Laws.[147]

More recently, in May 2009, the American Law Institute (ALI) approved a set of Principles of the Law of Software Contracts, which are designed to be legal principles to guide courts in deciding disputes involving transactions in software and to guide the drafting of software contracts.[148] These contain provisions dealing with what the Principles term 'standard form licenses' – that is, licences covering standard transfers of a small number of copies, or right of access to small number of users. The term is designed to cover end-user licence agreements (EULAs), and would apply to all kinds of software licences, including open source, shareware, and freeware. Section 2.02(b) covers the formation of standard-form transfers of generally available software, and states that a contract will be formed and the transferee is bound if a reasonable transferor would believe the transferee to be bound. Section 2.02(b) then sets out what is termed a 'safe harbor', which will ensure enforcement of a licence. This includes that:

- the standard-form licence is available prior to the transfer of the software;
- the licensee has reasonable access to the standard-form licence prior to the payment (or completion of the transaction if no payment is received);
- for electronic transactions, the licensee must signify agreement at the end of, or next to, the electronic standard-form licence;
- for standard-form licences printed on, or attached to a package, or separately wrapped from the software, the licensee must fail to return the unopened packaged software for a full refund within a reasonable period of time; and
- the licensee must be able to store and reproduce a copy of the standard-form licence, if it is only available electronically.

143 Robert W Gomulkiewicz, 'The Federal Circuit's licensing law jurisprudence: Its nature and influence' (2009) 84 Wash L Rev 199, citing Mark Lemley, Peter S Menell, and Robert P Merges, *Software and Internet Law*, 3rd edn, 2006, New York: Aspen Law & Business, p 337: 'Since ProCD, a majority of courts have enforced shrinkwrap licenses.'

144 *Uniform Computer Information Transactions Act* (UCITA), available online at: www.uniformlaws.org/shared/docs/computer_information_transactions/ucita_final_02.pdf

145 In fact, UCITA was originally envisioned as a new §2B of the Uniform Commercial Code.

146 See, e.g., David A Szwak, 'Uniform Computer Information Transactions Act (UCITA): The consumer's perspective' (2002) 63 Louis L Rev 27.

147 See Gomulkiewicz, above, 208–13.

148 The ALI began working on the Principles of the Law of Software Contracts in 2004. The official text of this project was published by the ALI in 2010 as *Principles of the Law of Software Contracts: Official Text*. See further Robert A Hillman and Maureen A O'Rourke, 'Principles of the law of software contracts' (2010) 53(9) J Commun ACM 26–8.

Section 2.02(e) places the burden of proving that these requirements have been met on the licensor. In addition to the terms of the 'safe harbor', the principles require that the standard-form licence terms must be 'reasonably comprehensible', such that a 'person of average intelligence and education can understand the language with ordinary effort', and that a standard-form licence will still be subject to public policy, unconscionability, and other invalidating defence. Standard-form licences may also not require advance agreement from the licensee to contract modifications (Section 2.03).

The ALI principles are designed to be 'soft law' – that is, to be used as guidance and not as a template for state laws. However, due to their source, they are likely to be influential in US courts as demonstrating good practice in software contracting.

In the UK, there has been a dearth of commentary on shrink-wrap (and clickwrap) licences in academic and practitioner circles, and no further judicial discussion, since *Beta v Adobe*, in the courts. This may be because:

- consumers have adjusted to the concept of shrink-wrap licences (if they were aware of them and their content in the first place);
- software producers (or their distributors) have been willing to negotiate settlement of disputes with consumers outside the courts;
- consumers are more aware of the abilities and limitations of the software that they are purchasing due to the availability of online information; or
- the net cost of bringing a case claiming the invalidity of all or part of a shrink-wrap licence is prohibitive compared to the cost of much consumer software.

Whatever the reasons, initiatives such as the ALI Principles of the Law of Software Contracts suggest that the time may be ripe for reconsideration of the issue of shrink-wrap licences in the UK – if only to ensure that US-centric legal interpretations of such licences are parsed for compatibility with UK contract law, intellectual property law, and conflict-of-laws obligations.[149]

## Resale of software licences

The delivery of software from licensor to licensee is increasingly divorced from a tangible means of transfer, e.g. floppy disks, CD-ROMs etc, with software being 'digitally delivered' by means of download from an internet-based server (either that of the licensor, or of an authorised third party). As noted above, this has implications for the classification of software as a 'good' or a 'service'. However, it also raises questions about the extent to which a licensor of software can use contractual licence terms to control/prevent resale or redistribution of software, thereby avoiding the doctrine of 'exhaustion' or 'first sale' – i.e. the principle that limits the rightsholder's exclusive right to distribute a protected work following the first (authorised) sale of the work.[150]

---

149 See further, Michael L Rustad and Maria Vittoria Onufrio, *The Exportability of the Principles of Software: Lost in Translation?*, 2009, Stetson University College of Law Research Paper No 2009–03/Suffolk University Law School Research Paper No 09–45; available online at: http://ssrn.com/abstract=1466875

150 The application of 'exhaustion' or 'first sale' principle to digital content generally is an ongoing area of legislative and judicial development, and it is clear that various jurisdictions are adopting different policy-driven approaches that vary not just according to the perceived role of exhaustion, but also depending upon the nature of the digital works in question. Compare, for example, the CJEU's ruling in Case C-419/13 *Art & Allposters International BV v Stichting Pictoright*, 22 January 2015, with that of *UsedSoft v Oracle* (below). See further, Louise Longdin and Pheh Hoon Lim, 'Inexhaustible distribution rights for copyright owners and the foreclosure of secondary markets for used software' International Review of Intellectual Property and Competition Law (2013) 44(5): 541–68. As regards the US, see *Vernor v Autodesk* 621 F.3d 1102 (9th Cir. 2010) (software); *Capitol Records LLC v ReDigi Inc* 934 F.Supp.2d 640 (2013) (SDNY) (digital music).

This issue was addressed by the CJEU in *UsedSoft GmbH v Oracle International Corp*,[151] where Oracle licensed particular software which was primarily distributed by download to the licensee (licensees could opt to receive the software on CD-ROM or DVD). The terms of the licence were that in exchange for a one-off fee, the licensee received, exclusively for their internal business purposes 'for an unlimited period a non-exclusive non-transferable user right free of charge for everything that Oracle develops and makes available to [the licensee] on the basis of the agreement'. Under a separate maintenance agreement, licensees could also download updates and patches from Oracle's website.

UsedSoft, a German company, purported to sell 'used' licences for the software. It claimed that the licences it sold were valid, as the maintenance agreement between the initial licence holder and Oracle remained in force, and it provided notary certificates stating that the initial licence holder lawfully owned the licences, had ceased using the software, and had paid the entire initial purchase price. Oracle sought to prevent UsedSoft from engaging in this activity on the grounds that the actions of UsedSoft and its customers infringed Oracle's exclusive right of permanent or temporary reproduction of computer programs under Art 4(1)(a) of the Software Directive.[152] UsedSoft argued that, in fact, Oracle's right was exhausted as Art 4(2) states that the first sale of a copy of a program exhausts distribution rights over that copy, and that under Art 5(1) the parties to which it sold the 'used' licenses were 'lawful acquirers' able to undertake any reproduction necessary to use the software in question for its 'intended purpose'. On appeal, UsedSoft having lost both prior hearings, the German Bundesgerichtshof referred a series of questions to the CJEU.[153]

The focus of those questions was, in essence, to call into question what Moon called the '"law merchant" . . . underpinning current software transactions'[154] – that is, the software industry's understanding that where software was sold online (and thus not in tangible medium) it was subject to control through IP licensing, permitting the use of licence restrictions on re-use or sellingon.[155] This understanding about the nature and control of digital works permeates the Information Society Directive,[156] and if the approach in the InfoSoc Directive was followed, this would have clearly torpedoed UsedSoft's claims.[157] The CJEU, however, decided to prioritise the Software Directive over the InfoSoc Directive – perhaps, surprisingly, for as Gillen notes:

> The Software Directive . . . a codification/reiteration of Directive 91/250/EEC, and therefore originally written for the software on a disk paradigm, favours the idea of exhaustion but envisages it within a physical context, whereas the information Society Directive [is] designed for the post broadband era . . . with the prevention of the piracy of multimedia goods as its key goal.[158]

---

151 C-128/11 *UsedSoft GmbH v Oracle International Corp* [2012] All ER (EC) 1220. See also Martina Gillen, 'The software Proteus – UsedSoft changing our understanding of software as "saleable goods"' (2014) International Review of Law Computers & Technology 28(1): 4–20; Paul L.C Torremans, *The Future Implications of the UsedSoft Decision*, CREATe Working Paper 2014/2 (February 2014); Andrew Nicholson, 'Old habits die hard?: UsedSoft v Oracle' (2013) 10(3) SCRIPTed 389, available online at: script-ed.org/?p=1167

152 Directive 2009/24/EC of the European Parliament and of the Council of 23 April 2009 on the legal protection of computer programs: OJ 2009 L 111, p 16.

153 C-128/11 *UsedSoft GmbH*, above, [34]

154 Moon, above, 407.

155 See, e.g., the US case of *Vernor v Autodesk* 621 F.3d 1102 (9th Cir. 2010), 'a software user is a licensee rather than an owner of a copy where the copyright owner, in the documents included with the software packaging, (1) specifies that the user is granted a license; (2) significantly restricts the user's ability to transfer the software; and (3) imposes notable use restrictions'.

156 Directive 2001/29/EC of the European Parliament and of the Council of 22 May 2001 on the harmonisation of certain aspects of copyright and related rights in the information society: OJ L 167, 22/06/2001 p 10–19.

157 See, e.g., Recital 29: 'The question of exhaustion does not arise in the case of services and on-line services in particular. This also applies with regard to a material copy of a work or other subject-matter made by a user of such a service with the consent of the rightholder. Therefore, the same applies to rental and lending of the original and copies of works or other subject-matter which are services by nature. Unlike CD-ROM or CD-I, where the intellectual property is incorporated in a material medium, namely an item of goods, every on-line service is in fact an act which should be subject to authorisation where the copyright or related right so provides'.

158 Gillen, above, 8.

The court began by noting that Art 4(2) of Directive 2009/24/EC states that the first sale in the EU of a copy of a computer program by the rightholder, or with his consent, exhausts the distribution right within the EU in respect of that copy. It noted also that in the absence of a definition of 'sale' in Directive 2009/24/EC the court had to apply a uniform interpretation of the term 'sale' in order to avoid differing national protection for copyright holders under Directive 2009/24/EC. It adopted the following definition: 'an agreement by which a person, in return for payment, transfers to another person his rights of ownership in an item of tangible or intangible property belonging to him'. It rejected Oracle's submission that neither the making available of a copy free of charge nor the conclusion of the user licence agreement added up to a transfer of the right of ownership of that copy. It held that, taken as a whole, that combined process did constitute the transfer of the right of ownership of the copy in question, regardless of the medium by, or in which, the transfer took place:

> The making available by Oracle of a copy of its computer program and the conclusion of a user licence agreement for that copy are . . . intended to make the copy usable by the customer, permanently, in return for payment of a fee designed to enable the copyright holder to obtain a remuneration corresponding to the economic value of the copy of the work of which it is the proprietor.[159]

If 'sale' were to be given a narrower definition, the suppliers would merely have to call the contract a 'licence' rather than a 'sale' in order to circumvent the rule of exhaustion.

With regard to the apparent clash between the provisions of the InfoSoc and Software Directives, the CJEU declared that Directive 2009/24/EC, being specifically concerned with the legal protection of computer programs, constituted a *lex specialis*[160] in relation to Directive 2001/29/EC. If exhaustion only applies to tangible objects under the InfoSoc Directive, but the Software Directive states that exhaustion applies in relation to both tangible and intangible copies of software, then to square that circle it is necessary to assume that the EU legislature intended, in the specific case of software, that tangible and intangible copies were to be treated identically/equally.[161] If this is the case, then exhaustion of the distribution right takes effect after the first sale in the European Union of a copy of a computer program by the copyright holder or with his consent, regardless of whether the sale relates to a tangible or an intangible copy of the program. Such exhaustion applies even if the software is updated or patched under a separate agreement, after the initial sale, as the original licensee would be able to continue to use the amended software in perpetuity.[162]

Following from this, if the rightholder's rights in a copy of the software were exhausted after first sale, then regardless of contractual terms prohibiting a further transfer, they could not oppose the resale of that copy. If that was the case, then the second acquirer of that copy and any subsequent acquirer are 'lawful acquirers' of it within the meaning of Art 5(1) of Directive 2009/24. The rightholder cannot prevent the effective use of any used copy in which his distribution right has been exhausted under Art 4(2) of Directive 2009/24, by relying on his exclusive right of reproduction in Art 4(1)(a), as this would render the exhaustion of the distribution right under Art 4(2) ineffective.

159 C-128/11 *UsedSoft GmbH*, above, [45].
160 *Ibid*, [51], [56]. Where two laws govern the same factual situation, a law governing a specific subject matter (*lex specialis*) overrides a law which only governs general matters (*lex generalis*).
161 *Ibid*, [59]–[61].
162 *Ibid*, [64]–[68].

In principle, the outcome of the CJEU's ruling in *UsedSoft* is that the resale of software licences is lawful if the seller can demonstrate that:

- the computer program in question has been put on the market in the EEA with the consent of the rightsholder;[163]
- the rightsholder has granted a perpetual licence to the initial acquirer/licensee;
- the rightsholder has received reasonable remuneration;
- the initial acquirer has deleted their program copies upon the sale of the licence.

The eventual outcome of the *UsedSoft* litigation might be seen to indicate that the CJEU's rulings may not be as far reaching as was initially thought. UsedSoft are reported to have withdrawn its legal action and signed an undertaking to cease and desist in early 2015. The precise reason for this is unclear, but commentators have suggested that the company may not have been able to meet the evidential burdens posed by the CJEU and the Bundesgerichtshof.[164] However, since the *UsedSoft* decision, there have been a number of national cases that suggest both that there is potential for a further development and expansion in software resales, and that national courts are comfortable with the application of the CJEU's rulings.[165]

A rightsholder could potentially limit the scope for resale by licensing their software for a fixed term – perhaps of ten years; or prohibiting transfer of their maintenance and support agreements. However, in the former case, switching to term licences be unattractive to customers; and in the latter case, given that the support costs of software may exceed the initial licence fees, there may be incentives for rightsholders to continue to support software that has been transferred. The software industry's shift towards providing software via cloud services (see 'Software as a service' (SaaS) below) with access to software provided on a subscription basis, allows for a scenario where no software is delivered to the subscriber, and a rightsholder should thus be able to rely on the provisions of the InfoSoc Directive (2001/29/EC), wherein the provision of services over the internet will not result in exhaustion.

# Free and open source software licensing (F/OSS)[166]

As was noted at the beginning of this chapter, when computers entered the commercial marketplace in the 1950s, software was not considered as an item to be sold separately. As Campbell-Kelly and Garcia-Swartz note in their longitudinal analysis of IBM's changing policy towards supply of software, companies such as IBM initially bundled basic software with their hardware, and actively collaborated with their customers in developing software specific to their customers' needs. During this period, there were essentially no independent software producers, so if IBM wanted to sell (or lease) its computers, it either had to produce the software itself, or rely on its customers to

163 The EU practices 'regional exhaustion', therefore software that has not been put on the market in the EEA with the consent of the rightsholder can legitimately be prevented from being resold, i.e. resale of software licences sourced from the US would not be permissible, as these would not have previously been put on the market in the EEA with the rightsholder's consent. The US does not currently have a similar resale right for software, and the ruling in *Capital Records v Redigi Inc* 934 F.Supp.2d 640 suggests that there is no US first sale/exhaustion defence for digital files.

164 Anon. 'The end of the UsedSoft case and its implications for "used" software licences', *Osborne Clarke* (May 2015), available online at: www.osborneclarke.com/connected-insights/publications/end-usedsoft-case-and-its-implications-used-software-licences/

165 See, e.g., *SusenSoftware v SAP LG Hamburg* 315 O 449/12, October 25, 2013; *Straton IT-consulting v Saga Consulting, RIcha and CTAC*, Brussels Court of Appeal, 11 September 2015. See further Robin Fry, 'Reselling software licences' (2015) 26(4) Computers & Law 20; Maša Savič, 'The legality of resale of digital content after *UsedSoft* in subsequent German and CJEU case law' (2015) 37(7) EIPR 414.

166 See further, van R Wendel de Joode, JA de Bruijn, and MJG van Eeten, *Protecting the Virtual Commons: Self-organizing Open Source and Free Software Communities and Innovative Intellectual Property Regimes*, 2003, The Hague: TMC Asser Press; Rod Dixon, *Open Source Software Law*, 2003, Norwood MA: Artech House; Lawrence Rosen, *Open Source Licensing: Software Freedom and Intellectual Property Law*, 2004, London: Prentice Hall; and Mikko Välimäki, *The Rise of Open Source Licensing: A Challenge to the Use of Intellectual Property in the Software Industry*, 2005, Helsinki: Turre, available online at: lib.tkk.fi/Diss/2005/isbn9529187793/isbn9529187793.pdf

generate it using the basic software utilities that IBM provided. In order to facilitate this, IBM provided the source code for all its programs to its end-users – the source code was 'open'.[167] Gradually, for IBM, that model began to change during the 1960s, as it moved away from collaborative software production and began to produce its own bundled programs; however, the source code remained open, because customers still needed to customise software according to their needs.

However, by the 1970s, IBM, faced with pressure from competitors in the computer market alleging that its bundling practices were anti-competitive, began to unbundle its software and market it separately from the hardware. While the source code still remained open to customers, IBM was now beginning to use licences and copyright to restrict third-party access.[168] This process was facilitated by the US Copyright Act of 1976, which explicitly provided copyright protection to computer programs. Finally, in the early 1980s, IBM moved to an 'object code only' policy, whereby customers were not supplied with the source code. This was driven in part by the threat of competitors' hardware being used to run competing programs derived from analysis of IBM source code. There was also the fact that, as the computing marketplace became more competitive, the cost of hardware was declining and IBM was beginning to generate a significant proportion of its revenue from software. Maintaining that revenue appeared to require the closing of the company's source code.[169]

## Free software

IBM's journey from open source to closed source was largely mirrored across the computer industry, led by the software development houses. However, this change was not always well received. Initially, for example, the software industry sought to retain access to IBM's source code, claiming the need for access to maintain effective interoperability of their programs with those of IBM (while this may seem illogical, it is worth bearing in mind just how dominant a player IBM was in the computer marketplace at the time).[170] Equally annoyed, however, were a large number of 'hackers'[171] based at companies and universities, who were used to being able to access the source code of the computers that their institution operated, and to making such modifications, upgrades, and code fixes as they felt necessary. It is from this group that the concept of 'free software' arose.

The essential concept underlying free software is that users should have the 'freedom to run, copy, distribute, study, change and improve'[172] software. It does not mean that software should not be capable of being paid for: '"Free software" is a matter of liberty, not price. To understand the concept, you should think of "free" as in "free speech," not as in "free beer."'[173] The leading light in the free software movement was (and is) a computer programmer called Richard Stallman. According to Stallman, while he was working at the Massachusetts Institute of Technology (MIT) Artificial Intelligence Laboratory (AI Lab) in the late 1970s and early 1980s, two incidents occurred that made him question the direction that the software industry was taking. The first was the deliberate use of 'timebomb' coding[174] by a fellow programmer to control the ability of end-users to use

---

167 Martin Campbell-Kelly and Daniel D Garcia-Swartz, 'Pragmatism, not ideology: Historical perspectives on IBM's adoption of open-source software' (2009) 21 (3) Inform Econ Pol 229, 233.
168 *Ibid*, 235–7.
169 *Ibid*, 237–9. Interestingly, Campbell-Kelly and Garcia-Swartz go on to describe how, since the late 1990s, in some areas of its operations, IBM has begun to embrace open sources again – notably the open source operating system Linux.
170 *Ibid*, 238.
171 'Hacker' has not always had the primarily pejorative meaning that is usually placed on it today. In the early days of computing, the term appears to have been mainly used to denote skilful or quick programmers. However, its precise etymology remains disputed: see Guy L Steele and Eric S Raymond (eds), *The New Hacker's Dictionary*, 3rd edn, 1996, Cambridge, MA: MIT Press.
172 Free Software Foundation, 'The Free Software Definition', available online at: www.gnu.org/philosophy/free-sw.html
173 *Ibid*.
174 A software timebomb is a software routine that causes the program in which it is embedded to stop functioning, or to function in a restricted fashion, after a pre-determined time. Such timebombs were often used by software companies as a means of 'renting' their software for particular periods. Modern licences have largely superseded such mechanisms, although 'trialware' – software obtained on a trial basis by end-users – may contain such routines. 'Timebombs' and 'logic bombs' have been increasingly associated with computer misuse – see Chapter 7 – which may also have led to their decline in popularity in legitimate circumstances.

particular software; the second was the denial of source code to a program used to run the AI Labs Xerox® laser printer under a non-disclosure agreement.[175] Both of these developments, Stallman felt, meant that commercial imperatives were destroying the cooperative environment in which programmers had worked, to the detriment of both programmers and the effective development of software.[176] Shortly afterwards, in 1982, the AI Lab itself moved from its existing open mainframe computer operating system to a proprietary system. This left Stallman with a dilemma: he could stay and work within a software development system in which he did not believe, or he would have to strike out in a different direction.[177]

In 1984, Stallman left employment at MIT and began work on a project to develop a new operating system called GNU, designed to be compatible with, but eventually replace, the proprietary Unix operating system. This project involved the development not only of the base operating system or 'kernel', but also of a range of programs including command processors, assemblers, compilers, interpreters, debuggers, text editors, and mailers.[178] Stallman intended that GNU would remain open, and 'free' – that is, that users would have the freedom to:

● run the program, for any purpose;
● modify the program to suit their needs, meaning access to the source code;
● redistribute copies, either gratis or for a fee; and
● distribute modified versions of the program, so that the community could benefit from their improvements.[179]

The problem with granting these freedoms to other users was that they came with no obligation for those users to offer the same terms to others. Thus a software company could incorporate 'free' software source code into its proprietary products and then sell the result only as object code, under a proprietary licence, including non-disclosure agreements. Even if some element of control was kept over the 'free' source code, for example, requiring the 'free' source code to be provided to users by the software company, there was also the issue of circumstances in which a company had made non-trivial modifications to that code, or incorporated it into larger, more complex programs – in principle, it would be able to withhold those improvements to the original 'free' code from other programmers.[180]

Stallman's innovative solution was hinted at in his article 'The GNU Manifesto' in 1985,[181] in which he wrote that:

> GNU is not in the public domain. Everyone will be permitted to modify and redistribute GNU, but no distributor will be allowed to restrict its further redistribution. That is to say, proprietary modifications will not be allowed. I want to make sure that all versions of GNU remain free.

What Stallman proposed was to use a copyright licensing strategy to ensure that his freedoms applied not only to the original source code provided, but also to any source code created using that original source code, such as where the original source code was incorporated into a larger

175 See Sam Williams, *Free as in Freedom: Richard Stallman's Crusade for Free Software*, 2002, Sebastopol, CA: O'Reilly Media, ch 1, available online at: www.oreilly.com/openbook/freedom/ch01.html
176 See Richard M Stallman, 'The GNU operating system and the free software movement' in Chris DiBona, Sam Ockman, and Mark Stone, *Open Sources: Voices from the Open Source Revolution*, 1999, Sebastopol, CA: O'Reilly Media, available online at: www.oreilly.com/openbook/opensources/book/stallman.html
177 Ibid.
178 Ibid.
179 See, GNU, 'The Free Software Definition', available online at: www.gnu.org/philosophy/free-sw.html
180 Ibid.
181 Richard M Stallman, 'The GNU Manifesto' (1985) 10(3) *Dr Dobb's Journal of Software Tools* 30, available (annotated) online at: manybooks.net/titles/stallmanother05gnumanifesto.html

piece of source code, or where the original source code was improved or extended. In other words, by accepting Stallman's licence, a programmer would be agreeing to distribute his or her new, improved, or expanded source code under the same or an equivalent licence. This would mean him or her giving up certain rights that would otherwise be exclusively reserved to him or her by copyright as the copyright holder. Such licences have become known as 'copyleft' licences, because the copyright holder 'leaves' what would otherwise be exclusive rights available to others. It is important to remember, when discussing 'free' software licences (and open source software licences), that they are still copyright licences and that to grant such a licence requires a person or organisation to have the right under copyright law to do so, for example, as a creator, employer, or assignee. The first copyleft software licence that Stallman created was the Emacs General Public Licence (GPL);[182] this was to form the basis of the widely used GNU GPL. In 1985, Stallman set up the Free Software Foundation (FSF), a non-profit organisation that today sponsors the GNU project, holds copyright on a large proportion of the GNU operating system and other free software, and publishes a range of free software licences, including the GNU GPL, the GNU Lesser General Public Licence (GNU LGPL), the GNU Affero General Public Licence (GNU AGPL), and the GNU Free Document Licence (GNU FDL).

Stallman was not alone in seeking to make software source code widely available, although others were not as concerned that their source code remain outside what Gomulkiewicz[183] terms the 'binary use' software model (that is, software that is only distributed in object/binary code, such as Microsoft Office). A team of programmers at the University of California at Berkeley also tackled the issue of 'freeing' the Unix operating system. Unlike Stallman, they did not start from scratch, but rather evaluated the existing software and replaced any source code elements that were not authored by members of the project. These 'free' source code programs were released from 1989 onwards under the Berkeley Software Distribution (BSD) Licence.[184] This licence, and others modelled on it, like the MIT Licence[185] and Apache licence,[186] simply aimed to encourage reuse of the source code provided, and contained no copyleft requirement with regard to circumstances in which the original source code was incorporated into a larger piece of source code, or in which the original source code was improved or extended. Because of this degree of latitude permitted to end-users as to reuse, even in proprietary products, these licences became known as 'permissive' licences.

### A permissive licence: The modified BSD licence

It has been estimated that variations on the BSD 'permissive' licence[187] are used for roughly 6 per cent of open source software projects, placing it fourth on the list of most popular free licences behind the GPL and associated LGPL, which are used by around 64 per cent of open source software projects.[188] The BSD licence, in its 'modified' form below, permits a licensee to:

- use, copy and distribute the unmodified source or binary forms of the licensed program; and

---

182  Robert W Gomulkiewicz, 'General Public License 3.0: Hacking the Free Software Movement's Constitution' (2005) 42(4) Hous L Rev 1015, 1024; see the Emacs General Public License, available online at: www.free-soft.org/gpl_history/emacs_gpl.html

183  Ibid, 1021.

184  Paul B de Laat, 'Copyright or copyleft? An analysis of property regimes for software development' (2005) 34(10) Research Policy 1511, 1519; Marshall Kirk McKusick, 'Twenty years of Berkeley Unix: From AT&T-owned to freely redistributable' in Chris DiBona, Sam Ockman, and Mark Stone (eds), Open Sources:Voices From the Open Source Revolution, 1999, Sebastopol, CA: O'Reilly, pp 31–46.

185  The MIT License, available online at: www.opensource.org/licenses/mit-license.html

186  Apache License, Version 2.0, available online at: www.opensource.org/licenses/apache2.0.php

187  The BSD licence has gone through three iterations: the original BSD licence, which contained a clause on advertising (four clauses); the 'modified' version with the advertising clause removed (three clauses); and the 'simplified' version, which removes the 'no-endorsement' clause (two clauses): see below.

188  See statistics provided at Black Duck Software, 'Top 20 Most Commonly Used Licenses in Open Source Projects', available online at: www.blackducksoftware.com/compliance/top-20-open-source-licenses

- use, copy and distribute modified source or binary forms of the licensed program. It requires only that the licensee ensure that—
- all distributed copies are accompanied by the licence; and
- the names of the previous contributors are not used to promote any modified versions without their written consent.

The 'permissive' non-copyleft nature of the BSD licence means that source code licensed under it can be used in both 'open source' and 'closed source' software: for example, Microsoft Windows has used BSD-derived code in its implementation of TCP/IP. Would-be licensors wishing simply to see their source code used as widely as possible, and who do not require either a financial return or that licensees make improved and extended versions of the code, or other code in which the licensed code is included, available upon public distribution of the object code, are likely to use this licence.

### The modified BSD license template[189]

Copyright (c), <YEAR>, <OWNER>
    All rights reserved.
    Redistribution and use in source and binary forms, with or without modification, are permitted provided that the following conditions are met:
    Redistributions of source code must retain the above copyright notice, this list of conditions and the following disclaimer.
    Redistributions in binary form must reproduce the above copyright notice, this list of conditions and the following disclaimer in the documentation and/or other materials provided with the distribution.
    Neither the name of the ←ORGANIZATION→ nor the names of its contributors may be used to endorse or promote products derived from this software without specific prior written permission.
    THIS SOFTWARE IS PROVIDED BY THE COPYRIGHT HOLDERS AND CONTRIBUTORS 'AS IS' AND ANY EXPRESS OR IMPLIED WARRANTIES, INCLUDING, BUT NOT LIMITED TO, THE IMPLIED WARRANTIES OF MERCHANTABILITY AND FITNESS FOR A PARTICULAR PURPOSE ARE DISCLAIMED. IN NO EVENT SHALL THE COPYRIGHT HOLDER OR CONTRIBUTORS BE LIABLE FOR ANY DIRECT, INDIRECT, INCIDENTAL, SPECIAL, EXEMPLARY, OR CONSEQUENTIAL DAMAGES (INCLUDING, BUT NOT LIMITED TO, PROCUREMENT OF SUBSTITUTE GOODS OR SERVICES; LOSS OF USE, DATA, OR PROFITS; OR BUSINESS INTERRUPTION) HOWEVER CAUSED AND ON ANY THEORY OF LIABILITY, WHETHER IN CONTRACT, STRICT LIABILITY, OR TORT (INCLUDING NEGLIGENCE OR OTHERWISE) ARISING IN ANY WAY OUT OF THE USE OF THIS SOFTWARE, EVEN IF ADVISED OF THE POSSIBILITY OF SUCH DAMAGE.

A key problem with 'permissive' licences is the issue of 'freeriding'. This is where 'the product of open source contributors' efforts is monetised by a party that did not contribute to the project . . .'.[190] While this is not a problem wholly restricted to 'permissive' licences, it is sometimes cited as a reason why such licences are not more widely used.[191] However, it is worth noting that the range of motivations for developing free and open source software (F/OSS), for both individual developers and companies, are complex and certainly much wider in scope than simple direct financial gain.

---

189 The BSD License (modified), available online at: www.opensource.org/licenses/bsd-license.php
190 See Oded Nov and George Kuk, 'Open source content contributors' response to free-riding: The effect of personality and context' (2008) 24(6) Comp Hum Behav 2848.
191 For example, Brian Fitzgerald and Nic Suzor, 'Legal issues for the use of free and open source software in government' (2005) 29(2) Mel U L Rev 412, 413.

For developers, issues such as talent signalling, reputation gain, learning, and altruism are perceived as motivations. For companies, broad external input, improved software quality, and (as with IBM, above) wider consumer choice for particular hardware all play a part.[192]

### An inheritable licence: The GPL/GPL v.3

The GNU GPL, like the BSD licence, has been through several iterations. The original version was drafted in 1989 by Richard Stallman, to provide a unified licence for all GNU 'free' software.[193] The second version was released in 1991[194] with relatively minor changes, bar what Stallman refers to as the 'liberty or death' clause, designed to limit the impact of software patents on GNU licensed source code.[195] The current version was released in 2007 after considerable amendment.[196] The last two versions will be considered here.

The second version of the GPL (GPL v.2) permits a licensee to:

- copy and distribute unmodified copies of the licensed program;[197]
- modify a copy or copies of the licensed program or any portion of it, and copy and distribute such modifications;[198]
- copy and distribute the program or a work based on it, in object code or executable form.[199]

These permissions are subject to the licensee providing:

- on both modified and unmodified copies of the program, an appropriate copyright notice and disclaimer of warranty, all of the notices that refer to the GPL and to the absence of any warranty, and a copy of the GPL v.2;[200]
- where the program has been modified, a modification notice, including the date of modification.[201]

He or she must also ensure that:

- any work containing the source code licensed under the GPL v.2 that is distributed or published by the licensor is licensed as a whole under the GPL v.2;[202]
- where any work is distributed in object code or as an executable program, the complete corresponding machine-readable source code is also supplied, or is made available to third parties by reasonable alternative means.[203]

Licensees breaching GPL v.2 lose their rights under it, but this does not void the rights of those who have received properly licensed copies of the GPL v.2 licensed source code, and who have themselves not breached the GPL v.2.[204] Modification or distribution of GPL v.2 licensed source code is taken to

---

192  See Nov and Kuk, above; Andrea Bonaccorsi and Cristina Rossi, 'Comparing motivations of individual programmers and firms to take part in the open source movement: From community to business' (2006) 18(4) Knowledge, Technology & Policy 40.

193  Free Software Foundation Europe (FSFE), 'Transcript of Richard Stallman at the 2nd International GPLv3 Conference, 21 April 2006', available online at: fsfe.org/campaigns/gplv3/fisl-rms-transcript.en.html

194  The GNU General Public License, Version 2 (GPLv2), available online at: www.opensource.org/licenses/gpl-2.0.php

195  FSFE, above; see section 7 of GPLv2, ibid.

196  The GNU General Public License, Version 3 (GPLv3), available online at: www.opensource.org/licenses/gpl-3.0.html

197  GPL v.2, section 1.

198  Ibid, section 2.

199  Ibid, section 3.

200  Ibid, sections 1 and 2.

201  Ibid, section 2(a).

202  Ibid, section 2(b).

203  Ibid, section 3(a) and (b).

204  Ibid, sections 4 and 6.

indicate acceptance by a licensor of the GPL v.2 terms.[205] Where legal conditions, including patent restrictions, are imposed on, or agreed by, a distributor/licensee of a GPL v.2 licensed program, this will breach the terms of the GPL v.2 and, in such circumstances, the licensee may not distribute the GPL v.2 program.[206] The GPL v.2 also includes an express exclusion of any warranty of merchantability or fitness for purpose, as far as any applicable law permits.[207] It should be noted that the requirement on a licensee to make any modified source code available applies only if the licensee distributes, or otherwise makes available, the software to the public. If the software is modified for use solely by the licensee, then there is no obligation to make the source code publicly available.

The latest version of the GPL, version 3 (GPL v.3), is drafted in a more legalistic form, is more precise (and less US law-specific) in its definitions,[208] and is considerably longer than its two predecessors.[209] It attempts to address issues that have arisen from the GPL v.2, as well as issues that have developed out of changes in the technological environment. At its core, however, the GPL v.3 retains the key elements of the GPL v.2. It permits a licensee to:

- run the unmodified program, and to make, run, and propagate 'covered works' (that is, 'the unmodified Program or a work based on the Program') that are not 'conveyed' (which refers to 'any kind of propagation that enables other parties to make or receive copies') – in-house modifications and modifications made by third parties at the direction of the licensee, which are not made available outside that arrangement, fall within this category;[210]
- copy and distribute unmodified copies of the licensed program (that is, convey verbatim copies);[211]
- modify a copy or copies of the licensed program or any portion of it, and copy and distribute such modifications (that is, convey modified source versions);[212]
- copy and distribute the program or a work based on it, in object code or executable form (that is, convey non-source forms).[213]

These permissions are subject to the licensee providing:

- on both modified and unmodified copies of the program, an appropriate copyright notice and disclaimer of warranty, all of the notices that refer to the GPL and to the absence of any warranty, and a copy of the GPL v.3,[214] including any other 'additional permissions' (that is, terms additional to the GPL v.3 that make exceptions from one or more of its conditions) allowed under section 7 of the GPL v.3;[215]
- where the program has been modified, a modification notice, including the date of modification.[216]

The licensee must also ensure that:

- any work containing the source code licensed under the GPL v.3 that is distributed or published by the licensor is licensed as a whole under the GPL v.3,[217] including any other

205 Ibid, section 5.
206 Ibid, section 7.
207 Ibid, sections 11 and 12.
208 GPL v.3, section 0.
209 See further John Tsai, 'For better or worse: Introducing the GNU General Public License Version 3' (2008) 23(1) Berk Tech LJ 547.
210 GPL v.3, section 2.
211 Ibid, section 4.
212 Ibid, section 5.
213 Ibid, section 6.
214 Ibid, sections 4 and 5.
215 See the exhaustive list, ibid, section 7(a)–(f).
216 Ibid, section 5(a).
217 Ibid, section 5(c).

'additional permissions' (that is, terms additional to the GPL v.3 that make exceptions from one or more of its conditions) allowed under section 7 of the GPL v.3;

- where any work is distributed in object code or as an executable program, the complete corresponding machine-readable source code is also supplied or is made available to third parties by reasonable alternative means.[218]

The GPL v.3 also retains:

- termination for breach of the licence, but softens the position under GPL v.2 by permitting a licensee to avoid termination by remedying a breach within 30 days of reasonable notice of violation of the GPL v.3 by a relevant copyright holder;[219]
- the position that a licensor is deemed to have accepted the licence by virtue of modifying or propagating (but not receiving or running) a covered work;[220]
- automatic licensing of downstream recipients, whereby each new recipient automatically receives a licence from the original licensors to run, modify, and propagate that work, subject to the GPL v.3,[221] and that this remains even if a conveyor or licensor upstream of them has had their licence terminated for breach;[222]
- the requirement that a licensor cannot limit the freedoms of others by accepting conditions that contradict the GPL v.3 (in such circumstances, the licensor may not convey the covered work);[223]
- a disclaimer of any warranties and exclusion of liability to the extent permitted by applicable laws.[224]

Significant policy changes from the GPL v.2 can be seen in a number of key areas. First, the GPL v.3 tackles the issue of software patents much more directly. It is clear that, the copyright provisions of the GPL notwithstanding, the use of software patents could hinder the four freedoms that the GPL aims to protect (see above). The GPL v.2 appeared to suggest that use of source code under the GPL v.2 licence created an implied licence of any software patent in added source code for downstream users.[225] The GPL v.3, on the other hand, contains a dedicated section on patents.[226] This requires that:

- anyone conveying software under the GPL v.3, whether newly written or a modified source version, in which they have a patent claim, must provide every recipient with any patent licences necessary for them to exercise the rights granted via the GPL v.3 – that is, if a company combines any GPL v.3 licensed software into software for which it has a patent, it must grant all downstream users a licence in relation to that patent;
- if a distributor conveys a covered work, knowingly relying on his or her own licence of a patent held by a third party that could be used to prevent downstream users from exercising the rights granted via the GPL v.3, via infringement proceeding threats from the third party,

---

218 Ibid, section 6(a)–(e).
219 Ibid, section 8.
220 Ibid, section 9.
221 Ibid, section 10.
222 Ibid, section 8.
223 Ibid, section 12.
224 Ibid, sections 15 and 16.
225 See GPL v.2, Preamble: 'We wish to avoid the danger that redistributors of a free program will individually obtain patent licenses, in effect making the program proprietary. To prevent this, we have made it clear that any patent must be licensed for everyone's free use or not licensed at all.'
226 GPL v.3, section 11.

then the distributor must ensure that downstream parties are also granted appropriate licence rights;

● where a third party is indirectly granted a patent licence that grants rights to source code in a GPL v.3 covered work, then those rights must be granted to all other GPL v.3 licensees of the covered work.

Second, and somewhat controversially, the GPL v.3 addresses the issue of digital rights management (DRM), by requiring that no covered work can be deemed to be part of an 'effective technical measure' under Art 11 of the World Intellectual Property Organization (WIPO) Copyright Treaty. Article 11 requires treaty signatories to 'provide adequate legal protection and effective legal remedies against the circumvention of effective technological measures' that are used by authors, performers, and producers of phonograms to restrict acts with respect to their copyrighted works that are not authorised by the rights holders, or permitted by law. When a GPL v.3 licensee enables other parties to make or receive copies of a covered work, he or she must waive any legal right that he or she has to prevent the circumvention of technological measures, in as far as that circumvention occurs as a result of downstream parties exercising GPL v.3 rights with regard to the covered work, and disclaim any restrictions on the operation or modification of the covered work that would allow the licensee or third parties to enforce prohibitions on the circumvention of technological measures.[227] In effect, this means that any DRM system released under the GPL v.3 (or containing GPL v.3 software) could be circumvented by a program without constituting a violation of laws implementing Art 11 of the WIPO Copyright Treaty. These would include the US Digital Millennium Copyright Act of 1998 (DMCA 1998),[228] and EU Member State legislation implementing the EU Copyright Directive,[229] including s 264 of the CDPA 1988.

Third, the GPL v.3 tackles the issue of 'tivoisation'. This concept, popularised by Richard Stallman, refers to the use of GPL v.2 software by the popular model of digital video recorder (DVR), the TiVo, which allows users to capture television programming to internal hard disk storage for viewing later. The TiVo uses a GNU/Linux-based operating system that, because Linux is licensed under the GPL v.2, requires the TiVo's manufacturers to make the source code of its program available. The manufacturer has duly made the source code available online, or by post.[230] However, if a TiVo user downloads the software and modifies it, and then attempts to upload it to his or her TiVo, he or she will discover that the machine has been set up to reject such modified code. It does this by performing digital signature checks in hardware that require the modified software to contain codes known only to the manufacturer. This was perceived by the FSF as contrary to the spirit, if not to the letter, of the GPL v.2, and the GPL v.3 was thus drafted to attempt to prevent future efforts at 'tivoisation'. The GPL v.3 does not prevent a vendor licensee from using software containing GPL v.3 licensed code on hardware that has been designed so that an executable requires a specific key signature in order for it to operate, but the licensee must provide the necessary signature key, or other necessary elements, so that the hardware will accept and run any modified executables.[231]

Like the DRM provisions, the 'anti-tivoisation' measures are controversial in as much as they appear to move the GPL into a more political sphere than simply the protection of the four freedoms. Critics have suggested that sections aimed at promoting the FSF's opposition to DRM and to

---

227 *Ibid*, section 3. For application of Art 11 to proprietary software see Chapter 11.

228 *Digital Millennium Copyright Act of 1998* (DCMA 1998), s 103 of which adds a new Ch 12 to Title 17 USC. USC §1201 implements the obligation to provide adequate and effective protection against circumvention of technological measures used by copyright owners to protect their works.

229 Directive 2001/29/EC of the European Parliament and of the Council of 22 May 2001 on the harmonisation of certain aspects of copyright and related rights in the information society: OJ 2001 L167/10.

230 TiVo, GNU/Linux Source Code, available online at: www.tivo.com/linux/

231 GPL v.3, section 6.

hardware-based code lockdowns have no place in a software licence.[232] It is worth remembering, however, that the GPL v.3 is one of a range of licences available for F/OSS projects, and that the impact of both the DRM and 'anti-tivoisation' sections in the GPL v.3 can thus be avoided by not using GPL v.3 licensed source code, such as by 'forking' existing GPL v.2 code.[233] Many existing F/OSS projects may not wish to move from GPL v.2 to GPL v.3, or may not feel able to do so – for example, Linus Torvalds, who directs the development of the Linux kernel, has indicated that there are no plans to adopt the GPL v.3.[234]

Finally, the GPL v.3 attempts to bring some clarity to the issue of licence incompatibility. There are a wide range of F/OSS licences currently available,[235] and they are often incompatible in some regard – that is, they contain requirements that mean that code licensed under them cannot be used with code licensed under a different licence. This incompatibility causes problems for programmers attempting to create software using source code under different licences and potentially 'balkanises' F/OSS-licensed code. While a number of solutions have been suggested to the problem and a number of organisations provide services to help to avoid problems caused by licence incompatibilities (for example, Koders.com by Black Duck Software is a source code search engine that permits developers to limit their code search to specific licences[236]), this is a continuing issue. The GPL v.2 did not permit any modification of its terms, which led to incompatibility with other F/OSS licences and also potential problems in countries other than the USA where the wording of warranty disclaimers and limitation of liability clauses differed from those of the USA. The GPL v.3 allows for limited modifications to reduce these problems, including, for material added to a covered work:

- disclaiming warranty or limiting liability differently from the terms of sections 15 and 16 of the GPL v.3;
- requiring preservation of specified reasonable legal notices or author attributions in that material or in the appropriate legal notices displayed by works containing it;
- prohibiting misrepresentation of the origin of that material, or requiring that modified versions of such material be marked in reasonable ways as different from the original version;
- limiting the use for publicity purposes of names of licensors or authors of the material;
- declining to grant rights under trade mark law for use of some trade names, trade marks, or service marks;
- requiring indemnification of licensors and authors of that material by anyone who conveys the material (or modified versions of it), with contractual assumptions of liability to the recipient for any liability that these contractual assumptions directly impose on those licensors and authors.[237]

The net result of these permitted modifications is that the GPL v.3 is compatible with a wider range of other F/OSS licences, including the Apache licence, MIT licence, and later versions of the BSD

232 For example, Douglas Ferguson, 'Recent development, syntax errors: Why Version 3 of the GNU General Public License needs debugging' (2006) 7(2) NC JL & Tech 397.

233 Software forking is when developers take a copy of the source code of a program and start independent development on it, creating a new piece of software, based on, but different from, the existing piece. This is easily done with F/OSS, because no permissions are required to take and modify the source code. If future Linux kernel developments were licensed under the GPL3, then TiVo could take code created under the GPL2 (in which there is no 'anti-tivoisation' clause) and develop their own line of GPL2 source code, without needing to use GPL3 licensed source code. However, this would restrict both the range of source code and programmer base available to TiVo in the future.

234 'The Linux kernel is under the GPL version 2. Not anything else. Some individual files are licenceable [sic] under v3, but not the kernel in general. And quite frankly, I don't see that changing': Linus Torvalds, 25 January 2006, online communication.

235 The Open Source Initiative (see below) recognises approximately 70 F/OSS licences.

236 Cited in DM German and AE Hassan, 'License integration patterns: Addressing license mismatches in component-based development', Paper read at 31st International Conference on Software Engineering, 16–24 May 2009, Vancouver.

237 GPL v.3, section 7(a)–(f).

licence. What this means in practice is that where a licensee wishes to combine code licensed under another open-source licence, with GPL v.3-licensed code, the licensee can now usually license the entire work, as a whole, under the GPL v.3 licence without breaching the other licences. There remains the problem that GPL v.2 is, by itself, not compatible with GPL v.3 – that is, there is no legal way to combine code under GPL v.2 with code under GPL v.3 in a single program. This was a recognised issue with GPL v.2 and has been addressed by the FSF in two ways:

- the use of contributor agreements assigning copyright to the FSF, thus allowing the FSF to relicense as copyright owner;
- encouraging GPL v.2 licensors to license under a specific version or 'any later version', thus allowing existing source code licensed under GPL v.2 or 'any later version' to be relicensed under GPL v.3 without direct contributor approval.[238]

## Dual licensing

It is important to remember that the holder of a copyright in the source code of a computer program can, like any other copyright holder, license his or her exclusive rights in his or her work to different licensees under different licence terms. It is possible, therefore, for the copyright holder of the source code in a computer program to make it available for licensing under a proprietary fee-based licence option, as well as an open source licence option, such as one of the versions of the GPL (GPLx). In such cases, a licensee choosing the GPLx licence option would be required to release the full source code with any distribution of object code/executable that contained the GPLx licensed code. In contrast, a licensee choosing the proprietary fee-based licence option would be able to distribute the object code/executable alone, and would have no obligation to release his or her source code.[239]

## Open source software

There has been a tendency over time, particularly in the popular media, to refer to all software released under licences such as the modified BSD licence and the GPLx family of licences, as 'open source software'. This catch-all phrase tends to disguise the fact that there are several distinct schools of thought on the nature of software development. The split between the permissive ethos of those who created the BSD licence and the activist ethos of the Stallman/FSF is one example of this. The other key split is between the 'free software' purists (such as Stallman/FSF), and the 'open source software' school, who feel that the politicised nature of the FSF's approach hinders the uptake of 'open' programming in the business environment. Indeed, it appears to have been this concern that led to the adoption of the phrase 'open source software' as a more commercially friendly alternative to 'free software'. Stallman himself has noted the differences between 'open source' and 'free software' rooted in their different premises – namely, that whereas:

> open source is a development methodology; free software is a social movement. The latter focuses on the social problem of nonfree software and the ethical imperative of free software. The open source movement, on the other hand, emphasises the ability to improve the software creating a better, more effective solution to a practical problem than nonfree software.[240]

---

238 Tsai, above, 579.
239 See Mikko Välimäki, 'Dual licensing in open source software industry' (2003) 8(1) Systèmes d'Information et Management 63, available online at: papers.ssrn.com/sol3/papers.cfm?abstract_id=1261644; Robert W Gomulkiewicz, 'Entrepreneurial open source software hackers: MySQL and its dual licensing' (2004) 9(1) CLRTJ 203.
240 Richard M Stallman, 'Why open source misses the point of free software' (2007; 2010), available online at: www.gnu.org/philosophy/open-source-misses-the-point.html

This divergence of opinion helps to explain some of the opposition to the FSF's introduction of the GPL v.3, which was seen by a significant number of those in the open source community as dealing with issues that were outwith the remit of a software licence.

## The Open Source Initiative (OSI)

The Open Source Initiative (OSI) was established in 1998 as a California public benefit corporation.[241] Its establishment came about as a result of the decision of Netscape Communications to release the source code of its popular Netscape Web browser as free software in January 1998. This, it is claimed, was inspired by the publication of the classic paper about the impact of 'free software' development (the phrase was changed by its author to 'open source software' in later iterations) The Cathedral and the Bazaar[242] in 1997. Its aim was 'to dump the moralizing and confrontational attitude that had been associated with "free software" in the past and sell the idea strictly on the same pragmatic, business-case grounds that had motivated Netscape'.[243]

In many respects, the FSF and OSI appear to have similar goals. However, the OSI is not ideologically opposed to closed-source software and, broadly speaking, is disinclined to involve itself in the campaigning that the FSF has adopted against both DRM technology and 'tivoisation'. It has significant interaction with traditional software companies, such as IBM, Hewlett Packard, and Sun, as well as with smaller companies working within an open source business model, such as Red Hat and Mandrake.

The two key roles that the OSI has played in the F/OSS community take the form of the creation and maintenance of the Open Source Definition (OSD), and its (self-appointed) community role as the body that reviews and approves licences as OSD-conformant.[244]

## The Open Source Definition

The OSI OSD was based on an existing set of free software principles known as the Debian Free Software Guidelines.[245] It was adopted in revised form by the OSI in February 1998, and has remained largely unchanged since 2004, when the OSI added clause 10 to address issues surrounding click-wrap licensing. In principle, any software licence creator who wishes his or her licence to be recognised as an 'open source' licence by the 'open source community' will have to ensure that it meets the requirements of the OSD, and passes the OSI's approval process.

*The open source definition*[246]

### Introduction

Open source doesn't just mean access to the source code. The distribution terms of open-source software must comply with the following criteria:

### 1. Free Redistribution

The license shall not restrict any party from selling or giving away the software as a component of an aggregate software distribution containing programs from several different sources. The license shall not require a royalty or other fee for such sale.

---

241  In October 2009, the OSI's corporate status was suspended by the state of California, apparently on the grounds of failure to file required material with the state authorities. It was reinstated in February 2010.

242  Eric S Raymond, The Cathedral and the Bazaar: Musings on Linux and Open Source by an Accidental Revolutionary, 1999, Sebastopol, CA: O'Reilly Media.

243  Open Source Initiative, 'History of the OSI', available online at: www.opensource.org/history

244  Open Source Initiative, 'The Licence Review Process', available online at: www.opensource.org/approval

245  Debian is a free operating system based on the Linux kernel and tools from the GNU project. It was one of the early free software projects, beginning in 1993. The Debian Free Software Guidelines form part of the 'Debian Social Contract', online at www.debian.org/social_contract.html

246  Open Source Initiative, 'The Open Source Definition', online at www.opensource.org/docs/osd

2. **Source Code**
The program must include source code, and must allow distribution in source code as well as compiled form. Where some form of a product is not distributed with source code, there must be a well-publicized means of obtaining the source code for no more than a reasonable reproduction cost preferably, downloading via the Internet without charge. The source code must be the preferred form in which a programmer would modify the program. Deliberately obfuscated source code is not allowed. Intermediate forms such as the output of a preprocessor or translator are not allowed.

3. **Derived Works**
The license must allow modifications and derived works, and must allow them to be distributed under the same terms as the license of the original software.

4. **Integrity of The Author's Source Code**
The license may restrict source-code from being distributed in modified form only if the license allows the distribution of 'patch files' with the source code for the purpose of modifying the program at build time. The license must explicitly permit distribution of software built from modified source code. The license may require derived works to carry a different name or version number from the original software.

5. **No Discrimination Against Persons or Groups**
The license must not discriminate against any person or group of persons.

6. **No Discrimination Against Fields of Endeavor**
The license must not restrict anyone from making use of the program in a specific field of endeavor. For example, it may not restrict the program from being used in a business, or from being used for genetic research.

7. **Distribution of License**
The rights attached to the program must apply to all to whom the program is redistributed without the need for execution of an additional license by those parties.

8. **License Must Not Be Specific to a Product**
The rights attached to the program must not depend on the program's being part of a particular software distribution. If the program is extracted from that distribution and used or distributed within the terms of the program's license, all parties to whom the program is redistributed should have the same rights as those that are granted in conjunction with the original software distribution.

9. **License Must Not Restrict Other Software**
The license must not place restrictions on other software that is distributed along with the licensed software. For example, the license must not insist that all other programs distributed on the same medium must be open-source software.

10. **License Must Be Technology-Neutral**
No provision of the license may be predicated on any individual technology or style of interface.

The OSD is broad enough to cover an array of licences, including both the modified BSD and the GLPx family of licences. While it does not mandate the type of copyleft/reciprocity conditions (also known as 'viral', 'infectious', or 'hereditary' conditions) found in the GLPx licences, neither does it prohibit them.[247] In October 2015, there were 72 licences approved by the OSI as 'open source'. The 'proliferation' of F/OSS licences has brought concerns that there are too many licences available and that incompatibilities between different licences will cause confusion. The OSI has suggested that it will seek to reduce the number of licences on its list of approved licences, but has made little headway beyond labelling some of the OSD-compliant licences as 'redundant' or 'superseded'.[248]

## Open source developments

While 'community' pressure is clearly a significant factor in both individual and organisational compliance with the terms of a F/OSS licence,[249] the acid test for F/OSS licences is, of course, whether they can be relied upon to achieve the licensor's goals when subjected to judicial scrutiny. At the present time, there is no case law relating to F/OSS licences in England and Wales (or Scotland). There have been several successful cases brought for infringement of the GPL in Germany,[250] a case in France in which the court appears (as part of a broader contract discussion) to view the GPL positively,[251] and a number of cases addressing aspects of F/OSS licences in the USA.

As with other jurisdictions, the majority of US cases brought alleging infringement of F/OSS licences have settled out of court. The Software Freedom Law Center (SFLC)[252] has brought numerous cases, primarily on behalf of the principal developers of BusyBox, a software application that works with the Linux kernel and which is often used with embedded devices such as wireless connectivity devices. Busybox is licensed under the GPL v.2. To date, virtually all of these cases have settled out of court.[253] Until recently, therefore, US courts have only tended to consider the legality of the GPL and other F/OSS licences tangentially, indicating a willingness to consider the GPL and similar licences to be valid, but not actually providing a clear decision on the matter.[254] In *Wallace v IBM*,[255] the plaintiff alleged that the GPL v.2 violated US anti-trust law in that 'IBM, Red Hat, and Novell have conspired among themselves and with others (including the Free Software Foundation) to eliminate competition in the operating system market by making Linux available at an unbeatable price'.[256] The court was unpersuaded by this argument, noting that:

> the GPL keeps price low forever and precludes the reduction of output that is essential to monopoly . . . antitrust laws forbid conspiracies 'in restraint of trade', . . . the GPL does not restrain trade . . . Nor does it help to call the GPL 'price fixing'. Although it sets a price of zero, agreements to set maximum prices usually assist consumers and therefore are evaluated

---

247 However, recent F/OSS developments – notably the recognition of the GPL3 as an OSI approved licence – have caused some controversy, as both the GPL3 measures against DRM/TPM and 'tivoisation' are arguably discriminatory under cl 6. Controversy has also surrounded Microsoft's application for OSI approval for its Public (Ms-PL) and Reciprocal (Ms-RL) licences (both granted).

248 Open Source Initiative, *Report of License Proliferation Committee and draft FAQ* (2006), available online at: https://opensource.org/proliferation-report. See further Robert W Gomulkiewicz, 'Open source license proliferation: Helpful diversity or hopeless confusion' (2009) 30 Wash U JL & Pol'y 261.

249 Richard Kemp, 'Current developments in open source software' (2009) 25(6) CLSR 569, 580–1.

250 For example, *Welte v Deutschland GmbH Landgericht München I (LG)* (Munich District Court) 9 May 2004, No 21 06123/04; *Welte v D-Link Germany GmbH, Landgericht Frankfurt Am Main (LG)* (Frankfurt Am Main District Court) 6 September 2006, No 2–6 0224/06; *Welte v Skype, Landgericht München I (LG)* (Munich District Court) July 2007, No 7 05245/07. Harald Welte founded gpl-violations.org in 2004 to raise awareness about past and present violations of the GPL. He has been responsible for over a hundred settlements of GPL infringements, including several successful legal actions.

251 *SA Edu4 v Associations AFPA*, 04/24298 (Cour D'Appel de Paris, 16 September 2009).

252 The Software Freedom Law Center, available online at: www.softwarefreedom.org

253 Cases were filed against, then settled with: Monsoon Multimedia; Xterasys Corporation; High-Gain Antennas, LLC; Verizon Communications, Inc; Bell Microproducts, Inc; Super Micro Computer, Inc; Extreme Networks, Inc. In December 2009, the SFLC filed further cases against 14 consumer electronics companies, including Best Buy, Samsung, Westinghouse, and JVC. No further litigation appears to have been commenced by the SFLC since 2010.

254 See, e.g., *Progress Software Corp v MySQL AB* 195 F Supp 2d 328 (D Mass 2002), in which the Federal Court in Massachusetts assumed that the GPL was enforceable (case settled before trial); *Computer Associates International v Quest Software Inc* 333 F Supp 2d 688 (ND Ill 2004), in which the federal court in the Northern District of Illinois analysed the Bison licence (a licence similar to the GPL) and assumed that it was enforceable.

255 *Wallace v IBM* 467 F 3d 1104 (7th Cir 2006).

256 *Ibid*, 1106.

under the Rule of Reason . . . The GPL and open-source software have nothing to fear from the antitrust laws.[257]

However, the most important US case concerning F/OSS licences to date did not concern the GPL, but instead a rather more obscure F/OSS licence known as the Artistic License version 1.0 (ALv1).[258] The ALv1, which has now been superseded by the ALv2, permits licensees to copy, modify, and distribute the software provided that they place certain notices in those works as attribution to its original author and, where necessary, identify that they have changed the software, to preserve the original author's reputation.[259] In *Jacobsen v Katzer*,[260] the case was brought by a model railway hobbyist, who managed and contributed code to an open source project, the Java Model Railroad Interface Project (JMRI). The JMRI developed software that controlled model trains and which was distributed under the ALv1. A company run by the defendant had taken software created by the JMRI and included it in its proprietary software. It did not, however, comply with the attribution requirements of the ALv1. Amongst other things, it did not include with the modified and distributed software:

- the authors' names;
- the JMRI copyright notices;
- references to the terms of the Artistic License;
- an identification of SourceForge,[261] or JMRI, as the original source of the definition files; and
- a description of how the files or computer code had been changed from the original source code.

Jacobsen thus sought a preliminary injunction against Katzer for infringement of his copyright, because of Katzer's failure to observe the terms of the ALv1. However, the district court refused the preliminary injunction, holding that a non-exclusive licence such as the ALv1 provided a waiver of the licensor's right to sue for infringement while the licensee's use of the work remained within the scope of the licence – thus Katzer did not commit copyright infringement by copying and redistributing the JMRI software source code files. The court further held that the licence provisions requiring attribution did not constitute a restriction on the scope of the licence. Thus, Katzer's failure to include the information required by the ALv1 did not mean that Katzer was doing something that the licence did not permit (that is, acting outside the scope of the licence); rather it was a breach of the terms of the licence. The court was thus minded to treat the notice requirements in the Artistic License as being a contractual covenant, which in turn led it to treat the issue as one of contractual breach, rather than copyright infringement. As damages were the traditional remedy for breach of contract, the court refused the preliminary injunction.[262]

On appeal to the Federal Circuit Court of Appeals,[263] the court reassessed the issue of copyright infringement/contractual breach and considered in particular whether the terms of the Artistic License were conditions of, or merely covenants to, the copyright licence. The district court's

---

257 *Ibid*, 1107–8.
258 Artistic License version 1.0 (ALv1), available online at: https://opensource.org/licenses/Artistic-1.0
259 See Lawrence Rosen, 'Bad facts make good law: The Jacobsen Case and open source' (2009) 1(1) IFOSS L Rev 27, available online at: www.ifosslr.org/ifosslr/article/view/5
260 See further Erich M Fabricius, 'Jacobsen v Katzer: Failure of the Artistic License and repercussions for open source' (2008) 9 NC JL & Tech 65, discussing the lower court decision; Robert W Gomulkiewicz, 'Conditions and covenants in license contracts: Tales from a test of the Artistic License' (2009) 17(3) *Tex Intell Prop LJ* 335, discussing the Circuit Court of Appeal decision.
261 SourceForge is a web-based source code repository that offers free access to hosting and tools for F/OSS developers, available online at: http://sourceforge.net/about
262 *Jacobsen v Katzer*, WL 2358628, 6–7 (ND Cal, 17 August 2007).
263 *Jacobsen v Katzer* 535 F 3d 1373 (Fed Cir 2008).

analysis had clearly treated the ALv1 licence limitations as covenants rather than conditions, and this interpretation was firmly rejected by the Court of Appeals. The licence stated that the document created conditions; further, these conditions were vital to ensure compliance with the requirement to retain the reference to the original source, and maintain knowledge of subsequent uses and the collaborative effort involved. The explicit restrictions placed on the right to modify and distribute the work were both 'clear and necessary' to accomplish the objectives of the open source licensing collaboration.[264] The Court underlined the right of copyright holders to control the modification and distribution of copyright material; this was not only a question of economic benefits and monetary payments.

> Copyright holders who engage in open source licensing have the right to control the modification and distribution of copyrighted material . . . Copyright licenses are designed to support the right to exclude; money damages alone do not support or enforce that right. The choice to exact consideration in the form of compliance with the open source requirements of disclosure and explanation of changes, rather than as a dollar-denominated fee, is entitled to no less legal recognition. Indeed, because a calculation of damages is inherently speculative, these types of license restrictions might well be rendered meaningless absent the ability to enforce through injunctive relief.[265]

Having clearly identified the ALv1 conditions as being copyright licence conditions, the Court of Appeals then remanded the case back to the district court for reconsideration of the appropriateness of injunctive relief. This was again refused by the district court,[266] on the grounds that Jacobsen had not provided adequate admissible evidence to show: that he was likely to succeed on the merits, that he was likely to suffer irreparable harm in the absence of preliminary relief, that the balance of equities tipped in his favour, and that an injunction would be in the public interest.[267] The case eventually settled in Jacobsen's favour, with a permanent injunction against Katzer reproducing the software and the settlement agreement requiring a payment of US$100,000 to the open source movement.[268]

The *Jacobsen* case thus represents a positive result for the F/OSS community, in as much as it is a recognition (at least in California) both that breach of a F/OSS licence term can be copyright infringement and that the most appropriate remedy in such circumstances is likely to be injunctive relief: either negative, in terms of removing the licensee's ability to distribute an infringing work; or positive, in terms of forcing the licensee to release source code, or properly attribute the authors. Some issues remain: for example, the Court of Appeals clearly looked carefully at the licence terms when determining whether they were to be deemed licence conditions or contractual covenants, and the unclear terminology in some F/OSS licences may pose future problems in their interpretation. The GPL v.2, however, explicitly uses conditions, not covenants: it permits redistribution 'provided that' the user meets a list of 'conditions'.

As far as UK law is concerned, commentators both prior to[269] and after[270] the US Court of Appeals ruling in the *Jacobsen* case seem agreed that a F/OSS licence would be enforceable in the UK

---

264 *Ibid*, 1381.
265 *Ibid*, 1381–2.
266 *Jacobsen v Katzer* 609 F Supp 2d 925 (ND Cal 2009).
267 Per *Winter v Natural Resources Defense Council, Inc* 129 S Ct 365 (2008).
268 *Jacobsen v Katzer* 2010 WL 2985829 (ND Cal 2010); see Suzanne K Nusbaum, 'Copyright cases' (2010) 66 Bus Law 205, 207.
269 For example, Andrés Guadamuz Gonzalez, 'Viral contracts or unenforceable documents? Contractual validity of copyleft licenses' (2004) 26(8) EIPR 331.
270 For example, Mark Henley, 'Jacobsen v Katzer and Kamind Associates: An English legal perspective' (2009) 1(1) IFOSS L Rev 41, available online at: www.ifosslr.org/ifosslr/article/view/4; Andrew Katz, 'United Kingdom' in *The International Free and Open Source Software Law Book* (2011), available online at: ifosslawbook.org/uk; Kemp Little LLP, *Open Source Software – Freedoms, Responsibilities and Governance*, version 4 (March 2013), available online at: www.kemplittle.com/cms/document/Kemp_Little_Open_Source_White_Paper__March_2013_.pdf

courts, although there is some uncertainty as to whether the UK courts would treat such a licence as either a 'bare licence' or a fully contractual licence. As with the Jacobsen case, the importance of such distinctions may lie not so much in the determination of whether the bare or contractual licence has been breached, as in what remedy is available. Henley suggests that if a situation such as that in Jacobsen were to arise in England and Wales, it would be likely that no contract would be found and that the Artistic License would be treated as a bare licence. Nonetheless, if it were deemed to be a contract, Henley envisages a similar approach to that in Jacobsen depending on whether the breach involved a condition or a less critical term. In either case, use of the software in breach of the licence could still constitute copyright infringement for which an interim injunction might be available.[271]

A concern for those using F/OSS licences, should they be deemed to be contractual licences rather than bare licences, is that this classification would potentially open licensors to actions by licensees (and the licence itself to deeper judicial scrutiny and broader contractual interpretation).[272]

# Software as a service (SaaS)

The future development of software licensing, and the concomitant legal perspectives on issues such as whether software is a good or a service, whether access may be granted to object and/or source code, and whether users should be permitted to make back-up copies or to decompile for error correction, are likely to depend on business and end-user decisions about the most efficient and cost-effective ways for them to access and utilise software.

Presently, for many home end-users, the primary way in which they utilise software is by purchasing a software package and a licence to install that software on one or more machines that they own. In the corporate environment, purchased software may be installed across individual machines within a company, or programs may be run on a company server that can be accessed by individual workstations. In both home and corporate circumstances, the licence for such software is usually either:

- a 'perpetual' licence that is paid once and does not need to be renewed annually – normally valid for the software version supplied at the time of purchase, with full version upgrades (as opposed to minor upgrades and bug fixes) likely to require an additional payment;
- a 'subscription' licence valid for a set period of time, at the end of which, if the licence is not renewed, the software ceases to work – typically including any upgrades provided by the vendor during the lifetime of the licence.[273]

Additionally, the licence is usually restricted in terms of the number of iterations of the software that can be run simultaneously. Home computing licences often restrict installation to one machine, although the use of portable computers has led some vendors to permit multiple installations. In a corporate environment, there are a variety of licensing/pricing options available, the most popular being:[274]

- per seat – the company pays a licence fee per machine on which the software is installed, or per server via which it can be accessed by workstations (use being restricted to specific machines);

---

271 Ibid, 43–4; see also Kemp, above, 578.
272 Henley, above, 44.
273 Software companies will often choose to offer their products under both types of licence.
274 Acresso Software, 2008 Key Trends in Software Pricing and Licensing, available online at: www.softsummit.com/library/reports/2008KeyTrendsSurvey.pdf

- floating user/concurrent user – the company pays a licence fee based on the number of people able to access the software simultaneously;
- named user – the licence fee is paid in relation to a specific user rather than a specific machine;
- per metric – the licence fee is dependent upon metrics, such as actual usage, or financial targets, etc;
- per central processing unit (CPU) – the licence permits an unlimited number of end-users to use the software running on a single CPU (usually applied to server-based software).

All of these options require both home and corporate software users to install the software on their own machines, and to maintain and where necessary upgrade the software. Corporate users will often incur significant hardware and technical support costs in ensuring that software is properly licensed, such as that the company is not under or over-licensed, and that systems are effectively maintained, such as that server/network maintenance, hardware compatibility checks, and installation of software patches are carried out. Home users also often struggle with installation and upgrading of even basic software packages.

## Application service provision (ASP), cloud computing, and SaaS

As noted in the previous section, the traditional model for software use has been for an individual or company to purchase a software package, along with a software licence appropriate to its intended use. This places the burden of maintaining both the necessary hardware and software, as well as ensuring compliance with often quite complex licence conditions, upon the users. Even where licensees are willing to comply with the licences, it may be difficult and costly, particularly in the corporate environment, for them to gauge accurately the extent of their compliance (or for the licensor to enforce licensee compliance).

These issues have led to a number of possible solutions being offered that aim to reduce both the technical overheads imposed on users and the complexities of existing licensing practices. This section will briefly outline three key developments with relevance to software licensing that have seen significant media coverage over the past decade – application service provision (ASP), cloud computing, and Software as a Service (SaaS) – and their interrelationship.[275] All three terms relate to ways of removing the need to install software on a user's machine by hosting it at a service provider, with the user then able to utilise the software remotely via a network.

As a term, ASP has the longest history; it appears to have diminished in use partly because of technological changes, but also because new providers have sought to distinguish their services from previous (and sometimes failed) examples. An early, 'general business' ASP provider would:

- host standard software packages that would otherwise be based on a customer's machines or servers – but the software packages were usually not specifically designed for this method of delivery and thus the ASP vendor would often be reselling or renting legacy applications;
- provide access to the software via a network, such as a dedicated line, virtual private network, or the internet, through which a customer's users could then log on to the ASP's application server to run the software;

---

275 As with many other areas of developing information technology, the area of 'outsourced' software provision is replete with jargon. Some of the jargon is created by vendors and interest groups, and some by the media. Terms are often used by different parties to mean different things and theoretically distinct terms are often used interchangeably. There is no agreed version of any of the terms.

- manage the licensing process, regardless of whether the rights to the software were owned by the vendor or a third party, which might entail taking over the licences previously granted to the customer by a third-party software company;
- manage and maintain a standardised version of the software, including upgrades and bug fixes; and
- provide the service on a subscription basis, such as on a per use basis or on a monthly/ annual fee basis.

Such general business ASP providers often faced difficulties in pricing their services, handling licensing issues, and dealing with customer demands for integration of different software and services, and for customer support. They also struggled to supply services that demanded high bandwidth in a technological environment in which access to such bandwidth, even amongst corporate customers, was limited.[276] As a result, many fell victim to the dot.com crash.

However, the principle of 'software as a service' has endured, particularly in the form of enterprise[277] and vertical market[278] ASP vendors. As technology has improved and businesses have increasingly seen outsourcing of non-core operations as a high priority, more opportunities have opened up for provision of such services. Contemporary SaaS providers tend to provide their own software solutions rather than third-party applications, and both the software itself and the hardware supporting it tend to be optimised for network (usually internet) delivery. Applications are usually designed as 'multi-tenant', allowing multiple customers to share the same application, running on the same operating system, on the same hardware, with the same data storage mechanism, but segregating each customer's data. The fact that the application is maintained by the SaaS provider on its own server(s) means that upgrading and optional enhancements can be rapidly made available to the entire user base of a customer. The concept of SaaS is rapidly developing in the consumer and small-to-medium-sized enterprise (SME) marketplace, with developments such as Gmail and Google Apps. When a user uses Google Apps, the 'data and the applications themselves are served from Google's highly secure, scalable, and reliable data centers'.[279] This means that a user can access and use his or her data from anywhere that he or she can access the internet.

The concept of 'cloud computing' takes matters one step further. It describes a situation in which a range of services, including some types of SaaS, can be provided via the internet (which is often represented by a cloud in diagrams and flowcharts), from:

> massively scalable datacentres running hundreds of thousands of CPUs as a single computer engine, using virtualisation technology. That approach means workloads are distributed across multiple machines – which can also be located in multiple datacentres – and capacity can be allocated or scaled back according to a customer's needs.[280]

In essence, when a user accesses an application 'in the cloud', they are connecting not only to a single remote server, but potentially to any of a number of machines, which may be located in one or more data centres, in more than one country. If a corporate customer has a fluctuating number of users, or fluctuating patterns of usage, a cloud computing system is capable of adjusting the computer capacity available to the customer at any point. A SaaS vendor using a cloud computing

276 Sushil K Sharma and Jatinder ND Gupta, 'Application service providers: Issues and challenges' (2002) 15(3) Logistics Information Management 160, 164–7.
277 Enterprise ASP vendors (e.g., Oracle) supply high-end software applications, such as enterprise resource planning (ERP), customer relationship management (CRM), and supply chain management (SCM) software.
278 Vertical market ASP vendors (e.g., Portera Systems) supply software applications to a particular industry or industries.
279 Google Apps, available online at: www.google.com/work/apps/business/
280 Cath Everett, 'Five cloud computing myths exploded' (2009) ZDNet.co.uk, 2 February. See further, Renzo Marchini, Cloud Computing: A practical introduction to the legal issues, 2nd edn, 2015, London: BSI; Christopher Millard, Cloud Computing Law, 2013, Oxford: OUP.

model supplies the hardware infrastructure and the software product, and interacts with the user through a front-end portal. It may own its own data centres, but equally may obtain some or all of its data centre capacity from a range of third parties.

## Licences or service level agreements?

In most circumstances in which a customer is using a SaaS service, he or she will be doing so without ever receiving a copy of the software, which remains entirely under the control of the vendor. He or she will purchase access to the software on a subscription basis, and expect the vendor to ensure that the software is available during the term of subscription, is maintained and updated, and, in the case of some software, is customised to his or her requirements. The role of the traditional software licence in this environment is thus largely redundant; what replaces the licence is usually a service level agreement (SLA) between the vendor and the customer.[281]

## SaaS, F/OSS, and the Affero GPL

The increasing popularity of the SaaS model, whereby the user does not receive a copy of a software program for installation locally, but accesses the functionality of the software over the internet, causes some problems for the F/OSS model described above. In particular, the copyleft provisions of the GPL v.2 only come into play where there is distribution of a work containing the licensed code.

*GPL v.2*

### Preamble

. . . if you *distribute* copies of such a program, whether gratis or for a fee, you must give the recipients all the rights that you have. You must make sure that they, too, receive or can get the source code. And you must show them these terms so they know their rights.

. . .

### Terms and conditions for copying, modification and distribution

. . .

    2. . . .

    (b)        You must cause any work that you *distribute* or publish, which in whole or in part contains or is derived from the Program or any part thereof, to be licensed as a whole at no charge to all third parties under the terms of this License.

The GPL v.2 thus does not take account of the server-based/web services business model. It is therefore possible for an SaaS vendor (for example, Google) to take code covered by the GPL v.2, make a modified version of that software, and provide public access to it via its service, and yet not be obliged to release the modified source code.[282]

---

281 See Helen Eliadis and Adrian Rand, *Setting Expectations in SaaS: The Importance of the Service Level Agreement to SaaS Providers and Consumers*, 2007, Washington, DC: Software & Information Industry Association; Li et al, above.

282 See Kemp, above, 579; Mikko Välimäki, 'GNU General Public License and the distribution of derivative works' (2005) 1 JILT, available online at: www2.warwick.ac.uk/fac/soc/law/elj/jilt/2005_1/valimaki/

This is seen by many in the free software movement both as 'freeriding' and contrary to the free software ethos, because SaaS vendors could use F/OSS code, but contribute little, or nothing, back to the F/OSS community. As a result, an attempt was made during the early drafting of the GPL v.3 to close this apparent loophole by adding a clause covering use of GPL licensed code in networked services. This, however, sparked considerable opposition, not least from companies such as Google, which provide several SaaS offerings incorporating GPL code. The furore caused the FSF to rethink its position and instead simply to clarify the relationship of the GPL v.3 licence with regard to SaaS:

*GPL v.3*

**Preamble**

. . . if you distribute copies of such a program, whether gratis or for a fee, you must pass on to the recipients the same freedoms that you received. You must make sure that they, too, receive or can get the source code. And you must show them these terms so they know their rights.

. . .

**Terms and conditions**

**0. Definitions**

. . .

To 'convey' a work means any kind of propagation that enables other parties to make or receive copies. Mere interaction with a user through a computer network, with no transfer of a copy, is not conveying.

While the FSF accepted that placing a direct clause in the GPL v.3 might damage the licence's chances of significant uptake, it has provided software developers with another alternative. This takes the form of the Affero GPL v.3 (AGPLv3).[283] This licence, which is OSI-approved, is broadly similar to the GPL v.3, with the addition of a clause explicitly requiring that where a program licensed under the AGPLv3 is modified by a licensee and made available to users who interact with it remotely through a computer network, the source code of the modified program must be made available to users from a network server at no charge.

Both the AGPLv3 and the GPL v.3 also contain clauses that make the two licences compatible.

*AGPLv3*

**Terms and conditions**

**13. Remote Network Interaction; Use with the GNU General Public License.**
Notwithstanding any other provision of this License, if you modify the Program, your modified version must prominently offer all users interacting with it remotely through a computer network (if your version supports such interaction) an opportunity to receive the Corresponding Source of your version by providing access to the Corresponding Source from a network server at no charge, through some standard or customary means of facilitating copying of software. This Corresponding Source shall include the Corresponding Source for any work covered by

---

version 3 of the GNU General Public License that is incorporated pursuant to the following paragraph.

Notwithstanding any other provision of this License, you have permission to link or combine any covered work with a work licensed under version 3 of the GNU General Public License into a single combined work, and to convey the resulting work. The terms of this License will continue to apply to the part which is the covered work, but the work with which it is combined will remain governed by version 3 of the GNU General Public License.

*GPL3*

### Terms and conditions

### 13.  Use with the GNU Affero General Public License.

Notwithstanding any other provision of this License, you have permission to link or combine any covered work with a work licensed under version 3 of the GNU Affero General Public License into a single combined work, and to convey the resulting work. The terms of this License will continue to apply to the part which is the covered work, but the special requirements of the GNU Affero General Public License, section 13, concerning interaction through a network will apply to the combination as such.

## Conclusions

The field of computer software licensing is one that constantly gains in complexity. While new technological developments add to the ways in which licensors seek to exploit their software, and consumers demand new ways to access, share, and use software, many of the pre-existing methods will survive for the foreseeable future. While increased bandwidth may encourage consumers to download even large programs, such as Microsoft's Windows 10 and Office 2013, via the internet, software is still bought on tangible media such as CDs and DVDs, so knowledge of shrink-wrap and browse-wrap licences (and their legal uncertainties) is still important. While the uptake of SaaS is on the increase, there are many reasons why potential users may shy away from adopting SaaS solutions across the board: lack of confidence in SaaS suppliers' performance, lack of adequate SaaS services to meet particular user needs, limited customisation, privacy, and business confidentiality concerns, to name but a few. As such, the 'in-house' or 'on-premise' model of software use, in which customers purchase mass-market software packages or commission bespoke software solutions for their own private use, is likely to remain a significant model. Developments, such as the *UsedSoft* decision in the EU may, however, see software firms accelerate their move towards cloud-based provision of software across the board.

The diverse motivations of both software licensors and licensees, exemplified in, but not exclusive to, the development of F/OSS licensing, also complicate matters for those seeking to advise parties on the legal implications of particular forms of software licensing. Increasing recent litigation around F/OSS licences, combined with licensing conditions targeting particular business methods, such as DRM, 'tivoisation', and SaaS, suggest interesting times ahead as lawyers and lawmakers seek to establish workable mechanisms for protecting reasonable licensor requirements, preventing unfair terms being placed on licensees, and maintaining a viable environment for future software development.

To date, the history of software licensing displays a considerable degree of pragmatism, not to say utilitarianism, on the part of legislators and the courts. Whether evaluating the nature of software as a good, a service or as digital content, the ownership of intellectual property rights in commissioned software, the validity of shrink-wrap and browse-wrap licences, the effect of the shift from software provided on tangible media to software provided via the internet on licensing terms, or the form and purpose of F/OSS licences, the courts appear to have trodden a careful path with regard to the rights and responsibilities of the parties, keeping a weather eye towards any undue impact on the future development of software.

## Further reading

Richard Morgan and Kit Burden, *Morgan and Burden on Computer Contracts*, 9th edn, 2013, London: Sweet & Maxwell

Maša Savič, 'The legality of resale of digital content after *UsedSoft* in subsequent German and CJEU case law' (2015) 37(7) EIPR 414.

Andrew Katz, 'United Kingdom' in *The International Free and Open Source Software Law Book* (2011), available online at: ifosslawbook.org/uk

Renzo Marchini, *Cloud Computing: A practical introduction to the legal issues*, 2nd edn, 2015, London: BSI

# Index